D1249453

HUMAN DEVELOPMENT

A LIFE-SPAN APPROACH

HUMAN DEVELOPMENT

A LIFE-SPAN APPROACH

F. PHILIP RICE

University of Maine

MACMILLAN PUBLISHING COMPANY

New York

MAXWELL MACMILLAN CANADA

Toronto

Editor: **Christine Cardone**
Production Supervisor: **Charlotte Hyland and Andrew Roney**
Production Manager: **Valerie Sawyer**
Text Designer: **Eileen Burke**
Cover Designer: **Jane Edelstein**
Cover Illustration: **Scott Barrow, Inc./Superstock**
Photo Researcher: **Chris Migdol** and **Ray Segal**
Illustrations: **York Graphic Services**

This book was set in Palatino by Waldman Graphics, Inc., and printed and bound by R. R. Donnelley & Sons Company. The cover was printed by Lehigh Press, Inc.

Copyright © 1992 by Macmillan Publishing Company, a division of Macmillan, Inc.

Printed in the United States of America

All rights reserved. No part of this book may be reproduced or transmitted in any form or by any means, electronic or mechanical, including photocopying, recording, or any information storage and retrieval system, without permission in writing from the Publisher.

Macmillan Publishing Company
866 Third Avenue, New York, New York 10022

Macmillan Publishing Company is part of the Maxwell Communication Group of Companies.

Maxwell Macmillan Canada, Inc.
1200 Eglinton Avenue East
Suite 200
Don Mills, Ontario M3C 3N1

Library of Congress Cataloging-in-Publication Data

Rice, F. Philip.
    Human development : a life-span approach / F. Philip Rice.
        p.   cm.
    Includes bibliographical references and index.
    ISBN 0-02-399765-6
        1. Life cycle, Human—Social aspects.   2. Life cycle, Human
    —Psychological aspects.   3. Human biology—Social aspects.
    I. Title.
    HQ799.95.R53   1992
    304.5—dc20   91-539
                                                        CIP

Photo credits appear on page 533, which constitutes a continuation of the copyright page.

Printing: 2 3 4 5 6 7   Year: 2 3 4 5 6 7 8

**TO
IRMA ANN RICE
WITH DEEPEST LOVE**

PREFACE

The story of human development is an exciting portrayal of life in the process of becoming. From conception to death, the drama unfolds, revealing an ever more complex being in the making. This story is about you and me as well as others: how we began, how we grew and changed before we were born, our infancy, childhood, adolescence, and our adult years. As you read this story, you will be asked to examine your own life, to learn as much as possible about the various influences that fashioned you into the person you are today. You may be encouraged not only to think about who you are and how you became you, but to set new sights for the future, to adjust your life course, so your development proceeds in the new directions you chart for yourself.

DIVISIONS

This life-span development text is divided into five major parts as follows:

Part I introduces a life-span development perspective, the periods of development, research methods in the study of life-span development, and theories of development.

Part II discusses hereditary and environmental influences on development, prenatal development, childbirth, and the characteristics of the neonate.

Part III examines child development and includes physical, cognitive, emotional, and social development from infancy to puberty.

Part IV covers adolescent development and includes physical, cognitive, emotional, and social development from puberty through age 19.

Part V covers adult development and includes physical, cognitive, emotional, and social development from age 20 to death.

ORGANIZATION

There are two basic ways to write about and to teach the subject of human development. One is the *chronological approach*: to present all aspects of development during each separate stage of life. The other is the *topical approach*: to discuss each aspect of development through the entire life span. This text combines the best features of both approaches. The life span is divided into broad chronological age divisions: childhood, adolescence, and adulthood. Under each major age division, four topics are discussed: physical, cognitive, emotional, and social development. The topical presentation within each age division allows the text to be used in courses emphasizing either a topical or a chronological format.

BALANCED PRESENTATION

Following the two introductory parts, five chapters are devoted to child development, five to adolescent development, and six to adult development. This fairly equal allocation of space among the three age groups reflects the emphasis on development throughout the life span. The expanded focus on the whole life avoids emphasizing the child at the expense of the adolescent and the adult.

SOLID RESEARCH BASE

The text uses the findings of over 2,000 references, which are incorporated into the body of the narrative and provide a solid factual basis for the discussion.

COMPREHENSIVENESS

This book encompasses a very broad range of subject matter, as much as is feasible within the confines of one text. The approach enables the student to be exposed to a wide range of topics, emphases, and issues.

EMOTIONAL DEVELOPMENT

A special feature of this text is the inclusion under each age division of a separate chapter on emotional development.

RELATIONSHIPS

Since development is so influenced by relationships, they are emphasized throughout the discussion. Parent–child, sibling, peer, family, and other social relationships are highlighted.

ECLECTIC APPROACH

The discussion emphasizes not just one but many developmental theories, reflecting an eclectic approach. The emphasis here is on presenting the most important and various approaches to human development.

PRACTICAL AND PERSONAL DIMENSIONS

The teaching and counseling experiences of the author as well as those of other teachers and therapists are used as real-life examples to illustrate situations and relationships under discussion. Case studies, anecdotal material, and quotations from students and clients are intended to add human interest. Personalized discussion questions help students to apply principles being examined to their own lives and can well result in individual growth and change.

SPECIAL BOXED SECTIONS

Parenting Issues are discussed in boxed sections and present practical problems in raising children and adolescents. **Living Issues** highlight everyday problems and issues faced by adolescents and adults and enable students to see the relevance of the discussion to their own lives. **Focus** sections include research findings, opinions, and viewpoints about specific subjects and issues that need to be clarified.

LEARNING AIDS

Each chapter contains a detailed outline at its beginning. At the end of each chapter are a summary, a list of key terms, questions for discussion, and suggested readings. Within each chapter, the key terms are printed in boldfaced type; they are defined next to the text and again in the glossary at the end of the book. Key thoughts and phrases in selected paragraphs are italicized throughout. The text includes a full bibliography of references as well as an author and subject index.

VISUAL AIDS

The textbook includes over 100 photographs, 105 diagrams and graphs, and 51 tables. These facilitate the learning process and add greatly to visual appeal.

PEDAGOGICAL AIDS

An *Instructor's Manual* is provided to the teacher. The Manual includes learning objectives, extended lecture outlines, teaching strategies, individual and classroom activities, and suggested video tapes and 16-mm film for each chapter. Test questions are available in book form and on computer disk in an easy-to-use test generation system for IBM-compatible, Macintosh, and Apple computers. Transparency masters are also available and can be used to illustrate classroom lectures. A *Student Study Guide*, by Roberta Kestenbaum of the University of Michigan, provides chapter outlines, learning objectives, key terms, applications' exercises, and self-test questions.

ACKNOWLEDGMENTS

I would particularly like to thank the following reviewers for their helpful suggestions and comments: David S. Dungan, Emporia State University; Kathleen V. Fox, Salisbury State University; Carole A. Martin, Rutgers University; Dr. Edward A. Nicholas, University of Iowa; Joe M. Tinnin, Richland College of the Dallas County Community College District; Karen K. Colbert, Iowa State University; Elaine Purcell, Midwestern State University; Philip Mohan, University of Iowa; Karen Caplovitz Barrett, Colorado State University; Sally Carr, Lakeland Community College; William S. Gnagey, Illinois State University; Donald H. Wykoff, Slippery Rock University; James A. Blackburn, University of Wisconsin-Milwaukee; and Nancy Snyder, Northeastern University.

I would also like to give special thanks to Allyn and Bacon, Inc., for permission to use material on adolescence which was adapted from the author's textook: *The Adolescent: Development, Relationships, and Culture*, 6th ed. (1990). Copyright © 1990 by Allyn and Bacon.

My appreciation is extended to the Macmillan staff who helped me on this project: Christine Cardone, senior editor; Sui Mon Wu, editorial assistant; Charlotte Hyland and Andrew Roney, production supervisors; and John Sollami, managing editor.

F. PHILIP RICE

BRIEF CONTENTS

DETAILED CONTENTS

2

THEORIES OF DEVELOPMENT

PART TWO

THE BEGINNINGS OF HUMAN LIFE

3

HEREDITY, ENVIRONMENTAL INFLUENCES, AND PRENATAL DEVELOPMENT

4

CHILDBIRTH AND THE NEONATE

PART THREE

CHILD DEVELOPMENT

5

PERSPECTIVES ON CHILD DEVELOPMENT

PHYSICAL DEVELOPMENT

COGNITIVE DEVELOPMENT

EMOTIONAL DEVELOPMENT

SOCIAL DEVELOPMENT

PART FOUR

ADOLESCENT DEVELOPMENT

10

PERSPECTIVES ON ADOLESCENT DEVELOPMENT

11

PHYSICAL DEVELOPMENT

12

COGNITIVE DEVELOPMENT

13

EMOTIONAL DEVELOPMENT

14

SOCIAL DEVELOPMENT

PART FIVE

ADULT DEVELOPMENT

15

PERSPECTIVES ON ADULT DEVELOPMENT

17

COGNITIVE DEVELOPMENT

16

PHYSICAL DEVELOPMENT

18

EMOTIONAL DEVELOPMENT

19

SOCIAL DEVELOPMENT

20

DEATH, DYING, AND BEREAVEMENT

BOXES

HUMAN DEVELOPMENT

A LIFE-SPAN APPROACH

PART ONE

THE STUDY OF
HUMAN DEVELOPMENT
OVER THE LIFE SPAN

1

A Life-Span
Developmental Perspective

INTRODUCTION TO THE STUDY OF HUMAN DEVELOPMENT

Scope

Congratulations on enrolling in this course in human development! You should find it a fascinating and intriguing subject, primarily because it is about people: ourselves and others. *This course is about the changes that take place in our lives:* in our bodies, our personalities, our ways of thinking, our feelings, our behavior, our relationships, and in the roles that we play during different periods of our lives.

In this course, we seek to *describe* the changes that take place from conception through adulthood. Information about these changes comes primarily from scientific research that accurately observes, measures, records, and interprets so that objective data are obtained. For example, one researcher may want to understand better the changes that take place in sexual behavior during childhood, adolescence, and adulthood. Another researcher may want to trace physical growth and development; another may want to measure changes in cognitive thinking.

In addition to describing the changes, we will seek to *explain* the changes insofar as possible. Why have they occurred? What roles do heredity and environment play in causing these changes?

Explaining the reasons for changes is vitally important. A parent may ask: "Why has my preschool child developed so many fears?" An adolescent may wonder: "Why have I become so self-conscious?" The wife of a 40-year-old man may complain:

> I don't understand what's happening to my husband. He used to be so dependable and conservative. He'd come home for supper every night. We spent most evenings together at home. Now, he dresses in loud clothes, bought a sports car, and has been arrested twice for speeding. He stops off at a lounge after work, and sometimes doesn't get home until 9 or 10 o'clock. He's even talking about what it would be like not to be married, and to be free again. (Author's counseling notes)

This woman needs some explanation of her husband's changed behavior.

Human developmental psychology also seeks to *predict* changes that may occur. What types of parent–child relationships are most conducive to the development of emo-

Husbands and wives may have to adjust to significant changes during a lifetime together.

tional security or positive self-esteem in children? What health habits are more conducive to lowering the probability of heart attacks? If an adolescent achieves a particular score on an SAT, what is the statistical probability of academic success in college?

Each of these questions seeks to predict future behavior. We need to remember, however, that general research evaluates statistical probability of something happening under a given set of conditions. The findings do not suggest that every individual is affected in the same way or to the same extent. No research predicts with 100% accuracy what happens to every individual in a group.

Once we are able to describe, explain, and predict changes, the last step is to be able to *influence* changes. If we know, for example, that we have been raised in an alcoholic family, what can we do to overcome possible negative effects? We may decide to go for therapy or join an Al-Anon group for adult children of alcoholics. Our goal is to try to initiate positive changes that would be helpful in our lives.

The goal of life-span developmental psychology is to help us live meaningful, productive lives. The more we can learn about how and why we grow and change, and the more control we can have over the process, the more positive influences we can exert on the lives of our children, our adolescents, and ourselves.

LIVING ISSUES

Changing Ourselves

One of the ways that people develop understanding of the changes needed in their lives, and are able to make these changes, is through psychotherapy. Psychotherapy can facilitate growth.

When people go to therapists, several questions are usually uppermost in their minds: "Will therapy do any good?" "Can the situation be changed?" Or spouses ask: "Do you think my husband (or wife) will ever change?" These questions reflect the fact that a favorable outcome of therapy depends partially on change. Either the situation has to be changed or the people in it need to change.

As a therapist, I cannot predict ahead of time whether the situation can be changed or whether the people will change. Much depends upon the insight they are able to achieve, their own flexibility and adaptability, their motivation to succeed, and their willingness to assume personal responsibility. I can counsel some people for months, and they don't make any changes. Other people institute significant changes in a relatively short time.

Some people want their spouses to change, but don't want to change themselves. A wife will say: "You have to get my husband straightened out and everything will be all right." A husband will complain: "If my wife would only stop getting so upset, we could get along a lot better." These husbands and wives feel that the fault lies with their spouse, not themselves, and that the way to make the situation better is for the spouse to stop the offensive behavior. As a consequence, they consistently pressure the spouse to change and may use every power tactic they can think of to make this happen.

Realistically, we really can't change another person's behavior unless that person wants to change. In many cases,

One of the purposes of therapy is to help people make changes in themselves.

we probably shouldn't try. This is really saying: "I can like you only if you change." But what is most helpful and possible is to gain some control over ourselves. *We can change ourselves, if we want to and need to, although sometimes it may take therapeutic help to make these changes.* By changing ourselves, we may find that our whole situation and our relationships have changed as well. (A composite of the author's counseling experiences)

PERIODS OF DEVELOPMENT

For ease of discussion, the life span is usually divided into three major developmental periods: child development, adolescent development, and adult development. The first and last of these two are divided into subdivisions. Child development includes the prenatal period, infancy, early childhood, and middle childhood. Adult development includes early adulthood, middle adulthood, and late adulthood. The developmental framework includes the following periods and age divisions:

Child development
    Prenatal period: conception through birth
    Infancy: the first two years
    Early childhood: 3 to 5 years
    Middle childhood: 6 to 11 years
Adolescent development: 12 to 19 years
    Early adolescence: 12 to 14 years
    Middle or late adolescence: 15 to 19 years
Adult development
    Early adulthood: 20s and 30s
    Middle adulthood: 40s and 50s
    Late adulthood: 60 and over

The age ranges within specific periods differ slightly, particularly during adulthood, depending on the preferences of the individual psychologist.

Prenatal Period (Conception Through Birth)

Prenatal period—
the period from
conception to birth

The **prenatal period** includes the developmental process from conception through birth, during which time the human organism grows from a fertilized cell to billions of cells. During this period, the basic body structure and organs are formed. Both heredity and environment influence development. During the early months, the organism is more vulnerable to negative environmental influences than during any other period of growth.

Infancy (The First Two Years)

Infancy—the first
two years of life

Infancy, which extends from childbirth through toddlerhood—usually the second year of life—is a period of tremendous changes. Infants grow in motor ability and coordination, and develop sensory skills and an ability to use language. They form attachments to family members and other caregivers, learn to trust or distrust, and to express or withhold love and affection. They learn to express basic feelings and emotions and develop some sense of self and independence. Already, they evidence considerable differences in personality and temperament.

Early Childhood (3 to 5 Years)

During the **early childhood** preschool years (from ages 3 to 5), children continue their rapid physical, cognitive, and linquistic growth. They are better able to care for themselves, begin to develop a concept of self and of gender identities and roles, and become very interested in play with other children. The quality of parent–child relationships is important in the socialization process that is taking place.

Early childhood—
the preschool pe-
riod of develop-
ment from 3 to 5
years

Middle Childhood (6 to 11 Years)

During **middle childhood**, children make significant advances in their ability to read, write, and do arithmetic; to understand their world; and to think logically. Achievement becomes vitally important, as does successful adjustment with parents. Both psychosocial

Middle child-
hood—the elemen-
tary school years,
from 6 to 11 years

During early childhood children begin to develop a concept of self.

and moral development proceed at a rapid rate. The quality of family relationships continues to exert a major influence on emotional and social adjustments.

Adolescence
(12 to 19 Years)

Adolescence—the period of transition from childhood to young adulthood, from about 12 to 19 years of age

Adolescence is the period of transition between childhood and adulthood during which sexual maturation takes place, formal operational thinking begins, and preparation for entering the adult world occurs. The formation of a positive identity is an important psychosocial task. As adolescents seek greater independence from parents, they also want increased contact and a closer sense of belonging and companionship with their peers.

Early Adulthood
(20s and 30s)

Early adulthood—the young adult years, including the 20s and 30s

Achieving intimacy, making career choices, and attaining vocational success are important challenges of **early adulthood**. Young adults face other decisions such as whether to marry, the selection of a mate, and whether to become parents. Some face the prospects of divorce and remarriage, which can result in a reconstituted family. Many of the decisions made during this period set the stage for later life.

During middle age adults begin to feel a time squeeze as their social and biological clocks continue ticking away.

Middle Adulthood
(40s and 50s)

During **middle adulthood**, many people begin to feel a time squeeze as their social and biological clocks tick away. This stimulates a mid-life crisis in some, during which they reexamine many facets of their lives. For those parents who have launched their children, the middle years may be a time of increased freedom, because the parents are

Middle adulthood—middle age, including the 40s and 50s

Late adulthood requires increasing attention to health care to maintain vigor and well-being.

Adolescents turn to their peers to find belonging and companionship.

freer to pursue their own interests. This is a period during which many people achieve maximum personal and social responsibility and vocational success. However, adjustments need to be made to changing bodies and changing emotional, social, and job situations.

Late Adulthood (60 and Over)

Late adulthood— age 60 and over

Late adulthood is a time of adjustment, particularly to changing physical capacities, personal and social situations, and relationships. Increasing attention to health care is needed to maintain physical vigor and well-being. The persistence of verbal abilities allows some to continue to grow in knowledge and cognitive skills. Relationships with adult children, grandchildren, and other relatives take on a new meaning, especially for the widowed. Maintaining and establishing meaningful friendships with peers is especially important to well-being. According to Reker, Peacock, and Wong (1987), people in this stage of life report a high degree of happiness and life satisfaction, and little fear of death.

LIVING ISSUES

Rethinking Who Is Old

Life expectancy continues to increase. Since 1920, the average life expectancy from birth has increased from 54 to 75 years of age (U.S. Bureau of the Census, 1990). As a consequence, the proportion of older people in the United States continues to increase. By the year 2020, approximately 22% of the country's population will be 60 and older. Larger and larger percentages are over 75 or 85. This means we need to begin to rethink the concept of who is old. At what age do you consider people old: 50? 60? 70? 80? Market Facts, Inc. asked 1,000 adults of all ages how old they felt. Regardless of their actual age, most people said they felt and acted as if they were in their mid 30s. Men said that old age began in the late 60s, but

women said old age began in the 70s (Age: All in your head, 1989). Neugarten (1989) has suggested that our biological and social clocks have changed: puberty comes earlier; menopause comes later. The ages for completion of education and for marriage and parenthood are all increasing. People start new jobs and families at 50 or 60. It is a mistake, therefore, to categorize people by age brackets. Grandparents may be 35; students may be 70. The 35-year-old grandparent is certainly not old, but the 70-year-old student—by tomorrow's standards—may not be old either (Neugarten & Neugarten, 1987).

FIGURE 1.1 Expectation of life at birth, United States: 1920–1990.

From *Statistical Abstract of the United States, 1990* (p. 72) by U.S. Bureau of the Census, 1990, Washington, DC: U.S. Government Printing Office.

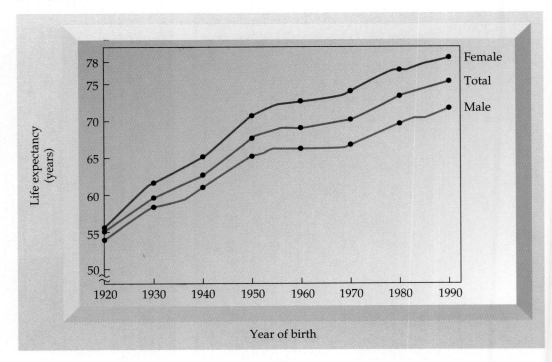

A PHILOSOPHY OF LIFE-SPAN DEVELOPMENT

The science of life-span development has slowly evolved over the years as longevity has increased and people begin to realize the importance of every age period of life. A large body of research has also evolved that sheds increasing light on the developmental process. Gradually, there has emerged a philosophy of life-span development that reflects this increasing knowledge (Baltes, 1987). The most important elements of this philosophy are discussed here.

Development Is Multidimensional and Interdisciplinary

Biological development

Cognitive development

Emotional development

Social development

Human development is a complex process which is generally divided into four basic dimensions: **biological, cognitive, emotional, and social development.** These four dimensions are discussed in this book under each of the major age periods. Though each dimension emphasizes a particular aspect of development, there is considerable interdependency among the areas. Cognitive skills, for example, may depend on physical and emotional health and social experience. Social development is influenced by biological maturation, cognitive understanding, and emotional reactions. In effect, each dimension reflects the others. Figure 1.2 outlines the four dimensions.

In describing all four of these areas, life-span development has become a multidisciplinary science, borrowing from biology, physiology, medicine, education, psychology, sociology, and anthropology (Baltes, 1987). The most up-to-date knowledge available is taken from each of these disciplines and used in the study of human development.

Development Continues Through the Life Span

For years, psychologists accepted what now seems an incredible notion: that development starts prenatally and stops with adolescence. In the past, it was assumed that most aspects of development (physical, cognitive, emotional, and social) reached their zenith in late adolescence and somehow magically stopped after that point. Although some aspects of physical growth stop, development in terms of change and adaptation continues throughout life (Datan, Rodeheaver, & Hughes, 1987). Even in the physical sense, persons who were sickly during childhood and adolescence may become healthy adults. Emotional maturation continues, as does the socialization process. Some measures of intelligence indicate that cognitive development continues past age 60. Some findings suggest that even scores on tests of performance-type tasks requiring speed and motor coordination can be improved with practice during late adulthood (Beres and Baron, 1981). The notion that adults cannot or will not learn is a fallacy.

FIGURE 1.2　The dimensions of human development.

Human Development			
Biological Development	Cognitive Development	Emotional Development	Social Development
Biological development includes genetic foundations for development; the physical growth of all the components of the body; changes in motor development, the senses, and in bodily systems; plus related subjects such as health care, nutrition, sleep, drug abuse, and sexual functioning.	Cognitive development includes all changes in the intellectual processes of thinking, learning, remembering, judging, problem solving, and communicating. It includes both heredity and environmental influences in the developmental process.	Emotional development refers to the development of attachment, trust, security, love, and affection; and a variety of emotions, feelings, and temperaments. It includes development of concepts of self and autonomy, and a discussion of stress, emotional disturbances, and acting-out behavior.	Social development emphasizes the socialization process, moral development, and relationships with peers and family members. It discusses marriage, parenthood, work, and vocational roles and employment.

FOCUS

Adults in Elderhostels

An elderhostel is an innovative educational program for older adults held on college and university campuses. A survey of 496 participants in the program in 14 colleges and universities in Virginia during the summer of 1981 investigated their motivations for enrolling in the program. The participants came from 35 different states. Their mean age was 66.8 years. The five most important motivational factors for attending the elderhostel (in decreasing order of importance) were

Learning new things
Trying something new
Catalog course descriptions
Visiting new places
Meeting new people.

It is interesting to note that acquiring new experiences was the most important motive for enrolling in the program. Who said you can't teach an old dog new tricks? (Romaniuk & Romaniuk, 1982)

Development Reflects Both Continuity and Discontinuity

Some developmental psychologists emphasize that development is a gradual, continuous process of growth and change. Physical growth and language development, or other aspects of development, show smooth, incremental changes. Other developmental psychologists describe development as a series of distinct stages, each preceded by abrupt changes that occur from one phase to another.

Continuous development is illustrated by the growth of an acorn. After planting, it sprouts and gradually grows as an oak tree. Growth is quantitative. Discontinuous development is illustrated by the life cycle of a frog. It begins as an egg, which then hatches into a tadpole, and then fairly abruptly changes into an amphibious frog (see Fig. 1.3). Growth takes place as a sequence of stages, each qualitatively different from the other. Psychologists who emphasize continuous development tend to emphasize the importance of environmental influences and social learning in the growth process. Psychologists who emphasize discontinuous development or stage theories of development tend to stress the role of heredity (nature) and maturation in the growth sequence.

Today, many psychologists do not ally themselves with either extreme point of view. They recognize that some aspects of development are continuous, whereas others show stagelike characteristics (Fischer & Silvern, 1985). Environment continuously affects people, but because people grow and develop from within, in stages, they can in turn influence their environment. (The nurture–nature issue is discussed later.) Several psychologists have combined the two points of view by emphasizing the way individuals experience and negotiate the various stages (Neugarten & Neugarten, 1987; Rosenfeld & Stark, 1987).

Development Is Cumulative

We all recognize that our lives today are affected by what has happened before. Psychoanalysts especially emphasize the influence of early childhood experiences on later adjustment. Block, Block, and Keyes (1988) were able to show that girls who were undercontrolled by parents during their nursery school years—that is, raised in unstructured, laissez-faire homes—were more likely to use drugs during adolescence than those whose parents exerted more control. In a study of 206 females and 192 males, ages 30–31, Dubow, Huesmann, and Eron (1987) showed that children of parents who were accepting, used nonauthoritarian approaches to punishment, and were closely identified with their children, showed higher levels of adult ego development 22 years later. Both studies emphasized the influence of early childhood experiences on later life.

Does this mean that if we have an unhappy childhood, we are condemned to maladjustment and unhappiness as adults? A traumatic incident or abusive childhood may have serious consequences, but neither is 100% predictive of later adjustment. Countless people have emerged from dysfunctional family backgrounds and found nurturing environments that enable them to lead productive, meaningful lives.

Development Reflects Both Stability and Change

We have already suggested that the study of human development investigates the changes that occur over the life span (Sroufe, Egeland, & Kruetzer, 1990). The question

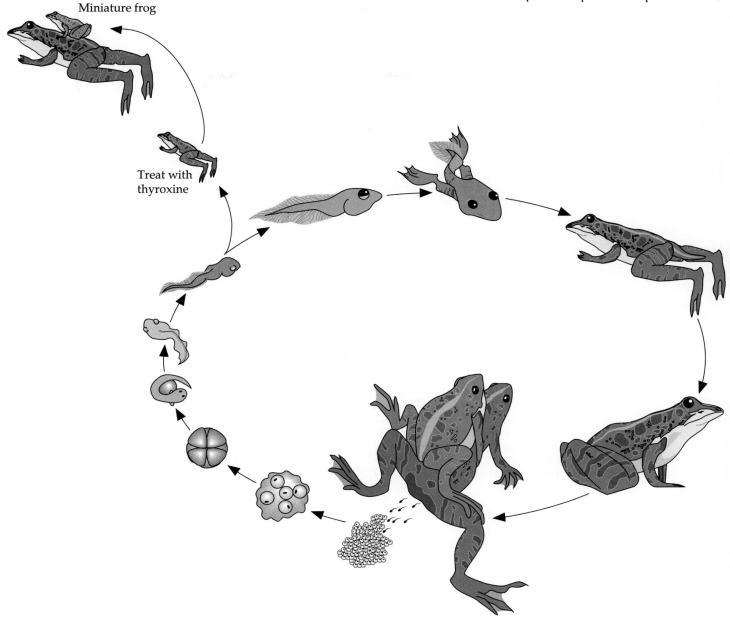

Miniature frog

Treat with thyroxine

FIGURE 1.3 The life cycle of the frog includes fertilization of the eggs (bottom); development into an aquatic, fishlike tadpole; growth of the tadpole; and ultimately metamorphosis into an adult frog. Metamorphosis is triggered by a surge of thyroxine from the tadpole's thyroid gland. If a young tadpole is injected with extra thyroxine, it will metamorphose ahead of schedule into a miniature adult frog.

arises: "Are there elements of personality that remain stable? If a person manifests certain personality characteristics during childhood, will these persist into adolescence or adulthood?" One longitudinal study of 75 white, middle-class children from infancy to adolescence revealed that children who were excessively aggressive and hostile and who showed negative emotional states (anxiety, depression, or rejection) in early childhood showed poorer emotional and social adjustment as adolescents (Lerner, Hertzog, Hooker, Hassibi, & Thomas, 1988). The researchers were able to predict adolescent adjustment through emotional behavior in early childhood. They also suggested that early intervention might ameliorate later behavior and adjustment problems.

FOCUS

Childhood Environment and Adult Outcomes

George Vaillant (1977a, 1977b), a psychiatrist teaching at Harvard Medical School, made a longitudinal study of 94 males who were among 268 college sophomores carefully selected for the Grant Study begun in 1938. The average age in 1969 was 47. Childhood histories were obtained from parental interviews. Physical, physiological, and psychological examinations were conducted each year until 1955, and every two years after that. A social anthropologist conducted in-depth home interviews with each subject between 1950 and 1952. Vaillant interviewed each man in 1967, usually at home, using identical interview questionnaires.

One of the study's most interesting aspects was the comparison of the childhoods, family backgrounds, and earlier years of the men who, in their 50s, were labeled *Best Outcomes* and *Worst Outcomes*. One-half of the men who had experienced unsatisfactory (poor) childhood environments were among the 30 *Worst Outcomes*. Twenty-three of these men whose childhoods had been bleak and loveless showed four characteristics: (1) they were unable to have fun, (2) they were dependent and lacking in trust, (3) they were more likely to have become mentally ill, and (4) they were lacking in friends. However, 17% with poor childhood environments were among the 30 *Best Outcomes*, indicating that childhood environment was not the sole determinant of adult success.

Psychologists are not in agreement as to how much personality change can take place and how much remains stable. Will the child who is shy and quiet ever become an outgoing, extroverted adult? Sometimes this happens. Will the child who is a mediocre student become a brilliant scholar in college? Sometimes this happens. The adolescent who earns a reputation for being wild and irresponsible can sometimes settle down to become a responsible, productive adult. Not all students who are voted "most likely to succeed" make it. Some who are overlooked capture top honors later in life. All we can say for certain is that there is evidence for personality stability in some people, and change of personality in others. Sometimes external events of a traumatic nature completely change the course of a person's life.

Development Is Variable

Growth is uneven. Not all dimensions of the personality grow at the same rate. A child may be exceptionally bright, but lag in physical growth and development. Most adolescents become physically mature before they are emotionally mature or socially responsible. An adolescent boy who is physically mature with the body of a man, may be childish and immature in behavior and actions, leading his parents to ask: "When is he going to grow up?" Similarly, an adolescent girl who develops early may have the body of a woman, the social interests of an adult, but the emotions of a child. Her parents may feel very confused about her behavior because she acts childish in some ways and adultlike in other ways.

Development Is Sometimes Cyclical and Repetitive

There may be some repetition of adjustment phases during anyone's life. A person may

Some psychologists emphasize that development is a continuous process of growth and change.

face an identity crisis during adolescence, and another at middle age. Adolescents may go through a period of value conflict, and adults may go through another years later. Entering the 30s may involve reevaluating one's life, but so does entering the 40s (Levinson, 1978). Likewise, vocational adjustments are necessary when one enters or retires from employment.

In addition to repetition in an individual life, there may be a repetition of similar phases occurring at different times in the life cycle of other individuals. Different persons may experience similar stages of life, but with individual and cultural differences. Different influences shape each life, producing alternate routes (one may marry and another may remain single). A variety of factors speed up and slow down the timetable, or even stop the development process altogether. But where similarities in developmental phases do exist, we can learn from the experiences of others. This fact makes a life-span approach meaningful.

Development Reflects Individual Differences

Whereas there is some repetition of developmental sequences from one person to another, *there is also a wide range of individual differences*. Individuals differ in timing and rates of development; in such factors as height, weight, body build, physical abilities, and health; and in cognitive characteristics, emotional reactions, and personality characteristics. They differ in social abilities, leisure-time preferences, relationships with friends, vocational interests, job competence, marriage and family situations, and life-styles. When discussing development, one must refer to averages: average height or weight, or average vocabulary at a certain age. However, these averages do not reflect the wide range of individual differences. Be careful not to assume that everyone must conform to these averages.

Both Heredity and Environment Influence Development

For years, psychologists have tried to sort out the influences of heredity and environment on development (Himelstein, Graham, & Weinter, 1991). If heredity plays the primary role, the human race would be im-

proved through genetic counseling to eliminate genetic faults. If environment plays the primary role, the task would be to determine what positive influences enhance development, and to control these influences toward the desired results. Actually, both **nature** (heredity) and **nurture** (environment) exert important influences. Some aspects of development seem to be influenced more by heredity; others by environment (Coll, 1990). Most are influenced by both. Children inherit their physical constitutions that enable them to stand, walk, and play as maturation proceeds. Poor diet, illness, drugs, and physical restriction can retard the process. Because some children are not very strong or well-coordinated, they have poor athletic ability, but practice may overcome these deficiencies. Children are born with the capacity to love, but must learn how to express it.

The critical question is not *which* factor—heredity or environment—is responsible for our behavior, but how these two factors interact and how they may be controlled so that optimum development takes place. *Both nature and nurture are essential to development.*

The Locus of Control Is Both External and Internal

Locus of control means the center of control in one's life. Do we have personal, internal control of our lives, or are we controlled primarily externally by other people or events? The answer is that we are controlled by both. We are influenced by events and by other people over whom we have little control, but most of us retain some control over our own development. Cognitive psychologists emphasize that it is not only what happens to us but also how we react to events that is important. Two people can go through a similar divorce experience. One is devastated and never really recovers. The other person learns from the experience and uses it as a beginning to increase happiness and life satisfaction. Part of being a mature person is to take responsibility for our own development. We cannot continue to blame our parents for our problems.

Positive mental health depends partially on our maintaining some individual power. This seems to be true throughout life. One study of 92 adults ranging in age from 69 to 100 years old and residing in a retirement community revealed that optimism about their lives (belief that good things would happen regardless of their situation) was cor-

Nature—biological and genetic factors that influence development

Nurture—the influence of environment and experience on development

Locus of control—the center of control of our lives, whether internal or external

related positively with internal locus of control measures. The more control these older adults retained, the greater their optimism about life (Guarnera & Williams, 1987).

RESEARCH IN HUMAN DEVELOPMENT: THE SCIENTIFIC METHOD

Scientific method—a series of steps used to obtain accurate data; these include formulating the problem, developing a hypothesis, testing the hypothesis, and drawing conclusions that are stated in the form of a theory

Psychologists use scientific methods to obtain information on human development (Scarr, 1985). The **scientific method** involves four major steps:

1. Formulate the problem to be solved or the question to be answered.
2. Develop a hypothesis in the form of a proposition to be tested.
3. Test the hypothesis through research to determine the truth or fallacy of the proposition.
4. Draw conclusions and state them in the form of a theory that explains the data or facts observed.

The conclusions of the study are usually published in scientific journals. Other scientists may seek to replicate the findings of the study, or to clarify the conclusions to further increase their knowledge about the subject.

DATA COLLECTION METHODS AND CONSIDERATIONS

Before a hypothesis can be tested, the researcher must gather as much data about it as possible. The primary data-gathering techniques are naturalistic observation, interviews, questionnaires, case studies, and standardized testing.

Naturalistic Observation

Naturalistic observation involves watching people in natural environments (such as at home, in school, in a neighborhood, in a park, in a shopping center, or at a party), and then recording their behavior without making any effort to manipulate the situation. This approach provides information about what is happening, but not why or how it is happening, or how the behavior might change under a different set of circumstances. Because observers make no effort to influence what is happening, they are limited to recording what they see.

Naturalistic observation—research conducted in a natural setting by watching and recording behavior

Interviews

Because **interviews** are conducted face-to-face, much detailed and personal information can be obtained with probing follow-up questions to clarify responses. Interviews

Interviews—a research method conducted face-to-face between an interviewer and subject where information is obtained through recorded responses to questions

One way of gathering data is by observing people in natural environments such as at home and school, or in neighborhoods and parks.

review feelings, emotions, and attitudes, which are sometimes more important than factual information. Another advantage is that it is a flexible method so that a broad range of subjects may be explored, depending on the needs of the interviewer. Questions may be predetermined and the same ones asked of everyone to be certain to obtain information on the same topic from each person.

This technique has some disadvantages. Interviews are time consuming, expensive, and usually involve only a limited number of subjects. The success of the interview depends on the ability of the interviewer to establish a rapport with the subject and encourage self-disclosure.

Some subjects are less verbal than others, making it difficult for the interviewer to obtain information. Sometimes subjects give false data, simply because they don't remember accurately. Interviewers need training in how to be both objective and professional. Because of biases, an interviewer might distort or misunderstand a subject's responses. In spite of this disadvantage, the technique continues to be a rich source of information for researchers.

Questionnaires

Questionnaires—a research method whereby the subject writes out answers to written questions

One frequently used method in human development research is the survey method, by which one gathers information through **questionnaires**. Questionaires are carefully designed to obtain relevant information, and are then given or mailed to people to complete anonymously. Sometimes subjects are asked to fill out a questionnaire that is then followed by a person-to-person interview. One advantage of questionnaires is that large numbers of people may be surveyed fairly easily, at a minimum expense, and data are standardized and easy to summarize. Another advantage is that questionnaires assure anonymity, so people usually respond honestly. However, questions can be misunderstood and wrong answers can be obtained. If the researchers omit significant questions, they may not receive some important information.

Case Studies

Case studies—a research method involving in-depth, longitudinal investigations and records of individuals

Case studies involve longitudinal investigations of individuals rather than groups of subjects. Clinical psychologists use case studies extensively in gathering data as a foundation for the treatment of emotionally disturbed individuals. However, the method is also used to do in-depth studies of normal individuals. The primary drawback of this approach is that data obtained about individuals may not be applicable to other persons. Conclusions about groups of people cannot be made from a sample size of one person.

Standardized Testing

Tests—research instruments used to measure specific characteristics such as intelligence, aptitude, achievement, vocational interests, personality traits, and so forth

Validity

Reliability

Psychologists have developed a wide variety of **tests** to measure specific characteristics. Tests include those for intelligence, aptitude, achievement, vocational interests, and personality; there are also diagnostic tests, and a wide variety of others. Tests have a high **validity** if they measure what they claim to measure. If a test is supposed to measure intelligence, it has a high validity if it predicts performance on tasks that most people agree require intelligence. A test has high **reliability** if the same scores are obtained when the test is administered on two or more occasions, or by two or more examiners. If the scores change from one testing to the next, the test may not be a reliable means of evaluation.

Tests are usually used in addition to other means of obtaining data. Tests can be a valuable source of information, but are most helpful when supplemented by data from other sources. Many colleges require scores on SATs as a basis for admission, but they also evaluate high school grades, class standings, letters of recommendation, interviews, and essays.

Sampling

Sample

Random sample

Representative sample

The **sample** (the group of subjects chosen) is an important consideration in research. **Random samples** are often taken from groups enlisted for study. A truly **representative sample** of a population includes the same percentages of people from the different cultural, ethnic, socioeconomic, and educational backgrounds as contained in the population. In addition, sufficient numbers are necessary to be representative of a much larger group. Practical considerations often prohibit such a sampling. However, researchers have to be careful not to apply their findings to groups that are different from those studied.

EXPERIMENTAL METHODS

Procedure

Experimental methods—methods of gathering scientific data, in which procedures are closely controlled and the experimenter manipulates variables to determine how one affects the other

Experimental methods are closely controlled procedures whereby the experimenter manipulates variables to determine how they affect one another. Changes are compared with those in control groups that have not been exposed to the variables. Because the experimenter changes the variables, a link between cause and effect is more easily established than by other methods. Experiments can be conducted in a laboratory, in the field, or as part of a subject's everyday experience. Laboratory experiments are usually easiest to conduct because they permit a high degree of control over the situation.

Suppose, for example, we wanted to observe attachment behavior and separation anxiety in three different ages of children attending nursery school for the first time. The population of 15 children is divided into three age groups—2-year-olds, 3-year-olds, and 4-year-olds—and each separate group of 5 children is brought into the nursery room along with their parents. We might want to keep changing the situation, or altering the variables, as follows:

Observe the children with both parents present.

Observe the children with only the mother present.

Observe the children with only the father present.

Observe the children with no parent present, but with a teacher that they know present.

Observe the children with only a stranger present.

Observe the children when the mother leaves the room.

Observe the children when the father leaves the room.

Observe the children when both parents leave the room.

We might compare the behavior of these children with a control group that had attended the nursery school continuously for one month. We might want to compare the behavior of the boys and girls. And we certainly would want to compare the behavior of the children of different age groups. A great variety of variables might be introduced. Would the physical setting of the room make any difference? How might the behavior of the parents affect the reactions of the children? For example, would there be any difference in the reaction of the children whose parents sneaked out without telling them, compared with children whose parents explained that they were going to leave?

Independent and Dependent Variables

Note that in the previous example, both independent and dependent variables are used. The **independent variable** is the variable over which the experimenter has direct control. The **dependent variable** is so named because it changes as a result of changes in the independent variable. In this case, the independent variable is the changing situation under which the children are observed—both parents present, only the mother present, and so forth. The dependent variable in the example is the behavior and separation anxiety experienced by the children. The purpose of the experiment is to change the independent variable to determine how that change affects the dependent variable (the behavior and separation anxiety of the children).

In another example, suppose that an experimenter wants to sort out social and demographic factors that increase or decrease the probability of divorce (Breault & Kposowa, 1987). The experimenter decides to test a selected number of independent variables: age, religion, race, socioeconomic status, geographic area of residence, and parental divorce. By looking at one independent variable at a time, and establishing correlations with the dependent variable, the researcher is able to show the relationship of each independent variable to the dependent variable (the probability of divorce). By changing one variable at a time while holding the others constant, the researcher can sort out the variables that exert the most influence.

Establishing Relationships: Correlational Studies

One way of evaluating data, once obtained, is to establish the degree of **correlation** between variables. When a correlation exists, there is a relationship, or association, between the variables. Correlation is indicated statistically from −1.0 to +1.0. Minus 1 indicates a completely negative association: When one variable increases, the other decreases. Plus 1 indicates a completely positive association: When one variable increases, the other also increases. Zero means there is no correlation or relationship at all. Correlation coefficients are expressed in r values from −1 to +1. A correlation of +.8 is not twice the correlation of +.4 (because

Independent variable—in an experiment, a factor that is manipulated or controlled by the experimenter to determine its effect on the subjects' behavior

Dependent variable—in an experiment, a factor that is influenced by the independent or manipulated variable

Correlation—the extent to which two factors are associated or related to one another

the relationships are not linear), but it would indicate a high degree of positive association.

Researchers have established a great number of correlations relating to human development. There is a positive correlation between children's exposure to violence on television and showing aggression themselves (Toot, 1985). There is a negative correlation between the degree of religiousness of adolescents and premarital sexual permissiveness (Fisher & Hall, 1988). There is a positive correlation between education and income of adults (U.S. Bureau of the Census, 1989).

Correlation is an important concept, but it does not indicate causation. A relationship between A and B does not mean that A causes B, or B causes A. Both A and B may be caused by other factors. For years, for example, psychologists showed a relationship between broken homes and delinquency. But does this mean that divorce causes delinquency? Not necessarily. There may be other variables that need to be taken into consideration. For example, divorce may follow family conflict. And there has been research indicating that family conflict contributes to delinquency, whether divorce has occurred or not (Demo & Acock, 1988). In addition, there are many other factors that may accompany divorce. After divorce, some mothers with custody of their children may be forced to live in poverty, in poor sections of town with high crime rates. The mothers have to go out to work and leave their children unsupervised. Their children are not as likely to complete their education as they woud be in intact families. Any one of these factors, and not the divorce alone, may have some relationship to delinquency. We need to be careful, therefore, not to assume that because there are correlations, causes are also established (Scarr, 1985).

RESEARCH DESIGNS

Age, Cohort, and Time of Testing

Researchers often want to sort out the effects of age, cohort, and time of testing on findings. If changes are noted as people age, is aging responsible or are there other causes? One cause may relate to a cohort. A **cohort** consists of a group of people born during the same time period, for example, during 1960–1965. There may be significant differences among people born at different time periods, not because of differences in their

Cohort—a group of subjects born during the same time period

ages, but because of the different economic and social conditions under which they grew up. Similarly, time of testing may influence results. If we were to measure life satisfaction of an older group of adults during a recession, and later were to measure life satisfaction of a younger group of adults during an economic boom, and found that the younger group reported higher life satisfaction than the older group, is this a result of the younger age or of the differences in time of testing? Researchers seek to sort out exact causes.

The four basic research designs are (1) cross-sectional studies, (2) longitudinal studies, (3) time lag studies, and (4) sequential studies. Each design has its own characteristics.

Cross-Sectional Studies

A **cross-sectional study** compares one age group, or cohort, with another age group at one time of testing. For example, a cross-sectional study conducted in 1990 might compare four groups of cohorts: those born in 1930, with those born in 1935, 1940, and 1945. As illustrated in Figure 1.4, group D (45-year-olds born in 1945) would be compared with group G (50-year-olds born in 1940) with group I (55-year-olds born in 1935) with group J (60-year-olds born in 1930). This method measures the different age groups during one testing period and compares these groups to determine differences. As shown, comparisons of groups C, F, and H during 1985, or groups B and E during 1980 would also represent cross-sectional studies.

Cross-sectional study—comparing one age group with others at one time of testing

Longitudinal Studies

Longitudinal research studies one group of people repeatedly over a period of years. For example, a select group might be studied at ages forty-five, fifty, fifty-five, and sixty. Referring to Figure 1.3, if the group of adults born in 1930 were studied during 1975, 1980, 1985, and 1990 (those groups labeled A, E, H, J), the study would be longitudinal. Similarly, a study of the 1935 cohort during 1980, 1985, and 1990 (groups B, F, I), at ages 45, 50, and 55, or of the 1940 cohort during 1985 and 1990 (groups C, G), would be longitudinal as well.

Cross-sectional studies confound age and cohort effects; that is, they fail to differentiate whether differences in age or differences due to time of birth are responsible for change. *Longitudinal studies confound age and time of*

Longitudinal research—the repeated measurement of a group of subjects over a period of years

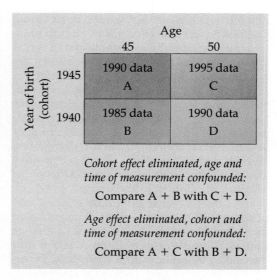

Cross-Sectional Studies

1990 Study: DGIJ
1985 Study: CFH
1980 Study: BE

Longitudinal Studies

Groups AEHJ in 1975, 1980, 1985, and 1990
Groups BFI   in 1980, 1985, and 1990
Groups CG   in 1985, and 1990

Time-Lag Studies

Compare ABCD
Compare EFG
Compare HI

FIGURE 1.4   Research designs.

FIGURE 1.5   Cohort-sequential design.

testing; that is, they fail to differentiate whether age differences or differences that relate to time of testing are responsible for change.

Time Lag Studies

> **Time lag study**—using intervals in time measurements during which people of different cohorts are examined

A third type of design, the **time lag study**, uses an interval in the time measurements during which people of different cohorts are examined. This design eliminates age effects (all the subjects are the same age), but confounds cohort and time measurements (it fails to separate the effects of each). Thus, in Figure 1.4, groups A, B, C, and D constitute a time lag comparison. Similarly, comparisons of groups E, F, and G, or of groups H and I, are time lag studies.

Ideally, time lag, cross-sectional, and longitudinal studies might all be conducted. Although each design is confounded by two sources of variation, examining the results of the three approaches can yield a more accurate picture.

Sequential Studies

A fourth pattern of research is the **sequential study**. The **cohort-sequential study** is probably the best sequential design for separating the effects of different ages and cohorts. The simplest cohort-sequential study is illustrated by Figure 1.5. Two age groups (45 and 50) representing two cohort groups (born in 1945 and 1940) are measured three different times (1985, 1990, and 1995). By comparing A + B with C + D, age and time measurements are confounded (that is, the effects of each are not sorted out), but cohort effect is eliminated. By comparing A + C with B + D, cohort and time measurements are confounded (the effect of each is not determined), but age effect is eliminated. *Of all the assumptions that can be made in developmental research, the assumption that time of testing is unimportant may be the most tenable.* If the effect of time of the study is discounted, the effects of age and cohort are sorted out, and they can be meaningfully compared in research design. Of course, the longer the total time span of the study, the greater will be the effect of time of measurement.

> **Sequential study**—a combination of cross-sectional and longitudinal research designs that attempts to sort out age, cohort, and time effects. Age changes are not measured.

> **Cohort-sequential study**—the best sequential design for separating the effects of age and cohorts

Advantages and Disadvantages of Research Designs

Each type of study design has advantages and disadvantages. The primary purpose of a *cross-sectional study* is to compare age groups.

But this method makes it difficult to determine the exact cause of any detected age differences. For example, if intellectual decline is found, is it due to physical and mental deterioration with age, or to the life situation of the older groups? Up to now, older adults generally have less education and also perform less effectively on intellectual tests than do younger adults. Because of this difference in education between the two groups, cross-sectional studies exaggerate intellectual decline with age. What cross-sectional studies often attribute to age may in fact be due to cohort effects. Furthermore, comparing a sampling of 20-year-olds with a sampling of persons over 40 fails to show changes occurring in the intervening years. Are those changes gradual, sudden, or concentrated at specific ages?

The chief advantage of the cross-sectional approach is that data for different age groups can be obtained over the same time period, usually a brief one. Therefore, it is easier to obtain information and conclude the study fairly quickly.

A *longitudinal study* periodically compares the same group of people over the years. Obvious difficulties are the amount of time and money necessary to complete the study. In addition, researchers might die or lose interest. And subjects might move, leaving no address, or otewise become unavailable. Some might even die before the study is completed. There is therefore a selective subject dropout and availability factor: Subjects who tend to perform poorly become less available over time than those who perform well. As time passes, the most competent subjects remain, tending to minimize any effect of age on intellectual decline. Thus, the combination of random and selective availability factors can easily lead to invalid conclusions.

The primary advantage of a longitudinal study is that it eliminates cohort effects. Because the same people are studied, change with age or time really is due to these factors.

Time lag studies eliminate age effects but confound cohort and time measurements. If the time between testing periods is short, then cohort effect may be partially determined. This method will not yield age differences (each group of subjects is the same age at the time of testing), but it does help differentiate other effects.

Cohort-sequential studies come closest to separating differences due to age from those related to cohort effects, but only if you assume that the time of testing has no effect.

Ethical Issues in Research

A number of ethical issues are important in human development research. The ethical standards of the *American Psychological Association (APA)* and the *American Sociological Association (ASA)* insist upon two fundamental principles: *informed consent* and *protection from harm* (APA, 1982). Informed consent entitles subjects to a complete explanation of the nature, purpose, and methods of the research before the study begins. Subjects also must be told exactly what will happen and what they agree to do if they participate. They must be informed of their right to choose not to participate and of their freedom to withdraw from the research at any time.

Researchers must be careful to minimize physical and psychological stress during the procedures in order to protect their subjects from harm. If subjects are to suffer electrical shock, for example, it should be moderate and necessary. If subjects are to be asked certain questions that will cause emotional stress, questions must be carefully selected and worded, and must be asked in ways to minimize the upset. For example, if abused wives are being interviewed, this may be an extremely stressful experience for them. In

FOCUS

Research With Children

The *Society for Research In Child Development* has issued a set of guidelines for research with children (Cooke, 1982). Research on children raises sensitive issues since minor children have a limited ability to give informed consent. *The Belmont Report* of the Department of Health and Human Services (1979) identifies three elements of adequate informed consent: *information, comprehension,* and *voluntariness*. Children of very young ages cannot meet the criteria of informed consent. One ethics panel has stated that children age 7 or over should be asked for their consent and should be overruled only if the research promises direct benefit to the child (National Commission for the Protection of Human Subjects of Biomedical and Behavioral Research, 1978). When parents and guardians are empowered to decide whether minors will be used as research subjects, they must decide what is in the best interests of the children. Researchers, too, have a responsibility to proceed objectively and as humanely as possible. They have a responsibility for the welfare of the children (Heatherington, Friendlander, & Johnson, 1989).

any case, interviewers need to take the subjects' stress into account, to ask questions tactfully, and to provide therapeutic help if required.

Protection from harm includes keeping the confidentiality of subjects. Exposure might result in embarrassment, ridicule, or conflict within relationships. Thus, data on individuals may be assigned code numbers as well as be restricted and kept in locked places. All possible means of identifying individuals with the findings of a study should be eliminated.

Universities have special committees to review planned research projects before they are begun. If particular ethical questions arise, the committee may ask the researchers to withdraw their proposal or to modify it to meet required standards.

SUMMARY

1. Life-span human development seeks to describe, explain, predict, and influence the changes that take place from conception through adulthood. The ultimate goal of life-span developmental psychology is to help people live meaningful, productive lives.

2. Human development over the life span is divided into three major periods of development: child development, adolescent development, and adult development.

3. Child development may be subdivided into the prenatal period (from conception to birth), infancy (the first two years), early childhood (3 to 5 years), and middle childhood (6 to 11 years).

4. Adolescent development extends from approximately 12 to 19 years of age.

5. Adult development may be divided into early adulthood (20s and 30s), middle adulthood (40s and 50s), and late adulthood (60 and over).

6. Because of increasing life expectancy, people stay young longer, so we need to rethink the concept of who is old.

7. A philosophy of life-span development includes the following important elements:
   Development is multidimensional and interdisciplinary and includes four dimensions: biological, cognitive, emotional, and social development.
   Development continues through the life span; it does not stop at adolescence.
   Development reflects both continuity and discontinuity.
   Development is cumulative, although what happens early is not 100% predictive of what happens later.
   Development reflects both stability and change.
   Development is variable, so that not all dimensions of the personality grow at the same rate.
   Development is sometimes cyclical and repetitive.
   Development reflects individual differences.
   Both heredity and environment influence development.
   The locus of control is both external and internal.

8. Research in human development utilizes scientific methods to obtain information. Both nonexperimental and experimental research methods are used.

9. Data collection methods include naturalistic observation, interviews, questionnaires, case studies, and standardized testing. Sampling, the selection of subjects, is an important element in data collection. Size of sample is also important.

10. Experimental methods manipulate variables to see how one affects the others. By changing variables, a link between cause and effect is more easily established than in nonexperimental methods. An independent variable is one over which the experimenter has control. A dependent variable is dependent on the independent variable. Correlational studies show the relationship between the independent variables and the dependent variables.

11. In developmental research, experimenters seek to sort out the relative influences of age, cohorts, and time of testing.

12. Research designs are of four basic types: cross-sectional studies, longitudinal studies, time lag studies, and sequential studies. Each has advantages and disadvantages.

13. Ethical standards governing research insist upon two fundamental principles: informed consent and protection from harm.
14. Research with children raises sensitive issues. For example, to what extent can minor children give informed consent? If they cannot, parents, guardians, and researchers must decide issues according to what is in the best interests of children.

KEY TERMS

Adolescence *p. 7*
Biological development *p. 9*
Case studies *p. 15*
Cognitive development *p. 9*
Cohort *p. 17*
Cohort-sequential study *p. 18*
Correlation *p. 16*
Cross-sectional study *p. 17*
Dependent variable *p. 16*
Early adulthood *p. 7*
Early childhood *p. 6*
Emotional development *p. 9*
Experimental methods *p. 15*
Independent variable *p. 16*
Infancy *p. 6*
Interviews *p. 14*
Late adulthood *p. 8*
Locus of control *p. 13*

Longitudinal research *p. 17*
Middle adulthood *p. 7*
Middle childhood *p. 6*
Naturalistic observation *p. 14*
Nature *p. 13*
Nurture *p. 13*
Prenatal period *p. 6*
Questionnaires *p. 15*
Random sample *p. 15*
Reliability *p. 15*
Representative sample *p. 15*
Sample *p. 15*
Scientific method *p. 14*
Sequential study *p. 18*
Social development *p. 9*
Tests *p. 15*
Time lag study *p. 18*
Validity *p. 15*

DISCUSSION QUESTIONS

1. Have you ever known anyone who changed a lot during his or her lifetime? How did the person change? What were the causes of the changes?
2. Do you have parents or grandparents whom you consider elderly? How old are they? What characteristics do they possess that makes them old in your eyes? At what age do you consider that people are old?
3. Can people continue to develop physically, cognitively, emotionally, and socially during their entire lifetime? Why? Why not? What factors may prevent continued development in any of these areas?
4. Do you believe that development is continuous or that it occurs in stages? Give examples.
5. To what extent is your life now partially a product of what has happened to you before? Explain. Have you faced any traumatic or unusual incidents that have changed the course of your life? Describe.
6. In what ways are you the same person today that you were five years ago? Explain with examples. How are you different, and why? Explain.
7. The text says that development is variable, that not all aspects of our lives develop at the same rate. Can you describe a person you know whose personality structure shows uneven development?
8. What aspects of development do you believe are more controlled by heredity, and which are more controlled by environment?
9. To what extent do you have control over your life? What aspects of your life are controlled internally, and what aspects of your life are controlled externally? Give examples.
10. If you had to select a subject for a research study, what would it be? What method or methods would you use to obtain information? Whom would your subjects be, and how would you select them? Would you prefer a cross-sectional or longitudinal study? Why?

SUGGESTED READINGS

American Psychological Association. (1982). *Ethical principles in the conduct of research with human participants.* Washington, DC.: American Psychological Association. A basic guidebook.

Brim, O. G., & Kagan, U. (Eds.). (1980). *Constancy and change in human development.* Cambridge, MA: Harvard University Press. A book of readings by experts on how stable or changeable are our lives throughout the life span.

Cohen, D. H., & Stern, V. (1983). *Observing and recording the behavior of young children* (3rd ed.). New York: Teachers College Press.

Eckardt, G., Bringman, W. G., & Sprung, L. (Eds.). (1985). *Contributions to a history of developmental psychology.* Berlin: Morton. A series of article by experts.

Irwin, D. M., & Bushnell, M. M. (1980). *Observational strategies of child study.* New York: Holt, Rinehart and Winston. Observational techniques for studying children along with applications in the class situation.

Kagan, J. (1984). *The nature of the child.* New York: Basic Books. Argues against the irreversibility of early experience and emphasizes the capacity to change throughout life.

Kegan, R. (1982). *The evolving self: Problems and process in human development.* Cambridge, MA.: Harvard University Press. Humans organize their world in meaningful ways so that their lives make sense to themselves and others.

McClusky, K. A., & Reese, H. W. (Eds.). (1985). *Life-span developmental psychology: Historical and cohort effects.* New York: Academic Press. How historical events and year of birth affect life-span development.

Ray, W. J., & Ravizza, R. (1988). *Methods toward a science of behavior and experience* (3rd ed.). Belmont, CA: Wadsworth. Scientific methods in conducting experimental research and in writing research articles.

2

Theories of Development

THE ROLES OF THEORIES

One of our human characteristics is that we seek logical explanations of things that happen. We ask "What happened?" or "How did it happen?" or "Why did it happen?" Last summer a house in our neighborhood caught fire. The owner, an elderly gentleman who lived alone, was found dead in his chair in the living room. Apparently he had been asleep and had been overcome by smoke inhalation before he could wake up and get out of the house. Everyone in our neighborhood sought an explanation of what, how, and why it happened. Investigators were called in to make an official report.

We all seem to have been born with a natural curiosity and with logical minds that seek to make sense out of events. Most of us have said at one time or another, "I have a theory about that"—meaning, "I think I have a logical explanation." Human development theories are really one expression of the human tendency to want to explain things. As we've seen, the scientific method involves formulating a problem, developing a hypothesis, testing it, and then drawing conclusions that are stated in the form of a **theory**. *A theory organizes the data, ideas, and hypotheses and states them in coherent, interrelated, general propositions, principles, or laws.* These propositions, principles, or laws are

Theory—a tentative explanation of facts and data that have been observed

The scientific method involves formulating a problem, developing a hypothesis, testing it, and then drawing conclusions in the form of a theory.

useful in explaining and predicting phenomena, now and in the future. Theories are particularly useful because they look beyond detailed data and give broad, comprehensive views of things.

A human development theory may focus on only one aspect of development, such as cognitive development, or may emphasize development of the total self. A theory may focus on only one time period: adolescence, for example, or it may cover the entire life span.

In this chapter, we will examine some of the major theories that researchers have developed to explain human development. The theories may be arranged into five categories: *psychoanalytic theories, learning theories, humanistic theories, cognitive theories,* and *ethological theories.*

PSYCHOANALYTIC THEORIES

Freud: Psychoanalytical Theory

Sigmund Freud (1856–1939) was the originator of **psychoanalytical theory** (Freud, 1917). *This theory emphasizes the importance of early childhood experiences and unconscious motivations in influencing behavior.* Many instinctual urges and memories of traumatic experiences are repressed early in life. They are driven out of conscious awareness into the unconscious mind, where they continue to cause anxiety and conflict and to influence behavior.

Freud was a Viennese physician in the Victorian era. He became interested in neurology, the study of the brain, and in nervous disorders. At first, he used *hypnosis* in treating these nervous disorders, but became interested in delving further into his patients' thoughts to uncover the causes of emotional disturbances. In a method he called **free association**, he asked patients to lie down on a couch and to talk about anything that came to mind. Freud sat behind his patients so they couldn't see his facial reactions. His patients would gradually reveal repressed thoughts and urges that were the causes of their conflicts. Freud also used *dream interpretation* to delve into the unconscious.

Freud felt that sexual urges and aggressive instincts and drives were the primary determinants of behavior. The individual was motivated by the **pleasure principle**, the

Psychoanalytical theory—Freud's theory that the structure of personality is composed of the id, ego, and superego, and that mental health depends on keeping the balance among them

Free association—a method of treatment in which the patient is encouraged to say anything that comes to mind, allowing unconscious thoughts to slip out

Pleasure principle—the motivation of the id to seek pleasure and avoid pain, regardless of the consequences

Sigmund Freud was the originator of psychoanalytical theory.

personality is composed of three components: the id, ego, and superego. The **id** is present from birth and consists of the basic instincts and urges that seek immediate gratification, regardless of the consequences. Left unchecked, the id places the individual in deep conflict with other people and society.

The second element of personality structure is the **ego**, which begins to develop during the first year of life. The ego consists of mental processes, the powers of reasoning and common sense, that seek to help the id find expression without getting into trouble. The ego operates according to a *reality principal.*

The third element of personality structure is the **superego**, which develops as a result of parental and societal teaching. It represents those social values that are incorporated into the personality structure of the child. It becomes the conscience that seeks to influence behavior to conform to social expectations. The id and superego are often in conflict, causing guilt, anxiety, and disturbances. The ego strives to minimize the conflict by keeping the instinctual urges and societal prohibitions in balance.

According to Freud, one of the ways people relieve anxiety and conflict is by employing **defense mechanisms**, which are mental devices that distort reality to minimize psychic pain. Defense mechanisms are employed unconsciously and become pathological only when used in excess to impair effective functioning. The defense mechanisms include the following:

Id—the inborn instinctual urges that a person seeks to satisfy

Ego—the rational part of the mind, which uses the reality principle to satisfy the id

Superego—the socially induced moral restrictions that strive to keep the id in check and help the individual attain perfection

Defense mechanisms—according to Freud, unconscious strategies used by the ego to protect itself from disturbance and to discharge tension

desire to achieve maximum pleasure and to avoid pain. However, sexual and aggressive instincts put people in direct conflict with social mores, especially during the Victorian era, when prudishness and social convention were emphasized. The conflict within the individual between these instinctual urges and societal expectations was the primary cause of emotional disturbances and illnesses.

In outlining his theory, Freud developed an explanation of the basic structure of personality (Singer, 1984). His theory states that

PARENTING ISSUES

The Overly Developed Superego

Five-year-old Stephen was a very quiet, shy, inhibited child. In kindergarten, he usually sat in a chair, watching the other children play. When given finger paint, the typical five-year-old will put the fingers in, then the whole hand, then the other hand, then smear it all over the paper, and if not supervised, may smear it over the table, wipe it on the clothes, or on the clothes of another child nearby.

In one-half hour, Stephen had barely put the end of one finger in the paint and had quickly withdrawn it. Stephen was obviously a very inhibited child.

The teacher discussed the situation with the parents. The parents were very strict and were pleased that Stephen was such a ''good boy,'' but they were willing to admit that per-

haps they had been too strict in disciplining him. At the teacher's suggestion, both the parents and teacher agreed to encourage more initiative and spontaneity.

A year later Stephen was more relaxed and far happier, willing to try new things and to enter into all activities along with the other children.

Keeping the id and superego in balance is not always easy. Some children are undercontrolled; others, like Stephen, overcontrolled with a too highly developed superego. Either extreme can cause problems for individuals who need to learn to consider both their own desires and needs and those of other individuals as well. (Author's counseling notes)

Repression—dealing with unacceptable impulses by pushing them down into the unconscious mind, where they continue to cause conflict and exert powerful influences over our behavior.

Regression—reverting to earlier, childish forms of behavior when confronted with anxiety. For example, an older child reverts to bed-wetting or to thumb sucking.

Sublimation—replacing distasteful, unacceptable behavior with behavior that is socially acceptable. For example, a man filled with anger and hostility and aggression participates in competitive sports, lest he explode into violence (Kohn, 1988).

Displacement—transferring strong emotions from a source of frustration and venting them on another object or person who becomes the scapegoat. An example would be a child who becomes angry at her parents and takes out her hostile feelings on a pet dog.

Reaction formation—acting completely opposite of the way one feels to hide unacceptable feelings or tendencies. A person might crusade against child sexual abuse (pedophilia) because he or she has such tendencies.

Denial—protecting oneself from anxiety by refusing to acknowledge that a situation exists. One example might be to refuse to acknowledge that a child is mentally retarded.

Rationalization—making up excuses for behavior that would otherwise be unacceptable.

Freud not only developed a theory of personality structure, but he outlined a **psychosexual theory** of development as well. According to Freud, the center of sensual sensitivity, or *erogenous zones*, shifts from one body zone to another as children mature. The stages of psychosexual development according to Freud are as follows:

Oral stage—first year of life, during which the child's chief source of sensual gratification centers around the mouth. The infant's chief source of pleasure and gratification is through sucking, chewing, and biting. Such activity increases security and relieves tension.

Anal stage—ages 2, 3, during which the child's principle source of greatest pleasure is through anal activity. This is the age when the child becomes very interested in eliminative functions, toileting activities, and training.

Phallic stage—ages 4, 5. The center of pleasure shifts to the genitals as children explore their bodies through self-manipulation.

Freud also taught that boys experience *castration anxiety* and that girls develop *penis envy* because of a lack of phallus. Freud said that penis envy in girls becomes a major source of what he termed women's sense of inferiority (Simon, 1988). Also, during this period boys develop an **Oedipal complex** and fall in love with their mothers, becoming jealous of their fathers as they compete for their mother's love and affection. Gradually, they repress their incestuous feelings and begin to identify with their father during the next stage of development. Meanwhile, during this period, girls develop an **Electra Complex** and fall in love with their fathers, becoming jealous of their mother as they compete for their father's love and affection. They also blame their mother for the fact that they have no penis. They are ready for the next stage when they are able to repress their incestuous feelings for their father and identify with their mother.

Latency stage—age 6 to puberty, during which time the child represses sexual urges and devotes time and energy to learning and physical and social activities. The source of pleasure shifts from self to other persons as the child becomes interested in cultivating the friendship of others.

Genital stage—begins with sexual maturation, after which the young person seeks sexual stimulation and satisfaction from a member of the opposite sex. This stage continues through adulthood.

Freud said that if children receive too much or too little gratification at any given stage, they become **fixated** at that stage, so their psychosexual development is incomplete (Phares, 1984). Thus, if children receive too little oral gratification during that stage, they may continue to try to find oral gratification later in life through smoking, eating, kissing, drinking, or chewing. Children who become fixated at the latency stage seek to repress sexual feelings and continue to identify with the same-sex parent, never moving on to make mature heterosexual adjustments.

Psychosexual theory—Freud's theory in which the center of sensual sensitivity shifts from one body zone to another in stages as children mature

Oedipal complex—according to Freud, the unconscious love and sexual desire of male children for their mother

Electra complex—according to Freud, the unconscious love and sexual desire of female children for their father

Fixated—according to Freud, remaining at a particular psychosexual stage because of too much or too little gratification

Erik Erikson developed a psychosocial theory that divided the developmental process into eight stages.

Erikson: Psychosocial Theory

Erik Erikson (b. 1902) studied under a Freudian group in Germany before coming to the United States in 1933. He became a U.S. citizen and taught at Harvard University. Erikson disagreed with Freud on several points. For example, he felt that Freud placed too much emphasis on the sexual basis for behavior. In contrast to Freud, Erikson concluded in his **psychosocial theory** that there are other psychosocial motivations and needs that become the driving forces in human development and behavior. Erikson accepted Freud's emphasis on early experiences but rejected Freud's neglect of the adult years (Erikson, 1982). Also, Erikson rejected Freud's cynical view of human nature and his belief that humans are unable to deal with their problems. Erikson said that humans can resolve their difficulties and conflicts as they arise.

Erikson divided human development into eight stages and said that the individual has a psychosocial task to master during each stage. The confrontation with each task produces conflict with two possible outcomes. If the task during each stage is mastered, a positive quality is built into the personality and further development takes place. If the task is not mastered, and the conflict is unsatisfactorily resolved, the ego is damaged because a negative quality is incorporated in it. The overall task of the individual is to acquire a positive identity as he or she moves from one stage to the next.

Psychosocial theory—the term used to describe Erikson's stage theory of development in which there are psychosocial tasks to master at each level of development

The positive solution of each task and its negative counterpart are shown in Figure 2.1 for each period (Erikson, 1950, 1959). The stages are as follows:

Trust vs. distrust (0–1 year). Infants learn that they can trust caregivers for sustenance, protection, comfort, and affection, or they develop a distrust because their needs are not met.

Autonomy vs. shame and doubt (1 to 2 years). Children gain control over eliminative functions, learn to feed themselves, are allowed to play alone and to explore the world (within safe limits), and develop some degree of independence, or if too restricted by caregivers, develop a sense of shame and doubt about their own abilities.

Initiative vs. guilt (3 to 5 years). Children's motor and intellectual abilities continue to increase; they continue to explore the environment and to experience many new things, assuming more responsibility for initiating and carrying out plans. Caregivers who cannot accept children's developing initiative instill a feeling of guilt over misbehavior.

Industry vs. inferiority (6 to 11 years). Children learn to meet the demands of home and school, and develop a feeling of self-worth through accomplishment and interaction with others, or they come to feel inferior in relation to others.

Identity vs. role confusion (12 years to 19 years). Adolescents develop a strong sense of self, or become confused about their identity and their roles in life.

Intimacy vs. isolation (young adulthood: 20s & 30s). Young adults develop close relationships with others or remain isolated from meaningful relationships with others.

Generativity vs. stagnation (middle adulthood: 40s & 50s). Middle adults assume responsible, adult roles in the community, at work, and in teaching and caring for the next generation, or they become personally impoverished, self-centered, and stagnant.

Integrity vs. despair (late adulthood: 60 and over). Late adults evaluate their lives, and accept them for what they are, or they despair because they cannot find meaning in their life.

Table 2.1 shows a comparison between Freud's and Erikson's stages of development.

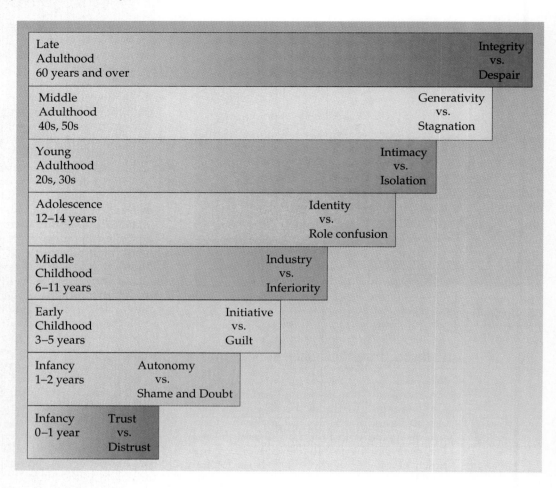

FIGURE 2.1 Erikson's eight developmental stages.

Evaluation of Psychoanalytical Theories

Freud's psychoanalytical theory is an influential one (Hofer, 1981). His emphasis on unconscious motivations and ego defense mechanisms has been particularly valuable for psychotherapists in gaining insight into the mental health or illnesses of their clients. Freud's method of treatment was unique, and became the foundation for subsequent development of a variety of treatment techniques. Freud also made parents and professionals realize how important the experiences of the early years can be. His emphasis on environmental influences placed the responsibility for development directly into the hands of all caregivers of children.

Freud's psychosexual theory of development is limited in scope, with an overemphasis (according to some) on sexual motivations as the basis of behavior, and the resolution of psychosexual conflict as the key to healthy behavior. Freud developed his theory on the basis of treatment of adult patients, so the theory was not tested on children. In fact, much of Freud's ideas are not easily tested by research. Freud also had a very cynical view of human nature that certainly does not explain the motivations of countless millions who act out of genuine care and concern.

TABLE 2.1 Comparison of Freud's and Erikson's Stages of Development

Approximate Age	Freud	Erikson
Birth to 1 year	Oral Stage	Trust vs. Distrust
1–2 years	Anal Stage	Autonomy vs. Shame and Doubt
3–5 years	Phallic Stage	Initiative vs. Guilt
6–11 years	Latency Stage	Industry vs. Inferiority
12–Young Adulthood	Genital Stage	Identity vs. Role Confusion
Early Adulthood	Genital Stage	Intimacy vs. Isolation
Middle Adulthood	Genital Stage	Generativity vs. Stagnation
Late Adulthood	Genital Stage	Industry vs. Despair

Freud has been criticized recently because he suppressed his original belief that his patients' parents had maltreated and sexually abused them (Masson, 1984; Tribich & Klein, 1986). He claimed instead that children are naturally seductive, that as victims they are to blame, a point of view that has encouraged society to overlook the extent of child abuse.

Erikson's theory is much broader than Freud's, focusing on the importance of both maturational and environmental factors in development and on the importance of a variety of psychological motivations for behavior. In addition, Erikson's theory encompasses the entire life span, outlining the stages that occur. Erikson also emphasized individual responsibility during each stage of development and the opportunity to achieve a positive and healthy resolution of the identity crisis. In Erikson's view, it's the ego and not the id that is the life force of human development (Hamachek, 1988). Erikson has also been criticized for his antifemale bias and his failure to take into account different social and cultural influences in the lives of men and women. Erikson's descriptions of development are validated by a considerable body of research findings.

LEARNING THEORIES

Behaviorism

Behaviorism—the school of psychology that emphasizes that behavior is modified through conditioning

The theory of development known as **behaviorism** emphasizes the role of environmental influences in molding behavior. For the behaviorist, *behavior becomes the sum total of learned or conditioned responses to stimuli.* Such a view is labeled **mechanistic** or **deterministic**.

Mechanistic or deterministic—as applied to behaviorism, is a criticism that behavior is a result of mindless reactions to stimuli

Behaviorists are not interested in unconscious motives for behavior. Furthermore, they see learning as progressing in a continuous manner, rather than in a sequence of stages, as in psychoanalytical theory.

Conditioning—a simple process of learning

The process of learning, according to behaviorist theory, is called **conditioning**. There are two types of conditioning: classical conditioning and operant conditioning.

Pavlov: Classical Conditioning

The Russian physiologist Ivan Pavlov (1849–1936) first discovered the link between stimulus and response. He was doing research on salivation in dogs and noticed that a dog

would begin to salivate not only at the sight of food, but also at the sound of the approaching attendant. The dog began to associate the sound of the approaching attendant with being fed.

Pavlov then began a series of experiments to test what was happening. He presented a clicking metronome to the dog, then blew a small amount of meat powder into the dog's mouth to elicit salivation. Eventually, after some repetition, he found that the sound of the metronome alone elicited salivation. The dog began to associate the sound of the metronome with the subsequent presentation of food. The best results were obtained when the metronome preceded the food powder by about half a second. This type of learning through association has been called **classical conditioning**. Figure 2.2 shows the apparatus used by Pavlov.

Learning through classical conditioning always involves a series of stimuli and responses: an unconditioned stimulus (UCS), an unconditioned response (UCR), a conditioned stimulus (CS), and a conditioned response (CR). In the case of Pavlov and his dogs, the stimuli and responses were as follows:

Classical conditioning—a form of learning through association, in which a previously neutral stimulus is paired with an unconditioned stimulus to stimulate a conditioned response that is similar to the unconditioned response

FIGURE 2.2   Apparatus used by Pavlov in his studies of conditioning.

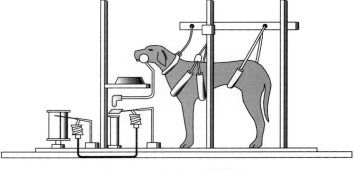

Unconditioned stimulus (UCS)—was the meat powder in the dog's mouth that elicited the response of salivation without any learning.

Unconditioned response (UCR)—was salivation in response to meat powder in the mouth, an inborn reaction

Conditioned stimulus (CS)—was the metronome, which, when associated with the meat powder, acquired the ability to elicit a response

Conditioned response (CR)—was salivation in response to the metronome alone.

Classical conditioning is a form of learning because an old behavior can be elicited by a new stimulus.

Some years later in the United States, John Watson (1878–1958) and his associate Rosalie Rayner tested this idea by teaching fear to a young child named Albert. Albert was first allowed to play with a white laboratory rat and was not in the least afraid of it. Then Watson began striking a steel bar with a hammer just behind Albert's head as he played with the rat. The loud noise made Albert cry. After seven such pairings, Albert showed fear of the rat when it was placed near him. He had been conditioned to fear it. Furthermore, his fear responses became generalized; that is, Albert became afraid of other white, furry objects as well. The conduct of this experiment raises some serious ethical issues about research with children and would not be permitted today (Watson and Rayner, 1920). Watson made no effort to extinguish Albert's fears after the experiment was over. Nevertheless, this example illustrates how a series of responses may be conditioned in children.

Skinner: Operant Conditioning

Operant conditioning—learning from the consequences of behavior so that the consequences change the probability of the behavior's reoccurrence

Positive reinforcement—a consequence of behavior that leads to an increase in the probability of its occurrence

The second type of conditioning is **operant conditioning**, which is learning from the consequences of behavior. According to B. F. Skinner (1904–1990), who originated the term, our behavior operates on the environment to produce consequences: either rewards or punishments. The nature of the consequences determines the probability of the behavior's reoccurrence. Put very simply, if our behavior results in a reward (a **positive reinforcement**), the probability that the behavior will reoccur is increased. If our behavior results in punishment, the consequence decreases the probability that the behavior will reoccur. In summary, *operant conditioning*

B. F. Skinner originated the concept of operant conditioning.

is learning in which the consequences of behavior lead to changes in the probability of that behavior's occurrence. This principle has numerous applications in child rearing and in adult learning (Skinner, 1953).

In a classical study in the 1960s, a group of preschool teachers decided to help a young girl overcome her shyness with other children (Allen, Hart, Buell, Harris, & Wolf, 1964). The teachers were concerned that the girl spent too little time playing with other children and too much time with adults, so they decided to give her praise only when she was playing with another child. When she was doing anything else, they paid very little attention to her. As a result of the positive reinforcement of the praise and attention, the little girl's frequency of playing with other children increased considerably.

Many kinds of behavior can be encouraged with positive reinforcement. Even pain can be a learned response. After minor surgery at the Johns Hopkins Children's Center, 2-year-old Adam was woozy but ready to go home. The surgeon told his mother: "Be cheerful and optimistic, compliment him when he moves around without whimpering or crying. Don't ask him if it hurts. Give him a baby aspirin only if he really complains about pain. But he won't."

After a full night's sleep Adam toddled downstairs for breakfast—slowly, but without complaints of pain (Rodgers, 1988, p. 26).

PARENTING ISSUES

Learned Helplessness in Children

Unfortunately, undesirable behavior can also be learned by reinforcement. One of the things that can be learned is help-lessness. If, for example, children who do poorly in school learn to attribute their failure to external factors rather than to lack of effort, they have learned helplessness and tend to show even more decrements in performance (Licht & Dweck, 1984). Fincham, Hokoda, and Sanders (1989) found a relationship between learned helplessness in third grade (as measured by lack of effort) and achievement test scores in the fifth grade. Once students begin to get an idea that they can't do anything about their poor academic performance, they quit trying, and of course, this lowers their test scores even more. Their concept of being unable to do the work encourages their lack of motivation, which further lowers their performance scores, thus reinforcing their poor self-concept.

Bandura: Social Learning Theory

Social learning theory—a view of learning that emphasizes that behavior is learned through social interaction with other persons

Social learning theorists accept the view of behaviorists that behavior is learned and that development is influenced by the environment, but they reject the mechanistic view that altered behavior is a mindless response to stimuli. **Social learning theory** emphasizes the role of both cognition and environmental influences in development. We are all thinking creatures with some powers of self-

Albert Bandura developed social learning theory.

determination, not just robots that show B response when A stimulus is introduced. We can think about what is happening, evaluate it, and alter our responses accordingly.

Albert Bandura (1977, 1986), Stanford University psychologist, is one of the most important contemporary exponents of social learning theory. Bandura says that children learn by observing the behavior of others and by **modeling** their behavior after them. Thus, a child may watch another play baseball: how to hold the bat and swing it, how to run the bases, how to catch and throw a ball. The child learns the fundamentals of the game through watching others. When given the opportunity, he or she then tries to imitate, or model, what was seen. Children are great imitators: They imitate parents caring for the baby; imitate them mowing the lawn; or imitate them in learning how to eat, talk, walk, or dress.

Modeling—learning through observing and imitating the behavior of others

In his classic study, Bandura let children observe a film in which an adult kicked, hit, and sat on a blow-up Bobo doll (Bandura, Ross, & Ross, 1963). When the children were placed in a playroom with a Bobo doll, they were significantly more aggressive toward the Bobo doll than a group of children who had not seen the film. They learned to act more aggressively through modeling.

Once modeled, behavior can be strengthened or weakened, depending upon whether it is rewarded or punished. Behavior can also be influenced by seeing others rewarded or punished. Suppose, for example, the children had seen the adult rewarded for hitting the Bobo doll. Their own aggressive behavior would be increased through **vicarious reinforcement**. If the adult's aggressive behavior had been punished, the children's similar behavior would decrease because of **vicarious punishment**. So children learn to behave both by modeling and by observing the consequences of their own behavior and the behavior of others.

Vicarious reinforcement—observing the positive consequences of another's behavior increases the probability of the behavior in the observer

Vicarious punishment—observing the punishment of another's behavior decreases the probability of the same behavior in the observer

Evaluation of Learning Theories

Learning theorists have contributed much to the understanding of human development. Their emphasis on the role of environmental influences in shaping behavior patterns has put the responsibility for creating positive environments for child development directly in the hands of parents, teachers, and other care givers. The principles of social learning through modeling and reinforcement have also made adults very aware of the example they set in teaching children and youth.

When psychologists concluded that much behavior is caused and learned, they began to develop many *behavioral modification* programs to eliminate problem behaviors such as phobias, explosive tempers, compulsions, or drug addiction. Behaviorist approaches to treating problem behaviors are among the most successful of the treatment approaches. They are based on a very optimistic view of the ability to control and change behavior.

Social learning theories have been criticized for leaving out the role of unconscious, psychodynamic factors and of underlying feelings in influencing behavior. As a result, social learning theorists tend to focus on surface behavior and to deemphasize the search for causes. They also neglect the role of biology and maturation in development. In spite of these criticisms, learning theories have contributed much to the overall understanding of human development.

HUMANISTIC THEORIES

Humanistic theory—psychological theory that emphasizes the ability of individuals to make the right choices and to reach their full potential

Humanistic theory has been described as the third force in modern psychology. It rejects both the Freudian determinism of instincts and the environmental determinism of learning theory. Humanists have a very positive, optimistic view of human nature. The humanistic view states that *humans are free agents with superior ability to use symbols and to think in abstract terms*. Thus, people are able to make intelligent choices, to be responsible for their actions, and to realize their full potential as self-actualized persons. Humanists hold a **holistic view** of human development, which sees each person as a whole, unique being of independent worth. In the holistic view, a person is more than a collection of drives, instincts, and learned experiences. Three of the most famous leaders of humanistic psychology were Charlotte Buhler (1893–1974), Abraham Maslow (1908–1970), and Carl Rogers (1902–1987).

Holistic view—emphasizes the functioning of the total individual to try to grow, improve, and reach his or her full potential

Buhler: Developmental Phase Theory

Charlotte Buhler, a Viennese psychologist, was the first president of the Association of Humanistic Psychology. Buhler rejected the contention of psychoanalysts that restoring psychological *homeostasis* (equilibrium) through release of tensions is the goal of human beings. According to Buhler's theory, *the real goal of human beings is the fulfillment*

TABLE 2.2 Buhler's Developmental Phases of Life

Phase	Development
Phase One: 0 to 15 Years	Progressive biological growth; child at home; life centers around narrow interest, school, family
Phase Two: 16 to 27 Years	Continued biological growth, sexual maturity; expansion of activities, self-determination; leaves family, enters into independent activities and personal relations
Phase Three: 28 to 47 Years	Biological stability; culmination period; most fruitful period of professional and creative work; most personal and social relationships
Phase Four: 48 to 62 Years	Loss of reproductive functions, decline in abilities; decrease in activities; personal, family, economic losses; transition to this phase marked by psychological crises; period of introspection
Phase Five: 63 Years and over	Biological decline, increased sickness; retirement from profession; decrease in socialization, but increase in hobbies, individual pursuits; period of retrospection; feeling of fulfillment or failure

Adapted from "The Curve of Life as Studied in Biographies" by C. Buhler, 1935, *Journal of Applied Psychology, 19*, pp. 405–409.

they can attain by accomplishment in themselves and in the world (Buhler, 1935). The basic human tendency is **self-actualization**, or self-realization, so that the peak experiences of life come through creativity. Buhler emphasized the active role that humans play through their own initiative in fulfilling goals.

Buhler (1935) analyzed 400 biographies of individuals from various nations, classes, and vocations, plus additional data from clinical interviews. Three types of data were collected: the external events surrounding a person's life, the internal reactions to these events, and the accomplishments and production of each person. From these data, Buhler outlined five phases of the life span and showed the parallels between biological and psychological development during each phase (Buhler & Massarik, 1968). Table 2.2 illustrates the phases outlined by Buhler (1935). In the last phase of life, most human beings evaluate their total existence in terms of fulfillment or failure.

Self-actualization—according to Buhler, the drive of individuals to try to grow, improve, and reach their full potential

Maslow: Hierarchy of Needs Theory

Abraham Maslow was one of the most influential leaders in humanistic psychology. He was born into an Orthodox Jewish family in New York, and earned his PhD in psychol-

Abraham Maslow said that human behavior can be explained as motivation to satisfy needs.

ogy from Columbia University in 1934. According to him, human behavior can be explained as motivation to satisfy needs. Maslow arranged human needs into five categories: *physiological needs, safety needs, love and belongingness needs, esteem needs,* and *self-*

actualization needs (Maslow, 1970). Figure 2.3 shows the hierarchy of needs as arranged by Maslow.

In Maslow's view, our first concern as human beings is to satisfy basic needs for survival: food, water, protection from harm. Only when these needs are satisfied can we direct our energy to more exclusively human needs: for love, acceptance, and belonging. The satisfaction of these needs makes possible our concern about self-esteem: We need to gain recognition, approval, and competence. And finally, if we grow up well-fed, safe, loved, and respected, we are more likely to become self-actualized persons who have fulfilled our potential. According to Maslow, *self-actualization is the highest need, and the culmination of life.*

Like other humanists, Maslow was very optimistic about human potential: "Healthy children enjoy growing up and moving forward, gaining new skills, capacities, and powers. . . . In the normal development of the healthy child . . . if he is given a full choice, he will choose what is good for his growth" (Maslow, 1968).

Rogers: Personal Growth Theory

Carl Rogers was raised in a very religious family in the midwest and became a Protestant minister, graduating from Union Theo-

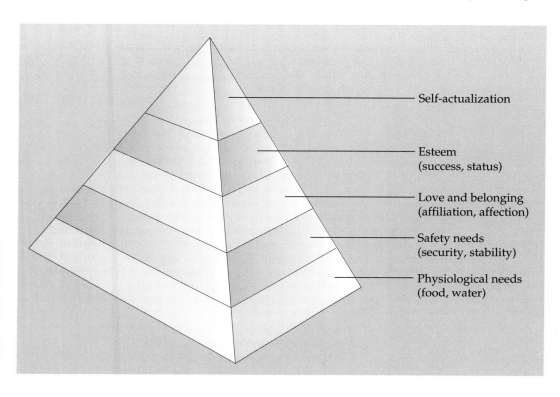

FIGURE 2.3 Maslow's hierarchy of needs.

FOCUS

The Self-Actualized Person

There are a number of characteristics of a self-actualized person as described by Maslow (1971). They include the following:

Realistic orientation
Self-acceptance and acceptance of others and the natural world as they are
Spontaneity
Problem-centered rather than self-centered
Air of detachment and need for privacy
Autonomous and independent
Fresh rather than stereotyped appreciation of people and things
Generally has had profound mystical or spiritual, though not necessarily religious, experiences

Identification with humankind and a strong social interest
Tendency to have strong, intimate relationships with a few special, loved people rather than superficial relationships with many people
Democratic values and attitudes
No confusion of means with ends
Philosophical rather than hostile sense of humor
High degree of creativity
Resistance to cultural conformity
Transcendence of environment rather than always coping with it

From: A. Maslow (1971). *The Farther Reaches of Human Nature.* © 1971 by Bertha G. Maslow. Reprinted by permission.

Client-centered therapy—Rogers's approach to humanistic therapy, in which the discussion focuses on the client's thoughts and feelings and the therapist creates an atmosphere of acceptance

logical Seminary in New York (Rogers, 1961). During his career as a minister, Rogers became more and more interested in counseling and therapy as a means of ministering to people with problems, for whom he developed a specialized form of therapy called **client-centered therapy** (Rogers, 1951). His theory is based on the humanistic principle that if people are given freedom and emotional support to grow, they can develop into fully functioning human beings. Without criticism or direction, but encouraged by the

The humanist Carl Rogers developed client-centered therapy.

accepting and understanding environment of the therapeutic situation, people will solve their own problems and develop into the kind of individuals they wish to become.

Rogers said that each of us has two selves: the self that we perceive ourselves to be (the "I" or "me" that is our perception of our *real self*), and our *ideal self* (which we would like to be). Rogers (1961) taught that each of us is a victim of **conditional positive regard** that others show us. We can't have the love and approval of parents or others unless we conform to rigid parental and social standards. We are told what we must do and think. We are criticized, called names, rejected, or punished when we don't live up to the standards of others. Too often we fail, so we develop low self-esteem, we devalue our true self, and lose sight of who we really are.

Rogers said that when we have a very poor self-image, or are behaving badly, we need the love, approval, companionship, and support of others even more. We need **unconditional positive regard**, not because we deserve it, but because we are human beings of worth and dignity. With it, we can find self-worth and the ability to achieve our ideal self. Without unconditional positive regard we cannot overcome our faults and become fully functioning persons (Rogers, 1980).

Rogers taught that the healthy individual, the fully functioning person, is one who has achieved a congruence between the real self and ideal self, a situation that results in

Conditional positive regard—giving love, praise, and acceptance only if the individual conforms to parental or social standards

Unconditional positive regard—giving acceptance and appreciation of the individual regardless of socially unacceptable behavior

freedom from internal conflict and anxiety. When there is a merger between what people perceive themselves to be and what they want to be, they are able to accept themselves, be themselves, and live as themselves without conflict.

Evaluation of Humanistic Theories

Humanists teach people to believe in themselves and to assume responsibility for developing their full potential. They also emphasize that people have very real human needs that must be met for growth and development. Adults are also taught to respect the uniqueness of each child. This places an obligation to meet these needs on those who are responsible for directing the development of growing children.

Humanists are sometimes criticized for having a view of human nature that is too optimistic. Children don't always choose what is best for them. They need some direction and guidance. Nevertheless, humanism has exerted a very positive influence on the whole mental health movement, especially in relation to counseling and therapy.

COGNITIVE THEORIES

Cognition—the act of knowing

Cognition is the act or process of knowing. There are three basic approaches to understanding cognition. One is the *psychometric approach*, which measures quantitative changes in intelligence as people mature. The second approach is the *Piagetian approach*, which emphasizes the qualitative changes in the way people think as they develop. The third approach is the *information-processing view*, which examines the progressive steps, actions, and operations that take place when people receive, perceive, remember, think about, and use information. The Piagetian and information-processing approaches are discussed here in relation to developmental theory. The psychometric approach is discussed in Chapters 7, 12, and 17.

Piaget: Cognitive Development

Jean Piaget (1896–1980) was a Swiss developmental psychologist who became interested in the growth of human cognitive capacities. He began working in Alfred Binet's Paris laboratory, where modern intelligence

Jean Piaget studied how children's thinking changes as they develop.

testing originated. Piaget rejected Binet's view that intelligence is innate and fixed, and began to explore how children grow and develop in their thinking abilities. He became more interested in how children reach conclusions than in whether their answers were correct. Instead of asking questions and scoring them right or wrong, Piaget questioned children to find the logic behind their answers. Through painstaking observation of his own and other children, he constructed his theory of cognitive development (Piaget, 1950; Piaget & Inhelder, 1969; Rice, 1990).

Piaget taught that cognitive development is the combined result of maturation of the brain and nervous system and adaptation to our environment. He used five terms to describe the dynamics of development. A **schema** represents a mental structure, the original pattern of thinking that a person uses for dealing with a specific situation in the environment. For example, infants see an object they want, so they learn to grasp what they see. They form a schema that is appropriate to the situation. **Adaptation** is the process by which children adjust their thinking to include new information that furthers their understanding. Piaget (1954) said that children adapt in two ways: assimilation and

Schema—the original patterns of thinking that people use for dealing with the specific situations in their environment

Adaptation—the process by which individuals adjust their thinking to new conditions or situations

Assimilation—acquiring new information by using already existing structures in response to new stimuli

Accommodation—adjusting to new information by creating new structures when the old ones won't do

Equilibrium—a balance between schemas and accommodation, a state in which children feel comfortable because what they find in their environment is compatible with what they have been taught to believe

Sensorimotor stage—Piaget's first stage of cognitive development (birth–2 years), during which the child coordinates motor actions with sensory experiences

Preoperational stage—Piaget's second stage of cognitive development (2–7 years), during which the child gains some conquest over symbols

Concrete operational stage—Piaget's third stage of cognitive development (7–11 years), during which the child gains some mastery over classes, relations, and quantities

accommodation. **Assimilation** means acquiring new information by using already existing structures in response to new environmental stimuli. **Accommodation** involves adjusting to new information by creating new structures when the old ones won't do. Children may see dogs for the first time (assimilation), but learn that some dogs are safe to pet and others aren't (accommodation). As children acquire more and more information, they construct their understanding of the world differently.

Equilibrium means achieving a balance between schemas and accommodation, a state in which children feel comfortable because what they find in their environment is compatible with what they have been taught to believe. Disequilibrium arises when there is conflict between children's reality and their comprehension of it, when assimilation won't work and accommodation is necessary. Children resolve the conflict by acquiring new ways of thinking, to make what they observe agree with their understanding of it. The desire for equilibrium becomes a motivating factor that pushes children upward through the stages of cognitive development.

Piaget outlined four stages of cognitive development.

During the **sensorimotor stage** (birth to 2 years), children learn to coordinate sensory experiences with physical, motor actions. Infants' senses of vision, touch, taste, hearing, and smell bring them into contact with things with various properties. They learn how far to reach to touch a ball, to move their eyes and head to follow a moving object, to move their hand and arm to pick up an object. Elkind (1970) labels the principal cognitive task during this period the *conquest of the object*.

Through the **preoperational stage** (2 to 7 years), children acquire language, and learn that they can manipulate these symbols that represent the environment. Preoperational children can deal with the world symbolically, but still cannot perform mental operations that are reversible. That is why Piaget (1967) called this stage the preoperational stage of thought. Elkind (1970) labels the principal cognitive task during this period the *conquest of the symbol*.

Children in the **concrete operational stage** (7 to 11 years) show a greater capacity for logical reasoning, though this is limited to things actually experienced. They can perform a number of mental operations. They can arrange objects into *hierarchical classifications*; they can understand *class inclusion re-*

LIVING ISSUES

Cognitive Development and the Use of Birth Control

Large numbers of adolescents are becoming sexually involved at young ages (Hofferth, Kahn, & Baldwin, 1987). Unfortunately, about a third of sexually active 15- to 19-year-old, unmarried females or males never used contraceptives whenever they had intercourse, according to one study. Another third only sometimes used some method of contraception (Zelnick & Kantner, 1980). One of the reasons may be that these adolescents had not yet achieved formal operational thinking. Effective contraceptive use requires (1) acceptance of one's sexuality, (2) acknowledgment that one is sexually active, (3) anticipation in the present, and (4) the ability to view future sexual encounters realistically, so they can be prepared for. Adolescents who were functioning only at a concrete operational stage of cognitive development were not able to project themselves into the future and to prepare themselves for sexual encounters (Pestrak & Martin, 1985).

lationships, *serialization* (grouping objects by size or alphabetical order), and the principles of *symmetry* and *reciprocity* (two brothers are brothers to each other). They understand the principle of *conservation*, that you can pour a liquid from a tall to a flat dish without altering the total volume of the liquid. Elkind (1970) calls the major cognitive task of this period *mastering classes, relations, and quantities*.

In the **formal operational stage** (11 years and up), adolescents move beyond concrete, actual experiences to think in more abstract, logical terms. They are able to use systematic, *propositional logic* in solving hypothetical problems and drawing conclusions. They are able to use *inductive reasoning* to systemize their ideas and to construct theories about them. They are able to use *deductive reasoning* to play the role of scientist in constructing and testing theories. They can use *metaphorical speech* and *algebraic symbols* as symbols for symbols. They can move from what is real to what is possible, and they can think about what might be, projecting themselves into the future and planning for it.

Information Processing

The **information-processing** approach to cognition emphasizes the progressive steps, actions, and operations that take place when

Formal operational stage—Piaget's highest stage of cognitive development (11 years and up), during which individuals are able to use logic and abstract concepts

Information-processing approach—an approach to cognition that emphasizes the steps, actions, and operations by which persons receive, perceive, remember, think about, and utilize information

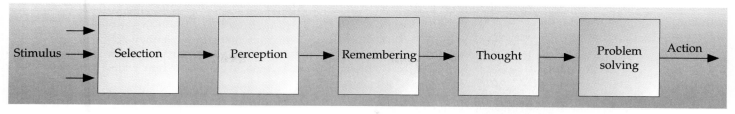

FIGURE 2.4   Steps in information processing.

the person receives, perceives, remembers, thinks about, and uses information. The steps in information processing are illustrated in Figure 2.4. The diagram shows the information flowing in one direction, but there may be some flow backward also. A person may take information in and out of memory to think about it for a time before making a decision. Nevertheless, the steps shown help us to understand the total process.

The process begins with our being bombarded with stimuli that are received through our senses. Because we are interested in some happenings more than others, we select that which is of value to us. However, the information is not just photocopied by our mind; it is interpreted and evaluated according to our perception of it, which, in turn, depends partly on our past experience. If information seems of value, it is then stored in our memory for future use. When needed, the information is retrieved from memory stores. We think about it, seek to relate it to our own present situation, and use it as a basis for solving our problems. In subsequent discussions in this book, we talk about the development of information-processing skills during various phases of the life span (Rice, 1990).

Evaluation of Cognitive Theories

Piaget has exerted more influence on cognitive theory and applications than any other person. He has revolutionized developmental psychology by focusing attention on mental processes and their role in behavior. He has made us aware that children think differently than adults, and that children can only do what they can understand at different stages. Piaget has helped educators, parents, and researchers understand the capabilities of children at different stages. Many school curricula have been redesigned based on Piagetian findings.

Piaget has been criticized for several points. He underestimated the role of the school and home in fostering cognitive development, because he stressed biological maturation rather than environmental influences. However, he did teach that each child should be given learning materials appropriate to each stage of growth. Piaget's depiction of stages as universal is not always true. Many persons never reach the higher stages of development. In fact, formal operational thinking may have limited usefulness in adult life. For example, a carpenter needs the ability to do concrete operational thinking, whereas an architect needs formal operational abilities. Furthermore, people may advance to a certain cognitive level in one aspect of their lives, but not in others. The separation of stages is not always distinct. Growth then is uneven (Flavell, 1985).

The information-processing approach has stimulated much research on learning, memory, and problem solving. It is a useful concept in describing mental processes. However, both the Piagetian and information-processing approaches emphasize mental processes at a conscious level, completely ignoring any unconscious, psychodynamic causes of behavior. They minimize the importance of motivation and emotions in learning, both of which are vital to the process.

ETHOLOGICAL THEORIES

Lorenz: Imprinting

Ethology emphasizes that behavior is a product of evolution and is biologically determined. Each species learns what adaptations are necessary for survival, and through the process of natural selection, the fittest live to pass on their traits to their offspring.

Konrad Lorenz (1965), a Nobel Prize-winning ethologist, studied the behavior patterns of graylag geese and found that goslings were born with an instinct to follow their mothers. This behavior was present from birth and was part of their instinct for

Ethology—the view that behavior is a product of evolution and biology

Konrad Lorenz's goslings developed an attachment to him, a process which he called imprinting.

survival. Lorenz also found that if goslings were hatched in an incubator, they would follow the first moving object that they saw, believing that object to be their mother. Lor-

enz stood by when the lid of one incubator was lifted. He was the first person the goslings saw, so from that point on they followed Lorenz as they would their mother. The goslings would even follow him when he went swimming.

Lorenz called this process **imprinting**, which involved rapidly developing an attachment for the first object seen. Lorenz found that there was a critical period, shortly after hatching, during which imprinting would take place.

Imprinting—a biological ability to establish an attachment on first exposure to an object or person

Bonding and Attachment Theories

Efforts have been made to apply the principles of ethology to human beings. While there is no human equivalent to imprinting, bonding shows some similarities. There is some evidence to show that parent–infant contacts during the early hours and days of life are important to later parent–child relationships (Klaus & Kennel, 1982). Studies at Case-Western Reserve University in Cleveland confirmed the maternal feeling that the emotional bonds between mother and infant are strengthened by intimate contact during the first hours of life (Klaus & Kennel, 1982). One group of mothers was allowed 16 extra hours of intimacy during the first three days of life—an hour after birth and five hours each afternoon. When the babies were one month of age and a year old, these mothers were compared with a control group that had gone through the usual hospital routine. The mothers who had had more time with their babies fondled them more, sought close eye contact, and responded to their cries. The researchers concluded that keeping the mother and baby together during the first hours after birth strengthened a mother's "maternal sensitivities" and that prolonged infant–mother separation during the first few days would have negative effects.

Although early parent–infant contact is important, other studies fail to confirm Klaus and Kennel's finding that there is a critical period during which **bonding** must take place, and that if it does not, harmful effects will be felt and lasting (Goldberg, 1983). In contrast, Egeland and Vaughn (1987) found no greater incidence of neglect, abuse, illness, or adjustment problems among infants who had been separated from their mothers for a time after birth. The point is that the importance of a few crucial hours immediately after birth has not yet been conclusively established.

Bonding—the formation of a close relationship between a person and a child through early and frequent association

FOCUS

King, the Guard Duck

A number of years ago I raised Labrador retrievers for hunting and field trial work. Part of the training procedure was to teach the dogs to retrieve live birds. I was able to find two white ducks, newly hatched, at a nearby farm. Apparently, the ducks thought I was their mother because they developed a very special attachment to me. The male, who we named King, would follow me around the yard of our camp. He became very protective of me and would attack any person who tried to come into the yard. If someone tried to come too close to me when I was swimming, King would dive underwater, swim to the outsider, and bite the person's legs and toes. King became the terror of the neighborhood. Even the Labrador retrievers were afraid of him. So King lived in style, king of our castle, until he died.   (From the author's experience)

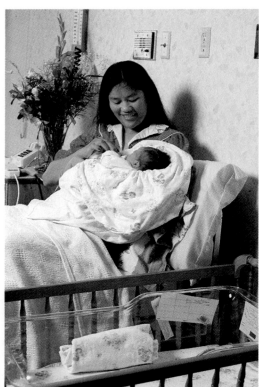

Emotional bonds between mother and infant are strengthened during the first hours of life.

It is evident, however, that there must be a powerful genetic predisposition in the child that encourages the formation of a relationship. However, no emotional bond ties the infant to its mother immediately at birth. Infants taken from their mother can form a bond with another person. However, Schaffer (1984) pointed out that the infant has certain biological biases and tendencies that facilitate the development of a bond with someone.

John Bowlby (1969) shed a great deal of light on the subject in his discussion of **attachment theory**. Infants are not born with attachment to anyone: mother, father, or others. However, since the infant's survival depends upon a loving care giver, the infant needs to develop attachments. Bowlby suggested that during the first six months, infants' attachments are quite broad. Infants become attached to people in general, so they seem to have no particular preference who cares for them. However, from six months on, attachments become more specific. The child may develop multiple attachments, but these are with individuals—the mother, father, a baby-sitter—so that the child is upset when left with an unfamiliar care giver.

Attachment theory—the description of the process by which infants develop close emotional dependence on one or more adult care givers

Hinde: Sensitive Periods of Development

Ethologist Robert Hinde (1983), professor of psychology at Cambridge University, England, prefers the term **sensitive period** to "critical period" in reference to certain times of life when the organism is more affected by particular kinds of experiences. The term *sensitive period* seems broader and is a more flexible concept than the narrow concept of critical period. With human children, there seem to be particularly sensitive periods for development of language, emotional attachments, or social relationships (Bornstein, 1987). When deficits occur during these sensitive periods, the question remains whether they can be made up during subsequent periods of development. Much depends on the extent of the early deprivation and the degree to which later environmental influences meet important needs (Werner & Smith, 1982).

Sensitive period—a period during which a given effect can be produced more readily than at other times

Evaluation of Ethological Theories

Ethological theories have emphasized the role of evolution and biology in human development and behavior, an emphasis that deserves serious attention. Although ethological emphasis on critical periods of development is too rigid and narrow, the principle of sensitive periods of development is a helpful one. Even then, the theories overlook the importance of positive environmental influences in overcoming the deficits of early deprivation. Biology has a marked influence on behavior, but it is not destiny. People are more than a combination of genes and chromosomes; they are developing human beings, influenced by a wide variety of environmental experiences over many years.

AN ECLECTIC THEORETICAL ORIENTATION

The point of view of this book is that no one theory completely explains human developmental processes or behavior. Taken together, the theories represent a collage of ideas that are closer to the whole truth than any one theory alone. For this reason, the book presents an *eclectic* theoretical orientation. This means that no one point of view has a monopoly on the truth, and that each theory has contributed an element of understanding to the total, complex process of human development over the life span.

SUMMARY

1. The scientific method involves formulating a problem, developing a hypothesis, testing it, and drawing conclusions that are stated in the form of a theory. A theory organizes the data, ideas, and hypotheses and states them in coherent, interrelated, general propositions, principles, or laws.

2. Freud's psychoanalytical theory emphasizes the importance of early childhood experiences and unconscious motivations in influencing behavior. Freud thought that sexual urges and aggressive instincts and drives were the primary determinants of behavior, or that people operated according to the pleasure principle.

3. Freud said that the basic structure of the personality consists of the id, ego, and superego, and that the ego strives to minimize the conflict within by keeping the instinctual urges (the id) and societal prohibitions (the superego) in balance.

4. According to Freud, one of the ways people relieve anxiety and conflict is by employing defense mechanisms: repression, regression, sublimation, displacement, reaction formation, denial, and rationalization.

5. According to Freud's psychosexual theory, the center of sensual sensitivity shifts from one part of the body to another as development proceeds through the following series of stages: oral stage (to age 1); anal stage (ages 2, 3); phallic stage (ages 4, 5); latency stage (age 6 to puberty); and genital stage (puberty on).

6. Erikson thought that Freud placed too much emphasis on the sexual basis for behavior and that his view of human nature was too cynical. Erikson divided human development into eight stages and said that the individual has a psychosocial task to master during each stage.

7. The eight stages, according to Erikson, are trust vs. distrust (0–1 year); autonomy vs. shame and doubt (1–2 years); initiative vs. guilt (3–5 years); industry vs. inferiority (6–11 years); identity vs. role confusion (12–19 years); intimacy vs. isolation (young adulthood: 20s and 30s); generativity vs. stagnation (middle adulthood: 40s and 50s); and integrity vs. despair (late adulthood: 60 and over).

8. Freud's psychoanalytical theory is an influential one. His emphases on unconscious motivations and defense mechanisms, as well as on environmental influences, and his treatment methods have made a real contribution to psychological theory and practice. Some feel his psychosexual theory of development is limited in scope, with overemphasis on sexual motivations and aggressive instincts as the basis of behavior. He has also done a disservice to women by blaming the survivors—the female victims themselves—for incest.

9. Erikson's theory is much broader than Freud's and encompasses the entire life span, with emphasis on a greater variety of motivational and environmental factors.

10. Behaviorism emphasizes the role of environmental influences in molding behavior. Behavior becomes the sum total of learned or conditioned responses to stimuli, a view that is somewhat mechanistic.

11. According to behaviorists, learning takes place through conditioning. There are two types of conditioning: classical conditioning, which is learning through association, and operant conditioning, which is learning from the consequences of behavior.

12. Social learning theory says that children learn by observing the behavior of others and by modeling their behavior after them.

13. Learning theorists have contributed much to the understanding of human development by emphasizing the role of environmental influences in shaping behavior. However, learning theories have been criticized for being too mechanistic, and for neglecting the role of biology and maturation in development.

14. Humanism takes a very positive view of human nature and says that people are free to use their superior abilities to make intelligent choices and to realize their full potential as self-actualized persons.

15. Buhler said that the real goal of humans is fulfillment through accomplishment.

16. Maslow said that human behavior can be explained as motivation to satisfy needs, which can be classified into five categories: physiological needs, safety needs, love and belongingness needs, esteem needs, and self-actualization needs. Self-actualization is the highest need and the culmination of life.

17. Carl Rogers reflected the humanistic philosophy that if people are given freedom to grow and emotional support (which he called unconditional positive regard), they can develop into fully functioning human beings.

18. Humanists have taught people to believe in themselves and in human nature, but are sometimes criticized for having a too optimistic view of human nature.

19. Cognition is the act or process of knowing. The Piagetian approach to cognitive development emphasizes the qualitative changes in the way people think as they develop.

20. Piaget divided the process of cognitive development into four stages: sensorimotor stage (birth to 2 years), preoperational stage (2 to 7 years), concrete operational stage (7 to 11 years), and formal operational stage (11 years and up).

21. The information-processing approach to cognition emphasizes the progressive steps, actions, and operations that take place when a person receives, perceives, remembers, thinks about, and utilizes information.

22. The cognitive theorists have made a real contribution by focusing attention on mental processes and their role in behavior. Piaget has been criticized for stressing biological maturation and minimizing the importance of environmental influences. Both Piagetian and information-processing approaches emphasize mental processes at a conscious level, ignoring any unconscious, psychodynamic causes of behavior.

23. Ethology emphasizes that behavior is a product of evolution and is biologically determined. Imprinting, bonding, and attachment theory are examples of this emphasis. Ethologist Robert Hinde prefers the term *sensitive period*, referring to certain times of life when the organism is more affected by particular kinds of experiences.

24. This book presents an eclectic theoretical orientation.

KEY TERMS

Accommodation   *p. 38*
Adaptation   *p. 37*
Anal stage   *p. 28*
Assimilation   *p. 38*
Attachment theory   *p. 41*
Autonomy vs. shame and doubt   *p. 29*
Behaviorism   *p. 31*
Bonding   *p. 40*
Classical conditioning   *p. 31*
Client-centered therapy   *p. 36*
Cognition   *p. 37*
Concrete operational stage   *p. 38*
Conditional positive regard   *p. 36*
Conditioning   *p. 31*
Defense mechanisms   *p. 27*
Denial   *p. 28*
Displacement   *p. 28*
Ego   *p. 27*
Electra complex   *p. 28*
Equilibrium   *p. 38*
Ethology   *p. 39*
Fixated   *p. 28*
Formal operational stage   *p. 38*
Free association   *p. 26*
Generativity vs. stagnation   *p. 29*
Genital stage   *p. 28*
Holistic view   *p. 34*
Humanistic theory   *p. 34*
Id   *p. 27*

Identity vs. role confusion   *p. 29*
Imprinting   *p. 40*
Industry vs. inferiority   *p. 29*
Information-processing approach   *p. 38*
Initiative vs. guilt   *p. 29*
Integrity vs. despair   *p. 29*
Intimacy vs. isolation   *p. 29*
Latency stage   *p. 28*
Mechanistic or deterministic   *p. 31*
Modeling   *p. 33*
Oedipal complex   *p. 28*
Operant conditioning   *p. 32*
Oral stage   *p. 28*
Phallic stage   *p. 28*
Pleasure principle   *p. 26*
Positive reinforcement   *p. 32*
Preoperational stage   *p. 38*
Psychoanalytical theory   *p. 26*
Psychosexual theory   *p. 28*
Psychosocial theory   *p. 29*
Rationalization   *p. 28*
Reaction formation   *p. 28*
Regression   *p. 28*
Repression   *p. 28*
Schema   *p. 37*
Self-actualization   *p. 34*
Sensitive period   *p. 41*
Sensorimotor stage   *p. 38*
Social learning theory   *p. 33*

Sublimation *p. 28*
Superego *p. 27*
Theory *p. 26*
Trust vs. distrust *p. 29*

Unconditional positive regard *p. 36*
Vicarious punishment *p. 33*
Vicarious reinforcement *p. 33*

DISCUSSION QUESTIONS

1. Give examples of human behavior that support Freud's view of human nature and motivations. Give examples that do not support Freud's view of human nature and motivations.
2. What do you think of Freud's theory of psychosexual development? Which points do you agree with? Which do you disagree with? Give examples.
3. If you have children of your own, or if you teach children or care for them, give examples of their behavior that support Erikson's descriptions of one or more stages of psychosocial development.
4. Describe and give examples of learning through:
   a. Classical conditioning
   b. Operant conditioning
   c. Modeling
   d. Vicarious reinforcement
5. Do you agree or disagree with Buhler that the real goal of humans is fulfillment that is attained through accomplishment? Explain your views.

6. Is it possible to find self-actualization without first having the needs for love and belonging and esteem met? Explain.
7. According to humanistic theory, if children are given freedom and emotional support, they will make right choices and develop into fully functioning people. According to this view, do children need parental guidance? Why or why not? What are your views?
8. Compare formal operational thinking with the scientific methods of discovering truth.
9. Do you believe that bonding between a mother and her baby shortly after birth is a prerequisite for a satisfying parent–child relationship later in life? Explain.
10. Give examples of sensitive periods for optimum development of particular characteristics, skills, habits, or relationships in the lives of children. Describe.

SUGGESTED READINGS

Bandura, A. (1986). *Social foundations of thought and action*. Englewood Cliffs, NJ: Prentice-Hall. Bandura's social learning view of development.

Erikson, E. H. (1980). *Identity and the life cycle*. New York: W. W. Norton. Erikson's basic views on identity development.

Flavell, J. H. (1985). *Cognitive development* (2nd ed.). Englewood Cliffs, NJ: Prentice-Hall. A helpful summary.

Ginsburg, H., & Opper, S. (1979). *Piaget's theory of intellectual development* (2nd ed.). Englewood Cliffs, NJ: Prentice-Hall. Outline of Piaget's research on infancy through adolescence.

Loevinger, J. (1987). *Paradigms of personality*.

New York: W. H. Freeman. General summary and comparison of major theories.

Miller, P. (1983). *Theories of developmental psychology*. New York: W. H. Feeman. Overview of major theories.

Salkind, N. J. (1985). *Theories of human development* (2nd ed.). New York: Wiley. General discussion of theories.

Schwartz, B., & Lacey, H. (1982). *Behaviorism, science, and human nature*. New York: Norton. Conditioning theories.

Thomas, R. M. (1985). *Comparing theories of child development* (2nd ed.). Belmont, CA: Wadsworth.

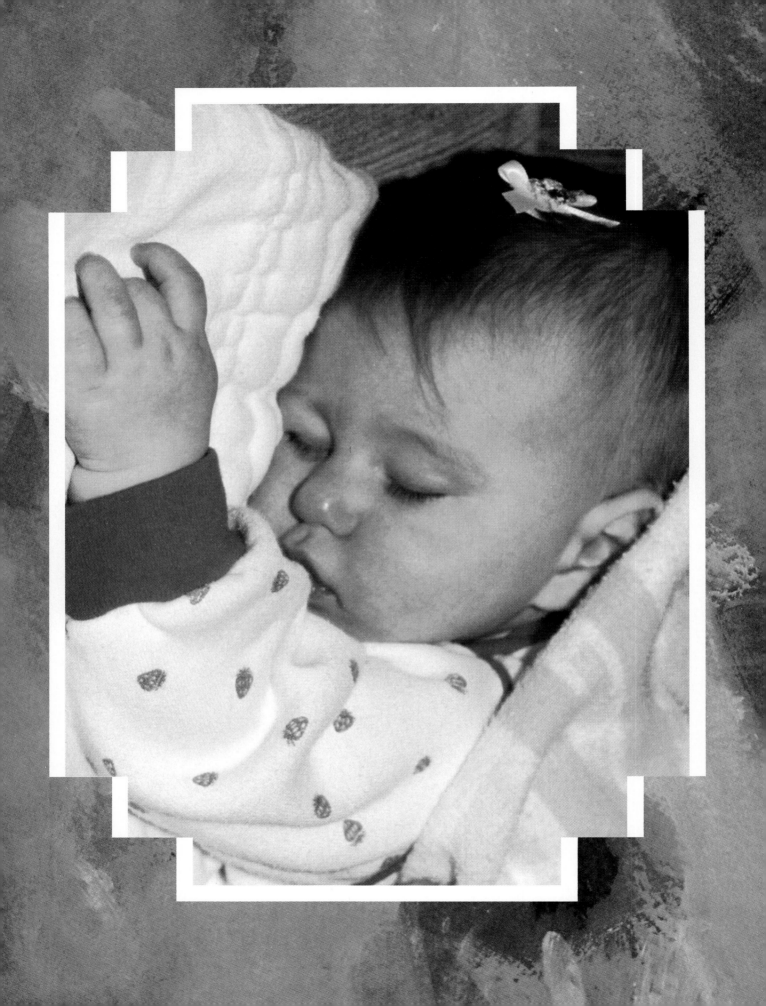

PART TWO

THE BEGINNINGS OF HUMAN LIFE

3

Heredity, Environmental Influences, and Prenatal Development

REPRODUCTION

Gametes—Sex cells

Two kinds of sex cells, or **gametes**, are involved in human reproduction: the male gamete, or sperm cell, and the female gamete, or ovum. Reproduction begins when a sperm cell fuses with an ovum to form a single new cell called a **zygote**. But let's begin at the beginning.

Zygote—A fertilized ovum

Spermatogenesis

Spermatogenesis—Process by which sperm are produced

Meiosis—Process of cell division by which gametes reproduce

Spermatogenesis refers to the process of sperm production that takes place in the *testes* of the male after he reaches puberty. Through a repeated cell division called **meiosis**, about 300 million sperm are produced daily and then stored in the *epididymis*, a system of ducts located at the back of the *testis*. Ordinarily, 200 million to 500 million sperm are released at each ejaculation. Some of these sperm are abnormal or dead, but for the sperm count to be normal, a minimum of 20 million healthy sperm per milliliter of *semen* need to be present (Jones, 1984). Sperm are microscopic in size—only about 1/500th of an inch long. About 10 to 20 ejaculations contain as many sperm as there are people on the planet. The sperm has a *head*, containing the cell nucleus that houses the chromosomes; a *midpiece*; and a *tail*. The midpiece produces chemical reactions that provide energy for the tail to lash back and forth, to propel the sperm along.

During intercourse, millions of sperm are ejaculated into the *vagina* during male orgasm, and begin a fantastic journey up the

Two hundred to 500 million sperm are released at each ejaculation.

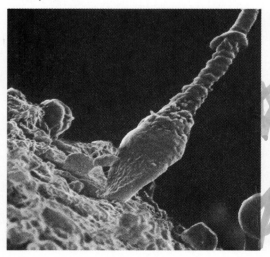

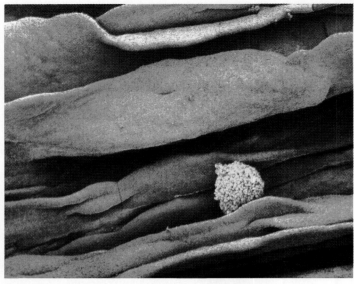

Ordinarily, at the time of ovulation, only one ovum ripens and is released during each menstrual cycle.

vagina, into the *uterus*, and up the *fallopian tubes*. When fertilization occurs, only a single sperm gains entrance to each available ovum.

Oogenesis

Oogenesis is the process by which female gametes, or egg cells called **ova**, are ripened in the *ovaries*. All of the egg cells that will ever be in the ovaries are present at birth, though undeveloped. Beginning at puberty, ordinarily only one ovum ripens and is released each 28 days or so (depending on the length of the menstrual cycle).

Oogenesis—Process by which ova mature

Ova—Female egg cells

The ovum is the largest cell of the body, about 1/200th of an inch in diameter, large enough to be visible. In this cell, a clear thin shell encloses a liquid composed of hundreds of fat droplets and proteins in which a nucleus containing the chromosomes is found.

Conception

After the ovum is released (a process called **ovulation**), fingerlike projections of the fallopian tube sweep the egg into it. Inside the tube, hairlike projections called *cilia* propel the ovum toward the uterus. The journey from the ovary to the uterus usually takes about 3 to 4 days, but fertilization must take place within 48 hours after ovulation. **Fertilization**, or **conception**, normally takes place in the third of the fallopian tube nearest the ovary. Eventually, a few sperm reach the egg, but a sperm cannot penetrate the egg's

Ovulation—Process by which the mature ovum separates from the ovarian wall and is released from the ovary

Fertilization, or **conception**—Union of sperm and ovum

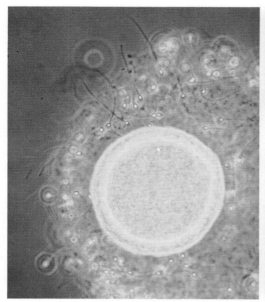

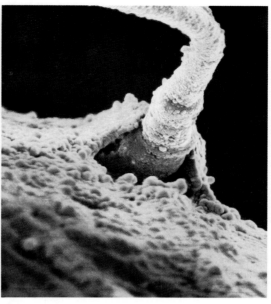

Millions of sperm attempt to fertilize the ovum, but only one will be able to penetrate the wall.

This sperm is penetrating the ovum.

outer wall without the help of chemical *enzymes* released from the head of the sperm. The enzymes dissolve the wall of the ovum, allowing one sperm to penetrate. Immediately, the outer layer of the egg hardens so the other sperm cannot enter (Schatten & Schatten, 1983). The tail of the sperm drops off and its nucleus unites with the nucleus of the ovum so that the first single new cell is formed (Grobstein, 1989; Silber, 1980).

PRENATAL DEVELOPMENT*

Periods of Development

Prenatal development takes place during three periods:

Germinal period

Embryonic period

Fetal period

1. the **germinal period**—from conception to implantation (attachment to the uterine wall)—about 14 days;
2. the **embryonic period**—from 2 weeks to 8 weeks after conception; and
3. the **fetal period**—from 8 weeks though the remainder of the pregnancy.

Figure 3.1 shows the early stages of the germinal period.

*Part of the material in this section is based on the author's book *Human Sexuality*, 1989. Used by permission of the publisher, Wm. C. Brown.

Germinal Period

The fertilized ovum is called a **zygote** (see Figure 3.2), which continues to be propelled through the fallopian tube by the cilia. About 30 hours after fertilization, the process of cell division begins. One cell divides into two, two into four, four into eight, and so on, the collection forming a **morula** (from the Latin word meaning "mulberry"). Every time the cells divide they become smaller, allowing the total mass, called the **blastula**, to pass through the fallopian tube. The result of the repeated cell dividing is the formation of a hollow inner portion containing fluid.

Three to 4 days after fertilization, the newly formed blastula enters the uterus and floats around for another 3 to 4 days before the inner layer, called the **blastocyst**, begins to attach itself to the inner lining of the uterus (the *endometrium*) in a process called **implantation**. The implanting blastocyst releases an enzyme that literally eats a hole in the soft, spongy tissue of the endometrium until it completely buries itself in the uterine wall. By about 10 days after the blastula enters the uterus, implantation of the blastocyst is complete.

Sometimes the blastocyst implants itself in the fallopian tube or elsewhere in the body cavity. Such a condition is called an **ectopic pregnancy**. An embryo that begins forming in this way, outside the uterus, usually dies or has to be removed surgically.

Morula—Zygote after a number of cell divisions have taken place; resembles a mulberry

Blastula—Zygote after the cells have divided into 100–150 cells

Blastocyst—Inner layer of the blastula that develops into the embryo

Implantation—Attachment of the blastocyst to the uterine wall

Ectopic pregnancy—Attachment and growth of the embryo in any location other than inside the uterus

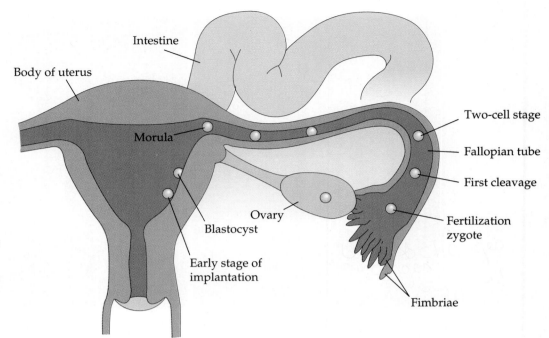

Intestine

Body of uterus

Morula

Two-cell stage

Fallopian tube

First cleavage

Ovary

Blastocyst

Fertilization
zygote

Early stage of
implantation

Fimbriae

FIGURE 3.1   From zygote to implanted blastocyst. From the time of ovulation, it takes about two weeks before the fertilized egg is completely implanted in the wall of the uterus. In the meantime, the ovum divides and subdivides, forming the *morula* and then the *blastocyst*.

Embryonic Period

As stated previously, *about 14 days after conception, the blastocyst implants itself in the uterine wall*. The embryonic period begins at the end of the second week. The embryo develops from a round layer of cells across the center of the blastocyst. At 18 days, the em-

bryo is about 0.0625 (¹⁄₁₆) of an inch long. During its early weeks, human embryos closely resemble those of other vertebrate animals, as Figure 3.3 illustrates. The embryo has a tail and traces of gills, both of which soon disappear. The head develops before the rest of the body. Eyes, nose, and ears are not yet visible at one month, but a backbone

Embryo—Growing baby from the end of the second week to the end of the eighth week after conception

FIGURE 3.2   Early development from zygote to blastocyst.

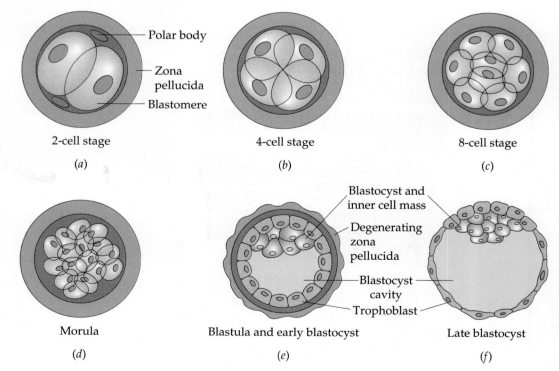

Polar body

Zona pellucida

Blastomere

2-cell stage

(a)

4-cell stage

(b)

8-cell stage

(c)

Blastocyst and inner cell mass

Degenerating zona pellucida

Blastocyst cavity

Trophoblast

Morula

(d)

Blastula and early blastocyst

(e)

Late blastocyst

(f)

The blastocyst facilitates its landing on the uterine wall with leglike structures composed of sugar molecules.

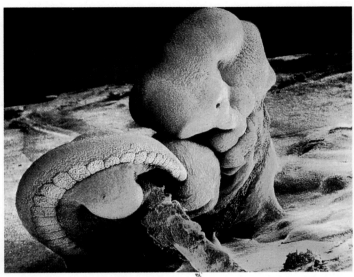

By 4½ weeks a rudimentary heart and an early eye have formed. The tail will disappear, leaving behind shrunk vertebrae which remain.

and vertebral canal have formed. Small buds that will develop into arms and legs appear. The heart forms and starts beating; other body systems begin to take shape.

FIGURE 3.3   Development of human embryo from the third week to the eighth week after conception. The embryo grows from about 1 inch in length after the third week to 1¼ inches at the end of the eighth week.

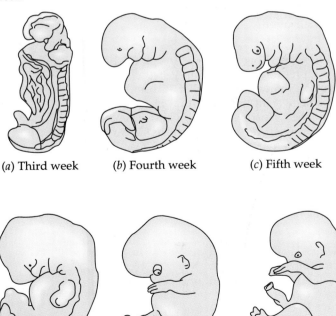

(a) Third week   (b) Fourth week   (c) Fifth week

(d) Sixth week   (e) Seventh week   (f) Eighth week

Fetal Period   *8 weeks*

By the end of the embryonic period (2 months), the **fetus** has developed the first bone structure and distinct limbs and digits that take on human form. Major blood vessels form, and internal organs continue to develop. By the end of the first **trimester** (one-third the length of pregnancy, or 12.7 weeks), the fetus is about 3 inches long; most major organs are present, a large head and face are well formed, and a heartbeat can be detected with a stethoscope. Figure 3.4 shows embryonic and fetal sizes from 2 to 15 weeks following conception.

By the end of the fourth or fifth month, the mother can usually feel fetal movement. The skin of the fetus is covered with a fine hair, usually shed before birth. At the end of the fifth month, the fetus weighs about 1 pound and is about 12 inches long. It sleeps and wakes, sucks, and moves its position. At the end of the sixth month, eyes, eyelids, and eyelashes form. The fetus's eyes are light sensitive, and he or she can hear uterine sounds.

The head and body of the fetus become more proportionate during the third trimester. Fat layers form under the skin. By the end of the eighth month, the fetus weighs about 5 pounds and is about 18 inches long. By the end of the ninth month, the nails have grown to the ends of the fingers and toes. The skin becomes smoother and is covered with a protective waxy substance called *vernix caseosa*. The baby is ready for delivery (Tortora & Anagnostakos, 1981).

Fetus—Growing baby from the beginning of the third month of development to birth

Trimester—One-third of the gestation period, or about 12.7 weeks

before 37 weeks of age is considered premature to be 28-30 weeks for lungs tested

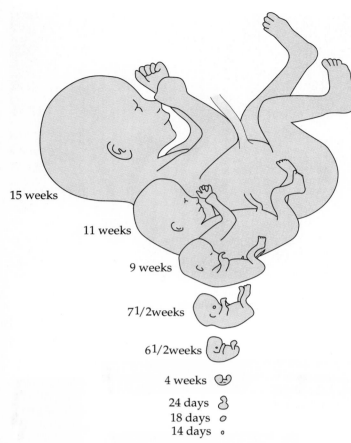

15 weeks

11 weeks

9 weeks

7 1/2 weeks

6 1/2 weeks

4 weeks

24 days
18 days
14 days

FIGURE 3.4 Embryonic and fetal development from 2 to 15 weeks following conception.

PRENATAL CARE

Medical and Health Care

Ordinarily the fetus is well protected in its uterine environment, but as soon as a woman suspects she is pregnant, she needs to receive good prenatal care. Time is of the essence because the first 3 months of fetal development are crucial to the optimum health of the child. Initial prenatal visits include a complete physical examination. Because the prospective father is involved and concerned as well, it is helpful for him to accompany his partner on prenatal visits. The examiner will take a complete medical history, perform various tests, and make recommendations regarding health care during pregnancy. Sexual relations, minor complications of pregnancy, and danger signs to

watch for in avoiding major complications will be discussed to allay the couple's fear and anxieties (Rice, 1989).

Minor Side Effects

No pregnancy is without some discomfort. Expectant mothers may experience one or several of the following to varying degrees: *nausea (morning sickness), heartburn, flatus (gas), hemorrhoids, constipation, shortness of breath, backache, leg cramps, uterine contractions, insomnia, minor vaginal discharge,* and *varicose veins.* The care giver, or examiner, will suggest the best ways in which each woman can minimize her discomforts (Rice, 1989).

breast changes
changes in
energy level

Major Complications of Pregnancy

Major complications of pregnancy arise infrequently; however, when they do, they more seriously threaten the health and life of the woman and the developing embryo or fetus than do the usual minor discomforts of pregnancy.

PERNICIOUS VOMITING.   This is prolonged and persistent vomiting, which may dehydrate the woman and rob her of adequate nutrients for proper fetal growth. One woman in several hundred suffers from vomiting to the extent that she requires hospitalization.

TOXEMIA.   This is characterized by high blood pressure; waterlogging of the tissues (edema), indicated by swollen face and limbs or rapid weight gain; albumin in the urine; headaches; blurring of vision; and eclampsia (convulsions). If not treated, toxemia can be fatal to mother and embryo or fetus. Most commonly it is a disease of neglect because proper prenatal care is lacking. Toxemia during pregnancy ranks as one of three chief cause of maternal mortality (Guttmacher, 1983).

THREATENED ABORTION.   The first symptoms are usually vaginal bleeding. Studies reveal that about one in six pregnancies is spontaneously aborted before the fetus is of sufficient size to survive. Most spontaneous abortions occur early in pregnancy. Three out of four happen before the 12th week, and only one in four occurs between 12 and 28 weeks (Guttmacher, 1983).

LIVING ISSUES

Abortion and the Question of Viability

On January 22, 1973, the United States Supreme Court ruled that a state could not inhibit or restrict a woman's right to obtain an abortion during the first trimester of pregnancy (12.7 weeks) and that the decision to have an abortion was the woman's own in consultation with her doctor (*Roe v. Wade*, 1973). In a 5–4 decision announced on July 3, 1989, the court overthrew the trimester provisions of *Roe v. Wade*, and said that a doctor, before aborting a fetus believed to be at least 20 weeks gestation, will determine if the fetus is **viable** and perform tests that establish the fetus's gestational age, weight, and lung maturity (*Webster v. Reproductive Health Services*, 1988). The majority opinion in this decision said the statement was interpreted to mean that only those tests that are necessary to determine viability be performed.

Several comments need to be made.

1. Determination of viability through tests is expensive and, because of their costs, prevent women who cannot afford them from having an abortion.

2. The tests sometimes impose health risks for both the pregnant woman and the fetus.
3. The tests are sometimes unreliable and inaccurate.
4. At 20 weeks of age, no fetus is viable or can be made viable by any foreseeable new scientific techniques (Rosoff, 1989).
5. Tests of lung maturity cannot provide the necessary information until the fetus is at least 28–30 weeks gestation. Any tests before these ages are imprecise ("The Court Edges," 1989).
6. Using viability tests as a basis for decision eliminates the woman's right to choose whether she will have an abortion or not.

For these reasons, many thoughtful persons are opposed to viability tests as one determinant of whether a woman can have an abortion.

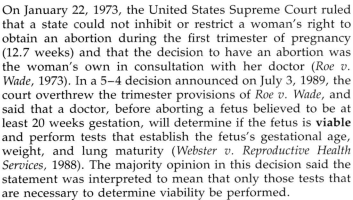

PLACENTA PRAEVIA. *Placenta praevia* refers to the premature separation of the placenta from the uterine wall, usually because the placenta grows partially or entirely over the cervical opening. One in 200 pregnant women suffers from this problem, which usually occurs in the third trimester. If they are given proper treatment, 80% to 85% of the babies will survive. About 60% are delivered by cesarean section.

TUBAL PREGNANCY. Tubal pregnancy occurs when the fertilized ovum attaches itself to the wall of the fallopian tube and grows there rather than within the uterus. Sometimes the pregnancy, termed *ectopic*, is situated in the ovary, abdomen, or cervix. Such pregnancies have to be terminated by surgery. Surveys indicate that the number of ectopic pregnancies has been climbing steadily. Possible causes may be the postponement of childbearing, during which time the fallopian tubes age; previous abortion; pelvic inflammatory disease (PID); sexually transmitted diseases (STDs); frequent douching with commercial preparations; and previous surgery. Any condition that affects the fallopian tubes can impede transport of the fertilized ovum, thus contributing to an ectopic preg-

nancy. ("Increasing Rates," 1984, p. 14). Despite the increase in ectopic pregnancies, which must always be terminated, fetal mortality rates have fallen because women are getting prompter and better treatment (Rice, 1989).

RH INCOMPATIBILITY. This involves an expectant mother with Rh negative blood who carries a fetus with Rh positive blood (Rice, 1989).

INFERTILITY

Causes

About 15% of all couples are **infertile** and would not be able to have children without medical help (Porter & Christopher, 1984). About half of those with problems are able to conceive with medical help (Collins, Wrixon, James, & Wilson, 1983).

About 20% of infertility cases involve both partners. Both are "subfertile": they have too frequent or too infrequent intercourse; they have intercourse only during those times of the month when the woman is least likely to get pregnant; they use Vaseline or some other vaginal lubricant that injures sperm

Infertile—Unable to conceive or to effect pregnancy

cells or acts as a barrier preventing the sperm from entering the *cervix*; or they are too old or in poor health.

About 40% of infertility cases involve the man. To impregnate a woman a man must meet four biological requirements. He must

1. produce healthy live sperm in sufficient numbers;
2. secrete seminal fluid in proper amounts and with the right composition to transport sperm;
3. have an unobstructed throughway from the testile to the end of the penis, allowing the sperm to pass; and
4. be able to achieve and sustain an erection in order to ejaculate sperm within the vagina.

A number of physical and psychological factors may cause male infertility (Boyarsky & Boyarsky, 1983; Crocket & Cosentino, 1984; Witkin & Toth, 1983).

About 40 percent of infertility cases involve the woman. To be capable of pregnancy, a woman also must meet several basic biological requirements. She needs to be ovulating, the passage through the fallopian tubes needs to be clear, and the cervical mucus must allow passage of the sperm (Ansbacher & Adler, 1988). Several additional factors may affect female fertility: Abnormalities of the uterus sometimes prevent conception or full-term pregnancy (Malinak & Wheeler, 1985); the climate of the vagina may be too acid, thus immobilizing the sperm; and the age of the mother may also be a factor (Bongaarts, 1982). Fertility decreases gradually after age 35 and ceases completely after menopause.

Alternate Means of Conception

ARTIFICIAL INSEMINATION.   If other medical treatments for infertility don't succeed, several techniques may permit couples to have children (Cushner, 1986). One technique is **artificial insemination**. In this procedure, the sperm are injected into the woman's vagina or uterus for the purpose of inducing pregnancy. If the husband's sperm are used, the process is called **homologous insemination**, or **AIH** (artificial insemination husband). If the husband's sperm count is low, the sperm may be collected, frozen, and stored until a sufficient quantity is available, then thawed and injected. Generally, AIH is effective in only 5% of the cases, because the

sperm was incapable of effecting pregnancy in the first place (Pierson & D'Antonio, 1974). Using sperm from a donor is called **heterologous insemination**, or **AID** (artificial insemination donor) (Tagatz, Gibson, Schiller, & Nagel, 1980).

SURROGATE MOTHER.   Sometimes a woman not able to bear a child still wants to have one by her partner, so together they find a consenting woman who acts as a **surrogate mother**. The surrogate mother agrees to be inseminated with the semen of the male member of the couple, to carry the fetus to term, and then to give the child (and all rights to it) to the couple. When 70 women were questioned regarding their motives for serving as surrogate mothers, they gave the following reasons: money, compassion for the childless couple and desire to help them, or enjoyment of pregnancy (Sobel, 1981). Half the surrogate mothers were married and already had children of their own. There are many unsettled legal questions relating to the rights to the child and to the legitimacy of surrogate agreements.

IN VITRO FERTILIZATION.   This is the procedure whereby a "test tube baby" is conceived. It is used when the fallopian tubes are blocked so the sperm never reaches the ovum. The egg is removed from the mother, fertilized in the laboratory with the partner's sperm, grown for several days until the uterus is hormonally ready, then implanted in the uterine wall (Zimmerman, 1982). The procedure is opposed by those who feel it is immoral and tampering with nature.

Artificial insemination—Injection of sperm cells into the vagina or uterus for the purpose of inducing pregnancy

Homologous insemination (AIH)—Artificial insemination with the husband's sperm

Heterologous insemination (AID)—Artificial insemination using the sperm from a donor

Surrogate mother—Woman whose services are obtained by a couple. She agrees to be inseminated with the man's sperm, to carry the resulting baby until birth, and then to give the baby and all rights to it to the couple

In vitro fertilization—Removal of the ovum from the mother and fertilizing it in the laboratory, then implanting the zygote within the uterine wall

In *in vitro* fertilization, scratching the surface of the ovum allows the sperm to penetrate more easily.

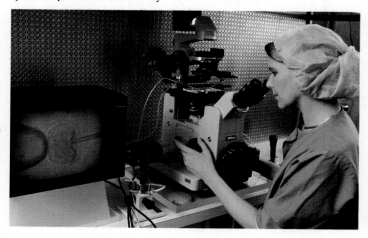

Gamete intra-fallopian transfer (GIFT)—Inserting sperm cells and an egg cell directly into the fallopian tube, where fertilization is expected to occur

GAMETE INTRAFALLOPIAN TRANSFER (GIFT).   This involves inserting a thin, plastic tube carrying the sperm and egg directly into the fallopian tube, where the gametes unite just as they would in normal conception. "GIFT is what nature really does, with a little help from us," says Dr. Ricardo Asch, professor of obstetrics and gynecology at the University of California at Irwin (Ubell, 1990). The success rate is 40%—double that of in vitro fertilization.

Embryo transplant—Insemination of a female with the sperm of an infertile woman's partner; the resulting zygote is transferred, about 5 days later, into the uterus of the mother-to-be, who carries the child during pregnancy

EMBRYO TRANSPLANT.   This procedure is even more controversial (Dunn, Ryan, & O'Brien, 1988). In this procedure, a volunteer female donor is artificially inseminated with the sperm of the infertile woman's partner. After about 5 days, the zygote is removed from the donor and transferred into the uterus of the mother-to-be, who carries the child during pregnancy. Embryos may even be frozen and stored prior to implantation in a uterus. At present, the procedure is experimental, costly, and has a low success rate.

FOCUS

Treatments for Infertility

Generally speaking, if couples are younger than 35 years of age, they should wait for a full year of attempting pregnancy before consulting a physician. This gives enough time for conception to take place if the couple are fertile. If they are older than 35, they should see a doctor after 6 months of unsuccessful attempts. Older couples should get help sooner because psychological and physical factors that work against conception grow stronger with time. For the younger couple, waiting for a reasonable period of time (1 year) improves the chances of fertility (Rice, 1990).

Genes are made up of numerous molecules called deoxyribonecleic acid or **DNA**. The DNA molecule looks like a double helix, or a spiral staircase, with a phosphate–sugar structure on the outside framework and with

DNA—Complex molecules in genes that form the basis for the genetic structure, deoxyribonucleic acid

HEREDITY

Chromosomes, Genes, and DNA

Chromosomes—Rodlike structures in each cell, occurring in pairs, that carry the hereditary material

Genes—The hereditary material of the chromosomes

Chromosomes are rodlike structures in the nucleus of each cell. The chromosomes carry the hereditary material called **genes**, which control physical characteristics that are inherited. The genes do this by directing the physical changes in the body throughout its development. Each body cell, except the sex cells, or gametes, contains 23 pairs of chromosomes, and each chromosome has between 20,000 and 100,000 genes. The gametes contain only half the number of chromosomes present in other body cells. Instead of 23 pairs, each sperm or ovum has 23 single chromosomes. *When the sperm and ovum unite, the 23 single chromosomes within the nucleus of each gamete combine in pairs with those in the other gamete to produce 46 chromosomes in the resulting zygote.* Figure 3.5 shows the process. After fertilization takes place and the one-celled zygote begins to divide and subdivide, the 46 chromosomes each split in half with each cell division, so that each daughter cell contains the same 23 pairs of chromosomes. This means that each new cell produced contains the same 23 pairs of chromosomes with their genes.

Body cells of men and women contain 23 pairs of chromosomes.

Man   Woman

At maturity, each sex cell has only 23 single chromosomes. Through meiosis, a member is taken randomly from each original pair of chromosomes.

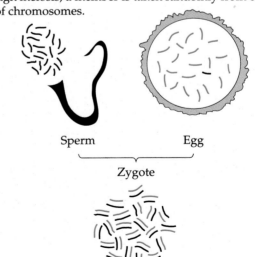

Sperm   Egg

Zygote

At fertilization, the chromosomes from each parent pair up so that the zygote contains 23 pairs of chromosomes—half from the mother and half from the father.

FIGURE 3.5   Hereditary composition of the zygote.

four *base* molecules (*adenine, thymine, guanine,* and *cystosine*) occurring in pairs that form the steps of the staircase on the inside. The bases are labeled A, T, G, and C, as shown in Figure 3.6. One strand of DNA may continue for thousands of base pairs, and the number of different strands that can be made is almost infinite. Each section of DNA is a separate gene, and the vertical sequence of the base pairs acts as a code to direct the cells as they reproduce and manufacture proteins that maintain life. Each cell of the body has the same DNA code and the same genes that direct growth. The particular code that we inherit from our parents directs our growth as humans rather than other creatures, and is responsible for all the physical characteristics we develop.

The Twenty-third Pair and Sex Determination

Each sperm cell and each ovum contains 23 chromosomes. Twenty-two of these are labeled **autosomes** and are responsible for most aspects of the individual's development. Figure 3.7 illustrates the twenty-third pair, the **sex chromosomes**, which determine whether the offspring will be male or female. As shown in Figure 3.8, the man produces two types of sperm: one type with an X chromosome, having a larger head and shorter tail; another type with a Y chromosome, having a smaller head and longer tail. The woman produces ova with only X chromosomes. If a sperm containing an X chromosome unites with the ovum (producing an XX combination), a girl is conceived. If a sperm containing a Y chromosome unites with the ovum (producing an XY combination), a boy is conceived. Because the Y-carrying sperm have a longer tail and a lighter head, they swim faster and may reach the egg cell sooner. For this reason, there is a conception ratio of 160 males to 100 females. However, the male zygote is more vulnerable, so the ratio is reduced to 120 males to 100 females by the time of implan-

Autosomes— Twenty-two pairs of chromosomes that are responsible for most aspects of the individual's development

Sex chromosomes— Twenty-third pair of chromosomes that determine the gender of the offspring

FIGURE 3.6   DNA molecule.

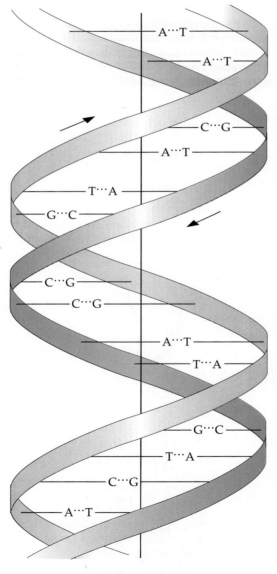

FIGURE 3.7   The twenty-third pair of chromosomes.

1	2	3	4	5	6
7	8	9	10	11	12
13	14	15	16	17	18
19	20	21	22	♀ XX	♂ XY

23

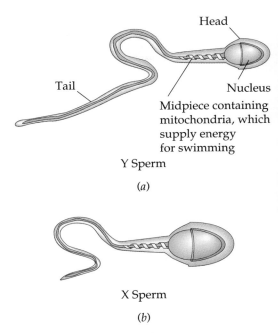

Head

Tail

Nucleus

Midpiece containing mitochondria, which supply energy for swimming

Y Sperm

(a)

X Sperm

(b)

FIGURE 3.8   Two types of sperm.

Identical twins are called monozygotic twins because they develop from one egg.

tation; to 110 males to 100 females by full term; and to 105 males to 100 females born live (Rice, 1989).

PARENTING ISSUES

Selecting the Sex of Your Child

Various techniques have been used to try to control the sex of the child that is conceived. Sperm carrying Y chromosomes are more fragile than X-carrying sperm, and all sperm are more viable in an alkaline environment. So if a male baby is desired, one theory suggests that everything possible be done to keep the Y-carrying sperm alive and healthy: use an alkaline douche; have intercourse two days or so after ovulation (so the sperm can reach the egg easily); use deep penetration during intercourse; and have the female orgasm precede male ejaculation (so the sperm are not squirted out during female orgasm). The opposite measures would be taken if a female baby is desired. Some researchers have found this total approach to sex selection reliable (Karp, 1980; Simcock, 1985).

A more promising technique is to separate the Y and X sperm and through artificial insemination to inject the type needed, depending on the sex desired (Glass & Ericsson, 1982).

Multiple Births

Twins may be of the same sex or of both sexes, depending on whether they start from one egg, as **monozygotic (identical) twins**, or from two eggs, as **dizygotic (fraternal) twins**. *Identical twins result when an ovum fertilized by one sperm divides during development to produce two embryos.* The embryos have the same heredity, are always of the same sex, and usually share a common *placenta*. If the two developing embryos do not completely separate, **Siamese twins** result. *Fraternal twins result when two ova are fertilized by two separate sperm.* They may be of the same sex or different sexes and will be as different in heredity as are any other siblings. They develop with separate placentas, as shown in the corresponding photo. Triplets, quadruplets, and so forth may be all identical (from one ova), all fraternal (from separately fertilized ova), or a combination. Two of three triplets may be identical, for example, with the third fraternal. In this case, two ova are fertilized by two sperm, and one of the resulting zygotes divides after fertilization to produce two embryos.

Simple Inheritance and Dominant–Recessive Inheritance

An Austrian monk named Gregor Mendel (1822–1884) first discovered the laws that govern inheritance. He experimented by crossing garden pea plants with one another, and noticed that various traits such as yellow or green color, wrinkled or smooth seeds, tall

Monozygotic (identical) twins—One-egg, or identical, twins

Dizygotic (fraternal) twins—Two-egg, or fraternal, twins

Siamese twins—Monozygotic twins where complete separation did not occur during development

or short height appeared or disappeared from one generation to the next.

The peas that Mendel used for his experiments came in two colors: yellow or green. When Mendel crossed purebred plants producing yellow peas with other purebreds containing yellow peas, he noticed that all the resulting offspring plants produced yellow peas. When he crossed two purebred plants with green peas, the result was always plants with green peas. However, when he crossed purebred plants producing yellow peas with those producing purebred green peas, all the offspring plants produced yellow peas. If he then bred these hybrids, 75 percent of the offspring had yellow peas and the remaining 25 percent had green peas. Mendel explained this result by formulating the **law of dominant inheritance**. The law says that when an organism inherits competing traits (such as green and yellow colors), only one trait will be expressed. The trait that is expressed is *dominant* over the other, which is recessive. The dominant trait is written with a capital letter, the *recessive* with a lowercase letter.

The diagrams in Figure 3.9 illustrate possible results when peas are crossed.

Let's see how **dominant genes** and **recessive genes** work. Genes that govern alternate expressions of a particular characteristic (such as skin color) are called **alleles**. An organism receives a pair of alleles for a given characteristic, one from each parent. When

Law of dominant inheritance

Dominant gene

Recessive gene

Alleles

Gregor Mendel discovered the laws that govern inheritance by crossing garden pea plants with one another.

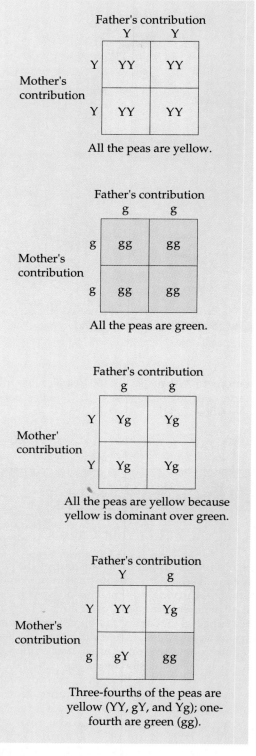

FIGURE 3.9   Mendalian inheritance in peas.

both alleles are the same, the organism is **homozygous** for the trait; when the alleles are different, the organism is **heterozygous** for the characteristic. When the alleles are

Skin color is an example of polygenetic inheritance since it is controlled by a number of genes.

Heterozygous

Homozygous

Phenotype

Genotype

heterozygous, the dominant allele is expressed. Thus, in Figure 3.9, YY or gg alleles are **homozygous**, and gY or Yg are heterozygous. Only when there is a pairing of recessive alleles (gg) can the recessive trait be expressed.

An observable trait (like seed color) is called a **phenotype**, while the underlying genetic pattern is called a **genotype**. Organisms may have identical phenotypes but different genotypes. For example, the plants that produce yellow peas (the phenotype) may have different genotypes (YY, Yg, or gY).

The same principle holds true in humans. Brown eyes, for example, are dominant over blue eyes. If we let B = brown eyes, and b = blue eyes, and pair a brown-eyed man with heterozygous alleles with a blue-eyed woman with homozygous alleles,

we get the possible results shown in Figure 3.10. In this case, half the offspring would have brown eyes (bB and bB) because B is always dominant over b, and half would have blue eyes (bb and bb) because two recessive genes would have to be paired to produce blue eyes.

Table 3.1 shows a variety of dominant and recessive human characteristics.

FIGURE 3.10   Inheritance for eye color.

		Father's contribution	
		B	b
Mother's contribution	b	bB	bb
	b	bB	bb

One-half the offspring have brown eyes (bB and bB); one-half have blue eyes (bb and bb).

TABLE 3.1 Dominant and Recessive Traits in Humans

Dominant	Recessive
Brown eyes	Blue or hazel eyes
Long eyelashes	Short eyelashes
Near- or farsightedness	Normal vision
Dark hair	Light or red hair
Curly hair	Straight hair
Cataract	Normal vision
Skin pigmentation	Albinism
Glaucoma	Normal eyes
Color vision	Color blindness
Free earlobes	Attached earlobes
Normal metabolism	Phenylketonuria
Broad lips	Thin lips
Scaly skin (Ichthyosis)	Normal skin
Polydactylism (extra fingers & toes)	Normal
Dwarfism (Achondroplasia)	Normal
Huntington's disease	Normal
Normal hearing	Deafness

Codominance

Sometimes one allele is not completely dominant over the other. This phenomenon is known as **incomplete dominance**, or **codominance**. An example is *sickle-cell anemia*, a condition common among blacks. In this condition, the red blood cells of a person are sickle- or crescent-shaped instead of circular, and they tend to clog the blood vessels, restricting blood circulation, causing tissue damage and even death. Also, the spleen tries to destroy the blood cells, causing anemia. Sickle-cell anemia occurs only in persons who carry homozygous genes for that trait. The result for these people is that both sickle-cell genes direct the body to manufacture the abnormal blood cells. Other people are heterozygous with respect to the sickle-cell trait, having one sickle-cell gene and one normal one. The result is that neither gene is dominant or recessive, so the person has a mixture of two types of blood cells: part normal and part sickle-cell. Such a person functions all right except at high altitudes, where oxygen is scarce. Interestingly, people with sickle-cells are protected against malaria because the malaria parasite apparently doesn't thrive in blood containing these cells.

Polygenic Inheritance

In many instances, traits do not result from a single gene pair, but from a combination of many gene pairs. For example, numerous genes or gene pairs are involved in body height, weight, and shape. When gene pairs interact, one gene pair may inhibit or allow the expression of the other gene pair. A system of interacting gene pairs is called a **polygenic system of inheritance**. Such systems produce a wide variety of phenotypes that may differ from those of either parent.

One example is skin color, which is the result of the action of a number of genes. A light-skinned person and a dark-skinned person usually have children with skin tone between their own because half the genes come from each parent. However, the child may also have a lighter or darker skin than either parent, with the child inheriting only the light- or dark-skin genes from the parents.

Many other characteristics, including personality traits such as intelligence, sociability, and temperament, are a result of polygenic inheritance. Even then, inheritance only predisposes us toward certain traits. We inherit a range of possibilities called the **reaction range**, which is the range of phenotypes for each genotype (Scarr, 1984). Envi-

ronmental influences may enhance or detract from the inherited possibilities.

Some genotypes seem to produce characteristics that persist regardless of environmental influences. A child who seems to have a predisposition toward superior intelligence, for example, may evidence this characteristic in spite of adverse environmental circumstances (Kagan, 1984). This tendency for a trait to persist is called **canalization**.

Sex-Linked Traits

Some defective, recessive genes are carried on only the twenty-third pair of chromosomes, the sex chromosomes, to produce what are called **sex-linked disorders**. One example is *hemophilia*, a disorder characterized by inability of the blood to clot. If a woman inherits a defective, recessive, hemophilic gene on the X chromosome she receives from her mother, and a second, normal, dominant gene on the X chromosome she receives from her father, she will not be a hemophiliac but will be a carrier (because she has one defective gene). However, if she has a son, and passes the defective, recessive gene on the X chromosome to him, there is no corresponding dominant, healthy X chromosome to counterbalance the defective gene, so the son inherits hemophilia. Figure 3.11 shows the possible combinations and results when a woman who is a carrier has children. *Color blindness, baldness,* some *allergies, Duchenne's*

FIGURE 3.11   Sex-linked inheritance.

		Father's contribution	
		X	Y
Mother's contribution	X.	X.X Girl (carrier)	X.Y Boy (hemophiliac)
	X	XX Girl (normal)	XY Boy (normal)

The odds for a male child being a hemophiliac are 50%; the odds for a female child being a carrier are 50%.
The odds for having a male child who is also a hemophiliac are 25%; the odds for having a female child who is also a carrier are 25%.

X. = defective chromosome.

Incomplete dominance, or codominance—When one paired allele is not completely dominant over the other

Polygenic system of inheritance—A number of interacting genes that produce a phenotype

Reaction range—Range of possible phenotypes given a particular genotype and environmental influences

Canalization—Tendency for inherited characteristics to persist along a certain path regardless of environmental conditions

Sex-linked disorders—Disorders carried only by the mother, through defective, recessive genes on the X chromosome

muscular dystrophy, and other diseases are examples of sex-linked traits that are inherited. A woman cannot inherit such a trait unless she received two defective genes, one from her mother who is a carrier, and one from her father who manifests the defect.

HEREDITARY DEFECTS

Causes of Birth Defects

The majority of babies coming into the world are healthy and normal. Occasionally, however, a child is born with a **congenital deformity**: a defect that is present at the time of birth. Currently, 1 in 16 infants is born with some sort of serious defect (National Foundation for the March of Dimes, 1977).

Birth defects result from three causes: (1) hereditary factors, (2) faulty environments that prevent the child from developing normally, and (3) birth injuries. Only 20% of birth defects are inherited. The other 80% are caused by a faulty environment, birth injuries, or a combination of causes. Let's concentrate here on defects that are inherited due to faulty genes.

Genetic Defects

Some defects are inherited via a single, dominant, defective gene. McKusick's catalogue of genetic diseases lists 1,172 dominant gene disorders, 618 recessive gene disorders, and 124 sex-linked disorders (McKusick, 1986). *Huntington's disease* is a common example of a dominant gene disorder. The disease causes a gradual deterioration of the nervous system, physical weakness, emotional disturbance, mental retardation, and eventually, death. The symptoms do not appear until after 30 years of age (Pines, 1984).

Large numbers of diseases are caused by pairs of recessive genes. These include *cystic fibrosis, phenylketonuria (PKU), Tay-Sachs disease*, and many others (Welsh, Pennington, Ozonoff, Rouse, & McCabe, 1990). Babies born with cystic fibrosis lack an enzyme. This lack causes mucous obstructions in the body, especially in the lungs and digestive organs. Treatments have improved, but death is still inevitable. PKU is caused by an excess of *phenylalanine*, an amino acid, which causes mental retardation and neurological disturbances. The disease is treatable with diet regulation. Tay-Sach's disease is caused by an enzyme deficiency. It is characterized by progressive retardation of development, paral-

ysis, dementia, blindness, and death by age 3 or 4. It is most common in families of Eastern European Jewish origin (Berkow, 1987). Carriers of both cystic fibrosis and Tay-Sachs disease can be detected through genetic counseling. All three diseases can usually be detected through prenatal examinations.

A large number of defects have multiple factors as causes. The defects do not become apparent until a faulty prenatal or postnatal environment triggers their onset. *Cleft palate* or *cleft lip* is one example. It may be related to hereditary factors, to the position of the embryo in the uterus, to the blood supply, or to some drugs taken during pregnancy. *Spina bifada* is another example, characterized by incomplete closure of the lower spine. Both hereditary defects and environmental factors play a causative role. Recent data points to a vitamin deficiency as a contributing factor (Berkow, 1987).

Chromosomal Abnormalities

Chromosomal abnormalities are of two types: sex chromosomal abnormalities and autosomal chromosomal abnormalities (Money, 1968). Five of the most common sex-linked chromosomal abnormalities are summarized in Table 3.2 (Berch & Bender, 1987). These abnormalities arise during meiosis. When an ova or sperm are formed, the 46 chromosomes divide unevenly, producing a gamete that has too few or too many chromosomes (Moore, 1982).

Sometimes problems result from abnormalities in the autosomes rather than the sex chromosomes. One of the most common of these is *Down's syndrome.* Down's children have an extra chromosome: 47 instead of 46. The overall incidence is about 1:700 live births, but the rate rises to about 1:40 live births in mothers over age 40 (Adams, Oakley, & Marks, 1982). There is also a greater risk when the father is over age 45. Characteristics include a flattened skull; folds of skin over the eyes; a flattened bridge of the nose; protruding tongue; short, broad hands and fingers; and short stature. Congenital heart disease is common. Both physical and mental development are retarded; mean IQ is about 50. Most individuals without a major heart disease survive to adulthood.

Genetic Counseling

Couples who have inherited disabilities themselves, or who have a family history of some types of disability, should get genetic counseling to dis-

---

Congenital deformity—Defect present at birth, which may be the result of hereditary factors, conditions during pregnancy, or damage occurring at the time of birth

TABLE 3.2 Common Sex-Linked Chromosomal Abnormalities

Name	Chromosome Combination	Characteristics	Incidence
None	XYY	Tall stature; subnormal intelligence; severe acne; impulsive and aggressive behavior, which may stem from psychosocial problems	1 in 1,000 males
Kleinfelter's Syndrome	XXY	Feminine appearance; small penis and testicles; infertile; low sexual drive; decreased body hair; prominent breasts; tendency toward mental impairment	1 in 1,000 males
Fragile X	Usually XY	X chromosome is not influential. Some persons normal, others are retarded. Males may have enlarged testicles.	1 in 1,000 males; 1 in 5,000 females
Turner's Syndrome	XO	Lack of functioning ovaries; incompletely developed internal and external sex organs; loose skin; webbed neck; widely spaced nipples; short stature; deafness and mental deficiency are common (McCauley, Kay, Ito, & Treder, 1987).	1 in 10,000 females
None	XXX	Characteristics vary; some women are normal, fertile; others are sterile, suffer mental retardation	1 in 1,000 females

cover the possibility of passing on the defect to a child yet to be conceived. Once the couple know the odds of passing on a defect, they are faced with making a decision regarding whether or not to risk having children. After pregnancy occurs, there are various procedures for discovering defects.

Amniocentesis—Removal of cells from the amniotic fluid to test for abnormalities

AMNIOCENTESIS. **Amniocentesis** can be performed between the 15th and 16th weeks of gestation. It involves inserting a hollow needle into the abdomen to obtain a sample of *amniotic fluid* containing fetal cells. The cells are cultured for genetic and chemical

studies (Hook, Cross, & Schreinemachers, 1983). One disadvantage of this procedure is that it can be performed only in the second trimester of pregnancy, after the fetus is fairly well developed. Another disadvantage is it results in fetal loss in 1 in 200 amniocenteses. Some of these fetuses are normal and would have survived if the test had not been done.

SONOGRAM. A **sonogram** uses high-frequency sound waves to obtain a visual image of the fetus's body structure, to see if growth is normal or if there are any malformations (Hill, Breckle, & Gehrking, 1983). It is often used to confirm or deny the presence of fetal defects indicated by an elevation of a-Fetoprotein in the amniotic fluid (Berkow, 1987).

Sonogram—Visual image of fetus, produced from sound waves, used to detect fetal abnormalities

FETOSCOPE. A **fetoscope** is passed through a narrow tube that is inserted through the abdomen into the uterus to observe the fetus and placenta directly.

Fetoscope

CHORIONIC VILLI SAMPLING (CVS). The **chorionic villi** are threadlike protrusions from the membrane enclosing the fetus. The test involves inserting a thin catheter through the vagina and cervix into the uterus, from which a small sample of the chorionic villi is removed for analysis (Cadkin, Ginsberg, Pergament, & Verlinski, 1984). The real advantage of the procedure is that it can be performed in the eighth week of pregnancy.

Chorionic villi sampling (CVS)—Removal of a sample of chorionic villi from the membrane enclosing the fetus, to be analyzed for possible birth defects

Down's Syndrome is the most common chromosomal disorder resulting in physical and mental retardation.

PARENTING ISSUES

The Process of Decision Making in Cases of Possible Defects

Genetic counseling provides information with which couples can make informed decisions in cases of possible defects. Couples can find out before pregnancy the risk of having a baby with a genetic defect, so they can decide whether to take the risk of having a child at all. After pregnancy has occurred, couples can find out if a defect is present, and—if it is—make a decision regarding the course of action to take. The flow chart shown in Figure 3.12 traces the decision-making process involved.

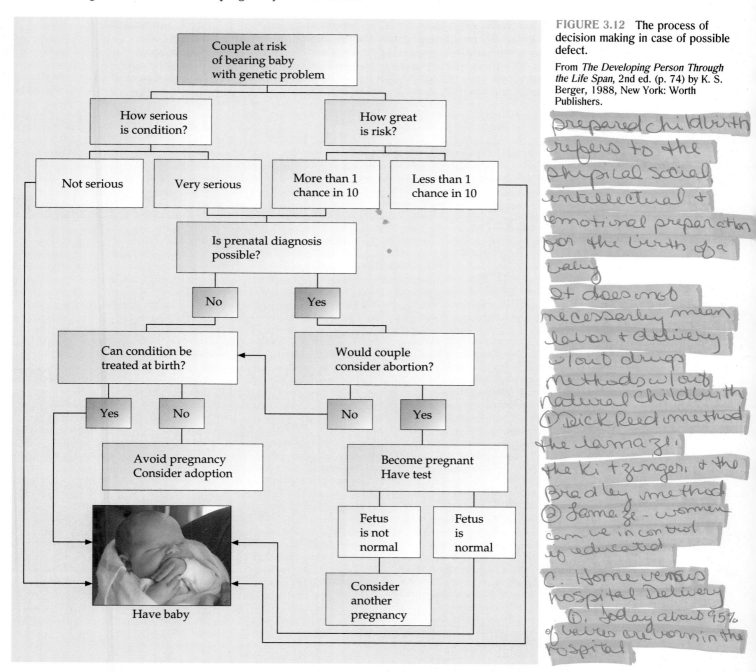

FIGURE 3.12 The process of decision making in case of possible defect.

From The Developing Person Through the Life Span, 2nd ed. (p. 74) by K. S. Berger, 1988, New York: Worth Publishers.

[handwritten margin notes:] Prepared childbirth refers to the physical social intellectual + emotional preparation for the birth of a baby. It does not necessarily mean labor + delivery w/out drugs methods w/out natural childbirth ① Dick Reed method the lamaze, the Kitzinger, + the Bradley method ② Lamaze - women can be in control if educated. C. Home versus hospital Delivery ① Today about 95% of babies are born in the hospital

PRENATAL ENVIRONMENT AND INFLUENCES

Following conception, the environment in which the fetus grows is crucial to healthy development. Let's focus now on the environment to which the pregnant mother is exposed.

Teratogens

Teratogen—Harmful substance that crosses the placenta barrier and harms the embryo or fetus and causes birth defects

Teratogens are any substance that cross the placental barrier, harm the embryo or fetus, and cause birth defects. The timing of exposure to teratogens is particularly important because there is a critical period during which organs and body parts develop, and during which exposure to teratogens is most damaging. Figure 3.13 shows the most sensitive periods. As can be seen, the first 8 weeks of development are most critical, but damage to the central nervous system (including the brain), the eyes, and the genitals may occur during the last weeks of pregnancy as well.

DRUGS. Doctors now recommend that the pregnant mother not take any medication, even aspirin, without medical approval. The list of harmful drugs continues to grow. The list includes drugs that are commonly used and abused. This section contains a brief discussion of the effects on offspring associated with some of the most used drugs.

Narcotics, sedatives, and analgesics are all central nervous system depressants. These include heroine and other forms of narcotics, barbiturates, aspirin, and other substances.

FIGURE 3.13 Sensitive periods of development.

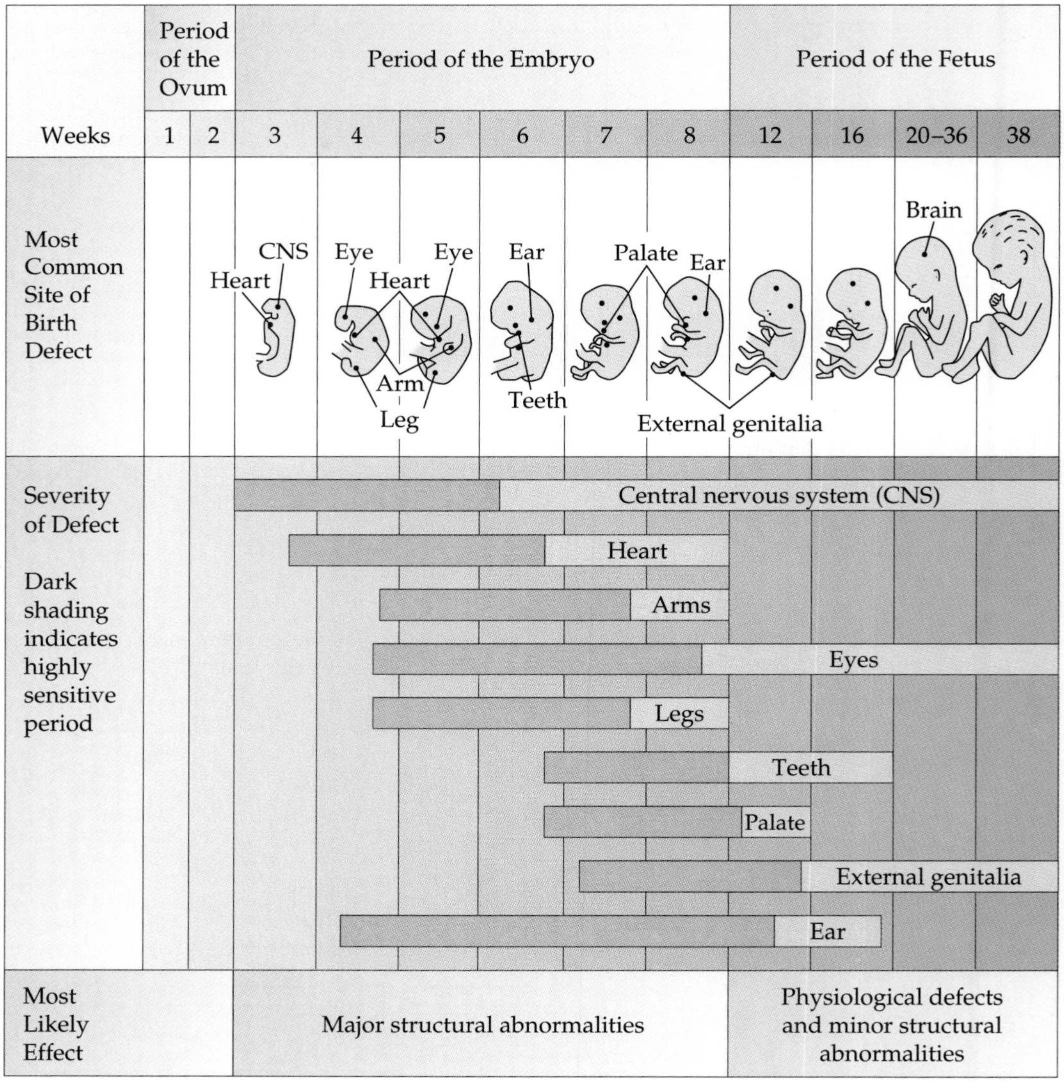

If a mother is a heroine addict, the baby will be born an addict also. Large doses of aspirin may cause prepartal and postpartal bleeding.

Alcohol is a particular cause for concern. *Fetal alcohol syndrome* is seen in babies born to mothers who are heavy drinkers (National Institute on Alcohol Abuse and Alcoholism, NIAAA, 1986). Consuming one or two drinks a day substantially heightens the risk of growth malformation, as well as physical and mental retardation (Mills, Graubard, Harley, Rhoades, & Berendes, 1984).

Tranquilizers and antidepressants have been associated with congenital malformation.

Nicotine is clearly a factor in low birth weight. The mean birth weight of infants of mothers who smoke during pregnancy is 6 oz. less than that of infants born to nonsmoking mothers. Growth retardation occurs when mothers smoke five or more cigarettes a day (Nieburg, Marks, McLaren, & Remington, 1985). The incidence of spontaneous abortion, stillbirth, and neonatal death is increased. Also, children of mothers who smoke 10 or more cigarettes per day run 50% greater risk of developing cancer during

childhood (Stjernfeldt, Berglund, Lindsten, & Ludvigsson, 1986).

Cocaine use may produce spontaneous abortion, stillbirth, a malformed baby, or sudden infant death syndrome (Bingol, Fuchs, Diaz, Stone, & Gromisch, 1987; Chassnoff, Burns, Schnoll, & Burns, 1985).

Marijuana use has been associated with premature birth and low birth weight (Fried, Watkinson, & Willan, 1984). Lester and Dreher (1989) have labeled marijuana as a behavioral teratogen because it affects the functioning of infants after birth. They found that marijuana smoking during pregnancy affected a newborn infant's cry, suggesting respiratory involvement. Other studies have shown a relationship between prenatal risk factors and various developmental outcomes (Lester, 1987).

CHEMICALS, HEAVY METALS, ENVIRONMENTAL POLLUTANTS.   In recent years, authorities have become concerned about chemicals, heavy metals, and environmental pollutants as a source of birth defects. Herbicides containing *dioxin*, called Agent Orange in Vietnam and labeled 2,4,5-T in this country, have been associated with an alarming rate of miscarriages, malformed infants, and cancer. The herbicide has now been banned in this country. However, health authorities in Maine recently found unsafe levels of dioxin in the flesh of fish found in several major Maine rivers. These are rivers into which paper companies discharge their wastes.

Industry is still a major source of pollution in many states (Miller, 1985). *PCB* (an industrial chemical, now banned) was found in Lake Michigan fish. Infants of mothers who ate the fish showed developmental deficits at birth and after (Jacobson, Jacobson, Fein, Schwartz, & Dowler, 1984; Raloff, 1986). *Lead* is a particularly toxic metal, and mothers who are exposed to it may bear infants with low birth weight, slow neurological development, and reduced intelligence (Bellinger, Leviton, Watermaux, Needleman, & Rabinowitz, 1987; Raloff, 1986). This is one reason why tetraethyl lead has been removed from gasoline for automobiles. Women workers who are exposed to *gaseous anesthetics* in hospitals have an increased number of spontaneous abortions and congenital malformations (Bronson, 1977).

Radiation

Exposure to *radiation* may also endanger the fetus. Survivors of the atomic bombing of Hiroshima and Nagasaki in Japan showed

---

LIVING ISSUES

Reproductive Results Associated With Smoking Cigarettes During Pregnancy

Preconception
  Infertility
  Cardiovascular disease associated with oral contraceptive use
Pregnancy
  Abruptio placentae—premature detachment of the placenta from the wall of the uterus
  Vaginal bleeding
  Premature rupture of membranes
  Fetal death
  Birth weight deficits
Lactation
  Higher levels of pesticide residues in breast milk
Infants
  Neonatal death
  Sudden infant death syndrome
  Linear growth deficit
  Possible emotional/intellectual deficits

From ''Fetal Tobacco Syndrome and Other Problems Caused by Smoking During Pregnancy'' by N. M. McLaren and P. Nieburg, August 1988, *Medical Aspects of Human Sexuality*, 22, p. 70.

PARENTING ISSUES

Pregnancy and Hot Tubs

Too much heat can also harm a fetus. If a pregnant woman immerses herself in very hot water, the temperature of the fetus may be raised enough to damage its central nervous system. As little as 15 minutes in a hot tub at 102 °F or 10 minutes at 106 °F may cause fetal damage. Studies have shown that some women gave birth to malformed babies after spending 45 minutes to 1 hour in hot tubs (Harvey, McRorie, & Smith, 1981).

great increases in stillbirths, miscarriages, and birth of babies with congenital malformations. Researchers found prenatal chromosome malformations in children in West Germany, which they believed were associated with the nuclear power plant disaster at Chernobyl in Russia (West Berlin Human Genetic Institute, 1987). The whole area around Chernobyl is now deserted because of the continued hazard of radiation. Prenatal exposure to *X rays*, especially in the first 3 months of pregnancy, has the potential of harming the fetus if the level of radiation is too high (Kleinman, Cooke, Machlin, & Kessel, 1983). Even radiation from video display terminals (VDTs) used in industry may be a factor in high miscarriage rates of pregnant women working on them (Meier, 1987).

Maternal Diseases

Many bacteria and viruses cross the placental barrier, so if a pregnant woman is infected, her baby becomes infected also. A variety of maternal illnesses during pregnancy cause birth defects. The extent of the damage depends on the nature and timing of the illness.

RUBELLA.   In the case of rubella, or German measles, if the mother is infected with the virus before the 11th week of pregnancy, the baby is almost certain to be deaf and to have heart defects and visual and intellectual deficiencies. The chance of defects is 1 in 3 for cases occurring between 13 and 16 weeks, and almost none after 16 weeks (Miller, Cradock-Watson, & Pollock, 1982). For these reasons, immunization against rubella is recommended for all children (age 15 months and older) and for adults who show no evidence of rubella immunity. Pregnant women

should not receive the vaccine; adult women should not become pregnant for 3 months after immunization (Berkow, 1987).

TOXOPLASMOSIS.   Toxoplasmosis is a parasite found in uncooked meat and in fecal matter of cats and other animals. The pregnant mother should not change the cat's litter if blood tests reveal that she is not immune. The parasite affects the nervous system of the fetus, resulting in retardation, deafness, and blindness (Larsen, 1986).

SEXUALLY TRANSMITTED DISEASES. These are a major cause of birth defects. *Congenital syphilis* is contracted by the fetus of the pregnant woman when the spirochete crosses the placental barrier. If the disease is diagnosed and treated before the fourth month of pregnancy, the fetus will not develop syphilis (Dubroff & Papalian, 1982). Later in pregnancy the fetus may suffer bone, liver, or brain damage (Grossman, 1986). If a woman is not treated in the primary or secondary stage of the disease, her child is likely to die before or shortly after birth.

Genital herpes, gonorrhea, and chlamydial infections are STDs transmitted to infants when they pass through the birth canal, so doctors recommend a cesarean section if the woman has an infection. Between 50% and

FOCUS

AIDS and Fetal Development

One of the most serious of the sexually transmitted diseases is *acquired immunodeficiency syndrome (AIDS)*. A person who has been exposed to the virus may become a carrier prior to actually having the disease. The AIDS virus can cross the placental barrier, so if the mother is a carrier, there is a substantial risk she will give birth to children with the disease. Infected infants have head and face abnormalities; small heads, boxlike foreheads, short, flattened noses, slanting eyes, "scooped out" profiles, fat lips, and growth retardation (Iosub et al., 1987; Marion, Wiznia, Hutcheon, & Rubinstein, 1986). The virus is present in mother's breast milk, and, although rare, transmission through this means has been implicated (Rogers, 1985). Approximately one-third of babies born to AIDS-infected mothers will also become infected (Koop, 1986). Most of the infected babies will eventually develop the disease and die (Cowan, Hellman, Chudwin, Wara, Chang, & Ammann, 1984).

60% of newborns who contract *herpes* die, and half of the survivors suffer brain damage or blindness (Subak-Sharp, 1984; Vontner, 1982). Infants of infected mothers may get *gonorrhea* of the eyes when passing through the birth canal and, if not treated with silver nitrate or antibiotics, can become blind. Some babies born to infected mothers contract the *chlamydia bacterium* when passing through the birth canal and become subject to eye infections, pneumonia, and sudden infant death syndrome (Faro, 1985). Chlamydia is the greatest single cause of preventable blindness (Crum & Ellner, 1985). The best precaution against birth defects caused by STDs is to make sure the woman is not exposed before or during pregnancy.

OTHER DISEASES.   Large numbers of other diseases may cause birth defects. *Poliomyelitis, diabetes, tuberculosis,* and *thyroid disease* have all been implicated in problems of fetal development.

Other Maternal Factors

MATERNAL AGE.   At first glance, maternal age seems to be associated with the well-being of the fetus. *Younger teenage mothers are more likely to have miscarriages, premature birth, and stillbirths than are mothers in their 20s.* The infants are more likely to be of low birth weight, to have physical and neurological defects, and to be retarded than are babies born to women over 20 (Smith, Weinman, & Malinak, 1984). However, it is not necessarily the mother's age that is the problem, but the fact that many of these babies are born out of wedlock to low socioeconomic status

More and more women in their late 30s and early 40s are having babies.

mothers who do not receive adequate nutrition and prenatal health care ("Social Factors," 1984).

The statistics indicate that women over 35 run progressively greater risks during pregnancy. These include greater risks of miscarriages, of complications during pregnancy and delivery, a greater chance of having twins and of developmental abnormalities than for women under 35. Here again, however, age may not be the causative factor but the fact that the older mother may not be in as good health as the younger. She is more likely to be obese, have high blood pressure, or have diabetes than is the younger woman. *Modern health care has made it possible for older women to deliver healthy full-term babies.* The risks of pregnancy for women over 40 have not been found to be greater than those for women 20 to 30, particularly when such factors as maternal weight, health condition, and cigarette smoking are taken into account (Kopp & Kaler, 1989). However, if any woman has health problems, she is certainly at greater risk.

NUTRITION.   *Lack of vitamins, minerals, and protein* in the diet of the expectant mother may affect the embryo adversely. Nutritional

PARENTING ISSUES

Maternal Stress and Infant Hyperactivity

Most expectant mothers experience some stress during pregnancy. A moderate amount of stress probably has no harmful effects on the fetus, but persistent, excessive stress does. When the mother is anxious, afraid, or upset, adrenaline is pumped into the blood stream, which increases heart rate, blood pressure, respiration, and levels of blood sugar, and diverts blood away from digestion to the skeletal muscles to prepare the body for emergency action. The emergency mobilization leaves the body exhausted afterward, severely disrupting bodily functioning.

The physical changes that occur in the mother's body take place in the fetus as well, since *adrenaline* passes through the placenta and enters the blood of the fetus. The fetus becomes hyperactive for as long as the mother is stressed. Furthermore, the stress is associated with low birth weight, infant hyperactivity, feeding problems, irritability, and digestive disturbances. Furthermore, the overly stressed mother is more likely to have complications during pregnancy and labor (Istvan, 1986).

deficiencies have been associated with still-births, miscarriages, and major deformities. The extent of damage depends on the time during the pregnancy, and on the duration and severity of the deficiencies. A lack of vitamin A or calcium in the mother may result in improperly developed teeth in the infant. A serious protein deficiency may cause mental retardation, premature birth, low resistance to infections, or low fetal birth weight (Guttmacher, 1983).

HEREDITY–ENVIRONMENT INTERACTION

Studying the Influence of Heredity and Environment

For years, psychologists have been trying to sort out the relative influences of heredity and environment on development and behavior. There are two principal methods of doing this: studies of twins and studies of adopted children.

TWIN STUDIES.   Identical twins share the same heredity, but if they are reared apart they would be subject to different environmental influences. Any shared traits that are still similar, therefore, would be caused by heredity and not environment. Fraternal twins are as different in heredity as are any other brothers or sisters. Comparisons are sometimes made between fraternal twins and identical twins, or between fraternal twins or other siblings and adopted children raised in the same family. Such comparisons

TABLE 3.3 The Degree of Similarity (Correlation) Between Monozygotic Twins, Dizygotic Twins, Siblings, and Unrelated Children on Measures of Intelligence

Relationship	Correlation
Monozygotic twins	.86
Same-sex dizygotic twins	.60
Siblings	.47
Unrelated children (raised in different homes)	.00

Adapted from "Family Studies of Intelligence: A Review" by T. J. Bouchard and M. McGue, 1981, *Science, 212,* pp. 1055–1059.

help to sort out environmental versus hereditary influences. Table 3.3 gives a summary of the degree of similarity between monozygotic twins, dizygotic twins, and siblings on measures of intelligence (comparisons of twins and of siblings are of children raised in the same home). The findings are summaries of a number of studies (Bouchard & McGue, 1981).

ADOPTION STUDIES.   Studies of adopted children enable researchers to try to disentangle the relative contributions of heredity and environment. In the Texas Adoption Project, researchers have found that the influence of heredity on intelligence is a strong one (Horn, 1983; Loehlin, 1985). *Children*

Twin studies help psychologists examine the influences of heredity and environment.

FOCUS

Twins Reared Apart

Jack Yufe and Oskar Stohr are identical twins. They were separated at 6 months of age from their parents and reared apart. Jack was raised in Israel as a Jew, and he spent time in an Israeli kibbutz and in the navy. Oskar was brought up in Germany as a Catholic and was involved in Hitler's youth movement. When they were brought together at age 47 by University of Minnesota researchers, they had similar personality profiles, and they both did well in sports, had trouble with math, had mustaches, wore wire-rimmed glasses, and read magazines from back to front (Bouchard, 1984). The researchers concluded that at least half the similarities in a wide range of personality characteristics were caused by heredity.

TABLE 3.4 IQ Correlations in the Texas Adoption Project

Pairing	Number of Pairs	Observed Correlations
SHARE GENES ONLY		
Adopted child and biological mother	297	0.28
SHARE ENVIRONMENT ONLY		
Adopted child and adoptive mother	401	0.15
Adopted child and adoptive father	405	0.12
All unrelated children	266	0.18
SHARE GENES AND ENVIRONMENT		
Natural child and mother	143	0.21
Natural child and father	144	0.29
Natural child and natural child	40	0.33

From "The Texas Adoption Project" by J. M. Horn, 1983, *Child Development*, 54, pp. 268–275.

reared away from their biological parents are still more similar in IQ to their biological mother than to their adoptive parents. As seen in Table 3.4, the strongest correlations of intelligence were between natural children and their father or between natural siblings. The weakest correlations were between adopted children and their adopted parents, indicating that the influence of environment alone was not high.

In one longitudinal Minnesota adoption study, black children adopted into white homes were still more closely related in intelligence to their biological parents than to their adoptive parents, indicating that genetics had more influence than environment (Scarr & Weinberg, 1983). However, these adopted black children had higher average intelligence test scores than their biological parents, indicating that performance had been improved by environmental influences.

Influences on Personality and Temperament

Heredity not only has an important influence on intelligence, but it also exerts a strong influence on personality and temperament. Intensive studies of 348 pairs of identical twins at the University of Minnesota, including 44 pairs who were reared apart, revealed that heredity was a stronger influence than environment on a number of key personality traits (Goleman, 1986; Leo, 1987). Figure 3.14 shows the extent to which selected personality traits were found to be inherited. A 60% figure would mean that 60% of the trait is due to heredity, and 40% to environmental influences.

The influence of heredity can be seen in identifiable characteristics that seem to be present in very young infants. Infants' temperament, for example, is strongly influenced by genetics, as indicated by their level of activity, irritability, sociability, and sleep patterns (Wilson & Matheny, 1983). Goldsmith (1983) found that identical twins were more similar than fraternal twins in personality traits such as emotionality: in the expression of anger and aggressive feelings, in activity level and sociability, and in work habits in school such as task persistence. In the New York Longitudinal Study, 133 children were followed from infancy into early adulthood (Thomas & Chess, 1984). The researchers investigated various characteristics: activity level, regularity of biological functioning, sensory sensitivity, intensity of responses, readiness to accept new people and situations, adaptability, distractibility, persistence, and cheerfulness or unhappiness. Individuals varied greatly in these characteristics, and differences remained into early adulthood. However, differences in parental handling and in other experiences did modify these behavioral characteristics somewhat.

Goldsmith and Gottesman (1981) found that, as infants got older, the relative influence of heredity on temperament usually declined, whereas environmental influences became more important (Riese, 1990). Kagan and his associates studied the development of inhibited and uninhibited 2- to 3-year-old children for 6 years to discover the relative stability of the tendency to be shy or not shy (Kagan, Reznick, Clarke, Snidman, & Garcia-Coll, 1984; Reznick, Kagan, Snidman, Gersten, Baak, & Rosenberg, 1986). About 5% to 10% of the children seemed to be born with a biological predisposition to be fearful of unfamiliar people, events, or objects. After $5\frac{1}{2}$ years, 40% of the originally inhibited children—usually boys—had become much less inhibited. However, 10% had become more timid. Some parents had helped their shy children overcome timidity by bringing playmates into the home, offering encouragement and support, and through other means. Other parents made matters worse by undermining their children's confidence. Certainly then, the quality of nurturing experiences exerted strong modifying influences on children's temperament and behavior. Of course, children also exerted strong influences on parents. Children who are different tax the patience of parents, but if parents start to become rejecting, critical, and punishing, they may make matters worse.

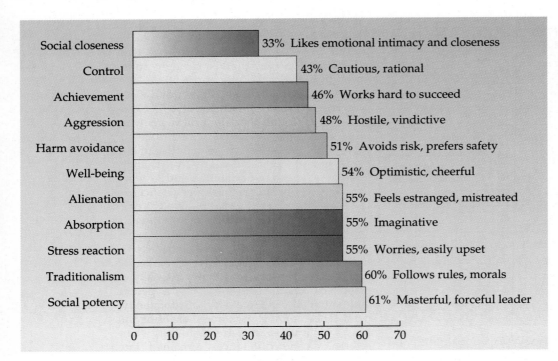

FIGURE 3.14 The extent to which different personality traits are inherited.

From "Major Personality Study Finds That Traits Are Mostly Inherited" by D. Goleman, December 2, 1986, *The New York Times*, pp. 17, 18.

The children who are hardest to love are the ones who need love, acceptance, and encouragement the most.

Some Disorders Influenced by Heredity and Environment

Not only are some superior traits inherited and then enhanced or minimized through environmental influences, but also various disorders with genetic origins can either be promoted or counteracted to some degree by environment. Several of these disorders are the focus in this section.

ALCOHOLISM.   Alcoholism runs in families and develops because of a combination of genetic and environmental factors. The evidence for genetic factors in alcoholism is convincing: (1) the concordance rate for alcoholism between identical twins is twice that between fraternal twins; (2) sons of alcohlics are four times as likely as sons of nonalcoholics to become alcoholics themselves, even if they are adopted at birth, and regardless of whether the adoptive parents are alcoholics; and, (3) children whose natural parents are nonalcoholics, but whose adoptive parents are, do not appear to have an un-

FOCUS

The Nobel Prize Winners' Sperm Bank

Robert Graham of Escondido, California, has founded a sperm bank with the intent of producing geniuses. He accepts only the sperm of Nobel Prize-winning scientists and then offers it free of charge to healthy and intelligent women of good breeding whose husbands are infertile. The second child born through the sperm bank, a boy named Doran, had a mental age of 4 when he was only 1 year old. His genetic father had a math score of 800 on the SATs. However, the father also passed on to Doran a 30 percent chance of inheriting hemorrhoids. It's too early to say how many of the children sired

through the sperm bank become creative geniuses. Certainly, a genius has other attributes besides a high IQ.

The bank offers a life-giving service to couples where the husband is unable to conceive a child. The bank is severely criticized, however, by those who are set against scientific breeding of any kind. Others emphasize that brighter is not necessarily better. One of the donors, Burton Richter, a Nobel Prize winner in physics from Stanford University, reports that his students ask him if he supplements his salary with stud fees. He is not amused (Garelik, 1985).

Alcoholism runs in families because of a combination of genetic and environmental factors.

usually high risk themselves (Schuckit, 1985, 1987). Alcoholics tend to inherit an ability to metabolize alcohol differently, and thus to find drinking more pleasurable, than nonalcoholics do. In contrast to alcoholics, some people can't drink because their bodies can't tolerate alcohol (Zucker & Gomberg, 1986). There is some evidence, also, that male alcoholics exhibit different brain wave patterns than nonalcoholics prior to exposure to alcohol (Porjesz & Begleitner, 1985).

Environmental influences are also a factor in alcoholism. In families where there is a lack of closeness, love, and recognition or trust; where there is parental rejection, hostility, conflict, inadequate role models or discipline; or where children do not learn coping skills from parents, the children are more prone to become alcoholics or abusers of other drugs than are those brought up in a more positive home environment (Jurich, Polson, Jurich, & Bates, 1985).

SCHIZOPHRENIA.   Schizophrenia is another disorder that has both and hereditary and environmental causes. The incidence of schizophrenia in the general population is about 1%, but if one parent has it, about 12% of their offspring will be affected. If both parents are schizophrenic, 39% of their children will be afflicted (Kinney & Matthysse, 1978). One study found that 48% of the monozygotic twins of schizophrenic individuals also had schizophrenia, whereas only 10% of the dizygotic twins of a schizophrenic parent had the disease (Farmer, McGuffin, & Gottesman, 1987). However, the fact that the majority of children were not affected indicates that children do not inherit the disease, per

se. Rather, some inherit a predisposition toward it. Schizophrenia seems to be particularly sensitive to the action of *dopamine*, which is a neurochemical transmitter that speeds nerve transmission. In schizophrenia, the rapid speed of transmission between neurons or nerve cells causes incoherent, bizarre behavior. Administering the drugs called *phenothiazines* inhibits the effect of dopamine on nerve transmission and is an effective treatment (Uhr, Stahl, & Berger, 1984). Environmental influences, such as coming from a dysfunctional family situation, tend to increase the chances of developing the illness.

DEPRESSION.   Depression is another disorder that may be caused by biological factors including a genetic predisposition. Identical twins have a 70% concordance rate; fraternal twins, other siblings, and parents and their children have about a 15% concordance rate, indicating a genetic influence (U.S. Department of Health and Human Services, 1981). Depression seems to be accompanied by an excess of *acetylcholine*, a chemical that inhibits the transmission of messages between nerve cells (Nadi, Nurnberger, & Gershon, 1984). Here again, depression may be triggered by stressful life events, such as the sudden loss of love. However, some people apparently have a predisposition to the illness.

INFANTILE AUTISM.   Infantile autism is first noticed in early infancy, with a diagnosis confirmed by age 2 or 3 (Rutter & Schopher,

FOCUS

Treatment of Depression

The most common medical treatment for depression is the administration of *antidepressant drugs* that elevate mood and reduce self-blame and suicidal thoughts. *Psychotherapy* is also helpful and effective, especially when used in combination with the drugs. *Electroconvulsive therapy (ECT)* is now employed as a treatment of last resort with severely depressed patients for whom drug treatment and psychotherapy have failed. It is believed that ECT affects the metabolism and storage of neurotransmitters implicated in depressive disorders. *Exposing patients to large amounts of sunlight or to intense light from banks of light panels* has been found to be a very effective treatment of depression. No wonder that people like to go to sunny climates for the winter!

1987). The word *autism* comes from *auto*, meaning "self." Autistic children are self-involved, oblivious to other people; they don't cuddle, smile, or make eye contact when greeted (Kasari, Sigman, Mundy, & Yirmiya, 1988). Autistic children may spend hours performing repetitive motions such as clapping their hands or turning a ball over and over. They may scream in terror when something in the environment is changed. They are often mute, but may echo, word for word, things that they hear, such as a television ad (Wetherby & Prutting, 1984). About one-third have IQs of 70 or more. One in six makes fair adjustment and is able to work as an adult.

Autism is very rare (about 3 cases per 10,000 people). One study found a concordance of 96% among identical twins and 23% among fraternal twins; the evidence suggested that autism is an inherited neurobiological disorder passed on through recessive genes, and that environmental influences as causes are minimal (Ritvo, Freeman, Mason-Brothers, Mo, & Ritvo, 1985).

Paternal Factors in Defects

Advanced *paternal age* is also associated with reduced fertility and several hereditary defects (Evans, 1976). Negative environmental influences in the life of the father also contribute to birth defects. *Chronic marijuana use* suppresses the production of the male hormone testosterone, reduces sexual desire, interferes with erectile responses, and inhibits sperm production and motility (Relman,

1982; U. S. Department of Health and Human Services, June 1980). Sperm from *alcoholic men* have been found to be highly abnormal (Lester & Van Theil, 1977). Exposure to *radiation, lead, tobacco, arsenic, mercury, some solvents,* and *various pesticides* may contribute to male infertility, to lower sperm count, or genetic abnormalities in sperm cells (Meier, 1987; Brody, 1981). Wives of oral surgeons and dentists exposed to *anesthetic gas* for 3 hours or more a week were found to have a 78% higher incidence of spontaneous abortions than did other wives (Bronson, 1977). Even passive exposure of the fetus to *smoking* by the father reduces fetal birth weight and interferes with lung development of the fetus (Rubin et al., 1986). Another study at a University of North Carolina hospital revealed a twofold increase in risk for developing cancer during their lifetime among children of men who smoked (Sandler, Everson, Wilcox, & Browder, 1985). This may have been due to prenatal or postnatal exposure or both.

We do know that excessive heat is detrimental to sperm production and viability. Sperm are most effectively produced and most healthy when the temperature in the testes is 5.6 °F below body temperature. This lower temperature is achieved because the testes hang outside the body cavity in the scrotum. But when sperm are exposed to sources of artificial heat, their temperature rises, which is very detrimental.

As can be seen, the great majority of birth defects are preventable. Every effort needs to be made to keep them from happening.

FOCUS

Does Marijuana Smoking by Men Cause Birth Defects?

We know that marijuana smoking by men interferes with male potency and fertility, but does it contribute to birth defects? The answer is not conclusive.

Dr. Susan L. Dalterio, assistant professor of pharmacological research at the University of Texas Health Science center at San Antonio, has been giving oral dosages of THC (the active ingredient in marijuana) to mice. Giving THC to pregnant female mice has resulted in increased fetal losses, and has reduced testosterone in male fetuses, which has interfered with their sexual development.

When adult male mice were given THC, they had more difficulty impregnating the females. If pregnancy occurred, many male fetuses died before full term and before weaning. An examination of the testes of fathers and sons revealed abnormal sex chromosomes that were transmitted from one generation to the next.

Confirmation or rejection of these findings in humans can be obtained only when third-generation offspring of marijuana users can be tested (Dalterio, 1984). To date, there is no proof of chromosomal damage in humans.

SUMMARY

1. Reproduction begins when the male gamete, or sperm cell, fuses with the female gamete, or ovum.

2. Spermatogenesis refers to the process of sperm production; oogenesis is the process by which ova are ripened in the ovary.

3. Conception, or fertilization, normally takes place in the upper third of the fallopian tube.

4. Prenatal development may be divided into three periods: (1) the germinal period—from conception to completion of implantation, about 14 days; (2) the embryonic period—from 2 weeks to 8 weeks after conception; and (3) the fetal period—from 8 weeks through the remainder of pregnancy.

5. Many thoughtful people object to viability tests as determinants of whether a woman can have an abortion, because the tests are expensive, impose health risks for the mother and fetus, and are sometimes unreliable and inaccurate, especially if performed between 20 and 30 weeks.

6. The expectant mother ought to get prenatal medical care as early in her pregnancy as possible.

7. Minor side effects may cause varying degrees of discomfort during pregnancy. Major complications of pregnancy include pernicious vomiting, toxemia, threatened abortion, placenta praevia, tubal pregnancy, and Rh incompatibility.

8. About 20% of infertility cases involve the couple, about 40% the man, and about 40% the woman.

9. Alternate means of conception include artificial insemination (both homologous insemination and heterologous insemination), use of a surrogate mother, in vitro fertilization, gamete intra fallopian transfer (GIFT), and embryo transplant.

10. Chromosomes carry the hereditary material called genes that direct the physical changes in the body throughout development. When the sperm and ovum unite, the 23 single chromosomes within the nucleus of each gamete combine in pairs with those in the other gamete to produce 46 chromosomes in the resulting zygote.

11. Genes are made up of molecules called DNA. Each cell of the body has the same DNA code and the same genes that direct growth.

12. In the zygote, twenty-two of the chromosomes from each gamete are labeled autosomes; the twenty-third pair are sex chromosomes, which determine whether the offspring will be male or female. An XY chromosome pairing produces a male; an XX combination produces a female.

13. Twins may be identical (monozygotic, or one-egg) twins, or fraternal (dizygotic, or two-egg) twins.

14. Mendel formulated the law of dominant inheritance, which says that when an organism inherits competing traits, the trait that is expressed is dominant over the other, which is recessive. An organism may be homozygous or heterozygous for a trait.

15. A trait that is observable in an organism is called a phenotype, while the underlying genetic pattern is called a genotype.

16. When one allele is not completely dominant over the other, the phenomenon is known as incomplete dominance. Polygenic inheritance is when numerous interacting genes produce a trait.

17. We inherit a range of possibilities for many traits. This is known as the reaction range. Canalization is the tendency for a trait to persist regardless of environment.

18. Sex-linked disorders are inherited by being passed on through defective recessive genes on the X chromosome.

19. Birth defects result from three causes: (1) hereditary factors, (2) faulty environments, and (3) birth injuries. Some genetic diseases are inherited through dominant genes, others through recessive genes.

20. Chromosomal abnormalities are of two types: sex chromosomal abnormalities and autosomal chromosomal abnormalities.

21. Couples who have inherited disabilities themselves, or who have a family history of such disabilities, should get genetic counseling to discover the possibility of passing on a defect.

22. Procedures for discovering defects include amniocentesis, sonogram, fetoscope, or chorionic villus sampling (CVS).

23. Adverse prenatal environmental influences include various teratogens, drugs, chemicals, heavy metals; and environmental pollutants, radiation, and exces-

sive heat. The earlier in development the embryo or fetus is exposed, the greater the possibility of harm. Thus, there are sensitive periods when exposure is most harmful.

24. There are also many maternal diseases that can affect the development of the unborn child.

25. Other maternal factors that need to be taken into account are maternal age, nutrition, and stress.

26. There are two principal methods for sorting out the relative influence of heredity versus environment: twin studies and adoption studies. Heredity seems to have a greater influence on intelligence than do environmental influences. Heredity exerts a strong influence on personality and temperament also.

27. Some disorders are influenced by both heredity and environment. These include alcoholism, schizophrenia, depression, and infantile autism.

28. Paternal factors important in defects include paternal age; use of some drugs; and exposure to radiation, lead, arsenic, mercury, some solvents, and various pesticides or gases.

KEY TERMS

Alleles *p. 60*
Amniocentesis *p. 64*
Artificial insemination *p. 56*
Autosomes *p. 58*
Blastocyst *p. 51*
Blastula *p. 51*
Canalization *p. 62*
Chorionic villi sampling (CVS) *p. 64*
Chromosomes *p. 57*
Congenital deformity *p. 63*
Dizygotic (fraternal) twins *p. 59*
DNA *p. 57*
Dominant gene *p. 60*
Ectopic pregnancy *p. 51*
Embryo transplant *p. 57*
Embryo *p. 52*
Embryonic period *p. 51*
Fertilization or conception *p. 50*
Fetal period *p. 51*
Fetoscope *p. 64*
Fetus *p. 53*
Gamete intro fallopian transfer (GIFT) *p. 57*
Gametes *p. 50*
Genes *p. 57*
Genotype *p. 61*
Germinal period *p. 51*
Heterologous insemination (AID) *p. 56*
Heterozygous *p. 60*

Homologous insemination (AIH) *p. 56*
Homozygous *p. 60*
Implantation *p. 51*
In vitro fertilization *p. 56*
Incomplete dominance, or codominance *p. 62*
Infertile *p. 55*
Law of dominant inheritance *p. 60*
Meiosis *p. 50*
Monozygotic (identical) twins *p. 59*
Morula *p. 51*
Oogenesis *p. 50*
Ova *p. 50*
Ovulation *p. 50*
Phenotype *p. 61*
Polygenic system of inheritance *p. 62*
Reaction range *p. 62*
Recessive gene *p. 60*
Sex chromosomes *p. 58*
Sex-linked disorders *p. 62*
Siamese twins *p. 59*
Sonogam *p. 64*
Spermatogenesis *p. 50*
Surrogate mother *p. 56*
Teratogen *p. 66*
Trimester *p. 53*
Viable *p. 55*
Zygote *p. 51*

DISCUSSION QUESTIONS

1. What do you think about each of the following alternate means of conception?
   Artificial insemination: AIH, AID
   Using a surrogate mother
   Gamete intra fallopian transfer (GIFT)
   In vitro fertilization
   Embryo transplant

2. If you wanted a child of a particular sex, would you try to employ means to determine your child's sex? Explain.

3. Do any members of either side of your family have inherited defects, or might they be carriers of defects? Has any member of your family received genetic counseling? With what results?

4. What do you think of the Nobel Prize

Winners' Sperm Bank? Explain your feelings about it.

5. Do you know of anyone who has borne defective children because of exposure to teratogens, radiation, heat, or maternal diseases?

6. Regardless of whether you are now a parent, would you want to consider having children when you are over 35 years of age? Why or why not?

7. Do you know any mothers who are nervous, hyperactive people? Were they that way during pregnancy? Compare their children with children of mothers who are calm, easygoing persons who do not get upset easily. Do you notice any difference in the temperament of the children? Is a nervous temperament inherited or due to environmental influence?

8. To women who are mothers: Did you have any minor discomforts during your pregnancy? What bothered you the most? What did you do about it? Did you have any of the major complications of pregnancy that are mentioned in the text? Explain.

9. To men who are fathers: How did you feel about your wife becoming pregnant? In what ways were you able to assist her? What bothered you the most during her pregnancy?

SUGGESTED READINGS

Abel, E. L. (1984). *Fetal alcohol syndrome and fetal alcohol effects.* New York: Plenum. An enlightening book on this subject.

Anderson, G. R. (1986). *Children and AIDS: The challenge for child welfare.* Washington, DC: Child Welfare League of America. Implications of AIDS for social workers.

Anthony, E. J., & Cohler, B. J. (Eds.). (1987). *The invulnerable child.* New York: Guilford Press. A book of readings on how children are resistant to unfortunate environments.

Baker, R., & Mednick, B. R. (1984). *Influences on human development.* Boston: Kluwer-Nijhoff.

Corea, G. (1986). *The mother machine.* New York: Harper & Row. Ethics of new reproductive technologies.

Farber, S. (1981). *Identical twins reared apart: A reanalysis.* New York: Basic Books. Summary of findings of studies.

Glass, R., & Ericsson, R. J. (1982). *Getting pregnant in the 1980s.* Berkeley: University of California Press. A nontechnical presentation of pregnancy and birth control.

Kelly, T. E. (1986). *Clinical genetics and genetic counseling* (2nd ed.). Chicago and London: Yearbook Medical Publishers. A textbook on genetics and its clinical applications.

Kevles, D. J. (1985). *In the name of eugenics.* New York: Knopf. A thought-provoking discussion.

Norwood, C. (1980). *At highest risk: Environmental hazards to young and unborn children.* New York: McGraw-Hill.

Rubin, S. (1980). *It's not too late for a baby.* Englewood Cliffs, NJ: Prentice-Hall. Pregnancy and child rearing concerns for the parent over 35.

Schwarz, R. H., & Yaffe, S. J. (Eds.). (1980). *Drug and chemical risks to the fetus and newborn.* New York: Alan R. Liss.

Shapiro, H. J. (1983). *The pregnancy book for today's woman.* New York: Harper & Row. Issues during pregnancy.

Snyder, L. A., Freifelder, D., & Hartl, D. L. (1985). *General genetics.* Boston: Jones and Bartlett. A textbook.

4

Childbirth and the Neonate

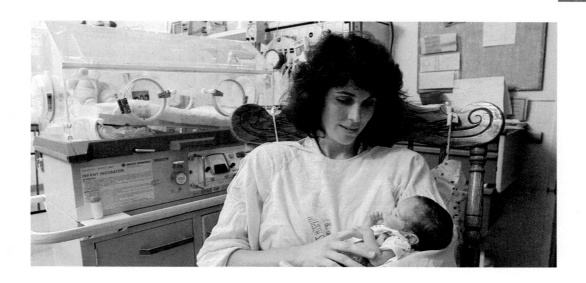

CHILDBIRTH*

Prepared Childbirth

**Prepared child-
birth**—the physical,
social, intellectual
and emotional
preparation for the
birth of a baby

The term **prepared childbirth** here refers to the physical, social, intellectual, and emotional preparation for the birth of a baby. Good physical care of the body provides a favorable environment for the growing fetus, and physical conditioning readies the body for labor and childbirth. Social preparation of the home and family provides a secure environment in which the child can grow. Intellectual preparation ensures adequate instruction in and understanding of the birth process, prenatal and postnatal hospitalization, and infant and child care (Hicks & Williams, 1981). Emotional preparation minimizes fear and tension so that childbirth can be as pleasant and painless as possible.

Prepared childbirth, as used in this context, does not necessarily mean labor and delivery without medication, although these may be drug free if the mother so desires. Emphasis is not just on natural childbirth (in a sense all childbirth is natural), but on the

*Part of the material in this section and in the sections on labor, delivery, and postpartum are based on excerpts from the author's book, *Human Sexuality*, 1989. Used by permission of the publisher, Wm. C. Brown.

overall preparations a woman and her partner can make for the experience of becoming parents.

Methods of Natural Childbirth

DICK-READ METHOD.   Dr. Grantley Dick-Read (1953), an English obstetrician, pioneered the concept of prepared childbirth with an article published in 1933, then later with his book, *Childbirth Without Fear*. He believed that fear causes tension that inhibits the process of childbirth. According to him, if women could be educated to understand what was happening to their bodies, they could eliminate their tension and fear. If they could also be conditioned for the experience, pain during childbirth could be eliminated without medication in all but a minority of cases. Women who took no drugs during labor and delivery had perfectly healthy babies and were able to resume their duties sooner after delivery than those who had anesthesia (Bean, 1974).

These are three important elements of the **Dick-Read method:**

1. Education about birth, including deconditioning from earlier fears, myths, and misconceptions

**Dick-Read
method**—a natural
childbirth method
emphasizing child-
birth without fear

Couples need to be prepared for childbirth and the experience of becoming parents.

2. Physical conditioning and exercises, including voluntary muscle relaxation and proper breathing
3. Emotional support from the partner, family, nurses, and physician during pregnancy, labor, and delivery

The Read approach is a fairly passive method, emphasizing relaxation and proper breathing as each contraction comes.

Lamaze method— a natural childbirth method emphasizing education, physical conditioning, controlled breathing, and emotional support

LAMAZE METHOD.   The **Lamaze method** originated in Russia and was introduced to the Western world in 1951 by Dr. Fernand Lamaze (1970), a French obstetrician. The following are important elements of the Lamaze method:

1. Education about birth, including the ability to relax muscles not involved in the labor and delivery process
2. Physical conditioning through exercises
3. Controlled breathing, providing the psychological technique for pain prevention and the ability to release muscular tension by "letting go"
4. Emotional support during labor and delivery, primarily through instruction of the partner in coaching and supportive techniques

The Lamaze method emphasizes the man–woman relationship and communication. In this method, as well as in the Dick-Read method, attendance of the partner or another support person in childbirth education classes is essential (Bean, 1974). The underlying feature of the Lamaze method is its focus on teaching the woman that she can be in control during the experience (Felton & Segelman, 1978).

KITZINGER METHOD.   The **Kitzinger,** or psychosexual, **method** was developed by Dr. Sheila Kitzinger in England. Kitzinger's approach is called psychosexual because it shows the partner how to help the pregnant woman relax by his touching various parts of her body. This approach also teaches women prescribed exercises to gain better control over their pelvic and vaginal muscles, thus allowing facile descent and delivery of the baby.

Kitzinger method—a psychosocial method of natural childbirth emphasizing relaxation and muscle control

BRADLEY METHOD.   The **Bradley method,** or "husband-coached childbirth method," was developed by Robert Bradley, a Denver obstetrician. This approach focuses on the couple's relationship: marital communication, sexual relationship, and parental roles, as well as on relaxation exercises and proper nutrition. The couple are encouraged to discuss various issues with their physician, such as their desire for a birth at home or in a hospital.

Bradley method—a husband-coached natural childbirth method

CRITIQUE.   Prepared childbirth, by whatever method, is not without its critics, especially if a particular advocate emphasizes a drug-free labor and delivery. Medical opin-

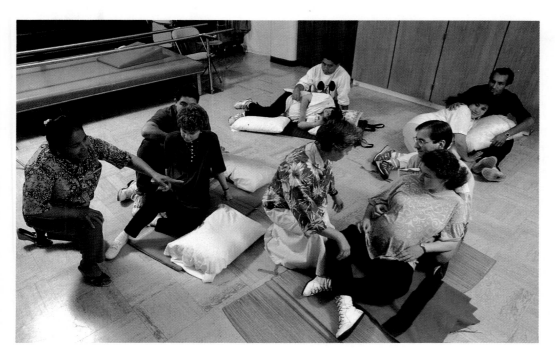

Both prospective fathers and mothers attend childbirth education classes.

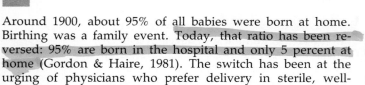

PARENTING ISSUES

Home versus Hospital Delivery

Around 1900, about 95% of all babies were born at home. Birthing was a family event. Today, that ratio has been reversed: 95% are born in the hospital and only 5 percent at home (Gordon & Haire, 1981). The switch has been at the urging of physicians who prefer delivery in sterile, well-equipped, more convenient hospital settings.

Some expectant parents are concerned about hospital practices being too rigid, impersonal, and expensive. They object to the separation of family members and want more control over the childbirth process. Some parents seek midwives to perform home deliveries. Midwives should be certified nurse-midwives (CNMs) who practice in conjunction with physicians, referring problem pregnancies to them and calling upon them as needed. The American College of Nurse-Midwives certifies members who have completed a one-year course at such places as the University of Miami or Georgetown University. Two organizations, the Association for Childbirth at Home (ACAH) and the Home Oriented Maternity Experience (HOME), offer classes to prepare couples for home birth (Parfitt, 1977).

Studies of nurse-midwifery practice, past and present, consistently show delivery outcomes as good as or better than those with physicians. Births through nurse-midwives result in fewer forceps deliveries, cesarean sections, episiotomies, stillbirths, and low-birth-weight babies (Boston Women's Health Book Collective, 1984; Tew, 1978). Similarly, a study of paired samples of 1,146 home and hospital births revealed no differences in infant mortality rates, but lower rates of infant and maternal disease and birth injuries in home births (Mehl & Peterson, 1981; Tew, 1978).

One reason for the high success rate of home births is that a prospective candidate for home delivery must be screened carefully. The National Association of Parents and Professionals for Safe Alternatives in Childbirth (NAPSAC) recommends certain standards to ensure maternal and infant health. The woman must live less than 10 miles from the hospital and be willing to go there in case of complications. She must be educated about birth, learn to identify birth and labor complications, and agree to prepare her home for delivery. She also must locate a pediatrician who will see the infant soon after birth.

The NAPSAC advises against home birth if the woman

1. is not in good health;
2. has a history of previous birth complications;
3. has chances of a premature, breech transverse, or multiple birth;
4. has a blood incompatibility with the baby; or
5. has a pelvic size insufficient for normal passage of the baby's head.

Many physicians will not deliver babies at home. Even those who approve may lose hospital privileges or insurance coverage. Many couples also find that their health insurance policies will not cover home deliveries.

Even with careful screening, there are risks and disadvantages to home births. The couple must weigh the benefits against the risks.

---

ion is changing gradually in relation to the role of the father. Because fathers are encouraged to attend classes with their partners and to act as coaches during labor and delivery, many couples are insisting that the father be present during the entire process, even during the delivery. Certainly, a partner's willingness to participate in childbirth can be critical to the physical comfort and satisfaction of his mate's experience (Block, Norr, Meyering, Norr, & Charles, 1981). One study revealed that fathers who were present at delivery showed more interest in looking at and talking to their infants than fathers who did not attend the birth (Miller & Bowen, 1982). To avoid misunderstanding, the issue of the father's presence during delivery needs to be worked out between the couple and physician beforehand.

A majority of obstetricians accept most concepts of prepared childbirth and think they are advantageous. The combined benefits of psychological suggestion and physical conditioning can enhance the woman's comfort and happiness throughout the labor and delivery process.

Birthing Rooms and Family-Centered Care

Birthing rooms are lounge-type, informal, pleasantly decorated rooms with homelike settings within the hospital itself. Medical equipment is present but unobtrusive. Both labor and delivery take place in the birthing room, attended by the father and a nurse-midwife or obstetrician. The woman can be moved into another room if complications arise. The mother is encouraged to keep her baby with her after delivery to encourage bonding (Parker, 1980).

Birthing centers are another alternative to the standard hospital setting. They are separated from, but near, a hospital. They seek to combine the advantages of delivery in a homelike environment with the medical backup of a hospital. Birthing centers provide complete prenatal and delivery services to families. They emphasize childbirth as a family-centered event, giving both parents maximum involvement (Eakins, 1986). One big advantage of birthing centers is that new parents learn about infant care while still at the center.

LABOR

Beginning

Labor—rhythmic muscular contractions of the uterus that expel the baby through the birth canal

Real **labor** is rhythmic in nature, recurring at fixed intervals, with uterine contractions usually beginning about 15 to 20 minutes apart and then decreasing to 3- to 4-minute intervals when labor is well under way. In addition, the total length of each contraction increases from less than ½ minute to more than 1 minute. The **show**, or discharge of the blood-tinged mucus plug sealing the neck of the uterus, may precede the onset of labor by as much as 72 hours. At other times, it is an indication that labor has begun (Berkow, 1987).

Show—blood-tinged mucus expelled from the cervix, usually when labor contractions begin

Today few deliveries take place at home and are attended by a midwife. Dilation is the longest of labor's three stages.

Sometimes the first sign of impending labor is rupture of the **amniotic sac** (bag of waters), followed by a gush or leakage of watery fluid from the vagina. In one-eighth of all pregnancies, especially in first pregnancies, the amniotic membranes rupture *before* labor begins. When this happens, labor will commence 6 to 24 hours later if the woman is within a few days of term. If she is not near term, doctors try to delay labor until the fetal lungs are mature. Bed rest in the hospital is usually prescribed, or medication is necessary. The real problem is the risk of infection. If infection is suspected or fetal maturity is reached, delivery is accomplished (Berkow, 1987). About half the time, however, the bag of waters does not rupture until the last hours of labor.

Amniotic sac (bag of waters)—sac containing the liquid in which the fetus is suspended during pregnancy

Duration

Bean (1974) studied 10,000 patients who delivered at Johns Hopkins Hospital. The study encompassed length of labor and delivery of each patient from onset of the first contraction until extrusion of the afterbirth. The median length of labor for *pripara* (first labor) women was 10.6 hours; for *multipara* (refers to all labor subsequent to the first) women, 6.2 hours. One woman in 100 may anticipate that her first child will be born in less than 3 hours. Every ninth woman requires more than 24 hours.

Stages

The actual process of labor can be divided into three stages. The first and longest is the *dilation stage,* during which the force of the uterine muscles pushing on the baby gradually opens the mouth of the cervix. The cervix increases from less than 0.8 (⅘) inch in diameter to 4 inches. The woman can do nothing to help except relax as completely as possible, allowing the involuntary muscles to do their work. Dilation progresses faster if the mother is not tense. Dilation is complete when the baby's head can start to pass through the cervix.

Upon complete dilation of the cervix, the second stage of labor begins, during which *the baby passes through the birth canal.* When hard contractions come, the woman alternatively pushes and relaxes to help force the baby through the vagina. After the baby is born and tended to, the obstetrician again turns his or her attention to the mother to assist in the third stage of labor.

Passage of the placenta, or afterbirth, occurs during the third stage.

Use of Anesthesia

To alleviate pain in childbirth, **general anesthesia** or **local or regional anesthesia** may be used. General anesthesia affects the body by acting on the whole nervous system; it can slow or stop labor and lower the mother's blood pressure (Wilson, Carrington, & Ledger, 1983). It crosses the placental barrier and affects the fetus as well, decreasing the responses of the newborn infant. Local or regional anesthesia blocks pain in specific areas; some types have a minimal effect on the baby. Table 4.1 describes various types of anesthesia under each category.

Fetal Monitoring

Electronic fetal monitoring, with external devices applied to the woman's abdomen, detects and records fetal heart tones and uterine contractions. Internal leads may also be used, with an electrode attached to the fetal

TABLE 4.1 Types of Anesthesia Used in Childbirth

General Anesthesia	Effects

Inhalation anesthesia
  nitrous oxide
  ether
  halothane
  thiopental
	In sufficient quantities, renders woman unconscious. Used only in advanced stages of labor. May cause vomiting and other complications; leading cause of maternal death. Depresses infant's nervous system and respiration. Nitrous oxide may delay infant motor skill development.

Barbiturates
  Nembutal
  Seconal
  Amytal
  Sodium Pentothal
	Usually taken orally, except for Sodium Pentothal. Reduce anxiety and cause drowsiness. Pentothal is injected intravenously to induce sleep. All types may slow labor and depress infant's nervous system and respiration.

Narcotics
  Demerol
  Dolophine
  Nisentil
	Reduce pain, elevate mood; may inhibit uterine contractions; may cause nausea and vomiting; depress infant's nervous system and respiration.

Tranquilizers
  Valium
  Vistaril
  Sparine
  promethazine
	Induce physical relaxation, relieve anxiety, may reduce pain. Have minimal effect on infant.

Amnesics
  scopolamine
  atropine
	Do not reduce pain, but induce "twilight sleep" or forgetfulness. May cause physical excitation. Have minimal effect on infant.

Local or Regional Anesthesia	Effects
Pudendal: local injection of novocaine in vulval-perineal area	Blocks pain in vulva and perineum in 50 percent of cases. Has minimal effect on infant.
Paracervical: local injection of novocaine into cervix and uterus	Blocks pain in cervix and uterus for short duration; not effective late in labor. Can lower mother's blood pressure, cause complications, slow fetal heartbeat, precipitate fetal death.
Spinal: regional injection into space around spinal column	Used during delivery to anesthetize entire birth area from abdomen to toes. Stops labor, motor functions. Requires forceps delivery. Generally does not affect infant unless misadministered; then can cause heart and respiratory failure and death.
Epidural: regional injection administered continuously through a tiny catheter and a needle in the back	Effectively numbs area around perineum, lower uterus, and belly to knees. Can cause serious drop in mother's blood pressure and seizures. May require forceps delivery. Used frequently for cesarean sections.
Caudal: regional injection administered continuously through a catheter and needle in the back	Requires larger doses than epidural. Carries greater risk to infant and mother. May cause sudden drop in mother's blood pressure and lack of oxygen to infant.

scalp and a catheter through the cervix into the uterus to measure amniotic fluid pressure. The external devices are generally employed for normal pregnancies, and the internal methods for high-risk or problem pregnancies. External fetal monitoring is routinely used in all labors by many obstetricians. Other obstetricians feel it is not always necessary and restricts the mother's movement. If a problem occurs or has been previously identified, internal monitoring is used to provide more reliable information about fetal heart patterns and uterine contraction patterns (Berkow, 1987).

DELIVERY

Normal Delivery

In normal delivery, the baby's head is delivered first, the baby's body then rotates so that one shoulder then the other is delivered, and then the rest of the baby's body is delivered without difficulty. The baby's nose, mouth, and pharynx are aspirated with a bulb syringe to remove mucus and fluid and help establish breathing. The umbilical cord is double clamped, cut between the clamps, and tied. Normally, obstetricians recommend that an **episiotomy** be performed on almost all patients having their first baby, or on those who have had a previous episiotomy (Berkow, 1987). An episiotomy involves a surgical incision to prevent excessive stretching or tearing of the tissues of the **perineum**. It is easily stitched up after birth and heals more easily than a tear.

Episiotomy—a surgical incision of the perineum to allow for passage of the baby from the birth canal without tearing the mother's tissue

Perineum—area of skin between the vagina and anus

Stress on the Infant

Giving birth produces stress on the baby as well as on the mother. The powerful muscles of the uterus squeeze the baby, usually head first, through the birth canal. Contractions may compress the *placenta* and *umbilical cord* periodically, causing some oxygen deprivation during those times. Furthermore, the infant passes from its dark, warm, secure environment into the outside world with bright lights, cool temperatures, and noises.

Research has revealed that the stress of birth produces large amounts of *adrenaline* and *noradrenaline* in the baby's blood. These are the same hormones that prepare the adult to flee or fight in situations of danger or emergency. The hormones in the infant have a stimulating affect on breathing, heart action, and all organs and cells of the body.

FOCUS

Induced or Accelerated Labor?

There are various reasons why physicians sometimes induce labor: Rh incompatibility problems, diabetes, toxemia, rupture of the bag of waters, cessation of labor, overdue baby, or unavailability of trained personnel located near the mother's home. In 1978 the Federal Drug Administration took a stand against elective induction (that which is solely for the woman's or physician's convenience). Elective induction is rare and is usually used when patients live long distances from the hospital and when weather would make transportation difficult. Risks of induced labor include internal hemorrhaging, uterine rupture, hypertension, oxygen deprivation to the fetus, premature birth, or excessive labor pain.

The most successful and safest method for induction is giving dilute intravenous oxytocin, using an infusion pump for precise control. External fetal monitoring is essential. Internal monitoring is performed as soon as the membranes can be safely ruptured (Berkow, 1987).

As a consequence, the baby is usually born alert. Babies delivered by **cesarean section** before labor has begun lack these high levels of hormones, which is one reason why these babies may have problems breathing right after birth (Lagercrantz & Slotkin, 1986).

Cesarean section—removal of the fetus through a surgical incision of the abdominal and uterine walls

Delivery Complications

Complications during delivery may include vaginal bleeding during the first stage of labor, abnormal fetal heart rate, a disproportion in size between the fetus and the pelvic opening, or abnormal fetal presentations and positions. Abnormal presentations include a *face presentation, brow presentation, shoulder presentation*, or *breech presentation* (when the buttocks present rather than the head). Sometimes feet are presented before the buttocks. All of these abnormal presentations require expert attention. Sometimes delivery by cesarean section is essential to protect the infant.

Anoxia and Brain Injury

Two of the most serious delivery complications are **anoxia** (oxygen deprivation to the brain) and *brain injury*. Anoxia may result

Anoxia—oxygen deprivation to the brain

Prolapsed cord—
squeezing of the
umbilical cord be-
tween the baby's
body and the wall
of the birth canal
during childbirth,
causing oxygen
deprivation to the
fetus

from a **prolapsed umbilical cord** (the cord is squeezed between the baby's body and the birth canal). It also may result from placental insufficiency, premature labor, severe maternal bleeding, maternal hypotension, toxemia, neonatal pulmonary dysfunction, placental passage of maternal analgesics or anesthetics, or because of malformations (Berkow, 1987). The result of anoxia may be permanent damage to the infant's brain cells or even death. The brain can also be injured during difficult deliveries, especially when forceps are used improperly during the procedure.

POSTPARTUM

Leboyer Method

Leboyer method—
ideas for gentle
birth procedure

In his book *Birth Without Violence*, the French obstetrician Dr. Frederick Leboyer (1975) emphasized gentle, loving treatment of the newborn. His ideas, combined in the **Leboyer method**, include the use of dim lights, gentle voices, and delay in cutting the cord until the naked newborn is soothed, massaged, and stroked while resting on the mother's abdomen. After the cord is cut, the baby is bathed in water of similar tempera-

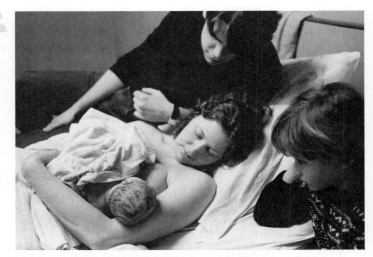

Birthing centers emphasize childbirth as a family-centered event.

ture to the amniotic fluid in which he or she lived for 9 months. American obstetricians do not accept all of Dr. Leboyer's ideas.

The theory behind the Leboyer method is that bringing a newborn into a world of blinding lights and loud voices, where it is jerked upside down, spanked, treated roughly, and immediately separated from its

FOCUS

Too Many Cesareans?

As discussed, cesareans can be a life-saving procedure in many emergency situations. Cesarean sections now account for up to 18% of all births (Pritchard, Mac-Donald, & Grant, 1985). The rapid increase in their use has led some to cry out that too many cesareans are being performed without sufficient cause, although numerous reasons account for the increase.

1. Obstetrician anxiety, the doctor's fear of being sued if a baby is born less than perfect. Physicians think that cesarean procedures cover them legally.
2. Once a cesarean, always a cesarean. However, in 1982 the American College of Obstetricians and Gynecologists reversed its 75-year-old policy and said that some women who had previously had a cesarean could have a vaginal delivery (Gellman et al., 1983; Lavin, Stephens, Miodovnik, & Barden, 1982; Porreco & Meier, 1983).
3. Obstetrician unwillingness or inability to perform difficult deliveries.

4. Improved obstetrical technology, which detects fetal distress that requires cesarean intervention.
5. Improved training, which reduces the surgical risks.
6. Obstetrical practices making cesarean intervention more necessary, for example, a complication arising from labor induction.
7. Belief that cesareans mean better babies.
8. Patient pressure: Some women want to avoid labor.
9. Medical enthusiasm for cesareans: "What's so great about delivery from below? . . . You don't want the baby squeezed out like toothpaste in a tube. . . . You might say we're helping women to do what nature hasn't evolved to do for herself" (Boston Women's Health Collective, 1984, p. 386).
10. Financial incentives: Physicians and hospitals make more money, and many insurance companies reimburse most of the cost of cesareans, though they cover only a small portion of the cost of vaginal delivery.

mother, is a terrifying, traumatic experience after the secure, warm world of the womb. Leboyer explained why we do this: "Because we never really thought of the infant as a person. The newborn is a sensitive, feeling human being, and in the first few moments after birth, he should be treated that way. We must introduce him to the world gradually" (Braun, 1975, p. 17). Advocates of the Leboyer method are highly enthusiastic.

Results of research to date do not offer substantial proof that the benefits are as great as claimed. One research study found that infants delivered by the Leboyer method were only slightly more contented and easier to care for than those delivered by other methods (Maziade, Boudreault, Cote, & Thivierge, 1986). However, the emphasis on gentle treatment is a positive one, and the mother is happier that her baby has received special care.

Evaluating Neonatal Health and Behavior

APGAR SCORE. After delivery, the physician will evaluate the health status of the neonate. The most common method is a widely used system developed by Virginia Apgar in 1952 called the **Apgar Score**. The system has designated values for various neonatal signs and permits a tentative and rapid diagnosis of major problems (Apgar, 1953). The neonate is evaluated at 1 minute and 5 minutes after birth.

There are five signs of the baby's physical condition that compose the Apgar Score: *heart rate, respiratory effort, muscle tone, reflex response* (response to breath test and to skin stimulation of the feet), and *color*. Each sign is given a value of 0, 1, or 2, as shown in Table 4.2 (Greenberg, Bruess, & Sands, 1986). The maximum score on all five scales is 10, and is rare. A score of 0–3 indicates the infant is very weak; 4–6, moderately weak; and 7–10, in good condition.

BRAZELTON ASSESSMENT. Dr. T. Berry Brazelton (1984) developed the **Brazelton Neonatal Behavior Assessment Scale**, which is used to evaluate both the neurological condition and the behavior of the neonate (Brazelton, 1990). The scale is a useful indicator of central nervous system maturity and of

Apgar score— method of evaluating the physical condition of the neonate

Brazelton Neonatal Behavior Assessment Scale— method of evaluating the neurological condition of the neonate

---

TABLE 4.2 Apgar Score

The Apgar scoring, developed in 1952 by Dr. Virginia Apgar, is an index to the health status of the newborn infant. The scoring system was developed to predict survival, to compare various methods of resuscitation, to evaluate certain obstetrical practices (such as inducing labor, maternal anesthesia, cesarean section), and to ensure closer observation of the infant during the first minutes of life.

Five signs of a baby's physical condition at birth were chosen for measurement: heart rate, respiratory effort, muscle tone, reflex response (response to breath test and to skin stimulation of the feet), and color. Each sign is given a score of 0, 1, or 2, as shown in the table.

Sign	0	1	2
Heart rate	Absent	Slow (below 100)	Over 100
Respiratory effort	Absent	Weak cry, hypoventilation	Good strong cry
Muscle tone	Limp	Some flexion of extremities	Well-flexed
Reflex response Response to catheter in nostril (tested after pharynx is clear)	No response	Grimace	Cough or sneeze
Tangential feet slap	No response	Grimace	Cry and withdrawal of foot
Color	Blue, pale	Body pink, extremities blue	Healthy skin with no discoloration

The Apgar Score is the sum of the five values and ranges from 0 to 10, with 10 being the optimum. A score of 0–3 indicates that the infant is very weak; 4–6, moderately weak; and 7–10, in good to excellent condition. One-minute and five-minute scoring are done. The one-minute score indicates the condition at birth; the five-minute score combines the condition at birth and the results of care given during the first five minutes.

From "A Proposal for a New Method of Evaluation of a Newborn Infant" by Virginia A. Apgar, 1975, *Anesthesia and Analgesia*, 32. Copyright © 1975 International Anesthesia Research Society. Reprinted by permission.

social behavior and is helpful in predicting subsequent developmental problems (Behrman & Vaughan, 1983). The scale assesses four areas of infant behavior:

Motor behaviors (reflexes, hand-to-mouth coordination, and muscle tone)
Interactive, adaptive behavior (alertness, cuddliness)
Response to stress (startle reaction)
Physiological control (ability to calm down after being upset)

Altogether, the scale looks at 26 specific behaviors as well as the strength of various reflexes (Brazelton, 1984).

Postpartum Blues

The period following childbirth is one in which conflicting feelings may surface (Leifer, 1980). The long pregnancy is over, which brings a feeling of relief. If the baby is wanted and healthy, the family experiences considerable happiness and elation. Within several days after delivery, however, the woman may suffer varying degrees of "baby blues," or **postpartal depression**, characterized by feelings of sadness, periods of crying, depressed mood, insomnia, irritability, and fatigue (Hopkins, Marcues, & Campbell, 1984).

Numerous causes precipitate postpartal depression. The mother may have been under emotional strain while she anxiously awaited her baby. Once the baby comes, feelings of exhaustion and depression may result from a letdown of tension. Childbirth itself may impose considerable physical strain on a woman's body, which requires a period of rest and recovery. Estrogen and progesterone levels decline rapidly following delivery, which may have an upsetting, depressive effect on her (Waletzky, 1981).

Upon returning home, the mother may feel the strain of "trying to do everything right" in caring for the baby. One young

Postpartal depression—feelings of sadness, crying, depression, insomnia, irritability, and fatigue commonly experienced by the mother several days after her baby is born

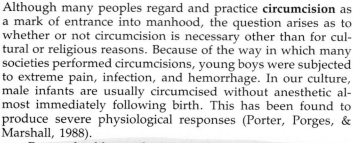

PARENTING ISSUES

Circumcision Pros and Cons

Although many peoples regard and practice **circumcision** as a mark of entrance into manhood, the question arises as to whether or not circumcision is necessary other than for cultural or religious reasons. Because of the way in which many societies performed circumcisions, young boys were subjected to extreme pain, infection, and hemorrhage. In our culture, male infants are usually circumcised without anesthetic almost immediately following birth. This has been found to produce severe physiological responses (Porter, Porges, & Marshall, 1988).

From a health standpoint, medical professionals are divided concerning the necessity of circumcision. Those in favor contend that it reduces the incidence of *carcinoma* (cancer) of the penis, as well as urinary tract infections and *cervical cancer* in women sex-partners (Green, 1977). Proponents also contend that a circumcised penis is easier to keep clean and improves sexual sensation and fulfillment. When the foreskin is too tight and cannot be retracted, circumcision is necessary.

The latest research is inconsistent in relation to these arguments. Wallerstein (1980) compiled and analyzed the data available and found no causal relationship between circumcision or lack of it and any kind of cancer. But carcinoma of the penis is more likely to occur in men who do not thoroughly and regularly cleanse themselves. If the glans is kept clean, whether the foreskin has to be retracted or not, cancer is less likely to occur. Similarly, the presence or absence of a foreskin does not cause urinary tract infections or cervical cancer in men's sexual partners; however, the lack of penile cleanliness does (Rotkin, 1973).

Opponents of the procedure contend that circumcision does not increase sexual satisfaction. During erection, the foreskin retracts from the glans so sensation is not affected. Some authorities even feel that circumcision reduces sexual sensitivity because the penis constantly rubs on clothing. However, there is really no evidence to substantiate whether circumcision affects sexual function one way or the other (Masters & Johnson, 1966).

Because routine circumcision has been practiced for so many years, the custom is hard to break. A national survey of several hundred pediatricians and obstetricians revealed that 38% of the pediatricians and 60% of the obstetricians supported routine circumcision for sound medical reasons (Herrera & Macaraeg, 1984). However, in strong opposition to the view of most obstetricians, the American Academy of Pediatrics concluded in 1975 that if there was no medical need for circumcision of the newborn, the procedure should not be performed routinely (Kirkendall, 1981). Canadian researchers recommended that government medical plans not pay for the procedure because no significant benefits could be demonstrated from routine circumcision (Cadman, Gafni, & McNamee, 1984).

mother remarked: "I never imagined that one small baby would require so much extra work. I'm exhausted" (Author's counseling notes). If the woman does not have much help from her partner, or if he or other children in the household continue to make personal demands upon her, she may become exhausted from the lack of sleep, and from the physical and emotional strain. Some women even return to their jobs outside the home very soon after having a baby. Clearly, the mother needs help and understanding. A conscientious partner will do everything he can to be a full partner in the process and to assume maximum responsibility in caring for her. He will share the responsibility of caring for the baby, and take full or increased responsibility in the care of other children and in managing the household during at least the first several months with a new baby.

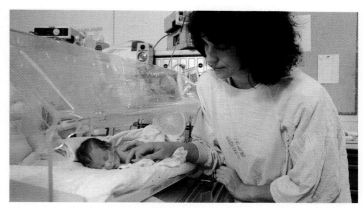

A premature infant is one whose gestational age is less than 37 weeks.

cartilage. Spontaneous activity and tone are at a minimum, and their extremities are not held in a fixed position. The testes are undescended in males; the labia majora do not cover the labia minora in females.

PREMATURE AND SMALL-FOR-GESTATIONAL-AGE (SGA) INFANTS

Classifications

Full-term infant

Premature infant

Postmature infant

Each newborn may be classified as full-term, premature, or postmature. A **full-term infant** is one whose gestational age is 37 to 42 weeks. A **premature infant** is one whose gestational age is less than 37 weeks (Duffy, Als, & McAnulty, 1990). A **postmature infant** has a gestational age of over 42 weeks. The neonate may also be classified as of appropriate size and weight for gestational age, small for gestational age, or large for gestational age. Figure 4.1 represents intrauterine growth based on birth weight and gestational age of liveborn, single, white infants (Sweet, 1979).

Premature Infants

A premature infant is one who is born before 37 weeks gestation. Previously, any infant weighing less than 2.5 kg (5.5 lb) was termed premature, but this definition was inappropriate because many newborns weighing less than 2.5 kg are actually mature or postmature but small for gestational age (SGA) and have different appearance and problems than premature infants (Berkow, 1987). However, most premature infants are also small, weighing less than 2.5 kg, and have thin, shiny, pink skin with underlying veins that are easily seen. They have little fat, hair, or external ear

FIGURE 4.1 Intrauterine growth of liveborn, white infants. Baby A is premature, whereas baby B is mature but small for gestational age. Curves show growth of infants in 10th and 90th percentiles. Adapted from "Classification of the Low-Birth-Weight Infant" by A. Y. Sweet, in *Care of the High-Risk Neonate,* 2nd ed., 1979 by M. H. Klaus and A. A. Fanaroff. Copyright 1979 by W. B. Saunders Co.

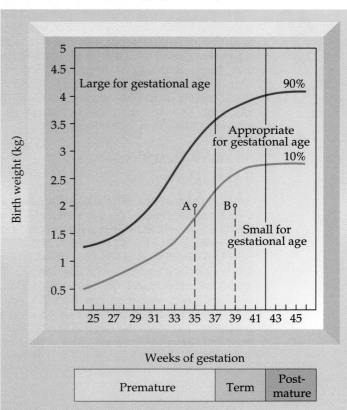

Problems with premature infants relate to immaturity of the organs. Premature infants have various kinds of respiratory difficulties. They may have inadequate sucking and swallowing reflexes; they may have a small stomach capacity and may have to be tube fed or fed intravenously. They often suffer from colitis and other gastrointestinal problems. They have lower immunity and are more subject to various infections than full-term infants. They exhibit various signs of metabolic difficulties: hypothermia (below normal body temperature); hypoglycemia (low blood glucose levels); hypocalcemia (low calcium levels); and hypernatremia (high sodium concentrations) are common. Renal function is immature, so the kidneys are less able to excrete fluids. Premature infants are also more prone to cerebral hemorrhage and injury (Sostek, Smith, Katz, & Grant, 1987).

Assuming there have been no significant abnormalities, and assuming proper medical, emotional, and social care and attention, preterm infants can often make up deficits in cognitive, language, and social development during the first 3 years of life (Greenberg & Crnic, 1988). When there are developmental deficits, it is usually because of significant medical complications. Altogether only 10% to 15% of all preterm infants have major intellectual impairment or neurological problems (Kopp, 1983), but as many as 100% of survivors in the lowest birth weight categories (less than 800 g, or 1.8 lbs) may be neurologically impaired (Britton, Chir, Fitzhardinge, & Ashby, 1981; Murray, 1988). Infants with birth weights less than 1.5 kilograms (3.3 lb) are at special risk (Rose, Feldman, McCarton, & Wolfson, 1988).

Small-for-Gestational-Age (SGA) Infants

An *SGA infant* is one whose weight is below the 10th percentile for gestational age, whether premature, full-term, or postmature (Achenbach, Phares, & Howell, 1990). Despite their small size, SGA infants have physical characteristics and behavior similar to normal-size infants of the same gestational age. An infant weighing less than 2.5 kilograms, but born between 37 and 42 weeks gestation, may have the same skin, ear, genital, and neurologic development as any other full-term infant. If low birth weight is due to prenatal malnutrition, such infants catch up quickly when given an adequate caloric intake (Berkow, 1987).

Perinatal (near the time of birth) *asphyxia*

Only 10% to 15% of all preterm infants have major intellectual impairment or neurological problems.

(lack of oxygen) is the greatest problem of these infants. If intrauterine growth retardation is due to placental insufficiency, asphyxia during labor is common, so a rapid delivery, sometimes by cesarean section, is needed. An infant who does not breathe spontaneously requires immediate resuscitation to sustain life and avoid brain damage. If asphyxia can be avoided, the neurologic prognosis is good. *Hypoglycemia* (low blood sugar) is also common due to inadequate glycogen storage (Berkow, 1987).

Assuming there have been no serious complications, the question still arises regarding the effects of low birth weight on health during subsequent childhood. In 1981, 15,400 interviews were carried out among the parents of children age 17 or younger that year. This study, known as the Child Health Supplement (CHS), was part of the National Interview Survey (Overpeck et al., 1989). About 8% of the children in the CHS sample were of low birth weight. (No distinction was made between prematurity and low birth weight.) Overall, 7% of the white children and 15% of the black children were of low birth weight. The study found that throughout childhood, but especially during the first 6 years, children who had been of low birth weight had a greater number of chronic conditions, were hospitalized more often, and generally exhibited a pattern of poorer health than did children who were of normal birth weight. The most common chronic condition was *respiratory illness* (Overpeck et al., 1989).

Parental Roles and Reactions

Ordinarily, the birth of a full-term infant is a positive event bringing happiness and close-

Preterm infants are critically dependent on parents to provide an adequate care-giving environment.

ness to family members. The birth of a preterm infant is a stressful event, leaving family members unsure of their roles and how to respond. Grandparents, for example, may need to grieve over the loss of their idealized grandchild. Rituals such as showers and birth announcements may be eliminated or postponed, leaving other family members in the dark. The anxiety and stress of the parents is increased when they don't find positive social supports. Furthermore, parents often find preterm infants less attractive, more irritating, and less likable (Easterbrooks, 1989). Mothers of preterm infants have been found to have lower maternal sensitivity to their infants than do mothers of full-term babies (Zarling, Hirsch, & Landry, 1988). The mother's reduced sensitivity interferes with the infant's total development because preterm infants are critically dependent on parents to provide an adequate care-giving environment, social enrichment, and encouragement (Levy-Shiff, Sharir, & Mogelner, 19889).

Intervention programs for parents of low-birth-weight, preterm infants are needed to help parents gain more self-confidence and satisfaction with parenting and to develop more positive perceptions of their infants (Affleck, Tennen, Rowe, Roscher, & Walker, 1989). Such programs usually consist of a series of teaching sessions in the hospital and follow-ups in the parents' home after the infant is discharged (Rauh, Achenbach, Nurcombe, Howell, & Teti, 1988).

THE NEONATE

Physical Appearance and Characteristics

At birth, the average full-term baby in the United States is about 20 inches long (50.8 cm) and weighs about 7 pounds (3.2 kg). Males tend to be larger and heavier than females, and size at birth bears a relationship to size during childhood. Most newborns lose 5% to 10% of their birth weight in the first few days of life because of fluid loss, and until they take in and digest enough food to begin gaining weight (Berkow, 1987).

Some newborns are not very attractive (Ritter, Casey, & Longlois, 1991). The *head* may be long, pointed, or misshapen from being squeezed through the birth canal. The ears and nose may be flattened for the same reason. The head is disproportionately large in relation to the rest of the body, and too heavy for the neck muscles to support it. The *legs and buttocks* are small in proportion to the rest of the body. The face, especially the flesh around the eyes, is usually puffy; the brow is wrinkled. The skin of the baby is covered with a protective cheeselike substance: **vernix caseosa**. Some babies have fuzzy body hair that drops off in a short time. Underweight babies look like wrinkled old people.

Vernix caseosa— waxy substance covering the skin of the neonate

Physiological Functioning

Although most neonates will not win any beauty contests, they are remarkable creatures with their own independently functioning systems. They must *breathe* on their own

A newborn's skin is covered with a protective cheeselike substance: *vernix caseosa.*

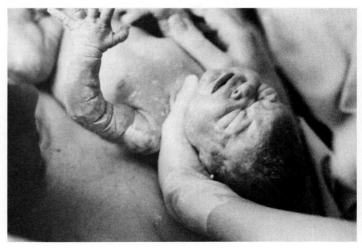

FOCUS

Kilogram Kids and Intensive Neonatal Care

Remarkable advances have been made in caring for pre-term infants. Highly specialized neonatal intensive-care units (NICUs) have been developed to take over various functions of organ systems of the body that are not sufficiently mature to sustain life on their own. The NICU is a series of blinking lights, numbers, monitors, and alarms, all of which are connected by tubes, catheters, and electrodes to the tiny infant. The NICU monitors brain waves, heartbeat, respiration, and other vital signs, and provides food, oxygen, and medicines. The infant lies on an undulating water bed in an incubator that carefully controls temperature and humidity.

Researchers have found that, even when confined to incubators, these tiny infants need normal skin contacts, handling, cuddling, talking, singing, and rocking from care givers and parents. Such contacts facilitate development (Scafidi, 1986; Zeskind & Iacino, 1984).

The survival rate of premature infants closely correlates with their birth weight. Kilogram infants weigh 1,000 grams (2.2 lb). In the best hospitals, 80% to 85% of infants 2.2 to 3.2 pounds (1 kg to 1.5 kg) survive. Remarkably, about a fourth of those weighing 1.6 pounds (750 g) survive (Davis, 1986; Fincher, 1982). Intensive care of these smallest infants poses a real dilemma, however. They may survive, but up to 100% of 750-gram babies are neurologically impaired. Costs for

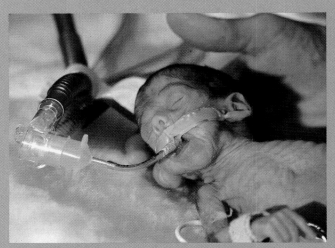

Intensive care of kilogram infants (2.2 lbs) poses a real dilemma: The majority survive but are neurologically impaired.

intensive care in the hospital may run from $100,000 to $200,000, leaving a family poverty-stricken. The question remains: How much care is too much? At what point should infants be allowed to die, rather than be saved to live with such severe impairments that they can never have a chance for a normal life?

---

as soon as they emerge into the air. In the beginning, breathing may be rapid, shallow, and irregular, but it gradually settles into a more regular rhythm. The infant can cough and sneeze to clear mucus from air passages.

The baby has had an *independent circulatory system*, with a heart pumping blood to the embryo, since the end of the sixth week of gestation (Witters & Jones-Witters, 1980). At birth, the heartbeat is still accelerated at about 120 to 150 beats per minute. Blood pressure begins to stabilize in about 10 days.

The baby has a strong *sucking reflex* to be able to take in milk. However, the mother's breasts don't begin secreting milk for 2 to 3 days after birth. In the meantime, a thin, watery, high-protein liquid called **colostrum** is produced, which is nutritionally rich and contains antibodies that enable the baby to fight infections. Some babies develop *physiological jaundice* for a while because of the immaturity of the liver. The condition is characterized by a yellowish tinge to the skin

and eyeballs. The condition is not serious and is treated by exposure to fluorescent light, which helps the action of the liver.

Because newborns lack fat layers under their skin, they lose heat very quickly, so they have difficulty maintaining stable body temperature. Crying and physical activity help them control the temperature.

The Senses and Perception

At one time it was thought that newborns' senses were not very well developed. Now it is recognized that *neonates are seeing, hearing, feeling, smelling, touching, tasting creatures who respond to a variety of stimuli, including pain.*

VISION.   Vision is the least developed of the senses. Newborns can see clearly objects between 7 and 15 inches away. Their eyes cannot focus properly at closer or farther distances. They have poor *visual acuity*: the

Colostrum—high-protein liquid secreted by the mother's breasts prior to her milk coming in; contains antibodies to protect the nursing infant from diseases

ability to distinguish details of objects. Their visual acuity at distances has been estimated to be between 20/150 and 20/800. (Normal vision is 20/20.) This means the neonate can see details of objects at 20 feet no more clearly than adults with normal vision would see them at 150 to 800 feet. However, at close distances, newborns can discriminate among circles, crosses, squares, and rectangles (Bronson, 1991; Slater, Morison, & Rose, 1983). They prefer looking at faces to looking at objects, and by 1 month of age can distinguish their mother's face from those of others (Ludemann, 1991; Maurer & Salapatek, 1976). They can tell the difference between different facial expressions and even imitate some of them (Field, Woodson, Greenberg, & Cohen, 1982).

By 6 months of age, visual acuity is about normal (Banks & Salapatek, 1983). The irises of babies' eyes open and close as lights go from dim to bright. Some infants have *binocular vision* at birth; that is, they use both eyes to focus on an object. It is not known whether they can see colors immediately, although this ability can be demonstrated by a few months of age (Bornstein, 1985).

HEARING.   Infants can hear sounds while still in the uterus. They respond to various loud noises such as cars honking (Birnholz & Benacerraf, 1983). In fact, they can probably distinguish between their mother's voice and the voices of others (Aslin, Pisoni, & Jusczyk, 1983). After birth, their hearing is only slightly less sensitive than that of adults (Acredolo & Hoke, 1982). They seem to be able to discriminate among sounds of different intensity, pitch, and duration; are more sensitive to higher-pitched than lower-pitched sounds; and are most sensitive to human voices (Aslin, Pisoni, & Jusczyk, 1983; Spetner & Olsho, 1990). They can also detect the direction from which sound comes and turn their head toward it (Brody, Zelago, & Chaika, 1984). Like adults, neonates can get bored with the continuous presentation of a sound, but when presented with a new sound, such as a bell ringing, will pay attention or even show a startle response to it (Madison, Madison, & Adubato, 1986; Weiss, Zelazo, & Swain, 1988).

SMELL.   Human neonates are responsive to various odors, including odors from their mother's breast. Within several days after birth, breast-feeding infants respond preferentially either to breast or axillary odors from their own mother when paired with comparable stimuli from an unfamiliar lactating fe-

Human neonates are responsive to various odors, including odors from the mother's breast.

male (Cernoch & Porter, 1985). In another experiment, 2-week-old bottle-feeding girls with no prior breast-feeding experience found the breast odors of lactating females especially attractive (Makin & Porter, 1989).

TASTE.   Newborns can also discriminate among various taste stimuli. Rosenstein and Oster (1988) demonstrated that within 2 hours of birth, infants with no prior taste experience differentiated sour and bitter stimuli as well as sweet versus nonsweet taste stimuli. The responses to the sour, salty, and bitter stimuli were all characterized by negative facial actions in the brow and mid-face regions. This study and others showed clearly that newborns also have an innate preference for sweet solutions (Beauchamp & Cowart, 1985).

TOUCH AND PAIN.   There is strong evidence of touch sensitivity in neonates, with no discernable differences between the sexes. If you stroke the cheeks of newborns, they will turn their head in that direction. Stimulate the soles of infants' feet, and they flex their toes. Every parent knows that one way to soothe infants is to hold and stroke them. Recent studies indicate that infants are also sensitive to pain and that this sensitivity increases during the first 5 days of life (Haith, 1986).

Reflexes

Reflexes—unlearned behavioral responses to particular stimuli in the environment

Reflexes are unlearned behavioral responses to particular stimuli in the environment. Table 4.3 describes some of the reflexes of the neonate. Some of these reflexes, such as the *rooting and sucking reflex*, are critical to the infants' survival. Others evolved during evolutionary development. For example, *Palmar's grasp* was necessary to keep babies from falling when their mothers carried them around all the time. The *Moro reflex* could help infants to grasp something when in danger of falling. Other reflexes, such as blinking or the rage reflex, help protect the baby from physical discomfort. Only the *blinking, knee jerk,* and *sneezing reflexes* are permanent for a lifetime. The rest of the reflexes gradually disappear and are replaced by more deliberate, voluntary movements, as development proceeds.

Brain and Nervous System

Neurons—nerve cells

The nervous systems are composed of **neurons,** or nerve cells, which transmit messages. A neuron contains a *cell body; dendrites,* which receive neural messages; and an *axon,* which passes along the neural messages, in the form of electrical impulses, to the dendrites of the next neuron. The axon is insulated with a *myelin sheath,* which prevents the electrical impulses from leaking out. Figure 4.2 shows a typical neuron.

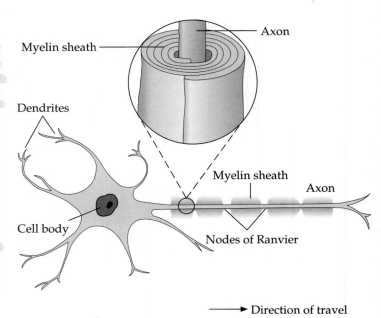

FIGURE 4.2   Neuron. The neurons are wrapped in an insulation substance called myelin. The myelin sheath also speeds transmission through the neuron by preventing the electrical charge from escaping.

There are several differences between the brain and neurons of a neonate and those of a mature adult. (1) The neonate continues to form new nerve cells, a process that continues until about the second month after birth (Lipsitt, 1986). (2) The billions of nerve cells that are present continue to mature. Especially the dendrites grow and develop,

TABLE 4.3 Reflexes of the Neonate	
Reflex	Stimulus and Response
Babinski	Stimulate the sole of the foot; the infant's toes fan out and upward.
Babkin	Apply pressure to both palms of the infant's hands; the infant's eyes close, mouth opens, and the infant turns its head.
Blinking	Flash on a light, or move an object toward the infant's eyes; they blink.
Knee jerk	Tap on the kneecap; the foot kicks upward.
Moro	Make a sudden loud noise or suddenly remove body support; the infant's arms and legs fling outward and toward the body as if to hold onto something.
Palmar grasp	Place an object or finger in the infant's palm; the infant grasps tightly and may even be lifted to a standing position.
Rooting	Touch the infant's cheek; the baby turns toward the touch and attempts to suck.
Rage	Restrain the infant's movements or put a cloth over its mouth; the baby cries and struggles.
Sneezing	Stimulate or tickle the nasal passages; the infant sneezes to clear the passages.
Stepping	Hold the infant upright with feet on the ground; the baby attempts to step as in walking.
Sucking	Put object in infant's mouth; infant begins rhythmic sucking.
Swallowing	Put food in mouth; the neonate swallows it.
Swimming	Place infant on its stomach; its arms and legs fan out and move as in swimming.

increasing their efficiency in receiving messages. (3) Many of the neurons in the newborn are not yet *myelinated*, or enclosed in a sheath, which allows electrical impulses to escape and results in inefficient nerve transmission, jerky responses, and lack of coordination (Morell & Norton, 1980). Myelination continues until adolescence (Guthrie, 1980). (4) The brain of the newborn is noticeably immature, with large areas dysfunctional. Brain activity is concentrated in the *brain stem*, which controls automatic physiological functions such as breathing, digestion, and a variety of reflexes. The *cerebral cortex*, or upper levels of the brain that control more complex functions, is quite immature in newborns. Growth of the cortex as the infant matures allows more flexible, complex motor and intellectual functioning as time goes by (Chugani & Phelps, 1986).

SUMMARY

1. Prepared childbirth refers to the physical, social, intellectual, and emotional preparation for the birth of a baby. In this context, it does not necessarily refer to labor and delivery without medication.

2. Methods of natural childbirth include the Dick-Read method, the Lamaze method, the Kitzinger method, and the Bradley method.

3. About 95% of babies are delivered in the hospital. If couples consider a home delivery, they ought to follow certain standards as outlined by the NAPSAC. Even with careful screening, home delivery has risks and disadvantages.

4. Birthing rooms and centers provide homelike settings where birth takes place and where the mother, and sometimes the whole family, may take care of the infant afterward. These settings seek to combine the advantages of delivery in a homelike environment with the medical backup of a hospital.

5. Real labor is rhythmic in nature and may be divided into three phases: the dilation phase; the childbirth phase; and passage of the placenta, or afterbirth, during the third phase.

6. General anesthesia or local or regional anesthesia may be used to alleviate pain during childbirth. General anesthesia affects the body by acting on the whole nervous system. It crosses the placental barrier and affects the fetus as well. Local anesthesia blocks pain in specific areas; some types have minimal effect on the baby.

7. Electronic fetal monitoring is used to provide information about fetal heartbeat and condition during labor and delivery.

8. There are various reasons why physicians sometimes induce labor, but elective induction solely for the woman's or the physician's convenience is restricted by the Federal Drug Administration.

9. In normal delivery the baby's head is delivered first. Complications during delivery may include vaginal bleeding, abnormal fetal heart rate, a disproportion in size between the fetus and pelvic opening, or abnormal fetal presentations and positions.

10. Birth is a stress on the baby, but the infant produces large amounts of adrenaline and noradrenaline, which have a stimulating affect on the infant and help it to breathe immediately after birth.

11. One of the most serious delivery complications is anoxia (oxygen deprivation to the brain) from a prolapsed umbilical cord or other causes. The result may be permanent damage to the infant's brain cells or even death. Brain injury can also occur during difficult deliveries, especially when forceps are used improperly.

12. A cesarean section can be a life-saving procedure when rapid delivery is needed, but some authorities complain that cesareans are being performed unnecessarily.

13. The Leboyer method of childbirth emphasizes gentle, loving treatment of the newborn, including the use of dim lights and gentle voices as well as soothing, massaging, and stroking the baby while it rests on the mother's abdomen. American obstetricians as well as research do not always support the validity of Leboyer's claims, but the emphasis on gentle treatment is a positive one.

14. After delivery, the physician evaluates the health status of the neonate and gives it an Apgar Score. The Brazelton Neonatal Behavior Assessment Scale is also used to evaluate both the neulogical condition and the behavior of the neonate.

15. Postpartal depression is common following childbirth. The mother needs help and understanding.

16. There are pros and cons regarding circumcision, but the American Academy of Pediatrics indicates there is no medical need for routine circumcision of the newborn.

17. Newborns may be classified as full-term (37 to 42 weeks gestation), premature (less than 37 weeks gestation), and postmature (over 42 weeks gestation). Premature infants may have problems because of the immaturity of their organs.

18. Small-for-gestational age (SGA) infants weigh below the 10th percentile for gestational age, whether premature, full-term, or postmature. They have physical characteristics and behavior similar to normal-size infants of the same gestational age. Perinatal asphyxia (lack of oxygen) is the greatest problem of these infants. However, throughout childhood, especially the first 6 years, they have poorer health than normal-size infants.

19. The birth of a preterm infant is stressful to the parents, who may be less sensitive to an infant who is less attractive, more irritating, and less likable.

20. Remarkable advances have been made in intensive neonatal care for preterm infants. However, intensive care of the very smallest infants, especially those less than 1.6 pounds (750 rams), poses a special dilemma. These infants may survive, but up to 100% are neurologically impaired. How much intensive care is too much? Costs may run from $100,000 to $200,000.

21. The average full-term neonate is about 20 inches long and weighs about 7 pounds. Some are not very attractive.

22. However, the neonate is a remarkable creature. It must breathe on its own; it has had an independent circulatory system operating since the sixth week of gestation. It has a strong sucking reflex to take in milk. It may have problems for a few days with physiological jaundice and may have some trouble regulating body temperature.

23. Neonates possess all the senses, though not all of these are well-developed. Vision is the least developed. Newborns can see clearly objects between 7 and 15 inches away, but have difficulty at closer or farther distances. By 6 months of age, visual acuity is about normal.

24. Infants can hear sounds while still in the uterus. After birth, their hearing is only slightly less sensitive than that of adults.

25. Human neonates are responsive to various odors, including odors from their mother's breast. They can also discriminate among various taste stimuli. There is strong evidence of touch sensitivity.

26. Reflexes are unlearned behavioral responses to particular stimuli in the environment. Reflexes help the infant to survive, to protect itself from harm and from physical discomfort. Only the blinking, knee jerk, and sneezing reflexes are permanent. The rest of the reflexes gradually disappear and are replaced by more deliberate, voluntary movements.

27. The nervous systems are composed of neurons, or nerve cells. The cells in neonates continue to multiply for about the first 2 months. The existing cells become more mature and more capable of transmitting messages. The brain also continues to develop, especially in the cerebral cortex, or higher levels. Growth of the cortex allows more flexible, complex motor and intellectual functioning as time goes by.

KEY TERMS

Amniotic sac (bag of waters) *p. 83*
Anoxia *p. 85*
Apgar score *p. 87*
Bradley method *p. 81*
Brazelton Neonatal Behavior Assessment Scale *p. 87*
Cesarean section *p. 85*
Circumcision *p. 88*
Colostrum *p. 92*
Dick-Read method *p. 80*
Episiotomy *p. 85*

Full-term infant *p. 89*
General anesthesia *p. 84*
Kitzinger method *p. 81*
Labor *p. 83*
Lamaze method *p. 81*
Leboyer method *p. 86*
Local or regional anesthesia *p. 84*
Neurons *p. 94*
Perineum *p. 85*
Postmature infant *p. 89*
Postpartal depression *p. 88*

DISCUSSION QUESTIONS

1. What do you think of the Lamaze method of natural childbirth? What are some advantages and disadvantages? Have you known any parents who used the Lamaze method or a similar method for having their baby? How did it work out?
2. For yourself, what do you think about having both parents participate actively in the labor and delivery process? About both parents being present in the delivery room when the baby is born? Explain your answers.
3. Do you know anyone who had induced labor? Delivery by cesarean section? With what results?
4. Do you know any couple who had a premature baby? What were some of their reactions? What problems did they encounter?
5. Assume you had a 750-gram baby that was premature. Would you want the doctor to try to save the life of your baby if it would be severely mentally retarded afterward?
6. To you who have had a child: What was your first feeling and reaction when you saw your baby? What pleased you the most? What troubled you the most? Explain.

SUGGESTING READINGS

Brazelton, T. B., & Lester, B. M. (1982). *New approaches to developmental screenings of infants*. New York: Elsevier. Brazelton method of neonatal evaluation and other new approaches.

Goldberg, S., & Divitto, B. A. (1983). *Born too soon: Preterm and early development*. San Francisco: Freeman. Focus on the first 3 years of life of preterm infants.

Henig, R. M., with Fletcher, A. B. (1983). *Your premature baby*. New York: Rawson. Guide for parents.

Klaus, M. H., & Klaus, P. H. (1985). *The amazing newborn: Making the most of the first weeks of life*. Reading, MA: Addison-Wesley. Latest scientific findings. Profusely illustrated.

Korte, D., & Scaer, R. (1984). *A good birth, a safe birth*. New York: Bantam. Options for delivery, including natural childbirth.

Lamaze, F. (1981). *Painless childbirth: The Lamaze method*. New York: Pocket. Full explanation.

Leach, P. (1983). *Babyhood* (2nd ed.). New York: Knopf. Covers infancy.

Restak, R. M. (1986). *The infant mind*. Garden City, NY: Doubleday. Early brain development.

Sagov, S. E., Feinbloom, R. I., Spindel, P., & Brodsky, A. (1984). *Home birth: A practitioner's guide to birth outside the hospital*. Rockville, MD.: Aspen Systems Corporation.

Sumner, P., & Phillips, C. (1981) *Birthing rooms: Concept and reality*. St. Louis: C. V. Mosby. Experiences of 13 couples.

PART THREE

CHILD DEVELOPMENT

5

Perspectives on Child Development

CHILD DEVELOPMENT AS A SUBJECT OF STUDY

Child develop-ment—all aspects of human growth from birth to adolescence; the study of this growth

Child development is a specialized discipline devoted to the understanding of all aspects of human development from birth to adolescence. It is a relatively new field of study. Sara Wiltse (1894), the first secretary to the child study section of the National Education Association, remarked that child study really began in America and that "previous to 1888, practically no scientific observations of child life had been done. . . . One searched libraries in vain to find what the average child could either know or do at a given age" (p. 191). Child development leader Margaret Schallenberger (1894) of Stanford University wrote that children were "among the last of nature's productions to become the privileged subjects of scientific study" (p. 87).

Child development is a specialized discipline devoted to understanding all aspects of human development from birth to adolescence.

HISTORICAL PERSPECTIVES

Children as Miniature Adults

One reason that interest in child development was so long in happening is that, *during the Middle ages and until several hundred years later, childhood was not considered a separate stage of life.* Children were permitted a few short years of dependence, then expected to be little adults. Aries (1962) reported that as soon as children outgrew their swaddling clothes (which were wrapped around their bodies), they were dressed like adult men and women. They played adult games, drank with adults, and worked beside them in fields and shops. Children could be married, crowned as monarchs, or hanged as

Paintings during the Middle ages portrayed children as miniature adults.

FOCUS

Paintings of Children

Art before recent times portrayed children as little adults. Their bodily proportions and appearances were shown to resemble those of grown-ups, and certainly the clothing they wore would not permit them to run and play like today's children.

criminals. Medieval law made no distinction between childhood and adult crimes (Borstelmann, 1983). No effort was made to protect their innocence in sexual matters. For example, Louis XIV of France became king at age 5 and played sexual games with his nursemaids. Because childhood was not considered a special stage, and because children were treated as little adults, no effort was made to consider them special in any way.

Children as Burdens

Before modern birth control was available, many of the children brought into the world were really not wanted. Children were considered a burden rather than a blessing. Each child born meant one more body to clothe and look after, and one more mouth to feed. While infanticide was a crime during the Middle Ages and after, it was probably the most frequent crime in all of Europe until about 1800 (Piers, 1978). Unwanted babies were sometimes abandoned or drowned. In the 1300s, Pope Innocent III established the first foundling home in Italy when he became upset at the sight of so many infants' bodies floating down the Tiber River. Some parents, not wanting to kill their infants, sent them to the country to be wet-nursed, or they put them in orphanages where they most likely died. As late as the nineteenth century, one

Irish orphanage had admitted 10,272 children, of which only 45 survived (Thompson & Grusec, 1970, p. 603). Conditions were not any better in the United States. One 1915 study in Baltimore, Maryland, revealed that 90% of children admitted to foundling homes and orphanages in the city died within one year of admission (Gardner, 1972).

Utilitarian Value of Children

Until the 20th century, child labor was an accepted practice. Like animals and slaves, children were forced to work at a variety of arduous tasks for the economic benefit of the family. During the Middle Ages, children were farmed out as apprentices to tradespeople and farmers. With the beginning of the industrial revolution in the 18th century, children were employed in textile mills, mines, and other industries for 12 hours a day, 6 days a week. The work was dangerous, dirty, exhausting, and unhealthy. Children as young as 5 or 6 crawled into the narrow, dark passages of mines to sit alone for 12 hours a day while they tended the doors that sealed off the shafts. Older children were "hurriers," whose job was to haul coal out of the narrow tunnels. They were harnessed to sleds that they pulled like draft animals. Figure 5.1 shows the process. One child recalls:

In the early 1900s, most children admitted to orphanages died within a year after admission.

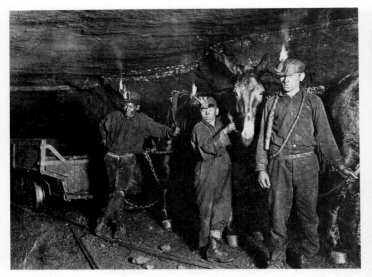

FIGURE 5.1   During the Industrial Revolution in the 18th century, children as young as 5 to 6 years of age were employed to work in mines for 12 hours a day.

These spindle boys in a Georgia cotton mill were exposed to the dangers of turning spindles and whirling machinery.

I went into a pit at seven years of age. When I drew with the girdle and chain the skin was broken and blood ran down. . . . If we said anything, they would beat us. I have seen many draw at six [years]. They must do it or be beat. They cannot straighten their backs during the day. I have sometimes pulled till my hips have hurt me so that I have not known what to do with myself (Bready, 1926, p. 273).

Children working in textile mills fared only a little better. Small children 5 years old had to crawl into the looms to retie threads. Older children were loom operators, exposed to turning spindles and whirling machinery. The following photo gives some idea of the dangers involved.

England passed the first child labor laws in 1832. Ten years later laws to regulate the use of children in mines were passed. Girls were not allowed to work underground and boys had to be at least 10 years of age. However, the widespread use of child labor continued abroad and in the United States. Not until the 20th century were laws passed to really regulate child labor, require children to get an education, and to prosecute parents for child abuse. Gradually, societies for prevention of cruelty to children, children's aid societies, and various social programs were established to further the welfare of children (Siegel & White, 1982). In addition, machines were used increasingly to replace people, and the first to be freed were the children who worked in factories and mills.

EARLY PHILOSOPHIES REGARDING THE MORAL NATURE OF CHILDREN

Original Sin

Historically, there were three major philosophies regarding the moral nature and development of children. One view was the Christian doctrine of **original sin**. According to this view, children were born sinful and rebellious, depraved in nature and spirit, and were in desperate need of redemption. They were unable to save themselves; their only hope lay in conversion and surrender to God, who would save them from eternal damnation. In the meantime, the role of parents and teachers was to break the rebellious spirit of children, to employ strict punishment and discipline, and to guide them toward virtue and salvation. *The New England Primer*, originally published in puritan America in 1687, began: "A—In Adam's fall we sinned all." This was the child's first reader. In school, the three Rs—reading, 'riting, and 'rithmetic—were taught to the tune of the hickory stick, which was routinely used to beat disobedient pupils.

Original sin—the Christian doctrine that, because of Adam's sin, a sinful nature has been passed on to succeeding generations

Schoolmasters often employed strict punishment and discipline to break the rebellious spirit of children.

Not all adults agreed with this philosophy. Many were reluctant to use harsh measures and sought to achieve a balance between discipline and kindness (Moran & Vinovskis, 1986). Horace Bushnel (1888) in his book *Christian Nurture*, first published in 1861, objected to raising children in an atmosphere of unchristian love, in which parents did nothing positive while they prayed for their children's salvation. *Bushnell said that the family as a social group influences the life and character of children, and that God's love and grace are mediated through caring parents.* "The child must not only be touched with some gentle emotions toward what is right, but he must love it [what is good] with a fixed love, love it for the sake of its principle, receive it as a vital and formative power" (Bushnell, 1888). Bushnell further observed that "infancy and childhood are the ages most pliant to good" (p. 14). Bushnell's view was certainly the forerunner of modern concepts of child development and of the family's role in the socialization of children.

In the late 1800s, Horace Bushnell said that God's love and grace are mediated through caring parents.

Tabula Rasa: John Locke

Regarding the moral nature and development of children, *the second major philosophy was that of John Locke (1632–1704), who said that children are morally neutral.* Locke said that children are a **tabula rasa**, a "blank slate" in the literal translation. According to this view, children have no inborn tendencies. They are neither good nor bad, and how they turn out depends on what they experience while growing up. Locke said that parents could mold their children in any way they wished through the use of associations, repetitions, imitations, rewards, and punishments (Locke, 1892). Locke suggested parents reward their children with praise and approval. He objected to physical punishment because he said it does not foster self-control and only teaches fear and anger. Locke was a forerunner of modern behaviorism and encouraged treating children with kindness and love.

Tabula rasa—literally, a blank slate; refers to John Locke's view that children are born morally neutral

Noble Savages: Jean-Jacques Rousseau

The third major philosophy reflecting the moral nature and development of children was espoused by Jean-Jacques Rousseau (1712–1778). *Rousseau (1762/1955) said that children are* **noble savages**, *endowed with a sense of right and wrong.* They will develop positively according to nature's plan because they have an innate moral sense. Rousseau felt that any attempt by adults to provide indoctrination and training would only interfere with children's development and corrupt them. Rouseau outlined four stages of development: *infancy, childhood, late childhood,* and *adolescence,* and said that adults should be responsive to the child's needs at each stage of development. Rousseau was the first to emphasize **maturation**—the unfolding of the genetically determined patterns of growth and development, which reflect unique patterns of thought and behavior at each stage of growth (Crain, 1980).

Noble savages—beings endowed with a sense of right and wrong; a term used by Jean-Jacques Rousseau to describe his view of children

Maturation—the unfolding of the genetically determined patterns of growth and development

EVOLUTIONARY BIOLOGY

Origin of the Species: Charles Darwin

Charles Darwin (1809–1882) published *On the Origin of Species* in 1859 (Darwin, 1936). He emphasized that the human species had evolved over millions of years through the

Charles Darwin emphasized natural selection and the survival of the fittest.

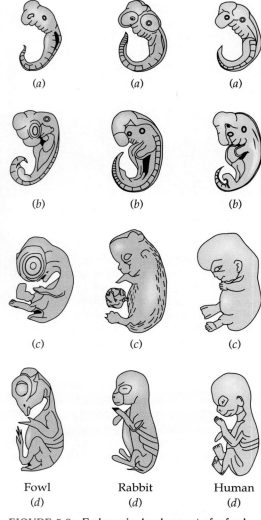

FIGURE 5.2 Embryonic development of a fowl, rabbit, and human shown in four parallel stages.

Natural selection

Survival of the fittest

process of **natural selection** and the **survival of the fittest**. Natural selection means that certain species were selected to survive because they had characteristics that helped them adapt to their environment (implying that the human species has evolved from lower life forms). Survival of the fittest means that only the fittest live to pass on their superior traits to future generations. Gradually, higher and more adaptable forms of life evolved. Darwin also observed that the embryos of many species were very much alike during certain stages of their development, indicating that they had evolved from common ancestors.

Recapitulation Theory: G. Stanley Hall

Darwin's idea concerning natural evolvement and maturation clearly influenced the subsequent work of G. Stanley Hall (1846–1924), who was the first PhD in psychology in the United States and the founder of the child study movement in North America. *Hall said that the development of the growing child parallels the evolution of the human species* (Hall, 1904). He outlined four major stages:

1. Infancy (to age 4), during which the child reenacts the animal stage of development

2. Childhood (age 5 to 7), which corresponds to the cave-dwelling, hunting-fishing epoch of human history (children play survival games and use toy weapons)

3. Youth (age 8 to 12), the preadolescent stage of development during which the child recapitulates the life of savagery but begins to be civilized by learning to read, write, draw, calculate, and learn language, music, and so on

4. Puberty (age 13 to 24), the period of adolescence, during which the child grows into adulthood

Elements of Darwin's theory are also evident in Piaget's ideas. Piaget said that childrens' development is an effort to adjust their behavior to societal demands. Etholo-

G. Stanley Hall made the first normative study of children's development during different stages.

gists also compare animal and human behavior. For example, they compare imprinting and bonding behavior to better understand how human children develop.

BABY BIOGRAPHIES

During the late 19th and early 20th centuries attempts were made to study children by keeping biographical records of their behavior. Darwin (1877) himself kept an account of the development of his young son. Milicent Shinn (1900) published *The Biography of a Baby*, which recorded the growth of her young niece during her first year of life. The baby biographies did not yield very much objective, scientific information about child development, but they were the forerunners of later observations that tried to describe normal growth patterns during various stages of development.

NORMATIVE STUDIES

The Contents of Childrens' Minds: G. Stanley Hall

G. Stanley Hall attempted to record facts concerning childrens' development during different stages. His approach launched the movement to make normative studies of children, to find out what to expect during each

age regarding their growth and behavior. Hall made up elaborate questionnaires that were distributed to schoolchildren. The questionnaires asked the children to describe almost everything in their lives: their interests, play, friendships, fears, and so forth. Hall's stated purpose was to "discover the contents of childrens' minds" (Hall, 1891). The casual data-collecting procedures left sample characteristics undetermined. The results were difficult to summarize and the usefulness of the data was doubtful, but this approach spawned several decades of more sophisticated normative research.

Growth Patterns: Arnold Gesell

Arnold Gesell (1880–1961) was one of Hall's pupils. He devoted a major part of his career to observing infants and children and to collecting normative information on them. He wrote volumes describing typical motor skills, social behavior, and personality traits to help parents and professionals know what to expect at each stage (Gesell & Ilg, 1943; Gesell & Ilg, 1946; Gesell & Ames, 1956). Gesell's books became the bibles of child development during the 1940s and 1950s. Actually, Gesell drew his conclusions from samples of boys and girls of favorable socioeconomic status in school populations in

Arnold Gesell, founder of the Gesell Institute of Child Development in New Haven, Connecticut.

New Haven, Connecticut, where the Gesell Institute of Child Development is located. Gesell contended that such a homogeneous sample would not lead to false generalizations. However, to try to correct the deficiencies of the earlier studies, the Gesell Institute has since conducted new normative studies of diverse samples of preschool children from different socioeconomic groups (Ames, Gillespie, Haines, & Ilg, 1978).

Gesell's theory is a biologically oriented one, in which maturation is mediated by genes and biology that determine behavioral traits and developmental trends. Since development is bio-logically determined, there is very little that parents and teachers can do to alter its progress. Gesell felt that acculturation can never transcend the primary importance of maturation. In spite of genetically determined individual differences, Gesell considered many of the principles, trends, and sequences to be universal among humans.

Although it is interesting, Gesell's normative theory has generally been discounted today by behaviorists and social learning theorists, who tend to emphasize the importance of experience and environmental influences on childrens' development.

FOCUS

Gesell's Behavior Profile of the 2-Year-Old

At two years the child cuts his last milk teeth. He is no longer an infant though compared with a 3 year old child he is still very immature. There is danger of overestimating his capacities, simply because he is sturdy on his feet and is beginning to put words together. . . .

He does not yet walk erect. There remains a little of the angularity of the ancient man in his posture. . . . When he picks up something from the floor, he half bends at the waist as well as at the knees; whereas at 18 months he squatted. Stooping is more advanced behavior than squatting. But the 2 year old still leans forward as he runs. . . .

To get up from a sitting position on the floor, he leans forward, pushes up buttocks first, and head second, instead of raising an erect trunk as he will later. He goes up and down stairs mark-time fashion, without alternating his feet. . . .

He is still geared to gross motor activity, and likes to run and romp, lug, push and pull, but with better coordination than at 18 months. His fine motor control also has advanced. . . . He also likes to take things apart and fit them together again.

The muscles of eyes and face are more adept. He moves his eyes more freely and is sensitive to marginal fields, whereas at 18 months he ran headlong as though he had blinders on. He stops and engages in long periods of looking. . . .

The whole linguistic apparatus, mouth, lips, tongue, larynx and thorax is undergoing rapid organization. Jargon is dropping out, sentences are coming in. Soliloquy is taking the place of the babbling of the 6 month old child, as though on an advanced level the 2 year old is under a similar compulsion to exercise his vocal abilities, to repeat words, to name things, to suit words to action and action to words. Vocabularies vary enormously in size from a half dozen to a thousand words. . . .

The third year is also the year when the sphincter muscles of bladder and bowel are coming under voluntary control. . . .

The action system of the 2 year old is not yet sufficiently advanced to effect delicate and long sustained interpersonal relations. He still prefers solitary play to parallel play and seldom plays cooperatively. He is in the pre-cooperative stage; watching what others are doing rather than participating. He cannot share; he cannot as a rule let someone else play with what is his own. He must learn "It's mine" first. He does so by holding on and by hoarding. . . . The hitting, patting, poking, biting, hairpulling, and tug of war over materials so characteristic of Two need to be handled with understanding and sensible techniques on the part of parent and guidance teacher. . . .

So to sum him up, what are his dominating interests? He loves to romp, flee and pursue. He likes to fill and empty, to put and to pull out, to tear apart and to fit together, to taste (even clay and wood), to touch and rub. He prefers action toys such as trains, cars, telephones. He is intrigued by water and washing. Although he is not yet an humanitarian, he likes to watch the human scene. He imitates the domesticities of feminine laundry work and doll play. He has a genuine interest in the mother–baby relationship (Gesell & Ilg, 1943, pp. 159–161).

Intelligence Testing: Lewis Terman

Lewis Terman (1877–1956) was another student of Hall's. A professor at Stanford University, he published in 1916 the first widely used intelligence test for children in the United States. He called it the *Stanford-Binet Intelligence Scale*, which was a revision of Binet's test that had been developed earlier in Paris. Binet's test had been used to identify retarded children in the Paris school system and to sort out children of varying scholastic abilities. Terman also conducted the first longitudinal study of children of superior intelligence. Terman followed more than 1,500 children with IQs averaging 150 and above from 1921 into mature adulthood to determine the relationship between intelligence and social adjustment, emotional stability, professional and marital success, health, and other characteristics. Generally, *he found intellectually gifted children to be superior in other ways as well* (Terman, 1925; Terman & Oden, 1959). Daniel Goleman (1980) has since reported on follow-up studies of Terman's subjects, now in their 60s and 70s. Terman's work produced a useful instrument for measuring intelligence and launched the whole intelligence test movement. Contemporary studies focus on the relative roles of genetics versus environmental influences on intellectual abilities, as was discussed in Chapter 3.

MODERN CONTRIBUTIONS TO CHILD DEVELOPMENT

Research Centers

By the beginning of the 20th century, thousands of adults working with children began to demand public and government intervention to help protect children who were under their care. The first White House Conference on Child Health and Protection was held in 1909. The conferences became yearly events and led to the establishment of the U.S. Children's Bureau in 1912 (McCullers & Love, 1976).

Interest in research in child development blossomed during the years following World War I. In 1917, the Iowa legislature allocated $50,000 for an Iowa Child Welfare Research Station. This effort was the first of its kind and was followed by the establish-

Lewis Terman published the first widely used intelligence test for children in the United States.

ment of the Teachers College Child Development Institute (at Columbia University), the Yale University Psycho-Clinic (later called the Yale Clinic of Child Development and still later the Gesell Institute of Child Development), the University of Minnesota Institute of Child Welfare, and the University of California Institute of Child Welfare (at Berkeley). In the early period, most of the money for the child-research institutes was provided by the Laura Spellman Rockefeller Memorial Fund. Federal funds became available after World War II. Today, there are hundreds of universities and organizations involved in child development research. One of the most prestigious organizations is the Society for Research in Child Development located in Chicago.

Today, there are child-development research centers scattered throughout the United States.

Medical and Mental Health Practitioners

Substantial information on child development has also been provided by medical and child guidance practitioners. *Pediatrics* was developed as a medical specialty, and pediatricians have made tremendous strides in treating acute illnesses and diseases of children. Pediatricians have also been called upon by concerned parents to answer their questions about normal development as well as about behavior problems. Benjamin Spock's *Commonsense Book of Baby and Child Care*, first published in 1946, has sold millions of copies and has become many modern parents' bible of child rearing (Spock, 1946; Spock & Rothenberg, 1985). Dr. T. Berry Brazelton's (1974, 1983) books for parents of infants and toddlers are also popular. Numerous child psychologists, one of whom is Dr. Lee Salk (1974), have published popular guidebooks for parents.

Recently, child development specialists and pediatricians have collaborated to share their knowledge, which has resulted in the emergence of a new field, **developmental pediatrics**, which integrates medical and psychological understanding, health care, and parental guidance.

Child guidance professionals who are psychiatrists, social workers, clinical and/or child psychologists, or child development specialists have always been concerned especially with the mental health and the intellectual, emotional, and social development of children. Behavioral misconduct, school failure, social maladjustments, or problems in parent or peer relationships are better understood than ever before. Hundreds of child guidance clinics now provide assessment of children's problems and guidance for parents, teachers, and other concerned adults.

Today

Interest in child development continues. Research studies by the thousands pour out of universities and child development centers. These studies provide a wealth of information on all aspects of child care, growth, and development. Countless organizations seek to apply this knowledge in ways that will benefit the children they serve. Medical and psychological help for children with problems is more accurate than ever before, but is often unavailable to those who need it the most. Conscientious parents seek to improve their parenting skills whenever possible.

Numerous problems remain. There is still tremendous need for adequate child care for working parents. Public attention continues to be focused on physical and sexual

Developmental pediatrics—a new field of study that integrates medical knowledge, psychological understanding, health care, and parental guidance in relation to children

---

PARENTING ISSUES

Changing Child Rearing Philosophies in the Government's Bulletin on Infant Care

One thing that has been evident throughout the study of child development is how much the philosophies and emphases in child rearing have changed over the years (Young, 1990). This is especially evident in the government's bulletin on *Infant Care* (Arkin, 1989). This booklet was first published in 1914, has gone through many editions, and has been completely rewritten numerous times. Between 1914 and 1921, the dangers of thumb sucking and masturbation were emphasized: Parents were advised to bind their children to the bed, hand and foot, so they would not suck their thumbs, touch their genitals, or rub their thighs together. Between 1929 and 1938, autoerotic impulses were not considered dangerous, but lack of proper bowel training and improper feeding habits were. The emphasis was on rigid schedules, strictly according to the clock. Bowel training was to be pursued with great determi-

nation. Weaning and the introduction of solid foods were to be accomplished with firmness, never yielding to the baby's protests for one instant, for fear the infant would dominate the parents.

Between 1942 and 1945, the views expressed in the bulletin changed drastically. The child was then thought to be devoid of dominating impulses. Mildness was advocated in all areas. Thumb sucking and masturbation were not to be discouraged. Weaning and toilet training were to be put off until later and to be accomplished more gently.

At the present time, *Infant Care* has a fairly permissive attitude toward thumb sucking, weaning, discipline, and bowel and bladder training. It is evident that child-rearing philosophies change from one generation to the next, so that parents often have to sort out conflicting advice.

abuse of children. All too many children, born in and out of wedlock, do not receive the necessary physical and emotional care to grow into healthy, happy individuals. Infant mortality in the United States is one of the highest in the Western world, reflecting the lack of prenatal and postnatal care of mothers and their infants. Too many children suffer the consequences of their parents' drug abuse, or of the growing incidence of AIDS and other sexually transmitted diseases. Thousands of children are born unplanned and unwanted—and thus suffer the lack of proper care. It is vital that all caring people join in the effort to provide the kind of environment in which children can be cared for and loved, and to deliver necessary services to those needing extra care.

SUMMARY

1. Child development is a specialized discipline devoted to the understanding of all aspects of human development from birth to adolescence. It is a relatively new field of study.

2. One reason that interest in studying child development was so long in happening is that, during the Middle Ages and until several hundred years later, childhood was not regarded as a separate stage of life. Children were expected to be little adults.

3. Before modern birth control, many children were unwanted and were considered a burden rather than a blessing. Unwanted children were killed, abandoned, or put in foundling homes, where most of them died.

4. Until the 20th century, the use of child labor was an accepted practice. Children had to work in shops, fields, mines, and mills for 12 hours a day, 6 days a week.

5. Historically, there were three major philosophies regarding the moral nature and development of children. The first of these, the Christian doctrine of original sin, held that children were born sinful and rebellious. The role of parents was to break the rebellious spirit of children and to pray for their salvation. Opposing this philosophy, Horace Bushnell held that God's love and grace are mediated through caring parents who should raise their children in an atmosphere of Christian love.

6. Representing the second major philosophy of child development, John Locke said that children are a tabula rasa, a blank slate; that they are morally neutral, and how they turn out depends on how they are raised. In effect, that parents can mold their children in any way they wish.

7. In the third major philosophy concerning children, Jean-Jacques Rousseau said that they are noble savages, endowed with a sense of right and wrong, and that they will develop positively according to nature's plan if parents don't interfere with their development and corrupt them.

8. Charles Darwin was the first of the evolutionary biologists. He taught that the human species evolved over millions of years through the process of natural selection and the survival of the fittest.

9. G. Stanley Hall said that the development of the growing child parallels the evolution of the human species.

10. During the late 19th and early 20th centuries, attempts were made to study children by keeping biographical records of their behavior.

11. G. Stanley Hall made the first attempt to study children's behavior during different stages. His effort launched the movement to make normative studies of children.

12. Arnold Gesell of Yale University devoted a major part of his career to observing infants and children and collecting normative information on them. Gesell's theory is biologically oriented and states that maturation is mediated by genes and biology, which determine behavioral traits and developmental trends. Gesell felt that acculturation can never transcend maturation.

13. Lewis Terman of Stanford University published the Stanford-Binet Intelligence Scale, the first widely used intelligence test for children in the United States. He also conducted the first longitudinal studies of intellectually gifted individuals.

14. Early in the 20th century, numerous organizations and research centers were established to study child development and to discover how best to protect and guide children.

15. Substantial contributions to understanding child development have also been made by pediatric and child guidance practitioners. Developmental pediatrics integrates medical and psychological understanding, health care, and parental guidance. Hundreds of child guidance clinics now provide assessment of children's problems and guidance for parents, teachers, and other concerned adults.

KEY TERMS

Child development   p. 102
Developmental pediatrics   p. 110
Maturation   p. 105
Natural selection   p. 106

Noble savages   p. 105
Original sin   p. 104
Survival of the fittest   p. 106
Tabula rasa   p. 105

DISCUSSION QUESTIONS

1. Historically, children were considered miniature adults. Can you give any evidence or examples of this view still being held today? Explain.
2. Unwanted children were considered burdens and were killed, abandoned, or given to orphanages. What do you think should be done about the problem of unwanted children today?
3. It is hard for us to imagine the extent to which child labor was exploited before laws were passed outlawing it. Do you think that children today are exploited, *or* not given enough work to do? Explain your views.
4. Of the three philosophies—that children are born sinful and rebellious, that they are born neutral, that they are born with an innate sense of right and wrong—with which do you most agree? Why? Are there elements of truth in all three views? Explain.
5. What might be some of the values of Gesell's normative studies? What might be some disadvantages? Why are his findings discounted by behaviorists and social learning theorists? From a cognitive point of view, how would you evaluate Gesell's findings?
6. According to Terman, is intelligence innate? What are some advantages and disadvantages of IQ tests? Would you want your children to know their IQ scores? Explain.
7. Have you had any contacts with child guidance clinics, child development specialists, or child psychologists? Under what circumstances? With what results?
8. To parents: What do you like about your child's pediatrician, and what don't you like? Should pediatricians give advice to parents about child rearing?
9. In what ways are your views of child rearing similar to and different from those of your parents? What do you like about your parents' views, and what do you disagree with?

SUGGESTED READINGS

Aries, P. (1962). *Centuries of adulthood: A social history of family life* (R. Baldick, Trans.). New York: Knopf (original work published 1960). The status of children throughout history.

Borstelmann, L. J. (1983). Children before psychology: Ideas about children from antiquity to the late 1800s. In P. H. Mussen (Ed.), *Handbook of child psychology* (4th ed., Vol. 1). New York: Wiley. His-

torical views of children from ancient times.

Eckardt, G., Bringman, W. G., & Sprung, L. (Eds.). (1985). *Contributions to a history of development psychology*. Berlin: Morton. The status of children throughout history.

Grant, J. P. (1986). *The status of the world's children*. New York: Oxford University Press. Written by the executive director of the United Nation's Children's Fund, it summarizes the horrible plight of children around the world.

Kessen, W. (1965). *The child.* New York: Wiley. The child as viewed by Rousseau, Darwin, Baldwin, Freud, Piaget, and others.

Sommerville, J. (1982). *The rise and fall of childhood.* Beverly Hills, CA: Sage. The status of children at different times in history.

Physical Development

PHYSICAL GROWTH

Body Height and Weight

Growth from birth to adolescence occurs in two different patterns. The first pattern (from birth to age 1) is one of very rapid but decelerating growth; the second (from age 1 to before the onset of puberty) shows a more linear and steadier annual increment. Typically, the infant's increase in length is approximately 30% up to 5 months of age and greater than 50% by 1 year of age. Height doubles by age 5. Figure 6.1 shows median heights by age of boys and girls. Boys and girls have little difference in size and growth rates during infancy and childhood. Note the very rapid increase in height from birth to age 1, followed by a gradual slowing of increase until about age 10 for girls and age 12 for boys.

Figure 6.2 shows the rates of increase in height in boys and girls. Ages 10 to 12 represent the onset of puberty in girls; ages 12 to 14, the onset of puberty in boys. The growth spurts are evident during these pe-

Physical growth after the first year shows a fairly linear and steady annual increment.

riods. If puberty is delayed, growth in height may virtually cease.

Infants' increases in weight are even more dramatic than their early growth in length. The infant doubles in weight by 5 months of age, triples in 1 year, and almost quadruples by age 2. Annual increases are fairly constant from ages 2 to 6, and then are slower until the onset of puberty. (See Figure 6.3.)

FIGURE 6.1   Median heights (by age) of boys and girls.

Adapted from *The Merck Manual*, 15th ed. (p. 1821) by R. Berkow, Ed., 1987, Rahway, NJ: Merck Sharp and Dohme Research Laboratories.

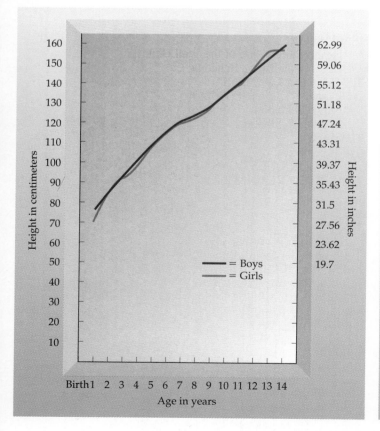

FIGURE 6.2   Rates of increase in height in boys and girls.

Adapted from *The Merck Manual*, 15th ed. (p. 1821) by R. Berkow, Ed., 1987, Rahway, NJ: Merck Sharp and Dohme Research Laboratories.

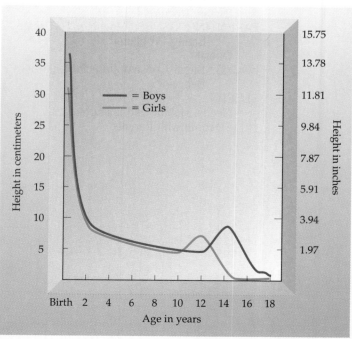

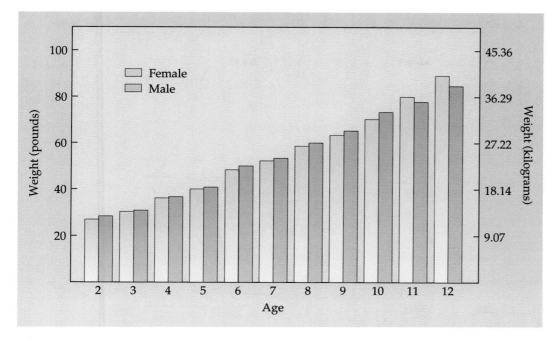

FIGURE 6.3 Weight at 50th percentile for U.S. children, by age.

Individual Differences

There are wide individual differences in growth patterns. At 36 months, boys in the 5th to the 95th percentiles may be 36 to 41 inches in length and weigh between 27 and 38 pounds. At the same age, girls in the 5th to the 95th percentiles may be 35½ to 40 inches in length and weigh between 25½ and 36½ pounds. Growth differentials depend upon heredity, nutrition and eating habits, and total health care. Children from upper-class, better-educated families are taller than lower-class children, primarily because of superior nutrition and health care that allows them to grow as tall as their genes permit (Vaughn, 1983).

There are wide individual differences in growth patterns.

Cultural and ethnic differences also influence growth (Widmayer et al., 1990). In the United States, black children tend to have longer legs and be taller than white children who, in turn, are taller than Asian-American children (Meredith, 1978). Canada's English-speaking children tend to be taller than French-speaking children (Shephard, 1976).

Children with slower physical maturation suffer social disadvantages. They may be the last ones selected on teams for games and sports, may have some difficulty in establishing friendships, and may be lonely and unhappy because they are "different" (Hartup, 1983).

Body Proportions

Not all parts of the body grow at the same rate. Development follows the **cephalocaudal principle**; that is, it proceeds downward from the head to the feet. Growth comes first in the head region, then in the trunk, and finally in the leg region. From birth to adulthood, the head doubles in size, the trunk trebles, the arms and hands quadruple in length, and the legs and feet grow fivefold (Bayley, 1956). At birth, the newborn's head is about one-fourth of the total body length, compared to one-eighth of the body length in adults. The legs of the newborn are one-quarter of the total body length, but about one-half of the body length in adults. (See Figure 6.4.)

Cephalocaudal principle—downward distribution of physical growth, starting in the head and proceeding, by stages, down the body to the feet

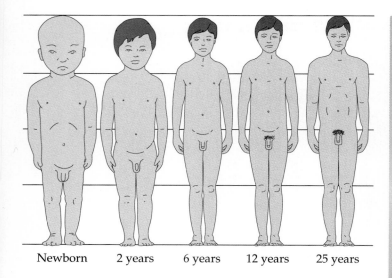

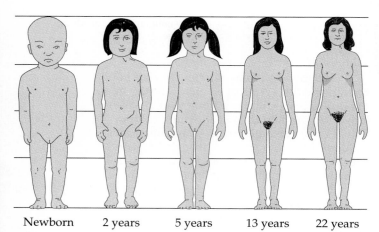

FIGURE 6.4   Bodily proportions at different ages.

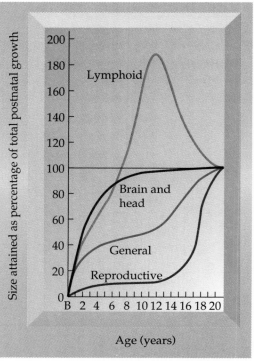

FIGURE 6.5   Growth patterns of different organ systems. These curves are based on the percentage of a person's total growth attained by age twenty. Thus, size at age twenty is 100 on the vertical scale. The lymphoid system includes the thymus and lymph nodes. The curve labeled "Brain and head" includes the brain, the skull, and the spinal cord. The curve labeled "General" covers the skeletal system, lungs, kidneys, and digestive organs. The reproductive system covers testes, ovaries, prostate, seminal vesicles, and Fallopian tubes.

From "The Measurement of the Body in Childhood" by Richard E. Scammon, 1930, in *The Measurement of Man* (Figure 73, p. 193) by J. A. Harris, C. M. Jackson, D. G. Paterson, and R. E. Scammon, Eds., Minneapolis: University of Minnesota Press. Reprinted by permission.

Proximodistal principle—outward distribution of physical growth, starting in the center of the body and proceeding out to the extremities

Development also follows the **proximodistal principle**; that is, it proceeds from the center of the body outward to the extremities. This is why large-muscle development in the trunk, arms, and legs precede small-muscle development in the hands and fingers. Infants are able to run and jump before they can perform detailed manual and grasping movements.

Organ Systems

Three organ systems do not follow the general pattern of growth of the rest of the body and organs. The *lymphoid system* grows fairly constantly and rapidly during childhood, so that at puberty the adolescent has almost twice the lymphoid tissue of the adult. After puberty, the lymphoid size recedes. The *reproductive system* shows little growth until puberty. Most of the growth of the *central*

nervous system occurs during the early years of life. At birth, the brain is 25% of adult size; at 1 year it is 75% of adult size. Growth gradually slows down, but the brain has reached 80% of adult size by 3 years, and 90% by age 7 (Berkow, 1987). Figure 6.5 shows the growth patterns of the different systems.

Brain Growth and Nerve Maturation

Not only does the brain grow in size, but increasingly complex nerve pathways and connections among nerve cells develop so the central nervous system is able to perform

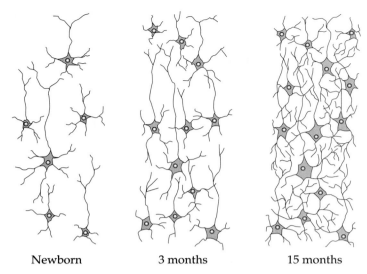

Newborn   3 months   15 months

FIGURE 6.6   The development of nerve cell connections.

70% of the neurons in the central nervous system. It is divided into two hemispheres, with the left side of the brain mainly controlling the right side of the body and the right side of the brain controlling the left side of the body. The two hemispheres are connected by a band of fibers called the corpus callosum.

The two sides of the brain each perform specialized functions. The *right hemisphere* is superior in music, drama, fantasy, intuition, and art. It is superior in recognizing patterns, faces, and melodies, and in visualizing spatial relationships. Thus, it is better in arranging blocks in a pattern, completing a puzzle, or drawing a picture. The *left hemisphere* is superior in logic, mathematics, language, writing, and judging time. About 95% of all adults use the left hemisphere in speaking, writing, and understanding language (Levy, 1985). In addition, 97% of right-handed people use the left hemisphere more than the right. They are said to be left-hemisphere dominant. About 60% of left-handed people are right-hemisphere dominant. Right- or left-handedness begins to be evident by 6 or 7 months of age (Ramsey, 1985) and is reasonably well established by age 2 (Ramsey & Weber, 1986). Four-year-olds who have not yet established a dominant hand appear to be uncoordinated and delayed in their motor development. Dyslexic children have difficulty learning to read and show a type of abnormal lateralization, with spatial functions being directed from both hemispheres (Tan, 1985).

Lateralization is the preference for using one side of the body more than the other in performing special tasks. Lateralization may be biologically programmed from the day a baby is born. It is a tendency that occurs throughout childhood, becoming stronger over time, and is not complete until puberty. Recognizing shapes by touch is a spatial ability controlled by the right hemisphere, and is most easily accomplished with the left hand. Rose (1984) found that 1-year-olds are not especially proficient at recognizing shapes with either hand, but 3-year-olds are already better at recognizing shapes with their left than with their right hand.

more complex functions. Figure 6.6 shows the development of nerve-cell connections from birth to 15 months.

MYELINIZATION.   Another important change is the increase in **myelinization** of individual neurons (discussed in Chapter 4). Myelinization is the process by which neurons become coated with a fatty insulating substance called myelin, which helps to transmit nerve impulses faster and more efficiently. The myelinization process parallels the maturation of the nervous system. The pathways between the brain and sense organs are partly myelinated at birth, so the neonate's senses are in fairly good working order. As neural pathways between the brain and skeletal muscles myelinate, the child becomes capable of more complex motor activities. Though myelinization proceeds rapidly for the first few years of life, some areas of the brain are not completely myelinated until the late teens or early adulthood (Guthrie, 1980).

Multiple sclerosis results when the myelin sheaths begin to disintegrate. As the condition worsens, the person loses muscular control and may become paralyzed or die. Myelinization is very important, therefore, in the development of the total nervous system.

CEREBRAL CORTEX.   The **cerebral cortex** is the largest structure of the forebrain and contains the higher brain centers controlling intellectual, sensory, and motor functions. The cerebral cortex is larger in proportion to total body weight and is more highly developed in humans than in any other animals. In humans, the cerebral cortex accounts for

CORTICAL FUNCTIONS.   The control of particular functions is located in various areas of the cerebral cortex. Figure 6.7 shows the location of several major functions in the left cerebral hemisphere. The development of these functions results from brain and nervous system maturation combined with experience and practice. Neurons that are

Myelinization—the process by which neurons become coated with an insulating, fatty substance called myelin

Cerebral cortex—two large hemispheres of the forebrain, which control intellectual, motor, and sensory functions

Lateralization—the preference for using one side of the body more than the other in performing special tasks, depending on which hemisphere is dominant for the task

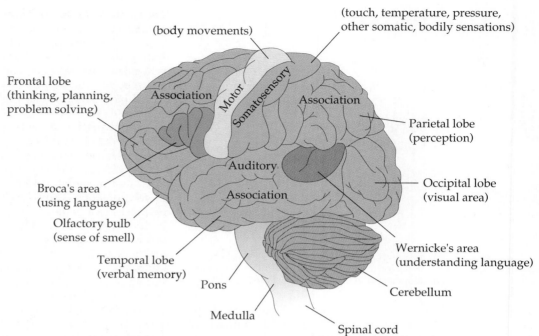

FIGURE 6.7 Location of major functions in the left cerebral hemisphere.

Association regions process and combine information from different senses.

stimulated continue to grow new dendrite branches and myelin sheaths, increasing synaptic connections and the efficiency of nerve transmission. Thus, the growth of the brain and nervous system is influenced by both heredity and environment.

Different regions of the cortex mature at different rates. The first area to mature is the *motor area*, followed by the *sensory area*. The *association areas* are the last to mature, continuing their growth into the twenties or thirties (Spreen, Tupper, Risser, Tuokko, & Edgell, 1984). The higher functions of thinking, planning, and problem solving, performed by the frontal lobes, take years to develop. Adults with frontal lobe damage show decreased emotionality, altered personalities, and an inability to reason or to plan. They repeat the same wrong answers over and over (Springer & Deutsch, 1985). Injury to the left hemisphere of the frontal lobe of adults may produce either depression or increased aggression (Miller, 1988). When brain damage occurs during childhood, lost abilities are sometimes regained, depending on the extent of the damage.

Two areas of the cortex are related to language. The *Broca's area* is involved in using language, the *Wernicke's area* in understanding it. Injury to either area can cause *aphasia*, an impaired ability to use language.

Growth of cortical structures depends partly upon environmental influences (Greenough, Black, & Wallace, 1987). Partic-

ularly during the third trimester of pregnancy, during which development of the central nervous system is proceeding at an astounding pace, malnutrition can lead to a permanent loss in brain weight, a reduction in the number of brain cells, and serious mental retardation. Sensory deprivation in the early years of life can lead to degenerative changes in the cortex. Light deprivation for a brief period of 3 or 4 days can cause degenerative changes in the visual cortex of a 4-week-old kitten.

PARENTING ISSUES

Maturation and Toilet Training

The importance of both maturation and learning in development can be illustrated by discussing the task of toilet training. Experience plays an important role in toilet training—children must be taught to use the toilet. However, maturation also plays an important part. In a classic study, McGraw (1940) began training one identical twin, Hugh, when he was only 50 days old. No progress was achieved until Hugh was about 650 days (21 months) of age. Training of the other twin, Hilton, began at 700 days (23 months) of age. Hilton's progress was rapid from the beginning. Both children learned, but only when they reached a particular level of maturation. Figure 6.8 illustrates the progress of the twins.

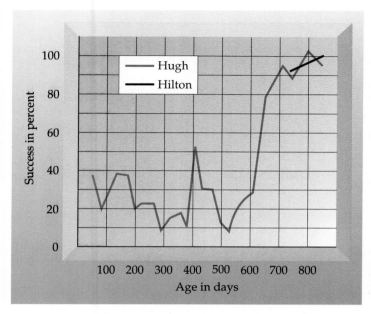

FIGURE 6.8   Maturation and achievement of bladder control.

Adapted from "Neural Maturation as Exemplified in Achievement of Bladder Control" by M. B. McGraw, 1940, *Journal of Pediatrics, 16*, pp. 580–590.

Teeth Eruption Times

The timing of teeth eruption is somewhat variable, depending on family factors (both heredity and nutrition). Occasionally, teeth eruption is significantly delayed because of *hypothyroidism. Deciduous teeth* (baby teeth) eruption is similar in both sexes; *permanent teeth* tend to appear earlier in girls. Deciduous teeth are smaller than their permanent

counterparts. Table 6.1 shows average teeth eruption times.

The first permanent molars (so-called 6-year molars, which erupt between the ages of 5 and 7 years) come in farther back than the baby molars. The first baby teeth to be lost are the *incisors*, followed by the *molars*, and *canines* (*cuspids*). The permanent teeth that take the place of the baby molars are called *bicuspids*. The 2nd molars (or 12-year molars, which erupt between the ages of 11 and 13 years) come in behind the 6-year molars, with the 3rd molars (18-year molars, also called wisdom teeth) coming behind the 12-year molars. Figure 6.9 identifies the location of different teeth.

MOTOR DEVELOPMENT

Gross-Motor Skills and Locomotion During Infancy

Children's motor development is dependent primarily on overall physical maturation, especially on skeletal and neuromuscular development. To a lesser extent, motor development is also influenced by the opportunities children have for exercise and practice. Infants spend a great deal of time in *rhythmic motor activity*— kicking, waving, bouncing, rocking, banging, rubbing, swinging, twisting, thrusting, and scratching. These rhythmic activities are an important transition between uncoordinated activity and more coordinated, complex motor behavior (Thelen, 1981).

Figure 6.10 shows the sequence of motor development in average infants as they

TABLE 6.1 Teeth Eruption Times					
Deciduous Teeth[1] (20 in number)	Number	Time of Eruption[2] (in months)	Permanent Teeth (32 in number)	Number	Time of Eruption[2] (in years)
Lower central incisors	2	5–9	First molars[3]	4	5–7
Upper central incisors	2	8–12	Incisors	8	6–8
Upper lateral incisors	2	10–12	Bicuspids	8	9–12
Lower lateral incisors	2	12–15	Canines (cuspids)	4	10–13
First molars[3]	4	10–16	Second molars[3]	4	11–13
Canines (cuspids)	4	16–20	Third molars[3]	4	17–25
Second molars[3]	4	20–30			

[1]The average child should have 6 teeth at age 1 year, 12 teeth at 1½ years, 16 teeth at 2 years, 20 teeth at 2½ years.

[2]Varies greatly.

[3]Molars are numbered from the front to the back of the mouth.

From *The Merck Manual* (15th ed., p. 1822) by R. Berkow (Ed.), 1987, Rahway, NJ: Merck, Sharp, and Dohme Research Laboratories.

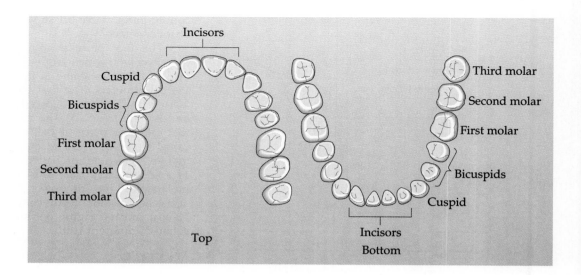

FIGURE 6.9   Permanent teeth.

finally develop the ability to walk alone. Note that they can raise their chin up by 1 month, sit with support at 3 months, sit alone at 6 months, creep at 8 months, pull to a standing position holding onto furniture by 10 months, climb stairs at 11 months, and walk alone at 13 months. However, there are variations in abilities with different individuals. Table 6.2 shows age norms for motor skills according to the Denver Developmental Screening Test (Frankenburg, Frandal, Sciarillo, & Burgess, 1981). According to the table, by 20 months of age half the infants could kick a ball forward, but not until 24 months had 90% of them mastered this skill.

Fine-Motor Skills During Infancy

Fine-motor skills involve the smaller muscles of the body used in reaching, grasping, manipulating, pincering, clapping, turning, opening, twisting, pulling, or scribbling (Mathew & Cook, 1990). Table 6.3 shows the age in months at which 90% of a normal sample of infants could accomplish each of the designated tasks according to the Denver Developmental Screening Test (Frankenburg, Frandal, Sciarillo, & Burgess, 1981). Note that 90% of the infants were 4 months old before they could grasp a rattle, 15 months

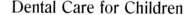

PARENTING ISSUES

Dental Care for Children

Parents sometimes think they don't have to take a small child to a dentist because all the baby teeth are going to fall out anyway. This is unwise thinking. Decayed teeth may cause pain to the child, or lead to a jaw infection. If a baby tooth is so painful it has to be pulled, nearby teeth tend to grow into the space and out of position, so there isn't enough room for the permanent tooth when it's ready to come through. The last baby teeth are not lost until around 12 years of age. This is a long time to go without dental care.

Children should be given a toothbrush and be taught to brush their teeth beginning at about age 2. They aren't very efficient brushers at first, but they enjoy imitating parents,

and early training in dental hygiene is important. Ordinarily, regular trips to the dentist—every 6 months to a year—may begin at about age 3. Tooth decay may start early, and the time to fill cavities is when they are small. Even if the child has no cavities, getting used to going to the dentist without fear is important. Dentists need to be consulted about jaw malformations or malaligned teeth. However, teeth that come through crooked or out of place often straighten out later. Permanent teeth often erupt behind baby teeth and later move forward. A dentist will help to determine whether any special treatments are needed for these conditions.

Newborn
Fetal posture

1 month
Chin up

2 months
Chest up

3 months
Reach and miss

3 months
Sit with support

5 months
Sit on lap
Grasp object

6 months
Sit on high chair
Grasp dangling object

6 months
Sit alone

6 months
Stand with help

7 months
Stand holding furniture

8 months
Creep

9 months
Walk when led

10 months
Pull to stand by furniture

11 months
Climb stairs, steps

12 months
Stand alone

13 months
Walk alone

FIGURE 6.10 Sequences of motor development in average infants.

before they could grasp a raisin with a neat pincer grasp, and 25 months before they could scribble spontaneously.

Gross-Motor Skills of Preschool Children

Preschool children between 2 and 5 years of age make important advances in motor development. With stronger bones, muscles, lung power, and neuromuscular coordination between the arms, legs, senses, and central nervous system, these children show in-creased skill and mastery of their bodies in performing physical feats that would have been impossible before. Table 6.4 shows some gross-motor skills of preschool children of different ages. Notice the skills of 5-year-olds. They can skip smoothly; broad jump up to 3 feet; jump 1 foot high; hop on one foot a distance of 16 feet; start, turn, and stop effectively in playing games; descend a long stairway unaided, alternating the feet; walk a balance beam; throw a ball with one leg stepping forward on the same side as the throwing arm; and catch a ball using their hands only.

TABLE 6.2 Age Norms for Motor Skills (in Months)

Skill	When 50% Master the Skill	When 90% Master the Skill
Lifts head 90° when lying on stomach	2.2	3.2
Rolls over	2.8	4.7
Sits propped up (head steady)	2.9	4.2
Sits without support	5.5	7.8
Stands holding on	5.8	10.0
Walks holding on	9.2	12.7
Stands momentarily	9.8	13.0
Stands alone well	11.5	13.9
Walks well	12.1	14.3
Walks backward	14.3	21.5
Walks up steps	17.0	22.0
Kicks ball forward	20.0	24.0

From ''The Newly Abbreviated and Revised Denver Developmental Screening Test'' by W. K. Frankenburg, A. Frandal, W. Sciarillo, and D. Burgess, 1981, *Journal of Pediatrics, 99*, pp. 995–999.

Gross motor development is dependent primarily on overall physical maturation.

Fine-Motor Skills of Preschool Children

Fine-motor skills involve a high degree of small-muscle and eye–hand coordination. With small muscles under control, children gain a sense of competence and independence because they can do a lot of things, such as eating or dressing, for themselves. Table 6.5 shows some small-muscle motor skills of average preschool children of different ages. For eating, note that 2-year-olds can hold a glass with one hand, and 3-year-olds can eat with a spoon and pour from a pitcher. For dressing, 2-year-olds can put on simple clothing, 4-year-olds can dress themselves, and 5-year-olds may be able to manage a zipper, fasten buttons, or even tie shoelaces. For other small-muscle activities, 2-year-olds will scribble; 3-year-olds can copy a circle or draw a straight line; 4-year-olds can draw simple figures, cut on a line with scissors, and make crude letters; and 5-year-olds can copy squares, which takes considerably more manipulative skill and eye–hand coordination than drawing a circle.

Fine-motor skills involve a high degree of small-muscle and eye–hand coordination.

TABLE 6.3 Age Norms for Fine-Motor Skills When 90% of Infants Could Accomplish a Task

Fine-Motor Task	Months
Hands together	3.7
Grasps rattle	4.2
Reaches for objects	5.0
Sits, takes 2 cubes	7.5
Transfers cube hand to hand	7.5
Thumb–finger grasp	10.6
Neat pincer grasp of raisin	14.7
Scribbles spontaneously	25.0

From ''The Newly Abbreviated and Revised Denver Developmental Screening Test'' by W. K. Frankenburg, A. Frandal, W. Sciarillo, and D. Burgess, 1981, *Journal of Pediatrics, 99*, pp. 995–999.

TABLE 6.4 Large-Muscle Motor Skills of Average Preschool Children

2-Year-Olds	3-Year-Olds	4-Year-Olds	5-Year-Olds
Jump 12 inches	Broad jump 15 to 24 inches	Broad jump 24 to 34 inches	Broad jump 28 to 36 inches
Throw ball overhand, body stationary	Balance on 1 foot, 1 second	Can gallop	Can skip smoothly
Cannot turn or stop smoothly or quickly	Hop up to three times	Hop up to 6 steps on one foot	Hop on 1 foot a distance of 16 feet
Kick a large ball forward	Can propel a wagon with 1 foot	Catch a bounced ball	Can catch small ball using hands only
	Ascend a stairway unaided, alternating the feet		Descend a long stairway unaided, alternating feet
	Pedal a tricycle		Jump 1 foot high
	Basket catch of ball using body		Can start, turn, and stop effectively in games
			Can walk a balance beam
			Can catch small ball using hands only

Changes During the School Years

Elementary school-age children gradually increase in motor ability as their bodies continue to grow. Muscles increase in size and coordination continues to improve, so that most children can run, hop, skip, and jump with agility. Most 6-year-olds can ride a bicycle, jump rope, skate, climb trees, and scale fences if given the opportunity to learn.

Fine-motor skills also increase. Most 8- or 9-year-olds can learn to hammer, saw, use garden tools, sew, knit, draw in proportion, write, print, and cut fingernails.

There are inconsistent gender differences in motor development between boys and girls during middle childhood. Girls are more physically mature than same-age boys; that is, girls have reached a greater percentage of their adult height than same-age boys (Eaton & Yu, 1989). This means that in comparing boys and girls of the same chronological age, developmental studies often compare developmentally more mature girls to less mature boys. This ignores substantial sex differences in maturational tempo.

In general, older children are less active than younger ones, with activity level decreasing with maturational age (Kendall & Brophy, 1981). Boys are thought to be superior in physical skills requiring strength and

TABLE 6.5 Small-Muscle Motor Skills of Average Preschool Children

2-Year-Olds	3-Year-Olds	4-Year-Olds	5-Year-Olds
Scribble spontaneously	Copy a circle	Draw shapes, simple figures	Copy squares
Imitate vertical line within 30°	Draw a straight line	Draw man, 3 parts	String beads
Put on simple clothing	Can eat with a spoon	Can dress self	Can fasten buttons that are visible to the eye
Construct tower of 6 to 8 blocks	Smear and daub paint	Make crude letters	
Hold a glass with 1 hand	Pour from a pitcher	Use blocks to build buildings	Can manage zipper
Turn pages of a book singly		Cut on a line with scissors	May tie shoelaces

gross-motor performance, such as football. Girls are considered superior in physical skills requiring grace, flexibility, and agility, such as gymnastics. However, prior to puberty, many of these differences are due to differential expectations and experiences of boys and girls. A group of third-, fourth-, and fifth-grade boys and girls who had been in coeducational physical education classes for at least a year were compared on scores on sit-ups, shuttle run, 50-yard dash, broad jump, and 600-yard walk-run. The girls scored as well as the boys on most measures. In the third year of the program, the girls performed better than the boys on a number of tests (Hall & Lee, 1984). *The American Academy of Pediatrics has said that there is no reason to separate prepubertal boys and girls for physical activities.* After puberty, girls are lighter, and their smaller frames make them more subject to injury in heavy collision sports (American Academy of Pediatrics Committee on Pediatric Aspects, 1981).

One important factor in motor skills is reaction time, which depends partly on brain maturation. One study of reaction time of children aged 5 through 14 found that older children were almost twice as fast as younger ones (Southard, 1985). In another study, none of the children 7, 9, or 11 years old did as well as any adults, even 75-year-olds, in pressing a button in response to a flash of light (Stern, Oster, & Newport, 1980). Seven-year-olds took twice as long as the typical adult to react to the flash of light. Nine-

Adults have a decided advantage over younger children in sports that require quick reactions.

year-olds were better than 7-year-olds, and 11-year-olds were even better. Thus, *older children have a decided advantage over younger children in sports that require quick reactions. Adults are better still.* This is one reason why so many children have trouble in catching balls. By the time they close arms, hands, or mitts, the ball has fallen through or bounced out. Also, throwing or batting balls efficiently requires distance judgment, eye–hand coordination, and quick reaction times, all skills that young elementary children may not possess. Many sports that adults play are not ideal for children.

Physical Fitness

Today's schoolchildren are less physically fit than were children in the 1960s (*National Children and Youth Fitness Study*, 1984). They have more body fat; they are less fit in terms of heart rate, muscle strength, lung capacity, and physical endurance. Many have high levels of cholesterol, or high blood pressure.

The reason is they are not active enough. Only about half of all children are involved in physical education classes twice a week. They spend too much time watching television. One survey indicated that the average American child aged 2 to 11 views television 27.5 hours per week (Tooth, 1985). Or, physical activities in or out of school emphasize competitive sports or games rather than teaching lifetime fitness activities such as walking, running, bicycling, skating, swimming, golf, tennis, or bowling, which they can continue to enjoy in the adult years.

One health education and fitness program involving 24,000 children in Michigan

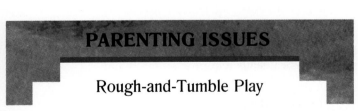

PARENTING ISSUES

Rough-and-Tumble Play

Rough-and-tumble play is a part of the motor activities of many preschool children, especially after they have been sitting for a period of time. It's a way of releasing excess energy, of enjoying social contact, and of having fun (Di Pietro, 1981). All children need frequent periods of physical activity.

Rough-and-tumble play is not the same as aggression, but it sometimes gets out of hand, especially among children who are used to roughhousing at home. Hank, a big 5-year-old in our preschool class, was used to roughhousing with his dad. He and his father seldom played without vigorous, but playful, physical contact. As a result, Hank was usually too rough when he played with smaller children in his class. He was not a bully, but he often hurt other children only because he had learned to be so rough (Author's teaching experience).

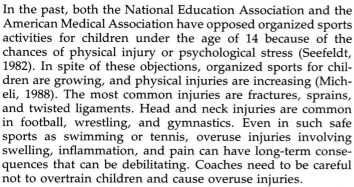

PARENTING ISSUES

Organized Sports

In the past, both the National Education Association and the American Medical Association have opposed organized sports activities for children under the age of 14 because of the chances of physical injury or psychological stress (Seefeldt, 1982). In spite of these objections, organized sports for children are growing, and physical injuries are increasing (Micheli, 1988). The most common injuries are fractures, sprains, and twisted ligaments. Head and neck injuries are common in football, wrestling, and gymnastics. Even in such safe sports as swimming or tennis, overuse injuries involving swelling, inflammation, and pain can have long-term consequences that can be debilitating. Coaches need to be careful not to overtrain children and cause overuse injuries.

The possibility of psychological stress is even greater if the emphasis is on winning rather than just having fun (Mar-

tens, 1988). Little League coaches, or parents who pressure their children to win, cause considerable stress. Sports are supposed to build character and improve self-esteem. But how can the child who consistently does poorly, or whose team is at the bottom of the Little League standing, have a positive self-image if the measure of success is competence and victory?

Benjamin Spock (1990) told Yale University graduates that one of the worst ailments of American society is excessive competitiveness. One of his recommendations was to abolish Little League baseball because "it takes the fun out of athletics at an early age—we ought to raise our children with quite a different spirit." Not all adults would agree with Spock, but most would agree that children ought to come first and winning second.

schools taught children what foods to eat; how to measure their own blood pressure, heart rate, and body fat; and how to resist unhealthy foods and drugs. It also encouraged them to participate in activities and games that build fitness. An analysis of the effects of the program on 360 second-, fifth-, and seventh-graders revealed that the children had lowered their cholesterol levels, blood pressure, and body fat, and had improved their time for running a mile (Fitness Finders, 1984). Children's fitness can be improved through carefully designed programs.

NUTRITION

Breast-Feeding Versus Bottle-Feeding

Another way to improve physical health is through good nutrition. The question arises whether children are healthier being breast- or bottle-fed. Breast-feeding declined rapidly in popularity during the early years of this century and up until about 1970. This decline occurred not only in the United States but in countries all over the world. By the early 1970s, fewer than one in four mothers in North America breast-fed their babies (Eiger & Olds, 1987). Lathan (1977) reports that breast-feeding of infants in Chile declined from 90% in 1960 to less than 10% in 1968; the breast-feeding of infants in Mexico de-

clined from 95% in 1960 to 40% in 1966; the breast-feeding of infants in Singapore declined from 80% in 1951 to 5% in 1971. Whenever this occurred in developing countries, infant mortality rates increased because commercial formula was diluted with contaminated water that transmitted intestinal diseases to infants (Hinds, 1982). As a consequence, the World Health Organization is urging women in these countries to return to breast-feeding and is discouraging the distribution of formula.

The downward trend in the popularity of breast-feeding has been reversed, especially among middle- and upper-class mothers, so that today between 55% and 60% of new mothers breast-feed their babies and they are more likely to nurse their babies until at least the fifth or sixth month (Eiger & Olds, 1987; Martinez, Dodd, & Samaltgedes, 1981). Breast-feeding continues to be less common among black women, women with less than a high school education, economically poor women, and women who have never worked outside the home (U.S. Bureau of the Census, 1988, p. 64).

ADVANTAGES.   Breast-feeding has some distinct advantages. It is the *best food* available for infants and is nutritionally superior to formulas and to cow's milk (Eiger, 1987). It contains the right proportion of fats, calories, proteins, vitamins, and minerals. In relation to cow's milk, it contains several additional amino acids necessary for neural development. It also contains more iron and vitamins A and C. It is more digestible than cow's milk. Breast-fed babies have fewer cases of digestive upsets, allergies, coughs, respiratory difficulties, gastrointestinal infections, and diarrhea (Palti, Mansback, Pridan, Adler, & Palti, 1984; Short, 1984). Breast milk is clean and always at body temperature. Breast-fed babies gain weight more rapidly than bottle-fed babies, and yet Kramer (1981) suggests that breast-fed babies are less prone to subsequent obesity. One big advantage is that breast milk *contains antibodies* derived from the mother's body that immunize the infant from disease and infection. Another advantage is that nursing *helps shrink the uterus* back to normal size more quickly.

In some respects, breast-feeding is also *convenient and practical.* There are no bottles to sterilize, no formulas to mix, no refrigeration required, no bottles to warm. In those ways, it saves time and money. And parents don't have to bring along as much equipment when they go on a trip.

There are also some *psychological advantages.* Many nursing mothers gain a great deal of satisfaction from breast-feeding: from giving good nutrition to their baby, from seeing their devotion, and from the feeling of closeness.

Infants also gain emotional satisfaction and security from the closeness of breast-feeding, from feeling the mother's warmth, and from the experience of sucking. All infants need to suck. Usually, they have to suck harder and longer during breast feeding than during bottle-feeding to get enough milk. This fulfills their psychological needs as well as providing nutrition. Parents need to recognize, however, that babies can achieve the same emotional security from bottle feeding as from breast-feeding, provided they are held and cuddled during feeding. All infants need physical contact and warmth, the sound of a pleasant voice, and the sight of a happy face. A warm, accepting parent who is bottle-feeding the baby can help the infant feel more secure and loved. The important consideration is the total parent–infant relationship, not just the method of feeding.

DISADVANTAGES.   There are also some disadvantages to breast-feeding and some advantages to bottle-feeding. One of the most-frequent criticisms of breast-feeding is that *it is too confining, that it limits the mother's physical freedom, and that it is inconvenient,* especially for the mother who works outside the home. Few working mothers can take time

off during the day to nurse the baby, unless the infant is being cared for nearby or in a child-care center at the place of business, and the business allows time during the day for the mother to nurse. Even mothers who do not work must leave the home, at which time they have to either find a time and place to nurse their babies, or hurry home in time for feeding. Before bottle-feeding was widespread, nursing mothers used to feel free to nurse in public—while shopping, on buses, even in church—but as nursing became less acceptable, the practice gradually declined.

Nursing a baby also means that baby-sitters cannot be employed during feeding times. One answer, of course, is to use a breast pump and keep the milk in a relief bottle for the care giver to feed the baby when the mother is out of the house. Formula may also be used in a relief bottle. Spock and Rothenberg (1985) suggest that the baby be introduced to the bottle at about 6 weeks of age, only after the flow of milk has become well established.

Some fathers object to breast-feeding because they are excluded from feeding the baby themselves. Insecure fathers may be jealous of the time and attention given the baby. Of course, the father can hold the baby as well as the mother can, apart from feeding times.

One disadvantage of breast-feeding is that *some drugs and chemicals are passed to the baby through the breast milk.* Some drugs are not passed in large enough quantities to affect the baby. Other drugs, such as alcohol and narcotics, come through in sufficient amounts to cause addiction. The mother needs to check with her doctor to determine what medication she is allowed to take. Some diseases, such as AIDS, may also be transmitted through the mother's milk (Rogers, 1985).

Some mothers do not produce enough milk to satisfy the baby. There are various possible reasons for this. At the outset, it may take extra time for the milk to begin flowing. The colorless liquid called colostrum, produced by the breasts the first couple of days after birth, supplies liquid and antibodies to the baby; and nervous upset may curtail the milk's "coming in" for a longer time. The mother may need to consume more liquids to increase the supply. Breast size is not a factor because the number of mammary glands, which produce the milk, is usually about the same in all women.

For some, breast-feeding becomes a painful experience. The nipples get dry and cracked. The baby bites the nipple and makes it sore. Spock and Rothenberg (1985) suggest putting the entire areola in the baby's mouth so their gums squeeze the areola rather than the nipple. The baby gets more milk this way also. Other mothers complain that nursing is *too fatiguing* and that it takes too much out of them. They certainly do need proper diet and rest.

PERSONAL CHOICE.   One of the most important considerations is the mother's attitude toward nursing itself. Breast-feeding requires a personal choice. Some women find breast-feeding to be a challenge, and they become very upset if they can't manage it. Others really want to breast-feed but let other people dissuade them. In these cases, the father's support can be a crucial positive contribution. Individual mothers can follow their best instincts and do what they really want to do and what seems to be best for the baby. If needed, they can receive support and consultation from La Leche League, an organization that promotes breast-feeding and offers help to nursing mothers, which has chapters all over the world.

Dietary Requirements

As children get older, a balanced diet is vitally important for their good health and vigor. Their bodies need protein, minerals, vitamins, carbohydrates, fats, roughage, and water. These nutrients are derived from four basic food groups: *milk and dairy products, meat, fruits and vegetables,* and *breads and cereals.* Children can be taught to eat foods from the four basic food groups every day as the best way of assuring good nutrition.

Obesity

Obesity may be a health problem as children get older and it is a distinct disadvantage to children in a society that places a social stigma on being fat (Kolata, 1986). Even young children have negative attitudes toward obesity (Reaves & Roberts, 1983). Because fat children tend to become fat adults, obesity presents a future health hazard to them (Brownell, 1982).

Several factors influence obesity. One is *heredity.* If parents are obese, children tend to be obese also, and not just because the parents teach their children to overeat (Stunkard, Foch, & Hrubec, 1986). Obese children tend to be born with more and larger fat cells than slim children, and the number of fat cells increases even more if there is excess weight gain before the age of 12 (Krieshok & Karpowitz, 1988). Another theory is that obese people have longer intestines than slim people, allowing more calories to be absorbed (Power, 1980). Of course, appetite is partly inherited. From birth, some children

PARENTING ISSUES

When Are Solid Foods Introduced?

Sometimes conflict develops between the mother and the pediatrician over the age at which solid foods are to be introduced to the child. Some pediatricians insist that infants do not need solid foods before 6 months of age. Some mothers prefer to give solid foods after several months of age because they say "it helps the baby sleep through the night."

There are several important considerations. Infants must develop a new movement of the tongue and mouth to swallow solid foods. Neurologic development has progressed sufficiently for this to happen at about 3 to 4 months of age. Infants can swallow foods at a younger age only if the food is placed on the back of the tongue, but this represents a kind of force-feeding. Some infants rebel and develop feeding problems later.

The time to start solid foods depends partially on the infant's needs and readiness. An infant who has loose bowels may not tolerate solid foods as easily. Certainly, babies do best with breast milk or formula, rather than cow's milk, until at least 6 months of age (AAP Committee on Nutrition, 1986). If there are not other problems, infants can benefit from beginning to eat cereal at about 4 months of age. Cereal has a high iron content that babies need. Fruit is usually started after babies have become used to cereal, followed by vegetables, then strained meat at about 6 months of age. Parents need to avoid too many "dinners" (combination foods) with large amounts of starch, cellulose, and sodium. Puddings and other desserts contain large quantities of cornstarch and sugar that are not advisable for children, especially for obese children or for those not getting enough other nutrients. By 6 months of age most babies are eating cereal and a variety of fruits, vegetables, and meats (Spock & Rothenberg, 1985). Wheat, eggs, and chocolate should be avoided until the child is 1 year of age to prevent unnecessary food sensitivities (Berkow, 1987).

PARENTING ISSUES

How Not to Create Eating Problems

Feeding problems most often develop because overly zealous parents try to make their children eat well, because careless parents don't feed them properly, or because overindulgent parents give children anything they want, including too many sweets. The following suggestions will help to avoid eating problems:

1. Avoid force-feeding children, or use of excessive urging to get them to eat. And avoid fighting with them over food. When pushed too hard, children will rebel and refuse to eat.

2. Recognize that children's appetites vary. Sometimes they eat a lot, sometimes a little. The amount usually evens out over time. Serve small portions—less than they will eat, not more—giving seconds as needed. This way, you can avoid hostility about their finishing their meals.

3. Use a gradual introduction to new foods, giving only small amounts at first and allowing the child time to learn to like them. Sometimes children will never accept a particular food, but as long as other foods provide the basic nutrients, there is no problem. Most adults admit there are foods they now eat that they didn't like as children.

4. Keep mealtimes happy and pleasant, avoiding arguments, controversy, and threats.

5. Serve balanced meals, avoiding excess sweets and fats. Some parents complain that their children will not eat vegetables. These parents may dislike vegetables and seldom serve them.

6. When children are old enough to eat adult table food, serve the same food to the whole family; don't cook separately for the children. It's certainly all right to serve children's favorites now and then, but not in addition to or as a substitute for food eaten by the rest of the family.

7. Generally avoid asking children what they want to eat. It may be all right occasionally or for special occasions, but if you do it on a regular basis, you'll be forever catering to their whims. Some children ask for one food, then when given it, don't want it and prefer something else. Letting children dictate their diets is really asking for trouble.

8. Don't bribe children to eat by promising a reward of any kind, whether it is a piece of candy, a gold star, or any other prize. The less fuss about eating, the better.

One major problem that contributes to becoming overweight is the habit of eating junk food.

seem to have voracious appetites. Others appear less interested in food.

Another factor in obesity is *eating habits* (Olvera-Ezzell, Power, & Cousins, 1990). Obese children do not necessarily eat more food, but they prefer calorific foods high in fats, starches, and sugars (Keesey & Pawley, 1986). When they eat such foods, their level of insulin increases, which, in turn, further increases hunger and food consumption. It's a vicious circle (Rodin, 1982).

One major problem that contributes to obesity is the habit of eating junk food—potato chips, sweets, and sodas—which are high in calories from fats and sugars, but low in nutritional value. The fat content and calorie ratings of foods from various fast-food restaurants is shown in Table 6.6 (CSPI, 1990). The American Heart Association recommends that the percentage of calories from fat should be no more than one-third. This means no more than 15 teaspoons of fat per day for women and 20 teaspoons of fat per day for men. As seen in Table 6.6, most of the foods from fast-food restaurants are high in fat.

TABLE 6.6 Fat, Calorie, and Sodium Content of Selected Fast-Food Meals

Selected Meal	Calories	Fat (tsp.)	Sodium Content
Burger King Whopper, medium fries, chocolate shake	1,312	15	1,301
McDonalds Big Mac, medium fries, iced cheese danish	1,070	16	1,520
Kentucky Fried Chicken, original recipe, two-piece dinner	1,002	12	2,362
Arby's regular roast beef sandwich, two potato cakes, side salad with light Italian dressing	607	6	1,270
Wendy's bacon swiss burger, small fries, medium Frosty	1,470	17	1,771
Dairy Queen double hamburger, onion rings, chocolate-dipped large cone	1,320	15	1,045
Hardee's big country breakfast with sausage, juice, milk	1,050	14	2,110
Burger King croissan'wich (sausage, egg, cheese), milk	665	10	1,107

Adapted from *CSPI's Fast Food Eating Guide* (1990). Center for Science in the Public Interest, Washington, D.C. Used by permission of the publisher.

Activity level also affects obesity. Obese children tend to be less active, which reduces metabolism and the amount of food burned up, thus increasing fat accumulation. There is a similar link between television watching and obesity. A study of 7,000 children between the ages of 6 and 11 and of 6,500 adolescents found that every hour per day spent watching television increases the prevalence of obesity by 2% (Dietz & Gortmacher, 1985). The reason is that television watching reduces physical activity and increases snack consumption. *Psychological factors* may also be a cause of obesity. Children may eat as a means of relieving tension or gaining security when they are tense, unhappy, or lonely.

The important question is what to do about obesity. Parents must try to prevent it in the first place by regulating the diet and eating habits of children while they are young. They should serve nutritious foods, low in calories from fat, starches, and sugars. As infants fat children may look cute, but they will feel bad about themselves when they are older.

Parents should not put their obese children on crash diets. Children may lose weight, but not permanently. *There are two principal ways to help children reduce their weight.* The first way is to gradually help them change their eating habits. Avoid keeping junk foods in the house, for example, and serve only healthy foods. The second way is to increase children's physical activity so they will use up more calories—for example, enroll children in groups emphasizing physical activities. Parents also can exercise with their children, acting as good role models and having fun as well. And they can encourage their children to cut down on TV.

SLEEP

Needs, Habits, and Disturbances

If they are made comfortable, get enough food to eat, and have plenty of fresh, cool air, most infants will get the amount of sleep they need. In the early months, most infants sleep from feeding to feeding, although,

FOCUS

Sugar Consumption and Children's Behavior

Not only is excessive sugar consumption unhealthy, but it also may be associated with behavior problems. Many parents feel that candy, cookies, and other sweets transform children into overactive and irrational hellions, furniture-destroying versions of their former selves (Chollar, 1988). There is evidence to show that high sugar consumption increases aggression, hyperactivity, and inattentiveness, especially in unstructured situations when children are bored (Goldman, Lerman, Contors, & Udall, 1986). The negative effects can be greater when snacks or meals already consumed have been very high in carbohydrates. When the child's basic diet contains high amounts of carbohydrates, sugar consumption increases inappropriate behavior; but if balanced with necessary proteins, the added sugar has less effect. If children's blood sugar is low, as when they have not had breakfast, additional carbohydrates may have a calming effect (Chollar, 1988).

from the beginning, some are wakeful during certain times of the day. By the end of the first year, most infants take only two naps a day, after the breakfast and lunch feedings. Between 1 and 1½ years they usually give up one of these (Spock & Rothenberg, 1985). If naps are too long in the afternoon, children don't want to go to bed at night.

Infants will take the sleep they need. Two-year-olds won't. They may be kept awake by overexcitement, conflicts, tenseness, or fears of various kinds. Resistance to going to bed generally peaks between 1 and 2 years of age. Children cry when left alone in the crib, or climb out and seek their parents. The cause is usually **separation anxiety**, or an effort to control their environment. When children get out of bed, the best way for parents to handle the situation is to put them back in the crib, and then wait in the hallway to make sure the children stay in bed. Parents need to avoid: (1) letting the children stay up; (2) lying down in bed with them; (3) reading more stories and allowing more play; or (4) taking children into bed with them. Once children learn that they will not be allowed out of their own bed and cannot entice parents for some stories or play, they will usually settle down and go to sleep (Berkow, 1987).

Separation anxiety—anxiety experienced by children when they are separated from care givers to whom they are emotionally attached

It is up to parents to see that children get the sleep they need. The average 2-year-old child needs 12 hours of sleep at night plus 1 to 2 hours of nap. Naps are gradually discontinued over several years. From age 6 to 9, children need about 11 hours sleep; 10- to 12-year-olds need about 10 hours. Some children need more or less than these averages.

There are several things that parents can do to develop regular sleeping habits for their children.

1. Put children to bed at the same time every night.

2. Develop a relaxed bedtime routine: Get washed and undressed, put pajamas on, have a snack, put the doll to bed, read a story, get tucked in, give a goodnight kiss. Children thrive on routine and are upset by variations. Routines help to give them security and condition them to settle down to sleep. Also, it's easier to put them to sleep in their own bed than in strange places, which requires extra effort and attention.

3. Avoid excessive stimulation before bedtime. Rough play, disturbances in the parent–child relationship, or tension in the home cause wakefulness. Parents can't let children roughhouse and then expect them to settle down and go to sleep immediately.

4. Keep bedtime relaxed and happy. It's far more pleasant to carry children to bed lovingly than to angrily order them to bed, or to spank them for not obeying instantly.

5. Avoid sending children to bed as a means of discipline. They will come to associate going to bed with punishment, which makes it harder to get them to bed at other times.

6. Avoid frightening stories or television programs, which may precipitate **nightmares**, especially in 3- to 4-year-olds, who cannot distinguish fantasy from reality. **Night terrors** are characterized by sudden awakening, panic, and screaming. They are most common between ages 3 and 8 years. **Sleepwalking** is estimated to occur in 15% of children between 5 and 12 years of age. Stressful events may trigger an episode of sleepwalking (Bowker, 1987). If these difficulties persist, psychological help may be necessary.

Nightmares

Night terrors

Sleepwalking

Sleeping with Parents

At some time or another, most children want to sleep with their parents, either in the same room, or actually in bed with them. The question arises whether this is a good idea. Many parents want their newborn in a crib, but in the same room with them so they can hear the baby cry. This may be a good idea up until about 6 months of age. If the practice continues too long, however, it can be hard to get children to sleep anywhere else. Also, even infants may be upset by the sounds of parents having intercourse, which they don't understand. An alternative arrangement is to put an electronic monitor (a microphone) in the baby's room, with the speaker in the parent's room so they can hear the infant at all times and be alerted if there is trouble.

Some parents feel that it's better not to take children into bed with them, even if the child wakes up frightened at night. Once established, the habit is hard to break. Children need to be taken back to their own bed and comforted. However, letting children come into bed for a cuddle in the morning is a different situation. It's a loving, reassuring thing to do.

HEALTH CARE

Health Supervision of the Well Child

Proper health supervision of the well child will help to promote optimum development of infants and children. Such supervision by

TABLE 6.7 Health-Care Schedule

	Infancy						Early Childhood					Late Childhood					Adolescence			
	By 1 mo	2 mo	4 mo	6 mo	9 mo	12 mo	15 mo	18 mo	24 mo	3 yr	4 yr	5 yr	6 yr	8 yr	10 yr	12 yr	14 yr	16 yr	18 yr	20+ yr
Age[1] History																				
Initial/Interval	•	•	•	•	•	•	•	•	•	•	•	•	•	•	•	•	•	•	•	•
Measurements																				
Height and weight	•	•	•	•	•	•	•	•	•	•	•	•	•	•	•	•	•	•	•	•
Head circumference	•	•	•	•	•	•														
Blood pressure										•	•	•	•	•	•	•	•	•	•	•
Sensory Screening																				
Vision	S	S	S	S	S	S	S	S	S	O	O	O	O	O	S	O	O	S	O	O
Hearing	S	S	S	S	S	S	S	S	S	S	O	O	S²	S²	S²	O	S	S	O	S
Development/Behavioral Assessment[3]	•	•	•	•	•	•	•	•	•	•	•	•	•	•	•	•	•	•	•	•
Physical Examination[4]	•	•	•	•	•	•	•	•	•	•	•	•	•	•	•	•	•	•	•	•
Procedures[5]																				
Hereditary/Metabolic screening[6]	•																			
Immunization[7]		•	•	•			•	•				•					•			
Tuberculin test						•			•[8]					•[8]					•[8]	
Hematocrit or Hemoglobin[9]					•				•					•					•	
Urinalysis[10]				•					•					•					•	
Anticipatory Guidance[11]	•	•	•	•	•	•	•	•	•	•	•	•	•	•	•	•	•	•	•	•
Initial Dental Referral[12]										•										

● = to be performed, **S** = subjective, by history, **O** = objective, by a standard testing method.

[1]If a child comes under care for the first time at any point on the schedule, or if any items are not accomplished at the suggested age, the schedule should be brought up to date at the earliest possible time.

[2]At these points, history may suffice; if problem suggested, a standard testing method should be used.

[3]By history and appropriate physical examination; if suspicious, by specific objective developmental testing.

[4]At each visit, a complete physical examination is essential, with infant totally unclothed, older child undressed and suitably draped.

[5]These may be modified, depending on entry point into schedule and individual need.

[6]PKU and thyroid testing should be done at about 2 weeks. Infants initially screened before 24 hours of age should be rescreened.

[7]Schedule(s) per Report of Committee on Infectious Diseases, ed. 18, 1982.

[8]The Committee on Infectious Diseases recommends tuberculin testing at 12 months of age and every 1 to 2 years thereafter. In some areas, tuberculosis is of exceedingly low occurrence and the physician may elect not to retest routinely or to use longer intervals.

[9]Present medical evidence suggests the need for reevaluation of the frequency and timing of hemoglobin or hematocrit tests. One determination is therefore suggested during each time period. Performance of additional tests is left to the individual practice experience.

[10]Present medical evidence suggests the need for reevaluation of the frequency and timing of urinalyses. One determination is therefore suggested during each time period. Performance of additional tests is left to the individual practice experience.

[11]Appropriate discussion and counseling should be an integral part of each visit for care.

[12]Subsequent examinations as prescribed by dentist.

NOTE: Special chemical, immunologic, and endocrine testing are usually carried out upon specific indications. Testing other than newborn (e.g., inborn errors of metabolism, sickle disease, lead) are discretionary with the physician.

Guidelines for child health supervision. Recommendations approved by the Executive Board of the American Academy of Pediatrics in March 1982. Modified from "Guidelines for Health Supervision," *News and Comment,* American Academy of Pediatrics, May 1982. Used with permission.

medical personnel ought to include: (1) instruction of parents in child rearing, health maintenance, accident prevention, and nutrition; (2) routine immunizations for the prevention of disease; (3) early detection of disease through interview and examination; and (4) early treatment of disease. To meet these objectives, parents and children should be seen by their doctor at regular intervals throughout the early years of life. The frequency of subsequent visits will vary, depending upon children's age and condition and the population served (Bowker, 1987).

The American Academy of Pediatrics has recommended the preventative health-care schedule which is found in Table 6.7. This schedule is for children who have not manifested any important health problems and who are growing and developing satisfactorily. More frequent and sophisticated visits are necessary for children with special problems.

FOCUS

Immunization Schedule

During the first 6 months of life, infants are given diphtheria, tetanus, pertussis (whooping cough), and polio vaccines. Vaccinations against measles, mumps, and rubella viruses are given at 15 months. Booster shots for diphtheria, tetanus, pertussis, and polio vaccines are repeated at various intervals, but ought to occur at or before school entry. *Hemophilus influenzae* b (flu) vaccine is given at 24 months. Adult tetanus and diphtheria toxoid are given between 14 and 16 years of age and repeated every 10 years throughout life. Table 6.8 shows the recommended schedule for normal infants and children.

TABLE 6.8 Recommended Schedule for Active Immunization of Normal Infants and Children

Age[1]	Vaccine(s)[2]	Comments
2 months	DTP-1[3]; OPV-1[4]	Can be given earlier in areas of high endemicity
4 months	DTP-2; OPV-2	Interval of 6 weeks to 2 months desired between OPV doses to avoid interference
6 months	DTP-3	An additional dose of OPV at this time is optional for use in areas with a high risk of polio exposure
15 months[5]	MMR[6]	
18 months[5]	DTP-4; OPV-3	Completion of primary series
24 months	Hib	*Hemophilus influenzae* b vaccine
4–6 years[7]	DTP-5; OPV-4	Preferably at or before school entry
14–16 years	Td[8]	Repeat every 10 years throughout life

[1]These recommended ages should not be construed as absolute; i.e., 2 months can be 6 to 10 weeks, etc.

[2]For all products used, consult manufacturer's package enclosure for instructions for storage, handling, and administration. Immunobiologics prepared by different manufacturers may vary, and those of the same manufacturer may change from time to time. The package insert should be followed for a specific product.

[3]DTP, diphtheria and tetanus toxoids and pertussis vaccine.

[4]OPV, oral, attenuated poliovirus vaccine contains poliovirus types 1, 2, and 3.

[5]Simultaneous administration of MMR, DTP, and OPV is appropriate for patients whose compliance with medical care recommendations cannot be assured.

[6]MMR, live measles, mumps, and rubella viruses in a combined vaccine.

[7]Up to 7th birthday.

[8]Td, adult tetanus toxoid and diphtheria toxoid in combination, contains the same dose of tetanus toxoid as DTP or pediatric diphtheria and tetanus toxoid (DT) and a reduced dose of diphtheria toxoid.

Modified from *Morbidity and Mortality Weekly Report*, January 14, 1983, vol. 32, no. 1, Centers for Disease Control, Atlanta, Georgia.

SEXUAL DEVELOPMENT

Infancy

The infant's capacity for sexual response begins early. Ultrasound pictures reveal that erections occur in developing male fetuses several months before birth (Calderone, 1983). Many male babies have erections even before the umbilical cord is cut or in the first few months after birth. Erections can occur with or without penile stimulation, and they often occur during feeding and sleep. Apparently, the warmth and softness of the mother's body, along with the stimulation of sucking, are pleasurable sensations that stimulate sexual reflexes.

Female infants also exhibit sexual response, evidenced by the presence of vaginal lubrication and clitoral erection during the first 24 hours of life (Langfeldt, 1981). Vaginal lubrication can also occur during nursing. Although their sexual reflexes respond to emotional and physical stimuli, both male and female infants are too young to consciously be aware of the encounters; therefore, they cannot be considered sexually awakened (Martinson, 1976).

Infants begin to discover their bodies

during the first year of life. During their exploration, they randomly touch their genitals. Later, as their motor abilities develop, children deliberately touch and rub their genitals. In the process, they discover that such touching brings pleasant sensations.

Early Childhood

Preschool children are curious about everything. This curiosity extends to their own bodies, which they continue to explore. Most masturbate at some time or another. Both boys and girls are fascinated with toileting procedures. They also develop curiosity about other children's bodies and about boy–girl differences. As a result, they peek at one another's bodies to see what they look like. "Doctor" games are one method of body exploration.

Parents need to recognize that some exploration, peeking, and touching is fairly common behavior that results from children's curiosity. If sexual exploration during play becomes too frequent, however, children may require greater supervision. In addition, parents need to be concerned about protecting younger children from advances of those who are older. They should teach children to report sexual requests from older children or adults, such as solicitations to take off their clothes or to touch their genitals.

Middle Childhood

Society becomes less accepting of children's sexual interests during middle childhood, so sexual activities take place more covertly than during the preschool years. Sexual experimentation does not cease or decrease. In fact, it may become more frequent. In one survey, parents of 6- and 7-year-old children reported that 83% of their sons and 76% of their daughters had participated in sexual play with siblings or friends of the same sex (Kolodny, 1980). Hunt (1974) found that one-third of females and two-thirds of males who responded to a questionnaire reported that they masturbated by age 13.

Children remain fascinated with sex and with facts concerning sexual development, human reproduction, and sexual intercourse. The delightful thing about children of school age is that they are not embarrassed to ask detailed questions, given the opportunity. An ideal time to teach children all the basic facts about sex is before they reach puberty and become self-conscious about discussing the subject openly.

SUMMARY

1. Physical growth from birth to adolescence manifests two different patterns: (1) very rapid but decelerating growth from birth to age 1, and (2) linear and steady annual increments after age 1. Increases both in height and weight are dramatic during the first year of life.
2. There are wide individual, cultural, ethnic, and socioeconomic class differences in growth patterns.
3. Body parts grow at different rates. They grow according to the cephalocaudal principle, from the head to the feet, and according to the proximodistal principle, from the center of the body outward.
4. Three organ systems—the lymphoid system, the reproductive system, and the central nervous system—do not follow the general patterns of growth of the rest of the body and organs.
5. Brain growth and nerve maturation include increased myelinization and the development of increasingly complex nerve pathways.
6. The cerebral cortex is the largest structure of the forebrain and contains the higher brain centers controlling intellectual, sensory, and motor functions.
7. The cerebral cortex is larger in proportion to total body weight and is more highly developed in humans than in any other animals.
8. The cerebral cortex is divided into two hemispheres; the left side of the brain controls mainly the right side of the body and the right side of the brain controls mainly the left side of the body.
9. Right- or left-handedness is reasonably well established by age 2. Lateralization is the preference for using one side of the body more than the other in performing specific tasks.
10. The right hemisphere specializes in music, drama, fantasy, intuition, and art; in recognizing patterns, faces, and melodies; and in visualizing spatial relationships. The left hemisphere specializes in logic, mathematics, language, writing, and judging time.
11. The motor, sensory, and association areas of the cortex each control particular functions.

12. The Broca's area of the cortex is involved in using language, the Wernicke's area in understanding language.

13. Both maturation and learning are important in the development of cortical structures and in learning such functions as toilet training.

14. The eruption of deciduous teeth (baby teeth) begins at about 5 months and is completed by 30 months of age. The eruption of permanent teeth begins at 5 years of age and is completed by age 25. Children need dental care of baby teeth as well as permanent teeth.

15. Gross-motor skills develop in infancy before fine-motor skills. The average infant can walk alone by 15 months of age, and can scribble spontaneously by 25 months.

16. Five-year-olds can perform a variety of physical feats, involving both gross-motor skills and fine-motor skills, that would have been impossible several years earlier.

17. Most differences between elementary school boys and girls in motor abilities are due to differential expectations and experiences. Children exposed to the same physical education classes show few gender differences in abilities.

18. Reaction time of children decreases with age. This is an important factor in many games children play.

19. Many authorities disapprove of organized sports for children under the age of 14 because of the chances of physical injury and psychological stress.

20. Today's children are less physically fit than were children in the 1960s.

21. Breast-feeding and bottle-feeding both have advantages and disadvantages, but most authorities would say that breast-feeding is superior from a health standpoint alone. The chief disadvantage of breast-feeding is that is hard to manage for mothers who work.

22. Generally speaking, solid foods are introduced about 4 months of age so that by the 6th month babies are eating cereal, fruits, vegetables, and meat.

23. It is vitally important for children to eat a balanced diet derived from four basic food groups daily: milk and dairy products, meat, fruits and vegetables, and breads and cereals.

24. Obesity is a distinct disadvantage to children and has multiple causes: heredity; eating habits that involve eating a lot of high-calorie food; low activity level; and using eating to ease tension or gain security.

25. Excessive sugar consumption makes children hyperactive if the basic diet is unbalanced or if the sugar is not combined with sufficient protein.

26. Most infants will take the amount of sleep they need; 2-year-olds won't. It is up to parents to see that children get the required sleep.

27. Some authorities discourage having children sleep with parents on a regular basis.

28. Health supervision of the well child ought to include: (1) instruction of parents in child rearing, health maintenance, accident prevention, and nutrition; (2) routine immunizations; (3) early detection of disease through interview and examination; and (4) early treatment of disease.

29. The American Academy of Pediatrics has a recommended schedule for child health supervision and a recommended schedule for immunizations.

30. Children's capacity for sexual responses begins in infancy.

31. Both preschool and grade-school children engage in body exploration and masturbation, and are interested in matters pertaining to sex.

KEY TERMS

Cephalocaudal principle   *p. 117*
Cerebral cortex   *p. 119*
Lateralization   *p. 119*
Myelinization   *p. 119*
Nightmares   *p. 132*

Night terrors   *p. 132*
Proximodistal principle   *p. 118*
Separation anxiety   *p. 132*
Sleepwalking   *p. 132*

DISCUSSION QUESTIONS

1. Do you know any children who are smaller or larger than average for their age group? Describe them. What are some of the social and psychological consequences for them?
2. Should parents play an active role in helping children develop gross-motor skills and fine-motor skills? Explain. Does it help? What might be some of the possible negative results? Should parents help children to learn sports?
3. What do you think of having boys and girls in the same physical education classes at school? Explain.
4. Have you breast-fed or have you been the father of a breast-fed baby? How did you get along? What do you think of it? What are your attitudes toward breast-feeding versus bottle-feeding?
5. Have you bottle-fed a baby, or do you know someone who does? What were the results?
6. What should parents do about children who are obese? Were you obese as a child? If so, how did it affect you and your relationships with others? If not, what were your experiences or friendships with children who were obese? How did obesity affect their behavior and attitudes as you saw them?
7. What do you or would you do about children who won't go to bed at night? Explain your choices.
8. Did you sleep with your parents while you were growing up? How do you feel about it now? How did it affect you? Do you think it encourages sexual stimulation, guilt, and anxiety? Why or why not?
9. What do you think of the recommended health-care schedule for well children that is found in the book? Are there any aspects you object to? What do you think of taking a child who is not sick to the doctor? Why do some people never want to take their children to the doctor, while others run at every little illness?

SUGGESTED READINGS

Brown, E. W., & Franta, C. F. (Eds.). (1988). *Competitive sports for children and youth.* Champaign, IL: Human Kinetics. A series of articles summarizing research and issues.

Caplan, F. (1981). *The first twelve months of life.* New York: Bantam. A summary, easily read.

Caplan, J., & Caplan, F. (1983). *The early childhood years: The 2- to 6-year-old.* New York: Putnam. Physical, cognitive, social, and emotional growth during the years 2 to 6.

Collins, A. (Ed.). (1984). *Development during middle childhood: The years from 6 to 12.* Washington, DC: National Academy Press. All aspects of development during these years.

Dodson, F., & Alexander, A. (1986). *Your child: Birth to age 6.* New York: Fireside. Summary.

Haywood, K. M. (1986). *Life span motor development.* Champaign, IL: Human Kinetics. Summary of development over the life span.

Lamb, M. E., & Bornstein, M. C. (1987). *Development in infancy.* New York: Random House. Description by two leading researchers.

Spock, B., & Rothenberg, M. B. (1985). *Dr. Spock's baby and child care.* New York: Pocket Books. Updated revision of this best-seller.

7

Cognitive Development

LANGUAGE

Language and Communication

All animals have evolved some method of communication. Whales apparently have meaningful ways of communicating through the use of various sounds. A dog can say a lot by wagging its tail or growling. A group of crows was observed circling overhead, squawking away in a very disturbed manner. The object of their upset was a red fox that was running into the woods carrying a dead bird. The crows were definitely communicating, expressing their upset and warning one another of the potential danger below.

Some insects also have developed methods of communication. If a honeybee discovers nectar within 100 meters of the hive, it does a round dance, first turning in a circle in one direction, then in another, as shown in Figure 7.1. Swarms of bees then fly out in all directions within 100 meters of the hive, looking for the nectar. If the nectar is 200 to 300 meters away, the honeybee does a tail-wagging dance in the form of a figure eight. The direction of the nectar is communicated through the angle of the middle part of the figure eight relative to the sun. The distance is communicated by the rate of turning, the

All animals have evolved some method of communication.

rate of tail wagging, and the sound made by the vibration of the wings (von Frisch, 1953). The bees are able to communicate messages very efficiently, but the extent of their communication is limited by their inheritance.

Long before they can use spoken words, human infants can communicate. The *rooting reflex* indicates an ability to suck and to eat. Various types of cries indicate upset, pain, or tiredness. *Nonverbal body language* includes such things as posture, facial expressions, still or tense muscles, movement, tears, sweating, shivering, or quivering. Alert parents learn to interpret these body signs and to give correct meaning to their expression.

Language, therefore, represents only one method of communication. It is certainly the most important, however. With it humans are able to transmit information, ideas, attitudes, and emotions to one another. Without it, what we think of as meaningful human relationships would be impossible. Language enables humans to transcend space or time, to pass on the knowledge of millions of years gone by to future generations. Language has a *generative function* also. It can be used to originate new ideas and thoughts by reordering words and phrases in combinations that have not been expressed before. Language goes beyond concrete experiences by using symbols to represent reality, yet in such a way that reality is understood. Above all, through thousands of words, language is an efficient way of communicating unlimited pieces of information, thoughts, ideas, and feelings from one person to others.

FIGURE 7.1   Bees communicating through their dance.

Adapted from D. von Frisch (1953), *The Dancing Bees: An Account of the Life and Senses of the Honeybee.* New York: Harcourt, Brace, and World.

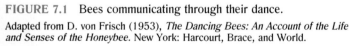

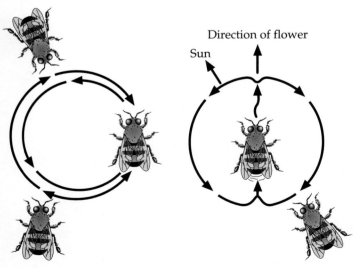

Direction of flower

Sun

Round Dance   Tail-Wagging Dance

[handwritten: John Locke - mind is blank slate]

FOCUS

Ape Talk

Beatrix and Allen Gardner (1971) argued that chimpanzees are not able to learn to speak a human language because they have incomplete control of their vocal cords, which makes speech impossible. They insisted, however, that the lack of spoken language was not a result of inadequate mental abilities. To prove their point, they raised a young chimp, named *Washoe*, to whom they taught *American Sign Language (ASL)*, used by the deaf. Washoe acquired a vocabulary of over 150 signs and was able to use them in combinations. She signed "listen" and "dog" when she heard a barking dog, or "water" and "bird" for duck. She could also make requests like "gimmee sweet drink." Washoe was also given a young male chimpanzee to adopt. She immediately began teaching sign language to her pupil. She taught him the sign for "come" by making the sign and then pulling him. Eventually, he learned over 50 signs from his adopted mother (Gardner & Gardner, 1986).

Penny Patterson (1977) taught over 600 signs to Koko, a gorilla who uses a sign language more spontaneously and generatively than Washoe. She has made a number of novel constructions, including the signs "bottle match" for cigarette lighter, "white tiger" for zebra, "look mask" for viewmaster, "eye hat" for mask, and "finger bracelet" for ring. She can also use signs to express anger. She signed "red mad gorilla" when she was upset. Although the word order of sign language

Does Koko, a gorilla, have her own rules of language?

is relatively free, Koko orders her signs consistently and in some cases differently from her teachers. For example, she consistently places adjectives after nouns, saying "bean green" and "baby mine." Her teachers usually use English word order as they speak and sign simultaneously. This indicates Koko may be generating her own rules rather than passively imitating her human companions. However, some researchers feel that in spite of Koko's novel word combinations, nothing she does seems to resemble the rigid syntactic rules that apply to human language (Greenfield & Savage-Rumbaugh, 1984).

Elements and Rules of Language

In accurately fulfilling its functions, language contains a finite set of elements that are used according to set rules. The basic elements of language include *phonemes, morphemes, syntax and grammar, semantics,* and *pragmatics.*

Phoneme—the smallest unit of sound in a language

PHONEMES. A **phoneme,** derived from the Greek word meaning "sound," is the smallest unit of sound in a language. There may be 20 to 60 phonemes, depending on the language. In English, everything we say is made up of only 44 phonemes; that is, our language is generated from only 44 basic sound distinctions. There are more phonemes than letters of the alphabet, because some letter combinations, such as *ch* and *th,* stand for different phonemes.

MORPHEMES. **Morphemes** are the smallest units of meaning in a language. They may be single words, such as *word* or *help,* or they may exist in combination with other morphemes, such as *anti-biotic* or *push-ed.* Combinations of morphemes always occur in particular sequences according to set rules. We wouldn't say *biotic-anti,* for example. In developing language, children come to know thousands of morphemes.

Morpheme—the smallest unit of meaning in a language

SYNTAX. **Syntax** is the system of rules by which phonemes are combined in morphemes and morphemes are combined in words and words are combined in phrases and sentences to form acceptable utterances. In English, we would say, "Mr. Jones went to town." We would not say, "Mr. Jones gone to town" or "Mr. Jones to town went." The formal description of syntactical rules comprises the grammar of the language.

Syntax—the grammatical rules of a language

Semantics—the meaning of words and sentences

SEMANTICS.   **Semantics** deals with the meanings of words and sentences. It assures proper word usage. Thus, a child learns that a pair of puppies is "two puppies," not "too puppies," or that *mother* is not synonymous with *woman*.

Pragmatics—the practical use of language to communicate with others in a variety of social contexts

PRAGMATICS.   **Pragmatics** refers to the practical use of language to communicate with others in a variety of social contexts (Capelli, Nakagawa, & Madden, 1990). Children learn appropriate choices of words and intensity of tone of voice when talking with their parents. They may use other words or vocal expressions when talking to their peers. These are practical applications of language. Pragmatics also refers to the ability to engage in meaningful conversation, to describe an event, or to explain something to a teacher. It's not enough to be able to know the correct usage of words and sentences. Children must be able to apply this knowledge in specific situations. This is the science of pragmatics.

Theories of Language Development

One of the most amazing aspects of human development is how quickly children learn language. Infants progress from simple cooing and babbling of sounds to the acquisition of a vocabulary of thousands of words, plus an understanding of the basic rules of syntax and grammar. How can we explain this very rapid development of language?

Basically there are four different theories of language development: *biological theory, learning theory, cognitive theory,* and *interactionist theory.*

BIOLOGICAL THEORY.   Biological theory (called the **nativist view**) says that children inherit a predisposition to learn language at a certain age (Chomsky, 1968). Chomsky (1980) and McNeill (1970) maintained that infants are born into the world with a **language acquisition device** (LAD) that enables them to listen to speech and to imitate sounds and sound patterns. The LAD enables them to produce phonemes at about 6 months, the first word at about 1 year, and the first sentences at about 2 years, regardless of the child's language, race, ethnic origin, or nationality. The development of language parallels neurological changes that occur as a result of maturation (Lenneberg, 1973). In a sense, this biological view does not explain the origins of language. All it says is that children learn language because they have the neurological structure and biological equipment to learn it. If children are not exposed to a particular language, they don't learn it.

LEARNING THEORY.   Learning theory suggests that language is learned like other behavior is learned: through *imitation, conditioning, association,* and *reinforcement* (Skinner, 1957; 1983). Children hear others talk, they imitate the sounds. Parents point to objects, name them, and children repeat the words. Examples would be naming articles of cloth-

Nativist view says that children have a predisposition to learn language at a certain age

Language acquisition device—the inherited characteristics that enable children to listen to and imitate speech sounds and patterns

The biological theory of language development says that children inherit a predisposition to learn language at a certain age.

ing: "shoes," "shirts," "pants," and "socks" as each is put on. At other times when children repeat words, their behavior is reinforced with a positive response. If they say "mama" or "dada" and are greeted with smiles, appreciation, and laughter, they are encouraged to repeat the word again. Not only do they learn to associate "mama" or "dada" with their parent, but calling mama or dada may bring food, a clean diaper, or cuddling. Their use of the word is *positively reinforced* because the repetition of it attracts their parents' attention and care. Similarly, they learn to say "bottle" when they want their milk, or they learn that saying "cookie" may bring a sweet.

Learning theory goes a long way in explaining the acquisition of language, but it does not explain everything. Children create sounds, words, phrases: "Mr. Fester, Dester, Mester, Pester." Children seem to like the sounds they create. Or they make up words for things if they don't know the correct names. A pacifier becomes a "gully." They can compose sentences that they have never heard before: "Daddy, bye bye, big truck."

COGNITIVE THEORY.   Cognitive theory emphasizes that language develops out of mental images, that it is a direct result of cognitive development.* Piaget (1926) said that children form a mental scheme and then apply linguistic labels to it. For example, Eskimos have several different words for snow. It seems plausible that they first learned to perceive different consistencies among types of snow, and then invented a vocabulary for talking about them to others. Children do the same thing. They begin to form concepts of things and actively construct their own grammar to express their thoughts. Children begin to master language near the end of the sensorimotor stage and near the beginning of the preoperational stage of cognitive development, when they use symbols to represent the environment.

INTERACTIONIST THEORY.   Interactionist theory emphasizes the equal importance of both biological maturation and the role of environmental influences and experiences in language development. Clearly the role of biology is important, but developing structures must have an environment in which they can be expressed.

*Another theory, the Whorfian hypothesis, says that language influences thought rather than the other way around. This hypothesis has not been validated with research.

Sequence of Language Development

PRELINGUISTIC PERIOD.   Children the world over seem to follow the same timetable and sequence of language development. Table 7.1 shows the sequence through 48 months of age. During the prelinguistic period, before children actually verbalize, they seem to understand far more than they can express (Kuczaj, 1986). Even newborns come to recognize their mother's voice.

TABLE 7.1 Sequence of Language Development

Age in months	Language
2	Begins making vowel-like cooing sounds
4	Smiles, coos pitch-modulated, makes vowel-like sounds interspersed with consonant sounds
6	Begins babbling (one-syllable utterances), vowels interspersed with consonants
8	Often uses two-syllable utterances such as "mama" or "baba," imitates sounds
10	Understands some words, gestures (may say "no" and shake head); uses holophrases (single words with different meanings)
12	Understands some simple commands; uses more holophrases such as "baby," "bye-bye," and "hi"; may imitate sounds of dog: "bow-wow"; some control over intonation
18	Vocabulary of 3 to 50 words; may use 2-word utterances; still babbles; uses words with several syllables with intricate intonation pattern
24	Vocabulary over 50 words; 2-word phrases; interested in verbal communication
30	Rapid increase in vocabulary; uses 3- to 5-word phrases; many grammatical errors; some children hard to understand; excellent comprehension
36	Vocabulary of 1,000 words, of which 80 percent intelligible; colloquial grammar; fewer syntactic errors
48	Well-established language; style may differ some from adult speech

Adapted from *The First Twelve Months of Life* by F. Caplan, 1973, New York: Grosset and Dunlap, and *Biological Foundations of Language* (pp. 128–130) by E. H. Lenneberg, 1973, New York: Wiley.

FOCUS

Is There a Critical Period for Learning Language?

One major question in language development research is whether there is a critical period during which human beings are especially receptive to acquire language. As we have seen in Chapter 6, brain lateralization (or localization) of language functions takes place in the left hemisphere of the brain (Kee, Gottfried, Bathurst, & Brown, 1987). One point of view is that because language lateralization in the left hemisphere begins during the early years of life, language itself must also be acquired early or it becomes impossible or difficult to learn (Witelson, 1987).

Studies of severely abused and neglected children who are not exposed to language early in childhood lend some support for this hypothesis. Historically, there have been about 60 recorded cases of children who were abandoned in the wild at an early age, but who survived and were eventually returned to human society. Among the 60 cases, 11 children (ranging in age between 4 and 18) acquired some but very immature language ability. The rest of the children never learned any language (Reich, 1986).

The most famous modern case was *Genie*, who was a normal, alert, responsive baby until 20 months of age. At that time she was isolated naked in the back room of her parents' home, harnessed to a potty-chair, and only able to move her hands and feet. At night, she was laced in a kind of straight jacket and enclosed in a wire cage. She was fed sparingly by her brother, who was not permitted to talk to her. She only heard her father's doglike barking when he beat her for crying or making noise.

When she was discovered at age 13 in 1970, she had no bowel or bladder control, could not stand erect, could not chew solid food, and could neither speak nor understand language. After her release, doctors at Los Angeles Children's Hospital took care of her bodily needs and nursed her back to health. Psychologists were called in to evaluate her mental and emotional state and begin socialization, including teaching language.

Genie made some limited progress in language development. After 7 years, she learned as much language as a normal child learns in 2 to 3 years. By age 24, she lacked some of the language skills of 5-year-olds. She developed a fairly large vocabulary, could comprehend everyday conversation, but had limited knowledge of grammar, could not use some syntactic forms such as pronouns, showed poor pitch control, and was not able to use intonation to express meaning. Neurolinguistic assessments revealed that Genie used the right hemisphere of her brain to process linguistic information. Apparently, the developmental period had passed during which specialized language areas in the left hemisphere could facilitate language learning (Curtis, 1977). Nonlanguage areas in the right hemisphere were forced to take over language functioning, but never efficiently, particularly with grammar. The case of Genie gives some support to the critical period hypothesis, although it is impossible to determine the extent to which malnutrition, physical and mental abuse, and social isolation played a part in Genie's language retardation (Pines, 1981).

Cooing—the initial vowel-like utterances by young infants

Babbling—one-syllable utterances containing vowels and consonants in combination

Holophrases—single words that infants use to convey different meanings, depending on the context in which they are used

Crying is the first major sound uttered by the newborn. **Cooing** begins at about 2 months of age. It consists of squeals, gurgles, or vowel-like sounds of short duration such as "ahhh." Babbling begins at about 6 months of age. **Babbling** is one-syllable utterances, usually containing vowels and consonants in combinations, for example, "ma-ma-ma-ma." Most babbling is of sounds without meaning. Even deaf infants babble, so they are not imitating sounds they hear.

FIRST SPOKEN WORDS.   At about 10 months of age, infants use **holophrases,** which are single words that convey different meanings, depending on the context in which they are used. Only the parents may understand what the child is saying. By 12 months of age most infants are speaking 1 or 2 words that are recognizable language. "Mama" or "dada" may be the first words spoken. By 18 months, the average toddler knows 3 to 50 words, usually naming objects—"car"; animals—"doggie"; items of clothing—"shoes"; a part of the body—"eye"; or an important person—"mama" (Clark, 1983). Action words such as "bye-bye," adjectives such as "hot," or adverbs such as "no" may also be included (Barrett, 1986; Nelson, 1981). The number of new words that children learn depends a lot on the extent of parent–child interaction. Some parents talk to their infants all the time. They name objects, repeat single words and phrases, ask questions, speak in short sentences, and converse with them whenever they are together.

This tendency of adults to adjust their

Motherese—baby talk that adults use in speaking to infants

Duos—two-word utterances

Telegraphic speech—several-word utterances that convey meaning

speech when talking to children is called **motherese** (D'Odorico & Franco, 1985; Lederberg, 1982). When speaking to young children, adults usually use a slower rate of speech, try to speak correct grammar, usually use a higher and more varied pitch, and use more present-tense words (Cooper & Aslin, 1990). When parents say "tum-tum" for stomach, or "choo-choo" for train, they are speaking motherese. Such interaction facilitates the development of understanding and the ability to communicate. It encourages children to talk about things they are experiencing.

TWO-WORD UTTERANCES. Two-word utterances (**duos**) usually begin when children are from 18 to 24 months of age. Children begin to combine words to express ideas that they want to communicate with others: "Amanda cry," "milk gone," "mama bye-bye." These expressions indicate knowledge of subject–predicate order. Other constructions are not acceptable English sentences: "More water," "no up," "mama hat," "allgone soup." Two-word utterances represent attempts of children to express themselves through their own unique language (Clark, Gelman, & Lane, 1985).

Children begin to use literally hundreds of two-word utterances, expressing many different meanings. Table 7.2 shows some of the meanings possible with two-word utterances.

TELEGRAPHIC SPEECH. **Telegraphic speech** consists of two-, three-, or several-word utterances that convey meaning but exclude any unnecessary words such as articles, auxiliary verbs, conjunctions, preposi-

Adults tend to speak at a slower rate, with correct grammar, when talking to young children.

tions, or other connectives. The speech is telegraphic, like a telegram that omits any unnecessary words, but still conveys meaning. "Daddy give Billy money" is an example of telegraphic speech. By 30 months of age, children are using three- to five-word phrases. Vocabulary may have grown to 1,000 words by age 3.

SENTENCES. From 2½ to 4 years of age, children are using multiple-word sentences (three to five words are common), each with a subject and predicate and with fewer grammatical errors. The syntax may still differ from adult speech, but improvement continues. The following are examples (Wood, 1981).

"She's a pretty baby"
"Read it, my book"
"Where is daddy?"
"I can't play"
"I would like some milk"
"Take me to the store"
"Ask what time it is"

Between the ages of 4 and 5, children's sentences average four to five words. They can use prepositions like *over, under, in, on,* and *behind,* and they use more verbs than nouns. Between ages 5 and 6, sentences consist of six to eight words, including some conjunctions, prepositions, and articles. By ages 6 and 7, children's speech resembles that of adults. They can use correct grammar, all parts of speech, and can construct compound and complex sentences.

Vocabulary and Semantics

Preschool and early school-age children seem to soak up new words like a sponge. Their vocabu-

TABLE 7.2 Meanings Conveyed in Two-Word Utterances

Meaning	Utterances
Identification	"See kittie"
Location	"Table there"
Repetition	"More juice"
Nonexistence	"Allgone milk"
Negation	"Not doggie"
Possession	"Katy dress"
Attribution	"Big house"
Agent action	"Baby eat"
Action object	"Hurt daddy"
Action location	"Sit potty"
Question	"Where car?"

lary grows from over 50 words at age 2 to between 8,000 and 14,000 words at age 6 (Carey, 1977). Estimates of the size of children's vocabulary vary widely (Nagy & Anderson, 1984). We do know that vocabulary growth continues at a high rate well through adolescence and adulthood. Children learn nouns before verbs, followed by adjectives, adverbs, conjunctions, and interrogatives (Waxman & Kosowski, 1990). Basic nouns such as *cars* are learned before specific nouns such as *Porsches* or more inclusive nouns such as *vehicles* (Matlin, 1983). The first interrogatives are usually "where?" and "what?", followed by "who?", "how?", and "why?" (Bloom, Merkin, & Wooten, 1982).

One of the difficulties in obtaining an accurate assessment of the size of vocabulary is in finding an acceptable definition of what it means to "know a word." Does it mean being able to comprehend the word, to define it, or to use it in a sentence? Usually children comprehend a word before they can define it or speak it. However, their knowledge may be only partial or incorrect. Because some words have several meanings, comprehension of meanings is built slowly, usually through repeated exposure (Mezynski, 1983). Children learn new words by noticing how they are used, the context in which they are found, and their relationships

to other words (Nagy, Herman, & Anderson, 1985). A single exposure teaches little about a word's many meanings and the subtleties of its use. Children learn new words through conversation and through reading. The more others talk and read to children, and the more children read themselves, the more opportunities they have of learning new vocabulary (Wilson, 1985).

Grammar

Grammar is the formal description of structure and rules that a language uses to communicate meaning. Grammar defines word form (such as singular or plural of nouns or verbs); word order in sentences; the relationship of words to one another; the use of modifiers; the use of clauses and phrases; tenses of verbs; the use of suffixes and prefixes; the subjective, objective, and possessive forms of pronouns; and the use of interrogatives and negatives. Grammar includes the correct pronunciation of words and proper intonations. Grammar is all-important in understanding language. It makes a difference whether we are told "Billy hit Johnny" or "Johnny hit Billy." Our knowledge of grammar enables us to understand who hit whom.

Grammar—the formal description of structure and rules that a language uses to communicate meaning

---

PARENTING ISSUES

When Your Child Uses Bad Language

By the age of 2 to 4, most children have picked up a number of words their parents prefer they not use in polite company. Children seem to delight in bathroom language: "poo-poo," "ca-ca," and "wee-wee" (and large numbers of other words). They enjoy repeating them at the most inappropriate times, and soon learn that such words bring giggles from other children and that they can be used to shock parents and get their immediate attention. If parents swear, children pick up this language also.

With young children (preschool age), the less fuss made about such words, the better. If parents pay too much attention, and act shocked, the attention children receive acts as positive reinforcement and only encourages their using the language even more.

As children get older, they will hear a variety of sexual words and swear words from other children and adults. Four-letter slang words for sexual parts or functions sound indecent when repeated by 10-year-old children.

There are several things parents can do.

1. They need to avoid using the language themselves. If parents say it, children will say it.
2. They need to avoid being shocked. If children can shock parents, they may try to do it even more.
3. They can use correct language for sexual parts and functions. Certainly, *penis, vagina, anus,* or *urinate* doesn't have the negative connotations of the slang counterparts.
4. Parents need to let children know that they and other parents disapprove of the language. Parents don't need to accept "dirty talk" from children. Sometimes children use words but don't know the real meaning. Parents need to explain the meaning and why they disapprove. Usually, by discussing the issues of language with their children, and setting up a few guidelines, the cooperation of children can be obtained.

Children do not use adult syntactic structures immediately, but they do start showing some knowledge from the time they begin to combine words into sentences (MacWhinney, 1982). They learn to put the subject before the verb and the verb before the object. They learn singular and plural forms, verb tenses, and interrogatives such as: "Where are you going?" Their understanding of negatives progresses from "no nap" to "I don't want to go to sleep because I am not tired." They learn which words can modify nouns and in what order. They will make increasing use of adjectives to describe nouns, and adverbs to modify verbs, adjectives, or other adverbs. They will say: "That's a very beautiful bicycle," for example. School-age children continue to learn increasingly complex structures, such as those with conjunctions and difficult clauses: "Although Wednesday was a school day, George did not go because he was sick." They learn to sort out ideas in clauses that are embedded in sentences: "The man who is 75 years old finished painting the house."

Children younger than school age have difficulty in understanding the use of verbs in the passive voice. Children are used to the subject of the sentence acting upon an object, and not the subject being acted upon. During the elementary school years, they learn the difference between saying "The ball was hit by the boy" and "The boy hit the ball." They learn that the ball didn't do the hitting. Romaine (1984) found that compared with 6-year-olds, 8-year-olds used the passive voice 2½ times more frequently, and 10-year-olds 3½ times more frequently.

Pragmatics

Pragmatics, the practical ability to use language to communicate with others in a variety of social contexts, is an aspect of language use that develops during the elementary school years. Preschool and young school-age children may talk a lot, but they sometimes have difficulty in making themselves understood. They often begin by getting attention: "Guess what?" They may stop to see if others are listening or if they are understood. "Are you listening?" They may pause, start again, repeat themselves, correct themselves, or change subjects. However, they do learn to take turns in talking and to show by various means that they are listening. Parents try hard to teach them to say "please" and "thank you," not to interrupt others, and to speak respectfully to adults.

Pragmatics is the practical ability to use language to communicate with others.

The following is a conversation among second-graders (Dorval & Eckerman, 1984):

1. Well, we . . . uh . . . have paper plates . . . with turkey on it and lots of (unintelligible). You know.
2. Doo-doo-doo-doo-doo (singing)
3. I don't know what you're talking about.
4. You know what? My uncle killed a turkey.
5. Not frying pan?
6. No.
7. I seen a frying pan at Hulen's store!

Children's conversation can be quite disjointed, shifting off topic and often containing many false starts ("The car . . . it was . . . uh . . . the door . . . the kid he pushed on the door . . . They . . . uh . . . he pushed . . . he closed it hard.")

Contrast this conversation with that of fifth graders (Dorval & Eckerman, 1984, p. 22):

1. Be quiet! Start off, Billy, what if you was the teacher?
2. OK. If I was the teacher, I'd give us less work and more time to play . . . and I'd be mean to y'all, too.
3. OK. Ann (meaning that it is her turn).
4. If I was the teacher, I'd do work . . . um. I'd sit around and watch TV. I wouldn't assign no papers . . . umm . . .
5. I'd let y'all watch TV stories.
6. I'd turn the TV on Channel 4 at 9:30 to watch "Popeye"!

One characteristic of children's conversation at this age is that it stays with a topic.

Bilingualism

One half of the world's population is *bilingual*. In North America, millions of children grow up in bilingual families or in families where English is not the dominant or preferred language. Many questions arise regarding bilingualism. What effect does a second language have on the first? When should a second language be taught?

From some children in groups where their first language is a minority language, a second language may be a subtractive influence. That is, the minority children become less fluent in their first language as their language skills improve in the second. Because the second language is the dominant language, the one others speak and the one used in the community and the media, the children come to prefer it. The first language receives little support and attention outside the home; it is not taught in school, so the children have little opportunity to read or write it (Landry, 1987). As a result, competence in the minority language suffers.

For children whose first language is the majority language, learning a second language is largely an additive experience (Cummins & Swain, 1986). Thus, English-speaking children enrolled in French- or Spanish-language programs can develop linguistic skills in the second language without interfering with their competence in English (Genesee, 1985). Good bilingual programs not only develop proficiency in a second language, but also can strengthen the first language.

Research indicates, however, that *instruction for minority group children should be primarily in the minority language*, with English learned as the second language. One study showed that when French minority group children were taught in French, with English taught as the second language, their French not only became better than that of French children who were taught primarily in English, but their English became better as well (Cummins, 1986). When a person learns two languages, the process does not involve competition for mental resources (Hakuta & Garcia, 1989). Research has also shown that formal instruction in the second language can be introduced in the early elementary grades, provided the children are already proficient in their majority language, that the teachers are bilingual and trained and skilled in language teaching, that the language to be learned and the native language are both of relatively high status in the culture, and that parents and the community are supportive of the program (McLaughlin, 1985).

APPROACHES TO THE STUDY OF COGNITION

There are three basic approaches to the study of cognition during childhood. One is the

---

PARENTING ISSUES

Stuttering

In the past, stuttering was considered a symptom of disturbed interpersonal relationships and emotional maladjustment. As a consequence, parents bore a burden of guilt for their child's problem. Currently, except in cases of a traumatic event or illness, stuttering appears to have a genetic base with environmental factors either aggravating the predisposition to stutter or helping children to overcome it. If one identical twin stutters, there is a 77% chance the other will too. Only 1 out of 3 fraternal twins of stutterers also stutter. Stuttering seems to result from difficulty in coordinating respiration, larynx functioning, and articulation.

There are several ways parents can help.

1. Speak slowly and simply, giving children the feeling that they have more time to talk.

2. Before responding to the child's speech, allow more time after he or she talks, so children feel more relaxed and less hurried.
3. Minimize stress in the home because anxiety and stress can trigger stuttering.
4. Find a quiet time during the day to talk with the children.
5. Don't overreact to early speech problems or temporary lapses in fluency. Many young children stutter over words or repeat phrases, particularly when tired or excited.
6. If the problem persists, seek professional help during the period of most rapid speech development, between ages 2 and 7. It's better to correct the problem before children become neurotic about their speech (Chollar, 1988).

8 60% of children will Not in a 1 parent home

Piagetian approach—the approach to the study of cognitive development emphasizing the qualitative changes in the way children think, created by Jean Piaget

Information-processing approach—examines the progressive steps, actions, and operations that take place when a child receives, perceives, remembers, thinks about, and uses information

Psychometric approach—the approach to the study of cognitive development that measures the quantitative changes in children's intelligence

Piagetian approach, which emphasizes the qualitative changes in the ways children think. A second is the **information-processing approach,** which examines the progressive steps, actions, and operations that take place when the child receives, perceives, remembers, thinks about, and utilizes information. The third approach is the **psychometric approach,** which measures quantitative changes in children's intelligence. Each of these approaches is discussed in this chapter.

A PIAGETIAN PERSPECTIVE

As discussed in Chapter 2, the Swiss developmental psychologist Jean Piaget outlined four stages of cognitive development: the *sensorimotor stage* (birth to 2 years), the *preoperational stage* (2 to 7 years), the *concrete operational stage* (7 to 11 years), and the *formal operational stage* (11 years and up). The formal operational stage is discussed in the sections of this book on adolescence.

Sensorimotor Stage (Birth to 2 Years)

Piaget (1954; 1963) labeled the first stage of cognitive development the sensorimotor period because it involves learning to respond through motor activity to the various stimuli that are presented to the senses. The child not only hears and sees a rattle, but learns how to grasp it, shake it, or suck on it. *The task is learning to coordinate sensorimotor sequences to solve simple problems.* Piaget has subdivided the sensorimotor period into six substages.

1. *Stage one (0 to 1 month)—exercising reflexes.* Infants use their inborn reflexes and gain some control over them. For example, they suck whatever is near their mouth or grasp whatever touches their palm. They practice these and other reflexes repeatedly and become more proficient, but they can't reach out to deliberately suck or grasp the object.

2. *Stage two (1 to 4 months)—primary circular reactions.* Infants repeat pleasurable behavior that occurs by chance (such as thumb sucking). By chance, a child's thumb touches the mouth, which triggers the sucking reflex, which results in a pleasurable sensation, which leads to a repetition of the response. This circular reaction is called *primary* because it involves the child's own body.

3. *Stage three (4 to 8 months)—secondary circular reactions.* The child accidentally does something interesting or pleasing, like moving an overhead mobile. The action is then deliberately repeated to obtain the same result. (The action-reaction is circular.) It is called *secondary* because it happens outside the child's own body.

4. *Stage four (8 to 12 months)—purposeful coordination of secondary schemes.* Behavior is more deliberate and purposeful as infants coordinate motor activities with sensory input. Thus, infants will look at and grasp a rattle, or see a toy across the room and crawl to it. They begin to anticipate events and to try out previous schemes to solve problems in present situations.

5. *Stage five (12 to 18 months)—tertiary circular reactions.* In this stage, babies begin to experiment with novel actions to see what will happen rather than merely repeating behavior patterns they have already learned. They use trial and error to find the most efficient way of reaching new goals. The stage is called *tertiary reactions* because their purpose is to explore. For example, a child will crawl into a box, then lie down in the box, then put it on his or her head, or try to put the cat into the box.

6. *Stage six (18 to 24 months)—mental solutions.* Children begin to think about problems to find mental solutions; that is, they begin to internalize actions and their consequences, no longer relying exclusively on trial and error. Thus, they begin to develop insight into how to solve simple problems. This development is accompanied by a growing ability to use word symbols (language) in dealing with people and situations.

The sensorimotor period of cognitive development involves learning to respond to various stimuli through motor activity.

OBJECT PERMANENCE. One of the accomplishments during the sensorimotor stage is the development of a concept of **object permanence**—the knowledge that an object continues to exist independent of our seeing, hearing, touching, tasting, or smelling it (Piaget, 1954). According to Piaget, during stage three (4 to 8 months), infants will search for a partially hidden object that is already present. During stage four (8 to 12 months), infants will search for objects that have disappeared, but only in the place previously found, even if they saw it moved to a new place. During stage five (12 to 18 months), toddlers will follow a series of object displacements and will search for the object, but only where they have observed it being hidden. They can't imagine it being moved without their seeing it. And finally, during stage six, object permanence is fully developed. Toddlers can figure where an object might be, and will look for it, though they didn't see it placed there.

According to some modern researchers using different and more refined techniques, the acquisition of object permanence comes at younger ages than Piaget claimed (Harris, 1983). Baillargeon (1987) found that infants as young as 3½ months seemed to hold some primitive and short-lived memories of absent objects. But this does not mean that the infants would search for objects that had not been present recently. So there was no real sense of object permanence.

IMITATION. Another characteristic of the sensorimotor stage is **imitation,** or copying the behavior of another. Meltzoff and Moore (1977; 1979) found that 2-week-old infants will imitate adults sticking out their tongue or opening their mouth wide. In more recent studies, Reissland (1988) in an experiment with 12 neonates in the first hour after birth found that when adults bent over the infants and either widened their lips or pursed them, the neonates moved their lips in a similar manner. Kaitz, Meschaulach-Sarfaty, Auerbach, and Eidelman (1988) found that infants 10 to 51 hours old demonstrated modeling of tongue protusion but not of facial expressions.

Piaget (1962) maintained that imitation is not likely to occur before 9 to 12 months of age, but he was talking about **deferred imitation**—imitating someone or something no longer present. A 2-year-old who diapers her dolly in the absence of her mother is exhibiting deferred imitation. Meltzoff (1988) had a model perform 6 different actions with 6 different objects in the presence of a group of 14-month-old infants. The infants were not allowed to interact with the model and objects. One full week later, when showed the same objects, the infants showed a tendency to imitate the behavior of the model. This means the infants had the ability to make mental images of the behavior, to remember it, and to do it 1 week later. This ability is important to language development and to many aspects of learned behavior.

Preoperational Stage (2 to 7 Years)

Piaget called the second stage preoperational thinking because a mental operation involves logical thought, and children at this stage do not yet have this ability to think logically. Instead, children develop the ability to deal with the world *symbolically*, or *representationally*. That is, they develop the ability to imagine doing something, rather than actually doing it. For example, a child in the sensorimotor stage of development learns how to pull a toy along the floor. A child reaching the preoperational stage of development develops a mental representation of the toy and a mental picture of pulling the toy. If the child can use words to describe the action, it is accomplished mentally and symbolically through the use of words. One of the major accomplishments during this period is the development of language, the ability to think and communicate by using words that represent objects and events.

SYMBOLIC PLAY. **Symbolic,** or pretend, **play** also becomes more frequent each year of the preoperational period (Rubin, Fein, & Vandenberg, 1983). A 2-year-old child may use one object (such as a teddy bear) to symbolize another (such as a mommy). As children get older, they will pretend a series of events: going shopping, cooking dinner, playing house; or they will play doctor and have mommy or daddy go off to the hospital. Much of the symbolic play of 5- or 6-year-olds involves other children: playing store or army, for example (Corrigan, 1983).

TRANSDUCTIVE REASONING. **Transductive reasoning** occurs when the child proceeds from particular to particular, without generalization, rather than from the particular to the general (**inductive reasoning**) or from the general to the particular (**deductive reasoning**). For example, the dog Sport jumps on you because he has, and Blackie will jump on you because he is frisky like

Object permanence—the concept that an object continues to exist independent of our perceiving it

Imitation—copying the behavior of another

Deferred imitation—imitating someone or something no longer present

Symbolic play—using one object to represent another in play

Transductive reasoning—proceeding from particular to particular in thought, without making generalizations

Inductive reasoning—gathering individual items of information and putting them together to form a hypothesis or conclusions

Deductive reasoning—beginning with a hypothesis or premise and breaking it down to see if it is true

PARENTING ISSUES

Offering Environmental Stimulation

One important requirement for mental growth is that children be reared in an intellectually stimulating environment (Pellegrini, Perlmutter, Galda, & Brody, 1990). Infants begin to get acquainted with their world from the moment of birth. If they have a variety of objects to see, touch, or taste; different sounds to hear; or different odors to smell; they learn more than if their exposure is quite limited. Sensory stimulation encourages motor learning and coordination as infants reach out to grasp or as they toddle forward. Auditory stimulation, especially exposure to words, encourages language development and speech.

But what children learn, and how much, depends not only on the amount of stimulation but also on its type, variety, intensity, regularity, duration, and timing. Children who are regularly given appropriate materials are going to learn more from their play activities over periods of time than children whose exposure is more limited. Children who are encouraged to explore the environment around them will learn faster than those who are not given much opportunity to move about. Children whose parents handle them, talk to them, and play with them will learn more than children who are left alone for long periods of time without social contacts. Parents who take their children out with them are going to increase their knowledge and understanding of the world to a greater extent than parents who never permit their children out of their own yard.

Maximum mental growth takes place when children are stimulated mentally from infancy on, year after year. No one year, experience, or situation is as important as what happens over several years of growth. Mental growth may accelerate when children are exposed to an enriching environment, such as that provided by a superior teacher, but growth then stops or even reverses when children are educationally and intellectually deprived for a period of time.

Of course, it is entirely possible to expose children to excessive stimulation or to experiences inappropriate to their age level. In face-to-face interactions with their infants, some parents try too hard to get their attention, resulting in an information overload that causes infants to avert their gaze and turn away. Children can tolerate only a certain amount of stimulation, after which they want to escape and not respond. The same principle holds true in the classroom. The teacher who tries to expose the students to too much material in too short a time causes them to become uninterested in further learning. The maximum learning takes place when teachers or parents take their cues from their children and expose them to as much as they can assimilate at a time and no more.

Sport, but Rex will not jump on you because he is too big (when in fact he may). An error in judgment is made because the general concept that dogs jump on you is never developed (Rice, 1990).

Syncretism—trying to link ideas together that are not always related

SYNCRETISM.   **Syncretism** involves making errors of reasoning by trying to link ideas that are not always related. Mother had a baby last time she went to the hospital, so the next time she goes to the hospital, she is mistakenly expected to bring home another baby (Rice, 1990).

Egocentricism—the inability to take the perspective of another, to imagine the other person's point of view

EGOCENTRISM.   **Egocentrism** is the inability to take the perspective of another, to imagine the other person's point of view. Children get upset, for example, when they cannot convince their mother not to wash their dirty rag doll. They gain security from it, and that is the important thing to them, whereas to their mother the important thing is that the doll is dirty. Children are also egocentric in their attitudes about other things.

Space and time are focused on them: When they walk, the moon follows them. Gradually, however, children learn to conceive of a world in time and space existing independently of themselves and, through social interaction, they learn to take into account the viewpoints of others (Rice, 1990).

ANIMISM.   **Animism** is ascribing lifelike qualities to inanimate objects. Children will usually ascribe life to objects that represent figures that are alive in real life: stuffed animals, toy people, and so on. They know that rocks, chairs, or beds are not alive, although they blame these objects for accidents: "The chair made me fall down"; "The ball was naughty—it hit me." They may be confused about things in nature—flowers, trees, the wind, or the moon—and talk to them or about them as though they could hear. Animism probably reveals incomplete knowledge and understanding of the world, but it is also a reflection of children's vivid imagination (Bullock, 1985; Dolgin & Behrend, 1984).

Animism—ascribing lifelike qualities to inanimate objects

Centration—focusing attention on only one aspect, or detail, of a situation

Conservation—the idea that properties of objects such as weight and mass stay the same regardless of how the shape or arrangement changes

CENTRATION.   Part of the reason that pre-operational children can't think logically is that they focus attention on one aspect of a situation, or on one detail, and are unable to take into account other details. This tendency is called **centration**—meaning to center on only one idea at a time. For example, our 6-year-old grandson knew his mother was coming home this morning, so he woke us up an hour earlier than usual. When told it was too early to get up, he replied, "But mommy is coming home." Or, the other day he wanted to go to the beach. When told it was cloudy, wet, and misty, he insisted it was not and that we should go to the beach. Children of this age will get an idea in their head and completely ignore other thoughts.

CONSERVATION.   The tendency to practice centration is revealed in tasks of **conservation.** For example, children may conclude there is more water in a shallow dish than in a glass because the dish is wider, even though they have already seen all the water poured from the glass into the dish. Figure 7.2 shows that the child has ignored the greater height of the glass and the demonstration of pouring. As a result of their inability to maintain more than one relationship in their thinking at a time, children make errors of judgment, give inadequate or inconsistent explanations, show a lack of logical sequence in their arguments, and a lack of comprehension of constants. Similarly, other tests of conservation of numbers, volume, length, or area are beyond the cognitive ability of preschoolers (Rice, 1990).

FIGURE 7.2   Understanding the principle of conservation of volume. (a) The child agrees that glasses A and B have the same amount of water. (b) The water from B is poured into the dish. The child is unable to understand that glass A and the dish still have the same amount of water, because the dish appears broader even though it is shallower. The child is unable to retain one aspect (the amount) when another aspect changes (the height of the water column and the width of the column).

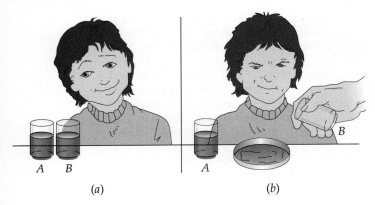

A   B

(a)

A

B

(b)

Classification—arranging objects into categories or classes

Irreversibility—failure to recognize that an operation can go both ways

CLASSIFICATION.   **Classification** means that objects can be thought of in terms of categories or classes. Preoperational children are limited in their ability to classify objects according to categories (Waxman, Shipley, & Shepperson, 1991). Suppose children are shown 7 cats of different breeds: 4 Siamese, 1 Persian, 1 tiger, and 1 coon. The examiner makes certain the children know they are all cats, and that the children can name each breed. The children are then asked: "Are there more Siamese or more cats?" Until about 7 or 8 years of age, most children will reply: "More Siamese." They cannot segregate the concept of cats from the subclassification "Siamese."

IRREVERSIBILITY.   Preoperational children also make errors in their thinking because of **irreversibility**, that is, their inability to recognize that an operation can go both ways. For example, they do not understand that if water is poured from a tall container into a flat container, it can also be poured back again, keeping the same amount of water. Preoperational children cannot mentally accept that the original state can be regained (Rice, 1990).

Concrete Operational Stage (7 to 11 Years)*

During the concrete operational stage, children show a greater capacity for logical reasoning, though still at a very concrete level (Jacobs & Potenza, 1991). The child's thinking is still linked to empirical reality (Piaget, 1967). Inhelder and Piaget (1958) wrote: "Concrete thought remains essentially attached to empirical reality. . . . Therefore, it attains no more than a concept of 'what is possible,' which is a simple (and not very great) extension of the empirical situation" (p. 250). Children have made some progress toward extending their thoughts from the actual toward the potential (Elkind, 1970), but the starting point must still be what is real because concrete operational children can reason only about those things with which they have had direct, personal experience. When children have to start with any hypothetical or contrary-to-fact proposition, they have difficulty. Elkind (1967) also pointed out that one of the difficulties at this stage is that the child can deal with only two classes, relations, or quantitative dimensions at the

*Part of the material in this section is adapted from the author's book *The Adolescent* (1990), 6th ed. Used by permission of the publisher, Allyn and Bacon.

same time. When more variables are present, the child flounders.

However, concrete operational children are able to arrange objects into **hierarchical classifications** and comprehend **class inclusion relationships** (the inclusion of objects in different levels of the hierarchy at the same time). This gives children the ability to understand the relations of the parts to the whole, the whole to the parts, and the parts to the parts. Suppose children are given a randomly organized array of yellow and red squares and black and white circles. If they understand inclusion relationships, they discover there are two major collections (squares and circles) and two subtypes of each (yellow versus red squares and black versus white circles). There is a hierarchy whose higher level is defined by shape and whose lower level is defined by color. This enables the children to say that all squares are either yellow or red, that there are more squares than yellow squares, that there are more squares than red squares, that if you take away the red squares, the yellow ones are left, and so on.

Concrete operational children are capable also of **serialization**, serial ordering. They learn that different objects may be grouped by size, or by alphabetical order.

Conservation refers to the recognition that properties of things such as weight or volume are not altered by changing their container or shape. Conservation tasks involve some manipulation of the shape of matter without altering its mass or volume (Piaget & Inhelder, 1969). A typical conservation problem is represented by the ball of clay in Figure 7.3.

Muuss (1988) summarizes four concrete operations the child is able to perform:

1. **Combinativity**. This represents the ability to combine two or more classes into one larger, more comprehensive class. For example, all men and all women equals all adults; A is larger than B and B is larger than C can be combined into a new statement that A is larger than C.

2. **Reversibility**. This is the concept that every operation has an opposite operation that reverses it. Supraclasses can be taken apart, so that the effect of combining subclasses is reversed. All adults except all women equals all men.

3. **Associativity**. The child whose operations have become associative can reach a goal in various ways . . . but the results obtained . . . remain the same. For example, (3 plus 6) plus 4 equals 13, and 6 plus (3 plus 4) equals 13.

Hierarchical classification—arranging objects into categories according to level

Class inclusion relationships—the inclusion of objects in different levels of hierarchy at the same time

Serialization—arranging objects into hierarchy of classes

Combinativity—ability to combine two or more classes into one larger class

Reversibility—the concept that every operation has an opposite operation that reverses it

Associativity—the understanding that operations can reach a goal in various ways

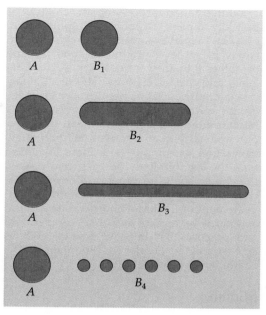

FIGURE 7.3 Conservation of mass. In this example, the child is asked to confirm that A and B_1 are the same size. Then B_1 is changed to B_2, then to B_3, then to B_4. The child is asked to compare A with B_2, then with B_3, and with B_4, each time stating whether A and B are still the same. Children in the preoperational stage are guided by the shapes they see. Children in the concrete operational stage preserve recognition of the equal quantity between A and B that transcends their physical shape.

4. **Identity or nullifiability**. This is the understanding that an operation that is combined with its opposite becomes nullified, resulting in no change. An example is that to give 3 and take away 3 results in null (p. 185).

Identity or nullifiability—the understanding that an operation that is combined with its opposite becomes nullified

INFORMATION PROCESSING

The *Piagetian approach* to cognition describes the stages involved in the development of logical thinking. The *information-processing approach* describes the way children obtain information, remember it, retrieve it, and use it in solving problems.

Information processing has often been compared to the actions of a computer. Information is coded and fed into a computer in an organized way, and then it is stored in the memory banks. When any of that information is required, the computer is asked to produce it. The machine searches for the relevant information and reproduces or prints out the items requested.

Information processing by children is basically similar but far more sophisticated. The child receives information, organizes it, stores it, retrieves it, thinks about it, and combines it to answer questions, solve problems, and make decisions. The most elaborate computer used in creating *artificial intelligence* cannot match the capacity of the human mind and nervous system in the input and output of information. Each new generation of computers is more advanced than the last. Similarly, as each year passes, the child's ability to process information increases, partly because of the continued development of the brain and nervous system, and partly because of the learning experience and practice that improve mental abilities and strategies (Teyler & Fountain, 1987; Goodman & Haith, 1987).

Stimuli

Before information can be processed it must be received. Children are constantly bombarded with stimuli. Their senses are their receptors, their contacts between themselves and the world outside, and the method by which they learn. *Research has shown the importance of stimulation in the learning process.* Maternal stimulation during the first year has been associated with infants' 1-year vocabu-

lary size (Bornstein, 1985), 2-year cognitive/language competence (Olson, Bates, & Bayles, 1984), 3-year language performance (Bee et al., 1982), 4-year intelligence test performance (Bornstein, 1985), and 6-year school performance (Coates & Lewis, 1984).

Habituation

Stimulation is important to cognitive development, but researchers also have found that when infants get used to a sound or sight, it loses its novelty, and the infants do not pay as much attention to it, a process called **habituation**. Infants can become habituated to every type of sensory stimulation (Rovee-Collier, 1987b). Furthermore, this tendency becomes increasingly developed during the first 3 months of life (Lipsitt, 1986). It is important in parent–infant interaction that parents repeat stimuli to facilitate learning, but once children stop responding, the parents need to stop or change the type of stimulation (Rosenblith & Sims-Knight, 1985).

Habituation is important because it has been used to measure infants' sensory perception, memory, and neurological health. It can have important implications for a child's present and future cognitive, emotional, and social development (Dunham, Dunham, Hurshman, & Alexander, 1989). For example, habituation in the first 6 months of life has been reported to explain 59% of the variance in indexes of childhood intelligence between 2 and 8 years (Bornstein & Sigman, 1986; Tamis-LeMonda & Bornstein, 1989). Babies with low Apgar scores, brain damage, or Down's syndrome show impaired habituation.

Habituation—the tendency to adapt to a repeated stimulus and to lose interest in it

Selective Attention

Another important factor in learning is that children don't pay equal amounts of attention to everything. *They attend selectively to stimuli, with dramatic increases in selectivity with age.* The older the children, the more they develop a selective strategy, that is, they are better able to sort out relevant from nonrelevant information, and to learn more efficiently (DeMarie-Dreblow & Miller, 1988; Woody-Ramsey & Miller, 1988).

Memory

The ability to remember is basic to all learning. Without memory, we would never be able to recall or recognize what we have already experienced. We would not be able to accumulate a body of useful knowledge, to learn

FOCUS

Distractibility

Every parent knows that young children are easily distracted by competing stimuli (Pillow, 1988). Toddlers may start to do one thing, be attracted to something else, and turn their attention to the second thing. As a result, it is hard to get them to focus their attention on any one activity for very long (Ruff, Lawson, Parrinello, & Weissberg, 1990). In contrast, preschool children may be able to focus their attention for much longer periods. In one experiment, 3- and 5-year-old children were observed as they watched a 58-minute "Sesame Street" program on television. They were distracted during the program by the presentation of attractive pictures projected through colored slides. Altogether, the children watched the television during 43% of the program, with older children paying more visual attention (47%) than younger children (35%) (Anderson, Choi, & Lorch, 1987). The attention span of children increases even more dramatically with age between early preschool and early elementary school age (Kail & Bisanz, 1982).

from past mistakes, or to think and reason intelligently. Memory is a central part of information processing.

INFANT MEMORY.   Studies of infants reveal some memory ability from the early weeks of life (Borovsky & Rovee-Collier, 1990; Perris, Myers, & Clifton, 1990). Newborns can distinguish different speech sounds and odors, and by one month of age can distinguish their mother's face from others. These abilities are evidence of memory (Cernoch & Porter, 1985; Maurer & Salapatek, 1976; Rovee-Collier, 1987). Rovee-Collier (1987) hung a mobile over an infant's crib and attached a ribbon from the mobile to one of the baby's legs. The 6-week-old infant quickly learned which leg would move the mobile. Two weeks later the child was put into the crib and, as a "reminder," was allowed to look at the mobile without having the ribbon attached. The next day, with the ribbon reconnected, the infant kicked to move the mobile as it had learned to do two weeks before. Obviously, it had remembered the behavior previously taught (Linde, Morrongiello, & Rovee-Collier, 1985).

The memory of infants is fairly short-lived, however. Without a repetition of the stimuli, the memory trace fades fairly quickly (Hayne, Rovee-Collier, & Perris, 1987). Infants have to be over 7 months of age before

The infant quickly learned which leg kicked the mobile and two weeks later remembered how to make the mobile move.

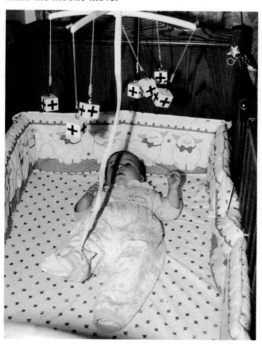

they will search for objects that have disappeared. One mother reported that her 9-month-old daughter was looking for ribbons. She looked first in the old drawer from which they had been removed. She then looked in other drawers until she found them. The next day she went directly to the new drawer to find the ribbons (Ashmead & Perlmutter, 1979).

These early memories are not permanent, however. *Very few people can recall events that happened prior to 3 years of age.* We don't remember being born; we don't remember nursing, crawling, starting to walk, or the birth of a sibling 2 or 3 years younger than us. I have a sister who is 4 years younger than I am. I can remember my mother nursing her. I can remember my first day in kindergarten at age 5, but very little before that. This phenomenon is known as **infantile amnesia**, the essential lack of memory of events experienced before 3 years of age (Sheingold & Tenney, 1982).

MEMORY CAPACITY AND STORAGE.   The process of remembering involves a series of steps. The most widely accepted model is a three-stage one: **sensory storage**, **short-term storage**, and **long-term storage**. Information is seen as passing from one compartment to another, with decreasing amounts passed on at any one time to the next stage (Rice, 1990). Figure 7.4 illustrates the three-stage model of memory. Information is held only briefly (as little as a fraction of a second) in sensory storage before the image begins to decay or is blocked out by other incoming sensory information. Information that has not already faded from the sensory storage is read out to the short-term storage, where it may be held for up to 30 seconds. Because of the limited capacity of the short-term storage, information to be held longer must be rehearsed and transferred to the relatively permanent long-term storage. For all practical purposes, long-term storage capacity is infinite. In the process of retrieval, stored information is obtained by searching, finding, and remembering, either through **recall** (remembering without cues) or **recognition** (remembering with cues). Memory efficiency depends on all three of these processes.

SENSORY STORAGE.   In sensory storage, no cognitive processing takes place. Our senses of vision, hearing, taste, smell, or touch are momentarily stimulated. We pay attention to some of the stimuli, then the sensation fades. Some significant information is passed on to the short-term storage.

Infantile amnesia—the lack of memory of events experienced before age 3

Sensory storage—the process by which information is received and transduced by the senses, usually in a fraction of a second

Short-term storage—the process by which information is still in the conscious mind and being rehearsed and focused on

Long-term storage—the process by which information is perceived and processed deeply so it passes into the layers of memory below the conscious level

Recall—remembering without cues

Recognition—remembering after cues have been given

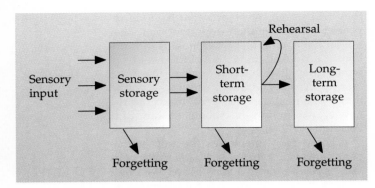

FIGURE 7.4   Three-stage model of memory.

SHORT-TERM STORAGE.   Short-term storage involves very little processing of information. As a result, it is not remembered for longer than about 30 seconds. Furthermore, it involves the equivalent of only about 7 digits—the same amount of data as in a local telephone number. Siegler (1989) suggests that children are often unable to solve certain problems because they can't keep all the relevant information in mind long enough. Obviously, they have not rehearsed it long enough to put it in long-term storage.

Short-term memory ability increases during childhood (Raine, Hulme, Chadderton, & Bailey, 1991). One way to measure short-term memory is to ask subjects to repeat a series of digits that they have heard repeated at a fairly rapid rate. In one study, 2- to 3-year-old children were able to remember 2 digits. By 9 years of age, the children were able to repeat 6 digits. After that, the number remembered continued to increase, but at a much slower rate, so that 12-year-olds could repeat 6½ digits and adults could repeat about 7 (Dempster, 1981). As mentioned, short-term memory capacity is usually about 7 digits. *The short-term memory span is fairly constant throughout adolescence and adulthood* (Kail, 1979).

LONG-TERM STORAGE.   Long-term memory contains information that is processed deeply (for example, it is rehearsed and repeated until it is thoroughly familiar) and stored on a fairly permanent basis. Unlike short-term memory, *long-term memory increases fairly rapidly with age during middle and late childhood; it continues to increase until young adulthood* (Price & Goodman, 1990).

A life-span study of memory for pictures was conducted for 7-year-olds, 9-year-olds, young adults, and older adults over 68 (Pez-

dek, 1987). Subjects were presented simple and complex line drawings and then tested with the same and changed forms of these pictures, at both 5-second and 15-second presentation rates. For each test picture the experimenter asked: "Is this picture the same as a picture you saw before, or are there some changes in the picture?" The questions were asked long enough after the picture was presented (3 minutes) to ensure that the test measured long-term memory. Figure 7.5 shows examples of pictures in both simple and complex forms. Figure 7.6 shows the percentage correct, by age group, when the test pictures presented were complex forms of simple pictures. The graph shows the results of both 5-second and 15-second presentation rates. As can be seen, the ability of subjects to remember the pictures increased from age 7 to college age, then declined in older adults over 68 years of age. For all age groups, pictures presented in their simple

FIGURE 7.5   Examples of pictures in both simple and complex forms.

From: "Memory for Pictures: A Life-Span Study of the Role of Visual Detail" by K. Pezdek, 1987, *Child Development, 58,* pp. 807–815.

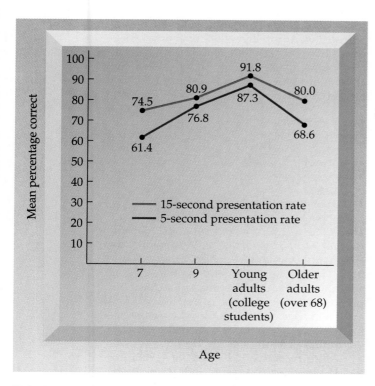

FIGURE 7.6   Memory for pictures by age of subject.

Data from "Memory for Pictures: A Life-Span Study of the Role of Visual Detail" by K. Pezdek, 1987, *Child Development, 58*, pp. 807–815.

dren often use codes to make maps or posters. A code may also be audible, such as the ringing of a timer bell to remind a child it's bedtime.

Another mnemonic device is to provide children with *memory cues*: for example, the letters representing notes on a music staff, shown in Figure 7.7. The letters F A C E refer to the notes between the lines. The letters E G B D F are the first letters of the words in the phrase: "Every Good Boy Does Fine." These letters represent the notes on the lines.

Another way to remember material is by *visualizing position or place*: the so-called **method of loci**. Children often remember material they have read by visualizing its position on a page of their textbook. Children are also better able to remember material that is *meaningful and familiar*. They would have more trouble remembering the letters NOTGNIHSAW than they would the letters WASHINGTON, unless they were able to recognize that NOTGNIHSAW is WASHINGTON backwards. If children are motivated to learn material because it is *interesting*, or if it is *important*, it's surprising how much they can learn and remember (Lorch, Bellack, & Augsbach, 1987). They may never learn material that they are not interested in. In support of this assertion, it has been found that preschool children have extremely good memories for stories or for social or family events (Mandler, 1983). In one study, children were told a detailed story about two boys who had lunch at McDonald's. The children were later asked to identify which words from a list were in the story. The memory of these children was extremely accurate (Mistry & Lange, 1985). Researchers have found that the use of *mnemonic devices* increases from preschool years through adolescence (Brown, Bransford, Ferrara, & Champione, 1983; Flavell, 1985).

Method of loci— remembering by visualizing the position of something

form were recognized more accurately than pictures presented in their complex form. Also, memory for pictures increased as the exposure duration per picture increased. Longer study intervals allowed for greater efficiency in encoding and storing the information on picture details.

METAMEMORY.   Metamemory consists of knowledge of memory strategies people employ to learn and remember information. There are a number of **mnemonic**, or memory-aiding, strategies that are useful. One is *rehearsal*, the repetition of information to be remembered. This helps to process information deeply and to store it in long-term memory. Another way to aid memory is through *organization*. Material can be arranged by categories (for example, animals), alphabetically, or in some other logical order. **Chunking** consists of dividing material into meaningful parts. Thus, it is easier to remember the telephone number 1-516-799-4362 than it is to remember 15167994362. Material can also be *coded*: for example, by color. A map with its symbols is a good illustration of visual representation of roads, cities, railroads, rivers, highways, and so forth. Chil-

Metamemory— knowledge of memory strategies people employ to learn and remember information

Mnemonic— memory-aiding

Chunking—dividing material into meaningful parts to remember it

FIGURE 7.7   Cues to remember notes on a music staff.

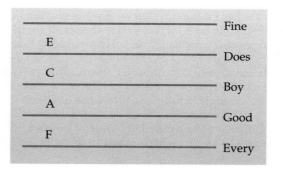

INTELLIGENCE

So far we have discussed two approaches to the study of cognition: the *Piagetian approach* and the *information-processing approach*. The third approach, discussed here, is the *psychometric approach*. This is a quantitative approach, concerned with the level of intelligence as measured by test scores.

Views of Intelligence

To measure successfully the quantity or level of intelligence, it is necessary to know what intelligence is. Unfortunately, psychologists are not in complete agreement as to what constitutes intelligence.

One of the first persons to address the problem was *Alfred Binet* (1857–1911), a professor of psychology at the Sorbonne, the University of Paris. In the 1890s, he was asked by the Paris Ministry of Education to develop a test to sort out those children who were slow learners, who could not benefit from regular classroom instruction. The result was the creation of an intelligence test that was later revised and translated in America to become the current, widely used *Stanford-Binet Intelligence Scale*. To Binet, intelligence was a general capacity for comprehension, reasoning, judgment, and memory (Binet & Simon, 1916). Binet described this capacity as **mental age (MA)**: the level of development in relation to **chronological age (CA)**. The higher MA is in relation to CA, the brighter the child. The German psychologist *William Stern* originated the term **IQ, intelligence quotient**, which is calculated as follows:

$$IQ = \frac{MA}{CA} \times 100$$

If MA is equal to CA, IQ is 100. If MA is greater than CA, then IQ is over 100. If MA is less than CA, the IQ is under 100.

In England, *Charles Spearman* (1863–1945) advanced a **two-factor theory of intelligence** (Spearman, 1927). He concluded that there is a *general intellectual factor* that he labeled *g*, and a number of *specific abilities*—*s* factors—that are useful for different tasks, for example, arithmetic or spatial relations.

This concept of many kinds of intelligence was expanded by *Louis Thurstone*, a mathematician who worked in Thomas Edi-

son's laboratory. Thurstone believed that if persons were intelligent in one area, they were not necessarily intelligent in other areas (Thurstone, 1938). Thurstone's research enabled him to identify seven distinct **primary mental abilities**:

1. verbal meaning
2. perceptual speed
3. logical reasoning
4. number
5. rote memory
6. word fluency
7. a spatial or visualization factor

These factors were tested separately in the *Primary Mental Abilities Test*. A version was eventually developed for young schoolchildren (Thurstone & Thurstone, 1953). After additional research, Thurstone found that his primary mental abilities correlated moderately with one another, so he eventually acknowledged a *g* factor as well as the individual primary factors.

More recently, *J. P. Guilford* (1967) expanded the idea of specific abilities by identifying 120 factors in intelligence. Other psychologists agree that there are different kinds of intelligence, but disagree as to the number. *Howard Gardner* (1983) divides intelligence into seven dimensions:

1. Linguistic intelligence—verbal abilities.
2. Logical mathematical intelligence—ability to reason logically and to use mathematical symbols.
3. Spatial intelligence—ability to form spatial images and to find one's way around in an environment. The sailors in the Caroline Islands of Micronesia navigate among hundreds of islands using only the stars and their bodily feelings.
4. Musical intelligence—ability to perceive and create pitch and rhythmic patterns. There are individuals who are otherwise mentally retarded who can play a song on the piano after hearing it once.
5. Body-kinesthetic intelligence—the gift of graceful motor movement as seen in a surgeon or dancer.
6. Interpersonal intelligence—understanding of others, how they feel, what motivates them, and how they interact.
7. Intrapersonal intelligence—individual's ability to know himself or herself and to develop a sense of identity.

Gardner's concept is unique because he claims independent existences for different intelligences in the human neural system. He

Mental age (MA)—describes the intellectual level of a person

Chronological age (CA)—age in years

Intelligence quotient—MA divided by CA × 100

Two-factor theory of intelligence—concept that intelligence consists of a general factor—"g"—and a number of specific abilities—"s" factors

Primary mental abilities—seven basic abilities described by Thurstone

would like to stop measuring people according to some unitary dimension called intelligence. Instead he would like to think in terms of different intellectual strengths.

Robert Sternberg (1985) and his colleagues at Yale University arranged abilities into the following three major groupings in describing intelligence. His theory is called the **triarchic theory of intelligence**.

COMPONENTIAL INTELLIGENCE. Componential intelligence includes the ability to acquire and store information, general learning and comprehension abilities such as good vocabulary and high reading comprehension; ability to do test items such as analogies, syllogisms, and series; and ability to think critically. This is the traditional concept of intelligence as measured on tests.

EXPERIENTIAL INTELLIGENCE. Experiential intelligence (intelligence based on experience), includes ability to select, encode, compare, and combine information in meaningful ways to create new insights, theories, and ideas.

CONTEXTUAL INTELLIGENCE. Contextual intelligence includes adaptive behavior in the real world, such as the ability to get along with other people, size up situations, achieve goals, and solve practical problems (Sternberg & Wagner, 1986).

In an effort to include the influence of both heredity and environment in the development of intelligence, *Raymond Cattell* (1963) described two dimensions of intelligence: *crystallized* and *fluid*. **Crystallized intelligence** includes knowledge and skills measured by tests of vocabulary, general information, and reading comprehension. It arises out of experience and represents the extent of acculturation and education. **Fluid intelligence** is a person's ability to think and reason abstractly as measured by reasoning tests, such as figural analogies and figural classifications. It involves the processes of perceiving relationships, deducing correlates, reasoning inductively, abstracting, forming concepts, and solving problems as measured by tasks with figural, symbolic, and semantic content. Fluid intelligence has a hereditary base in neurophysiological structures; therefore it is not influenced as much as crystallized intelligence by intensive education and acculturation.

Intelligence Tests

STANFORD-BINET.   Revisions of Binet's tests were made by *Lewis Terman* of Stanford University and became the Stanford-Binet test. It is used with individuals from age 2 through adulthood. The fourth edition of the Stanford-Binet was published in 1985 (Thorndike, Hagan, & Sattler, 1985) and yields scores in four areas: *verbal reasoning, quantitative reasoning, abstract/visual reasoning,* and *short-term memory*. It also provides a composite score that can be interpreted as an *Intelligence Quotient (IQ)* that reflects overall intelligence. Figure 7.8 shows a normal distribution of intelligence test scores on the Stanford-Binet. Note that 68.26% of individuals have scores between 85 and 115. Only 2.28% score above 130 and below 70.

THE WECHSLER SCALES.   The Wechsler Scales, developed by *David Wechsler*, are also widely used. There are three scales: the *Wechsler Adult Intelligence Scale—Revised (WAIS-R)*, the *Wechsler Intelligence Scale for Children—Revised (WISC-R)* for use with children ages 6 to 16, and the *Wechsler Preschool and Primary Scale of Intelligence (WPPSI)* for use with children ages 4 to 6½ (Wechsler, 1967, 1974, 1981). The Wechsler Scales yield a composite IQ score, plus a verbal IQ from the six verbal subscales, and a performance IQ from the six performance subscales. Table 7.3 describes the various subtests in the WISC-R.

FIGURE 7.8   Normal distribution of IQ scores.

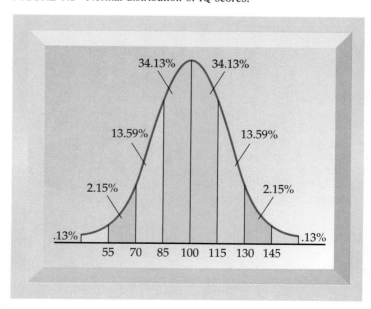

Triarchic theory of intelligence—three components of intelligence described by Sternberg

Crystallized intelligence—Cattell's concept that knowledge and skills arise out of acculturation and education

Fluid intelligence—Cattell's concept of inherited ability to think and reason abstractly

TABLE 7.3 The Wechsler Intelligence Scale for Children Revised (WISC-R)

Verbal Scale	Performance Scale
1. *General information.* Questions relating to information most children in our society have the opportunity to acquire.	1. *Picture completion.* Child indicates what is missing in pictures; measures visual alertness and ability to organize visually.
2. *General comprehension.* Questions designed to assess child's judgment and common sense.	2. *Picture arrangement.* Series of pictures must be arranged to tell a story; ability to think logically and meaningfully.
3. *Arithmetic.* Oral arithmetic problems: addition, subtraction, multiplication, division.	3. *Block design.* Child is required to copy exactly a design with colored blocks; visual–motor coordination, perceptual organization, spatial visualization.
4. *Similarities.* Child thinks logically and abstractly to determine how certain things are alike.	4. *Object assembly.* Puzzles to be assembled by the child; visual–motor coordination and spatial visualization.
5. *Vocabulary.* Child gives meanings of words of increasing difficulty.	5. *Coding.* Child pairs symbols with digits following a key; visual–motor coordination and speed of thought.
6. *Digit span.* Child repeats orally presented sequence of numbers forward and backward; measures short-term memory.	6. *Mazes.* Child traces way out of mazes with pencil; an optional scale.

Critique of IQ and IQ Tests

IQ, SCHOOL PERFORMANCE, JOB AND PERSONAL SUCCESS.   IQ tests were designed initially to predict school performance. They do a pretty good job of this. Correlations between measured IQ and grades in school usually average about +.65 (Stevenson, Hall, Klein, & Miller, 1968). This accounts for about 45% of the variance in school grades. Still, over one-half of the variance in school grades is not predicted by IQ. Future school success is better predicted by past and present school success than by IQ. IQ tests are more predictive of job success in some occupations (for example, stockbroker) than they are in others, such as police officer (Ghiselli, 1966). If a job requires academic skills, an IQ test will be a fairly good predictor of success on that kind of job. However, IQ scores tell us nothing about the ability to get along with other people; flexibility and the ability to adapt to different situations; work habits, motivation, interest, and effort; or emotional factors such as self-esteem, emotional security, or emotional stability. Yet, these are all important factors in job success or in interpersonal relationships.

STABILITY OF IQ.   As is covered in a subsequent discussion of infant intelligence testing, tests given in infancy (at about age 2) are almost worthless in predicting later IQ scores. By age 5, future IQ scores are more predictable. By age 10, scores are even more stable. However, there are wide individual variations in patterns even after this age. For some children, IQ may remain fairly constant. Correlations between tests in middle childhood and later scores are generally quite high (about +.7 or more). In other children, IQ scores may increase, decrease, or go up and down like a bouncing ball (Francois, 1990). Pinneau (1961) reanalyzed the data from the *Berkeley Growth Study* and converted all the scores to deviation IQs. He found that

FOCUS

Terman's Study of Gifted Men*

A follow-up of 52 superintelligent men from a study begun in 1921 at Stanford University by Lewis Terman revealed some interesting results (Hagan, 1983). Sixty years after the initial study began, the men with the highest IQs could scarcely be distinguished from the general population in relation to marriage, family, and domestic relations. However, the majority had received advanced degrees and were successful and superior achievers in their professions, though those with IQs of 150 were as successful as those with IQs of 180. IQ at best taps only a few facets of intelligence and prerequisites for success in life (Trotter, 1986).

*One of the criticisms of Terman's research is that it did not include women.

children tested at 5 years and at subsequent ages up to 17 years showed median changes from 6 to 12 points, with the range of individual changes from 0 to 40 points. Eichorn, Hunt, and Honzik (1981) found a correlation of +.80 between IQ in adolescence and IQ in middle age. However, 11% of the persons showed IQ gains of 13 points or more between adolescence and middle age. Another 11% showed IQ drops of 6 points or more. Overall, there was a 4-point gain in IQ between adolescence and middle age. IQ scores, therefore, are not fixed norms. They can vary, depending on many factors.

PERSONAL FACTORS INFLUENCING TEST RESULTS.   Test results may be influenced by such personal factors as *test anxiety, motivation* and *interest* in the tasks, or *rapport* with the *test giver*. A prime example is that of a 10-year-old in the Boston school system who would not answer test questions and whose record subsequently contained this entry: "The child's IQ is so low, she is not testable." After a young psychologist talked with the child and established rapport with her, he tested her and found she achieved an IQ score of 115 ("Aptitude Test Scores," 1979).

CULTURAL BIAS.   The chief criticism of intelligence tests is that they are biased in favor of white, middle-class children. Tests to measure IQ were originally designed to measure "innate" general intelligence apart from environmental influences. But research over a long period has shown that sociocultural factors play a significant role in the outcome of the tests (Carmines & Baxter, 1986). Children reared in stimulus-rich environments may show superiority in intelligence, whereas those reared under intellectually sterile conditions may not reach their full intelligence capacities (Scarr & Weinberg, 1978). Furthermore, the test language, illustrations, examples, and abstractions are middle-class, and thus are designed to measure intelligence according to middle-class standards. Many children from low socioeconomic backgrounds grow up in a nonverbal world or a world where words used are so different that to understand middle-class expressions on an intelligence test is difficult. These children do poorly not because they are less intelligent but because they do not comprehend language foreign to their backgrounds and experiences. Children from minority groups who are also from lower socioeconomic families experience greater difficulties (Roberts & DeBlossie, 1983). Native American children and others from rural areas who have been raised in an environment free from considerations of time do poorly on tests with a time limit. When allowed to do the test at their own rate, they score much higher.

Efforts to develop culturally unbiased tests have been very frustrating. The general approach has been to use language familiar to the particular minorities for which the test is designed. But the major problem is how to evaluate their accuracy. Most have been measured against IQ scores, which continue to reflect a cultural bias (Rice, 1979).

A more promising approach is known as *SOMPA (System of Multicultural Pluralistic Assessment)*, which consists of the Wechsler IQ test; an interview in which the examiner learns the child's health history; a "sociocultural inventory" of the family's background; and an "adaptive-behavior inventory" of the child, which evaluates the child's nonacademic performance in school, at home, and in the neighborhood. A complete medical exam evaluates the child's physical condition, manual dexterity, motor skills, and visual and auditory ability. The final score on the SOMPA is obtained from not only the IQ test but also from the other inventories. Thus, a child who receives 68 on the Wechsler may earn an *adjusted IQ* of 89 when scores on the sociocultural and the adaptive-behavior inventories are taken into account (Rice, 1979). Thus, SOMPA measures potential rather than current ability.

FOCUS

The Kaufman Assessment Battery for Children (K-ABC)

This test was developed by Alan and Nadeen Kaufman in the early 1980s, in part to eliminate racial differences. The test cuts the IQ differences between blacks and whites by 50% (to about 7 points) and eliminates the differences between Hispanic and white children, thus reducing cultural bias.

The K-ABC has been found to correlate well with achievement tests (Childers, Durham, Bolen, & Taylor, 1985; Valencia, 1985). This means that the K-ABC distinguishes between those who have acquired knowledge and those who haven't, without reflecting a racial or ethnic bias.

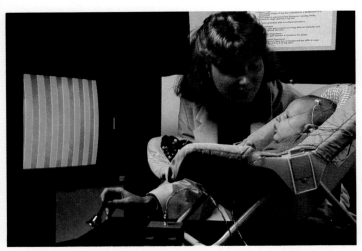

It is difficult to test the intelligence of infants because they are easily distracted.

Infant Intelligence and Measurement

For a number of years, psychologists have been interested in testing the intelligence of infants. If measurements could be made accurately, this would be of considerable help in matching adoptive parents and children, or in planning educational activities. The problem is that infants are less verbal than older children, so they are tested on the basis of what they do, not what they say. However, infants are distractible; it's hard to get their attention to test them. If they don't do something, is it because they don't know how to do it, don't feel like doing it, or because they don't know what is expected?

DEVELOPMENTAL QUOTIENT (DQ). Arnold Gesell (1934) developed a measure that was used to sort out babies for adoption. The Gesell test divided behavior into four categories: *motor, language, adaptive,* and *personal-social*. The scores in these four areas could be combined into a **developmental quotient (DQ)**. The problem is that DQs during infancy do not correlate highly with IQs in later childhood, so any efforts to predict IQs of normal children before age 2 are practically worthless.

BAYLEY'S SCALES OF INFANT DEVELOPMENT. The *Bayley Scales of Infant Development* were developed by Nancy Bayley (1969). The three scales assess the developmental status of children from 2 months to 2½ years of age in three areas: *mental abilities* such as memory, learning, perception, and

Development quotient (DQ)— score developed by Gesell to evaluate an infant's behavioral level in four categories: motor, language, adaptive, and personal-social

verbal communication (for example, infants are asked to imitate simple actions or words); *motor abilities*, including both gross- and fine-motor skills; and *infant behavior record* (during mental and motor assessments). Separate scores are given for each scale. Unfortunately, the scores for infants are highly unreliable in predicting later IQ in childhood and adolescence. However, the closer children are to their 5th birthday when tested, the higher the correlation between their intelligence scores and those in later childhood (Bornstein & Sigman, 1986). It's easier to predict the future IQ of a handicapped infant than of one with normal intelligence, but some of those who are handicapped as infants improve greatly as they get older (Kopp & McCall, 1982).

Parental IQ and educational level is a much more reliable predictor of childhood IQ (Kopp & McCall, 1982). Also, measures of *habituation or dishabituation* in infancy have been found to be a much better predictor of intelligence in childhood than the developmental scales (Bornstein & Sigman, 1986), as was discussed previously in this chapter in the section on habituation.

Early Intervention

Can early intervention through remedial programs increase the intelligence of young children (Wasik, Ramey, Bryant, & Sparling, 1990)? The general consensus seems to be that *high-quality programs for educationally deprived children can have lasting and valuable effects* (Casto & Mastropieri, 1986). The best example comes from research on *Head Start* programs, which were designed to help disadvantaged preschool children do better in school as they grow older (Lee, Brooks-Gunn, Schnur, & Liaw, 1990). An 18-year study of the progress of 123 children, beginning when they were 3- and 4-year-olds, at Perry Elementary School in Ypsilanti, Michigan, showed that those who had been in the Head Start program scored higher on reading, math, and language achievement tests than children in a control group. The Head Start children also showed fewer antisocial and delinquent tendencies as they grew up.

If programs are well funded and teachers are competent, Head Start children show "improved intellectual performance during early childhood, better scholastic placement and improved scholastic achievement during elementary school years, and, during adolescence, a lower rate of delinquency and higher rates of both graduation from high school and employment at age 19" (Schweinhart &

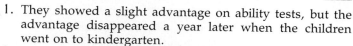

PARENTING ISSUES

Pushing Preschoolers

Programs like Head Start have been found to help children from economically disadvantaged homes overcome disparity in their backgrounds. But what is the effect of providing accelerated, academically enriched programs for preschool children from middle-class families? Two psychologists, Dr. Marion Hyson at the University of Delaware and Dr. Leslie Rescoria at Bryn Mawr College, compared 85 children who had gone to academically enriched preschools with those who went to preschools where they simply played. Accelerated activities included learning numbers, letters, computer instruction, social studies, and foreign languages. When tested at age 4, in comparison to those in other preschools, those in the accelerated program tended to share the following characteristics:

1. They showed a slight advantage on ability tests, but the advantage disappeared a year later when the children went on to kindergarten.
2. They knew their numbers and letters better, but there was no difference in other cognitive skills that contributed to academic success.
3. Their parents tended to push them and to have higher academic expectations. These parents tended to be more controlling, critical, and emotionally negative.
4. The net result emotionally was that the children tended to be more anxious, less critical, and less positive toward school (Goleman, 1989).

Weikert, 1985, p. 547). These are significant findings.

An important part of Head Start is the involvement of parents: giving them information and training in child development and care, home management, family relationships, nutrition, health, and other topics. Parents are involved in planning their own programs. In one study, trained mothers gave their children more instruction, information, and praise; more encouragement to think and talk; were more emotionally responsive, sensitive, and accepting of their children; and were less critical than mothers in a control group (Andrews et al., 1982). Overall, parent–child relationships are important factors in cognitive development.

SCHOOL

Early Childhood Education

The numbers of children in some kind of early childhood education program have grown tremendously. There are several reasons for this trend. In 1988, 24% of all families with children at home were maintained by one parent. The comparable figures for black families were 54% (U.S. Bureau of the Census, 1990). Furthermore, in 1988, 57% of married women with the youngest child under age 6 were employed outside the home (U.S. Bureau of the Census, 1990). These circumstances necessitated parents' placing their children under some kind of child-care

arrangement. In addition, many parents, whether they work or not, have come to recognize the benefits of preschool education for their children. Table 7.4 shows the primary child-care arrangements used by employed mothers for children under 5 (U.S. Bureau of the Census, 1987). Note that about a third (32%) of these children were cared for

TABLE 7.4 Primary Child Care Arrangements Used by Employed Mothers for Children Under 5, 1986

Form of Care	Percent of Mothers Making Arrangement
Care in child's home:	31.0
By father	15.7
By grandparent	5.7
By other relative	3.7
By nonrelative	5.9
Care in another home:	37.0
By grandparent	10.2
By other relative	4.5
By nonrelative	22.3
Organized child care facilities	32.0
Day or group care center	14.0
Nursery school or preschool	9.1
Kindergarten or grade school	0.8
Parent caring for child*	8.1

*Includes mothers working at home or away from home.

From U.S. Bureau of the Census, 1990.

in organized child-care facilities: a day-care center, group-care home, nursery school, or other preschool.

NURSERY SCHOOLS. Nursery schools are usually for children after age 2½ to 3, after they have been toilet trained. They typically operate 3 to 5 half days a week, so do not meet the needs of parents working full-time. The best schools offer college-trained teachers, and enriched intellectual and social experiences in informal settings.

MONTESSORI SCHOOLS. These schools for children 3 to 7 are named after their founder, Dr. Maria Montessori, an Italian physician. They are expensive private schools featuring a prepared environment and carefully designed, individually paced, self-taught, self-correcting materials. The teacher arranges the environment, but otherwise does not interfere with the learning process.

GROUP-CARE HOME. The best of these are licensed by the state to accommodate a small number of children—usually in the home of the teacher. Teachers are not usually as well trained as those in larger day-care centers, but if they are warm, caring persons who love children, the effect on the children may be quite positive.

DAY-CARE CENTERS. Day-care centers are licensed by the state, and are open year round, all day, five or more days a week. They are deliberately planned to meet the needs of children of working parents. Day-care centers vary tremendously in quality. The best centers are characterized by the following (AAP, 1986; Belsky, 1984; Bredekamp, 1987; Howes & Rubenstein, 1985):

1. Have a low child-to-adult ratio: 3 to 4 infants and toddlers per adult, or 7 to 9 3- to 5-year-olds per adult.
2. Have workers who are trained in early childhood education and who are affectionate, sensitive, and responsive to the needs of children.
3. Have teachers who encourage self-control, set clear limits, reward expected behavior, and redirect troublesome children to more acceptable activities.
4. Provide a safe, clean, and healthy environment both indoors and outdoors that affords optimum physical development.
5. Offer an environment that encourages children to select from a variety of activities, to master cognitive and language skills, to learn to think and to do, and to solve problems.
6. Encourage children's curiosity, creativity, and self-development at their own pace.
7. Foster children's social skills, respect for others, and ability to get along with others.
8. Foster children's self-esteem, emotional development, and security.
9. Promote cooperation and communication with parents and assist them in parenting skills.

A good day-care program helps parents meet the needs of children, helps enrich children's lives, and can strengthen the family rather than simply separate parent and child. The key lies in the quality of service that is provided. A growing number of businesses are offering in-house child care for children of employees.

American Education

We periodically hear outcries that American education is in trouble. In 1983, the National Commission on Excellence in Education (1983) pointed to a "rising tide of mediocrity" in the schools. In 1986, the U. S. Secretary of Education said that education in the first three grades was in "pretty good shape," but that large numbers of schools were failing to teach the more complicated subject matter beginning around the fourth grade (Bennett, 1986). The reports pointed to poor achievement test scores; the long-term decrease in SAT scores for college admission; declining enrollments and achievement in science and math; poor abilities in communication, writing, and thinking skills; and the need for remedial education and training to prepare students for jobs.

Successful Schools

Before we condemn all U.S. schools as inferior, we need to point out that there are tremendous differences among schools in this country. The American schools in Stevenson's study were from the Minneapolis area, chosen primarily to eliminate ethnicity, because there were few minority children in Minneapolis. These schools were neither the best nor the worst. There are schools that are vastly superior. So our task here is to delineate some of the factors that make schools great.

One of the most important characteristics of successful schools is that *they emphasize academic excellence.* They have high expectations of their students, give regularly assigned and graded homework (Rutter, 1983), and devote a high proportion of classroom

FOCUS

How American Children Compare with Asian Children

Japanese and Chinese (Taiwanese) students outperform their American counterparts in mathematics and science (Stevenson, Lee, Chen, & Lummis, 1990). These differences begin early. By the first grade, American children's scores in math are significantly below those of both Japanese and Chinese children. By fifth grade, the differences are even greater. According to Stevenson and his colleagues, the average score of fifth-grade children in the highest scoring American classroom was below that of all Japanese classrooms and of all but one Chinese classroom (Stevenson, Lee, & Stigler, 1986). Table 7.5 shows the results.

Several reasons have been given for the discrepancies.

- Asian culture places more emphasis on education and hard work than does American culture. Asian parents have higher educational expectations. Pressure is placed on young children to do well on examinations that are required for admission to upper grades.

- Asian children go to school between 230 and 240 days per year versus an average of 174 days in the United States. Asians go to school 5½ days per week, and the school day is ½ hour to 2 hours longer.
- Educational policy is centralized in Taiwan and Japan. The Ministry of Education selects the curriculum and textbooks, placing more emphasis on math and science than do boards of education in the United States.
- Asian children devote more time to academic activities and to studying arithmetic.
- Asian children receive more instruction from teachers, pay more attention in class, spend less time in irrelevant activities, and less time in transitions from one class to another. American children are frequently left to work alone on material they do not understand, so spend larger amounts of time in irrelevant activities, more time in transition periods, and remarkably little time paying attention to their teachers (Stigler, Lee, & Stevenson, 1987).

TABLE 7.5 Mathematic Achievement in the U.S., Japan, and Taiwan

	Mean Number of Math Questions Answered Correctly	Percent of Class Time Spent on Math	Percent of Time Spent on Academic Activities	Percent of Time Students Paid Attention in Class
First Grade				
United States	17.1	13.8	69.8	45.3
Japan	20.1	24.5	79.2	66.2
Taiwan	21.2	16.5	85.1	65.0
Fifth Grade				
United States	44.4	17.2	64.5	46.5
Japan	53.8	23.4	87.4	64.6
Taiwan	50.8	28.2	91.5	77.7

Statistics from "Mathematics Achievement of Chinese, Japanese, and American Children" by H. W. Stevenson, S. Y. Lee, and J. W. Stigler, 1986, *Science, 231*, pp. 693–699.

time to active teaching. Teachers are expected to plan lessons carefully, and they are adequately supervised to see that this is done. The administration supplies the equipment and materials so teachers can do a good job. Students are encouraged to have pride in their work and their school.

Successful schools *pay attention to the needs of individual students*. Students who have low reading scores, or who are below level in other subjects, are given individual help to bring their achievement up. Staff and

teaching personnel are encouraged to build good relations with students, and to be alert to provide assistance with personal problems (Solorzanol, Hogue, Peterson, Lyons, & Bosc, 1984). Teachers are expected to respect their students and to help them have pride in themselves.

Another characteristic of successful schools is *the emphasis on no-nonsense discipline*. Teachers are not left to their own devices to discipline students. They receive the guidance and support they need from the administration, so it is easier for them to keep order, and they have more time to devote to teaching (Jensen, 1986).

Great teachers are also important in building great schools. Great teachers are well trained, intelligent persons who know the subjects they are teaching. They have superior understanding of instructional knowledge and skills. They keep up to date in their field and are willing to spend time in preparation for class. They are also personable, mature adults who like the students they teach and have a genuine interest in their welfare. The best teachers have a real understanding of children, their developmental needs, interests, problems, and adjustments. They show genuine concern, tolerance, and friendliness, and tremendous respect and love for their pupils.

One study demonstrated the power of a teacher to influence her pupils for the rest of their lives. Miss "A" was a first-grade teacher of disadvantaged children. Her former pupils scored higher on occupational status, type of housing, and personal appearance than did other graduates of the same school (Pederson, Faucher, & Eaton, 1978). There were several reasons for Miss A's success. She believed in her children's ability and encouraged them to work hard. She stayed after school to give extra time to pupils who needed it. She was affectionate, caring, and unselfish, sometimes sharing her lunch with those who had forgotten theirs. Even 20 years later, she remembered her pupils by name! She succeeded because she cared about her pupils and their success, and worked to help them accomplish their goals.

Achievement

HEREDITY.   Educators have spent a lot of time and energy sorting out the reasons why some pupils achieve in school and others do not. As discussed in Chapter 3, one most important factor is heredity. Success is not inherited, but heredity is an important factor in intelligence, and intelligence is an important factor in achievement (Bouchard & McGue, 1981).

PHYSICAL FACTORS.   Some of the reasons for underachievement are physical: *poor hearing, poor eyesight*, and *various physical illnesses or handicaps*. One child did poorly in school for 3 years before the parents found out that she was seeing images upside down. Another was found to be so *deaf* that he could not hear most of what the teacher was saying. Some children suffer from brain impairments, such as *dyslexia*, which causes reading problems. Others are *hyperkinetic* because of brain injuries. Is the child doing poorly in school because of mental retardation or because of other physical impairments? Parents and teachers need to seek expert advice to see if there are physical causes for problems before they assume that the child is "just lazy" or "not trying."

ACHIEVEMENT MOTIVATION.   Another important factor is achievement motivation, or the desire to succeed. Individuals vary in the strength of this desire. Studies of 348 pairs of identical twins at the University of Minnesota showed that heredity accounted for 46% of the variance (or differences) in the motivation to work hard to succeed (Goleman, 1986). Some children seem to be born with the desire to succeed; others are more laid back and seem not to care.

However, part of achievement motivation is instilled in children by parents, teachers, or other influential persons. I was brought up with two brothers and a sister. My parents were both from poor families, were college graduates who worked their way through school, and were successful as professional persons. My parents assumed we would go to college and work hard. We were motivated by these expectations. Three of us earned doctorates and one a master's degree. There is no question that our family background was a primary motivator in our achievement.

In contrast, the parents of some of my students actively discouraged achievement motivation. These parents took very little interest in their children's progress in school during the grade-school years. They could not wait until their children were old enough to leave school and go to work. These parents actively discouraged their children from going to college. Some of the children had to wait until they were on their own to return

Great teachers are intelligent, well-trained, and have an understanding of the needs, interests, problems, and adjustments of children.

to school to get their degree. Their motivation came from within, in spite of the negative influence of parents.

DYSFUNCTIONAL FAMILY RELATIONSHIPS AND DIVORCE. Dysfunctional family relationships have a negative effect on school achievement. Family conflict and tension, physical or emotional abuse, parental rejection and neglect, criticism, or hostility undermine children's sense of security and self-esteem, creating anxieties, tensions, and fears that interfere with school achievement. Divorce itself is perceived as a negative event that can stimulate painful emotions, confusion, and uncertainty in children (Jellinger & Slovik; Kalter, 1983). Many children regain their psychological equilibrium in a year or so and resume normal intellectual growth and development, but the initial upset may create substantial emotional and social upheaval that affects schoolwork (Wallerstein & Kelly, 1980). The long-term effects on social, emotional, and cognitive growth are not clear and continue to be studied (Kalter, 1983).

ONE-PARENT FAMILIES. At the present time, 24% of families with children living at home are maintained by one parent (U.S. Bureau of the Census, 1990). However, this is the percentage of one-parent families at the time of the survey. Projections show that nearly 60% of all children born in 1986 may be expected to spend a large part of a year or longer in a one-parent family before reaching the age of 18 (Norton & Glick, 1986). One comparison of 559 youths in the seventh, eighth, and ninth grades showed that children from single-parent homes had the lowest grades and lowest occupational aspirations (Rosenthal & Hansen, 1980). But simple cause-and-effect relationships have not been established. Many of these children came from minority and low socioeconomic groups. Lower achievement and vocational aspirations are often a result of the financial status of the family. Blechman (1982) has suggested that a number of studies of children's academic performances are based on teacher evaluations and ratings, which reflect prejudices against those from one-parent families: "He comes from a broken home." Teachers' ratings do not always agree with objective evaluations.

SOCIOCULTURAL INFLUENCES. Many of the studies of achievement of minority groups indicate lower achievement levels of blacks, Hispanics, and others (Stevenson, Chen, & Uttal, 1990). Table 7.6 shows the percentage of people age 25 or older with designated years of schooling, by race and

Nearly 60 percent of those born in 1986 may spend a year or longer in a one-parent family.

ethnic origin for 1987 (U.S. Bureau of the Census, 1989). As can be seen, 41% of Mexican Americans age 25 or older had only an elementary education. This contrasts with 18% of blacks and 12% of whites. However, there are many reasons for this low achievement of Mexican-Americans. There is often a language problem if parents do not speak English at home. Teachers may be poorly trained, may not speak Spanish, or may be prejudiced against Hispanics. The schools they attend are more often poorly funded, and educational programs are inferior (Casas & Ponterotto, 1984). Many parents do not value education or give their children the support they need for academic success. Under these circumstances, it is not surprising that scholastic performance is poor.

However, many of the studies of minority groups do not take into account socioeconomic status (which is determined by the combination of education, occupation, and income). In

TABLE 7.6 Percentage of People Age 25 or Older with Designated Years of Schooling, by Race and Ethnic Origin, 1987

Number of Years of Schooling	White	Black	Mexican
Elementary: 0–8	12.0	18.4	40.6
Four years of high school or more	76.9	63.5	44.9
Four years or more of college	20.5	10.7	5.8

From U.S. Bureau of the Census. (1989). *Statistical Abstract of the United States, 1989* (109th ed.). Washington, DC: U.S. Government Printing Office, 38.

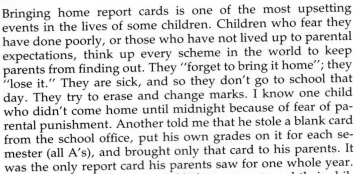

PARENTING ISSUES

Report Cards

Bringing home report cards is one of the most upsetting events in the lives of some children. Children who fear they have done poorly, or those who have not lived up to parental expectations, think up every scheme in the world to keep parents from finding out. They "forget to bring it home"; they "lose it." They are sick, and so they don't go to school that day. They try to erase and change marks. I know one child who didn't come home until midnight because of fear of parental punishment. Another told me that he stole a blank card from the school office, put his own grades on it for each semester (all A's), and brought only that card to his parents. It was the only report card his parents saw for one whole year.

Report cards should be of help to parents and their children, not a major source of family disaster. But how? One, parents should be very cautious about how they react to a poor report. Some parents become violently upset, and resort to severe punishments, physical or verbal thrashings, or threats of disciplinary measures that are excessive or unwise. "Grounding" children every night and weekend for a whole semester, for example—not letting them have any social life at all—may create a lot of resentment and may not accomplish the purpose of stimulating better study habits or grades. No child can study all the time. Nervous, upset children may do far better when they are studying if they have a chance to relax and have fun in between study times. I've known par-

ents to try to force an overactive child to remain inactive and study for long hours at a time. It just doesn't improve grades sometimes. Other parents may try to push a child of average ability to do better than he or she is capable of doing. I know one family where the parents won't let their 10-year-old son watch television until he makes the honor roll. It's been two years and the boy hasn't made it—and he may never make it. In fact, such achievement may be beyond his capabilities.

Two, parents should interpret a report card as an evaluation of achievement and progress and as an indication of strengths and weaknesses. They should give praise and recognition for strengths as well as thoughtful consideration for weaknesses. Do parents compliment their children on the good marks and evaluations? Or do they only notice the low ones? Most children need encouragement, morale building, and emotional support in overcoming problems. Poor marks may indicate the need for tutoring, counseling, or remedial attention of some kind.

Three, report cards are more helpful if followed up by parent–teacher conferences to discuss the reasons for the marks and the child's individual needs, and to decide on a course of remedial action, if needed. If children are having trouble, what will help the most? What should the parents' role be? (Author's counseling notes)

---

many instances, socioeconomic status is a better predictor of achievement than race (Graham, 1986). For example, middle-class blacks have a similar achievement orientation as middle-class whites. Many times, as blacks grow up, their overall achievement is lower than whites, but this is because of prejudices that prevent them from getting ahead, not a lack of motivation to succeed. Middle- and upper-class blacks—like comparable classes of whites—have high expectations of success.

SUMMARY

1. Language is only one of many methods of communication.
2. Apes can't talk because they don't have the vocal equipment, but they can be taught sign language.
3. The basic elements of language include phonemes, morphemes, syntax and grammar, semantics, and pragmatics.
4. Theories of language development include biological theory, learning theory, cognitive theory, and interactionist theory.
5. There is considerable support for the theory that there is a critical period for language development.

6. The sequences of language development are: prelinguistic period, first spoken words, two-word utterances, telegraphic speech, and sentences.
7. The vocabulary of preschool and early school-age children grows from over 50 words at age 2 to 8,000 to 14,000 words at age 6.
8. Grammar is the formal description of structure and rules that a language uses in order to communicate meaning.
9. Pragmatics is the practical ability to use language to communicate with others in a variety of social contexts.
10. For children in groups where their first

language is a minority language, a second language may be a subtractive influence. For children whose first language is the majority language, learning a second language is largely an additive experience.

11. Stuttering appears to have both a genetic base and to be influenced by environment.

12. There are three approaches to the study of cognition: the Piagetian approach, the information-processing approach, and the psychometric approach.

13. Piaget divided the stages of cognitive development into four stages: the sensorimotor stage (birth to 2 years), the preoperational stage (2 to 7 years), the concrete operational stage (7 to 11 years), and the formal operational stage (11 years and up).

14. During the sensorimotor stage children learn to respond through motor activity to stimuli.

15. During the sensorimotor stage children develop the concept of object permanence. They also develop the ability to imitate.

16. The parental role is to offer a stimulating intellectual environment so children can grow cognitively.

17. During the preoperational stage, children develop the ability to deal with the world symbolically and representationally. They acquire language, reason transductively, make errors of reasoning because of syncretism, and may be characterized as exhibiting egocentrism, animism, centration, and lack of comprehension of conservation. They are limited in their classification ability and make errors because their thinking is irreversible.

18. During the concrete operational stage, children show some ability to do logical thinking, but only at a concrete level. They are capable of classification and serialization, understand conservation, and can perform tasks involving combinativity, reversibility, associativity, and identity or nullifiability.

19. The information-processing approach to cognition describes the way children obtain, remember, retrieve, and utilize information in solving problems.

20. Stimulation is important to the learning process; when infants get used to a particular stimulation, they don't pay any attention to it, a process called habituation. Children are very distractible and attend selectively to stimuli.

21. The ability to remember, which begins in infancy, is basic to all learning. However, few people can remember events that happened before they were 3 years old.

22. The process of remembering involves three stages: sensory storage, short-term storage, and long-term storage. Short-term memory ability increases during childhood. Long-term memory increases fairly rapidly to young adulthood.

23. Metamemory consists of knowledge of memory strategies people employ to learn and remember information. Mnemonic, or memory-aiding, strategies include: rehearsal, organization, chunking, using memory cues, using the method of loci, and being motivated to learn material because it is interesting and important.

24. The psychometric approach to the study of cognition is concerned with the level of intelligence as measured by test scores.

25. Different psychologists discuss differing views of intelligence. Some of the more important views were those introduced by Binet (mental age versus chronological age), Spearman (two-factor theory of intelligence), Thurstone (primary mental abilities), Guilford (120 factors), Gardner (seven frames of mind), Sternberg (triarchic theory of intelligence), and Cattell (crystallized and fluid intelligence).

26. The two most important intelligent tests used with children are the Stanford-Binet and the Wechsler Scales.

27. IQ is correlated with school grades, but still only accounts for 45% of the variance in grades. Present school success is a better predictor of future school grades than is IQ.

28. IQ is more predictive of job success in some occupations than in others.

29. By age 10, IQ scores are fairly stable, but there are still wide individual variations in patterns even after this age.

30. There are many personal factors influencing test results: text anxiety, motivation and interest, and rapport with the test giver.

31. The chief criticism of intelligence tests is that they are culturally biased in favor of white, middle-class families.

32. SOMPA is a more promising approach in eliminating cultural bias in measuring IQ. The Kaufman Assessment Battery for Children (K-ABC) was also developed to eliminate racial differences.

33. Trying to predict the intelligence of infants by testing before 2 years of age is practically worthless in predicting later

IQ. The closer the child is to age 5, the more valid a test becomes. The two principal tests used with the infant are Gesell's Developmental Quotient (DQ) and Bayley's Scales of Infant Development.

34. Parental IQ and educational level and habituation are more reliable predictors of childhood IQ than the developmental tests.

35. High-quality programs for economically deprived children can have lasting and valuable effects.

36. The numbers of children in some kind of early childhood education program continue to rise. The principal programs are nursery schools, Montesorri schools, group-care homes, and day-care centers. Programs differ tremendously in quality.

37. Periodically, reports emphasize that American education is in trouble. When our children are compared to Asians in science and math, our children score considerably lower.

38. Not all American schools are mediocre, however. Successful schools emphasize academic excellence, pay attention to the needs of individual children, emphasize no-nonsense discipline, and have great teachers.

39. There are a number of factors that influence achievement: heredity, physical factors, achievement motivation, family background and relations, and sociocultural influences. However, many of the studies of minority groups don't take into account socioeconomic status.

KEY TERMS

Animism   *p. 151*
Associativity   *p. 153*
Babbling   *p. 144*
Centration   *p. 152*
Chronological age (CA)   *p. 158*
Chunking   *p. 157*
Class inclusion relationships   *p. 153*
Classification   *p. 152*
Combinativity   *p. 153*
Conservation   *p. 152*
Cooing   *p. 144*
Crystallized intelligence   *p. 159*
Deductive reasoning   *p. 150*
Deferred imitation   *p. 150*
Developmental quotient (DQ)   *p. 162*
Duos   *p. 145*
Egocentrism   *p. 151*
Fluid intelligence   *p. 159*
Grammar   *p. 146*
Habituation   *p. 154*
Hierarchical classification   *p. 153*
Holophrases   *p. 144*
Identity or nullifiability   *p. 153*
Imitation   *p. 150*
Inductive reasoning   *p. 150*
Infantile amnesia   *p. 155*
Information-processing approach   *p. 149*
Intelligence quotient (IQ)   *p. 158*
Irreversibility   *p. 152*

Language acquisition device   *p. 142*
Long-term storage   *p. 155*
Mental age (MA)   *p. 158*
Metamemory   *p. 157*
Method of loci   *p. 157*
Mnemonic   *p. 157*
Morpheme   *p. 141*
Motherese   *p. 145*
Nativist view   *p. 142*
Object permanence   *p. 150*
Phoneme   *p. 141*
Piagetian approach   *p. 149*
Pragmatics   *p. 142*
Primary mental abilities   *p. 158*
Psychometric approach   *p. 149*
Recall   *p. 155*
Recognition   *p. 155*
Reversibility   *p. 153*
Semantics   *p. 142*
Sensory storage   *p. 155*
Serialization   *p. 153*
Short-term storage   *p. 155*
Symbolic play   *p. 150*
Syncretism   *p. 151*
Syntax   *p. 141*
Telegraphic speech   *p. 145*
Transductive reasoning   *p. 150*
Triarchic theory of intelligence   *p. 159*
Two-factor theory of intelligence   *p. 158*

DISCUSSION QUESTIONS

1. Have you ever known a young preschool child who did not talk? What were the reasons?
2. Have you ever known an infant who seemed to be advanced in language development? Describe. What were the reasons for this advanced development?
3. What can parents do to stimulate the cognitive development of their children?
4. Why has the influence of Piaget been so

felt in the psychological world? What are some of the characteristics of his theories that you like? What are some of your major criticisms of his viewpoints?

5. In what ways is the distractibility of young children a handicap to parents? In what ways is it a help?

6. Can you give examples of the memory ability of children you know?

7. What are the advantages and disadvantages for parents and teachers of knowing the IQ scores of children? In what ways are IQ test results misused?

8. Do you know any children who go to nursery school, Montesorri school, a group-care home, or a day-care center? What are some of the benefits? What are some of the negative effects or problems?

9. Describe your experiences as a child when you brought your report card home. What do you think of parents giving the child money for good grades? What should parents do and not do when their child brings home a poor report card?

SUGGESTED READINGS

Anastasi, A. (1988). *Psychological testing* (6th ed.). New York: Macmillan. Intelligence tests for children.

Anisfield, M. (1984). *Language development from birth to three.* Hillsdale, NJ: Erlbaum.

Brainerd, C. J., & Pressley, M. (Eds.) (1985). *Basic processes in memory development: Progress in cognitive development research.* New York: Springer-Verlag. Methods and findings. Research and theory.

Bruner, J. (1983). *Child talk.* New York: Norton. Language development of children.

Carroll, D. W. (1986). *Psychology of language* (2nd ed.). Pacific Grove, CA: Brooks/Cole. Language Development.

Case, R. (1985). *Cognitive development: A systematic reinterpretation.* New York: Academic Press. Research.

Clark, B. (1983). *Growing up gifted: Developing the potential of children at home and at school* (2nd ed.). Columbus, OH: Charles E. Merrill. Fostering excellence at home and school.

Cummins, J., & Swain, M. (1986). *Bilingualism in education: Aspects of theory, research, and practice.* London: Taylor and Fry. Current discussion.

Eysenck, H. J., & Kamin, L. (1981). *The intelligence controversy.* New York: Wiley.

Flavell, J. H. (1985). *Cognitive development* (2nd ed.). Englewood Cliffs, NJ: Prentice-Hall. Piaget's theories.

Forman, G. E. (Ed.). (1982). *Action and thought: From sensorimotor schemes to symbolic operations.* New York: Academic Press. Research-based articles.

Furth, H. G. (1981). *Piaget and knowledge* (2nd ed.). Englewood Cliffs, NJ: Prentice-Hall. Simplified discussion of Piaget.

Garvey, C. (1984). *Children's talk.* Cambridge, MA: Harvard University Press. Research on language of children.

Gross, T. F. (1985). *Cognitive development.* Monterey, CA: Brooks/Cole. A basic textbook.

Kail, R. (1984). *The development of memory in children.* San Francisco: W. H. Freeman. Changes in children's memory.

Kessel, F. (Ed.). (1988). *The development of language and language researchers.* Hillsdale, NJ: Erlbaum. Chapters by experts.

McDaniel, M. A., & Pressley, M. (1987). *Imagery and related mnemonic processes.* New York: Springer-Verlag. Strategies, especially imagery, for improving memory.

Sattler, J. M. (1981). *Assessment of children's intelligence and special abilities* (2nd ed.). Newton, MA: Allyn and Bacon. Tests and testing.

Siegel, M. G. (1987). *Psychological testing from early childhood through adolescence: A developmental and psychodynamic approach.* Madison, CT.: International Universities Press. Common psychological tests.

Sternberg, R. J. (1984). *Mechanisms of cognitive development.* New York: W. H. Freeman.

Sternberg, R. J. (1985). *Beyond IQ: A triarchic theory of human intelligence.* New York: Cambridge University Press. Sternberg's theory.

Emotional Development

ATTACHMENT*

Meaning and Importance

Attachment—the feeling that binds a child to a parent or care giver

Attachment means the feeling that binds a parent and child together. It is the emotional link between them, the desire to maintain contact through physical closeness, touching, looking, smiling, listening, or talking (Pipp & Harmon, 1987). Young children who have developed a close attachment to their parents run to them when frightened, seek the comfort of their arms when upset, and otherwise derive pleasure and security from just being near them or from being able to see or communicate with them.

All infants need to form a secure emotional attachment to someone: a mother, father, other family member, or a substitute care giver (Bowlby, 1982). To feel emotionally secure, children need warm, loving, stable relationships with a responsive adult on whom they can depend (Kochanska, 1991). If for some reason parents can't be close, the child needs to form a similar attachment to whoever is the primary care giver.

The formation of such attachments is vitally important to children's total development (Main & Cassidy, 1988; Sroufe, 1985). It gives them security, a developing sense of self, and makes their socialization possible (Cassidy, 1986). They are better able to get along with other children, both siblings and those outside the family (Jacobson & Willie, 1986; Park & Waters, 1989; Teti & Ablard, 1989). Children begin to identify with, imitate, and learn from the person(s) to whom they feel closest. And it is through these contacts that children learn what society expects of them. Such relationships become the basis for personality and character formation. We know, too, that mental growth is accelerated if children have secure relationships from which to reach out to explore and learn (Bus & Ijzendoorn, 1988; Frankel & Bates, 1990).

Multiple Attachments

Children can develop close attachments to more than one person (Fox, Kimmerly, & Schafer, 1991; Goossens & van Ijzendoorn, 1990). Most studies show that young children can and often do become equally attached to their mother and father (Dickstein & Parke, 1988; La Rossa, 1988; Ricks, 1985). This rep-

Securely attached infants have affectionate, loving, attentive, and responsive caregivers.

resents two significant attachments. Then, if there are other relatives, such as a grandparent or older children in the home, strong attachments may also be developed with these persons. Anthropologists have emphasized that in some societies children are regularly cared for by a number of persons and that these children enjoy healthy interpersonal relations with all the family members. In fact, in such families, the loss of the mother is not completely disastrous because the child has already become closely attached to other adults. The same thing holds true in our own society in extended families. One woman said that when her father deserted the family, she was not very upset because she had her grandmother, grandfather, aunt, mother, and older sisters and brothers in the household, all of whom were very close to her (Author's counseling notes).

Because children can form multiple attachments does not mean that care givers can be constantly changed. Stability of care, whether by a parent, relative, or baby-sitter, is one of the most important elements in the maintenance of emotional security. It *is* upsetting to a child who has formed a close attachment to one person to have that person leave and be replaced by another person and then by another. One of the hardest problems working parents face is to get dependable substitute care that will not be changing continually, yet this is one of the most important keys to the overall effect of substitute care on children. It is also important that the child, before he or she is separated from the primary attachment figure, first has a chance to form a close attachment with the substitute (Belsky, 1977).

*Part of the material in this section and that on development of trust and security is adapted from the author's book *Working Mothers Guide to Child Development* (1979). Used by permission of the publisher, Prentice-Hall.

The important factor in attachment development is the total dialogue that goes on between parent and child (Isabella & Belsky, 1991). Some parents are supersensitive to their children's needs (Smith & Pederson, 1988). They seem tuned to their children's signals and respond fairly promptly and appropriately to their babies' cries (Pederson, Moran, Sitko, Campbell, Ghesquire, & Acton, 1990). They are able to interpret behavioral cues to discover what their infants are trying to communicate. They like their babies, are interested in them, spend time interacting with them, and are understanding in their responses to them (Lamb, Frodi, Hwang, & Frodi, 1983). As a result, their babies often smile, bounce, and vocalize in interaction with their parents, and show in other ways that they enjoy the social contacts with them (Lewis & Feiring, 1989).

Specific Attachments

On the average, attachments to specific persons do not develop until about 6 or 7 months of age. Before this age, we find no upset at separation, whether it is a major one, such as hospitalization, or a minor one, such as the mother leaving the room. It is true that babies left alone in a room may begin to fret, but they may be comforted by anyone. They seek attention in general rather than the attention of a specific person. Consider the following two observations:

> A 10-week-old baby is lying in her crib. Her mother, tidying the blankets, leans over her, talking and smiling, while the baby coos and "talks" back. The mother leaves the room to greet a visitor. The baby cries. The visitor, who has not seen the baby before, comes over, leans down, smiles, and talks to the baby. The baby stops crying and smiles as the visitor picks her up.
>
> An 8-month-old baby is playing on his mother's knee, when his mother puts him down and leaves the room to answer the door. As the visitor enters, the baby cries. When the visitor attempts to comfort him by picking him up, the baby cries more frantically until the mother returns and holds him. Then the baby calms down. From his mother's lap he first stares and later smiles at the visitor (Dunn, 1977, p. 29).

The two situations demonstrate a crucial change. Both the 10-week-old and the 8-month-old babies protested at being left, but the older child protested at his *mother's* departure. The visitor seemed to upset him more. He no longer treats people as interchangeable companions; separation from his mother has taken on new meaning because he is now attached to *her*.

MATURATION.   Before attachment to parents can take place, three things must occur. *One*, infants must learn to distinguish human beings from inanimate objects in the environment. This ability comes early. By 3 weeks of age, a live human face elicits more excitement from an infant than a drawing of a face. Babies will smile readily at the sight of a human face by 5 or 6 weeks of age. *Two*, infants must learn to distinguish between different human beings so that they can recognize their parents as familiar and strangers as unfamiliar. Some infants are able to recognize their parents by 1 month of age; 81% can do so by 3 months; and all normal infants can by 5 months (Fagan, 1977). *Three*, infants must develop a specific attachment to one person. As suggested, infants develop attachments to persons in general before they develop attachments to individuals. Before specific attachments develop, children can accept equally the care of a loving, attentive baby-sitter or of their parent. Although infants know their parents, they are still content with the attention offered by others.

DECREASES IN ATTACHMENT BEHAVIOR. *From 12 to 18 months of age is probably the most vulnerable time, when specific attachments are at their maximum* (Vaughn & Waters, 1990). Generally, we see a decrease in the attachment behavior of children over the course of the second year, indicating increasing independence and maturity. Also, the need for contact, which is sought primarily through physical closeness and touching at 1 year of age, gradually expands to the social realm. At 3 years, children want contact by looking and talking across a distance. Nursery school children may want to be close to their parents or teachers, but they also seek other forms of comfort, reassurance, and attention. The older children get, the more they seek verbal soothing and reinforcement. Also, as their social contacts expand, so do the number of attachments they form.

Nonattached Children and Insecure Attachment

Some young children whose parents reject them are distant and unemotional, and they don't even seem to notice when their parents come home in the evening or have taken a trip. Of course, sometimes children don't notice because they are preoccupied with their own activities, but if this happens frequently, it may indicate a lack of attachment to the

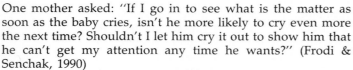

PARENTING ISSUES

Response to Crying

One mother asked: "If I go in to see what is the matter as soon as the baby cries, isn't he more likely to cry even more the next time? Shouldn't I let him cry it out to show him that he can't get my attention any time he wants?" (Frodi & Senchak, 1990)

Social-learning theorists would agree with this parent: Responding promptly to babies' cries rewards their crying and encourages them to cry more. *Attachment theorists* believe just the opposite. They say that babies whose crying is ignored early in life tend to cry more persistently thereafter. Furthermore, this persistent crying aggravates the parents and discourages response (Bisping, Steingrueber, Oltmann, & Wenk, 1990; Donovan & Leavitt, 1989).

Who is right? Both are. This is not as confusing or impossible as it sounds. Generally speaking, a sensitive and prompt response by the parent to the baby promotes a harmonious relationship with a child who is secure and content. Parents who respond promptly to distress tend to have children who are among the least fretful. This view supports the attachment theorists. However, overanxious parents who respond unnecessarily when the baby really doesn't need them are encouraging excessive crying and demands. In other words, some of the most fretful babies may have parents who are overly anxious about responding. This view supports the social-learning theorists.

As in many other instances, avoiding extremes in raising children is often the wisest thing. If a parent never responds to the baby's cries of distress, one reaction is for the child to give up crying entirely and become withdrawn, but no one would say such a quiet child is well adjusted. The other extreme is for the parent to respond anxiously to every whimper.

Nonattached children—children who have not developed a close emotional relationship with parents or care givers

Insecurely attached—children who are overly dependent on parents or care givers because of insufficient attachment

parents. Young children may show marked differences in the degree of attachment. **Nonattached children**, or those whose attachment development is delayed, may make no distinction between their own parents and other members of the household or a caretaker. They accept the attention of any person as readily as they accept that of their own parents. They do not cry when the parents leave the room nor do they attempt to follow them, and they are sometimes precociously independent. This is not normal behavior for children who are old enough to have developed attachments to their parents.

At the other extreme are children who are **insecurely attached**, who are so dependent on their parents that they won't let them out of their sight at all (Lieberman, Weston, & Pawl, 1991). If parents have to leave, the children scream. The clinging, dependent behaviors of these children are symptoms of their insecurities. Insecurely attached infants are fussy babies. They cry not only when they are parted from their parents, but also when they are in close proximity. They cry to be picked up, or they cry when their parents put them down. They seek almost continuous physical contact and are unable to tolerate even a little distance from their parents.

There are various reasons for this overdependent behavior (Egland & Farber, 1984). Children who receive insufficient food and who are chronically hungry may develop these symptoms. Children who are chronically ill may become overly dependent. Children who are rejected and neglected may develop an excessive need for attachment. If parents are highly anxious, nervous, or neurotic persons, this anxiety is felt by their children, who seek reassurance as a result. Also, parents who become depressed, mentally ill, or preoccupied with their own personal problems are not able to give their children the attention and assurance they need. Any one or a combination of these conditions may result in children who are overly dependent and insecurely attached (Lyons-Ruth, Connell, & Grunelbaum, 1990).

Separation Anxiety

SYMPTOMS. Signs of separation anxiety vary somewhat according to individual children, their ages, and the length of time they are separated from the attachment figure (Lollis, 1990). After infants develop attachments to specific persons, they begin to show signs of distress when these persons leave them (Bridges, Connell, & Belsky, 1988). The simplest manifestation is a baby crying when a parent leaves the room (Vaughn, Lefever, Seifer, & Barglow, 1989). Observers have found that some babies as young as 15 weeks will cry when parents leave. Most babies certainly will by 30 weeks.

In the movie "Home Alone," the parents mistakenly left on vacation without their child.

The most common separation is a parent leaving a child alone in a room and closing the door. Infants may cry, and their play may cease soon after the parent leaves. If they are old enough to creep or walk, they may try to follow. If the parent leaves the room but the child can observe the parent in the adjacent room, anxiety is minimized. One observer discovered that young children in a park commonly "froze" when their mothers kept in sight while walking away from them, but they did not cry or attempt to follow. However, a group of infants in a laboratory experiment played contentedly for several minutes and then tried to follow their mothers, who had walked out of sight (Corter, 1976).

EFFECTS OF LONG-TERM SEPARATION. If separation continues for very long, usually over a period of days, symptoms become more serious. The initial phase of protest and searching is followed by a period of despair, during which children become quiet, apathetic, listless, unhappy, and unresponsive to a smile or coo. Finally, if separation continues, the children enter a period of detachment and withdrawal when they seek to sever the emotional ties with the attachment figure. They appear to have lost all interest in the person to whom they were formerly attached. In extreme cases, they seem to lose interest in almost everything going on around them. There is no attempt to contact a stranger and no brightening if strangers contact them. Their activities are retarded. They often sit or lie in a dazed stupor. They lose weight and catch infections easily. There is a sharp decline in general development (Bowlby, 1980).

The trauma of long-term separations without an adequate substitute attachment figure is best illustrated by the following description of a 2-year-old child who had a good relationship with his parents at the time he was hospitalized. He was looked after by the same mother substitute and visited daily by his parents during the first week. However, his behavior deteriorated when the parents reduced their visits to twice a week and then gave up visiting him.

> He became listless, often sat in a corner sucking and dreaming; at other times he was very aggressive. He almost completely stopped talking. . . . He sat in front of his plate eating very little, without pleasure, and started smearing his food over the table. At this time, the nurse who had been looking after him fell ill, and Bobby did not make friends with anyone else, but let himself be handled by everyone without opposition. A few days later he had tonsillitis and went to the sickroom. In the quiet atmosphere there he seemed not quite so unhappy, played quietly but generally gave the impression of a baby. He hardly ever said a word, had entirely lost his bladder and bowel control, sucked a great deal. On his return to the nursery he looked very pale and tired. He was very unhappy after rejoining the group, always in trouble and in need of help and comfort. He did not seem to recognize the nurse who had looked after him at first (Bowlby, 1973).

The trauma of extensive separation without an adequate substitute can be quite severe.

AGE FACTORS. Generally speaking, distress over separation is greatest after 6 months and until about 3 years of age. It is most evident in young children who have had a close relationship with their parents and who are separated suddenly without an adequate substitute care giver provided to whom the child has already become attached. Protest over temporary separation begins to decline most sharply around age 3. The decline in anxiety accompanies the increase in the power of recall: Children are able to remember their parents and a promise that they will return; also, increasing autonomy and mobility make them less dependent.

Preschool children from 3 to 5 years of age can still experience a great deal of separation anxiety, however, as every nursery school teacher knows. The older children become, the less they are upset at separation, partially because they are more independent and partially because they will take more readily to mother substitutes. Between the

PARENTING ISSUES

When a Child Goes to the Hospital

One parent asks: "My 4-year-old may have to go to the hospital for a major operation, and he will probably have to stay a week. What should I do to minimize the emotional upset?" It is helpful if one parent can stay with the child, making arrangements to sleep in the same room, if possible. If one parent can't stay all the time, the other parent, older relatives, and/or teenagers can rotate so that a family member is present all the time. Such arrangements can be made in many hospitals and are vitally important to the child's emotional health. Going to the hospital is frightening enough, but having to stay there for a week is far more upsetting than most children, even the best-adjusted ones, can handle. All of the symptoms of separation anxiety are frequently seen after a few days of hospitalization. In addition, children fear being hurt or mutilated or being left alone. Also, they may interpret being sent to the hospital as punishment for wrongdoing. "I will be good, don't make me go" is the way some children feel. One 7½-year-old boy who had been in the hospital three times since the age of 3 recalled: "I thought I was never coming home again because I was only 6 years old. I heard my sister

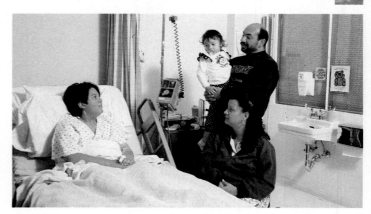

Familial comfort, attention, and support diminish a child's fears of staying in a hospital.

say they were going to dump me and that I'd never come home again" (Bowlby, 1982).

ages of 5 and 8, the risks of upset decrease even further. Contrary to what we find in younger ages, the children of this age who have the happiest relationships with their parents are better able to tolerate separations than those who are only insecurely attached. A happy child, secure in parental love, is not made unbearably anxious. The insecure child, already anxious in his or her attachments, may become even more troubled by forced separation (Ainsworth, 1988).

School-age children or even adolescents are not untouched by separations. Surveys of children between the ages of 5 and 16 who were evacuated from the city of London during World War II confirm the finding that children are not yet emotionally self-supporting. Teachers reported that homesickness was prevalent; that the power of concentration on schoolwork declined; and that bedwetting, nervous symptoms, and delinquency increased. In most cases, there were no serious aftereffects following the children's return home, but in others, the problems persisted for a while afterward (Bowlby, 1982). Young people as old as college age may go through a period of extreme homesickness when first away from home. They get over it, but it's very upsetting for a while.

Reunion Behavior

Investigations of reunion behavior of children reveal various reactions (Bowlby, 1982). Some children become very dependent and possessive, clinging, whining, crying for attention, and placing great demands on their parents. In such cases, it is helpful if the parents can devote themselves exclusively to their children after they get home, otherwise their attachment behavior may increase.

Some children are quite angry at their parents and resist (at least initially) their efforts to hug them and to pay attention to them. It is evident that they have ambivalent feelings toward their parents. On the one hand, they want their love and attention. On the other hand, they resist it because they are angry and fearful. If a separation has been long and upsetting, any withdrawal behavior of children is their effort to keep from being rejected or deserted again.

Sometimes, on reunion, children are emotionally cold, unable to speak or express their feelings until tearful sobs finally burst forth, accompanied by accusing questions: "Why did you leave me?" The worse children behave, the more evident it is that they have been upset by the parent's being away.

Strangers

Fear of strangers ordinarily begins at about 6 or 7 months of age, and increases to about 2 years, after which it declines (Fagot & Kavanagh, 1990). Usually, this fear begins after the onset of specific attachments. Children who are very frightened may cry or cling to their parents. Less upsetting reactions include general wariness or active turning away and avoidance (refusing to be picked up, refusing to speak, or running away).

Children differ considerably in their reactions to strangers (Thompson, Connell, & Bridges, 1988). Some never seem to show much fear at all. They smile readily, seldom turn away from being approached, and may even approach the strangers after only a few minutes of contact. Individual differences relate to how secure children are and to their background of social experiences. Some children are more accustomed to having pleasant experiences with a variety of persons. However, children who have suffered repeated and upsetting exposures to strangers become even more wary and frightened the next time they are approached.

If children are with their parents at the same time that they are in the presence of strangers, they are less frightened than when they are alone with strangers. Children are less frightened of strangers in familiar surroundings. This means that parents who invite friends over to their own home and let the children stay around during the socializing are helping the children get used to other people in an environment that is not stressful. Or, if parents stay with their children when they go out among strangers, they are getting their children used to other persons at the same time that they are giving them the security of their presence. The most frightening situation is to leave the children with strangers in an unfamiliar setting. Also, it is wise to avoid separations and frightening experiences at a time when the fear of strangers is developing or is at its peak. From 1 to 2 years of age is an especially bad time. Either before fears develop or after children begin to lose their fear of strangers is a better time to expose children to new people.

Baby-Sitters and Substitute Care Givers

Leaving a child with a baby-sitter can be a very upsetting experience, but it need not affect the child negatively at all if the proper arrangements are made. The arrangement considered the least upsetting is care by the other parent in the child's own home while the one parent is gone, or substitute care by a close, dependable relative in the child's own home. If neither of these alternatives is possible, the next alternative is a dependable, capable baby-sitter in the child's own home, provided that the child has become acquainted with the sitter over a period of days before the parent has to leave. It is perhaps a good idea to help children become attached to several substitute care givers in case one cannot show up. It is often worse for the parents to surprise the child with a complete stranger and then leave for several days or longer without warning.

The question of the long-term effects of substitute care on children is a very controversial one (Belsky, 1990; Rapp & Lloyd, 1989). Some studies find no association between a mother's work status and the quality of the infant's attachment to her (Chase-Lansdale & Owen, 1987). Belsky and Rovine (1988) have concluded that when infants are 12 and 13 months of age and exposed to 20 or more hours of substitute care per week, they are more likely to be insecurely attached than are infants cared for less than 20 hours per week. However, leaving a child daily in the care of a baby-sitter so that both parents

PARENTING ISSUES

Introduction to Nursery School

If parents are sending a child to nursery school, it is helpful to introduce the child to the school gradually. The best schools allow the parent to first bring the child to the room to play when no other children are around. If the child can become used to the room and become attached to a familiar toy, then he or she will feel more secure the next time. Also, it's important for the child to become acquainted with the teacher, so when school opens the child knows that Ms. Smith is going to be there. Also, having shortened sessions during the opening few days of school can help, as does the practice of allowing the parent to stay for the first few mornings. The parent's presence helps to alleviate the child's anxiety. Gradually, children begin leaving their parents' sides and entering in the play; they forget that they are in a new situation. There is no need for the introduction to nursery school to be a frightening experience. Some parents become so anxious themselves that they transfer this anxiety to their children (Hock, McBride, & Gnezda, 1989). If properly handled, separation anxiety can be kept to a minimum, and the child can very much look forward to going to school.

can go to work, even over a period of years, is far different from leaving a child to be cared for by a procession of baby-sitters with whom the child has only superficial attachments. Also, leaving a child in a well-run, well-staffed infant-care center is far different from leaving a child in an overcrowded, understaffed nursery where care is inadequate and the personnel cannot give sufficient attention to each child. The biggest problem is finding dependable, high-quality care (Meredith, 1986; Trotter, 1987b). Even then, some authorities object to group care for infants and prefer individual care by a person to whom the child is attached.

DEVELOPMENT OF TRUST AND SECURTY

Theoretical Perspectives

Erik Erikson (1963, 1968) suggested that the "cornerstone of a vital personality" is formed in infancy as the child interacts with parents or other care givers. This cornerstone is one of basic trust as infants learn that they can depend on the care givers to meet their needs for sustenance, protection, comfort, and affection. If these needs are not met, the infants become mistrustful and insecure.

Margaret Mahler, a clinical psychologist, emphasizes the importance of the mother–child relationship (Mahler, Pine, & Bergman, 1975). From birth to 2 months, infants go through an **autistic phase** during which their only awareness of the mother is as an agent to meet their basic needs. Then from 2 to 5 months, they enter a second phase, **symbiosis**, during which they estab-

Autistic phase—age during which children are aware of their mother only as an agent to meet their basic needs

Symbiosis—a period in which children establish a close dependency on their mothers, to the extent that there is almost a fusing of personalities

lish dependency on their mother, building a solid foundation for later growth and independence. Mothers who are sensitive and responsive encourage a symbiotic relationship with their infants. A less sensitive mother can frustrate the infant's need to fuse with her, causing the infant to be insecure. The basic psychosocial task, therefore, is to build trust and security through dependency and need fulfillment.

Requirements for the Development of Trust and Security in Infants

There are a number of requirements if trust and security are to be developed. One is for children to receive regular and adequate feedings. The chronically hungry child becomes an anxious child (Valenzuela, 1990).

A second requirement for the development of trust and security is for babies to get sufficient sucking. Most need several hours a day in addition to their nutritional requirements. Since sucking is a source of comfort and emotional security, feeding time needs to be a relaxed, unhurried experience, allowing the baby ample opportunity to suck. Most babies can empty the mother's breast in a short time, but they continue to suck for a period afterward (Schaffer, 1977). A pacifier is a helpful way of meeting children's emotional needs.

Another important emotional need of children is for cuddling and physical contact (Anisfeld, Casper, Nozyce, & Cunningham, 1990). Children have an emotional need for fondling, touching, stroking, warmth, the sound of a pleasant voice, and the image of a happy face.

The most important requirement for the development of trust and security in children is for parents to show them that they love them. Parents need to convey through attitude, word, and deed that they adore their children.

Some Causes of Distrust and Insecurity

PARENTAL DEPRIVATION.   As already discussed, once children have formed close emotional attachments to a parent or parent substitute, any extended separation has negative effects. The longer the deprivation continues, the more pronounced the effects. Such children are typically described as emotionally withdrawn and isolated, with an air of coldness and an inability to show warmth and sincere affection or to make friends in

Sensitive mothers encourage a symbiotic relationship with their infants.

LIVING ISSUES

Learning to Express Affection

A frequent complaint of both men and women is that their partner is not affectionate enough (Kaplan, 1979). By affection, they do not always mean sexual intercourse; they mean touching, hugging, cuddling, holding, kissing. In a response to a challenge from one of her readers, Ann Landers (1985) asked women to reply to this question: "Would you be content to be held close and treated tenderly and forget about the act?" Over 100,000 replies poured in. Yes, answered 72% of the respondents. Of the total, 40% were under 40 years of age. Whatever else the replies indicated, they revealed that these women wanted to feel cared about, that they wanted tender words and loving embraces more than intercourse with an inexpressive partner. The fortunate women were those who received both emotional expressions of affection and complete physical satisfaction as well.

Shere Hite (1981), in her report on male sexuality, discovered that men wanted more than mechanical sex. They wanted physical affection—touching, hugging, kissing, back rubs, and stroking. They also wanted friendship, communication, emotional closeness, warmth, and genuine affection.

Although the need for affection is inborn, learning ways of expressing it are not (Money, 1980). Some children grow up in families in which hugging, kissing, and demonstrations of affection are a part of everyday life. The parents hold children on their laps, cuddle with them, hug and kiss them, tuck them in bed at night, tell them they love them, and show it in word and deed. Other children grow up in families that are not at all demonstrative. If they love one another, they never say or show it in intimate ways. Children from these families may grow up embarrassed to express affection and feelings (Montagu & Matson, 1979). When they marry, they may have the same hesitancy in being demonstrative.

---

a caring way. One woman, who adopted a 5½-year-old girl who had been shifted from one relative to another, described her daughter as not being able to show affection. The mother complained that she "would kiss you, but it would mean nothing." The adoptive father explained that "you just can't get to her." A year and a half after the adoption, the mother remarked: "I have no more idea today what's going on in that child's mind than I knew the day she came" (Bowlby, 1971, p. 37).

What is significant is that some children can remain with parents and be similarly deprived if their parents are not able to fulfill their needs for affection, for loving care, for understanding and approval, or for protection from harm. Parents who have babies they don't want and who reject them or fail to care for them properly are exposing their children to parental deprivation just as surely as if they went away and left them.

TENSION.   Another important cause of emotional insecurity is to be cared for by parents who are tense, nervous, anxious, and irritable (Crnic & Greenberg, 1990; Holden & Titchie, 1991). Parents need to be aware that quarreling between family members upsets children, especially if the quarrels are frequent and violent. A husband and wife start to shout at one another; the baby begins to cry. Even the dog hides under the table. Children who are forced to listen to repeated parental fights become more and more anxious themselves.

EXPOSURE TO FRIGHTENING EXPERIENCES.   The effects of isolated exposure to frightening experiences are usually temporary, unless the experience is quite traumatic. Many adults can recall frightening experiences: being locked in a closet, being chased by a dog, getting lost on the way home from school. Sometimes such experiences are traumatic enough or repeated often enough to cause long-term upset. Children who are sexually molested may be deeply affected psychologically, depending on the situation.

CRITICISM.   Frequent disapproval and criticism may make children unsure of themselves. Actually, some disapproving parents are showing their children that they resent them or even hate them. Two psychiatrists describe the life of a boy whose parents hate him.

From the time he awakens in the morning until he goes to bed at night he is nagged, scolded, and frequently slapped. His attempts at conversation are received with curt, cold silence or he is told to be quiet. If he attempts to show any demonstration of affection, he is pushed away and told not to bother his parents. He receives no praise for anything he does no matter how well he has

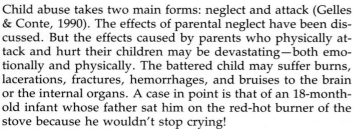

PARENTING ISSUES

Child Abuse

Child abuse takes two main forms: neglect and attack (Gelles & Conte, 1990). The effects of parental neglect have been discussed. But the effects caused by parents who physically attack and hurt their children may be devastating—both emotionally and physically. The battered child may suffer burns, lacerations, fractures, hemorrhages, and bruises to the brain or the internal organs. A case in point is that of an 18-month-old infant whose father sat him on the red-hot burner of the stove because he wouldn't stop crying!

Battered children are often unplanned, premature, or sickly children who make extra demands on parents who are not able to cope (Zucavin, 1988). Parents who batter their children expect and demand behavior from them that is far beyond the children's ability. Such parents are immature themselves, with poor impulse control, and in great need of love (Kugler & Hansson, 1988). In some cases they are emotionally ill (Walker, Downey, & Bergman, 1989). Often they were neglected and abused while growing up. One such example is that of Kathy, the mother of a 3-week-old boy, Kenny: "I have never felt loved in all my life. When the baby was born, I thought he would love me, but when he cried all

the time, it meant he didn't love me. So I hit him" (Smart & Smart, 1972, p. 178). Not only do battered children suffer the pains of physical abuse, but they are also deeply scarred emotionally by the rage and hatred directed at them. Pathological fear, deep-seated hostility or cold indifference, and an inability to love others are often the results. And the possibility for success of emotional rehabilitation will depend upon the damage done. There are cases of battered children blossoming into happy persons after being adopted by loving parents.

Some parents who were abused while growing up resolve never to abuse their own children. Unfortunately, other parents who have been abused themselves as children are likely to abuse their own children. This is why it is vitally important to get help, so that the cycle of abuse can be broken. One study found that abused mothers who were able to break the cycle of abuse were likely to have received emotional support from a nonabusive adult during childhood; to have received therapy; and to have married a stable, emotionally supportive mate with whom they had a satisfying relationship (Egeland, Jacobovitz, & Sroufe, 1988).

---

done it. If he walks with his parents, and lags a little, his arm is seized and he is yanked forward. If he falls, he is yanked to his feet. . . . At meal times he is either ignored or his table manners and inconsequential food fads are criticized severely. He is made to finish whatever is on his plate. . . . The child soon realizes that he can expect nothing but a hurt body or hurt feelings from his parents, and instead of feeling love for them, he feels fear, loathing, and hatred (English & Pearson, 1945, p. 108).

Frequent criticism can be devastating, resulting in deep-seated insecurities and poor self-esteem.

OVERPROTECTION.   Parents who are filled with anxieties themselves and who are fearful for the safety and well-being of their children, may not permit any activities in which there is an element of danger. One girl remarked: "My parents would never let me go to dances because they were afraid I'd get involved with boys." Overprotected children, whose parents never let them develop autonomy, may become so fearful of making decisions or of doing things on their own that they have difficulty establishing themselves as independent adults.

OVERINDULGENCE.   One of the chief causes of insecurity in children is poor impulse control on their part, resulting in guilt and anxiety over their own behavior. Children who are permitted every satisfaction and liberty, whether these things are good for them or not, are inadequately prepared to face the frustrations and disappointments of life. Such children are not disciplined or taught to consider others, so they become selfish and demanding. Anxiety results when these persons get into the world and discover that other people resent them or dislike them because of their selfish behavior. They are puzzled that others don't indulge them as their parents have done, and they become more and more anxious that they won't be successful in their social relationships.

DEVELOPMENT OF EMOTIONS

Components

Psychologists have attempted to explain emotions in various ways. One book quotes over 30 different definitions of emotions

Psychologists have identified four components of emotions: stimuli, feeling, physiological arousal, and behavioral response.

Epinephrine—hormone secreted by the adrenal glands that produces physiological arousal

(Strongman, 1987). Most of the descriptions include a sequence of four basic components of emotions:

1. Stimuli that provoke a reaction
2. Feelings—positive or negative conscious experiences of which we become aware
3. Physiological arousal produced by the hormonal secretions of the endocrine glands
4. Behavioral response to the emotions

To retrace the sequence, suppose that a child

1. is confronted by a growling dog and interprets this as danger;
2. reacts with fear;
3. experiences physiological arousal from the adrenal hormone secretion **epinephrine**, which produces an increase in heartrate, blood pressure, blood flow, sugar in the blood, respiration, and other changes; and
4. trembles and runs away.

Psychologists are not in complete agreement as to whether (a) the child trembles and runs because of feeling afraid, or (b) becomes afraid only after experiencing the bodily reactions, or (c) experiences both the fear and the physiological arousal simultaneously. Cognitive theorists would disagree with all these explanations and say that emotional reactions depend upon how the children would interpret the stimuli from the environment (the dog growling), and how they would interpret the internal bodily stimuli (Schacter & Singer, 1962). Whatever the explanation, all emotions involve the same four basic components: stimuli (which are interpreted cognitively), feelings, physiological arousal, and behavioral response.

Functions

Emotions play a number of important functions in our lives (Barrett & Campos, 1987). They play *an adaptive function* to ensure survival. The fear that children may feel because of a growling dog motivates them to want to get away from the danger. Emotions are also *a means of communication* (Russell, 1990). When children are sad or angry, they are transmitting the message that something is wrong. When they are happy, they are telling others that all is right with their world. Emotions also are extremely *important in social relationships*. They are operative in forming social bonds and attachments, or in keeping other people at a distance. Emotions *are also powerful motivators* and have a significant influence on behavior. Children tend to act out what they feel, be it love or anger. A boy may become hostile toward all women because he has an abusive, rejecting, cruel mother. His hostility influences his relationships with other women, especially with those who remind him of his mother. Or, a girl may become hostile toward all men because of an abusive, rejecting, cruel father.

Emotions are also *a source of pleasure or of pain*. Children who feel joyful and happy are able to enjoy the luxury of these positive feelings. In the same way, negative emotions of anger, disgust, fear, or sadness create disturbing feelings that can be very painful to endure. Yet, without feelings, either positive or negative, life would be colorless and dull. Children who have learned to repress their feelings are emotionally dead. Being able to feel is what adds spice to life.

Basic Emotions

Psychologists have sought to identify and separate different emotions. Ekman (1972) and his colleagues found that people from all over the world were able to distinguish six basic emotions by distinctive facial expressions: *happiness, sadness, anger, surprise, disgust,* and *fear*. Carroll Izard (1977, 1980) has specialized in studying the emotional development of children. Like Ekman, she says that each emotion has its own distinctive facial expression. Eight of Izard's basic emotions are shown by the facial expressions in the accompanying photo.

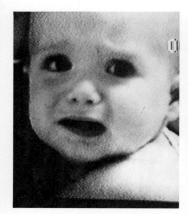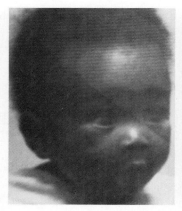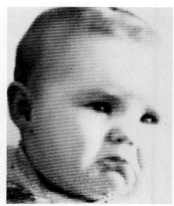

Infants' emotions (left to right): **Fear**—brows level, drawn in and up, eyelids lifted, mouth retracted. **Surprise**—brows raised, eyes widened, mouth rounded in oval shape. **Joy**—mouth forms smile, cheeks lifted, twinkle in eyes. **Sadness**—inner corners of brows raised, mouth corners drawn down.

TABLE 8.1 Timetable of Development of Infant Emotions

Emotion	Time of Emergence
Interest	Present at birth
Distress	Present at birth
Disgust	Present at birth
Joy (social smile)	4–6 weeks
Anger	3–4 months
Surprise	3–4 months
Sadness	3–4 months
Fear	5–7 months
Shame, shyness	6–8 months
Contempt	Second year of life
Guilt	Second year of life

Timetable of Development

Izard also said that emotions develop according to a biological timetable. Interest, distress, and disgust are present from birth; joy (social smile) develops from 4 to 6 weeks; anger, surprise, and sadness are experienced at 3 to 4 months; and fear at 5 to 7 months. Shame and shyness (Broberg, Lamb, & Hwang, 1990) are experienced after the infant develops self-awareness at 6 to 8 months; contempt and guilt are felt during the second year of life. Table 8.1 shows the chronology.

Not all psychologists agree with this timetable. Campos, Barrett, Lamb, Goldsmith, & Stenberg (1983) believe that all emotions are experienced at birth, but observers are not always aware that these various feelings are being expressed. Also, the feelings that are being expressed depend a lot on what is experienced and when.

Abused children develop fear and sadness earlier than others (Gaensbauer & Hiatt, 1984).

Environmental and Biological Influences in Development

Hyson and Izard (1985) agree that emotional responses are partly learned; for example, infants are affected by their mother's moods and emotional expressions. Infants tend to model their mother's emotional expressions. One study found that 3- to 6-month-old infants of depressed mothers also showed depressed behavior and that this behavior carried over in their interactions with other adults who were nondepressed (Field, Healy, Goldstein, Perry, & Bendell, 1988). Another study showed that when 1½-year-old infants smiled, and when their mothers or mother substitutes were attentive and smiled back, the infants' frequency of smiling increased (Jones & Raag, 1989). Thus, open channels of social communication promote the outward expression of internal feelings.

Izard also emphasizes that emotional expressions have a biological component, because they seem to be fairly constant and stable (Trotter, 1987a). Kagan and colleagues found that behavioral inhibition in children may be due to the lower threshold of physical responsivity, so some children don't react as readily to stimuli (Kagan, Rezneck, & Snidman, 1987). Kagan and colleagues also found that children who were inhibited or uninhibited at 21 months of age showed the same characteristics of inhibition and lack of inhibition at 4, 5½, and 7½ years of age (Kagan, Reznick, Snidman, Gibbons, & Johnson, 1988). Thus, *emotional expression and behavior in infancy tell us something about the personality of the child later in life* (Izard, Hembree, & Huebner, 1987). Biology defines the broad outlines and limits of emotional development; environmental influences stimulate and modify that evolution. Part of the task of being a parent or teacher is *socialization:* influencing the feelings and behavior of children so they conform to societal expectations (Malatesta, Grigoryev, Lamb, Albin, & Culver, 1986). This would be impossible if feelings and behavior were only biologically determined.

DIFFERENCES IN TEMPERAMENT

Personality and Temperament

Psychologists make a distinction between personality and temperament. **Personality** is the sum total of the physical, mental, emotional, and social characteristics of an individual. Personality is a global concept and includes all those characteristics that make every person an individual, different from every other person. Personality is not static; it is developed over the years and is always in the process of becoming.

Temperament refers to relatively consistent, basic dispositions inherent in people, which underlie and modulate much of their behavior (McCall, in Goldsmith et al., 1987). Rothbart defines temperament as "relatively stable, primarily biologically based individual differences in reactivity and self-regulation" (Rothbart in Goldsmith et al., 1987, p. 510). *Reactivity* means excitability or arousability. *Self-regulation* means inhibition (Rothbart, 1988). So temperament involves differences in excitability and inhibition. Goldsmith identifies temperament as "individual differences in the probability of experiencing and expressing the primary emotions and arousal" (Goldsmith et al., 1987, p. 510).

Temperament is comprised primarily of inherited biological factors, so basic dispositions comprising temperament are present

Personality—the sum total of the physical, mental, social, and emotional characteristics of an individual

Temperament—the relatively consistent, basic dispositions inherent in people that underlie and modulate much of their behavior

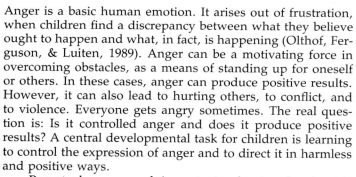

PARENTING ISSUES

When Your Child is Angry

Anger is a basic human emotion. It arises out of frustration, when children find a discrepancy between what they believe ought to happen and what, in fact, is happening (Olthof, Ferguson, & Luiten, 1989). Anger can be a motivating force in overcoming obstacles, as a means of standing up for oneself or others. In these cases, anger can produce positive results. However, it can also lead to hurting others, to conflict, and to violence. Everyone gets angry sometimes. The real question is: Is it controlled anger and does it produce positive results? A central developmental task for children is learning to control the expression of anger and to direct it in harmless and positive ways.

Parents have several important roles to play in this regard.

1. They can represent positive models for their children; that is, they can show restraint in their own expressions of anger, so that children learn acceptable, helpful means of expression. Children who grow up in a house where there is a lot of anger are more likely to learn negative means of expression themselves (Cummings, 1987).

2. Parents can help children control anger by letting them know that certain expressions of anger such as temper tantrums, hitting, biting, or screaming are not acceptable. Children learn to control their emotions by parents' helping them to exercise control: "I know you're angry, but I can't let you bite your brother. You'll have to sit in the chair for awhile."

3. Parents can help children to dissipate anger through physical activity, verbalization, and directed play. "Go out and play in the yard until you're not angry." "Let's talk about why you're mad." "Maybe if we played with the puppets it would help you with your anger." (Then have the child use various puppets that represent the angry one and the one the child is expressing anger toward.)

4. Parents can tell children they recognize their being angry, and that anger feelings are normal, but that children have to learn to control and redirect their reactions to their feelings. Spock and Rothenberg (1985) wrote:

> It helps children to realize that their parents know they have angry feelings, and that their parents are not enraged at them or alienated from them on account of them. This realization helps them get over their anger and keeps them from feeling too guilty or frightened because of it (p. 402).

5. If anger becomes excessive and persistent, parents need to get at the root causes of the anger and to correct situations that cause it, if possible. If parents don't seem to make progress themselves, it is helpful if they will get counseling for themselves and their child.

early in life (Goldsmith, 1983). However, as development proceeds, the *expression* of temperament becomes increasingly influenced by environmental factors (Goldsmith & Campos, 1990). (Hereditary factors in personality and temperament were discussed in Chapter 3.) A child's activity level, for example, is influenced by heredity, but the environment either permits or inhibits such a level of activity.

Components and Patterns of Temperament

Buss and Plomin (1984) specify three traits as constituting temperament. The first is *emotionality*, which is the intensity of emotional reactions. This dimension varies from an almost stoic lack of reaction to very intense, agitated reactions (Mangelsdorf, Gunnar, Kestenbaum, Lang, & Andreas, 1990). The second trait is *activity*, which has tempo and vigor as its two major components. Individuals vary from lethargy to almost mania. The third trait is *sociability*, which is the preference for being with others rather than being alone.

In the New York Longitudinal Study of 133 children discussed in Chapter 3, Thomas and Chess (1977) followed their subjects from infancy into early adulthood and identified these nine components of temperament:

1. Rhythmicity—the regularity of biological cycles of eating, sleeping, and toileting
2. Activity level—energy level as expressed by the degree of movement
3. Approach or withdrawal from new stimuli—how a person reacts to new stimuli
4. Adaptability—ability to adjust to change
5. Sensory threshold—sensitivity to sensory stimuli
6. Predominant quality of mood—whether a person is predominantly happy or unhappy
7. Intensity of mood expression—the degree to which a person responds
8. Distractibility—how easily an added stimulus can capture a person's attention
9. Persistency and attention span—how long a person focuses on one activity and pursues it.

The researchers also grouped the children they studied into three categories, or temperament patterns: the *easy child*, the *difficult child*, and the *slow-to-warm-up child* (Chess & Thomas, 1986). Table 8.2 shows the temperament characteristics of each of these categories of children. Some of the components of temperament would not be identified with any one cluster. These are indicated by the dashes in some sections of the table.

TABLE 8.2 Three Temperament Patterns

Component of Temperament	Easy Child	Difficult Child	Slow-to-Warm-Up Child
Rhythmicity	Regular eating, sleeping, toileting schedules	Irregular schedules	—
Activity level	—	High activity level	Low activity level
Approach or withdrawal	Easily approaches new situations, people	Suspicion of new situations, strangers	Mildly negative initial response to new stimuli
Adaptability	Adjusts easily to new routines, circumstances. Accepts most frustrations without fuss	Adjusts slowly. Temper tantrums when frustrated	Gradually likes new after unpressured repeated exposure
Sensory threshold	—	—	—
Quality of mood	Positive moods	Negative moods	—
Intensity of mood expression	Mild to moderate intensity of mood	High mood intensity. Loud laughter, crying	Low intensity of mood
Distractibility	—	—	—
Persistency, attention span	—	—	—

Adapted from "Genesis and Evolution of Behavioral Disorder: From Infancy to Early Adult Life" by A. Thomas and S. Chess, 1984, *American Journal of Orthopsychiatry, 141,* pp. 1–9.

FOCUS

The Hyperactive Child

Hyperactivity, known as **attention deficit disorder** (ADD), appears in about 3% of elementary school children (American Psychiatric Association, 1987). Boys are 10 times more likely to have the problem than girls (Moffitt, 1990). Those afflicted have 3 major symptoms: *excessive activity*, *inattentiveness*, and *impulsivity*. ADD children engage in almost continuous talking, fidgeting, climbing, crawling, or running. They have difficulty remaining seated in the classroom or playing quietly, and often engage in physically dangerous activities. They have difficulty in sustaining attention, do not seem to listen to what is being said, are easily distracted, shift from one uncompleted activity to another, have difficulty following through on instructions, and often lose clothes, school supplies, or notes from school. They have a low frustration tolerance, difficulty in taking turns, and poor peer adjustments; they blurt out answers to questions before they have been completed; and interrupt or intrude on others, butting into conversations and groups (Clark et al., 1988; Landau & Milich, 1988). Age of onset must be before age 7 to differentiate it from disorders that might arise because of stress. The American Psychiatric Association (1987) stipulates a duration of at least one year to distinguish it from disorders due to stress.

There are many possible causes: *Genetic, neurological, biochemical,* or *environmental factors* are all possibilities. Birth injury, prenatal exposure to teratogens such as alcohol or other drugs, prematurity, infections that affect the brain, lead poisoning, vitamin deficiencies, food allergies, or reactions to food additives and colorings have all been suspected. A delay in maturation of the central nervous system seems likely in some cases because some children outgrow the problem (Connors, 1980; Hadley, 1984; Hartsough & Lambert, 1985; Jacobovitz & Sroufe, 1987; Ross & Ross, 1982; and Streissguth et al., 1984).

It's hard to treat the problem when the cause is not certain. In general, there are various treatment methods.

1. *Ritalin.* This drug is a stimulant that has a reversal effect on hyperactive children. Its results are remarkable for some children (Sprague & Ullman, 1981; Whalen, Henker, Castro, & Granger, 1987). Sometimes, however, the drug produces adverse side effects such as appetite loss, growth retardation, sleeping difficulties, and lethargy in the classroom (Nemeth, 1990). The drug should never be used as a one-step solution; it should always be given in conjunction with other treatment programs.

2. *Diet management.* If nutritional deficiencies, food allergies, food additives, or colorings are suspected, these are eliminated through diet control. Diets free of additives and food colorings help only a small number of hyperactive children (Ross & Ross, 1982).

3. *Psychotherapy* for families and children. This is used to help parents and siblings deal with their resentment and anger. *Behavior-modification techniques* are used as teaching devices to help hyperactive children gain some control over their behavior (Ross & Ross, 1982). Parents need training in how to manage the hyperactive child (Dubey, O'Leary, & Kaufman, 1983). Parents can also receive help from a nationwide support group called Children With Attention Deficit Disorders (C.H.A.D.D.).

4. *Educational planning.* This is needed to offer ADD children the optimum educational environment. Teachers need to be taught how *not* to make the problem worse. The best teachers are flexible in allowing minor disruptions and some physical activity in the classroom, but still provide some structure and guidance. Teachers can help children break up work into small, manageable units (Nemeth, 1990) and to channel excess activity into appropriate instrumental motor and attention responses (Zentall & Meyer, 1987).

DEVELOPMENT OF SELF, AUTONOMY, SELF-CONCEPT, AND SELF-ESTEEM

Self-Awareness

The development of self-awareness means that children begin to understand their separateness from others and other things. In the first few months of life, babies discover their arms and hands appearing and disappearing.

They see them move and are fascinated by what they see. Imagine coming into the world and never having seen an arm and hand before! At this time, however, infants are not aware that the hand is part of them. It comes in and out of view by accident. Sometime later, they also discover feet and toes. But they still don't associate them with themselves.

The sense of self emerges gradually. At about 1 year of age, infants become aware that other children are distinct persons they can see, hear, and touch, and who may take

Babies start reaching toward their mirror image at about 4 months of age.

a toy. At about 18 months of age, infants are able to recognize their own reflection in a mirror and to develop a sense of *me* and *mine*. As they become aware of themselves, they begin to develop a sense of possessiveness: "my hair," "my chair," "my bed," as distinct from "mama's hair," "mama's chair," or "daddy's bed." Feelings of jealousy, anger, or guilt are possible as a result of increased self-awareness and the need to protect the self from other selves (Campos et al., 1983). This new awareness of others also allows the development of affection toward them and rebellion against them.

Autonomy

Erikson (1950, 1959) said that the chief psychosocial task between 1 and 2 years of age is the development of autonomy. As the self emerges, children also want some degree of independence: to feed themselves, to explore the world, to do what they want to do without being too restricted by care givers. If they aren't permitted to do some things (within reasonable limits), they develop a sense of shame and doubt about their abilities. According to Freud, part of the conflict over autonomy centers around toilet training. Parents who are too strict during this anal stage of development create shame and doubt. Children's increasing mobility, however, gets them in trouble, or can endanger lives, so reasonable controls are necessary to keep them safe and to help them manage their actions and emotions.

Separation-Individuation

In a previous section, we discussed Margaret Mahler's concept of the period of *symbiosis*, during which infants develop a strong dependency on the mother to such an extent that there is some fusing of personalities. However, at about 5 months of age, lasting until about age 3, Mahler says a new period begins: a period of **separation-individuation**, during which infants gradually develop a self apart from the mother (Mahler, Pine, & Bergman, 1975). Infants are still dependent on their mothers. But as they gradually develop greater physical and psychological separation, they need to achieve a balance in their dependent–independent conflict while developing a sense of self. They want to be independent, yet they are frightened of too great a separation. The development of autonomy is vital to their later development as an independent adult. However, too much autonomy may produce an inconsiderate, selfish person who has no regard for the rights and needs of others, or an insecure person with excessive fears, anxieties, and doubts about self.

Separation-individuation—a period during which the infant gradually develops a self apart from the mother

Self-Definition and Self-Concept

As children begin to develop real awareness, they also begin to define themselves, to develop a concept of self, to develop an identity (Spencer & Markstrom-Adams, 1990). For a full discussion of children from minority groups see *Child Development* (April, 1990) 61, Number 2. *By 3 years of age, personal characteristics are defined in childlike terms, and are usually positive and exaggerated.* "I'm bigger, strong, the fastest runner; can jump high, can skip, can sing pretty songs." Two researchers found that even when preschool children have just scored low on a game, they predicted they would do very well the next time (Stipek & Hoffman, 1980). Other research indicates that preschool children usually have a very high opinion of their physical and intellectual abilities (Harter & Pike, 1984; Stipek & MacIver, 1989).

By the middle elementary grades, most children begin to develop a more realistic concept of self and admit that they are not as capable in some areas as in others (Butler, 1990). "I'm a good reader, but I don't like arithmetic"; "I'm good in baseball, but I can't run" (Harter, 1983). Markus and Nurius (1984) emphasize that as children enter middle childhood, they begin to develop truer self-understanding; to become aware of their

PARENTING ISSUES

Freedom Versus Control

One of the questions that parents face, at all stages of their children's development, is how much autonomy and freedom to allow and still ensure the safety, well-being, and socialization of their children. I once heard a psychiatrist say in a speech to a group that he lived at the top of a steep cliff, but that he wouldn't think of fencing in his yard, because his 2-year-old son had to learn to avoid the danger. Most of us would not be willing to go this far in allowing autonomy and in teaching responsibility. How controlling or permissive to be is one of the difficult dilemmas of parenting (Remley, 1988).

However, the degree of control is not the only important factor to consider. Another one is the attitude of parents toward their children, whether loving or hostile. In our culture, children seem to thrive best in a loving and democratic environment, where there are rules of conduct and social restrictions on behavior, but where the children are also held in high esteem, and are encouraged to explore, to try new things, and to do things themselves (Denham, Renwick, & Holt, 1991). As they get older, they are given opportunities to participate in decision making. Children in this environment tend to be independent, self-confident, assertive, outgoing, and active. Children who are loved in a dominating way tend to be dependent, polite, submissive, and obedient, but lack initiative and self-confidence. Children whose par-

Parents often face the task of how much autonomy and freedom to allow their children.

ents are overly permissive and hostile toward them tend to be rebellious, disobedient, angry, aggressive, and delinquent. Children reared by hostile but controlling parents tend to be sullen and socially withdrawn. They are not allowed to express their anger outwardly, so it may erupt sometimes in violence, or turn inward, resulting in self-recrimination (Remley, 1988).

---

achieved characteristics and their own values, norms, and goals; and to develop standards for their own behavior (Eder, 1990). They begin to be more specific and realistic about themselves and to realize that they do sometimes try to fool themselves (Eder, 1989).

There are, however, children who are highly competent, but who fail to acquire positive perceptions of their abilities. Phillips (1987) found that in these cases, children's self-perceptions of competence are influenced more by their parents' negative appraisals than by objective evidence of their achievements. There are also children with only average abilities who have an inflated perception of themselves because of exaggerated views instilled by parents.

Self-Reference and Self-Efficacy

Self-reference has to do with ourselves, our estimates of our abilities, and how capable

and effective we are in dealing with others and the world (Ruble & Flett, 1988). Estimates of our effectiveness have been termed **self-efficacy.** Self-efficacy is not so much our actual skill and effectiveness in dealing with situations and with others. Rather, it is our *perceptions* of these things.

Perceptions of self-efficacy are important because they influence children's relationships, their willingness to undertake difficult tasks, and their feelings about themselves: their self-worth and competence (Schunk, 1984).

Harter (1982) developed a *Perceived Competence Scale for Children.* The scale measures competence in four areas:

- General self-worth—being happy with self the way I am
- Social skills—having friends, being liked
- Cognitive skills—being good at schoolwork, having a good memory
- Physical skills—being able to do well in sports

Self-reference— estimates of our abilities and of how effectively we deal with others and the world

Self-efficacy—our perceptions of our actual skill and personal effectiveness

Note that this scale measures perceived competence and does not represent others' judgments of the child. Some children have very high opinions of their competence, regardless of others' opinions to the contrary. The important consideration is how they perceive themselves.

Bandura (1986) suggests that children's judgment of personal efficacy stems from four main causes:

First, self-efficacy depends upon personal accomplishments and children's judgments about these accomplishments. Children who do well in school or in sports are more likely to feel self-efficacious than those who fail. Bandura calls this sense of self-efficacy *enactive* because it is based on the outcome of actions. Erikson has said that the chief psychosocial task during the 3- to 5-year-old period is *initiative versus guilt.* Children seek to become more assertive and to pursue a variety of activities, yet in ways that bring praise rather than reprimand. If they fail, their efforts result in criticism or self-blame, so they feel guilty. Similarly, the chief psychosocial task during the school years is *industry versus inferiority.* Children strive for competence and proficiency. Failure results in feelings of inferiority.

Second, self-efficacy is derived partly from children's comparison of themselves with others. Ten-year-olds may compare their skill in a game with the skills of others. If they discover they do very well, they feel very good about themselves. Bandura calls this a *vicarious* source of self-efficacy (based on comparison of personal performance with that of others).

Third, self-efficacy is also influenced by persuasion. "You can do it, you're capable." Positive persuasion increases self-efficacy, whereas negative persuasion—"don't try it"—decreases self-efficacy. Bandura calls this the *persuasory* source of self-efficacy.

The fourth source of influence on judgments of self-efficacy is the person's arousal level: the level of physiological and emotional arousal. High arousal can affect judgments—either positively or negatively. For example, if a child is very aroused and excited before being in a school play, this emotional state may lead to a superior performance if it motivates effort, or to a poor performance if nervousness prevents the child from doing his or her best. Bandura calls this an *emotional* source of self-efficacy.

Self-Esteem

Self-esteem is closely related to self-concept and self-efficacy. When children perceive

their worth, their abilities, their accomplishments, do they view themselves positively or negatively? Everyone needs to feel loved, liked, accepted, valued, capable, and competent. How children feel about themselves is their self-esteem (Damon, 1983). It is their liking and respect for themselves.

There are four primary sources of self-esteem: children's emotional relationships with parents, their social competence with peers, their intellectual prowess at school, and the attitudes of society and community toward them. Children who are *loved and wanted,* whose parents are warm, supportive, concerned, interested, and active in their guidance, tend to develop positive self-esteem (Abraham & Christopherson, 1984; Felson & Zielinski, 1989). As children develop, *social competence* becomes an increasing component of self-esteem (Waters & Sroufe, 1983). *School success* is also related to high self-esteem (Entwisle, Alexander, Pallas, & Cadigan 1987). It's hard to feel good about oneself while doing poorly in school (Coopersmith & Gilberts, 1982). And finally, *the attitudes of society* influence self-esteem. Children of some minority groups have trouble in developing a positive self-image if they feel that others look down on them because of their racial or ethnic origin (Rotheram-Borus, 1990a,b). However, society's attitudes are not always enough to produce low self-esteem. Children brought up in families that teach pride in their race or background, where they develop a strong ethnic identity and social pride, are able to maintain high self-esteem despite some of the prejudices they encounter from others.

A number of self-esteem inventories have been developed to evaluate self-esteem of school-age children (Chiu, 1988). Some of these inventories are self-rating. The *Coopersmith Self-Esteem Inventories* (CSEI) contain short statements such as "I'm a lot of fun to be with" to which children respond positively or negatively (Coopersmith, 1981). The *Culture-Free Self-Esteem Inventories (SEI) for Children and Adults* is a Canadian instrument containing short statements such as "I often feel ashamed of myself." Children are to answer "yes" or "no" (Battle, 1981). The *Piers-Harris Children's Self-Concept Scale (CSCS)* is for children in grades 4–12 and contains statements such as "I can be trusted" to which respondents are to check "yes" or "no" (Piers, 1984).

Other self-esteem scales are for teachers to rate pupils. The *Behavior Academic Self-Esteem (BASE)* scale is designed to measure the academic self-esteem of children in preschool through the eighth grade. It consists

Self-esteem—our perception of our worth, abilities, and accomplishments; our view of ourselves, negative or positive

of 16 statements such as "This child adapts easily to changes in procedures." Teachers respond on a 5-point scale from *never* to *always* (Coopersmith & Gilberts, 1982). Similarly, the *Self-Esteem Rating Scale for Children (SERSC)* (Chiu, 1987) is for use with children in kindergarten through ninth grade. It consists of 12 statements such as "Hesitates to speak in class." Teachers evaluate these items for each child on a 5-point scale ranging from *never* to *always*.

Together, these instruments can be valuable diagnostic tools when evaluation of self-esteem of children is of major concern.

Conclusions

Self-definition, self-concept, self-reference, self-efficacy, and self-esteem are all similar concepts. Self-definition and self-concept are our self-perceived identity. Self-reference and self-efficacy are our estimates and perceptions of our self-worth, abilities, and accomplishments. Self-esteem is our overall perception of our self-worth and abilities. How children feel about themselves is crucial to their mental health, and to their later relationships and successes in life.

SUMMARY

1. Attachment is the feeling that binds a parent and child together. The formation of attachment is vitally important to children's total development.

2. Children can develop close attachments to more than one person. Attachments to specific persons do not develop until about 6 or 7 months of age, after infants can distinguish among different human beings. Specific attachments are at their maximum from 12 to 18 months of age.

3. Nonattached children are very unemotional and distant; insecurely attached children are overly dependent.

4. Separation anxiety varies with individual children, depending on their age and the length of the separation. The effects of long-term separation can be serious.

5. Children show various forms of reunion behavior. Some children are very dependent; others are angry; others are emotionally cold.

6. Fear of strangers begins at about 6 or 7 months of age and increases until about 2 years, after which it declines.

7. Parents need to let the child develop attachment to baby-sitters or substitute care givers before leaving the child with them alone. Much depends upon the quality of the substitute care. Similarly, parents need to select nursery schools carefully and to introduce the child to them gradually.

8. Erickson has said that the basic psychosocial task of infancy is the development of trust. Mahler says that infants need to establish a symbiotic relationship with their mother.

9. Development of trust and security is aided by the following: regular and adequate feedings, sufficient sucking, and cuddling and physical contact. Their most important requirement is for parents to show children their love.

10. Children learn to express affection by having affection shown them.

11. There are a number of causes of distrust and insecurity: parental deprivation, tension in the home, exposure to frightening experiences, child abuse, criticism, overprotection, and overindulgence.

12. There are four basic components of emotions: (1) stimuli, (2) feelings, (3) physiological arousal, and (4) behavioral response.

13. Emotions play a number of important functions in our lives: they play an adaptive function, are a means of communication, are important in social relationships, are powerful motivators, and are a source of pleasure or of pain.

14. Ekman and colleagues found six basic emotions: happiness, sadness, anger, surprise, disgust, and fear. Emotions develop according to a biological timetable. Some psychologists say that all emotions are present at birth.

15. Emotional responses have a biological basis and are partly learned.

16. Temperament refers to relatively consistent, basic dispositions inherent in people, which underlie and modulate much of their behavior. Temperament is primarily inherited, so basic dispositions are present early in life; expression of temperament is progressively affected by environment.

17. Different researchers have identified different components of temperament: emotionality, activity level, sociability, rhythmicity, approach or withdrawal from new stimuli, adaptability, sensory threshold, quality of mood, intensity of mood expression, distractibility, and persistency and attention span. Some children are easy to take care of, others difficult, others in between, depending upon temperament.

18. Hyperactive children, those with attention deficit disorder (ADD) have 3 major symptoms: excessive activity, inattentiveness, and impulsivity.

19. The development of self-awareness means that children begin to understand their separateness from others and other things. The sense of self emerges gradually.

20. Erikson said that the chief psychosocial task between 1 and 2 years of age is the development of autonomy. One of the parenting tasks is to decide how much freedom to allow and how much control to exercise.

21. Mahler says that after 5 months and until age 3, children go through a period of separation-individuation during which they develop a self apart from the mother.

22. Children also begin to develop real awareness and definition of the self and a self-concept. Preschoolers describe themselves in exaggerated and positive terms. By the middle elementary grades, most children begin to develop a more realistic concept of self. Children's self-perceptions are influenced greatly by their parents' appraisals.

23. Self-reference has to do with our estimates of our abilities; self-efficacy is our perceptions of our effectiveness in dealing with situations and with others.

24. Harter developed a *Perceived Competence Scale for Children* that measures competence in four areas: general self-worth, social skills, cognitive skills, and physical skills.

25. Bandura says that self-efficacy stems from four main causes: Personal accomplishments and perceptions of them; comparison of self with others; persuasion by others; and arousal level.

26. Self-esteem is how children view themselves: positively or negatively. There are four primary sources of children's self-esteem: relationships with parents, social competence, intellectual prowess at school, and the attitudes of society and community toward them.

27. A number of self-esteem inventories have been developed to evelute self-esteem of school-age children.

KEY TERMS

Attachment   *p. 174*
Attention deficit disorder   *p. 187*
Autistic phase   *p. 180*
Epinephrine   *p. 183*
Insecurely attached   *p. 176*
Nonattached children   *p. 176*
Personality   *p. 185*

Self-efficacy   *p. 189*
Self-esteem   *p. 190*
Self-reference   *p. 189*
Separation-individuation   *p. 188*
Symbiosis   *p. 180*
Temperament   *p. 185*

DISCUSSION QUESTIONS

1. Describe the attachment behavior of a child you know. Does this child manifest separation anxiety? What suggestions do you have for minimizing separation anxiety?

2. Do you know a child who had to go to the hospital? Describe the experience. How did it affect the child emotionally?

3. Describe the experience of a child you know who went to nursery school or kindergarten for the first time.

4. How can separation anxiety be minimized when employing a baby-sitter?

5. Will family arguments cause children to become distrustful and insecure? Explain.

6. Have you ever known a child who had been physically abused? Describe. What were the effects? Would you report parents whom you knew were abusing their child? Why? Why not?

7. Can you experience emotion without physiological arousal? Explain.

8. Are emotions present from birth, or are they developed? Explain.

9. What might parents do when their child has temper tantrums?

10. Psychologists feel that temperament is inherited. How do you feel about that statement? Compare your temperament now with your temperament when you were younger.

11. Have you ever known a child who was difficult to care for? Have you ever

known a child who was easy to care for? Can two children in the same family be this different?

12. Have you ever known a child who was hyperactive? Describe. What were the causes? What did the parents do?

13. What might happen if children are not allowed to develop autonomy when young? Effects depend not only upon the degree of control but whether parents are loving or hostile. Explain.

14. What are the most important factors in the development of self-esteem?

15. What helps the most in helping children to develop self-efficacy?

SUGGESTED READINGS

Bowlby, J. (1982). *Attachment and loss* (Vol. 1). New York: Basic Books. Mother–infant interaction and attachment.

Collins, W. A. (Ed.). (1984). *Development during middle childhood: The years from 6 to 12.* Washington, DC: National Academy Press. All aspects of development.

Finkelhor, D. et al. (Eds.). (1986). *A sourcebook on child sexual abuse.* Beverly Hills, CA: Sage. A guide for parents and leaders of children.

Izard, C. E. (1982). *Measuring emotion in infants and children.* New York: Cambridge University Press. Classic study on how to assess emotions of infants and children.

Johnson, J. H. (1986). *Life events as stressors in childhood and abolescence.* Beverly Hills, CA: Sage. Effects of major changes in the lives of children and adolescents.

Kellerman, J. (1981). *Helping the fearful child: A parents' guide.* New York: Warner Books.

Sroufe, L. A., & Fleeson, J. (1986). Attachment and the construction of relationships. In W. Hartup and Z. Rubin (Eds.), *Relationships and development.* Hillsdale, NJ: Erlbaum. Attachment theory and applications.

Social Development

SOCIOCULTURAL INFLUENCES

Children do not develop in a vacuum. They develop in the context of their family, neighborhood, community, country, and world. In this context, children are influenced by parents, siblings, other relatives, friends and peers; other adults with whom they come in contact; and by the school, the church, and the groups of which they are a part. They are influenced by the media: newspapers, magazines, radio, and TV. They are influenced by community and national leaders, by the culture in which they are growing up, and even by things going on in the world. They are partly a product of social influences.

Bronfenbrenner (1977, 1979, 1987) developed an ecological model for understanding social influences. As can be seen in Figure 9.1, social influences are seen as a series of systems extending beyond the child. The child is at the center of the model. The most immediate influences are within the **microsystem** and include those with which the child has immediate contact. The **mesosystem** involves the reciprocal relationships among microsystem settings. For example, what happens at home influences what happens at school and vice versa. Thus, the child's social development is understood best when the influences from many sources are considered, and in relation to one another.

The **exosystem** includes those settings in which the child usually does not have an active role as a participant, but that influence the child indirectly through their effects on the microsystem. For example, what happens to the parents at work influences them and they in turn influence their child's development. Also, community organizations provide family support that affects child rearing.

The **macrosystem** includes the ideologies, values, attitudes, laws, mores, and customs of a particular culture. Cultures may differ among countries or among racial, ethnic, or socioeconomic groups. There are also differences within each group (Gutierrez, Sameroff, & Carrer, 1988). In Sweden, for example, it is against the law for parents to hit children, yet the practice is condoned by some groups in the United States. Middle-class parents in this country often have goals and philosophies of child rearing different from those in low socioeconomic status groups (Gutierrez & Sameroff, 1990; Harrison, Wilson, Pine, Chan, & Buriel, 1990; McLoyd, 1990; Slaughter-Defoe, Nakagawa, Takanishi, & Johnson, 1990). Rural families may have parenting values different from those of urban families (Coleman, Ganong, Clark, & Madsen, 1989). All such value-related and setting-related elements have different effects on children. In talking about social development, therefore, we have to discuss issues and concerns in the contexts in which children are growing up.

Microsystem—the child's immediate contacts

Mesosystem—social influences involving reciprocal relationships

Exosystem—social settings in which the child usually is not an active participant, but that influence the child indirectly through their effects on the microsystem

Macrosystem—influences of a particular culture

Numerous sociocultural influences play a part in children's development

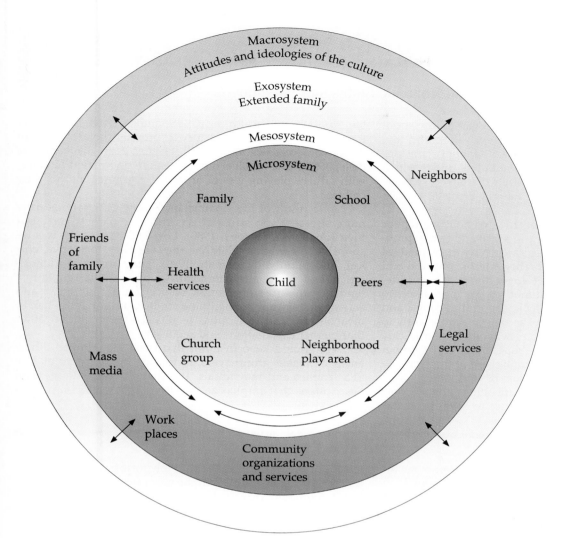

FIGURE 9.1 Bronfenbrenner's ecological model for understanding social influences.

Data from U. Bronfenbrenner (1979), "Contexts of Child Rearing: Problems and Prospects." *American Psychologist* 34, 844–850.

THE FAMILY AND SOCIALIZATION*

The Family's Role

In the discussion here, a **family** may be defined as "any group of persons united by the ties of marriage, blood, or adoption or any sexually expressive relationship, in which (1) the people are committed to one another in an intimate, interpersonal relationship, (2) the members see their identity as importantly attached to the group, and (3) the group has an identity of its own" (Rice, 1990, p. 4).

The following are some of the different types of families.

*Part of the material in this section is excerpted from the author's book *Intimate Relationships, Marriages, and Families* (1990). Used by permission of the publisher, Mayfield Publishing Co.

A **single-parent family** consists of a parent (who may or may not have been married) and one or more children (McLanahan, Wedemeyer, & Adelberg, 1981).

A **nuclear family** consists of a father, mother, and their children. This type of family as a proportion of all families has been declining in recent years (White & Tsui, 1986).

The **extended family** consists of one person, a possible mate, any children they might have, and other relatives who live with them in their household. More broadly, the extended family can include relatives living in close proximity to or those who are in frequent contact with a household's members.

The **blended or reconstituted family** is formed when a widowed or divorced person, with or without children, remarries another person who may or may not have been married before and who may or may not have children (Dowling, 1983). If either the remar-

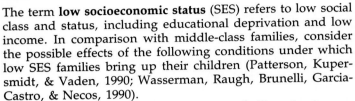

PARENTING ISSUES

Low Socioeconomic Status and Parenting

The term **low socioeconomic status** (SES) refers to low social class and status, including educational deprivation and low income. In comparison with middle-class families, consider the possible effects of the following conditions under which low SES families bring up their children (Patterson, Kupersmidt, & Vaden, 1990; Wasserman, Raugh, Brunelli, Garcia-Castro, & Necos, 1990).

Low income means inadequate, crowded housing in poor neighborhoods, where crime rates and social and family problems are greater. Low SES families often have poor medical care, higher mortality rates, and higher rates of physical and mental illnesses. The incidence of accidental death, suicide, and homicide is higher. Expectant mothers are more likely to be young and unmarried, to use alcohol and other drugs, and to receive inadequate prenatal care; so they are more likely to deliver premature and difficult babies who are harder to care for and love. One consequence is that child abuse is higher (Young & Gately, 1988). Low SES families are at the mercy of life's unpredictable events: sickness, loss of work, injury, legal problems, and school and family difficulties. Low income means less likelihood of having insurance to cover property,

life, disability, or health. Low SES families strive for security to protect themselves, and just to provide themselves with the basic necessities of life (Dill, Field, Martin, Beukemia, & Belle, 1980). The families more often are one-parent families, with fathers playing less of an active role in caring for their children.

As a result of life circumstances, low SES parents have more stresses, and stress affects the way parents carry out their functions (Maccoby, 1980). Low SES parents are less responsive toward their children; they are more restrictive, critical, and punitive (Zussman, 1980). They are more authoritarian and issue more imperatives and absolutes, with a tendency to stress obedience, respect for all authority, and staying out of trouble. Discipline tends to be impulsive, harsh, inconsistent, and to emphasize physical punishment rather than verbal explanations and requests.

We should keep in mind that these class-linked differences represent group averages that do not apply to all low SES families and individuals. But they are accurate, general descriptions that emphasize the effects of low SES on parenting behavior.

---

ried husband or wife has children from the former marriage, a **stepfamily** is formed.

A **binuclear family** is an original family divided into two by divorce. It consists of two nuclear families, the maternal nuclear family headed by the mother, and the paternal family headed by the father. The families include whatever children have been in the original family. Each new family may be headed by a single parent or by two parents if former spouses remarry (Ahrons & Rodgers, 1987).

A **communal family** consists of a group of people who live together and share various aspects of their lives. They can be considered a family if the group falls within the preceding general definition. Some communal groups are not families in this sense.

A **homosexual family** consists of adults of the same sex who live together, with their children, and who share sexual expression and commitment.

A **cohabiting family** consists of two people of the opposite sex who live together, with or without children, and who share sexual expression and commitment to their relationship without formal legal marriage.

When talking about the family, then, we need to specify which type we are referring

to. With such a wide variety of family forms, we can no longer assume that the word *family* is synonymous with nuclear family. When families are so different in structure and composition, the influence of different family members is variable. Grandparents or great-grandparents may have considerable influence on children in an extended family, but very little in some nuclear families (Pearson, Hunter, Ensminger, & Kellam, 1990; Tolson & Wilson, 1990). Or, a noncustodial father may have a limited role in socializing his children in a single-parent family where the children are living with the mother. *Total influence varies with family forms* (Stevens, 1988).

Overall, however, the family is the principal transmitter of knowledge, values, attitudes, roles, and habits that one generation passes on to the next (Thornton, Chatters, Taylor, & Allen, 1990). Through word and example the family shapes children's personality and instills modes of thought and ways of acting that become habitual (Kochanska, 1990). Peterson and Rollins (1987) refer to this process as **generational transmission**.

Socialization is the process by which persons learn the ways of society or social groups so that they can function within it or them (Kalmuss & Seltzer, 1989). A dictionary

Generational transmission—transmitting of knowledge, values, attitudes, roles, and habits from one generation to the next

Socialization—the process by which persons learn the ways of society or social groups so they can function within them

says it is "to make fit for life in companionship with others." Children are taught the ways and values of their society through contact with already socialized individuals, initially the family (Rice, 1990).

The process takes place partly through *formal instruction* that parents provide their children and partly by the efforts of parents to control children through *rewards and punishments*. Learning also takes place through *reciprocal parent–child interaction* as each influences and modifies the behavior of the other in an intense social process (Stryker, 1980). Learning also occurs through *observational modeling*, as children observe, imitate, and model the behavior that they find around them (Bandura, 1976). It is not only what parents say that is important, but it is also what children actually perceive parents to believe and do that most influences them.

Not all children are influenced to the same degree by their families. The degree of parental influence depends partly on the frequency, duration, intensity, and priority of social contacts that parents have with their children. Parents who are emotionally close to their children, in loving relationships, for long periods of time, exert more influence than do those not so close and who relate to their children less frequently (Russell & Russell, 1987).

Another factor in determining the influence of the family is the difference in individual children (Chess, 1984). Not all children react in the same way to the same family environment, because of differences in heredity, temperament, cognitive perception, developmental characteristics, and maturational levels. Because A happens does not mean that B will inevitably result. When children are brought up in an unhappy, conflicting family, it is more difficult for them to establish happy marriages themselves (Fine & Hovestadt, 1984). However, some do. Not all children are influenced by their families to the same degree, and not all react the same way to the same environment.

Patterns of Parenting

Just as there are differences in families, there are also various patterns of parenting (McNally, Eisenberg, & Harris, 1991). These patterns partly reflect differences in parental values (Luster, Rhoades, & Haas, 1989). For example, some parents value conformity in children; others value self-direction (Mills & Rubin, 1990). Diana Baumrind (1971, 1978, 1980) examined the way that parenting styles affected the social characteristics of preschool children from 300 families. Baumrind was particularly concerned with the patterns of control that parents used, and identified three general styles of parenting: authoritarian, permissive, and authoritative.

AUTHORITARIAN.   Authoritarian parents emphasize obedience, using force to curb children's self-will, keeping children subordinate, restricting autonomy, and discouraging verbal give and take (Kochanska, Kuczynski, & Radke-Yarrow, 1989). This type of parenting tended to produce withdrawn, fearful children who exhibited little or no independence and were generally irritable, unassertive, and moody.

PERMISSIVE.   Permissive parents free children from restraint, accept their impulses and actions without trying to shape their behavior. Some of these parents are protective and moderately loving, but others let children do what they want as a way of avoiding responsibility for them. These children tend to be rebellious, self-indulgent, aggressive, impulsive, and socially inept.

AUTHORITATIVE.   Authoritative parents seek to direct their children's activities in a rational manner, encouraging discussion and also exerting firm control when children disobey, but without being overly restrictive. These parents recognize children's individual needs and interests, but set standards of conduct (Kochanska et al., 1989). These children are the best adjusted of the three groups; they are the most self-reliant, self-controlled, self-confident, and socially competent.

On the basis of her research, Baumrind concluded that *authoritative parenting, which is firm but reasonable,* and *which is warm, nurturing, and loving, works best in the socialization of children* (Donovan, Leavitt, & Walsh, 1990).

Research by Schaefer (1959) emphasized both the pattern of control—the autonomy versus control dimension—and the degree of affection—the love versus hostility dimension (Amato, 1990). These dimensions interact to form four patterns: *love–autonomy, love–control, hostility–autonomy,* and *hostility–control*. Of course, there are degrees within each pattern. The four dimensions are shown in Figure 9.2. The secret of successful parenting seems to be to show the maximum amount of love (children are never spoiled by love) and the right balance between autonomy and control. Autonomy without any control is permissiveness and overindulgence. Hostility without any control results

PARENTING ISSUES

Parental Control Techniques

Smith (1988) has given a helpful summary of seven control techniques that are used by parents.

- *Power-assertive discipline*—physical punishment, deprivation, and threats. Harsh physical punishment especially has been associated with physical aggression in children who model their parent's behavior (Dishion, 1990; Hart, Ladd, & Burleson, 1990; Kandel, 1990).
- *Command*—imperative statements not accompanied by punishment or overt threat of punishment. The success of this technique depends upon the child's acceptance of parental authority.
- *Self-oriented induction*—reasoning in pointing out gains or costs children might experience as a result of their behavior. This technique produces positive effects on children.
- *Other-oriented induction*—reasoning in pointing out religious or ethical principles, altruism, or personal obligations and reasons for children to change their behavior. This technique helps in internalizing values and acceptable behavior.
- *Love withdrawal*—temporary coldness or rejection to gain compliance. This method may threaten children's security.
- *Advice*—suggesting how children might accomplish what is desired by the parent. The success of this technique depends on the children's recognition of parents' expert power.
- *Relationship maintenance*—striving to build and maintain a positive relationship with children at the same time that influence is being exerted.

FIGURE 9.2 Dimensions of parenting: autonomy vs. control and love vs. hostility.

From: E. S. Schaefer (1959), "A Circumplex Model for Maternal Behavior." *Journal of Abnormal and Social Psychology* 59, 226–235.

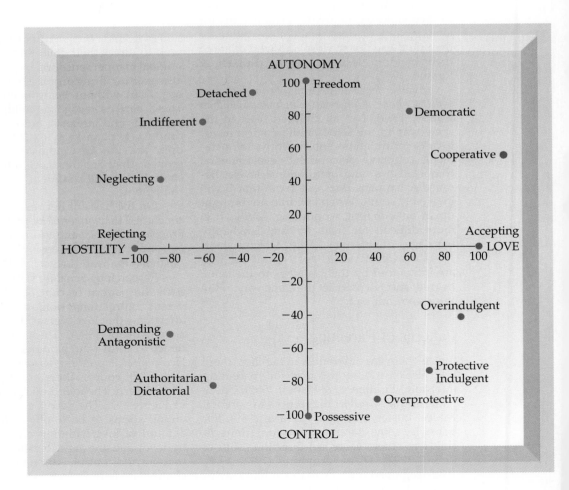

FOCUS

China's Patterns of Socialization

David Ho (1989) of the University of Hong Kong has summarized research on China's patterns of socialization in Taiwan and on the China mainland and has found the following distinguishing characteristics (Lin & Fu, 1990):

1. Parents tend to be highly lenient or even indulgent in their attitudes toward the infant and young child, in contrast to the strict discipline they impose on older children.
2. Traditionally, the transition from childhood through adolescence to adulthood takes place gradually and smoothly. A marked departure from this pattern of continuity is evidenced by intergenerational conflicts and increasing rates of juvenile delinquency.
3. Traditionally, sex roles are clearly and sharply differentiated.
4. Traditionally, parental roles between the father and mother are clearly differentiated; the mother is the agent of nurturance; the father assumes the role of disciplinarian when the child grows older.
5. Disciplinary training tends to be more severe for boys than for girls, very likely reflecting the fact that boys present more behavioral problems than girls.
6. The social class and rural–urban patterning of socialization is similar to that observed in other countries. Greater departures from the traditional pattern of parenting are found among younger, better-educated, and urban parents.
7. In traditional Chinese society, the downward social mobility of prominent families resulted in large

Despite some changes, traditional patterns of socialization are preserved in many Asian-American families today.

measure from the progressive degeneracy of the sons and their descendants. Given the wealth and status of their families, the children were not required to be prepared for having to work for a living in adulthood.
8. Despite important variations across geographical boundaries, common features that are distinctively Chinese in character may be discerned; and despite undeniable changes over time, continuity with the traditional pattern of socialization is preserved among the Chinese of today.

---

in a high rate of aggression. Hostility with a high degree of control may produce extreme hostility and anger that sometimes erupt in destructive ways. Of course, children are different and sometimes are affected differently by a specific pattern of parenting. Also, these findings were determined from the study of middle-class populations in the United States. Firm control patterns in some Asian countries are usual, and may produce less reactionary results (Rohner & Rohner, 1981).

Other research has attempted to relate specific child-care practices to children's socialization and personality development. In the 1950s, Sears, Maccoby, and Levin (1957) interviewed mothers of 379 kindergarten children, rated each on more than 100 child-rearing practices. They looked at the relationships between these practices, and at the per-

sonalities of the children. McClelland and colleagues did a follow-up on 78 of these subjects, who were then 31 years of age (McClelland, Constantian, Regalado, & Stone, 1978). They drew an interesting conclusion:

> Wide variations in the way parents reared their children didn't seem to matter much in the long run. Adult interest and beliefs were by and large not determined by the duration of breast-feeding, the age and severity of toilet training, strictness about bedtimes, or indeed any of these things (p. 46).

This does not mean that parents can do anything they want, and it has no effect on children. What McClelland and his associates (1978) did find was that *the one parenting variable that was most related to adjustment was*

PARENTING ISSUES

Children's Chores

A study of 790 Nebraska homes in which there were children revealed some interesting data on the extent to which children were regularly required to do chores around the house or yard. Apparently, assigning chores was a developmental process. In some households, chores were assigned to very young children (about a third of boys and girls 4 years of age or under were assigned work). The older children became, the more work was assigned, so that by age 9 or 10, well over 90% of the children were involved in regular chores. The median number of hours spent on chores was 4 hours per week. Even among the older, hardest workers, only 6 hours per week were required (White & Brinkerhoff, 1981).

In the beginning, children were responsible for themselves, picking up their own toys, making beds, cleaning their rooms. By 10 years of age, children moved beyond self-centered chores and were now required to help the family.

Parents gave five types of reasons for assigning chores.

In many families, children help their parents with household chores.

Developmental—doing chores builds character, develops responsibility, helps children learn.
Reciprocal obligation—it is children's duty to help the family.
Extrinsic—parents need help.

Task learning—children need to learn to do these tasks.
Residual—miscellaneous reasons, including earning an allowance or needing to keep busy (White & Brinkerhoff, 1981).

---

love. Parents who genuinely loved their children provided them with the most important requirement for successful socialization (Jakab, 1987).

Discipline

Discipline—a process of learning by which socialization takes place; its purpose is instruction in proper conduct

The word **discipline** comes from the same root as does the word disciple, which means "a learner." *Discipline, therefore, is a process of learning, of education, a means by which socialization takes place.* Its purpose is to instruct in proper conduct or action rather than to punish (Petersen, Lee, & Ellis, 1982). The ultimate goal of discipline is to sensitize the conscience and to develop self-control, so that individuals live according to the standards of behavior and in accord with the rules and regulations established by the group.

In the beginning, control over the child is established by external authority; but gradually children are encouraged to develop internal controls so that the standards they strive to follow become a part of their own lives, not because they have to, but because they want to. When this happens, these internalized truths become their own standards of conduct.

If discipline is to accomplish its goal of developing inner control, there are a number of principles that, if followed, enhance this development (Schneider-Rosen & Wenz-Gross, 1990). These are summarized here (Rice, 1990).

1. Children respond more readily to parents within the context of a *loving, trusting relationship of mutual esteem.* Children who receive nurturance and emotional support from parents show lower levels of aggression than do those who do not receive this support (Zelkowitz, 1987).

2. Discipline is more effective when it is *consistent rather than erratic.* It is helpful if parents agree on discipline (Deal, Halverson, & Wampler, 1989; Vaughn, Block, & Block, 1988).

3. Learning is enhanced if responses involve *rewards and punishments.*

4. Discipline is more effective when applied *as soon after the offense as possible.*

5. *Do not use discipline that inflicts pain.* This means avoiding spanking. Severe punishment, especially if it is cruel and abusive, is counterproductive because it stimulates resentment, rejection, and similar harsh, cruel behavior on the part of children (Herzberger & Tennen, 1985). Sweden has laws making spanking of children a crime.

6. *Discipline becomes less effective if it is too strict or too often applied.* A parent who continually criticizes a child no matter what the child does is teaching the child that it is impossible to please the parents.

7. All children want and need external controls in the beginning because they are not yet mature enough to exert self-control over their own behavior. Appropriate methods of discipline will vary according to the child's age and level of understanding. However, *extremes of either permissiveness or authoritarianism are counterproductive.* At very young ages, discipline may be accomplished through wise management: providing interesting toys and activities; equipping sections of the residence as a playroom, play yard, or play area; and child-proofing the house by keeping dangerous things out of reach. Young children may be disciplined through distraction and offering substitute activities (Holden & West, 1989). Sometimes the wisest discipline is through environmental manipulation: removing the child from the situation or the situation from the child. Parents can discuss issues with older children and arrive at joint decisions, whereas instruction to preschoolers necessarily involves more imperatives. Even then, explanations and reasons are helpful, depending upon the children's level of understanding.

8. *Methods of discipline to be avoided are those that threaten the child's security or development of self-esteem.* In some cases, parents threaten to give children away if they aren't good or to call a policeman to put them in jail. Similarly, threats to withdraw love if children aren't good are harmful means of disciplining, but are often employed by middle-class parents to try to control their children's behavior. They are devastating to children's security if regularly employed (Rice, 1990).

One-Parent Families

Between 1970 and 1987, there was a 187% increase in the number of one-parent families in the United States (U.S. Bureau of the Census, 1990). Of this total number, 88% were maintained by mothers, but only 12% were maintained by fathers. (See Figure 9.3.) High divorce and illegitimacy rates mean that both the number and total percentage of these families will continue to increase. The one-parent family, therefore, represents a major segment of the population, especially among black families and especially among the poor. Among blacks, 51% of all children under 18 are currently living with a lone mother, as compared with 16% among whites (U.S. Bu-

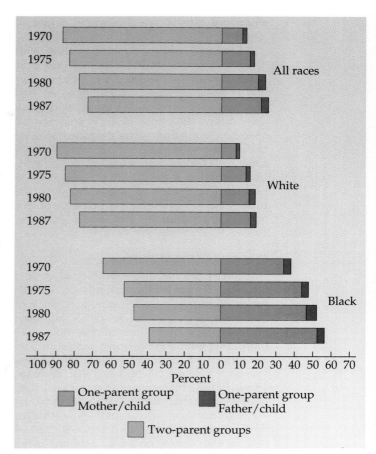

FIGURE 9.3 Change in composition of family groups with children, by race: 1970 to 1987.

From "Household and Family Characteristics, March 1985" by U.S. Bureau of the Census, 1986, in *Current Population Reports*, ser. p-20, no. 411, p. 10, Washington, DC: U.S. Government Printing Office; and *Statistical Abstract of the United States, 1990* (p. 53) by U.S. Bureau of the Census, 1990, Washington, DC.

reau of the Census, 1990). Large numbers of these single mothers have never been married (Campbell, Breitmayer, & Ramey, 1986).

THE FEMALE-HEADED FAMILY.   One of the most important problems of the female-headed family is *limited income* (Blechman, 1982; Pett & Vaughn-Cole, 1986). The median income of families headed by a woman is 50% of the income of families with a male head (Duncan & Rodgers, 1987). These women often have to cope with problems such as inadequate child care (Turner & Smith, 1983). Mothers who are left alone to bring up their children themselves may have *difficulty performing all family functions well* (Burden, 1986; Sanik & Mauldin, 1986). There may be little time or energy left to perform household tasks, which means either the house is less clean, less time is available for food preparation, or the physical and emotional care of the children is neglected (Quinn & Allen, 1989).

Several studies have shown that, after divorce, many custodial mothers have *more trouble communicating with their children, showing as much affection, controlling them,* and *spending as much time with them.* Because of demands on their time, mothers are often too absorbed with their own problems to help their children (Hetherington, Cox, & Cox, 1982; Colletta, 1985; Dornbusch et al., 1985; McLanahan & Booth, 1989). Some of these problems in mother–child relationships improve and stabilize after the first year or two following separation (Wallerstein & Kelly, 1980).

THE MALE-HEADED FAMILY.   Solo fathers face many of the same problems as solo mothers. However, they usually do not suffer poverty to the same extent as do solo mothers (Norton & Glick, 1986), although *financial pressure* is still one of the most common complaints. Also, most single fathers are concerned about not *spending enough time with their children* (Pichitino, 1983; Resman, 1986). If the children are of preschool age, fathers are faced with the same dilemmas as are solo mothers who must work: that of finding adequate child-care services. Part of their stress arises because they are often *forced to change their circle of friends* and to rebuild their social life (Greif, 1988).

EFFECTS OF PATERNAL ABSENCE ON SONS.   The important question that plagues both parents and professionals is whether children grow up to be maladjusted because of the lack of two parents in the home (Blechman, 1982). The findings reveal that *the earlier a boy is separated from his father and the longer the separation is, the more affected the boy will be in his early years* (Stanley, Weikel, & Wilson, 1986). One study of fifth-grade boys who were father-absent before age 2 found them to be less trusting, less industrious, and to have more feelings of inferiority than did boys who became father-absent between the age of 3 and 5 (Santrock, 1970a). *Father absence may also affect the development of masculinity.* As boys grow older, however, the earlier effects of father absence decrease (Santrok & Wohlford, 1970). By late childhood, lower-class father-absent boys appear to score as high as their father-present counterparts on certain measures of sex role preference and sex role adoption.

There is one fairly certain difference between boys raised in single-parent and dual-parent families. Those in single-parent families have a *lower level of educational attainment*

FOCUS

Father Hunger

Psychiatrist Alfred Messer (1989) identifies a new syndrome described by child psychiatrists: **father hunger**, found in boys 18 to 36 months of age, which consists primarily of sleep disturbances that begin 1 to 3 months after the father leaves. The syndrome evolves from the abrupt loss of a father during a young boy's critical period for gender development. The absent father deprives the boy of

- A grown male with whom to identify
- A feeling of protection and security
- Emotional support for completion of the separation-individuation phase of development
- A role model for learning how to handle aggressive and erotic impulses and for learning gender-appropriate social behavior

and consequent lower income as adults (Krein & Beller, 1988; Mueller & Cooper, 1986; Nock, 1988).

The effect of father absence is dependent partially on whether boys have surrogate male models. Father-absent boys with a father substitute such as an older male sibling are less affected than those without a father substitute (Santrock, 1970b). Young father-absent male children seek the attention of older males and are strongly motivated to imitate and please potential father figures.

EFFECTS OF PATERNAL ABSENCE ON DAUGHTERS.   Some researchers contend that the effect of paternal absence on daughters is not as great as on sons (Stevenson & Black, 1988). The reasoning has been that children make a same-sex identification, and so daughters would be affected less by the father's absence than would sons. Some girls aren't affected as much when they are young, but they may be affected more during adolescence. *Lack of meaningful male–female relationships in childhood can make it more difficult to relate to the opposite sex.* In one study of a group of girls who grew up without fathers, Eberhardt and Schill (1984) found few effects during preadolescence; but during adolescence the girls of divorced parents who had lived with their mothers were inappropriately assertive, seductive, and sometimes sexually promiscuous. Having ambivalent feelings about men because of their negative memories of their fathers, they pursued men in inept and inappropriate ways. They began dating early and were likely to engage in sexual intercourse at an early age. Hepworth, Ryder, and Dreyer (1984) reported two major effects of parental loss on the formation of intimate relationships: avoidance of intimacy and accelerated courtship. In summary, therefore, fathers appear to play a significant role in encouraging their daughters' feminine development (Heilbrun, 1984). The father's acceptance and reinforcement of his daughter's femininity greatly facilitates the development of her self-concept. Interaction with a competent father also provides the girl with basic experiences that help in her relationships with other males.

Nevertheless, *a father-present home is not necessarily always better for the children than a father-absent home*. Some fathers, though home, spend little time in caring for their children or relating to them (Levant, Slattery, & Loiselle, 1987). In such families, father absence would not have as much effect as in homes where the father spent more time with his children. Some fathers are also inappropriate models. If there is a father at home who is rejecting, paternal deprivation may be a significant cause of emotional problems and/or antisocial behavior.

The effect of paternal absence on the mother is crucial in determining the influence on the children. Many father-absence studies have failed to take into account the mother's changed position following a divorce, separation, or the death of her husband. If the mother is quite upset, if her income is severely reduced, if she must be away from home frequently because she has to work, or if she has inadequate care for her children when she is gone, the children are going to be affected—not because of the father's absence, as such, but because of the subsequent effect on their mother and their relationship with her. Furthermore, the presence of surrogate father figures exerts a modifying influence on both boys and girls.

Divorce and Children

A growing number of clinicians emphasize that children perceive divorce as a major, negative event that stimulates painful emotions, confusion, and uncertainty (Jellinger & Slovik, 1981; Kalter, 1983). Some clinicians feel that the majority of children regain psychological equilibrium in a year or so and resume a normal curve of growth and development (Hetherington, Cox, & Cox, 1979). Others feel that for a substantial portion of children, the upheaval in their lives will result in interferences in wholesome, social-emotional growth (Amato, 1991; Giudubaldi & Perry,

1985; Wallerstein & Kelly, 1980). However, children are individuals and react differently to the same experience (Hetherington, 1989). We do know that children of divorced parents are more likely to marry at an early age, and to get divorced themselves (Amato, 1988; Glenn & Kramer, 1987). Overall, the long-term impact on social, emotional, and cognitive growth is not clear and continues to be studied and debated (Kalter, 1983).

Short-term reactions have been fairly well described. Children go through a period of *mourning and grief*, and the mood and feeling may be one of sadness, depression, and dejection. One 7-year-old described divorce as "when people go away" (Rice, 1990, p. 613). Other common reactions are a *heightened sense of insecurity and anxiety* about their future. Children feel that "if you really loved me, you wouldn't go away and leave me." Some become very possessive with the parent (Kalter, 1983). One mother remarked: "Since the divorce, Tommy has been very upset when I go to work or when he goes to school. I think he's afraid that he'll come home and not find me there" (Rice, 1990).

Another common reaction is for children to *blame themselves*. If one major source of couple conflict is over the children, the children feel that the departing parent is abandoning them because they haven't been "good boys or girls." Another common reaction is *preoccupation with reconciliation*, to try to bring their parents together. They "wish that everyone could live together and be happy." The longing for a reunited family may go on for a long time, until children fully understand the realities of the situation and the reason for the separation.

After children get over the initial upset of divorce, one common reaction is *anger and resentment*, especially against the parent they blame for the divorce. Sometimes this is directed against the father—especially if they feel he has deserted the family. The child feels: "I hate you because you have gone off and left me." The resentment or hostility may also be directed at the mother, especially if the children blame her for the divorce. One 5-year-old blamed her mother for her father's absence: "I hate you, because you sent my daddy away." (Actually, the mother hadn't wanted the divorce.) An older girl, age 12, asked her mother, "Why did you leave my father all alone?" It was obvious that the girl did not understand the reason for the divorce (Author's counseling notes).

Children have other adjustments to make. *They have to adjust to the absence of one parent.* Older children may be required to assume more responsibility for homemaking.

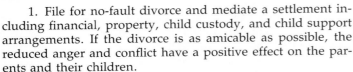

PARENTING ISSUES

Minimizing the Harmful Effects of Divorce

1. File for no-fault divorce and mediate a settlement including financial, property, child custody, and child support arrangements. If the divorce is as amicable as possible, the reduced anger and conflict have a positive effect on the parents and their children.

2. Make it clear to the children that you are divorcing your spouse, not the children, that you will always be their parents, continue to take care of them and see them. One primary goal is to reduce children's anxiety and insecurity.

3. If you are the noncustodial parent, arrange for open access to your children. This means living close to them and seeing them regularly. The primary negative effect of divorce is loss of contact with a parent (Kurdek & Berg, 1983). Predictable and frequent contact with the noncustodial parent is associated with better adjustment unless the father is poorly adjusted or extremely immature (Seltzer, 1990; Warshak, 1986). Adjustment of the children is enhanced if the custodial mother approves of the father's continued contact and rates the relationship positively (Giudubaldi & Perry, 1985).

4. If you are the custodial parent, your psychological adjustment is of great significance in determining the adjustment of your child (Kitson & Morgan, 1990; Umberson, 1989). If you're disturbed, your child is more likely to be disturbed. Get help if you can't make a happy adjustment yourself (Giudubaldi & Perry, 1985; Wallerstein & Kelly, 1980).

5. Keep conflict with your ex-spouse to a minimum (Kline, Johnstone, & Tschann, 1991). Reduced conflict after divorce has a major positive effect on children (Demo & Acock, 1988; Tschann, Johnston, Kline, & Wallerstein, 1989). Continued conflict has a negative effect (Emery, 1982; Kelly, 1988).

6. Custody arrangements, whether maternal, paternal, or joint custody, are not as important an issue as the degree of interparental conflict (Leupnitz, 1982). Joint custody is a satisfactory arrangement if ex-spouses get along with one another, but detrimental if it leads to conflict (Kolata, 1988; Irving, Benjamin, & Trume, 1984; Maccoby, Depner, & Mnookin, 1988; Schwartz, 1987).

7. Parents report high levels of satisfaction with shared (joint) physical custody, and the results run positive for children (Steinman, Zemmelman, & Knoblauch, 1985). This requires that parents reside in the same school district if children are of school age.

8. Don't use children to hurt your spouse or get back at him or her. Children become especially upset if they are used as pawns in angry power plays between divorcing spouses. Don't ask children to take sides or try to turn children against the other parent. Children love them both; whose side are they supposed to be on?

9. Share in financial child support as much as you are able. It is one way of assuring that your children have the necessities of life and are not affected by the custodial parent's having to live in poverty.

Money is tight. *Special adjustments are necessary when the parents get emotionally involved with other persons.* Now the children must share their parents with another adult. If the parent remarries, as the majority do, the children are confronted with a total readjustment to a stepparent (Baylar, 1988; Rice, 1990).

Stepfamilies

Approximately 83% of divorced men and 76% of divorced women remarry (Fine, 1986). Today, 46% of marriages involve an adult who has been married before (U.S. Bureau of the Census, 1990). Most of these adults have children. This means that 16% of all American children live in stepfamilies (Coleman & Ganong, 1990).

Many couples enter into stepfamily relations expecting relationships similar to those of primary families (Mills, 1984). They are soon disappointed, surprised, and bewildered when they find few similarities (Skeen, Covi, & Robinson, 1985).

One reason for disappointment is that *stepparents have unrealistically high expectations* of themselves and what to expect (Turnbull & Turnbull, 1983). After all, they have been married before and have been parents before. They expect they will be able to fit into the stepparent role very nicely. They are shocked when they discover their stepchildren don't take to them the way they do to biological parents. This creates anxiety, anger, guilt, and low self-esteem. They either blame the children or begin to feel there is something wrong with themselves (Visher & Visher, 1979). They need to realize it may take several years before satisfactory relationships are worked out. Over a period of time, love and affection may develop.

Parents and stepparents enter into their new family with a great deal of guilt and regret over

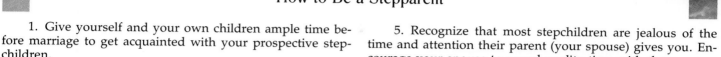

PARENTING ISSUES

How to Be a Stepparent

1. Give yourself and your own children ample time before marriage to get acquainted with your prospective stepchildren.

2. Don't try to take the place of your stepchildren's parent. Psychologically, children can only accept one father or mother at a time. Children often reject the stepparent as an intruder if the stepparent tries to compete with the child's natural parent for the child's loyalty.

3. Don't expect instant love. Any affection that develops arises only gradually. In many cases, it takes several years to develop a good relationship. The older the stepchildren, the longer it takes (Hobart, 1987).

4. Winning the friendship of your stepchildren is an important first step. If you can be good friends and learn to like one another, you will have come a long way toward developing a close relationship.

5. Recognize that most stepchildren are jealous of the time and attention their parent (your spouse) gives you. Encourage your spouse to spend quality time with them.

6. Let the children's natural parent take the lead in guidance and discipline, then you support the effort. If you as a stepparent try to change the way stepchildren are being taught, they will resent your efforts, especially if they can get their own parent to take their side.

7. Don't try to buy the affection and loyalty of your own children or stepchildren. They will learn to manipulate you to win approval and favors.

8. All stepchildren are different, so you have to deal with them as individuals.

their failed marriage and divorce. They feel sorry for their children, whom they have put through an upsetting experience. This has several effects. Usually, parents tend to be overindulgent, not as strict as they might otherwise be, and have more trouble guiding and controlling the children's behavior (Amato, 1987). Often they try to buy the children's affection and cooperation.

A stepparent's role is ill-defined (Hobart, 1988). Stepparents are neither parents nor just friends. Their efforts to try to be parents may be rejected by older children. Stepparents are required to assume many of the responsibilities of parents, yet they have none of the privileges and satisfactions of parenthood. In the beginning, being a stepparent seems all give and no receive. It's frustrating.

Fairly tales and folklore have developed the stereotype of the cruel stepmother, a myth that is hard to overcome (Radomski, 1981). Most studies indicate that the stepmother role is more difficult than that of stepfather, primarily because the mother has more responsibilities for direct care of the children (Brand & Clingempeel, 1987; Sauer & Fine, 1988).

Stepparents confront the necessity of attempting to deal with children who have already been socialized by another set of parents (Kompara, 1980). Stepparents may disagree with the way that their stepchildren are being brought up. But any attempt on their part to

suddenly step in and try to change things is deeply resented.

Stepparents expect gratitude and thanks for what they do, but often get rejection and criticism instead. They were expected to support and care for their own biological children, but feel they are being very generous and helpful by offering the same to stepchildren. Yet, stepchildren seem to take help for granted and ask for more, offering little thanks or appreciation for what is done for them.

Stepparents are faced with unresolved emotional issues from the prior marriage and divorce. They need to resolve some of the hostilities that were created through the process of separation and divorce, so that they can make a fresh start.

They must also deal with a network of complex kinship relationships: with their own biological family members, with their former spouse's family members, with their new spouse's family members, plus their own children and stepchildren. This adds a more difficult dimension to their family involvements (Berstein & Collins, 1985).

Stepparents must cope with stepsibling feelings and relationships. Stepchildren are rarely helpful to each other in coping with the strains of the divorce period. Instead, there may be stepsibling rivalry and competition for the attention of parents (Amato, 1987).

Family cohesion tends to be lower in stepfamilies than in intact families. Life in divorced and reconstituted families tends to be chaotic and stressful during the years following remarriage (Wallerstein & Kelly, 1980). However, as far as the marriages themselves are concerned, in comparison to first-married couples, one study found that if both spouses remarried, stepfather families reported *higher* relationship quality and stronger intrinsic motivations to be in the relationship (Kurdek, 1989).

THE DEVELOPMENT OF PEER RELATIONSHIPS

Psychosocial Development

Autosociality—a stage of psychosocial development during the first year or so of life, during which infants' interests, pleasures, and satisfactions are themselves

Childhood heterosociality—a stage when children seek the companionship of others regardless of sex

Homosociality—a stage during which children prefer to play with others of the same sex

The development of friendships with peers is one of the most important aspects of social development of children. In the process of psychosocial development, all normal children pass through four stages:

1. **Autosociality**—infancy and toddler stage of development, in which children's interests, pleasures, and satisfactions are themselves. Toddlers want to be in the company of others, but they play *alongside* of others, not *with* them. A child who is a loner has not yet progressed beyond this stage of psychosocial development.

2. **Childhood heterosociality**—ages 2–7, during which children seek the companionship of others regardless of sex.

3. **Homosociality**—ages 8–12, or primary school period of development, during which children prefer to play with others of the same sex (not for sexual purposes, but for friendship and companionship). There is some antagonism between the sexes.

4. **Adolescent and adult heterosociality**—age 13 and over, or the adolescent and adult stage of psychosocial development, in which the individual's pleasure, friendships, and companionship are found with those of both sexes. Adolescent boys and girls begin to pair off; most begin dating.

Early Childhood

INFANTS AND TODDLERS. Babies' first social experiences are usually with parents and siblings (Fiese, 1990; Vandell & Wilson, 1987). Observations of babies and toddlers indicate that they interact with one another from about 5 months onward. Their first social response is simply to notice one another and to smile at one another. When they are able to move around, they crawl all over one another. When they can stand up, they occasionally knock one another down. Studies of 6-month-olds reveal little conflict or fussing when infants touch one another's toys, touch one another, or even find themselves trapped beneath a partner (Hay, Nash, & Pedersen, 1983). By 9 months of age, they offer a toy to others and oppose toys being taken away. They also comfort others in distress and pick up the ones who get pushed over. Personal aggression increases with age, but cooperation also increases as children become more experienced in relating to one another. Observation of children in infant centers indicates that helpfulness is more apparent than are efforts to dominate. By the time children are toddlers, they have learned much about fending for themselves in a group and about how to find satisfaction there. They have made a strong beginning in establishing group relations that are a main source of emotional security and orientation.

TWO-YEAR-OLDS. Children of this age enjoy playing alongside one another, rather than with one another, since cooperative play is not very evident, at least in the beginning. However, 2-year-olds begin to show some preferences in playmates. Individuals interact more with familiar play partners (Brownell, 1990). Twins interact more with one another than with unfamiliar peers (Vandell, Owen, Wilson, & Henderson, 1988). Social interchange becomes more frequent; friendly behavior gradually replaces negative behavior (Brownell & Carriger, 1990; Ross & Lollis, 1989). Sex preferences are not yet evident.

Toddlers are not as forbearing as infants when their toys are touched or taken (Shants, 1987). Two-year-olds do a lot of

Adolescent and adult heterosociality—a stage of psychosocial development during which those ages 13 and over find pleasure, friendship, and companionship with those of both sexes

Between the ages of 8 and 12, a period of homosociality, children prefer to play with others of the same sex.

grabbing, hitting, and pushing, not usually with an intent to hurt, but for the purpose of protecting their own toy or getting a toy someone else has. Since they are egocentric, they are not aware of the effect that their own actions have upon others, nor of the moods and feelings of others. They think in terms of "my ball" or "my book," and they protest when denied what they want. As a result, they inevitably run into conflict from their social interactions. They need supervision and experience in considering the needs and interests of others.

THREE-YEAR-OLDS.   As children grow older, they engage in fewer solitary activities, do less passive watching of other children, and become less inclined toward isolated play. Friendly contacts occur with increasing frequency, and cooperative behavior also increases (Ladd, Price, & Hart, 1988). Children may select one friend, sometimes two, with whom they identify for short periods of time. Aggressive behavior gradually declines (Cummings, Iannotti, & Zahn-Waxler, 1989).

We see the beginning of group play and activity. The development of language makes communication possible, so that when two children play together they talk about what they are making in the sand, about dressing up their dolls, or about pretending to be a mother or a baby. Group membership, however, is constantly changing, with children moving in and out of a group.

Three-year-olds are likely to be victims of aggression by other children in nursery school, so teachers have to provide supervision and be careful to reinforce socially acceptable acts.

FOUR- AND FIVE-YEAR-OLDS.   Children ages 4 and 5 gradually develop more socially competent interactions with their peers (Guralnick & Groom, 1987). They begin to depend less on parents and more and more on peers for companionship and social interaction. They now share affection and tangible objects. They offer approval and make demands on one another. Best friends in a group will pair off. Groups of three children are quite common. Occasionally, up to five or six children will form a group and spend most of their playtime with one another.

Their behavior varies. One moment they are aggressive, the next moment cooperative. Conflict occurs more often between friends than with nonfriends, but the conflict with friends is less intense and resolved more quickly, insuring that the children's re-

lationships will continue once the disagreement ends (Hartup, Laursen, Stewart, & Eastenson, 1988). Children's behavior is affected a lot by the attitude of others at home or in school. If cooperation is stressed, children become less competitive. If competition is encouraged, rivalry becomes a strong motivator of behavior, and jealousy is quite common. For this reason, most experts try to discourage competitive activities for this age group.

Children vary greatly in their social competence and acceptance by peers (Denham, McKinley, Couehoud, & Holt, 1990; Ladd & Price, 1987). Social status and peer interaction depend partly on children's communication skills (Hazen & Black, 1989). Children develop definite preferences in playmates. Some children in a group become leaders and are quite popular with nearly everyone. Other children are content to be followers. There is still much intermingling between the sexes. There is little prejudice in evidence. Children choose friends without regard for race, color, ethnic origin, or social class.

As preschool children interact with other children of the same age, they gradually discover that they come from a variety of family situations. Some have siblings, others none. Some have young parents, others old parents, and some only have one parent at home. These initial engagements with peers are broadening experiences that stimulate children to ask numerous questions. "How come I don't have any brothers or sisters?" "Why can't I have a big bike like Mary has?" "Why doesn't Johnny have any daddy?"

Research has revealed that experiences in the family have a definite effect on the development of social competence. One study of economically disadvantaged 4- and 5-year-olds in a Midwestern community revealed the following factors were detrimental to the development of social skills:

- Exposure to aggressive models in the home and parents' endorsement of aggression as a means of solving conflicts.
- Restrictive discipline, in which parents used a high degree of constriction.
- Parents' hostile reactions to provocation by the child.

In contrast with these negative factors, the study found that parents who used preventative teaching and gave their children opportunity for direct peer experience contrib-

FOCUS

Preschooler's Play

Preschooler's play has been classified in a number of ways. In a classic study, Mildred Parten (1932) observed the play of children in a nursery school setting and established categories of play according to the degree of the children's social involvement. This study is as pertinent today as it was 60 years ago. Parten identified six categories of play involvement:

- *Unoccupied play*—children are not really playing, they are looking around, engaging in random activities.
- *Solitary play*—children play with toys by themselves, making no effort to relate to other children.
- *Onlooker play*—children watch others play, and are talking to them, but do not join the play.
- *Parallel play*—children play alongside of others, not *with* them, but mimic others' behavior.
- *Associative play*—children interact with others, borrowing or lending toys, following or leading one another in similar activities.
- *Cooperative play*—organized groups of children engage in play, such as a game.

Play may also be classified according to the type of activity.

1. *Sensory play*—play that involves sensory experiences such as splashing water, digging in the sand, banging pots and pans, plucking flower petals, or blowing bubbles. Children learn about the world through these sensory experiences (Athey, 1984).

2. *Motor play*—play that involves physical motion such as running, jumping, skipping, or swinging. This type of play helps to develop muscles and motor coordination, and to release pent-up energy.

3. *Rough-and-tumble play*—motor play that involves mock-fighting and the controlled release of aggression. Children learn to control their impulses and feelings, and to express them in socially acceptable ways. The development of this type of play is often influenced by the way fathers play with their children at home (Levine, 1988). Sometimes this type of play gets out of hand, gets too rough, and children are hurt.

4. *Cognitive play*—play that involves language, the repetition of sounds and words because they sound funny, or playing word games, or asking riddles. This play gives children a chance to master word sounds and grammar, to think, and to develop cognitive skills (Galda & Pellegrini, 1985; Schwartz, 1981).

5. *Dramatic play or pretend play*—play that involves modeling activities and role-playing, such as playing house, firefighters, nurse or doctor, baby, astronaut, army, or truck driver. This play gives children a chance to recreate experiences and to try out roles (Fein, 1986; Howes, Unger, & Seidner, 1989). It is also called *symbolic play* (Slade, 1987; Wooley & Wellman, 1990).

6. *Games and competitive sports*—play that may involve board games such as checkers, games of skill such as darts, or outdoor games and sports such as tag, hide and seek, or baseball. Children learn to follow rules, to take turns, to be able to accept losing or winning, and to cooperate with other children in the group (Kamii & DeVries, 1980).

---

uted positively to the development of social skills of their children (Pettit, Dodge, & Brown, 1988).

Middle Childhood

FRIENDSHIPS. *The older children become, the more important companionship with friends becomes* (Buhrmester & Furman, 1987). By the time children start first grade, they are no longer interested in being alone so much of the time. They want to be with friends (Ladd, 1990). They still seek out a special companion, but their circle of friends is widening. During the preschool period, most of their friends were confined to the immediate neighborhood, but now children meet many friends from other areas served by the school. Some of these persons are different from the ones the children are used to playing with. This makes it harder for children to get acquainted and to learn to get along, but it is a broadening experience and helps them to mature.

Parents become concerned about the kinds of friends their children want to bring home or want to visit. They worry, and with justification, about the influence of these friends upon their children. Parents want to know: "What kind of persons are these children?" Parents are wise to be concerned, because peer-group influence over children becomes more and more important. Certainly, parents need to spell out some ground rules about how far away and where children are allowed to play, about what time to come in, and about the types of activities that are permitted. Grade-school children need some supervision, so it is helpful if there are concerned parents nearby.

However, *some parents are overprotective* and won't allow their children to do what others do or allow them to play with other children in the usual way. This is especially likely to happen if children are frail or sickly. The parents try to protect their children from germs, noise, and rough-and-tumble play, but as a result, they keep their children from making friends or from learning how to do what others do.

Others expect too much of their children, try to push them too fast, and are very critical when their children don't measure up. Such attitudes undermine their children's self-confidence. The children become afraid of failure, of rejection, of ridicule, and of criticism, and they react by trying to avoid social groups where they are embarrassed. Thus, in socialization as in other areas, parents need to balance supervision and guidance with freedom and encouragement. Generally speaking, parents who are sociable, agreeable, and who have positive feelings toward their children have children who are sociable, agreeable, and have positive attitudes toward others (Putallaz, 1987).

POPULARITY.   Children differ in the degree to which they strive for or achieve popularity. If a group of children are asked individually to name other children whom they most like or with whom they would most like to be associated, it is possible to discover which children are most and least popular (Boulton & Smith, 1990). Usually, such surveys show that even those children who are rated most popular have a few acquaintances who are indifferent to them or dislike them, and those who are least popular are rarely unpopular with everyone.

Nevertheless, since children place such emphasis on being popular, it is helpful to sort out those qualities of personality and character that make for popularity or unpopularity (Gelb & Jacobson, 1988). What types of children are most popular? Generally speaking, popular children (Chance, 1989):

- Are socially aggressive and outgoing (Dodge, Cole, Pettit, & Price, 1990).
- Have a high energy level that they use in activities approved by the group.
- Have positive self-perceptions (Boivin & Begin, 1989).
- Actively participate in social events enthusiastically.
- Are friendly and sociable in relation to others.

- Accept others, are sympathetic, protective, and comforting toward them.
- Are cheerful, good natured, have a good sense of humor.
- Are above average in intelligence and school performance, but not too high above others.

There are some social and sex differences in the qualities considered important to popularity. Boys need to show physical prowess, athletic ability, and skill in competitive games. In some antisocial groups, the most popular boys show superior fighting ability. In the upper elementary grades, girls are rated most popular who are considered physically attractive and socially sophisticated and mature. Middle-class children put greater emphasis on scholastic achievement than do lower-class children. A lower-class boy who excels in schoolwork risks alienation from his peers. A lower-class girl can be a good student without alienating her friends.

What types of children are considered least popular (French, 1990)? Generally speaking, the least popular children (Chance, 1989; Rogosch & Newcomb, 1989):

- Are self-centered and withdrawn.
- Are anxious, fearful, and moody.
- Are more likely to be emotionally disturbed (Altmann & Gotlib, 1988; Asarnow, 1988).
- Are impulsive, with poor emotional control (French, 1988).
- Show a lack of sensitivity to others and to social situations.
- Behave in inappropriate ways (Gelb & Jacobson, 1988).
- Are hostile and overaggressive.
- Behave considerably younger or older than their age groups.
- Are different looking or unconventional in behavior.
- Are more likely to be of low intelligence.

There is a difference between children who are *unliked* and those who are *disliked*. Unliked children are socially invisible. They are loners (Coie & Dodge, 1988). Research reveals, however, that as children get older, even shy, withdrawn children are increasingly accepted and liked by their peers, whereas overly aggressive children are disliked at all ages (Younger & Piccinin, 1989). Disliked children are quite visible, and they behave in obnoxious, socially unacceptable ways.

GANGS AND CLUBS.   *Ages 10 and 11 are when children begin joining clubs and gangs.*

These groups arise out of children's need to be independent from parents and to be with peers. Children form play clubs, neighborhood gangs, fan clubs, and secret societies with special rules, observances, passwords, and initiation rites. They make plans to build a fort or clubhouse and to do things in groups. Members are obliged to participate in the group's activities, and outsiders are excluded.

Gangs are usually organized along sex lines. The boys will have their gangs, and the girls their social clubs. Whether groups are helpful or harmful depends upon their nature, purpose, and membership. Gangs of delinquents in tough neighborhoods provide some semblance of protection for individual members, but the members themselves may engage in fighting, stealing, or drinking, or in pushing and using drugs.

The same drive that impels children into gang activities can be channeled into well-organized, supervised clubs where individuals can give acceptable expression to their social needs. This is the age for *Cub Scouts, Brownies, YMCA, YWCA, Police Athletic Leagues,* and many other groups for a variety of general and particular interests. Parents would be wise to encourage their children to join and participate in worthwhile groups.

COMPETITION.   One of the problems of some groups is that they place undue emphasis on competition. In our society, individuals are encouraged to compete with one another to see who can be the strongest or the fastest, have the largest collection of baseball cards, or win the game. Some groups encourage this competitiveness by their emphasis on winning, regardless of the effect of this competition on individuals. The American Academy of Pediatrics and many other *authorities feel that it is unwise to push preadolescents into highly competitive sports.* Young school-age children are not ready physically, psychologically, or socially for highly competitive games. The urge to win is so strong that the experience stimulates too much tension and anxiety, and defeat becomes a real blow to self-esteem.

Children ought to be encouraged to compete with themselves. Thus, a Cub Scout or Brownie can be encouraged to work for the next achievement rather than to become involved in stiff competition with other youngsters or groups. Those who are physically inept, unathletic, or unskilled at competitive games suffer terribly if they are excluded from teams or group activities. The purpose of such activities should be enjoyment, recreation, and the enhancement of self-esteem and self-worth, not the destruction of these.

CRUELTY AND AGGRESSION.   Some children of this age can be very cruel (Perry, Williard, & Perry, 1990). They callously exclude one another from their groups, or say things that shame or belittle others. Bullies who pick on those who are younger or weaker are a problem (Roberts, 1988). Their primary motive seems to be to gain control of others as a means of feeling important themselves (Boldizar, Perry, & Perry, 1989). Because of their own angry feelings, they

PARENTING ISSUES

The Bully

I remember counseling with one mother who—because of her religious upbringing—strongly objected to fighting. She had taught her 9-year-old son never to fight; in fact, she had taught him literally to turn the other cheek and never to hit back if someone hit him. Unfortunately, one bully at school found this out and would daily hit, abuse, and taunt this boy each afternoon on the way home from school. The youngster came home battered, bruised, and crying, but he obeyed his mother and would not fight back. Of course, the more he refused to fight, the more the bully called him a "sissie" and picked on him. After several sessions of counseling, the mother became convinced that she could not let her son take any more punishment, so she told him never to start a fight or to hit first, but if the bully hit him, to hit him back. The next day her son came home triumphant: "I really hit him, Mom, I knocked him down and made him cry. He won't pick on me again." And he didn't.

Of course, the best way to deal with bullies is not to have anything to do with them, but if they insist on trouble, children have to be prepared to deal with the situation. However, younger and smaller children can't handle bullies themselves. They need to enlist the aid of teachers, parents, and of older, stronger friends (Author's counseling notes).

often attribute hostile intentions to the actions of others when none exist (Dodge & Somberg, 1987). Under these circumstances, other children need to learn to stand up for themselves and to protect themselves (Ferguson & Rule, 1988).

Social Cognition

Social cognition— the capacity to understand social relationships

Social cognition is the capacity to understand social relationships. In children, it is the ability to understand others: their thoughts, their intentions, their emotions, their social behavior, and their general point of view. Social cognition is basic to all human interactions. To know what other people think and feel is necessary to understand them and to get along with them (Feldman & Ruble, 1988; Gnepp & Chilamkurti, 1988).

Yet, this ability develops very slowly. Robert Selman (1977, 1980) has advanced a theory of social cognition outlining predictable stages in **social role taking**. To Selman, social role taking is the ability to understand the self and others as subjects, to react to others as like the self, and to react to the self's behavior from the other's point of view.

Selman's five stages of development are:

Social role taking

Egocentric undifferentiated stage— the stage of awareness when another person is seen egocentrically, undifferentiated from the self's own point of view

STAGE 0.   Egocentric undifferentiated stage (age 0 to 6). Until about age 6, children cannot make a clear distinction between their own interpretation of a social situation and another's point of view, nor can they understand that their own perception may not be correct (Yaniv & Shatz, 1990). When they are asked how someone else feels in a particular situation, their responses reflect how *they* feel, not how *others* feel (Lewis & Osborne, 1990).

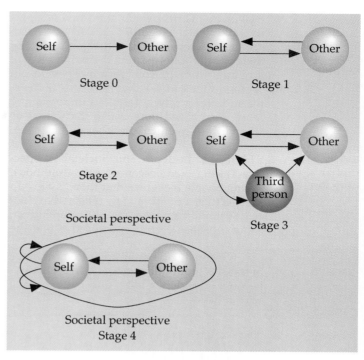

FIGURE 9.4   Selman's five stages of social role taking. *Stage* 0. The other person is seen egocentrically, or undifferentiated from the self's own point of view. *Stage* 1. The other is seen as different from the self, but the other person's perception of the self is still undifferentiated. *Stage* 2. The self can take the perspective of another person and becomes aware that the other person can also take the perspective of the self. *Stage* 3. The self can view the self–other interaction from the perspective of a neutral third person. *Stage* 4. The self can take a generalized societal perspective of the self–other interaction.

From *Theories of Adolescence*, 5th ed. (pp. 249, 251, 254, 256, 258) by R. E. Muuss, 1988, New York: McGraw Hill Publishing Company. Copyright © McGraw Hill Publishing Company. Used by permission.

rect, not realizing that people may hide their true feelings.

Differentiated or subjective perspective-taking stage— the stage of awareness when the other is seen as different from the self, but the other person's perception of the self is still undifferentiated

STAGE 1.   Differentiated or subjective perspective-taking stage (age 6 to 8). Children develop an awareness that others may have a different social perspective, but they have little understanding of the reasons for others' viewpoints (LeMare & Rubin, 1987). Children believe that others would feel the same way if they had the same information. Perspective taking is a one-way street; children cannot accurately judge their own behavior from the perspective of the other person. They do begin to distinguish between intentionality and unintentionality of behavior and to consider causes of actions (Miller & Aloise, 1989). They are capable of inferring other peoples' intentions, feelings, and thoughts, but base their conclusions on physical observations that may not be cor-

STAGE 2.   Self-reflective thinking or reciprocal perspective-taking stage (age 8 to 10). A child develops reciprocal awareness, realizing that others have a different point of view and that others are aware that he or she has a particular point of view. The principal change from stage 1 to stage 2 is children's ability to take the perspective of others; to reflect about their own behavior and their own motivation as seen from the perspective of another person. This ability includes an awareness of relativity, that no individual's social perspective is necessarily correct or valid in an absolute sense. Another person's point of view may be as correct as one's own. This awareness also means that individuals may take other persons' points of view into account (Dizon & Moore, 1990).

Self-reflective thinking or reciprocal perspective-taking stage— the stage of awareness when the self can take the perspective of another person and know that the other person can also take the perspective of the self

Third-person or mutual perspec-tive-taking stage—when children see their own perspective, their partner's, plus a third person's perspective

STAGE 3.   **Third-person or mutual perspec-tive-taking stage** (age 10 to 12). Children can see their own perspective, the perspective of their partner, plus assume the perspective of a neutral third person. As third-person observers, they can see themselves as both actor and object. Thus, they can understand a more generalized perspective that might be taken by an "average" member of the group.

In-depth and so-cietal perspective-taking stage—the stage of social awareness when the self can take a generalized societal perspective of the self–other interaction

STAGE 4.   **In-depth and Societal Perspec-tive-Taking** (adolescence to adulthood). Young people recognize that there is a group perspective, a point of view reflected in a social system. Law and morality depend on some consensual group perspective that the individual must take into account.

Obviously, the more advanced the stage of social cognition, the more capable children become in understanding and getting along with others.

TELEVISION AS A SOCIALIZING INFLUENCE

Viewing Habits

Today, 98% of the households in the United States own at least one television set (Christopher, Fabes, & Wilson, 1989). According to a 1985 Nielson report, schoolchildren between the ages of 6 and 11 spend an average of 26 hours and 34 minutes per week watching television (National Audience Demographics Report, 1985). Preschool children spend an average of 28 hours, 20 minutes per week. By age 18, children will have watched

Adults have become concerned with the effects on children of their watching television for long hours.

television approximately 20,000 hours, compared with 11,000 hours in the classroom. Singer and Singer (1983) pointed out that children spend more time watching television than they spend in conversation with adults or siblings. They spend more time watching television than engaging in any other activity (including playing and eating) except sleeping (Institute for Social Research, 1985). These figures are startling, so the real question is: *What effect does watching so much television have on children, on their development and relationships?*

Violence and Aggression

A most important concern has been the influence of television as a stimulus of aggressive behavior in children. There is certainly no doubt of the extent of violence on TV. By the time children are in the eighth grade, they will have watched 18,000 human beings killed on television, and violent acts committed against thousands more. Thomas Radicki, a psychiatrist who is head of the National Coalition on Television Violence, reports a deluge of high-action violent cartoon shows (Tooth, 1985). In examining a typical Saturday morning program of the *Bugs Bunny–Roadrunner* cartoon, one analysis revealed an average of 50 violent acts per hour (Zimmerman, 1983). The classic research by Bandura on the relationship between television violence and aggressive behavior in children found that children were less likely to imitate the violent behavior of cartoon models than they were the violence of real-people models (Bandura, Ross, & Ross, 1963). Nevertheless, violent cartoons had a negative effect. One study found that television shows with rapid changes of scene and high action, such as cartoons, increase children's aggression, regardless of content, because the sensory excitement stimulates the children to act without reflection (Greer, Potts, Wright, & Huston, 1982).

Real-life models of violence are not hard to find. The National Coalition on Television Violence reports that violent acts on television increased 65% from 1981 to 1985. The violent acts to which children are exposed on television include war, assassination, murder, shooting, knifing, beating, punching, torture, kicking, choking, burning, rape, cruelty to animals, robbery, violent accidents, and property destruction. While precise cause and effect relationships are hard to establish, extensive research indicates that *television violence is associated with increased aggressive behavior in children who watch it*. After reviewing the research on the subject, the National Institute of Mental Health (NIMH) (1982) concluded that children who see violence on the screen behave more aggressively, regardless of their geographical location or socioeconomic level. This is true of both boys and girls, and of normal children as well as those with emotional problems. The NIMH report concludes that television encourages aggressive behavior in two ways: *Children model and imitate what they see, and they come to accept aggression as appropriate behavior*.

This finding seems to hold true internationally, also. Huesmann and Eron (1986) summarized research from 5 countries: the United States, Finland, Israel, Poland, and Australia. The conclusion was the same as that reached in other studies: television violence does have an adverse affect on children. Furthermore, *the effect is interdependent. Aggressive children select more violent television programs and view more of them, and those who watch more violent programs tend to be more aggressive*. Other research substantiates that the effect of violence is interactive and cumulative. Children who watch violence on television are more aggressive than children who do not, and children who are aggressive are likely to watch a lot of TV violence (Friedrich-Cofer & Huston, 1986). The effects may be long lasting. One study concluded that the amount of television violence watched by children when they were in elementary school was associated with how aggressive they were at age 19 and at age 30 (Eron, 1987). Of course, this still does not prove cause and effect.

Family Interaction

Critics argue that television watching has other negative effects on children. One of the effects is felt by the whole family (Fabes, Wilson, & Christopher, 1989). *Extensive viewing has been associated with a decrease in family interaction, social communication, and interpersonal conversation*. Of course, families interact differently depending on the program being watched. Some families talk less but touch more while watching television (Brody & Stoneman, 1983). Interaction is certainly decreased in those families with more than one television set. The parents watch one program, the children another, in separate locations of the house. Experiments with families that decided to give up television viewing for a period of time revealed that the children played together more, family activities increased, mealtimes were longer, the children read more, and bedtimes were earlier (Chira, 1984).

Increased television viewing has also been associated with lower socioeconomic status families (Huston, Siegle, & Bremer, 1983), dysfunctional families, and increased parent–child conflict (Price and Feshbach, 1982). However, it is likely that increased television viewing is the result of trouble in the family, not the cause. *Children use television as an escape from the stress of the home environment*. One study found that lack of parental empathy, sensitivity, and adaptive role expectations was related to heavy viewing of violent, fantasy-oriented television content (Tangney, 1988).

Cognitive Development

Heavy television viewing has also been associated with lower school achievement (Rubenstein, 1983), including lower reading comprehension (Singer & Singer, 1983), poorer language usage, and neglect of homework. Certainly, if their parents will let them, many children will stay up until all hours to watch television rather than do their homework. Interestingly, however, *heavy TV viewing by children of low socioeconomic status has been associated with higher scholastic achievement and reading comprehension* (Morgan & Gross, 1982) *and at the same time with lower abilities among children of high socioeconomic status*. Apparently, television has a leveling effect. The fact remains that any time spent watching television decreases the amount of time that children spend on other activities, whether it be playing, engaging in hobbies, reading, or talking with friends or family members. Some authorities feel that television makes children less creative, less verbal, less social, and less independent.

Commercials

The question also arises regarding the effects of television commercials on children. *There is no question that television advertising is influential*. Part of the effects are positive. Television warns against smoking and the use of drugs, encourages children to brush their teeth to avoid cavities, and encourages them to eat their cereal. However, one study found that a significant portion of commercials advertised food products high in sugar, and the consumption of these products increased because of television advertising (Barcus, 1978).

Television is used to sell every conceivable type of new toy also (Dorr, 1986). Children see a toy advertised, want it, and request it from their parents. If parents refuse, parent–child arguments follow. In one study, when children were presented with a hypothetical scenario of a father refusing to purchase a toy his son had requested, less than 40% of the children who had been exposed to an advertisement of the toy felt the boy would still want to play with his father, whereas over 60% of the children who had not viewed the commercial thought the boy would still want to play with his father (Goldberg & Gorn, 1977). Television is not simply an innocuous form of family entertainment. It is a powerful force.

Positive Effects

Not all effects of television are negative. One of the most watched educational programs is "Sesame Street." Viewing is highest by children between ages 3 and 5, with a peak between 3½ and 4 and a decline between ages 5 and 7 (Pinon, Huston, & Wright, 1989). A series of studies found the following positive benefits: Viewers showed increased abilities to recognize and name letters, to sort different objects, to name body parts, and to recognize and label geometric forms. However, "Sesame Street" has not reduced the difference between the advantaged and disadvantaged in terms of cognitive functioning (Cook, Appleton, Conner, Shaffer, Tamkin, & Weber, 1975). In fact, already advantaged children tend to benefit more. Another children's program, "Mr. Rogers' Neighborhood," was found to increase prosocial behavior in children (Tower, Singer, Singer, & Biggs, 1979).

There are many other potential benefits of carefully designed children's programs. Children can be taught cooperation, sharing, affection, friendship, control of aggression, coping with frustration, and the necessity of completing tasks. They can be presented models of harmonious family relationships, and of cooperative, sympathetic, and nurturant behavior. As they get older, they can be exposed to greatness; to various ethnic and cultural groups; to world geography and history; to the world of nature; to a wide variety of interpersonal experiences; to literature and the classics; and to science, art, music, and drama. The potentials are unlimited. Unfortunately, television programs have fallen far short of their potential (*Television and Your Children*, 1985).

THE DEVELOPMENT OF GENDER ROLES

Meaning

One of the negative effects of television is that it sometimes portrays stereotypical gender roles. **Gender** refers to our biological sex, whether male or female. **Gender roles** are outward expressions of masculinity or femininity in social settings. They are how we act and think as males or females. They are our sex roles.

Sex roles are molded by three important influences: *biological*, *cognitive*, and *environmental*.

Gender—our biological sex

Gender roles—our outward expressions of masculinity or femininity in social settings

Influences on Gender Roles*

BIOLOGICAL.   The biological bases for gender have already been discussed in Chapter 3. If an ovum is fertilized by a sperm carrying an X chromosome, a female is conceived. If the ovum is fertilized by a sperm carrying a Y chromosome, a male is conceived. *The chromosomal combination is the initial controlling factor in the development of gender.*

*Part of the material in this section is taken from the author's book *Intimate Relationships, Marriages, and Families* (1990). Used by permission of the publisher, Mayfield Publishing Co.

Gender roles which are outward expressions of masculinity or femininity in social settings are in a state of flux and transition.

PARENTING ISSUES

Nintendo

Nintendo is the new video game craze that has swept the nation. By the end of 1989, Nintendo was in 20 million American homes. Forty million of the game devices had been installed around the world. Fifty million of the game cartridges were sold in 1989 alone. There are more than 100 different Nintendo game cartridges available. The archetypical Nintendo game portrays the adventures of *Mario*, an indomitable, mustached man in a red cap whose goal is to rescue a princess. Mario runs through a stylized landscape while the computer sends hazards toward him. The farther he goes, the more clever his enemies become, until at last he either rescues the princess or dies on the screen with an electronic gurgle. Some players play for weeks or months without ever seeing the princess. In *Super Mario 2*, Mario and his brother Luigi go over hill, dale, and waterfall, through tunnel, and by magic carpet to defeat the evil Wart. In the *Legend of Zelda*, the hero Link searches the mystical labyrinths of the Underworld to find the lost pieces of the golden Triforce of Wisdom. In *Rad Racer*, a Ferrari 328 Twin Turbo competes with Corvettes, Lamborghinis, and Porsches in a 200 km/hr cross-country race. In *Punch Out*, Little Mac, a teenage battler from the Bronx, fights his way up the ranks until he earns a fight against Mike Tyson (Adler, 1989).

Sixty percent of players are males between 8 and 15. For some children and adolescents, Nintendo becomes a compulsion. It seems to speak to primordial and powerful urges. It arouses warrior instincts. As one 14-year-old said:

> You just want to play and play it until you beat it. You get so nervous near the end. You perspire. Your heart rate is up. Afterward you just want to drop dead (Adler, 1989, p. 65).

To assist players in mastering the games, the manufacturer has installed hotlines in a room in Redmond, Washington, where 100 "counselors" answer 50,000 calls a week to offer players hints on how to deal with evil knights or bottomless pits ("Trapped by Mutilator Troy?" . . . , 1990).

Nintendo stimulates children to do extreme things. One 14-year-old boy from West Palm Beach, Florida, played continuously for 2 days straight. A female school aide from Hammond, Indiana, played it for 4 months, 4 hours a night, until her doctor gave her a thumb splint for her "Nintendonitis" and told her to lay off video games. She started playing with her palms.

Nintendo is the new video game craze that has swept the nation.

This craze is causing some reactions among adults. One antiviolence group has rated 70% of the games "harmful for children." Many parents, seeing their kids play *Super Mario 2* for hours on end, are asking what this nonstop diet of video games is doing to impressionable young minds ("Dr. Nintendo," 1990). Combat on Nintendo is not always conducted according to the Geneva convention. Karate kicks, maces and swords, and bludgeoning are popular. In *Renegade*, the object is to slaughter a gang of muggers before they throw you on the railroad tracks. The body count by the end of the *Double Dragon* is 50, including the hero's own brother, who has stolen the hero's girlfriend (Adler, 1989). As a result, some parents limit Nintendo to only 1 hour a night, or to Saturday mornings, or to rainy days. Nintendo has become a principal means of discipline: "No Nintendo until you've done your homework." "Just for that you can't play Nintendo for a whole week."

Peggy Charren, president of Action for Children's Television, considers Nintendo pretty bland compared to such TV programs as "Nightmare on Elm Street." Perhaps to buy some respect, but nevertheless to get more information, Nintendo has donated $3 million to MIT's Media Laboratory to study "how children learn while they play." No doubt, some new and better games will be created ("Dr. Nintendo," 1990).

Testosterone—the masculinizing hormone

Estrogen—the feminizing hormone

Gender development is also influenced by sex hormones. **Testosterone** is the masculinizing hormone secreted by the testes; **estrogen** is the feminizing hormone secreted by the ovaries. If human females are exposed to excessive *androgenic* (masculinizing) influences

prenatally, after birth they become more physically vigorous and more assertive than other females. They prefer boys rather than girls as playmates and choose strenuous activities over relatively docile play. Similarly, boys born to mothers who receive estrogen and progesterone during pregnancy tend to exhibit less assertiveness and physical activity and may be rated lower in general masculine-typed behavior (Ehrhardt & Meyer-Bahlburg, 1981). The studies suggest that *changes in prenatal hormonal levels in humans may have marked effects on gender-role behavior.* After birth, hormonal secretions stimulate the development of masculine or feminine physical characteristics, but have minimal effect on gender-role behavior, usually only accentuating behavior already manifested.

COGNITIVE.   Cognitive theory suggests that *sex-role identity has its beginning in the gender cognitively assigned to the child at birth and subsequently accepted by him or her while growing up.* At the time of birth, gender assignment is made largely on the basis of genital examination. The assignment of gender influences everything that happens thereafter (Marcus & Overton, 1978). Kohlberg (1966), the chief exponent of this view, emphasized that the child's self-categorization (as a boy or girl) is the basic organizer of the sex-role attitudes that develop. A child who recognizes that he is a male begins to value maleness, and a child who recognizes that she is a female begins to value femaleness and to act consistently with gender expectations (Martin & Little, 1990). The child begins to structure experience according to the accepted gender and to act out appropriate sex roles. Sex differentiation takes place gradually as children learn to be male or female according to culturally established sex-role expectations and their interpretations of them. It is important to emphasize that according to this theory *girls do not become girls because they identify with or model themselves after their mothers; they model themselves after their mothers because they have realized that they are girls.* They preferentially value their own sex and are motivated to appropriate sex-role behavior.

ENVIRONMENTAL.   Environmentalists reason differently. In their view, *a child learns sex-typed behavior the same way he or she learns any other type of behavior: through a combination of rewards and punishment, indoctrination, observation of others, and modeling.* From the beginning, boys and girls are socialized differently. Boys are expected to be more active and aggressive. When they act according to these expectations, they are praised; when they refuse to fight, they are criticized for being "sissies." Girls are condemned or pun-

ished for being too boisterous or aggressive and are rewarded when they are polite and submissive (Williams, 1988). As a consequence, boys and girls grow up manifesting different behaviors.

Traditional sex roles and concepts are taught in many ways as the child grows up (Brody and Steelman, 1985; Roopnarine, 1986). *Giving children gender-specific toys may have considerable influence on vocational choices.* Such toys influence boys to be scientists, astronauts, or football players and girls to be nurses, teachers, or stewardesses. Without realizing it, *many teachers still develop traditional masculine–feminine stereotypical behavior in school.* Studies of teachers' relationships with boys and girls reveal that teachers encourage boys to be more assertive in the classroom (Sadker & Sadker, 1985). When the teacher asks questions, the boys call out comments without raising their hands, literally grabbing the teacher's attention. Most girls sit patiently with their hands raised, but if a girl calls out, the teacher reprimands her: "In this class, we don't shout our answers; we raise our hands." The message is subtle but powerful; boys should be assertive academically; girls should be quiet.

Children also find appropriate sex roles through a process of identification, especially with parents of the same sex. Parental identification is the process by which the child adopts and internalizes parental values, attitudes, behavioral traits, and personality characteristics (Weisner & Wilson-Mitchell, 1990). When applied to sex-role development, parental identification theory suggests that children develop sex-role concepts, attitudes, values, characteristics, and behavior by identifying with their parents, especially with the parent of the opposite sex (Hock & Curry, 1983). Identification begins immediately after birth because of the child's early dependency on parents. This dependency in turn normally leads to a close emotional attachment. Sex-role learning takes place almost unconsciously and indirectly in this close parent–child relationship. Through example and through daily contacts and associations (McHale, Bartko, Crouter, & Perry-Jenkins, 1990), children learn what a mother, a wife, a father, a husband, a woman, or a man is.

Peer groups also exert tremendous influence on children in sex-role development. Boys are condemned as "sissies" if they manifest feminine characteristics. Girls are labeled "tomboys" if they are unladylike. Day after day, children are taught to be boys or girls according to the definitions prevalent in their culture.

Age and Gender-Role Development

By *2 years of age* most children are aware that there are boys and girls, mommies and daddies, that daddies have a penis and mommies have breasts. They use the pronouns *he* and *she* to refer to brothers and sisters and begin to be aware of what constitutes masculine and feminine dress and behavior. Men wear shirts, trousers, suits, and they shave; women wear slacks, dresses, skirts, and blouses, and they put on makeup. Both wear jeans. Children begin to be aware of sex-typed roles. If a person drives a truck and is a firefighter, that person must be a man. If someone washes dishes, cooks, or irons clothes, that person must be a woman. By *3 years of age* children choose gender-typed toys—dolls or cars—and perform sex-typed roles—nurses versus doctors (Weinraub et al., 1984). Yet, at this age, they are unaware that most of the toys they choose are considered appropriate for their gender. There is considerable switching of stereotypical gender-related toys and roles. Three-year-old boys will pretend to be babies, fathers, mothers, or monsters. They will wear mother's high heels or father's cowboy boots. They will play dolls as comfortably as girls.

By *age 5*, this has usually changed. A boy who wants to dress a doll, or a girl who wants to be a space warrior, is criticized by the family (Roopnarine, 1984). Boys will pretend to be monsters or superman; girls pretend to be princesses or sisters (Paley, 1984).

Sex differences become evident in play. Boys play outdoors more; use more physical space; engage in more rough-and-tumble, noisy play; more often wrestle, run, push, and tease. Girls more often engage in helping, nurturant play, and more often play house, care for babies, cook, clean, and dress up in hats and other clothes (Pitcher & Schultz, 1983). There is still considerable intermingling of the sexes during play, with some preferences for same-sex companionship becoming evident. By *age 7* children have developed a sense of **gender constancy**: the understanding of which gender they are and the knowledge that their own sex remains constant. Once a girl, always a girl.

Stereotypes

Gender stereotypes are common concepts and assumed characteristics of what boys and girls, or men and women, are supposed to be like within the context of the culture in which they live. In our society, when we talk about a "real boy" or a "masculine man" we are expressing value judgments based on an assessment of those personal and behavioral characteristics of "maleness" according to the defined standards of our culture. Similarly, when we are talking about "a little lady" or a "feminine woman" we are labeling her according to culturally defined criteria for "femaleness."

Although the standards of maleness and femaleness are undergoing change, *there is still much evidence of traditional stereotypes.* Table 9.1 lists the traditional stereotypes of boys and girls in our culture. These concepts are commonly held by boys and girls themselves (Martin, Wood, & Little, 1990).

There are numerous problems with stereotypes. *One*, they are inaccurate descriptions of those boys and girls who don't fit the stereotypes. To say that all boys are bigger and stronger than girls, or that girls are littler and weaker than boys is simply not true. *Two*, stereotypes define what it means to be a boy or girl within narrowly defined limits, and those who don't match the descriptions are criticized, or even persecuted because they are different. *Three*, stereotypes tend to perpetuate traditional characteristics, many of which may be undesirable. To say that real boys are rough and aggressive and like to fight, that girls are passive, gentle, and don't hit, creates numerous problems. Boys may become too physical and girls too passive. A world full of hostile, aggressive males leads to fighting and wars. A world full of passive females leads to exploitation. Similarly, one of the problems between the sexes is that those very traits of sensitivity and emotionality that women are supposed to exhibit and men are supposed to repress exposes women to the hurts and upsets of intimate living and isolates men from being able to understand why their partners are so upset in the first place. It's difficult for men and women to become real friends and companions.

Four, stereotypes limit the roles that men and women play both at home and work. If women are expected to be breadwinners, as the majority are, then men need to be expected to be homemakers and babytenders. Stereotypes also limit the occupations and professions open to men and women. Men can make good nurses and elementary school teachers (and men elementary school teachers are very much needed) and women can make good scientists and engineers. The important thing is for children to be brought up free to choose their profession.

Gender constancy—the understanding of the gender that one is, and the knowledge that gender is going to remain the same: usually achieved by 7 years of age

Gender stereotypes—widespread, assumed gender characteristics of what boys and girls are like

TABLE 9.1 Stereotypes of Boys and Girls

	Boys	Girls
Physical characteristics	Bigger stronger, muscular, hard Wear trousers, shirts, suits Short hair	Weaker, softer, littler, delicate Wear dresses, skirts, blouses, makeup, jewelry Long hair, curls, ribbons
Play	Play war, army, fireman, policeman, cowboy, astronaut, build things Play with blocks, cars, trucks, airplanes, boats, soldiers, bulldozers, cranes, tools, space-age toys, video games More physical play, sports: football, soccer, hockey, baseball	Domestic play: play house, wash dishes, cook, iron, sweep, tend babies Play with dollhouses, dolls, kitchen set, pots, stoves, doll carriage, cooking utensils, pots and pans, board games More interest in art, drawing, music
Domestic work	Mow lawn, build and fix things	Domestic chores, housekeeping, care for children, laundry
Behavior	Rough, aggressive, forceful, tough, daring, brave, competitive, like to fight Loud, noisy, naughty Not a sissy, unemotional, not cry, self-confident, independent	Passive, nurturant, helping, caring, compassionate, sympathetic, gentle, kind, scared, like to kiss, don't hit or fight Talk a lot Emotional, high-strung, cry, frivolous, impractical, dependent
Cognitive	Better in math, science, visual-spatial skills, mechanical aptitude	Better in verbal skills, grammar, reading, spelling, languages, history

Androgyny

Gender-role concepts are changing slowly. What seems to be developing is a gradual mixing of male and female traits and roles to produce **androgyny** (male and female in one). Male traits emphasize *self-assertion*: leadership, dominance, independence, competitiveness, and individualism. Female traits emphasize *integration*: sympathy, affection, and understanding. Children who possess neither masculine nor feminine characteristics are labeled undifferentiated. Androgynous children have a high degree of both self-assertion and integration: of male and female traits (Ford, 1986). Thus, we have four classifications of gender-role types: *masculine, feminine, undifferentiated,* and *androgynous.* Figure 9.5 shows the possible combinations. A person who is high in both self-assertion and integration is androgynous. Similarly, a person who is high in self-assertion and low in integration is masculine; low in self-assertion and high in integration, feminine; and low in both self-assertion and integration, undifferentiated. *Androgynous persons are not sex-typed with respect to roles (although they are distinctly male or female in gender).* They match their behavior to the

situation rather than being limited by what is culturally defined as male or female. An androgynous male feels comfortable cuddling and caring for a young baby; an androgynous female feels comfortable pumping gas and changing the oil in her car. Androgyny expands the range of human behavior, allowing individuals to cope effectively in a variety of situations (Flake-Hobson, Skeen, & Robinson, 1980).

FIGURE 9.5 Classifications of gender-typed roles.

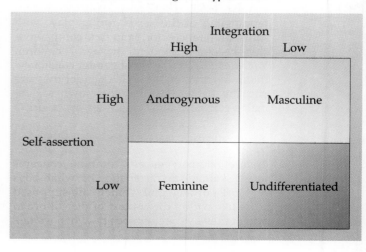

Androgyny—a mixing of male and female traits in one person

PARENTING ISSUES

Parental Roles in Androgynous Development

There are many things that parents can do to encourage development of androgyny in their children (Katz & Walsh, 1990).

- Become androgynous role models for children to imitate. If parents can manifest both self-assertive and integrative traits, and exemplify both masculine and feminine roles in the family, children are likely to adopt both traits and roles themselves.
- Eliminate separating "men's work" and "women's work" in the family, with the whole family performing "our work."
- Encourage children to play games and use toys without regard for traditional sex-typed associations.
- Encourage boys to be integrative and girls to be self-assertive. Let boys know it's all right to have tender feelings and to express emotion, and let girls know they can assert their individualism and independence.
- Teach children that both men and women can engage in traditionally male or traditionally female professions. A woman doesn't have to be a secretary; she can have a secretary.

MORAL DEVELOPMENT

The process by which children develop moral judgment is extremely interesting (Walker & Taylor, 1991). The most important early research on the development of moral judgment of children is that of Piaget (1948, 1969). Piaget emphasized the development of moral judgment as a gradual cognitive process, stimulated by increasing social relationships of children as they get older.

Piaget's (1948) work is reported in four sections. The *first section* discusses the attitudes of children to the rules of the game when playing marbles. The *second and third* sections report the results of telling children stories that require them to make moral judgments on the basis of the information given. The *last section* reviews his findings in relation to social psychology, particularly to the work of Durkheim (1960), who argues that the sanctions of society are the only source of morality.

In studying children's attitudes to the rules of the game, Piaget concluded that there is, first of all, a **morality of constraint**. In the early stages of moral development,

Morality of constraint—conduct coerced by rules or by authority

children are constrained by the rules of the game. These rules are coercive because children regard them as inviolable and because they reflect parental authority. Rules constitute a given order of existence and, like parents, must be obeyed without question. (In actual practice, children's attitudes and behavior don't always coincide, however.) Later, according to Piaget, children learn from social interaction a **morality of cooperation**, that rules are not absolute but can be altered by social consensus (Gabennesch, 1990; Helwig, Tisak, & Turiel, 1990). Rules are no longer external laws to be considered sacred because they are laid down by adults, but social creations arrived at through a process of free decision and thus deserving of mutual respect and consent. Children move from *heteronomy* to *autonomy* in making moral judgments (Piaget, 1948).

Piaget also discusses the motives or reasons for judgments. He says there are, first, judgments based solely on the consequences of wrongdoing (**objective judgments**) and, second, judgments that take into account intention or motive (**subjective judgments**). Piaget (1948) claims there is a growing pattern of operational thinking, with children moving from objective to subjective responsibility as they grow older. Piaget would insist that although the two processes overlap, the second gradually supersedes the first. The first stage is superseded when children deem motive or intention more important than consequences.

Morality of cooperation—conduct regulated by mutual respect and consent

Objective judgments—judgments based solely on the consequences of wrongdoing

Subjective judgments—judgments that take into account intention or motives

> The child finds in his brothers and sisters or in his playmates a form of society which develops his desire for cooperation. Then a new type of morality will be created in him, a *morality of reciprocity* and not of *obedience*. This is true morality of intention (p. 133).

Piaget (1948) is careful to note that obedience and cooperation are not always successive stages but nevertheless are formative processes that broadly follow one another: "The first of these processes is the moral constraint of the adult, a constraint which leads to heteronomy and consequently to *moral realism*. The second is cooperation which leads to autonomy" (p. 193). (By moral realism Piaget means submitting meekly to the demands of law.)

Before moral judgment moves from the *heteronomous* to the *autonomous* stage, the self-accepted rules must be internalized. This happens when, in a reciprocal relationship and out of mutual respect, people begin to feel from within the desire to treat others as they themselves would wish to be treated. They pass from *preoperational* to *operational thinking*, from premoral to moral judgment as they internalize the rules they want to follow.

In the third section of his report, Piaget discusses the child's concept of justice as the child moves from moral restraint to moral co-operation. Two concepts of punishment emerge. The first results from the transgression of an externally imposed regulation; this Piaget calls **expiatory punishment**, which goes hand in hand with constraint and the rules of authority. The second is self-imposed punishment, which comes into operation when the individual, in violation of his or her own conscience, is denied normal social relations and is isolated from the group by his or her own actions. Piaget (1948) calls this the **punishment of reciprocity**, which accompanies cooperation. An ethic of mutual respect, of good as opposed to duty, leads to improved social relationships that are basic to any concept of real equality and reciprocity.

In the last section of his work, Piaget (1948), following Durkheim, asserts that "society is the only source of morality" (p. 326). Morality, to Piaget, consists of a system of rules, but such rules require a sociological context for their development. Thus, "whether the child's moral judgments are heteronomous or autonomous, accepted under pressure or worked out in freedom, this morality is social, and on this point, Durkheim was unquestionably right" (p. 344).

Expiatory punishment—punishment that results from an externally imposed regulation; associated with morality of constraint

Punishment of reciprocity—Self-imposed punishment; associated with morality of cooperation

One of the important implications of Piaget's views is that the changes in the moral judgments of children are related to their cognitive growth and to the changes in their social relationships. At first children judge the severity of transgressions by their visible damage or harm. They also develop the concept of **imminent justice**: the child's belief that immoral behavior inevitably brings pain or punishment as a natural consequence of the transgression (Jose, 1990). "If you do wrong, you will certainly be punished." Furthermore, children judge the appropriateness of this punishment by its severity rather than by its relevance to the transgression. Only as children get older are they likely to recommend that the transgressor make restitution or that punishment be tailored to fit the wrong done.

As an example, if 6-year-olds are told the story of a little boy who has accidentally dropped a sweet roll in the lake, they are likely to respond: "That's too bad. But it's his own fault for being so clumsy. He shouldn't get another." For them, the punishment implies a crime, and losing a roll in the lake is clearly a punishment in their eyes. They are incapable of taking extenuating circumstances into account. Adolescents, however, make moral judgments on the basis of what Piaget calls **equity**, assigning punishments in accordance with the transgressors' abilities to take responsibility for their crimes.

Imminent justice—the child's belief that immoral behavior inevitably brings pain or punishment as a natural consequence of the transgression

Equity—assignment of punishments in accordance with transgressors' ability to take responsibility for a crime

PARENTING ISSUES

Taking Small Children to Adult Worship Services

Some parents say: "I'm going to take my children to worship from the time they are young. Then they will get in the habit of going." Other adults say: "I was forced to go when I was growing up and I hated it. I'm never going to do that to my children." Assuming that parents want to give their children a firm foundation of religious teaching, what's the wisest approach?

There are some negative aspects of taking small children to adult worship services. The most important consideration is that children are bored; they don't understand what is going on; they are learning to be inattentive, so they either do something else or fall asleep. They are conditioned not to like going to adult worship services and not to get anything out of them.

Letting children stay home until they are old enough to understand adult services is not the answer either. This teaches them that church, synagogue, mosque, or temple is not important and they miss out on religious instruction during many of their formative years.

One positive approach is to enroll children in religious classes that meet during the adult service. These should be classes that are divided according to age groups with programs appropriate for each age level. If children like to go and they are learning from the experience, they not only are growing in understanding, but they are also developing positive attitudes and feelings toward going that carry over into adulthood. One mother commented: "Every time we go by the church, my two-year-old says: "Horsey, horsey." The child had made an association between the church and riding on the horsey in the nursery, where she was learning one of the most important religious lessons of all: how to get along with other children. She was getting a helpful beginning.

Another important implication of Piaget's view is that changes in judgments of children must be related to the changes in their social relationships. As peer-group activity and cooperation increase and as adult constraint decreases, the child becomes more truly an autonomous, cooperative, moral person.

SUMMARY

1. Children do not develop in a vacuum. They are influenced by their social relationships in their family, neighborhood, community, country, and the world.

2. Bronfenbrenner developed an ecological model for understanding social influences in the microsystem, mesosystem, exosystem, and macrosystem.

3. There are differences in the way that children are socialized according to socioeconomic status, setting, and ethnic or national background.

4. Socialization is the process by which persons learn the way of society and social groups so they can function within them.

5. The family is the chief socializing influence on children, but there are many family types, each of which may have a somewhat different influence on children.

6. The influence of the family is also variable because of differences in individual children.

7. There are three major styles of parenting in our culture: authoritarian, permissive, and authoritative. Authoritative control seems to work best in our culture.

8. Parental control techniques may be divided into seven categories: power-assertive discipline, command, self-oriented induction, other-oriented induction, love withdrawal, advice, and relationship maintenance.

9. Parental relationships with children can also be divided into four categories according to the degree of control and of affection. These four categories are love-autonomy, love-control, hostility-autonomy, and hostility-control. Successful parenting seems to depend upon the maximum amount of love and the right balance between autonomy and control.

10. The one parenting variable that is most related to adjustment is love.

11. The Chinese pattern of parenting seems to follow traditional practices of firm control.

12. The primary purpose of discipline is to teach, not to punish. The ultimate goal is to sensitize the conscience and to develop self-control.

13. The number of one-parent families is on the increase. The majority are female-headed families. The primary problems of the female family are limited income and pressures to perform all functions well. Like females, single males heading families are concerned about income, not spending enough time with their children, child care, and changes in their social life.

14. Father absence affects boys emotionally, affects their development of masculinity, and affects the level of education they are able to attain. The effect depends partially on the availability of male surrogate models.

15. Father absence affects girls also, but especially during adolescence, when girls may develop difficulty with their heterosexual adjustments and with forming a positive and feminine self-concept.

16. Father-absent homes are not always worse for children than father-present homes.

17. Divorce is often a major, negative event that stimulates painful emotions, confusion, and uncertainty in children. Many children are able to regain psychological equilibrium in a year or so.

18. Parents can do much to minimize the harmful effects of divorce.

19. The problems of children become more complicated when parents remarry and a stepfamily is formed.

20. Stepfamilies have their own unique set of problems, different from those of primary families.

21. There are many things parents can do to learn to be good stepparents.

22. The psychosocial development of children and youth can be divided into four stages: autosociality, childhood heterosociality, homosociality, and adolescent and adult heterosociality.

23. Children move through progressive stages of social development as they get older.

24. Similarly, the play of preschoolers has been divided into six categories of play involvement: unoccupied play, solitary play, onlooker play, parallel play, associative play, and cooperative play.

25. Play may also be divided into categories according to the type of activity: sensory play, motor play, rough-and-tumble play, cognitive play, dramatic or pretend play, and games and competitive sports.
26. The older children become, the more important companionship with friends becomes. Popularity, gangs and clubs, competition, and cruelty and aggression all become important considerations during middle childhood.
27. Social cognition is the capacity to understand social relationships, an ability that is very important in getting along with others.
28. Robert Selman outlined 5 stages of development of social cognition: the egocentric undifferentiated stage, differentiated or subjective perspective-taking stage, self-reflective thinking or reciprocal perspective-taking stage, third-person or mutual perspective-taking stage, and the in-depth and societal perspective-taking stage.
29. Television is an important socializing influence. Experts are particularly concerned about its effect on childhood aggression, family interaction, and cognitive development; and about the effects of commercials and video games.
30. Television, especially well-designed children's programs, can have a positive effect on children.

31. Gender refers to our biological sex; gender roles are outward expressions of masculinity or femininity.
32. There are three important influences on gender-role development: biological, cognitive, and environmental.
33. Gender-role development begins at birth and continues for many years. Children reach gender-role constancy by age 7.
34. Gender stereotypes are inaccurate descriptions of all boys and girls; boys and girls who don't match the descriptions are criticized; stereotypes tend to perpetuate undesirable characteristics; and they limit the roles that men and women play at home and at work.
35. Androgyny is a gradual mixing of male and female traits. Male characteristics emphasize self-assertion; female emphasize integration. Androgynous persons manifest both sets of traits.
36. According to Piaget, children develop moral judgment in a series of steps. They move from a morality of constraint to a morality of cooperation; from heteronomy to autonomy; from making objective judgments to making subjective judgments; from a morality of obedience to a morality of reciprocity; and from a concept of expiatory punishment to one of punishment of reciprocity. They also move from a concept of imminent justice to a concept of equity.

KEY TERMS

DISCUSSION QUESTIONS

1. From your own experience, compare authoritarian, permissive, and authoritative patterns of parenting.
2. What methods of discipline do you believe work the best and why? Take children's ages into account.
3. Were you brought up in a one-parent family, or do you know someone who was? What were the effects on you or other children?
4. Were your parents divorced while you were growing up, or have you been divorced? What were the effects on you while growing up, or on your children now? What effects have you noticed on friends whose parents were divorced or who are now divorced themselves?
5. What are the major advantages and disadvantages of stepfamilies?
6. What are the principal problems of social development of preschoolers, and of elementary school-age children?
7. What are your views on the effects of television on children?
8. What stereotypes of masculine men or feminine women do you think are helpful; what ones do you object to and why?
9. What do you think of androgynous personalities? Would you want your child to be androgynous in personality development?
10. What can parents do to raise their children as moral persons? How do you feel about enrolling your children in religious school activities from the time they are little? How do you feel about taking young children to adult worship services?

SUGGESTED READINGS

Adams, P. L., Milner, J. R., & Schrepf, N. A. (Eds.). (1984). *Fatherless children.* New York: Wiley. Effects of father absence.

Askew, W., & Ross, C. (1988). *Boys don't cry: Boys and sexism in education.* Philadelphia: Open University Press. Sexism and how it can be overcome.

Gilligan, C. (1982). *In a different voice.* Cambridge, MA: Harvard University Press. Pioneering work on women and their moral development.

Gottman, J. M., & Parker, J. G. (Eds.). (1987). *Conversations of friends.* New York: Cambridge University Press. Children's friendships.

Greif, G. L. (1985). *Single fathers.* Lexington, MA: D. C. Heath. Implications of single fatherhood.

Huesmann, L. R., & Eron, L. D. (Eds.). (1986). *Television and the aggressive child: A cross-national comparison.* Hillsdale, NJ: Erlbaum. TV violence and aggression in children.

Lamb, M. E. (1987). *The father's role: Cross-cultural perspectives.* Hillsdale, NJ: Erlbaum. Fathers' roles in different cultures.

Liebert, R. M., & Sprakin, J. N. (1988). *The early window: Effects of television on children and youth* (3rd ed.). Elmsford, NY: Pergamon. Updated research on subject.

Maccoby, E. E. (1980). *Social development: Psychological growth and the parent-child relationship.* New York: Harcourt Brace. General discussion.

Mitchell, A. (1985). *Children in the middle.* New York: Tavistock. Effects of divorce.

Paley, V. G. (1984). *Boys and girls: Superheroes in the doll corner.* Chicago: University of Chicago Press. Kindergarten children learn what it means to be a boy or girl.

Reinisch, J. M., Rosenblum, L. A., & Sanders, S. A. (Eds.). (1987). *Masculinity/femininity.* New York: Oxford University Press. A collection of articles.

Rubin, Z. (1980). *Children's friendships.* Cambridge, MA: Harvard University Press. Helpful account.

Schaffer, H. R. (1984). *The child's entry into a social world.* New York: Academic Press. Development in social context, especially the family.

Selman, R. L. (1980). *The growth of interpersonal understanding.* New York: Academic Press. Social cognition.

Stein, S. B. (1983). *Girls and boys: The limits of nonsexist childrearing.* New York: Charles Scribner's Sons. Child-rearing practices and sexism.

Winn, M. (1985). *The plug-in drug* (rev. ed.). New York: Viking. Harmful effects of TV.

PART
FOUR

ADOLESCENT
DEVELOPMENT

10

Perspectives on
Adolescent Development

INTRODUCTION

In this chapter we are concerned with describing adolescence and a number of terms related to it: maturity, puberty, pubescence, juvenile, and youth. This chapter begins with a discussion of these concepts.

Another way to understand adolescence is to approach it from various points of view: from the studies of the psychobiologist, psychiatrist, psychologist, social psychologist, and anthropologist. This chapter presents the views of theorists from each of these disciplines: psychobiological view—G. Stanley Hall; psychoanalytical view—Anna Freud; sociopsychoanalytical view—Erik Erikson; psychosociological view—Robert Havighurst; and anthropological view—Margaret Mead. By understanding different theories of adolescence, the student can gain a more comprehensive view.

THE MEANING OF ADOLESCENCE*

Adolescence

The word *adolescence* comes from the Latin verb *adolescere*, which means "to grow up" or "to grow to maturity" (Golinko, 1984). Adolescence is a period of growth beginning with puberty and ending at the beginning of adulthood; it is a transitional stage between childhood and adulthood (Matter, 1984). The period has been likened to a bridge between childhood and adulthood over which individuals must pass before they can take their places as grown adults (see Fig. 10.1). In general, the total period of adolescence has been prolonged in industrial societies as the time span of dependency has increased. The transition from childhood to adulthood is complicated (Hammer & Vaglum, 1990), and the amount of time one takes to pass through this stage is variable, but most adolescents eventually complete the passage.

Maturity

Maturity is that age, state, or time of life at which a person is considered fully developed socially, intellectually, emotionally, physically, and spiritually. Maturity is not reached

*Portions of this chapter are adapted from the author's book, *The Adolescent: Development, Relationships, and Culture.* 6th ed. Copyright © 1990 by Allyn and Bacon. Used by permission of the publisher.

Adolescence is a period of growth beginning with puberty and ending at the beginning of adulthood.

in all of these characteristics at the same time. Youths who become physically mature at age 12 are usually not mature in other ways. A person may be mature socially, but still be immature emotionally.

Puberty and Pubescence

Puberty is the period or age at which a person reaches sexual maturity and becomes capable of having children.

Pubescence is used to denote the whole period during which physical changes relative to sexual maturation are taking place. Literally, it means becoming downy or hairy, describing the growth of body hair that accompanies sexual maturation.

FIGURE 10.1 Adolescence as a bridge between childhood and adulthood.

Puberty—the period or age at which a person reaches sexual maturity and becomes capable of reproduction

Pubescence—the whole period during which the physical changes related to sexual maturation take place

Maturity—the time in life when one becomes an adult physically, emotionally, socially, intellectually, and spiritually

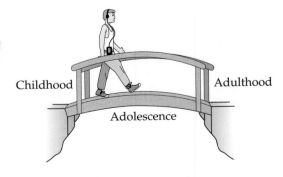

Childhood   Adulthood

Adolescence

Juvenile

Juvenile—one who is not yet considered an adult in the eyes of the law

The word **juvenile** is a legal term describing an individual who is not accorded adult status in the eyes of the law. In most states, this is a person under 18 years of age. The legal rights of 18-year-olds vary from state to state, however. The 26th Amendment gave them the right to vote. They may obtain credit in their own names at some stores or banks, whereas others require cosigners. This depends on the degree to which they have established a good credit rating in their own names. Many landlords will not rent to minors. Youths have to be 21 years of age to purchase alcoholic beverages. In some states, 18-year-olds can marry without parental consent; in other states they have to wait until they are older. In Colorado, adolescents can leave home at age 16, but do not attain full legal rights until age 21. The net result is confusion over their status. When do they fully become adults? Some authorities feel that adolescents have to wait too many years to "get into the club" ("Legal Rights . . . 1976).

Keniston (1970) suggested the law recognize an intermediate legal status between age 15 and 18 when adolescents are accorded more rights than children but fewer than those of adults. Keniston conceptualized a new stage of life, that of *youth*, which he defined as a developmental period that would follow adolescence. In general, his suggestion was never adopted. In modern terminology, however, youth refers to the younger generation, usually adolescence (Sebald, 1984). It is used in this latter sense in this book.

ADOLESCENCE AND PSYCHIC DISEQUILIBRIUM

Storm and Stress

G. Stanley Hall (1904), the founder of the child-study movement in North America and the first Ph.D. in psychology in the United States, first described adolescence as a period of great "storm and stress," corresponding to the time when the human race was in a turbulent, transitional stage on the way to becoming civilized. Hall said the causes of this storm and stress in adolescents are biological, resulting from changes at puberty. *Puberty represents a time of emotional upset and instability* in which the adolescent's moods oscillate between energy and lethargy, joy and depression, or egotism and self-depreciation. The end of adolescence marks a birth of adult traits, corresponding to the beginning of modern civilization. Although Hall was a psychologist, his explanation of the changes at adolescence was biological.

Psychic Conflict

Anna Freud (1946), daughter of Sigmund Freud, also characterized adolescence as a period of psychic disequilibrium, emotional

FOCUS

Rites of Passage

In some cultures, when a child reaches puberty, ceremonies are conducted to celebrate the passage from childhood to maturity. Once the child successfully passes the prescribed tests, he or she is accepted as a member of adult society.

The ceremonies are often stressful and painful. The most common rite for boys is *circumcision*, usually performed with a sharp stone knife. A tribe in the South Pacific requires that boys leap headfirst from a 100-foot-high platform built in a tree, with nothing but 90-foot-long vines tied to their feet. The vine catches them up short just before their head hits the ground. Sometimes, miscalculations result in permanent injury or death. If the boy is brave enough to go through this experience, he is considered worthy to be an adult. The Mandan Indian tribe, living on the plains of the United States, tested the endurance of their pubertal sons by piercing their pectoral muscles under their breasts with sharp sticks and then suspending the boys from the lodge poles by ropes attached to the sticks. Boys who could endure the longest were considered the bravest.

Initiation rites for girls center around the attainment of reproductive capabilities as marked by the onset of menstruation. The girls are prepared ahead of time by instruction on domestic and parental duties, sexual matters, and modes of dress. Some ceremonies are designed to ensure their fertility. In some Arab cultures, a girl's clitoris is removed. In other societies, a girl is scarred while cutting beauty features into the skin.

conflict, and erratic behavior. On the one hand, adolescents are egotistic and self-centered, and they believe that everyone's attention is focused on them. On the other hand, they are capable of forgetting themselves while they focus on the needs of others and engage in charitable projects. They can become involved in intense infatuations, but can fall out of love just as suddenly. They sometimes want to be with others in their social group, but the next day seek solitude. They oscillate between rebellion and conformity. They are not only selfish and materialistic, but also morally idealistic. They are ascetic, yet hedonistic; inconsiderate and rude, yet loving and tender. They fluctuate between overflowing confidence and fearful self-doubt; between indefatigable enthusiasm and tired indifference (Freud, 1946).

According to Anna Freud, the reason for this conflicting behavior is sexual maturation at puberty, which causes psychic disequilibrium (Blos, 1979). At puberty, there is a marked increase in the instinctual drives (the *id*), including a greater interest in genitality and sexual impulses. There is also a rise in other instinctual drives at puberty: exhibitionism and rebelliousness increase; physical hunger intensifies; oral and anal interests reappear; and habits of cleanliness give way to dirt and disorder. Instinctual forces that have remained latent since early childhood reappear at puberty (Freud, 1946, p. 159).

The increasing demands of the id during adolescence create conflict with the *superego* that the *ego* tries to resolve. The task of the ego is to allow the instinctual drives of the id to be satisfied, within the limits of societal expectations as represented by the superego. The ego is a person's power of reasoning. The superego is the conscience that results from internalizing the social values of one's parents and society, according to Anna Freud. The increase in instinctual drives during adolescence directly challenges the reasoning abilities and the powers of conscience of the individual. Open conflict breaks out between the id and superego, and the ego has trouble keeping the peace. If the ego takes the side of the id, "no trace will be left of the previous character of the individual and the entrance into adult life will be marked by a riot of uninhibited gratification of instinct" (Freud, 1946, p. 163). If the ego sides only with the superego, the id impulses are confined within the narrow limits prescribed for a child. Keeping instinctual forces suppressed requires constant expenditure of psychic energy, because defense mechanisms and other measures are used to hold the id in check. *If this id–ego–superego conflict is not resolved during adolescence, emotional disturbance results.*

Anna Freud described the methods of defense (the *defense mechanisms*) the ego employs to remain in control. The ego denies, rationalizes, or projects the instincts on to others to allow the id to have its way. If conflict over behavior remains, anxiety may result, causing phobias and hysterical symptoms. The appearance of asceticism and intellectualism during adolescence is symptomatic of the mistrust of all instinctual impulses. The rise of neurotic symptoms and excessive inhibitions during adolescence may be a sign of the success of the ego and superego at the expense of the individual.

Anna Freud suggests, however, that *harmony among the id, ego, and superego is possible and does occur finally in most normal adolescents.* The superego needs to be developed during the latency period—but not to the extent that it inhibits the instincts too much, causing extreme guilt and anxiety. The ego needs to be sufficiently strong and wise to mediate the conflict (Freud, 1946).

ADOLESCENCE AND IDENTITY ACHIEVEMENT

Components of Identity

According to Erikson (1950, 1959) *the chief psychosocial task of adolescence is the achievement of identity* (Archer, 1990a,b; Bilsker & Marcia, 1991; Raskin, 1990; Rotheram-Borus, 1990a; Waterman, 1990). Identity has many components (Rogow, Marcia, & Slugoski, 1983) —*sexual, social, physical, psychological, moral, ideological,* and *vocational* characteristics—that make up the total self (Grotevant, Thorbecke, & Meyer, 1982; Waterman, 1982). Thus, individuals may be identified by their physical characteristics, looks, and build; by their biological sex and enactment of gender roles; by their skills in social interaction and membership in groups; by their career choice and achievement; by their political alignment, religious affiliations, morals, values, and philosophies; and by their ethnic identity (Phinney & Alipuria, 1990), personality characteristics, psychological adjustment, and mental health. Identity is personal and individual: it is not only the "I," but also, socially and collectively, the "we" within groups and society (Adams, 1977). Adolescents who are able to accept themselves, who have developed a positive identity, are more

Sexual identity is only one of many components that make up the total self.

likely to be mentally healthy than those who have a negative identity or do not like themselves (Goldman, Rosenzweig, & Lugger, 1980).

Some components of identity are established before others (Dellas & Jernigan, 1990). Physical and sexual components of the self seem to be formulated earliest. Early adolescents are concerned with their body image and sexual identity. Later they become concerned about choosing a vocation and about moral values and ideologies. Similarly, they must deal with their social identities fairly early in their development (Waterman & Nevid, 1977).

Vocational, ideological, and moral identities are formulated gradually (Logan, 1983). After adolescents reach the formal operational stage of cognitive growth and development, they are able to explore alternative ideas and vocations in systematic ways. The exploration of occupational alternatives is the most immediate and concrete task as adolescents select their high school program and decide whether to continue their education after high school. Political and religious ideologies are usually examined during late adolescence, especially during the college years, but may be formulated over a period of many years of adulthood (Raphael, 1979).

Psychosocial Moratorium

Erikson invented the term **psychosocial moratorium** to describe a period of adolescence during which the individual may stand back, analyze, and experiment with various roles without assuming any one role. According to Erikson (1968), the length of adolescence and the degree of emotional conflict experienced by adolescents will vary among different societies. However, failure to establish identity during this time causes self-doubt and role confusion that may trigger previously latent psychological disturbances. Some individuals may withdraw or turn to drugs or alcohol to relieve anxiety. Lack of a clear identity and lack of personality integration can also be observed in the chronic delinquent (Muuss, 1988).

ADOLESCENCE AND DEVELOPMENTAL TASKS

Meaning

Robert Havighurst (1972) sought to develop a psychosocial theory of adolescence by combining consideration of societal demands with individuals' needs (Klaczynski, 1990). What society demands and individuals need constitute **developmental tasks**. These tasks are the knowledge, attitudes, functions, and skills that individuals must acquire at certain points in their lives through physical maturation, personal effort, and social expectations. Mastery of the tasks at each stage of development results in adjustment, preparation for the harder tasks ahead, and greater maturity. Failure to master the developmental tasks results in social disapproval, anxiety, and inability to function as a mature person.

Psychosocial moratorium—a socially sanctioned period between childhood and adulthood during which the individual is free to experiment to find a socially acceptable identity and role

Developmental tasks—the skills, knowledge, functions, and attitudes that individuals have to acquire at certain points in their lives in order to function effectively as mature persons

One of the psychosocial tasks of adolescence is to achieve mature relations with age-mates of both sexes.

Eight Major Tasks

Havighurst (1972) outlined eight major psychosocial tasks to be accomplished during adolescence as follows:

1. Accepting one's physique and using the body effectively
2. Achieving emotional independence from parents and other adults
3. Achieving a masculine or feminine social-sex role
4. Achieving new and more mature relations with age-mates of both sexes
5. Desiring and achieving socially responsible behavior
6. Acquiring a set of values and an ethical system as a guide to behavior
7. Preparing for an economic career
8. Preparing for marriage and family life

These eight developmental tasks need to be interpreted. What did Havighurst say about them?

1. *Accepting one's physique and using the body effectively.* Adolescents become extremely self-conscious about the changes occurring in their bodies at puberty. Adolescents are concerned about body build, image, and appearance (Newell, Hammig, Jurich, & Johnson, 1990). They need to understand the patterns of growth of their own bodies, to accept their own physiques, to care for their health, and to use their bodies effectively in athletics, recreation, work, and everyday tasks (Havighurst, 1972).

2. *Achieving emotional independence from parents and other adults.* Some adolescents are too emotionally dependent on their parents; others are estranged from their parents. Part of the task of growing up is to achieve au-

tonomy from parents and establish adult relationships with them at the same time (Brown & Mann, 1990; Daniels, 1990). Adolescents who are rebellious and in conflict with their parents need help in understanding the situation and learning how to improve it.

3. *Achieving a masculine or feminine social–sex role.* What is a woman? What is a man? What are women and men supposed to look like? How are they supposed to act? What roles are they required to play (Kissman, 1990)? Part of the maturing process for adolescents is to reexamine the changing sex roles of their culture and to decide what roles they can adopt (Havighurst, 1972; Nelson & Keith, 1990).

4. *Achieving new and more mature relations with age-mates of both sexes.* One of the tasks of adolescents is to establish heterosocial friendships, as opposed to the same-sex friendships that are more prevalent in middle childhood (Verduyn, Lord, & Forrest, 1990). Maturing also means developing the social skills necessary to get along with others and to participate in social groups.

5. *Desiring and achieving socially responsible behavior.* This goal refers to sorting out social values and goals in our pluralistic society, which also includes assuming more responsibility for community and national affairs. Some adolescents are disturbed by the injustices, social inequities, and problems they see around them. Some become radical activists; others work in quieter ways to make a difference; others simply refuse to act. Many adolescents struggle to find their niche in society in a way that gives meaning to their lives (Havighurst, 1972).

6. *Acquiring a set of values and an ethical system as a guide to behavior.* This goal includes the development, adoption, and application of meaningful values, morals, and ideals in one's personal life (Harding & Snyder, 1991; Zern, 1991).

7. *Preparing for an economic career.* Determining life goals, choosing a vocation, and preparing for that career are long-term tasks that begin at adolescence (Berzonsky, Rice, & Neimeyer, 1990; Green, 1990; Harding & Snyder, 1991; Steel, 1991).

8. *Preparing for marriage and family life.* The majority of youths consider a happy marriage and parenthood to be important goals in life. However, they need to develop the social skills, positive attitudes, emotional maturity, objective knowledge, and empathetic understanding to make marriage work. This preparation and development begins in adolescence.

Havighurst feels that many modern youths have not found direction in their lives and therefore suffer from aimlessness and uncertainty. He says that during the first half of the 20th century, the primary method of identity achievement (especially for boys) was through an occupation. Work was the focus of life. Today, however, many adolescents would say that expressive values have become more important. Identity is established through close, meaningful, and loving relationships with other persons.

ANTHROPOLOGISTS' VIEWS OF ADOLESCENCE

Developmental Continuity versus Discontinuity

Anthropologists look at adolescence somewhat differently. *They generally reject age and stage theories of development, which say that children go through various stages of development at different ages.* Instead, anthropologists emphasize continuity of development. Margaret Mead said, for example, that Samoan children follow a relatively continuous pattern of growth with relatively little change from one age to the other. Children are not expected to behave one way and adults another. Samoans never have to abruptly change their ways of acting or thinking as they move from childhood to adulthood, so adolescence as a transition from one pattern of behavior to another is practically nonexistent. This principle of continuity of development may be illustrated with three examples by Mead (1950).

First, the submissive role of children in Western culture is contrasted with the dominant role of children in primitive society. Children in Western culture are taught to be submissive, but as adults they are expected to be dominant. Mead (1950) showed that the Samoan child is not expected to become dominant on reaching adulthood after being taught submission as a child. On the contrary, the Samoan girl dominates her younger siblings and in turn is dominated by the older ones. The older she gets, the more dominating she becomes and the fewer girls who dominate her (the parents never try to dominate her). When she becomes an adult, she does not experience the conflict of dominance and submission that is found among adolescents in Western society.

Second, the nonresponsible roles of children in Western culture are contrasted with the responsible roles of children in primitive societies. Children in Western culture must assume drastically different roles as they grow up; they shift from nonresponsible play to responsible work and must do it rather suddenly. In contrast, children in primitive societies learn responsibility quite early. Work and play often involve the same activity. By "playing" with a bow and arrow, a boy learns to hunt. His youthful hunting "play" is a prelude to his adult hunting "work."

Third, dissimilarity of sex roles of children and adults in Western culture is contrasted with similarity of sex roles of children and adults in primitive cultures. In Western culture, infant sexuality is denied and adolescent sexuality is repressed. When adolescents mature sexually, they must unlearn earlier attitudes and taboos and become sexually responsive adults. Mead indicates that the Samoan girl experiences no real discontinuity of sex roles as she passes from childhood to adulthood. She has the opportunity to experiment and become familiar with sex with almost no taboos (except against incest). Therefore, by the time maturity is reached, she is able to assume a sexual role in marriage very easily.

Storm and Stress and Cultural Conditioning

Anthropologists say that storm and stress during adolescence is not inevitable. For example, whether or not menstruation is a disturbing experience depends on its interpretation. One tribe may teach that the menstruating girl may dry up the well or scare the game; another tribe may consider her condition a blessing (a priest could obtain a blessing by touching her, or she could increase the food supply). A girl who is taught that menstruation is a curse will react and act differently from a girl who is taught that it is a positive thing. Therefore, the strains and stresses of pubescent physical changes may be caused by negative teachings of the culture and not by any inherited biological tendencies.

Generation Gap

Although anthropologists deny the inevitability of a generation gap (Mead, 1974), they describe the many conditions in Western culture that create such a gap. Those conditions include pluralistic value systems, rapid social change, and modern technology that make the world appear too complex and too unstable to adolescents to provide them with a stable frame of reference. Furthermore, early physiological puberty and the prolongation of adolescence allow many years for the development of a peer-group culture in which adolescent values, customs, and mores may be in conflict with those of the adult world (Finkelstein & Gaier, 1983). Mead (1950) felt that parent–adolescent conflict and tension can be minimized by giving adolescents more freedom to make their own choices and to live their own lives, by requiring less conformity and less dependency, and by tolerating individual differences within the family. Also, Mead felt that youth can be accepted into adult society at younger ages. They should be allowed to have sex and to marry, but parenthood should be postponed. Adolescents should be given greater responsibility for community life. These measures would allow for a smoother, easier transition to adulthood by eliminating discontinuities in development.

CRITIQUE

What about the various perspectives on adolescence? Which views are most plausible? Each view adds something to a more complete understanding. Anna Freud made a significant contribution in her emphasis on sexual and psychic drives. Her explanation of the psychic disequilibrium of adolescents helps us understand possible causes of erratic behavior. It is important to remember, however, that not all adolescents go through a period of psychic disequilibrium. Some do, but the majority are not in turmoil, deeply disturbed, at the mercy of their impulses, or rebellious. A survey of 6,000 adolescents from 10 nations found few adolescents who were alienated from their parents. Only 7% said they thought their parents were ashamed of them or would be disappointed in them in the future (Atkinson, 1988).

Erikson's explanation of the adolescent's need for identity and the process by which identity is formed has had a marked influence on adolescent theory and research for years. Although Erikson discusses identity achievement as the principal psychosocial task of adolescence, he emphasizes that the process neither begins nor ends with adolescence. It is a lifelong process.

Havighurst's outline of the developmental tasks of adolescence can help youth to discover some of the things they need to accomplish to reach adulthood. The outline can also help adults who seek to guide adolescents on their road to maturity.

Anthropologists have emphasized that there are few universal patterns of development of behavior, so that general conclusions about adolescents should be formulated to take into account the cultural differences. By making cultural comparisons, anthropologists enable us to see some of the positive and negative elements in each culture that help or hinder the adolescent. In our culture, it is evident from an anthropological point of view that adolescence is a creation, an increasingly prolonged period of transition from childhood to adulthood, during which the individual is educated and socialized to take his or her adult place in society. In urban, industrialized societies, the process of achieving adulthood is more complicated and takes longer than in primitive cultures. There is fear in the minds of some parents that their adolescents are "never going to grow up." As one father said: "My son is 25 years old and I'm still supporting him." This process does take a long time, especially when years of higher education are involved. Nevertheless, parents can play an important role in the preparatory process as long as they remember that the ultimate goal is mature adulthood.

One perspective of adolescence gives only a partial picture; after all, adolescents are biological creations who are psychologically and sociologically conditioned by the family, community, and society of which they are members. One must stand in many places and look from many points of view to develop the fullest understanding of adolescents (Mead, 1974).

SUMMARY

1. Adolescence means to grow to maturity. Maturity is that age, state, or condition of life in which a person is fully developed physically, emotionally, socially, intellectually, and spiritually. Puberty is the age or period during which a person reaches sexual maturity. Pubescence is the whole period during which sexual maturation takes place. A juvenile is not yet considered an adult in the eyes of the law.

2. Some tribes have specific initiation ceremonies, or rites of passage, to celebrate the transition from childhood to maturity.

3. G. Stanley Hall said that puberty is a time of upset, emotional maladjustment, and instability that corresponds to the

transition of mankind from savagery to civilization.

4. Anna Freud characterized adolescence as a period of internal conflict, psychic disequilibrium, and erratic behavior. The disequilibrium is caused by the increase of instinctual urges (the id) at the time that sexual maturation takes place. The increase in the id presents a direct challenge to the ego and superego, which seek to curtail the id's expression. Only when the id–ego–superego conflict is resolved is psychic equilibrium restored. The ego employs defense mechanisms to protect itself, but excessive use of them is detrimental to the individual.

5. According to Erikson, the chief psychosocial task of adolescence is the achievement of identity. Identity has many components: sexual, social, vocational, moral, ideological, and psychological. Some aspects of identity are more easily formed than others.

6. According to Erikson, adolescence is a period of psychosocial moratorium during which the individual can try out various roles. The adolescent who fails in the search for identity will experience self-doubt, role diffusion, and role confusion.

7. Havighurst outlined eight major psychosocial tasks that need to be accomplished during adolescence: accepting one's physique and using the body effectively, achieving new and more mature relations with age-mates of both sexes, achieving a masculine or feminine social-sex role, achieving emotional independence from parents and other adults, preparing for an economic career, preparing for marriage and family life, desiring and achieving socially responsible behavior, and acquiring a set of values and an ethical system as a guide to behavior.

8. Anthropologists challenge the basic truths of all age and stage theories of child and adolescent development. They say that in some cultures, children follow a relatively continuous growth pattern, with adult roles evolving as a continuation of the roles they learned as children. In our culture, particular roles are learned as children, and other roles as adults. This discontinuous development results in the creation of a period of adolescence during which roles have to be relearned.

9. Anthropologists also challenge the inevitability of the storm and stress of adolescence and of the generation gap.

10. No one view incorporates the total truth about adolescence. To understand adolescence, one must stand in many places and look from many points of view.

KEY TERMS

Developmental tasks *p. 233*
Juvenile *p. 231*
Maturity *p. 230*

Psychosocial moratorium *p. 233*
Puberty *p. 230*
Pubescence *p. 230*

DISCUSSION QUESTIONS

1. Think back to your adolescence. Was this a period of storm and stress and psychic conflict for you? Why or why not?

2. Which one of Havighurst's developmental tasks was hardest for you when you were an adolescent? Explain.

3. Name as many rites of passage as you can that mark a transition from childhood into adulthood in our culture. Which one of these was most important to your growing up? Why?

4. Who was the most important person to you in your identity development? In what ways was that person most helpful?

5. Why do some people develop a negative identity? What can they do to form a more positive view of themselves? Which components of identity are most difficult to establish and why?

6. What do you think of Mead's concepts of continuity and discontinuity of development? Is it possible to eliminate the discontinuity of development experienced by children in our culture? Explain.

7. When you were an adolescent, was there a generation gap between you and your parents? In what respects? Is there a generation gap between you and your parents now? Explain.

SUGGESTED READINGS

Bilby, R. W., & Posterski, D. C. (1985). *The emerging generation: An inside look at Canada's teenager*. Toronto: Irwin. A summary of what 3,000 teenagers said.

Elkind, D. (1984). *All grown up and no place to go: Teenagers in crisis*. Reading, MA: Addison-Wesley. Pressures placed on today's adolescents.

Erikson, E. H. (1968). *Identity: Youth and crisis*. New York: Norton. A classic.

Kaplan, L. J. (1984). *Adolescence: The farewell to childhood*. New York: Simon and Schuster. The conflicts in letting go of childhood in becoming an adult.

Kett, J. F. (1977). *Rites of passage: Adolescence in America, 1790 to the present*. New York: Basic Books. Historical view of adolescence.

Offer, D. O., Ostrov, E., Howard, K., & Atkinson, R. (1988). *The teenage world: Adolescents' self-image in ten countries*. Answers to questions from 6,000 teenagers in 10 countries.

Rice, F. P. (1990). *The adolescent: Development, relationships, and culture* (6th ed.). Boston: Allyn and Bacon. The author's comprehensive textbook.

Sebald, H. (1984). *Adolescence: A social psychological analysis* (3rd ed.). Englewood Cliffs, NJ: Prentice-Hall. Social relationships, generational conflicts, teen cultures, and adolescent activism.

Physical Development

THE ENDOCRINE GLANDS AND HYPOTHALAMUS*

Endocrine glands—ductless glands that secrete hormones

Hormones—biochemical substances secreted into the bloodstream by the endocrine glands that act as an internal communication system telling the different cells what to do

An **endocrine gland**, as shown in Figure 11.1, is a gland that secretes **hormones** internally. Because the hormones are secreting into the bloodstream, they reach every cell of the body. However, each hormone has target organs its influences, telling those organs what to do and when to act.

Only three glands of the endocrine system are discussed here: the *pituitary gland*, the *adrenal glands*, and *the gonads*. The *hypothalamus*, which is a part of the brain, is discussed here as well because it regulates the pituitary secretions.

Pituitary Gland

Pituitary gland—master gland of the body, located at the base of the brain, that produces hormones to regulate growth

Gonadotropic hormones—sex hormones secreted by the gonads

The **pituitary gland** is only about ½ inch long, weighs less than ½ gram (1/56 oz), and is located in the base of the brain. Its primary identification is a master gland producing hormones that regulate growth. The best known hormones secreted by the pituitary gland are discussed here along with their functions.

Gonadotropic hormones are secreted by the anterior pituitary gland and influence gonad (or sex gland) functioning. There are two gonadotropic hormones. **Follicle-stimulating hormone** (FSH) and **luteinizing hormone** (LH) stimulate the growth of egg cells in the ovaries and sperm in the testes. In the female, FSH and LH control the production and release of the feminizing hormone estrogen and of the hormone progesterone. Both are produced in the ovaries. In the male, LH controls the production and release of the masculinizing hormone testosterone by the testes (Rice, 1989).

Human growth hormone (HGH)—a pituitary hormone that regulates overall body growth

The growth hormone, referred to as **human growth hormone** (HGH) or somatotrophic hormone (SH), affects the overall growth and shaping of the skeleton. A deficiency causes dwarfism; an excess causes giantism.

Prolactin—pituitary hormone that stimulates the secretion of milk by the mammary glands

The pituitary gland also secretes a lactogenic hormone, luteotropic hormone (LTH), that contains the hormone **prolactin**, which influences the secretion of milk by the mammary glands of the breast.

*Part of the material in this chapter is adapted from the author's book, *The Adolescent: Development, Relationships, and Culture.* 6th ed. (1990). Used by permission of the publisher, Allyn and Bacon.

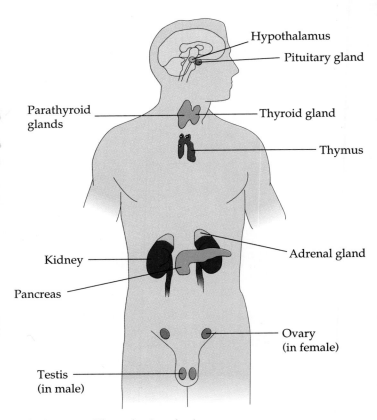

FIGURE 11.1 The endocrine glands.

Adapted from John W. Hole, Jr., *Human Anatomy and Physiology*, 5th ed. Copyright © 1990 Wm. C. Brown Publishers, Dubuque, IA. All rights reserved. Reprinted by permission.

Gonads

The **gonads**, or sex glands, include the ovaries in the female and testes in the male. The ovaries in the female secrete a whole group of hormones known as **estrogens** that stimulate the development of the sexual organs themselves and of female secondary sexual characteristics, such as the growth of pubic hair and breasts, and the distribution of fat on the body.

The ovaries also secrete the female hormone **progesterone**. This hormone is produced following the rupture of the **ovum** from the ovarian follicle. When an egg cell is discharged from a follicle in ovulation, the remaining follicular cells multiply rapidly and fill the cavity. This new cell growth becomes the **corpus luteum** ("yellow body"), and secretes progesterone during the later part of the menstrual cycle. If the ovum has not been fertilized, the corpus luteum disintegrates, and progesterone secretion ceases until the next cycle. Progesterone is of primary importance in preparing the uterus for

Gonads—the sex glands: testes and ovaries

Estrogens—female hormones produced by the ovaries and to some extent by the adrenal glands in both males and females

Progesterone—female sex hormone produced by the corpus luteum of the ovary

Ovum—egg cell

Physical growth and development is an important part of the maturation process during adolescence.

pregnancy and for maintaining the pregnancy itself.

Under the stimulation of LH from the pituitary, the testes in the male begin the production of the androgenic hormone, testosterone. This male hormone is responsible for the development of the male sex organs: the penis, scrotum, epididymis, prostate gland, and seminal vesicles. Both FSH and LH secretions from the pituitary gland stimulate the production and growth of sperm cells. Testosterone is also responsible for the development and preservation of masculine secondary sexual characteristics, including muscular and skeletal development, voice changes, and facial and body hair.

As the ovaries mature, ovarian estrogenic hormone levels increase dramatically and begin to show the cyclic variation in level during various stages of the menstrual cycle. The level of androgens in girls' bloodstreams increases only slightly. As the testes mature in the male, testosterone production increases dramatically, whereas the level of the estrogens increase only slightly. Figure 11.2 shows the increase in hormones at puberty. The ratio of the levels of the male to the female hormones is partly responsible for the development of male or female characteristics. When ratios are not normal in a growing child, deviations occur in the development of

expected masculine or feminine physical traits. A male with an androgen deficiency and an excess of estrogens may evidence decreased potency and sex drive and an enlargement of the breasts. A female with an excess of androgens may grow body and facial hair, develop masculine musculature and strength, or develop an enlarged clitoris or other masculine characteristics.

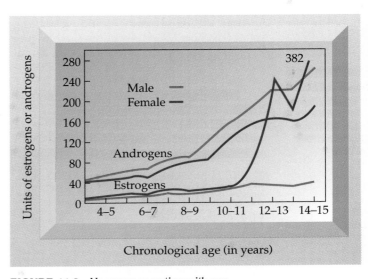

FIGURE 11.2   Hormone secretion with age.

LIVING ISSUES

Use of Steroids by Athletes

Attention has been focused in recent years on the use of **anabolic steroids** by athletes of all ages. A steroid is the male hormone testosterone. Fuller and LaFountain (1987) interviewed 50 athletes, ages 15 to 45 years, who admitted to steroid use. The athletes included both high school and college weight lifters, track stars, body builders, wrestlers, and football players. These athletes said they used the drugs to be competitive.

> We should be allowed to take them because all those other countries take them . . . the women too. You have no choice if you want to compete in the big time (Fuller & LaFountain, 1987, p. 971).

Steroids increase performance, strength, and muscle mass, and reduce fat deposits and fluid retention by the body. They also increase aggression and hostility. This increase may result in sexual aggression, fights and arguments with others, and beating up girlfriends or boyfriends.

Steroids may cause serious physical harm. Athletes can suffer damage to the stomach, reproductive system, liver, and heart. Liver tumors, stomach ulcers, sterility, and heart attacks are common, in addition to emotional instability. Although the illegal use of steroids has even disqualified some athletes from competition, many continue to use them for the sake of improved performance.

Adrenals and Hypothalamus

Adrenal glands— ductless glands that secrete androgens and estrogens, as well as adrenalin, in both men and women

The **adrenal glands** are located just above the kidneys. In the female, they produce low levels of both androgens (masculinizing sex hormones) and estrogen (feminizing sex hormone), and they partially replace the loss of ovarian estrogen after menopause. Although the adrenals secrete both androgens and estrogens in the male, androgens are produced in greater amounts.

Hypothalamus—a small area of the brain controlling motivation, emotion, pleasure, and pain in the body

The **hypothalamus** is located in a small area of the forebrain about the size of a marble. As the motivational and emotional control center of the brain, it regulates such functions as lactation (milk production), pregnancy, menstrual cycles, hormonal production, drinking, eating, and sexual response and behavior. Since it is the pleasure and pain center of the brain, electrical stimulation of the hypothalamus can produce sexual feelings and thoughts (Delgardo, 1969).

GnRH (gonadotropin-releasing hormone)—controls the production and release of FSH and LH from the pituitary

The hypothalamus plays an important role in hormonal production and regulation. A chemical called **gonadotropin-releasing hormone (GnRH)** is produced to control the secretion of FSH and LH from the pituitary.

MATURATION AND FUNCTIONS OF SEX ORGANS

Male

The primary male sex organs are the **penis, scrotum, testes, prostate gland, seminal vesicles, epididymis, Cowper's glands, urethra,** and **vas deferens**. They are depicted in Figure 11.3. Important changes occur in these organs during adolescence. The testes and scrotum begin to grow faster at about age 11½, with the growth becoming fairly rapid after age 13½, and slowing thereafter. These ages are averages. The testes increase 2½ times in length and about 8½ times in weight during this period. The penis doubles in length and girth during adolescence, with the most rapid growth taking place between ages 14 and 16. Both the prostate gland and the seminal vesicles mature and begin secreting semen. The Cowper's glands mature at this time and begin to secrete the alkaline

LIVING ISSUES

Penis Size and Sexuality

Adolescent boys are often concerned about the size of their penises, for they associate masculinity and sexual capability with penis size (Henker, 1982). In reality, the size of the erect penis has little to do with sexual capability. The vagina has few internal nerve endings, and female excitation comes primarily from stimulation of the external genitalia (Rowan, 1982). Therefore, the degree of pleasure experienced by both the man and woman has nothing to do with the size of the male organ. Moreover, the size of the flaccid penis has little to do with the size of the erect penis, because a small penis enlarges much more in proportion to its size than does a large penis.

Can affect self esteem

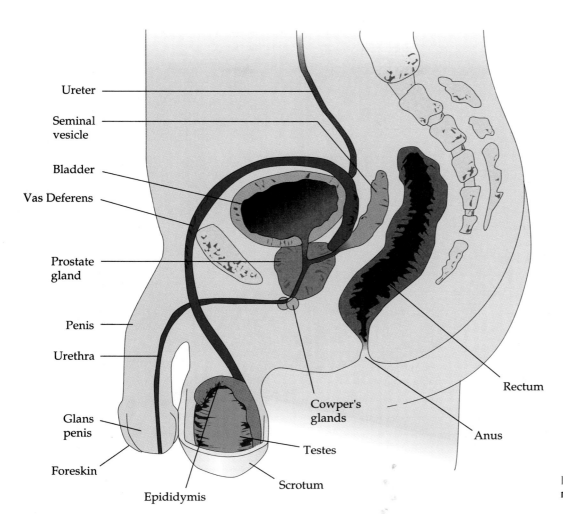

Ureter

Seminal
vesicle

Bladder

Vas Deferens

Prostate
gland

Penis

Urethra

Glans
penis

Foreskin

Epididymis

Cowper's
glands

Testes

Scrotum

Rectum

Anus

FIGURE 11.3 The male
reproductive system.

fluid that neutralizes the acidity of the urethra and lubricates it for safe and easy passage of the sperm. This fluid appears at the
opening of the urethra during sexual excitement and before ejaculation. Because this
fluid contains sperm in about 25% of the
cases examined, conception is possible
whenever intercourse occurs, even if the
male withdraws prior to ejaculation (McCary
& McCary, 1982).

The most important change within the
testes is the development of mature sperm
cells, which occurs when FSH and LH from
the pituitary stimulate their production.
The total process of spermatogenesis, from
the time the primitive spermatogonium is
formed until it grows into a mature sperm,
is about 10 days. After production, the sperm
ripen and mature and are stored in the epididymis for as long as 6 weeks until ejaculated through the vas deferens and urethra
or until absorbed into the body.

Adolescent boys may become concerned
about **nocturnal emissions**, or so-called wet

dreams. Kinsey (1948) reported that almost
100% of men have erotic dreams, and about
83% of them have dreams that culminate in
orgasm. These dreams occur most frequently
among males in their teens and twenties, but
about half of all adult men continue to have
them. Adolescents should be reassured that
such experiences are normal, that no harm
comes from them, and that they can be accepted as part of their sexuality. Anxiety may
be prevented if adolescents are prepared for
nocturnal emissions before they occur (Pad-
dac, 1987).

Female

The primary internal female sex organs are
the **vagina**, **fallopian tubes**, **uterus**, and **ovaries**. The external female sex organs are
known collectively as the **vulva**. They include the clitoris, the labia majora (major or
large outer lips), the labia minora (small inner lips), the mons veneris (mons pubis),
and the **vestibule** (the cleft region enclosed

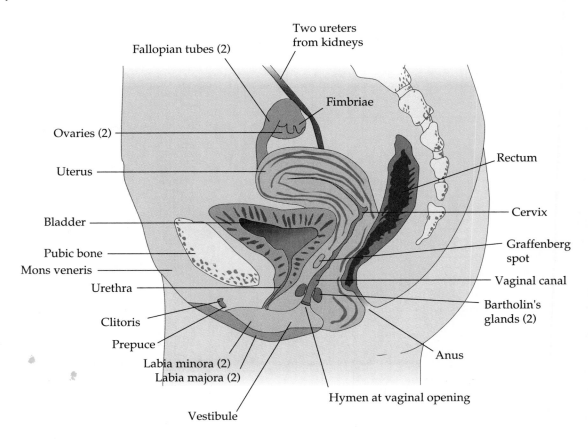

Two ureters from kidneys

Fallopian tubes (2)

Fimbriae

Ovaries (2)

Rectum

Uterus

Cervix

Bladder

Graffenberg spot

Pubic bone

Mons veneris

Vaginal canal

Urethra

Bartholin's glands (2)

Clitoris

Prepuce

Anus

Labia minora (2)

Labia majora (2)

Hymen at vaginal opening

Vestibule

FIGURE 11.4 The female reproductive system.

by the labia minora). The **hymen** is a fold of connective tissue that partly closes the vagina in the virginal female. The **Bartholin's glands**, situated on either side of the vaginal orifice, secrete a drop or so of fluid during sexual excitement.

At puberty, the vagina increases in length, and its mucous lining becomes thicker and more elastic, and turns a deeper color. The inner walls of the vagina change their secretion from the alkaline reaction of childhood to an acid reaction in adolescence. The Bartholin's glands begin to secrete their fluids.

The **labia majora**, practically nonexistent in childhood, enlarge greatly, as do the **labia minora** and the **clitoris**. The **mons veneris** becomes more prominent through the development of a fatty pad. The uterus doubles in length, showing a straight-line increase during the period from 10 to 18 years of age. The ovaries increase greatly in size and weight. They show a fairly steady growth from birth to age 8, some acceleration of growth from age 8 to the time of ovulation (age 12 or 13), and a very rapid increase after sexual maturity is reached. This is a result, no doubt, of the maturation of the follicles (the structures that produce the eggs) within

the ovaries themselves. Every infant girl is born with about 400,000 follicles in each ovary. By the time she reaches puberty, this number has declined to about 80,000 in each ovary. Ordinarily, one follicle produces a mature ovum about every 28 days for a period of about 38 years, which means that fewer than 500 ripen during the woman's reproductive years (McCary & McCary, 1982).

Menstruation

The adolescent girl begins menstruating at an average age of 12 to 13 years, although she may mature considerably earlier or later (from age 9 to age 18 years is an extreme range). **Menarche** (the onset of menstruation) usually does not occur until maximum growth rates in height and weight have been achieved. Because of superior health care and nutrition, girls start menstruating earlier today than in former generations (Bullough, 1981). The average age has decreased from age 14 in 1905 to about age 12½ today (Gilger, Geary, & Eisele, 1991). An increase in body fat may stimulate menarche, whereas vigorous exercise tends to delay it (Stager, 1988). The menstrual cycle may vary in length from 20 to 40 days, with an average

Menarche—first menstruation

of about 28 days (Vollman, 1977). However, there is considerable difference in the length of the cycle when different women are compared, and any one woman may show widespread variations. A regular cycle is quite rare.

The exact time ovulation occurs is an important consideration. *The time of ovulation is ordinarily about 14 days before the onset of the next menstrual period,* which would be on the 12th day of a 26-day cycle and on the 16th day of a 30-day cycle. There is some evidence that women have become pregnant on any one day of the cycle, including during menstruation itself, and that some women may ovulate more than once during a cycle, possibly because of the stimulus of sexual excitement itself.

Menarche can be a traumatic event for some girls who are not prepared ahead of time (Pillemer, Koff, Rhinehart, & Rierdan, 1987). Other girls are able to accept menstruation because they have been taught the basic facts (McGrory, 1990). The young girl's attitudes and feelings about menstruation are very important (Buchanan, 1991). A study of menarche experiences of 95 women from 23

countries revealed that negative reactions to first menstruation were very common (Logan, 1980). Many girls from Asian countries had heard little about menstruation, and 50% of these females reported embarrassment when it began. Some 50% of Japanese women reported being surprised by menarche. Only half of the Asian mothers spoke to their daughters prior to menarche; over one-half of the daughters felt inadequately prepared for their first period. Table 11.1 shows the emotional reactions to menarche of all 95 of the foreign women. The more knowledgeable girls are prior to menarche, the more likely they are to report a positive initial experience (Kogg, Rierdan, & Sheingold, 1982; Ruble & Brooks-Gunn, 1982; Skandhan, 1988).

(Education + response)

PHYSICAL GROWTH AND DEVELOPMENT

Development of Secondary Sexual Characteristics

Sexual maturation at puberty also includes development of **secondary sexual characteristics.** These include the development of mature female and male body contours, voice changes, the appearance of body hair, and other minor changes.

The sequence of development for boys and girls is given in Table 11.2. The development of the **primary sexual characteristics** is also included in the table. Primary sexual characteristics are marked with an asterisk. The ages given are averages; actual ages may extend several years before and after these ages (Akinboye, 1984; Westney, Jenkins, Butts, & Williams, 1984). The average girl matures about 2 years before the average boy, but the time of development is not always consistent. An early-maturing boy may be younger than a late-maturing girl. The mean age for the first ejaculation of semen is 13.7 years. The mean age of menarche is 12.5 years. However, the age of sexual maturity extends over such a wide range (ages 9 to 18 are not unusual) that any age within the range should be considered normal.

Secondary sexual characteristics—changes in the body at the time of sexual maturation that do not involve the sex organs themselves

Primary sexual characteristics—changes that involve the sex organs at the time of sexual maturation

TABLE 11.1 Emotional Reactions of the Foreign Women to Their Menarche

Reaction	Percentage Showing Reaction
Surprised	32
More grown up	24
Embarrassed	23
Sick	15
Frightened	15
Happy	15
More feminine	13
Different	13
Afraid everyone would know	12
Unclean	11
Proud	10
Worried about what to do	10
Sad	8
Closer to mother	5

The number of subjects from each of the 23 countries was as follows: Brazil—6, Burma—1, Chile—1, Colombia—4, El Salvador—2, France—2, Germany—2, Hong Kong—1, India—1, Indonesia—5, Iran—15, Italy—2, Japan—16, Mexico—3, Peru—5, Samoa—1, Spain—1, Switzerland—1, Taiwan—1, Thailand—1, Venezuela—16, Vietnam—1, and Zambia—3.

From "The Menarche Experience in Twenty-Three Foreign Countries" by D. D. Logan, 1980, *Adolescence, 15* (Summer), p. 254.

Growth in Height and Weight

A growth spurt in height begins in early adolescence, accompanied by an increase in weight and changes in body proportions. The combined data from longitudinal studies of individual adolescents provide a compos-

LIVING ISSUES

Menstrual Irregularity in Athletes

Extensive research has established that **amenorrhea** or irregular menstruation is common in female athletes: swimmers, distance runners, ballet dancers, and others (Calabrese et al., 1983; Frisch et al., 1981; Baker et al., 1981). The reason is that extensive exercise reduces body fat, which influences the menses. The current evidence, from both anecdotal and investigative sources, suggests that exercise-induced amenorrhea rapidly reverses once training is discontinued (Stager, 1984; Stager, Ritchie, & Robertshaw, 1984). When physical training is reduced or stopped, as a result of either an injury or taking a vacation, amenorrheic athletes report a resumption of normal menstrual periodicity.

In comparing current runners with ex-collegiate distance runners and sedentary controls, a study showed that current runners reported significantly fewer menses than either of the other two groups. The ex-runner and the control group were similar in terms of the number of menses in the previous 12 months. Further, the ex-runners who experienced menstrual irregularity during training reported that they resumed normal menstruation on an average of 1.7 months after training was terminated. No relationship was established between length of amenorrhea and the time of resumption of regular menses (Stager, Ritchie, & Robertshaw, 1984).

Sexual maturation at puberty includes the development of secondary sexual characteristics.

TABLE 11.2 Sequence of Development of Primary and Secondary Sexual Characteristics

Boys	Age Span		Girls
Beginning growth of testes, scrotum, pubic hair	11.5–13	10–11	Height spurt begins
			Slight growth of pubic hair
Some pigmentation, nodulation of breasts (later disappears)			Breasts, nipples elevated to form "bud stage"
Height spurt begins			
Beginning growth of penis*			
Development of straight, pigmented pubic hair	13–16	11–14	Straight, pigmented pubic hair
			Some deepening of voice
Early voice changes			
Rapid growth of penis, testes, scrotum, prostate, seminal vesicles*			Rapid growth of vagina, ovaries, labia, uterus*
First ejaculation of semen*			Kinky pubic hair
Kinky pubic hair			Age of maximum growth
Age of maximum growth			Further enlargement, pigmentation, elevation of nipple, areola to form primary breasts
Beginning growth of axillary hair			
			Menarche*
Rapid growth of axillary hair	16–18	14–16	Growth of axillary hair
Marked voice change			Filling out of breasts to form adult conformation, secondary breast stage
Growth of beard			
Indentation of frontal hair line			

Note. Primary sexual characteristics are marked with an asterisk.

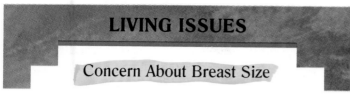

LIVING ISSUES

Concern About Breast Size

Many adolescent girls are concerned about the size and shape of their breasts. Some girls who are flat chested feel self-conscious because they are influenced by society, which emphasizes fullness of breasts as a mark of beauty and sexuality. Some adolescent girls wear padded bras or tight jerseys or sweaters, or even get medical help to enlarge their breasts. Such girls may also be swayed by misleading advertising promises to ''put inches on your bosom in only a few days.'' In contrast, some girls who have large breasts are made to feel self-conscious when they suffer unkind remarks and stares.

ite picture of growth trends in groups of children.

Boys grow fastest in height and weight at approximately 14 years of age; girls grow fastest at approximately 12 years of age, as shown in Figure 11.5 (Tanner, 1962, 1972). Because girls start to mature earlier, between the ages of 12 and 14 they average slightly taller than boys, and between the ages of 10

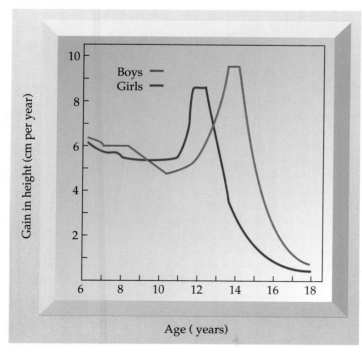

FIGURE 11.5   Increase in height.

From J. M. Tanner (1962), *Growth at Adolescence*, 2d ed. Courtesy of Charles C. Thomas, publisher, Springfield, IL.

and 14 girls are heavier than boys. Whereas girls have reached 98% of adult height at 16¼ years, boys do not reach 98% of their adult height until 17¾ years. These rates vary for different individuals.

One of the most important factors in determining the total mature height of the individual is *heredity* (Eveleth & Tanner, 1976; Gertner, 1986). Short parents tend to have short children; tall parents tend to have tall children. *Nutrition* is the most important environmental factor (Tanner, 1970). Children who receive better diets during the growth years become taller adults than do less well-nourished children. The age when sexual maturation begins also affects the total height finally achieved. Girls and boys who are early maturers tend to be shorter as adults than those who are late maturers. The reason is that a late maturer has a longer time to grow before the sex hormones stop the pituitary from stimulating further growth.

Furthermore, the *growth achieved before puberty is of greater significance to total adult height than is the growth achieved during puberty*. The adolescent growth spurt contributes, in absolute terms, relatively little to the postadolescent skeletal dimensions and only moderately to strength and weight.

The total process of growth is speeding up. Children and adolescents today experience the growth spurt earlier, grow faster, attain a greater total adult height, and attain this height at an earlier age than did children and adolescents 60 or 70 years ago.

EARLY AND LATE MATURATION

Figure 11.6 shows the considerable variations in stage of physical development at a given age for each sex. Intensive investigations have been made on the effect of early or late physical maturation on psychological and social adjustments. The results of these studies are important to understanding adolescents who differ from the norm in the timing of their development (Collins & Propert, 1983).

Early-Maturing Boys

Early-maturing boys are large for their age, more muscular, and better coordinated than late-maturing boys, so they enjoy both athletic and social advantages. They are better able to excel in competitive sports (Blyth, Bulcroft, & Simmons, 1981). Their superior development and athletic skills enhance their social prestige and position. They participate

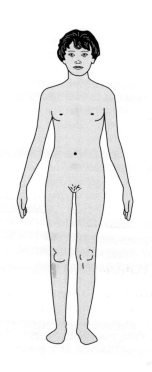
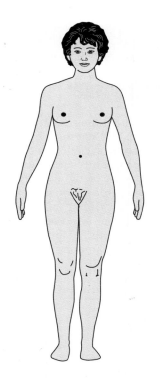
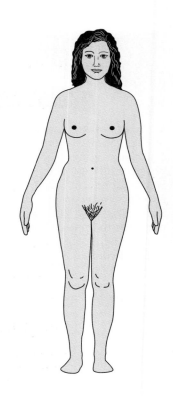
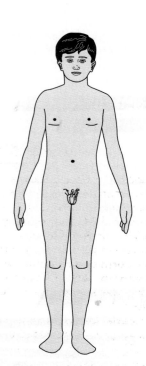
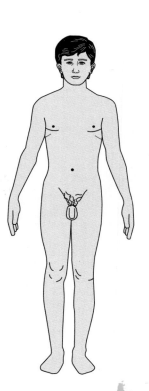
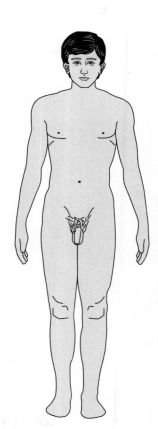

FIGURE 11.6 Variations in pubescent development. All three girls are 12¾ years and all three boys are 14¾ years of age but in different stages of puberty.

Adapted from J. M. Tanner (1973), "Growing Up." *Scientific American,* September, p. 38. Copyright © 1973 by Scientific American, Inc. All rights reserved.

Girls 12
Boy 16 '14

more frequently in extracurricular activities in high school (Pomeranz, 1979). They are often chosen for leadership roles; their peers tend to give them greater social recognition by appointing them to positions of leadership in school. They tend to show more interest in girls and to be poular with them because of their adult appearance and sophisticated social interests and skills. Early sexual maturation may thrust them into early heterosexual relationships.

Adults, too, tend to favor early-maturing boys by rating them as more physically attractive, better groomed, and more masculine than late-maturing boys (Hamachek, 1976). However, adults tend to expect more of them in terms of adult behavior and responsibilities, which gives early-maturing boys less time to enjoy the freedom that comes with childhood.

Early-Maturing Girls

Girls who mature early are at a disadvantage during their elementary school years. They are taller and more physically developed, and they tend to feel self-conscious and awkward. They enjoy less prestige at this age than do prepubertal girls.

However, early-maturing girls come into their own socially by the time they reach junior high and high school age. They tend to look grown up and are envied by other girls because of their looks. They also begin to attract the attention of older boys and to start dating earlier than normal (Phinney, Jensen, Olsen, & Cundick, 1990). However, parents may begin to worry because of their daughters' emerging heterosexual interests and strive to curtail their social activities. The girls may find themselves emotionally unequipped to deal with sexual enticement, and with sophisticated social activities (Udry & Cliquet, 1982). Parental restriction and these outside pressures may create stress, so for some this is a period of upset and anxiety. Nevertheless, usually by the time early-maturing girls have reached 17 years of age, they score higher on tests of total personal and family adjustments, have more positive self-concepts, and enjoy better personal relations than do later maturers (Hamachek, 1976). However, the net positive effect of early maturation does not seem to be as pronounced for girls as for boys.

Late-Maturing Boys

Late-maturing boys suffer a number of social disadvantages and may develop feelings of inferiority as a result (Apter, Galatzer, Beth-

Halachmi, & Laron, 1981). At age 15 they may be 8 inches shorter and 30 pounds lighter than early-maturing males, so they may have less strength and show poorer motor performance, coordination, and reaction time than those who mature earlier. Physical size and motor coordination play an important role in social acceptance, so later maturers may develop negative self-perceptions. They have been characterized as less popular; less well-groomed; less attractive physically; more restless and affected; bossy and rebellious against their parents; and as being dependent, with feelings of inadequacy and rejection. They often become self-conscious and withdraw because of their social rejection (Dreyfus, 1976).

Late-Maturing Girls

Late-maturing girls of junior high or senior high school age are often socially handicapped (Apter et al., 1981). They look and are treated like "little girls." They may not get invited to boy–girl parties and social activities. One study in New York City showed that those who first menstruated at ages 14 to 18 tended to be late daters (Presser, 1978). They are often jealous of their friends who are more developed, but have much in common with normal-maturing boys and look on them as friends. However, their activities reflect the interests of those of younger age groups with whom they spend their time.

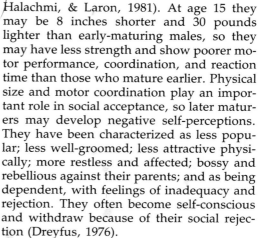

FOCUS

Precocious Puberty

Precocious puberty means early sexual maturation. A recent example is that of 9-year-old Maria Eliana Jesus Mascarenhas, who gave birth to a healthy 7-pound daughter in March 1986. She named the girl Diana. The daughter of illiterate Brazilian farmhands, Maria delivered via cesarean section in the rural town of Jequie, 800 miles north of São Paulo. Dr. Fernando Prata Goes, the obstetrician who performed the surgery, explained: "Maria was scared and confused, and so was the father of the baby" ("Mom, Nine, Doing Fine," 1986, p. 15).

Maria suffers from an imbalance of hormones that produce premature puberty. At the time she gave birth, her physical age was estimated to be between 13 and 14. Since making worldwide headlines, Maria has returned to her parents' farm, where she is learning how to be a mother (Rice, 1989, p. 70).

One advantage for late-maturing girls, compared with those who develop early, is that they may not be criticized by parents and other adults. The chief disadvantage for late maturers seems to be the temporary loss of social status because of their relative physical immaturity.

BODY IMAGE AND PSYCHOLOGICAL IMPACT

Physical Attractiveness

Physical attractiveness is important in several ways. It affects the adolescent's positive self-esteem and social acceptance (Koff, Rierdan, & Stubbs, 1990; Thornton & Ryckman, 1991). It affects personality, interpersonal attraction, and social relationships (Shea & Adams, 1984). Attractive adolescents are thought of in positive terms: intelligent, desirable, successful, friendly, and warm (Lerner, Delaney, Hess, Jovanovic, & Von Eye, 1990). Partly as a result of differential treatment, attractive adolescents appear to possess a wider variety of interpersonal skills, to be better adjusted socially, and to have higher self-perceptions and healthy personality attributes (Adams, 1980; Cash & Janda, 1984; Reis, Nezlek, & Wheeler, 1980).

Concepts of the Ideal

Adolescents are influenced by the concepts of the ideal build that are accepted by our culture (Cok, 1990; Collins, 1981). Most adolescents would prefer to be of medium build (Ogundari, 1985). Adolescents who are tall and skinny are unhappy with their builds, as are those who are short and fat. Because Western culture overemphasizes the importance of being slim, the obese adolescent female is especially miserable (Bozzi, 1985; Lundholm & Littrell, 1986). It is partly because of this obsession with slimness that **anorexia nervosa** and **bulimia** develop among adolescents (Grant & Fodor, 1986). If a girl does not have a slim figure, she is less likely to have dates. Social rejection is hard to live with. This means that self-satisfaction and self-esteem are closely related to acceptance of the physical self (Jaquish & Savins-Williams, 1981; Littrell & Littrell, 1990; Padin, Lerner, & Spiro, 1981; Pomerantz, 1979; Stewart, 1982).

Studies of males provide further proof of the social importance of possessing an

Anorexia nervosa—an eating disorder characterized by an obsession with food and being thin

Bulimia—an eating disorder characterized by binging and purging

LIVING ISSUES

The Problem of Acne

At the onset of puberty, because of an increase in the secretion of androgens in the bloodstream, the glands of the skin increase their activity. Three kinds of skin glands cause problems for the adolescent:

1. *Apocrine sweat glands*, located in the armpits and in the mammary, genital, and anal regions.
2. *Merocrine sweat glands*, distributed over most of the skin surfaces of the body.
3. *Sebaceous glands*, oil-producing glands of the skin.

After puberty, the apocrine and merocrine sweat glands secrete a fatty substance causing body odor. The sebaceous glands develop at a greater speed than the skin ducts through which they discharge their skin oils. As a result the ducts may become plugged and turn black as the oil oxidizes and dries upon exposure to the air, creating a blackhead. This in turn may become infected, causing a pimple or **acne** to form. The acne may be fairly mild with spontaneous remission occurring. Deep acne requires medical management to prevent scarring. A variety of treatment options are available.

average physique and of physical attractiveness. Men with muscular body builds are more socially accepted than those with other types of builds (Tucker, 1982). Tall men with good builds are considered more attractive than short men (Feingold, 1982). College-age men with muscular builds are more likely to feel comfortable and confident in interacting with others than those who are skinny or obese (Tucker, 1983). In another study, adolescents who rated themselves as unattractive were also likely to describe themselves as lonely (Moore & Schultz, 1983).

NUTRITION AND WEIGHT

Caloric Requirements

During the period of rapid growth, adolescents need greater quantities of food to take care of bodily requirements. As a consequence, they develop voracious appetites. The stomach increases in capacity to be able to digest the increased amounts of food. The

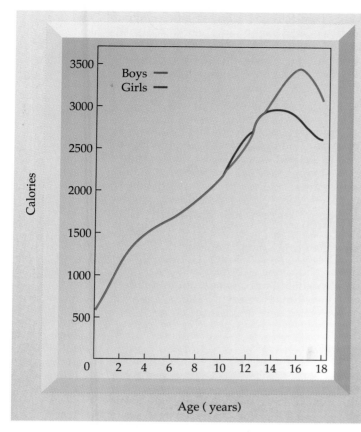

FIGURE 11.7 Daily caloric requirements for both sexes from birth to eighteen years.

Redrawn from "Energy Requirements" by E. L. Holt, Jr., 1972, in H. L. Barnett and A. H. Einhorn (Eds.), *Pediatrics*, 15th ed., p. 130. By permission of Appleton-Century-Crofts.

caloric requirement for girls may increase on the average by 25% from ages 10 to 15. The caloric requirement for boys may increase on the average by 90% from ages 10 to 19 (Figure 11.7 shows the increase). As a result, the adolescent boy finds it almost impossible to get enough to eat.

Importance of Nutrition

Health maintenance depends partly on proper eating habits (Carruth & Goldberg, 1990). Attainment of maximum height, strength, and physical well-being depends on proper nutrition. Nerve, bone, muscle, and other tissue growth requires body-building foods. Nutritional deficiencies are related to emotional instability, premenstrual tension (in females), lower resistance to infection, reduced stamina, and physical and mental retardation. Good nutrition also is extremely important during pregnancy.

Deficiencies

Many adolescents have inadequate diets (U.S. Departments of Agriculture and of Health and Human Services, 1985). When present, the principal deficiencies are as follows:

1. Insufficient thiamine and riboflavin.
2. Insufficient vitamins—especially A and C—caused primarily by lack of fresh vegetables and fruit in the diet.
3. Insufficient calcium—caused primarily by an inadequate intake of milk.
4. Insufficient iron—especially true in females.
5. Insufficient protein—usually true only in females.

Overweight and Underweight

Adolescents often worry about being overweight (Cook, Reiley, Stallsmith, & Garretson, 1991; Steele, 1980). From 10% to 15% of all adolescents are obese (at least 20% overweight or more), girls more than boys (Storz, 1982; U.S. Department of Commerce, 1987). Being overweight affects the adolescent's emotional adjustment, ego identity development, self-esteem, and social relationships. It also is a future health hazard because obesity is related to gynecological disorders, joint disease, hypertension, and cardiovascular disease (Shestowsky, 1983; Stein, 1987).

Underweight adolescents have the opposite condition: They are burning up more calories than they are consuming. Males especially worry about being too skinny or "not having a good build." In one study of 568 adolescent males, over half were dissatisfied with their body, and 71% reported eating to gain weight (Fleischer & Read, 1982). Underweight adolescents need to increase the consumption of fattening foods and overcome a poor appetite. They also can conserve energy by spending more hours in bed and omitting strenuous exercise.

Anorexia Nervosa

Anorexia nervosa is a life-threatening emotional disorder characterized by an obsession with being slender (Gilbert & DeBlassie, 1984). About 5% to 10% of cases are male, and the remainder are females, usually between ages 12 and 18 (Svec, 1987). The major symptoms are a constant preoccupation with dieting; body image disturbance (Mallick, Whipple, & Huerta, 1987); excess weight loss (at least 15% below

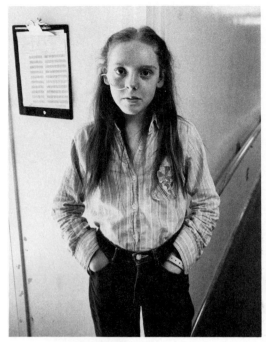

The majority of anorexic victims are female. How would you explain this?

optimal body weight); hyperactivity (excessive exercise); extreme moodiness, loneliness, depression, helplessness, and inadequacy; strong feelings of insecurity; social isolation; and amenorrhea (American Psychiatric Association, 1987). Anorexia is associated with numerous medical conditions: abdominal distress, constipation, metabolic changes, electrolyte abnormalities, hypothermia, dehydration, low blood pressure, slow heartbeat, and cardiac arrest (which is a frequent cause of death). The anorexic feels cold, even though the body grows fine silky hair to conserve body heat. Kidney malfunction may occur because of a potassium deficiency (Muuss, 1985).

Anorexics become thin and emaciated in appearance once the illness has developed. Treichel (1982) found that malnutrition causes brain abnormalities, impaired mental performance, and lengthened reaction time and perceptual speed. Medical problems associated with malnutrition cause death in 5% to 10% of anorexics. Obsession with dieting combined with a compulsion to exercise leads to social isolation and withdrawal from friends and family. Hunger and fatigue are usually denied, and any attempt to interfere with the regime is angrily resisted. Anorexics are very hard to treat (Grant & Fodor, 1984).

Bulimia

Bulimia is a binge–purge syndrome. It is characterized by a compulsive and rapid consumption of large quantities of high-calorie food followed by efforts to eliminate the food (Stein & Reichert, 1990). According to one study, bulimic clients in an outpatient setting revealed an average of 13.7 hours spent in binge eating each week, with a range of 15 minutes to 8 hours for each episode (Mitchell, Pyle, & Eckert, 1981). Binging and purg-

FOCUS

Five Theories About Causes of Anorexia

Biological theory. A disturbance in the hypothalamus causes anorexic behavior.

Psychobiologic regression hypothesis. Once body weight drops below a critical level because of inadequate diet, neuroendocrine functions are impaired, which reverses the developmental changes of puberty. The anorexic regresses to a prepubertal stage of development (Muus, 1985, pp. 526, 527).

Psychosexual theory. The fact that anorexia appears at puberty after the development of sexual characteristics suggests that sexual conflict is a central issue in the illness (Romeo, 1984). The anorexic is unwilling to accept her role as a woman and her feminine sexuality. She fears sexual intimacy, so she uses the disorder to delay or regress her psychosexual development.

Social theory. Anorexics are brainwashed by a culture that emphasizes being slim, so they become obsessed with food and diet (Hertzler & Grun, 1990).

Family systems theory. Anorexics often have disturbed relationships with their parents (Eisele, Hertsgaard, & Light, 1986). The families are often rigid and overprotective, with a hypochondriacal concern for the child's health (Brone & Fisher, 1988). Often a power struggle develops between the adolescent girl and her parents, particularly with her mother (Goldstein, 1981; Levin, Adelson, Buchalter, & Bilcher, 1983). This desire to guide and control becomes more evident as parental concern grows. The more the parents try to change the pattern, the more intense the power struggle becomes (Russell, Halasz, & Beumont, 1990).

ing could occur many times daily. Caloric consumption ranged from 1,200 to 11,500 calories per episode, with carbohydrates as the primary food. Many clients could not perceive a sense of fullness. Episodes took place secretly, usually in the afternoon, evening, or at night. Induced vomiting was the most common purging method. Other times bulimics used amphetamines, enemas, diuretics, laxatives, compulsive exercising, or fasting to offset the huge food intake (LeClair & Berkowitz, 1983).

Bulimics feel a compulsion to eat, but because of concern about their weight, purge afterward. Binges usually follow periods of stress and are accompanied by anxiety, depressed mood, and self-depreciating thoughts during and after the episode. The illness is most common in college-age females or those in their early 20s (Lachenmeyer & Muni-Brander, 1988), although frequency of occurrence is increasing among high school females (Johnson, Lewis, Love, Lewisk & Stuckey, 1984).

Bulimics have low self-esteem, are anxious and depressed, and have strong moral beliefs (Baird & Sights, 1986; Brouwers, 1988). They wish to be perfect, yet have negative self-worth and a poor self-image, are shy, and lack assertiveness (Holleran, Pascale, & Fraley, 1988). They are often preoccupied with fear of rejection in sexual relationships and with not being attractive enough to please a man (Van Thorre & Vogel, 1985). Because of the drive for perfection, anxiety builds up, which is relieved through lapses of control during binging and purging episodes. This is followed by feelings of guilt and shame, which contribute to the sense of low self-esteem and depression (Pyle, Mitchell, & Eckert, 1981). Bulimics are often difficult to treat because they resist seeking help or they sabotage treatment. Both bulimics and anorexics need short-term intervention to restore body weight and to save their life, followed by long-term therapy to ameliorate personality and family problems.

SUMMARY

1. The endocrine glands are ductless glands that secrete hormones directly into the bloodstream. The hormones tell different cells what to do and when to act.
2. The three most important glands related to sexuality are the pituitary gland, the adrenal glands, and the gonads.
3. The pituitary secretes HGH, which regulates growth; gonadotropic hormones (FSH and LH) that stimulate the gonads (ovaries and testes) to function; and LTH, which stimulates milk production.
4. The ovaries secrete estrogen, which is responsible for sexual maturation, and progesterone, which is active in the menstrual cycle.
5. The testes secrete testosterone, which is responsible for sexual maturation in males.
6. Both feminizing and masculinizing hormones (estrogens and androgens) are present in both boys and girls. The ratio of male to female hormones is partly responsible for the development of male or female characteristics.
7. The adrenal glands also secrete both androgens and estrogens in both males and females.
8. The hypothalamus secretes GnRH, which acts on the pituitary to trigger the secretion of the gonadotropic hormones that act on the gonads (the testes and ovaries).
9. The primary sex organs of the male are the testes, scrotum, epididymis, seminal vesicles, prostate gland, Cowper's glands, penis, vas deferens, and urethra, all of which mature at puberty. The most important change within the testes is the production of mature sperm cells. Boys begin ejaculating semen and sperm cells at the mean age of 13.7. Boys need to be prepared for nocturnal emissions.
10. The primary internal female sex organs that develop during puberty are the ovaries, fallopian tubes, uterus, and vagina. The external female organs are known collectively as the vulva, and include the mons veneris (mons pubis), labia majora, labia minora, clitoris, vestibule, and hymen.
11. On the average, females begin menstruating at 12 to 13 years of age. Girls need to be prepared in a positive way for menarche (first menstruation).
12. Sexual maturation also includes the development of secondary sexual characteristics.
13. One of the earliest signs of the physical changes of adolescents is the growth spurt that begins early in adolescence. A

number of factors are important in determining the total mature height achieved: heredity, nutrition, age of sexual maturation, and total height achieved before puberty.

14. Some girls and boys are early or late maturers. Early-maturing boys have a physical and social advantage, although parents tend to expect more of them at this age. Some early-maturing girls are at a disadvantage in elementary school, but come into their own in junior high school, enjoying many social advantages.

15. Late-maturing boys tend to suffer social inferiority because of their delayed growth and development. Late-maturing girls also tend to be at a distinct social disadvantage.

16. Precocious puberty means early sexual maturation.

17. Adolescents are very concerned about their body image and physical attractiveness. They have been influenced by images of the ideal build as taught in our culture, which emphasizes medium builds.

18. Acne is a problem for some adolescents.

19. Good nutrition is very important to good health. Common deficiencies include calcium, iron, and protein; and vitamins A, C, thiamine, and riboflavin.

20. Being either overweight or underweight is a problem.

21. The two most serious eating disorders are anorexia nervosa and bulimia, both of which can be life-threatening diseases, and both of which are hard to treat.

KEY TERMS

Acne *p. 252*
Adrenal glands *p. 244*
Amenorrhea *p. 248*
Anabolic steroids *p. 244*
Anorexia nervosa *p. 252*
Bartholin's glands *p. 246*
Bulimia *p. 252*
Clitoris *p. 246*
Corpus luteum *p. 242*
Cowper's glands *p. 244*
Endocrine glands *p. 242*
Epididymis *p. 244*
Estrogens *p. 242*
Fallopian tubes *p. 245*
FSH (follicle-stimulating hormone) *p. 242*
GnRH (gonadotropin-releasing hormone) *p. 244*
Gonadotropic hormones *p. 242*
Gonads *p. 242*
HGH (human growth hormone) *p. 242*
Hormones *p. 242*
Hymen *p. 246*
Hypothalamus *p. 244*
Labia majora *p. 246*

Labia minora *p. 246*
LH (luteinizing hormone) *p. 242*
Menarche *p. 246*
Mons veneris (mons pubis) *p. 246*
Nocturnal emissions *p. 245*
Ovaries *p. 245*
Ovum *p. 242*
Penis *p. 244*
Pituitary gland *p. 242*
Precocious puberty *p. 251*
Primary sexual characteristics *p. 247*
Progesterone *p. 242*
Prolactin *p. 242*
Prostate gland *p. 244*
Scrotum *p. 244*
Secondary sexual characteristics *p. 247*
Seminal vesicles *p. 244*
Testes *p. 244*
Urethra *p. 244*
Uterus *p. 245*
Vagina *p. 245*
Vas deferens *p. 244*
Vestibule *p. 245*
Vulva *p. 245*

DISCUSSION QUESTIONS

1. Should athletes be allowed to take steroids to improve their ability? Have you ever known anyone who did? What were the results?

2. To men: When you had your first nocturnal emission, did you understand what was happening? Were you prepared for it? How did you feel?

3. To women: When you first started to menstruate, did you understand what was happening? Were you prepared for it? How did you feel?

4. Comment on the attitudes in American culture toward female breasts and male penis size. What effect do these attitudes have on adolescents?
5. Do you know anyone who matured early? Late? What were the effects?
6. What can be done if a person has acne?
7. What factors prevent some adolescents from getting a balanced diet?

8. What can be done if a person is overweight? What helps the most? What can be done if a person is underweight? What helps the most?
9. Do you know anyone who suffered from anorexia nervosa? Describe. What were the results? Do you know anyone who was bulimic? Describe. What were the results?

SUGGESTED READINGS

Katchadourian, N. (1977). *The biology of adolescence*. New York: W. H. Freeman.

Lerner, R. M., & Foch, T. T. (Eds.). (1987). *Biological-psychological interactions in early adolescence*. Hillsdale, NJ: Erlbaum. Series of articles.

Rice, F. P. (1989). *Human sexuality*. Dubuque, IA: Wm. C. Brown. The author's comprehensive college text on human sexuality. Includes all age groups.

Rice, F. P. (1990). *The adolescent: Development, relationships, and culture* (6th ed.). Boston: Allyn and Bacon. The author's comprehensive textbook on adolescence.

12

Cognitive Development

FORMAL OPERATIONAL THOUGHT*

As we have seen in Chapter 7, Piaget outlined four stages of cognitive development: the *sensorimotor stage* (birth to 2 years), the *preoperational stage* (2 to 7 years), the *concrete operational stage* (7 to 11 years), and the *formal operational stage* (11 years and up). The formal operational stage is discussed in this section on the cognitive development of adolescents.

Characteristics

During the formal operational stage of development, the thinking of adolescents begins to differ radically from that of children (Barenboim, 1977; Piaget, 1972). Children perform concrete operations and arrange things into classes, relations, or numbers, making logical "groupings" and classifications. However, they never integrate their thought into a single, total, logical system. Adolescents, however, are able to use propositional logic. In formal operations, they are able to reason, systematize their ideas, and construct theories. Furthermore, they can test these theories scientifically and logically, considering several variables, and are able

*Part of the material in this chapter is adapted from the author's book, *The Adolescent: Development, Relationships, and Culture.* 6th ed. (1990). Boston: Allyn and Bacon. Used by permission of the publisher.

to discover truth scientifically (Inhelder & Piaget, 1958). Adolescents are able to assume the role of scientists because they have the capacity to construct and test theories (Okun & Sasfy, 1977). Elkind (1967) called the formal operational stage *the conquest of thought.*

Piaget conducted an interesting experiment to discover the strategies adolescents use in solving problems. This experiment involved a pendulum suspended by a string (see Figure 12.1). The problem was to find out what would affect the oscillatory speed of the pendulum. The subjects were to investigate four possible effects: starting the pendulum with various degrees of force, releasing the pendulum from various heights, changing its weight, or changing the length of the pendulum. The subjects were free to solve the problem in any way they chose.

The adolescents showed three basic characteristics in their problem-solving behavior. *First*, they planned their investigations systematically. They began to test all possible causes for variation in the pendulum swings: various degrees of force or push, high or low height, light or heavy weight, and long or short string. *Second*, they recorded the results accurately and objectively. *Third*, they formed logical conclusions.

For example, they first observed that both the force and the height of the drop of the pendulum had no effect on oscillatory speed. They next tried different combinations of weight and found out that the oscillation speed remained the same regardless of

During the formal operational stage of development, the thinking of adolescents begins to differ radically from that of children.

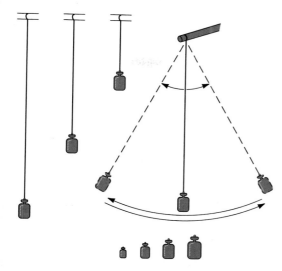

FIGURE 12.1   The pendulum problem. The pendulum problem utilizes a simple apparatus consisting of a string, which can be shortened or lengthened, and a set of varying weights. The other variables that at first might be considered relevant are the height of the release point and the force of the push given by the subject.

From *The Growth of Logical Thinking from Childhood to Adolescence* by Bärbel Inhelder and Jean Piaget, translated by Anne Parsons and Stanley Milgram. Copyright © 1958 by Basic Books, Inc. Reproduced by permission of Basic Books, Inc., Publishers.

the weight. They did discover that changing the string length (the pendulum length) alone determined the speed of oscillation. Other researchers have replicated this experiment many times.

By trial and error, children may come up with the right answer but they fail to use systematic procedures to find the answer and give logical explanations of the solutions. They often form conclusions that are premature and false because they have not considered all of the important facts and are not able to reason logically about them. Children tend to hold tenaciously to their initial opinions even when presented with contrary evidence. They even try to make the circumstances fit their preconceived notions:

> In summary, three interrelated characteristics of adolescent thought have emerged. These are the ability to derive a proposition from two or more variables or a complex relationship; the ability to suggest mentally the possible effect of one or more variables; and the capacity to combine and separate variables in a hypothetical-deductive framework ("if this is so, this will happen") so that a reasonable possibility is recognized before

the test is made in reality. The fundamental property of adolescent thought is this reversible maneuvering between reality and possibility (Gallager & Noppe, 1976, p. 202).

To do formal operational thinking, adolescents are able to be *flexible*. They can be quite versatile in their thoughts, and can devise many interpretations of an observed outcome, without relying on preconceived ideas. In contrast, younger children are confused by unexpected results that are inconsistent with their simple preconceptions.

Preoperational children begin to use symbols, but *the formal operational adolescents now begin to use a second symbol system: a set of symbols of symbols.* For example, algebraic signs and metaphorical speech are symbols for numbers and/or words. The capacity to identify symbols makes the adolescent's thought much more flexible than the child's. Words can now carry double or triple meanings. Cartoons can represent a complete story that would otherwise have to be explained in words. Junior high school youth have no difficulty understanding religious symbols or political cartoons that younger children cannot comprehend. Algebra may be understood by adolescents but not by elementary school children.

Adolescents are also able to orient themselves toward what is abstract and not immediately present. This facility enables them to distinguish possibility from present reality, to project themselves into the future, and to think about what might be (Bart, 1983). Adolescents have not only the capacity to accept and understand what is given, but also the ability to conceive of what might occur. Because they can construct ideas, they have the ability to elaborate on these ideas and generate new thoughts. They become inventive, imaginative, and original in their thinking, and "possibility dominates reality." "The adolescent is the person who commits himself to possibilities . . . who begins to build 'systems' or 'theories' in the largest sense of the term" (Baker, 1982; Inhelder & Piaget, 1958).

In summary, formal thinking, according to Piaget, involves four major aspects: *introspection* (thinking about thought), *abstract thinking* (going beyond the real to what is possible), *logical thinking* (being able to consider all important facts and ideas and to form correct conclusions, such as the ability to determine cause and effect), and *hypothetical reasoning* (formulating hypotheses and examining the evidence for them, considering numerous variables).

FOCUS

Comparison of Childhood and Adolescent Thought

The way children approach problems and the logical, systematic way adolescents approach problems is described below:

E. A. Peel . . . asked children what they thought about the following event: "Only brave pilots are allowed to fly over high mountains. A fighter pilot flying over the Alps collided with an aerial cableway and cut a main cable, causing some cars to fall to the glacier below. Several people were killed." A child at the concrete-operational level answered: "I think the pilot was not very good at flying." A formal-operational child responded: "He was either not informed of the mountain railway on his route or he was flying too low. Also his flying compass may have been affected by something before or after take-off, thus setting him off course causing collision with the cable."

The concrete-operational child assumes that if there was a collision the pilot was a bad pilot; the formal-operational child considers all the possibilities that might have caused the collision. The concrete-operational child adopts the hypothesis that seems most probable or likely to him. The formal-operational child constructs all possibilities and checks them out one by one (Kohlberg & Gilligan, 1971, pp. 1061, 1062).

Effects on Personality and Behavior

IDEALISM.   Adolescents' power of reflective thinking enables them to evaluate what they have learned as children (Schmidt & Davison, 1983) and to become more capable of moral reasoning (Steinberg, Greenberger, Jacobi, & Garduque, 1981). Their ability to distinguish the possible from the real enables them to imagine what the adult world might be like under ideal circumstances. They compare the possible with the actual, recognize that the actual is less than ideal, and so become idealistic rebels (White, 1980).

For awhile, some adolescents develop the equivalent of a messianic complex, seeing themselves in a major effort to reform the world. Usually the efforts of young adolescents are confined to verbal discussion, but some older adolescents get caught up in group movements that seek the utopian reconstruction of society. By late adolescence, attention shifts from egocentrism to a newfound **sociocentrism** (Enright, Shukla, & Lapsley, 1980).

So adolescents also become champions of the underdog. Shapiro (1973) believed that adolescents' own inner conflicts account for their empathetic capacities for the suffering of others. They can easily identify with the oppressed, the victims of selfish society, the poor, and the weak. They perceive that social injustices mirror their own internal, individual struggles.

Sociocentrism—a focus of attention on social problems and the concerns of society

HYPOCRISY.   Adolescents are sometimes accused of hypocrisy because of the discrepancy between what they say and what they actually do. Elkind (1978) illustrated this tendency with two examples. *First,* his son lamented about his brother's going into his room and taking his things. He berated his father for not punishing the culprit; yet the same boy felt no guilt about going into his father's study, using his calculator and typewriter, and playing his music on his father's stereo without permission. *Second,* a group of young people were involved in a "Walk for Water" drive, in which sponsors were paid for each mile walked. The money was for pollution control. The next day, however, a drive along the route the youths had walked revealed a roadside littered with fast-food wrappers and beverage cans. City workers had to be hired to clean up the mess. The question was: Did the cost of cleaning up amount to more money than was collected? And weren't these adolescents hypocritical? They objected to pollution, yet they were among the chief offenders in defacing their environment (Elkind, 1978).

The behavior of these adolescents reveals the discrepancy between idealism and behavior. Early adolescents have the capacity to formulate general principles such as "Thou shalt not pollute" but lack the experience to see the application of these general rules to specific practice. Youths believe that if they can conceive and express high moral principles, they have attained them, and that nothing concrete need be done. This attitude upsets and confuses adults, who insist that ideals cannot be attained instantly and that one must work for them (Elkind, 1978).

Adolescents can manifest hypocrisy in another way. They pretend to be what they are not (Mitchell, 1980). They are expected to conform to parental viewpoints and beliefs even when they do not agree with them. They are expected to be open and honest but are chastised when they are. They are expected to like school but rarely do. They are expected not to be hurt or angry when they really are. They are expected not to engage in behavior that will hurt or disappoint parents, so they do not talk to them about important things. They are expected to pretend to be what they are not. They are pressured not to be, not to feel, and not to desire. They are expected to deny the self and so behave hypocritically.

SELF-CONSCIOUSNESS AND EGOCENTRISM.   Formal operational thinking also results in the development of a new form of egocentrism (Adams & Jones, 1982; Enright, Lapsley, & Shukla, 1979; Enright, Shukla, & Lapsley, 1980; Hudson & Gray, 1986; de Rosenroll, 1987). The capacity to think about their own thoughts makes adolescents become acutely aware of themselves. As a result, they become egocentric, self-conscious, and introspective. They become so concerned about themselves that they may conclude that others are equally obsessed with their appearance and behavior (Peterson & Roscoe, 1991). "It is this belief that others are preoccupied with his appearance and behavior that constitutes the egocentrism of the adolescent" (Elkind, 1967, p. 1029). Adolescents feel they are "on stage" much of the time, so that much of their energy is spent "reacting to an imaginary audience." As a result, they become extremely self-conscious. Whether in the lunchroom or on the bus going home, youths feel they are the center of attention.

Elkind (1967) also discusses what he terms **personal fable**—adolescents' beliefs in the uniqueness of their own experiences. Because of their beliefs that they are important to so many people, they come to regard themselves as special and unique. This may be why so many adolescents believe that misfortunes such as unwanted pregnancies or accidents happen only to others, never to them.

Self-consciousness and egocentrism have other manifestations. Adolescents believe everyone is looking at them, but they feel totally alone, unique in a vast, uncaring universe. To always be on stage, scrutinized but rarely understood, imposes a terrific emotional strain. As a result, they employ numerous psychological mechanisms to protect their frail egos. They become critical and sarcastic, partly as a defense against their own feelings of inferiority and as a way of making themselves look good (Elkind, 1975). Those with low self-esteem tend to present a false front to others and to mask their true feelings by fabricating an image (Elliot, 1982; Hauck & Loughhead, 1985). The intellectualization and newfound asceticism of college students have been explained as just such a defense mechanism.

Whereas adolescents are often self-centered, they are frequently self-admiring, too. Their boorishness, loudness, and faddish dress reflect what they feel others admire. The boy who stands in front of the mirror for two hours combing his hair is probably imagining the swooning reactions he will produce from his girlfriend.

CONFORMITY.   One would expect that adolescents who are capable of logical reasoning processes would also be creative (Torrance, 1974). But investigations of the relationship of adolescent thinking processes to creative behavior suggest a negative relationship: Adolescents become less creative, not more so (Wolf, 1981). The reason is not because they are less capable of being crea-

Personal fable— beliefs in the uniqueness of one's own experience

FOCUS

Formal Operational Thinking and Self-Concept

The capacity to think about themselves is necessary in adolescents' process of developing self-concept and identity. In doing this, they have to formulate a number of postulates about themselves, such as "I am physically attractive" or "I'm smart in school" or "I'm popular." These postulates are based on a number of specifics, such as "I'm attractive because I have pretty hair, a nice figure, or the boys notice me." Because of formal operational thinking they are able to entertain a number of simultaneous ideas and to test each one by, for example, asking a friend: "What do you think of my hair?" or "Do you think I have ugly hair?" *Gradually they begin to sort out what they feel is truth from error about themselves and to formulate total concepts of self.*

tive. They have a greater potential than before. But in actuality they are less creative because of the pressures on them to conform—from both their peers and society in general. The price they pay for acceptance is conformity. As a result, they squelch their individuality and begin to dress, think, and act like others in groups to which they want to belong. One study emphasized that adolescents who rate highest in self-trust (who believe in themselves) are more willing to risk doing things that are imaginative and creative (Earl, 1987).

DECENTERING AND A LIFE PLAN. In the process of becoming adults, adolescents gradually begin to develop more cognitive objectivity and perspective. They begin to cure themselves of their idealistic crises and to return to the reality that is the beginning of adulthood. Piaget and Inhelder (1969) go on to emphasize that "the focal point of the decentering process is the entrance into the occupational world or the beginning of serious professional training. The adolescent becomes an adult when he undertakes a real job. It is then that he is transformed from the idealistic reformer into an achiever" (p. 346).

Piaget refers to the importance of adolescent work in the community as a facilitator of human growth. He states that work helps the adolescent meet the storm and stress of that period. Work experience can also stimulate the development of social understanding and socially competent behavior (Miller, 1978; Steinberg, Greenberger, Jacobi, & Garduque, 1981). True integration into society comes when the adolescent begins to affirm a life plan and adopt a social role.

Critique of Piaget's Formal Operational Stage

AGES AND PERCENTAGES. Since Piaget formulated his concept of a formal operational stage of cognitive development, researchers have been examining various components of the formulation. The age at which the formal operational stage replaces the concrete operational stage is one question that has to be raised. Piaget (1972) himself advanced the possibility that in some circumstances, the appearance of formal operations may be delayed to 15 to 20 years of age and "that perhaps in extremely disadvantageous conditions, such a type of thought will never really take shape" (p. 1012). Piaget (1971) acknowledged that social environment can accelerate or delay the onset of formal opera-

tions. Research has shown that fewer economically deprived adolescents achieve formal thought than do their more priviledged counterparts and that there is a complete absence of formal operations among the mentally retarded (Gaylor-Ross, 1975).

Parents, teachers, and other adults need to realize that not all same-age adolescents are at the same stage of development. Some have not yet achieved formal operations. To ask these youths to make decisions from among numerous alternatives or variables that cannot be grasped simultaneously is to ask the impossible. Very few youths may make the transition to formal operations by age 10 or 11, but only about 40% have progressed beyond concrete operations by high school graduation (Bauman, 1978).

TEST CRITERIA. The measured percentages of people reaching formal operational thinking depend partially on the criteria for formal thinking that are established and the tests employed to evaluate that criteria. Piaget distinguished between an easy level of tests (III-A) and a more advanced level (III-B). Arlin (1975) and Kuhn (1979) observed that only approximately 50% of the adult population actually attain the full stage of formal thinking (III-B). Piaget (1980) readily admitted that the subjects of his study were "from the better schools in Geneva" and that his conclusions were based on a "privileged population." However, he still maintained that "all normal individuals are capable of reaching the level of formal operation" (Piaget, 1980, p. 75) as long as the environment provides the necessary cognitive stimulation. Actually, not all adolescents or adults reach the formal level, but there is still a significant increase in the use of formal operational thinking among adolescents between ages 11 and 15.

MATURATION AND INTELLIGENCE. Maturation of the nervous system plays an important role in cognitive development, because the nervous system must be sufficiently developed for any real thought to take place. This is one reason why a greater percentage of older adolescents exhibit formal thought than do younger adolescents (Ross, 1974). Webb (1974) tested very bright 6- to 11-year-old children (IQs of 160 and above) to determine their levels of thinking. All subjects performed the concrete operational tasks easily, showing that they were cognitively at their developmental age, but only 4 males, age 10 and older, solved the formal thought problems, indicating that re-

Sociocultural and environmental factors influence the development of formal operational thought.

Educational experiences can be geared to teaching scientific methods of problem solving.

gardless of high intelligence, a degree of maturation was necessary for movement into the next stage of cognitive development. Other research helps explain further the relationship among development, intelligence, and cognition. Other things being equal, individuals with high IQs are more likely to develop formal thought sooner than those with low IQs, but *it is the interaction of age and intelligence that contributes to cognitive ability* (Cloutier & Goldschmid, 1976).

CULTURE AND ENVIRONMENT. Formal thought is, however, more dependent on social experience than is sensorimotor or concrete operational thought (Carlson, 1973). Adolescents from various cultural backgrounds show considerable variability in abstract reasoning abilities. Some cultures offer more opportunities to adolescents to develop abstract thinking than others do, by providing a rich verbal environment and experiences that facilitate growth by exposure to problem-solving situations.

Social institutions such as the family and school accelerate or retard the development of formal operations. Parents who encourage academic excellence, ideational explorations, exchanges of thoughts, and the attainment of ambitious educational and occupational goals are fostering cognitive growth. Schools that encourage students to develop problem-solving skills and to acquire abstract reasoning enhance cognitive development.

Adolescent Education and Formal Operational Thought

Many students are used to traditional methods of instruction that involve lectures, memorization, and so forth, so they have difficulty adjusting to methods designed to en-

courage free thinking (Maroufi, 1989). However, development of abstract thinking and formal operations problem solving can be encouraged in a number of ways (Danner & Day, 1977). Discussion groups, debates, question periods, problem-solving sessions, and science experiments are approaches that encourage the development of formal thinking and problem-solving abilities. Teachers need to be prepared to handle group discussion and stimulate interchange and feedback. Experimental or problematic situations can be presented that allow students opportunities to observe, analyze possibilities, and draw inferences about perceived relationships. Teachers who use authoritarian approaches rather than social interchange stifle real thinking. Some students develop higher cognitive abilities at a relatively slow pace (Arons, 1978), so teachers must be willing to give explicit help and encouragement and allow the necessary time for reasoning capacities to develop.

Piaget (1972) sets forth two goals of education that incorporate this philosophy.

The principal goal of education is to create men who are capable of doing new things, not simply of repeating what other generations have done—men who are creative, inventive, and discoverers. *The second goal of education is to form minds which can be critical, can verify, and not accept everything they are offered* . . . We need pupils who are active, who learn early to find out by themselves, partly by their own spontaneous activity and partly through material we set up for them, who learn early to tell what is verifiable and what is simply the first idea to come to them (p. 5).

Beyond Formal Operations

Progressive changes in thought structure may extend beyond the level of formal operations. The suggestion is that cognitive growth is continuous; there is no end point limiting the possibility for new thought structures to appear. Researchers continue to seek these new structures (Arlin, 1975; Arlin, 1977; Commons, Richards, & Kuhn, 1982).

There is some evidence that a fifth stage of development can be differentiated. It has been labeled a **problem-finding stage** (Arlin, 1975). This new stage represents an ability to discover problems not yet delineated, to describe these problems, or to raise general questions from ill-defined problems.

Only some people in the problem-solving stage reach the problem-finding stage. Arlin (1975), in her research with college seniors, found that all subjects who scored high in problem finding had reached formal operational thinking, but not all subjects who had reached formal thinking scored high in problem finding. However, sequencing of development was evident: Formal operations had to be accomplished before persons could move on to the next stage.

SCHOLASTIC APTITUDE

SAT

The **Scholastic Aptitude Test** (SAT) is one of the most widely used tests in the United States. It is a multiple-choice exam with two parts, a verbal section and a math section, which are each scored on a scale of 200–800. The SAT is the predominant college entrance exam in 22 states, and 88% of all colleges use it (Franco, 1983). Over 1 million high school seniors took the test in 1990. The combined verbal and math scores often determine eligibility not only for admission but also for financial aid and scholarships. The Educational Testing Service (ETS), which produces the test, claims that when combined with high school records, the SAT is a better predictor of students' first-year performance in college than any other measurement. Nevertheless, the complaints over the use or misuse of the test grow louder (Rice, 1979; Robinson, 1983).

The test is supposed to measure basic abilities acquired over a student's lifetime and is thus supposed to be immune to last-minute cramming and "coaching." But a study by the Federal Trade Commission's Bureau of Consumer Protection showed that special coaching can improve SAT scores for each part by an average of 25 points out of the possible 800 (Rice, 1979). In one nationwide chain, more than 80 coaching schools tutored 30,000 students in one year, and improved scores on the average by 25 points. In individual cases, these schools claim they can improve scores up to 100 points. The author talked to a lawyer who, as a student, wanted to raise his verbal score on the LSAT (law school aptitude test) before applying to law school. He studied a vocabulary list of the 5,000 most-used words and was able to raise his verbal score by 60 points.

The basic question is: If coaching can raise a student's score, should the test be relied on as a basic measure of scholastic aptitude and as a standard for college admission? In all fairness, the College Entrance Examination Board warns against making admission decisions on the basis of the SAT scores alone. The ETS itself has said that an individual's score can vary plus or minus 30 to 35 points, which is a spread of 60 to 70 points. For these reasons, some of the best schools may rely more on class rank, high school grades, interviews, student essays, and other admission procedures (Chance, 1988). Even high marks from high school may be questioned, for standards vary from school to school. Also, grading standards have become more lenient so the number of students with A averages has increased so rapidly that there are now as many A students as there are those with C averages.

Some authorities suggest that achievement tests would be a better way of predicting college success than SATs. (See the following section on the ACT.) Such tests have several advantages. They evaluate a student's mastery of a particular subject area. They encourage high schools to offer more rigorous courses. They also encourage students to work harder in these courses because they would have to pass tests on the subjects to get into college (Chance, 1988).

The SAT score averages by college-bound seniors dropped until 1980, after which they increased until 1985. Since 1985, math scores have held steady, and verbal scores have declined. Figure 12.2 shows score averages from 1963 through 1990. As can be seen, average scores from the 1989–1990 school year on the verbal section of the SAT fell to 424, the lowest since 1980. Math scores averaged 476.

Declining scores have led to increased

Problem-finding stage—a fifth stage of cognitive development characterized by the ability to create, to discover, and to formulate problems

Scholastic Aptitude Test (SAT)—the most widely used test for youths to determine their aptitude for college work

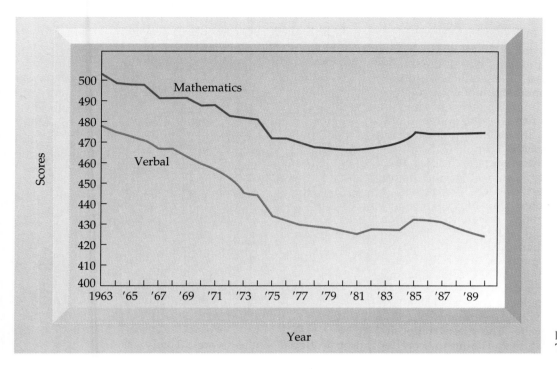

FIGURE 12.2   Scholastic Aptitude Test average scores.

criticism of the schools for relaxing teaching standards and not teaching the basics. College Board president Donald M. Stewart commented:

> Students must pay less attention to video games and music videos and begin to read more. The requirement to read through homework has been reduced. Students don't read as much because they don't have to . . . . Reading is in danger of becoming a lost art among too many American students—and that would be a national tragedy (Mitgang, 1990, pp. 1A, 4A).

Part of the blame for the drop was attributed to changes and problems in the family, increased television viewing, and such problems as turbulence in national affairs (Zuckerman, 1985). Males continue to score somewhat higher than females, especially on math scores, probably reflecting differences in cultural conditioning (Denno, 1982; Mills, 1981). On the positive side, in the 1989–1990 school year women's math scores reached their highest levels in 16 years; scores of Native Americans rose a combined 13 points, and African-American test-takers continued a 15-year trend as the most improved ethnic group.

Proposed Revisions of the SAT

The College Board has recently approved changes in the SAT that will take effect in 1994. The test will be known as the Scholastic Assessment Test, with the mandatory section labeled SAT I. Some educators wanted to require a written essay, but others said such a section would discriminate against minorities, so the essay was made optional in a separate part known as the SAT II. Also, scoring millions of essays would require enormous amounts of time and money.

The new SAT I has both a verbal part and a math part. The verbal section includes longer critical reading passages about which students must answer questions. The antonyms section has been deleted. But the greatest changes are in the math section. Students may use calculators for solving problems, rather than select answers from multiple-choice slots. There is a new emphasis in the whole test on critical reasoning and "real-life" problem solving. Although the new test will still be "coachable," proponents claim it will be less coachable than the old test. Maximum scores will still be 1600, or 800 for each of the two parts.

ACT

ACT Assessment Program (American College Testing program)—the second most widely used college admissions test

The **ACT Assessment Program (American College Testing program,** 1986) is the second most widely used college admissions test, administered to more than a million students each year. The ACT Assessment Program consists of three parts: (a) the *Student Profile Section (SPS)*, (b) the *ACT Interest Inventory*, and (c) the *Academic Tests*. The Academic Tests are the Natural Sciences Reading Test, the Social Studies Reading Test, the Mathematics Usage Test, and the English Usage Test. The ACT Interest Inventory is a survey of students' vocational preferences based on Holland's typology (Kifer, 1985). The Student Profile Section (SPS) is a 192-item inventory of demographics, high school activities and accomplishments, and academic and extracurricular plans for college.

The ACT Academic Tests yield standard scores of 1 to 36, which are averaged to create the ACT Composite. The mean composite score in 1987 was 18.7. The mean score for males was 19.5, and for females it was 18.1. The scores for the four academic tests— English, Math, Social Studies, and Natural Sciences—for both males and females held remarkably steady when compared to 1986 scores. However, there has been a drop in composite scores between 1970 and 1987, for both males and females, with the biggest drop in Math scores, and the next biggest drop in Social Studies scores. There was a modest rise in Natural Sciences scores between 1970 and 1987, especially for males. Table 12.1 shows the scores.

The SPS has been shown to be valid, with follow-up studies showing a 69% to 70% match between students' choices of major on the SPS and actual choices at the end of the freshman year of college (Laing, Valiga, & Eberly, 1986).

TABLE 12.1 American College Testing (ACT) Composite Achievement Scores, 1970 and 1987

Subject	1970	1987	Differential
English	18.5	18.4	−.1
M	17.6	17.9	+.3
F	19.4	18.9	−.5
Math	20.0	17.2	−2.8
M	21.1	18.6	−2.5
F	18.8	16.1	−2.7
Social Studies	19.7	17.5	−2.2
M	20.3	18.4	−1.9
F	19.0	16.7	−2.3
Natural Sciences	20.8	21.4	+0.6
M	21.6	22.8	+1.2
F	20.0	20.1	+.1

Adapted from *High School Profile Report*. Annual, 1987. Iowa City, IA: The American College Testing Program.

FOCUS

Gender Differences in Spatial Abilities and Achievement

For a number of years, a variety of tests have shown gender differences in some specific abilities and achievements. Boys generally score higher in spatial and math tests, and girls score higher in reading and verbal tests. This has been attributed primarily to differences in sex-role socialization. Boys are encouraged to excel in math and spatial skills, but not in reading and verbal skills. Although girls are expected to perform well academically in all subjects, they have not been encouraged to excel in math, or in experiences thought to enhance spatial abilities (e.g., sports). Butcher (1986) reported that girls in grades 6 through 10 ranked "getting good grades" as their primary aspiration at school, well above the choice of "being good at sports." Gender differences may indeed reflect two different sex-role socialization processes (Pearson & Ferguson, 1989).

SCHOOL

Trends in American Education

PROGRESSIVES VERSUS TRADITIONALISTS. The emphasis in American education has shifted from one extreme to the other. **Progressives** have argued that the goal of education is to prepare students for all phases of life: effective personality growth, the effective use of leisure time, physical health, a vocation, home and family living, and citizenship. **Traditionalists** have argued that the goal of education is to teach the basics—foreign languages, history, math, science, and English—to increase student knowledge and intellectual powers.

There are some authorities who insist that education plays an important role in reforming society and addressing social issues. Schools design new programs to deal with social problems as they arise. Driver education was introduced when traffic fatalities rose. Family life and sex education followed a rise in premarital pregnancies, sexually transmitted diseases, and divorce rates. African-American studies and school busing were introduced in response to demands for racial integration. Women's studies were introduced in part as a response to women's demands for equality. New social problems courses were offered when crime rates rose. Because social needs change from time to time, the educational pendulum has been pushed first in one direction and then in another.

RISE OF PROGRESSIVE EDUCATION. Traditionalism was the dominant emphasis in American schools until the 1930s. When the Depression came, there were no jobs for adolescents, so many stayed in school instead of seeking employment (Ravitch, 1983). Many of these youths were not bound for college or interested in traditional academic subjects, so they needed special programs. Progressive educators like John Dewey said the schoolroom should be a laboratory of living, preparing students for all of life. As a consequence, many schools introduced vocational and personal service courses, restricting most academic courses to the college preparatory program. These courses included life adjustment education centered around personal concerns, health, leisure activities, vocations, and community problems. Principals boasted that their programs helped students adjust to the demands of real life, freeing them from dry academic studies. Developing an effective personality became as important as improving reading skills (Ravitch, 1983; Wood, Wood, & McDonald, 1988).

SPUTNIK AND AFTER. When the Soviet Union launched Sputnik, the first space satellite, in the 1950s, our nation became obsessed with the failure of our schools to keep pace with the technological advances of the Soviet Union. Critics accused the schools of offering a watered-down curriculum that left American youth unprepared to challenge a communist country. Congress passed the *National Defense Education Act* and appropriated nearly $1 billion in federal aid to education, which supported the teaching of science, math, and foreign languages. Schools modernized their laboratories, and courses in math and physical sciences were rewritten by leading scholars to reflect advances in knowledge.

1960s AND 1970s. The Cold War had abated by the mid-1960s, but the United States was disturbed by increasing racial tension, social unrest, and antiwar protests. The schools were called on to rescue a society that was in trouble. Major school aid legislation was passed as part of the Johnson administration's "War on Poverty." Once more there was a clamor for educational relevance. Educators demanded that adolescents spend time not only in the classroom, but also in community and work settings. Career and experimental education replaced academic programs so that adolescents could receive "hands-on" experience. Elementary schools

Progressives—educators emphasizing that education is to prepare pupils for life

Traditionalists—educators who argue that the purpose of education is to teach the basics

Progressive schools include instruction in the use of computers.

knocked down classroom walls, adopted open education, and gave students more choices of what to study. High schools lowered graduation requirements. Enrollments in traditional subjects such as math, science, and foreign language fell and gave way to student-designed courses, independent study, and a flock of electives. By the late 1970s, over 40% of all high school students were taking a general rather than a college preparatory or a vocational course of study, and 25% of their educational credits came from remedial coursework and courses aimed at personal growth and development (National Commission on Excellence in Education, 1983).

1980s AND 1990s. By 1980, many people became alarmed at the steady, slow decline in academic indicators. SAT scores had shown a steady decline from 1963. Verbal scores fell over 50 points and average math scores 35 points. Parental and public outcry grew, resulting in the appointment of the National Commission on Excellence in Education (1983). The commission's findings were as follows:

- The number and proportion of students demonstrating superior achievement on the SATs (those with math or verbal scores of 650 or higher) had declined.
- Scores on achievement tests in such subjects as physics and English had declined.
- There was a steady decline in science achievement scores of 17-year-olds by national assessments in 1969, 1973, and 1979.
- Average achievement of high school students on most standardized tests was lower than when Sputnik was launched.
- Nearly 40% of 17-year-olds could not draw inferences from written material; only one-fifth could write a persuasive essay, and only one-third could solve a mathematics problem requiring several steps.
- About 13% of all 17-year-olds were functionally illiterate.

Economic competition from Western Europe and Japan made officials fear that the nation was losing its competitive edge in world markets. Educational reformers demanded more required courses, particularly in math and science; longer school days; more academic rigor in the schools; and tougher standards for graduation. The pendulum began to swing back to a more traditionalist position.

Enrollment in High School

Prior to 1870, free secondary education was not available to all American youths. There were only 800 public high schools in the whole country. Most youths who were preparing for college attended private secondary schools, then called *preparatory schools*. The now-accepted principle that public education need not be restricted to the elementary schools was established by the famous Kalamazoo decision in 1874. Secondary education began to grow. In 1950, only 33% of those 25 and over had completed 4 or more years of high school. By 1989, the number was 76%. Figure 12.3 shows the rise since 1950.

FIGURE 12.3 Percentage of adults who have completed four years of high school or more: 1950–1989.

From *Statistical Abstract of the United States, 1990* (p. 38) by U.S. Department of Commerce, Bureau of the Census, 1990, Washington, DC: U.S. Government Printing Office.

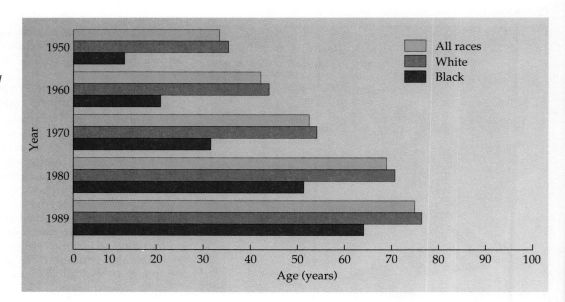

pregnancy + marriage most common reason for girls

Dropouts

Figure 12.4 shows the percentage of dropouts from school by age and race during 1989. Through age 17, attendance figures are very high, with little difference between whites and blacks. Most dropouts occur during the high school years, especially after age 17, with a greater percentage of blacks than whites leaving school. The total number of dropouts is considerable, though the rate has been decreasing over the years. During 1988, 4.3 million youths dropped out of school. The overall dropout rate in 1988 was 10.9% (U.S. Bureau of the Census, 1990).

WHO DROPS OUT AND WHY.   There are numerous reasons for youths dropping out of school or underachieving (Zarb, 1984). Lack of interest in school, low marks, school failure, misconduct, reading disability, intellectual difficulties or retardation, health problems, financial problems, social maladjustments (Buhrmester, 1990), personality problems, parental influence and relationships, family background (Sarigiani, Wilson, Petersen, & Viocay, 1990), racial and ethnic prejudice and discrimination, and socioeconomic factors were listed (Kupersmidt & Coie, 1990). Usually problems accumulate over the years until withdrawal occurs, after the legal requirements of the number of years of schooling and age have been met. The actual circumstance or event that results in withdrawal may be minor: a misunderstanding with a teacher, a disciplinary action, a misunderstanding at home, or difficulty with peers. One boy was refused admittance to a class until a late excuse was obtained from his gym teacher in the prior period. The gym teacher would not give an excuse; the boy got angry, walked out of school, and never returned. Another boy withdrew in the last semester of his senior year because his foster parents would not buy him a suit for graduation. In many cases, a whole series of prior events leads to final withdrawal: social maladjustment or isolation, strained family relationships, conduct problems at school, grade retardation, or poor marks. There are a number of factors that correlate with early school withdrawal (Tidwell, 1988).

FAMILY RELATIONSHIPS.   The quality of family relationships has a significant impact on school success (Hurrelmann, Engel, Holler, & Nordlohne, 1988; Snodgrass, 1991). Bright, high-achieving high school students are more likely to describe their parents as less restrictive or severe in discipline, encouraging (but not pressuring) with respect to achievement, affectionate, trusting, approving, understanding, and typically sharing recreation and ideas. Youth from conflict-

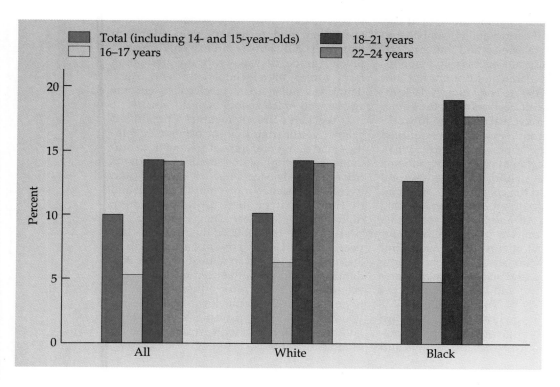

FIGURE 12.4 High school dropouts from 14 to 24 years old, by race and age, 1989.

Statistics from *Statistical Abstract of the United States, 1990* (p. 150) by U.S. Department of Commerce, Bureau of the Census, 1990, Washington, DC: U.S. Government Printing Office.

oriented family environments are more likely to be underachievers and school dropouts than those who come from cohesive, non-conflicting families (Wood, Chapin, & Hannah, 1988).

PREGNANCY AND MARRIAGE.   Pregnancy and marriage are among the most common reasons for girls dropping out of school (De-bolt, Pasley, & Kreutzer, 1990), although it is seldom a reason for boys to drop out (Up-church & McCarthy, 1989).

EMPLOYMENT AND MONEY.   Even high school is expensive. This factor, plus financial pressures at home, forces some adolescents to leave school to go to work. For other students, there is the lure of being financially independent. The desire to have money for social activities, a car, or clothes lures many youths to leave school to accept early employment.

SOCIAL ADJUSTMENT AND PEER ASSO-CIATIONS.   Most adolescents want to do what their friends are doing. A student may be persuaded to leave school if friends are dropping out to get jobs earning "big money" or to get married.

SCHOOL   APATHY,   DISSATISFACTION, AND FAILURE.   A number of scholastic factors are correlated with dropping out of school (O'Sullivan, 1990). Among these are low IQ or mental retardation, low or failing marks, misplacement, grade retardation and repetition, poor reading ability, inability to get along with teachers, and misconduct. Some students are not necessarily emotionally or socially maladjusted but are not motivated (Elmen, 1991). They simply lack interest in schoolwork, feel it is a waste of time, and would rather get married or go to work. Sometimes such students have been placed in the wrong type of program (Knoff, 1983). A switch to a vocational course that students find appealing is helpful to the adolescent wrongly placed in the college prep program. Students who have to repeat grades, causing them to miss friends and feel like social misfits, may develop an intense dislike for school and lose all interest in learning. Similarly, students who have a history of low marks and failure find school to be an unrewarding experience and cannot wait to get out (Deci, 1985).

Many students do not drop out; they are either thrown out or given a temporary suspension and never come back. Teachers and administrators often breathe a sigh of relief when the student does not come back. In the case of expulsion, the student has no choice and is not allowed to return.

PERSONALITY CHARACTERISTICS.   Drop-outs are more likely to be emotionally immature and less well adjusted than high school graduates. They manifest symptoms of defective ego functioning: emotional instability; excessive fear and anxiety; feelings of inferiority; low self-esteem; deep-seated feelings of hostility and resentment; and rebellion, negativism, and alienation (Cairns, Cairns, & Neckerman, 1989). What is so often described as lack of willpower or laziness may actually be resentment toward punitive parents, unfair treatment at school, or social rejection, all of which can cause such feelings of rebellion that the adolescent refuses to do anything demanded by authority. Some of these students develop a real phobia about school (Paccione-Dyszlewski & Contessa-Kislus, 1987). Five traits have been identified as common among underachievers: (1) overprotectiveness, (2) boredom, (3) anxiety, (4) inferiority, and (5) negativism (Stevens & Phil, 1987).

SOCIOECONOMIC FACTORS.   Low socioeconomic status correlates positively with early withdrawal from school (Manaster, 1977). There are a number of reasons why this is so. The role models presented by parents may not be conducive to finishing school. Many low socioeconomic parents want their children to have more education than they did, but if parents only finished seventh grade, they may consider graduating from junior high school sufficient. Also, daughters still tend to receive less encouragement to finish school than do sons.

Teachers   are   sometimes   prejudiced against youth from low socioeconomic families, and show preferential treatment to students from high-status families. Students from a low socioeconomic background tend to receive less encouragement to do well and to stay in school than do students from higher-status families. They often do not possess the verbal skills of their middle-class peers. This in itself presents a handicap in learning to read and in almost all other academic work. Peer influences on low socioeconomic youth are often antischool and delinquency prone. Some low socioeconomic youths reject adult institutions and values, and become involved with groups composed of jobless dropouts.

ETHNIC IDENTITY. <u>Students from minority groups, especially those from inner-city schools, have a much higher dropout rate than do white students</u> (U.S. Bureau of the Census, 1989). The value orientation and the familial, social, and economic conditions under which they live tend not to be conducive to continuing education. Youths from poor neighborhoods are frequently truant and tend to drop out as soon as they reach age 16. However, race, per se, is not the important factor in the high dropout rate of minority students. Low economic status is what makes the difference (Nettles, 1989). For example, the dropout rate among black adolescents in poverty is 33%, compared with 13% for middle-class black adolescents (Children's Defense Fund, 1988).

INTERVENTION. Intervention programs can reduce the dropout rate considerably. This means the conditions that cause the student to drop out need to be corrected (Caliste, 1984). One study of juvenile delinquents and school dropouts revealed four factors that predicted school dropout: poor relationships with parents, negative influence of peers, disliking school, and misbehavior in school (Dunham & Alpert, 1987). Specific in-

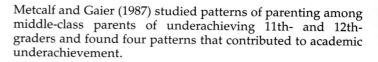

PARENTING ISSUES

Middle-Class Parenting and Underachievement

Metcalf and Gaier (1987) studied patterns of parenting among middle-class parents of underachieving 11th- and 12th-graders and found four patterns that contributed to academic underachievement.

- Conflicted parents—parents disagree on childrearing.
- Indifferent parents—parents set no consistent limits or standards, and show little interest.
- Overprotective parents—parents are perfectionists, domineering, overdirecting, overrestrictive, and constantly expect their children to do better.
- Upward-striving parents—parents criticize, nag, and pressure adolescents to get good marks.

terventions are needed to correct these conditions if the likelihood of dropping out is to be reduced (Block, 1989; Kammer, Fouad, & Williams, 1988).

SUMMARY

1. According to Piaget, the fourth stage of cognitive development is the formal operational stage, achieved by some during adolescence and adulthood.

2. During the formal operational stage, adolescents are capable of introspection (thinking critically about their thoughts); logical thinking (considering all important variables and forming correct conclusions); abstract thinking (going beyond the real to the possible); and hypothetical reasoning (formulating hypotheses, examining the evidence for them, and determining if they are correct). They are able to use symbols of symbols, so that words can carry double or triple meanings, and their thinking is flexible.

3. As a result of formal operational thinking, adolescents' thoughts and behavior are characterized by idealism and sociocentrism, hypocrisy, egocentrism and self-consciousness, and conformity. Gradually adolescents become decentered as they enter into the adult world and begin an occupation.

4. There are several considerations in relation to Piaget's views: The ages and percentages are not precise and not all adolescents or adults achieve formal operations. The test criteria for operational thinking depend partly on the level of the tests employed; environmental influences, as well as maturation, play a role in cognitive development. There is considerable variability in abstract reasoning abilities, depending upon cultural background. Social institutions such as the family and school accelerate or retard the development of formal operations.

5. The development of formal operational thinking can be encouraged in a number of ways by school programs that stimulate students to think.

6. There is some evidence of a fifth stage of development known as a problem-finding stage. This stage represents an ability to discover and formulate new problems.

7. One of the most widely used tests in the United States is the SAT—a two-part test consisting of a verbal part and a math

part, each scored from 200 to 800. The Educational Testing Service insists that in combination with high school records, the SAT is a better predictor of a student's first-year performance in college than any other measurement. Objections to the test center around the fact that students can be taught through coaching to do better on the test, and it is not fair, therefore, to use it as the sole basis for college admission. Actually, the test should not be used as the exclusive basis, but in combination with other factors such as high school grades, essays, interviews, class rank, and other admission procedures.

8. SAT score averages of college-bound seniors dropped until 1980 and increased after that until 1985, with the math scores holding steady and the verbal scores declining since that time. A revision of the SAT, to take effect in 1994, will place increased emphasis on critical reasoning and "real-life" problem solving.

9. Some authorities feel that achievement test scores are a more valid measure of scholastic aptitude. The most widely used test of this type is the ACT Assessment Program.

10. Aptitude tests reveal gender differences in abilities. Boys generally score higher in spatial and math abilities, and girls

higher in reading and verbal skills. Such differences are due primarily to differences in sex-role socialization.

11. During the past 50 years, the emphasis in American education has shifted from one extreme to another: from traditionalism to progressivism and back again. Until the 1930s, traditionalism was the dominant emphasis in American schools. Then came the Depression and the shift to progressive education. After Sputnik, the call was to return to basics: especially math, science, and foreign languages. In the 1960s and 1970s, the call was to do something about social problems and to achieve relevancy. During the 1980s, the cry was to return to basics again.

12. The percentage of youths attending high school continues to increase, but the percentage of those dropping out is still high, especially among nonwhites.

13. There are a number of factors that correlate with early school withdrawal: low socioeconomic status, quality of family relationships, personality, social adjustments and peer associations, financial considerations, school failure, apathy and dissatisfaction, and pregnancy and marriage.

14. Schools that establish intervention programs can reduce the dropout rate considerably.

KEY TERMS

ACT Assessment Program (American College Testing Program)   *p. 268*
Personal fable   *p. 263*
Problem-finding stage   *p. 266*

Progressives   *p. 269*
Scholastic Aptitude Test (SAT)   *p. 266*
Sociocentrism   *p. 262*
Traditionalists   *p. 269*

DISCUSSION QUESTIONS

1. Give some examples of adolescents you know who are self-conscious and egocentric.
2. Do adolescents think logically? Why or why not? Give some examples.
3. How does the idealism of adolescents compare to that of adults?
4. What evidence is there that adolescents are hypocritical?
5. Comment on the statement: "Adolescents are able to escape the concrete present and think about the abstract and the possible."

6. Why do adolescents tend to be conformists?
7. When you were in high school, did your teachers encourage original thinking? Give example of ways they did and ways they did not.
8. What do you think of the SAT? Should it be used as a basis for admission to college? What criteria would you use for selection?
9. What do you think of requiring certain performance on achievement tests as a basis for college admission?

10. In your opinion, what are the principal reasons for pupils dropping out of school?
11. What can schools do to reduce the number of dropouts?
12. Should pupils be required by law to stay in school through the 12th grade? Why or why not?
13. What can and should parents do if their adolescent is not doing well in school?

SUGGESTED READINGS

Chipman, S. F., Segal, J. W., & Glaser, R. (Eds.). (1985). *Thinking and learning skills,* vol. 2: *Research and open questions.* Hillsdale, NJ: Erlbaum. Current approaches to cognition.

Elkind, D. (1981). *Children and adolescents: Interpretive essays on Jean Piaget* (3rd ed.). New York: Oxford University Press. A helpful explanation.

Flavell, J. H. (1977). *Cognitive development.* Englewood Cliffs, NJ: Prentice-Hall. New insights into Piaget's ideas and beyond.

Lipsitz, J. (1984). *Successful schools for young adolescents.* New Brunswick, NJ: Transaction Books. Factors that contribute to effective education of young adolescents and examples of successful schools.

13

Emotional Development

ADOLESCENTS' EMOTIONS*

The Components of Emotions

Emotions are subjective feelings an individual experiences in response to stimuli. The word *emotion* literally means "the act of being moved out, or stirred up." An **emotion** is a state of consciousness that is felt as an integrated reaction of the total organism. As discussed in Chapter 8, emotions are accompanied by physiological arousal and result in behavioral responses. Emotional growth and development refer to the development of subjective feelings and to the conditioning of physiological and behavioral responses to these feelings.

Emotion—a state of consciousness, or a feeling, felt as an integrated reaction of the total organism, accompanied by physiological arousal, and resulting in behavioral responses

The kinds of feelings that develop, the intensity with which they are felt, and the period of time they persist are important for several reasons. *The emotional state of being affects physical well-being and health.* The entire body participates in and reacts to an emotional experience. The autonomic nervous system, the system that is not under voluntary control, carries stimuli to the adrenal glands, which, in turn, secrete adrenalin that acts on the internal organs—the heart, lungs, stomach, intestines, colon, kidneys, liver, pancreas—and glands such as the tear glands, salivary glands, the gonads, and the genitals. Through this network of connections, emotional stimuli can inhibit or increase the rate of respiration or heartbeat. They can contract the blood vessels, dilate the pupils of the eyes, release blood sugar from the liver, secrete perspiration from the glands of the skin, tense the muscles, cause the skin to blush, result in loss of bladder control, or produce a wide variety of other physical reactions. The more intense the emotional stimulus and the longer it persists, the greater and longer the physical reactions will be. Furthermore, emotional states that persist over long periods of time either enhance or destroy physical well-being and health. For example, intense emotional stimuli that cause the stomach to secrete large amounts of acidic fluids over a long period of time may eventually result in those acids' eating away the inner lining of the stomach.

*Part of the material in this chapter is adapted from the author's book, *The Adolescent: Development, Relationships, and Culture*, 2nd ed. (1978) and 6th ed. (1990). Boston: Allyn and Bacon. Used by permission of the publisher.

Emotions are subjective feelings and individual experiences in response to stimuli.

Emotions are also important because they affect behavior in relationships with others (Wintre, Polivy, & Murray, 1990). How people feel partially controls how they act. People who feel loving, consciously or unconsciously, act more kindly toward others. People who feel angry may strike out at others or hurt them. People who feel fearful may try to run away or escape.

The behavior of adolescents can be partly understood by studying and understanding their emotions and feelings. Behavior is caused, in part, by feeling and emotion. In this sense, emotions are a source of motivation; that is, they drive the individual to action. Fear of failure can result in the adolescent's striving for achievement; excessive fear may result in paralysis and prevent action. Emotions, therefore, may have either a positive or negative effect on behavior, depending on the type of emotion and its intensity.

Emotions are important because they can be sources of pleasure, enjoyment, and satisfaction. They can add color and spice to living. A feeling of joy or happy excitement makes an otherwise routine day bearable. The warmth of love and affection, given or received, gives inner satisfaction and genuine pleasure. The individual who can feel may also fully appreciate the beauty and joy that life can offer.

As seen in Chapter 8, emotions are classified into different types of categories. One helpful classification is to divide them in three categories according to their effect and result:

Joyous states—positive emotions of affection, love, happiness, and pleasure.

Inhibitory states—fear or dread, worry or anxiety, sadness or sorrow, embarrassment, regret or guilt, and disgust.
Hostile states—anger, hatred, contempt, and jealousy.

Each person experiences these three states at some time, but the ones that predominate are going to be the ones that have the most influence over the person's behavior and life. And the choice of which ones predominate depends, in turn, on the events and people to which one is exposed as a child.

Joyous States

Children are born with an unlimited capacity to love, but the actual development of warm, affectionate, caring and optimistic, happy feelings comes from a secure environment, pleasurable events, and close interpersonal relationships. According to Maslow (1970), children first need to satisfy physiological needs and the need for physical protection from harm. As these needs are supplied, children experience positive feelings of comfort, satisfaction, and well-being. However, the basic needs of children are not only physical, but also emotional and social. They need love and affection, companionship, approval, acceptance, and respect. If these emotional supports are supplied, their capacity to show positive feelings toward others grows, and they become loving, affectionate, friendly, sociable, approving, accepting, and respecting people. Whether

or not children are joyous, happy, and loving will depend on the events taking place around them and on the influence of the people with whom they relate. The continued repetition of pleasant experiences and relationships builds positive emotions, whereas the continued repetition of unpleasant experiences and relationships builds negative emotions.

The important point is that *by the time children reach adolescence they already exhibit well-developed patterns of emotional responses to events and people.* They may already be described as warm, affectionate, and friendly, or as cold, unresponsive, and distant. The pattern of emotional response shown during adolescence is only a continuation of the pattern that has been emerging slowly during childhood.

Adolescents who become warm, affectionate, and friendly people have some distinct advantages (Paul & White, 1990). They not only derive far greater potential satisfaction from human relationships, but they also engage in social relationships that are more harmonious. Love encourages a positive response from others; it minimizes the individual's aggressive behavior; it acts as a therapeutic force in healing hurts; and it is a creative power in individual accomplishment and in social movements. Love stimulates human vitality and longevity; it is the driving force in positive biological and social relationships in marriage. For adolescents, it is necessary as a binding power in their friendships or in relationships with their parents.

LIVING ISSUES

Is It Love or Infatuation?

An adolescent can develop very intense feelings for another person. But, there is a difference between infatuation, which is an emotional crush on another person, and a deep love. Some of the differences are the following:

- Infatuation is associated with immaturity, and is more frequent among young adolescents than mature adults (Rubenstein, 1983).
- Infatuation may develop toward someone the adolescent doesn't even know. The romance may be entirely fantasized. Mature love is based on knowledge of the other individual.

- Infatuation may be felt toward an unsuitable person; love more likely develops in relation to an appropriate partner.
- Infatuation may cause frustration, insecurity, upset, and anguish; love is more likely to result in fulfillment and happiness (Hatfield and Sprecher, 1986).
- Infatuation is more likely to arise very quickly; love grows slowly. Infatuation can fade as quickly as it arises. Love is more lasting.
- Infatuation centers on intense emotion and strong sexual feelings; love involves the whole personality and includes friendship, admiration, care, and concern as well as sexual attraction.

Inhibitory States

FEAR.   Fear is one of the most powerful negative human emotions. The psychologists Watson and Raynor (1920) observed that the infant, by nature, shows fear responses to only two types of situations: when threatened with loss of support or falling, and when startled with a loud noise. They found that children do not naturally fear the dark, fire, snakes, or strangers without either having had frightening exposure to them or having been otherwise conditioned to fear them.

Many of the fears children develop carry over into adolescence. Sometimes, however, the nature and content of fears change as one gets older.

Fears may be divided into four categories:

Fear of material things and natural phenomena—bugs, snakes, dogs, storms, strange noises, fire, water, closed spaces, heights, trains, airplanes, and the like.
Fear relating to the self—failure in school, inadequacy in vocational situations, illness, being hurt, death, personal inadequacy, immoral drives or wrongdoings, or temptations.
Fear involving social relationships—parents, meeting people, loneliness, personal appearance, crowds, the opposite sex, adult groups or situations, dates, parties, certain types of people, speaking before a group, or other situations arising when in social groups.
Fear of the unknown—supernatural phenomena, world events, unpredictable future, or tragedies.

Generally, as children grow they lose some of their fears of material things and natural phenomena (although usually not all of them), but develop other fears such as the fear that parents are angry, fear of failure, or fear of particular social situations, persons, or groups. Adolescents become more concerned with the effect they have on others, with what others think of them, and of being disliked or rejected by others. Being ignored by a group, or being put on the spot in front of a class is a terrifying experience for some adolescents.

Phobia—an anxiety disorder characterized by excessive, uncontrolled fear of objects, situations, or living creatures of some type

PHOBIAS.   A **phobia** is an irrational fear that exceeds normal proportions and has no basis in reality. The *Diagnostic and Statistical Manual of Mental Disorders III-R* (American Psychiatric Association, 1987) divided phobias into three categories: (1) simple phobias, (2) social phobias, and (3) agoraphobia. *Simple phobias* include *acrophobia*, fear of high places, and *hematophobia*, fear of blood. Other simple phobias are *hydrophobia*, fear of water, and *zoophobia*, fear of animals (usually a specific kind).   *public speaking*

Social phobias are characterized by fears of social situations, such as meeting strangers, going to a party, or applying for a job. This kind of phobia limits social relationships, so it can interfere with normal living.

Agoraphobia means literally "fear of open spaces" and involves fear of going outside one's own home. It can include fear of going shopping, to church, to work, or to any kind

TABLE 13.1 Types of Phobias

Name	Object or Situation Feared
Acrophobia	Heights
Agoraphobia	Open places
Algophobia	Pain
Anthophobia	Flowers
Astraphobia	Storms, thunder, lightning
Cardiophobia	Heart attack
Claustrophobia	Enclosed spaces or confinement
Cyberphobia	Computers
Decidophobia	Making decisions
Ergophobia	Work
Gephydrophobia	Crossing bridges
Hematophobia	Blood
Hydrophobia	Water
Iatrophobia	Doctors
Lalophobia	Public speaking
Monophobia	Being alone
Mysophobia	Contamination or germs
Nyctophobia	Darkness
Ochlophobia	Crowds
Ombrophobia	Rain
Pathophobia	Disease
Peccatophobia	Sinning
Phobophobia	Fear
Photophobia	Light
Pyrophobia	Fire
Syphilophobia	Syphilis
Taphophobia	Being buried alive
Thanatophobia	Death
Toxophobia	Being poisoned
Trichophobia	Hair
Xenophobia	Strangers
Zoophobia	Animals (usually a specific kind)

of public place because of a fear of crowds. For this reason it is a very handicapping phobia. Table 13.1 lists some common phobias.

WORRY AND ANXIETY.   Worry and anxiety are closely allied to fear, but they may arise from imagined unpleasant situations as well as from real causes (Moore, Jensen, & Hauck, 1990). The mind imagines what might happen. Many times the worst never happens, so the worry has been unnecessary.

Some worry is directed to a specific person, thing, or situation. Adolescents may worry about what their parents will do because the car battery ran down; they may worry about an examination or about having to give a speech in front of the class. Other causes of adolescent anxiety include not being asked to dance, friends criticizing their dress, or friends making fun of the braces on their teeth. These worries arise out of specific things, but the imagined "happening" has not yet occurred or maybe never takes place. Table 13.2 shows what some young women worry about the most as revealed in one study from the University of Maine (Rice, 1989). The number one concern was school. Parents, future vocation and employment, and social relationships were also of some concern. It is interesting that few of the young women were worried about marriage or sex.

There are wide variations in the extent to which adolescents worry. Some adolescents are more resistant to worry than others. Some are fairly worry free, not only because of constitutional and hereditary factors, but also because of an environment in which they have had little to worry about as they were growing up. All of their physical needs were supplied; they were loved, accepted, respected, and admired by their parents. They had normal opportunities for companionship, social contacts, and new experiences. They received the necessary guidance and discipline to help them become socialized people. They found success in school experiences, learned acceptable standards of conduct, and adjusted well to society. They did not have to be anxious.

Some adolescents are reared in conditions that are just the opposite. They learned early they could not depend on their parents to supply their basic needs for food, protection from harm, or physical contact. They were never really loved, accepted, praised, or encouraged. Instead, they were rejected, criticized, belittled, or ignored. These experiences stimulated repeated doubts about

TABLE 13.2 Causes of Worry in 136 College Females (Sophomores, Juniors, Seniors) Attending the University of Maine

Number of Responses	Worry
47	School
18	Grades, doing well on exams
16	Meeting deadlines; doing assignments, work on time
9	Schoolwork, studies (general)
2	Getting through school
2	Scholarship, student teaching
23	Family, Parents
6	General, family, parents
3	Stability of parents' marriage; divorce, separation
3	Emotionality of parents; highstrung, upset parents
3	Relationship with parents, independence, obligations
3	Mother
3	Health of parents
2	Future of brothers, sisters
22	Vocation, Employment
17	Getting good job, employment; finding job I enjoy; deciding what to do after graduation
5	Being able to accomplish what I want; realizing potential, doing as well as I want
15	Social Relationships
8	Being accepted, liked; what others think; feeling shy, inferior
3	Boyfriends, meaningful relations with them
2	General or social relations
2	Fear of hurting others; worry about others not arriving
9	Money
6	Money to graduate, pay bills
3	Money in years ahead
9	Future (in general)
6	General
3	Stable, happy, secure future
6	Marriage
3	Getting married; meeting man I can love, can love me
2	Future family happiness; being a good wife
1	Wedding in June
3	Sex
1	Abstaining from premarital sex
1	Mother finding out I'm on pill
1	Sex obligation in future
2	Overweight
136	Total

From [Causes of worry in college females attending the University of Maine] by F. P. Rice, 1989. Unpublished study.

their self-worth and their own capabilities and talents. They were denied opportunities for ego building and for fulfilling social experiences and relationships. School was a disaster, and friendships were lacking. Tension, turmoil, and conflict in the family were almost continual and extremely upsetting (Stern & Zevon, 1990).

Under these circumstances, adolescents grow up in an almost constant state of tension and anxiety (Daniels & Moos, 1990). Worry has become a way of life, so much so that they overreact to everyday frustrations or happenings and are anxious about everything that is going to happen. They doubt themselves, other people, and the outcomes of most situations. Whether people or circumstances justify it or not, these adolescents bring anxiety with them to their relationships and to the events they encounter (Frydenberg & Lewis, 1991).

Hostile States

ANGER.   Hostile states may be manifested as anger, hatred, contempt, or jealousy. They have been classified as hostile states because there is a natural tendency to express these emotions through various forms of hostility: fighting, swearing, arguing, or temper tantrums. Adolescents may seek to express their hostility in physical activity, such as work or sports. Sometimes they hold in their feelings, but sulk, become withdrawn, or get moody. At other times, their anger results in aggressive acts of violence in which damage is inflicted on inanimate objects, the self, or others. In fits of rage, adolescents will vent their anger by attacking family furniture, school property, a teacher, or a helpless victim. Figure 13.1 illustrates some typical responses to anger-producing stimuli during the adolescent years.

Some time ago, newspapers carried headlines of a father and his 12-year-old son who had been shot by a 16-year-old boy. Their bodies were covered over with leaves in the woods. The father had been shot 32 times. What prompted such rage and violence? Later investigation revealed that the boy who committed the murders was deeply disturbed emotionally and in desperate need of psychiatric help.

Hartocollis (1972) described the quieter, but still destructive expression of anger of a group of four young patients from the mental ward of a hospital.

Generalized Anxiety Disorder

Anxiety is not a mental illness. However, when anxiety becomes so intense and persistent that it interferes with everyday functioning, it is an illness called generalized anxiety disorder. Symptoms of **generalized anxiety disorder** include extreme worry about the smallest mishap, dread that something terrible is going to happen, and anxiety when there is no reason for it to exist. Adolescents suffering from this disorder do not think rationally, so one cannot calm their feelings by presenting all the facts and reasons why they have nothing to worry about. Such intense anxiety may be accompanied by somatic symptoms such as digestive or respiratory disturbances, tearfulness, sweating, shaking and trembling, nervousness, sleep disturbances, feelings of inferiority, or an increase in activity to try to cover up or escape the fear. It may also result in behavior disturbances.

FIGURE 13.1   Responses to anger-producing stimuli during the adolescent years.

Adapted from *Adolescent Development and Adjustment*, 2nd ed. (p. 146) by L. D. Crow and A. Crow, 1965, New York: McGraw-Hill Book Company. Used by permission.

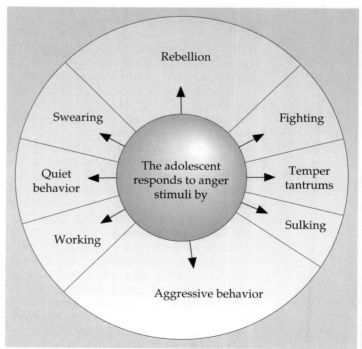

One night after bedtime and when nearly everybody had retired . . . four young patients, three boys and a girl, gathered in front of the nurses' central station. They sat down in a circle and, pouring some coke on the carpet, proceeded to deposit the ashes of their cigarettes on the round wet spot as if it were an ashtray. They did this casually, without saying much, as if performing a ritual, smiling in a mocking way at the nurses who were inside the station (p. 483).

Whenever excessive or uncontrollable anger builds up and is not expressed in socially constructive ways, it takes impulsive, irrational, and destructive forms, and the adolescent becomes a menace (Hart, 1990). This is one explanation for the wanton violence and vandalism found in many communities. Anger that turns into destructive violence usually builds up through a person's repeated and long-standing negative involvement with other people. A father may reject, belittle, and treat his son cruelly for years before the son's anger finally explodes in an act of violence.

Anger in adolescents has many causes. They may get angry when restricted in physical movement or social activity. They become especially resentful when denied opportunities for social life; for example, when they are not allowed to go out on a date or when they are denied the use of the car. They become angry at any attack on their ego, status, or position. Criticism (especially if they feel it is unjust or unfair), shaming, belittling, or rejection arouses their anger, partly because any such negative stimulus is a real threat to an already overly sensitive ego and a precarious social position. Anger stimuli in adolescents are mostly social. People—their personalities and behavior—stimulate anger responses more often than do things. Hypocritical, inconsiderate, intolerant, dishonest, unfair, nosy, selfish, irresponsible people who ridicule, criticize, hurt, snub, boss, gossip about, or take advantage of other people are the major cause of anger.

To a lesser extent, situations as well as things may cause anger. Situations may include such things as injustices in the world, war, and on-the-job frustrations. Petty situations cause anger: A car or lawnmower won't start, a flashlight won't work, the weather turns unfavorable and interrupts a planned picnic, a guitar string breaks, a baked cake falls, or a low door causes a blow to the head. Males are usually more angered by things that don't work than are females. Most females tend to be angered by people and social situations.

Adolescents' anger is sometimes aroused because of their own inability to perform a task or do something they are trying to do. They become angry at their own mistakes, frustrated when they can't paint a picture they imagine or achieve a school grade they desire. They're angry because they receive a low score on a test or because they are unable to hit a tennis ball the way they feel they should.

HATRED. Hatred can be a more serious emotion than anger (at least temporary anger), because it can persist over a longer period of time and can be a result of repeated exposure to a particular person or persons. Adolescents who grow up with parents who do things they detest may develop hatred toward them that is not easy to overcome. Hatred is difficult to hide and almost impossible to suppress over a period of time. The feelings are there, and may be expressed in subtle ways through words or actions, or in violent ways through explosive, aggressive behavior.

SELF-CONCEPT AND SELF-ESTEEM

Definitions

SELF-CONCEPT.   The **self** has been defined as a person's perception of his or her nature, character, and individuality. **Self-concept** is the view or impression people have of themselves; it is their "self-hypothesized identity," which develops over a period of many years (Hodgon & Fischer, 1978). Self-concept is the cognitive perceptions and attitudes people have about themselves. It is the sum total of their self-descriptions or self-appraisals (Chassin & Young, 1981).

Self-concept is multidimensional, with each dimension describing different roles (Griffin, Chassin, & Young, 1981). A person may rate himself or herself as a husband or wife, professional person, community leader, relative, friend, and so forth. These different aspects of the self describe the total person.

Individuals may have different self-concepts that change from time to time and that may or may not be accurate portrayals of their real selves. Self-concepts are constantly being formulated depending on the circum-

Self—overall perception of one's personality, nature, and individuality

Self-concept—an individual's conscious, cognitive perception and evaluation of self; one's thoughts and opinions about oneself

The self is a person's perception of his or her nature, character, and individuality.

stances and relationships confronting the individual (Palazzi, deVito, Luzzati, Guerrini, & Torre, 1990).

A number of years ago, in *Becoming: Basic Considerations for a Psychology of Personality*, Gordon W. Allport (1950) said that personality has some stability, but it never remains exactly the same; it is always in transition, undergoing revisions. Allport used the word **proprium**, which is defined as "all aspects of personality that make for inward unity." This is one's personal identity, one's self that is developing over a period of time.

Ruth Strang (1957) said there are four basic dimensions of the self. *First*, there is a general self-concept, which is an adolescent's overall "perceptions of his abilities and his status and roles in the outer world" (p. 68).

Second, there are temporary or changing self-concepts, which are influenced by current experiences. A critical remark from a teacher may produce a temporary feeling of deflated self-worth.

Third, there are adolescents' social selves: their selves in relationships with others, and their selves that others react to (Lackovic-Grgin & Dekovic, 1990). As one adolescent said: "I like the way others respond to me; it makes me feel good about myself." Some adolescents think of themselves only in negative ways because they feel others don't like them. One important influence on self-concept is the way adolescents feel in social groups.

Fourth, adolescents would like to be their conceptualized ideal self. These projected images may or may not be realistic. Imagining themselves to be selves they never

Proprium—the self's core of identity that is developing in time

can be sometimes leads to frustration and disappointment. At other times, adolescents project an idealized self and then strive to be that person. Those who are in the healthiest emotional state are those whose real selves approximate their projected ideal selves, and who are able to accept the selves they are.

SELF-ESTEEM. Self-esteem is the value individuals place on the selves they perceive. If their self-appraisal leads to self-acceptance and approval, to a feeling of self-worth, they have high self-esteem. If they view themselves negatively, their self-esteem is low. At various times, adolescents make a thorough assessment of themselves, comparing not only their body parts, but also their motor skills, intellectual abilities, talents, and social skills with those of their peers and their ideals or heroes. If their self-appraisal is negative, it may result in self-conscious, embarrassed behavior. They become unhappy because they can't measure up to their ideal selves (Handel, 1980). Hopefully, they learn to accept themselves as they are, to formulate a positive view of themselves, and to integrate their goals into their ideal selves.

Correlations

RELATIONSHIPS WITH OTHERS. Those who can accept themselves are more likely to be able to accept others and be accepted by them. There is a positive correlation between self-acceptance and social adjustment.

Low self-concept and self-esteem affect social relationships in a number of ways. Adolescents with low self-esteem more often develop feelings of isolation and are more often afflicted with pangs of loneliness. They often feel awkward and tense in social situations, which makes it more difficult for them to communicate with others (Ishiyama, 1984). Because they want to please others, they are more easily led and influenced by them.

EMOTIONAL WELL-BEING. Self-esteem grows out of human interaction in which the self is considered important to someone. The ego grows through small accomplishments, praise, and success. Individuals with low self-esteem often manifest a number of symptoms of emotional ill-health (Brennan & O'Loideain, 1980; Ehrenberg, Cox, & Koopman, 1991; Koenig, 1988). They may evidence psychosomatic symptoms of anxiety and stress (Youngs, Rathge, Mullis, & Mullis, 1990). Low self-esteem has also been found to be a factor in drug abuse (Reardon

& Griffing, 1983) and in pregnancy among unwed mothers (Black & deBlassie, 1985; Blinn, 1987; Horn & Rudolph, 1987; Patten, 1981). In fact, pregnancy among unwed mothers may be an effort on the part of young women to enhance their self-esteem (Streetman, 1987).

Sometimes adolescents with low self-esteem try to compensate and overcome the feeling of worthlessness by putting on a false front to convince others that they are worthy (Elliott, 1982). "I try to cover up so that others won't know I'm afraid." But putting on an act is a strain. To act confident, friendly, and cheerful when one feels the opposite is a constant struggle. The anxiety that one might make a false step and let his or her guard slip creates considerable tension.

Adolescents with low self-esteem are vulnerable to criticism, rejection, or any other evidence in their daily lives that testifies to their inadequacy, incompetence, or worthlessness. They may be deeply disturbed when laughed at, scolded, blamed, or when others have a poor opinion of them. The more vulnerable they feel themselves to be, the higher are their anxiety levels. Such adolescents report: "Criticism hurts me terribly" or "I can't stand to have anyone laugh at me or blame me when something goes wrong." As a result, they feel awkward and uneasy in social situations and avoid embarrassment whenever they can.

ACHIEVEMENT.   There is a correlation between self-concept and achievement in school (Bell & Ward, 1980). A high self-concept contributes to school success, and scholastic achievement builds a positive self-concept. The relationship is reciprocal (Roberts, Sarigiani, Petersen, & Newman, 1990).

This relationship between school achievement and self-concept begins in the early grades. Those who already have negative self-images before they enter school feel they may not be able to do well, so consequently they do not. Older siblings, close friends, fathers, mothers, grandparents, teachers, and school counselors can have an important influence on students' academic self-concepts. If these people manifest positive attitudes in relation to the academic ability of students, the students are more likely to have confidence in their abilities and do well in school (Johnsen & Medley, 1978).

GOALS.   There is a positive correlation between the degree of self-esteem and the level of vocational aspirations (Chiu, 1990). Adolescents with either low or high self-esteem consider it important to get ahead, but those with low self-esteem are less likely to expect they will succeed. They are more likely to say: "I never get any breaks, which is why I don't get ahead, but I really don't care anyhow." Underneath, they are afraid they don't possess those qualities essential to success. Women who aspire to have both marriage and a career tend to have higher self-esteem than those who desire to be homemakers only. Men who have a strong sense of self-worth are more likely to get ahead than those with negative self-perceptions. Not only do they aspire to get ahead, but they have more confidence that they can do so. For these reasons, they are more likely to succeed.

ACTING OUT BEHAVIOR.   Juvenile delinquency and low self-esteem seem to be related (Lund and Salary, 1980). In fact, delinquency is sometimes an attempt to compensate for lower self-esteem (Bynner, O'Malley, & Bachman, 1981). The theory is that those who have low self-esteem sometimes adopt deviant patterns of behavior to reduce self-rejecting feelings. By making their behavior match their low self-concept, they confirm their own rejection of themselves (Kaplan, 1978). In these instances, adolescents ally themselves with deviant groups that give them the recognition that society does not give (Rosenberg and Rosenberg, 1978). Those who see themselves as "nondelinquents" or "good people" don't have to prove their own inner worth by becoming delinquent (Krueger & Hansen, 1987).

Parental Roles in Development

PARENT–ADOLESCENT RELATIONSHIPS. A number of family variables are related to the development of self-concept and self-esteem (Demo, Small, & Savin-Williams, 1987; Gecas & Schwalbe, 1986; Hoelter & Harper, 1987; Openshaw, Thomas, & Rollins, 1983). Adolescents who identify closely with parents strive to model their personality and behavior after them. Erikson (1968) said, however, that too close an identification with parents stifles the ego and retards identity development. However, children with minimal parental identification will also have poor ego development. Overall, the degree of maternal identification is related to self-concept (Offer, Ostrov, & Howard, 1982).

Self-concept and self-esteem are influenced partly by identification with parents.

Thus, ego identity of girls is weak if they have poor maternal identification and weak again if there is overidentification.

Fathers also influence identity development. Girls who have a warm relationship with their fathers are more comfortable with their own femininity and with their relationships with other men. They are able to make more mature heterosocial adjustments. Similarly, if the adolescent boy identifies closely with his father and also has very positive, warm feelings toward his mother, his relationships with other women are more likely to be positive.

DIVIDED FAMILIES.   There are a number of factors that mediate the influence of divorce on a growing child (Sessa & Steinberg, 1991). If the mother has custody of the children, the mother's age at the time of divorce is important. If the mother is young at the time of divorce, the effect on the children will be more negative than if the mother is older because younger mothers are less able to cope with the upset of divorce. The child's age at the time of the marital rupture is also a factor. Young children are more negatively influenced than are older children. Remarriage also influences self-esteem. In one study, children whose parents remarried ("reconstituted families") evaluated themselves more positively than children whose parents had divorced but not remarried (Parish & Dostal, 1980). However, children who did not get along with their stepparents tended to evaluate themselves more negatively than children whose mothers did not remarry. Children from intact families tend to have the most positive self-esteem of all (Parish, 1991; Parish & Taylor, 1979).

In one study, no significant differences in self-concept scores were found in third-, sixth-, and eighth-grade children from intact,

PARENTING ISSUES

Parental Control and Adolescent Self-Esteem

The warmth, concern, and interest parents show adolescents is important in helping youth build a positive ego identity. Parents who show interest and care are more likely to have adolescents who have high self-esteem. Furthermore, parents who are democratic but not permissive are also more likely to have adolescents with high self-esteem. The best parents are strict consistently, demanding high standards, but they are also flexible enough to allow necessary deviations from rules as needed (Graybill, 1978). There seems to be a combination of firmness and emotional warmth. The parent–adolescent relationship is characterized by ties of affection, strong iden-

tification, and good communication. Parents who are often inconsistent in expectations and discipline are more likely to have adolescents with low self-esteem.

Some parents are too restrictive or critical of their children. For example, adolescents who are under excessive pressure from their parents to achieve in school are likely to have low self-esteem and feel they are incapable of reaching the goals set for them by their families (Eskilson, Wiley, Muehlbauer, & Dodder, 1986). Certainly adolescents who are physically abused by their parents develop low self-esteem (Hjorth, 1982).

single-parent, and reconstituted families (Raschke & Raschke, 1979). However, children who reported higher levels of family conflict also had significantly lower self-concept scores regardless of family type. Thus, the quality of interpersonal relationships is more important than the type of family structure. Parish and Parish (1983) also found that whether a child came from an intact, reconstituted, or single-parent family was not as important as whether the existing family was happy or unhappy. Conflicts between parents or between children and parents often result in lower self-esteem in the children (Cooper, Holman, & Braithwaite, 1983). Amato (1986) also found lower self-esteem among adolescents from conflicting families and from those where the parent–adolescent relationship was poor.

One significant finding is that loss of self-esteem when parents divorce may or may not be temporary (Parish & Parish, 1991). Amato (1988) found little correlation between adult self-esteem and the experience of parental divorce or death during childhood. However, in a longitudinal study of 60 divorced families, Wallerstein (1989) found that more than half of the adolescents entered adulthood as underachieving, self-deprecating, and sometimes angry young men and women. They showed high levels of delinquency, promiscuity, and alcohol abuse both 10 and 15 years after the divorce. Not surprisingly, they had trouble with intimacy in relationships.

Unfortunately, Wallerstein did not study a control group from intact families for a comparison of her findings. The findings were predicated on the assumption that these problems would not occur as often in intact families. Also, her findings were from an affluent sample living in Marin County, California. The findings might not apply to those of other groups. However, Wallerstein's provocative study has shattered the complacent feeling that divorce never has long-term consequences for children.

Socioeconomic Variables

Socioeconomic status (SES) has an inconsistent effect on self-esteem. Generally, students with higher SES have higher self-esteem than those with lower SES. However, in their study of 11th-grade students from three North Carolina high schools, Richman, Clark, and Brown (1985) found that females with higher SES had lower self-esteem than those with middle or low SES. In this instance, females with higher SES felt pressured to excel in social activities, physical attractiveness, academics, and so on. Perceived failure in any one of these areas led to feelings of inadequacy and loss of self-esteem. Females with lower SES were more used to failure, so it was not as traumatic for them as for those with higher SES.

Socioeconomic status of the parents alone does not produce a specific level of self-esteem (Martinez & Dukes, 1991). Families with low SES can raise high self-esteem children if the parents have high self-esteem. Similarly, parents from minority groups can raise high self-esteem children if the parents have high self-esteem. One example is that of Jewish adolescents, who, though they come from a minority religious group in American society, tend to have high self-esteem, probably because of the high self-esteem of the Jewish parents and the generally adequate parent–child relationship, measured by the concern and care Jewish parents show for their children.

Racial Considerations

Self-esteem among blacks has risen, partly as civil rights and black consciousness movements have encouraged racial pride. A study of public high school black and white adolescents from Tennessee showed that the black students had significantly higher levels of self-esteem than did the white students (Rust & McCraw, 1984). Richman, Clark, and Brown (1985) found this same thing in North Carolina. However, when blacks are exposed to white prejudices, their self-esteem declines. If black adolescents are surrounded by those with similar social class standing, family background, and school performance, they rate themselves much higher in self-esteem than when surrounded by prejudiced white people (Simmons et al., 1978).

Understandably, some black adolescents have high self-esteem and others have low self-esteem. According to one study, black early adolescents who had established close friendships and achieved some degree of intimacy had high self-concepts and felt good about themselves (Paul & Fischer, 1980). This finding emphasizes an important factor in self-esteem. Social adjustments are important to adolescents' developing high self-concepts. Those who have difficulty maintaining close friendships and gaining group acceptance also show signs of low self-concepts.

Short-Term and Longitudinal Changes

The self-esteem of adolescents is affected by important changes and events in their lives (Balk, 1983). Adolescents who get involved with the wrong crowd and begin to adopt deviant behavior may show less self-respect and an increase in their own self-derogation (Kaplan, 1977). One study found that high school juniors had a lower self-concept after they had moved with their families a long distance to another town (Kroger, 1980). Another study showed that self-esteem was lowest at around 12 years of age (Protinsky & Farrier, 1980). By applying careful statistical controls, researchers showed that the onset of puberty itself was not the determining factor. Twelve-year-olds in junior high school had lower self-esteem, higher self-consciousness, and greater instability of self-image than did 12-year-olds in elementary school. When differences in race, socioeconomic class, or marks in school were considered, none of these variables was found to be conclusive. The one factor that was significant was whether the students had entered junior high school. The move from a protected elementary school, where a child had one set of classmates and few teachers, to a more impersonal and larger junior high school, where classrooms, classmates, and teachers were constantly shifting, was disturbing to the self-image. Males, particularly, were much more likely to be harassed or beaten up after they entered junior high school (Blyth et al., 1978). This study clearly illustrates that self-image can be affected, at least temporarily, by disturbing events.

Different schools have a different effect on self-concepts (Tierno, 1983). If pupils aren't doing well in one school, transferring them to another school sometimes changes their behavior, attitudes, and self-concepts. Transferring pupils to different schools is, however, more effective with junior high school pupils than with those in senior high schools (Strathe & Hash, 1979).

Self-image and self-esteem can also be improved by helpful events. Positive summer camp experiences can improve the self-concepts of young adolescents (Flynn & Beasley, 1980). Stake, DeVille, and Pennell (1983) and Waksman (1984a, 1984b) offered assertion training to secondary school and college-level students who were timid and withdrawn. Good results were reported by Stake and colleagues (1983) at 3-month follow-up, and by Waksman at 7-week follow-up, in helping students to maintain eye contact, talk to others, greet them, ask questions, refuse some requests, and express their feelings when they dealt with other students, teachers, or relatives. Ratherarm and Armstrong (1980) also reported significant increases in assertiveness of 9th- and 12th-grade girls after 10 weeks of assertion training. Wehr and Kaufman (1987) report improved assertiveness of 9th-grade boys and girls after only four hours of training.

Overall, self-concept gradually stabilizes (Chiam, 1987; Ellis & Davis, 1982). A 10-year longitudinal study of adolescents, beginning in grades 5 and 6 and continuing until they

LIVING ISSUES

Perfectionism

The wish to excel is an admirable attribute. However, there is a difference between normal and neurotic perfectionism. Normal perfectionists derive a real sense of pleasure from painstaking effort, but feel free to be less precise if needed. Neurotic perfectionists pursue excellence to an unhealthy extreme. Their standards are far beyond reach or reason; they strain unremittingly toward impossible goals and measure their own worth in terms of productivity and accomplishment. They are plagued by self-criticism. When faced with "imperfect" actions, their self-worth is lowered. Recurrent and persistent dissatisfaction with themselves leaves perfec-

tionists feeling unrelenting stress. They fear and anticipate rejection when they are judged imperfect; they are overly defensive when criticized. When contradicted, they become angry. Their behavior alienates others who show the very disapproval that the perfectionist fears. Thus, the irrational belief is reinforced that they must be perfect to be accepted.

Perfectionism evolves from interactions with perfectionistic parents. In a desperate pursuit of parental love and acceptance, the children strive to be flawless. When they are less than perfect, they feel terrible, so they are caught up in compulsively striving to avoid failure (Halgin & Leahy, 1989).

were out of high school, showed only a slight increase in positive self-concept. For the majority of youth, those who had a negative self-concept in early adolescence entered adulthood with the same negative feelings (Barnes & Farrier, 1985).

EMOTIONS AND BEHAVIORAL PROBLEMS

Sometimes negative emotions result in behavioral problems. Three such problems discussed here are drug abuse, delinquency, and running away.

Drug Abuse

COMMONLY ABUSED DRUGS.   The drugs most commonly abused may be grouped into a number of categories: alcohol, nicotine, narcotics, stimulants, depressants, hallucinogens, marijuana, and inhalants. Out of these groups, the most frequently used drugs in the United States are alcohol, tobacco, and marijuana, in that order. Table 13.3 shows the percentage of high school seniors having ever used various types of drugs in 1984, 1987, and 1988.

Drug abuse education tries to prevent children and youths from starting to use drugs.

TABLE 13.3 Lifetime Illicit Drug Usage of High School Seniors 1984, 1987, 1988 (percent used)

Drug	1984	1987	1988
Used alcohol	92.6	92.2	92.0
Used cigarettes	69.7	67.2	66.4
Used marijuana	54.9	50.2	47.2
Used stimulants (not under doctor's orders)	27.9	21.6	19.8
Used tranquilizers (not under doctor's orders)	12.4	10.9	9.4
Used other sedatives	13.3	8.7	7.8
Used hallucinogens	13.3	10.6	9.2
Used cocaine	16.1	15.2	12.1
Used crack cocaine	N/A	5.6	4.8
Used inhalants	19.0	18.6	17.5
Used opiates (other than heroin) (not under doctor's orders)	9.7	9.2	8.6
Used heroin	1.3	1.2	1.1

Adapted from *Drug usage: America's high school students* (1988). National Institute on Drug Abuse: University of Michigan Institute for Social Research.

ADDICTION AND DEPENDENCY.   A distinction must be made between **physical addiction**, or physical dependency, and **psychological dependency**. An addictive drug is one that causes the body to build up a chemical dependency to it, so that withdrawal results in unpleasant physical symptoms (Ralph & Morgan, 1991). Psychological dependency is the development of a powerful psychological need for a drug resulting in a compulsion to take it (Capuzzi & Lecoqu, 1983). Drugs become a means of finding relief, comfort, or security. Some individuals become psychologically dependent on drugs that are also physically addicting, such as crack cocaine, barbiturates, alcohol, heroin, and nicotine. Dependence is strongly reinforced by the desire to avoid the pain and distress of physical withdrawal. Sometimes physical dependency is broken, but individuals go back to the drug because of psychological dependency on it. It is a mistake, therefore, to assume that the only dangerous drugs are those that are physically addictive.

Physical addiction—the body's chemical dependency on a drug built up through its use

Psychological dependency—an overpowering emotional need for a drug

TRENDS IN DRUG ABUSE.   Youths are trying drugs at young ages. It is not unusual for children 8 to 10 years old to use drugs.

An elementary school official in Washington, D.C., complained that he had not been able to keep one third-grader from smoking marijuana every day at recess. Threats of expulsion did not help because the child insisted he could not break the habit. He did refuse to share his cigarettes with classmates because, he said, "the habit is dangerous" ("Drug Pushers," 1979). One longitudinal study in the San Francisco area showed that socially precocious females were more likely to become involved with drugs earlier than were males, although for both boys and girls, the transition to junior high school played an important role in initiating drug use (Keyes & Block, 1984).

PATTERNS OF DRUG USE.   Five patterns of drug use may be identified (Pedersen, 1990):

1. *Social-recreational use* occurs among acquaintances or friends as a part of socializing. Usually this use does not include addictive drugs and does not escalate in either frequency or intensity to become uncontrolled use.

2. *Experimental use* is motivated primarily by curiosity or by a desire to experience new feelings on a short-term basis. Users rarely use any drug on a daily basis, and tend not to use drugs to escape the pressures of personal problems. However, if users experiment with physically addictive drugs they may become addicted before they realize it.

3. *Circumstantial–situational use* is indulgence to achieve a known and desired effect. A person may take stimulants to stay awake while driving, or may take sedatives to relieve tension and go to sleep. Some persons use drugs to try to escape problems (Paton & Kandel, 1978). The danger is that such use will escalate to intensified use.

4. *Intensified drug use* generally involves using drugs at least once daily over a long period of time to achieve relief from a stressful situation or a persistent problem. Drugs become a customary part of the daily routine. Use may or may not affect functioning depending on the frequency, intensity, and amount of use.

5. *Compulsive drug use* involves both extensive and frequent use for relatively long periods, producing psychological dependence and physiological addiction with discontinuance resulting in psychological stress or physiological discomfort. The threat of psychological and physical discomfort from withdrawal becomes the motivation for continued use. Users in this category include not only the skid-row alcoholic and street "junkie" but also the crack-dependent adolescent, the alcohol-dependent businessman, the barbiturate-dependent housewife, and the opiate-dependent physician, and the habitual smoker.

FAMILY ORIGINS.   The following family factors correlate closely with excessive drug use by adolescents while growing up (Bettes, Dusenbury, Kerner, James-Ortiz, & Botvin, 1990; Rees and Wilborn, 1983). In comparison to nonabusers:

- Abusers are usually not as close to their parents, are more likely to have negative adolescent–parent relationships, and have a low degree of parental support.
- Abusers are more likely to have parents who drink excessively and/or use other psychotropic drugs (McDermott, 1984; Wodarski, 1990).
- Abusers are more likely to come from broken homes or not to live with both parents (Doherty & Needle, 1991; Johnson, Shontz, & Locke, 1984; Stern, Northman, & Van Slyck, 1984).
- Abusers are more likely to be dissatisfied with parents and experience parental deprivation (Hundleby & Mercer, 1987).
- Abusers' parents less often praise, encourage, and counsel and set limits to adolescents' behavior (Coombs & Landsverk, 1988; Hauser, Bornan, Jacobson, Powers, & Noam, 1991).
- Parental conflict in childrearing practices, inconsistent discipline, restrictive discipline, and maternal rejection are all associated with marijuana and alcohol use in older adolescents (Vicary & Lerner, 1986).
- Abusers are likely to experience parental physical and sexual abuse, which leads to self-derogation (Dembo, Dertke, LaVoie, Borders, Washburn & Schmeidler, 1987).
- The family relationships of adolescents who abuse drugs are similar to those of adolescents who are emotionally disturbed.

These types of family situations create personality problems that cause individuals to be more likely to turn to drugs. Numerous other studies associate drug addiction and dependency with disturbed family relationships (Shaver, 1983) and personality problems (Page, 1990).

LIVING ISSUES

How Can You Tell If You're an Alcoholic?

A distinction must be made between chronic alcoholism and alcohol abuse. **Chronic alcoholism** is characterized by compulsive drinking, so that the person does not have voluntary control over the amount consumed (McMurran & Whitman, 1990). As a result of chemical and psychological dependence on alcohol, the person drinks too much. Chronic alcoholics may go on binges of heavy drinking followed by a long period of sobriety. Or they may drink heavily only on weekends, or may drink large amounts daily. Drinking patterns vary.

Alcohol abuse is the use of alcohol to a degree that causes physical damage; impairs physical, social, intellectual, or occupational functioning; or results in behavior harmful to others.

Warning Signs. The following are some of the warning signs that a drinking problem is developing:

You drink to relieve feelings of inadequacy, anxiety, depression, or boredom.

You have begun to drink to relieve stress or when problems build up.

You drink before or after others start or are finished with drinking.

You have begun to drink alone.

You drink the "morning after" to counteract the effects of a previous night's drinking.

You get drunk on important occasions.

You indulge in drinking bouts followed by hangovers.

You get drunk when you do not want to, drink more than you plan, and lose control of your drinking.

You want to drink less but cannot.

You feel guilty about your drinking behavior.

You lie about your drinking and deny that you are drinking.

You often regret what you have done or said while you were drinking.

You begin to criticize people who do not drink.

Your drinking is affecting your relationships with family and friends.

You pass out or have memory blackouts while drinking.

You have been absent from school or work because of drinking.

Delinquency

INCIDENCE.   Of all persons arrested in 1988, 16% were juveniles—under age 18; an additional 31% were age 18 to 24. Figure 13.2 shows the percentages. *This means that 47% of all arrests during 1988 were of people under age 25.* As seen in Figure 13.3, the incidence of delinquency among males under 18 is 3½ times that among females of the same age (U.S. Bureau of the Census, 1990).

PSYCHOLOGICAL CAUSES.   In general, the causes of delinquency may be grouped into three major categories (Farrington, 1990): psychological factors that include emotional and personality factors and difficulties in interpersonal relationships; sociological factors that include societal and cultural influences; and biological factors that include the effects of organic and physical elements.

There have been efforts to determine whether certain personality factors predispose the adolescent to delinquency (Bernstein, 1981; Thornton, 1982). Generally speaking, no one personality type is related to delinquency, but those who become delinquent are more likely to be impulsive, destructive, suspicious, hostile, resentful, ambivalent to authority, defiant, socially assertive, and lack self-control (Ashford & LeCroy, 1990; Serok & Blum, 1982; Thompson and Dodder, 1986).

Delinquency is sometimes a manifestation of hostilities, anxieties, fears, or of deeper neuroses. One important cause is love deprivation while growing up (Walsh & Beyer, 1987). In other instances, delinquency occurs in basically healthy adolescents who have been misled by others. In some cases, delinquency is the result of poor socialization that results in adolescents' not developing proper impulse controls (Eisikovits & Sagi, 1982; Stefanko, 1984). The psychodynamics of delinquents' behavior are different, although the results of that behavior are similar (Hoffman, 1984).

SOCIOLOGICAL CAUSES.   Family factors, such as strained family relationships and lack of family cohesion, are important sources of delinquency (Anolik, 1980; Anolik, 1981; Fischer, 1980; Kroupa, 1988; Madden & Harbin, 1983; Tolan, 1988; Tygart, 1991). Broken homes have been associated with delin-

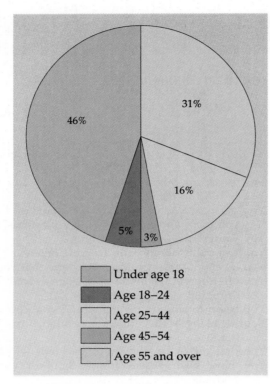

FIGURE 13.2 Age distribution of all people arrested, 1989.

From *Statistical Abstract of the United States, 1990* (p. 177) by U.S. Bureau of the Census. Department of Commerce, 1990, Washington, DC: U.S. Government Printing Office.

cents from intact but unhappy homes, the effects on adolescents are similar, indicating that family environment is more important in delinquency than family structure (LeFlore, 1988).

Juvenile delinquency is distributed through all socioeconomic status levels (Lempers & Clark-Lempers, 1990). In fact, as great an incidence of some forms of delinquency among adolescents of middle classes exists as among those of lower classes. Tygart (1988) found, for example, that youths of high socioeconomic status (SES) were more likely to be involved in school vandalism than youths of low SES. One big difference is that middle-class adolescents who commit delinquent offenses are less often arrested and incarcerated than are low-class youths.

Community and neighborhood influences are also important. Most larger communities have areas in which delinquency rates are higher than in other neighborhoods. A larger than average percentage of adolescents growing up in these areas becomes delinquent because of the negative influence of the neighborhood.

Some adolescents become delinquent because of antisocial influences of peers (Covington, 1982; Mitchell & Dodder, 1980; Zober, 1981). A high degree of peer orientation is sometimes associated with a high level of delinquency.

Modern youths are also influenced by affluent and hedonistic values and life-styles in our culture. Youths may be encouraged to keep late hours, get into mischief, and become involved in vandalism or delinquent acts just for kicks (Riener, 1981; Wasson, 1980).

Violent youths may have been influenced by the violence they see in our culture

quency, but are no worse than, and sometimes not as detrimental as, intact but unhappy or disturbed family relationships. Studies of delinquency often compare the rates for adolescents from broken homes with those from intact happy homes. However, if comparisons are made between adolescents from broken homes with adoles-

FIGURE 13.3 People arrested, by sex and age, 1987.

Statistics from *Statistical Abstract of the United States, 1989* by U.S. Bureau of the Census, Department of Commerce, 1989, Washington, DC: U.S. Government Printing Office.

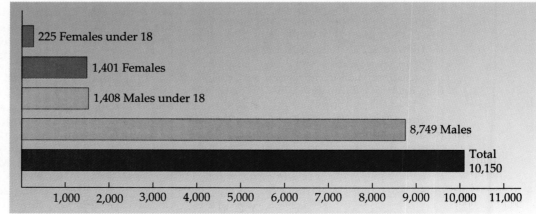

and in the media (Snyder, 1991). May (1986) found that youths who behave in a violent manner give more selective attention to violent cues. They tend to choose to attend movies that are more violent, and imitate what they have seen and heard. Today's adolescents are also living in a period of unrest, disorganization, and rapid cultural change, all of which tend to increase delinquency rates.

Dawkins and Dawkins (1981) found that drinking was strongly associated with serious delinquency among both white and black youths, especially when other factors such as drug use, association with drug users, and previous arrests were present (Watts & Wright, 1990). Stuck and Glassner (1985) emphasized the strong correlation between criminal activity and drug use.

The level of school performance is also correlated with delinquency (Grande, 1988). Inability getting along with teachers and administrators, difficulty adjusting to the school program, classroom misconduct, poor grades, and a lack of school success are associated with delinquency.

BIOLOGICAL CAUSES. Biological causes may play a role in delinquency (Anolik, 1983). Mednick and Christiansen (1977) showed that the autonomic nervous system (ANS) in criminals recovers more slowly from environmental stimulation as compared to that of noncriminals. Slow recovery time reduces the ability to alter their behavior through punishment; thus, it becomes more difficult to unlearn delinquent behavior.

There is a possibility that a maturational lag in the development of the frontal lobe of the brain results in neurophysiological dysfunction and delinquent behavior (Voorhees, 1981). Juveniles are not able to act on the basis of the knowledge they have.

We know also that certain personality characteristics, such as temperament, are partly inherited, so that a child may have a predisposition to behave poorly. If the parents do not know how to cope, the problem is compounded because the child develops a psychological disturbance (Schwarz, 1979).

According to Sheppard (1974), at least 25% of delinquency can be blamed on organic causes. He cited the case of a 15-year-old girl whose blood sugar level was too low because of an excess of insulin. The girl was fidgety, jumpy, restless, and unable to think or act rationally. Proper diet and medication corrected the difficulty. Sheppard cited other examples of delinquency caused by abnormal brain wave patterns, hyperactivity from hy-

perthyroidism, and hearing impairment. Other research indicates a definite relationship between delinquency and health problems such as neurological, speech, hearing, and vision abnormalities. Prenatal and perinatal complications may also be the cause of later behavior problems.

PREVENTION. Those who work with delinquents are very concerned about prevention. One of the ways to prevent delinquency is to identify children (such as hyperactive ones) who may be predisposed to getting into trouble, and then plan intervention programs to help them. Another preventative measure is to focus on dysfunctional family relationships and assist parents in learning more effective parenting skills. Antisocial youths may be placed in groups of prosocial peers, such as at day camps, where their behavior is influenced positively. Young children may be placed in preschool settings before problems arise. Older children need help with learning disabilities before they develop behavior problems. Hurley (1985) wrote: "A partial list of the links to crime includes television, poor nutrition, eyesight problems, teenage unemployment or employment, too little punishment, too much punishment, high or low IQ, allergies and fluorescent light" (p. 680). Great commitment is required to sort out the various links to crime and to correct these causes.

Running Away

INCIDENCE. Over 700,000 youths, ages 10 to 17, run away from home for at least one night without adult consent. Almost 60% of these youths are females, many of whom are assisted by boyfriends. An analysis of the youths served under the *National Runaway Youth Program* across the United States revealed the following profile (U.S. Dept. of HHS, 1980).

Race/ethnic origin: White (74%)
Age: 16 years (25%)
Sex: Female (59%)
Living situation past 3 years: Home with parents or legal guardians (82.4%)
Length of stay: Less than 14 days (84.1%)
Juvenile justice system involvement: No involvement (59.4%)
Reasons for seeking services: Poor communication with parent figures (51.8%)
Parent participation: One or both parents (51.9%)
Disposition: Home with parents or legal guardian (30.4%)

Some adolescents who run away from home become street kids.

These youths come from a variety of social classes and home backgrounds indicating that the reasons for running away are not a result of any one cause (Adams & Munro, 1979).

CLASSIFICATION.   Roberts (1982) made a helpful classification of different types of runaways according to the degree of conflict with parents. Figure 13.4 illustrates the categories. The 0–1 categories include youths who wanted to travel and received permission from parents. Runaway explorers wanted adventure and to assert their independence. They left their parents word about where they had gone, and then left without permission. They generally returned home on their own if they were not picked up by the police. Social pleasure seekers usually had conflict with parents over such issues as dating a certain person, attending an important event, grounding, or an early curfew. They sneaked out to engage in the forbidden activity and then either sneaked back or stopped by a friend's house overnight. They

usually telephoned the parents the next morning to ask to come home.

Runaway manipulators tried to manipulate parents by running away to force them to permit return on the runaways' own terms. They had serious conflict with parents over choice of friends, home chores, and other issues.

Runaway retreatists came from families where there was conflict, hitting or throwing objects, frequent yelling, and other manifestations of tension. Some of the homes were broken. In addition, the majority of adolescents had one or more school problems, or problems with alcohol or other types of drugs. They and their families needed counseling help to correct the situations that resulted in running away in the first place.

Endangered runaways left to escape abusive parents or stepparents. These youths often used drugs and had drinking problems. A beating or the threat of a beating may have precipitated running away (Roberts, 1982). Physical or sexual abuse of both males and females is often a reason for running away (Janus, Burgess, & McCormack, 1987). For this reason, many didn't want to return home.

The simplest classification of runaways is to divide them into two groups: the running from and the running to (Miller, Eggertson-Tacon, & Quigg, 1990; Roberts, 1982). The running from adolescents could not tolerate one or both parents, or their home situation. The running to adolescents were pleasure seekers, running to places or people providing exciting and different activities. Some enjoyed running away and liked the friends they met on the way. They usually did not return until picked up by the police.

Not all runaways are the same or leave home for similar reasons (Hier, Korboot, & Schweitzer, 1990). However, clusters of personal or situational variables appear repeatedly in their case histories. One study in

FIGURE 13.4 Formulation of the degree of parent-youth conflict continuum.

From "Adolescent Runaways in Suburbia: A New Typology" by A. R. Roberts, Summer 1982, *Adolescence, 17*, pp. 379–396.

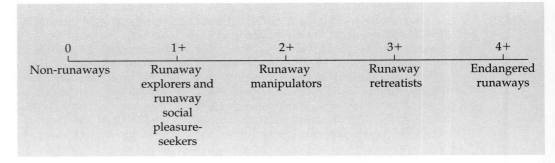

0	1+	2+	3+	4+
Non-runaways	Runaway explorers and runaway social pleasure-seekers	Runaway manipulators	Runaway retreatists	Endangered runaways

Hawaii found that children from single-parent families had less chance of becoming chronic runaways than those from intact families (Matthews & Ilon, 1980). This is because there was much more quarreling in the two-parent families that the child felt powerless to prevent and from which escape seemed the only solution.

ASSISTANCE.   The *National Runaway Youth Program*, with the U.S. Youth Development Bureau, has promoted nationwide assistance to youths who are vulnerable to exploitation and to dangerous encounters. The program offers a national toll-free communication system to enable youths to telephone their families and/or centers where they can get help. Most of the individual programs throughout the United States have developed different services to meet various needs. Social service agencies and juvenile justice/law enforcement systems also use their services to assist runaways and their families (U.S. Department of Health and Human Services, 1980).

SUMMARY

1. Emotions are subjective feelings an individual experiences in response to stimuli, accompanied by physiological arousal, and which result in behavioral responses.

2. Emotions affect physical well-being and behavior, and are important sources of pleasure and satisfaction.

3. Emotions may be classified into three categories: joyous states including affection, love, happiness, and pleasure; inhibitory states including fear or dread, worry or anxiety, sadness or sorrow, embarassment, regret or guilt, and disgust; and hostile states including anger, hatred, contempt, and jealousy.

4. By the time children reach adolescence, they already exhibit well-developed patterns of emotional responses to events and people. They may already be described as warm, affectionate, and friendly, or cold, unresponsive, and distant.

5. Fear may be divided into four categories: fear of material things and natural phenomena, fear relating to the self, fear involving social relationships, and fear of the unknown.

6. A phobia is an excessive, uncontrolled fear. Phobias may be divided into three categories: simple phobias, social phobias, and agoraphobia.

7. Worry and anxiety are closely allied with fear but may arise from imagined unpleasant situations as well as from real causes.

8. A study of college females at the University of Maine revealed that the number one worry was school, followed by parents and family, vocation and employment, social relationships, money, the future, marriage, sex, and being overweight, in that order.

9. Some adolescents have grown up in a worry-free environment; others under conditions that cause constant worry and tension.

10. Generalized anxiety disorder is when anxiety becomes so pervasive and tenacious that it interferes with normal functioning.

11. Hostile states may be manifested as anger, hatred, contempt, or jealousy.

12. Anger in adolescents has many causes: restrictions on social life, attacks on their ego or status, criticism, shaming, rejection, or the actions or treatment of other people. Situations, and the adolescents' own ineptitude, also cause anger.

13. Hatred can be more serious than anger because it persists over a long period of time, is difficult to suppress, and may be expressed through words or actions in violent, aggressive, explosive ways.

14. Self-concept may be defined as a person's perception of his or her nature, character, and individuality.

15. Ruth Strang said there are four basic dimensions of the self: the basic, overall self-concepts; transitory or temporary self-concepts; social selves; and ideal selves.

16. Self-esteem is the value people place on themselves.

17. A positive self-esteem is important to interpersonal competence and social adjustments, and to emotional well-being, progress in school, and vocational aspirations. Negative self-esteem is related to delinquency.

18. A number of factors are important to the development of a positive self-concept: the quality of parent–adolescent relationships, the type of parental control, the atmosphere of the home—whether happy or unhappy, the self-esteem of

the parents, and the quality of social relationships and friendships.

19. Self-concept gradually stabilizes during adolescence, although adolescents are sensitive to important events and changes in their lives.

20. Neurotic perfectionists pursue excellence to an unhealthy extreme, are plagued by self-criticism and low self-worth, and by the stress of having to be perfect.

21. The most frequently abused drugs are alcohol, tobacco, and marijuana, in that order.

22. A physically addictive drug is one that builds up a chemical craving for it, so that denial results in withdrawal symptoms. Psychological dependence is the development of a persistent, psychological need for a drug. Those who use physically addictive drugs may develop a chemical dependency before they realize it. Those who use nonaddictive drugs to solve emotional problems become psychologically dependent on them.

23. Youths are trying drugs at younger ages.

24. Drug use may be divided into five patterns: social–recreational use, experimental use, circumstantial–situational use, intensified use, and compulsive use.

25. There is a correlation between drug addiction and dependency and disturbed family relationships.

26. Alcoholism is dependence on alcohol, uncontrolled, compulsive, and excessive drinking leading to functional impairment. Alcohol abuse is the use of alcohol to a degree that causes physical damage or impairs functioning.

27. Forty-seven percent of all arrests during 1988 were of people under age 25. Delinquency among males under age 18 is 3½ times that among females of the same age.

28. The causes of delinquency may be grouped into three categories: psychological, sociological, and biological.

29. Psychological causes include emotional and personality factors.

30. Sociological causes include family background influences, socioeconomic status levels, neighborhood and community influences, peer group involvement, affluence and hedonistic values and lifestyles, violence in our culture, cultural change and unrest, drinking and drug use, and school performance.

31. Biological or organic factors may also be involved in delinquency.

32. Any efforts to curb delinquency need to focus on prevention.

33. Adolescents who run away from home have been classified along a continuum as runaway explorers, social pleasure seekers, runaway manipulators, runaway retreatists, and endangered runaways. The simplest classification is to divide them into two groups: the running from and running to. Thus, not all runaways leave home for the same reasons.

34. The National Runaway Youth Program has been developed to provide multiple-service assistance to runaways.

KEY TERMS

Alcohol abuse *p. 291*
Chronic alcoholism *p. 291*
Emotion *p. 278*
Generalized anxiety disorder *p. 282*
Phobia *p. 280*

Physical addiction *p. 289*
Proprium *p. 284*
Psychological dependency *p. 289*
Self *p. 283*
Self-concept *p. 283*

DISCUSSION QUESTIONS

1. What sort of things make you the happiest? most afraid? most worried? most angry?

2. Do you have any phobias? Describe. How did they arise? What do you do about them?

3. Why do some adolescents hate their parents? What can or should they do about these feelings?

4. Do you have a positive or negative self-concept? What factors have been most influential in molding your ideas about yourself?

5. If you could be any type of person you wanted, what would you be like?

6. Is there any possibility you can become your ideal self? Explain why or why not.

7. Do you have a different self-concept from when you were younger? Explain.

8. What role have your parents played in influencing your self-esteem?

9. Do you accept what your friends say about you? Why? or Why not?

10. Who have been the most significant others in your life in influencing your self-conception?

11. Does parental divorce or remarriage influence self-esteem? Explain with personal examples.

12. Did you or your friends use drugs when you were in high school? With what effects?

13. What type of drug education programs in high school would help the most?

14. If you were a parent and discovered your adolescent was using alcohol, tobacco, marijuana, narcotics, or cocaine, what would you do?

15. To those who have stopped smoking: What helped the most in being able to stop?

16. Why do far fewer females than males become delinquent?

17. If you were a parent, would you forbid your adolescent to run around with a friend who was a convicted delinquent? How would you handle the situation?

18. What factors are most important in causing delinquency?

19. Do you have any firsthand knowledge of gangs in the town where you live, or in which you grew up? Describe.

20. Have you or has a member of your family ever run away from home? Why? What happened?

SUGGESTED READINGS

Johnston, L. L., O'Malley, P. M., & Bachman, J. G. (1987). *National trends in drug use and related factors among American high school students and young adults, 1975–1986*. Ann Arbor: Institute for Social Research, University of Michigan. Trends in adolescent drug use.

Offer, D., Ostrov, E., & Howard, K. J. (1981). *The adolescent: A psychological self-portrait*. New York: Basic Books. Descriptive.

Perkins, W. M., & McMurtrie-Perkins, N. (1986). *Raising drug-free kids in a drug-filled world*. Austin, TX: Hazelden. Advice for parents.

Quay, H. C. (Ed.). (1987). *Handbook of juvenile delinquency*. New York: Wiley. Series of articles on description, causes, and prevention of delinquency.

14

Social Development

ADOLESCENTS IN THEIR FAMILIES*

The family is the chief socializing influence on adolescents. This means that the family is the principal transmitter of knowledge, values, attitudes, roles, and habits that one generation passes on to the next. Through word and example the family shapes adolescents' personality and instills modes of thought and ways of acting that become habitual. But what adolescents learn from parents depends partly on the kinds of people the parents are (McKenry, Kotch, & Browne, 1991). Just as a starter, what kinds of parents do adolescents say they want and need?

What Adolescents Expect of Parents

The following is a compilation of research findings. These findings indicate that youths want and need parents who

"Treat us as grown-ups, not like children."
"Have faith in us to do the right things."
"Love us and like us the way we are."
"We can talk to."
"Listen to us and try to understand us."
"Are interested in us."
"Guide us."
"Are fun and have a sense of humor."
"We can be proud of."

These characteristics need closer examination (Williamson & Campbell, 1985).

REASONABLE FREEDOM AND PRIVILEGES.   One of the complaints of adolescents is that their parents treat them like kids. Most adolescents push as hard as they can for adult privileges and freedom (Fasick, 1984). They want to feel they can make their own decisions and run their own lives, without their parents always telling them what to do (Pardeck, 1990). However, adolescents need parents who will grant them autonomy in slowly increasing amounts as they learn to use it responsibly (Dornbusch, Ritter, Mont-Reynaud, & Chen, 1990; Gavazzi & Sabatelli, 1990). In his research with adolescent boys, Steinberg (1981) found that assertiveness increases from early puberty to middle adolescence, after which it tapers off as adolescents

The family is the chief socializing influence on adolescents.

begin to exert more influence in family decision making (Ellis, 1991; Papini, Roggman, & Anderson, 1990). Too much freedom granted too early may make them think that the parents aren't interested. Youth want freedom—but do not want it all at once. Those who have it suddenly worry about it because they realize they do not know how to use it. Adolescents who have good relationships with their parents still look to them for guidance and advice (Greene & Grimsley, 1990).

FAITH.   Adolescents say

"My parents don't trust me. They always seem to expect the worst. I even have trouble getting them to believe me when I tell them where I'm going or what I'm going to do. I might as well not do right; they already accuse me anyhow. If they could expect me to do the right thing, I wouldn't disappoint them."

Some parents seem to have more trouble than others in trusting their adolescents. They tend to project their own guilt, anxieties, and fears onto the adolescent. They worry most about problems that they experienced while growing up.

APPROVAL.   All adolescents want their parents to like them, approve of them, and accept them in spite of faults. Adolescents don't want to feel that they have to be perfect before they receive their parents' approval. No adolescent can thrive in an atmosphere of constant criticism and disapproval.

*Part of the material in this chapter is adapted from the author's book, *The Adolescent, Development Relationships, and Culture,* 6th ed. (1990). Boston: Allyn and Bacon. Used by permission of the publisher.

WILLINGNESS TO COMMUNICATE. Many of the problems between parents and adolescents can be solved if both are able to communicate with one another (Masselam, Marcus, & Stunkard, 1990; Papini, Farmer, Clark, Micka, & Barnett, 1990). Parents complain that their adolescents never listen to them. Adolescents say their parents lecture them or preach to them rather than discuss issues with them. One adolescent comments:

> "My parents aren't really willing to listen to what I have to say. They don't understand me. I'm not even allowed to express my point of view. They will tell me to be quiet and not to argue. That's the end of the discussion."

When parents show respect for adolescents' opinions, conflict is minimized and the atmosphere of the home is enhanced. Some parents don't give their adolescents a chance to express their feelings or point of view. This builds up resentment and tension (Thompson, Acock, & Clark, 1985).

PARENTAL CONCERN AND SUPPORT. Adolescents want their parents to be interested in what they are doing and to give moral support when necessary (Northman, 1985). One boy, a baseball player, was angry because his parents never attended a game to see him play ball. Adolescents especially resent parents who are so involved with their own activities that they don't have time for their children or are not around when they are needed (Gullotta, Steven, Donohue, & Clark, 1981; Jensen & Borges, 1986). The term "latchkey" children applies to youth who have to let themselves in the house after school because parents are working outside the home. For a full discussion of parental employment and adolescents see *The Journal of Adolescence* (Volume 10, August 1990).

GUIDANCE. All adolescents need guidance and discipline, but some methods work better than others (Holmbeck & Hill, 1991; Nurmi & Pulliainen, 1991). Research generally indicates that parental explanations and reasoning (induction) are strongly associated with adolescents' internalizing ethical and moral principles. To talk with adolescents is the most frequent disciplinary measure used and the one considered best for the age group (de Turck & Miller, 1983; McKenry, Price-Bonham, & O'Bryant, 1981; Smith, 1983). The parents and adolescents who are most successful at conflict resolution are those who show mutual respect and exchange and high regard for the needs of one another, and who exchange ideas and information (McCombs, Forehand, & Smith, 1988). Use of physical punishment, deprivation, and threats (power-assertive discipline) is associated with children's aggression, hostility, and delinquency (Feldman & Wentzel, 1990). It impedes the development of emotional, social, and intellectual maturity (Portes, Dunham, & Williams, 1986).

The authoritative but democratic home, where parents encourage individual responsibility, decision making, initiative, and autonomy but still exercise authority and give guidance, has a positive effect upon adolescents (Kelly & Goodwin, 1983). The home atmosphere has the character of respect, appreciation, warmth, and acceptance. This type of home, where there is warmth, fairness, and consistency of discipline, is associated with conforming, trouble-free, nondelinquent behavior for both boys and girls.

Inconsistent or sporadic parental control also has a negative effect on adolescents. Adolescents become insecure and confused when they lack boundaries and clear guidelines. Such youths may show antisocial, delinquent behavior and rebel against conflicting expectations.

A HAPPY HOME. The most important contribution parents can make to their adolescent children is to create a happy home environment in which to bring them up (Fauber, Forehand, Thomas, & Wierson, 1990; Parish, 1990; Parish, Dostal, & Parish, 1981). One adolescent remarked:

> "I love it at home because we always have such a good time together. Mom and Dad are always laughing and joking. We seldom argue, but when we do, we get over it quickly. No one holds a grudge. We are really happy together."

In contrast to this, some families live in a home climate of anger, unhappiness, and hostility, all of which has a negative effect on everyone (Forsstrom-Cohen & Rosenbaum, 1985). The best-adjusted adolescents are those who grow up in happy homes where children and parents spend pleasurable time together (McMillan & Hiltonsmith, 1982).

GOOD EXAMPLE. Adolescents say they want parents who "make us proud of them," "follow the same principles they try to teach us," "set a good example for us to follow," and "who practice what they preach." They want parents they can admire. As one adolescent expressed it: "It's good to feel our parents are trying to teach us right from wrong and set a good example for us to follow" (Clark-Lempers, Lempers, & Ho, 1991).

Parent—Adolescent Disagreements

Most parents get along fairly well with their adolescent children (Stefanko, 1984). When disagreement occurs, it usually is in one or more of the following areas (Hall, 1987; Leslie, Huston, & Johnson, 1986; Smetana, Braeges, & Yau, 1991).

MORAL, ETHICAL BEHAVIOR.   Parents are concerned about their adolescents' going to church, synagogue, or temple; obeying the law and staying out of trouble; sexual behavior, honesty; language and speech; drinking, smoking, and use of drugs.

RELATIONSHIPS WITH FAMILY MEMBERS.   Disagreements arise over the amount of time adolescents spend with the family (Felson & Gottfredson, 1984; Jurich, Schumm, & Bollman, 1987), relationships with relatives, especially with aged grandparents in the home, quarreling with siblings, the general attitude and level of respect shown to parents, and temper tantrums and other manifestations of childish behavior.

Adolescent social activities probably create more conflict with parents than any other areas of concern.

ACADEMICS.   Parents are concerned about adolescents' behavior in school, general attitudes toward school studies and teachers, regularity of attendance, study habits and homework, and grades and level of performance.

FULFILLING RESPONSIBILITIES.   Most parents expect adolescents to show responsibility in the following areas: use of family property or belongings, furnishings, supplies, tools, and equipment; use of the telephone; use of the family automobile; care of personal belongings, clothes, and room; earning and spending money; and performance of family chores (Grief, 1985; Light, Hertsgaard, & Martin, 1985; Sanik & Stafford, 1985).

SOCIAL ACTIVITIES.   Adolescents' social activities probably create more conflict with parents than any other areas of concern. The most common sources of friction are the following:

Choice of clothes and hair styles; going steady and age allowed to date, ride in cars, and participate in certain events; curfew hours and where they are allowed to go; how often they are allowed to go out, going out on a school night, or frequency of dating; and choice of friends or dating partners.

WORK OUTSIDE THE HOME.   Most parents expect adolescents to do some work outside the home to earn money, and most do, but sometimes the amount of work is excessive so that the adolescent neglects the family and school and is away from home too much.

CORRELATIONS WITH CONFLICT.   A number of factors relate to the focus and extent of conflict with parents.

The type of *discipline* that parents use has an effect on conflict (Johnson, Shulman, & Collings, 1991). Authoritarian discipline results in more conflict with parents over home chores, activities outside the home, friends, and spending money than does a democratic approach to guidance.

The *socioeconomic status* of the family influences the focus of conflict. Parents of low socioeconomic status are more often concerned with respect, politeness, and obedience, whereas middle-income families are more concerned with developing initiative and independence. Parents of low socioeconomic status worry about keeping children out of trouble at school, whereas middle-class parents are more concerned about achievement and grades (McKenry, Kotch, & Browne, 1991).

The *number of children* in the family is a significant factor, at least in middle-class families (Kidwell, 1981). The more children in the middle-class family, the more parent–youth conflict and the more parents use physical force to control adolescents (Bell & Avery, 1985).

The *stage of development* of adolescents is another factor. From age 12 on, girls are increasingly in conflict with parents over boyfriends, with the peak years being 14 and 15. The peak age of boys for conflict with parents over girlfriends is around age 16.

The *gender* of the adolescent relates to conflict. Boys report fewer problems with family than do girls, which is an indication of gender differences in the extent of difficulty. The gender of the parent also relates to conflict. Adolescents are usually closer to their mothers than to their fathers (Cicirelli, 1980; Paulson, Hill, & Holmbeck, 1990; Rubin, 1982). As a result, they usually get along better with their mothers and the mothers exert more influence over them in such areas as educational goals (Smith, 1981). Most adolescents report more difficulties getting along with their fathers than with their mothers (Miller & Lane, 1991).

The variables associated with parent–adolescent conflict are numerous (Flanagan, 1990), but the ones discussed here are representative. Not all parents and adolescents quarrel about the same things or to the same extent.

Relationships With Siblings

The relationships between brothers and sisters have a considerable influence on the social development of the adolescent (Buhrmester & Furman, 1990). This development is affected in a number of ways (Blyth, Hill, & Thiel, 1982).

Siblings often provide friendship and companionship and meet one another's needs for meaningful relationships and affection. They act as confidants for one another, share many experiences, and are able to help one another when there are problems. However, this is not as true if siblings are 6 or more years apart in age.

On the negative side, if there is less than 6 years' difference in their ages, siblings tend to be more jealous of one another than if they are farther apart in age. Also, sibling rivalry is greater during early adolescence than later. As adolescents mature, conflicting relationships with siblings tend to subside (Goodwin & Roscoe, 1990).

Older siblings often serve as confidants, playmates, teachers, caretakers, and surrogate parents. Pleasant relationships can contribute to younger children's sense of acceptance, belonging, and security. Rejecting, hostile relationships may create deep-seated feelings of hostility, resentment, insecurity, or anxiety that may be carried into adulthood. Many adolescents learn adult responsibilities and roles by having to care for younger sisters and brothers while growing up. However, some adolescents are given too much responsibility, and provide most of the care that parents ought to be providing. They may grow to resent this responsibility, which prevents them from having any free time of their own. Older siblings represent masculine or feminine personalities and behavior to younger siblings. Through appearance, character, and overall behavior, they exemplify a type of person the younger child might become. This can have either a positive or negative effect, depending on the example set.

SOCIAL RELATIONSHIPS

Friendships of Young Adolescents

Adolescents' need for close friends is different from that of children (Pombeni, Kirchler, & Palmonari, 1990; Yarcheski & Mahon, 1984). Children need playmates of their own

Adolescents turn to their friends for companionship and emotional fulfillment.

age to share common activities and games. However, they do not depend primarily on one another for love and affection. They look to their parents for filling their emotional needs and seek praise, affection, and love from them. Only if they have been rejected and unloved by parents will they have turned to parent substitutes and friends for emotional fulfillment.

Needs change with the advent of puberty. The adolescent desires emotional independence and emancipation from parents and emotional fulfillment from friends (Larson & Richards, 1991; Quintana & Lapsley, 1990). Peers now provide part of the emotional support formerly provided by families (DuBois & Hirsch, 1990; Howes & Wu, 1990; Sebald, 1986).

Young adolescents begin to form a small group of friends, and often choose one or several very best friends. Usually these best friends are of the same sex in the beginning (Benenson, 1990). Adolescents attend school, get to athletic events, and share in recreational activities with these friends (Zarbatany, Hartmann, & Rankin, 1990). Best friends strive to dress alike, look alike, and act alike. After spending all day together, they may come home and talk for additional hours on the telephone.

Early adolescent friendships are sometimes upsetting if expectations are not fulfilled (Yarcheski & Mahon, 1984). The more intense and narcissistic the emotions that drive adolescents to seek companionship, the more likely it is that sustained friendships will be difficult and tenuous. Once disappointed, the frustrated, immature, and unstable adolescent may react with excessive emotions, which may disrupt friendships at least temporarily.

Heterosocial Development

Heterosociality means forming friendships with those of both sexes (Goff, 1990). Getting to know and feel comfortable with the opposite sex is a difficult process for some adolescents (Miller, 1990). Here are typical questions of adolescents who are trying to form heterosocial relationships:

"Why is it that I'm so shy when I'm around girls?"
"How can you get a girl to like you?"
"How old do you have to be before you can start dating?"
"How can I get boys to think of me as more than a friend?"

"If a girl likes a boy, should she tell him?"
"How can I become more sexy?"
"How can I overcome my fear of asking a girl out?"
"How do you go about talking to a girl?"

Puberty brings on a biological and emotional awareness of the opposite sex, the beginning of sexual attraction, and a decline in negative attitudes. The girl who was looked on before as a giggly kid now becomes strangely alluring. On the one hand, the now-maturing male is attracted and fascinated by this young woman; on the other hand he is perplexed, awed, and terrified. No wonder he ends up asking: "How do you go about talking to a girl?" Girls, who used to feel that boys were too rough and ill-mannered, now feel a strange urge to be near them: "If a girl likes a boy, should she tell him?"

Some boys show their interest through physical contact and teasing: by pulling the girl's hat off, putting snow down her neck, or chasing after her. Girls, too, find ways of attracting attention. Gradually, these initial contacts are replaced by more mature behavior: attempts at conversation, considerate acts to win favor, or other means of expressing interest. The effort is to act more grown up and mannerly in social situations. The group boy–girl relationships change into paired relationships, and these deepen into affectionate friendships and romance as the two sexes discover one another.

Group Involvement

NEED TO BELONG TO A GROUP.   Finding acceptance in social groups also becomes a powerful motivation in the lives of adolescents (Woodward & Kalyan-Masih, 1990). A primary goal of adolescents is to be accepted by members of a group or clique to which they are attracted. At this stage, adolescents are sensitive to criticism or to others' negative reaction to them. They are concerned about what people think because they want to be accepted and admired by them. Also, their degree of self-worth is partly a reflection of the opinions of others.

The following questions are real-life examples of questions asked by adolescents in the seventh, eighth, and ninth grades. The questions reflect adolescents' concern about group involvement.

"What do you have to do to become a member of a group you like?"

"Why are some kids not friendly? Is there something wrong with me?"

"When other kids ignore you, what do you do?"

"Are kids born popular or do they learn to be that way?"

"If you are too fat, will other kids not accept you?"

SOCIAL ACCEPTANCE.   Considerable evidence shows that personal qualities and social skills such as conversational ability, ability to empathize with others, and poise are the most important factors in social acceptance (Meyers & Nelson, 1986). One study of 204 adolescents in the 7th, 9th, and 12th grades revealed that personal factors such as social conduct, personality, and character traits were more important in social acceptance than either achievement or physical characteristics. This was true of adolescents at all grade levels (Tedesco & Gaier, 1988). But achievement, which included academic success and athletic prowess, also contributed to popularity. And physical characteristics, including appearance and material things such as money or autos, also affected social acceptance. However, the older they became, the more adolescents emphasized personal factors and deemphasized achievement and physical characteristics in friendship. Other research also emphasizes the importance of personal qualities as a criterion of popularity.

Thus, one of the primary ways adolescents find group acceptance is by developing and exhibiting personal qualities that others admire and by learning social skills that ensure acceptance (Miller, 1991; Wise, Bundy, Bundy, & Wise, 1991). In general, popular youths are accepted because of their character, sociability, and personal appearance. They have good reputations and exhibit qualities of moral character that people admire. They usually possess high self-esteem and positive self-concepts. They are appropriately groomed and dressed according to the standards of their group. They are acceptable-looking youths who are friendly, happy, fun-loving, outgoing, and energetic; who have developed a high degree of social skills (Adams, 1983); and who like to participate in many activities with others (Gifford & Dean, 1990). They may be sexually experienced but are not promiscuous (Newcomer, Udry, & Cameron, 1983).

DEVIANT BEHAVIOR.   So far we have been talking about youths who are in the mainstream of group participation. There are other adolescents, however, who find acceptance in deviant groups by conforming to the antisocial standards adopted by their members (Downs & Rose, 1991). Whereas delinquent or antisocial behavior may be unacceptable in society as a whole, it may be required as a condition of membership in a ghetto gang. What might be considered causes of a bad reputation in the local high school (sexual promiscuity, antisocial behavior, being uncooperative, making trouble, or fighting) might be considered causes of a good reputation among a group of delinquents. One study of 12- to 16-year-old boys who were overaggressive and who bullied younger and weaker youths showed that the bullies enjoyed average popularity among other boys (Olweus, 1977); those who were the targets of aggression were far less popular than the bullies. These findings illustrate that standards of group behavior vary with different groups and that popularity depends not so much on a fixed standard as on group conformity.

Sometimes peer groups are formed because of hostility to family authority and a desire to rebel against it. When this happens, the peer groups may become antisocial gangs that are hostile to all established authority, yet supportive of the particular deviancy accepted by the group (Bensman & Liliesfield, 1979).

Dating

Dating in American culture is not equivalent to courtship, at least during the early and middle years of adolescence. Traditionally, courtship was for purposes of mate sorting and selection. Today, however, dating has other purposes in the eyes of adolescents (McCabe, 1984; Roscoe, Diana, & Brooks, 1987).

VALUES.   One major purpose of dating is to have *fun*. Dating provides amusement; it is a form of recreation and a source of enjoyment; it can be an end in itself. Wanting the *friendship, acceptance, affection, and love* of the opposite sex is a normal part of growing up. Dating is also used to achieve and *maintain status*. However, adolescents of higher socioeconomic status more often use dating as a symbol of their status than do those of lower socioeconomic status. Membership in certain cliques is associated with the status-seeking aspects of dating. Dating is also a *means of social and personal growth*. It is a way of learning to get along with others and to know and understand many different types of people.

Dating has become more *sex oriented* as increasing numbers of adolescents have sexual intercourse. Dating is sometimes used to have sex; at other times sex develops out of dating experiences. Most research indicates that men want sexual involvement in a relationship sooner than women, with the discrepancy a source of potential conflict (Knox & Wilson, 1981).

One of the major purposes of dating is to find *intimacy*. Intimacy is the development of affection, respect, loyalty, mutual trust, sharing, openness, love, and commitment (Roscoe, Kennedy, & Pope, 1987). Some adolescent relationships with friends are superficial. Other relationships are close ones, in which adolescents are sensitive to the innermost thoughts and feelings of their partner and are willing to share personal information, private thoughts, and feelings. Heterosocial relationships vary greatly in intensity of feeling and in depth of communication. Dating can provide the opportunity for intimacy, but whether it develops varies with the individuals and with different pairs. Boys who are socialized to hide feelings may have trouble developing intimate relationships with girls.

As youths get older, dating becomes more a means of *mate sorting and selection*, whether the motive is conscious or not. Those who are similar in personality characteristics are more likely to be compatible than those who are dissimilar in social characteristics, psychological traits, and physical attractiveness (Till & Freedman, 1978). Thus, dating can result in sorting out compatible pairs and can contribute to wise mate selection (Cote & Koval, 1983).

DATING CONCERNS.   A study of 107 men and 227 women, who comprised a random sample of students at East Carolina University, sought to identify dating problems (Knox & Wilson, 1983). Table 14.1 shows the problems experienced by the men. The most frequently mentioned problems of the men were communication, where to go and what to do on dates, shyness, money, and honesty/openness, in that order. By honesty and openness the men meant how much to tell about themselves and how soon, and getting their partner to open up (Knox & Wilson, 1983). The most frequent problems expressed by the women (see Table 14.2) were unwanted pressure to engage in sexual behav-

ior, where to go and what to do on dates, communication, sexual misunderstandings, and money, in that order. An example of sexual misunderstandings was leading a man on when the woman did not really want to have intercourse. Some of the women complained that the men wanted to move toward a sexual relationship too quickly.

The problem of communication was mentioned frequently by both women and men. Students complained that they didn't know what to talk about and that they ran out of things to say. After they had discussed school, classes, teachers, jobs, or the weather, the conversation lagged and they had trouble filling in long gaps of silence.

Both college women and men look for honesty and openness in a relationship. Part of the problem is caused by the fact that both the man and woman strive to be on their best behavior. This involves a certain amount of pretense or play acting called **imaging,** to present oneself in the best possible manner.

Imaging—being on one's best behavior to make a good impression

TABLE 14.1 Dating Problems Experienced by 107 University Men

Problem	Percentage
Honesty, openness	8
Money	17
Shyness	20
Place to date	23
Communication with date	35

Adapted from "Dating Problems of University Students" by D. Knox and K. Wilson, 1983, *College Student Journal*, *17*, pp. 225–228.

TABLE 14.2 Dating Problems Experienced by 227 University Women

Problem	Percentage
Money	9
Sexual misunderstandings	13
Communication with date	20
Places to go	22
Unwanted pressure to engage in sexual behavior	23

Adapted from "Dating Problems of University Students" by D. Knox and K. Wilson, 1983, *College Student Journal*, *17*, pp. 225–228.

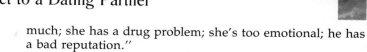

PARENTING ISSUES

When Parents Object to a Dating Partner

Since our system of courtship emphasizes individual freedom, the question arises as to how much influence parents have in the dating process. In a study of 334 university students by Knox and Wilson (1981), women were significantly more likely than men to report that their parents tried to influence their choice of dates. About 60% of the women, compared with 40% of the men, said parental influence was involved. Daughters also were more likely than sons to say that parents interfered with dating relationships. However, daughters were also more likely than sons to say it was important to them that they dated the kinds of people their parents approved of. About 30% of men versus 10% of women said they didn't care what their parents thought.

Parental objections are usually based on one or more of the following:

- *The parents don't like the person* because "he's rude; she's impolite; she has a bad reputation; he's not a nice person." These objections are based on dislike of the other's personality.
- *The parents feel the other person has a problem:* "He drinks too much; she has a drug problem; she's too emotional; he has a bad reputation."
- *The other person's family is different from the parents' family.* "His family are rather common people; he's not of our religion; why couldn't he have picked some fine Italian (or Irish, Jewish, or Spanish) girl?"
- *There is a significant age difference.* "He's too old for her."
- *Parents object because they are too possessive of their offspring and are unwilling to let them grow up.* In this case, the parents might object no matter whom their child wanted to go out with.

There are several approaches adolescents can take. They can try to get their parents to like their choice. If objections are based on a lack of knowledge, they can invite the person over to get acquainted. Sometimes parents end up approving. At other times, parents object even more. Parents are not always wrong. The situation needs to be discussed, employing the aid of a counselor if the parents and adolescent are not able to find a solution.

PREMARITAL SEXUAL BEHAVIOR

Sexual Interests

Intensified interest in sex accompanies sexual maturation (Weinstein & Rosen, 1991). At first this interest focuses on the adolescent's bodily changes and observable happenings. Most adolescents spend time looking in the mirror and examining body parts in minute detail. Accompanying this self-centered concern is the desire to develop an acceptable body image.

Gradually young adolescents become interested not only in their own development, and that of others of the same gender, but also in the opposite sex (Frydenberg & Lewis, 1991). Curiosity motivates them to try to learn as much as possible about the sexual characteristics of the opposite sex. Adolescents also become fascinated with basic facts about human reproduction. Both boys and girls gradually become aware of their own developing sexual feelings and drives and how these are aroused and expressed. Most adolescents begin some experimentation:

touching themselves, playing with their genitals, or exploring various parts of the body. Often by accident they experience orgasm through self-manipulation. From that time on, interest in sex as erotic feeling and expression increases. Adolescents begin to compare their ideas with those of others and spend a lot of time talking about sex, telling jokes, using sex slang, and exchanging sex-oriented literature. Adults are sometimes shocked at the language and jokes. Many parents have been horrified at finding sex-related books hidden under the mattress. But these activities are motivated by a desire to understand human sexuality; they are a means of understanding, expressing, and gaining control over sexual feelings. Wise parents can play a positive role in the sex education of their children (Mueller & Powers, 1990).

Masturbation

One of the common practices of adolescents is **masturbation,** which is any type of self-stimulating that produces erotic arousal, whether or not arousal results in orgasm.

Masturbation—self-stimulation for purposes of sexual arousal

After adolescents discover that they can sexually arouse themselves through self-manipulation, masturbation may become a regular part of their self-expression. The incidence of masturbation varies somewhat among studies. At the University of Northern Iowa, a study of undergraduate students in a class titled Human Relationships and Sexuality revealed that 64% of the females and 90% of the males had masturbated (Story, 1982).

Practically all authorities now say that masturbation is a normal part of growing up and does not have any harmful physical and mental effects. Masturbation provides sexual release and serves a useful function in helping the individual to learn about his or her body, to learn how to respond sexually, and to develop sexual identity (Wagner, 1980). The only ill effect that masturbation may stimulate is guilt, fear, or anxiety stemming from the belief that the practice will do harm or create problems (Parcel & Luttman, 1981). Negative emotions concerning masturbation can lead to great anxiety if a youth continues to practice it and feel guilty about it.

Premarital Sexual Intercourse

The most recent survey of premarital sexual behavior of adolescent females 15 to 19 years of age is the *National Survey of Family Growth* (NSFG) conducted in 1988 (Forrest & Singh, 1990; Olsen, Jensen, & Greaves, 1991). (See Figure 14.1.)

The survey is significant because figures are calculated for the years 1971, 1976, 1979, 1982, and 1988 (Hofferth, Kahn, & Baldwin, 1987). A trend toward an increase in premarital sexual intercourse during this period is evident. The percentage of U.S. teenage women who had premarital sexual intercourse rose from 32% in 1971 to 39% in 1976, 43% in 1979, 47% in 1982, and 53% in 1988. Virtually all growth in the incidence of **coitus** between 1979 and 1988 was accounted for by the growth in sexual activity among never-married white adolescent females. The rate among black adolescent females declined (Pete & DeSantis, 1990). Unfortunately, comparable figures were not obtained for teenage men (Ensminger, 1990).

Coitus—sexual intercourse

Use of Contraceptives

With large numbers of adolescents having premarital sex (DiBlasio & Benda, 1990), the rate of use of contraceptives becomes important (Zabin, 1981). What percentage of these young people are using some form of protection against pregnancy? Results from a 1979 Zelnik and Kantner (1980) nationwide study showed that 27% of 15- to 19-year-old unmarried females *never* used contraception whenever they had intercourse, only 39% *sometimes* used contraception, and only 34% of these teenage girls *always* used contraception. The NSFG in 1988 revealed that only 35% of 15- to 19-year-olds used any methods

FIGURE 14.1 15- to 19-year-old females who ever had premarital intercourse, by year.

Statistics from "Premarital Sexual Activity among U.S. Teenage Women Over the Past Three Decades" by S. L. Hofferth, J. R. Kahn, and W. Baldwin, 1987, *Family Planning Perspectives, 19,* pp. 46–53; and from "The Sexual and Reproductive Behavior of American Women, 1982–1988" by J. D. Forrest and S. Singh, *Family Planning Perspectives, 22,* pp. 206–214.

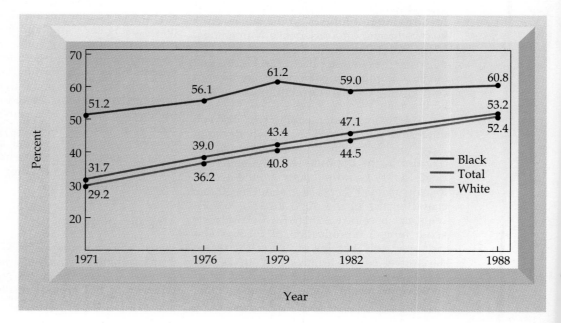

LIVING ISSUES

Is Sex Becoming Depersonalized?

The question arises regarding the meaning attached to sexual relationships experienced by adolescents: Do adolescents have premarital sexual intercourse as an expression of emotional intimacy and loving feelings accompanied by commitment?

Past studies have shown that the preferred sexual standard for youth has been permissiveness with affection. However, there is a significant number of adolescents today who engage in coitus without affection or commitment (Wilson & Medora, 1990). Figure 14.2 shows the results of a survey among 237 (male and female) undergraduate students enrolled in 1986 at Illinois State University (Sprecher, McKinney, Walsh, & Anderson, 1988). The students ranged in age from 18 to 47, with a mean age of 20. All four undergraduate classes were represented. About 90% of the respondents were white,

8% black, and 2% other. About 49% were Catholic, 22% Protestant, 3% Jewish, and the remainder either another religion or no religion.

As indicated, 45% agreed that heavy petting was acceptable on a first date, 28% agreed that sexual intercourse was acceptable on a first date, and 22% found oral-genital sex to be acceptable on a first date. For those engaged in casual dating, 61% approved of heavy petting, 41% approved of intercourse, and 37% approved of oral-genital sex. The largest increase in acceptability for various types of sexual behavior occurred between the casual and serious dating stages. Surprisingly, there were no significant differences according to gender, although there were differences according to age. The 18-year-olds were less sexually permissive than those 21 years of age.

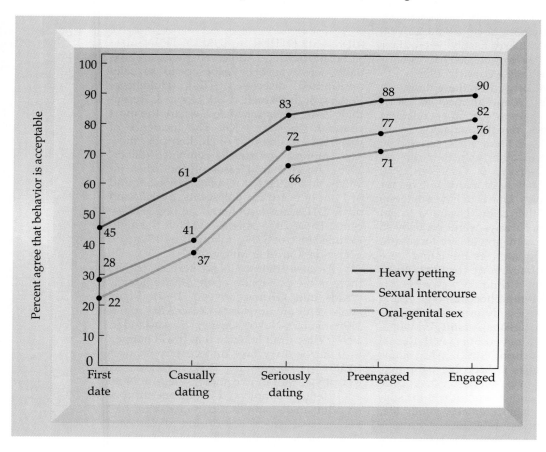

FIGURE 14.2 Acceptance of sexual activity by relationship stage.

From "A Revision of the Reiss Premarital Sexual Permissiveness Scale" by S. Sprecher, K. McKinney, R. Walsh, and C. Anderson, August 1988, by *Journal of Marriage and the Family, 50,* pp. 821–828. Copyrighted 1988 by the National Council on Family Relations, 1910 West County Road B, Suite 147, St. Paul, Minnesota 55113. Reprinted by permission.

of contraception (including withdrawal) at first intercourse (Forrest & Singh, 1990). These figures indicate large numbers of adolescents are not protected against unwanted

pregnancy. As a result, 1 out of every 10 women age 15 to 19 becomes pregnant each year in the United States (Trussell, 1988), and 4 out of 5 of these young women are unmarried. Among teenage men and women who use contraceptives, the most popular method is the pill, followed by the condom (Beck & Davies, 1987; Segest, Mygind, Jergensen, Bechgaard, & Fallov, 1990). Withdrawal and rhythm, both relatively ineffective methods, are the next most commonly used methods. Only small percentages of adolescents use the diaphragm, sponge, IUD, or foam.

Potential Problems

TEENAGE PREGNANCY.   The net increase in premarital sexual intercourse accompanied by a lack of efficient use of contraceptives has resulted in an increase in the incidence of out-of-wedlock pregnancies, now estimated at 1 million each year among women 15 to 19 years of age (Jemmott & Jemmott, 1990; Paikoff, 1990). Of this number, 115,000 are miscarriages or stillbirths, 420,000 (42%) are induced abortions, and the remaining 465,000 babies are born alive. About 225,000 expectant mothers marry hastily before their babies are born, leaving 240,000 babies born out of wedlock in 1988 (Trussell, 1988).

Over 90% of unwed mothers decide to keep their babies (Alan Guttmacher, 1981). Some let their parents or other relatives adopt their babies, but the remainder want to raise their children themselves, assisted by whatever family or other help they can get (Culp, Culp, Osofsky, & Osofsky, 1991; Hanson, 1990). They have many motives for keeping their babies. One is to have someone to love. One mother said: "I wanted to get pregnant because I always wanted a baby so that I could have someone to care for and to care for me." Other motives are to find identity, a feeling of importance, or to try to be an adult by having a child.

Ummarried motherhood among young teenage girls is a tragedy in most instances (Christmon, 1990; Kellam, Adams, Brown, & Ensminger, 1982; Moore & Stief, 1991; Roosa, Fitzgerald, & Carlson, 1982). The single mother who decides to keep her baby may become trapped in a self-destructive cycle consisting of dependence on others for support, failure to establish a stable family life, repeated pregnancies, and failure to continue her education (Blinn, 1990). Marriage is not the answer because only 20% of those who marry are still together after five years. Only a minority complete their high school education and are able to get a good job to support themselves and their family, so most are likely to require welfare assistance for years (Dillard & Pol, 1982).

Education is an important tool for young unmarried mothers.

AIDS AND OTHER SEXUALLY TRANSMITTED DISEASES.   Adolescents who are sexually active may be exposed to sexually transmitted diseases (STDs) (Holmbeck, Waters, & Brookmen, 1990; Moore & Rosenthal, 1990). *Chlamydial infections* are the most common (Judson, 1985). The incidence of *gonorrhea* exceeds that of chicken pox, measles, mumps, and rubella combined (Silber, 1986). About 1 in 4 cases of gonorrhea involves an adolescent. *Genital herpes* is found in 1 out of every 35 adolescents. *Syphilis* and other STDs are also found among adolescents. Those 20 to 24 years old have the highest incidence of STDs, followed by 15- to 19-year-olds (Carrol & Miller, 1982).

Because adolescents are sexually active, there is the possibility of an *AIDS* epidemic ("Kids and Contraceptives," 1987). Many adolescents are unrealistic (Roscoe & Kruger, 1990; Slonim-Nevo, Ozaga, & Auslander, 1991). They can't imagine that it will happen to them, so they take unnecessary chances (Andre & Bormann, 1991; Peterson & Murphy, 1990). In one study, one-fifth of an adult female sample and about one-third of an adult male sample reported having had homosexual experience during adolescence (Petersen, Kretchner, Nellis, Lever, & Hertz, 1983). Those adolescents who are most heterosexually active, who are intravenous drug users, or who engage in homosexual contacts comprise a high-risk group for contracting AIDS. They can easily become infected and transmit the disease to others, if they do not take necessary precautions.

Because the incubation period for AIDS may be from a few years to up to 10 years (Wallis, 1987), adolescents can be exposed to the virus and carry it for years without knowing it if blood tests have not been done. During this period they can transmit the disease to others. Because of the long incubation period, few cases of active AIDS are reported during adolescence itself.

UNWANTED SEXUAL ACTIVITY.   One study of 507 university men and 486 university women revealed that 97.5% of the men and 93.5% of the women had experienced unwanted sexual activity (Muehlenhard & Cook, 1988). More men than women experienced unwanted intercourse. More women than men were likely to have engaged in unwanted kissing. The ten most important reasons given for engaging in unwanted sexual activity were verbal coercion, physical coercion, threat to terminate the relationship, sex-role concern (afraid of appearing unmasculine or unfeminine), peer pressure, reluctance (felt obligated, under pressure), intoxication, inexperience (desire to build experience), altruism (desire to please partner), and enticement by partners. Reported incidents of physical coercion were generally of a nonviolent nature.

Another survey of 275 undergraduate single women at Arizona State University revealed that over 50% of the participants reported being pressured into oral contact with their partners' genitals, genital and breast manipulation, and kissing (Christopher, 1988). Both the use of physical force and the verbal threat of force were uncommon. However, persistent attempts and verbal pressure were frequent.

Strategies that women use for rejecting advances include (Perper & Weis, 1987): threats ("I'm going home if you don't stop"), delaying tactics ("Wait until I know you better"), physical rejection, excuses ("I have to get up early tomorrow"), diversion and distraction, ignoring sexual signals the man gives, avoiding intimate situations, and avoiding enticing behavior.

Adolescent Marriage

FREQUENCY.   Figure 14.3 gives a detailed picture of U.S. statistics on marriage ages between 1890 and 1988. The median age at first marriage stopped declining for males in 1959 and for females in 1956, and has been increasing slowly since. The median age at first marriage in 1988 was 23.6 for females and 25.9 for males. It appears that the steady drop in median age at marriage that was especially noticeable in the 1940s has been arrested. However, there are still numbers of youth, especially females, who are marrying young. Census figures for 1988 show that 5.8% of females and 1.8% of males age 15 to 19 are (or have been) married (U.S. Bureau of the Census, 1990).

SUCCESS RATES.   To evaluate whether adolescent marriage is desirable or undesirable, one must ask how successful these marriages are. There is no cause for concern if these marriages are strong, happy, and satisfying; but if they are weak, unhappy, and frustrating, causing much personal suffering and numerous social problems, there is ample cause for concern.

Using divorce statistics as the measure of success, adolescent marriages do not work out well (Bishop & Lynn, 1983; Booth & Edwards, 1985). Numerous studies indicate that the younger people are when married, the greater the chance of unhappy marriage and of divorce (Teti, Lamb, & Elster, 1987). The older the couple is at first marriage, the more likely that the marriage will succeed. But this direct correlation between age at first marriage and marital success diminishes for men at about age 27, when the decline in divorce

FOCUS

School Birth Control Clinics

Faced with a desperate situation, some high school administrators offer contraceptive education services in birth control clinics right on the school premises. This idea is shocking to many people. Opponents insist that providing such services condones teenage sex, but advocates say that such programs in high schools are responses to emergency situations. A clinic in DeSable High School in Chicago was established after more than one-third of the 1,000 female students in the school became pregnant each year (Plummer, 1985). A 50% dropout rate from school resulted from the high rate of pregnancies. One of the most important services of the clinic was to keep pregnant girls in school to continue their education. Similar programs have been established in other cities across the country. This approach is pragmatic. Its purpose is to protect adolescents against unwanted pregnancy and from sexually transmitted diseases, without necessarily reducing sexual activity (Zellman, 1982).

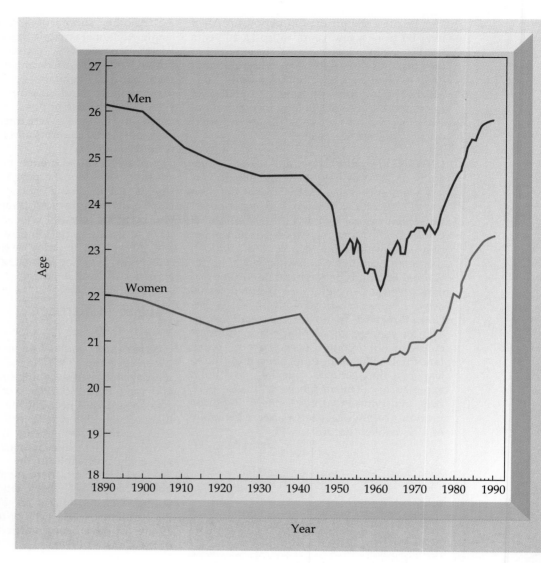

FIGURE 14.3 Median age at first marriage, by sex: 1890 to 1988.

Statistics from *Statistical Abstract of the United States, 1990* by U.S Bureau of the Census, 1990, Washington, DC: U.S. Government Printing Office.

rates with advancing age slows considerably. For women, the divorce rate declines with each year they wait to marry until a gradual leveling off occurs at about age 25. Therefore, strictly from the standpoint of marital stability, men who wait to marry until at least age 27 and women who wait until about age 25 are old enough to maximize their chances of success (Booth & Edwards, 1985).

MOTIVATIONS.   The most influential motivations for adolescents to marry young are

Overly romantic, glamorous views of marriage
Social pressure
Early dating, acceleration of adult sophistication
Sexual stimulation and unwed pregnancy
Escape; attempt to resolve personal or social problems.

THE PROBLEM OF IMMATURITY.   Many of the adjustments young couples must make become more difficult because of the immaturity of the couple. The less mature are less likely to make a wise choice of mate. The less mature are less likely to evidence the ultimate direction of their personality growth. They change as they get older and so have nothing in common with their partners after awhile. The less mature are less likely to be able to deal with the complex adjustments and problems of marriage. They are immature and insecure, oversensitive, unstable, and rebellious against authority, characteristics that make it harder for them to get along with their mate and to solve problems that arise. Booth and Edwards (1985) found that the principal sources of marital dissatisfaction among couples who married young were lack of faithfulness, presence of jealousy, lack of understanding, disagreement,

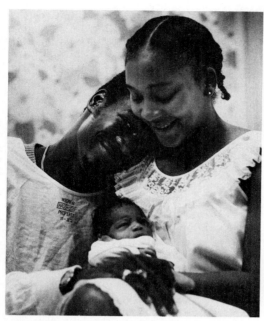

Family, friends, and counseling services can help prevent adolescent marriages from failing.

and lack of communication. Attempts by one partner to dominate or a refusal to talk made communication difficult.

Most youths have not become responsible enough for marriage. One of the major problems of early marriage is financial worry. The primary difficulties are inadequate income and the fact that income has not reached the level expected. Little education, inexperience, and youth do not bring high wages (Grindstaff, 1988). Some couples marry without any income. In many cases, education is interrupted or terminated, so the young person never achieves as much as the person who is able to continue an education.

Another real problem in early marriage is that it often results in *early parenthood* (Kellam, Adams, Brown, & Ensminger, 1982). A majority of teenage brides are pregnant at the time of marriage. In fact, the earlier the age at marriage, the greater is the percentage of brides who are premaritally pregnant, and the sooner they start having children. Yet marriage because of pregnancy has a poor prognosis of success.

DEVELOPMENT OF MORAL JUDGMENT

An important part of social development is developing the ability to make moral judgments or decisions. The process by which children and youths develop moral judgment is extremely interesting. Two major theories, those of Lawrence Kohlberg and Carol Gilligan, are discussed in this section. Both theories emphasize that the development of moral judgment is a gradual cognitive process, stimulated by increasing, changing social relationships of children as they get older. For a new theory of morality for everyday life, see the discussion by Shelton and McAdams (1990).

Lawrence Kohlberg

Lawrence Kohlberg has made a lasting contribution to the study of the development of moral judgment in children and youth (Kohlberg, 1963, 1966, 1969, 1970; Kohlberg & Gilligan, 1971; Kohlberg & Kramer, 1969; Kohlberg & Turiel, 1972).

Initially, Kohlberg (1963) studied 72 boys aged 10, 13, and 16. Boys in the different age groups were all similar in IQ with half of them from upper middle classes. Ten moral dilemmas were presented to each subject. Each dilemma presented a choice of whether to obey authority figures even though the action violated legal-social rules, or to do what was best for the welfare of others and meet human needs. The choices were taped and the subjects were then questioned about the reasons for their choices. Kohlberg's technique and material were Piagetian in form. In this study, Kohlberg was concerned not with behavior, but with moral judgment and the process of thought by which the individual made a judgment. There were no wrong or right answers expected; the individual was scored according to modes of reasoning, regardless of the direction of the given response.

Kohlberg (1970) identified three major levels of development of moral judgment, each level with two types of motivation. The levels and subtypes are listed in Table 14.3. Kohlberg found that *Level I* of premoral thinking declined sharply from the younger to the older age groups. *Level II* thinking increased until age 13, then stabilized. *Level III* thinking also increased markedly between 10 and 13 years of age, with some additional increase between ages 13 and 16.

Kohlberg cautioned that each type should not be equated with only one age. Individuals of different ages are at different levels of development in their moral thinking: Some are advanced, others are retarded. No person fits neatly into any one of the 6 types. Kohlberg (1970) indicated that moral thought develops gradually as the individual

TABLE 14.3 Kohlberg's Levels of Development of Moral Thought

Level I. *Premoral level*

Type 1. *Punishment and obedience orientation*
(Motivation: to avoid punishment by others)

Type 2: Naive instrumental hedonism
(Motivation: to gain rewards from others)

Level II. *Morality of conventional role conformity*

Type 3. Good-person morality of maintaining good relations with and approval of others
(Motivation: to avoid disapproval of others)

Type 4. Authority-maintaining morality
(Motivation: to maintain law and order and because of concern for the community)

Level III. *Morality of self-accepted moral principles*

Type 5. Morality of democratically accepted laws
(Motivation: to gain the respect of an individual community)

Type 6. Morality of individual principles of conduct
(Motivation: to avoid self-condemnation for lapses)

From Kohlberg, L. (1963). The development of children's orientations toward a moral order. I: Sequence in the development of thought. *Vita humana, 6,* pp. 11–33. Used by permission.

passes through a sequence of increasingly sophisticated moral stages.

At Level I, the **premoral level,** children respond to the definitions of good and bad provided by parental authority figures. Decisions are made on the basis of self-interest; children interpret acts as good or bad in terms of physical consequences. There are two types under Level I. *Type 1* obeys rules to avoid punishment. *Type 2* conforms to obtain rewards or have favors returned.

Level II, the level of **morality of conventional role conformity,** comprises *type 3* and *type 4* and is less egocentric and more sociocentric in orientation, and is based on a desire to justify, support, and maintain the existing social structure (Muuss, 1988). *Type 3* under this level is the good boy–nice girl orientation in which the child conforms to avoid disapproval and dislike by others; *type 4* conforms because of a desire to maintain law and order or because of concern for the larger community.

Level III, the level of **morality of self-accepted moral principles,** is made up of individuals who accept democratically recognized principles of universal truths, not because they have to but because they believe in the principles or truths. *Type 5* under this

level conforms to maintain mutual respect with another person or group. At this stage, the individual defines moral thinking in terms of general principles such as mutual obligations, contractual agreement, equality, human dignity, and individual rights. Finally, *type 6* conforms to avoid self-condemnation. The motivation is to uphold universal principles of justice that are valid beyond existing laws, peer mores, or social conditions.

Kohlberg's stage concept implies sequence: Each child must go through successive levels of moral judgment. Kohlberg also said that the sequence of development of his stages is universal, even under varying cultural conditions. Developing moral judgment is not merely a matter of learning the rules of a particular culture; it reflects a universal process of development. Kohlberg (1966) tested and validated his theory with boys aged 10, 13, and 16 in a Taiwanese city, in a Malaysian (Atayal) aboriginal tribal village, and in a Turkish village, as well as in the United States, Canada, and Great Britain.

Kohlberg (1966) found that the sequence of development was similar in all cultures, but that the last two stages of moral thought did not develop clearly in tribal and preliterate communities. Data from the U.S. showed that the great majority of American adults never reached Level III either, even by age 24.

Kohlberg (1966) tested his hypothesis with boys and girls of different classes and religions, and with popular and socially isolated children. The same general stages of development were found among all groups, with middle-class children of all ages in advance of the working-class children. Middle-class children moved faster and farther in development compared to working-class children. Working-class children had less understanding of the broader social order and had less participation in it; thus, their development of moral judgment was retarded. This explanation is further substantiated by the fact that children with extensive social participation advance considerably more quickly through the successive stages of development.

Moral judgment also correlates highly with *IQ,* indicating that it is partly cognitive in nature. Children who participate in social groups lose some of their cognitive naivete and adopt a more sophisticated view of authority and social relationships (Berkowitz, Gibbs, & Broughton, 1980). They acquire a greater capacity for moral thinking, but whether such knowledge leads to better behavior depends on emotional and social in-

Premoral level—the first level of development of moral judgment, based on rewards and punishments, according to Kohlberg

Morality of conventional role conformity—the second level of development of moral thought, based on a desire to conform to social convention, according to Kohlberg

Morality of self-accepted moral principles—the third level of development of moral thought, based on adherence to universal principles, according to Kohlberg

fluences in their backgrounds and relationships (Kupfersmid & Wonderly, 1980). The point is, the ability to make moral judgments does not always result in more moral behavior.

Carol Gilligan

Kohlberg conducted his research on moral development on male subjects. His scoring method was developed from male responses, with the average adolescent female attaining a rating corresponding to type 3 (the good boy–nice girl orientation). The average adolescent male was rated as type 4 (the law-and-order orientation).

Carol Gilligan (1977), an associate of Kohlberg, found that females approach moral issues from a different perspective (Linn, 1991). Women emphasize sensitivity to others' feelings and rights, and show concern and care for others. Women emphasize care of human beings rather than obedience to abstract principles. Men emphasize justice—preserving principles, rules, and rights. Thus, women and men speak with two different voices (Gilligan, 1982). In summarizing six studies, including four longitudinal ones, Gilligan (1984) revealed that women rely on an interpersonal network of care orientation, and men rely more heavily on a justice orientation (Muuss, 1988a).

As a result of the difference in the way women and men think, Gilligan proposed a female alternative to Kohlberg's stages of moral reasoning. Table 14.4 compares Kohlberg and Gilligan.

At *Level I*, women are concerned with survival and self-interest. Gradually, they become aware of the differences between what they want (selfishness) and what they ought to do (responsibility). This leads to *Level II*, in which the need to please others takes precedence over self-interest. Women begin sacrificing their own preferences and become responsible for caring for others. They begin to wonder whether they can remain true to themselves while fulfilling the needs of others. Still, they place others' needs before their own. At *Level III*, which many never attain, women develop a universal perspective, in which they no longer see themselves

TABLE 14.4 Kohlberg's Versus Gilligan's Understanding of Moral Development

Kohlberg's Levels and Stages	Kohlberg's Definition	Gilligan's Levels
Level I. Preconventional morality Stage 1: Punishment orientation	Obey rules to avoid punishment	*Level I. Preconventional morality* Concern for the self and survival
Stage 2: Naive reward orientation	Obey rules to get rewards, share in order to get returns	
Level II. Conventional morality Stage 3: Good-boy/good-girl orientation	Conform to rules that are defined by others' approval/disapproval	*Level II. Conventional morality* Concern for being responsible, caring for others
Stage 4: Authority orientation	Rigid conformity to society's rules, law-and-order mentality, avoid censure for rule-breaking	
Level III. Postconventional morality Stage 5. Social-contract orientation	More flexible understanding that we obey rules because they are necessary for social order, but the rules could be changed if there were better alternatives	*Level III. Postconventional morality* Concern for self and others as interdependent
Stage 6. Morality of individual principles and conscience	Behavior conforms to internal principles (justice, equality) to avoid self-condemnation, and sometimes may violate society's rules	

From *Half the Human Experience* by J. S. Hyde, 1985, Lexington, MA: D. C. Heath. Reprinted with permission.

as powerless and submissive, but as active in decision making. They become concerned about the consequences for all, including themselves, in making decisions.

Obviously, Gilligan's and Kohlberg's stages are parallel. Gilligan does not contend that her theory should replace Kohlberg's. She insists only that her theory is more applicable to the moral reasoning of females and that the highest form of moral reasoning can interpret, use, and combine the female emphasis on responsibility and care with the male emphasis on rights and justice (Muuss, 1988a).

WORK

Another important part of socialization is to learn to work and hold responsible positions. Of today's high school seniors, 75% hold a part-time job during the school year (Bachman, Johnston, & O'Malley, 1987; Johnston, O'Malley, & Bachmen, 1987). The proportion of high school students who work has been rising steadily. Generally speaking, teachers, social scientists, and parents have encouraged students to work. The conventional wisdom seems to argue: "Working is good for them" (Otto, 1988).

Among high school seniors one of four females works at least 20 hours a week, and among males, one of three does the same (Bachman et al., 1987). These students are working half time while going to school full time.

Some authorities, however, are beginning to say that some adolescents are devoting too much time to jobs and not enough to

Seventy-five percent of today's high school seniors hold a part-time job during the school year.

school. Greenberger and Steinberg (1981) emphasize that when high school students work more than 15 to 20 hours a week, the disadvantages include diminished involvement with peers, family, and school and increased use of marijuana, alcohol, cigarettes, and other drugs (Steinberg, Greenberger, Garduque, Ruggiero, & Vaux, 1982).

Some adolescents today grow up so used to working after school and on weekends that they never have time for fun with peers, healthy recreation, or for extracurricular activities. They become adult workaholics who have never learned how to play or relax. Such habits can be detrimental to personal health and marital and family relationships.

SUMMARY

1. Adolescents want parents who will treat them like adults, have faith in them, love and like them the way they are, whom they can communicate with, who are interested in them, who will guide them, who are fun and have a sense of humor, and whom they can be proud of.
2. Adolescent–parent conflict usually revolves around six areas: values and morals, family relationships, school, responsibilities, social activities, and work outside the home.
3. A number of variables affect conflict: home environment, discipline, socioeconomic status, family size, and age and sex of the adolescent.
4. Relationships with brothers and sisters are vitally important because they have a considerable influence on the development of the adolescent. Older siblings provide companionship; serve as surrogate parents, acting as caretakers, teachers, playmates, and confidants; and they can serve as role models.
5. The need for close friendships becomes crucial during adolescence. Young adolescents choose a best friend, a chum or two, usually of the same sex in the

beginning. Early adolescent friendships are emotional, intense, sometimes conflicting.

6. One of the most important social goals of mid-adolescence is to achieve hetero-sociality in which the individual's pleasure and friendships are found with those of both sexes.

7. Adolescents become increasingly aware of their need to belong to a group and to find peer acceptance. Personality and social skills have been found to be very important in gaining social acceptance.

8. Some youths gain social acceptance by joining deviant groups.

9. Dating has many purposes: It provides amusement, enjoyment, friendship, affection; is a means of achieving social status and personal and social growth; provides sexual intimacy and emotional intimacy; and is a means of mate sorting and selection.

10. The most frequent dating problems reported in one study of college women were: unwanted pressure to engage in sex, where to go and what to do on dates, communication, sexual misunderstandings, and money. The most common dating problems reported in one study of college men were: communication, where to go and what to do on dates, shyness, money, and honesty/openness. Both men and women report problems in communication, due partly to imaging—presenting oneself in the best possible manner.

11. Parents sometimes object to their adolescent's selection of a dating partner because they don't like the person, they feel the person has a problem, the other person's family is different from the parents' family, or there is a significant age difference.

12. The onset of puberty is accompanied by an increasing interest in sex.

13. Masturbation is commonly practiced by both adolescent men and women and is a normal part of growing up.

14. Premarital sexual intercourse among white, teenage women has been increasing.

15. Results from the Zelnik and Kantner study indicate that only 39% of 15- to 19-year-old unmarried women sometimes used contraception, only 34% always did, and 27% never did when they had intercourse.

16. There is some evidence that sex among many adolescents is becoming deper-sonalized, without affection or commitment.

17. The net result of the increase in premarital sexual intercourse accompanied by a lack of efficient use of contraceptives has been an increase in out-of-wedlock pregnancies, now estimated at over 1 million per year.

18. Authorities are also concerned about the increase in sexually transmitted diseases among adolescents: especially chlamydia, gonorrhea, genital herpes, syphilis, and AIDS.

19. One of the problems faced by both adolescent boys and girls is unwanted sexual activity.

20. Faced with the rising tide of teenage pregnancies and the threat of AIDS, some schools offer birth control clinics on the school premises. The high rate of pregnancies is partly responsible for high dropout rates. One of the goals of the clinic programs is to keep pregnant girls in school.

21. The median age at first marriage has been increasing, but there are still large numbers of adolescents who marry. The prognosis of success is poor. Many young marrieds express deep dissatisfaction with their marriage.

22. There are a number of reasons for adolescent marriage: sexual stimulation and pregnancy, early dating and acceleration of adult sophistication, social pressure, overly romantic views of marriage, desire to escape problems, and affluence and prosperity.

23. Many of the problems of early marriage are due to the immaturity of the couple.

24. Lawrence Kohlberg has made a lasting contribution to the study of the development of moral judgment of children and youth.

25. Kohlberg has identified three levels of moral development. Level I is the premoral level; Level II is a morality of conventional role conformity; Level III is a morality of self-accepted moral principles.

26. Although Kohlberg's findings show a similar sequence of development in all cultures, not all persons reach the higher levels of development. This is true in preliterate communities, and among youth from various socioeconomic classes, especially among the working classes of adolescents.

27. The development of moral judgment also correlates highly with IQ.

28. Carol Gilligan emphasized that women approach moral issues from a different perspective than do men. Men rely more heavily on a justice orientation; women on an interpersonal network or care orientation.

29. Gilligan outlined three levels of development: Level I—self-interest, Level II—caring for the needs of others, and Level III—a universal perspective that takes into account consequences for all people.

30. Most adolescents dislike helping parents around the house but work at jobs outside the home. The proportion of high school students working has been rising steadily.

31. Among high school seniors, one of three males, and one of four females work at least 20 hours a week, leading some authorities to feel that many adolescents are devoting too much time to work and not enough to school.

KEY TERMS

Coitus   *p. 308*
Imaging   *p. 306*
Masturbation   *p. 307*
Morality of conventional role conformity
   p. 314

Morality of self-accepted moral principles
   p. 314
Premoral level   *p. 314*

DISCUSSION QUESTIONS

1. When you were growing up how did you get along with your parents? Explain.
2. What did you like about your parents? What did you dislike?
3. When adolescents disobey their parents, what should the parents do?
4. How many brothers and sisters did you have? How did you get along with them?
5. How can an adolescent get over being shy in groups?
6. What qualities are most important in being popular and accepted by others?
7. At what age should adolescents be allowed to start dating?
8. What do you think of going steady in high school?
9. Should seventh-graders be allowed to go to school dances? Explain.
10. Should girls initiate dates? How do boys feel about girls asking them out?
11. Is it all right to date several persons at once?
12. Is it necessary for a girl to be sexually responsive to be popular with boys? Will boys ask a girl out if she is not willing to go all the way?
13. What should a 15-year-old girl do if her parents object to her going out with a boy who is 18?
14. Have sexual attitudes and behavior become more liberal since you were in high school? How or how not?
15. Why don't more sexually active adolescents use contraceptives?
16. What can be done to reduce the number of unwed pregnancies?
17. Should adolescents marry because of premarital pregnancy? What are some alternatives? Which would you choose?
18. What sort of sex education did you receive from parents when you were growing up? Describe.
19. Should school teach sex education? Why or why not? Are there any sex subjects that high schools should not teach? Why?
20. What do you think about having birth control clinics in high schools?
21. Explain Kohlberg's three levels of moral development.
22. Do you agree or disagree with Gilligan's idea that the level of moral judgment of women ought to be evaluated differently from that of men?
23. How do you feel about adolescents working 20 or more hours per week when in high school?

SUGGESTED READINGS

Byrne, D., & Fisher, W. (Eds). (1983). *Adolescents, sex, and contraception.* Hillsdale, NJ: Erlbaum. About adolescent sexuality.

Burkhart, K. (1981). *Growing into love.* New York: Putnam. Interviews with teenagers.

Gilligan, C. (1983). *In a different voice: Psychological theory and women's development.* Cambridge, MA: Harvard University Press. The patterns of moral thought of women as compared to men.

Group for the Advancement of Psychiatry, Committee on Adolescence (1986). *Crises of adolescence: Teenage pregnancy, impact on adolescent development.* New York: Brunner/Mazel.

Sugar, M. (Ed.). (1984). *Adolescent parenthood.* New York: SP Medical and Scientific Books. Adolescent parenting and programs available.

Youniss, M., & Smollar, J. (1985). *Adolescent relations with mothers, fathers, and friends.* Chicago: University of Chicago Press. Parent–teen relationships.

PART FIVE

ADULT DEVELOPMENT

15

Perspectives on Adult Development

DEMOGRAPHICS

Age Periods

For purposes of analysis in this book, the span of adulthood has been divided into three age periods: *early adulthood* (the 20s and 30s), *middle adulthood* (the 40s and 50s), and *late adulthood* (age 60 and over). There is no general agreement among researchers as to when adolescence ends and early adulthood begins, or when middle age begins and ends. So the divisions proposed here are somewhat arbitrary. However, Levinson and colleagues describe middle adulthood as 40 to 59 years of age and late adulthood as age 60 and over (Levinson, Darrow, Klein, Levinson, & McKee, 1978). These age groupings are adopted in this book.

Population Trends

Figure 15.1 shows the population distribution in the United States, by age, in 1988 (U.S. Bureau of the Census, 1990). As can be seen, people 19 and younger are 29% of the population, early adults comprise 33% of the total, middle adults 21%, and those 60 and over 17%. *The median age of the U.S. population continues to increase as life expectancy increases.* Though it seems almost unbelievable, in 1850 the median age of people in this country was only 18.9 years. As shown in Figure 15.2, the comparable figure was 32.3 years in 1988 (U.S. Bureau of the Census, 1989). As seen on the graph, the decline in median age between 1950 and 1970 was due to the huge cohort of babies born during the post–World War II years. By the year 2000, the median age is expected to increase to 35.5 years (Kii, 1982).

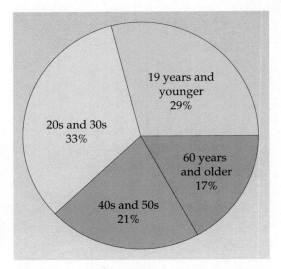

FIGURE 15.1   Distribution of resident population by age, U.S., 1988.

Statistic from *Statistical Abstract of the United States, 1990* (p. 13) by U.S. Bureau of the Census, 1990, Washington, DC: U.S. Government Printing Office.

Figure 15.3 shows the birthrates in the United States between 1910 and 1990. This graph reveals several major cycles. The high birthrate during the early 1900s was followed by a sharp decline from the mid-1920s to mid-1930s, during the Great Depression. This was followed by a baby boom after World War II, between the years 1945 and 1960.

Implications

The birthrate cycles have important implications. The small cohort born between 1930 and 1945 (the depression- and war-period

Middle-age adults, in their 40s and 50s, comprise 21 percent of the population, and adults over 60 comprise 17 percent.

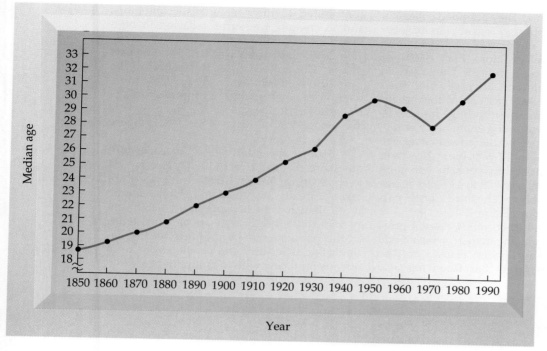

FIGURE 15.2 Median age of the population, U.S.

Statistics from *Statistical Abstract of the United States, 1990* (p. 13) by U.S. Bureau of the Census, 1990, Washington, DC: U.S. Government Printing Office.

babies) were 45 to 60 years old in 1990. As a generation they enjoyed little job competition and an exceptionally high degree of prosperity and social stability. They succeeded, primarily because of their small numbers and superior opportunities.

But the teeming ranks of **baby boomers** have had a more difficult time. They were the restless generation in the 1960s and early 1970s, the activists, protestors, and hippies rebelling against society and unwilling to accept the status quo handed down by their

Baby boomers— the huge cohort of babies born during the postwar period between 1945 and 1960

FIGURE 15.3 Birthrates: 1910–1990, United States.

From U.S. Bureau of the Census.

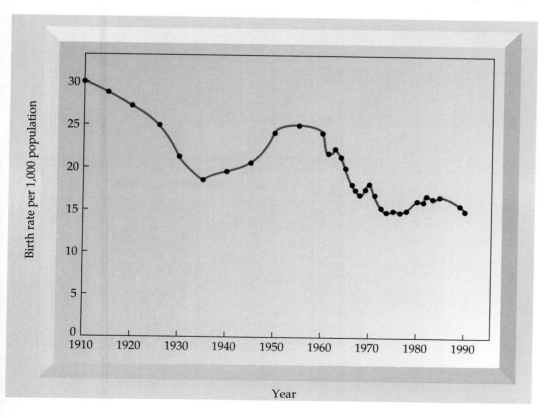

prosperous parents. They attended college in huge numbers, but had to compete for jobs. Many remained underemployed, forced to accept lower-level positions than those for which they had been trained. They married later than their parents, often not until their late 20s or early 30s. Because of their sheer numbers, they have borne a huge number of children. The pressure on elementary school enrollments has been especially intense. The population of 5- to 17-year-olds shown in Figure 15.4 are the children of baby boomers. The baby boomers were 28 to 43 years of age in 1988; as also shown, they are a large portion of the total population.

Once married, this cohort exerted great pressure on the housing market, which made rents and housing prices skyrocket. The competition this group has faced has also contributed to their materialistic ambitions and to creating pressures reflected in high divorce rates and continued drug use. In the year 2010, this group will be 50 to 65 years of age. The projection for this cohort in the year 2010 is, as shown in Figure 15.4, to remain large. As the entire group reaches age 60 and over (in the year 2020), the prospects are staggering (Butler, 1983). (See Figure 15.5.)

Because the elderly get a disproportionate share of health care, medical costs will keep soaring unless drastic measures are taken. Already, people 65 and older consume more than half of tax-supported health expenditures, although they are only one-tenth of the population. The pressure on the nation's Social Security and pension systems is already surfacing with the retirement of large

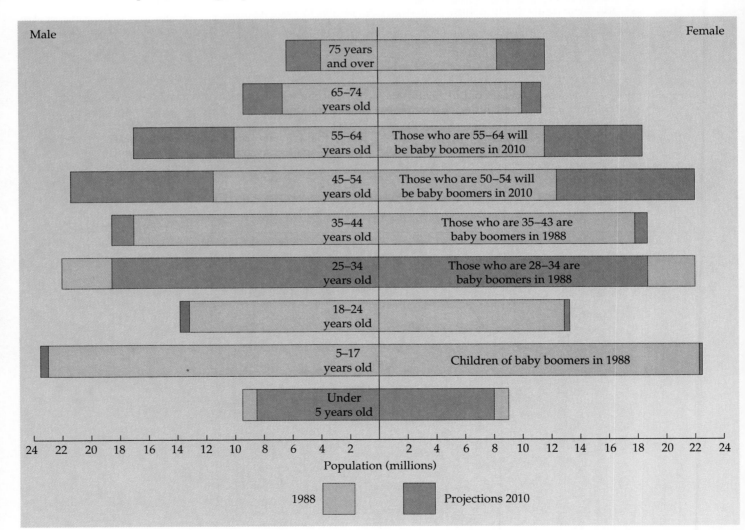

FIGURE 15.4   Total U.S. population by age, 1988 and 2010.

Statistics from *Statistical Abstract of the United States, 1989* (p. 15) by U.S. Bureau of the Census, 1989, Washington, DC: U.S. Government Printing Office.

The large cohort born between 1945 and 1960 is known as the baby boomers.

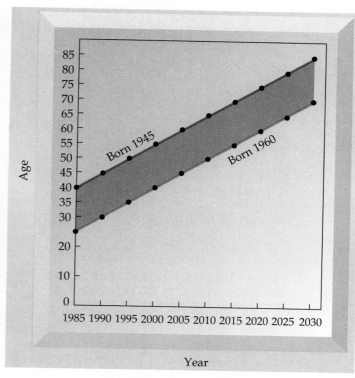

FIGURE 15.5   Aging of the postwar baby boom generation.

numbers of people born before the Depression of the 1930s. What will happen to the system when the postwar baby-boom generation retires? In 1990, one beneficiary drew Social Security for every three workers paying into the system. By 2030, that ratio will decrease to one beneficiary for every two workers paying into the system under the present law (*Aging in America*, 1989). If revenue sources remain unchanged, the Social Security tax rate, already high, would become exorbitant.

To reduce slightly the extent of these tax rate increases, Social Security amendments in 1983 increased the retirement age for full benefits to 66 in the year 2008 and to age 67 in the year 2027 (Chen, 1987).

Another way to look at the situation is through examining dependency ratios. The **dependency ratio** is the number of dependents for each person in the labor force. This includes both child and elderly dependents. In 1990, that ratio was 1.02 dependents for each person working. In the year 2025, the ratio will be 1.20 to 1 (Crown, 1985). The only reason it won't increase more is that the large increase in elderly dependents will be partially offset by a decrease in child dependents.

As large numbers of Americans move into older adulthood, the problem will intensify because their political power will in-

Dependency ratio—the number of dependent persons for each person in the labor force

crease (Hudson, 1987). If society tries to infringe on their rights or reduce their benefits and services, they will present formidable opposition. Because a greater percentage of the elderly vote than do younger adults, they already exhibit considerable power. The *American Association of Retired Persons* (AARP) currently has 12 million members. Other senior citizens' groups have increased their total political power. This generation has always fought for its rights and will continue to do so. However, as high expectations collide with reality, some degree of frustration is bound to set in.

Some Positive Developments and Challenges

DEVELOPMENTS.   As a result of the demographic and social and political forces shaping our lives, some positive changes are also taking place. The *divorce rate,* which peaked in 1979, has leveled off and is decreasing slightly as the baby-boom generation moves through the crucial early years of marriage. The aging of the population has caused a shift from a youth-oriented culture to an adult-centered society. *Clothing* styles are increasingly geared to the needs of young and middle-aged adults. Demands for *auto-*

FOCUS

Dependency Ratios

As mentioned, the dependency ratio is the number of dependents for each person in the labor force. As seen in Table 15.1, the number of dependents includes people from four groups: children 1 to 15 years of age, youth and adults 16 to 64 who are not working, and those 65 and over who are not working. The number of child dependents is expected to decrease as the birthrate declines. The number of adult male dependents is expected to increase as a result of declining male labor force participation rates. *At the same time that child de-* pendency decreases and male dependency increases, female dependency will decrease as female labor force participation increases. Thus, the burden of responsibility for supporting dependents is shifting from male to female. As seen in the table, the total dependency burden in the year 2000 is projected to be 1.042 dependents for each person in the labor force. By the year 2050, there will be 1.238 dependents for each person in the labor force. This represents a 19% increase from the total dependency ratio for the year 2000.

TABLE 15.1 Dependents Relative to Total Labor Force by Age and Sex: Historical Data and Projections

Age by sex	Historical				Projections
	1950	1960	1970	1979	2000
Male					
1 to 15	.344	.415	.367	.264	0.222
16 to 64	.079	.073	.069	.096	0.130
65 +	.053	.073	.073	.077	0.093
Male dependency contribution	.476	.561	.509	.437	0.445
Female					
1 to 15	.332	.401	.354	.253	0.212
16 to 64	.484	.429	.373	.281	0.229
65 +	.093	.114	.124	.129	0.156
Female dependency contribution	.909	.944	.851	.663	0.597
Total dependency ratio	1.385	1.505	1.360	1.100	1.042

Sources. Historical data: U.S. Bureau of the Census (1980). *Social Indicators III.* Washington, DC: U.S. Government Printing Office. Derived from Table 715, p. 350. Projections: Tables 3 and 4.

mobiles reflect the practical requirements of adults and their families. Even tastes in *music* have changed, with increasing emphasis on the big-band sound and the love ballads of the 1940s and 1950s. The *food* industry, which for years catered to the demands of the young, now courts middle-aged and older adults who want to stay healthy and trim and add years to their lives. *Aerobic classes and fitness centers* enroll adults by the millions. The *recreational industry,* after emphasizing the sports pursuits and leisure-time activities of the young, now appeals to adults to take up tennis, golf, fishing, and skiing; to rent or buy a recreational home; or to engage in aerobics, jogging, or other physical fitness activities. *Travel agencies* cater to adults who prefer tours or more leisurely cruises. Because of increasing *housing* costs, more and more adults are moving into condominiums and other group housing arrangements. This frees them from some of the responsibilities of home ownership, allows them more time for leisurely pursuits, and offers companionship and camaraderie to those who enjoy social living.

Colleges, which experienced a drop in enrollments because of the declining numbers of teenagers, have expanded their continuing education and other programs for adults. As a result, the average level of education of adults continues to rise. Adults can now upgrade their knowledge and skills and even retrain themselves for a second or third career. The more educated they become, the less likely they are to face obsolescence, and the greater their chances to continue working throughout life.

CHALLENGES. Some real challenges remain. *One is to alter our age-appropriate norms of behavior and make the necessary psychological adjustments to living a longer, more active life* (Branch, Guralnik, Foley, Kohout, Wetle, Ostfeld, & Katz, 1991; Manton & Stallard, 1991). The stages of the life cycle have been delayed. Adolescence is prolonged; entry into adulthood comes later; and the ages of vocational establishment, marriage, and parenthood have been delayed. Yet, America still suffers from a "rocking chair syndrome," a notion that disengagement should come early, even though poor health and death come later. A man conditioned toward early retirement, who decides to retire at age 60, still has an average of 18 more years to live; a woman has 23. These are long periods of time to live without working regularly and to be supported by the rest of society. Society will not be able to support the whole generation of baby-boom dependents. For the most part, they will have to continue to struggle to look after themselves.

Society needs a new orientation to the concept of who is old. A person of 60 should no longer be considered old. Perhaps 80 is old, but in a short span of time, this concept may be outdated and 80-year-olds may be considered "young-old." We know that sexual enjoyment can continue into this age, that a high proportion of intellectual capacity is retained, that an ability to learn remains, and that many health problems of late adulthood are being cured, allowing the majority of people to be healthy, active, and productive throughout their lives. Therefore, we need to revise our age norms, or our social age clock. We have to rethink the time schedule of our life—the time to go to school, the time to work, the time to marry, and the time to die (Horn & Meer, 1987).

MEANING OF ADULTHOOD

Adulthood means different things to different people. To a child, it means special privileges like staying up late or not having to go to school. To a child's parents, being an adult means acting grown up and assuming responsibility. To an adolescent, adulthood means being on one's own, having an apartment and freedom from parental control.

Social Dimensions

Whatever else it is, *the primary meaning of adulthood is social.* One cannot declare oneself an adult; one is perceived as such. Inevitably this perception reflects a mature, rational, and responsible person. It is unthinkable to call an undisciplined, irrational, undependable, socially irresponsible person an adult.

Biological Dimensions

Dictionaries define an adult as one who has attained *full size and strength; a fully grown person.* This definition implies biological maturity, reaching the limits of physical development and attaining reproductive capacity. But this biological definition alone is inadequate. Adolescents in our culture may attain their full height and strength and become sexually mature but still behave childishly and dependently, with nebulous identities and undetermined stations in life.

Emotional Dimensions

Being an adult also includes *emotional maturity.* It implies a high degree of emotional stability, including good impulse control, a high frustration tolerance, and freedom from violent mood swings. Another requirement of adulthood is to break childish dependency ties with parents and to function autonomously.

Legal Dimensions

Laws attempt to differentiate who should and should not be *accorded adult rights and responsibilities.* They designate chronological ages at which privileges are granted and duties required. Thus, the 26th Amendment to the U.S. Constitution established the legal voting age as 18. Child labor laws partially define whether one is permitted to be gainfully employed, and the type of work one is allowed to perform at age 16, 18, or 21. Federal law restricts the age for military service and for obtaining contraceptives. Constitutional law limits election to the U.S. House of Representatives to people 25 and over, to the Senate to people age 30 and over, and to the presidency of the United States to those 35 and over.

The states retain the privilege of deciding at what age to grant some other rights; for example, the age a person may purchase alcoholic beverages, obtain a driver's license, or marry without parental consent. States also decide the legal age for making binding contracts, obtaining credit, disposing of property, or being tried in court as an adult. Whatever age legislatures select, the decision also affects when adolescents may make decisions without parental consent and when they no longer are legally entitled to financial support from parents.

One problem of deciding adult status by law is that chronological age is not always the best determinant of capability. An 18-year-old may be eligible to vote but be completely unqualified to do so. The only positive value of automatic entitlement at 18 is that all persons are treated equally. Although the law can bestow adult status in one way, the person may not be an adult in other ways.

TRANSITION TO ADULTHOOD

Difficulties

Becoming an adult is a complicated process, especially in the pluralistic and highly industrialized society in which we live. Different segments of society seek to protect their own interests by erecting barriers to admission. Trade unions may require long periods of apprenticeship; businesses may require employees to have years of formal education. Until one fulfills the preparatory requirements of a group, one is denied adult membership in that society. As these requirements become more stringent, the age of admission to the adult labor force is delayed and the period between childhood and adulthood lengthens (Modell, Furstenberg, & Hershberg, 1976).

Passages and Rites

In our culture, numerous rites of passage take place before adulthood can be reached. They include religious confirmations, Bar or Bas Mitzvahs, driver's license tests, and school graduation ceremonies. Unlike primitive cultures, however, each rite in our culture is only one small part of the process of reaching adulthood. Even if various tests are passed, there may still be some question whether an individual is an adult in other ways (Rice, 1990). This makes the passage more ambiguous and lengthy than in primitive societies.

Socialization

An important part of becoming an adult is the accompanying socialization. *Socialization involves learning and adopting the norms, values, expectations, and social roles required by a particular group.* It is the process that grooms a person for life in companionship with others.

Part of socialization is anticipatory: preparing for certain tasks. Education for a specific profession is one example. At other times, resocialization is required. An adult must relearn something or learn something new in anticipation of a new task or role. Thus, a college graduate may have to return to school before taking a job requiring additional knowledge. Resocialization may be necessitated by role changes, occupational transfers, changes in family structure, relocation, retirement, or other reasons. Socialization does not happen only to children and adolescents in preparation for adulthood; it occurs throughout adulthood, particularly during periods of transition and preparation for new experiences.

DEVELOPMENTAL TASKS

Becoming an adult also involves the successful completion of a number of developmental tasks. A *developmental task* is a "task which arises at or about a certain period of life of the individual, successful achievement of which leads to his happiness and to success with later tasks, while failure leads to unhappiness in the individual, disapproval by society, and difficulty with later tasks" (Havighurst, 1972, p. 2). Each society defines what tasks must be accomplished and at what ages. Once these tasks are completed, the individual can enter another period or phase of life. Developmental tasks of early, middle, and late adulthood are shown in Table 15.2 and are discussed in detail in the following sections.

The Twenties and Thirties

Detaching oneself from parents is an important step in becoming an adult (Fasick, 1984). During their teens, adolescents turn to their peers for companionship, emotional fulfillment, and guidance. This step helps break the close parental ties. *Establishing a separate residence,* whether in a dormitory room at school or an apartment in the community, also helps in achieving autonomy. *Achieving emotional autonomy* is even more important than physical separation. The task is to break the close, dependent emotional ties that have been formed, realigning those ties on the basis of equality—one adult to another.

In detaching themselves from their families, adolescents gain an opportunity to *form their personal identities.* Separation at least provides the opportunity to become a unique person. However, Erikson (1968) suggests that identity formation neither begins nor

TABLE 15.2 Developmental Tasks of Adulthood

EARLY ADULTHOOD
1. Achieving autonomy
2. Molding an identity
3. Developing emotional stability
4. Establishing and consolidating a career
5. Finding intimacy
6. Becoming part of congenial social groups and of a community
7. Selecting a mate and adjusting to marriage
8. Establishing residence and learning to manage a home
9. Becoming a parent and rearing children

MIDDLE ADULTHOOD
1. Adjusting to the physical changes of middle age
2. Finding satisfaction and success in one's occupational career
3. Assuming adult social and civic responsibility
4. Launching children into responsible, happy adulthood
5. Revitalizing marriage
6. Reorienting oneself to aging parents
7. Realigning sex roles
8. Developing social networks and leisure-time activities
9. Finding new meaning in life

LATE ADULTHOOD
1. Staying physically healthy and adjusting to limitations
2. Maintaining an adequate income and means of support
3. Adjusting to revised work roles
4. Establishing acceptable housing and living conditions
5. Maintaining identity and social status
6. Finding companionship and friendship
7. Learning to use leisure time pleasurably
8. Establishing new roles in the family
9. Achieving integrity through acceptance of one's life

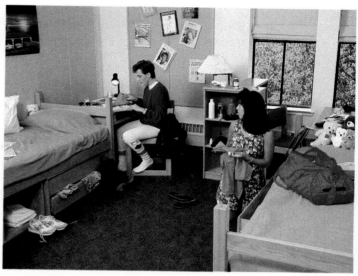

Establishing a separate residence, whether it is a dormitory room or an apartment in the community, is an important step for young adults in achieving autonomy.

ends with adolescence. It is a lifelong process of selection and assimilation of parental, peer, social, and self-perceptions and expectations. Becoming an adult involves integrating various aspects of identity, resolving conflicts among them, and developing a complete personality.

A major task in becoming a mature adult is *developing the capacity to tolerate tensions and frustrations.* Frustrations are recognized as a part of life and are either overcome or accepted without undue hostility and aggression. The ability to control emotions is one measure of the degree of maturity achieved (Douglas & Arenberg, 1978).

Young adults are also involved in *making an occupational commitment,* completing their education, entering the work world, gaining proficiency in their work, and becoming economically independent. Career success provides a sense of fulfillment and worth. Enjoyable work contributes to personal happiness and adds meaning to life.

Erikson (1968) says that the chief psychosocial task of early adulthood is the *achievement of intimacy.* "Intimacy includes the ability to experience an open, supportive, tender relationship with another person, without fear of losing one's own identity in the process of growing close" (Newman & Newman, 1984, p. 384). Intimacy suggests the capacity to give of oneself, to share feelings and thoughts, and to establish mutual empathy. It may involve expressing sexual feelings; it does involve giving up isolation and complete independence and developing some dependent emotional ties. *Participation in congenial social groups,* another psychosocial need of young adults, begins in childhood, continues during adolescence, and is consolidated during young adulthood.

In 1990, the median age for *marriage* was 24 for females and 26 for males. This means that half of all persons who marry do so in their early 20s, often finding themselves unprepared for the responsibilities (U.S. Bureau of the Census, 1990). The earliest years of marriage are the most difficult, requiring extensive adjustments and readjustments as couples learn to live together harmoniously (Schumm & Bugaighis, 1986).

Young adults must also decide where and in what type of housing to live. More young adults are moving to the West and South than to other sections of the United States. First, they must choose among urban, suburban, and rural areas. About 60% of the total population live in urban areas, but not necessarily in the inner city (U.S. Bureau of the Census, 1990). Second, depending partly on the type of area, they need to select an apartment or other rented unit, a mobile home, condominium, single-family home, or multiple-family dwelling. As the price of single-family homes skyrockets, more couples are forced to rent or buy into multiple-family dwellings. *Learning to manage and maintain their own residence* is a new experience for most young adults. It often requires years of experience before they can do it efficiently.

The numbers of persons remaining voluntarily childless are increasing, but they are only about 4% of married couples (Rice, 1990). The others turn their attention to *becoming parents and raising a family*. This task requires major economic, social, and emotional adjustments as family responsibilities increase and marital roles are realigned (Miller & Sollie, 1980). Because of the increasing pressures, marital satisfaction declines, usually reaching its lowest point when the children reach school age (Anderson, Russell, & Schumm, 1983; Spanier, Lewis, & Cole, 1975). The majority of couples are between their late 20s and mid-30s during this period. Once these years pass, family responsibilities decline and pressures ease.

Middle Age

Middle age presents a number of challenges or developmental tasks. If these challenges are met and the conflicts resolved, middle age can be a time of continued growth, personal satisfaction, and happiness. If these psychosocial tasks are not accomplished, however, the period can be one of stagnation and increasing disillusionment (Erikson, 1959). Again, Table 15.2 lists the developmental tasks.

The day comes when many adults realize they are out of shape; they cannot run as fast, lift as much, or perform as much physical work without tiring. Some women equate their loss of reproductive capacity at menopause with a loss of sexuality and youthfulness. These *physical changes require psychological adjustments and adjustments in lifestyle and health habits* to keep as fit and healthy as possible.

Middle age can be a time of continued growth, personal satisfaction, and happiness if the psychosocial tasks of the period are accomplished.

Ordinarily, middle age is the most fruitful period of *professional and creative work*. Middle-agers become the senior persons at the office, who receive a certain amount of respect and deference because of experience and seniority. But several things can happen. They may find that their superiors take them for granted and pass them over for promotions. Or, they may become bored or disillusioned with their work. Middle age may be a time of unfulfilled expectations. The realization that the dreams of earlier years are not going to come true comes as quite a shock.

A more positive awareness may also develop. Realizing they no longer find their work interesting and challenging, adults begin to rethink what they want to do for the second half of their lives. They modify their dreams in terms of new directions or locations in their present occupation, or in terms of a completely different career.

Adults 40 to 60 years old have been called "the ruling class" or "the command generation" (Stevenson, 1977). Although they make up only one-fifth of the population, they control our society and social institutions. They are the norm bearers, the decision makers, and the office holders. Their *participation in community life* is essential for society's progress. Ordinarily, community concerns and participation increase during these years.

When men marry at the median age of 26 and women at the median age of 24, the average father is 50 and the average mother 48 when the last child leaves home (Rice, 1990). But before this day occurs, there are long years preparing dependent children for independent adult living. Ordinarily, children's dependency on parents gradually lessens and parental control slowly wanes, until the children are capable of managing their own lives. Part of the developmental task at this point is to *let go of the responsibility, as well as the control, for the children.*

Marital needs depend on what the marriage has experienced over the years. It is common for marital satisfaction to decline during the early and middle years of the life cycle (Schram, 1979). A couple whose children are independent now have only one another (Swensen, 1983). They face the task of working out problems, eliminating resentments, getting reacquainted, and being close all over again. Goldstine (1977) suggests that there are three cycles in most marriages— falling in love, falling out of love, and falling back in love—and that the last cycle is both the most difficult and the most rewarding. Many people whose marriages failed during early adulthood have since remarried. The challenge is to *revitalize troubled, intact marriages* (Appleton, 1983). Some cannot be revitalized, and the couple may *divorce* in mid-life, often *remarrying* and starting over. Only a small percentage of people are widowed during middle adulthood and have to *adjust to living without a spouse.*

By the time adults reach 40, their parents are anywhere from 58 to 80 years of age, with 65 to 70 being most common. Therefore, during middle adulthood children watch their parents grow old, retire, perhaps become ill, and die. *Middle-agers become more responsible for providing assistance to aging parents:* economic support, personal care, transportation, food, companionship, medical help, housekeeping or yard care, or a place to live. However, only 10% of married elderly couples and 17% of widows and widowers actually live with married children.

Once children are independent, *crossing of adult sex roles* becomes more apparent. Women are freer after the children are launched; they are not as tied down; some who have not worked before take jobs outside the home. This increasing personal and economic independence gives them more authority, and the husband is called on to perform more services formerly provided by the wife. Some husbands object to their wives' independence and to their own revised roles (Baruch, Barnett, & Rivers, 1983).

Middle age brings a shift in the focus of social activities. Parents previously involved in family-centered social activities find an *increasing need for couple-centered activities.* Teenagers go out with friends. Grown children move out of the house, leaving the couple to their own resources. As a result, adult friendships assume greater importance.

Mid-life may bring *increased interest in having fun, in pursuing one's own interests and hobbies, or in developing entirely new leisure-time pursuits.* It is not unusual for middle-agers to explore interests that they ignored during their child-rearing years. Some travel to places they always longed to visit.

One goal of the middle years is to find new meaning in life. This can be a period of introspection, in which to examine one's feelings, attitudes, values, and goals. There is a need to redefine one's identity, and to answer the questions: Who am I? Where do I go from here? These years can be a time of rejuvenation of the self and enrichment of one's life.

Late Adulthood

As adults enter late adulthood, they are faced with a number of developmental tasks. The task of *staying physically healthy* becomes more difficult as people age (Speare, Avery, & Lawton, 1991). Older people dread physical problems that impair mobility, their senses, and the capacity to take care of themselves (Longino, Jackson, Zimmerman, &

Pleasurable activities, such as collecting model trains, can enhance life satisfaction in late adulthood.

Bradsher, 1991; Quinn, 1983). As a consequence, maintaining good health is one of the most important predictors of life satisfaction in the elderly (Baur & Okun, 1983).

Many adults face the problem of *having adequate income* in their old age. One study revealed that the elderly who felt they were better off financially than their relatives reported higher life satisfaction than did those who were not so well off (Usui, Keil, & Durig, 1985). Most older adults want financial independence, but this requires careful long-term planning (Strate & Dubnoff, 1986). Retirement at age 65 is no longer compulsory, but many workers must retire at 70. Forced retirement has been ranked among the top ten crises in terms of the amount of stress it causes the individual (Sarason, 1981). People who elect retirement, plan for it, and look forward to it feel they have directed their own lives and are not being pushed or manipulated (Kilty & Behling, 1985, 1986). Those most satisfied with retirement are those who have been preparing for it for a number of years (Evans, Eberdt, & Bosse, 1985). Certainly, retirement should be retirement to, not from. Retirees who are most satisfied seem to be those most involved in meaningful activity following retirement (Hooker & Ventis, 1984).

For some of the elderly, *being able to keep their own home is of great importance* (Worobey & Angel, 1990). It allows them independence and usually more satisfactory relationships with their children (Hoyt, Kaiser, Peters, & Babchuk, 1980). Statistics from 1986 revealed that almost 3 out of 4 households maintained by persons 65 years old and over were owned by them. In the remaining households, the elderly were renting. Of course, about 1 out of 10 men and 1 out of 5 women 65 and older are not heads of household because they go to live with married children (U.S. Bureau of the Census, 1980).

The elderly have high status and prestige in primitive societies because they possess the greatest knowledge of traditions and ceremonies considered essential for group survival. The elderly also have high status in agricultural societies because they control the property, have the greatest knowledge of farming skills, are able to perform useful tasks, and are the leaders of the extended family. But as our society becomes more industrialized and modern, the elderly lose their economic advantages and their leadership roles in industry and the extended family. Consequently, they lose their *status and prestige* (Balkwell & Balswick, 1981; Ishii-Kuntz & Lee, 1987).

Part of the loss of status comes when people retire. People find status through their occupation (Hurst & Guldin, 1981). When they leave that role, they have the feeling that they have lost their main identity. As Bell (1975) said, "A former mechanic is no longer a mechanic—he is occupationally nothing" (p. 332). Those who are able to develop a meaningful identity through avocations, social life, their marriage, their children, or other activities adjust more easily.

Loneliness is one of the most frequent complaints of some older people, especially of the formerly married (Creecy, Berg, & Wright, 1985; Essex & Nam, 1987). Their challenge is to *find meaningful relationships with others*. Developing and maintaining friendships with peers seems to be more important to the emotional well-being of the elderly than interaction with kin (Lee & Ellithorpe, 1982). Late adulthood offers most people an opportunity to enjoy themselves. As work roles decline, more leisure time is available for preferred pursuits. Life satisfaction in late adulthood is very much dependent on social activity. People need *worthwhile, pleasurable activities* to help them feel good about themselves and about life in general (Glass & Grant, 1983; McClelland, 1982).

Several events bring about the *adjustment of family roles:* children marrying and moving away, grandparenthood (Miller & Cavanaugh, 1990), retirement, the death of a spouse, or becoming dependent on one's children. All of these circumstances require major adjustments and a realignment of family roles and responsibilities.

Erikson (1959) says that *the development of ego integrity* is the chief psychosocial task of the final stage of life. This includes life review, being able to accept the facts of one's life without regret, and being able to face death without great fear. It entails appreciating one's own individuality, accomplishments, and satisfactions, as well as accepting the hardships, failures, and disappointments one has experienced. Ultimately, it means contentment with one's life as it is and has been (Reker, Peacock, & Wong, 1987; Ryff, 1982).

THEORIES OF ADULT DEVELOPMENT OVER THE LIFE SPAN

In addition to outlining the various developmental tasks of early, middle, and late adulthood, another approach to the study of adult development is to divide the process into a series of phases or stages of life. Several psychologists have sought to divide life into phases, to outline the transitions from one phase to another, and to define the major adjustments required during these different stages. Three theories have been selected for discussion here: those of *Gould* (1972, 1978), *Levinson et al.* (1976, 1977, 1978), and *Vaillant* (1977a, 1977b).

Gould—Phases of Life

Psychiatrist Roger Gould (1972, 1978) reported on two studies. One was a descriptive report of cross-sectional observations of psychiatric outpatients divided into 7 age-homogeneous groups. At the end of 6 months, a second set of 7 groups was constituted. Each of the 14 groups was observed continuously over a period of months. The second study was based on questionnaire answers of 524 middle-class adults not in psychotherapy.

Gould's seven arbitrary age groupings and descriptions were:

Ages 16 to 18. Desire for autonomy, to get away from parents, for deep, close relationships with peers.

Ages 18 to 22. Desire not to be reclaimed by family, for intimacy with peers, to re-create with peers the family they are leaving; real living is just around the corner.

Ages 22 to 29. Engage in work of being adults, in proving competence as adults; now is the time for living as well as growing and building for future; on guard against extreme emotions.

Ages 29 to 35. Role confusion; question self, marriage, career; begin to question what they are doing; weary of devoting themselves to the task of doing what they are supposed to do; desire to be what they are, to accept their children for what they are becoming.

Ages 35 to 43. Increasing awareness of time squeeze; realignment of goals, increasing urgency to attain goals; realization that control over children is waning.

Ages 43 to 50. Acceptance of finite time as reality, settling-down stage, acceptance of one's fate in life; desire for social activities and friends, need for sympathy and affection from spouse; watchful of young adult children's progress.

Ages 50 to 60. Mellowing, warming, more accepting of parents, children, friends, past failures; also renewed questioning about meaningfulness of life; hunger for personal relationships.

Gould admitted the dangers in reporting cross-sectional data because changing cultural values, rather than age, could influence results. Gould's reported fluctuations are not necessarily age specific for one individual. That is, changes occurring over certain periods of time do not necessarily occur at the same ages in all individuals. He acknowledged that his studies were designed to cancel out individual differences to highlight sameness existing in an age group. But he defended his findings on the basis that many of them were supported by other studies using different methodologies and populations.

Some findings from his second study are illustrated in Figure 15.6. In this study, the subjects were asked to respond to a series of statements in a questionnaire. Gould concluded his discussion by stating that strong evidence indicated that a series of distinct stages could be demarcated.

Levinson—Seasons of Life

Daniel Levinson (1978), a social psychology professor from Yale, and his associates made a cross-sectional study of 40 men between 35 and 45 years of age over a period of several years. The subjects were divided into four groups: 10 hourly workers, 10 Ph.D biologists, 10 novelists, and 10 executives from two companies. Of the 40 men, 70% had completed college, all had married at least once, 20% were divorced, 80% had children, and 50% were Protestants. Subjects were interviewed weekly for several months, with a follow-up interview after two years. The interviews were taped and interpretations made from the data. The interviews included much retrospective data from childhood on, as well as information about the present. *Thematic Apperception Test* pictures were used to recall personal experiences. Most of the subjects' wives were interviewed once. Extensive biographical information was also used in interpreting the data.

Levinson proposed a model of adult development that included periods of relative stability (periods of structure building) interspersed with periods of transition (periods of structure changing) (Kanchier & Unruh, 1988). Figure 15.7 shows the developmental periods outlined by Levinson.

The periods can be described as follows:

Ages 17 to 22. Early adult transition: Leaving the family and adolescent groups, going to college, military service, marrying.

Ages 22 to 28. Entering the adult world: Time of choices, defining goals, establishing

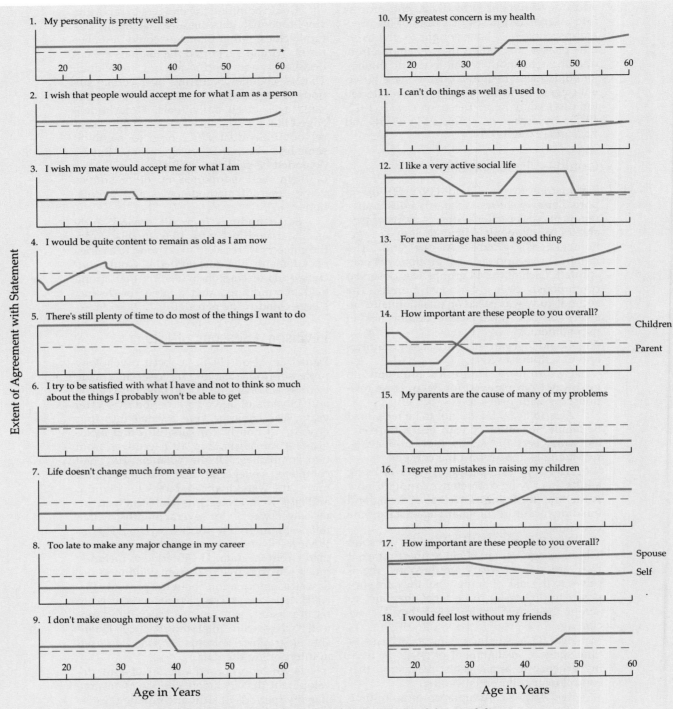

1. My personality is pretty well set
2. I wish that people would accept me for what I am as a person
3. I wish my mate would accept me for what I am
4. I would be quite content to remain as old as I am now
5. There's still plenty of time to do most of the things I want to do
6. I try to be satisfied with what I have and not to think so much about the things I probably won't be able to get
7. Life doesn't change much from year to year
8. Too late to make any major change in my career
9. I don't make enough money to do what I want

10. My greatest concern is my health
11. I can't do things as well as I used to
12. I like a very active social life
13. For me marriage has been a good thing
14. How important are these people to you overall?   Children   Parent
15. My parents are the cause of many of my problems
16. I regret my mistakes in raising my children
17. How important are these people to you overall?   Spouse   Self
18. I would feel lost without my friends

Age in Years

Age in Years

Extent of Agreement with Statement

*The horizontal dashed line is placed arbitrarily to help show the trends of the graph lines.

FIGURE 15.6   Sample curves associated with the time boundaries of the adult life span.

Reprinted from "The Phases of Adult Life: A Study in Developmental Psychology," by R. J. Gould, 1972, *The American Journal of Psychiatry, 129* (November), pp. 521–531. Copyright, 1972, in American Psychiatric Association. Reprinted by permission.

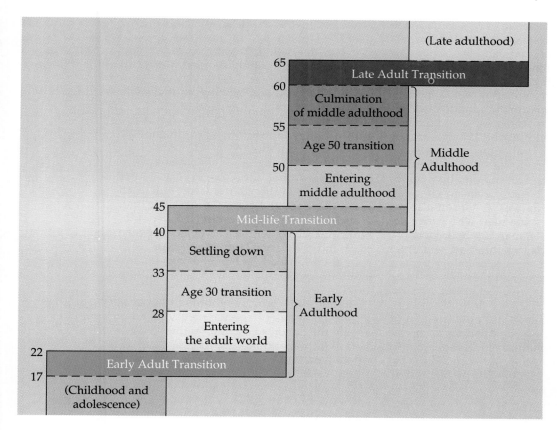

FIGURE 15.7 Developmental periods in early and middle adulthood.

Reprinted from *The Seasons of a Man's Life* by D. J. Levinson et al., 1978, New York: Ballantine Books. Copyright © 1978 by Daniel J. Levinson. Reprinted by permission of Alfred A. Knopf, Inc.

occupation and marriage; conflict between desire to explore and desire to commit.

Ages 28 to 33. Age 30 transition: Period of reworking, modifying life structure; smooth transition for some, disruptive crisis for others; growing sense of need for change before becoming locked in because of commitments.

Ages 33 to 40. Settling down: Accepting a few major goals, building the structure around central choices; establishing one's niche, working at advancement.

Ages 40 to 45. Mid-life transition: Mid-life crisis, link between early and middle adulthood; review and reappraise early adult period; modify unsatisfying aspects of life structure; adjust psychologically to the final half of life; intense reexamination causes emotional upset, tumultuous struggles with self, questioning every aspect of life.

Because Levinson's (1978) original groups were younger than 45, his descriptions basically end with the mid-life transition. However, he does give some brief and tentative descriptions of subsequent periods based primarily on speculation.

Ages 45 to 50. Entering middle adulthood: End of reappraisal, time of choices, forming a new life structure in relation to oc-

cupation, marriage, locale; wide variations in satisfactions and extent of fulfillment.

Ages 50 to 55. Age 50 transition: Work further on the tasks of mid-life transition and modification of structure formed in the mid-40s; crisis if there was not enough change during mid-life transition.

Ages 55 to 60. Culmination of middle adulthood: Building a second middle adult structure; time of fulfillment for those who can rejuvenate themselves and enrich their lives.

Ages 60 to 65. Late adult transition: Conclude efforts of middle adulthood, prepare for era to come; major turning point in life cycle.

Ages 65 and over. Late adulthood: Confrontation with self, life: need to make peace with the world.

Levinson also observed that the entire period after age 65 is often regarded as a single era, primarily because of a lack of research data. However, with many people living to well past 80, there is a period of late-late adulthood that can be either a period of further psychosocial development or of senescence.

Levinson emphasized that periods are defined in terms of developmental tasks, not in terms of such concrete events as marriage or retirement. Each stable life period has certain developmental tasks and life issues crucial to the evolution of that period. A period ends when its tasks lose their primacy and new tasks emerge, initiating a new period. Transitional periods are the times to question and reappraise, to search for new possibilities in the self and the world. Furthermore, there are ranges of variations when periods begin or end. Thus, the age 30 transition can start between 26 and 29 and end between 30 and 34. The exact ages Levinson cited are averages for his samples. Levinson also acknowledged that some men who suffer defeats (such as in their marriage or occupation) in previous periods lack the inner and outer resources to create even minimally adequate structures. Their lives lack meaning and they face future periods with feelings of constriction and failure.

Levinson is soon to publish a book about women: *Seasons of a Woman's Life*. He contends that women have life stages similar to those experienced by men, but that women face more serious life problems than men during the transition periods at 22, 40, and 60. Levinson gives several reasons. *One,* women's lives are harder than men's. Women place a great deal of emphasis on intimacy, yet many don't have intimacy—either in marriage or with other women. Wives and their husbands are so busy with work and family that they don't have time for one another. When the children leave, they have to begin to get to know one another again.

Two, women often do "women's work": as secretaries, clerks, salespersons, teachers, nurses, and so on. Their jobs are primarily lower-paid jobs that don't go anywhere, so because their work is less satisfying, their life crises are deeper and more profound than those experienced by men. Work is at the center of life. It is partly how people justify their existence, but because women often don't feel good about their work, they often find unhappiness when they begin to question their lives during periods of transition (Ferriss, 1989).

Vaillant—Adaptation to Life

George Vaillant (1977a, 1977b), a psychiatrist teaching at Harvard Medical School, conducted a longitudinal study of 94 males who had been graduated from Harvard College between 1942 and 1944. These white males were among 268 college sophomores who had been carefully selected for the *Grant Study*, begun in 1938. The average age in 1969 was 47. The average income was $30,000, 95% had married, 15% were divorced, and 25% were doctors and lawyers. Most had served in World War II, 71% viewed themselves as liberals, and most were "extremely satisfied" with their professions.

A variety of research methods were used. Childhood histories were obtained by interviewing parents. Physical, physiological, and psychological examinations were conducted during the college years. After graduation, questionnaires were sent each year until 1955, and every 2 years after that. A social anthropologist conducted in-depth, home interviews with each subject between 1950 and 1952. Vaillant interviewed each man in 1967, usually at home, using identical interview questionnaires with each (Muson, 1977).

This study provides thorough histories of the life cycles of specific men who were among the nation's best and brightest. It is a long view of maturational processes, ego development, and coping strategies and adaptation mechanisms, as these men reacted to life's challenges. Some succeeded, while others remained locked in patterns of defeat. Vaillant (1977b) also said the study confirmed the principal developmental tasks in Erikson's life stages, especially those of adolescence (identity), young adulthood (intimacy), and middle adulthood (generativity).

One of the study's most interesting aspects was the comparison of the childhoods, family backgrounds, and earlier years of the men who, in their 50s, were labeled *Best Outcomes* and *Worst Outcomes*. Table 15.3 presents the results (Vaillant, 1977a). The table shows that *about one-half of the men who had experienced unsatisfactory (poor) childhood environments were among the 30 Worst Outcomes. However, 17% with poor childhood environments were among the 30 Best Outcomes,* indicating that childhood environment was not the sole determinant of adult success.

Some details were surprising. Fingernail biting, early toilet training, and mental illness failed to predict adult emotional illness. However, the comparison of 23 men whose childhoods were bleak and loveless with 23 men whose childhoods were happy and fortunate yielded four conclusions. Men with unhappy childhoods were (1) unable to play, (2) dependent and lacking in trust, (3) more likely to become mentally ill, and (4) lacking friends.

Similarly, it was difficult to predict successful mid-life adaptation from negative traits seen during adolescence. Descriptions

TABLE 15.3 Comparison of Best and Worst Outcomes in the Grant Study

	The 30 Best Outcomes	The 30 Worst Outcomes
Poor childhood environment	17%	47%
Pessimism, self-doubt, passivity, and fear of sex at 50	3%	50%
In college, personality integration put in bottom fifth	0%	33%
Career choice reflected identification with father	60%	27%
Dominated by mother in adult life	0%	40%
Failure to marry by 30	3%	37%
Bleak friendship patterns at 50	0%	57%
Current job has little supervisory responsibility	20%	93%
Children admitted to father's college	47%	10%
Children's outcome described as good or excellent	66%	23%
Average yearly charitable contribution	$3,000	$500

Reprinted from G. E. Vaillant, *Adaptation to Life* (Boston: Little, Brown, 1977). Copyright © 1977 by George E. Vaillant. By permission of Little, Brown and Company.

such as shyness, ideation, introspection, and lacking purpose and values did not predict the Worst Outcomes. Rather, these traits were merely characteristic of many adolescents. However, late adolescents labeled "well-integrated" and "practical and organized" were best adapted at 50, whereas those labeled "asocial" were least likely to be Best Outcomes (Vaillant, 1977b).

The study underlined the importance of achieving intimacy during young adulthood. The majority who married between 23 and 29 were happily married, and 28 of the 30 Best Outcomes had achieved a stable marriage before age 30 and remained married at 50, whereas 23 of the 30 Worst Outcomes had either married after 30 or separated from their wives before 50. Those who married before 23 (before developing a capacity for intimacy) and those who delayed marriage until after 30 were both likely to have the worst marriages (Vaillant, 1977b).

Between 25 and 35, the men tended to work hard, consolidate their careers, and devote themselves to the nuclear family. The most frequent psychological complaints of the men in their 20s reflected a retreat from intimacy, whereas the emotional complaints of those in their 30s reflected conflicts about success (occupational overachievement or neurotic defeat). Many found nonparental role models or mentors during this period of career consolidation.

At 40 (plus or minus 10 years), men left the compulsive, unreflective busywork of their occupational apprenticeship and once more explored the world within. The pain of this age was preparation for a new life stage. Some men who were bland and colorless during adolescence became vibrant and interesting.

> In his early 40s, one man took up underwater archaeology and deep-sea diving in the Mediterranean. Another built a dramatic, shamelessly exhibitionistic house. A third man whose projective tests at 24 suggested an inner life like "some Brazilian jungle spilling out onto a North Dakota plain" was at 50 finally able to let the Brazilian jungle emerge into his conscious life, yet, he was the last man that the study ever expected to have an exciting love affair (Vaillant, 1977b, p. 41).

The enrichment of these years also extended into the lives of the most successful businessmen. Their career patterns suddenly broadened in middle life; they assumed tasks for which they were untrained. The men who enjoyed the best marriages and richest friendships became the company presidents.

Vaillant continued to study these men in their *50s.* Most of them reported having attained a certain tranquility, perhaps suffused with a mild undercurrent of regret.

Comparison and Critique of Studies

Table 15.4 compares the results of the Gould, Levinson, and Vaillant studies. It must be emphasized that *Gould* purposely used arbitrary age grouping to organize the outpatients into age-homogeneous groups. Although he divided them into seven groups with particular age ranges, he could have used fewer or more groups, changing the age range of each. The age ranges, therefore, are themselves not important.

Levinson used five time periods (5 to 6 years each) between the ages of 17 and 45. Each major time period, which is a period of settling down and becoming established, was interspersed with an unsettling, restless period of transition and change. The beginning and end of the age periods were averages for Levinson's samples; he acknowledged that for individuals the beginning and end of each period may differ. Levinson also projected 5-year age periods to 65 and over, interspersing main periods with transition periods.

TABLE 15.4 Stages or Phases of the Life Cycle

Age in Years	Gould	Levinson	Vaillant
60	Mellowing, warming; acceptance of parents, friends, past failures; but renewed questions about life's meaning; hunger for personal relationships		Middle adulthood: mild mid-life crisis around 40, inner exploration, reassessment, reawakening of instinctual urges including sex, throwing off some overrestraint of 30s, intergenerational conflict, establishing generativity versus stagnation.
50	Settling down stage; acceptance of one's life, finite time; desire for social activity, friends; need for spousal affection; watch children		
		Mid-life transition: crisis, review, reappraisal, modify life, emotion turmoil, upset	
40	Time squeeze, realignment of goals, urgency to attain goals; realization that control over children is waning.	Settling down: acceptance of a few major goals, central choices, establish niche, work at advancement	Young adulthood: achieve intimacy, career consolidation
30	Role confusion, question self, marriage, career; waning of duty, desire to be self; accept children as are	Age 30 transition: reworking, modifying life structure, need for change now	
	Working, proving competence as adults; living, growing for future; control of emotions	Entering adult world: choices, defining goals, occupation, marriage, explore versus commit	
20	Getting away from parents; desire for intimacy with peers	Early adult transition: leaving family, adolescent groups, college, service, marriage	
16	Desire for autonomy		Adolescence: search for identity

Adapted from R. L. Gould, "The Phases of Adult Life: A Study in Developmental Psychology," *American Journal of Psychiatry* 129 (November 1972): 33–43; D. J. Levinson *et al.*, *The Seasons of a Man's Life* (New York: Knopf, 1978); G. E. Vaillant, *Adaptation to Life* (Boston: Little, Brown, 1977).

Vaillant used much broader life periods in seeking to confirm Erikson's description of the psychosocial task of each life stage. Young adulthood is a period of intimacy achievement and career consolidation. But although Vaillant related restlessness and desire for change with the age of 40, he said that some individuals experience this as much as 10 years earlier or later. Again, the exact age is not as important as the actual step in development.

All three researchers described a period of transition between adolescence and early adulthood, a period according to Levinson in which "The Dream" is formed. The Dream is a concept of what one wishes to accomplish. Some envision riches and fame, others a home and children.

These researchers also described a period of struggle, achievement, and growth as individuals in their 20s enter the adult world, striving to succeed in their occupations and in marriage.

One question that arises when comparing these studies is whether there are dual crisis periods during early and middle adulthood; one during the age 30 transition, followed by a period of settling down, and a mid-life crisis as one enters the 40s. For Gould, there was one period from 29 to 43 of role confusion and realignment, and questioning of oneself, one's marriage, and one's career plans. Gould gave the impression that this entire period was devoted to reworking and adjusting one's life. Levinson (1978) made the clearest distinction between an age 30 transition period, about 7 years of settling down, and another transition period in the early 40s. But he also found that only 62% of the men experienced a moderate or severe crisis during the age 30 transition period. The rest did not report a crisis at age 30. Vaillant described no age 30 transition period; for him, the period from 20 to 40 was one of intimacy and career consolidation.

All three described a mid-life crisis. For Gould, it occurred between 35 and 43, for Levinson between 40 and 45, and for Vaillant at 40 (give or take a decade). Gould and Levinson reported a marked crisis. According to Vaillant, severe crises were rare. Mild upsets occurred that created some anxiety, which often resulted in new challenges and vigor. One man of 47 commented:

> I am into a whole new life, a personal renaissance, which has got me excited most of the time. If I can make it pay adequate to my family responsibility, I will "really be livin'," man (Vaillant, 1977a, p. 221).

Psychologically healthy adults were able to reorganize their life patterns during their 40s and emerge with a new sense of personal happiness and fulfillment.

These findings were derived primarily from studies of middle- and upper-middle-class segments of the population. Gould's subjects included two groups: psychiatric outpatients and middle-class adults. Levinson's subjects included only 10 hourly workers. The remaining 30 were all professional people. Vaillant's subjects were 94 males, all of whom had graduated from Harvard College. *Furthermore, of the three studies, only Gould's included women.* Levinson's and Vaillant's populations were all men.

Whether the findings apply to lower socioeconomic status adults, especially to those of minority groups, and to women of different backgrounds and ages, is uncertain. As mentioned, Levinson has been subsequently involved with studying the life stages of women. Nevertheless, there is a great need for longitudinal studies of adults of a variety of socioeconomic, racial, and ethnic groups to shed light on the changes and challenges they face as they go through various phases of the life cycle.

CAUSES OF CHANGE AND TRANSITION

The theories just described help us to understand what happens during various life stages, but they don't deal with the basic question of why these changes and transitions take place. There are basically two theoretical models that explain the causes of change and transition in our lives (Baltes, Reese, & Lipsett, 1980).

Normative-Crisis Model

One model is called the **normative-crisis model**. This model describes human development in terms of a definite sequence of age-related biological, social, and emotional changes. The three theories already discussed come under this category. Thus, Gould, Levinson, and Vaillant all describe a mid-life crisis around age 40. Because the majority of persons experienced this crisis, it could be called a normative happening. Some normative crises are biologically based. Thus, puberty and menopause are determined by a **biological time clock**, which includes a specific range of ages for everyone.

Other normative crises occur because of social norms that define what is appropriate for people to do at various ages. Each society establishes a **social clock** that specifies when various life events and activities are supposed to happen. There is a best age to go to college, to marry, to begin a vocation, to have children. However, social clocks are not set the same for everyone in our culture, or in different cultures. Low socioeconomic status people in our society generally leave school, begin work, marry, and become parents at younger ages than those of higher socioeconomic status. Similarly, it may be appropriate for a woman in some other cultures to marry much younger than women in our country. When people do things earlier or later than society prescribes, pressures are put on them to conform to expectations.

The normative-crisis model also takes into account emotional factors that influence behavior and changes. People must be emotionally ready to make changes or to accept various responsibilities, such as going to college, getting married, or becoming parents.

As seen in the following Focus topic, there has been a dramatic decline in consensus regarding the "right time" for various things to happen.

Normative-crisis model—a model based on a definite sequence of age-related changes

Biological time clock—life events regulated by maturation and biological changes

Social clock—a society's specification as to when various life events and activities are supposed to happen

Counseling often helps people deal with important changes in their lives.

FOCUS

The Right Time for Life Events

Two surveys asked Americans 20 years apart (late 1950s and late 1970s) what's the right age for various major events and achievements of adult life. A dramatic decline occurred in the consensus among middle-class, middle-aged people.

TABLE 15.5 Concepts of "The Right Time"

Activity/Event	Appropriate Age Range	Late '50s Study (% Who Agree)		Late '70s Study (% Who Agree)	
		Men	Women	Men	Women
Best age for a man to marry	20–25	80%	90%	42%	42%
Best age for a woman to marry	19–24	85	90	44	36
When most people should become grandparents	45–50	84	79	64	57
Best age for most people to finish school and go to work	20–22	86	82	36	38
When most men should be settled on a career	24–26	74	64	24	26
When most men hold their top jobs	45–50	71	58	38	31
When most people should be ready to retire	60–65	83	86	66	41
When a man has the most responsibilities	35–50	79	75	49	50
When a man accomplishes most	40–50	82	71	46	41
The prime of life for a man	35–50	86	80	59	66
When a woman has the most responsibilities	25–40	93	91	59	53
When a woman accomplishes most	30–45	94	92	57	48

Source: Adapted from "Age Norms and Age Constraints Twenty Years Later" by P. Passuth, D. Maines, and B. L. Neugarten. Paper presented at the Midwest Sociological Society meeting. Chicago, April 1984.

Timing-of-Events Model

Timing-of-events model—a model of development based on responses to the occurrences and timing of normative and nonnormative events—typified by Neugarten

The **timing-of-events model** says that development is not the result of a set plan or schedule of crises but is a result of the time in people's lives when important events take place. People develop in response to specific events that occur at various times in their lives. Neugarten, the chief exponent of this view, suggests that this results in much variation in the time when events happen (Neugarten, Moore, & Lowe, 1965; Neugarten & Neugarten, 1987).

Normative influences—expected life events that occur at customary times

Generally speaking, life events that are expected (**normative influences**) create few problems for people. If people have time to prepare for a job or for marriage or parenthood, they are usually able to make the transition more easily. But unexpected events (**nonnormative or idiosyncratic events**) are the ones that create the most stress. Thus, an unexpected divorce, job layoff, automobile accident, heart attack, or death may create a great deal of stress. There is no time to prepare for these nonnormative influences, yet these critical events may define a turning point in one's life.

Some events are *sociohistorical*. These would include wars, economic depression, revolutions, or epidemics. They would also include events in the physical world such as fires, hurricanes, earthquakes, or volcanic eruptions. These events may alter significantly the lives of many people.

Sociohistorical events affect different age cohorts significantly. A small child during the Great Depression of the 1930s may have been largely unaware of unemployment and financial hardships that caused his father

Nonnormative or idiosyncratic influences—life events that occur at unexpected times or that are unusual, both of which have a major impact on development

TABLE 15.6 How Sociohistorical Events Affect Different Age Cohorts

Historical Event	Year Born						
	1930	1940	1950	1960	1970	1980	1990
1930 Depression	Born	—	—	—	—	—	—
1940 World War II Social Security	Age 10	Born	—	—	—	—	—
1950 Korean War Baby Boom	Age 20 College Draft age Single	Age 10	Born	—	—	—	—
1960 Affluence Civil Rights Movement	Age 30 Marriage, Divorce, Parenting, Career	Age 20 College Single	Age 10	Born	—	—	—
1970 Vietnam War Economic stagnation	Age 40 Mid-life crisis	Age 30 Marriage, Divorce, Parenting, Career	Age 20 College Draft age Activism	Age 10	Born	—	—
1980 Recession and Inflation; Economic recovery	Age 50 Empty-nest years	Age 40 Mid-life crisis	Age 30 Marriage, Divorce, Parenting, Career	Age 20 College Single	Age 10	Born	—
1990 Middle East Crisis AIDS Epidemic	Age 60 Begin late adulthood	Age 50 Empty-nest years	Age 40 Mid-life crisis	Age 30 Marriage, Divorce, Parenting, Career	Age 20 College Single	Age 10	Born

and mother to lie awake nights worrying about how they were going to make ends meet. Similarly, a 21-year-old who was subject to the draft in 1968 during the Vietnam War was affected far differently from his 75-year-old grandfather. Table 15.6 shows how sociohistorical events have a different influence on different age cohorts.

SUMMARY

1. The span of adulthood may be divided into three age periods: early adulthood (20s and 30s), middle adulthood (40s and 50s), and late adulthood (60 and over).
2. The median age of the population continues to increase and was 32.3 years in 1988.
3. Graphs of birthrates reveal a large cohort born during the early 1900s, a small cohort of depression babies born between 1930 and 1945, and a large cohort of baby boomers born after World War II, between 1945 and 1960. Because of their large numbers, the baby boomers have had to struggle for jobs, have had large numbers of children, have exerted great pressure on the housing market, and have reacted to the stress with high divorce rates and drug use. When they age, medical and Social Security costs will be staggering. They will exert con-

siderable political power in demanding their rights.
4. As the dependency ratio increases, the burden of responsibility for supporting dependents is great, and is partially shifting from men to women.
5. As a result of these demographics, there are various positive developments that are taking place: a leveling off of divorce rates and society turning its attention from a youth-oriented to an adult-conscious culture.
6. We must alter our age-appropriate norms to take into account that people are living longer, more active lives.
7. Adulthood means different things to different people, but has social, biological, emotional, and legal dimensions; its primary meaning is social.
8. The transition to adulthood is a complicated process in our highly industrial-

ized society, with individuals having to go through various rites of passage as they become socialized (learning and adopting the norms, values, expectations, and social roles of their group).

9. Becoming an adult means the successful completion of a number of developmental tasks. Development continues and the tasks change during early, middle, and late adulthood.

10. Early adults face the tasks of achieving autonomy, molding an identity, developing emotional stability, establishing a career, finding intimacy, becoming part of social groups, selecting a mate and adjusting to marriage, establishing and managing a residence, becoming parents and rearing children.

11. Middle-aged adults are faced with the tasks of adjusting to physical changes, finding satisfaction in their career, assuming social and civic responsibilities, launching children, revitalizing marriage, reorienting to aging parents, realigning sex roles, developing social networks and leisure-time activities. Their overall goal is to find new meaning in life.

12. Late adults are faced with the tasks of staying physically healthy and adjusting to limitations, maintaining an adequate income, adjusting to revised work roles, establishing acceptable housing and living conditions, maintaining identity and social status, finding companionship, learning to use leisure time pleasurably, establishing new roles in the family, and achieving integrity through acceptance of one's life.

13. Three major theories of adult development over the life span are discussed here: those of Roger Gould, Daniel Levinson, and George Vaillant.

14. Gould used seven homogeneous age groups to define the changes and adjustments required as people go through various life phases.

15. Levinson proposed a model of adult development that outlines periods of relative stability interspersed with major periods of transition beginning at ages 17,

40, and 60, and lesser transitions at 30 and 50.

16. Vaillant made a longitudinal study of the histories of the life cycles of men who were among the nation's best and brightest. One important contribution was the comparison of childhood background with adult success. Half the men who had poor childhood environments were among the 30 Worst Outcomes, and 17 with poor childhood environments were among the 30 Best Outcomes, indicating that childhood environment alone was not the sole determinant of adult success. However, those with unhappy childhoods were: (1) unable to play, (2) dependent and lacking in trust, (3) more likely to become mentally ill, and (4) lacking friends.

17. It was difficult to predict successful adaptation from negative traits during adolescence. The study revealed the importance of achieving intimacy during young adulthood in terms of later marital success.

18. The age divisions in the three studies are purely arbitrary. All three researchers described a period of transition between adolescence and early adulthood, and a mid-life crisis around age 40.

19. Two theoretical models describe the causes of change and transition in life: the normative-crisis model and the timing-of-events model.

20. The normative-crisis model describes normative happenings according to a biological time clock and a social clock. These happenings result in changes in our lives. This model also takes into account emotional factors that influence behavior and change.

21. The timing-of-events model says that development is a result of the times in people's lives when important events take place. Some events are normative; others are nonnormative or idiosyncratic. In this model, the latter type of events are often the most critical to a person's development.

KEY TERMS

Baby boomers   *p. 325*
Biological time clock   *p. 341*
Dependency ratio   *p. 327*
Nonnormative or idiosyncratic influences   *p. 342*

Normative-crisis model   *p. 341*
Normative influences   *p. 342*
Social clock   *p. 341*
Timing-of-events model   *p. 342*

DISCUSSION QUESTIONS

1. When were you born, and how does your age cohort differ from others who are younger or older?
2. Were your parents part of the baby boomers' cohort? What difference might it have made in their lives?
3. What are some things that are likely to happen because of increasing dependency ratios? What is your reaction to the idea that the responsibility for taking care of dependents is shifting from men to women?
4. What are the most important qualities in an adult? Which rite of passage is most important to you in achieving adulthood?
5. To those in your 20s and 30s: Which developmental tasks are most important to you? Which ones are the most difficult?
6. To those in your 40s or 50s or 60s: Which developmental tasks are most important to you? Which ones are the most difficult?
7. Are any of your parents or grandparents age 60 and over? Which developmental tasks seem to be most important to them? Which are the most difficult?
8. Look at Figure 15.6 based upon Gould's findings. Which findings do you find most significant? Explain. Are there any findings that you find surprising? Are there any findings that seem different from those of your own experiences? Explain.
9. What do you think of Levinson's theory? What aspects do you feel are most important? Which ones agree with your own experience? Which do you disagree with? Explain.
10. Think about your own childhood background. How has it affected you in the process of becoming an adult? In what ways have you been handicapped by your childhood background? In what ways have you been helped by your childhood background?
11. Why do some people overcome the effects of being brought up in a dysfunctional family and others do not? What factors are important in overcoming the negative effects?
12. Is it possible to have too happy a childhood as far as later adult success is concerned?
13. In what ways has your biological time clock affected your life? In what ways has your social clock affected your life?
14. What events in your life have been most significant in influencing change and transitions? Describe.

SUGGESTED READINGS

Aging in America: The federal government's role. (1989). Washington, DC: Congressional Quarterly. Special edition on aging in America with emphasis on implications for Social Security, Medicare, Medicaid, catastrophic costs, and long-term care.

Baruch, G., & Brooks-Gunn, J. (Eds.). (1984). *Women in midlife.* New York: Plenum. A collection of articles on women during the middle years.

Block, M., Davidson, J., & Grambs, J. (1981). *Women over forty: Visions and realities.* New York: Springer Publishing. Research on life circumstances, images, and stereotypes of older women.

Breytspraak, L. M. (1984). *The development of self in later life.* Boston: Little, Brown. Personal experience of aging.

Filene, P. (1981). *Men in the middle.* Englewood Cliffs, NJ: Prentice-Hall. How men at middle age can cope.

Gould, R. L. (1978). *Transformations: Growth and change in adult life.* New York: Simon and Schuster. Gould's model of adult development.

Kegan, R. (1982). *The evolving self: Problems and process in human development.* Cambridge, MA: Harvard University Press. The process of making life meaningful.

Levinson, D. (1978). *Seasons of a man's life.* New York: Ballantine Books. Levinson's model of adult development as revealed in the biographies of 40 men.

McCrae, R., & Costa, P. (1984). *Emerging lives, enduring dispositions: Personality in adulthood.* Boston: Little, Brown. Longitudinal studies on personality during adulthood.

Sherman, E. (1987). *Meaning in mid-life transitions.* Albany: State University of New York Press. Case studies of individuals making the transitions during middle age.

Skinner, B. F., & Vaughan, M. E. (1983). *Enjoy old age: A program of self-management.* New York: Norton. A positive message for those getting older by B. F. Skinner, the famous psychologist, and his colleague.

Trolls, L. E. (1985). *Early and middle adulthood* (2nd ed.). Monterey, CA: Brooks/Cole. Textbook.

16

Physical Development

PHYSICAL ATTRACTIVENESS, ABILITIES, AND FITNESS

Growth and Aging

Sometime during the mid-20s, the human body is usually at the peak of its physical development. Height is at a maximum, bones and teeth are strong, muscles are powerful, the skin is supple, senses are keen, and the mind is sharp. Table 16.1 shows the ages of peak performance of athletes (Horn, 1988). Ironically, at the same time that peak performance is reached, aging is taking place. Every human being is born with a fantastic reserve of tissue and cells, but this reserve is gradually depleted with age. Some types of cells, such as liver and kidney cells, replace themselves over a long period of time. Other cells, such as muscle cells, have a limited replicative potential. All cells and tissue have limited lives, and the older a person gets, the weaker the regenerative process becomes. Slowly, almost imperceptibly for years, the human body ages.

One characteristic of middle age is a growing awareness of personal mortality accompanying the first physical signs of aging. Most young adults are concerned about their appearance because "they want to look nice," but middle-aged adults are concerned for a different reason. For the first time, they begin to look older, with noticeable alteration in appearance. However, the extent of changes depends partly on the individual. Superior nutrition and health care, with close

During the mid-20s, the body is at the peak of its physical development.

attention to exercise and physical fitness, help people look much younger than was the case a generation ago. Everyone eventually ages physically, but some people look 20 or 30 years younger than their actual age would suggest.

Attitudes of Society

Self-conciousness about one's changing physique is accentuated by society's attitudes. In the United States, attractiveness is equated with youthfulness. To be beautiful is to be young and slender. Female models of cosmetics and clothes are thin and sinewy; male models are slender and muscular. The middle-aged adults conclude from these ads that their bodies are crumbling. The roof is in trouble, the mortar is coming out of the joints, the floors are sagging, and the doors creak (Conway, 1978). As a result, some people will go to extreme lengths, including cosmetic surgery, to look more youthful (Hamburger, 1988). Those who have a poor concept of their body image, even if they are reasonably attractive, become self-conscious and socially inhibited and anxious because they can't accept the way they look (Cash & Butters, 1988).

Generally speaking, our society accepts a double standard for men and women (Berman, O'Nan, & Floyd, 1981). It helps if a man is slim and youthful, but it is practically obligatory for a woman. Most modern women reject this sexist philosophy, but many are still taught that physical attractiveness is their most valuable asset. As a result, women—in general—are less satisfied with their physical appearance than are men (Cash, Winstead, & Janda, 1986; Thompson, 1986).

TABLE 16.1 Ages of Peak Performance of Athletes

Sport	Age	
	Men	Women
Baseball		
Pitchers	27 years	
Batters	26.5–28	
Swimming	20	18
Short-Distance Running	23	22
Medium-Distance Running	24	24
Long-Distance Running	27	27
Tennis	24	24
Golf	31	30

Adapted from "The Peak Years" by J. C. Horn, 1988, *Psychology Today, 22,* pp. 62–63.

FOCUS

Ageism in Our Society

The term **ageism** was coined in 1968 by Robert Butler, a physician and former director of the National Institute of Aging. He used the word to describe profound, widespread prejudice against the elderly. Like sexism and racism, ageism represents discrimination of one group against another, in this case based on age. When applied to the elderly, it reflects negative attitudes toward them, unfair and false stereotyping, differential medical or employment treatment, and emotional rejection.

Ageism assumes many forms in our society. An examination of prescription drug advertising in two journals (*Medical Economics* and *Geriatrics*) generally showed the elderly as active people, but the written descriptions of them were negative. They were described as aimless, apathetic, debilitated, disruptive, hypochondriacal, insecure, needing insatiable reassurance, low in self-esteem, out of control, sluggish, reclusive, and temperamental (Smith, 1975).

Ageism is evident in various professions. One study of 69 graduate students in the fields of social work, law, and medicine showed that not one student registered a first-choice preference for working with the elderly (Geiger, 1978).

Television perpetuates a negative image of the elderly. Commercials portray nice 80-year-old grandmothers (today many are 40) in old-fashioned clothes. Most often they are shown buying laxatives or denture cleansers. The elderly are often pictured living in nursing homes, when actually only 6% of people over 65 are institutionalized (U.S. Bureau of the Census, 1989). There are a few exceptions to these negative images. Problems of the aged have become a more viable subject for television; they are now being shown as misunderstood by the young and perfectly capable of getting along without their children's help. In fact, the capabilities of the aged, especially as represented by national leaders and entertainment figures, are gaining recognition.

A number of studies have analyzed the humorous portrayal of the elderly in jokes, birthday cards, and cartoons. Birthday cards deal most often with the subject of age itself: the associated physical and mental characteristics, the inevitability of growing older, the concealment of age, aging as a state of mind, the aging of others but not oneself, and concern about age (Demos & Jache, 1981). The emphasis on decline in physical appearance is illustrated by the following quote from a greeting card:

> Another birthday? You're not old until you go to the beauty parlor on Tuesday, come home on Thursday . . . And still look like you did on Monday (Demos & Jache, 1981, p. 212).

Demos and Jache conclude their study by suggesting that birthday messages appear to reflect stereotypes about aging and consequently may reinforce ageist ideas.

An analysis of contemporary American poetry showed that a number of poems equate growing old with diminishment, whereas others express a striving for continued change, growth, and self-realization in old age (Clark, 1980). The elderly are sometimes portrayed as having a "vigor beyond their youth"; even though bones may creak, eyes grow bleary, and breasts wither, the aging are endowed with strength arising from their individuality. Age is referred to as "the hour for praise . . . praise that is joy." There is also a keen sense of the passage of years, and the desire in the time left, with the strength given, to do "that which is worthy of heaven." There is a realization, too, that age offers opportunities for love that are not available to the young.

> Ours is the late, last wisdom of the afternoon.
> We know that love, like light, grows dearer toward the dark (Clark, 1980, p. 190).

The aged are described negatively as having "no faces," "no voices," with "riches gone." The old are diminished in value "as merchandise marked down." They are "sitters by the wall," and the poet asks: "Is there a song left then for aged voices?" (Clark, 1980) Still, despite, the emphasis on loss, the retention of pleasant memories is often mentioned. The older person learns to become patient, placid, tranquil, content, and quiet. Some older people will weave "nets of dreams," laugh, and appreciate the beauty of nature; the fortunate even retain the poet's ability to "sing" (Sohngen & Smith, 1978, p. 183).

Physical Fitness and Health

CHRONOLOGICAL AGE VERSUS FUNCTIONAL AGE. Each person has a different biological time clock, some aging faster than others. Men age more quickly than women up to the age of fifty. Cross-cultural studies indicate wide variations. Differences also exist within a particular culture. Black males age faster than do white males (Morgan, 1968). Much depends on heredity, but diet, climate, exercise, and health habits are also

Cross-cultural studies indicate wide variations in the speed of aging. Functional age emphasizes the ability of the adult to perform regardless of age. Speed of aging depends on heredity, diet, climate, exercise, and health habits.

Functional age— age as measured by the ability to perform physical or mental functions

influential. This is why chronological age alone is a poor measure of physical condition or aging.

The important emphasis should be on **functional age**, that is, the ability of the adult to perform regardless of age. Some 40-year-olds act, think, and behave like 60-year-olds, and some at 60 live and perform better than those in their 20s. One study of 1,146 healthy men, ages 25 to 83, revealed a 42% differential between functional age and chronological age when personality factors, abilities, and blood chemistry were considered (Nuttal, Fozard, Rose, & Spencer, 1971). Other extensive studies attempted to measure different aspects of functional age, such as body chemistry, anthropometric descrip-

tions, perceptual and motor abilities, and other factors (Bell, Rose, & Danon, 1972). These measurements, along with subjective evaluations of age (how old people say they actually look, feel, think, and act), enable researchers to make more accurate age determinations than are possible with chronological evaluations (Kastenbaum, Derbin, Sabatini, & Artt, 1972).

REACTION TIME.   One measurement of functional ability in the older adult is **reaction time**, the interval between stimulation and response. If a person is driving a car and the traffic light turns red, reaction time is the interval between the time the light changes and the time the person steps on the car brake.

Reaction time— the interval between stimulation and response

Regular exercise is important in improving reaction time.

rior performance on tasks requiring accuracy without emphasizing speed.

MOTOR ABILITY, COORDINATION, DEXTERITY.   Other measurements of functional ability include motor ability, coordination, and dexterity. **Motor ability** implies the ability to move the fingers, hands, arms, legs, or other parts of the body. This ability requires muscular strength, coordination, dexterity, and proper functioning of the central nervous system, which carries the messages from the brain to the muscles. Motor skills vary from the mundane (walking, running, or dressing) to the dramatic (gymnastics or ballet). All of these abilities eventually decline with age, but *the decline is minimal during early adulthood. Most of the decline occurs after the 30s.* It becomes more difficult to compete in such sports as boxing, baseball, tennis, or basketball, which require good motor ability (Horn, 1988).

Psychomotor ability affects numerous skills, including writing skill. Research on writing speed in relation to age reveals some decline with age, but this depends partially on occupation. There is little decline in writing speed among clerical workers, indicating the importance of practice (LaRiviere & Simonson, 1965).

STRENGTH.   The potential of increases in strength remains until almost age 30. There is usually very little loss of muscular strength during the 30s. *Regular exercise can maintain power and even restore it to muscles that have gone unused.*

One study of the effect of exercise and training on improving the muscular strength of both young male subjects (mean age 22) and elderly male subjects (mean age 70) showed significant increases in strength in both age groups in response to a progressive weight-training program over an 8-week period (Moritani & deVries, 1980). The subjects were asked to flex their elbows while holding progressively heavier dumbbells. Figure 16.1 shows the maximum strengths attained by both subject groups and the percentage changes in maximum strength of these subjects. The strength of the older subjects increased somewhat faster than that of the younger subjects until the 7th week of training. The maximum weight the older subjects were able to flex was 75 pounds; the younger subjects reached a maximum of 114 pounds. Considering the nearly 50-year differential between the two age groups, a 52% differential in maximum strength does not appear

Motor ability—the ability to move fingers, hands, arms, legs, and other parts of the body in a useful, coordinated way

Numerous studies have been done to discover how this time interval changes as persons age. *In general, reaction time decreases from childhood to about age 20, remains constant until the mid-20s, and then slowly increases.* This increase has been estimated at approximately 17% between 20 and 40 years of age (Bromley, 1974). Whether this increase has any practical significance depends on the type of activity in which a person engages. Most active sports require quick reactions as well as good coordination. Consequently, most professional athletes in their 30s are considered old. However, those who play various sports for pleasure can continue to enjoy themselves and benefit from the activity.

Adults whose jobs involve physical skill, quick movements, and speed will slow down as they get older. However, they can often do as much work as younger adults because they work steadily and conscientiously. Older adults are also safer drivers than young adults, even though their reactions have slowed. Young adults respond more quickly in emergencies, but they can create problems by driving too fast.

Comparisons of athletes with nonathletes have shown the importance of regular exercise and practice in improving reaction time. Although older adults fatigue more easily than do young adults, suitable rest periods minimize fatigue and improve reaction time. Another reason older adults respond more slowly is that they are more cautious about making errors. They may show supe-

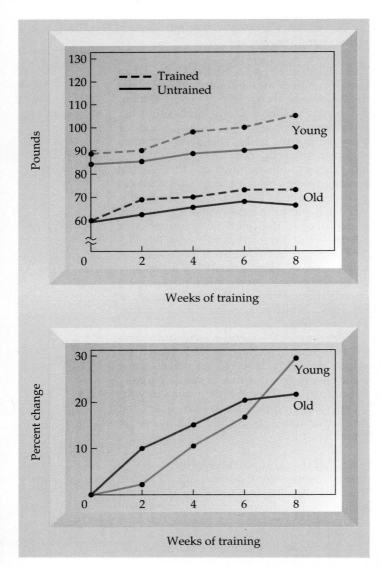

FIGURE 16.1 Effect of age and training on maximum strength.

Adapted from "Potential for Gross Muscle Hypertrophy in Older Men" by T. Moritani and H. A. deVries, 1980, *Journal of Gerontology, 35,* pp. 672–682. Reprinted by permission of *Journal of Gerontology.*

Exercise

BENEFITS. *Exercise is one of the best ways to prevent ill health and maintain body fitness* (Harris, 1988). One of the secrets of the abundance of energy and drive of the chief executive officers of America's top corporations is their devotion to exercise as well as to other good health habits such as not smoking, eating a good diet, and getting adequate sleep (Rippe, 1989). Many corporations have developed whole programs to encourage their workers to stay healthy. L. L. Bean in Maine has three fitness rooms, rewards persons who have logged 200 miles jogging, and gives gift certificates to those who attend exercise classes (Roberts & Harris, 1989). Without exercise, bodies literally waste away. Muscles grow weak, bones become more porous, arteries clog up, and the heart is pressed to cope with sudden demands. A study of 16,936 men (35 to 74) showed that those who took part in strenuous sports had fewer heart attacks than those who were sedentary (Boeckman, 1979). Exercise may be the most effective fountain of youth yet discovered (Doan & Scherman, 1987). Exercise improves respiration and feeds more oxygen to the whole body, increasing circulation and metabolism (Poehlman, Melby, & Badylak, 1991), nourishing the brain, improving digestion and bowel functioning, preserving the bones, toning the muscles, and relieving

Aerobic exercise helps to maintain cardiovascular and respiratory fitness.

considerable. The important point is that even a brief training program improved performance.

ENDURANCE AND FATIGUE. *The maximum work rate one can achieve without fatigue begins to decline at about 35,* as related to such activities as climbing stairs, using a treadmill, or cranking a wheel. The capacity for hard work at high temperatures falls off sharply by age 30. But here again, physical condition is an important factor causing abilities to overlap considerably over a broad age range. Some older adults do more physical work than younger adults half their age.

nervous tension, depression, and anxiety. Moderate exercise can even improve one's sex life (Whitten & Whiteside, 1989). Without exercise, the cardiovascular system's capacity to deliver oxygen to working muscles is reduced relatively early in the aging process, and the weakness and fatigability of the muscles advances rapidly (Gutmann, 1977).

HABITS.   According to one national survey, about one-half of young adults between 20 and 39 engage in some sort of regular exercise (at least once a week). Less than half (42%) of this country's middle adults, age 45 to 64, engage in any form of exercise at least weekly (U.S. Bureau of the Census, 1989). For those who exercise, walking is the most common and one of the best forms of exercise (Thayer, 1988). Calisthenics, swimming, and bicycle riding are about equal in popularity. Only a small percentage jog (8%) or lift weights (6%) (U.S. Bureau of the Census, 1989). Many adults of all ages become couch potatoes, spending long hours in front of the television set ("Couch Potato Physique," 1989).

PULSE RATE.   *One of the simplest measures of health and physical fitness is pulse rate.* **Pulse rate** is the number of times the heart beats per minute. It can be felt in various parts of the body, but the area commonly used is the wrist artery. Count the number of pulse beats for 6 seconds and then add a zero; or count the beats for 15 seconds and multiply

Pulse rate—the number of heartbeats per minute

by 4. This gives the heartbeats per minute. The pulse rate is the body's most important single indicator of well-being, stress, or illness (Morehouse & Gross, 1975). In the average adult male, the resting pulse rate averages 72 to 76 beats per minute. In adult females, the resting pulse rate averages 76 to 80 beats per minute. In general, the lower the resting rate, the healthier the person, unless there is a major heart problem. Resting pulse rates higher than 80 beats per minute suggest poor health and fitness; the heart is working hard just to maintain the circulation in the body. For example, the mortality rate for men and women with resting pulse rates of 92 is 4 times greater than for those with pulse rates lower than 67 (Morehouse & Gross, 1975).

The pulse rate goes up during exercise and indicates the intensity of exertion as well as one's fitness. A rate of about 120 per minute borders on intensive exertion. However, the more physically fit you are, the more strenuously you can exercise without increasing your pulse rate excessively. A person whose resting pulse is racing at 100 or 110 cannot tolerate much exertion; the heart is already strained. But a person who exercises strenuously and whose pulse rate rises very little is in excellent physical condition, unless significant problems are preventing the heartbeat from increasing. The healthy person's heart is already working strongly, pumping a large volume of blood with each beat, so the pumping rate does not have to

LIVING ISSUES

Monitoring Pulse Rate During Exercise

There are some indexes of how much the pulse rate should increase during exercise to make certain an individual is not exerting too much or too little (Blanding, 1982). For instance, take the figure of 220 beats per minute (the theoretical maximum pulse rate), subtract your age, and multiply by a percentage. People in poor physical condition should multiply by 60%, those in moderate condition by 70%, and those in good physical condition by 80%. The result is a target pulse rate.

Suppose a person is 40 years old and in moderate physical condition.

220 (maximum pulse rate)
−40 (age)
180 × .70 (for moderate condition) = 126 beats per minute

The target rate of 126 is the rate the person should strive to achieve while exercising. If the rate is not reached, more strenuous exercise is needed. If the rate is much higher, the exertion may be too great for one's fitness level. Furthermore, the target rate should be sustained for at least 15 to 30 minutes of continuous exercise. Some authorities advise exercise at least 3 or 4 times per week. Some recommend daily exercise to maintain cardiovascular fitness. As fitness improves, the target rate will increase, requiring one to exercise more strenuously to raise the pulse rate. Once a person is in good physical condition (using an 80% multiple), maintenance is achieved by raising the pulse rate to the target figure, or slightly above, during exercise.

rise much even under considerable exertion. Ordinarily, the more a person exercises over a period of time, the stronger the heart becomes, and the slower the pulse rate is at rest or under exertion.

Diet and Nutrition

REQUIREMENTS AND DEFICIENCIES. Proper nutrition is another important factor in maintaining good health (Hallfrisch, Muller, Drinkwater, Tobin, & Andres, 1990). It results in feelings of well-being, high energy levels to carry on daily activities, and maximum resistance to disease and fatigue. Poor nutrition may accelerate the aging process, accentuate physical handicaps, and result in generally poorer health. The saying, "You are what you eat," is certainly true.

Although energy requirements decrease with advancing age, middle-aged and older adults need as many nutrients as do younger adults. Thus, the older person's diet must provide foods of great **nutrient density,** relative to calories (Yearick, Wang, & Pisias, 1980). This means cutting back on fats and sugars, especially on fats (Brownell, 1989; Gurin, 1989; Simon, 1989).

Unfortunately, reduced caloric intake with age is sometimes accompanied by progressive decreases in the intake of necessary minerals, vitamins, and proteins. A number of different studies have indicated that calcium and iron are the minerals most likely to be deficient, primarily because of a low intake of milk and dairy products (Slesinger, McDivitt, & O'Donnell, 1980). Vitamins A, C, thiamin (Smidt, Cremin, Grivetti, & Clifford, 1991), riboflavin, and niacin are the vitamins most likely to be deficient (Yearick et al., 1980).

METABOLISM, EATING BEHAVIOR, AND OBESITY. The average adult in the United States is 20 or more pounds overweight (Meyers, Goldberg, Bleecker, Coon, Drinkwater, & Bleecker, 1991; Schwartz, Shuman, Bradbury, Cain, Fellingham, Beard, Kahn, Stratton, Cerqueira, & Abrass, 1990). Although the average 50-year-old woman weighs 154 pounds and the average 50-year-old man weighs 177 pounds, these are not ideal weights. Ideal weights range from 20 to 40 pounds less, depending on body frame.

Losing weight is difficult unless caloric intake is reduced. Figure 16.2 shows the daily caloric intake and expenditure in normal males. **Basal calories** are those metabolized by the body to carry on its physiological functions and maintain normal body tem-

Nutrient density—percentage of essential nutrients in food in relation to calories

Basal calories—energy metabolized by the body

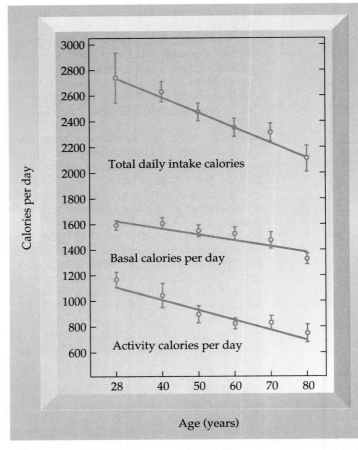

FIGURE 16.2   Daily caloric intake and expenditure in normal males.

Adapted from "Systems Integration" by N. W. Shock, 1977, in *Handbook of the Biology of Aging* (p. 644) by C. E. Finch and L. Hayflick, Eds., New York: Van Nostrand Reinhold Co.

perature. **Activity calories** are those expended through physical activities. Because of reduced exercise, the need for activity calories falls somewhat more rapidly than for basal calories, requiring a corresponding reduction in caloric intake to avoid weight gain (Shock, 1977). *In order to lose weight, either exercise must be increased or caloric intake reduced, preferably both* (Fisher, 1988). Rapid weight loss diets are usually followed by rapid weight gain once the diet is discontinued. Permanent reduction in weight requires a basic restructuring of eating habits (Brownell, 1988).

SPECIAL NEEDS OF ADULTS. Adults may require special diets; for example, diets low in **saturated fats** and **cholesterol** (Lowik, Wedel, Kok, Odink, Westenbrink, & Meulmeester, 1991), a chemical found in all animal fats (Roberts, 1989). Excesses of these substances in the bloodstream contribute to ath-

Activity calories—energy expended through physical activities

Saturated fats—animal fats

Cholesterol—chemical in all animal fats that is a major cause of atherosclerosis

erosclerosis by building up fatty deposits in the arteries (Fritzsche, Tracy, Speirs, & Glueck, 1990). The result is a higher incidence of heart disease and heart attack (Wohl, 1988).

Adults have other special nutritional needs. One of these needs is a *diet low in sodium*. Sodium from salt, sodium nitrates, sodium nitrites, and other sources encourages fluid retention and edema. This, in turn, may cause high blood pressure and other problems. One major treatment for hypertension is the administration of *diuretics,* which help the body eliminate excess fluids. Limiting sodium intake will minimize fluid retention.

Most adults get *too much sugar* in their diets. This is certainly a problem for diabetics, but everyone should be cognizant of sugar intake. Sugar is considered "empty calories" because it contains no proteins, vitamins, or minerals. More than that, it forms acids that deplete the body's source of calcium and destroy important B vitamins. Most people get enough sugar from fresh fruits and other natural foods. In addition, carbohydrates are converted into sugar during the process of digestion, so the body often gets too much sugar if the diet is rich in starches.

Rest and Sleep

PATTERNS.   Adequate amounts of sleep and rest help to stave off physical fatigue by replenishing energy burned up while awake. Rest also helps maintain maximum intellectual functioning. A positive correlation has been found, for example, between adequate rest and high scores on the *Wechsler Adult Intelligence Scale (WAIS)* (Prinz, 1977). Lack of sleep has also been correlated with an increase in accidents such as that at Three Mile Island (Adessa, 1988). Most adults regularly need 7 or 8 hours of sleep at night to stay healthy. *But sleeping habits change as one ages, and the rest received may not be adequate* (Reynolds, Mon, Hoch, Jennings, Buysee, Houck, Jarrett, & Kupfer, 1991). On the average, people over 50 sleep an hour less, and among the elderly, deep sleep generally disappears. Consequently, older adults sleep more fitfully and are more easily disturbed. Generally, the hours spent in bed are not as restful as they once were.

In addition, older adults usually wake earlier than when they were younger. One adult male in his 40s reported, "When I was younger, I used to stay in bed all morning on the weekends. Now, I can't sleep past 8 o'clock." If the adult goes to bed later than

LIVING ISSUES

Controlling Cholesterol

The best way to reduce cholesterol and saturated fat is to reduce the intake of animal fats and oils. The American Heart Association recommends a maximum of 300 mg of cholesterol daily. One medium chicken egg has 274 mg of cholesterol and 1.7 g of saturated fat. The following quantities are in a 3 oz serving of each food: Beef liver has 327 mg of cholesterol and 2.5 g of saturated fat. Of all the fish, squid has the highest cholesterol (152 mg) but only .4 g of saturated fat. There is not much difference in the amount of cholesterol in beef, pork, lamb, veal, and chicken, provided the meat is lean. But the total saturated fat content of red meat is considerably higher than that of poultry, and much higher than that of fish. Lean fish, clams, oysters, and scallops have the lowest amounts of overall cholesterol and saturated fat. Crabs, lobster, and shrimp have somewhat higher levels of cholesterol but are still very low in saturated fats. Saturated fats have been included in this discussion because they tend to raise the levels of harmful cholesterol.

The harmful cholesterol is **LDL (low-density lipoprotein).** Another type of cholesterol, known as **HDL (high-density lipoprotein),** plays a salutary role by helping to remove LDL from circulation and reducing the risk of heart disease. The higher the HDL in relation to LDL, the less risk of heart disease. Most physicians feel that a total cholesterol (LDL plus HDL) over 200 mg is too high and the person should cut back on fat and cholesterol consumption, and that a ratio of LDL to HDL ought to be 4.6 to 1 or lower.

Another way to reduce LDL is to increase the amount of fiber in the diet. Dr. Jon Story of Purdue University says, "LDL cholesterol can be reduced 20% in people with high levels just by consuming a cup of oat bran a day" (Wallis, 1984). Regular, sustained aerobic exercise is a healthy way to increase protective HDL.

usual, he or she may not get adequate sleep because of the tendency to wake up early.

INSOMNIA.   Researchers have documented at least five groups of factors that contribute to insomnia: (1) underlying biological predisposition, (2) psychological factors, (3) the use of drugs and alcohol, (4) disturbing environment and bad habits, and (5) negative conditioning (Hopson, 1986).

Some researchers believe that people can be *biologically predisposed to insomnia*. Wakefulness and sleep are controlled by two systems in the hypothalamus: an *arousal system* and a *sleep, or hypnagogic system*. Insomniacs seem to have an overly active arousal system and an underactive hypnagogic system. They are predisposed to be light sleepers and are more easily aroused. Plus, they may have various medical problems, such as physical pain, that contribute to their insomnia.

Psychological factors include a variety of emotional problems: anxiety, chronic anger, worry, or depression. Insomnia may be triggered by a variety of upsetting circumstances: death in the family or job loss. Emotional arousal causes physiological arousal that keeps people awake.

Alcohol and many other drugs are major causes of insomnia. Various stimulants, sedatives, antidepressants, thyroid drugs, contraceptives, and heart medicines may cause insomnia. Both sleeping pills and alcohol, while seeming to put one to sleep, actually lead to shallow, fragmented, disturbed sleep with shortened, abnormal REM-sleep periods and early morning awakening.

Bad sleep habits such as irregular bedtimes or awake times, frequent afternoon naps, going to bed too early, or sleeping too late in the morning, may confuse the sleeping mechanism so that insomnia results.

Negative conditioning may also cause insomnia. If a person doesn't fall asleep right away, and begins to worry and try too hard to sleep, the thought of going to bed triggers stress and fear of insomnia, which becomes a self-fulfilling prophecy.

The most effective insomnia treatment programs use a multidimensional approach, including initially a hypnotic drug to relieve the symptoms, counseling to improve sleep habits and environment, training in stress reduction and relaxation techniques, and psychology (Hopson, 1986).

Drug Abuse

PATTERNS.   Few social problems have caused more concern in recent years than drug abuse. Currently, *the greatest abusers of drugs are young adults between the ages 18 and 25*. Table 16.2 compares the use of various drugs by adults from different age groups (U.S. Bureau of the Census, 1990). The figures include the total percentages of those who ever used the drug and the percentages who used the drug within the past month.

As shown in Table 16.2, young adults 18 to 25 years of age have the greatest percentage of users in every drug category mentioned except heroin and cigarettes, which have been used by a slightly greater percentage of adults age 26 and over. Young adults also have the greatest percentage of current users (past month) in every drug category mentioned except inhalants, which are used by a slightly greater percentage of youth age 12 to 17. More than two-thirds of young adults 18 to 25 years of age report experience with an illicit substance.

DRUGS AND THE ELDERLY.   The figures cited describe the abuse of drugs for nonmedical purposes. But sometimes drugs are abused even when legally prescribed by a doctor for medical reasons. In addition, many over-the-counter drugs are taken for other reasons than intended, and in larger amounts or at more frequent intervals than prescribed.

Although national surveys show only small percentages of older persons taking drugs for nonmedical purposes, *these same*

FOCUS

Marital Happiness and Mismatched Sleep/Wake Cycles

Researchers have found that couples whose sleep/wake patterns are out of sync are more likely to have troubled marriages than couples whose patterns are similar. If one person wants to sleep while the other person reads in bed, or if one person is still sleeping while the other has been up for hours, couples report more arguments, less sex and serious conversation, and fewer shared activities. Asynchronous sleep/wake differences may be a cause or a symptom of marital problems. The two seem to be associated.

Larks and owls who are happily married are able to resolve the conflict by negotiation, by willingness to be flexible, and by compromise (Locitzer, 1989).

TABLE 16.2 Drug Use, by Type of Drug and Age Group: 1974 and 1988

Type of Drug	Percent of Persons 12–17 Years Old				Percent of Persons 18–25 Years Old				Percent of Persons 26 Years Old and Over			
	Ever Used		Current User		Ever Used		Current User		Ever Used		Current User	
	1974	1988	1974	1988	1974	1988	1974	1988	1974	1988	1974	1988
Marihuana	23.0	17.4	12.0	6.4	52.7	56.4	25.2	15.5	9.9	30.7	2.0	3.9
Inhalants	8.5	8.8	.7	2.0	9.2	12.5	(NA)	1.7	1.2	3.9	(NA)	.2
Hallucinogens	6.0	3.5	1.3	.8	16.6	13.8	2.5	1.9	1.3	6.6	(NA)	(NA)
Cocaine	3.6	3.4	1.0	1.1	12.7	19.7	3.1	4.5	.9	9.9	(NA)	.9
Heroin	1.0	.6	(NA)	(NA)	4.5	.4	(NA)	(NA)	.5	1.1	(NA)	(NA)
Analgesics[1]	(NA)	4.2	(NA)	.9	(NA)	9.4	(NA)	1.5	(NA)	4.5	(NA)	.4
Stimulants[1]	5.0	4.2	1.0	1.2	17.0	11.3	3.7	2.4	3.0	6.6	(NA)	.5
Sedatives[1]	5.0	2.4	1.0	.6	15.0	5.5	1.6	.9	2.0	3.3	(NA)	.3
Tranquilizers[1]	3.0	2.0	1.0	.2	10.0	7.8	1.6	1.0	2.0	4.6	(NA)	.6
Alcohol	54.0	50.2	34.0	25.2	81.6	90.3	69.3	65.3	73.2	88.6	54.5	54.8
Cigarettes	52.0	42.3	25.0	11.8	68.8	75.0	48.8	35.2	65.4	79.6	39.1	29.8

NA   not available. [1]Nonmedical use.

[Current users are those who used drugs at least once within month prior to this study. For **1988**, based on national samples of 8,814 respondents residing in households. Subject to sampling variability; see source]

From *Statistical Abstract of the United States* (p. 122) by U.S. Bureau of the Census, 1990, Washington, DC: U.S. Government Printing Office.

studies do indicate widespread drug abuse among the elderly who report taking them for medical reasons. These drugs are most commonly obtained through prescriptions. Or, they may be nonprescription drugs that are widely available.

The drugs most commonly prescribed for the elderly can be classified into five groups:

1. *Hypertensives and diuretics:* those used to control high blood pressure.
2. *Heart medicines:* those that act either on the heart itself or on the blood vessels.
3. *Psychotropics:* mood-altering drugs, such as tranquilizers, antidepressants, sedatives, hypnotics, or stimulants.
4. *Painkillers:* analgesics with codeine.
5. *Miscellaneous:* a variety of drugs, including antacids and antibiotics (tretracycline is one of the most popular).

Psychotropics— mood-altering drugs

The widespread use of **psychotropics** among the aged, especially among institutionalized patients, is causing concern. Either the aged in institutions have more psychological problems or develop more psychological problems while institutionalized, or the drugs are administered more for the benefit of the institutions. Certainly, too many institutions use drugs as chemical restraints in the absence of adequate help, to keep patients quiet and avoid trouble (Krupka & Vener, 1979).

All kinds of drugs are potentially more harmful for older persons than for younger persons. Older adults metabolize drugs more slowly, and because of decreased renal (kidney) and liver functions, the safety margin between therapeutic and toxic doses is considerably narrowed (Krupka & Vener, 1979). Drugs taken regularly can easily build up to toxic levels. For example, 24 hours after taking *Valium,* half the drug is still in the system. If another dose is taken at this time, the remaining Valium will escalate the action.

The greater the number of drugs taken, the greater the possibilities of adverse reactions. Some drugs are antagonistic to one another or heighten the action of other drugs.

Another factor leading to drug abuse is patients who use the services of different physicians and pharmacists. Prescriptions from several physicians may cause confusion about instructions for individual drugs. Multiple or conflicting explanations may lead to information overload, which could interfere with appropriate drug-taking behavior (Raffoul, Cooper, & Love, 1981). Many drugs the elderly abuse are nonprescription medicines bought over the counter and taken improperly. Such drugs may include *analgesics, bromides, antihistamines,* and *anticholinergics.*

Another common type of inappropriate drug use among the elderly is underuse. Some deliberately omit; others forget to take needed medication (Raffoul et al., 1981).

LIVING ISSUES

How to Stop Smoking

Recent research indicates that the only way to quit smoking is to stop completely. Cutting down doesn't work. Smokers who decide to have "just one" go right back to their former habit. One study showed that of 348 people who quit smoking on their own, 58% had relapsed by the end of the first month, 83% by year's end. One-quarter who relapsed during the first month smoked a single cigarette and then immediately resumed their previous level of smoking. About 42% reached their previous level gradually, but never abstained for more than 24 hours. About 30% experienced at least one period of more than 1 day of abstinence between their first cigarette and full resumption (Simon, 1988). The most likely candidates for quitting are those who are highly motivated to stop. Tell yourself that you can't smoke under any circumstances.

Here are some suggestions:

1. Accept the fact that if you have even so much as a puff, you're right back to smoking all over again.
2. Read all you an about the harmful effects of smoking. Look at a video on quitting smoking.
3. Use oral substitutes such as sugarless gum, mints, toothpicks, or dummy cigarettes (Bozzi, 1986).
4. Immerse yourself in activities such as sports, running, reading, working, or watching TV.

5. Don't keep any cigarettes or ashtrays or other cigarette-associated objects in the house or office. Not having them available helps you to stop. Resolve never to borrow from another smoker.
6. Join a support group or enlist in an antismoking clinic if you can't stop on your own.
7. While you're breaking the chemical dependency on nicotine, chew nicotine gum and gradually cut down on its use until you're off completely.
8. Remember that the first few weeks are the hardest. Resolve to avoid a relapse during these critical weeks. The craving will gradually subside so that not smoking becomes easier.
9. Don't use weight gain as an excuse to resume smoking. Most smokers who quit gain some weight, but do not "balloon," contrary to popular belief. Lick the smoking habit first, then deal with the weight (Meer, 1986).
10. Each week or month you abstain, reward yourself by buying something you want with the money you save by not smoking (Hall, 1986).
11. Once you've stopped, remember never to take a puff again, or you'll be right back to the habit.

SOME BODILY SYSTEMS AND THEIR FUNCTIONING

Nervous Systems

To understand what happens to various parts of the nervous systems as people grow older, let us first examine the *brain*. The largest part of the brain, the *cerebrum*, contains about 14 billion nerve cells (neurons) that are located in its outer layer (*cortex*). The cortex is associated with three major functions. The *motor cortex* coordinates voluntary movements of the body through direct action on the skeletal muscles. The *sensory cortex* is the center of perception, where changes in the environment, which are received through the senses of vision, hearing, smell, taste, touch, and pain, are interpreted. The *associational cortex* includes areas involved in cognitive functions (reasoning, abstract thinking, memory), as well as general consciousness.

As aging progresses, brain weight declines, but this is due to a decline in size of brain cells and not because of cell death. For some reason, the neurons shrink, resulting in fewer large neurons. This shrinkage may contribute to some loss of mental vigor, but normal elderly people are largely intact intellectually (Chollar, 1988).

The brain's efficiency depends primarily on the amount of blood and oxygen it receives. If **arteriosclerosis** (hardening of the arteries) occurs, or damage to the heart or vascular system diminishes the blood supply, the brain cannot work properly. If, however, the blood supply is gradually lowered, the brain reacts by growing additional and larger blood vessels. The adjustments result in an increased blood supply to the cerebral cortex during old age.

Almost all bodily functions slow down with age. As a result, people talk, read, write, walk, and jump more slowly as they get older. The most widely accepted explanation for this slowing down is that *nerve im-*

Arteriosclerosis—hardening of the arteries by a buildup of calcium in the middle muscle layer of arterial tissue, resulting in decreased elasticity

pulses are transmitted more slowly as people age. This is due primarily to an increase in the time required to transmit impulses across nerve connections (synapses) via the neurochemical transmitters. Information is also processed more slowly before appropriate impulses can be sent to areas of the body that must respond. Thus, older people become disproportionately slower than younger ones as tasks become more difficult and choices increase.

Cardiovascular System

The cardiovascular system consists of the *heart* and *blood vessels.* The heart itself is a muscular organ that works constantly throughout life. During a 70-year lifetime, the average human heart pumps about 900 million gallons of blood.

Several changes occur in the heart with age. Fat deposits form around the heart and at the entry points of the blood vessels. The number and size of heart muscles decline as muscle cells age and die. Collagen replaces more flexible tissues in valves and artery walls, causing hardening and thickening. Arterial walls become calcified, causing the arteries to dilate, lengthen, and lose elasticity. The walls of the aorta, the largest artery, become less elastic, producing a typical increase in **systolic blood pressure** (pressure produced by the heart forcing out blood). **Diastolic blood pressure** is the lower of the two blood pressure readings. It represents the pressure of the blood returning to the heart.

Changes in the heart and blood vessels cause a decline in the heart's pumping power and stroke volume (the amount of blood

If arteries become constricted, an increase in blood pressure may strain the heart and damage it.

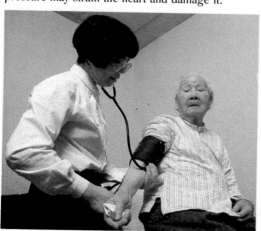

pumped out with each beat) (Kitzman & Edwards, 1990). In addition, the heartbeat rate (pulse rate) diminishes gradually. The net result is a decrease in cardiac output. From age 20 to 75, this output typically declines by only 30%. It must be emphasized, however, that cardiac output is not a function of age alone in all individuals. The described changes may not occur in the most physically fit individuals.

The heart can lose its ability to respond to stress, such as vigorous exercise (Schwartz, Gibb, & Tran, 1991). People in their 20s exhibit a greater increase in heart rate during vigorous exercise than do older persons. The younger heart can also pump more blood per heartbeat, enabling it to respond better to demands for an increased blood supply.

The health of the heart depends partially on the health of the blood vessels that transport the blood. Several types of conditions can impede the flow of blood (Mukerji, 1988). The arteries consist of three layers: a lining, a middle muscular layer, and an outer layer. In arteriosclerosis, progressive deposits of calcium in the middle muscular layer cause the arteries to become rigid (hardening of the arteries). Because they cannot expand as readily when blood is pumped through them, their cross-sectional volume is reduced.

As the arteries stiffen and peripheral resistance increases, hypertension, or elevated blood pressure, results as the heart works harder to force the blood through smaller openings. This puts additional strain on the heart and, in extreme cases, may cause enlargement of the heart and damage to it. This type of heart trouble is called **hypertensive heart disease.** In **atherosclerosis,** fatty deposits collect between the artery lining and the middle muscular layer. If these deposits break through into the artery, rough spots form on which blood may clot, reducing blood flow. When this happens in the coronary arteries, which supply the heart muscle with blood, the oxygen supply to the heart muscle is reduced (Williams & Spark, 1988). The heart struggles to get more oxygen, resulting in chest pains known as **angina pectoris** (Chun, 1988). A complete cutoff of the blood supply to any area of the heart, as with a blood clot, is called a **coronary occlusion with myocardial infarction** (heart attack). Since there are three major coronary arteries, an occlusion of one does not ordinarily cause death (12% die following a first heart attack). However, each succeeding attack becomes more risky. These types of **ischemic heart**

Systolic blood pressure

Diastolic blood pressure

Hypertensive heart disease—caused by high blood pressure

Atherosclerosis— a buildup of fatty deposits

Angina pectoris

Coronary occlusion with myocardial infarction

Ischemic heart disease

disease (that impede the flow of blood and oxygen to the heart) are the most common and serious heart diseases of the elderly.

Congestive heart failure is also common among the elderly (Benotti, 1988). Diminished cardiac output accompanied by increased blood pressure results in a buildup of fluid (**edema**) in other organs, particularly the lungs, liver, and legs. Symptoms include shortness of breath, severe discomfort when lying down, and swelling of the ankles.

Cardiac arrhythmias are irregularities in the normal heartbeat sequence (Sato, Hasegawa, Takahashi, Hirata, Shimomura, & Hotta, 1981). They can be dangerous when they alter the heart's normal contraction cycle. Irregular contractions may result in reduced pumping capacity and inadequate nourishment of the heart muscle, which leads to ischemia (inadequate oxygen supply) conditions (Vlay & Fricchione, 1987).

Heart disease is the number-one killer of the elderly. Furthermore, the incidence of heart disease increases with advancing age. However, rapid advances have been made in the treatment of heart and circulatory disorders, and the incidence of these diseases is declining (Roberts, 1988). With good medical care and proper health habits, the average older person can minimize the risks of heart problems (Harris, 1989; Krone & Hodson, 1988; Williams, 1989).

When the brain is the site of vascular disease (**cerebrovascular disease**), an accident can occur in the form of a **thrombosis** (blockage from any kind of undissolved material in the blood), an **embolism** (blockage from a blood clot), or a **hemorrhage** (a ruptured blood vessel). A **stroke** is a paralysis that occurs when the blood supply to the brain is cut off and affected brain cells die (Brackenridge, 1981). Loss of speech and paralysis commonly result, depending on the part of the brain affected. When a blockage of blood vessels to the lung occurs, **pulmonary thrombosis** results. A blockage due to a blood clot is called a **pulmonary embolism.**

Respiratory System

The respiratory system includes the *lungs* and related *air passageways*. Several significant things occur during aging to reduce lung efficiency. The rib cage and muscles become increasingly rigid, reducing the expansion and contraction capacity of the lungs. Air passageways become calcified and rigid. The result, together with changes in the rib cage, is a 55% to 60% reduction in maximum breathing capacity from 25 to 85 years of age.

Margin glossary terms

Congestive heart failure

Edema

Cardiac arrhythmias

Cerebrovascular disease

Thrombosis

Embolism

Hemorrhage

Stroke

Pulmonary thrombosis

Pulmonary embolism

Smoking is one of the greatest preventable hazards to health.

The breathing rate remains constant while breathing capacity declines. This means that the volume inhaled with each breath (**vital capacity**) declines considerably.

Vital capacity

Several other changes occur that reduce lung efficiency. The air sacs lose elasticity, hindering their ability to expand on inhalation and contract on exhalation. Furthermore, deterioration in the capillaries and air sacs reduces the effectiveness of gas exchange between the air sacs and their blood supply.

Various studies have shown that oxygen conductance in the elderly can be increased through intensive training efforts (Sidney & Shephard, 1977). Part of the improvement is due to improved blood circulation, which brings more oxygen to the lungs (Niinimaa & Shephard, 1978).

The changes just described commonly accompany aging. Various environmental factors can aggravate these changes. Long-term exposure to concentrations of air pollutants destroys the functional capability of the **alveoli** (lung cells) and capillaries. Acute respiratory distress and even death may result from such conditions. Such respiratory diseases as **tuberculosis, bronchial pneu-**

monia, and **pulmonary infections** are most frequent in persons over 65. Smoking is one of the greatest hazards. It is a principal cause of **emphysema** and of lung cancer.

Gastrointestinal System

The gastrointestinal system consists of the *mouth, esophagus, stomach, small intestine, large intestine, liver, pancreas,* and *gall bladder.*

The liver is the single most important organ in digestion. It is involved in the intermediate metabolism of all three nutrients: fats, proteins, and carbohydrates (which are reduced to sugars). It is also important in detoxifying drugs like morphine and steroids and in converting uric acid into urea, which then passes out of the body in urine.

The liver receives blood from the stomach and intestines and removes waste matter and poisons from it. It stores **glycogen** and emits it as sugar when the blood needs it. It stores vitamins A and D and those of the B-complex group, including vitamin B$_{12}$, which helps produce red blood cells and prevent **pernicious anemia**. The liver stores iron needed to produce **hemoglobin**, the red blood pigment. It also makes many blood proteins that prevent edema, provide resistance to disease, and ensure blood clotting to prevent extensive bleeding. The liver shrinks about 20% by age 75, yet half of the organ can be removed and it will still function effectively. It has remarkable power to grow new cells as needed.

The liver is subject to damage, disease, and infections. **Jaundice**, in which the skin tissues turn yellow, develops if the liver is not functioning properly. **Cirrhosis** is a condition in which the connective tissue thickens and then shrinks, causing the liver to become hard, lumpy, and shriveled. Alcohol, which irritates the liver, is a major cause of cirrhosis. Certain infections and poisons, an excess of fat, lack of protein in the diet, and lack of B-complex vitamins also can cause cirrhosis, the eighth leading cause of death among diseases of the elderly (U.S. Bureau of the Census, 1983).

Gall bladder trouble is also fairly common in old age. The gall bladder stores about 1½ ounces of **bile** at one time. It receives the bile from the liver and releases it when needed for digestion. Disease can block the bile duct and cause extreme pain. If the bile becomes highly concentrated, **gallstones** form that must be removed.

The pancreas is also important to digestion because it secretes enzymes and salts that help digest proteins, sugars, and fats. It also secretes **insulin** directly into the bloodstream. All body cells need insulin to help them use sugar (glucose), their main fuel. If the pancreas secretes too little insulin, as sometimes happens with advancing age, the cells cannot function properly. Sugar accumulates and is passed out of the body in urine. Sugar in urine is one of the primary symptoms of **diabetes mellitus**, the seventh leading cause of death among diseases of the elderly (U.S. Bureau of the Census, 1989). Cancer of the pancreas has only a 3% survival rate among those afflicted.

Older persons often complain of indigestion and gas. This may be a result of chronic inflammation of the stomach lining. This condition (**gastritis**) is also characterized by a reduced secretion of digestive juices. The incidence of stomach cancer increases with age. Although the frequency of gastric (stomach) ulcers increases in middle age, few new cases develop after age 60.

Urinary System

The urinary system includes the *kidneys,* the *bladder* (which stores the urine), the *ureters* (tubes that transport the urine from the kidneys to the bladder), and the *urethra* (excretory tube that passes urine to the outside). The overall functions of the system are to eliminate wastes from the blood, maintain the proper balance of water and salts in the body, and regulate the pH level (the measure of acidity or alkalinity) of body fluids, which should be slightly alkaline.

The kidneys filter the waste products of metabolism from the blood. They slowly lose their filtering ability and function less efficiently with advancing age. Filtration declines as much as 50% from 25 to 80 years of age, with very little change occurring before age 40 (Lindeman, 1975). However, the capacity is so great that if one kidney is removed, the other takes over completely. Therefore, most changes with age are not debilitating.

Diseases of the kidney can be serious, however, because poisons collect in the body if the kidneys function improperly. Various types of diseases and inflammations reduce kidney functioning, and if too many wastes accumulate in the blood, the result can be fatal.

The bladder's ability to store urine diminishes at advanced ages. Consequently, older people have to urinate more often. Almost one-third of adults over 65 become **incontinent**, losing bladder control, which results in bed wetting (Herzog, Diokno,

---

Glycogen—a starchlike substance stored by the liver and released when the body needs sugar

Pernicious anemia—a severe anemia with a great reduction in red blood cells

Jaundice

Cirrhosis

Gall bladder trouble—any kind of trouble that prevents the gall bladder from functioning properly; gallstones, for example

Insulin—a hormone secreted by the pancreas that regulates the blood sugar level

Diabetes mellitis—a disease characterized by excess sugar in the system due to insufficient insulin production

Gastritis—inflammation of the stomach lining

Incontinent—Unable to control passage of urine

Brown, Normolle, & Brock, 1990). This is most common after strokes and in cases of organic brain syndrome. About 3% of women and 13% of men over 65 lose all control of urination and void involuntarily. This symptom is often associated with prostate gland problems in men (Rockstein & Sussman, 1979).

Skeletal-Dental Systems

One of the most noticeable signs of advancing age is a change in stature and posture. Investigations have shown that white males lose approximately ½ inch in height every 20 years after age 30. This loss is accelerated in blacks (McPherson, Lancaster, & Carroll, 1978). It is also greater in females of both races than in males.

There are several reasons for this loss in stature. There is some loss of bone mass itself and a flattening of vertebral discs. Muscles shrink; ligaments and tendons lose elasticity, shrink, and harden. The result is a posture slump or stoop, with the head, neck, and upper torso bent forward. Accordingly, height diminishes with advancing age.

Osteoarthritis—a degenerative joint disease

One important disease that affects the skeletal systems of the elderly is **osteoarthritis** (Ehrlich, 1988). Osteoarthritis is a degenerative joint disease (Verbrugge, Kepkowski, & Konkol, 1991). It occurs in different bones, including weight- and nonweight-bearing types, but it seems more common in parts of the body bearing the greatest weight. Males seem to have the disease with greater severity than females, and blacks appear more susceptible than whites. The incidence and severity of osteoarthritis increases to the age of 80, with a striking decrease after 90. Hereditary factors may have some influence on the probability of the disease.

Rheumatoid arthritis—a chronic disease marked by painful inflammation and swelling of the small joints of the hands and wrists, and often accompanied by deformities

Rheumatoid arthritis, a second disease affecting the joints (Ehrlich, 1988), is less common than osteoarthritis. It characteristically affects the small joints of the hands and wrists, is marked by a swelling or disfigurement of the affected area, and is accompanied by a higher level of pain than most other types of arthritis. There is considerable evidence that the causes are partly psychosomatic, related to reactions to stress. At the present time, arthritis cannot be cured, but it can be managed, allowing people to function. Unfortunately, many older people seek out all kinds of quack cures that do not help (Shuman, 1980).

Years ago, women believed that they would lose at least one tooth for each child born. This often happened because nutritional demands of pregnancy and nursing depleted the mother's nutrients. Because these nutrients were not replaced through vitamin and mineral supplements, the mother's body suffered. Many older people resigned themselves to losing all their teeth by 65 and having to wear dentures. Even today, as many as 50% of people over 65 have lost all their teeth.

Without proper dental care, older people face greater dental problems.

FOCUS

Osteoporosis

Decalcification and loss of bone is called **osteoporosis**. It occurs in both sexes but is more extensive in females. Females show a 25% bone loss, as compared to a 12% loss in males, over a 30-year period. However, in the United States, black women have a lower rate of adult bone loss than do white women. In extreme cases of osteoporosis, the upper spinal vertebrae collapse, causing what is referred to in women as *dowager's hump*. The disease affects both men and women, but females are 4 times more likely to be affected with severe osteoporosis than are men (Wyshak, 1981). The wisest approach to osteoporosis is to try to prevent it through diet, hormonal supplements, exercise, and by the practice of other good health habits (Mitchell & Lyles, 1990).

Peridontal disease—a disease of the gums in which they become infected, swell, and shrink away from the teeth

Periodontal disease (formerly called pyorrhea) is a major reason for tooth loss. It is a disease in which the gums become infected, swell, and shrink away from the teeth. Tooth decay is also a significant factor in tooth loss in the elderly. Yet these diseases are not inevitable results of aging. They are primarily caused by neglect of the teeth and lack of proper dental care. Almost 70% of the elderly receive no dental care (Beck, Ettinger, Glenn, Paule, & Holtzman, 1979).

Dental health is important not only in preserving the teeth, but also in maintaining the body's health. Improperly chewed food affects digestion. People with sore gums become less interested in eating, thus receiving inadequate amounts of nutrients needed to maintain bodily health.

Reproductive System

MENOPAUSE.   **Menopause** is derived from two Greek words meaning "month" and "cessation," and it refers to the cessation of the monthly menstrual period. Common use of the term has given it a wider meaning that includes the entire period during which periodic menstrual flow stops.

Menopause—the permanent cessation of menstruation at midlife

The cessation of menstruation takes place over a period of years. The ovaries gradually atrophy, become less able to fulfill their double function of hormonal secretion and housing of egg cells. The pituitary gland continues to secrete FSH on a cyclic basis, but the ovaries are not able to respond to FSH, so ovulation ceases. The production of estrogen and progesterone gradually declines, the endometrium does not build or slough off, and the regular rhythmic cycle of menstrual bleeding gradually ceases (Cutler, Garcia, & McCoy, 1987).

Symptoms sometimes associated with menopause are hot flashes (Sherman, Wallace, Bean, Chang, & Schlabaugh, 1981), profuse perspiration, numbness or tingling of fingers and toes, headaches, dizziness, insomnia, fatigue, palpitations, weakness, gastrointestinal upset, joint pain, backaches, bladder difficulties, thickening and drying of the skin and relaxation of tissues under it, itching, and dryness of vaginal tissue causing pain during intercourse (Leiblum, Bachmann, Kemmann, Colburn, & Swartzman, 1983). There can also be nervous tensions, irritability, and depression (McCoy, Cutler, & Davidson, 1985; Schmitt, Gogate, Rothert, Rovener, Holmes, Talarcyzk, Given, & Kroll, 1991). These symptoms can also develop and exist independently of the hormonal imbalance characteristic of menopausal changes, so that they may not be due to menopause per se but become manifest at the age when menopause commonly occurs and are precipitated by other life events (King, 1989).

About 75% of menopausal women do not exhibit these symptoms at all (Goodman, Stewart, & Gilbert, 1977). Therefore, the symptoms are not inevitable results of the change. Neither are abnormal physiological conditions associated with the menopausal state per se. Menopause is neither a disorder nor a disease, but simply a normal change (Patterson & Lynch, 1988; Ritz, 1981). Almost one-half of all women having a natural menopause do so by 49.76 years of age. One hundred percent have gone through menopause by age 58.

MALE CLIMACTERIC.   The **climacteric,** derived from a Greek word meaning "rung of a ladder," implies the passage from one stage of life to another, and so can apply to any period of life. When applied to a man's middle years, it refers to the many changes he experiences during this period. The decline in reproductive function in the male is generally a gradual process. Sperm cells constantly replenish themselves from puberty to old age. Consequently, *reproduction is often possible into extreme old age.* Men as old as 94 have fathered children. About half of all men between 80 and 90 have viable sperm in their semen (Talbert, 1977).

Testosterone secretion decreases in some elderly men. The level remains constant until about age 60, after which it declines (Vermeulen, Rubens, & Verdonck, 1972). This may cause some decline in sexual drive and erectile ability; however, wide individual variations exist. Testosterone levels in some 80- and 90-year-olds are in the high-normal range. Levels fluctuate over a period of time, ranging from 3 to 30 days (Parlee, 1978). The male climacteric is sometimes associated with depression, anxiety, headache, insomnia, irritability, tremors, palpitations, and digestive and urinary disturbances. Many of the reactions men have toward aging are psychological.

Climacteric—often, a man's midlife changes; also, menopause or changes marking the transition from one stage of life to another

THE SENSES AND PERCEPTION

Visual Acuity

Visual acuity, the ability to perceive small details, reaches a maximum around age 20 and remains relatively constant to 40 (Sekuler & Blake, 1987). It then begins to decline. Al-

Visual acuity

Although most older people need eyeglasses, about 70% have fair to adequate visual acuity.

though most older people need eyeglasses, about 70% have fair to adequate visual acuity to age 80 and beyond.

Presbyopia

Accommodation

There are various kinds of visual impairments. One of the most common is **presbyopia** (farsightedness). As the lens becomes less elastic, it begins to lose some power of **accommodation** (the power to focus so that distinct vision is assured at both near and far distances). Accommodation declines from age 6 to 60, after which it levels off until extreme old age. Farsighted adults must wear corrective glasses for reading, writing, knitting, or other close work.

Adaptation—ability of the eye to adjust to different intensities of light

Another common problem is a decrease in pupil size, allowing less light to reach the retina (Shore, 1976). The pupil also declines in ability to open and close with changes in light intensity (loss of **adaptation**). This ability decreases linearly from age 20 to age 60. As a result, older people have difficulty seeing at night or in dimly lit places. At the same time, glare in intense light is a problem because the eye cannot close enough to block out the excess. **Peripheral vision,** or ability to see toward the sides when looking straight ahead, also begins to show meaningful decrements when people reach their 50s and 60s. Color vision is also affected by age. The lens gradually yellows and filters out the violet, blue, and green colors toward the dark end of the spectrum (Jacobs and Krohn, 1976). For this reason, older people see yellow, orange, and red colors more easily than darker colors.

Peripheral vision—ability to see objects to either side of the line of sight in front of one's face

Cataracts

Glaucoma

A number of diseases affect vision in old age. Among these are **cataracts** (clouding of the lenses); **glaucoma** (loss of vision from excess pressure inside the eyes); and **macular diseases** (of the retina) and damage to the cornea.

Macular diseases

Hearing Acuity

Hearing ability reaches its maximum around age 20. Hearing impairment associated with advancing age is called **presbycusis** (Sekuler & Blake, 1987). Usually, hearing loss occurs gradually from childhood on, with severe loss occurring first in the ability to hear high-pitched sounds (Potash & Jones, 1977). A 10-year-old, for example, can hear high-pitched sounds with upper frequencies of almost 20,000 cycles per second (Hz). But at 65, persons hear sound only up to about 8,000 Hz. They have more difficulty hearing high-pitched voices and perceiving certain high-frequency consonants, such as *z, s, g, f,* and *t*. The elderly person may hear *ave* instead of *save, ame* instead of *game, alk* instead of *talk,* or *pa* instead of *pat*. Such words as *gaze, first, stop,* or *grass,* with two or more high-frequency consonants, may not be understood at all (Sataloff & Vassallo, 1966).

Presbycusis—hearing impairment associated with advancing age

A noticeable decline begins in the 50s, and by 70 there is a loss in hearing at all frequencies, even those below 1,000 Hz (Bergman, Blumenfeld, Cascardo, Dash, Levitt, & Margulies, 1976). After 55, men show a greater incidence of hearing loss than do women. However, when speech is clear, undistorted, and presented without competing noise, most older subjects suffer very little loss in ability to understand (Warren, Wagener, & Herman, 1978). Distorted and noise-masked speech is difficult for many older people to decipher. Shouting at them usually does not help, because this involves raising the voice to higher pitches. Fortunately, some hearing problems are treatable or correctable. Approximately 10% of all hearing losses can be helped medically or surgically. Most of the remaining 90% can be helped with amplification: through the use of hearing aids. Most important, many hearing problems are preventable by avoiding overexposure to loud noises.

Taste and Smell

Eating is such an important part of our physical and social lives that any change in the ability to taste various foods is significant. Evidence indicates that the ability to perceive all four taste qualities—sweet, salt, bitter, and sour—declines in later life, although the decrement is small (Shore, 1976). Actually, taste buds continually replace themselves, but taste sensitivity shows some decline

FOCUS

New Hearing Aids

Different models of hearing aids are available for different types of loss. For mild to moderate losses, *All-in-ear (AIE)* aids are used. These are customized to fit inside the wearer's ear, with the microphone, speaker, and amplifier all in the case that is inside the ear. So-called *low-profile aids* have the same cases as regular AIE aids, but have inset face plates so that the microphone, battery cover, and volume control are recessed. Another variation is *canal aids*, which fit in the small shaped space at the beginning of the ear canal. They are the least visible of any aids. Nearly 60% of all aids recommended today are either AIE or canal aids.

Behind-the-ear (BTE) aids are designed to correct moderate to profound losses. The aid fits comfortably behind the ear and is attached by a tube to a custom earmold that carries the sound to the aid. Many can be modified with connections to external sound sources such as television.

A third type of aids are *body aids*, which consist of a pocket-size battery pack and amplifier attached to the earmold by a cord worn under clothing. They are used to assist individuals with severe to profound hearing losses.

An older type of aid was used with *eyeglasses* in which the parts of the aid were contained in the earpieces of the eyeglasses. Today body aids and eyeglass aids are used by only 2% of all subjects with losses that can be treated with amplification.

Some persons wear two hearing aids, one in each ear, and find much more satisfactory results than with wearing only one. *T-coils* can be put on some hearing aids; these pick up magnetic forces from some telephones and enable the wearer to hear better when talking over the phone. Other devices can be used to amplify directly the telephone signal.

(Weiffenbach, Tylenda, & Baum, 1990); the number of taste buds is not as crucial as are their responsiveness and ability to transmit taste sensations through the neurons to the brain (Moore, Nielsen, & Mistretta, 1982).

The taste for sweet and salty flavors declines faster than that for bitter and sour (Moore, Nielsen, & Mistretta, 1982). As a result, older people complain that their food tastes bitter and sour. Or, they require more highly seasoned food to experience the same taste satisfactions they had when younger (Sekuler & Blake, 1987).

Tactile Sensitivity: Touch, Temperature, and Pain

Tactile acuity—sensitivity of touch

Research reveals some decrease in **tactile acuity** with increasing age, but the loss is small, and a number of individuals over 60 retain high sensitivity. Temperature and pain sensitivity are impaired in only a small percentage of the elderly.

Thermoregulation

Thermoregulation—maintenance of correct body temperature during exposure to heat or cold

Thermoregulation is the maintenance of body temperature during exposure to heat or cold. Body temperature is usually regulated within narrow limits. Experiments have shown that young adults can regulate body heat under adverse temperature conditions, whereas older adults show significant

changes in body temperature. This is why older adults suffer more in extremes of hot or cold.

Sense of Balance

Hairlike projections in the inner ear that are activated by the flow of fluids as the body changes positions act as sensory perceptors that pick up and pass on information to the brain about body positions and orientations that constitute our sense of balance. A maximum sense of balance is achieved between 40 and 50, followed by decline. One consequence is that older people tend to fall more often. We are not certain exactly why balance declines. Inner ear tissues may deteriorate with age, but not always. Possibly a diminishing blood supply causes dizziness. Declines in nervous reflexes, psychomotor coordination, and muscular strength are undoubtedly factors. Or, failing eyesight and improper illumination may cause older adults to have more accidents.

BIOLOGICAL AGING

Senescence

Senescence is the term biologists, gerontologists, and others use to describe biological aging. It should not be confused with *senility*, which is a disease. Disease is not inevitable

Senescence—biological aging

as people age. Senescence describes the processes that lead to a decline in the viability of the human organism and increase its vulnerability. There is no known animal species whose individual members do not age. However, rates of senescence for most species vary from individual to individual. These individual variations increase with chronological age. Some persons exhibit traits similar to those chronologically older or younger than themselves (Borkan & Norris, 1980). Furthermore, senescence is not one process but many, with decline occurring in different parts of the body at different rates.

Theories of Biological Aging

Exactly why physical aging occurs has been the subject of much investigation and discussion. Do people have to age? Under ideal conditions, could they stay young forever? Or, does a built-in time clock control longevity, so that living much beyond an allotted time is impossible? There are no answers, but a number of different theories have attempted to explain the causes of physical aging.

HEREDITY THEORY.   The most obvious explanation is that the theoretical length of life is hereditary. The life span of a species is set by genetic characteristics that have evolved over countless years. Thus, each species has its own life expectancy. Elephants may live 60 years, hippopotamuses 50, and primates reach or exceed 30 years. Heredity also plays an important role in human longevity, so that children whose parents and grandparents are long lived may also live longer. Apparently, they inherit certain traits (e.g., increased resistance to disease) that contribute to a longer life.

CELLULAR AGING THEORY.   Some cells in the body, such as those in the brain and nervous system, never reproduce. Other cells reproduce, but only a finite number of times. Hayflick (1970) studied the aging of living cells maintained in cultures. He found that lung tissues, for example, multiply rapidly, at first doubling every 24 hours. But as the process progresses, the length of time between doublings increases; after about 50 doublings (about 6 months), the cells fail to double and start to die. Other cells of the body double fewer times. This fact suggests that aging is programmed by the limited capacity of cells to replace themselves (Lockshin & Zakeri, 1990).

WEAR-AND-TEAR THEORY.   The wear-and-tear theory emphasizes that the organism simply wears out, like a machine that has run for too many years. Metabolic rate seems to be a factor. Modestly underfed animals (including humans), or cold-blooded animals living at lower than normal temperatures, tend to live longer because metabolism slows down.

METABOLIC WASTE OR CLINKER THEORY.   The metabolic waste or clinker theory suggests that aging is caused by the accumulation of deleterious substances (by-products of cellular metabolism) within various cells of the body. The accumulation of these substances interferes with the normal tissue functioning. One such substance is collagen, a fibrous protein associated with connective tissue. It builds up slowly in most organs, tendons, skin, and blood vessels, and is eliminated gradually, if at all. It also stiffens with age. Therefore, tissues containing collagen lose elasticity, causing deterioration in organ functions.

AUTOIMMUNITY THEORY.   The autoimmunity theory of aging describes the process by which the body's immune system rejects its own tissues through the production of autoimmune antibodies. When foreign substances enter the body, it produces antibodies to neutralize their effects. The response to invasion is called an immune reaction. When antibodies respond to mutations within the body, their response is an autoimmune reaction. The net result is self-destruction. This promising theory may lead to the discovery of methods that retard this action and modify the aging process.

HOMEOSTATIC IMBALANCE THEORY.   The homeostatic imbalance theory emphasizes the gradual inability of the body to maintain vital physiologic balances. For example, the body gradually loses its ability to maintain the proper temperature during exposure to heat or cold; similarly, it loses its ability to maintain the proper blood sugar level. Older people have difficulty adapting to emotional stress. This is why many older persons die soon after their spouses. This loss of efficiency of the physiologic response to stress is perhaps the most general theory of aging and provides the closest link between the physiological, social, and psychological aspects of aging.

MUTATION THEORY.   The mutation theory describes what happens when more and more body cells develop mutations. Rates of genetic mutation increase with age. One cause is radiation, which damages the genetic material and shortens the organ's life span in direct proportion to the amount of genetic damage incurred. Cell functioning is controlled by the genetic material DNA (deoxyribonucleic acid), which is found in each cell. When mutations occur in DNA, subsequent cell divisions replicate them, and an appreciable percentage of an organ's cells become mutated. Since most mutations are harmful, mutated cells function less efficiently, and the organs made up of these cells become inefficient and senescent.

ERROR THEORY.   The error theory is a variation of the mutation theory. The error theory includes the cumulative effects of a variety of mistakes that may occur; mistakes in RNA (ribonucleic acid) production, which affect enzymic synthesis, which affects protein synthesis, and so on. Research indicates a loss of DNA from the cells of aging animals, which impairs the production of RNA and DNA. This, in turn, impairs cell functioning and eventually leads to cellular death (Johnson & Strehler, 1972).

WHICH THEORY?   No single theory proposed to date adequately explains the complex events that occur in aging. Aging involves a number of processes that produce time-dependent changes in an organism. In addition to hereditary factors and intrinsic changes (those occurring from within), environmental stresses, bacteria, viruses, and other influences affect the organism from without, sometimes modifying and reducing the abilities of various organs to continue functioning.

PROLONGEVITY

Possibilities

Longevity refers to the duration of life, usually implying a long or extended life. The term *prolongevity* was introduced in 1966 by Gerald J. Gruman, a physician and historian, to describe deliberate efforts to extend the length of life by human action (Gruman, 1966). Some prolongevitists have been optimistic in their predictions. They assert that the problems of death and aging can be overcome, virtually removing limits on the length of human life. More conservative prolongevitists have proposed a more limited increase in the length of life: usually to age 100 or over. They look forward to breaking the 110-year limit,

Mary E. Jones was a prolongevitist who lived to be 103 years old.

which is a formidable barrier. Dr. Roy Walford, professor of pathology at UCLA's medical school, asserts that by the end of this century we may be able to retard the rate of aging so people will live to be 100 years of age or more ("How People Will Live to be 100 or More," 1983).

Implications

The goal of prolongevitists is not simply to increase the maximum life span, but to retard both disease and the aging process. If people were physically young and healthy, even though advanced in years, heart disease, cancer, and diabetes would practically be eliminated. Instead of being sick, disabled, and dependent, people would have their health and vigor for years and live active, useful lives (Rothenberg, Lentzener, & Parker, 1991).

Equally important, the wisdom and experience amassed by the young-old could be used to solve societal problems and create a better life for all. There is no telling what a person might become or achieve given a significant number of extra years. Those who live a long time can not only learn more, but can also synthesize their learning in new ways to create new systems of thought and ideas. If the lives of some of the world's geniuses were prolonged, what might they achieve?

FOCUS

Facts on Aging. A Short Quiz

The following quiz by Erdman Palmore (1977) is designed to cover the basic physical, mental, and social facts and the most common misconceptions about aging. Take the quiz to find out those facts you may be unaware of. Circle T for true or F for false.

T F   1. The majority of old people (past age 65) are senile (i.e., defective memory, disoriented, or demented).

T F   2. All five senses tend to decline in old age.

T F   3. Most old people have no interest in, or capacity for, sexual relations.

T F   4. Lung capacity tends to decline in old age.

T F   5. The majority of old people feel miserable most of the time.

T F   6. Physical strength tends to decline in old age.

T F   7. At least one-tenth of the aged are living in long-stay institutions (i.e., nursing homes, mental hospitals, homes for the aged, etc.).

T F   8. Aged drivers have fewer accidents per person than drivers under age 65.

T F   9. Most older workers cannot work as effectively as younger workers.

T F 10. About 80% of the aged are healthy enough to carry out their normal activities.

T F 11. Most old people are set in their ways and unable to change.

T F 12. Old people usually take longer to learn something new.

T F 13. It is almost impossible for most old people to learn new things.

T F 14. The reaction time of most old people tends to be slower than reaction time of younger people.

T F 15. In general, most old people are pretty much alike.

T F 16. The majority of old people are seldom bored.

T F 17. The majority of old people are socially isolated and lonely.

T F 18. Older workers have fewer accidents than younger workers.

T F 19. Over 15% of the U.S. population are now age 65 or over.

T F 20. Most medical practitioners tend to give low priority to the aged.

T F 21. The majority of older people have incomes below the poverty level (as defined by the federal government).

T F 22. The majority of old people are working or would like to have some kind of work to do (including housework and volunteer work).

T F 23. Older people tend to become more religious as they age.

T F 24. The majority of old people are seldom irritated or angry.

T F 25. The health and socioeconomic status of older people (compared to younger people) in the year 2000 will probably be about the same as now.

Key: Odd-numbered items are false; even-numbered are true.

SUMMARY

1. During the mid-20s the human body is at the peak of its physical development, but at the same time, aging is already taking place.

2. Self-consciousness about one's changing physique is accentuated by society's attitudes that equate attractiveness with youthfulness.

3. Ageism is prejudice and discrimination against the elderly, which is so widely reflected in advertising, professional attitudes, television, humorous greeting cards, and poetry.

4. Since some people age more rapidly than others, the important emphasis should be on functional age, not chronological age.

5. Functional age is reflected in reaction time, motor ability, coordination, dexterity, strength, and endurance and fatigue.

6. Exercise is one of the best ways to prevent ill health and maintain body fitness, but about half of 20- to 39-year-old adults, and less than half of adults 45 to 64, engage in any form of exercise at least weekly.

7. Pulse rate is one of the simplest measures of health and physical fitness. It should be monitored during exercise so that the target rate is reached and maintained for periods of 15 to 30 minutes.

8. Proper nutrition is another important factor in maintaining good health. Older

adults need diets with greater nutrient density in proportion to the number of calories consumed. Weight gain occurs because fewer basal and activity calories are burned up in relation to those eaten.

9. Adults require diets low in saturated fats and cholesterol, sodium, and sugar.

10. Adequate amounts of sleep and rest maximize healthful functioning, but sleep patterns change with age, and some older adults do not get adequate rest.

11. There are 5 groups of factors that contribute to insomnia: biological, psychological, drugs and alcohol, disturbing environment and bad habits, and negative conditioning. The most effective insomnia treatments utilize a multidimensional approach.

12. Drug abuse is highest in young adults ages 18 to 25.

13. Many elderly abuse drugs that are prescribed for them for medical purposes. The elderly are especially susceptible to drugs because their bodies do not metabolize them readily and the drugs remain in their system. Also, the greater the number of drugs taken, the greater the possibility of adverse reactions as the drugs interact with one another.

14. Research has revealed that the only effective way to quit smoking is to give it up entirely, rather than trying to cut down.

15. As aging progresses, brain weight declines, arteriosclerosis may cut down on the blood supply, and nerve impulses are transmitted more slowly.

16. Significant changes may occur in the heart and blood vessels with age. The following cardiovascular and heart diseases are common: atherosclerosis, coronary occlusion with myocardial infarction, congestive heart failure, and cardiac arrhythmias. Heart disease is the number-one killer of the elderly.

17. Other vascular diseases include thrombosis, embolism, hemorrhage, and stroke. When the brain is the site of the vascular disease, it is called cerebrovascular. When the lung is the site, it is called a pulmonary thrombosis or pulmonary embolism.

18. Changes in the respiratory system with age include a decline in vital capacity of the lungs, and lower efficiency in air exchange and oxygen conductance. Important respiratory diseases include tuberculosis, bronchial pneumonia, emphysema, pulmonary infections, and lung cancer.

19. The liver is the most important organ in digestion, since it removes waste matter from the blood; stores glycogen and makes sugar available as needed; stores vitamins and iron; and makes many blood proteins that prevent edema, resist disease, and ensure blood clotting.

20. Jaundice, in which the skin tissues turn yellow, occurs when the liver is not functioning properly. Cirrhosis of the liver is the eighth leading cause of death among the elderly.

21. The gall bladder stores bile and releases it as needed for digestion. Gallstones form when the bile duct becomes blocked.

22. Diabetes mellitus occurs when the pancreas does not secrete enough insulin to regulate the sugar level in the blood. Diabetes is the seventh leading cause of death among diseases of the elderly.

23. Gastritis is a chronic inflammation of the stomach lining causing indigestion and gas.

24. The urinary system includes the kidneys, bladder, ureters, and urethra. The kidneys filter the waste products of metabolism. Since the body can live with one kidney, most changes in age are not debilitating, although various diseases reduce kidney functioning.

25. The bladder's ability to store and hold urine diminishes at advanced ages. One-third of adults over 65 become incontinent.

26. Common diseases of the skeletal system include osteoarthritis, rheumatoid arthritis, and osteoporosis.

27. Periodontal disease of the gums and tooth decay, along with neglect of the teeth, cause many elderly to lose some or all of their teeth.

28. Menopause is cessation of menstruation as the ovaries gradually atrophy and become less able to secrete hormones and develop egg cells. The median age of natural menopause is 49.76 years. About 75% of women do not exhibit the common symptoms of menopause.

29. The male climacteric is primarily psychological although the secretion of testosterone declines very slowly in some men as they age.

30. With age, changes occur in visual acuity, loss of accommodation, adaptation, and peripheral vision. Common diseases of the eye that affect vision are cataracts, glaucoma, macular diseases, and damage to the cornea.

31. Hearing acuity declines with age, especially in relation to high-pitched sounds. Ninety percent of losses can be corrected by amplification, by wearing a hearing aid.

32. Ability to taste declines somewhat with age, though the taste for sweet and salty flavors declines faster than that for bitter and sour.

33. Tactile acuity and temperature and pain sensitivity are impaired in only a small percentage of the elderly. Thermoregulation declines, as does the sense of balance.

34. Senescence refers to biological aging. Rates vary from individual to individual, with decline occurring in different parts of the body at various rates.

35. The principal theories of biological aging include the following: heredity theory, cellular aging theory, wear-and-tear theory, metabolic waste or clinker theory, autoimmunity theory, homeostatic imbalance theory, mutation theory, and error theory. No single theory adequately explains the complex events that occur in aging.

36. Longevity refers to the duration of life; prolongevity to efforts to extend the length of life. The goal is not simply to maximize the life span, but to retard the aging process itself.

KEY TERMS

Accommodation   *p. 364*
Activity calories   *p. 354*
Adaptation   *p. 364*
Ageism   *p. 349*
Alveoli   *p. 360*
Angina pectoris   *p. 359*
Arteriosclerosis   *p. 358*
Atherosclerosis   *p. 359*
Basal calories   *p. 354*
Bile   *p. 361*
Bronchial pneumonia   *p. 360*
Cardiac arrhythmias   *p. 360*
Cataracts   *p. 364*
Cerebrovascular disease   *p. 360*
Cholesterol   *p. 354*
Cirrhosis   *p. 361*
Climacteric   *p. 363*
Congestive heart failure   *p. 360*
Coronary occlusion with myocardial infarction   *p. 359*
Diabetes mellitus   *p. 361*
Diastolic blood pressure   *p. 359*
Edema   *p. 360*
Embolism   *p. 360*
Emphysema   *p. 361*
Functional age   *p. 350*
Gall bladder trouble   *p. 361*
Gallstones   *p. 361*
Gastritis   *p. 361*
Glaucoma   *p. 364*
Glycogen   *p. 361*
HDL (high-density lipoprotein)   *p. 355*
Hemoglobin   *p. 361*
Hemorrhage   *p. 360*

Hypertensive heart disease   *p. 359*
Incontinent   *p. 361*
Insulin   *p. 361*
Ischemic heart disease   *p. 359*
Jaundice   *p. 361*
LDL (low-density lipoprotein)   *p. 355*
Macular diseases   *p. 364*
Menopause   *p. 363*
Motor ability   *p. 351*
Nutrient density   *p. 354*
Osteoarthritis   *p. 362*
Osteoporosis   *p. 362*
Periodontal disease   *p. 363*
Peripheral vision   *p. 364*
Pernicious anemia   *p. 361*
Presbycusis   *p. 364*
Presbyopia   *p. 364*
Psychotropics   *p. 357*
Pulmonary embolism   *p. 360*
Pulmonary infections   *p. 361*
Pulmonary thrombosis   *p. 360*
Pulse rate   *p. 353*
Reaction time   *p. 350*
Rheumatoid arthritis   *p. 362*
Saturated fats   *p. 354*
Senescence   *p. 365*
Stroke   *p. 360*
Systolic blood pressure   *p. 359*
Tactile acuity   *p. 365*
Thermoregulation   *p. 365*
Thrombosis   *p. 360*
Tuberculosis   *p. 360*
Visual acuity   *p. 363*
Vital capacity   *p. 360*

DISCUSSION QUESTIONS

1. How do you feel about the aged? About getting old? Why does society equate worth with youthfulness? What evidence do you see of ageism in our society?

2. What can be done to change negative

feelings toward the elderly? What can the elderly do to help?

3. What factors do you feel are most important in maintaining physical fitness and health? What do you do to stay healthy? What habits do you have that are detrimental to your health?

4. What sort of exercise do you engage in? For what reasons? With what results?

5. What factors are important to you in maintaining proper nutrition? What factors prevent you from getting an adequate diet? Have you tried the liquid diets? What do you think of them? What factors have been most helpful to you in losing weight?

6. What drugs are abused most frequently among adults you know? Have you ever had serious problems with drug abuse? What happened and what did you do?

7. What factors helped you the most in stopping smoking? What factors prevent you from stopping smoking?

8. Have any members of your family had cardiovascular diseases, heart attacks, or brain disorders? Describe.

9. Do you know anyone who now has or has had tuberculosis? Lung cancer? Bronchial pneumonia? Emphysema? Describe.

10. Does any member of your family have liver disease? Cirrhosis of the liver? Gall bladder trouble? Diabetes? Stomach cancer? Describe.

11. Does any member of your family have kidney, bladder, or bowel problems? Describe. What can be done to help elderly people who are incontinent?

12. Does any member of your family have arthritis? osteoporosis? What can be done?

13. Is your mother or any female member of your family going through menopause? Describe. Is your father or any male member of your family going through a male climacteric?

14. Does any member of your family have problems with one or more of the following senses: vision, hearing, taste, smell, tactile sensitivity, thermoregulation, or sense of balance? Describe the condition, its consequences, and what is being done or can be done about it.

15. Of the various theories of aging, which ones have the greatest validity? Explain.

16. What do you think of trying to prolong the length and quality of life and of trying to delay the aging process? What are some of the implications of people living to be over 100 years old?

SUGGESTED READINGS

Boston Women's Health Book Collective. (1987). *Ourselves, growing older.* New York: Simon and Schuster. Women's health in middle and old age.

Brecher, E. M. (1984). *Love, sex, and aging.* Boston: Little, Brown. A Consumer's Union Report.

Carroll, C., & Miller, D. (1986). *Health: The science of human adaptation.* Dubuque, IA: Wm. C. Brown. College-level text.

Cooper, R. K. (1989). *Health and physical fitness excellence.* Boston: Houghton Mifflin. Stress, exercise, nutrition, fat control, wellness.

Coopers, K. H. (1988). *Controlling cholesterol.* New York: Bantam Books. An important book on this subject.

Fries, J., & Crapo, L. (1981). *Vitality and aging.* San Francisco: Freeman. Postponement of disease and death so people can live a vital life.

Gershoff, S. (1990). *The Tufts University guide to total nutrition.* New York: Harper and Row. An authoritative guide on all aspects of nutrition.

Kunz, J. R. M., & Finkel, A. J. (1987). *The American Medical Association family medical guide.* New York: Random House. Basic medical guide for the whole family.

Logue, A. W. (1986). *The psychology of eating and drinking.* New York: W. H. Freeman. Eating behavior, obesity, and weight loss.

Ostrow, A. C. (1984). *Physical activity and the older adult: Psychological perspectives.* Princeton, NJ: Princeton Book Co. Physical changes with age and need for exercise.

Rice, F. P. (1986). *Adult development and aging.* Boston: Allyn and Bacon. Basic college textbook by the author.

Spence A. P. (1989). *Biology of human aging.* Englewood Cliffs, NJ: Prentice-Hall. Theories plus changes in the bodily systems.

17

Cognitive Development

COGNITIVE DEVELOPMENT

Formal Operational Thinking

As discussed in Chapter 12, the achievement of formal operational thinking means the individual has developed the ability to engage in four distinct thought processes: (1) introspection (to think about thought); (2) abstract thinking (to go beyond the real to what is possible); (3) logical thinking (to gather facts and ideas to form correct conclusions); and (4) hypothetical reasoning (to formulate hypotheses and examine the truth of them considering numerous variables). According to Piaget (1972), the ability develops during adolescence from approximately age 11 to 15, although Piaget admits that the appearance of formal operations may be delayed until 15 to 20 years of age, and in disadvantaged conditions, may never take shape. According to other research using advanced criteria (Kuhn, 1979), *approximately half of the adult population may never attain the full stage of formal thinking.*

Some adults are able to use formal operational thinking in their particular field of specialization, but not in other fields. DeLisi and Staudt (1980) found that physics students could solve the pendulum problem easily, but had trouble in political-socialization tasks or in literary-styles tasks. English majors were successful in applying formal operations only in the literary-styles tasks. The years of formal education, intelligence level,

and numerous cultural factors also influence the development of formal operational thinking (Blackburn, 1984). Brodzinsky (1985) and Neimark (1981) suggested that cognitive style affects the ability to do well on Piagetian-type tasks. *Reflective people*, who are cautious and systematic in problem solving, and **field-independent people**, who can sort out relevant from irrelevant information, do well in such tasks, whereas those who are *impulsive* or who are **field-dependent** (who have trouble isolating the relevant information in solving a problem) do relatively poorly on Piagetian-type tasks.

There is some evidence that older adults approach problems at a lower level of abstraction than do adolescents or younger adults (Johnson, 1990). Hartley (1981) tested four age groups of adults on their abilities to solve a problem requiring deductive reasoning, or drawing specific conclusions from a premise. The younger adults (mean age 20) were enrolled in college. The middle-aged adults (mean age 41.4) were college graduates. The younger group of older adults (mean age 65.4) were also college graduates. The older, community-dwelling adults (mean age 71.5) had an average of 14.33 years of education. Figure 17.1 shows that a significantly smaller percentage of those in the older two adult groups were able to solve the problem. The older nonsolvers were less able to separate relevant from irrelevant information; they based solutions on hunches rather than on available evidence, processed information on only one dimension at a time, and generally showed a reduced ability to do formal operational thinking.

Other researchers generally find that *older adults do poorly on measures of formal reasoning ability, but this is because they approach problems differently* (Newman & Newman, 1983). Older adults tend to be more pragmatic, more attuned to social and economic realities (Labouvie-Vief (1985, 1986), so abstract questions don't seem meaningful or important. Older people tend to ignore some things as unimportant (Meer, 1986). They also tend to personalize learning tasks (Datan, Rodeheaver, & Hughes, 1987). Instead of applying logico-deductive methods, they rely more on subjective, intuitive thinking (Hartley & Anderson, 1983). Labouvie-Vief (1986) insisted that this is not inferior to formal logic; it is just different. She found that when older people are asked to summarize fables they have read, they excel at recalling the metaphorical meaning, whereas college students try to remember the precise text.

Field-independent people—people who sort out relevant from irrelevant information in solving problems

Field-dependent people—people who have trouble isolating relevant information in solving problems

About half of all adults are able to do formal operational thinking.

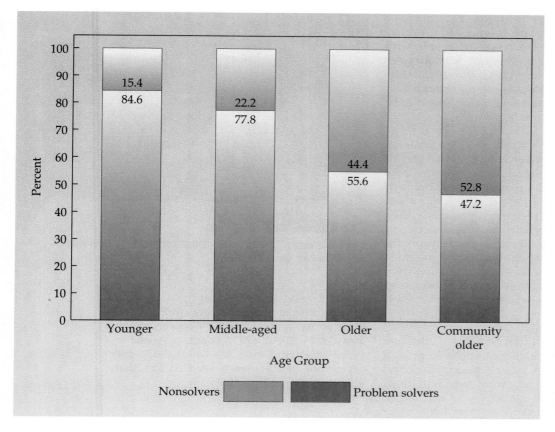

FIGURE 17.1   Percentage of
problem solvers as a function of
age group.

Adapted from "Adult Age Differences in
Deductive Reasoning Processes" by
A. A. Hartley, 1981, *Journal of
Gerontology, 36*, pp. 700–706.
Reprinted by permission.

Practical Problem-Solving Abilities

When adults over 65 were asked how they thought their abilities to reason, think, and solve problems had changed throughout their adult lives, 76% thought their abilities had increased with age, 20% reported no change, and only 4% reported that their abilities had declined with age (Williams, Denney, & Schadler, 1980). But these people were talking about practical problems of everyday living, not about abstract reasoning problems traditionally used in laboratory experiments.

Denney and Palmer (1981) found a diminution with age in capacity to do abstract problems but an improvement in ability to solve practical problems that might actually be encountered. They presented two types of problem-solving tasks to adults between 20 and 79 years of age. The first task was a 20 questions type of test typically used in problem-solving research. The test results showed that such ability peaked in the late 20s. The second task was designed to measure the ability to solve problems presented in real-life situations. The test results showed that the ability to solve practical problems increased during early adulthood and did not peak until the late 40s. The researchers cautioned that this was a cross-sectional study, so one must be careful about drawing strong conclusions with reference to age. Because cross-sectional studies usually overemphasize decline with age, the fact that the ability to solve practical problems actually increased is even more significant.

Other problem-solving research shows similar results. *Young adults do not appear to be solving the practical problems of everyday living as efficiently as older adults.* Problem-solving abilities may also be improved with training (Denney, 1980).

Comprehension

WORD FAMILIARITY.   A number of studies have been conducted to determine age-related abilities of adults to comprehend linguistic meanings of individual words, sentences, or paragraphs (Emery & Breslau, 1989). *Tests of word familiarity have shown that adults generally show performance improvement* to ages 50 through 59 (mean age 55), after which scores decline (Monge & Gardner, 1972). However, the scores of people with high education (above high school) were never as low as the scores of those with low education (high school or less), regardless of age. Thus, educational level was found to be more important than age itself.

SENTENCE COMPREHENSION.   Sentence comprehension research has revealed that *the ability to comprehend relativized sentences (complex sentences with a number of relative clauses) remains stable until the 60s, after which ability declines with age* (Feier & Gerstman, 1980). However, comprehension of sentences presented auditorily depends partially on the rate of presentation. Material presented either too rapidly or too slowly is not comprehended as readily as material presented at a normal rate (Schmitt & McCroskey, 1981).

PROSE   COMPREHENSION.   Belmore (1981) tested the ability of adults to process and comprehend linguistic meanings of short prose passages they were asked to read. *Older adults (mean age 66.5) were able to comprehend the meanings almost as well as younger adults (mean age 18.3).* The older subjects were correct on 83% of the trials, the younger subjects on 91% of the trials. However, when testing for levels of comprehension was delayed, older adults showed impairment in retaining the information over a period of time. They comprehended almost as well initially,

One advantage of getting older is that people develop pragmatic knowledge we call wisdom.

but they could not remember the material as long as the younger subjects could. In another study, both young (18–33 years of age) and old (65–80) adults were able to recall narrative passages better than expository passages, but older subjects recalled less than young subjects (Tun, 1989).

Wisdom

One of the advantages of getting older is that people develop pragmatic knowledge we call wisdom (Luszki & Luszki, 1985). Wisdom goes beyond book learning and factual knowledge. It involves the accumulation of a lifetime of expertise in dealing with life tasks, managing situations, and solving problems. Wisdom involves using sound judgment in the conduct of life. Wisdom is developing understanding through experience and the capacity to apply that understanding to the issues of life (Baltes, Smith, Staundinger, & Sowarka, 1988).

Problem Finding

In some ways, adulthood requires a different kind of thinking. Schoolchildren learn to solve teacher-determined problems. Adults need to learn to identify problems that exist, and to delineate those that need solving. This involves going beyond formal operational thinking to a fifth stage of development that has been labeled a *problem-finding stage* (Arlin, 1975). This fifth stage represents an ability to discover problems not yet delineated, to formulate these problems, and to raise general questions from ill-defined problems.

Investigations of the Piagetian stage of formal operations suggest that progressive

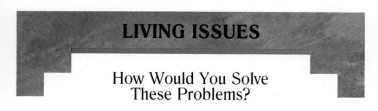

LIVING ISSUES

How Would You Solve These Problems?

The following are three examples of real-life situations. How would you solve these problems?

Let's say that one evening you go to the refrigerator and notice that it is not cold inside; rather, it's warm. What would you do?

Let's say that you live in a house with a basement. One night there is a flash flood and you notice that your basement is being flooded with water coming in the window wells. What would you do?

If you were traveling by car and got stranded out on an interstate highway during a blizzard, what would you do? (Denney & Palmer, 1981, p. 325).

changes in thought structures may extend beyond the level of formal operations. *The suggestion is that formal structures may not be the final equilibrium; they may be building blocks for new structures that might be identified.* The implication is that cognitive growth in adulthood is continuous; there is no end point beyond which new structures may appear. Researchers continue to seek these new structures (Arlin, 1977; Commons, Richards, & Kuhn, 1982).

Dialectical Thinking

A number of theorists have described an advanced form of adult thought that they call **dialectical thinking** (Basseches, 1984; Leadbeater, 1986; Riegel, 1975). According to this view, every idea, truth, or **thesis** implies an opposing idea or **antithesis**. *Dialectical thinking involves being able to consider both sides of an issue simultaneously,* and to be able to accept the existence of contradictions. Dialectical thinking sometimes leads to integrating one's beliefs and experiences with the inconsistencies and contradictions that are discovered, so that a continuously new view evolves. The new view recognizes that answers need to be constantly updated to take into account new information. At each stage, however, the dialectical theorist commits himself or herself to the best that is known, realizing that knowledge and values will change tomorrow. In other words, the unifying premise of dialectical thinking is that change itself is the universal truth.

Not only are adult dialectical thinkers more sensitive to contradictions—and more appreciative of opposing points of view—but they have learned to live with them. In marriage, dialectical thinkers can appreciate their spouses' viewpoints that are opposite to their own. They have an ability, not common in all people, to evaluate personal, social, and political viewpoints. *Although they can accept contradictions as a basic property of thought, they are sometimes able to synthesize new formulations of ideas that are superior to both opposites.* The result is a continuously evolving view of truths about the world.

Schaie's Stages of Adult Cognitive Development

One of the most interesting models of cognitive development was described by Schaie (1977–1978), who identified five stages people go through in acquiring knowledge and then in making increased use of it.

1. *Acquisitive stage* (childhood and adolescence)—learning information and skills without regard for their usefulness in one's life.
2. *Achieving stage* (late teens to early 20s or 30s)—recognition of the need to apply knowledge to achieve long-term goals.
3. *Responsibility stage* (late 30s to early 60s)—use of cognitive abilities in caring for family, for others on the job, and in the community.
4. *Executive stage* (another stage during the 30s or 40s through middle age)—development of the ability to apply complex knowledge at a number of different levels; becoming responsible for businesses, academic institutions, churches, government, and other organizations.
5. *Reintegrative stage* (late adulthood)—increasingly selective acquisition and application of knowledge to specific tasks: to interests and purposes one thinks have value; becoming less likely to expend effort to solve problems that have no meaning for them and that they do not personally face.

As can be seen, Schaie emphasized that *people typically switch from acquiring knowledge to applying knowledge in their own lives.*

INTELLIGENCE

Any attempt to measure intelligence with advancing age depends on the types of tests used, their research design, and what they purport to measure. Some intellectual functions increase with age; some peak early and are maintained well into old age; others show decline beginning in early adulthood. Clearly, conclusions regarding changes in intellectual ability will differ, depending on which functions are evaluated.

Scores on the WAIS as a Function of Age

The *Wechsler Adult Intelligence Scale (WAIS)* is the most widely used measure of adult intelligence (Wechsler, 1955). It includes 11 subtests. Of these, 6 of the tests, *Information, Comprehension, Arithmetic, Similarities, Digit Span,* and *Vocabulary,* comprise the verbal scores. The other 5 tests, *Digit Symbol, Picture Completion, Block Design, Picture Arrangement,* and *Object Assembly,* comprise the performance scores. In general, *verbal scores tend to*

Dialectical thinking—the view that every idea implies its opposite; the ability to consider opposing viewpoints simultaneously

Thesis—the principal point or idea

Antithesis—the idea or point directly opposing a stated idea, or thesis

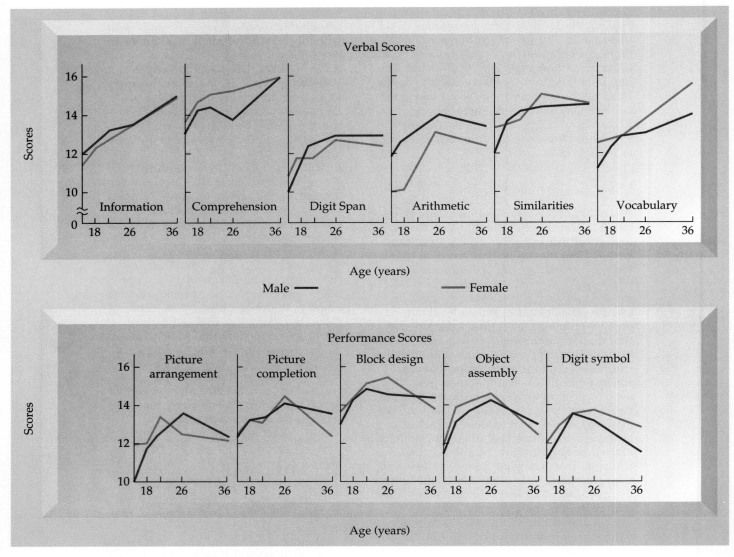

FIGURE 17.2 Curves of mean scores for young adults on the eleven Wechsler subtests, Berkeley Growth Study.

From "Behavioral Correlates of Mental Growth: Birth to Thirty-Six Years" by N. Bayley, 1968, *American Psychologist, 23*, pp. 1–17. Copyright 1968 by the American Psychological Association. Reprinted by permission of the publisher and author.

hold up with increasing age, whereas performance scores tend to decline after the mid-20s (Storandt & Futterman, 1982). The decline of performance scores is partially due to a loss of speed and psychomotor coordination (Erber, Botwinick, & Storandt, 1981).

Figure 17.2 shows the curves for young adults on the 11 Wechsler subtests (Bayley, 1968). The findings are taken from the longitudinal *Berkeley Growth Study* (Bayley, 1968). Because only 52 subjects were available for retesting at ages 16, 18, 21, 26, and 36, the findings must be interpreted cau-

tiously. As shown, scores on 5 of the first 6 subtests, representing verbal scores, tended to increase through age 36. The scores on Information and Vocabulary were still increasing rapidly at that age. Only the arithmetic subtest score peaked by age 26 and declined after that. However, all scores on the last 5 subtests, representing performance scores, peaked in the early or mid-20s and declined thereafter. A continuation of the study to age 40 showed that the average IQ increased 3.8 points between ages 18 and 40.

Cross-Sectional Versus Longitudinal Measurements

It must be emphasized that the results obtained from the Berkeley Growth Study were longitudinal measurements. As discussed in Chapter 1, longitudinal measurements tend to minimize intellectual decline with age, whereas cross-sectional measurements tend to maximize it. However, *longitudinal and cross-sectional measurements both show that verbal scores remain the most stable and performance scores decline the most*. Figure 17.3 shows the cross-sectional scores on the verbal and performance portions of the WAIS as a function of age (Wechsler, 1955). Scores on Information, Vocabulary, and Comprehension from the verbal section remained the most stable. Scores on Block Design, Object Assembly, and Digit Symbol from the performance section declined the most with age.

Some longitudinal studies emphasize that intellectual decline of a number of abilities is not inevitable, even by age 50 and over. Extreme care must be taken when interpreting the results of any testing, or faulty conclusions will be drawn (Hayslip & Brookshire, 1985). Figure 17.4 shows the full-scale WAIS scores of subjects who were aged 60 to 69 and 70 to 79 at the start of a longitudinal study (Eisdorfer & Wilke, 1973). The solid lines represent the scores of those tested 4 times during a 10-year period, and the dashed lines those of subjects tested 7 times during a 15-year period. Note that those available over a 15-year period showed no decline the first 10 years, whereas the group tested 4 times did. Those tested over 15 years apparently were healthier, because they were available 5 years beyond the initial 4 testings. Decline was not apparent until much later in life. As the longitudinal research continued, selective subject dropout obscured decline patterns that otherwise might have been present earlier.

Scores on the PMA as a Function of Age

Thurstone's (1949) *Primary Mental Abilities Test* (PMA) is constructed so scores are derived from 5 subtests: *World Fluency, Number, Reasoning, Space,* and *Verbal Meaning*. Each score represents a different mental ability relatively unrelated to the others. Schaie and colleagues (1973, 1974) used the PMA to test subjects so comparison could be made between cross-sectional and longitudinal results. The cross-sectional data were obtained by a single testing of 500 people, 50 in each of ten 5-year age spans. The results of the cross-sectional comparisons are given in Figure 17.5. *The scores peaked at age 35, with a very slight decline over the next 15 years. And the decline from age 50 to 70 was still only 22%.*

The longitudinal data were obtained by dividing the subjects into 7 age cohorts and testing them during a 14-year time span (in 1956, 1963, and 1970). The results of the longitudinal testing are shown in Figure 17.6.

FIGURE 17.3 Scaled scores on the verbal and performance portion of the WAIS as a function of age.

Reproduced by permission from the Manual for the Wechsler Adult Intelligence Scale. Copyright © 1955 by The Psychological Corporation. All rights reserved.

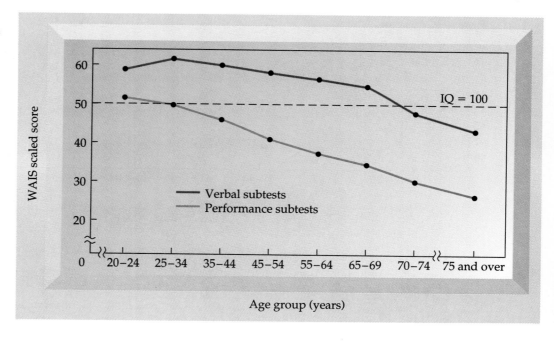

Age group (years)

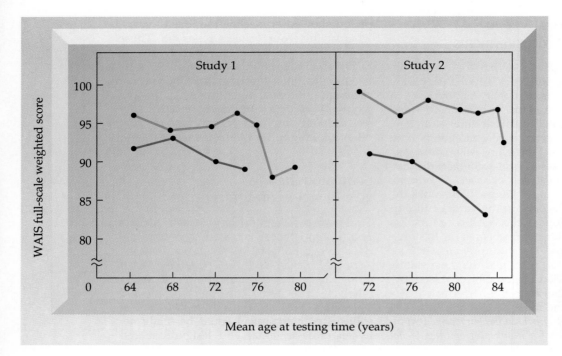

FIGURE 17.4 Full-scale WAIS scores of elderly subjects tested four times during a 10-year period and of subjects tested seven times during a 15-year period.

Adapted from "Intellectual Changes With Advancing Age" by C. Eisdorfer and F. Wilkie, 1973, in *Intellectual Functioning in Adults* (pp. 21–29) by L. F. Jarvik, C. Eisdorfer, and J. E. Blum, Eds., New York: Springer. Used by permission.

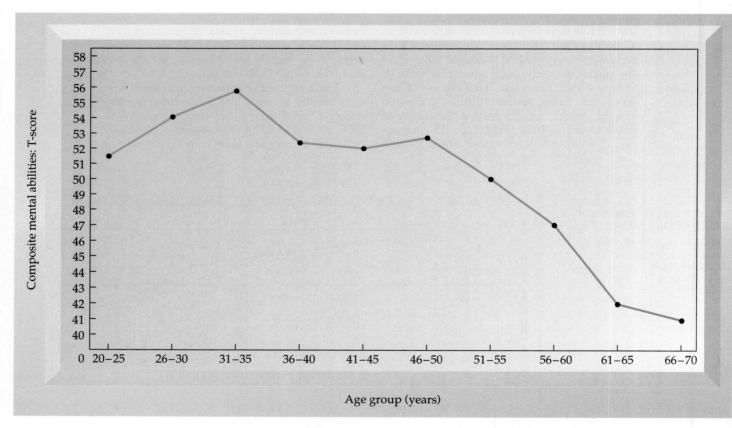

FIGURE 17.5   Composite primary mental abilities as a function of age (cross-sectional studies).

Adapted from "Generational Versus Ontogenetic Components of Change in Adult Cognitive Behavior: A Fourteen-Year Cross-Sequential Study" by K. W. Schaie and G. Labouvie-Vief, 1974, *Developmental Psychology, 10,* pp. 305–320; and "Generational and Cohort-Specific Differences in Adult Cognitive Functioning: A Fourteen-Year Study of Independent Samples" by K. W. Schaie, G. V. Labouvie, and B. U. Buech, 1973, *Developmental Psychology, 9,* pp. 151–166. Copyright 1973, 1974 by the American Psychological Association. Adapted by permission of the publisher and authors.

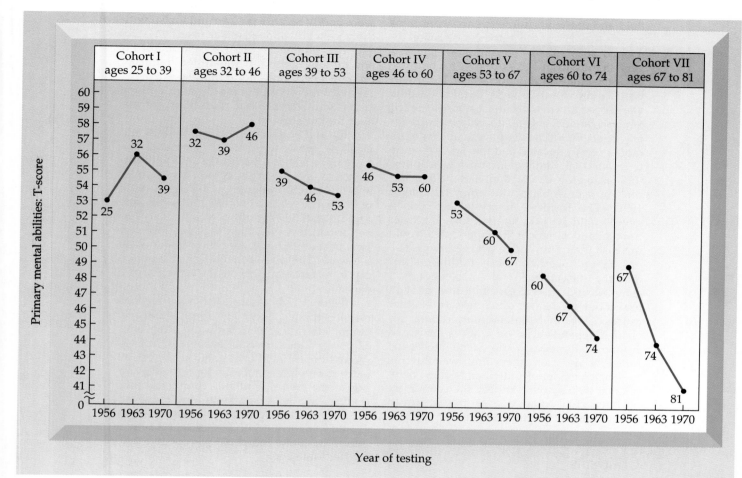

FIGURE 17.6 Composite primary mental abilities as a function of age (longitudinal studies).

Adapted from "Generational Versus Ontogenetic Components of Change in Adult Cognitive Behavior: A Fourteen-Year Cross-Sequential Study" by K. W. Schaie and G. Labouvie-Vief, 1974, *Developmental Psychology, 10*, pp. 305–320; and "Generational and Cohort-Specific Differences in Adult Cognitive Functioning: A Fourteen-Year Study of Independent Samples" by K. W. Schaie, G. V. Labouvie, and B. U. Buech, 1973, *Developmental Psychology, 9*, pp. 151–166. Copyright 1973, 1974 by the American Psychological Association. Adapted by permission of the publisher and authors.

The findings suggest no significant age decline at all in cohorts I through IV during the 14-year span. Decline began in the mid-50s and continued progressively in cohorts V through VII. The greatest decline was in the oldest cohort, ages 67 to 81, but it was still only 16% over the 14-year span. It is evident that *intellectual decline was less when measured longitudinally than when measured cross-sectionally. It is also apparent that decline does not always occur. When it does, it usually takes place after age 50.*

Fluid and Crystallized Intelligence

Horn and Cattell (1967) felt the reason that studies of the kinds made by Schaie and Labouvie-Vief (1974) show a plateau in intel-ligence test scores during the early adult years is that the studies do not separate the data for *fluid* and *crystallized intelligence. Horn and Cattell found that fluid intelligence declined after age 14 and that the sharpest decline came in early adulthood.* The decline in fluid intelligence was evidenced by poorer performance on tests requiring abstract thinking, inductive reasoning, relational thinking, and short-term memory, and on tests requiring figural classification, analogy, and the completion of logical series. Horn and Cattell also reported that *at least 20 studies, both cross-sectional and longitudinal, showed increases in crystallized intelligence through adulthood.* They reasoned that learning through experience and acculturation continues for many years. Therefore, intelligence, defined as knowledge, increases until at least age 60. However, when the scores on the tests for both fluid and crystallized intelligence were combined, the composite intelligence score remained substantially the same or increased very slightly from age 14 to 60.

Schaie (1978) did not accept Horn and Cattell's arguments as valid, because the data were based on cross-sectional studies. He felt *the apparent decline in fluid intelligence was due to generational differences*: Older subjects were more poorly educated and had less exposure to intellectual stimulation and fewer opportunities to grow during their lifetime than did the younger subjects (Cockburn & Smith, 1991). The increase in crystallized intelligence could be expected because a greater number and variety of life experiences would increase their knowledge over many years.

Taken together, these findings show that the measurement of intelligence is a complex undertaking and that it is difficult to sort out age-related differences from other causes. Whether intellectual capabilities change depends a lot on what is measured and how (Cornelius, 1984). Some intellectual functions decline; others improve. But the two-factor model of Cattell and Horn, helpful as it is, may oversimplify the complexity of intellectual change over the life span (Cunningham, Clayton, & Overton, 1975).

Criticisms

The WAIS and other tests have been criticized primarily on the basis that they are not relevant for the purposes for which the tests are used. Scores on the WAIS can be converted into IQ using a table in the test manual. But *IQ is only one important factor necessary to carry out responsible tasks.* To succeed, a successful businessperson needs drive and motivation, social adeptness, courage, patience, self-confidence, practical wisdom, organizational and administrative ability, and a variety of skills, in addition to intelligence. People should not be selected for a job on the basis of intelligence alone. It would be a mistake to assume that people of any age could be successfully evaluated for responsibility only by test scores.

Another criticism of adult intelligence tests is that the test items are *more familiar to children or very young adults* than to older adults. When tests are constructed comprising practical information items related more to the needs of adults, scores rise through the middle and older adult years. Furthermore, intelligence tests show a *cultural and economic bias.* They are more suited to middle-class adults than to minorities and low socioeconomic groups, who tend to score poorly because they are unfamiliar with the vocabulary and examples used.

The original WAIS (1955) is outdated and no longer used. It was tested originally on only a very small adult sample. The new, revised WAIS (1982) was tested on a much larger adult sample and is an improvement over the original.

IQ can be quite misleading. It does not measure innate capacity; it measures the score on a test at a particular time with reference to one's own age group. Thus, an IQ of 100 at age 50 indicates an average level of performance relative to other adults the same age. But the 50-year-old person actually has performed less well than a 20-year-old person, because an age correction is added to the score. The older person is given a handicap in expectation that his or her score will decline.

Figure 17.7 indicates the corrections made with age. Those age 20 to 24 have 10 points subtracted; people 75 and older have 32 points added to attain average IQs of 100 (Wechsler, 1955). If one matched the IQs of older and younger subjects for research purposes, the results would be completely misleading. Studies to ascertain absolute levels of intellectual functioning at different ages should use deviation IQs that reflect how a person has done compared with people who are the same age.

Factors Affecting Scores

How, by whom, to whom, and under what circumstances tests are administered can affect scores (Schaie, 1978). Adults score better if test items are *relevant* to their daily lives. For example, the Block Design subtest of the WAIS requires the rearranging of assorted red and white blocks according to a design on a printed card, while the examiner checks a stopwatch. If adults find this activity irrelevant, their scores will be lower than on tests they consider more meaningful.

Other factors, such as the *degree of motivation*, affect performance. Such *personality traits* as cautiousness, rigidity, or dogmatism negatively affect test scores. Self-confidence can improve scores, as can experience and practice in taking tests (Beres & Baron, 1981). *Physical factors*, such as physical fitness, cardiovascular health, brain functioning, overall health (Perlmutter & Nyquist, 1990), sleep, eyesight, hearing, motor ability, and reaction time, are especially important on subtests measuring performance (Elsayed, Ismail, & Young, 1980; Karasawa, Kawashima, & Kasahara, 1979; Manton, Siegler, &

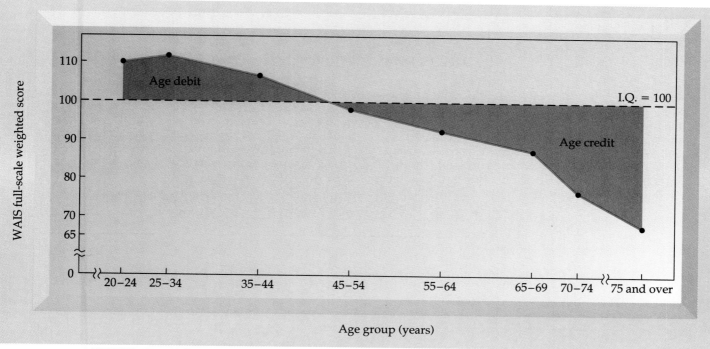

FIGURE 17.7   Full-scaled scores as a function of age.

Reproduced by permission from the Manual for the Wechsler Adult Intelligence Scale. Copyright © 1955 by The Psychological Corporation. All rights reserved.

Woodbury, 1986). Furthermore, *emotional factors* such as low morale, depression, learning apprehension, and tension may result in lower scores. One study showed that *hypertension* (Elias, Robbins, Schultz, & Pierce, 1990) had a more negative effect on the WAIS scores of young adults than on the scores of older subjects (Schultz, Elias, Robbins, Streeten, & Blakeman, 1986). One explanation for the decline of cognitive functioning of the aged, particularly verbal comprehension, is a decline in *hearing acuity*. Even a slight hearing loss imposes handicaps in receiving and understanding verbal messages. Many older people show poor intelligibility of fast speech and low-volume speech. Research has shown a fairly clear-cut relationship between auditory acuity and a decline in level of cognitive functioning (Sands & Meredith, 1989).

The relationship between the test administrator and the test takers also affects performance. In general, the administrator who develops good rapport, puts subjects at ease, and offers supportive comments can maximize test performance. *General intellectual level and years of school completed* are also related to test performance. People with superior intelligence and education show little decline or they show improvement, at least to age 60. Those of average intelligence and low educational level show increasingly poorer performance between 40 and 60.

Personality, Behavior, and Mental Abilities

To what extent is the decline in intellectual functioning with age related to personality factors? Unfortunately, only limited objective information is available to answer this question. Part of the problem is the difficulty of classifying and measuring personality types and trying to describe personality changes with age.

EMOTIONAL HEALTH.   In general, there is a positive relationship between mental health and cognitive ability. The emotionally healthy seem to show less cognitive decline with age than the emotionally ill. The extreme example is the seriously depressed person whose severe withdrawal precludes any type of testing. Kleban and associates (1976) found that in comparison to subjects exhibiting declines in functioning levels, stable subjects comprehended their situations better (more awareness, coherence, verbalization, better memory), were more socially reactive, manifested fewer neurotic conditions, and had greater control over impulses and aggression.

FOCUS

Heart Disease and Intelligence

The *Duke Longitudinal Study of Aging* sought to demonstrate a relationship between heart disease and brain impairment of aged persons (Wang & Busse, 1974). Figure 17.8 shows the relationship between heart disease and WAIS verbal and performance scores (Wang & Busse, 1974). Verbal and performance scores were significantly higher for persons with no heart disease than for those with compensated heart disease (those who have received remedial treatment) or decompensated heart disease. This difference in scores was due partly to the fact that subjects with heart disease were slightly older than those without. When age, race, and education differences were considered, however, WAIS scores of the diseased group were still slightly lower, particularly on performance tests.

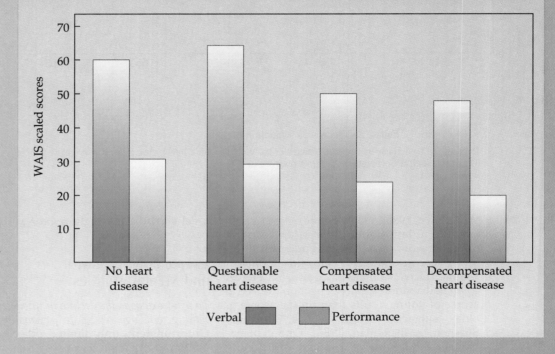

FIGURE 17.8 Mean WAIS verbal and performance scaled scores.

From: "Heart Disease and Brain Impairment Among Aged Persons" by H. S. Wang and E. W. Busse, 1974, in *Normal Aging II* by E. Palmore, Ed., Durham, NC: Duke University Press. Copyright © 1974 by Duke University Press.

PERSONALITY TYPES. Personality indirectly affects intellectual functioning by influencing life cycle changes (Karasawa et al., 1979). People who are more open and imaginative, outgoing and highly interactive socially, more open to new ideas, curious, and highly motivated to learn are likely to accumulate a great variety of cognitive experiences over a lifetime. Therefore, they score higher on measures dependent on accumulated knowledge and abilities, such as crystallized intelligence measures. If the elderly show negative personality changes with old age, becoming short-tempered, stubborn, or suspicious, these cause maladaptations that are often accompanied by distinct intellectual decline. Sometimes organic brain pathologies underlie such personality changes.

CAUTIOUSNESS AND RIGIDITY. Individuals become more cautious with advancing age. They take longer to answer questions on cognitive tests because they want to avoid mistakes. As their response time increases, they do progressively worse on timed tests. But, conversely, cautiousness in later life may be a function of intellectual decline, making either interpretation tenable.

Rigidity, or resistance to change, may have a negative effect on changes in one's ideas, attitudes, habits, and tasks. The rigid person refuses to relinquish attitudes, opinions, or tasks, despite plentiful evidence that this persistence is wrong or unrewarding.

There is no such thing as global rigidity, that is, inflexibility in all aspects of one's personality or life. The notion that one's whole being or life-style can be characterized as rigid or inflexible is not supported by research results. There are a variety of rigidities. An engineer who is very rigid in his ideas of marital roles can be very open-minded about the results of his scientific research. And a person with inflexible habits may show tolerance to new ideas.

The statement that rigidity increases with age is simplistic. Rigid behavior in older people tends to be marginal. Many studies that indicate increasing rigidity with age fail to differentiate among other deficits in cognitive performance. For example, older people have difficulty shifting from one task to another, but this is partially because of slowness and the increased time they need to switch tasks. This slowness results in higher rigidity scores. When the elderly are given step-by-step instructions regarding which function to perform next, their slowness in shift performance is minimized and they score higher.

Some studies also fail to consider cultural change factors. Cross-sectional studies comparing older and younger subjects show the former to be more rigid. But longitudinal studies fail to show consistent results or extensive rigidity (Schaie & Labouvie-Vief, 1974). Thus, rigidity may or may not be intrinsic to maturational age changes. Rigidity is influenced greatly by intelligence and educational level. *The person with more intelligence and education will exhibit less rigidity.*

EXPECTATIONS.   The maintenance of intellectual abilities with advancing age partly depends on what people expect will happen (Lachman & Jelalian, 1984). Those who believe they are becoming senile, whether they are or not, who believe they can't remember or learn, and who make little effort to find intellectual stimulation, may find their expectations have become self-fulfilling prophecy. They become less competent because of disuse, not because of any changes inherent in the aging process itself. Elderly people can often greatly improve their intellectual abilities if they can become convinced that cognitive loss is not inevitable (Perlmutter, 1987).

Socioenvironmental Effects

STIMULATING ENVIRONMENT.   Older adults who are exposed to intellectually stimulating environments maintain a higher level of cognitive ability with increasing age than those who are not. Social contacts with family, friends, social groups, or at work; interesting activities that provide a variety of experiences in different settings; and opportunities to look at books, magazines, art, or television all help maintain cognitive powers. A person who is isolated from other people, with little opportunity for meaningful interpersonal contacts, becomes generally divorced from social interaction. In all probability, that person's mental abilities will evidence decline.

EDUCATIONAL LEVEL AND SOCIOECONOMIC STATUS.   People with high education levels and superior socioeconomic status show less decline in cognitive abilities with age, especially verbal abilities, than do those with less education and lower socioeconomic status. Superior education and socioeconomic status are both causes and effects. The most educated people have superior intellectual abilities to start with, as measured by intelligence tests. This is true regardless of age. In fact, educational level is as important to intellectual functioning as is age. Those with high status and education are more likely to maintain an active interest in learning and to remain involved in various rewarding activities. They also have more opportunities and resources to participate. As a result, they manifest fewer signs of mental deterioration in old age. In fact, they may show improvement, at least to age 60. Although they decline in perceptual-integrative abilities and in performance functions, the extent of the decline is not enough to reduce them to the level of their less intellectually capable age peers (Kangas & Bradway, 1971).

LIFE CRISES AND STRESS.   Mental deterioration is also related to the frequency and intensity of people's life crises. The greater and more frequent the stress, the greater the probability of mental deterioration. Amster and Krauss (1974) found that elderly females from 65 to 95 who showed mental deterioration had been exposed to almost twice as many crises as the women in a control group who showed no deterioration.

TRAINING.   Efforts have been made to improve the cognitive abilities of older adults through training (Dittmann-Kohli, Lachman, Kliefl, & Baltes, 1991). Such efforts reflect the philosophy that reduced intellectual performance is an experiential or performance deficit that can be reduced by training in certain component skills. However, current opinion emphasizes that the extent to which different intellectual abilities are trainable differs markedly, depending on the degree to which abilities represent the effects of acculturation or of the individual's biological-maturational well-being. Those abilities most dependent on acculturation, such as the components of crystallized intelligence, are considered the most trainable.

To show, however, that other abilities may also be trainable, Labouvie-Vief and Gonda (1976) attempted to improve the scores of 60 females, ages 63 to 95, in solving complex problems requiring inductive reasoning. The results showed that training could produce significant increments in intellectual performance of the elderly, even with skills linked primarily with biological-maturational factors (i.e., fluid intelligence). Plemons and associates (1978) tried to determine to what extent fluid intelligence could be modified in subjects aged 59 to 85. A training program was devised to enhance the figural relations component of fluid intelligence. Posttraining assessments after one week, one month, and six months showed improved performance as a result of training. This improvement carried over to other tasks related to fluid intelligence. These significant findings suggest that *intellectual performance on fluid intelligence tests is more modifiable through short-term intervention than traditionally assumed* (Blackburn, Papalia-Finlay, Foye, & Serlin, 1988).

Several studies have also shown that *scores on performance-type tests requiring speed and motor coordination can also be improved with practice* (Grant, Storandt, & Botwinick, 1978). Beres and Baron (1981) administered the Digit Symbol Substitution subtest of the WAIS to older women (mean age 69) and to younger women (mean age 23) on each of 5 training days. The older women improved substantially, but equally large gains were made by the younger women. Therefore, age differences were not reduced by training when both groups were trained. However, as a result of training, scores of the older women on this subtest increased from the 19th to the 25th percentile, relative to norms for young adults in general. These scores were maintained during a follow-up test 10 days later.

The notion that adults cannot or will not learn, or that little can be done about the decline of cognitive abilities, is fallacious. The fact that a variety of performance deficits typically observed in the elderly are amenable to intervention suggests that *adult cognitive functioning can be more proficient if adequate environmental support is provided* (Sanders & Sanders, 1978). Moreover, the degree of plasticity revealed in intervention studies (Baltes & Schaie, 1976) has contributed to a deeper, more positive understanding of adult cognitive potential.

Terminal Decline

The theory of **terminal decline** holds that many human functions not only are primarily related to chronological age, but also show marked decline during a period of a few weeks to a few years before death (Johansson & Berg, 1989; Palmore & Cleveland, 1976). The theory assumes that whatever genetic and environmental factors cause death also cause marked functional decline prior to death.

Some evidence suggests that *within 1 to 7 years a decrement in intellectual performance is associated with death* (Siegler, Roseman, & Harkins, 1975). A drop in scores on the WAIS and WMS (Wechsler Memory Scale) have been found to be reliable indicators of distance from death (Siegler, McCarty, & Logue, 1982). The *Duke Longitudinal Study of Aging* (Wilkie & Eisdorfer, 1972) showed that survivors and nonsurvivors achieved the same WAIS scores in initial testing. However, two nonsurvivor groups (death occurred 13 to 24 months and 25 to 32 months after initial testing) showed significantly greater losses in scores between the first and second tests than did the survivor groups. These results partially support previous findings of terminal decline in intellectual performance.

An additional analysis of the Duke study attempted to distinguish between the relative effects of aging declines and terminal declines. The analysis showed substantial aging declines in intelligence and substantial terminal declines in physical functions. Longitudinal analysis showed no substantial terminal declines remaining after aging declines were controlled. Cross-sectional analysis, however, showed a small but significant terminal decline in intelligence after aging decline was controlled (Palmore & Cleveland, 1976). Although the reality of terminal decline was confirmed, it was much less than previously supposed when age was taken into account. *Age and physical condition were more important factors in intellectual decline than a person's distance from death.*

Terminal decline—marked decline in intellectual performance shortly before death; theory that genetic and environmental factors producing decline lead to marked functional decline prior to death

INFORMATION PROCESSING

Memory

WHAT MEMORY INVOLVES.   The ability to remember is basic to all learning and to intellectual and social functioning. Studies of memory during adulthood are extremely important because they enable us to determine what happens to this basic process throughout the adult life cycle. All studies of memory recognize three basic processes: **acquisition**, **storage**, and **retrieval**.

The process of acquisition begins with exposure to stimuli so information can be learned. It involves making an impression on memory receptors and registering and recording information. Acquisition is the learning or input phase of memory. Unless something is acquired, it cannot be remembered.

In the process of storage, information is cycled, processed, organized, rehearsed, and stored until needed. Retrieval is the process of recalling, or remembering, stored information. The most popular concept of memory storage is a threefold model: *sensory storage*, *short-term storage*, and *long-term storage*. These stores are also referred to as *sensory memory*, *short-term memory*, and *long-term memory*. Figure 17.9 illustrates this three-stage model of memory (Murdock, 1974).

Information is seen as passing from one compartment to another, with decreasing amounts passing to the next stage at any one time. Information is first received and transduced by the senses. It is held only briefly (as little as a fraction of a second) before the image begins to decay and/or is blocked out by other incoming sensory information. Information that has not already faded from the sensory store is read out to the short-term store. Because of the limited capacity of the short-term store, information to be held longer must be further rehearsed and transferred to the relatively permanent long-term store. For all practical purposes, long-term storage capacity is infinite.

In the process of retrieval, stored information is obtained by searching, finding, and remembering, either through recall or recognition.

Memory efficiency depends on all three of these processes. Loss of memory represents a decline with advancing age. This is true whether learning is measured in terms of speed (Hertzog, Raskind, & Cannon, 1986) or by the amount revealed or recognized. However, there are many exceptions to this generalization (Rebok, Montaglione, & Bendlin, 1988). *Age-related differences are not great* (McCarty, Siegler, & Logue, 1982). If ample time is given for registering, assimilating, coding, categorizing, rehearsing, and reinforcing short-term holdings, many older persons do as well as or better than younger ones. This is true even when no extra time is given for recall or recognition. Much depends on the neuropsychological health of the subjects being tested (Moehle & Long, 1989). In one national health survey, only 15% of adults age 55 and over reported having trouble remembering things during the past year. About 36% indicated having no trouble at all (Cutler & Grams, 1988). Most elderly adults feel they are not at all handicapped by forgetfulness (Erber & Rothberg, 1991; Sunderland, Watts, Baddeley, & Harris, 1986).

SENSORY MEMORY.   Sensory memory abilities of older adults depend partially on the extent to which their sensory receptors are functioning at normal levels. Those who show some decrement in visual or auditory functioning cannot be expected to remember what they have not acquired (Arenberg, 1982). Less information is passed from sensory to short-term stores.

Information received by the senses is held very briefly in one of several specific sensory stores. For example, auditory information is held in an *auditory sensory store*, and visual information is held in a *visual sensory store*. The auditory sensory store is referred to as **echoic memory**, the visual sensory store

Acquisition—the process by which information is recorded, encoded, and stored

Storage—the process by which acquired information is put away for later use

Retrieval—the process of recalling or of being able to remember or recognize information that has been stored

Echoic memory—the auditory sensory store

FIGURE 17.9   Three-stage model of memory.

Adapted from *Human Memory: Theory and Data* by B. Murdock, 1974, Potomac, MD: Lawrence Erlbaum Associates.

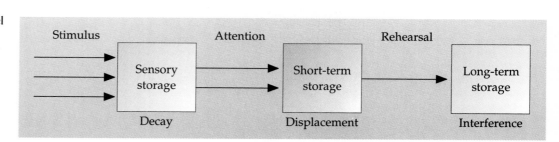

Iconic memory—
the visual sensory
store

Tactual memory—
memory of touch

as **iconic memory**. Other sensory stores include those for tactual information and for smell.

Most investigations of visual or iconic memory have shown a rapid decay in less than a second. But other studies have confirmed that the durability of a memory trace depends on how intensively the stimulus was presented and how deeply it was processed (Gilmore, Allan, & Royer, 1986). Studies of auditory, or echoic, memory as contrasted with visual, or iconic, memory and **tactual memory** show variable results (Riege & Inman, 1981; Zacks, Hasher, Doren, Hamm, & Attig, 1987). *All three sensory memory stores show some decline with age, but tactual memory seems to decline the fastest* (Riege & Inman, 1981). Figure 17.10 shows the average performances of groups of volunteers divided on the basis of age decades. *Visual sensory memory did not decline much before age 50, but did so fairly rapidly after that. It also declined after 60, whereas auditory memory did not.* This is particularly true in older subjects if any interference or disruption occurs while the stimuli are being presented. Visual memory tasks require close attention while the images are being presented; auditory inputs can be heard and held briefly whether they are attended to or not.

However, *the durability of an audio memory trace depends on the attention given it when heard, and therefore the depth at which the stimulus is processed* (Wingfield, Lahar, & Stine, 1989). When attention is diverted during a stimulus, older subjects in particular remem-

ber less because the information is processed less deeply. Thus, if they are asked to listen to two things at once, or to hold some information while reporting other information, or to receive some input while recalling and reporting information previously given, older subjects tend to concentrate on only one task. Performance on the other task deteriorates badly. Older subjects are penalized more when they must divide their attention.

SHORT-TERM, OR PRIMARY, MEMORY. There is some confusion in various studies about the difference between short-term and long-term memory. One helpful distinction was given by Waugh and Norman (1965). They used the terms **primary memory (PM)** and **secondary memory (SM)**. Primary memory, considered synonymous with short-term memory, involves information still being rehearsed and focused on in one's conscious mind. Secondary memory, or long-term memory, is characterized by how deeply the information has been processed, not by how long the information has been held. Deep processing, in which perceived information has been passed into layers of memory below the conscious level, constitutes secondary memory. For example, when a subject memorizes a word list, the words under immediate consideration are at the primary or short-term memory stage. Words already looked at, memorized, and tucked away are at the secondary, or long-term, memory level, even though they were learned only a short time before. Specific

Primary memory—short-term memory

Secondary memory—long-term memory

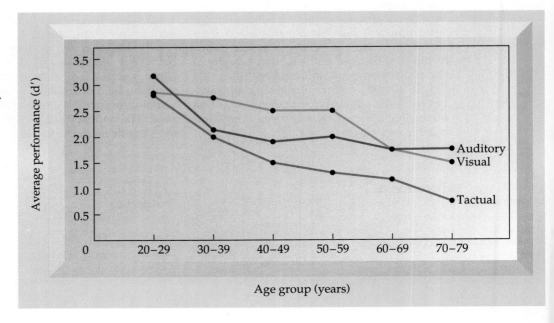

FIGURE 17.10 Average performances (d') on nonverbal recognition tests, by age group.

Adapted from "Age Differences in Nonverbal Memory Tasks" by W. H. Riege and V. Inman, January 1991, *Journal of Gerontology, 36*, pp. 51–58. Copyright 1991 by The Gerontological Society. Adapted by permission of the publisher.

words recalled several days or months later are recalled from secondary memory. Secondary memory can last for 30 seconds or for years. The terms *primary* and *secondary* memory are used synonymously in this discussion with short-term and long-term memory, even though some secondary memory stores may be recalled after relatively short time intervals.

In measuring primary memory, the subject is presented a short string of digits, letters, or words and then tested for the total that can be recalled immediately. When measured in this way, *primary memory span does not change with age or it decreases only slightly,* unless ability has been seriously impaired by physical deterioration (Friedman, 1974; Wright, 1982).

LONG-TERM, OR SECONDARY, MEMORY.

Many studies show that *older subjects perform less well than younger subjects when secondary memory is involved* (Allen & Coyne, 1989; Guttentag & Hunt, 1988). For example, if subjects are asked to recall a list of 12 to 30 words in any order, no age differences appear in the recall of the last four items (retrieved from primary memory). However, older subjects recall fewer words from the beginning and middle of the list, where secondary memory is involved.

It should not be assumed, however, that aging always brings memory deficits (Erber, 1989). Many factors can eliminate age differences. Overall *verbal ability* is a better predictor of prose recall than is age (Rice & Meyer, 1986). *Material organized, categorized, or associated* with what is already familiar is remembered more readily, because acquisition is enhanced (Mueller, Rankin, & Carlomusto, 1979; Sanders, Murphy, Schmitt, & Walsh, 1980; Wingfield, Aberdeen, & Stine, 1991). Also, if a list of words is presented in one category (for example, animals), age differences in recall are slight, suggesting that grouping words under one concept offers cues that enhance retrieval. Retrieval is also enhanced if the *same cues* are given at retrieval as given when the material was learned (Gerard, Zacks, Hasher, & Radvansky, 1991; Puglisi, Park, Smith, & Dudley, 1988). Furthermore, other *studies have shown greater age losses in free recall than in recognition performance,* suggesting that retrieval from storage without any cues constitutes a special problem for older subjects (Kausler & Puckett, 1981; Riege & Inman, 1981). Recognition does not require retrieval, because cues are given, so smaller age decrements are found in recognition than in recall (Harkins, Chapman, & Eisdorfer, 1979; Perlmutter, 1979). Figure 17.11 shows age-related differences in recall and recognition.

Older subjects are at their greatest disadvantage when materials to be learned are meaningless or unfamiliar, or cannot be associated with what is already known. For example, the spatial memory of older adults, measured by being asked to remember object location, depends partly on how meaningful are the objects that

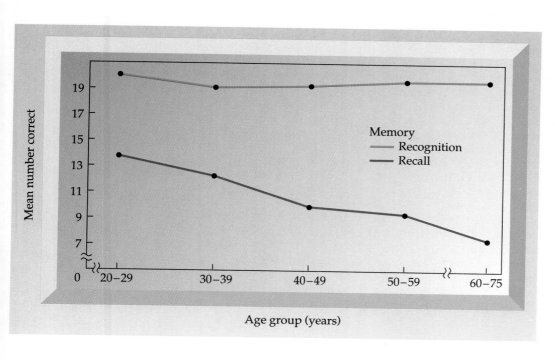

FIGURE 17.11 Mean recall and recognition scores as a function of age.

Adapted from "Memory Changes with Age" by D. Schonfield, 1965, *Nature 28,* p. 918. Reprinted by permission from *Nature,* Vol. 28, p. 918. Copyright © 1965 Macmillan Journals Limited.

they are expected to remember (Cherry & Park, 1989; Sharp & Gollin, 1988) and on the total context in which the objects are placed (Denney, Miller, Dew, & Levav, 1991; Sharp & Gollin, 1987). In general, however, memory for spatial information declines over age in adulthood (Bowling & Browne, 1991; Bruce & Herman, 1986). Also, it is more difficult to remember nonsense syllables than meaningful words. Similarly, if random materials can be sorted out or arranged in some logical order, such as alphabetically, they are easier to remember. However, *general recall ability decreases with age* (Hultsch, 1971).

MEMORY TRAINING.   Can training improve the memory of older adults (Menich & Baron, 1990)? Evidence indicates that it can (Hill, Storandt, & Simeone, 1990; LeBreck & Baron, 1987). Recall ability, in particular, can be improved if adults are trained in such recall strategies as repetition, association, and categorical material arrangement (Schmitt & McCroskey, 1981). In one experiment, training classes were held weekly for 4 weeks, during which institutionalized adults, 60 to 89 years of age, were exposed to 90-minute

training sessions (Zarit, Cole, & Guider, 1981). At the end of the training, retesting revealed considerable improvement in their ability to recall related items, names, and faces, and unrelated items. No improvement was found in the recall of paragraph material or in recognition performance. Training did cause some decline in subject complaints about their memory ability, regardless of whether performance improved. This finding indicates that elderly complaints about memory may not be related objectively to actual memory decrements.

Learning

Most people maintain the ability to learn through adulthood. Such capacity is vitally necessary because each new event in an adult's life requires new knowledge and abilities. Getting married, becoming parents, assuming a new job, moving to another house or community, retiring, and adjusting to a rapidly changing world all require learning.

LEARNING AND MEMORY.   Learning and memory are inextricably intertwined. Unless

FOCUS

Extremely Long-Term Memory

The ability to remember over a long period of time depends partially on how often the material is recalled and used in the intervening years (Botwinick & Storandt, 1980). For example, if words are periodically recalled, held in working memory, and then tucked away again, they can be remembered more easily than if they were never used after initial learning took place (Howard, Lasaga, & McAndrews, 1980). Retrieval from very long-term memory is also enhanced if the information is familiar. In one experiment, 20-year-olds remembered the names of unique contemporary pictures faster than the older subjects, but the 65-year-old group retrieved the names of unique but dated pictures faster. The speed of 50-year-old subjects fell between that of the two other groups (Poon & Fozard, 1978). Each age group recalled best pictures with which they were familiar.

It is commonly assumed that older people are not good at recalling recent events, but that their memory for remote events is unimpaired. One flaw in this assumption is that childhood events usually have been recalled many times since they occurred; the older person is remembering from the time of the last rehearsal, not from 40 years before (Rabinowitz & Craik, 1986).

Even so, objective studies show that *older subjects are poorer than younger controls at recalling and recognizing events from the past* (Bahrick, Bahrick, & Wittlinger, 1975; Holding, Noonan, Pfau, & Holding, 1986). Performance declines with the remoteness of events and with increasing age.

It must be emphasized, however, that decline is very slow. Warrington and Silberstein (1970) found that adults under 40 were able to recall 32% of the news items 1½ years after they had happened. Adults over 55 were able to recall 26% of the items. No differences were found in recognition performance between the two different age groups.

The ability to recall may depend partially on the subjects' age when the events occurred. Botwinick and Storandt (1974) found that *subjects of all ages (20 to 79) could best remember sociohistoric events that occurred when the subjects were 15 to 25 years old.* This agrees with the findings of Hyland and Ackerman (1988). These ages may be the most impressionable years, so persons of 60 remember events that occurred 35 to 45 years earlier better than they recall events that happened before or after.

Most people maintain the ability to learn throughout adulthood.

individuals learn well, they have little to recall. Conversely, if their memory is poor, they cannot learn much. Learning is the acquisition of knowledge; memory is the storage, processing, and retrieval of knowledge. Each ability depends on the other.

A distinction must be made between learning as an internal process and performance as an external act. If performance declines, we assume, often incorrectly, that learning has decreased. Performance, not learning ability, may decline because of many environmental factors, lack of motivation, or psychological disturbances. Before making definitive statements about changes in learning ability as one ages, it is necessary to sort out factors that affect performance. Much of what was previously regarded as learning ability deficiency in later life is now seen as a problem in the ability to express learned information—as a difficulty older people have in adapting to a task and demonstrating what they know. There is little disagreement regarding performance declines in later life, but controversy exists about the extent to which learning ability declines with age.

Paired-associate learning—learning to make associations between pairs of items

Serial-learning tasks—learning items in a list in the exact order of presentation

VERBAL LEARNING RESEARCH.
Verbal learning research uses two different types of tasks: **paired-associate learning** and **serial learning tasks.** In paired-associate learning tasks, subjects must learn associations between pairs of verbal items (for example, *book-car*), and then be able to supply the correct word to complete the pair when a particular stimulus word is given. Paired-associate verbal learning ability is measured by the number of trials required for perfect recitation, or to reach a designated level of proficiency, or by the number of errors made per trial. In serial learning tasks, subjects must learn a list of simple words, usually in the exact order presented. Learning ability is measured by the number of errors per trial or by the number of trials required for one or more perfect recitations of the list.

MOTIVATION, RELEVANCE, MEANING.
Every teacher knows that the desire to learn (the degree of motivation) is an important key to success. **Intrinsic motivation** comes from within, from physical and psychological drives. Thus, a person who has an emotional need to excel is driven to learn; so is a person who learns to achieve status. These people are driven by personal needs for ego satisfaction, and they strive harder than those who have lesser needs and desires.

Motivation is also enhanced through outside incentives (**extrinsic motivation**). The promise of promotion or increased financial rewards, or even verbal praise, may stimulate greater efforts. However, no amount of incentive works unless the subjects feel the rewards are attainable. Prizes seen as virtually unattainable result in lower performance scores because the subjects do not try. Even among students of high ability, there is no significantly different effect between virtually unattainable prizes and no prizes at all. Motivation is also enhanced if assigned tasks are more meaningful and personally relevant.

Intrinsic motivation—motivation coming directly from physical and psychological needs

Extrinsic motivation—motivation influenced by external rewards

ASSOCIATIVE STRENGTH.
The degree of association, or so-called **associative strength,** also affects learning. Some words go together naturally. For example, *table* goes with *chair* more than with *hat*. Thus, *table-chair* has greater associative strength. The higher the associative strength, and the more meaningful and familiar the word lists, the less likely older adults are to show a decline in learning ability.

Associative strength—degree of association, as between two words

AUTONOMIC AROUSAL.
Autonomic arousal is stimulation of the autonomic nervous system. The degree of autonomic arousal has been measured in a number of ways: by the level of free fatty acids (FFA) in the blood (the higher the level, the greater the degree of arousal) and by heart rate, blood pressure, and skin conductance. It was assumed in the past that older persons

Autonomic arousal—stimulation of the autonomic, or involuntary, nervous system—found to be positively associated with serial learning at all ages, particularly for learning simpler tasks

showed less autonomic arousal during learning tasks because they did not get as involved as younger persons. Consequently, they did not learn as much as younger subjects. Actually, just the opposite may occur. Powell and associates (1980) showed that the blood pressure of older subjects (between 55 and 70) increased during serial learning tasks, and that this increase was positively related to serial learning ability and better performance on the easier tasks. If, however, learning tasks became too complex, the positive relationship to an increase in autonomic arousal was obscured. Subjects did less well because of anxiety. Older adults can become so emotionally aroused and anxious that their energies are dissipated in undifferentiated, haphazard ways, and learning performance declines. When given a drug that suppresses the action of the autonomic nervous system (anxiety and upset), learning

performance inproves (Eisdorfer, Nowling, & Wilkie, 1970).

PACING, SPEED.   **Pacing** refers to the time intervals between stimuli. In paired-associate tasks, subjects must learn a series of paired words or letters, such as *ball-bat* or *boy-girl*. These paired associates may be presented at 2-second, 4-second, or longer intervals. It has been found that *older adults take more time to learn than do younger adults.* When older adults are allowed to study paired associates on a slower or self-paced schedule, their learning ability improves. The total time needed to learn continues to increase with advancing age.

Once the pairs are learned, older adults also take longer to respond to the stimulus word. Thus, if the word *ball* is presented, older adults take longer to respond with the correct word *bat.* Older adults need more

Pacing—time intervals between stimuli

FOCUS

Enhancing Learning

One purpose of research is to provide practical knowledge that can be used. The research on adult learning can be beneficial to adult education. People who teach adults and adults who seek to learn can benefit from understanding and practicing the following important principles:

1. Task performance and learning improve as adult anxiety regarding proficiency decreases. Establishing rapport and offering assurance, moral support, and assistance help reduce anxiety.
2. Adults need opportunities to express what they do know and to exhibit their talents. They often know and are capable of more than they show. A natural cautiousness about doing something wrong makes them wary of exhibiting their skills.
3. Careful instruction and directions help overcome adult cautiousness and stimulate performance.
4. Adults do much better with material and tasks that are relevant and meaningful to them. They can hardly be expected to show their intelligence on tests of tasks they consider stupid (Ridley, Bachrach, & Dawson, 1979; Barrett & Wright, 1981).
5. Adults are able to perform better with materials and tasks that are organized into logical categories or sequences. They benefit from organizational aids and suggestions that help them categorize and group materials into meaningful associations.

6. Motivation is increased if adults comprehend the reasons for learning or for performance. Offering explanations about the relevance of the material or task and providing rewards and incentives, within the realm of possibility, stimulate effort (Hartley & Walsh, 1980).
7. Because adults value accuracy more than speed, tasks must be paced to allow maximum learning and performance. Self-paced assignments are often accomplished more proficiently than those with severe time limitations.
8. Maximum and repeated exposure to material or tasks to be learned encourages deeper processing and enhances learning and performance.
9. Reducing all forms of interference and distracting stimuli enhances learning. If present materials and tasks are completely learned before new ones are introduced, interference effects are minimized and learning is enhanced (Arenberg, 1976; Parkinson, Lindholm, & Urell, 1980).
10. The use of both visual and auditory presentations in the teaching process enhances learning more than the use of only one method. When studying, repeating information out loud enhances learning (Rissenberg & Glanzer, 1986).
11. Adult performance declines as fatigue increases. Offering appropriate breaks and rest periods may actually improve learning and performance.

time to show what they have learned; otherwise it appears they have not learned as well as younger adults.

LEARNING AND AGE.   The most extensive body of longitudinal data on adult learning appears in the *Baltimore Longitudinal Study of Men* (Arenberg & Robertson-Tshabo, 1977). For the most part, these were well-educated men of high socioeconomic status. The data consisted of paired-associate and serial-performance learning data measured at two different speed intervals for each task. Cross-sectional analysis showed small age differences before age 60 and large age differences thereafter, particularly at the faster pacing speeds. Analysis of the longitudinal data for both the paired-associate and serial-performance learning tasks showed similar results: *The great increases in learning errors occurred after age 60, using both the slow- and fast-paced intervals.* The youngest group of men (initially between 30 and 38) either showed a slight improvement in scores or the smallest mean decline (depending on the speed of pacing) over a 7-year period. The two groups of men between 39 and 54 years of age showed moderate mean declines; the two oldest groups, initially 61 to 74, showed the largest mean declines. Even among men who learned at the slower pace, the earliest born cohorts showed the most decline and the latest born cohorts the least. Mean errors were consistently greater for older subsamples within each cohort, indicating that they performed less effectively than younger subsamples from the same cohort. *This evidence indicates a verbal learning deficit in the later years of life.*

CREATIVITY

Creativity in Late Adulthood

Much has been written about developing creativity in children but little about creativity in adulthood. Do educators and psychologists equate creativity with youthfulness? If so, the notion is fallacious. Outstanding contributions have been made by many people during late adulthood, as the following examples show.

- Will and Ariel Durant completed their 11-volume work *The Story of Civilization* when he was 90 and she was 77.
- Sophocles wrote *Oedipus Rex* at 75.
- Sigmund Freud wrote his last book at 83.
- Von Benden discovered the reduction of chromosomes at 74.

Many older adults are highly creative.

- Mahatma Gandhi launched his movement to gain India's independence at 72.
- Cecil B. DeMille produced *the Ten Commandments* at 75.
- Claude Monet began his *Water Lily* series at 73.

Creativity as Quality of Production

The lack of attention to creativity in adulthood has resulted in a paucity of research. The work by Lehman (1962, 1966) is usually cited as the most important on the subject, even though it is now more than 26 years old. Lehman is still cited because little subsequent research is available to supplement his work. Lehman measured creativity by the quality of work achieved by adults in the various fields of science, medicine, philosophy, psychology, art, invention, and other areas. His method was to tabulate by age groups the frequency with which high-quality productions were listed in historical accounts covering a period of more than 400 years. He found that in most fields people produced the greatest proportion of superior work during their 30s. After that there was a decline in high-quality production. About 80% of superior work was completed by age 50. The rate of lower-quality work peaked somewhat later. He also found some fields of endeavor peaked earlier than others. However, in all fields, individual variations were so great that Lehman emphasized that usefulness was not limited to age and that age was not always a causative factor in the decline of creative quality. *People made valuable contributions at all ages.*

Creativity as Quantity of Work

Lehman has had his critics. Dennis (1966) maintained that it is almost impossible to make objective judgments of the quality of a person's work. A person's early, pioneering work is more likely to be mentioned than later work. Older work is usually designated masterwork more often than recent work. Thus, investigations tend to show that earlier work at younger ages is superior. Besides, competition increases as the years pass, making it difficult for a person's later work to be labeled superior. Dennis (1966) maintained Lehman's analysis of quality through bibliographies and citations favored early work and distorted the findings. He insisted that quantity of output, not quality, is a far better measure of creativity.

Dennis's research revealed that peak performance years occurred much later than Lehman maintained, that the performance often continued over many years of the life cycle, and that *the quantity of output at each age varied depending on the field of endeavor.* Output in creative arts and science peaked in the 40s and declined thereafter, with artistic output declining the most and scientific output falling only a little. Output of adults in the humanities continued to rise from the 30s to the 60s, with little decline even through the 70s. Figure 17.12 shows the data presented by Dennis and represented graphically by Botwinick (1967).

Another study analyzed the productivity of scientists in the math, physics, and economics departments at the University of California at Berkeley, and in the math, physics, and chemistry departments at the University of Illinois at Urbana. Productivity was measured by the number of citations made in a year to all of the scientists' earlier work, as listed in the *Science Citation Index.* The mean peak age for the greatest number of citations was 59, but the ages ranged from 39 for the Berkeley physics professors to 89 for the Urbana math professors. The mean peak age of salaries of all of the professors was in the mid-60s (Diamond, 1986).

Individual Variations

Why individuals in the humanities remain creative into late adulthood, whereas the output of artists and scientists declines with age, remains a question. Certainly, individual variations exist in every field. Some people remain intellectually alive, active, and inventive, continuing to question, search, and participate fully in life. Others become stagnant at an early age. What happens depends partly on individual attitudes about oneself

FIGURE 17.12 Creative output of people in the humanities, sciences, and arts over the life cycle.

Adapted from *Cognitive Processes in Maturity and Old Age* by J. Botwinick, 1967, New York: Springer Publishing Co., Inc.

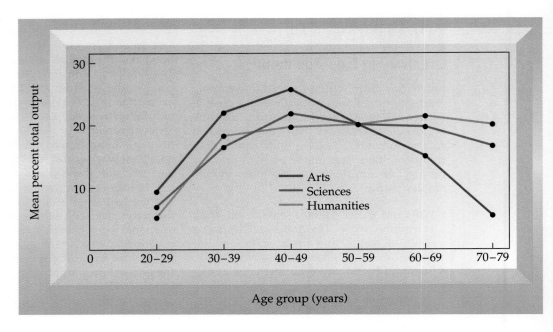

and the aging process. Life can be a fascinating challenge throughout the adult life span.

EDUCATION

Learning is a lifelong endeavor. There is no specific age at which people can or should cease learning.

> Learning is not something outside life. It is something within life waiting to be understood. Learning is a kind of big umbrella over everything else that happens to you. And it can help you whether you are buying a house, reading about heart trouble, studying your social security rates, or even trying to understand what's happening in Congress (Schuckman, 1975, p. 85).

Increasingly, serious consideration is being given to adult education. Many opportunities exist to learn through adult courses in high schools, vocational schools, community colleges, universities, and self-taught or directed home study programs. In addition, thousands of older adults attend regular university classes with younger students. Some universities provide gold card registrations that offer free tuition to people over 65. A variety of nonacademic organizations also offer courses for older people, notably *The Institute for Lifetime Learning*, sponsored by the *American Association for Retired Persons (AARP)* and the *National Retired Teachers' Association (NRTA)*.

In spite of the progress, the total number of older persons with a secondary or college education is limited. Figure 17.13 shows the percentages of people 55 and older who have completed various levels of education (U.S. Bureau of the Census, 1990). The number of older people taking some type of formal education is also limited. The major reasons older people give for not participating in educational courses are lack of interest, being too old, poor health, and lack of time. Other barriers are vision and hearing prob-

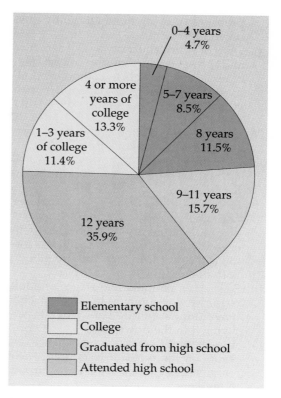

FIGURE 17.13 Years of school completed by adults, 55 years of age or older, 1988.

Statistics from *Statistical Abstract of the United States, 1990* (p. 134) by U.S. Bureau of the Census, 1990, Washington, DC: U.S. Government Printing Office.

lems, and lack of transportation. For handicapped adults, courses must be carefully planned, considering numerous learning, personality, and environmental factors.

The concept of lifelong education is taken seriously today by educators and administrators. Exposure to schooling throughout life enables adults to maintain their cognitive skills, morale, self-image, and abilities to deal with the complex problems of the future. The rate of change of our knowledge base in most fields is so rapid that workers need refresher and retraining courses several times during a career.

SUMMARY

1. About half the adult population attains the full stage of formal operational thinking. Some adults are able to use formal thinking in their field of specialization but not in others.
2. Like education, intelligence, and many cultural factors, cognitive style influences the ability to do Piagetian-type tasks.
3. Older adults approach problems at a lower level of abstraction than do young adults or adolescents.
4. Older adults approach problems differently; they tend to be more pragmatic and subjective, and to personalize learning tasks.
5. Older adults appear to solve practical

problems of living more efficiently than do younger adults.

6. Tests of word familiarity and of sentence and prose comprehension reveal that older adults are able to comprehend almost as well as younger adults, with comprehension declining some after age 60.

7. Older people develop pragmatic knowledge we call wisdom.

8. Some adults seem to go beyond formal operational thinking to reach a problem-finding stage.

9. Dialectical thinkers are able to consider opposing viewpoints simultaneously without need to resolve the inconsistencies, and they are sometimes able to formulate new ideas that are superior to both opposites.

10. Schaie has outlined five stages of adult cognitive development in which people move from acquiring knowledge to applying it in their own lives.

11. Any attempt to measure intelligence depends on the types of tests used, their research design, and what they purport to measure.

12. Verbal scores on the WAIS tend to hold up with increasing age, whereas performance scores tend to decline after the mid-20s.

13. Longitudinal measurements tend to minimize intellectual decline with age, whereas cross-sectional measurements tend to maximize it. Some longitudinal studies emphasize that intellectual decline is not inevitable even by age 50 and over.

14. Scores on the PMA also show that intellectual decline does not always occur, and when it does, it usually takes place after age 50.

15. Fluid intelligence seems to decline from early adulthood on, but this is probably due to generational differences and not to aging itself. Scores on crystallized intelligence increase through adulthood.

16. A chief criticism of intelligence tests is that IQ is only one important factor necessary to carry out responsible tasks. Other criticisms include the familiarity of test items to children and young adults, and the cultural and economic bias.

17. A large number of factors affect test scores: the circumstances of test administration, motivation, personality traits of the subjects, physical factors, emotional factors, sensory abilities, the relationship with the test administrator, and general intellectual level and years of school completed.

18. Socioenvironmental factors that influence intellectual abilities include educational level, socioeconomic status, stress, and training.

19. Intellectual performance can be modified by training.

20. Age and physical condition are more important factors in intellectual decline than is terminal decline (the person's distance from death).

21. Memory involves acquisition, storage, and retrieval of information.

22. There are three memory stores: sensory stores, short-term storage, and long-term storage. Information passes from one compartment to another.

23. Sensory memory stores show some decline with age, with tactual memory declining the fastest, visual memory declining the next fastest, and audio memory showing the least decline.

24. Primary memory, or short-term memory, does not change much with age, but secondary, or long-term, memory may decline some. There are greater losses in recall ability than in recognition ability.

25. Young adults have greater long-term memory ability than do older adults, but subjects of all ages remember best sociohistoric events that occurred when the subjects were 15 to 25 years old.

26. Memory training can enhance the memory of elderly adults.

27. Learning and memory are intertwined, but the performance of adults is not always indicative of what they have learned.

28. Learning research has revealed the importance of motivation, relevance, meaning, associative strength, autonomic arousal, and pacing and speed in learning ability.

29. Research reveals some decline in learning ability after age 60, particularly at faster pacing speeds.

30. Creative ability measured as quality of production shows that about 80% of superior work is completed by age 50, with the peak occurring during the 30s.

31. Creativity as quantity of production shows a peak in the 40s in the sciences and art, and in the 60s in the humanities. In another study, the mean peak age for the greatest number of science citations was 59, with age ranges from 39 to 89; however, there are wide individual variations.

32. Learning is a lifelong endeavor, so increasing attention is being given to education of adults throughout life.

KEY TERMS

Acquisition   *p. 387*
Antithesis   *p. 377*
Associative strength   *p. 391*
Autonomic arousal   *p. 391*
Dialectical thinking   *p. 377*
Echoic memory   *p. 387*
Extrinsic motivation   *p. 391*
Field-dependent people   *p. 374*
Field-independent people   *p. 374*
Iconic memory   *p. 388*
Intrinsic motivation   *p. 391*

Pacing   *p. 392*
Paired-associate learning   *p. 391*
Primary memory   *p. 388*
Retrieval   *p. 387*
Secondary memory   *p. 388*
Serial learning tasks   *p. 391*
Storage   *p. 387*
Tactual memory   *p. 388*
Terminal decline   *p. 386*
Thesis   *p. 377*

DISCUSSION QUESTIONS

1. Do you know any adults over 55 or 60? How does their thinking differ from your own? Do they have greater practical problem-solving abilities than younger adults?
2. How does your word comprehension now compare to your ability when you were younger?
3. Do you think people become wiser as they get older? Why or why not?
4. One of the tasks of marriage counselors is to try to get couples to identify their problems. What evidence do you have that some adults are better at problem finding than others?
5. What are some advantages and disadvantages of being able to think dialectically?
6. Schaie says that as people age they move from acquiring knowledge to using knowledge in their everyday lives. Do you think that all adults use their knowledge to the fullest? Explain. Give examples.
7. What do you think of evaluating the intellectual ability of people in terms of IQ? What are some pros and cons?
8. Why do cross-sectional measurements of intelligence maximize decline with age whereas longitudinal measurements minimize it?
9. Give some examples of fluid versus crystallized intelligence.
10. What personality factors do you feel are most important in affecting intelligence?
11. What socioenvironmental factors are most important in maintaining intellectual abilities as one ages?
12. Talk about the memory ability of some adult you know. Has this ability changed as the person has aged? How?
13. Do you agree that people best remember events that happen when they are 15 to 25 years of age? What events do you best remember that happened during this age period of your life?
14. To older students: Do you feel you can learn as well now as when you were younger? Discuss.
15. To younger students: Of the principles for adult learning outlined in the Focus: Enhancing Learning, which items are most important for people of all ages? for children? for older people? Discuss.
16. What helps you the most when you are trying to learn something?
17. Give examples of people whose greatest period of creativity was after they were 50 years or more old.

SUGGESTED READINGS

Commons, M. L., Richards, F. A., & Arnon, C. (Eds.). (1984). *Beyond formal operations: Late adolescent and adult cognitive development.* New York: Praeger. A fifth stage.

Rybash, J. M., Hoyer, W. J., & Roodin, P. A. (1986). *Adult cognition and aging.* New York: Pergamon. Formal operational and dialectical thinking.

Schooler, C., & Schaie, K. W. (Eds.). (1987). *Cognitive functioning and social structure over the life course.* Norwood, NJ: Ablex. Articles about cognitive development, change.

18

Emotional Development

SUBJECTIVE WELL-BEING

In this chapter, we are concerned with the emotional side of life: with how adults feel about themselves, about others, and about life in general. We are concerned especially with identifying what psychologists call **subjective well-being**, and with an understanding of the many factors that influence it (Stacey & Gatz, 1991).

A number of definitions of subjective well-being have been proposed. Horley (1984) defines it as "a self-perceived positive feeling or state" (p. 127). Liang (1985) describes subjective well-being as "an individual's cognitive as well as affective assessments about life as a whole" (p. 552). Most psychologists agree that subjective well-being is an abstract, multidimensional concept that can best be measured by specific indicators such as *life satisfaction, morale, happiness, congruence*, and *affect* (George, 1981; Liang, 1984). Let's look at some of these indicators.

Subjective well-being—a self-perceived positive feeling or state; a cognitive and affective assessment about life as a whole

Life Satisfaction

Neugarten, Havighurst, and Tobin (1961) conducted the most influential initial research on life satisfaction (Krause, 1991) and developed the *Life Satisfaction Index A (LSIA)* to measure it in older adults. The researchers viewed life satisfaction as having five dimensions:

1. *Zest versus apathy*—the degree of involvement in activity, with other persons, or with ideas.

Subjective well-being describes how adults feel about themselves, others, and life in general.

2. *Resolution and fortitude*—the extent to which persons take responsibility for their own lives.
3. *Congruence*—the extent to which goals are achieved.
4. *Self-concept*—the extent to which a person has a positive concept of self, physically, psychologically, and socially.
5. *Mood tone*—whether the person holds optimistic attitudes and happy feelings.

Thus, an individual possesses positive psychological well-being

> to the extent that he (a) takes pleasure from whatever round of activities that constitutes his everyday life; (b) regards his life as meaningful and accepts resolutely that which life has been; (c) feels he has succeeded in achieving his major goals; (d) holds a positive image of self; and (e) maintains happy and optimistic attitudes and mood (Neugarten, Havighurst, & Tobin, 1961, p. 137).

Research has only partially supported the LSIA as originally constructed as a valid measure of life satisfaction among older adults (Hoyt & Creech, 1983; Stock and Okun, 1982).

Sociodemographic Factors

The LSIA completely leaves out sociodemographic factors in measuring life satisfaction. The question arises as to the effect of such factors as race, residence, and socioeconomic status on life satisfaction. Let's look at these three variables.

RACE.   Several studies measure the effect of race on life satisfaction (Liang, Lawrence, & Bollen, 1987). One study showed that most factors influencing life satisfaction affected both whites and blacks, but that the negative effects of various physical impairments are considerably stronger among blacks than among whites (Usui, Keil, & Phillips, 1983).

SOCIOECONOMIC STATUS.   Cross-sectional studies consistently reveal a positive relationship between income and overall satisfaction with life (Larson, 1978). But longitudinal and cross-national studies reveal a more complex relationship. Life satisfaction in the United States does not automatically rise as income and consumption levels increase. Furthermore, persons in richer nations are not happier than those in poorer nations (Usui, Keil, & Durig, 1985).

The key seems to be the standard by which one judges satisfaction. People compare their own financial status to those of others. Their satisfaction then reflects the extent to which reality matches what is considered necessary or desirable. Fernandez and Kulik (1981) suggested that people compare their situation to the standard of others in their neighborhood, assuming that the neighborhood provides a relative basis for comparison. One study of persons 60 years and older living in Kentucky in 1980 showed that the adults compared themselves with the nearest or closest relatives (Usui, Keil, & Durig, 1985). If they felt they were better off than their relatives, their sense of well-being was heightened. Interestingly, comparison with close friends and neighbors did not seem to affect subjective well-being, but this was probably because neighbors and friends were usually similar to themselves in status. Certainly, if people feel they are considerably poorer than those in their neighborhood, most would feel some dissatisfaction. Other research on marital satisfaction has shown that *it is not the level of income that is important, but whether people are satisfied with the level they have reached* (Berry & Williams, 1987).

URBAN VERSUS RURAL LIVING.   Another study sought to sort out the effects of urban versus rural living on life satisfaction (Liang & Warfel, 1983). Even though no direct effect of urbanism on life satisfaction was found, *urbanism influenced life satisfaction indirectly and interactively because it influenced health, financial satisfaction, and social integration.* In general, the better the health, the greater the financial satisfaction; and the higher the social integration, the greater was life satisfaction. But the influence of the size of the city on these is variable. Some urban areas have better health care than do rural areas, but many rural residents see their services as more accessible. Income is lower in rural than in urban areas, but many rural residents don't see themselves as financially deprived. The level of social integration in urban areas is lower than in rural areas. Social relationships in rural communities tend to be more personal, so social integration in large cities may contribute less to life satisfaction. Overall, *the effects of urban living on life satisfaction are inconsistent.*

Morale

Subjective well-being has also been described in terms of **morale**, which is defined as one's moral or mental condition with respect to cheerfulness, confidence, zeal, and the like. The *Philadelphia Geriatric Center (PGC) Morale Scale* is the most commonly used instrument to measure morale among the elderly (Lawton, 1975). The PGC Morale Scale evaluates three components of morale.

Agitation—as revealed by such phrases as "Little things bother me more this year," "I worry so much that I can't sleep," "I am afraid of a lot of things," "I get mad more than I used to," "I take things hard," and "I get upset easily."

Dissatisfaction—as revealed by such phrases as "Life isn't worth living," "Life is hard for me," "How satisfied am I with life today?" and "I have a lot to be sad about."

Attitudes toward aging—as revealed by such phrases as "Things get worse as one ages," "I have as much pep as last year," "As one ages, he gets less useful," "Things are better/worse than I thought," and "I am as happy as when I was younger."

The *PGC Morale Scale* has been found to be a helpful measure of subjective well-being (Liang & Bolan, 1983). In slightly modified form, it has been found useful in comparing the morale of American and Japanese elderly (Liang, Asano, Boller, Kahana, & Maeda, 1987). The level of morale varies greatly, depending on the group studied.

Happiness

Happiness has been listed as another dimension of subjective well-being. It has been described as a quality or state characterized by pleasure, delight, joy, gladness, and contentment. In more technical terms, it has

Morale—one's moral or mental condition with respect to cheerfulness, confidence, zeal, and the like

Happiness—a quality or state characterized by pleasure, delight, joy, gladness, and contentment

Whether people live in urban or rural areas is not the key determinant of life satisfaction.

Happiness is a quality or state characterized by pleasure, delight, joy, gladness, and contentment.

been referred to as "a long-term positive affect or a cognitive measurement of positive affect" (Liang, 1985, p. 552). It is a sense of subjective well-being.

Much has been written about happiness: what it is and how to achieve it. Researchers have examined the role that genetics plays in happiness and unhappiness. Interestingly, twin studies have indicated a genetic predisposition for unhappiness that runs in families (Goldsmith, 1983; Goleman, 1986; Thomas & Chess, 1984). Some people seem to be born to be sad. However, happiness itself is not inherited; it is a capacity that must be developed.

What are the happiest years? One survey of 216 men and women, ages 16 to 67, showed that approximately 40% of the respondents regarded the 20s as the best age of life. About 18% chose the 30s. The middle years of life (the 40s and 50s) were considered best by 19%. Only 2% chose the 60s (Chiriboga, 1978). This finding agrees with other studies showing the young adult years to be the happiest.

When broken down into age groups, however, this same study indicated that *each group reported the present to be a satisfying time of life.* Most young adults felt that their age was the best age; but among those of pre-retirement age, 44% of the men and 61% of the women felt that the 40s and after were the best periods of life (Chiriboga, 1978). Because life expectancy at 40 is still more than 38 years, these individuals had nearly half a lifetime ahead. It is encouraging that most looked forward to those years with expectation and optimism.

Congruence

Congruence means that, when assessed cognitively, there is an agreement between a person's desired goals and the goals that have been, or are being, attained in life. Congruence begins with finding meaning in life,

Congruence—cognitive agreement between a person's desired goals and the goals that have been, or are being, attained in life

---

LIVING ISSUES

Who Is Happiest?

The following are a compilation of research findings on happiness (Swanbrow, 1989).

1. People who plan to be happier tend to be, by making happiness a priority in their lives.
2. People are happy who have control over their own lives (Aldwin, 1991; Heckhausen & Baltes, 1991).
3. Poverty makes people miserable; having enough money makes them happier, but having more than enough doesn't guarantee happiness.
4. Love and intimacy, sharing loving relationships, are important ingredients to happiness.
5. Maintaining a positive attitude of optimism toward life contributes to happiness.
6. Novelty, doing new things, contributes to happiness.
7. The frequency and duration of emotional highs contributes more to happiness than does the intensity of positive feelings.
8. Keeping busy at work that is enjoyable, and accomplishing it, contributes to happiness.
9. Altruism, doing good, enhances self-esteem, makes people feel good about themselves, and contributes to happiness.
10. Maintaining physical fitness through exercise and good health habits is an important road to happiness.
11. Having meaning and purpose in life is one component of a happy life.

making sense, order, or coherence out of one's existence, having a purpose and then striving toward a goal or goals (Reker, Peacock, & Wong, 1987). The search for meaning remains a significant and universal human motive. Meaninglessness in life, if left unresolved, can lead to symptoms of anxiety, depression, hopelessness, or physical decline.

Reker and Peacock (1981) developed a multidimensional measure of meaning and purpose in life called the *Life Attitude Profile (LAP)*. The LAP consists of seven dimensions as follows:

- *Life purpose*—zest for life, fulfillment, contentment, satisfaction.
- *Existential vacuum*—lack of purpose, lack of goals, free-floating anxiety.
- *Life control*—freedom to make life choices, exercise of responsibility.
- *Death acceptance*—lack of fear or anxiety about death.
- *Will to meaning*—striving to find meaning in personal existence.

- *Goal seeking*—desire to achieve new goals, be on the move.
- *Future meaning*—determination to make the future meaningful, acceptance of future potentialities.

Three hundred men and women, ages 16 to over 75, divided into five age groups, were given the LAP. The researchers emphasized that the results were cross-sectional data and yielded information on age differences, not age changes. Observed differences might be caused by factors confounded with age. The results of the study are shown in Figure 18.1. As can be seen, both *Life Purpose (LP)* and *Death Acceptance (DA)* increased with age. *Goal Seeking (GS)* and *Future Meaning (FM)* decreased with age. *Existential Vacuum (EV)* showed a curvilinear relationship with age. Significant sex differences were found for *Life Control (LC)* and *Will to Meaning (WM)*. Women viewed life as more under their control and expressed a stronger will to find meaning as compared with males. FM, LP, and LC were found to predict psycho-

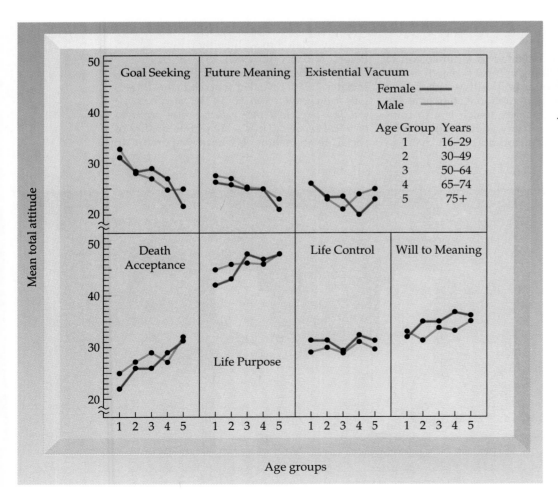

FIGURE 18.1 Age and sex differences in the seven dimensions of the Life Attitude Profile (LAP).

From "Meaning and Purpose in Life and Well-Being: A Life-Span Perspective" by G. T. Reker, E. J. Peacock, and P. T. P. Wong, 1987, *Journal of Gerontology, 42*, pp. 44–49.

logical and physical well-being. EV, GS, and DA predicted psychological and physical discomfort (Reker, Peacock, & Wong, 1987).

Older adults reported both an increasing sense of life purpose and an increasing acceptance of death. Young adults had a strong need to seek new goals and to look forward to future potentialities, whereas elderly people could look back at their past and find meaning in what they had already accomplished. The level of existential vacuum was curvilinear, higher among both the young and old, indicating a sense of futility and emptiness in absence of clear career goals in the young, and to a feeling of role loss, loss of friends and relatives, and reduction of active participation by the old. Middle-aged adults felt that they had found their niche in life, that they had arrived. Women of all ages viewed their lives as more under their control than did men. The stronger will to meaning among women may have been a consequence of dissatisfaction with the traditional women's role and an attempt to determine what to do with the rest of their lives (Reker, Peacock, & Wong, 1987).

Affect

Affect—one's feelings, whether positive or negative

Affect has been included as a dimension of subjective well-being in most research on the subject. Affect may be positive, which is a transitory feeling or emotional state of active pleasure. *Negative affect*, which is also transitory, includes anxiety, depression, agitation, worry, pessimism, and other distress-

ing psychological symptoms (Liang, 1985). The primary content of affect is emotion, feeling. On the *Affect Balance Scale (ABS)*, *positive affect* is described by such feelings as "excited," "pleased," "on top of the world," or "going my way" (Bradburn, 1969). Negative affect is described by such feelings as "restless," "very lonely," "bored," or "depressed." Affect has been found to be an important dimension of subjective well-being.

Social Networks

Subjective well-being has also been found to relate to the quality of **social networks**, that is, to the quality of social ties with children, family, and friends (Ward, Sherman, & LaGory, 1984). Past research has investigated the quality (number, frequency, and proximity) of relationships and has found that the number of ties and frequency of social interaction were relatively unimportant to life satisfaction (Bowling & Browne, 1991). Family availability and interaction particularly seemed to have little relation to the subjective well-being of older adults (Glenn & McLanahan, 1981). The quantity of friendship interaction was only a little more consistently related to well-being (Hoyt, Kaiser, Peters, & Babchuk, 1980).

More recent research by Ward and associates (1984) revealed that *whether older persons had enough social ties in the objective sense was less important than whether they perceived they had enough*. Thus a subjective quality of social relationships is more important to

Social networks—social ties with children, family, and friends

Subjective well-being is related to the quality of social relationships with children, family, and friends.

well-being than objective quantity (Krause, 1990). Children play an important role in social networks of older adults, but whether children are nearby and seen regularly is less important than whether they are seen enough and whether interaction with children has the quality desired by the older individual. The same is true in relation to friends and family. If adults expressed satisfaction with present levels and quality of social interaction and support, these social networks bore a strong association with subjective well-being.

Health

Numerous research studies point to health as one of the most important factors related to subjective well-being (George & Landerman, 1984; Okun, Stock, Haring, & Witter, 1984; Zautra & Hempel, 1984). Certainly, people who are sick or physically disabled are much less likely to express contentment about their lives (Revicki & Mitchell, 1990). Willits and Crider (1988) evaluated the relationship between health rating and other satisfaction measures of adults 50 to 55 years of age and found that health rating was significantly related to four satisfactions measures: life satisfaction, community satisfaction, job satisfaction, and marital satisfaction. Furthermore, these relationships held true regardless of gender, education, marital status, income, number of relatives in the area, number of friends nearby, or frequency of leisure involvement.

Stability of Subjective Well-Being

One question that arises is to what extent subjective well-being changes with age (Carp & Carp, 1983). How are different times of life perceived and evaluated? Is old age as bleak a period as younger people commonly assume? What changes take place in the affective (emotional) life of the adult? Is there a blunting of both positive and negative feelings, leading to tranquility or even emotional blandness?

One of the most important efforts to answer these questions was a research study known as the *National Health and Nutrition Examination Survey (NHANES) I Epidemiologic Follow-up Study* (Costa, Zonderman, McCrae, Cornoni-Huntley, Locke, & Barbano, 1987). This survey consisted of a 9-year longitudinal study of 4,942 men and women initially aged 25 to 74. This survey was supplemented by cross- and time-sequential analysis of an independent sample of 4,986 participants (ages 32 to 87) who were first administered the *General Well-Being Schedule (GWB)* at the time of follow-up. Although older participants tended to be lower in both positive and negative affect when measured cross-sectionally, longitudinal changes in these two measures were not found. Total well-being showed no significant age, birth cohort, or time effects in any of the analyses. Given the size and representativeness of the sample, *this is strong evidence of the stability of mean levels of psychological well-being in adulthood*, and points to the importance of enduring personality dispositions. It also suggests that many adults are able to adapt to varying circumstances of life so that levels of well-being stay fairly constant (Markides & Lee, 1990).

STRESS

Most people function adequately and positively during their lives. They may experience difficulty, however, when exposed to excessive stress.

Meaning

Stress is physical, mental, or emotional strain or tension caused by environmental, situational, or personal pressures and demands. A woman late for work becomes tense and anxious when caught in a traffic jam. She is needed for an important meeting and paces nervously until her arrival. Her children were upset that morning because she pushed them to dress in a hurry. Her husband became angry when he could not find a clean shirt. These stresses were minor and temporary and soon forgotten by those involved.

Other stresses involve more pressure, tension, strain, and upheaval for longer periods of time: A family member becomes critically ill or a soldier is exposed to violent combat over several months. The amount of stress depends partially on the severity of the circumstances and the duration of the exposure. Generally, more stress occurs when events happen suddenly than when the individual has advance warning and can make preparations. Unpredictable and uncontrollable events cause more stress than those over which individuals exercise more control.

Also, people react differently to stress. Some have a very high frustration tolerance, others a low one. Tolerance depends partially on one's hereditary makeup and past

Stress—physical, mental, or emotional strain

Type A personality—a personality characterized by intense competitiveness, hostility, overwork, and a sense of time urgency; one who has extreme bodily reactions to stress

experiences. A so-called **type A personality**, or one characterized by extreme competitiveness, overwork, hostility, and urgency, also seems to have extreme bodily reactions to stress, including increased heart rate, blood pressure, and blood flow to the muscles (Fischman, 1988). People raised in tense family environments over a period of years usually react more strongly to stressful situations. *The amount of stress experienced depends not only on the severity and duration of exposure, but also on one's previous conditioning.*

Causes

JOB RELATED.   Stress arises from various causes. Some stress is job related. Long hours, heavy responsibilities, and continued pressure can make a job stressful. However, these factors do not always cause stress. People who like their occupation, whose work offers opportunities to use their talents and skills and provides status, recognition, and pleasant associations, are less likely to experience job-related stress than those who are dissatisfied with their jobs.

Work that requires constant vigilance and exposes the worker to uncertainty or danger can result in stress. The work of air traffic controllers is one example. They never know when an accident is imminent. On the job, they must be alert at all times.

When the results of one's work are uncertain, stress is increased. Farm families never know if the weather will be favorable to their crops. Drought or floods can ruin a whole year's work (Davis-Brown & Salamon, 1987). Actors never know if the critics will give them good reviews or if the plays they are in will be a success. Writers never know if their works will sell, and how much their royalty checks will be. Workers who never know if

they will have a job tomorrow experience a great deal of stress.

ROLE STRAIN.   Stress can result from role strain. The busy homemaker and mother with four children, constantly under pressure from family members to run errands, provide personal services, supervise children's activities, stay up all night with a sick child, maintain a home, and give moral support to other family members, may find these demands exhausting and stressful over a long period of time.

> Mrs. L. prided herself on her ability to run her home, take care of her three children and her husband, and work at the same time. But then things began to pile up. Her aging mother became ill and required daily care and attention. Her boss expected overtime work until his accounts were caught up. Her youngest child became seriously ill and had to be hospitalized. After several weeks, Mrs. L. was physically and emotionally exhausted. She became nervous and distraught. She cried for no special reason. She became so distressed that she had to take a leave of absence from her job to remove part of the pressure on her (Author's counseling notes).

As long as people can manage their situations and feel in control, stress can be kept to a minimum. When the demands placed on one become too much to handle, stress develops (House et al., 1979).

INTERPERSONAL   RELATIONSHIPS. Stress is likely to arise out of interpersonal relationships that are unpleasant and conflicting over a period of time.

> Mr. and Mrs. S. were married young. She was only 16, he was 21 when she became pregnant. She dropped out of school to have her baby, and he worked at two jobs to try to make ends meet. After the baby was born, she had no car, little money, and no close friends where they lived. She would become particularly upset if her husband spent his time off going out with his friends, leaving her alone in their apartment to take care of the baby. If she tried to talk to him, he would accuse her of being a nag and storm out the door. They began to argue about everything. No matter what they discussed, it ended up in a fight.
>
> Mrs. S. began to show physical symptoms of the tension she was under. She was exhausted most of the time, frequently sick, and despondent and depressed. Many mornings she didn't feel like getting out of bed. One morning she was shocked when she found herself slapping the baby because he cried (Author's counseling notes).

The work of air traffic controllers involves a high degree of stress.

TRANSITION OR CHANGE.   Any kind of transition or change is also stressful for some people. They get along fine if life moves routinely on the same schedule, involving the same responsibilities, the same people, and familiar surroundings. But if something changes that routine, they become upset and confused.

Major transitions in the life cycle, such as going to school, getting a job, getting married, moving to a new community, becoming a parent, switching jobs, facing retirement, or similar transitions, may require considerable adjustment. Desired changes have a much different effect than do unwanted events. However, even happy events can cause stress. People have suffered heart attacks from good news as well as bad. Just recently an older man died of a heart attack after winning $10 million in the lottery. Having a baby can be a delightful experience, but it still causes stress, especially for the couple who did not plan on children.

LIFE CRISES.   Numerous life crises cause stress. A **crisis** may be defined as a drastic change in the course of events; it is a turning point that affects the trend of future events. It is a time of instability, necessitating decisions and adjustments. Sometimes the crisis develops because of *external events*: a hurricane, earthquake, flood (Phifer & Norris, 1989), war, national economic depression, or the closing of a plant where a person works (McCubbin, Joy, Cauble, Comeau, Patterson, & Needle, 1980). At other times, a crisis occurs within the family system: the loss of a family member, conflict that erupts in family violence, divorce, or alcoholism (Weigel, Weigel, & Blundall, 1987). *Internal crises* tend to demoralize a family, increasing resentment, alienation, and conflict. Sometimes a crisis develops out of a whole series of smaller external and internal events that build up to the point where people cannot cope (Lavee, McCubbin, & Olson, 1987). Broderick (1984) explained:

> Even small events, not enough by themselves to cause any real stress, can take a toll when they come one after another. First an unplanned pregnancy, then a move, then the big row with the new neighbors over keeping the dog tied up, and finally little Jimmy breaking his arm in a bicycle accident, all in three months, finally becomes too much (p. 310).

Broderick calls this situation **crisis overload**.

Sarason and colleagues (1978, 1981) developed a *Life Experience Survey* measuring the impact of various life events. People are asked to check events that occurred during the past year and to evaluate the effect of each on their lives, the extent to which they expected the event to happen, and the extent to which they had control over the event's occurrence. Some of the events, such as death of a spouse, were more stressful than others. People who experienced multiple events, whose troubles "came in bunches," became more depressed, anxious, hostile, and fatigued, performed more poorly, and experienced more of an increase in physical symptoms.

Crisis—a drastic change in the course of events; a turning point that affects the trend of future events

Crisis overload—a series of crises happening one after the other so that the person has difficulty in coping

FOCUS

Combat Fatigue

The combat experiences and reactions of soldiers during war have been the subject of much research. Soldiers must deal with the fear of death or injury. They witness other people blown up or maimed. There is the strain of combat vigilance against unexpected attack or capture. These situations, plus separation from family; loss of sleep; physical exhaustion; and exposure to hunger, heat, or cold, produce high levels of stress, sometimes over long periods. Long-term effects in the form of post-traumatic stress disorder may remain. Combat veterans report terrifying nightmares and other psychological disturbances years after the war ended for them.

Long-term effects of combat may remain in the form of post-traumatic stress disorder.

Effects of Stress

Stress produces physiological reactions within the body (Spiro, Aldwing, Levenson, & Bosse, 1990). According to Selye (1976), a Canadian physiologist, the body goes through three stages in adapting to stress. The first stage is an *alarm reaction*, in which the body prepares to cope. Large quantities of the hormones *adrenaline (epinephrine)* and *noradrenaline (norepinephrine)* are secreted into the bloodstream to prepare the body for action. This is accompanied by an increase in activity in the sympathetic nervous system, an increase in blood sugar, heart rate, blood pressure, and blood flow to the muscles.

If stress continues, the body enters a *resistance stage* during which it begins to recover from the initial stress and to cope with the situation. Secretion of adrenaline decreases, as do other body functions. During the final stage, a state of *exhaustion* is reached as bodily resources are depleted and the body begins to break down.

Repeated stress can result in physical damage, decline in health, and an increase in illness (Willis, Thomas, Gary, & Goodwin, 1987). High blood pressure (hypertension), some types of heart disease (Brodsky & Allen, 1988; Rubin, 1988), migraine headaches, respiratory problems such as asthma, gastrointestinal disorders such as peptic ulcers, rheumatoid arthritis, and skin disorders such as eczema and dermatitis are stress related. Stress can play a role in muscle cramps, backaches, and menstrual problems. It can cause a decrease in testosterone levels as men get older (Ottenweller, Tapp, Creighton, & Natelson, 1988). If this happens, it may play a role in decreased sexual functioning. Stress can adversely affect any part of the body. Stress can make people more subject to disease because it weakens the immune system (Stone, 1987). Even the incidence of cancer is higher in people who are exposed to stress they can't handle (Smith, 1988). Some people seem to have the type of personality that is cancer prone. These individuals exhibit two major features. *One* is an inability to express emotions such as anger, fear, and anxiety. The *other* is an inability to cope with stress and a tendency to develop feelings of hopelessness, helplessness, and finally depression (Eyseneck, 1988).

Stress can interfere with psychological functioning. Depression (Krause, 1986c), panic disorder (Roberts, 1988), anxiety, paranoia, aggression, painful guilt feelings, and insomnia are often post-traumatic stress reactions (Vinokur & Selzer, 1975).

Coping With Stress

TASK-ORIENTED APPROACH.   Adults deal with stress in various ways. In a task-oriented approach, they make a direct effort to alleviate the source of the stress. A person having financial problems gets an additional part-time job to earn extra money. The parent who is worried about a child consults a specialist for a solution. Couples with marital problems seek marriage counseling. In this way, stress can provide an opportunity for growth. The stressed person who believes that his or her own behavior makes a difference in the outcome of a stressful situation and then "takes charge" is pursuing an effective way of coping with stress (Preston & Mansfield, 1984). Individuals who perceive themselves as being "in control" become less demoralized in stress situations and are less likely to develop illness symptoms (MacFarlane, Norman, Sreiner, Ray, & Scott, 1980). There is one exception, however: When people who are in control fail and then blame themselves, stress is increased (Krause, 1986b).

The task-oriented approach requires reality testing, that is, being aware of what is going on, undistorted by anxiety, hostility, or other negative feelings. The first step in alleviating stress is to discover its roots. Then, constructive problem solving and objective evaluation must be used to discover methods that will relieve stress.

COGNITIVE EFFORT.   Another approach to stress is a deliberate, cognitive effort to change one's internal responses (Lohr, Essex, & Klein, 1988). Events alone do not determine the amount of stress. What people strive to do, what they tell themselves, and how they evaluate situations all influence the amount of anxiety they experience. Mind-set and expectations also have a great deal to do with the success that people have in accomplishing goals, or in overcoming a health problem (Langer, 1989).

Meichenbaum (1972) instituted a **cognitive modification program** to help students suffering from high test-taking anxiety. Worries about the test, fear of failure, and feelings of inadequacy kept these students from doing well on exams. Some would freeze and forget facts they actually knew. Meichenbaum explained to the students what their anxiety was doing to them. He helped them identify their negative thoughts and feelings: "I'm certain I'm going to flunk"; "I don't believe I know this stuff"; "If I don't do well, my parents will kill me." He instructed the

Cognitive modification program—a therapeutic program designed to teach restructuring of thought patterns, positive thinking, and focusing on immediate tasks; one such program, designed by Michenbaum helps students with high test-taking anxiety

students to restructure their thoughts, to think positively, and to direct their attention to the task at hand: "I can handle this"; "I've studied hard"; "All I have to do is quit worrying and pay attention to the questions"; "Relax, don't be afraid." During group instruction, the students had to imagine test situations and practice eliminating negative self-statements, focusing their attention on the task on hand. As a result, the students reported large decreases in anxiety and improved test performance.

RELAXATION TRAINING. **Relaxation training** is used widely to cope with stress. One approach is to lie down on a comfortable couch or bed, putting a small pillow under each knee and a large one under each arm. Arms should be slightly flexed alongside the body. Starting with the toes of each foot, make a deliberate effort to relax the muscles. Flex the muscles and relax them, telling each muscle to let go, to relax. Do the same thing with each foot, leg, thigh, and so on up the whole body, ending with the muscles of the neck, face, head, and scalp. By focusing attention on separate parts of the body, it is possible to relax each part and ultimately the whole body. Deep breathing during the process also helps one to relax. Deep relaxation has been used successfully in reducing headaches; in treating insomnia, high blood pressure, and body pains; and in natural childbirth. Some people use techniques like **transcendental meditation**, designed to direct one's consciousness away from thoughts and toward a state of relaxation, to accomplish the same purpose. Business executives are encouraged to take catnaps, lie down on the floor, or take a seventh-inning stretch between meetings (Executive Stress, 1979).

PHYSICAL ACTIVITY AND EXERCISE. Physical activity and exercise are wonderful ways to relieve stress. Dr. G., a dentist, finds his profession tiring and stressful. When he gets very tense, he takes time off to jog, often running 6 to 7 miles before beginning to relax. Other people walk or play tennis, racquetball, or other sports. Some climb mountains; others go fishing or hunting. Physical labor of any kind can be very relaxing after a tense day.

SUBLIMATION. Another way to deal with stress is to sublimate it through indirect means, such as psychotherapy, work, sex, hobbies, or recreation. Some people bury themselves in their work, paint the house, or work in the garden. Others escape through hobbies or through sexual release. One husband who was under great emotional strain at work joined a local theater group and relieved his pent-up emotions on stage. Another would hammer on an old metal water tank in his basement whenever he became upset.

MEDICATION. A common way of dealing with stress is to medicate it. Judging from the millions of tranquilizers and sedatives sold each year, this seems to be a popular source of relief. Reasonable medication on a temporary basis may provide appropriate and welcome relief. The danger is developing dependency or addiction that relieves symptoms but never gets to the root of the problem and ends up creating problems of its own.

SOCIAL INTEREST. Another way to minimize stress is to increase one's social interest—one's interest in and concern for others. Zarski, Bubenzer, and West (1986) found that there is a positive relationship between high social interest and life adjustment, and between high social interest and overall health, high energy level, and fewer somatic symptoms. Those adults who scored high on social interest were also lower on measures of day-to-day hassles and frustrations.

SOCIAL SUPPORT. Seeking social support helps in managing stress (Arling, 1987; Krause, 1986a, 1988). Family members, friends, or counselors who listen empathetically provide moral support and emotional assistance (Krause, 1991). Some people need support groups when they have problems, and groups like *Al-Anon, Parents Without Partners,* and *Divorce Perspectives* are very successful. People band together to learn how to cope and to overcome their difficulties.

HOSTILE REACTIONS. Hostile reactions to stress may or may not be helpful in relieving the stress (McCrae, 1982). If anger motivates people to do something positive about their situation, it can be very helpful, but if it leads to distrustful, hurtful behavior, it may make the situation worse and aggravate the stress.

OTHER COPING MECHANISMS. Generally speaking, middle-aged and older adults use more positive coping mechanisms in dealing with stress than do adolescents or young adults (McCrae, 1982). Positive mechanisms might include *direct confrontation, planful problem solving, positive reappraisal, seeking social support,* and sometimes *distanc-*

Relaxation training—techniques to relax the body in order to combat stress

Transcendental meditation—a technique to direct one's consciousness away from thoughts and toward a state of relaxation

ing, *self-controlling,* and *showing care and concern.* Negative coping mechanisms might include *escape-avoidance, some hostile reactions,* or *self-blame* (Irion & Blanchard-Fields, 1987).

PATTERNS OF FAMILY ADJUSTMENT TO CRISES*

A family crisis may be an important source of stress. There are definable stages to such crises (Boss, 1987; Hansen & Hill, 1964; Lavee, McCubbin, & Patterson, 1985; Walker, 1985). The stages of adjustment to a family crisis are shown in Figure 18.2 and discussed separately in this section.

First Stage: Definition and Acceptance

The *first stage* is the onset of the crisis and the increasing realization that a crisis has occurred. An initial reaction may include disbelief. Family members may define a situation

*The material in this section is excerpted from the author's book, *Intimate Relationships, Marriages, and Families.* Mountain View, CA: Mayfield Publishing Co., 1990. Used by permission of the publisher.

differently; what is a major crisis to one person may not be to another. In the case of a married couple having difficulties, for example, one spouse may be on the verge of a divorce; the other refuses to accept the fact that there is a problem, believing that the other is "making too big a deal out of it." The first step, therefore, involves defining the problem and gradually accepting that a crisis exists: for example, the gradual realization and acceptance of a child's disability. Therefore, the impact of the crisis will depend on the nature of the precipitating event and the interpretation and cognitive perception of it, the degree of hardship and stress the crisis produces, and the existing resources available to handle the problem.

Second Stage: Disorganization

The *second stage* of a crisis is a period of disorganization. Shock and disbelief may make it impossible to function at all or to think clearly in the beginning. "I don't know what I'm going to do" is a common reaction. The period of disorganization may last for only a few hours or it may stretch into days or weeks. During this period, the family's normal functioning is disrupted. Tempers are short, loyalties are strained, tensions fill the air, friction increases, and family morale de-

FIGURE 18.2 Family adjustment to a crisis.

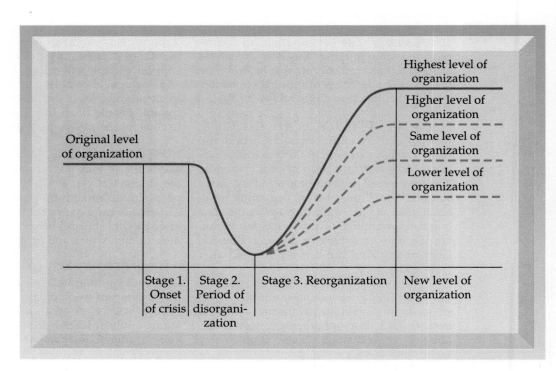

clines. When it occurs, child and spousal abuse is more likely to develop during the time of maximum disorganization than at any other time (Watkins & Bradbard, 1982). When Mount St. Helens erupted on May 18, 1980, thousands of people felt the stress. Associated Press reports from Washington after the eruption indicated that criminal assaults rose 25%, suicide threats and attempts doubled, and the number of cases of battered wives increased 45% (Blumenthal, 1980). The situation was particularly stressful because of the violence of the explosion (500 times the force of the atom bomb at Hiroshima) and the uncertainty of subsequent explosions. People did not know what would happen next or how long the catastrophe would last. The effects of stress were delayed, however. The greatest increase in cases of spouse abuse did not occur until about 30 days after the major eruption.

Other studies have shown that the use of alcohol and other drugs sharply increases during times of stress and may lead to a deeper level of disorganization or serve to handicap the family's capacity to bounce back from the crisis (Miller, Turner, & Kimball, 1981).

Third Stage: Reorganization

The *third stage* is one of gradual reorganization, during which family members try to take remedial action. If the crisis is a financial one (Larson, 1984), family members may borrow money, sell the family car, or cash in some savings. Other family members get temporary employment to help out, or a primary provider who is out of work starts drawing unemployment. If the financial crisis persists, the stock of resources begins to run out. The family has to think about a second mortgage, selling the house, or moving to another neighborhood.

Once the crisis "hits bottom," things begin to improve. The family providers get new jobs, and bills are gradually paid off; the family begins to recoup its emotional and physical resources. Eventually, after a period that may range from days to months, the family is reorganized at a new level. Sometimes the new level is never as satisfactory as the old one; at other times the level of organization is superior to the old. (In the case of a financial crisis, family money management improves and/or total income is higher). At any rate, the level is high enough and stable enough to mark the end of the period of crisis. (See Figure 18.2.)

MENTAL ILLNESS

Depression

SYMPTOMS.   **Depression** is the most common functional disorder of adults of all ages (Ponterotto, Pace, & Kavan, 1989). It exists in different degrees (Steuer, Bank, Olsen, & Jarvik, 1980). Major depressive episodes are characterized by a loss of interest and pleasure in almost all pastimes and activities. The person feels sad, hopeless, low, down in the dumps, and irritable, and these moods are dominant and persistent. To be diagnosed as suffering from major depression, a person must evidence depressed mood, plus at least half of the following symptoms every day for at least two weeks (American Psychiatric Association, 1987):

1. poor appetite or significant weight loss
2. insomnia or hypersomnia
3. psychomotor agitation or retardation
4. loss of interest or pleasure in usual activities or decrease in sexual drive
5. loss of energy and fatigue
6. feelings of worthlessness, self-reproach, or excessive guilt
7. diminished ability to think or concentrate, indecisiveness
8. recurrent thoughts of death or suicide, or a suicide attempt (Berry, Storandt, & Coyne, 1984)

Sometimes depression is accompanied by such psychotic features as delusions, hallucinations, or depressed stupor. Depression accompanied by melancholia is especially prevalent in mid-life, often in postmenopausal women. In melancholia, the depressed person is usually worse in the morning, often waking up two hours earlier than usual. There may also be marked psychomotor retardation or agitation, significant anorexia or weight loss, and excessive or inappropriate guilt.

MANIC PHASES.   Major depression can occur in a single episode, or be recurrent or bipolar (alternating with manic phases). The symptoms of manic episodes are the opposite of depression—the person is in an elevated, expansive, and irritable mood. At least three of the following symptoms must be present for the illness to be diagnosed as mania:

1. physical restlessness or an increase in activity socially, at work, or sexually

Depression—a functional disorder characterized by loss of interest in nearly all activities and by a predominance and persistence of sad, low, hopeless moods

2. more talkativeness than usual
3. racing thoughts and ideas
4. inflated self-esteem, grandiose behavior that may be delusional
5. decreased need for sleep
6. distractibility
7. excessive involvement in such activities as buying sprees, sexual indiscretions, reckless driving, or foolish business investments

Like depression, manic episodes may be accompanied by psychotic features.

When depression symptoms exist but are separated by periods of normal mood lasting months at a time, the person is not considered psychotic. The person who alternates between brief periods of depression and hypomania, or normal mood, suffers from what is now labeled a **cyclothymic disorder**. When the predominate mood is periodic depression, the illness is labeled **dysthymic disorder** (formerly called depressive neurosis).

Cyclothymic disorder

Dysthymic disorder

CAUSES.   No single theory explains the cause of depression. Some research suggests that depression has a *hereditary base* (U.S. Dept. of HHS, 1981). This view emphasizes a relationship to the body's chemical makeup. This theory suggests that depression is caused by insensitivity of receptors in the brain to the **monoamines** that act as neurotransmitters. Thus, the transmission of nerve impulses is retarded (Garver & Zelman, 1986). Mania is due to an oversensitivity of receptors to nerve transmission. This view is currently the best biological explanation for depressed or manic behavior. However, another line of biomedical research found a *hormonal or endocrine basis* for depression (Carroll, 1983).

Monoamines— neurotransmitters

Another theory is that depression is related to *medical conditions*. Elderly persons with medical problems appear to be at particularly high risk for developing depressive disorders (Borson, Barnes, Kukull, Okimoto, Veith, Inui, Carter, & Raskind, 1966). Sometimes a medical condition precipitates depression; at other times medical symptoms mimic depression. One study of 100 elderly patients with major depression revealed various medical conditions: electrolyte abnormalities, bacterial infections, medication reactions, endocrine disorders, thyroid disease, renal failure, Parkinson's disease, chronic obstructive lung diseases, and various other acute illnesses (Sweer, Martin, Ladd, Miller, & Karpf, 1988). Other studies report poorer health and more somatic complaints among the depressed than among those not depressed (Bolla-Wilson & Bleecker, 1989).

Learning theory emphasizes that depressed behavior is learned behavior. It may begin with a loss or stressful event causing temporary depression. Once people are depressed, their friends and family members feel anxious, depressed, and hostile in their presence, causing these persons to avoid them. This, in turn, reinforces the depressed behavior. Depressed persons begin to feel that nothing they do gains social reinforcement, so they withdraw further from activity, and the downward spiral continues. Furthermore, depressed people tend to be pessimistic—they are constantly foretelling doom or disaster. Nothing that happens is bright (Lewinsohn & Talkington, 1979).

Cognitive theorists suggest that the way persons interpret a situation is important in relation to depression. Their reaction is based not only on the situation, but also on their appraisal of it. They overgeneralize and use inexact labeling; then they respond to the labels and not the actual situation. They see the situation as bad, or they see themselves as stupid, inadequate, or guilty, and this makes them feel worse.

The more helpless people feel in situations, the more likely they are to feel depressed (Abramson, Seligman, & Teasdale, 1978; Foster & Gallagher, 1986). For example, if a student fails an examination but attributes the failure to a lack of preparation, the depressed mood may be temporary. However, if the student generalizes and attributes the failure to low intelligence, a feeling of helplessness pervades and depression may result. If the failure is attributed to an unfair test, the student reacts with anger, not depression. Thus, the interpretation of the situation is crucial to the emotional response. One study of dyadic response patterns of married couples showed that wives who were disgusted, angry, worried, or fearful about their situations and whose husbands were not, showed more depressed symptoms than other wives (Gruen, Folkman, & Lazarus, 1988). From this point of view, depression developed from the disturbed relationship and from the cognitive differences between the spouses.

Psychodynamic theories of depression emphasize overreactions to events based on early childhood experiences. Thus, prolonged depression following the death of someone close is often related to guilt feelings about earlier problems with the person.

Humanistic-existential theories of depression emphasize that it is caused by excessive strain, worry, and the loss of self-esteem (Keith, 1987). Persistent and disturbing troubles in the marital relationship have been associated with depression (Coyne, 1987; Whisman & Jacobson, 1989). The loss of a job, spouse (Breckenridge, Gallagher, Thompson, & Peterson, 1986), social status, or money creates anxiety and diminishes one's self-esteem. One study of elderly adults relates depression to having to care for a cognitively impaired spouse (Moritz, Kasl, & Berkman, 1989). Regrets over the past, accompanied by deep-seated feelings of anxiety, guilt, and unworthiness, trigger depression. The onset of a major illness can bring about depression. The realization that one has a debilitating illness, which may or may not be curable, is enough to trigger a major depression in some people (Rapp & Davis, 1989).

Actually, each of these theories contributes something to understanding the causes of depression. All or part of the circumstances, situations, or reactions described may be contributing factors. No one theory explains depression in every circumstance.

Organic Brain Syndromes

The discussion so far in this chapter has focused on depression. Depression may originate from emotional problems related to peoples' personalities and life experiences, or it may have a hereditary base, or it may be influenced by organic factors such as chemical balances of the body.

In other mental disorders, the primary cause is organic (related to disease, injury, or aging of tissues) (Rohling, Ellis, & Scogin, 1991). The most important are the **organic brain syndromes** (OBS), mental disorders caused by or associated with impairment of brain tissue function (Preston, 1986).

One syndrome is dementia, commonly called **senile dementia** in older people. The distinguishing features of dementia are: (1) disturbance and impairment of memory, (2) impairment of intellectual function or comprehension, (3) impairment of judgment, (4) impairment of orientation, and (5) lapse or change in these functions (Lawson, Rodenburg, & Dykes, 1977). These five signs may not appear together or in the same degree. The signs may be barely perceptible, with decline coming gradually or suddenly, depending on the cause. Some older persons evidence some impairment of mental functions, but their basic personality and behavior remain unchanged, and they cannot be classified as senile. They often sense what has happened to their intellectual abilities and make suitable adjustments, especially in the early stages of the illness. One example would be the older man who writes notes to remind himself to do things, who puts letters on the doorknob so he won't forget to mail them, or who attaches glasses to a chain around his neck so he won't misplace them.

Sometimes, intellectual functioning becomes so impaired that the person cannot live alone and requires constant care and attention. Memory deficits are the most noticeable symptom. The older person may remember past events but not what happened in the past few moments, today, or yesterday. Disorientation about the time of day or

Organic brain syndromes—disorders caused by or associated with brain tissue function impairment

Senile dementia—an organic brain disorder impairing brain function in older people

FOCUS

Light Therapy for Depression

An effective and innovative form of treatment for depression has evolved. It is light therapy, and involves exposing patients to intense levels of light under controlled conditions. The apparatus used is a set of fluorescent bulbs installed in a box with a diffusing screen to soften the light. The patient sits in a chair close to the light for 30 minutes to 3 hours, once or twice a day, depending on requirements. People vary in their response to light levels, so systems have been developed to deliver varying amounts of light. It is also critical that the light level match the level of light outdoors shortly after sunrise or before sunset. Some people respond best to treatment first thing in the morning; others do better with treatment in the evening.

Most people feel better after 4 or 5 days of treatment, but symptoms usually return after treatment is withdrawn, so users usually must establish a daily schedule in the fall and winter. Treatment can be withdrawn after the advent of spring.

The value of light therapy has been proven by researchers at the *National Institute of Mental Health*. The number of clinicians offering light therapy is increasing. People may also buy their own apparatus to use (Terman & Link, 1989).

year and the loss of a sense of place (where the person is) are common. In advanced stages, persons may not recognize family members or even know their own names.

OBS is sometimes accompanied by emotional symptoms and psychotic, neurotic, or behavior disorders that complicate the picture. Anxiety, irritability, and loss of inhibitions are often present, particularly in the early stages. Hallucinations, delusions of persecution, and severe depressive or manic manifestations are typical psychotic symptoms.

The reversible form of organic brain syndrome is called **reversible brain syndrome** (RBS), or acute brain syndrome. One symptom is a fluctuating awareness level, which can vary from mild confusion to stupor or active delirium.

Some persons with reversible brain syndromes recover completely if given proper and prompt treatment before permanent brain damage results. Some recover partially, whereas others die, usually from a serious physical illness that initially caused the syndrome.

Sometimes these disorders are called **chronic organic brain syndrome** (CBS) because of permanent brain damage. Often, all brain syndromes are categorized as such and left untreated when they could benefit from treatment (Barnes & Raskind, 1981). Even when damage is permanent and irreparable, some of the emotional and physical symptoms can be treated to improve functioning (Zeplin, Wolfe, & Kleinplatz, 1981).

The first of two major types of chronic brain syndrome is **senile psychosis**. This syndrome is caused by the atrophy and degeneration of brain cells, independent of vascular change, which causes an even and progressive decline in mental functioning (Yamaura, Ito, Kubota, & Matsuzawa, 1980). The disorder is more frequent in women, and the average age of onset is 75. Eventually fatal, senile psychosis has an average survival rate of 5 years beyond the onset of symptoms. Many persons can remain at home throughout most of the course of the illness if given adequate care and assistance.

The second major chronic brain syndrome is **psychosis associated with cerebral arteriosclerosis**. This is caused by a hardening and narrowing of the cerebral blood vessels, preventing sufficient oxygen and nutrients from reaching the brain. The onset of the disorder occurs in middle and late adulthood, between 50 and 70, with an average age of 66. Men are afflicted three times as often as women. The progress of the disease

is uneven and erratic, with symptoms more pronounced at various times. A person may be unable to remember one minute and regain total capacity the next. The degree of insight and judgment may be spotty, and hallucinations, deliriums, and paranoid reactions may occur when cerebral circulation is insufficient.

A related cause of senile dementia is a condition called **multi-infarct dementia**, which is the result of a number of tiny strokes that progressively kill brain cells. It is found in people with a history of high blood pressure, blood vessel disease, or a previous stroke (Edelson, 1991).

Alzheimer's Disease

Alzheimer's disease was first identified in 1907 by A. Alzheimer. It is characterized as a presenile dementia because it often afflicts people who are in their 40s and 50s. However, it also occurs in older people, with incidence increasing as people age (Heston & Mastri, 1982), accounting for perhaps one-half of the older people admitted to nursing homes (Butler, 1980). It is the single most common cause of dementia in the aged, and is currently the fourth leading cause of death in the United States (Shapira & Cummings, 1989). Individuals die on an average of 8 years after onset, although remissions occur occasionally so that death does not occur (White, McGue, & Heston, 1986). The cause of Alzheimer's disease is not definitely known, but the best-educated guess is that it is caused by a combination of genetic and environmental factors (Edelson, 1991). There is some evidence that a virus may be implicated (Fischman, 1988).

The disease is characterized by rapid deterioration and atrophy of the cerebral cortex. There is a characteristic neurofibril change in the nerve cells, which shrink and diminish in number. There is an increase of *plaque* (which are clusters of degenerating nerve cell endings) and *tangles* (which are masses of twisted filaments that accumulate in nerve cells), and *lipoid deposits* throughout the cortex (Kosik, 1989). The EEG shows significant slowing (Muller & Schwartz, 1978). The disease is associated with a defect in sympathetic nervous system function that is linked to cognition (Teri, Hughes, & Larson, 1990) and appears early in the course of the disease (Borson, Barnes, Veith, Halter, & Raskind, 1989).

In its early stages, as mental deficits and a tendency toward agitation appear, Alzheimer's disease can be mistaken for a be-

Margin glossary

Reversible brain syndrome—an acute brain syndrome that is treatable

Chronic organic brain syndrome—permanent impairment of brain function

Senile psychosis—a decline in mental functioning caused by the atrophy and degeneration of brain cells

Psychosis associated with cerebral arteriosclerosis—psychosis and degeneration of the brain cells caused by a hardening and narrowing of the blood vessels of the brain

Multi-infarct dementia—dementia caused by a series of small strokes that cut off blood supply to the brain

Alzheimer's disease—a presenile or senile dementia characterized by rapid deterioration and atrophy of the cerebral cortex

Aphasia

Agnosia

Apraxia

havioral disorder with symptoms of depression and anxiety (Lowestein et al., 1989). Gradually, the person loses memory ability (Ashford, Kolm, Colliver, Bekian, & Hsui, 1989; Fromholdt & Larsen, 1991); becomes more incoherent; and loses the ability to use or understand spoken or written language (**aphasia**), to recognize objects through use of the senses (**agnosia**), and to perform purposeful movements (**apraxia**). Falling be-

comes frequent (Morris, Rubin, Morris, & Mandel, 1987). The person develops a parkinsonian-like gait and convulsive seizures. Gradually, the person becomes rigid, unable to stand or walk, incontinent, and eventually helpless (Burger & Vogel, 1973). Continuous care is eventually needed (Cavanaugh et al., 1989; Motenko, 1989; Pruchno & Resch, 1989; Quayhagen & Quayhagen, 1989).

SUMMARY

1. Subjective well-being is a multidimensional concept that can best be measured by specific indicators such as life satisfaction, morale, happiness, congruence, and affect.
2. The Life Satisfaction Index A measures five dimensions of the concept: zest versus apathy, resolution and fortitude, congruence, self-concept, and mood tone.
3. Most factors influencing life satisfaction affect both blacks and whites, but the negative effects of impairments are considerably stronger among blacks than among whites.
4. Life satisfaction does not automatically increase as income rises. The key seems to be whether people are satisfied with the level of income they have reached.
5. Urbanism influences life satisfaction indirectly and interactively because it influences health, financial satisfaction, and social integration; however, the effects of urban living on life satisfaction are inconsistent.
6. Subjective well-being has also been described in terms of morale, which is one's mental or moral condition with respect to cheerfulness, confidence, zeal, and the like.
7. Happiness is listed as another dimension of subjective well-being. Genetics may play a role in unhappiness, but happiness itself is a capacity that must be developed. One study reported that each age group said that the present was a satisfying time of life.
8. Congruence is another element of subjective-well being. It means that there is an agreement between a person's desired goals and the goals that have been or are being attained. Congruence begins by trying to find meaning in life, establishing a purpose, and striving toward goals.
9. Results of testing a group of adults, age

16 to 75, with the Life Attitude Profile (LAP) showed that both life purpose and death acceptance increased with age; goal seeking and future meaning decreased with age; and existential vacuum showed a curvilinear relationship with age. Women scored higher on life control and will to meaning than men.
10. Affect is another dimension of subjective well-being. Positive affect (emotions) indicates well-being; negative affect indicates lack of well-being.
11. Social networks also relate to subjective well-being. The important consideration is not the quantity of such networks, but the quality, and whether adults perceive they have enough social ties with friends and family.
12. Numerous research studies point to health as one of the most important factors related to subjective well-being.
13. Subjective well-being is fairly stable throughout adulthood.
14. Stress is physical, mental, or emotional strain or tension caused by environmental, situational, or personal pressure and demands. The amount of stress experienced depends on the severity and duration of exposure, one's cognitive perception of it, one's previous conditioning, and one's hereditary makeup.
15. Stress may be job related or result from role strain; the degree of stress experienced depends on the degree of control people feel they have over their situations. Stress may arise from interpersonal relationships, be created by transition or change, or be precipitated by life crises. Crises may develop because of external events, or arise internally within the family.
16. There are three stages in adapting to stress: alarm reaction, resistance stage, and exhaustion.
17. Repeated stress can have a negative affect on health.

18. There are a variety of approaches in dealing with stress: a task-oriented approach, cognitive effort and modification, relaxation training, transcendental meditation, physical activity and exercise, sublimation, medication, increasing social interest, and seeking social support.

19. Hostile reactions may or may not be helpful in relieving stress.

20. A number of other positive mechanisms to cope with stress include: confrontation, planful problem solving, positive reappraisal, seeking social support, distancing, self-controlling, and showing care and concern.

21. Negative coping mechanisms include escape-avoidance, some hostile reactions, or self-blame.

22. There are three stages of family adjustment to a crisis: definition and acceptance of the crisis, disorganization, and reorganization.

23. Depression is the most common mental illness of adults of all ages. The most common overall symptom is depressed mood, but for it to be classified as a major depression, a person must exhibit half of eight symptoms outlined by the APA.

24. Depression may be bipolar, alternating with manic phases. Related, less severe disorders are called cyclothymic (brief periods of depression) or dysthymic (longer periods of depression).

25. No single theory explains the causes of depression, but the following are common theories: heredity; insensitivity of the body to neurotransmitters so that nerve impulses are slowed down; hormonal or endocrine imbalance; various medical conditions; learning theory; cognitive theory; psychodynamic theory; and humanistic-existential theory.

26. One innovative treatment for depression is light therapy.

27. Organic brain syndromes are mental disorders caused by or associated with impairment of brain tissue function. One most common syndrome is senile dementia.

28. A reversible form of organic brain syndrome is called reversible brain syndrome or acute brain syndrome.

29. Some organic brain syndromes are chronic. Two major types are senile psychosis and psychosis associated with cerebral arteriosclerosis. A related cause of senile dementia is multi-infarct dementia.

30. Alzheimer's disease may occur in the 40- to 50-year age group, but the incidence increases with age. It is the single most common cause of dementia in the aged, and is currently the fourth leading cause of death in the United States. The cause is not known but it may involve a combination of genetic and environmental factors. Death occurs on an average of 8 years after onset.

KEY TERMS

Affect *p. 404*
Agnosia *p. 415*
Alzheimer's disease *p. 414*
Aphasia *p. 415*
Apraxia *p. 415*
Chronic organic brain syndrome *p. 414*
Cognitive modification program *p. 408*
Congruence *p. 402*
Crisis *p. 407*
Crisis overload *p. 407*
Cyclothymic disorder *p. 412*
Depression *p. 411*
Dysthymic disorder *p. 412*
Happiness *p. 401*
Monoamines *p. 412*

Morale *p. 401*
Multi-infarct dementia *p. 414*
Organic brain syndromes *p. 413*
Psychosis associated with cerebral arteriosclerosis *p. 414*
Relaxation training *p. 409*
Reversible brain syndrome *p. 414*
Senile dementia *p. 413*
Senile psychosis *p. 414*
Social networks *p. 404*
Stress *p. 405*
Subjective well-being *p. 400*
Transcendental meditation *p. 409*
Type A personality *p. 406*

DISCUSSION QUESTIONS

1. To what extent do you feel positive, subjective well-being? What makes you most satisfied and happy? What makes you most dissatisfied and unhappy?

2. Identify a person you know who seems to be very happy and satisfied with life. Why is that person that way?
3. Identify a person you know who is never happy or satisfied. Why?
4. Can you be happier in the city or in rural areas? Explain.
5. How much of an income do you feel you need in order to be satisfied? Would you be happier if you won a million dollars in the lottery? Explain.
6. Describe your morale. Is it high, low, or medium? Why?
7. What factors do you feel are most important to happiness?
8. Why is it important to find meaning, purpose, and goals in life to be satisfied? What are your most important goals in life?
9. Do you know anyone who is always cheerful, pleased, and shows positive affect? Describe that person. Do you know anyone who seems to always show negative affect? Describe that person.
10. How do social networks relate to life satisfaction? Can you be happy without friends? Without seeing members of your family? Explain your feelings.
11. Do you know anyone who has poor health who is still happy? Describe.
12. What factors in your life have you found most stressful? What have you done or are you doing to relieve this stress? Does it help? Explain.
13. What factors cause you the most stress: school, job, interpersonal relationships with friends or with family, changes in your life, or life crises? Explain.
14. Describe a very stressful experience you have gone through and compare your reactions with the three stages in adapting to stress.
15. In your opinion, what are the most effective means of dealing with stress?
16. Describe a major crisis that occurred in your family, and the adjustments that were made to it.
17. Do you know anyone who seems to have the symptoms of major depression? Is the person receiving treatment? If so, what and with what results?
18. Do you know anyone who is a manic-depressive, who exhibits symptoms of mania? What does the person do, and how does the person react? Is the person receiving treatment? What, and with what effect?
19. What do you feel are the most important causes of depression in depressed people you have known?
20. Does the weather or the amount of sunlight affect your moods? Why or why not?
21. Do you know anyone who is suffering from senile dementia? Describe.
22. Do you know anyone who has Alzheimer's disease? Describe. If a member of your family developed Alzheimer's disease, would you want to put that person in a nursing home? Why or why not?

SUGGESTED READINGS

Brown, B. (1984). *Between health and illness.* Boston: Houghton Mifflin. The relationship between stress and health.

Campbell, A. (1981). *The sense of well-being in America: Recent patterns and trends.* New York: McGraw-Hill. Study of satisfaction and happiness in the United States.

Cartensen, L. L., & Edelstein, B. A. (Eds.). (1987). *Handbook of clinical gerontology.* New York: Pergamon. Alzheimer's disease and depression; treatment. Mental health problems.

Cooper, C. L. (Ed.). (1985). *Psychosocial stress and cancer.* New York: Wiley. The relationship between stress and cancer.

Figley, C. R., & McCubbin, H. T. (Eds.). (1983). *Stress and the family. Vol. II: Coping with catastrophe.* New York: Brunner-Mazel. Stress and crises.

Heston, L. L., & White, J. A. (1983). *Dementia: A practical guide to Alzheimer's disease and related disorders.* San Francisco: W. H. Freeman. Alzheimer's and organic brain syndromes.

Schwartz, J. (1982). *Letting go of stress.* New York: Pinnacle Books. A practical guide.

Taylor, S. E. (1986). *Health psychology.* New York: Random House. Overview of the field.

Social Development

SINGLEHOOD*

Marital Status and Delay

Figure 19.1 illustrates the marital status of the U.S. population, 18 years of age and older, in 1988. Overall, 62.7% were married, 21.9% were single (never married), 7.6% were widowed, and 7.8% were divorced. Obviously, the great majority of adults were married, and an additional number had been married at one time. Nevertheless, a bit more than 1 in 5 adults had never been married, but these were primarily in the youngest age groups.

The unmarried status of most in the singles group is only temporary because by age 45 to 54 only 5.6% of males and 5.1% of females have never been married. (See Figure 19.2.) However, the trend is for adults to get married at older ages than they used to.

Typology of Singles

There are various categories of single persons. Stein (1981) has developed a typology of single persons based on whether their status is voluntary or involuntary. Table 19.1 shows four major categories of singles according to Stein.

VOLUNTARY TEMPORARY SINGLES. This is a category that includes young persons who have never been married and are not currently looking, who are postponing mar-

People find both advantages and disadvantages in being single.

riage even though they are not opposed to the idea of marriage. It includes cohabitors who will eventually marry each other or someone else. It includes recently divorced or widowed persons who need time to be single, though they may eventually want to marry again. It also includes older never-marrieds who are not actively looking, but who would marry if the right person came along.

VOLUNTARY STABLE (PERMANENT) SINGLES. This is a category that includes never-marrieds and former-marrieds of all ages who have no intention of marrying or of remarrying.

INVOLUNTARY TEMPORARY SINGLES. Included in this category are young adults

---

*The material in this section and on marriage and family living is taken from the author's book *Intimate Relationships, Marriages, and Families,* 1990. Used by permission of the publisher, Mayfield Publishing Co.

FIGURE 19.1 Marital status of the population, 18 years old and over, 1988.

Adapted from *Statistical Abstract of the United States, 1990* (p. 43) by U.S. Bureau of the Census, 1990, Washington, DC: U.S. Government Printing Office.

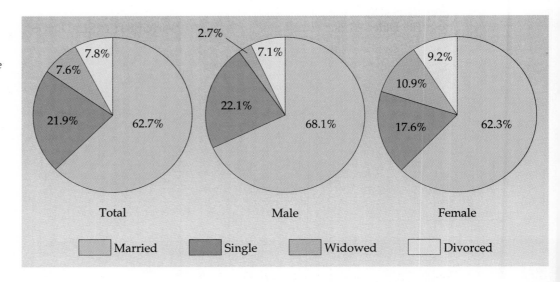

Total — 7.8%, 7.6%, 21.9%, 62.7%

Male — 2.7%, 7.1%, 22.1%, 68.1%

Female — 9.2%, 10.9%, 17.6%, 62.3%

Married   Single   Widowed   Divorced

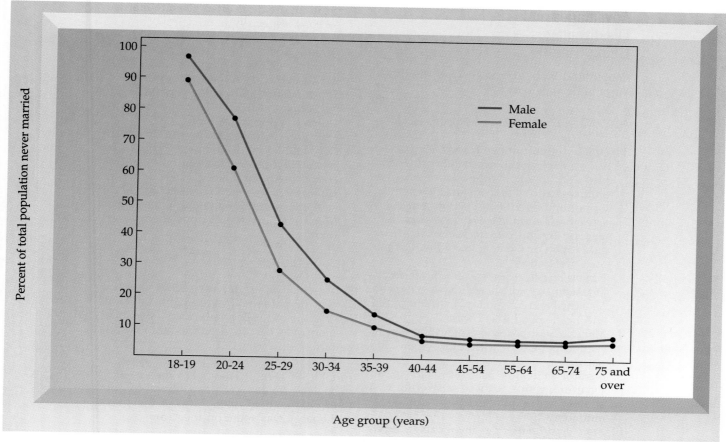

FIGURE 19.2   Never-married persons as percent of total population, 18 years old and older by age and sex, 1988.

Adapted from *Statistical Abstract of the United States, 1990* (p. 42) by U.S. Bureau of the Census, 1990, Washington, DC: U.S. Government Printing Office.

who have never been married but are actively seeking a mate, and divorced or widowed persons who want to remarry soon.

INVOLUNTARY STABLE (PERMANENT) SINGLES. This category includes never-married persons or widowed or divorced persons who wanted to marry or remarry and who have not found a mate; they have become reconciled to their single state. It also includes physically or mentally impaired persons.

TABLE 19.1   Typology of Singles

	Voluntary	Involuntary
Temporary	Never-marrieds and previously marrieds who are not opposed to the idea of marriage but are not currently seeking mates	Those who have actively been seeking mates but have not found them
Stable (permanent)	All those (never-marrieds and former-marrieds) who choose to be single	Never-marrieds and former-marrieds who wanted to marry, who have not found a mate, and who have more or less accepted being single

Adapted from *Single Life: Unmarried Adults in Social Context* by P. Stein, 1981, New York: St. Martin's Press. Used by permission of Haworth Press.

Advantages and Disadvantages of Being Single

People find both advantages and disadvantages in being single.

ADVANTAGES. Reputed advantages include:

1. Greater opportunities for *self-development and personal growth and fulfillment.* If singles want to take a course or travel, they are freer to do so than are married people.
2. Opportunities to *meet different people and develop and enjoy different friendships.* Singles are free to pursue friendships with either men or women, according to their own preferences.
3. *Economic independence and self-sufficiency.* One woman said: "I don't have to depend on a husband for money. I earn it myself and I can spend it as I want."
4. *More sexual experience.* Singles are free to seek experiences with more than one partner.
5. *Freedom to control one's own life,* to do what one wants without answering to a spouse; more psychological and social autonomy.
6. *More opportunities for career change, development, and expansion.* Singles are not locked in by family responsibilities and so can be more mobile and flexible in the climb up the career ladder.

Not all of these advantages can be applied to all singles. For example, not all singles have opportunities to meet different people. Not all are economically well off, nor are all free of family responsibilities. Nevertheless, some singles would list some of these or even all of these items as advantages for them.

DISADVANTAGES. Those who are not in favor of remaining single describe a number of disadvantages:

1. *Loneliness and lack of companionship.* This is one of the most pressing problems of singles.
2. *Economic hardship,* especially for single women. Single women earn less than single or married men and, without access to a husband's income, have a lower standard of living than do married men or women. Also, employers tend to feel that unmarried persons are less stable than are those who are married, so top positions are more often given to married persons, especially to men.
3. *Feeling out of place in many social gatherings* because social life is organized around married couples. In addition, singles may not be invited to some social events.
4. *Sexual frustration* for some persons.
5. *Not having children,* or lack of a family in which to bring up children.
6. *Prejudices* against single persons in our society and social disapproval of their lifestyles (Etaugh & Malstrom, 1981). This creates problems for singles if society considers them a threat to the established social order or to other people's marriages. Much pressure is put upon them to get married.

Life-Styles

Research on life-styles of singles reveals a variety of patterns. An in-depth study of never-married college-educated men and women over age 36 describes six life-style patterns (Schwartz, 1976).

PROFESSIONAL. These persons organized their lives around work and identified with their occupational roles. Most of their time and energy was spent on their careers.

SOCIAL. These persons had extensive social lives and many personal relationships. Friends and social activities were given priority over work. They were deeply involved in hobbies, organizations, and family activities.

INDIVIDUALISTIC. These persons focused their attention on self-growth. They enjoyed freedom, privacy, living alone, and not having to answer to anyone. They enjoyed hobbies, reading, and other solitary pursuits, along with classes on self-improvement.

ACTIVIST. The lives of these persons were centered on community and political causes. Work was important, but much time was devoted to trying to create a better world.

PASSIVE. These were loners who spent much free time alone, in solitary pursuits such as shopping or attending movies. They had negative outlooks on life and showed little initiative in using their lives creatively.

SUPPORTIVE. These persons spent their time in service to others. The few persons in this category were mostly women who were very satisfied with their lives.

FOCUS

Singles—Myths and Realities

Singles have often been described with stereotypical images, usually negative, that often lead to misunderstanding and discrimination against them (Etaugh & Malstrom, 1981). In their studies of singles, Cargan and Melko (1982) examined these stereotypes to discover which ones are myths and which ones approach reality. A summary of their findings is presented here.

Myth	Fact
Singles (especially men) are too attached to parents, so don't get married.	There is little difference between marrieds and singles in their perceptions of relations with parents.
Singles are rich.	On the whole, marrieds are better off financially.
Singles are happier.	On several measurements, singles are less happy than marrieds.
Singles are increasing in numbers.	This is true in the United States if we are considering numbers, but the percentage of singles has declined since World War II.
There is something wrong with singles.	This is a destructive and elusive myth. There is nothing wrong with being single.

Realities	Explanation
Singles are deviant.	Yes, but only because they are not following the norm, not because they are abnormal.
Singles have more free time.	Yes, they have more time to devote to activities of their own choosing.
Singles have more fun.	They are more involved in a variety of social activities than are marrieds, but don't necessarily have more fun.
Singles are swingers.	Singles have more variety of sexual partners; married people have more frequent sex.
Singles are lonely.	Sometimes, especially divorced persons.
Life for singles is changing for the better.	Yes, single life seems to be more rewarding and less frustrating than it used to be, although the alternative of marriage does not appear to have become less attractive.

Adapted from *Singles: Myths and Realities* (193–213) by L. Cargan and M. Melko, 1982, Beverly Hills, CA: Sage.

It is obvious that not all single adults fit into the same life-style. There is as great variation among members of this group as among other segments of the population, and so it is misleading to try to describe singles as a homogeneous group.

Living Arrangements

SINGLES COMMUNITIES. In the stereotyped fantasy, groups of singles occupy apartments or condominiums that cater especially to their needs. A case in point is Carl Sandburg Village in Chicago, transformed from a skid-row neighborhood with run-down apartments, greasy-spoon taverns, and transient hotels, into 9 high-rise buildings surrounded by townhouse and renovated apartments. Nearly three-quarters of the residents 18 and older are unmarried.

Occupants enjoy an indoor swimming pool, gymnasiums, restaurants, and other built-in amenities. Rents have skyrocketed, but people who cannot afford the leases often get roommates, increasing the number of unwed couples living together ("The Ways 'Singles' Are Changing U.S.," 1977).

SHARED LIVING SPACES. Although a large number of unmarrieds live in singles areas or apartments, more live with the general population. The majority occupy individual apartments, usually with roommates. The usual pattern is to share apartments and living expenses with one or more persons who provide emotional support and companionship.

LIVING WITH PARENTS. The percentage of young adults (18 to 29 years of age) who

TABLE 19.2 Young Adults Living With Their Parents, by Age, United States, 1988

	Percentage in Each Category	
	18–24 Years of age	25–34 Years of age
Total	54.4	11.6
Men	60.7	15.0
Women	48.4	8.3

From *Statistical Abstract of the United States, 1990* (p. 50) by U.S. Bureau of the Census, Washington, DC: U.S. Government Printing Office.

lived with parents reached a high in 1940, near the end of the economic depression. The percentage declined to a low point in 1960, near the end of the baby boom, and has risen modestly since then (Glick & Lin, 1986). The increase has occurred because of marriage postponement and high rates of college enrollment, unemployment, divorce and separation, and birth to unmarried mothers. Table 19.2 shows the percentages of young adult men and women of different ages living at home with parents. Note that greater percentages of men than women of all ages lived at home with parents.

LIVING ALONE.   Table 19.3 shows the percentage distribution, by age group, of singles living alone (U.S. Bureau of the Census, 1990). However, this table includes divorced, separated, or widowed people, as well as the never-married. As illustrated, greater numbers and percentages of males than females in the 15 to 24 and 25 to 44 age group live alone. With each succeeding age group (45

TABLE 19.3 Persons Living Alone, by Age and Sex, 1988

Age Group	Numbers of Persons (1,000)			Percentage Distribution		
	Both Sexes	Male	Female	Both Sexes	Male	Female
15–24	1,244	653	591	5.7	3.0	2.7
25–44	6,856	4,145	2,711	31.3	18.9	12.4
45–64	5,104	2,077	3,027	23.3	9.5	13.8
65 & over	8,683	1,913	6,770	39.7	8.7	30.9
All ages	21,889	8,788	13,101	100.0	40.1	59.9

Adapted from *Statistical Abstract of the United States, 1990* (p. 54) by U.S. Bureau of the Census, Washington, DC: U.S. Government Printing Office.

to 64 and 65 and over), the relative numbers and percentage of females living alone increase rapidly. This is because of the greater numbers of older females in the population.

Friendships and Social Life

COMPANIONSHIP.   One of the greatest needs of single people is to develop interpersonal relationships, networks of friendships that provide emotional fulfillment, companionship, and intimacy (Verbrugge, 1979). Single people value freedom and varied activities, but they also place a high value on enduring, close friendships.

When Cargan and Melko (1982) asked both marrieds and singles to describe the greatest advantage of being married, most replied in terms of shared feelings: "companionship and someone to share decisions with," "companionship," "love and companionship," "the opportunity to converse with someone every day," "being able to share your life with someone you love," "togetherness is very important to me," "love is caring and having children and sharing things, and doing things together." The concept that turned up most frequently was companionship.

LONELINESS.   Loneliness is a problem for a significant minority of never-marrieds (Cargan, 1981). Some evidence suggests that among single young adults, male–male friendships are less intimate and spontaneous than are female–female friendships. Single males are more isolated and have fewer intimate relationships than do single females (Tognoli, 1980). Although men sometimes exceed women in the number of voluntary associations in which they hold memberships, they spend less time in group activities and their participation is less stable. The norms of competition and fear of homosexuality have hindered the development of male friendships. Yet, *males as well as females need close, caring friendships* that develop into a sense of mutuality and constitute a major source of social support (Stein, 1978).

SOCIAL ACTIVITIES.   Is it true that singles have more leisure time and more fun than marrieds? It is easy for married persons to envy their apartment-dwelling single friends. But singles who work all week still have to clean their living quarters, make beds, cook, and do laundry. They go bicycling or to an art gallery, but if they want company, they may have to call friends and

One of the greatest advantages of being married is to be able to share companionship.

LIVING ISSUES

Nonmarital Cohabitation

The government now defines **cohabitation** as two unrelated adults of the opposite sex sharing the same living quarters in which there is no other adult present (Spanier, 1983). According to this definition, referred to as Persons of the Opposite Sex Sharing Living Quarters, or POSSLQ (S. Davidson, 1983), there were 2,588,000 unmarried cohabiting couples in the United States in 1988 (U.S. Bureau of the Census, 1990), a 63% increase since 1980. About 69% of these couples had some children in the household under 15 years of age. A little over half (54%) had never been married, about a third had been divorced, and a few (11%) were married to someone else or widowed. About 20% of all the householders were under 25 years of age; 63% were 25 to 44 years old; 13% were age 45 to 64; and 5% were 65 years or over.

One of the important questions is: To what extent has cohabitation resulted in greater satisfaction in subsequent marriage? Actually, *there is no evidence that premarital cohabitation weeds out incompatible couples and prepares people for successful marriage* (Macklin, 1983). Newcomb and Bentler (1980) conducted a longitudinal study examining the effects of premarital cohabitation on subsequent marital stability. After 4 years, they found no significant difference in marital stability between couples who had previously cohabited and those who had not.

The results seem to be affected partially by how long people have been married at the time of the evaluation. Most research indicates that a period of disillusionment in relation to marriage occurs after the initial glow and excitement have worn off and couples have settled down to daily living. Presumably, the longer couples have lived together before marriage, the earlier in the marriage relationship the period of disillusionment sets in. Thus, DeMaris and Leslie (1984) studied couples in the second year of marriage, and Watson (1983) evaluated them in the first year of marriage.

Comparisons of married couples who had and who had not cohabited showed that those who had lived together before marriage scored significantly lower in marital communication, consensus, and satisfaction. However, the researchers could not establish with clear cause and effect that cohabitation caused lower marital quality. There were too many other variables that might have influenced results. In fact, Watson and DeMeo (1987) did a follow-up in the fourth year of their marriages of couples who had earlier taken part in the original studies of Watson and found that the premarital relationships of the couples, whether of cohabitation or traditional courtship, do not appear to have had a long-term effect on the marital adjustment of intact couples. Watson and DeMeo (1987) were not able to determine the effects of cohabitation or noncohabitation on divorce, but what they did find was that *after 4 years of marriage, marital adjustment was no longer affected by the living arrangement in the months leading up to marriage.* Rather, the relationship the couple had subsequently built with one another was the important thing.

encounter some rejections before plans are completed, just as marrieds do.

In spite of this, *singles do have more time for optional activities.* They can make more choices and devote more time to leisure activities if they choose. Marrieds are more likely to have houses and children requiring time and attention (Cargan & Melko, 1982).

According to Cargan and Melko (1982), visiting friends was the preferred social activity of never-marrieds, followed (in declining order of preference) by going to movies, restaurants, nightclubs, theaters, visiting relatives, or going to social clubs. Couples married once preferred going to restaurants or visiting relatives. The entertainment preference of never-marrieds was more a preference of youth. Both never-marrieds and marrieds spent a lot of time watching television. Never-marrieds spent more time on hobbies.

Despite the fact that singles spent more time on social activities, *a greater percentage of marrieds than never-marrieds said they got a lot of fun out of life and that they were happy* (Cargan & Melko, 1982). Marrieds may derive happiness and fun in different ways. Gardening or taking the children on a picnic can be fun. When asked what was most important to their happiness, marrieds mentioned health first, then marriage, children, love, religion, and friends in that order. Only the category of friends was more important to singles than to marrieds. Surprisingly, success and money were not listed as important to happiness in either group (Cargan & Melko, 1982).

Dating and Courtship

ATTRACTION.   *The most important element in attraction—at least in initial encounters—is physical attractiveness.* We are attracted positively to those who are pleasing to look at, have good builds and well-proportioned bodies, and other physical characteristics that appeal to our aesthetic sensibilities. Study after study finds physical appearance to be one of the chief ingredients in early attraction (Adams, 1980; Reis, Nezlek, & Wheeler, 1980; Shea & Adams, 1984).

Factors other than physical appearance also attract people to one another. A study of 30 men and 30 women who were married (not to each other) for 2 to 8 years measured factors that the subjects found most attractive in their spouse (Whitehouse, 1981). The subjects were asked what attracted them to their spouse on first meeting, what attracted them after a few months, and what attracted

TABLE 19.4 Factors That Married Persons Found Attractive in Their Spouses

Category	Traits
Extroversion	Talkative
	Frank, open
	Adventurous
	Sociable
Agreeableness	Good-natured
	Not jealous
	Mild, gentle
	Cooperative
Conscientiousness	Fussy, tidy
	Responsible
	Scrupulous
	Persistent
Emotional stability	Poised
	Not nervous
	Calm
	Composed
	Not hypochondriacal
Culture	Artistic
	Sensitive
	Intellectual
	Polished, refined
	Imaginative

From "Toward an Adequate Taxonomy of Personal Attributes: Replicated Factor Structure in Peer Nomination Personality Ratings" by W. T. Norton, 1963, *Journal of Abnormal and Social Psychology, 66,* p. 577.

them at the time of the interview. The factors were divided into five categories: *extroversion, agreeableness, conscientiousness, emotional stability,* and *culture.* Various traits under each category are shown in Table 19.4. Upon initial meeting, the most important factor was extroversion: being talkative, frank, open, adventurous, and social. However, the importance of these traits declined with the years, while characteristics listed under agreeableness became much more important. The traits under conscientiousness also became slightly more important.

Other studies have confirmed that *personality traits and the way people act are significant factors in whether others find them attractive or not.* People who are generally warm, kind, generous, intelligent, interesting, poised, confident, or humorous, or who exhibit generally admired qualities, are more attractive than those who are rude, insecure, clumsy, insensitive, unstable, or irresponsible, or who manifest other negative traits. Orlofsky (1982) found that conformity to the cultural standards of approved femininity or masculinity was a powerful component of attractiveness.

LIVING ISSUES

Opening Lines

Psychologist Chris Kleinke asked several hundred students at colleges in California and Massachusetts to suggest opening lines that they might use to meet those of the opposite sex in general situations, at beaches, supermarkets, and bars. Kleinke divided approaches into three groups: "direct," "innocuous," or "cute/flippant." Men and women both claimed to prefer direct and innocuous approaches to cute/flippant ones. The top-rated openers were:

In general situations: "I feel a little embarrassed, but I'd like to meet you."   (direct)
At the beach: "The water is beautiful today, isn't it?" (innocuous)

At a supermarket: "Can you help me decide here? I'm a terrible shopper."   (direct)
At a bar: "What do you think of the band?"   (innocuous)

The least-favored of the cute/flippant openers were:

In general situations: "Is that really your hair?" "Your place or mine?" "You remind me of a woman I used to date."
At the beach: "Let me see your strap marks."
At a supermarket: "Do you really eat that junk?"
At a bar: "Bet I can outdrink you" (Rice, 1981).

FINDING AND MEETING DATES.   One of the major problems of those who want to date is where and how to meet prospective partners. Knox and Wilson (1981) surveyed a random sample of 334 students at East Carolina University to find out how they met, where they went, and what they did on dates. About a third of the students met their current dating partner "through a friend." The next most frequently mentioned way of meeting was "at a party." A lesser number met "at work" or "in class." Those not meeting in these ways checked "other," which included "I grew up with him/her" and "We met on the school newspaper" (p. 256).

GENDER ROLES IN DATING.   Male–female roles in the dating process are changing rapidly. Traditionally, males controlled initiation, planning, and paying for the date. This arrangement encouraged an unspoken agreement where females were expected to reciprocate for benefits received by allowing expressions of affection and sexual intimacies (Sprecher, 1985).

With the development of the feminist movement, women became increasingly aware of the inequalities between the sexes and suspicious of the power distribution in heterosexual relationships. They have sought to equalize control within the dating situation by initiating and paying for dates, thereby altering any alleged male sexual expectations and female sexual obligations on dates. In a study of 400 college women, Korman and Leslie (1982) found that approxi-

mately 55% of their sample reported that they helped pay the expenses of dates at least some of the time. Korman (1983) compared the initiation and expense-sharing behavior on dates of feminists and nonfeminists. The subjects were 258 unmarried, undergraduate women attending classes at a large Southeastern university. Feminists and nonfeminists were grouped according to summated scale scores on the *FEM Scale*. In comparison to nonfeminists, feminists were more likely to initiate dates and to share the financial obligations of women-initiated dates. However, their motives were to achieve more egalitarian relationships and not necessarily to reduce sexual obligations. Although both feminists and nonfeminists believed that men who paid for dates were more likely to expect

Present trends emphasize egalitarian relationships in dating while maintaining some desirable customs.

TABLE 19.5 Dating Problems
Experienced by 227 University Women

Problem	Percentage
Unwanted pressure to engage in sexual behavior	23
Places to go	22
Communication with date	20
Sexual misunderstandings	13
Money	9

Adapted from "Dating Problems of University Students" by D. Knox and K. Wilson, 1983, *College Student Journal*, 17, pp. 225–228.

sexual favors, both groups said they were unlikely to engage in unwanted sexual activity.

PROBLEMS IN DATING.   Dating is usually an important part of the social life of young people. Yet many haven't learned the social skills and developed the self-confidence to succeed. A survey of 3,800 undergraduates at the University of Arizona found that a third (37% of men and 25% of women) were "somewhat" or "very anxious" about dating. Half the students in a University of Indiana survey rated dating situations "difficult." Nearly a third of Iowa students said they feared meeting new people (Timnick, 1982).

Another study, this of 227 women and 107 men in a random sample of students at East Carolina University, sought to identify dating problems (Knox & Wilson, 1983). Table 19.5 shows the problems experienced by the women. The most frequent problems expressed by the women were *unwanted pressure to engage in sexual behavior, deciding where to go and what to do on dates, communication, sexual misunderstandings,* and *money.* An example of sexual misunderstandings was a man's thinking a woman was leading him on when the woman didn't really want to have intercourse and didn't mean to suggest she did.

The problems most frequently mentioned by the men (Table 19.6) were *communication, deciding where to go and what to do on dates, shyness, money,* and *honesty/openness.* By honesty/openness the men meant how much to tell about themselves and how soon, and getting their partner to reciprocate.

LIVING ISSUES

Date Rape

Date rape refers to rape that occurs on a voluntary, prearranged date or after a woman meets a man on a social occasion and voluntarily goes with him. This type of sexual aggression is very common. In a survey of 282 university women, 20% said that men tried to forcibly fondle their breasts, 31% reported that men tried to forcibly fondle their genitals, and 24% reported men tried to have coitus. A third of the coital attempts were completed (Kanin & Parcell, 1977). Over half of the coital attempts were initiated without foreplay, so these women certainly weren't leading the men on. One student writes:

Charlie and I went parking after the movie. He asked me to get in the back seat with him, which I did, because I trusted him and felt safe with him. We necked and petted awhile, and then he became violent. He ripped off my panties, pinned me down on the seat, and forced himself on me. I couldn't do anything about it, yet he had the nerve to ask me afterward if I enjoyed it (From a student paper).

Women are told frequently: "Don't go out with a man you don't know. If you do, you're taking a big chance." This is probably sound advice, but one of the purposes of dating is to get to know other people. And no matter how well you know an individual, problems can arise. Date rapes can occur in relationships where two people have gone together for a long period of time. As familiarity grows, the sexually aggressive male may become more insistent and try to coerce his partner into sexual activity that she finds objectionable.

This may reflect lack of communication and lack of understanding in the man–woman relationship. Some men are brought up to believe that when a woman says "no" she really means "yes," and it's up to the man to do what he feels she really wants to do anyhow. This reflects the same myth that exists in relation to other types of rape—the myth that women want to be forced. It also reflects the social learning in our culture: that men are supposed to be the sexual aggressors and overcome the reluctance and hesitancy of women. Men rape their dates out of anger, hostility, and contempt, as an expression of negative feelings, certainly not as an act of caring. Many such men engage repeatedly in acts of sexual aggression with a series of partners (Heilbrun & Loftus, 1986).

TABLE 19.6 Dating Problems Experienced by 107 University Men

Problem	Percentage
Communication with date	35
Place to date	23
Shyness	20
Money	17
Honesty/openness	8

Adapted from "Dating Problems of University Students" by D. Knox and K. Wilson, 1983, *College Student Journal,* *17,* pp. 225–228.

Sexual Behavior

According to a 1983 national survey of unmarried women, 82% of women age 20 to 29 had had sexual intercourse (Tanfer & Horn, 1985). *Hunt's (1974) survey of a national sample revealed that 97% of men had had sexual intercourse by 25 years of age.* The most sexually active singles are those who are divorced. Cargan and Melko (1982) reported that over half of divorced persons said they had intercourse twice a week or more. Only one-third of never-marrieds had intercourse twice a week or more (Cargan & Melko, 1982).

To what extent are single persons promiscuous; that is, to what extent do they have a variety of sexual partners? A study of 400 subjects in the Dayton, Ohio, area included never-married, first-married, divorced, and remarried individuals (Cargan, 1981). About 63% of never-marrieds claimed they had had 3 or fewer sexual partners in their sexual history and 15% said they had had 11 or more partners. In contrast, 31% of the divorced reported they had had 11 or more partners. Cargan concluded that only a minority of singles fit the sexual "swinger" stereotype and that this minority were more likely to be divorced and older than never-marrieds. He also found that both never-married and divorced persons were far less likely to be satisfied with their sex life than were married persons (Cargan, 1981).

The Older, Never-Married Adult

The major difference between younger and older adults who have never married is that most younger singles consider their status temporary, whereas older singles are often well adjusted to their situation. Older singles may or may not be interested in dating, but they usually have some social life and a variety of things to do with a few friends. A study of older singles between 60 and 94 found that they saw nothing special about being married; it was "just another way of life" (Gubrium, 1976). They valued being independent, were relatively

LIVING ISSUES

AIDS

AIDS is of special concern today not only because it is incurable, but also because it is always fatal once a person really contracts it. A blood test measures the presence of AIDS virus antibodies in the bloodstream. A person who tests positive for the AIDS virus antibodies has been exposed to the virus, is infected, can get it, and can transmit it to others (Wallis, 1987). Persons may spread the virus without knowing they are infected. The incubation period may be from several years to as long as 10 years.

The AIDS virus is found in semen, blood, urine, vaginal secretions, saliva, tears, and breast milk, and is transmitted from male to female, female to male, male to male, and female to female during the exchange of body fluids (Communicable Disease Summary, 1985). Transmission is through direct sexual contact, by getting HIV positive blood in an open wound or in the eyes, and by use of infected needles or syringes. The AIDS virus can also pass from mother to fetus during pregnancy and through breast milk to a nursing infant (Koop, 1986). Although the AIDS virus has been found in tears and saliva, no instance of transmission from these body fluids has been reported. However, physicians and dentists have transmitted the disease to patients and patients to them, through blood exchanges. AIDS is not transmitted through casual, nonsexual social contact such as occurs at home, in offices, restaurants, or schools (Friedland, Saltzman, Rogers, Kahl, Lesser, Mayers, & Klein, 1986). It is not transmitted through touching, holding, shaking hands, or playing together, nor by sneezing, breathing, or coughing, nor through food or biting insects, nor through towels, toilet seats, eating utensils, or water fountains ("Health Service," 1985). AIDS is a disease of heterosexuals as well as homosexuals and bisexuals. It also occurs frequently among intravenous drug users (Smilgis, 1987). The more sex partners one has, male or female, the greater the risk of becoming infected.

When older singles are satisfied with their activities, they tend to be happy.

isolated (but not lonely), and were generally satisfied with their activities. They did not have to face widowhood or divorce and tended to accept and take for granted their life-style. They were unique persons, not misfits, who had adjusted to life differently from most.

The following comments from a 71-year-old male are typical:

> I have been single all my life (71 years). I am living alone now and have a beautiful, well-furnished, two-and-a-half room apartment. I work at home and keep the apartment clean. I don't think I would like to live together presently. I'd rather not be married, even though I have plenty of opportunities (Hite, 1982, p. 266).

It's hard to find fault with this man's point of view or life-style. The important thing is that he is happy and satisfied.

In contrast to the situation of this man, other single adults who have never married are not completely happy with their situation. Keith (1986) found that a sizable minority of unmarried aged felt isolated from neighbors, friends, and relatives. Men were more likely to be isolated from family than were women. Divorced and never-married men and women were more isolated from family than were those who were widowed. Both never-married men and women, however, compensated for their isolation from relatives by maintaining more ties with friends.

Overall, however, *the happiness of these older adults was very dependent on satisfaction* *with their level of living and with their level of activity rather than just on the extent of social contacts.* Adequate financial resources permitted mobility and reciprocation in the development and maintenance of friendships. Also, if persons were satisfied with their level of activity even though they might be isolated from family or friends, they tended to express greater happiness.

MARRIAGE AND FAMILY LIVING

Marriage and Personal Happiness

Few married people would disagree with the thesis that the quality of marriage has a strong effect on their happiness and satisfaction with life (Zollar & Williams, 1987). Data from six national studies conducted in the United States revealed that *marital happiness contributed more to personal global (overall) happiness than did any other kinds of satisfaction, including satisfaction from work* (Glenn & Weaver, 1981). At the same time, an unhappy marriage can also have a negative effect on life satisfaction and subjective well-being (Haring-Hidore, Stock, Okun, & Witler, 1985). People who are having severe marital problems may not be able to eat properly; they often can't sleep; they may become debilitated and run-down during the period of upset.

The Family Life Cycle

STAGES.   One of the most helpful ways of examining marital relationships over periods of time is to look at them over various phases of the **family life cycle.** The family life cycle divides the family experience into phases or stages over the life span and seeks to describe changes in family structure and composition during each stage. The cycle can also be used to show the challenges, tasks, and problems that people face during each stage, and the satisfactions derived.

Figure 19.3 shows the family life cycle of a husband and wife in an intact marriage. The ages of the husband and wife are median ages for the U.S. population. Thus, the husband is married at 26, the wife at 24. They wait 2 years and have 2 children. The husband is 50 and the wife 48 when the youngest child is 20 and leaves home. The empty-nest years until retirement are from age 50 to 65 for the husband and age 48 to 65 for the wife.

Family life cycle— the family experience divided into phases or stages over the life span; a description of the changes in family structure and composition, and of the challenges, tasks, problems, and satisfactions involved during each stage

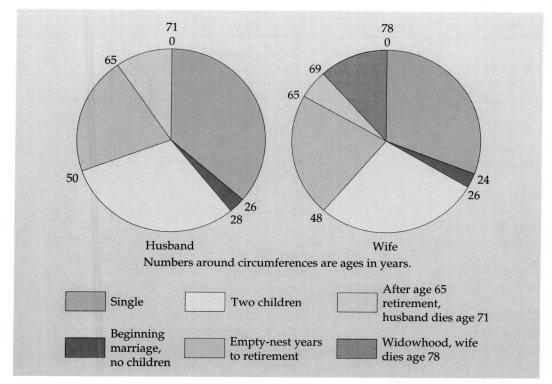

Husband

Wife

Numbers around circumferences are ages in years.

Single

Two children

After age 65 retirement, husband dies age 71

Beginning marriage, no children

Empty-nest years to retirement

Widowhood, wife dies age 78

FIGURE 19.3 Family life cycle—intact marriage.

Statistics from *Statistical Abstract of the United States, 1990* by U.S. Bureau of the Census, 1990, Washington, DC: U.S. Government Printing Office.

The wife lives to be age 78, the last 9 years as a widow (U.S. Bureau of the Census, 1990). The husband dies at 71.

MARITAL SATISFACTION OVER THE FAMILY LIFE CYCLE.   How does marital satisfaction change over various phases of the family life cycle? The studies are quite consistent in showing a decline in marital satisfaction during the early years of marriage, particularly following the birth of the first child and continuing to the end of the preschool or school-age period (Schumm & Bugaighis, 1986). A few studies show the decline extending to the end of the teenage period. Practically all studies show an overall increase in marital satisfaction after children have reached school age or finished their teenage years. Some also show another slight decline in satisfaction prior to retirement (Anderson, Russell, & Schumm, 1983; Feldman & Feldman, 1975; Lupri & Frideres, 1981; Rollins & Cannon, 1974; Spanier, Lewis, & Cole, 1975). *The general trend is for marital satisfaction to be somewhat curvilinear—to be high at the time of marriage, lowest during the child-rearing years, and higher again after the youngest child has passed beyond the teens.* Apparently, bearing and rearing children interferes with marital satisfaction (Anderson, Russell, & Schumm, 1983).

When the question is raised as to why marital satisfaction is at an ebb when the children are of school age, the most plausible explanation seems to be that the demands placed upon the couple during these years are at their greatest.

Adjustments Early in Marriage

All couples discover that their marriage never lives up to all of their expectations. As a result, couples go through a series of adjustments in which they try to modify their behavior and relationship to achieve the greatest degree of satisfaction with a minimum degree of frustration. The various areas of adjustment are called **marital adjustment tasks** and may be divided into 12 areas as shown in Table 19.7. The extent to which couples need to make adjustments after marriage depends partially on the extent to which some of these tasks are confronted during courtship.

Adjustments to Parenthood

"First pregnancy," says psychiatrist Eldred, "is a 9-month crisis. Thank God it takes 9 months, because a child's coming requires enormous changes in a couple's ways of adjusting to each other" (Maynard, 1974, p.

Marital adjustment tasks—areas of concern in marriage in which adjustments need to be made

TABLE 19.7 Marital Adjustment Tasks

Emotional fulfillment and support
Learning to give and receive affection and love
Development of sensitivity, empathy, closeness
Giving emotional support, building morale, fulfilling ego needs

Sexual adjustments
Learning to satisfy, fulfill one another sexually
Working out mode, manner, timing of sexual expression
Finding, using acceptable means of birth control

Personal habits
Adjusting to one another's personal habits, speech, cleanliness, grooming, manners, eating, sleeping, promptness
Reconciling differences in smoking, drinking, drug habits
Elimination or modification of personal habits that annoy one another
Adjusting to differences in body rhythms, schedules
Learning to share space, time, belongings, work

Sex roles
Establishing husband's and wife's roles in and outside the home
Working out sex roles in relation to income production, housekeeping, household maintenance, homemaking, caring for children
Agreement on division of labor

Material concerns, finances
Finding, selecting a residence: geographical area, community, neighborhood, type of housing
Equipping, maintaining a household
Earning adequate income
Managing money

Work, employment, achievement
Finding, selecting, maintaining employment
Adjustment to type, place, hours, conditions of employment
Working out schedules when one or both are working
Arranging for child care when one or both are working

Social life, friends, recreation
Learning to plan, execute joint social activities
Learning to visit, entertain as a couple
Deciding on type, frequency of social activities as individuals and as a couple
Selecting, relating to friends

Family, relatives
Establishing relationships with parents, in-laws, relatives
Learning how to deal with families

Communication
Learning to disclose and communicate ideas, worries, concerns, needs
Learning to listen to one another and to talk to one another in constructive ways

Power, decision-making
Achieving desired balance of status, power
Learning to make, execute decisions
Learning cooperation, accommodation, compromise
Learning to accept responsibility for actions

Handling conflict, solving problems
Learning to identify conflict causes, circumstances
Learning to cope with conflict constructively
Learning to solve problems
Learning where, when, how to obtain help if needed

Morals, values, ideology
Understanding and adjusting to individual morals, values, ethics, beliefs, philosophies, and goals in life
Establishing mutual values, goals, philosophies
Accepting one another's religious beliefs and practices
Decisions in relation to religious affiliation, participation

---

139). In recent years, there has been less of a tendency to refer to the addition of a first child as a crisis and more of an inclination to refer to it as a period of stress and transition (Bell, Johnson, McGillicuddy-Delishi, & Sigel, 1980; Boss, 1980; Miller & Sollie, 1980). The amount of stress will vary from couple to couple. *The more stressful a couple's marriage before parenthood, the more likely it is that they will have difficulty in adjusting to the first child.*

Sometimes stress arises if the pregnancy was not planned (Hobbs & Wimbish, 1977). Part of the stress comes from the fact that most couples are inadequately prepared for parenthood. As one mother states, "We knew where babies came from, but we didn't know what they were like." When their first child is born, many parents have absolutely no experience in caring for infants. One study showed that men who had been prepared for parenthood by attending classes, reading books, and so forth found far greater satisfaction in being a parent than did those who had not been so prepared (Russell, 1974).

Part of the stress arises, also, because of the abrupt transition to parenthood. Rossi (1968) wrote:

> The birth of a child is not followed by any gradual taking on of responsibility, as in the case of a professional work role. It is as if the woman shifted from a graduate student to a full professor with little intervening apprenticeship experience of slowly increasing responsibility. The new mother starts out immediately on 24-hour duty, with responsibility for a fragile and mysterious infant totally dependent on her care (p. 35).

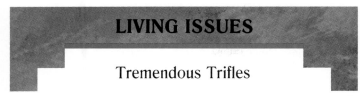

LIVING ISSUES

Tremendous Trifles

In the beginning, couples notice every minute detail about the way the other person walks, talks, dresses, eats, sleeps, bathes, and so on. Everything one does comes under the close scrutiny and observation of the other. The newness of the experience makes the two people very observant and sometimes critical. One husband complained because his wife never wanted to sleep with a window open, whereas he liked a lot of fresh air. One meticulous wife discovered that her husband never liked to take a bath or to use deodorant. Another discovered that her husband always threw his dirty socks and underwear in a corner of the room. Gradually, couples begin to get used to one another, to overlook some of these things, and to learn how not to annoy one another. Early in the marriage, however, these "tremendous trifles" can be quite aggravating.

For this reason, it is vital that the husband share the care with the mother. Direct assistance from relatives in the early days after birth can also reduce stress.

Stress will vary from child to child depending upon each child's temperament and how easy each child is to care for. Some children give a minimum of trouble. Others, such as hyperactive or sick children, require an abnormal amount of care (Balkwell & Halverson, 1980). How-

The amount of stress in child rearing varies, depending upon how easy each child is to care for.

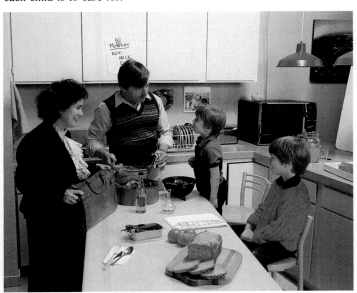

ever, all babies require considerable care, and significant stress necessarily occurs with every new baby.

Adjustments During Middle Adulthood

MARITAL ADJUSTMENTS.   As we have discussed, marital satisfaction tends to be at its lowest ebb when the children are of school age or in their teenage years. On the average, the wife is 41 and the husband is 43 when the youngest child is age 13. If the husband and wife have been busy working and raising children, and being active in community affairs, they may have drifted apart, spending less time communicating, playing, and being together (Swensen, Eskew, & Kohlhepp, 1981). It is easy to get so absorbed with other activities that the marriage suffers from lack of attention. Parents who stayed together until their children were grown now feel freer to dissolve their relationship. Some do get divorced.

For others, however, *middle age can become a time for revitalizing a tired marriage, for rethinking their relationship, and for deciding that they want to share many things in life together.* If the couple can learn to communicate and express tender feelings, especially feelings of love and affection that they have neglected, they can develop greater intimacy than they have experienced in a long time (Swensen, 1983). This improved communication can also uncover troublesome issues that have been denied. Once faced and resolved, they need no longer prevent improved companionship and togetherness (Appleton, 1983).

THE POSTPARENTAL YEARS.   The term **postparental years** usually refers to the ages after the last child leaves home and until the husband's and wife's retirement. If the woman gets married at the median age of 24 and has two children, she is 48 when the last child leaves home. The husband who married at age 26 and has two children will be 50 when the last child leaves. Some writers prefer the term the *empty-nest years;* for them, after children are born, one is always a parent.

The biggest adjustment for the wife if her whole life has been wrapped up in her children is in filling the gap after the children leave. However, *ever greater numbers of women breathe a sigh of relief after the last child leaves* (Cooper & Gutmann, 1987; Rubin, 1979). At last, these women are now free to live their own lives. Many husbands don't feel too great a loss when the children leave, espe-

Postparental years—the years after the last child leaves home and until the husband's and wife's retirement

cially if they have reasons to be proud of them and their accomplishments (Lewis, Freneau, & Roberts, 1979).

There is considerable evidence to show that adults in the postparental period are happier than are those earlier or later in life. The period has been described as "a time of freedom." One husband showed his relief at not having such a great financial burden: "It took a load off me when the boys left. I didn't have to support 'em anymore" (Deutscher, 1964, p. 55). It would appear, therefore, that while there are adjustments to be made during the empty-nest years, there are increased opportunities to enjoy life as a couple (Harkins, 1978).

One postscript needs to be added. The empty nest may not stay that way. High divorce rates and financial need have resulted in increasing numbers of adult children returning home to live with their parents. The fledglings are returning to the nest. This has important ramifications for parents, adult children, and grandchildren. Most parents do not welcome the return of their children and view their stay as a short-term arrangement (Clemens & Axelson, 1985). Sometimes the adult child reverts to the role of the dependent child, and the parents return to superordinate roles of earlier times. In these cases, increasing evidence points to a lessening of life satisfaction for all parties involved (Clemens & Axelson, 1985).

Adjustments During Late Adulthood

MARITAL STATUS. As health and longevity of the elderly increase, an increasing proportion of adults over age 65 are still married and living with their spouse. In 1989, 82% of men 65 to 74 years old and 70% of men 75 and older were married. Figures for women of comparable ages were 53% and 25% respectively. Obviously, there are far greater numbers of widowed women than men.

MARITAL SATISFACTION. For many older adults, marriage continues to be a major source of life satisfaction (Kozma and Stones, 1983). *Marital happiness and satisfaction usually increase during a second honeymoon stage after the children are launched and after retirement.* The spouses usually have more leisure time to spend together and with adult children and grandchildren. The adults may still be in good health. They depend more on one another for companionship (Zube, 1982). As one wife remarked: "I feel closer to Bill than

I have for years. We had forgotten what it meant to have real companionship" (Author's counseling notes).

Sometimes during the last stages of old age, marital satisfaction again declines (Gilford, 1984). Some wives complain that their husbands are always underfoot and expect to be waited on. Keating and Cole (1980) reported that wives were busier than ever completing and reorganizing household tasks, so they had little time to respond to their husband's needs as well. Some retired husbands take on a few additional household tasks, but others don't share more than when they were working (Arling, 1976). Much of a retired husband's time at home is spent in his own pursuits. So while the retired couple is together more, retirement does not ensure that the husband will spend much additional time in household chores.

NEW ROLES IN THE FAMILY. *There is some evidence that there is a reversal of sex roles in relation to authority in the family as people get older.* The man who retires loses some status and authority in family governance. The woman often assumes a more dominant role as an authority figure (Liang, 1982). This is especially true in relation to planning activities for herself and her husband and in assuming a nurturing role that has not been possible since the children were launched (Keating & Cole, 1980).

Declining physical health and financial resources begin to take their toll. The couple find it harder to cope with their life situation. Declining status and involuntary disengagement from society result in increasing discontent. Spouses now have fewer physical, social, and emotional resources to reward one another in mutual marital exchange (Dowd, 1980). Figure 19.4 shows the trend.

PARENT–ADULT CHILD RELATIONSHIPS. *The image of parents growing older without contact and concern of their adult children does not coincide with the facts* (Connidis & Davies, 1990; Montgomery, 1982). A national survey by Shanas (1980) revealed that half of the aged with children had seen one of them on the day of the interview or the day before. If the time period covered the previous week, the proportion of elderly parents in contact with children increased to three-fourths. Similar findings appear in a 1984 survey of the elderly (Kovar, 1986). Thus, "the finding that most older persons are not isolated from their children is well supported in the existing literature" (Bengtson, Cutler, Mangen, & Marshall, 1985, p. 319).

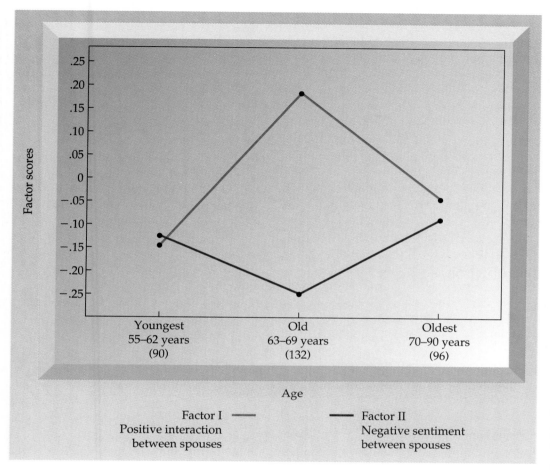

FIGURE 19.4 Mean levels of marital satisfaction by age group (N = 318). Group sample sizes are shown in parentheses.

From "Contrasts in Marital Satisfaction Throughout Old Age: An Exchange Theory Analysis" by R. Gilford, 1984, *Journal of Gerontology, 39*, p. 331.

Other studies have reported important factors in parent–adult child relationships (Hamon & Blieszner, 1990):

- The frequency of contact is not the key factor in satisfactory relationships; quality of contacts is.
- Emotional support is important and can be more significant than whether adult children provide financial support (Houser & Berkman, 1984).
- The morale of elderly individuals is higher if they feel they can reciprocate some of the help their children or friends give them (McCulloch, 1990; Stoller, 1985; Roberto & Scott, 1986).
- Providing extensive care for severely functionally impaired parents causes extreme stress and hardship for the caregivers. Community personal care services, day care, home nursing, and homemakers' services are needed (Archbold, 1983).

Widowhood

The greater longevity of women means that the number of widows exceeds widowers at all levels.

Table 19.8 shows the ratios at different ages (U.S. Bureau of the Census, 1990). Partly as a result of these ratios, the remarriage rates for widows is lower than for widowers. The younger a person is when a mate dies, the greater the chances of remarriage. The death of a spouse is recognized as one of life's most traumatic events. The survivor often confronts emotional, economic, and/or physical problems precipitated by the spouse's death (Bound, Duncan, Laren, & Oleinick, 1991; Smith & Zick, 1986).

TABLE 19.8 Ratio of Widows to Widowers at Different Ages

Age	Ratio of Widows to Widowers
45–54	4.7 to 1
55–64	5.0 to 1
65–74	5.3 to 1
75 years and over	4.7 to 1

Adapted from *Statistical Abstract of the United States, 1990* (p. 42) by U.S. Bureau of the Census, 1990, Washington, DC: U.S. Government Printing Office.

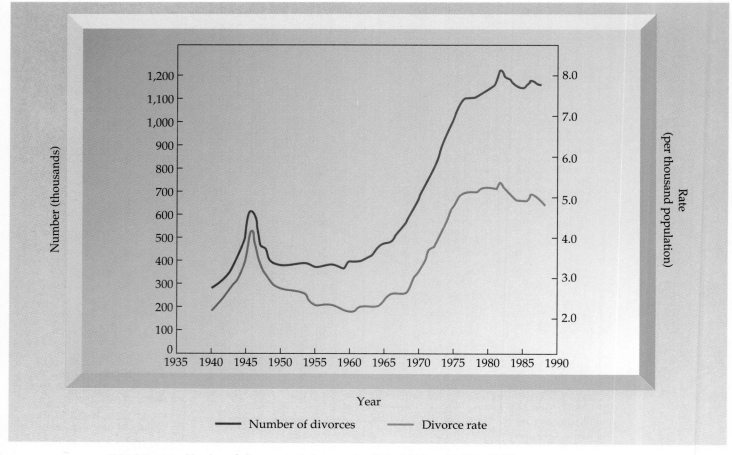

FIGURE 19.5   Number of divorces and divorce rate: United States, 1940 to 1987.

From *Statistical Abstract of the United States, 1990* by U.S. Bureau of the Census, 1990, Washington, DC: U.S. Government Printing Office.

Divorce

RATES.   *Divorce rates increased steadily from 1958 until 1979. After 1979, they leveled off and even declined.* (See Figure 19.5.) Whether rates will continue to decline remains to be seen. As they now stand, the high rates mean that a large number of marriages end in divorce. A survey in 1985 showed that nearly one-third of ever-married women aged 35 to 39 had ended a first marriage in divorce by the survey date and that a projected figure of 56% would eventually end a first marriage in divorce (Norton & Moorman, 1987). The proportion for this age group is greater than for women 10 years younger or older.

PROBLEMS MOST DAMAGING TO MARI-TAL RELATIONSHIPS.   A survey among 116 members of the *American Association of Marriage and Family Therapists* rates the frequency, severity, and treatment difficulty of 29 problems commonly experienced by distressed couples. The therapists were asked to choose and give the rank order of only the top 5 areas most damaging to the marital relationship and the 5 most difficult to treat successfully (Geiss & O'Leary, 1981). A value of 5 was assigned to an item for each first-place ranking it received, a value of 4 was given for each second-place ranking, and so on. These values were summed for each item. The 10 areas rated by respondents as having the most damaging effect on marital relationships were (Geiss & O'Leary, 1981, p. 516):

1. Communication (361)
2. Unrealistic expectation of marriage or spouse (197)
3. Power struggles (135)
4. Serious individual problems (126)
5. Role conflict (95)
6. Lack of loving feelings (92)
7. Demonstration of affection (90)
8. Alcoholism (81)
9. Extramarital affairs (80)
10. Sex (79)

FOCUS

Extramarital Affairs

The majority of Americans still enter marriage expecting and committed to sexual fidelity. Americans place a high value on sexual exclusiveness as important to a healthy marriage relationship (Stayton, 1983). In spite of these attitudes, the meager data available indicate an increase in extramarital sexual relationships since the 1960s (Elbaum, 1981; Reiss, 1973; Saunders & Edwards, 1984).

Extramarital affairs have varying effects on married people and their marriages. Some marriages are never the same afterward. Guilt, anger, jealousy, loss of respect, and the destruction of love and intimacy are common (Buunk, 1982; Elbaum, 1981). One wife remarked: "I don't know if I can ever trust him again. Every time he's out of town I wonder what he is doing and who he's with."

Sometimes, however, the crisis of an affair stimulates the couple to finally accept the fact that their marriage is in deep trouble and that they need help. One wife explained:

> I've been trying to tell my husband for years that I was unhappy in our marriage, but he didn't listen. Now, I've met someone else, and for the first time my husband is listening and is willing to go to a marriage counselor (Author's counseling notes).

In this case, the affair resulted in something positive.

There are some couples whose marriages are not affected very much by an affair. One of the spouses is having an affair, but the other doesn't care. These are often marriages where the emotional bonds between the couples are already broken, so the extramarital relationship is just evidence of the fractured marriage. These couples have either lost or have never had a meaningful relationship with each other (Voth, Perry, McCranie, & Rogers, 1982).

In some situations, a wife discovers that her husband is unfaithful but chooses not to confront him with his actions because they have children and she does not feel equipped to support herself and the children (Saul, 1983). Or, a husband discovers his wife is having an affair, but chooses not to confront her because he's afraid he'll lose her.

The affairs that are most threatening to the marriage are ongoing affairs that include emotional involvement as well as sexual relations (Thompson, 1984). Persons who believe that they have fallen deeply in love don't want to give up the affairs, which seem so meaningful and exciting. Some people report: "I haven't felt like this for years. I can't give up something that makes me feel alive again" (Author's counseling notes). Of course, what people don't realize in the beginning is that the intense emotional excitement tends to pass; and if the relationship is to endure, the couple needs to have many other things going in the relationship.

Based on these responses from marital therapists, lack of communication was ranked as having the most damaging effect. In a further analysis of data from the study, *communication problems were also rated as the most frequently occurring problems in distressed marriages.* These responses suggest the vital role that communication plays in well-functioning marriages.

ADULT ADJUSTMENTS AFTER DIVORCE. The problems of adjustment after divorce may be grouped into a number of categories.

▪ *Getting over the emotional trauma of divorce.* Under the best of circumstances, divorce is an emotionally disturbing experience (Plummer & Koch-Hattem, 1986; Thompson & Spanier, 1983). Under the worst conditions, it may result in a high degree of shock and disorientation. The trauma is greater when one spouse wants the divorce and the other doesn't (Huber, 1983), when the idea

comes unexpectedly, when one continues to be emotionally attached to the other after the divorce, or when friends and family disapprove of the whole idea. For most couples, the decision to divorce is viewed as an "end of the rope" decision, which is reached, on the average, over a period of about 2 years.

▪ *Dealing with the attitudes of society.* Part of the trauma of divorce is experienced because of the attitudes of society toward divorce and divorced persons. In the eyes of some, in spite of increasing liberal attitudes, divorce represents moral failure or evidence of personal inadequacy.

▪ *Loneliness and the problem of social readjustment.* Even if two married people did not get along, they kept one another company. Part of the time, at least, they knew that someone else was in the house. After divorce, they begin to realize what it is like to live alone. Numerous authorities suggest that the friendship and companionship of other people is one of the most essential ingredients for a successful readjustment after divorce, so getting involved with others is important (Leslie & Grady, 1985).

• *Finances.* In spite of some advances, women still receive only 62% of the income of males, assuming both have the same occupation, education, working experience, and hours. Furthermore, the mother still ends up with custody of the children in 9 out of 10 cases (Jencks, 1982). Some mothers get only a little or irregular support from their ex-husbands. As a result of these factors, most divorced mothers have to work, but do so at inadequate wages (Uhlenberg, Cooney, & Boyd, 1990). It is estimated that women who get divorced and do not remarry experience a 50% decline in family income (Jencks, 1982). The irony is that whereas divorce lowers the living standards of both mothers and children, it typically raises that of fathers (Pett & Vaughan-Cole, 1986).

• *Realignment of responsibilities and work roles.* The divorced person with children is faced with the prospect of an overload of work. Now that person must perform all family functions, which were formerly shared by two persons (Berman & Turk, 1981).

• *Sexual readjustments.* Research reveals that most divorced persons are sexually active. This does not mean, however, that all of these sexual contacts are emotionally satisfying. Some divorced persons speak of meaningless sex, using sex to find companionship, to prove sexual attractiveness, or as an escape from problems.

• *Contacts with ex-spouse.* The more upsetting the divorce has been and the more vindictive the spouse, the less the other person wants to have any postdivorce contact. This is particularly true in cases of remarriage.

• *Kinship interaction.* Divorce is a multigenerational process that affects grandparents and other kin as well as the divorcing couple and their children (Ferreiro, Warren, & Konanc, 1986).

Remarriage

Adults who remarry after divorce have some real advantages over those married for the first time. Remarrieds are older, more mature and experienced, and often highly motivated to make their marriages work (Goldberg, 1982). They ought to be able to make a better go of marriage the second time around. But divorce rates are about the same as for those in first marriages. However, Furstenberg and Spanier (1984) concluded that successful remarrieds stated that their new marriage was better than their first marriage. These people felt they had married the right person, "someone who allows you to be yourself" (p. 83). They felt they had learned to communicate and that they handled problems maturely. Better communication also led to better decision making. Both partners tended to feel they were more equal in remarriage and that the division of labor was more equitable.

All of these last comments came from those who had successful remarriages. *For others, remarriage introduces some complications*

LIVING ISSUES

Problems of Stepfathers

Although the situation is slowly changing, about 90% of children of divorced parents live with their mothers after divorce. If the mother remarries, the children inherit a stepfather. A summary of studies indicates that the most frequently cited problems of stepfathers include the following (Robinson, 1984; Stern, 1982):

1. Uncertainty about the degree of authority they have in the role of stepfather.
2. The amount of affection to give stepchildren and ways to show it. Stepfathers report feeling uncomfortable kissing their stepchildren.
3. The discipline of stepchildren and enforcement of rules.
4. Money conflicts.
5. Guilt over leaving children from a previous family.
6. Loyalty conflicts—how much time children spend with natural parents versus with stepparents.
7. Sexual conflict—the incest taboo is present but is not as strong in stepfather families as it is in biological families.
8. Conflict over surnames—different names of stepfathers and stepchildren may lead to problems, but some stepchildren and stepfathers don't want the same names (Robinson, 1984, p. 382).

LIVING ISSUES

Problems of Mothers in Remarriages

The mother in a remarriage has a whole set of problems that are unique to her situation.

1. She is often placed in the role of mediator between her own children and her husband. Her children want her to take their side; her husband wants her to take his side. The mother is drawn into the conflict and is in the middle, trying to please both.
2. Her children are often jealous of the time and attention given to the husband, resenting his intrusion into the family, and the fact that he takes their mother away from them. The mother is placed in a difficult situation. No matter whom she pleases, she displeases the other part of the family.
3. She has to adjust to the fact that her husband has other children and will be spending money for their support, money that she and her family may need; and that he will be seeing his children.
4. She may have to adjust to the fact that her husband was married to another woman before, and that he will be contacting her, especially when visiting the children or having them come to visit.
5. She has a difficult adjustment to make with her husband's children because she spends little time with them, and they may resent her taking their place in relation to their father.
6. She may have to mediate relationships between the stepsiblings, being careful not to show partiality (Author's counseling experience).

that were not present in first marriage. The biggest complication is children (Bridgwater, 1982). Children from prior marriages increase the likelihood of divorce among remarried couples (Fine, 1986). When remarrieds divorce, it is often because they want to get rid of the stepchildren, not the spouse (Meer, 1986). In a majority of cases, at least one partner already has children when the remarriage begins (Cherlin & McCarthy, 1985). Being a stepparent is far more difficult than being a natural parent, because children have difficulty accepting a substitute parental figure.

WORK AND CAREERS

Another major component of social adjustment is to successfully pursue a career. This section traces career development through early, middle, and late adulthood.

Career Establishment

VOCATIONAL IDENTITY.   Two major psychosocial tasks of early adulthood are to mold an identity and to choose and consolidate a career. These two goals are intertwined because vocational choice is one way to establish identity. Adults are associated with their work: "She is a branch manager of the bank." "He is superintendent of schools." Vocational achievement is important in a society that emphasizes individualism, personal fulfillment, and material success. Success and job satisfaction reaffirm one's identity and provide social recognition. One important task of this period, therefore, is to become established in an occupation (Levinson et al., 1978).

VOCATION AND LIFE SATISFACTION. Discontentment with jobs or money also affects other aspects of life. Rubenstein (1981) found that discontent with one's work is strongly associated with unhappiness at home. People most troubled about money or

Vocational achievement reaffirms identity and provides social recognition.

deriving little pleasure from their work are most unhappy with their love and sexual relationships.

ASPIRATIONS.   One goal of early adulthood is to succeed according to individual criteria with which one feels comfortable within the context of one's community. Everyone has to be somebody—somehow, somewhere, sometime. It is important to strive toward personalized goals and experience some success.

VOCATIONAL DEVELOPMENT.   During the years of early adulthood, primarily the 20s, adults can be grouped into five different categories according to the status of their vocational development.

One group consists of *vocational achievers*. They are highly involved in a vocation of their choice and are actively pursuing established career goals. They have completed their formal education and training and are applying their knowledge and skill in their work. They are fairly contented with their work and look forward to continued development.

A second group are the *vocationally frustrated*. They have in mind particular vocational goals they have not been able to attain, at least at present. This group includes a large number who want to go on to higher education or some type of postsecondary training, but they are hampered by economic, family, or personal circumstances. Also included are those who dropped out of school to get married and those locked into jobs they dislike because they cannot afford to leave them to pursue other goals.

A third group consists of the *noncommitted*: people who are still uncertain what they want to do. They are confused and anxious, unable to decide which direction to pursue (Marcia & Friedman, 1970). Some are still in school. They change majors frequently, trying a lot of different courses, but they cannot select a preference. Some of these persons are interested in so many things that they are unable to narrow down their interests to one program. Some are not particularly interested in any one thing. They take job after job but never find one type of work they prefer. They are concerned and confused. Some are so emotionally insecure that they have trouble making decisions about anything.

People in the fourth group are *vocational opportunists*. They do not have a clear-cut vocational plan or specific goals. They have not selected any particular occupation or profes-

sion, but instead accept jobs as opportunities arise. If they can get a job as a salesperson, they take it. If they find a better job doing factory work, they try that. Their employment record is usually erratic, with no real planning involved.

Members of the fifth group are *social dropouts*. Some of them do not care whether they work. They have no occupational goals and little personal ambition. Most of the time they are unemployed, or they work long enough to be eligible for unemployment and then get fired to collect. Some beg, some steal, some live off of others, some have drug problems. Others live at home, expecting their parents to support them. Certain people have a nonmaterialistic philosophy of life, rejecting the work ethic, or preferring to work as little as possible to maintain themselves. Some young adults move in with others who have adopted a "hang-loose" ethic. For many, this is a phase to be worked through before they become established members of society.

Mid-Life Careers and Employment

A TIME OF FRUITION.   For most people, middle adulthood is the fruition of a long period of professional work, when years of training and experience culminate in positions of maximum authority and responsibility (Buhler, 1977). People appointed to leadership positions usually achieve these positions by their early 50s. The important point is that the middle years of the 40s and 50s are years of high productivity. They can be quite satisfying years to those who gain widespread recognition of their accomplishments.

SECOND CAREERS.   Sometimes middle-aged people do not keep abreast in our increasingly technological society, where change is so rapid that they become completely outdated unless they attend refresher courses every several years. Companies are forced to hire new employees who are familiar with the latest technology.

When a person is shut out of a career or is at a dead end, one answer is to begin a second career. Thousands of middle-agers make midlife career changes, sometimes voluntarily after months or years of reevaluation and thought, or other times because of losing a job.

Opera star Beverly Sills gave up her active singing career at 50 to take on a second career as general director of the New York City Opera: "I may be considered old as an opera singer," she remarked, "but I'm thought of as a young manager. That's one of the corporate perks of this job" (Heymont, 1980, p. 64).

WORK AND EMOTIONAL STRESS. Whereas the middle years can be productive and rewarding for many, they can also be years of upset and anxiety for others. Job-related emotional problems are common among middle-agers. One source of stress, which was discussed earlier, is *being laid off or fired.* Although the economic impact of job loss may be severe, the emotional impact may be even more serious. Such psychosomatic symptoms as diarrhea, headaches, sleep disturbances, or depression are common. Middle-aged persons whose main gratifications in life came from work may panic when they find their primary source of emotional support terminated. The frustration of *unfulfilled expectations* is a source of stress for other people.

The Older Worker

JOB SATISFACTION. Most research has pointed to a high and positive correlation between job satisfaction and age; that is, *job satisfaction tends to increase with the worker's age* (Wright & Hamilton, 1978). There are several explanations for this satisfaction. The most plausible one is that older workers have better jobs with higher incomes, more occupational prestige, and greater skills. Also, older workers more likely have remained in jobs they liked and for which they were best suited (Phillips, Barrett, & Rush, 1978). They left unsatisfactory jobs earlier in their careers.

INCREASED NUMBERS. Because of increased longevity, better health care, and legislation extending the mandatory retirement age, the possible span of an adult's working life in the United States is increasing. The mandatory retirement age of 70 will allow millions of workers to remain on the job after age 65. Workers in certain types of jobs can remain even longer if they desire. It's still true that a lot of workers are taking early retirement (Gohmann, 1990), but many take other kinds of jobs (Myers, 1991). The gradual increase in age of retirement to draw maximum Social Security will have an influence in encouraging a longer work life. Accordingly, *the numbers of older workers in the work force may increase in the years ahead.*

RETIREMENT. *Forced retirement has been ranked among the top 10 crises in terms of the amount of stress it causes the individual* (Bosse, Aldwin, Levenson, & Workman-Daniels, 1991; Fritz, 1978; Sarason, 1981; Shapiro, 1977). People who elect early retirement, plan for it, and look forward to it feel that they have directed their own lives and are not being pushed or manipulated (Ferraro, 1990). They have some adjustment problems, but far fewer than those who retire unwillingly (Gibson, 1991). For people who want to continue working, forced retirement is a bitter pill to swallow. The resulting stress can precipitate various physical and emotional problems (Reitzes, Mutran, & Pope, 1991). Morale drops, the mortality rate rises as disillusionment sets in, and individuals who identified very closely with their work sometimes suffer prolonged depression and other ailments. Without the stabilizing influence of work, old emotional conflicts can re-emerge, and the person often acquires feelings of inadequacy and worthlessness that generate behavior sometimes regarded as "senile" (Brickfield, 1980).

The real issue of retirement is whether people have a choice (Miller, 1977). They should be able to decide for themselves. Actually, the earlier fears of industry that large numbers

LIVING ISSUES

Burnout

Burnout is a term that describes the condition of a person emotionally and physically exhausted from too much job pressure. Burnout can occur at any stage of adult life, but middle-aged people seem particularly prone. They have devoted their efforts to their careers and families, often not finding the replenishment they hoped for. Burned-out men and women describe their overwhelming depletion, saying: "I don't care any more," "I have nothing left to give," "I'm drained," or "I'm exhausted."

Job pressures often combine with personal and family circumstances to create an overload. Added together, family tensions and conflicts, financial pressures, illness, and problems with children or other family members can create stress. Poor health habits over a period of time can cause havoc. Unless people take time off for rest and relaxation and diversionary social activities, they forget how to relax and stress builds up. When burnout becomes advanced and prolonged and turns into severe depression or chronic anxiety, then psychotherapy or counseling is in order.

of less efficient workers would remain on the payrolls have not materialized. Workers with good health and superior performance are the ones most likely to stay on the job.

SOCIAL-PSYCHOLOGICAL THEORIES OF AGING

One task of social scientists is to develop theories explaining social phenomena. Theories of aging attempt to explain the process of aging in its many dimensions. The biological theories of aging were described in Chapter 16. This chapter discusses five social-psychological theories of aging.

Disengagement Theory

Disengagement theory—a theory of aging saying that aging people have a natural tendency to withdraw socially and psychologically from the environment, social activities, and other people

The **disengagement theory** of aging was originally formulated by Cumming and Henry (1961). The theory states that as people approach and enter old age, they have a natural tendency to withdraw socially and psychologically from the environment. According to the theory, older people tend to detach themselves voluntarily from outside social activities and to become less involved with other people. At the same time, they withdraw emotionally, turning inward to their own thoughts and feelings. This disengagement frees older people from the stress that arises from numerous role obligations and family and community responsibilities. It also allows them more time and opportunity to pursue those activities, values, and ideas they consider important. Thus, disengagement enhances their life satisfaction as they grow older.

Since its conception, disengagement theory has been criticized severely. *Critics argue that disengagement is not universal, inevitable, or inherent in the aging process.* Some older people never disengage; they remain active and productive all their lives. Benjamin Franklin was 70 when he helped draft the *Declaration of Independence.* Giuseppe Verdi, the distinguished Italian opera composer, was 73 when he composed *Othello,* and 80 when *Falstaff* was first performed in Milan. Karl Menninger, the outstanding psychiatrist who received countless awards, wrote the *Crime of Punishment* at 75. In his 80s, Arthur Fiedler was directing the Boston Pops Orchestra.

Critics also insist that the theory does not consider those individual differences in health and personality that influence activity. Further, it is continued activity, not disengagement, that produces the most life satisfaction for older people.

Activity Theory

Activity theory—a theory of aging suggesting that continuance of an active life cycle has a positive effect on the sense of well-being and satisfaction of older people

Activity theory suggests that continuance of an active life-style will have a positive effect on the sense of well-being and satisfaction of older people (Maddox, 1970). This personal satisfaction depends on a positive self-image, which is validated through continued participation in middle-aged roles. When these roles end, they must be replaced to avoid feelings of decline and uselessness.

Psychologists and social gerontologists give only partial support to this oversimplified theory (Lee & Markides, 1990). Simply engaging in activities does not automatically maintain one's feeling of self-worth, especially if those activities are less meaningful than the roles one has given up. Will a retired corporation president have as adequate a self-concept playing Bingo as he did when working? It is unlikely. Busywork alone is not the answer.

Another difficulty is that *activity theory neglects persons who cannot maintain middle-aged standards physically, mentally, or emotionally.* Some people are forced to shift roles for health or other reasons, yet still find great satisfaction. Not everyone must maintain a high level of activity to be happy. Overall, there is an association among morale, personality adjustment, and activity levels, but *different persons may prefer different types of activities and different degrees of participation to be satisfied* (Turner & Helms, 1979).

Continuing an active life-style contributes to a sense of well-being and satisfaction of some older people.

Personality and Life-Style Theory

Personality and life-style theory—a theory of aging that shows the relationship between personality type and patterns of aging

Because of individual differences in activity and disengagement, many gerontologists seek a **personality and life-style theory** to describe what constitutes successful aging. Neugarten (1968), who investigated older people between the ages of 70 and 79, identified four major personality types and categorized the role activities of those comprising the major types. Table 19.9 shows the four major personality types: *integrated, armored-defended, passive-dependent,* and *unintegrated.* The *integrated* include three subtypes. The *reorganizers* are those who substitute new activities for lost ones and engage in a wide variety of activities. The *focused* have integrated personalities with high life satisfaction. They are selective in their activities and derive major satisfaction from one or two role areas. The *disengaged* are integrated personalities with high life satisfaction but with low activity. They have voluntarily moved away from role commitments because of preference.

The *armored-defended* include two types: the *holding on* and the *constricted.* Aging is a threat to the holding-on group, so they maintain middle-age patterns as long as possible. They are successful in their attempts and maintain high life satisfaction at medium or high activity levels. They say, "I'll work until I drop" or "So long as you keep busy, you will get along all right" (Neugarten, 1968, p. 176). Those people in the *constricted* group deal with losses by constricting their social interactions and energies and by closing themselves off from experiences. This tactic works fairly well, giving them high or medium life satisfaction.

Those in the *passive-dependent* group are either *succorance-seeking* or *apathetic.* The succorance-seeking have high dependency needs and are fairly satisfied, as long as they have others to lean on who can meet their emotional needs. The apathetic are the "rocking chair types" who have disengaged, who have low role activity, and only medium or low life satisfaction.

The *unintegrated,* or *disorganized,* exhibit gross defects in psychological functions, loss of emotional control, and deterioration of thought processes.

Neugarten and associates concluded from their research that the activity and disengaged theories did not adequately explain what happened as people grow older. People are not at the mercy of their social environment or intrinsic processes. They continue to make choices, selecting in accordance with their long-established needs. Personality is "the pivotal dimension in describing patterns of aging and in predicting relationships between level of social role activity and life satisfaction" (Neugarten, 1968, p. 177). Other personality theorists group individuals into different categories.

Exchange Theory

Exchange theory—a theory that, as applied to the aged and their families, maintains that persons with the greatest needs lose the most power and those supplying needs gain power

Exchange theory rests on four basic assumptions:

1. Individuals and groups act to maximize rewards and minimize costs.
2. The individual uses past experience to

TABLE 19.9 Personality and Theories of Aging

Personality Type	Role Activity	Life Satisfaction	Number
1. Integrated	High	High	9
—Reorganizers	Medium	High	5
—Focused	Low	High	3
—Disengaged			
2. Armored-defended			
—Holding on	High or medium	High	11
—Constricted	Low or medium	High or medium	4
3. Passive-dependent			
—Succorance-seeking	High or medium	High or medium	6
—Apathetic	Low	Medium or low	5
4. Unintegrated			
—Disorganized	Low	Medium or low	7

Based on statistical material by B. L. Neugarten, R. J. Havighurst, and S. S. Tobin, in "Personality and Patterns of Aging" *Middle Age and Aging* (pp. 173–177) by B. L. Neugarten, Ed., 1968, Chicago: University of Chicago Press.

predict the outcome of similar exchanges in the present.

3. An individual will maintain an interaction if it continues to be more rewarding than costly.

4. When one individual is dependent on another, the latter accrues power.

According to this theory, social exchanges involve not only financial transactions but also psychological satisfaction and need gratification. *The person having the greater needs loses power; the other person gains power.* Power is thus derived from unequal needs or imbalances in social exchange.

Exchange theory was not formulated originally as a theory of aging. The first person to apply the theory to the aged was Martin (1971). He used the theory to describe visiting patterns among family members. The aged who have financial resources that younger persons need or who can offer valuable services such as baby-sitting hold positions of power and put their children in dependent positions. Those who have little to offer—who, for example, have to beg others to visit—are forced to pay a high price. Their relatives visit reluctantly and begrudgingly, demonstrating to the elderly that it is a chore or burden.

Social Reconstruction Theory

Kuypers and Bengtson (1973) have used the social breakdown model as developed by Zusman (1966) to show how our society causes negative changes in the self-concept of the aged. Four steps are involved (see Figure 19.6):

1. *Our society brings about role loss,* offers only sparse normative information and guidance, and deprives the elderly of reference groups, so that they lose the sense of who they are and what their roles are.

2. *Society then labels them negatively* as incompetent and deficient.

3. *Society deprives them of opportunities* to use their skills, which atrophy in the process.

4. The aged accept the external labeling, identify themselves as inadequate, and begin to act as they are expected to act, setting the stage for another spiral (Kuypers & Bengtson, 1973).

According to the **social reconstruction theory** of Kuypers and Bengtson, people can change the system and break the cycle through three types of action. *One,* we must eliminate the idea that work is the primary source of worth. The Protestant work ethic is inappropriate to old age. People need to be judged by their character, personality, and humanitarianism. *Two,* the social services, housing, health care, and financial status of the aged need to be improved. *Finally,* we must give the elderly greater powers of self-rule; they need to be the ones who determine the political and social policies and programs that affect them. In this way, they can develop greater self-confidence and feelings of self-worth and help maintain their personal competency and social power.

Social reconstruction theory—a theory of aging describing how society reduces the self-concept of the aged, and proposing ways to reverse this negative cycle

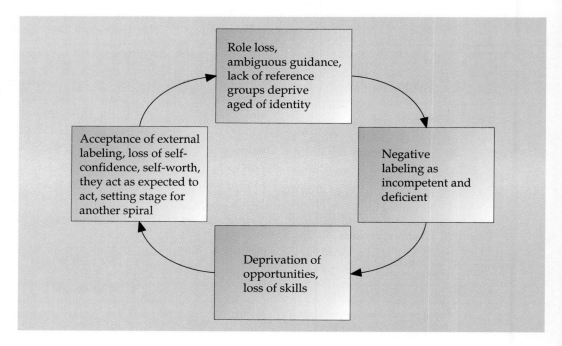

FIGURE 19.6 Social breakdown and the aged.

Adapted from "Social Breakdown and Competence: A Model of Normal Aging," by J. A. Kuypers and V. L. Bengtson, 1973, *Human Development, 16*, pp. 181–201.

Which Theory?

Each of these theories contributes something to the total understanding of the aging process. No one theory can explain the process in every individual. People are different; they live in different environments; their personalities and needs are different; and they act and react in different ways to social pressures. The more thoroughly we analyze these different determinants, the more clearly we will understand the process of aging in our culture. Finally, the better we understand our own needs and concerns as we age, the more likely we are to achieve satisfaction in our later years.

SUMMARY

1. A bit more than 1 in 5 adults over 18 years of age have never been married, but these are primarily in the youngest age groups. However, the unmarried status of most adult singles is only temporary because by age 45 to 54 only 5.6% of males and 5.1% of females have never been married.

2. Singles have been divided into four categories: voluntary temporary singles, voluntary permanent singles, involuntary temporary singles, and involuntary permanent singles.

3. There are both advantages and disadvantages in being single.

4. One study describes six life-stye patterns of singles: professional, social, individualistic, activist, passive, and supportive.

5. Some singles live in singles communities; others live in housing among the general population; others live with parents; others live alone.

6. The number of singles cohabiting with members of the opposite sex continues to increase, but there is no evidence that premarital cohabitation weeds out incompatible couples and prepares people for successful marriage.

7. One of the greatest needs of single people is for friendship and companionship. Loneliness is a problem for a significant majority.

8. Singles seem to have more time for optional activities than married couples, but married people report that they have more fun than singles.

9. The most important element in initial attraction is physical attractiveness, but personality factors become increasingly important as relationships develop.

10. One of the major problems for singles is finding and meeting dates. One survey reported that the most frequent way of meeting dates was through friends, at parties, at work or in class, and other ways (in decreasing order of frequency).

11. Gender roles in dating have been changing, with more females initiating dating and sharing part of the expenses. Among other things, this helps alter male–female sexual expectations.

12. Studies of university students reveal a great deal of anxiety about dating.

13. According to one study, the most frequent dating problems expressed by women were unwanted sexual pressure, where to go and what to do, communication, sexual misunderstanding, and money. The most frequently mentioned problems by the men were communication, where to go and what to do, shyness, money, and honesty/openness.

14. Date rape is a very common type of sexual aggression; it can occur in various kinds of relationships and it reflects the myth that women want to be forced and that it is up to the male to overcome female resistance. Of course, many men engage in such acts as an expression of anger, hostility, and contempt.

15. According to a national survey, 82% of unmarried women ages 20 to 29 had had sexual intercourse. Another survey revealed that 97% of men had had sexual intercourse by 25 years of age. However, studies suggest that neither men nor women are promiscuous; the great majority have only a few sexual partners in their sexual history.

16. AIDS is of special concern today because it is incurable and fatal.

17. The primary difference between older never-marrieds and younger ones is that the former are often well adjusted to their situation.

18. A minority of unmarried aged feel socially isolated. Their happiness depends a lot on their satisfaction with their level of living and their level of social activity.

19. Marital happiness contributes more to overall personal happiness than do any other kinds of satisfaction, including satisfaction from work.

The family life cycle divides the family experience into phases or stages over the life span. In general, marital satisfaction is curvilinear: high at the time of marriage, lowest during the child-rearing years, and higher again after the youngest child has passed beyond the teens.

21. All couples are faced with marital adjustment tasks early in marriage.

22. Adjustments to parenthood are less stressful if the marriage is not stressful, if parenthood was planned, if couples are prepared ahead of time, and if a child is easy to care for.

23. The task during middle adulthood may be to revitalize a tired marriage.

24. Some couples have trouble adjusting to the empty-nest years, but even greater numbers breathe a sigh of relief after the last child leaves. There is considerable evidence to show that adults in the postparental period are happier than are those earlier or later in life.

25. Marital satisfaction usually increases during a second honeymoon period after the children are launched and after retirement. However, during the last stages of old age, marital satisfaction may again decline.

26. Other adjustments during late adulthood are readjusting sex roles in the family, working out older parent–adult child relationships, contacts, and aid.

27. The greater longevity of women means that the number of widows exceeds widowers at all levels. Survivors often confront a variety of emotional, economic, and physical problems.

28. Divorce rates increased steadily from 1958 until 1979, and have since leveled off and declined. However, projections show that among women age 35 to 39, 56% may eventually divorce.

29. Surveys among marriage and family therapists show the following 10 areas as being most damaging to marital relationships (in decreasing frequency): communication, unrealistic expectations, power struggles, serious individual problems, role conflict, lack of love, demonstration of affection, alcoholism, extramarital affairs, and sex.

30. Extramarital affairs have varying effects on marriage: Some marriages are never the same afterward. Affairs sometimes stimulate the couple to seek help in solving unresolved problems. Sometimes affairs have no effect; at other times they hurt the wronged person who chooses not to make an issue. Other times, affairs result in divorce. The most damaging affairs are ongoing ones that include emotional involvement as well as sexual relations.

31. The most important adult adjustments after divorce are: getting over the emotional trauma, dealing with the attitudes of society, loneliness, finances, realignment of work responsibilities and sex roles, sexual readjustments, contacts with ex-spouse, and kinship interaction.

32. Adults who remarry have some real advantages over those married for the first time.

33. Remarriage introduces some complications not present in first marriage, the most important of which is stepchildren.

34. One of the major psychosocial tasks of young adulthood is to seek and find vocational identity, which is necessary to life satisfaction. It is important to aspire toward goals and to experience some success.

35. Adults have been grouped into five categories according to the status of their vocational development: vocational achievers, vocationally frustrated, noncommitted, vocational opportunists, and social dropouts.

36. Mid-life should be a time of vocational fruition. Some middle-agers lose their jobs because they do not keep abreast of their fields. Those who feel at a dead end in their career might start a second career.

37. Mid-life careers can also be a source of stress. One source is being fired. Too much job pressure and stress can result in burnout.

38. Job satisfaction tends to increase with a worker's age.

39. Because of increased longevity, raising of the mandatory retirement age and the age when workers can draw maximum social security, the numbers of older workers in the work force may increase in the years ahead.

40. Forced retirement has been ranked among the top 10 crises in terms of the amount of stress caused. Workers ought to have a choice in deciding when to retire.

41. Social-psychological theories of aging include disengagement theory, activity theory, personality and life-style theory, exchange theory, and social reconstruction theory.

KEY TERMS

Activity theory   *p. 442*
Burnout   *p. 441*
Cohabitation   *p. 425*
Date rape   *p. 428*
Disengagement theory   *p. 442*
Exchange theory   *p. 443*

Family life cycle   *p. 430*
Marital adjustment tasks   *p. 431*
Personality and life-style theory   *p. 443*
Postparental years   *p. 433*
Social reconstruction theory   *p. 444*

DISCUSSION QUESTIONS

1. What, in your view, are the greatest advantages and disadvantages to being single?
2. To singles: What are your greatest problems of adjustment? Describe.
3. What do you think of single young adults living with parents? living alone?
4. Describe the pros and cons of nonmarital cohabitation. Are you cohabiting with someone now? How is it working out? What are the biggest problems you have? Do you think that premarital cohabitation helps to sort out compatible mates? helps to prepare for a happy marriage? Explain.
5. To be happy, do you need close friends? a lot of social life? Do marrieds or singles have more fun? What are the greatest advantages to you of being married? What are the greatest disadvantages?
6. What are the biggest problems in dating?
7. To women: Have you ever been exposed to unwanted male sexual aggression? How has the experience affected you since then? What are the real issues in date rape? If you were date raped, would you go to the police? Explain.
8. To men: Are men today taught to believe that when women say no, they really mean yes, and that it is up to the man to overcome the woman's resistance? What can you do to ensure that you do not become guilty of date rape?
9. What particular problems are most associated with the high rate of premarital sexual intercourse? Would you marry a virgin? Explain your views.
10. Do you know any older, never-married adults? Describe. What are their reasons for not marrying? Are they happy? Are

you aware of any particular problems they face? Have you thought of never getting married? Explain your views.
11. In your opinion, what are the greatest adjustment problems early in marriage? during middle adulthood? parenthood? during late adulthood?
12. Are you a parent? What are your greatest problems in relation to parenthood? What are your greatest satisfactions?
13. Will you elect never to become a parent? Explain.
14. What are the greatest problems your parents face as married adults? Are any of your parents widowed? divorced? What are the most important problems they face?
15. If your spouse got involved in an extramarital affair, what would you do?
16. Was either of your parents remarried after divorce or widowhood? How did it work out? If you are a stepchild, what have been the most important adjustments you have had to make?
17. What are the primary problems and challenges you face in becoming established in your career?
18. Has either of your parents established a second career in mid-life? Describe. How has it worked out?
19. Have you ever known anyone who suffered from job burnout? Tell about it.
20. How do you feel about retirement at age 65? Is either of your parents retired? How has it worked out?
21. Which theory of aging best explains to you what happens as people get older?
22. What socioeconomic and political trends and conditions in America make growing old more difficult than it needs to be?

SUGGESTED READINGS

Ahrons, C. R., & Rodgers, R. H. (1987). *Divorced families*. New York: Norton. Divorce and its effects on adults.

Aldous, J. (Ed.). (1982). *Two paychecks: Life in dual earner families*. Beverly Hills, CA: Sage. Dual-career marriages and issues.

Brehm, S. S. (1985). *Intimate relationships.* New York: Random House. Intimate relationships from beginning to dissolution and how to improve them.

Einstein, E. (1982). *The stepfamily: Living, loving, and learning.* New York: Macmillan. A helpful guide.

Gilbert, L. A. (1985). *Men in dual-career families: Current realities and future prospects.* Hillsdale, NJ: Erlbaum. Comprehensive discussion.

Gilmour, R., & Duck, S. (Eds.). (1986). *The emerging field of intimate relationships.* Hillsdale, NJ: Erlbaum. Various types of intimate relationships and implications.

Hatfield, E., & Sprecher, S. (1986). *Mirror, mirror . . . : The importance of looks in everyday life.* Albany, NY: State University of New York Press. Looks and physical attractiveness.

Jorgensen, J. (1980). *The graying of America: Retirement and why you can't afford it.* New York: McGraw-Hill. All the reasons why people shouldn't retire completely.

Macklin, E. D., & Rubin, R. H. (1983). *Contemporary families and alternative lifestyles: Handbook on research and theory.* Beverly Hills, CA: Sage. Various life-style choices.

Parnes, H. S., Crowley, J. E., Haurin, R. J., Less, L. J., Morgan, W. R., Mott, F. L., & Nestel, G. (1985). *Retirement among American men.* Lexington, MA: Lexington Books. Retirement from different viewpoints.

Rice, F. P. (1990). *Intimate relationships, marriages, and families.* Mountain View, CA: Mayfield Publishing Co. Comprehensive look at all aspects.

Rubin, I. (1983). *Intimate strangers: Men and women together.* New York: Harper and Row. Differences between men and women and how these affect intimacy.

Scarf, M. (1987). *Intimate partners: Patterns in love and marriage.* New York: Random House. Love, relationships, and marriage, and the way earlier lives affect these.

Spanier, G. B., & Thompson, L. (1984). *Parting: The aftermath of separation and divorce.* Beverly Hills, CA: Sage. Research findings.

Voydanoff, P. (Ed.). (1984). *Work and family: Changing roles of men and women.* Palo Alto, CA: Mayfield. A series of articles.

Wilk, C. A. (1986). *Career women and childbearing: A psychological analysis of the decision process.* New York: Van Nostrand. Reconciling career with raising children.

20

Death, Dying, and Bereavement

LEADING CAUSES OF DEATH

Figure 20.1 shows the leading causes of death in the United States in 1987. *Heart disease was the number-one killer.* If all of the major cardiovascular diseases were added together (including heart diseases, hypertension, cerebrovascular disease, and atherosclerosis), these would account for 46% of all deaths. However, rapid progress in the treatment of these diseases has caused the associated death rate to decrease steadily (U.S. Bureau of the Census, 1990).

Cancer was the number-two killer, and in spite of advances in treatment, the death rate continues to rise. The rising death rate is due primarily to an increase among males, particularly those age 65 and over. Among females, deaths from cancer actively declined until 1970. Since then there has been a slight rise, but not comparable to the increase among older males. Cancer of the lungs has increased drastically in both men and women. Because deaths from most other forms of cancer have shown only very slight increases, the rise in lung cancer death is primarily responsible for the total increase.

Death rates from accidents declined 35% from 1970 to 1988. Death rates from homicides have stayed fairly constant over the same period. There is a marked difference in death rates among different groups of people:

1. Males die at a higher rate than females at all ages.
2. The nonwhite population has a higher death rate than the white population.
3. The death rate among nonwhite infants under 1 year of age is 2.4 times greater than among white infants.
4. Accidents are the leading cause of death among youths 15 to 24 years old.
5. Deaths from suicide reach a peak among adults in the 75- to 84-year-old age group.

FIGURE 20.1 Death rates by cause and sex, United States, 1987.

Statistics from *Statistical Abstract of the United States, 1990* (p. 81) by U.S. Bureau of the Census, 1990, Washington, DC: U.S. Government Printing Office.

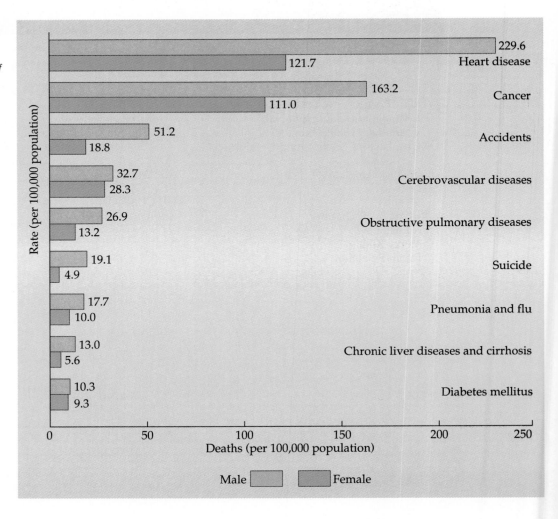

The causes of death have changed radically in the past 100 years. At one time, infectious diseases such as *influenza, pneumonia,* and *tuberculosis* were the leading causes of death (Hendricks & Hendricks, 1986). Childhood infections such as *diphtheria, whooping cough, measles, scarlet fever,* and *acute infectious gastroenteritis* claimed the lives of many children. Acute infectious gastroenteritis with vomiting and diarrhea is still the leading cause of death in children less than 4 years old in developing countries (Berkow, 1987).

ATTITUDES TOWARD DEATH AND DYING

Cultural Antecedents

The dominant feature of death in the 20th century is its invisibility. We try to solve the problems of death by hiding it or denying it. We lie to dying people about their condition because death is unmentionable. They, in turn, try to convince us that they are getting better. Or, we use machines to keep organs functioning, even when people are clinically dead. When people die, they are made to look healthy and alive, as though they were sleeping. We sometimes discourage mourning and the natural expression of grief at a time of great loss. The denial of death has become the orthodoxy of our culture (Robinson, 1981).

In earlier times, death was more a part of everyday life. People who were critically ill were usually cared for at home, with family members providing the service. Death often occurred at home. Relatives prepared the body for burial, built the coffin, and buried it. Services were by the graveside. The burial itself may have taken place in a family graveyard next to other relatives who had died. Death was stressful to all, but it was an accepted part of life.

Today, the critically ill usually die in the hospital with medical staff members attending them. The body is transported to the undertakers, where professionals prepare it for viewing in the funeral home. The undertaker feels proud if the deceased looks natural and seems to be sleeping. The graveside is prepared with plastic green carpet and flowers to hide the soil. Usually, the casket is not lowered into the grave until family members have left. Everything is done to hide the fact and reality of death.

Denial can be an important coping mechanism. The way that some people deal with loss is to believe it doesn't exist, but *it is this very denial, when carried to extremes, that*

There is a need for an expression of grief at a time of great loss.

prevents acceptance and positive adjustments. There are so many positive things that the dying want to do and say before they die. There are so many positive things that family members want to do and say, but when the living and dying both deny that death is taking place, the words are never spoken.

After death, one of the most important ways of dealing with grief is to be able to express it and talk about the loved one. When people try, they are hushed up, or the subject is changed. Death is considered too unpleasant a subject for polite conversation. Even children have to struggle to understand because their curiosity and questions are reprimanded or avoided. They are forced to try to cope as best they can (Kalish, 1985a).

Parents can help children to understand death by answering their questions.

FOCUS

The Cultural Meaning of Death

Aries (1981) has traced the cultural meaning of death in Western thought from the Middle Ages to the present. Before 1200, people accepted death as their destiny. Death was neither glorified nor avoided. From 1200 to 1700, the emphasis was on the art of dying, becoming personally reconciled to God in preparing for death. Death became important as an entrance into a better life. From 1700 to the late 1800s, a distinction was made between a "nonnatural" death, which was a punishment, and a "beautiful and edifying death," which was a natural transition. Death was romanticized and glorified. Then, beginning with the 20th century, death became culturally invisible and the effort was made to deny it. Physicians and hospitals were expected to prevent dying, or to deal with those who were dying. Funerals were institutionalized; mourning was discouraged.

Criticisms

Modern trends involving the denial of death have led to increasing examination of our philosophies of death and dying, to a deluge of courses on the subject, and to a flood of literature, much of it protesting modern practices. Tentler (1977) provided a comparative critique of writings about death in American culture, drawn from the fields of psychology, sociology, anthropology, religion, and literature. He observed a common theme in these essays: a "moralist, reformist approach" characterized by criticism of the denial of death. Dishonesty with dying people, lack of care for the aged, and American funeral practices are common subjects of scorn. *Currently, there is a swing away from the denial of death toward the notion of death with dignity.*

Attitudes Among Different Age Groups of Adults

Detailed studies of groups of adults reveal variations in attitudes toward death among different age groups. One study examined the attitudes toward death of black, white, and Mexican-American adults of low, medium, and high socioeconomic status, from three different age groups (45 to 54; 55 to 64; and 65 to 74). It revealed little variation in attitudes toward death with respect to race, socioeconomic status, or sex, but substantial differences according to age (Bengtson, Cuellar, & Ragan, 1977). *Middle-aged respondents age 45 to 54 expressed the greatest fear of death; the elderly, 65 to 74, reflected the least.* The researchers suggested that middle-aged adults are more frightened of death because they experience a middle-aged crisis and become aware of the finitude of their lives.

The researchers also indicated that in old age adults do resolve their death fear. This attitude is exemplified by a 67-year-old widower, who said: "I know I'm going to die, it's something that we all have to go through. When it happens, it happens, and there's nothing I can do. I'll cross that bridge when I come to it" (Bengtson et al., 1977).

Attitudes toward death depend partly on attitudes toward life. Keith (1979) surveyed 214 men and 254 women, median age 79, from small towns in a midwestern state, and found that those who experienced continuity in marital status, good health, church involvement, and informal contacts with family and friends viewed life and death more positively.

Attitudes Among the Elderly

The elderly are often more philosophical, more realistic, and less anxious about death than are others in our culture. Many studies underscore these attitudes. Questionnaires were administered to 40 voluntarily institutionalized ambulatory residents of the *Wyoming Pioneer Home* for senior citizens, and to 40 others who were noninstitutionalized ambulatory persons, members of the *Senior Citizen's Center* in Laramie, Wyoming, a center providing meals, nursing services, recreation, and social activities (Myska & Pasewark, 1978). Subjects ranged in age from 61 to 97. There were few differences between the institutionalized and noninstitutionalized in their views of death. Generally, fear of death was not suggested by the respondents (see Table 20.1).

Although they did not fear death, few of the elderly subjects indicated a resignation to or desire for death. Only 5% said they frequently wished for death. About 82% thought about things related to living and looked forward to the future. About 69% reported that they perceived death as rescuing them from pain and difficulty. However, only 33% looked forward to death for that reason. The one fear of the respondents was that death would be painful (45%), but only 6% believed this would be the case.

TABLE 20.1 Fear of Death Among Elderly Rural Residents

Attitude	Percent Affirming Attitude
Strong fear of death	1%
Absolutely unafraid of death	51%
Indifferent toward death	40%
Did not respond	8%

Reprinted with permission of authors and publisher from ''Death Attitudes of Residential and Non-residential Rural Aged Persons'' by M. J. Myska and R. A. Pasewark, December 1978, *Psychological Reports, 43*, pp. 1235–1238.

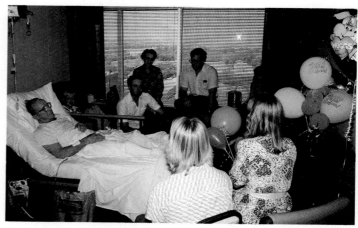

Sick and dying patients need the support and love of family members.

In relation to an afterlife, 62% believed it existed, but 94% said it did not worry them. About 75% reported they would not change their way of life even if they were certain there were no life after death (Myska & Pasewark, 1978). These results indicated an affirmation of life and a realistic acceptance of death, with little anxiety or preoccupation.

ASPECTS OF DEATH

What Is Death?

Physiological death—the ceasing to function of all the vital organs

Determining when a person is dead is not simple. A distinction is made between **physiological death** and **clinical death**. With physiological death, all the vital organs cease to function and the organism can no longer live, in any sense of the word. Deprived of oxygen and nutrients, the cells of the body gradually die. Clinical death is the cessation of all brain activity as indicated by an absence of brain waves. There is no consciousness, no awareness. The organism ceases to function as a self-sustaining, mind–body human, even though the heart and lungs can function with artificial support.

There are other aspects of death. **Sociological death** involves withdrawal and separation from the patient by others. This may occur weeks before terminus if patients are left alone to die. It happens when families desert the aged in nursing homes, where

Clinical death—the cessation of all brain activity

Sociological death—the withdrawal and separation by other people as though one were dead, often long before physiological death

FOCUS

Children's and Adolescents' Conceptions of Death

Maria Nagy (1948) conducted the first investigation of children's attitudes toward death. The following is a summary of her findings:

Ages 3 to 5. Children are curious about death, but they see it as temporary and reversible. The dead person will return.

Ages 5 to 9. Children gradually realize that death is final and permanent. They begin to realize they could die but they don't necessarily have to. Older people die because they can't run fast enough or hide from death the way younger, smaller people can.

Ages 9 to 10. Death is final, inevitable, and universal. They become concerned about how death affects them and their family. They can show a lot of anger, guilt, and grief over someone's dying (Schaefer & Lyons, 1986).

Adolescents. A few adolescents who have experienced the death of a close member of the family or of a close friend try to fathom its meaning and nature. For most, death is so remote that it doesn't have much relevance. Little thought is given to it because it is always something that happens to someone else.

older people may live for years as if dead. As a resident of one nursing home expressed it:

> What have I to live for? I have two children who don't care about me. They are so busy with their own lives that they haven't been in to see me in two years. My health is not good. I have arthritis, no appetite, and a weak heart. There is nothing to do here. It's the same old thing day after day. I might as well be dead.

Psychic death occurs when the patient accepts death and regresses into the self. Often this occurs long before physiological death. The psychic acceptance of death can

actually cause a person to die. Death comes through the power of suggestion because the will to live is gone.

Patterns of Death

Figure 20.2 illustrates five different patterns of death (Pattison, 1977). In *pattern one*, the terminal phase begins when the person starts to give up. There is still some element of desirable hope for life, but gradually other people withdraw (sociological death), the patient acquiesces (psychic death), the brain ceases to function (clinical death), and the body dies (physiological death).

Psychic death—the acceptance of death and regression into self, often long before physiological death

FIGURE 20.2   Patterns of death.

From the book *The Experience of Dying* by E. Mansell Pattison. © 1977 by Prentice-Hall, Inc. Published by Prentice-Hall, Inc., Englewood Cliffs, NJ 07632.

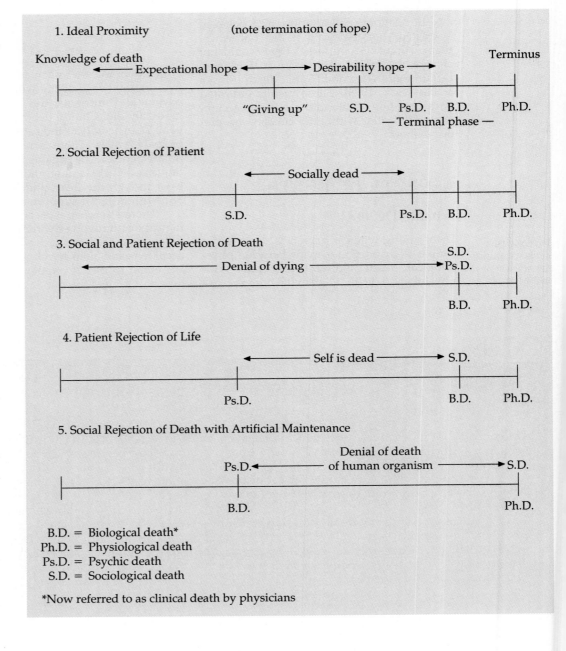

In *pattern two*, other people reject the patient and withdraw (sociological death) long before death occurs. This leads to psychic death, which ultimately results in clinical and physiological death.

In *pattern three*, both the patient and others refuse to accept impending death. When death comes, it may precipitate a shocked reaction. The same thing occurs when deterioration is sudden and death occurs contrary to expectations.

In *pattern four*, the patient rejects life and becomes psychically dead. This is met with social disapproval and efforts by family and friends to motivate the person to live.

Finally, in *pattern five* there is social denial of the fact that both psychic and clinical death have occurred, and the patient is kept physiologically alive by artificial means. The morality and ethics of such artificial procedures are currently the subject of much controversy.

VARYING CIRCUMSTANCES OF DEATH

Death, especially that of a spouse or other close relative, is among life's most stressful events. It creates considerable physical, mental, and emotional stress and tension, which may take a long period of time to subside.

There are various circumstances of death. These include:

1. *Uncertain death*
2. *Certain death*, either at a known or unknown time
3. *Untimely death*, which may be *premature, unexpected*, and/or *calamitous*

Each of these circumstances is discussed in this section.

Uncertain Death

Everyone will die, but the exact time is uncertain for most people. The circumstances of uncertain death can be very stressful if people have been badly injured and are in critical condition, or if they have had radical surgery with the result uncertain. During such times, the patient and family members must live through a continuing period of acute crisis.

> Harvey is lying in a hospital bed in the intensive care unit. He has just suffered a major heart attack. He is hooked up to a machine that beeps and registers a blip on a television screen every time his heart beats. His wife is beside him, holding his hand. He is receiving oxygen. He is scared. His wife is scared. They both know the days ahead are crucial (Rice, 1990b, p. 576).

The most difficult part about such uncertainty is the waiting: dreading something adverse; hoping for improvement; waiting anxiously for other family members to arrive. The patient needs to avoid panic, to relax, and to let healing take place. The wife and family need relief from the continued anxiety and worry; they need sleep and reassurance that their loved one will be all right.

The question of whether the patient will live or die is resolved eventually: "The next 48 hours will tell us whether she is going to make it or not." At other times, there are long-term uncertainties, as is the case with treatments of cancer that may or may not have arrested the disease. Ambiguity may remain for years: "If there is no return in 5 years, the outlook is very positive." Long years of waiting can be difficult. However, some people learn to go about being as happy and optimistic as possible and not to worry about what might happen.

Certain Death

Certain death requires a different adjustment. The approximate time of death may be known or unknown or can only be surmised. Such might be the case in a deadly disease such as cancer of the pancreas. Whether the approximate time of death is known or not, the adjustments to terminal illness are difficult.

KUBLER-ROSS: FIVE STAGES OF DYING. One of the best descriptions of the process of dying was given by Kubler-Ross (1969, 1974), a psychiatrist at the University of Chicago, who spent considerable time talking with 200 dying patients to try to understand and describe their reactions to terminal illness. She found considerable resistance among medical personnel to the idea of talking with patients about dying but she also found that the patients were relieved to share their concerns.

Kubler-Ross identified five stages of dying that did not necessarily occur in a regular sequence. She said: "Most of my patients have exhibited two or three stages simultaneously and these do not always occur in the same order" (1974). The five stages she identified are *denial, anger, bargaining, depression,* and *acceptance.*

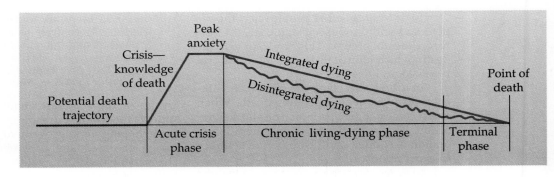

FIGURE 20.3 The living-dying trajectory.

Adapted from "The Experience of Dying" by E. M. Pattison in *The Experience of Dying* (pp. 43–60) by E. M. Pattison, Ed., Englewood Cliffs, NJ: Prentice-Hall. Used by permission of the publisher.

The *denial* response of patients is: "No, not me. It can't be true." Some accuse their doctor of incompetence, and some think a mistake was made in the lab or in diagnosis. Others seek the advice of other physicians or of faith healers, or look for miracle cures. Some simply deny the reality of impending death and proceed as if nothing were wrong. Only a few patients maintain denial to the very end; most accept reality gradually.

As they acknowledge reality, their next reaction is one of *anger*: "Why me? It's not fair it should be happening to me." Patients in this stage become very hostile, resentful, and highly irritable, often quarreling with doctors, nurses, and loved ones.

As terminally ill patients begin to realize that death may be coming, they try *bargaining* to win a reprieve. The patient propositions God, the staff, and family, sometimes just to live a while longer to attend a wedding or complete a task. The patient says to God: "If you give me 6 more months, I'll leave most of my money to the church." If the person lives beyond the requested period, however, the agreement is usually broken.

Once patients lose hope that life is possible and accept death as inevitable, *depression* may set in. Depression may be caused by regret at leaving behind everything and everybody that one loves. It may be caused by guilt over one's life. It may result from shame over bodily disfigurement or because of the inability to die with dignity. Some patients need to express their sorrow to overcome it. Others need cheering up and support to improve their morale and to regain their self-esteem.

The final stage of the dying process is *acceptance*. The patient has worked through denial, anger, bargaining, depression, and fear of death; he or she is now exhausted and weak. This is the time for friends or family members to sit quietly holding the patient's hands, to show that death is not such a frightening experience (Rice, 1986).

PATTISON: THE LIVING-DYING TRAJECTORY. Pattison (1977) presented the dying process in a little different way. He said that all of us project a trajectory of our life involving a certain anticipated life span within which we arrange our activities and our lives (see Figure 20.3). And then we are abruptly confronted with a crisis—the crisis of the knowledge of death. Our potential trajectory is suddenly changed. We shall die in days, weeks, months, or several years. Our life has been foreshortened. Our activities must be rearranged. We cannot plan for the potential; we must deal with the actual. The period between the "crisis and knowledge of death" and the "point of death" is the **living-dying interval**. This interval is divided into three phases: (1) *the acute crisis phase*, (2) *the chronic living-dying phase*, and (3) *the terminal phase*. Family members can help the person respond to the acute crisis so that it does not result in a chaotic disintegration of the person's life during the chronic living-dying phase. The following is an example of **disintegrated dying** during the living-dying phase.

Martha was told she had an incurable cancer. She shut herself up in her house, refused to talk to her family and friends or to see them. She never went out. Her husband couldn't stand to see her upset, so he went out most of the time. She spent most of her days depressed and crying. Finally, one afternoon her husband came home early and found that she had slashed her wrists in an effort to kill herself. Emergency treatment saved her life.

The following is an example of **integrated dying**, following psychiatric treatment that Martha received.

Martha alternated between feeling terrible (when she was given chemotherapy) and feeling fairly well at other times. Her husband began to stay home more and to pro-

Living-dying interval—period of time between the knowledge of the crisis of death and death itself

Disintegrated dying—going to pieces emotionally and not being able to function after learning of impending death

Integrated dying—being able to put one's life together, to make satisfactory adjustments to the dying process

vide moral support and companionship. Martha and her husband started to go out to dinner occasionally. She began to call family members and friends and let them come visit. She finally decided that she was going to make the best of her life during the time she had.

The last task of family members is to give the person comfort and support as the person moves inevitably into the terminal phase (Pattison, 1977).

NEEDS OF THE DYING. Dying people have a number of needs (Kalish, 1985b). They have the same need for food, clothing, shelter, rest, and warmth that we all have. In addition, they often have the need for freedom from pain. They also need reassurance that their close friends and family will not let them die alone.

The dying person usually has a number of tasks to complete. These include getting insurance and financial affairs in order, dealing with medical care needs, especially when alternate forms of treatment are proposed, arranging for distribution of possessions after death, making a will, and making funeral suggestions; some people even make their own funeral arrangements (Kalish & Reynolds, 1981).

TELLING PATIENTS THEY ARE DYING. Should patients be told they are dying? A survey among physicians, nurses, chaplains, and college students concerning their attitudes toward informing patients of their terminal condition revealed that all groups felt the patients had a right to be told (Carey &

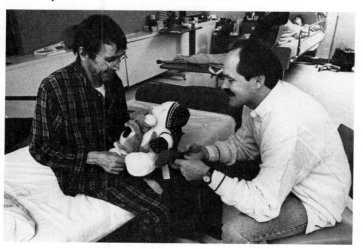

This AIDS patient who is dying needs reassurance that close friends and family members will not let him die alone.

Posavac, 1978–1979). Yet, there is a lack of socialization for dying in many hospitals. People are not oriented toward the process of dying and are left to cope with their problems in ambiguity and isolation (Rosel, 1978–1979). Moreover, not all patients should be approached and told in the same manner. There are no prescribed norms for dealing with dying patients. The basic intent should be to help, not harm, the patient (Gadow, 1980). There is no need for a long discussion about the severity of the illness with an acutely ill patient who is barely conscious. That person often knows death is imminent. Care and comfort are the primary concerns. But the patient who is experiencing physical deterioration and who is told there is nothing to worry about may say nothing but wonder much (Pattison, 1977). Some people absolutely do not want to know, and some would literally die of shock if they did know. *The goal is to ease the dying process, not to apply a dogma of always telling the truth.* Patients must be aware of the significance of their illness and helped to adjust. Respect for their feelings and the use of tact are extremely important (LeRoux, 1977).

Untimely Death: Premature Death

The psychological reactions to death are more extreme when death occurs in childhood or at a comparatively young age (Wass & Corr, 1984). People have trouble accepting a child's death or understanding it. It seems so unfair. The child has not had a chance at life. It is difficult to reconcile *what is* with what *might have been*. Parental reactions are variable. Many parents feel guilty: "If only I had not let him play in the front yard." "I should have watched her more carefully." "It's my fault for not taking him to the doctor sooner." "God is punishing me." Parents become angry and resentful and lash out at whomever they can blame for the loss: "I told him not to put the baby in the front seat." "If she had not been talking on the telephone, this would never have happened." Guilt and blame can destroy a family at the time they need one another's help. Sometimes blame is put on hospitals, doctors, and nurses. Medical personnel themselves get caught up in the struggle to save a child's life, and—when this fails—they are filled with sorrow and feelings of helplessness, or with self-recrimination for failure.

While the family is focusing on saving the dying child, other siblings may be overlooked. Siblings often are frightened, bewil-

South Africans attend the funeral of
this young child.

**Sudden infant
death syndrome—**
the sudden and
mysterious death
of infants in their
sleep, usually be-
tween 2 weeks and
1 year of age

dered, and jealous, and they may feel rejected. Parents need to keep them informed
about what's going on and pay attention to
them also (Wallinga, Paguio, & Skeen, 1987).

SUDDEN INFANT DEATH SYNDROME
(SIDS). **Sudden infant death syndrome**, or
when infants die mysteriously while asleep,

is the most common cause of death in infants
between 2 weeks and 1 year of age, accounting for 30% of all deaths in the age group.
SIDS is one type of unexpected death that
shocks and disorganizes the family system.
Survivors experience grief somatophysically
and as intense, subjective mental pain. Parents experience despondency, concentration

FOCUS

Hospice Care for the Terminally Ill

The hospice has emerged as a viable alternative to hospital deaths that are depersonalizing, lonely, and painful
experiences for dying persons and their families. The
term **hospice** means literally a "way station" to care for
travelers on their journey. In this case, the travelers are
on the way to dying.

Hospice care originated in London at St. Christopher's and spread to the United States in the early 1970s.
New Haven Hospice in New Haven, Connecticut, was the
first in the United States. Since then, thousands of hos-
pices have sprung up around the country. Hospice care
can take place at home or in the center. It includes phy-
sician-directed services, an interdisciplinary team, the
use of volunteers, 24-hour-a-day treatment for the patient and family, pain/symptom control, and bereavement follow-up of the family after death (Dubois, 1980;

Mor & Masterson-Allen, 1987). Patients have the same
rights to quality care as those receiving hospital care.
Medicare, Medicaid, and some other insurance plans
may pay part of the bill.

There are several other important features of hospice care. Bringing pain under control helps the dying
person face death comfortably. Family members are welcome, and keeping the dying patient and family together comforts the patient and minimizes the guilt and
anxiety of the family. The hospice permits patients and
family to make decisions and experience control over
their lives in a warm, caring atmosphere. They decide
family matters, funeral planning, wills, and *where*, with
whom, under *what* conditions, and *how* death will happen (Hayslip & Leon, 1988).

difficulties, time confusion, loss of appetite, or inability to sleep. They may dread being alone and fear the responsibilities of caring for other children. They feel helpless, angry, and guilty (Aadalen, 1980). Parents often blame themselves.

Research is being conducted on the best way to help families cope with the death of a child (Joyce, 1984). John Spinetta, professor of psychology at San Diego State University, has followed the course of bereavement in 120 families in which children have died of cancer, trying to distinguish the families that bounce back quickly from those that languish in grief. He asks whether the family can talk about or see reminders of the child without shedding tears, whether they have returned to normal activities like jobs, clubs, and hob-

bies. Are they still filled with questions about why it happened? It is hoped that some guidelines for the best ways to help grieving parents will be provided (Joyce, 1984).

Untimely Death: Unexpected Death

Unexpected death refers to the sudden death of a healthy person. The emotional impact on survivors is gauged by how vital, alive, and distinctive the person is at the time of death. The more vital and alive the person, the harder it is to imagine that person dead. When a young adult dies, relatives react with frustration, disappointment, and anger. Career, marriage, children, and home were probably yet to come. Unexpected death of

---

LIVING ISSUES

Involuntary Manslaughter

Involuntary manslaughter is the unintentional killing of another human being, most often while driving a car, less often in situations like hunting accidents.

> Mrs. A. was driving her car at night while very drunk. She swerved over the yellow centerline into an oncoming car, killing the woman driver. She was convicted of involuntary manslaughter and sentenced to 2 years in prison. During this period of time, her husband came for counseling as preparation for the time when his wife would be released from prison. After discharge from prison, the couple both came for therapy to try to put their lives back together (Author's counseling notes).

In this case, several factors were significant:

1. In the beginning, the husband gave his wife no moral support. During the 6 months' trial, the couple never talked about what had happened. The husband didn't want to. The husband slept on the couch; the wife described her pain as terrible. She wanted to reach out to her spouse, but he was not there when she needed him. The wife said she wanted a divorce. The husband finally broke down and cried and said he didn't want one. During the wife's imprisonment, the husband came for therapy.

2. The major problem in the marriage was the wife's chronic alcoholism. The wife agreed to enter a treatment and educational program for her alcoholism while she was in prison. She was successful in recovering from her disease.

3. Following her release from prison, the wife was ecstatic for 2 weeks, going through a psychedelic high. Following the high, she suffered a **posttraumatic stress disorder**. She cried daily, lay in bed, and couldn't force herself to go to work. The simplest task—like going shopping at a grocery store—overwhelmed her. Through therapy she was able to

Accidents are the leading cause of death among people 15 to 34 years of age.

relive some of her experiences and overcome them. Jail had been a nightmare for her. There were 25 other women, who were rough and tough, who never said hello, who were never nice to her, and who were always planning drug deals. In the beginning, she was petrified and scared; then she became disgusted. It took her 6 months to accept the fact that she was in prison.

4. Three months after the wife's discharge from prison, the husband–wife communication had improved. The husband had become more loving and attentive. The wife was off antidepressants and entered an educational program for Certified Nurses' Aides. The lives of the two people were slowly coming together (Author's counseling notes).

a middle-aged person can also be tragic, but for different reasons. The middle-aged person has assumed responsibilities for family, job, and home, as well as in the community. Financial obligations are at a peak. There is extensive involvement with spouse, children, relatives, business associates, and friends. Death leaves the survivors with continuing obligations and no one to assume the responsibilities. Coping with dying involves coping with obligations already assumed.

Untimely Death: Calamitous Death

Calamitous death is not only unpredictable, but it can be violent, destructive, demeaning, and even degrading. It includes *accidents, involuntary manslaughter, homicide,* and *suicide.* Accidents are the leading cause of death in the United States among people 15 to 34 years of age (U.S. Bureau of the Census, 1989). Most accidents have identifiable causes and are preventable, so family members are left with the knowledge that it need not have happened. The revelation of death comes as a shock, causing an extended period of disorganization before relatives can reorganize their lives to living without their loved one.

Calamitous Death: Homicide

Most of the stereotypes about murders and murderers have no foundation in fact. The following facts help to clear up the myths (Kastenbaum & Aisenberg, 1976).

- Most murderers are not mysterious strangers. In at least two-thirds of the cases of willful homicide and violent assault, the perpetrator and the victim were at least acquainted. A sizable minority of homicides are committed by relatives of the victim.
- Family members or acquaintances behave more violently toward their victims than do total strangers.
- Senseless assaults by complete strangers are rare.
- Policemen are more likely to be killed while investigating domestic disturbances than in any other type of duty.
- The incidence of violent crime decreases with increases in neighborhood income.
- In most cases of violence, the perpetrator and the victim are of the same race.

These facts suggest that homicide is most often an outgrowth of quarrels and violence among family members or friends. The quarrels get out of hand, resulting in people's slaying one another in the privacy of their own homes. Policemen who are summoned to quell domestic disturbances are sometimes killed themselves.

Calamitous Death: Suicide

Suicide is acting out behavior that is often an indication of severe emotional upset. The rate increases with advancing age, reaching a peak in males over 85 years of age and in females 45 to 54 (U.S. Bureau of the Census, 1989). Figure 20.4 shows the trends. Suicide is rare in children under age 15. Children are still dependent on love objects for gratification. They have not yet completed the process of identification within themselves; thus, the thought of turning hostility toward themselves is too painful and frightening. Only as children find more self-identity can they be independent enough to commit suicide.

As can be seen in the figure, the rate among males is far greater than among females. *Females attempt suicide much more frequently than do males, but many more males than females are successful in completing the suicide.* Males more frequently use violent means—hanging, jumping from heights, shooting, or stabbing themselves—whereas females more often use passive and less dangerous methods, such as taking pills. Females more often make multiple threats but less often want to kill themselves or actually do it (The Suicide Prevention Center, 1984).

There are a variety of motivations and reasons for suicide among the elderly. Many senile persons kill themselves in such a way that intention cannot be proven. They forget to light the gas stove after turning it on, or they overdose with medicine, having forgotten how much they have already taken. Sometimes the elderly make a deliberate and rational decision to end their lives, rather than die a slow death or live alone and penniless. Married couples may make a pact to commit suicide together or to commit mercy killing and suicide.

More single males commit suicide than married ones. Often they have been forced into unwanted retirement. Poor planning for retirement and poor adjustment to it are major factors in the suicides of older men (Miller, 1978). Very low income seems to have a significant impact on elderly white males who commit suicide (Marshall, 1978).

Older people who attempt suicide fail much less often than younger people, and any threats or symptoms must be taken seriously. Relatives and friends should be especially alert to signs of

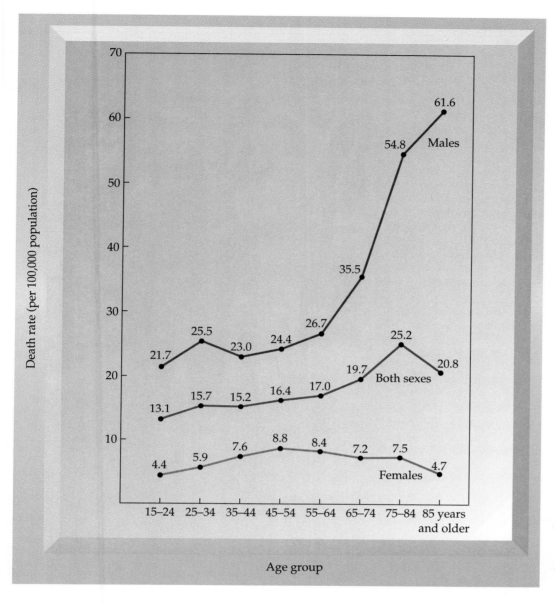

FIGURE 20.4 Suicide rates, 1986, United States, by age and sex.

Statistics from *Statistical Abstract of the United States, 1990* (p. 81) by U.S. Bureau of the Census, 1990, Washington, DC: U.S. Government Printing Office.

depression or suicidal preoccupation. Few human beings can sustain a meaningless life, and suicide is evidence of that fact. Some people do not attempt to take their lives with one act; rather they neglect themselves, refuse to eat, or show other self-destructive behavior as an alternative to suicide (Nelson & Farberow, 1980).

Suicide is one of the most upsetting of family crises because it leaves family members feeling so remorseful, so guilty, so confused and hurt. Survivors inevitably ask:

Why did he or she do it?
Why didn't I sense that something was wrong?
Why didn't I do something to prevent it?

Survivors who are left with dependent children, large financial responsibilities, and other obligations are also justifiably resentful.

How could he or she do such a thing?
I hate him or her for doing this and leaving me all the responsibility of caring for the children.

If family members blame themselves for letting suicide happen, or for not preventing it from happening, or for causing it to happen, it may take considerable therapy to get over the self-incrimination.

FOCUS

Factors Contributing to Adolescent Suicide

The following situations or factors contribute to suicide among adolescents (Greuling & DeBlassie, 1980; Rice, 1990a).

- Suicidal adolescents tend to come from *disturbed family backgrounds* (Wright, 1985). There may have been much conflict between the parents or between the parents and children, considerable family violence, or the parents may have manifested negative, rejecting attitudes toward the children (Wade, 1987).
- Other studies relate adolescent suicide with *frequent parental absence* because of employment (Stack, 1985). As a consequence, there is often an absence of any warm, parental figure with whom to identify and a sense of emotional and social isolation (Stivers, 1988).
- The background of *social isolation* makes these adolescents particularly vulnerable to a loss of love object, which may trigger the suicide attempt (Neiger & Hopkins, 1988).
- One frequent component of suicidal tendencies is *depression* (Cosand, Bourque, & Kraus, 1982).
- The risk of suicide among adolescents is increased with *alcohol and drug abuse* (Sommer, 1984). Or adolescents sometimes overdose and kill themselves without intending to do so (Gispert, Wheeler, Marsh, & Davis, 1985).
- Some suicidal adolescents have been categorized as *immature personalities* with poor impulse control.
- Other suicidal adolescents have been shown to be highly *suggestible* in following the directions or examples of others (Robbins, 1983).
- Suicide may be a direct result of *mental illness* (Cosand, Bourque, & Kraus, 1982). Some adolescents experience hallucinations that tell them to kill themselves.
- *Guilt* and/or anger and *hostility* are important emotional components of suicide. The adolescents may be in the terminal stages of a romance. Girls may believe they are pregnant. Guilt and shame over an out-of-wedlock pregnancy can be powerful motivating factors in suicides.
- Suicide is a cry for help to get *attention* or *sympathy* or is an attempt to manipulate other people.

Suicide is rare among children under age 15.

Contrary to common opinion, suicide attempts in a great majority of cases are considered in advance and weighed rationally against other alternatives. Having tried these alternatives and failed, the person turns to suicide attempts. Most adolescents who attempt suicide talk about it first (Pfeffer, 1987; Shafi, 1988). If others are alerted in time, and if they pay attention to these developments and take them seriously enough to try to remedy the situation, a death may be prevented (Fujimura, Weis, & Cochran, 1985; Gispert, 1987).

Socially Accelerated Dying

Socially accelerated dying—allowing any condition or action of society that shortens life and hastens death

In the broadest sense, **socially accelerated dying** is allowing any condition or action of society that shortens life and hastens death. This includes industrial pollution, unhealthy mine conditions that lead to black lung disease, asbestos or radiation exposure that causes cancer, and subsidizing tobacco farmers. In a narrow sense, it includes withholding health care from the elderly or abandoning them in nursing homes or other institutions. Hospitals that are unconcerned with geriatric medicine or curing illnesses in elderly people are socially accelerating the dying process.

In the *Northwestern Arnhem Land of Australia*, a doomed member of the *Murngin tribe* is socially rejected by other members. All relatives withdraw their sustaining support. Other tribe members change their attitudes, placing the sick member in a sacred, taboo category. No longer a member of the group, and alone and isolated, the person can only escape by death. The fact that the community has drawn away from him suggests in countless ways that the condition is irreversible. It takes little imagination to see that some institutionalized elderly suffer a similar fate. They too may feel cast aside with little support and condemned to die. No wonder that people relocated to a nursing home sometimes die quickly. About half the deaths take place in the first 3 months after admission (Watson & Maxwell, 1977).

Hospice care of the terminally ill can take place at home or in a center.

EUTHANASIA

Meaning

Some people want to die because they are crippled or in pain and have nothing left to live for, or because they are terminally ill or are being kept alive only by artificial life support. In such cases, questions arise as to the moral obligations of society, family, and medical personnel to keep them alive.

The word **euthanasia** conjures up many images, from so-called mercy killing to pulling the plug when there is no hope of recovery. Euthanasia is sometimes described as a positive/active process (forcing a person to die) or a negative/passive process (doing nothing, allowing death to come naturally). But as medical science advances, these distinctions are no longer clear. There is a difference between doing everything possible to cure a person's illness, but allowing death to come if the efforts fail, and using artificial means to prolong life even after ultimate death is certain.

Death With Dignity

Euthanasia includes three different concepts: death with dignity, mercy killing, and death selection. **Death with dignity** allows a terminally ill patient to die naturally without mechanized prolongation that could turn death into an ordeal. The concept rejects extraordinary means when a person has irrevocably entered the dying process. This is referred to as "pulling the plug." Some families refuse to do this, and physicians have sometimes been forbidden by courts to do it.

When asked whether they believed in the right of a patient and/or family to terminate medical care in the case of irreversible illness, three-fourths of 418 persons surveyed (ages 17 to 91) agreed with this right (Haug, 1978). There was a strong belief in the right of self-determination. This is why patients need to make their wishes known before they are no longer capable of making a reasoned decision.

Most medical and some church groups have no trouble accepting the concept of death with dignity (Ward, 1980). In March 1986, after two years of study, the *Council on Ethical and Judicial Affairs of the American Medical Association* issued the opinion that it is ethically permissible for doctors to withold all life-prolonging treatment, including artificial nutrition and hydration, from patients in irreversible comas and from dying patients.

Thirty-eight states plus the District of Columbia now have statutes that approve the use of a **living will**: Often a suggested form is included in the statute. And in every state, constitutional and common law support the right of any competent adult to refuse medical treatment in any situation (Annas & Desnsberger, 1984). Without a living will, however, it is sometimes hard to know what treatment a patient wants (Zweibel & Cassel, 1989).

Physicians are required to comply with living-will legislation or transfer the patient to a doctor who will. If a state has no living-will legislation, a person may still draw up such a document because court decisions give weight to individual choice (Sullivan, 1987).

Euthanasia—allowing a terminally ill patient to die naturally without life support; putting to death a person who suffers from an incurable disease (mercy killing); or killing a person who is no longer considered socially useful (death selection)

Death with dignity—allowing a terminally ill patient to die naturally without artificial life support that could turn death into an ordeal

Living will—a written request by a patient that life-sustaining procedures be withdrawn if there is no reasonable expectation of recovery or regaining a meaningful quality of life

LIVING WILL DECLARATION

To My Family, Doctors, and All Those Concerned with My Care

I, _____ , being of sound mind, make this statement as a directive to be followed if for any reason I become unable to participate in decisions regarding my medical care.

I direct that life-sustaining procedures should be withheld or withdrawn if I have an illness, disease or injury, or experience extreme mental deterioration, such that there is no reasonable expectation of recovering or regaining a meaningful quality of life.

These life-sustaining procedures that may be withheld or withdrawn include, but are not limited to:

SURGERY   ANTIBIOTICS   CARDIAC RESUSCITATION
RESPIRATORY SUPPORT   ARTIFICIALLY ADMINISTERED FEEDING AND FLUIDS

I further direct that treatment be limited to comfort measures only, even if they shorten my life.
You may delete any provision above by drawing a line through it and adding your initials.
Other personal instructions:

These directions express my legal right to refuse treatment. Therefore, I expect my family, doctors, and all those concerned with my care to regard themselves as legally and morally bound to act in accord with my wishes, and in so doing to be free from any liability for having followed my directions.

Signed _____ Date_____

Witness _____ Witness _____

PROXY DESIGNATION CLAUSE

If you wish, you may use this section to designate someone to make treatment decisions if you are unable to do so. Your Living Will Declaration will be in effect even if you have not designated a proxy.

I authorize the following person to implement my Living Will Declaration by accepting refusing and/or making decisions about treatment and hospitalization:
Name _____
Address _____

If the person I have named above is unable to act on my behalf, I authorize the following person to do so:
Name _____
Address _____

I have discussed my wishes with these persons and trust their judgment on my behalf.
Signed _____ Date_____
Witness _____ Witness _____

FIGURE 20.5 Living will declaration.
Used with permission of Society for the Right to Die, 250 West 57th Street, New York, NY 10107.

Living wills usually apply only when the person's condition is incurable. They direct in such cases that life-extending procedures be withdrawn or withheld. Living wills are not honored in situations when a person has a slow, degenerative disease, or when a very old person has "multiple systems failure."

A Living Will

Figure 20.5 shows a form that is used by persons who wish to have a living will.

Mercy Killing

Mercy killing— putting to death a person who suffers from an incurable disease

Mercy killing is positive, direct euthanasia, either voluntary or involuntary. Whereas death with dignity permits a natural death, mercy killing actively causes death or at least speeds up death; for example, by lethal injection (Sinnett, Goodyear, & Hannemann, 1989). The nurse who deliberately gives an overdose of medication because she does not want to see her patient suffer is using mercy killing.

Mercy killing also includes abandonment or withdrawal of ordinary medical care, that is, the withdrawal of any medical or surgical procedures commonly used to relieve suffering and problems caused by injuries or illness, based on the condition of the individual patient, the circumstances, and the available medical technology. As medical science advances, the interpretation of this principle becomes more confused. Artificial heart machines and respirators, artificial kidneys, intravenous feeding, and other advanced technologies can keep patients alive for weeks, months, or years. Not too long ago, these patients would have died much sooner. What constitutes ordinary care? Most persons insist that keeping a clinically dead person physiologically alive does not constitute ordinary care. Others feel that sustaining life indefinitely by artificial means should not be permitted.

Death Selection

Death selection— the involuntary mandatory killing of a person who is no longer socially useful

Opponents of euthanasia are especially concerned about **death selection**, that is, the involuntary or even mandatory killing of persons who are "no longer considered socially useful" or who are judged to be a burden on society. This type of euthanasia poses a real threat to many groups in our society, especially the aged, the severely handicapped, and the retarded. It is strongly opposed by all religious groups.

BEREAVEMENT

The loss of a loved one is among life's most stressful events. Loss is followed by a period of mourning for the deceased and grief over the departed. The grieving process may occur over a short period of time or it may never be finished. One 54-year-old woman comments:

> My husband died 18 years ago, and even though today I have a happy, full life, I still miss him. I am often reminded of what he is missing, especially at happy moments, such as the children's high school and college graduations, which are tinged with the wish that he were alive to share the joy (Howell, Allen, & Doress, 1987).

Grief Reactions

Grief reactions are dealt with on four levels:

1. Physical
2. Emotional
3. Intellectual
4. Sociological

PHYSICAL REACTIONS. A wide range of physical reactions accompany grief. These can include insomnia, loss of appetite or overeating, stomach upset, constipation or diarrhea, fatigue, headaches, shortness of breath, excessive perspiration, and dizziness. Stress from grief tends to lower immunologic effectiveness and to leave the bereaved less resistant to infection and disease (Norris & Murrell, 1987). This is why some studies show an increase in the number of sick days of survivors (Lundin, 1984) and a worsening of physical health following the death of a spouse (Thompson, Breckenridge, Gallagher, & Peterson, 1984). For adults who have been taking care of an elderly person during a long illness, the actual death may come as a relief. Health of the care giver may have deteriorated during care and then may improve after the actual death (George & Gwyther, 1984).

EMOTIONAL REACTIONS. Emotional reactions to grief include depression, despondency, crying, shock and disbelief, anger, guilt, anxiety, irritability, preoccupation with thoughts of the deceased, feelings of helplessness, difficulty concentrating, forgetfulness, apathy, indecisiveness, and withdrawal or feelings of aloneness. A study of grief among 162 health-care workers found these to be the two most common psychological grief reactions: About 92% reported thinking or talking about the patient, and 84% reported feelings of helplessness (Lerea & LiMauro, 1982).

INTELLECTUAL REACTIONS.   Intellectual reactions to grief include efforts to explain and accept the causes of death of the deceased and sometimes to rationalize, or try to understand, the reasons for the death. People want to know what happened and why. Sometimes, reasons concluded are never satisfactory, but people nevertheless try to find causes and meaning in the death.

Idealization—the attempt to purify the memory of the deceased

One common intellectual reaction to bereavement is **idealization**: the attempt to purify the memory of the deceased by mentally diminishing that person's negative characteristics. One woman who disliked her husband remarked: "My husband was an unusually good man." If this idealization continues, it can prevent the formation of new intimate friendships. Extended bereavement can result in a sentimentalized, nostalgic, and morose style of life.

SOCIOLOGICAL REACTIONS.   Sociological reactions to grief include the efforts of family and friends to band together to share the experience, and to offer support and aid to one another. Sociological reaction also includes all efforts to reorganize one's life after the loss: financial readjustments, reorientation of family and community roles, the return to work, resumption of social and community activities. Death may necessitate making a number of important decisions: taking a job or changing jobs, moving, or selling a house. Sometimes such decisions are made hastily while one is still in a state of shock. Hurried decisions made during the grieving period are often wrong decisions.

The Stages of Grief

There are usually three stages of grief (Hiltz, 1978). *The first is a short period of shock* during which the surviving family members are stunned and immobilized with grief and disbelief. The survivors frequently weep and become easily agitated. This stage occurs soon after death and usually lasts several days. *The second stage is a period of intense suffering* during which individuals show physical and emotional symptoms of great disturbance. There is a painful longing for the

FOCUS

Bereavement in Children

The reaction of children to loss depends partially on their age and understanding of what has taken place and how close they have been to the deceased. As mentioned in an earlier section, children under 5 believe that death is reversible and that the loved one will return. Because they do not see death as final, they are not too disturbed, but they become rather anxious about when the loved one will return.

I used to direct a nursery school and kindergarten and teach a class of 5-year-olds. The grandfather of one of the girls died and the mother asked me to break the news to the granddaughter. I explained to her that her grandfather had been sick, and that when our bodies become old and sick, they die. After my careful explanation, the girl turned to her mother and asked: "OK, can I go outside and play now?" The mother was devastated at her daughter's callous reaction. It was obvious the girl did not completely understand or accept the finality of death because for months afterward she would ask her mother when her grandfather was going to return home.

Unless they have been exposed to frightening experiences, young children are not afraid of bodies or funerals. I remember one girl whose brother had been killed by lightning while playing golf. She saw her brother's body in the casket, stroked his cheek very soothingly, but did remark that he seemed cold.

Young children are not completely grief stricken at death, partly because they don't understand the finality of it. However, when children begin to realize the permanence of death, they become more upset. Often 9- or 10-year-olds can show a lot of grief, anxiety, anger, and guilt, especially if in any way they believe that the death is their fault. They may become very upset as evidenced by nightmares, sleeping, eating, and academic problems. They may have temper tantrums, get in fights easily, and show other symptoms of emotional disturbance and physical upset. They sometimes show a great deal of anxiety about death itself, and, if one parent has died, about the other parent leaving. Also, the reactions of children depend partly on how upset other family members are with whom they are living. If children are not upset by funerals per se, they are upset by the crying and distress of the people there. Children can cope with death if they have the support of other loved ones (Furman, 1984; Horn, 1986).

dead, including memories and visual images of the deceased, sadness, insomnia, irritability, and restlessness. Beginning not long after the death of the family member, this stage often peaks in the second to fourth weeks following the death and may subside after several months, but can persist for 1 to 2 years.

During the third stage there is a gradual reawakening of interest in life. Stage three usually appears within a year after the death. This stage is marked by a resumption of ordinary activities, a greater likelihood that the deceased will be recalled with pleasant memories, and the establishment of new relationships with others.

Gender Differences

Most researchers say that men and women share equal feelings of pain and grief. However, there are important cultural differences in the way grief is expressed. *Men have been conditioned not to show their emotions.* They fear uncontrolled expression of emotion and appearing to be "unmanly" in front of other people. Men may put on a big show at the office, and then go home and stare at the walls. As a consequence, a widowed man often may become terribly isolated because his sole confidant had been his wife, who is now lost. Widowers are more likely to feel lonely and depressed than are widows, and they are less willing to talk about their feelings associated with their loss.

Women not only have more friends than men, but women more often use these friends as supports in time of loss. The pain of loss is eased by talking to others about the loss, and women seem to be better able to do this than men (Cole, 1988).

SUMMARY

1. In 1987, heart disease was the number-one cause of death; cancer was number two.

2. The causes of death have changed radically in the past 100 years. Infectious diseases used to be the primary killers.

3. The dominant feature of death in the 20th century is its invisibility; we try to solve the problem of death by denying it. In earlier times, death was more accepted as a part of everyday life. Currently, there is a swing away from the denial of death toward a notion of death with dignity.

4. Middle-agers express the greatest fear of death among different ages of adults; the elderly are less anxious about death than others.

5. Children under age 5 see death as temporary and reversible; between ages 5 and 9 they gradually realize that death is final and permanent; those 9 and over see it as final, inevitable, and universal. Adolescents usually give little thought to it, unless they have personal experience with someone's dying.

6. There are four aspects of death: physiological death, clinical death, sociological death, and psychic death.

7. Pattison outlined five different patterns of death.

8. Varying circumstances of death include uncertain death, certain death, and untimely death, which may be premature, unexpected, and/or calamitous.

9. Uncertain death is when a person has become seriously ill or injured and it is not known for certain if that person will live or die.

10. In certain death, the person is terminally ill and the approximate time of death may be known or unknown or can only be surmised. Kubler-Ross identified five stages of dying in terms of personal reactions: denial, anger, bargaining, depression, and acceptance.

11. Pattison outlined the living-dying trajectory that included three phases: the acute crisis phase, the chronic living-dying phase, and the terminal phase.

12. Disintegrated dying is when a person learns of pending death and goes all to pieces, unable to function. Integrated dying involves being able to put one's life together to make satisfactory adjustments to the dying process.

13. Dying people have the same need for food, clothing, shelter, rest, and warmth that we all have, plus the need for reassurance that family members will not let them die alone. The dying person also usually has a number of tasks to complete in making arrangements for death.

14. Many people want to be told they are dying; others do not. The goal is to ease the dying process and the adjustments that must be made, rather than to apply a dogma of always telling the truth.

15. Hospice care for the terminally ill is a viable alternative to hospital care.

16. The psychological reactions of adults to death are more extreme when a child or a comparatively young person dies.

17. Sudden infant death syndrome, or when infants die mysteriously while asleep, is the most common cause of death in infants between 2 weeks and 1 year of age. The syndrome often causes intense mental pain and disruption among the survivors.

18. Unexpected death is the sudden death of a normal and healthy person.

19. Calamitous death includes death from accidents, involuntary manslaughter, homicide, and suicide.

20. Involuntary manslaughter is the unintentional killing of another human being.

21. Most stereotypes about murders and murderers have no foundation in fact. A sizable minority of homicides are committed by relatives or acquaintances of the victim. Homicide is most often an outgrowth of quarrels and violence among family members or friends.

22. The rate of suicide increases with advancing age, reaching a peak in males over 85 years of age and in females 45 to 54. Females attempt suicide more frequently than males, but males more often succeed. Suicide is one of the most upsetting of family crises because it leaves family members feeling remorseful, guilty, confused, and hurt.

23. Socially accelerated dying is allowing any condition or action of society that shortens life and hastens death.

24. Euthanasia includes three different concepts: death with dignity, mercy killing, and death selection.

25. Death with dignity allows terminally ill patients to die naturally without mechanized prolongation.

26. Mercy killing is actively causing death or speeding it up rather than letting a patient suffer.

27. Death selection is involuntary or mandatory killing of persons who are no longer socially useful. It is considered a real threat to many groups in society, and it is opposed by all religious groups.

28. Grief reactions take place on four levels: physical, emotional, intellectual, and sociological.

29. There are usually three stages of grief: shock, intense suffering, and a gradual reawakening of interest in life.

30. Though feelings of pain and grief are equal among men and women, there are gender differences in the extent and ways of expressing grief practiced by men and women.

31. The reaction of a child to grief depends upon age, understanding of death, the reactions of family members, and the child's relationship with the deceased.

KEY TERMS

Clinical death p. 455
Death selection p. 467
Death with dignity p. 465
Disintegrated dying p. 458
Euthanasia p. 465
Hospice p. 460
Idealization p. 468
Integrated dying p. 458
Living-dying interval p. 458

Living will p. 465
Mercy killing p. 467
Physiological death p. 455
Posttraumatic stress disorder p. 461
Psychic death p. 456
Socially accelerated dying p. 464
Sociological death p. 455
Sudden infant death syndrome p. 460

DISCUSSION QUESTIONS

1. What do you think of the whole idea of making death as invisible as possible? Explain your views.

2. How do you feel about children attending funerals?

3. What are the differences between physiological death, clinical death, psychic death, and sociological death?

4. Have you or has any member of your family faced the prosect of uncertain death? What were the reactions, feelings, biggest problems?

5. Should terminally ill patients be told they are dying? Why? Why not?

6. Have there been any premature deaths, unexpected deaths, or calamitous deaths in your family? With what results?

7. How do you feel about the use of artificial life support systems to prolong the

life of a terminally ill patient? Under what circumstances would you pull the plug; under what circumstances would you not?

8. How do you feel about mercy killing, or giving a terminally ill patient who is suffering an injection to speed death?

9. When people are grieving for the loss of a loved one, what helps the most? What are the types of things that other people do or say that make things worse?

10. How do present funeral practices help or hinder people getting over their grief? Explain.

11. How do you feel about men weeping at a funeral?

12. How do you feel personally about death? About the fact that one day you will die? If you knew you were dying within one year, what would you do? How would you react?

SUGGESTED READINGS

Editors of Consumer Reports. (1977). *Funerals: Consumer's last rights; the consumers' union report on conventional funerals and burial . . . and some alternatives, including cremation, direct cremation, direct burial, and body donation.* New York: W. W. Norton.

Kubler-Ross, E. (1969). *On death and dying.* New York: Macmillan. Classic on the subject.

Levine, S. (1984). *Meetings at the edge: Dialogues with the grieving and the dying, the healing and the healed.* New York: Doubleday.

Maheady, J., & Reimer, R. (1985). *Comparative analysis of state statutes recognizing a patient's right to die a natural death.* Washington, DC: Congressional Research Service.

Mitford, J. (1979). *The American way of death.* New York: Fawcett. Discussion of the burial and funeral business.

Munley, A. (1983). *The hospice alternative: A new context for death and dying.* New York: Basic Books. The hospice movement and its benefits to patients and their families.

President's Commission for the Study of Ethical Problems in Biomedical and Behavioral Research. (1983). *Deciding to forgo life-sustaining treatment; ethical, medical, and legal issues in treatment decisions.* Washington, DC: U.S. Government Printing Office.

Saunders, D. C., & Baines, M. (1983). *Living with dying: The management of terminal diseases.* New York: Oxford University Press. Home health care for the dying.

Slagle, K. W. (1982). *Live with loss.* Englewood Cliffs, NJ: Prentice-Hall. Coping with grief.

Weizman, S. G., & Kamm, P. (1985). *About mourning: Support and guidance for the bereaved.* New York: Human Sciences Press. For mental health workers.

GLOSSARY

Accommodation according to Piaget, adjusting to new information by creating new structures when the old ones will not do (p. 38)

Accommodation the power of the eye's lens to focus (p. 364)

Acne pimples on the skin caused by overactive sebaceous glands (p. 252)

Acquisition the process by which information is recorded, encoded, and stored (p. 387)

ACT Assessment Program (American College Testing program) the second most widely used college admissions test (p. 268)

Activity calories energy expended through physical activities (p. 354)

Activity theory a theory of aging suggesting that continuance of an active life cycle has a positive effect on the sense of well-being and satisfaction of older people (p. 442)

Adaptation according to Piaget, the process by which individuals adjust their thinking to new conditions or situations (p. 364)

Adaptation ability of the eye to adjust to different intensities of light (p. 37)

Adolescence the period of transition from childhood to young adulthood, from about 12 to 19 years of age (p. 7)

Adolescent and adult heterosociality a period of psychosocial development during which those ages 13 and over find pleasure, friendships, and companionship with those of both sexes (p. 208)

Adrenal glands ductless glands located just above the kidneys that secrete androgens and estrogens in both men and women in addition to their secretion of adrenalin (p. 244)

Affect one's feelings, whether positive or negative (p. 404)

Ageism prejudice and discrimination against the elderly (p. 349)

Agnosia an impairment of the ability to recognize objects through the use of the senses (p. 415)

Alcohol abuse excessive use of alcohol so that functioning is impaired (p. 291)

Alcoholism *See* Chronic alcoholism

Alleles genes that govern alternate expressions of a particular characteristic (p. 60)

Alveoli air cells of the lungs (p. 360)

Alzheimer's disease a presenile or senile dementia characterized by rapid deterioration and atrophy of the cerebral cortex (p. 414)

Amenorrhea absence of menstruation (p. 248)

Amniocentesis removal of cells from the amniotic fluid to test for abnormalities (p. 64)

Amniotic sac (bag of waters) sac containing the liquid in which the fetus is suspended during pregnancy (p. 83)

Anabolic steroids the masculinizing hormone testosterone taken by athletes to build muscle mass (p. 244)

Anal stage Freud's second psychosexual stage of development (2–3 years), in which the child's chief source of pleasure is from anal activity (p. 28)

Androgyny a mixing of male and female traits in one person (p. 220)

Angina pectoris pain caused by constriction of blood vessels leading to the heart, causing an insufficient blood supply (p. 359)

Animism ascribing lifelike qualities to inanimate objects (p. 151)

Anorexia nervosa an eating disorder characterized by an obsession with food and being thin (p. 252)

Anoxia oxygen deprivation to the brain, causing neurological damage or death (p. 85)

Antithesis the idea or point directly opposing a stated idea, or thesis (p. 377)

Apgar score method of evaluating the physical condition of the neonate, developed by Dr. Virginia Apgar (p. 87)

Aphasia an impairment of the ability to understand or to use language (p. 415)

Apraxia an impairment of the ability to perform purposeful movements (p. 415)

Arteriosclerosis hardening of the arteries by a buildup of calcium in the middle muscle layer of arterial tissue, resulting in decreased elasticity (p. 358)

Artificial insemination injection of sperm cells into the vagina or uterus for the purpose of inducing pregnancy (p. 56)

Assimilation according to Piaget, the process of acquiring new information by using already existing structures in response to new stimuli (p. 38)

Associative strength degree of association, as between two words (p. 391)

Associativity the understanding that operations can reach a goal in various ways (p. 153)

Atherosclerosis a buildup of fatty deposits between the middle muscular layer and lining layer of arterial tissue (p. 359)

Attachment the feeling that binds a child to a parent or care giver (p. 174)

Attachment theory the description of the process by which infants develop close emotional dependence on one or more adult care givers (p. 41)

Attention-deficit disorder a child's hyperactivity, characterized by excessive activity, inattentiveness, and impulsivity (p. 187)

Autistic phase a period between birth and 2 months of age during which children are aware of their mother only as an agent to meet their basic needs (p. 180)

Autonomic arousal stimulation of the autonomic, or involuntary, nervous system—found to be positively associated with serial learning at all ages, particularly for learning simpler tasks (p. 391)

Autonomy vs. shame and doubt Erikson's second stage of psychosocial development (1–2 years), in which toddlers learn that they are capable of some independent actions, or they develop the fear that they are not capable (p. 29)

Autosociality a stage of psychosocial development during the first year or so of life, during which infants' interests, pleasures, and satisfactions are themselves, when they play alongside of others, not with them (p. 208)

Autosomes twenty-two pairs of chromosomes that are responsible for most aspects of the individual's development (p. 58)

Babbling one-syllable utterances containing vowels and consonants in combination (p. 144)

Baby boomers the huge cohort of babies born during the postwar period between 1945 and 1960 (p. 344)

Bartholin's glands glands on either side of the vaginal opening that secrete fluid during sexual arousal (p. 246)

Basal calories the energy metabolized by the body to carry on physiological functions and to maintain normal body temperature (p. 354)

Behaviorism the school of psychology emphasizing that behavior is modified through conditioning (p. 31)

Bile a liquid secreted by the liver which aids in the digestion and absorption of fats (p. 361)

Binuclear family an original family divided into two by divorce (p. 198)

Biological development the genetic foundations of development, the physical growth of all of the components of the body, their functioning and care (p. 9)

Biological time clock life events regulated by maturation and biological changes (p. 341)

Blastocyst inner layer of the blastula that develops into the embryo (p. 51)

Blastula zygote after the cells have divided into 100–150 cells (p. 51)

Blended or reconstituted family a family formed by any widowed or divorced person remarrying another person who may or may not have children (p. 197)

Bonding the formation of a close relationship between a person and a child through early and frequent association (p. 40)

Bradley method a husband-coached natural childbirth method developed by Robert Bradley, a Denver obstetrician (p. 81)

Brazelton Neonatal Behavior Assessment Scale method of evaluating the neurological condition and behavior of the neonate, developed by Dr. T. Berry Brazelton (p. 87)

Bronchial pneumonia an infectious disease of the bronchial tubes (p. 360)

Bulimia an eating disorder characterized by binging and purging (p. 252)

Burnout the situation of being emotionally and physically exhausted from too much job pressure (p. 441)

Canalization tendency for inherited characteristics to persist along a certain path regardless of environmental conditions (p. 62)

Cardiac arrhythmias irregular heartbeat (p. 360)

Case studies a research method involving in-depth, longitudinal investigations and records of individuals (p. 15)

Cataracts an abnormality of the eye in which the lens becomes cloudy and opaque (p. 364)

Centration focusing attention on one aspect of a situation, or one detail, and being unable to take into account other details (p. 152)

Cephalocaudal principle physical growth, which occurs first in the head and proceeds, by stages, down the body to the feet (p. 117)

Cerebral cortex two large hemispheres of the forebrain, which control intellectual, motor, and sensory functions (p. 119)

Cerebrovascular disease vascular disease in the brain (p. 360)

Cesarean section removal of the fetus through a surgical incision of the abdominal and uterine walls (p. 85)

Child development all aspects of human growth from birth to adolescence; the study of this growth (p. 102)

Childhood heterosociality a period of psychosocial development between ages 2 and 7, during which children seek the companionship of others regardless of sex (p. 208)

Cholesterol   a chemical occurring in all animal fats that is a major contributing cause of atherosclerosis (p. 354)

Chorionic villi sampling (CVS)   removal of a sample of chorionic villi from the membrane enclosing the fetus, to be analyzed for possible birth defects (p. 64)

Chromosomes   rodlike structures in each cell, occurring in pairs, that carry the hereditary material (p. 57)

Chronic alcoholism   chemical dependency on alcohol accompanied by compulsive and excessive drinking (p. 291)

Chronic organic brain syndrome   permanent impairment of brain function (p. 414)

Chronological age (CA)   age in years (p. 158)

Chunking   dividing material into meaningful parts to remember it (p. 157)

Circumcision   surgical removal of the foreskin of the penis (p. 88)

Cirrhosis   a disease of the liver in which the connective tissue becomes hard, lumpy, and shriveled (p. 361)

Classical conditioning   a form of learning through association, in which a previously neutral stimulus is paired with an unconditioned stimulus to stimulate a conditioned response that is similar to the unconditioned response (p. 31)

Classification   arranging objects into categories or classes (p. 152)

Class inclusion relationships   the inclusion of objects in different levels of hierarchy at the same time (p. 153)

Client-centered therapy   Rogers' approach to humanistic therapy, in which the discussion focuses on the client's thoughts and feelings and the therapist creates an atmosphere of acceptance so that the client can gain insight and grow toward his or her full potential (p. 36)

Climacteric   (literally, "rung of a ladder")—often, a man's mid-life changes; also, menopause or other changes marking the transition from one stage of life to another (p. 363)

Clinical death   the cessation of all brain activity (p. 455)

Clitoris   the small shaft containing erectile tissue located above the vaginal and urethral openings and that is highly responsive to sexual stimulation (p. 246)

Cognition   the act of knowing (p. 37)

Cognitive development   all the changes in the intellectual processes of thinking, learning, remembering, judging, problem solving, and communicating (p. 9)

Cognitive modification program   a therapeutic program designed to teach restructuring of thought patterns, positive thinking, and focusing on immediate tasks; one such program, designed by Michenbaum, to help students with high test-taking anxiety (p. 408)

Cohabitation   two unrelated adults of the opposite sex sharing the same living quarters in which there is no other adult present—according to the U.S. government; other adults may actually live with the couple (p. 447)

Cohabiting family   a family formed by two people of the opposite sex who live together, with or without children; who are committed to the relationship, without formal legal marriage, within the general definition in this book (p. 198)

Cohort   a group of subjects born during the same time period (p. 17)

Cohort-sequential study   the best sequential design for separating the effects of age and cohorts (p. 18)

Coitus   sexual intercourse (p. 308)

Colostrum   high-protein liquid secreted by the mother's breasts prior to her milk coming in; contains antibodies to protect the nursing infant from diseases (p. 92)

Combinativity   ability to combine two or more classes into one larger, more comprehensive class (p. 153)

Communal family   a group of people who live together and who qualify as a family according to the general definition in this book (p. 198)

Concrete operational stage   Piaget's third stage of cognitive development (7–11 years), during which the child gains some mastery over classes, relations, and quantities (p. 38)

Conditional positive regard   giving love, praise, and acceptance only if the individual conforms to parental or social standards (p. 36)

Conditioning   a simple process of learning (p. 31)

Congenital deformity   defect present at birth, which may be the result of hereditary factors, conditions during pregnancy, or damage occurring at the time of birth (p. 63)

Congestive heart failure   reduced cardiac output accompanied by increased blood pressure, which results in a buildup of fluids in the body (p. 360)

Congruence   cognitive agreement between a person's desired goals and the goals that have been, or are being, attained in life (p. 402)

Conservation   the idea that an object stays the same quantity regardless of how the shape changes (p. 152)

Cooing   the initial squeals, gurgles, or vowel-like sound utterances by young infants (p. 144)

Coronary occlusion with myocardial infarction   heart attack, a cutoff of blood from a coronary artery, causing death of a localized area (an infarct) of heart muscle (p. 359)

Corpus luteum   yellow body that grows from the ruptured ovarian follicle and becomes a mass of progesterone-secreting endocrine tissue (p. 242)

Correlation   the extent to which two factors are associated or related to one another (p. 16)

Cowper's glands   small twin glands in the male that secrete a fluid to neutralize the acid environment of the urethra (p. 244)

Crisis   a drastic change in the course of events; a turning point that affects the trend of future events (p. 407)

Crisis overload   a series of crises happening one after the other so that the person has difficulty in coping (p. 407)

Cross-sectional study   comparing one age group with others at one time of testing (p. 17)

Crystallized intelligence   knowledge and skills arising out of acculturation and education. Concept developed by Cattell (p. 159)

Cyclothymic disorder   a condition characterized by alternation between brief periods of depression, of hypomania, and normal mood (p. 412)

Date rape   forced sexual compliance on a person while on a date, whether or not intercourse occurs (p. 447)

Death selection   the involuntary mandatory killing of a person who is no longer considered socially useful (p. 467)

Death with dignity   allowing a terminally ill patient to die naturally without artificial life support that could turn death into an ordeal (p. 465)

Deductive reasoning   beginning with a hypothesis or premise and breaking it down to see if it is true (p. 150)

Defense mechanisms   according to Freud, unconscious strategies used by the ego to protect itself from disturbance and to discharge tension (p. 27)

Deferred imitation   imitating someone or something no longer present (p. 150)

Denial   a Freudian defense mechanism in which the individual refuses to admit that something exists (p. 28)

Dependency ratio   the number of dependent persons for each person in the labor force (p. 327)

Dependent variable   in an experiment, a factor that is influenced by the independent or manipulated variable (p. 16)

Depression   an affective emotional disorder characterized by loss of interest in nearly all activities and by a predominance and persistence of sad, low, hopeless moods (p. 411)

Developmental pediatrics   a new field of study that integrates medical knowledge, psychological understanding, health care, and parental guidance in relation to children (p. 110)

Developmental quotient (DQ)   a score developed by Gesell to evaluate an infant's behavioral level in four categories: motor, language, adaptive, and personal-social (p. 162)

Developmental tasks   the skills, knowledge, functions, and attitudes that individuals have to acquire at certain points in their lives in order to function effectively as mature persons (p. 233)

Diabetes mellitus   a disease characterized by excess sugar in the system due to insufficient insulin production in the pancreas (p. 361)

Dialectical thinking   the view that every idea implies its opposite; the ability to consider opposing viewpoints simultaneously (p. 377)

Diastolic blood pressure   the pressure produced when the chambers of the heart dilate and fill with blood (p. 359)

Dick-Read method   a natural childbirth method emphasizing childbirth without fear, developed by Dr. Dick-Read of England (p. 80)

Differentiated or subjective perspective-taking stage

the stage of awareness when the other is seen as different from the self, but the other person's perception of the self is still undifferentiated—stage 1 in Selman's theory (p. 213)

Discipline   a process of learning by which socialization takes place, whose purpose is instruction in proper conduct (p. 202)

Disengagement theory   a theory of aging saying that aging people have a natural tendency to withdraw socially and psychologically from the environment, social activities, and other people (p. 442)

Disintegrated dying   going to pieces emotionally and not being able to function after learning of impending death (p. 458)

Displacement   a Freudian defense mechanism in which an individual diverts aggressive, sexual, or disturbed feelings away from a primary object to something useful (p. 28)

Dizygotic (fraternal) twins   two-egg, or fraternal, twins (p. 59)

DNA   complex molecules in genes that form the basis for the genetic structure, deoxyribonucleic acid (p. 57)

Dominant gene   gene that exerts its full characteristic regardless of its gene pair (p. 60)

Duos   two-word utterances (p. 145)

Dysthymic disorder   periodic depression, a condition in which depression predominates over normal mood (p. 412)

Early adulthood   the young adult years, including the 20s and 30s (p. 7)

Early childhood   the preschool period of development from 3 to 5 years (p. 6)

Echoic memory   the auditory sensory store (p. 387)

Ectopic pregnancy   attachment and growth of the embryo in any location other than inside the uterus (p. 51)

Edema   retention of excess fluids in body tissues and cavities (p. 360)

Ego   according to Freud, the rational part of the mind, which uses the reality principle to satisfy the id (p. 27)

Egocentricism   the inability to take the perspective of another, to imagine the other person's point of view (p. 151)

Egocentric undifferentiated stage   the stage of awareness when the other person is seen egocentrically, undifferentiated from the self's own point of view—stage 0 in Selman's theory of development of social cognition (p. 213)

Electra complex   according to Freud, the unconscious love and sexual desire of female children for their father, after they blame the mother for the fact that they have no penis (p. 27)

Embolism   blockage from a blood clot (p. 360)

Embryo   growing baby from the end of the second week to the end of the eighth week after conception (p. 52)

Embryonic period   period from 2 weeks to 8 weeks after conception (p. 51)

Embryo transplant   insemination of a volunteer female

with the sperm of an infertile woman's partner, with the resulting zygote being transferred, about 5 days later, from the volunteer into the uterus of the mother-to-be, who carries the child during pregnancy (p. 57)

Emotion   a state of consciousness, or a feeling, felt as an integrated reaction of the total organism, accompanied by physiological arousal, and resulting in behavioral responses (p. 278)

Emotional development   the development of attachment, trust, love, feelings, temperament, concept of self, autonomy, and emotional disturbances (p. 9)

Emphysema   a degenerative disorder of the walls separating the air sacs in the lungs so they become distended, inelastic, and incapable of expelling stale air (p. 361)

Endocrine glands   ductless glands that secrete hormones (p. 242)

Epididymis   a system of ducts, running from the testes to the vas deferens, in which sperm ripen, mature, and are stored (p. 244)

Epinephrine   hormone secreted by the adrenal glands that produces physiological arousal (p. 183)

Episiotomy   a surgical incision of the perineum to allow room for passage of the baby from the birth canal without tearing the mother's tissue (p. 85)

Equilibrium   a Piagetian concept meaning a balance between schemas and accommodation, a state in which children feel comfortable because what they find in their environment is compatible with what they have been taught to believe (p. 38)

Equity   assignment of punishments in accordance with transgressors' ability to take responsibility for a crime (p. 222)

Estrogens   a group of feminizing hormones produced by the ovaries and to some extent by the adrenal glands in both males and females (p. 242)

Ethology   the view that behavior is a product of evolution and biology (p. 39)

Euthanasia   allowing a terminally ill patient to die naturally without life support; putting to death a person who suffers from an incurable disease (mercy killing); or killing a person who is no longer considered socially useful (death selection) (p. 465)

Exchange theory   a theory which, as applied to the aged and their families, maintains that persons with the greatest needs lose the most power and those supplying needs gain power (p. 443)

Exosystem   social settings in which the child usually is not an active participant, but that influence the child indirectly through their effects on the microsystem (p. 196)

Experimental methods   methods of gathering scientific data, in which procedures are closely controlled and the experimenter manipulates variables to determine how one affects the other (p. 15)

Expiatory punishment   punishment that results from an externally imposed regulation; associated with morality of constraint (p. 222)

Extended family   a family consisting of one person, a possible mate, their children, and other relatives who live with them in the household; more broadly, can include relatives living in close proximity or who are in regular or frequent contact with a household's members (p. 197)

Extrinsic motivation   motivation of behavior that is influenced by external rewards (p. 391)

Fallopian tubes   tubes that transport the ova from the ovaries to the uterus (p. 245)

Family   any group of persons united by the ties of marriage, blood, adoption, or any sexually expressive relationship, in which (1) people are committed to one another in an intimate, interpersonal relationship, (2) the members see their identity as importantly attached to the group, and (3) the group has an identity of its own (p. 197)

Family life cycle   the family experience divided into phases or stages over the life span; a description of the changes in family structure and composition, and of the challenges, tasks, problems, and satisfactions involved during each stage (p. 430)

Father hunger   an emotional disturbance, most common in boys from 18 to 36 months of age, brought about by the abrupt loss of a father, characterized by sleep disturbances (p. 204)

Fertilization, or conception   union of sperm and ovum (p. 50)

Fetal period   period of prenatal development from the beginning of the third month through the remainder of the pregnancy (p. 51)

Fetoscope   scope passed through a narrow tube inserted into the uterus to observe the fetus and placenta directly (p. 64)

Fetus   growing baby from the beginning of the third month of development to birth (p. 53)

Field-dependent people   people who have trouble isolating relevant information in solving problems (p. 374)

Field-independent people   people who sort out relevant from irrelevant information in solving problems (p. 374)

Fixated   according to Freud, remaining at a particular psychosexual stage because of too much or too little gratification (p. 28)

Fluid intelligence   a person's inherited ability to think and reason abstractly, concept developed by Cattell (p. 159)

Follicle   the structure in the ovary that nurtures the ripened ovum and releases it (p. 242)

Formal operational stage   Piaget's highest stage of cognitive development (11 years and up), during which individuals are able to use logic and abstract concepts (p. 38)

Free association   a method of treatment of Freud in which the patient is encouraged to say anything that comes to mind, allowing unconscious thoughts to slip out (p. 26)

FSH (follicle-stimulating hormone)   a pituitary hormone that stimulates the maturation of the follicles and ova in the ovaries and of sperm in the testes (p. 242)

Full-term infant an infant who is born with a gestational age between 37 and 42 weeks (p. 89)

Functional age age as measured by the ability to perform physical or mental functions (p. 350)

Gall bladder trouble any kind of trouble that prevents the gall bladder from functioning properly; gallstones, for example (p. 361)

Gallstones stones formed in the gall bladder or bile passages when the bile becomes overconcentrated (p. 361)

Gamete intra fallopian transfer (GIFT) inserting sperm cells and an egg cell directly into the fallopian tube, where fertilization is expected to occur (p. 57)

Gametes sex cells (p. 50)

Gastritis inflammation of the stomach lining (p. 361)

Gender our biological sex (p. 216)

Gender constancy the understanding of the gender that one is, and that it is going to remain the same: usually achieved by 7 years of age (p. 219)

Gender roles our outward expressions of masculinity or femininity in social settings; how we act and think as males or females, our sex roles (p. 216)

Gender stereotypes widespread, assumed gender characteristics of what boys and girls are like (p. 219)

General anesthesia a drug acting on the central nervous system and used to suppress pain during childbirth; affects the fetus also (p. 84)

Generalized anxiety disorder a mental illness involving fixated perceptions of catastrophe in the smallest mishap or in imagined events, an overexaggeration of anxiety out of proportion to the situation (p. 282)

Generational transmission transmitting of knowledge, values, attitudes, roles, and habits from one generation to the next (p. 198)

Generativity vs. stagnation Erikson's seventh psychosocial stage of development (middle adulthood), during which adults assume responsible, adult roles in their community and in caring for the younger generation, or they lead impoverished, self-centered lives (p. 29)

Genes the hereditary material of the chromosomes (p. 57)

Genital stage Freud's fifth psychosexual stage of development (puberty through adulthood), in which sexual urges are directed toward one's peers in a desire to relieve sexual tension (p. 28)

Genotype underlying genetic pattern of an individual (p. 61)

Germinal period the period from conception to 14 days later (p. 51)

Glaucoma a disease of the eye in which the fluid pressure within the eyeball increases, causing progressive vision loss (p. 364)

Glycogen a starchlike substance stored by the liver and released into the bloodstream when the body is in need of sugar (p. 361)

GnRH (gonadotropin-releasing hormone a hormone secreted by the hypothalamus that controls the production and release of FSH and LH from the pituitary (p. 244)

Gonadotropic hormones sex hormones secreted by the gonads (p. 242)

Gonads the sex glands: testes and ovaries (p. 242)

Grammar the formal description of structure and rules that a language uses in order to communicate meaning (p. 146)

Habituation the tendency to get used to a repeated stimulus and to lose interest in it (p. 154)

Happiness a quality or state characterized by pleasure, delight, joy, gladness, and contentment (p. 401)

HDL (high-density lipoprotein) a beneficial cholesterol that helps lower the level of LDL in the blood (p. 355)

Hemoglobin the red pigment of the blood (p. 361)

Hemorrhage copious blood flow, rapid loss of blood (p. 360)

Heterologous insemination (AID) artificial insemination using the sperm from a donor (p. 56)

Heterozygous having paired alleles that are different (p. 60)

HGH (human growth hormone) a pituitary hormone that regulates overall body growth (p. 242)

Hierarchical classification arranging objects into categories according to level (p. 153)

Holistic view emphasizes the functioning of the total individual to try to grow, improve, and reach his or her full potential (p. 34)

Holophrases single words that infants use to convey different meanings, depending on the context in which they are used (p. 144)

Homologous insemination (AIH) artificial insemination with the husband's sperm (p. 56)

Homosexual family a family formed by adults of the same sex who live together, with their children, and who share sexual expression and commitment according to the general definition in this book (p. 198)

Homosociality a period of psychosocial development during which children prefer to play with others of the same sex (p. 208)

Homozygous having paired alleles that are alike (p. 60)

Hormones biochemical substances secreted into the bloodstream by the endocrine glands that act as an internal communication system telling the different cells what to do (p. 242)

Hospice an institution committed to making the end of life free from pain and as comfortable and supportive as possible in a homelike environment with family members present (p. 460)

Humanistic theory psychological theory that emphasizes the ability of individuals to make the right choices and to reach their full potential (p. 34)

Hymen tissue partly covering the vaginal opening (p. 246)

Hypertensive heart disease heart trouble caused by high blood pressure (p. 359)

Hypothalamus a small area of the brain controlling mo-

tivation, emotion, pleasure, and pain in the body; that is, controls eating, drinking, hormonal production, menstruation, pregnancy, lactation, and sexual response and behavior (p. 244)

Iconic memory   the visual sensory store (p. 388)

Id   according to Freud, the inborn instinctual urges that a person seeks to satisfy (p. 27)

Idealization   the attempt to purify the memory of the deceased (p. 468)

Identity or nullifiability   the understanding that an operation that is combined with its opposite becomes nullified, and the element remains unchanged (p. 153)

Identity vs. role confusion   Erikson's fifth psychosocial stage of development (12–19 years), during which the adolescent develops a strong sense of self or becomes confused about identity and roles in life (p. 29)

Imaging   being on one's best behavior to make a good impression (p. 306)

Imitation   copying the behavior of another (p. 150)

Imminent justice   the child's belief that immoral behavior inevitably brings pain or punishment as a natural consequence of the transgression (p. 222)

Implantation   attachment of the blastocyst to the uterine wall (p. 51)

Imprinting   a biological ability to establish an attachment on first exposure to an object or person (p. 40)

Incomplete dominance, or codominance   when one paired allele is not completely dominant over the other (p. 62)

Incontinent   unable to control passage of urine (p. 361)

Independent variable   in an experiment, a factor that is manipulated or controlled by the experimenter to determine its effect on the subjects' behavior (p. 16)

In-depth and societal perspective taking stage   the stage of social awareness during which the self can take a generalized society perspective of the self–other interaction—stage 4 in Selman's theory (p. 214)

Inductive reasoning   gathering individual items of information and putting them together to form a hypothesis or conclusions (p. 150)

Industry vs. inferiority   Erikson's fourth psychosocial stage of development (6–11 years), during which children develop feelings of adequacy and self-worth for accomplishments or begin to feel inadequate (p. 29)

Infancy   the first two years of life (p. 6)

Infantile amnesia   the essential lack of memory of events experienced before 3 years of age (p. 155)

Infertile   unable to conceive or to effect pregnancy (p. 55)

Information-processing approach   an approach to cognition that emphasizes the steps, actions, and operations by which persons receive, perceive, remember, think about, and utilize information (p. 149)

Initiative vs. guilt   Erikson's third psychosocial stage of development (3–5 years), during which children are encouraged to assume responsibility for planning and carrying out actions, or are criticized and made to feel guilty for such actions (p. 29)

Insecurely attached   overly dependent on parents or care givers because of insufficient attachment (p. 176)

Insulin   a hormone secreted by the pancreas that regulates the blood sugar level (p. 361)

Integrated dying   being able to put one's life together, to make satisfactory adjustments to the dying process (p. 458)

Integrity vs. despair   Erikson's eighth psychosocial stage of development (late adulthood), in which adults evaluate their lives and either accept them for what they are, or despair because they have not found meaning in life (p. 29)

Intelligence quotient   MA divided by CA × 100 (p. 158)

Interviews   a research method conducted face-to-face between an interviewer and subject where information is obtained through recorded responses to questions (p. 14)

Intimacy vs. isolation   Erikson's sixth psychosocial stage of development (young adulthood), during which the young adult develops close relationships with others, or is unable to, resulting in feelings of isolation (p. 29)

Intrinsic motivation   motivation of behavior that comes directly from the satisfaction of needs through the inherent nature of activity and its consequences (p. 391)

In vitro fertilization   removal of the ovum from the mother and fertilizing it in the laboratory, then implanting the zygote within the uterine wall (p. 56)

Irreversibility   failure to recognize that an operation can go both ways (p. 152)

Ischemic heart disease   diseases that impede blood flow to the heart, resulting in inadequate oxygen supply (p. 359)

Jaundice   an abnormal liver condition causing increase in bile pigments in the blood and thus a yellowing of the skin and whites of the eyes (p. 361)

Juvenile   one who is not yet considered an adult in the eyes of the law (p. 231)

Kitzinger method   a psychosocial method of natural childbirth emphasizing relaxation and muscle control, developed by Dr. Kitzinger of England (p. 81)

Labia majora   the major or large lips of tissue on either side of the vaginal opening (p. 246)

Labia minora   the smaller lips of tissue on either side of the vagina (p. 246)

Labor   rhythmic muscular contractions of the uterus that expel the baby through the birth canal (p. 83)

Lamaze method   a natural childbirth method emphasizing education, physical conditioning, controlled breathing, and emotional support, developed by the French obstetrician Fernand Lamaze (p. 81)

Language acquisition device   the inherited characteristics that enable children to listen to and imitate speech sounds and patterns (p. 142)

Late adulthood   age 60 and over (p. 8)

Latency stage   Freud's fourth psychosexual stage of development (6 years to puberty), during which sexual interests are sublimated and concentrated on social and education activities (p. 28)

Lateralization   the preference for using one side of the body more than the other in performing special tasks, depending on which hemisphere is dominant for the task (p. 119)

Law of dominant inheritance   Mendel's law that says that when an organism inherits competing traits, only one trait will be expressed (p. 60)

LDL (low-density lipoprotein)   a harmful cholesterol that contributes to the buildup of fatty deposits in the arteries (p. 355)

Leboyer method   ideas for gentle birth procedure developed by the French obstetrician Frederick Leboyer (p. 86)

LH (luteinizing hormone)   a pituitary hormone that stimulates the development of the ovum and estrogen and progesterone in females and of sperm and testosterone in males (p. 242)

Living-dying interval   period of time between the knowledge of the crisis of death and death itself (p. 458)

Living will   a written request by a patient that life-sustaining procedures be withdrawn if there is no reasonable expectation of recovery or regaining a meaningful quality of life (p. 465)

Local or regional anesthesia   a drug injected into localized areas or regions to block pain during childbirth; some types may have little effect on the fetus (p. 84)

Locus of control   the center of control of our lives, whether internal or external (p. 13)

Longitudinal research   the repeated measurement of a group of subjects over a period of years (p. 17)

Long-term storage   long-term memory: the process by which information is perceived and processed deeply so it passes into the layers of memory below the conscious level—the third stage in a three-stage memory model (p. 155)

Low socioeconomic status   low social class, including cultural deprivation and low income (p. 198)

Macrosystem   influences of a particular culture (p. 196)

Macular diseases   diseases of the macula, the part of the retina that possesses maximum visual acuity (p. 364)

Marital adjustment tasks   areas of concern in marriage in which adjustments need to be made (p. 431)

Masturbation   self-stimulation for purposes of sexual arousal (p. 307)

Maturation   the unfolding of the genetically determined patterns of growth and development (p. 105)

Maturity   the time in life when one becomes an adult physically, emotionally, socially, intellectually, and spiritually (p. 230)

Mechanistic or deterministic   as applied to behaviorism, is a criticism that behavior is a result of mindless reactions to stimuli (p. 31)

Meiosis   process of cell division by which gametes reproduce (p. 50)

Menarche   first menstruation (p. 246)

Menopause   the permanent cessation of menstruation at mid-life (p. 363)

Mental age (MA)   term used by Binet to describe the intellectual level of a person (p. 158)

Mercy killing   putting to death a person who suffers from an incurable disease (p. 467)

Mesosystem   social influences involving reciprocal relationships among the child's microsystem settings; for example, reciprocal influences of the home and school (p. 196)

Metamemory   knowledge of memory strategies people employ to learn and remember information (p. 157)

Method of loci   remembering by visualizing the position of something (p. 157)

Microsystem   social influences with whom the child has immediate contact (p. 196)

Middle adulthood   middle age, including the 40s and 50s (p. 7)

Middle childhood   the elementary school years, from 6 to 11 years (p. 6)

Mnemonic   memory-aiding (p. 157)

Modeling   learning through observing and imitating the behavior of others (p. 33)

Monoamines   neurotransmitters (p. 412)

Monozygotic (identical) twins   One-egg, or identical, twins (p. 59)

Mons veneris (mons pubis)   the mound of flesh (mound of Venus) located above the vagina in the female, over which pubic hair grows (p. 246)

Morale   one's moral or mental condition with respect to cheerfulness, confidence, zeal, and the like (p. 401)

Morality of constraint   conduct coerced by rules or by authority (p. 221)

Morality of conventional role conformity   the second level of development of moral thought, based on a desire to conform to social convention, according to Kohlberg (p. 314)

Morality of cooperation   conduct regulated by mutual respect and consent (p. 221)

Morality of self-accepted moral principles   the third level of development of moral thought, based on adherence to universal principles, according to Kohlberg (p. 314)

Morpheme   the smallest unit of meaning in a language (p. 141)

Morula   zygote after a number of cell divisions have taken place, resembling a mulberry (p. 51)

Motherese   baby talk that adults use in speaking to infants (p. 145)

Motor ability   the ability to move fingers, hands, arms, legs, and other parts of the body in a useful, coordinated way (p. 351)

Multi-infarct dementia   dementia caused by a series of small strokes that cut off blood supply to the brain (p. 414)

Myelinization   the process by which neurons become

coated with an insulating, fatty substance called myelin (p. 119)

Nativist view   biological theory of language development (p. 142)

Naturalistic observation   research conducted in a natural setting by watching and recording behavior (p. 14)

Natural selection   Charles Darwin's concept that certain species have been selected to survive because of characteristics that help them adapt to their environment; part of the process implying that the human species has evolved from lower forms of life (p. 106)

Nature   biological and genetic factors that influence development (p. 13)

Neurons   nerve cells (p. 94)

Nightmares   frightening dreams during REM (rapid eye movement) sleep (p. 132)

Night terrors   upsetting nocturnal experiences during sleep that often cause children to wake up terrified and screaming (p. 132)

Noble savages   beings endowed with a sense of right and wrong, term used by Jean-Jacques Rousseau to describe his view of children (p. 105)

Nocturnal emissions   male ejaculations during sleep (p. 245)

Nonattached children   children who have not developed a close emotional relationship with parents or care givers (p. 176)

Nonnormative or idiosyncratic influences   life events that occur at unexpected times or that are unusual, both of which have a major impact on development (p. 342)

Normative-crisis model   a model of development based on a definite sequence of age-related changes—typified by Gould, Levinson, and Vaillant (p. 341)

Normative influences   expected life events that occur at customary times (p. 342)

Nuclear family   a family consisting of a mother, father, and their children (p. 197)

Nurture   the influence of environment and experience on development (p. 13)

Nutrient density   percentage of essential nutrients in food in relation to calories (p. 354)

Objective judgments   judgments based solely upon the consequences of wrongdoing (p. 221)

Object permanence   the concept that an object continues to exist independent of our perceiving it (p. 150)

Oedipal complex   according to Freud, the unconscious love and sexual desire of male children for their mother, and jealousy, hostility, and fear of the father (p. 28)

Oogenesis   process by which ova mature (p. 50)

Operant conditioning   learning from the consequences of behavior so that the consequences change the probability of the behavior's recurrence (p. 32)

Oral stage   Freud's first psychosexual stage of development (0–1 year), in which the child's chief source of pleasure is from oral activity (p. 28)

Organic brain syndromes   mental disorders caused by

or associated with impairment of brain tissue function (p. 413)

Original sin   the Christian doctrine that, because of Adam's sin, a sinful nature has been passed on to succeeding generations (p. 104)

Osteoarthritis   a degenerative joint disease (p. 362)

Osteoporosis   decalcification and loss of bone mass (p. 362)

Ova   female egg cells (p. 50)

Ovaries   female gonads, or sex glands, which secrete estrogen and progesterone and produce mature egg cells (p. 245)

Ovulation   process by which the mature ovum separates from the ovarian wall and is released from the ovary (p. 50)

Ovum   egg cell (p. 242)

Pacing   time intervals between stimuli (p. 392)

Paired-associate learning   learning to make associations between pairs of items (p. 391)

Penis   the male sexual organ for coitus and urination (p. 244)

Perineum   area of skin between the vagina and anus (p. 85)

Periodontal disease   a disease of the gums in which they become infected, swell, and shrink away from the teeth (p. 363)

Peripheral vision   ability to see objects to either side of the line of sight in front of one's face (p. 364)

Pernicious anemia   a severe anemia with a great reduction in red blood cells, an increase in their size, and the presence of large, primitive cells containing no hemoglobin (p. 361)

Personal fable   beliefs in the uniqueness of one's own experience (p. 263)

Personality   the sum total of the physical, mental, social, and emotional characteristics of an individual (p. 185)

Personality and life-style theory   a theory of aging that shows the relationship between personality type and patterns of aging (p. 443)

Phallic stage   Freud's third psychosexual stage of development (4–5 years), in which the child's chief source of pleasure is through exploration and self-manipulation of the genitals (p. 28)

Phenotype   observed characteristics of an individual (p. 61)

Phobia   an anxiety disorder characterized by excessive, uncontrolled fear of objects, situations, or living creatures of some type (p. 280)

Phoneme   the smallest unit of sound in a language (p. 141)

Physical addiction   the physical need for a drug; the body's chemical dependency on it built up through its use (p. 289)

Physiological death   the ceasing to function of all the vital organs, such as the lungs and heart (p. 455)

Piagetian approach   the approach to the study of cognitive development emphasizing the qualitative changes in the ways children think, created by Jean Piaget (p. 149)

Pituitary gland   master gland of the body, located at the base of the brain, that produces hormones (p. 242)

Pleasure principle   the motivation of the id to seek pleasure and avoid pain, regardless of the consequences (p. 26)

Polygenic system of inheritance   a number of interacting genes that produce a phenotype (p. 62)

Positive reinforcement   a consequence of behavior that leads to an increase in the probability of its occurrence (p. 32)

Postmature infant   an infant who is born with a gestational age over 42 weeks (p. 89)

Postparental years   the years after the last child leaves home and until the husband's and wife's retirement (p. 433)

Postpartal depression   feelings of sadness, crying, depression, insomnia, irritability, and fatigue commonly experienced by the mother several days after her baby is born (p. 88)

Posttraumatic stress disorder   a psychological disorder characterized by extreme emotional upset after a traumatic experience is over (p. 461)

Pragmatics   the practical use of language to communicate with others in a variety of social contexts (p. 142)

Precocious puberty   very early pubertal changes (p. 251)

Premature infant   an infant who is born with a gestational age less than 37 weeks (p. 89)

Premoral level   the first level of development of moral judgment, based on rewards and punishments, according to Kohlberg (p. 314)

Prenatal period   the period from conception to birth (p. 6)

Preoperational stage   Piaget's second stage of cognitive development (2–7 years), during which the child gains some conquest over symbols (p. 38)

Prepared childbirth   the physical, social, intellectual, and emotional preparation for the birth of a baby (p. 80)

Presbycusis   hearing impairment associated with advancing age (p. 364)

Presbyopia   farsightedness characterized by lack of clear focus at close distances (p. 364)

Primary memory   short-term memory (p. 388)

Primary mental abilities   seven basic abilities described by Thurstone (p. 158)

Primary sexual characteristics   changes that involve the sex organs at the time of sexual maturation (p. 247)

Problem-finding stage   a fifth stage of cognitive development characterized by the ability to create, to discover, and to formulate problems (p. 266)

Progesterone   female sex hormone produced by the corpus luteum of the ovary (p. 242)

Progressives   educators who emphasize that the purpose of education is to prepare pupils for all of life (p. 274)

Prolactin   pituitary hormone found in LTH that stimulates the secretion of milk by the mammary glands of the breast (p. 242)

Prolapsed cord   squeezing of the umbilical cord between the baby's body and the wall of the birth canal during childbirth, causing oxygen deprivation to the fetus (p. 86)

Proprium   the self's core of identity that is developing in time (p. 284)

Prostate gland   a gland that secretes a portion of the seminal fluid (p. 244)

Proximodistal principle   outward distribution of physical growth, which starts at the center of the body and proceeds outward to the extremities (p. 118)

Psychic death   the acceptance of death and regression into self, often long before physiological death (p. 456)

Psychoanalytical theory   Freud's theory that the structure of personality is composed of the id, ego, and superego, and that mental health depends on keeping the balance among them (p. 26)

Psychological dependency   an overpowering emotional need for a drug (p. 289)

Psychometric approach   the approach to the study of cognitive development that measures the quantitative changes in children's intelligence (p. 149)

Psychosexual theory   a theory developed by Freud in which development occurs in stages as the center of sensual sensitivity shifts from one body zone to another as children mature (p. 28)

Psychosis associated with cerebral arteriosclerosis   psychosis and degeneration of the brain cells caused by a hardening and narrowing of the blood vessels of the brain (p. 414)

Psychosocial moratorium   a socially sanctioned period between childhood and adulthood during which the individual is free to experiment to find a socially acceptable identity and role (p. 233)

Psychosocial theory   the term used to describe Erikson's stage theory of development in which there are psychosocial tasks to master at each level of development (p. 29)

Psychotropics   mood altering drugs (p. 357)

Puberty   the period or age at which a person reaches sexual maturity and becomes capable of reproduction (p. 230)

Pubescence   the whole period during which the physical changes related to sexual maturation take place (p. 230)

Pulmonary embolism   blockage of blood vessels to the lungs by a blood clot (p. 360)

Pulmonary infections   lung infections (p. 360)

Pulmonary thrombosis   blockage of blood vessels to the lungs (p. 361)

Pulse rate   the number of heartbeats per minute (p. 353)

Punishment of reciprocity   self-imposed punishment; associated with morality of cooperation (p. 222)

Questionnaires   a research method whereby the subject writes out answers to written questions (p. 15)

Random sample   research subjects selected at random (p. 15)

Rationalization a Freudian defense mechanism in which excuses are given for one's behavior (p. 28)

Reaction formation a Freudian defense mechanism in which an individual deals with an unacceptable impulse by overemphasizing the exact opposite in thought and behavior (p. 28)

Reaction range range of possible phenotypes given a particular genotype and environmental influences (p. 62)

Reaction time the interval between stimulation and response (p. 350)

Recall remembering without use of any cues (p. 155)

Recessive gene gene whose characteristic is masked by a dominant gene, and is expressed only when paired with a matching recessive gene (p. 60)

Recognition remembering after cues have been given (p. 155)

Reflexes unlearned behavioral responses to particular stimuli in the environment (p. 94)

Regression a Freudian defense mechanism in which there is a reverting to an earlier, childish form of behavior in response to anxiety (p. 28)

Relaxation training techniques to relax the body in order to combat stress (p. 409)

Reliability the extent to which a test reveals the same scores with repeated administration and when given by two or more examiners (p. 15)

Representative sample a population sample that includes the same percentage of people with specific personal or background characteristics as contained in the population studied (p. 15)

Repression a Freudian defense mechanism in which unpleasant thoughts are pushed down into the unconscious (p. 28)

Retrieval the process of recalling or of being able to remember or recognize information that has been stored (p. 387)

Reversibility the concept that every operation has an opposite operation that reverses it (p. 153)

Reversible brain syndrome an acute brain syndrome that is treatable (p. 414)

Rheumatoid arthritis a chronic disease marked by painful inflammation and swelling of the small joints of the hands and wrists, and often accompanied by deformities (p. 362)

Sample the group of subjects chosen for research (p. 15)

Saturated fats animal fats; fats saturated with hydrogen, such as oleomargarine (p. 354)

Schema a Piagetian term referring to mental structures, the original patterns of thinking that people use for dealing with the specific situations in their environment (p. 37)

Scholastic Aptitude Test (SAT) the most widely used test for youths to determine their aptitude to do college work (p. 266)

Scientific method a series of steps used to obtain accurate data; these include formulating the problem, developing a hypothesis, testing the hypothesis, and drawing conclusions that are stated in the form of a theory (p. 14)

Scrotum the pouch of skin containing the testes (p. 244)

Secondary memory long-term memory (p. 388)

Secondary sexual characteristics changes in the body at the time of sexual maturation that do not involve the sex organs themselves (p. 247)

Self the overall perception of one's personality, nature, and individuality of which one is aware (p. 283)

Self-actualization according to Buhler, the drive of individuals to try to grow, improve, and reach their full potential (p. 34)

Self-concept an individual's conscious, cognitive perception and evaluation of self; one's thoughts and opinions about oneself (p. 283)

Self-efficacy our perceptions of our actual skill and personal effectiveness in dealing with situations and others (p. 189)

Self-esteem our perception of our worth, abilities, and accomplishments; our view of ourselves: negative or positive (p. 190)

Self-reference our estimate of our abilities and of how capable and effective we are in dealing with others and the world (p. 189)

Self-reflective thinking or reciprocal perspective-taking stage the stage of awareness during which the self can take the perspective of another person and know that the other person can also take the perspective of the self—stage 2 in Selman's theory (p. 213)

Semantics the meaning of words and sentences (p. 142)

Seminal vesicles twin glands that secrete fluid into the vas deferens to enhance sperm viability (p. 244)

Senescence biological aging (p. 365)

Senile dementia an organic brain disorder impairing brain function in older people (p. 413)

Senile psychosis a decline in mental functioning caused by the atrophy and degeneration of brain cells (p. 414)

Sensitive period a period during which a given effect can be produced more readily than at other times (p. 41)

Sensorimotor stage Piaget's first stage of cognitive development (birth–2 years), during which the child coordinates motor actions with sensory experiences (p. 38)

Sensory storage sensory memory: the process by which information is received and transduced by the senses, usually in a fraction of a second—the first stage in a three-stage model of memory (p. 155)

Separation anxiety anxiety experienced by children when they are separated from care givers to whom they are emotionally attached (p. 132)

Separation-individuation a period during which the infant gradually develops a self apart from the mother, a concept of Mahler (p. 188)

Sequential study a combination of cross-sectional and longitudinal research designs that attempts to sort out age, cohort, and time effects. Age changes are not measured. (p. 18)

Serialization   arranging objects into a hierarchy of classes (p. 153)

Serial-learning tasks   learning items in a list in the exact order of presentation (p. 391)

Sex chromosomes   twenty-third pair of chromosomes that determine the gender of the offspring (p. 58)

Sex-linked disorders   disorders carried only by the mother, through defective, recessive genes on the X chromosome (p. 62)

Short-term storage   short-term memory: the process by which information is still in the conscious mind and being rehearsed and focused on—the second stage in a three-stage memory model (p. 155)

Show   blood-tinged mucus expelled from the cervix, usually when labor and contractions begin (p. 83)

Siamese twins   monozygotic twins where complete separation did not occur during development (p. 59)

Single-parent family   a family consisting of one parent and one or more children (p. 197)

Sleepwalking   walking and carrying on various activities during deep sleep (p. 132)

Social clock   a society's specification as to when various life events and activities are supposed to happen (p. 341)

Social cognition   the capacity to understand social relationships (p. 213)

Social development   the socialization process, moral development, and relationships with peers, family, and at work (p. 9)

Socialization   the process by which persons learn the ways of society or social groups so they can function within them (p. 198)

Social learning theory   a view of learning that emphasizes that behavior is learned through social interaction with other persons (p. 33)

Socially accelerated dying   allowing any condition or action of society that shortens life and hastens death (p. 464)

Social networks   social ties with children, family, and friends (p. 404)

Social reconstruction theory   a theory of aging describing how society reduces the self-concept of the aged, and proposing ways to reverse this negative cycle (p. 444)

Social role taking   the ability to understand the self and others as subjects, to react to them as like the self, and to react to the self's behavior from the other's point of view (p. 213)

Sociocentrism   a focus of attention on social problems and the concerns of society (p. 262)

Sociological death   the withdrawal and separation by other people as though one were dead, often long before physiological death (p. 455)

Sonogram   visual image of fetus, produced from sound waves, used to detect fetal abnormalities (p. 64)

Spermatogenesis   process by which sperm are produced (p. 50)

Stepfamily   a family formed when a remarried husband or wife brings children from a former marriage (p. 198)

Storage   the process by which acquired information is put away for later use (p. 387)

Stress   physical, mental, or emotional strain (p. 405)

Stroke   paralysis that occurs when the blood supply to part of the brain is cut off and affected brain cells die (p. 360)

Subjective judgments   judgments that take into account intention or motives (p. 221)

Subjective well-being   a self-perceived positive feeling or state; a cognitive and affective assessment about life as a whole (p. 400)

Sublimation   a Freudian defense mechanism in which a socially acceptable goal or action is substituted for an unacceptable, socially harmful one (p. 28)

Sudden infant death syndrome   the sudden and mysterious death of infants in their crib, usually between 2 weeks and 1 year of age (p. 460)

Superego   according to Freud, the socially induced moral restrictions that strive to keep the id in check and help the individual attain perfection (p. 27)

Surrogate mother   a woman whose services are obtained by a couple, who is to be inseminated with the man's sperm, to carry the resulting baby until birth, and then to give the baby and all rights to it to the couple (p. 56)

Survival of the fittest   Darwin's concept that only the fittest live to pass on their superior traits to future generations, thereby evolving into higher and higher forms of life (p. 106)

Symbiosis   a child's close dependency on the mother, to the extent that there is almost a fusing of personalities (p. 180)

Symbolic play   using one object to represent another in play (p. 150)

Syncretism   trying to link ideas together that are not always related (p. 151)

Syntax   the grammatical rules of a language (p. 141)

Systolic blood pressure   the pressure produced by the heart pumping blood out to the body (p. 359)

Tabula rasa   literally, a blank slate; refers to John Locke's view that children are born morally neutral (p. 105)

Tactile acuity   sensitivity of touch (p. 365)

Tactual memory   memory of touch (p. 388)

Telegraphic speech   several-word utterances that convey meaning (p. 145)

Temperament   the relatively consistent, basic dispositions inherent in people that underlie and modulate much of their behavior (p. 185)

Teratogen   harmful substance that crosses the placenta barrier and harms the embryo or fetus and causes birth defects (p. 66)

Terminal decline   marked decline in intellectual performance shortly before death; theory that genetic and environmental factors producing decline lead to marked functional decline prior to death (p. 386)

Testes   the male gonads that produce sperm and male sex hormones (p. 244)

Testosterone   the masculinizing hormone secreted by the testes (p. 217)

Tests   research instruments used to measure specific characteristics such as intelligence, aptitude, achievement, vocational interests, personality traits, and so forth (p. 15)

Theory   a tentative explanation of facts and data that have been observed (p. 26)

Thermoregulation   maintenance of correct body temperature during exposure to heat or cold (p. 365)

Thesis   the principal point or idea of a statement (p. 377)

Third person or mutual perspective-taking stage   the stage of social awareness during which the self can view the self–other interaction from the perspective of a neutral third person—stage 3 in Selman's theory (p. 214)

Thrombosis   blockage from any kind of undissolved material in the blood (p. 360)

Time lag study   using intervals in time measurements during which people of different cohorts are examined (p. 18)

Timing-of-events model   a model of development based on responses to the occurrences and timing of normative and nonnormative events—typified by Neugarten (p. 342)

Traditionalists   educators who argue that the purpose of education is to teach the basics (p. 269)

Transcendental meditation   a technique to direct one's consciousness away from thoughts and toward a state of relaxation (p. 409)

Transductive reasoning   proceeding from particular to particular in thought, without making generalizations (p. 150)

Triarchic theory of intelligence   three components of intelligence described by Sternberg (p. 159)

Trimester   one-third of the gestation period, or about 12.7 weeks (p. 53)

Trust vs. distrust   Erikson's first stage of psychosocial development (0–1 year) in which the infant learns that needs will be met or becomes anxious that needs will be frustrated (p. 29)

Tuberculosis   an infectious disease of the lungs (p. 360)

Two-factor theory of intelligence   concept developed by Spearman that intelligence consists of a general factor "g" and a number of specific abilities—"s" factors (p. 158)

Type A personality   a personality characterized by intense competitiveness, hostility, overwork, and a sense of time urgency; one who has extreme bodily reactions to stress (p. 406)

Unconditional positive regard   giving acceptance and appreciation of the individual regardless of socially unacceptable behavior (p. 36)

Urethra   the tube that carries urine from the bladder to the outside; in males it also carries the semen to the outside (p. 244)

Uterus   womb, in which the baby grows and develops (p. 245)

Vagina   canal from the cervix to the vulva that receives the penis during intercourse and acts as the birth canal through which the baby passes to the outside (p. 245)

Validity   the extent to which a test measures what it claims to measure (p. 15)

Vas deferens   the tubes running from the epididymis to the urethra that carry semen and sperm to the ejaculatory duct (p. 244)

Vernix caseosa   waxy substance covering the skin of the neonate (p. 91)

Vestibule   the opening cleft region enclosed by the labia minora (p. 245)

Viable   capable of living on its own (p. 55)

Vicarious punishment   observing the punishment of the behavior of another that decreases the probability of the same behavior in the observer (p. 33)

Vicarious reinforcement   observing the positive consequences of the behavior of another that increases the probability of the behavior in the observer (p. 33)

Visual acuity   the ability to see small details (p. 363)

Vital capacity   volume of air inhaled by the lungs with each breath (p. 360)

Vulva   a collective term for the external genitalia of the female (p. 245)

Zygote   a fertilized ovum (p. 50)

BIBLIOGRAPHY

Aadalen, S. (1980). Coping with sudden infant death syndrome: Intervention strategies and a case study. *Family Relations, 29*, 584–590.

Abraham, K. G., & Christopherson, V. A (1984). Perceived competence among rural middle school children: Parental antecedents and relations to locus of control. *Journal of Early Adolescence, 4*, 343–351.

Abramson, L., Seligman, M. E. P., & Teasdale, J. D. (1978). Learned helplessness in humans: Critique and reformulation. *Journal of Abnormal Psychology, 87*, 49–74.

Achenbach, T. M., Phares, V., & Howell, C. T. (1990). Seven-year outcome of the Vermont intervention program for low-birthweight infants. *Child Development, 61*, 1672–1681.

Acredolo, L. P., & Hake, J. L. (1982). Infant perception. In B. B. Wolman (Ed.), *Handbook of developmental psychology*. Englewood Cliffs, NJ: Prentice-Hall.

Adams, G. R. (1977, Summer). Personal identity formation: A synthesis of cognitive and ego psychology. *Adolescence, 12*, 151–164.

Adams, G. R. (1980). Social psychology of beauty: Effects of age, height, and weight on self-reported personality traits and social behavior. *Journal of Social Psychology, 112*, 287–293.

Adams, G. R. (1983). Social competence during adolescence: Social sensitivity, locus of control, empathy, and peer popularity. *Journal of Youth and Adolescence, 12*, 203–211.

Adams, G. R., & Jones, R. M. (1982, February). Adolescent egocentrism: Exploration into possible contributions of parent-child relations. *Journal of Youth and Adolescence, 11*, 25–31.

Adams, G. R., & Munro, G. (1979, September). Portrait of the North American runaway: A critical review. *Journal of Youth and Adolescence, 8*, 359–373.

Adams, M., Oakley, G., & Marks, J. (1982). Maternal age and births in the 1980s. *JAMA, Journal of the American Medical Association, 247*, 493–494.

Adessa, M. (1988). Sleep in and smell the coffee. *Psychology Today, 22*, 18.

Adler, J. (1989, March). The Nintendo kid. *Newsweek, 113*, 64–68.

Affleck, G., Tennen, H., Rowe, J., Roscher, B., & Walker, L. (1989). Effects of formal support on mother's adaptation to the hospital-to-home transition of high-risk infants: The benefits and costs of helping. *Child Development, 60*, 488–501.

Age: All in your head. (1989). *Psychology Today, 23*, 12.

Aging in America. (1989). Washington, DC: Congressional Quarterly.

Ahrons, C., & Rodgers, R. (1987). *Divorced families: A multidisciplinary view.* New York: W. W. Norton.

Ainsworth, M. D. S. (1988, August). *Attachment beyond infancy.* Paper presented at the meeting of the American Psychological Association.

Akinboye, J. O. (1984, Summer). Secondary sexual characteristics and normal puberty in Nigerian and Zimbabwian adolescents. *Adolescence, 19*, 483–492.

Alan Guttmacher Institute. (1981). *Teenage pregnancy.* New York: Alan Guttmacher Institute.

Aldwin, C. M. (1991). Does age affect the stress and coping process? Implications of age differences in perceived control. *Journal of Gerontology, 46*, P174–P180.

Allen, K. E., Hart, R. M., Buell, J. S., Harris, F. R., & Wolf, M. M. (1964). Effects of social reinforcement on isolate behavior of a nursery school child. *Child Development, 35*, 511–518.

Allen, P. A., & Coyne, A. C. (1989). Are there age differences in chunking? *Journal of Gerontology, 44*, 181–183.

Allport, G. W. (1950). *Becoming: Basic considerations for a psychology of personality.* New Haven, CT: Yale University Press.

Altmann, E. O., & Gottlieb, I. H. (1988). The social behavior of depressed children: An observational study. *Journal of Abnormal Child Psychology, 16*, 29–44.

Amato, P. R. (1986). Marital conflict, the parent-child relationship, and self-esteem. *Family Relations, 35*, 403–410.

Amato, P. R. (1987). Family process in one-parent, stepparent, and intact families: The child's point of view. *Journal of Marriage and the Family, 49*, 327–337.

Amato, P. R. (1988a). Long-term implications of parental divorce for adult self-concept. *Journal of Family Issues, 9*, 201–213.

Amato, P. R. (1988b). Parental divorce and attitudes toward marriage and family life. *Journal of Marriage and the Family, 50*, 453–461.

Amato, P. R. (1990). Dimensions of the family environment as perceived by children: A multidimensional scaling analysis. *Journal of Marriage and the Family, 52*, 613–620.

Amato, P. R. (1991). The "child of divorce" as a person prototype: Bias in the recall of information about children in divorced families. *Journal of Marriage and the Family, 53*, 59–69.

American Academy of Pediatrics. (1982, March). Guidelines for health supervision. *News and Comment*.

American Academy of Pediatrics. (1986). *Positive approaches to daycare dilemmas: How to make it work*. Elk Grove Village, IL: American Academy of Pediatrics.

American Academy of Pediatrics, Committee on Nutrition. (1986). Prudent life-style for children: Dietary fat and cholesterol. *Pediatrics, 78*, 521–525.

American Academy of Pediatrics, Committee on Pediatric Aspects of Physical Fitness, Recreation, and Sports. (1981). Competitive athletics for children of elementary school age. *Pediatrics, 67*.

American Psychiatric Association. (1987). *Diagnostic and statistical manual of mental disorders* (3rd ed., rev.). Washington, DC: American Psychiatric Association.

American Psychological Association (APA). (1982). *Ethical principles in the conduct of research with human participants*. Washington, DC: American Psychological Association.

Ames, L. B., Gillespie, C., Haines, J., & Ilg, F. L. (1978). *The Gesell Institute's child from one to six*. New York: Harper & Row.

Amster, L. E., & Krauss, H. H. (1974). Life crises and mental deterioration. *International Journal of Aging and Human Development, 5*, 51–55.

Anderson, D. R., Choi, H. P., & Lorch, E. P. (1987). Attentional inertia reduces distractibility during young children's TV viewing. *Child Development, 58*, 798–806.

Anderson, S. A., Russell, C. S., & Schumm, W. R. (1983). Perceived marital quality and family-life cycle categories: A further analysis. *Journal of Marriage and the Family, 45*, 227–239.

Andre, T., & Bormann, L. (1991). Knowledge of acquired immune deficiency syndrome and sexual responsibility among high school students. *Youth and Society, 22*, 339–361.

Andrews, S. R., Blumenthal, J. B., Johnson, D. L., Kahn, A. J., Ferguson, C. J., Lasater, T. M., Malone, P. E., & Wallace, D. B. (1982). The skills of mothering—a study of parent-child development centers. *Monographs of the Society for Research in Child Development, 47*(6, Serial No. 198).

Anisfeld, E., Casper, V., Nozyce, M., & Cunningham, N. (1990). Does infant carrying promote attachment? An experimental study of the effects of increased physical contact on the development of attachment. *Child Development, 61*, 1617–1627.

Annas, G., & Densberger, J. (1984). Competence to refuse medical treatment: Autonomy v. paternalism. *University of Toledo Law Review, 15*, 561–596.

Anolik, S. A. (1980, Winter). The family perceptions of delinquents, high school students and freshman college students. *Adolescence, 15*, 903–911.

Anolik, S. A. (1981, December). Imaginary audience behavior and perceptions of parents among delinquent and nondelinquent adolescents. *Journal of Youth and Adolescence, 10*, 443–454.

Anolik, S. A. (1983, Fall). Family influences upon delinquency: Biosocial and psychosocial perspectives. *Adolescence, 18*, 489–498.

Ansbacher, R., & Adler, J. P. (1988). Infertility workup and sexual stress. *Medical Aspects of Human Sexuality, 22*, 55–63.

Apgar, V. A. (1953). A proposal for a new method of evaluation of a newborn infant. *Anesthesia and Analgesia, 32*, 260–267.

Appleton, W. S. (1983). Women at middle age: Effects on marital relationships. *Medical Aspects of Human Sexuality, 17*, 188–194.

Apter, A., Galatzer, A., Beth-Halachmi, N., & Laron, Z. (1981, December). Self-image in adolescents with delayed puberty and growth retardation. *Journal of Youth and Adolescence, 10*, 501–505.

Aptitude test scores. Grumbling gets louder. (1979, May 14). *U.S. News and World Report*, pp. 76ff.

Archbold, P. B. (1983). Impact of parent-caring on women. *Family Relations, 39*, 309–320.

Archer, S. L. (1990a). Adolescent identity: An appraisal of health and intervention. *Journal of Adolescence, 13*, 341–344.

Archer, S. L. (1990b). The status of identity: Reflections on the need for intervention. *Journal of Adolescence, 13*, 345–360.

Arenberg, D. (1976). The effects of input condition on free recall in young and old adults. *Journal of Gerontology, 31*, 551–555.

Arenberg, D. (1982). Estimate of age changes on the Benton Visual Retention Test. *Journal of Gerontology, 37*, 87–90.

Arenberg, D., & Robertson-Tshabo, E. A. (1977). Learning and aging. In J. A. Bireen & K. W. Schaie (Eds.), *Handbook on the psychology of aging* (pp. 421–449). New York: Van Nostrand-Reinhold.

Aries, P. (1962). *Centuries of childhood: A social history of family life*. New York: Vintage Books.

Aries, P. (1981). *The hour of death*. New York: Alfred A. Knopf.

Arkin, E. B. (1989, July). *Infant care*. U.S. Department of HHS, Public Health Service, Health Resources and Services Administration, Bureau of Maternal and Child Health and Resources Development. Washington, DC: U.S. Government Printing Office.

Arlin, P. K. (1975). Cognitive development in adulthood: A fifth stage? *Developmental Psychology, 11*, 602–606.

Arlin, P. K. (1977). Piagetian operations in problem finding. *Developmental Psychology, 13*, 297–298.

Arling, G. (1976). The elderly widow and her family: Neighbors and friends. *Journal of Marriage and the Family, 38*, 757–768.

Arling, G. (1987). Strain, social support, and distress in old age. *Journal of Gerontology, 42*, 107–113.

Arons, A. B. (1987, Fall). Reasoning modes and processes arising in secondary and college level study of natural science, humanities, and the social sciences. *Andover Review, 5*, 3–8.

Asarnow, J. R. (1988). Peers status and social competence in child psychiatric inpatients: A comparison of children with depressive, externalizing, and concurrent depressive and externalizing disorders. *Journal of Abnormal Child Psychology, 16*, 151–162.

Ashford, J., & LeCroy, C. W. (1990). Juvenile recidivism: A comparison of three prediction instruments. *Adolescence, 25*, 441–450.

Ashford, J. W., Kolm, P., Colliver, J. A., Bekian, C., & Hsui, L. (1989). Alzheimer patient evaluation and the mini-mental state: Item characteristics curve analysis. *Journal of Gerontology, 44*, 139–146.

Ashmead, D. H., & Perlmutter, M. (1979, August). *Infant memory in everyday life*. Paper presented at the meeting of the American Psychological Association, New York City.

Aslin, R. N., Pisoni, D. P., & Jusczyk, P. W. (1983). Auditory development and speech perception in infancy. In P. H. Mussen, M. H. Haith, & J. J. Campos (Eds.), *Handbook of child psychology: Vol. 2. Infancy and developmental psychology*. New York: Wiley.

Athey, I. J. (1984). Contributions of play to development. In T. D. Yawkey & A. D. Pellegrini (Eds.), *Child's play*. Hillsdale, NJ: Erlbaum.

Atkinson, R. (1988). *Teenage world: Adolescent self-image in ten countries*. New York: Plenum.

Bachman, J. G., Johnston, L. D., & O'Malley, P. M. (1987). *Monitoring the future: Questionnaire responses from the nation's high school seniors, 1986.* Ann Arbor, MI: Institute for Social Research.

Bahrick, H. P., Bahrick, P. O., & Wittlinger, R. P. (1975). Fifty years of memory for names and faces: A cross-sectional approach. *Journal of Experimental Psychology: General, 104,* 54–75.

Baillargeon, R. (1987). Object permanence in 3½–4½-month-old infants. *Developmental Psychology, 23,* 655–664.

Baird, P., & Sights, J. R. (1986). Low self-esteem as a treatment issue in the psychotherapy of anorexia and bulimia. *Journal of Counseling and Development, 64,* 449–451.

Baker, C. C. (1982, June). The adolescent as theorist: An interpretative view. *Journal of Youth and Adolescence, 11,* 167–181.

Baker, E. R., Mathur, R. S., Kirk, R. F. et al. (1981). Female runners and secondary amenorrhea correlation with age, parity, mileage and plasma hormonal and sex hormone-binding globulin concentrations. *Fertility and Sterility, 36,* 183.

Balk, D. (1983, April). Adolescents' grief reactions and self-concept perceptions following sibling death: A study of 33 teenagers. *Journal of Youth and Adolescence, 12,* 137–161.

Balkwell, C., & Balswick, J. (1981). Subsistence economy, family structure, and status of the elderly. *Journal of Marriage and the Family, 43,* 423–429.

Balkwell, C., & Halverson, C. F., Jr. (1980). The hyperactive child as a source of stress in the family: Consequences of suggestions of intervention. *Family Relations, 29,* 550–557.

Baltes, P. B. (1987). Theoretical propositions of life-span developmental psychology: On the dynamics between growth and decline. *Developmental Psychology, 23,* 611–626.

Baltes, P. B., Reese, H. W., & Lipsitt, L. (1980). Life span developmental psychology. In M. Rosenzweig & L. Portor (Eds.), *Annual review of psychology* (Vol. 31). Palo Alto, CA: Annual Reviews.

Baltes, P. B., & Schaie, K. W. (1976). On the plasticity of intelligence in adulthood and old age: Where Horn and Donaldson fail. *American Psychologist, 31,* 720–725.

Baltes, P. B., Smith, J., Staudinger, V. M., & Sowarka, D. (1988). Wisdom: One facet of successful aging? In M. Perlmutter (Ed.), *Late-life potential.* Washington, DC: Gerontological Society of America.

Bandura, A. (1977). *Social learning theory.* Englewood Cliffs, NJ: Prentice-Hall.

Bandura, A. (1986). *Social foundations of thought and action: A social cognitive theory.* Englewood Cliffs, NJ: Prentice-Hall.

Bandura, A., Ross, D., & Ross, S. A. (1963a). Imitation of film-mediated aggressive models. *Journal of Abnormal and Social Psychology, 66,* 3–11.

Bandura, A., Ross, D., & Ross, S. A. (1963b). Imitation of film-mediated aggressive males. *Journal of Abnormal and Social Psychology, 67,* 601–607.

Banks, M. S., & Salapatek, P. (1983). Infant visual perception. In P. H. Mussen (Ed.), *Handbook of child psychology* (4th ed., Vol. 2). New York: Wiley.

Barcus, F. E. (1978). *Commercial children's television on weekends and weekday afternoons.* Newtonville, MA: Action for Children's Television.

Barenboim, C. (1977, December). Developmental changes in the interpersonal cognitive system from middle childhood to adolescence. *Child Development, 48,* 1467–1474.

Barnes, M. E., & Farrier, S. C. (1985, Spring). A longitudinal study of the self-concept of low-income youth. *Adolescence, 20,* 199–205.

Barnes, R. F., & Raskind, M. A. (1981). DSM-III. Criteria and the clinical diagnosis of dementia: A nursing home story. *Journal of Gerontology, 36,* 20–27.

Barrett, K. C., & Campos, J. J. (1987). A functionalist approach to emotions. In J. D Osofsky (Ed.), *Handbook of infant development.* New York: Wiley.

Barrett, M. D. (1986). Early semantic representations and early word-usage. In S. A. Kuczaj & M. C. Barett (Eds.), *The development of word meaning: Progress in cognitive developmental research.* New York: Springer-Verlag.

Barrett, T. R., & Wright, M. (1981). Age-related facilitation in recall following semantic processing. *Journal of Gerontology, 36,* 194–199.

Bart, W. M. (1983, Winter). Adolescent thinking and the quality of life. *Adolescence, 18,* 875–888.

Baruch, G., Barnett, R., & Rivers, C. (1983). *Life-prints: New patterns of love and work for today's women.* New York: McGraw-Hill.

Basseches, M. (1984). *Dialectical thinking and adult development.* Norwood, NJ: Ablex.

Battle, J. (1981). *Culture-free self-esteem inventories for children and adults.* Seattle, WA: Special Child Publications.

Bauman, R. P. (1978, Spring). Teaching for cognitive development. *Andover Review, 5,* 83–98.

Baumrind, D. (1971). Current patterns in parental authority. *Developmental Psychology Monographs, 1,* Pt. 2.

Baumrind, D. (1978). Parental disciplinary patterns and social competence in children. *Youth and Society, 9,* 239–276.

Baumrind, D. (1980). New directions in socialization research. *American Psychologist, 35,* 639–652.

Baur, P., & Okun, M. A. (1983). Stability of life satisfaction in late life. *Gerontologist, 23,* 261–265.

Baylar, N. (1988). Effects of parental separation and re-entry into union on the emotional well-being of children. *Journal of Marriage and the Family, 50,* 967–981.

Bayley, N. (1956). Individual patterns of development. *Child Development, 27,* 45–74.

Bayley, N. (1968). Behavioral correlates of mental growth: Birth to 36 years. *American Psychologist, 23,* 1–17.

Bayley, N. (1969). *Manual for the Bayley Scales of infant development.* New York: The Psychological Corporation.

Bean, C. (1974). *Methods of childbirth.* New York: Dolphin.

Beauchamp, G., & Cowart, B. (1985). Congenital and experiential factors in the development of human flavor preferences. *Appetite, 6,* 357–372.

Beck, J. D., Ettinger, R. L., Glenn, R. E., Paule, C. L., & Holtzman, J. M. (1979). Oral health status: Impact on dental students' attitudes toward the aged. *Gerontologist, 19,* 580–585.

Beck, J. G., & Davies, D. K. (1987). Teen contraception: A review of perspectives on compliance. *Archives of Sexual Behavior, 16,* 337–368.

Bee, H. L., Barnard, K. E., Eyres, S. J., Gray, C. A., Hammond, M. A., Spietz, A. L., Snyder, C., & Clark, B. (1982). Predictor of IQ and language skill from perinatal status, child performance, family characteristics, and mother-infant interaction. *Child Development, 53,* 1134–1156.

Behrend, D. A. (1990). The development of verb concepts: Children's use of verbs to label familiar and novel events. *Child Development, 61,* 681–696.

Behrman, R. E., & Vaughn, B. E. (Eds.). (1983). *Nelson textbook of pediatrics* (12th ed.). Philadelphia, PA: Saunders.

Bell, B., Rose, C. L., & Danon, A. (1972). The normative aging study: An interdisciplinary and longitudinal study of health and aging. *Aging and Human Development, 3,* 5–18.

Bell, C. S., & Ward, G. R. (1980, Winter). An investigation of the relationship between dimensions of self concept (DOSC) and achievement in mathematics. *Adolescence, 15,* 895–901.

Bell, C. S., Johnson, J. E., McGillicuddy-Delishi, A. V., & Sigel, I. W. (1980). Normative stress and young families: Adaptation and development. *Family Relations, 29,* 453–458.

Bell, N. J., & Avery, A. W. (1985). Family structure and parent-adolescent relationships: Does family structure really make a difference? *Journal of Marriage and Family Therapy, 47,* 503–508.

Bell, R. R. (1975). *Marriage and family interaction* (4th ed.). Homewood, IL: Dorsey.

Bellinger, D., Leviton, A. A., Watermaux, C., Needleman, H., & Rabinowitz, M. (1987). Longitudinal analyses of prenatal and postnatal lead exposure and early cognitive development. *New England Journal of Medicine, 316,* 1037–1043.

Belmore, S. M. (1981). Age-related changes in processing explicit and implicit language. *Journal of Gerontology, 36,* 316–322.

Belsky, J. (1984). Two waves of day care research: Developmental effects and condition of quality. In R. Ainslie (Ed.), *The child and the day care setting.* New York: Praeger.

Belsky, J. (1987, August). *Mother care, other care, and infant-parent attachment security.* Paper presented at the annual meeting of the American Psychological Association, New York.

Belsky, J. (1990). Parental and nonparental child care and children's socioemotional development: A decade in review. *Journal of Marriage and the Family, 52,* 885–903.

Belsky, J., & Rovine, M. J. (1988). Nonmaternal care in the first year of life and the security of infant-parent attachment. *Child Development, 59,* 157–167.

Benenson, J. F. (1990). Gender differences in social networks. *Journal of Early Adolescence, 10,* 472–495.

Bengston, V. L., Cuellar, J. B., & Ragan, P. K. (1977, January). Stratum contrasts and similarities in attitudes toward death. *Journal of Gerontology, 32,* 76–88.

Bengston, V. L., Cutler, N. E., Mangen, D. J., & Marshall, V. W. (1985). Generations, cohorts and relations between age groups. In R. H. Binstock & E. Shanas (Eds.), *Handbook of aging and social sciences* (pp. 304–338). New York: Van Nostrand-Reinhold.

Bennett, W. J. (1986). *First lessons: A report on elementary education in America.* Washington, DC: U.S Government Printing Office.

Benotti, J. R. (1988). Living with congestive heart disease. *Medical Aspects of Human Sexuality, 22,* 47–48.

Bensman, J., & Liliesfield, R. (1979). Friendship and alienation. *Psychology Today, 12,* 56ff.

Berch, D. B., & Bender, B. G. (1987). Margins of sexuality. *Psychology Today, 21,* 54–57.

Beres, C. A., & Baron, A. (1981). Improved digit symbol substitution by older women as a result of extended practice. *Journal of Gerontology, 36,* 591–597.

Bergman, M., Blumenfeld, V. G., Cascardo, D., Dash, B., Levitt, H., & Margulies, M. K. (1976). Age-related decrement in hearing for speech. *Journal of Gerontology, 31,* 533–538.

Berkow, R. (Ed.). (1987). *The Merck manual* (15th ed.). Rahway, NJ: Merck, Sharp and Dohme Research Laboratories.

Berkowitz, M., Gibbs, J., & Broughton, J. (1980). The relation of moral judgment stage disparity to developmental effects of peer dialogues. *Merrill-Palmer Quarterly, 26,* 341–357.

Berman, P. W., O'Nan, B. A., & Floyd, W. (1981). The double standard of aging and the social situation: Judgments of

attractiveness of the middle-aged woman. *Sex Roles, 7,* 87–96.

Berman, W. H., & Turk, D. C. (1981). Adaptation to divorce: Problems and coping strategies. *Journal of Marriage and the Family, 43,* 179–189.

Bernstein, R. M. (1981, Fall). The relationship between dimensions of delinquency and developments of self and peer perception. *Adolescence, 16,* 543–556.

Berry, J. J., Storandt, M., & Coyne, A. (1984). Age and sex differences in somatic complaints associated with depression. *Journal of Gerontology, 39,* 465–467.

Berry, R. E., & Williams, F. L. (1987). Assessing the relationship between the quality of life and marital income satisfaction. *Journal of Marriage and the Family, 49,* 107–116.

Berstein, B. E., & Collins, S. K. (1985). Remarriage counseling: Lawyer and therapists' help with the second time around. *Family Relations, 34,* 387–391.

Berzonsky, M. D., Rice, K. G., & Neimeyer, G. J. (1990). Identity status and self-construct systems: Process × structure interactions. *Journal of Adolescence, 13,* 251–264.

Bettes, B. A., Dusenbury, L., Kerner, J., James-Ortiz, S., & Botvin, G. J. (1990). Ethnicity and psychosocial factors in alcohol and tobacco use in adolescence. *Child Development, 61,* 557–565.

Bilsker, D., & Marcia, J. E. (1991). Adaptive regression and ego identity. *Journal of Adolescence, 14,* 75–84.

Binet, A., & Simon, T. (1916). *The development of intelligence in children.* Baltimore, MD: William & Wilkins.

Bingol, N., Fuchs, M., Diaz, V., Stone, R. K., & Gromisch, D. S. (1987). Teratogenicity of cocaine in humans. *Journal of Pediatrics, 110,* 93–96.

Birnholz, J. C., & Benacerraf, B. R. (1983). The development of human fetal hearing. *Science, 222,* 516–518.

Bishop, S. M., & Lynn, A. G. (1983). Multi-level vulnerability of adolescent marriages: An eco-system model for clinical assessment and intervention. *Journal of Marital and Family Therapy, 9,* 271–282.

Bisping, R., Steingrueber, H. J., Oltmann, M., & Wenk, C. (1990). Adults' tolerance of cries: An experimental investigation of acoustic features. *Child Development, 61,* 1218–1229.

Black, C., & deBlassie, R. R. (1985). Adolescent pregnancy: Contributing factors, consequences, treatment, and plausible solutions. *Adolescence, 20,* 281–290.

Blackburn, J. A. (1984). The influence of personality, curriculum, and memory correlates on formal reasoning in young adults and elderly persons. *Journal of Gerontology, 39,* 207–209.

Blackburn, J. A., Papalia-Finley, D., Foye, B. F., & Serlin, R. C. (1988). Modifiability of figural relations performance among elderly adults. *Journal of Gerontology, 43,* 87–89.

Blanding, F. H. (1982). *Pulse point plan.* New York: Random House.

Blechman, E. A. (1982, February). Are children with one parent at psychological risk? A methodological review. *Journal of Marriage and the Family, 44,* 179–195.

Blinn, L. M. (1987). Phototherapeutic intervention to improve self-concept and prevent repeat pregnancies among adolescents. *Family Relations, 36,* 252–257.

Blinn, L. M. (1990). Adolescent mothers' perceptions of their work lives in the future: Are they stable? *Journal of Adolescent Research, 5,* 206–221.

Bloch, D. P. (1989). Using career information with drop-outs and at-risk youth. *Career Development Quarterly, 38,* 160–171.

Block, C. R., Norr, K. L., Meyering, S., Norr, J., & Charles,

A. G. (1981, April). Husband gatekeeping in childbirth. *Family Relations, 30*, 197–204.

Block, J., Block, J. H., & Keyes, S. (1988). Longitudinally foretelling drug usage in adolescence: Early childhood personality and environmental precursors. *Child Development, 59*, 336–355.

Bloom, L., Merkin, S., & Wooten, J. (1982). Wh-Questions: Linguistic factors that contribute to the sequence of acquisition. *Child Development, 53*, 1084–1092.

Blos, P. (1979). *The adolescent passage: Developmental issues.* New York: International University Press.

Blumenthal, L. (1980, July 25). Upsurge in violence, stress, blamed on eruptions. *Seattle Times*, A1.

Blyth, D. A. et al. (1978, July). The transition into early adolescence: A longitudinal comparison of youth in two educational contexts. *Sociology of Education, 51*, 149–162.

Blyth, D. A., Bulcroft, R., & Simmons, R. G. (1981, August). *The impact of puberty on adolescents: A longitudinal study.* Paper presented at the annual meeting of the American Psychological Association, Los Angeles, CA.

Blyth, D. A., Hill, J. P., & Thiel, K. S. (1982). Early adolescents' significant others: Grade and gender differences in perceived relationships with familial and non-familial adults and young people. *Journal of Youth and Adolescence, 11*, 425–450.

Boeckman, C. (1979). Your health as you get older. *Dynamic Years, 14*, 24–27.

Boivin, M., & Begin, G. (1989). Peer status and self-perceptions among early elementary school children: The case of the rejected children. *Child Development, 60*, 571–579.

Boldizar, J. P., Perry, D. G., & Perry, L. C. (1989). Outcomes, values and aggression. *Child Development, 60*, 591–596.

Bolla-Wilson, K., & Bleecker, M. L. (1989). Absence of depression in elderly adults. *Journal of Gerontology, 44*, 53–55.

Bongaarts, J. (1982). Infertility after age 30: A false alarm. *Family Planning Perspectives, 14*, 75–78.

Booth, A., & Edwards, J. N. (1985). Age at marriage and marital instability. *Journal of Marriage and the Family, 47*, 67–75.

Borkan, G. A., & Norris, A. H. (1980). Assessment of biological age using a profile of physical parameters. *Journal of Gerontology, 35*, 177–184.

Bornstein, M. H. (1985a). How infant and mother jointly contribute to developing cognitive competence in the child. *Proceedings of the National Academy of Sciences of the U.S.A., 82*, 7470–7473.

Bornstein, M. H. (1985b). Human infant color vision and color perception. *Infant Behavior and Development, 8*, 109–113.

Bornstein, M. H. (1987). *Sensitive periods of development.* Hillsdale, NJ: Erlbaum.

Bornstein, M. H., & Sigman, M. D. (1986). Continuity in mental development from infancy. *Child Development, 57*, 251–274.

Borovsky, D., & Rovee-Collier, C. (1990). Contextual constraints on memory retrieval at six months. *Child Development, 61*, 1569–1583.

Borson, S., Barnes, R. A., Kukull, W. A., Okimoto, J. T., Veith, R. C., Inui, T. S., Carter, W., & Raskind, M. A. (1966). Symptomatic depression in elderly medical outpatients: I. Prevalence, demography, and health service utilization. *Journal of the American Geriatrics Society, 34*, 341–347.

Borson, S., Barnes, R. F., Veith, R. C., Halter, J. B., & Raskind, M. A. (1989). Impaired sympathetic nervous system response to cognitive effort in early Alzheimer's disease. *Journal of Gerontology, 44*, M8–M12.

Borstelmann, L. J. (1983). Children before psychology: Ideas about children from antiquity to the late 1800s. In P. H.

Mussen (Ed.), *Handbook of child psychology* (4th ed., Vol. 1). New York: Wiley.

Boss, P. B. (1987). Family stress. In M. B. Sussman & S. K. Steinmetz (Eds.), *Handbook of marriage and the family* (pp. 695–723). New York: Plenum.

Boss, P. B. (1980). Normative family stress: Family boundary changes across the life span. *Family Relations, 29*, 459–465.

Bosse, R., Aldwin, C. M., Levenson, M. R., & Workman-Daniels, K. (1991) How stressful is retirement? Findings from the normative aging study. *Journal of Gerontology, 46*, P9–P14.

Boston Women's Health Book Collective. (1984). *The new our bodies, ourselves.* New York: Simon & Schuster.

Botwinick, J. (1967). *Cognitive processes in maturity and old age* (1st ed.). New York: Springer-Verlag.

Botwinick, J. (1978). *Cognitive processes in maturity and old age* (2nd ed.). New York: Springer-Verlag.

Botwinick, J. (1984). *Cognitive processes in maturity and old age* (3rd ed.). New York: Springer-Verlag.

Botwinick, J., & Storandt, M. (1974). *Memory related functions and age.* Springfield, IL: Charles C. Thomas.

Botwinick, J., & Storandt, M. (1980). Recall and recognition of old information in relation to age and sex. *Journal of Gerontology, 35*, 70–76.

Bouchard, T. J., Jr. (1984). Twins reared together and apart: What they tell us about human diversity. In S. W. Fox (Ed.), *Individuality and determinism: Chemical and biological bases* (pp. 147–184). New York: Plenum.

Bouchard, T. J., Jr., & McGue, M. (1981). Familial studies of intelligence: A review. *Science, 212*, 1055–1059.

Boulton, M. J., & Smith, P. K. (1990). Affective bias in children's perceptions of dominance relationships. *Child Development, 61*, 221–229.

Bound, J., Duncan, G. J., Laren, D. S., & Oleinick, L. (1991). Poverty dynamics in widowhood. *Journal of Gerontology, 46*, S115–S124.

Bowlby, J. (1969). *Attachment and loss: Vol. 1. Attachment.* London: Hogarth.

Bowlby, J. (1971). *Child care and the growth of love.* Baltimore, MD: Pelican Books.

Bowlby, J. (1973). *Attachment and loss: Vol. 2. Separation.* London: Hogarth.

Bowlby, J. (1980). *Attachment and loss: Vol. 3. Loss, sadness, and depression.* London: Hogarth.

Bowlby, J. (1982). *Attachment and loss: Vol. 1. Attachment* (2nd ed.). London: Hogarth.

Bowling, A., & Browne, P. D. (1991). Social networks and emotional well-being among the oldest old in London. *Journal of Gerontology, 46*, S20–S32.

Boyarsky, R., & Boyarsky, S. (1983). Psychogenic factors in male infertility: A review. *Medical Aspects of Human Sexuality, 17*, 86H–86T.

Bozzi, V. (1985). Body talk. *Psychology Today, 19*, 20.

Bozzi, V. (1986). The stress alibi won't fly. *Psychology Today, 20*, 14.

Brackenridge, C. J. (1981). Daily variation and other factors affecting the occurrence of cerebrovascular accidents. *Journal of Gerontology, 36*, 176–179.

Bradburn, N. M. (1969). *The structure of psychological well-being.* Chicago, IL: Aldine.

Branch, L. G., Guralnik, J. M., Foley, D. J., Kohout, F. H., Wetle, T. T., Ostfeld, A., & Katz, S. (1991). Active life expectancy for 10,000 Caucasian men and women in three communities. *Journal of Gerontology, 26*, M145–M150.

Brand, E., & Clingempell, W. G. (1987). Interdependence of marital and stepparent-stepchild relationships and children's psychological adjustments: Research findings and clinical implications. *Family Relations, 36*, 140–145.

Braun, J. (1975, November 23). The struggle for acceptance of a new birth technique. *Parade.*

Brazelton, T. B. (1974). *Toddlers and parents.* New York: Delacorte Press.

Brazelton, T. B. (1983). *Infants and mothers.* New York: Delacorte Press.

Brazelton, T. B. (1984). *Neonatal behavior assessment scale.* Philadelphia, PA: Lippincott.

Brazelton, T. B. (1990). Saving the bathwater. *Child Development, 61,* 1661–1671.

Bready, J. W. (1926). *Lord Shaftesbury and social industrial progress.* London: Allen & Unwin.

Breault, K. D., & Kposowa, A. J. (1987). Explaining divorce in the United States: A study of 3,111 counties, 1980. *Journal of Marriage and the Family, 49,* 549–558.

Breckenridge, J. N., Gallagher, D., Thompson, L. W., & Peterson, J. (1986). Characteristic depressive symptoms of bereaved elders. *Journal of Gerontology, 41,* 163–168.

Bredekamp, S. (Ed.). (1987). *Developmentally appropriate practice* (pp. 50, 51). Washington, DC: National Association for the Education of Young Children.

Brennan, T. G., & O'Loideain, D. S. (1980, February). A comparison of normal and disturbed adolescents offer self-image questionnaire responses in an Irish cultural setting. *Journal of Youth and Adolescence, 9,* 11–18.

Brickfield, C. F. (1980, September–October). Can age discrimination laws be enforced? *Dynamic Years, 15,* 48.

Bridges, L. H., Connell, J. P., & Belsky, J. (1988). Similarities and differences in infant-mother and infant-father interaction in the strange situation: A composite process analysis. *Developmental Psychology, 24,* 92–100.

Bridgwater, C. A. (1982). Second marriages fare better with childless husbands. *Psychology Today, 16,* 18.

Britton, S., Chir, B., Fitzhardinge, P., & Ashby, S. (1981). Is intensive care justified for infants weighing less than 801 grams at birth? *Journal of Pediatrics, 99,* 939–943.

Broberg, A., Lamb, M. E., & Hwang, P. (1990). Inhibition: Its stability and correlates in sixteen- to forty-month-old children. *Child Development, 61,* 1153–1163.

Broderick, C. B. (1984). *Marriage and the family* (2nd ed.). Englewood Cliffs, NJ: Prentice-Hall.

Brodsky, M. A., & Allen, B. J. (1988). Stress-related sudden cardiac death. *Medical Aspects of Human Sexuality, 22,* 82–94.

Brody, C. J., & Steelman, L. C. (1985, May). Sibling structure and parental sex-typing of children's household tasks. *Journal of Marriage and the Family, 47,* 265–273.

Brody, G. G., & Stoneman, Z. (1983). The influence of television viewing on family interaction. *Journal of Family Issues, 4,* 329–348.

Brody, J. (1981, March 10). Sperm count found especially vulnerable to environment. *New York Times,* p. C1.

Brody, L., Zelago, P. R., & Chaike, M. (1984). Habituation-dishabituation to speech in the neonate. *Developmental Psychology, 20,* 114–119.

Brodzinsky, D. M. (1985). On the relationship between cognitive styles and cognitive structures. In E. Neimark & R. DeLisi (Eds.), *Moderators of competence.* Hillsdale, NJ: Erlbaum.

Bromley, D. B. (1974). *The psychology of human aging.* New York: Penguin Books.

Brone, R. J., & Fisher, C. B. (1988). Determinants of adolescent obesity: A comparison with anorexia nervosa. *Adolescence, 23,* 155–169.

Bronfenbrenner, U. (1977). Toward an experimental ecology of human development. *American Psychologist, 32,* 513–521.

Bronfenbrenner, U. (1979). *The ecology of human development.* Cambridge, MA: Harvard University Press.

Bronfenbrenner, U. (1987, August). *Recent advances in theory and design.* Paper presented at the meeting of the American Psychological Association, New York.

Bronson, G. (1977, March 1). Long exposure to waste anesthetic gas in peril to workers, United States safety unit says. *Wall St. Journal,* p. 10.

Bronson, G. W. (1991). Infant differences in rate of visual encoding. *Child Development, 62,* 44–54.

Brouwers, M. (1988). Depressive thought content among female college students with bulimia. *Journal of Counseling and Development, 66,* 425–428.

Brown, A. L., Bransford, J. D., Ferrara, R. A., & Champione, J. C. (1983). Learning, remembering, and understanding. In P. H. Mussen (Ed.), *Handbook of child psychology* (4th ed., Vol. 3). New York: Wiley.

Brown, J. E., & Mann, L. (1990). The relationship between family structure and process variables and adolescent decision making. *Journal of Adolescence, 13,* 25–38.

Brownell, C. A. (1990). Peer social skills in toddlers: Competencies and constraints illustrated by same-age and mixed-age interaction. *Child Development, 61,* 838–848.

Brownell, C. A., & Carriger, M. S. (1990). Changes in cooperation and self-other differentiation during the second year. *Child Development, 61,* 1164–1174.

Brownell, K. D. (1982). Obesity: Understanding and treating a serious, prevalent and refractory disorder. *Journal of Consulting and Clinical Psychology, 50,* 820–840.

Brownell, K. D. (1988). Yo-yo dieting. *Psychology Today, 22,* 20–23.

Brownell, K. D. (1989). When and how to diet. *Psychology Today, 23,* 40–46.

Bruce, P. R., & Herman, J. F. (1986). Adult age differences in spatial memory: Effects of distinctiveness and repeated experience. *Journal of Gerontology, 41,* 774–777.

Buchanan, C. M. (1991). Pubertal status in early-adolescent girls: Relations to moods, energy, and restlessness. *Journal of Early Adolescence, 11,* 185–200.

Buhler, C. (1935). The curve of life as studied in biographies. *Journal of Applied Psychology, 19,* 405–409.

Buhler, C. (1977). Meaningfulness of the biographical approach. In L. R. Allman & D. T. Jaffe (Eds.), *Readings in adult psychology: Contemporary perspectives* (pp. 20–27). New York: Harper & Row.

Buhler, C., & Massarik, F. (1968). *The course of human life: A study of goals in the humanistic perspective.* New York: Springer.

Buhrmester, D. (1990). Intimacy of friendships, interpersonal competence, and adjustment during preadolescence and adolescence. *Child Development, 61,* 1101–1111.

Buhrmester, D., & Furman, W. (1987). The development of companionship and intimacy. *Child Development, 58,* 1101–1113.

Buhrmester, D., & Furman, W. (1990). Perceptions of sibling relationships during middle childhood and adolescence. *Child Development, 61,* 1387–1398.

Bullock, M. (1985). Animism in childhood thinking: A new look at an old question. *Developmental Psychology, 21,* 217–225.

Bullough, V. L. (1981). Age at menarche: A misunderstanding. *Science, 213,* 365–366.

Burden, D. S. (1986). Single parents and the work setting: The impact of multiple job and homelife responsibilities. *Family Relations, 35,* 37–43.

Burger, P. C., & Vogel, F. S. (1973). The development of the pathologic changes of Alzheimer's disease and the senile dementia in patients with Down's syndrome. *American Journal of Pathology, 73,* 457–468.

Bus, A. B., & Ijzendoorn, M. H. (1988). Mother-child interaction, attachment, and emergent literacy: A cross-sectional study. *Child Development, 59,* 1262–1272.

Bushnell, H. (1888). *Christian nurture.* New Haven, CT: Yale University Press.

Buss, A. H., & Plomin, R. (1984). *Temperament: Early developing personality traits.* Hillsdale, NJ: Erlbaum.

Butcher, J. (1986). Longitudinal analysis of adolescent girls' aspirations at school and perceptions of popularity. *Adolescence, 21,* 133–143.

Butler, R. N. (1980). The alliance of advocacy with science, Kent lecture—1979. *Gerontologist, 20,* 154–162.

Butler, R. N. (1983, July/August). A generation at risk: When the baby boomers reach golden pond. *Across the Boards,* 37–45.

Butler, R. N. (1990). The effects of mastery and competitive conditions on self-assessment at different ages. *Child Development, 61,* 201–210.

Buunk, B. (1982). Strategies of jealousy: Styles of coping with extramarital involvement of the spouse. *Family Relations, 31,* 13–18.

Bynner, J. M., O'Malley, P. M., & Bachman, I. G. (1981, December). Self-esteem and delinquency revisited. *Journal of Youth and Adolescence, 10,* 407–441.

Cadkin, A., Ginsberg, N., Pergament, E., & Verlinski, Y. (1984). Chorionic villi sampling: A new technique for detection of genetic abnormalities in the first trimester. *Radiology, 151,* 159–162.

Cadman, D., Gafni, A., & McNamee, J. (1984). Newborn circumcision: An economic perspective. *Canadian Medical Association Journal, 131,* 1353–1355.

Caggiula, A. R., & Hoebel, B. G. (1966). Copulation-record site in the posterior hypothalamus. *Science, 153,* 1284–1285.

Cairns, R. B., Cairns, B. D., & Neckerman, H. J. (1989). Early school dropout: Configuration and determinants. *Child Development, 60,* 1436–1452.

Calabrese, L. H., Kirkendall, D. T., Floyd, M. et al. (1983). Menstrual abnormalities, nutritional patterns and body composition in female classic ballet dancers. *Physicians' Sports Medicine, 11,* 86.

Calderone, M. S. (1983). Fetal erection and its message to us. *SIECUS Report, II*(5/6), 9–16.

Campbell, F. A., Breitmayer, B., & Ramey, C. T. (1986). Disadvantaged single teenage mothers and their children: Consequences of free educational day care. *Family Relations, 35,* 63–68.

Campos, J., Barrett, K. C., Lamb, M. E., Goldsmith, H., & Stenberg, C. (1983). Socioemotional development. In P. H. Mussen, M. M. Haith, & J. J. Campos (Eds.), *Handbook of child psychology: Vol. 2. Infancy and developmental psychobiology.* New York: Wiley.

Capelli, C. A., Nakagawa, N., & Madden, C. M. (1990). How children understand sarcasm: The role of context and intonation. *Child development, 61,* 1824–1841.

Caplan, F. (1973). *The first twelve months of life.* New York: Grosset & Dunlap.

Capuzzi, D., & Lecoq, L. L. (1983, December). Social and personal determinants of adolescent use and abuse of alcohol and marijuana. *Personnel and Guidance Journal, 62,* 199–205.

Carey, R. G., & Posavac, E .J. (1978–1979). Attitudes of physicians on disclosing information to and maintaining life for terminal patients. *Omega: Journal of Death and Dying, 9,* 67–77.

Carey, S. (1977). The child as word learner. In M. Halle, J. Bresman, & G. A. Miller (Eds.), *Linguistic theory and psychological reality.* Cambridge, MA: MIT Press.

Cargan, L. (1981). Singles: An examination of two stereotypes. *Family Relations, 30,* 377–385.

Cargan, L., & Melko, M. (1982). *Singles: Myths and realities.* Beverly Hills, CA: Sage.

Carliste, E. R. (1984, Fall). The effect of a twelve-week dropout intervention program. *Adolescence, 19,* 649–657.

Carlson, J. S. (1973). *Cross-cultural Piagetian studies: What can they tell us?* Paper presented at the biennial meeting of the International Society for the Study of Behavioral Development, Ann Arbor, MI.

Carmines, E. G., & Baxter, D. J. (1986). Race, intelligence, and political efficacy among school children. *Adolescence, 22,* 437–442.

Carp, F. M., & Carp, A. (1983). Structural stability of well-being factors across age and gender, and development of scales of well-being unbiased for age and gender. *Journal of Gerontology, 28,* 572–581.

Carroll, B. J. (1983). Neuroendocrine diagnosis of depression: The dexamethasone suppression test. In P. J. Clayton & J. E. Barrett (Eds.), *Treatment of depression: Old controversies and new approaches.* New York: Raven Press.

Carroll, C., & Miller, D. (1982). *Health: The science of human adaptation* (3rd ed.). Dubuque, IA: Wm. C. Brown.

Carruth, B. R., & Goldberg, D. L. (1990). Nutritional issues of adolescents: Athletics and the body image mania. *Journal of Early Adolescence, 10,* 122–140.

Casas, J. M., & Ponterotto, J. G. (1984, February). Profiling an invisible minority in higher education: The Chicano. *Personnel and Guidance Journal, 62,* 349–353.

Cash, T. F., & Butters, J. W. (1988). Poor body image: Helping the patient to change. *Medical Aspects of Human Sexuality, 22,* 67–70.

Cash, T. F., & Janda, L. H. (1984, December). The eye of the beholder. *Psychology Today, 18,* 46–52.

Cash, T. F., Winstead, B. A., & Janda, L. H. (1986). The great American shape-up. *Psychology Today, 20,* 30–37.

Cassidy, J. (1986). The ability to negotiate the environment: An aspect of infant competence as related to quality of attachment. *Child Development, 57,* 331–337.

Casto, G., & Mastropieri, M. A. (1986). The efficacy of early intervention programs: A meta-analysis. *Exceptional Children, 52,* 417–424.

Cattell, R. B. (1963). Theory of fluid and crystallized intelligence: A critical experiment. *Journal of Educational Psychology, 54,* 1–22.

Cavanaugh, J. C., Dunn, N. J., Mowery, C., Feller, C., Niederehe, G., Bruge, E., & Volpendesta, D. (1989). *Gerontologist, 29,* 156–159.

Center for Science in the Public Interest. (1990). *CSPI's fast food eating guide.* Washington, DC: CSPI.

Centers for Disease Control. (1983, January 14). *Morbidity and mortality weekly report* (Vol. 32, No. 1). Atlanta, GA: CDC.

Cernoch, J. M., & Porter, R. H. (1985). Recognition of maternal axillary odors by infants. *Child Development, 56,* 1593–1598.

Chance, P. (1988). Testing education. *Psychology Today, 22,* 20–21.

Chance, P. (1989). Kids without friends. *Psychology Today, 23,* 29–31.

Chase-Lansdale, P. L., & Owen, M. T. (1987). Maternal employment in a family context: Effects on infant-mother and infant-father attachments. *Child Development, 58,* 1505–1512.

Chasnoff, I. J., Burns, W. J., Schnoll, S. H., & Burns, K. A. (1985). Cocaine use in pregnancy. *New England Journal of Medicine, 313,* 666–669.

Chassin, L. C., & Young, R. D. (1981, Fall). Salient self-conceptions in normal and deviant adolescents. *Adolescence, 16*, 613–620.

Chen, Y. (1987). Making assets out of tomorrow's elderly. *Gerontologist, 27*, 410–417.

Cherlin, A., & McCarthy, J. (1985). Remarried couple households: Data from the June 1980 current population survey. *Journal of Marriage and the Family, 47*, 23–30.

Cherry, K. E., & Park, D. C. (1989). Age-related differences in three-dimensional spatial memory. *Journal of Gerontology, 44*, 16–22.

Chess, S., & Thomas, A. (1986). *Temperament in clinical practice.* New York: Guilford.

Chess, T. A. (1984). The genesis and evolution of behavioral disorders: From infancy to early adult life. *American Journal of Psychiatry, 141*, 1.

Chiam, H. (1987). Changes in self-concept during adolescence. *Adolescence, 16*, 613–620.

Childers, J. S., Durham, R. W., Bolen, L. M., & Taylor, L. H. (1985). A predictive validity study of the Kaufman Assessment Battery for children taking the California Achievement Test. *Psychology in the Schools, 22*, 29–33.

Children's Defense Fund (1988). *A children's defense budget.* Washington, DC: Children's Defense Fund.

Chira, S. (1984, February 11). Town experiment cuts TV. *New York Times.*

Chiriboga, D. A. (1978). Evaluated time: A life course perspective. *Journal of Gerontology, 33*, 388–393.

Chiu, L. H. (1987). Development of the Self-esteem Rating Scale for Children (revised). *Measurement and Evaluation in Counseling and Development, 20*, 36–41.

Chiu, L. H. (1988). Measures of self-esteem of school-age children. *Journal of Counseling and Development, 66*, 298–301.

Chiu, L. H. (1990). The relationship of career goal and self-esteem among adolescents. *Adolescence, 25*, 593–598.

Chollar, S. (1988a). Older brains don't fade away. *Psychology Today, 22*, 22.

Chollar, S. (1988b, April). Food for thought. *Psychology Today, 22*, 30–34.

Chollar, S. (1988c, December). Stuttering: The parental influence. *Psychology Today, 22*, 12–16.

Chomsky, N. (1968). *Language and mind.* New York: Harcourt, Brace, World.

Chomsky, N. (1980). *Rules and representations.* New York: Columbia University Press.

Christmon, K. (1990). Parental responsibility of African-American unwed adolescent fathers. *Adolescence, 25*, 645–654.

Christopher, F. S. (1988). An initial investigation into a continuum of premarital sexual pressure. *Journal of Sex Research, 25*, 255–266.

Christopher, F. S., Fabes, R. A., & Wilson, P. M. (1989). Family television viewing and implications for family life education. *Family Relations, 38*, 210–214.

Chugani, H. T., & Phelps, M. E. (1986). Maturational changes in cerebral function in infants determined by FFG positron emission tomography. *Science, 231*, 840–843.

Chun, P. K. L. (1988). Angina pectoris. *Medical Aspects of Human Sexuality, 22*, 65–66.

Cicirelli, V. G. (1980). A comparison of college women's feelings toward their siblings and parents. *Journal of Marriage and the Family, 78*, 111–118.

Clark, E. V. (1983). Meaning and concepts. In P. H. Mussen (Ed.), *Handbook of child psychology* (4th ed., Vol. 4). New York: Wiley.

Clark, E. V., Gelman, S. A., & Lane, N. M. (1985). Compound nouns and category structure in young children. *Child Development, 56*, 84–94.

Clark, M. (1980). The poetry of aging: Views of old age in contemporary American poetry. *Gerontologist, 20*, 188–191.

Clark, M. L., Cheyne, J. A., Cunningham, C. E., & Siegel, L. S. (1988). *Journal of Abnormal Child Psychology, 16*, 1–15.

Clark-Lempers, D. S., Lempers, J. D., & Ho, C. (1991). Early, middle, and late adolescents' perceptions of their relationships with significant others. *Journal of Adolescent Research, 6*, 296–315.

Clemens, A. W., & Axelson, L. J. (1985). The not-so-empty nest: The return of the fledgling adult. *Family Relations, 34*, 259–264.

Cloutier, R., & Goldschmid, M. L. (1976, December). Individual differences in the development of formal reasoning. *Child Development, 47*, 1097–1102.

Coates, D. L., & Lewis, M. (1984). Early mother-infant interaction and infant cognitive status as predictors of school performance and cognitive behavior in six-year-olds. *Child Development, 55*, 1219–1230.

Cockburn, J., & Smith, P. T. (1991). The relative influence of intelligence and age on everyday memory. *Journal of Gerontology, 46*, P31–P36.

Cohn, D. A. (1990). Child–mother attachment of six-year-olds and social competence at school. *Child Development, 61*, 152–162.

Coie, J. D., & Dodge, K. A. (1988). Multiple sources of data on social behavior and social status in the school: A cross-age comparison. *Child Development, 59*, 815–829.

Cok, F. (1990). Body image satisfaction in Turkish adolescents. *Adolescence, 25*, 409–414.

Cole, D. (1988). Grief lessons: His and hers. *Psychology Today, 22*, 60–61.

Coleman, M., & Ganong, L. H. (1990). Remarriage and step-family research in the 1980s: Increased interest in an old family form. *Journal of Marriage and the Family, 52*, 925–940.

Coleman, M., Ganong, L. H., Clark, J. M., & Madsen, R. (1989). Parenting perceptions in rural and urban families. *Journal of Marriage and the Family, 51*, 329–335.

Coll, C. T. G. (1990). Developmental outcome of minority infants: A process-oriented look into our beginnings. *Child Development, 61*, 270–289.

Colletta, N. D. (1985). Stressful lives: The situation of divorced mothers and their children. *Journal of Divorce, 6*, 19–31.

Collins, J. A., Wrixon, W., Janes, L. B., & Wilson, E. H. (1983). Treatment-independent pregnancy among infertile couples. *New England Journal of Medicine, 309*, 1201–1209.

Collins, J. D. (1981, June). Self-recognition of the body and its part during late adolescence. *Journal of Youth and Adolescence, 10*, 243–254.

Collins, J. D, & Propert, D. S. (1983, Winter). A developmental study of body recognition in adolescent girls. *Adolescence, 18*, 767–774.

Commons, M. L., Richards, F. A., & Kuhn, D. (1982). Systematic and metasystematic reasoning: A case for level of reasoning beyond Piaget's stage of formal operations. *Child Development, 53*, 1058–1069.

Communicable disease summary. (1985, November). *AIDS update* (Vol. 34, pp. 1–3). Oregon Health Division.

Connidis, I. A., & Davies, L. (1990). Confidants and companions in later life: The place of family and friends. *Journal of Gerontology, 45*, S141–S149.

Connors, C. K. (1980). *Food additives and hyperactive children.* New York: Plenum.

Conway, J. (1978). *Men in mid-life crisis.* Elgin, IL: David C. Cook.

Cook, K. V., Reiley, K. L., Stallsmith, R., & Garretson, H. B.

(1991). Eating concerns on two Christian and two non-sectarian college campuses: A measure of sex and campus differences in attitudes toward eating. *Adolescence, 26,* 273–286.

Cook, T. D., Appleton, H., Conner, R. F., Shaffer, A., Tamkin, G., & Weber, S. J. (1975). *Sesame Street revisited.* New York: Russell Sage Foundation.

Cooke, R. A. (1982). The ethics and regulation of research involving children. In B. B. Wolman (Ed.), *Handbook of developmental psychology.* Englewood Cliffs, NJ: Prentice-Hall.

Coombs, R. H., & Landsverk, J. (1988). Parenting styles and substance use during childhood and adolescence. *Journal of Marriage and the Family, 50,* 473–482.

Cooper, J. E., Holman, J., & Braithwaite, V. A. (1983, February). Self-esteem and family cohesion: The child's perspective and adjustment. *Journal of Marriage and the Family, 45,* 153–159.

Cooper, K. L., & Gutmann, D. L. (1987). Gender identity and ego mastery style in middle-aged pre- and post-empty nest women. *Gerontologist, 27,* 347–352.

Cooper, R. P., & Aslin, R. N. (1990). Preference for infant-directed speech in the first month after birth. *Child Development, 61,* 1584–1595.

Coopersmith, S. (1981). *Self-esteem inventories.* Palo Alto, CA: Consulting Psychologists Press.

Coopersmith, S., & Gilberts, R. (1982). *BASE: Behavioral Academic Self-Esteem.* Palo Alto, CA: Consulting Psychologists Press.

Cornelius, S. W. (1984). Classic pattern of intellectual aging: Test familiarity, difficulty, and performance. *Journal of Gerontology, 39,* 201–206.

Corrigan, R. L. (1983). The development of representational skills. In K. W. Fischer (Ed.), *Levels and transitions of childhood development. New directions for child development* (No. 21). San Francisco, CA: Jossey-Bass.

Corter, C. M. (1976, September). The nature of the mother's absence and the infant's response to brief separations. *Developmental Psychology, 12,* 428–434.

Cosand, B. J., Bourque, L. B., & Kraus, J. F. (1982, Winter). Suicide among adolescents in Sacramento County, California, 1950–1979. *Adolescence, 17,* 917–930.

Costa, P. P., Zonderman, A. B., McCrae, R. R., Cornoni-Huntley, J., Locke, B. Z., & Barbano, H. E. (1987). Longitudinal analysis of psychological well-being in a national sample: Stability of mean levels. *Journal of Gerontology, 42,* 50–55.

Cote, R. M., & Koval, J. E. (1983). Heterosexual relationship development: Is it really a sequential process? *Adolescence, 18,* 507–514.

Couch potato physique. (1989). *Psychology Today, 23,* 8.

The court edges away from Roe v. Wade. (1989). *Family Planning Perspectives, 21,* 184–187.

Covington, J. (1982, August). Adolescent deviation and age. *Journal of Youth and Adolescence, 11,* 329–344.

Cowan, M., Hellman, D., Chudwin, D., Wara, D., Chang, R., & Ammann, A. (1984). Maternal transmission of acquired immune deficiency syndrome. *Pediatrics, 73,* 382–386.

Coyne, J. C. (1987). Depression, biology, marriage, and marital therapy. *Journal of Marriage and Family Therapy, 13,* 393–407.

Crain, W. C. (1980). *Theories of development.* Englewood Cliffs, NJ: Prentice-Hall.

Creecy, R. F., Berg, W. E., & Wright, R. (1985). Loneliness among the elderly: A causal approach. *Journal of Gerontology, 40,* 487–493.

Crnie, K. A., & Greenberg, M. T. (1990). Minor parenting stresses with young children. *Child Development, 61,* 1628–1637.

Crocket, T. H., & Consentino, M. (1984). The variocele. *Fertility and Sterility, 41,* 5–11.

Crow, L. D., & Crow, H. (1965). *Adolescent, development, and adjustment* (2nd ed.). New York: McGraw-Hill.

Crown, W. H. (1985). Some thoughts on reformulating the dependency ratio. *Gerontologist, 25,* 166–171.

Crum, C., & Ellner, P. (1985). Chlamydial infections: Making the diagnosis. *Contemporary Obstetrics and Gynecology, 25,* 153–159, 163, 165, 168.

Culp, R. E., Culp, A. M., Osofsky, J. D., & Osofsky, H. J. (1991). Adolescent and older mothers' interaction patterns with their six-month-old infants. *Journal of Adolescence, 14,* 195–200.

Cumming, E., & Henry, W. (1961). *Growing old: The process of disengagement.* New York: Basic Books.

Cummings, E. M. (1987). Coping with background anger in early childhood. *Child Development, 58,* 976–984.

Cummings, E. M., Iannotti, R. J., & Zahn-Waxler, C. (1989). Aggression between peers in early childhood: Individual continuity and developmental change. *Child Development, 60,* 887–895.

Cummins, J. (1986). Empowering minority students: A framework for intervention. *Harvard Educational Review, 56,* 18–36.

Cummins, J., & Swain, M. (1986). *Bilingualism in education: Aspects of theory, research, and practice.* London: Taylor & Fry.

Cunningham, W. R., Clayton, V., & Overton, W. (1975). Fluid and crystallized intelligence in young adulthood and old age. *Journal of Gerontology, 30,* 53–55.

Curtis, S. (1977). *Genie: A psychological study of a modern-day "wild child."* New York: Academic Press.

Cushner, I. M. (1986). Reproductive technologies: New choices, new hopes, new dilemmas. *Family Planning Perspectives, 18,* 129–132.

Cutler, S. J., & Grams, A. E. (1988). Correlates of self-reported everyday memory problems. *Journal of Gerontology, 43,* S82–S90.

Cutler, W. B., Garcia, C. R., & McCoy, N. (1987). Perimenopausal sexuality. *Archives of Sexual Behavior, 16,* 225–234.

D'Odorico, L., & Franco, F. (1985). The determinants of baby talk: Relationships and context. *Journal of Child Language, 12,* 567–586.

Dalterio, S. L. (1984, November). Marijuana and the unborn. *Listen,* pp. 8–11.

Damon, W. (1983). *Social and personality development.* New York: W. W. Norton.

Daniels, J. A. (1990). Adolescent separation-individuation and family transitions. *Adolescence, 25,* 105–116.

Daniels, D., & Moos, R. H. (1990). Assessing life stressors and social resources among adolescents: Applications to depressed youth. *Journal of Adolescent Research, 5,* 268–289.

Danner, F. W., & Day, M. C. (1977, December). Eliciting formal operations. *Child Development, 48,* 1600–1606.

Darwin, C. A. (1877). A biographical sketch of an infant. *Mind, 2,* 285–294.

Darwin, C. A. (1936). *The origin of species.* New York: Modern Library. (Original work published in 1859)

Datan, N., Rodeheaver, D., & Hughes, F. (1987). Adult development and aging. *Annual Review of Psychology, 38,* 153–180.

Davidson, S. (1983). Proliferating POSSLQ. *Psychology Today, 17,* 84.

Davis, B. (1986, April 25). Survival odds are improving for even smallest "preemies." *Wall Street Journal,* p. 19.

Davis-Brown, K., & Salamon, S. (1987). Farm families in crisis:

An application of stress theory to farm family research. *Family Relations, 36,* 368–373.

Dawkins, R. L., & Dawkins, M. P. (1983, Winter). Alcohol use and delinquency among black, white, and Hispanic adolescent offenders. *Adolescence, 18,* 799–809.

Deal, J. E., Halverson, C. F., & Wampler, K. S. (1989). Parental agreement on child-rearing orientations: Relations to parental, marital, family, and child characteristics. *Child Development, 60,* 1025–1034.

Debolt, M. E., Pasley, B. K., & Kreutzer, J. (1990). Factors affecting the probability of school dropout: A study of pregnant and parenting adolescent females. *Journal of Adolescent Research, 5,* 190–205.

deBrun, S. R. (1981, Winter). The psycho-social dimensions of preadolescence. *Adolescence, 16,* 913–918.

Deci, E. L. (1985, March). The well-tempered classroom. *Psychology Today, 19,* 52–53.

Delgardo, J. M. R. (1969). *Physical control of the mind.* New York: Harper & Row.

DeLisi, R., & Staudt, J. (1980). Individual differences in college students' performance on formal operational tasks. *Journal of Applied Developmental Psychology, 1,* 201–208.

Dellas, M., & Jernigan, L. P. (1990). Affective personality characteristics associated with undergraduate ego identity formation. *Journal of Adolescent Research, 5,* 306–324.

DeMarie-Dreblow, D., & Miller, P. H. (1988). The development of children's strategies for selective attention: Evidence for a transitional period. *Child Development, 59,* 1504–1513.

DeMaris, A., & Leslie, G. R. (1984). Cohabitation with the future spouse: Its influence upon marital satisfaction and communication. *Journal of Marriage and the Family, 46,* 77–84.

Dembo, R., Dertke, M., LaVoie, L., Borders, S., Washburn, M., & Schmeidler, J. (1987). Physical abuse, sexual victimization and illicit drug use: A structural analysis among high risk adolescents. *Journal of Adolescence, 10,* 13–33.

Demo, D. H., & Acock, A. C. (1988). The impact of divorce on children. *Journal of Marriage and the Family, 50,* 619–648.

Demo, D. H., Small, S. A., & Savin-Williams, R. C. (1987). Family relations and the self-esteem of adolescents and their parents. *Journal of Marriage and the Family, 49,* 705–715.

Demos, V., & Jache, A. (1981). When you care enough: An analysis of attitudes toward aging in humorous birthday cards. *Gerontologist, 21,* 209–215.

Dempster, F. N. (1981). Memory span: Sources of individual and developmental differences. *Psychological Bulletin, 80,* 63–100.

Denham, S. A., McKinley, M., Couehoud, E. Z., & Holt, R. (1990). Emotional and behavioral predictors of preschool peer ratings. *Child Development, 61,* 1145–1152.

Denham, S. A., Renwick, S. M., & Holt, R. W. (1991). Working and playing together: Prediction of preschool social-emotional competence from mother–child interaction. *Child Development, 62,* 242–249.

Denney, N. W. (1980). Task demands and problem-solving strategies in middle-aged and older adults. *Journal of Gerontology, 35,* 559–564.

Denney, N. W., Miller, B. V., Dew, J. R., & Levav, A. L. (1991). An adult developmental study of contextual memory. *Journal of Gerontology, 46,* P44–P50.

Denney, N. W., & Palmer, A. M. (1981). Adult age differences on traditional and practical problem-solving measures. *Journal of Gerontology, 36,* 323–328.

Dennis, W. (1966). Creative productivity between the ages of 20 and 80 years. *Journal of Gerontology, 21.*

Denno, D. (1982, Winter). Sex differences in cognition: A review and critique of the longitudinal evidence. *Adolescence, 17,* 779–788.

deRosenroll, D. A. (1987). Creativity and self-trust: A field of study. *Adolescence, 22,* 419–432.

deTurck, M. A., & Miller, G. R. (1983). Adolescent perceptions of parental persuasive message strategies. *Journal of Marriage and the Family, 34,* 533–542.

Deutscher, I. (1964). The qualities of postparental life: Definitions of the situation. *Journal of Marriage and the Family, 26,* 52–59.

Diamond, A. M. (1986). The life-cycle research productivity of mathematicians and scientists. *Journal of Gerontology, 41,* 520–525.

DiBlasio, F. A., & Benda, B. B. (1990). Adolescent sexual behavior: Multivariate analysis of a social learning model. *Journal of Adolescent Research, 5,* 449–466.

Dick-Read, G. D. (1973). *Childbirth without fear.* New York: Harper & Row.

Dickstein, S., & Parke, R. D. (1988). Social referencing in infancy: A glance at fathers and marriage. *Child Development, 59,* 506–511.

Dietz, W. H., & Gortmacher, S. L. (1985). Do we fatten our children at the television set? Obesity and television watching in children and adolescents. *Pediatrics, 75,* 807–812.

Dill, D., Feld, E., Martin, J., Beukema, S., & Belle, D. (1980). The impact of the environment on the coping effects of low-income mothers. *Family Relations, 29,* 503–509.

Dillard, K. D., & Pol, L. B. (1982). The individual economic costs of teenage childbearing. *Family Relations, 31,* 249–259.

DiPietro, J. B. (1981). Rough and tumble play: A function of gender. *Developmental Psychology, 17,* 50–58.

Dishion, T. J. (1990). The family ecology of boys' peer relations in middle childhood. *Child Development, 61,* 874–892.

Dizon, J. A., & Moore, C. F. (1990). The development of perspective taking: Understanding differences in information and weighting. *Child Development, 61,* 1502–1513.

Dittmann-Kohli, F., Lachman, M. E., Kliefl, R., & Baltes, P. B. (1991). Effects of cognitive training and testing on intellectual efficacy beliefs in elderly adults. *Journal of Gerontology, 46,* P162–P165.

Doan, R. E., & Scherman, A. (1987). The therapeutic effect of physical fitness on measures of personality: A literature review. *Journal of Counseling and Development, 66,* 28–36.

Dodge, K. A., Cole, J. D., Pettit, G. S., & Price, J. M. (1990). Peer status and aggression in boys' groups: Developmental and contextual analyses. *Child Development, 61,* 1289–1309.

Dodge, K. A., & Somberg, D. R. (1987). Hostile attributional biases among aggressive boys are exacerbated under conditions of threats to self. *Child Development, 58,* 215–224.

Doherty, W. J., & Needle, R. H. (1991). Psychological adjustment and substance use among adolescents before and after a parental divorce. *Child Development, 62,* 328–337.

Dolgin, K. B., & Behrend, D. A. (1984). Children's knowledge about animates and inanimates. *Child Development, 55,* 1646–1650.

Donovan, W. L., & Leavitt, L. A. (1989). Maternal self-efficacy and infant attachment: Integrating physiology, perceptions, and behavior. *Child Development, 60,* 460–472.

Donovan, W. L., Leavitt, L. A., & Walsh, R. O. (1990). Maternal self-efficacy: Illusory control and its effect on susceptibility to learned helplessness. *Child Development, 61,* 1638–1647.

Dornbusch, S. M., Ritter, P. L., Mont-Reynaud, R., & Chen,

Z. (1990). Family decision making and academic performance in a diverse high school population. *Journal of Adolescent Research, 5,* 143–160.

Dornbusch, S. M., Carlsmith, J. M., Bushwall, S. J., Ritter, P. L., Leidman, H., Historff, A. H., & Gross, R. T. (1985). Single parents, extended households, and the control of adolescents. *Child Development, 56,* 326–341.

Dorr, A. (1986). *Television and children.* Beverly Hills, CA: Sage.

Dorval, B., & Eckerman, C. O. (1984). Developmental trends in the quality of conversation achieved by small groups of acquainted peers. *Monographs of the Society for Research in Child Development, 49*(2, Serial No. 206).

Douglas, K., & Arenberg, D. (1978). Age changes, cohort differences, and cohort change on the Guilford-Zimmerman Temperament Survey. *Journal of Gerontology, 33,* 737–747.

Dowd, J. (1980). *Stratification among the aged.* Monterey, CA: Brooks/Cole.

Dowling, C. (1983). The relative explosion. *Psychology Today, 17,* 54–59.

Downs, W. W., & Rose, S. R. (1991). The relationship of adolescent peer groups to the incidence of psychosocial problems. *Adolescence, 26,* 473–492.

Dr. Nintendo. (1990, May 28). *Time, 135,* 72.

Dreyfus, E. A. (1976). *Adolescence: Theory and experience.* Columbus, OH: Merrill.

Drug pushers go for even younger prey. (1979, August 13). *U.S. News and World Report,* p. 31.

Drug usage: America's high school students. (1988). Ann Arbor: University of Michigan Institute for Social Research, National Institute on Drug Abuse.

Dubey, D. R., O'Leary, S. G., & Kaufman, K. F. (1983). Training parents of hyperactive children in child management: A comparative outcome study. *Journal of Abnormal Child Psychology, 11,* 229–246.

DuBois, D. L., & Hirsch, B. J. (1990). School and neighborhood friendship patterns of blacks and whites in early adolescence. *Child Development, 61,* 524–536.

Dubois, P. M. (1980). *Hospice way of death.* New York: Human Sciences Press.

Dubow, E. F., Huesmann, L. R., & Eron, L. D. (1987). Childhood correlates of adult ego development. *Child Development, 58,* 859–869.

Dubroff, L. M., & Papalian, M. M. (1982, June). Syphilis and gonorrhea in pregnant patients. *Medical Aspects of Human Sexuality, 16,* 85–90.

Duffy, F. H., Als, H., & McAnulty, G. B. (1990). Behavioral and electrophysiological evidence for gestational age effects in healthy preterm and full-term infants; studies two weeks after expected due date. *Child Development, 61,* 1271–1286.

Duncan, G. J., & Rodgers, W. (1987). Single-parent families: Are their economic problems transitory or persistent? *Family Planning Perspectives, 19,* 171–178.

Dunham, P., Dunham, F., Hurshman, A., & Alexander, T. (1989). Social contingency effects on subsequent perceptual-cognitive tasks in young infants. *Child Development, 60,* 1486–1696.

Dunham, R. G., & Alpert, G. P. (1987). Keeping juvenile delinquents in school: A prediction model. *Adolescence, 23,* 45–57.

Dunn, J. (1977). *Distress and comfort.* Cambridge, MA: Harvard University Press.

Dunn, P. C., Ryan, I. J., & O'Brien, K. (1988). College students' acceptance of adoption and five alternative fertilization techniques. *Journal of Sex Research, 24,* 282–287.

Durkheim, E. (1960). *Moral education.* New York: Free Press.

Eakins, P. S. (Ed.). (1986). *The American way of birth.* Philadelphia, PA: Temple University Press.

Earl, W. L. (1987). Creativity and self-thrust: A field of study. *Adolescence, 22,* 419–432.

Easterbrooks, M. A. (1989). Quality of attachment to mother and to father: Effects of perinatal risk status. *Child Development, 60,* 825–830.

Eaton, W. O., & Yu, A. P. (1989). Are sex differences in child motor activity level a function of sex differences in maturational status? *Child Development, 60,* 1005–1011.

Eberhardt, C. A., & Schill, T. (1984). Differences in sexual attitudes and likeliness of sexual behavior of black lower-socioeconomic father-present versus father-absent female adolescents. *Adolescence, 19,* 99–105.

Edelson, E. (1991). *Aging.* New York: Chelsea House.

Eder, R. A. (1989). The emergent personologist: The structure and content of 3½, 5½, and 7½-year-olds' concepts of themselves and other persons. *Child Development, 60,* 1218–1228.

Eder, R. A. (1990). Uncovering young children's psychological selves: Individual and developmental differences. *Child Development, 61,* 849–863.

Egeland, B., & Farber, E. A. (1984). Infant-mother attachment: Factors related to its development and changes over time. *Child Development, 55,* 753–771.

Egeland, B., Jacobvitz, D., & Sroufe, L. A. (1988). Breaking the cycle of abuse. *Child Development, 55,* 1080–1088.

Egeland, B., & Vaughn, B. (1981). Failure of "bond formation" as a cause of abuse, neglect, and maltreatment. *American Journal of Orthopsychiatry, 51,* 78–84.

Ehrenberg, M. F., Cox, D. N., & Koopman, R. F. (1991). The relationships between self-efficacy and depression in adolescents. *Adolescence, 26,* 361–374.

Ehrhardt, A., & Meyer-Bahlburg, H. (1981). Effects of prenatal sex hormones on gender-related behavior. *Science, 211,* 312–318.

Ehrlich, G. E. (1988). Sexual concerns of patients with arthritis. *Medical Aspects of Human Sexuality, 22,* 104–107.

Eichorn, D. M., Hunt, J. V., & Honzik, M. P. (1981). Experience, personality, and IQ: Adolescence to middle age. In D. Eichorn, J. Clausen, N. Haan, M. Honzik, & P. H. Mussen (Eds.), *Present and past in middle life.* New York: Academic Press.

Eiger, M. S. (1987). The feeding of infants and children. In R. A. Hoekelman, S. Blotman, S. B. Friedman, N. M. Nelson, & H. M. Siedel (Eds.), *Primary pediatric care.* St. Louis, MO: Mosby.

Eiger, M. S., & Olds, S. W. (1987). *The complete book of breastfeeding.* New York: Workman.

Eisdorfer, C., Nowling, J., & Wilkie, F. (1970). Improvement of learning in the aged by modification of autonomic nervous system activity. *Science, 170,* 1327–1329.

Eisdorfer, C., & Wilkie, F. (1973). Intellectual changes with advancing age. In L. F. Jarvik, C. Eisdorfer, & J. E. Blum (Eds.), *Intellectual functioning in adults* (pp. 21–29). New York: Springer.

Eisele, J., Hertsgaard, D., & Light, H. K. (1986). Factors related to eating disorders in young adolescent girls. *Adolescence, 82,* 283–290.

Eisikovits, Z., & Sagi, A. (1982, June). Moral development and discipline encounter in delinquent and nondelinquent adolescents. *Journal of Youth and Adolescence, 11,* 217–230.

Ekman, P. (1972). Universals in cultural differences in facial expressions of emotions. In J. K. Cole (Ed.), *Nebraska symposium on motivation* (Vol. 19). Lincoln: University of Nebraska Press.

Elbaum, P. L. (1981). The dynamics, implications and treatment of extramarital sexual relationships for the family therapist. *Journal of Marital and Family Therapy, 7,* 489–495.

Elias, M. F., Robbins, M. A., Schultz, N. R., & Pierce, T. W. (1990). Is blood pressure an important variable in research on aging and neuropsychological test performance? *Journal of Gerontology, 45,* P128–P135.

Elkind, D. (1967). Egocentrism in adolescence. *Child Development, 38,* 1025–1034.

Elkind, D. (1970). *Children and adolescents: Interpretive essays on Jean Piaget.* New York: Oxford University Press.

Elkind, D. (1975). Recent research on cognitive development in adolescence. In S. E. Dragastin & G. H. Elder, Jr. (Eds.), *Adolescence in the life cycle.* New York: Wiley.

Elkind, D. (1978, Spring). Understanding the young adolescent. *Adolescence, 13,* 127–134.

Elliott, G. C. (1982, April). Self-esteem and self-presentation among the young as a function of age and gender. *Journal of Youth and Adolescence, 11,* 135–153.

Ellis, D. W., & Davis, L. T. (1982, Fall). The development of self-concept boundaries across the adolescent years. *Adolescence, 17,* 695–710.

Ellis, N. B. (1991). An extension of the Steinberg accelerating hypothesis. *Journal of Early Adolescence, 11,* 221–235.

Elsayed, M., Ismail, A. H., & Young, R. J. (1980). Intellectual differences of adult men related to age and physical fitness before and after exercise program. *Journal of Gerontology, 35,* 383–387.

Elmen, J. (1991). Achievement orientation in early adolescence: Developmental patterns and social correlates. *Journal of Early Adolescence, 11,* 125–151.

Emery, O. B., & Breslau, L. D. (1989). Language deficits in depression: Comparisons with SDAT and normal aging. *Journal of Gerontology, 44,* M85–M92.

Emery, R. (1982). Interparental conflict and the children of discord and divorce. *Psychological Bulletin, 92,* 310–330.

English, O. S., & Pearson, G. H. J. (1945). *Emotional problems of living.* New York: W. W. Norton.

Enright, R. D., Lapsley, D. K., & Shukla, D. G. (1979, Winter). Adolescent egocentrism in early and late adolescence. *Adolescence, 14,* 687–695.

Enright, R. D., Shukla, D. G., & Lapsley, D. K. (1980, April). Adolescent egocentrism—sociocentrism and self-consciousness. *Journal of Youth and Adolescence, 9,* 101–116.

Ensminger, M. E. (1990). Sexual activity and problem behaviors among black, urban adolescents. *Child Development, 61,* 2032–2046.

Entwisle, D. R., Alexander, K. L., Pallas, A. M., & Cadigan, W. (1987). The emergent academic self-image of first graders: Its response to social structure. *Child Development, 58,* 1190–1206.

Ephron, N. (1975). *Crazy salad.* New York: Alfred A. Knopf.

Erber, J. T. (1989). Young and older adults' appraisal of memory failures in young and older adult target persons. *Journal of Gerontology, 44,* P170–P175.

Erber, J. T., Botwinick, J., & Storandt, M. (1981). The impact of memory on age differences in digit symbol performance. *Journal of Gerontology, 36,* 586–590.

Erber, J. T., & Rothberg, S. T. (1991). Here's looking at you: The relative effect of age and attractiveness on judgments about memory failure. *Journal of Gerontology, 46,* P116–P123.

Erikson, E. (1950). *Childhood and society.* New York: W. W. Norton.

Erikson, E. (1959). *Identity and the life cycle.* New York: International Universities Press.

Erikson, E. (1963). *Childhood and society* (2nd ed.). New York: W. W. Norton.

Erikson, E. (1968). *Identity: Youth and crisis.* New York: W. W. Norton.

Erikson, E. (1982). *The life cycle completed.* New York: W. W. Norton.

Eron, L. D. (1987). The development of aggression from the perspective of a developing behaviorism. *American Psychologist, 42,* 435–442.

Eskilson, A., Wiley, M. G., Muehlbauer, G., & Dodder, L. (1986). Parental pressure, self-esteem, and adolescent reported deviance: Bending the twig too far. *Adolescence, 21,* 501–515.

Essex, M. J., & Nam, S. (1987). Marital status and loneliness among older women: The differential importance of close family and friends. *Journal of Marriage and the Family, 49,* 93–106.

Etaugh, C., & Malstrom, J. (1981). The effect of marital status on person perception. *Journal of Marriage and the Family, 43,* 801–805.

Evans, G. (1976). The older the sperm . . . *Ms., 5,* 48–49.

Evans, L., Eberdt, D. J., & Bosse, R. (1985). Proximity to retirement and anticipatory involvement: Findings from the normative aging study. *Journal of Gerontology, 40,* 368–374.

Eveleth, P., & Tanner, J. (1976). *Worldwide variations in human growth.* New York: Cambridge University Press.

Executive stress: Keep it at bay. (1979). *Dynamic Years, 14,* 14.

Eysenck, H. J. (1988, December). Health's character. *Psychology Today, 22,* 28–35.

Fabes, R. A., Wilson, P., & Christopher, F. S. (1989). A time to reexamine the role of television in family life. *Family Relations, 38,* 337–341.

Fagan, J. F. III. (1977, March). Infant recognition memory: Studies in forgetting. *Child Development, 48,* 68–78.

Fagot, B. I., & Kavanagh, K. (1990). The prediction of antisocial behavior from avoidant attachment classifications. *Child Development, 61,* 864–873.

Farmer, A. E., McGuffin, P., & Gottesman, I. I. (1987). Twin concordance for DSM-III schizophrenia. Scrutinizing the validity of the definition. *Archives of General Psychiatry, 44,* 634–641.

Faro, S. (1985). Chlamydia trachomatic infection in women. *Journal of Reproductive Medicine, 30*(Suppl.), 273–278.

Farrington, D. P. (1990). Implications of criminal career research for the prevention of offending. *Journal of Adolescence, 13,* 93–114.

Fasick, F. A. (1984). Parents, peers, youth culture and autonomy in adolescence. *Adolescence, 19,* 143–157.

Fauber, R., Forehand, R., Thomas, A. M., & Wierson, M. (1990). A mediational model of the impact of marital conflict on adolescent adjustment in intact and divorced families: The role of disrupted parenting. *Child Development, 61,* 1112–1123.

Feier, C. D., & Gerstman, L. J. (1980). Sentence comprehension abilities throughout the adult life span. *Journal of Gerontology, 35,* 722–728.

Fein, G. G. (1986). Pretend play. In D. Gorletz & J. F. Wohlwill (Eds.), *Curiosity, imagination, and play.* Hillsdale, NJ: Erlbaum.

Feingold, A. (1982). Do taller men have prettier girlfriends? *Psychological Reports, 50,* 810.

Feldman, H., & Feldman, M. (1975). The family life cycle: Some suggestions of recycling. *Journal of Marriage and the Family, 37,* 277–284.

Feldman, N. A., & Ruble, D. N. (1988). The effect of personal relevance on psychological inference: A developmental analysis. *Child Development, 59,* 1339–1352.

Feldman, S. S., & Wentzel, K. R. (1990). The relationship between parenting styles, sons' self-restraint, and peer relations in early adolescence. *Journal of Early Adolescence, 10,* 439–454.

Felson, M., & Gottfredson, M. (1984). Social indicators of adolescent activities near peers and parents. *Journal of Marriage and Family, 46,* 709–714.

Felson, R. B., & Zielinski, M. A. (1989). Children's self-esteem and parental support. *Journal of Marriage and the Family, 51,* 727–735.

Felton, G., & Segelman, F. (1978). Lamaze childbirth training and changes in belief about personal control. *Birth and Family Journal, 5,* 141–150.

Ferguson, T. J., & Rule, B. G. (1988). Children's evaluations of retaliatory aggression. *Child Development, 59,* 961–968.

Fernandez, R. M., & Kulik, J. C. (1981). A multilevel model of life satisfaction: Effects of individual characteristics and neighborhood composition. *American Sociological Review, 46,* 840–850.

Ferraro, K. F. (1990). Cohort analysis of retirement preparation, 1974–1981. *Journal of Gerontology, 45,* S21–S31.

Ferreiro, B. W., Warren, N. J., & Konanc, J. T. (1986). ADAP: A divorce assessment proposal. *Family Relations, 35,* 439–449.

Ferriss, L. (1989, October 30). *Women's life crisis deepens says author.* Portland, ME: Portland Press Herald.

Field, T., Healy, B., Goldstein, S., Perry, S., & Bendell, D. (1988). Infants of depressed mothers show "depressed" behavior even with nondepressed adults. *Child Development, 59,* 1569–1579.

Field, T., Woodson, R., Greenberg, R., & Cohen, D. (1982). Discrimination and imitation of facial expressions by neonates. *Science, 218,* 179–181.

Fiese, B. H. (1990). Playful relationships: A contextual analysis of mother–toddler interaction and symbolic play. *Child Development, 61,* 1648–1656.

Finchan, F. D., Hokoda, A., & Sanders, R., Jr. (1989). Learned helplessness, test anxiety, and academic achievement: A longitudinal analysis. *Child Development, 60,* 138–145.

Fincher, J. (1982). Before their time. *Science, 82.*

Fine, M. A. (1986). Perceptions of stepparents: Variation in stereotypes as a function of current family structure. *Journal of Marriage and Family, 48,* 537–543.

Fine, M. A., & Hovestadt, A. J. (1984, April). Perceptions of marriage rationality by levels of perceived health in the family of origin, *Journal of Marital and Family Therapy, 10,* 193–195.

Finkelstein, M. J., & Gaier, E. L. (1983, Spring). The impact of prolonged student status on late adolescent development. *Adolescence, 18,* 115–129.

Fischer, J. L. (1980, October). Reciprocity, agreement, and family style in family systems with a disturbed and nondisturbed adolescent. *Journal of Youth and Adolescence, 9,* 391–406.

Fischer, K. W., & Silvern, L. (1985). Stages and individual differences in cognitive development. *Annual Review of Psychology, 36,* 613–648.

Fischman, B. (1988, November). Alzheimer's: To catch a thief. *Psychology Today, 22,* 14.

Fischman, J. (1988, September). Type A situations. *Psychology Today, 22,* 22.

Fisher, J. (1988). The "fitness factor" in individual and family health: One doctor's prescription. *Medical Aspects of Human Sexuality, 22,* 45–48.

Fisher, T. D., & Hall, R. G. (1988). A scale for the comparison of the sexual attitudes of adolescents and their parents. *Journal of Sex Research, 24,* 90–100.

Fitness Finders. (1984). *Feelin' good.* Spring Arbor, MI: Fitness Finders.

Flake-Hobson, C., Skeen, P., & Robinson, B. E. (1980, April). Review of theories and research concerning sex-role development and androgyny with suggestions for teachers. *Family Relations, 29,* 155–162.

Flanagan, C. A. (1990). Change in family work status: Effects on parent–adolescent decision making. *Child Development, 61,* 163–177.

Flavell, J. H. (1985). *Cognitive development* (2nd ed.). Englewood Cliffs, NJ: Prentice-Hall.

Fleischer, B., & Read, M. (1982, Winter). Food supplement usage by adolescent males. *Adolescence, 17,* 831–845.

Flynn, T. M., & Beasley, J. (1980, Winter). An experimental study of the effects of competition on the self-concept. *Adolescence, 15,* 799–806.

Ford, M. E. (1986). *Androgyny as self-assertion and integration: Implications for psychological and social competence.* Unpublished manuscript, Stanford University School of Education, Stanford, CA.

Forrest, J. D., & Singh, S. (1990). The sexual and reproductive behavior of American women, 1982–1988. *Family Planning Perspectives, 22,* 206–214.

Forsstrom-Cohen, B., & Rosenbaum, A. (1985). The effects of parental marital violence on young adults: An exploratory investigation. *Journal of Marriage and the Family, 47,* 467–472.

Foster, J. M., & Gallagher, D. (1986). An exploratory study comparing depressed and nondepressed elders' coping strategies. *Journal of Gerontology, 41,* 91–93.

Fox, N. A., Kimmerly, N. L., & Schafer, W. D. (1991). Attachment of mother/attachment to father: A meta-analysis. *Child Development, 62,* 210–225.

Franco, J. N. (1983, January). Aptitude tests: Can we predict their future? *Personnel and Guidance Journal, 61,* 263, 264.

François, G. R. (1990). *The lifespan* (3rd ed.). Belmont, CA: Wadsworth.

Frankel, K. A., & Bates, J. E. (1990). Mother–toddler problem solving: Antecedents in attachment, home behavior, and temperament. *Child Development, 61,* 810–819.

Frankenburg, W. K., Frandal, A., Sciarillo, W., & Burgess, D. (1981). The newly abbreviated and revised Denver Developmental Screening Test. *Journal of Pediatrics, 99,* 995–999.

French, D. C. (1988). Heterogeneity of peer-rejected boys: Aggressive and nonaggressive subtypes. *Child Development, 59,* 976–985.

French, D. C. (1990). Heterogeneity of peer-rejected girls. *Child Development, 61,* 2028–2031.

Freud, A. (1946). *The ego and the mechanism of defense.* New York: International Universities Press.

Freud, S. (1917). *A general introduction to psychoanalysis.* New York: Washington Square Press.

Fried, P. A., Watkinson, B., & Willan, A. (1984). Marijuana use during pregnancy and decreased length of gestation. *American Journal of Obstetrics and Gynecology, 150,* 23–27.

Friedland, G., Saltzman, G., Rogers, M., Kahl, P., Lesser, M., Mayers, M., & Klein, R. (1986). Lack of transmission of HLTLV-III/LAV infection to household contacts of patients with AIDS or AIDS-related complex with oral candidiases. *New England Journal of Medicine, 314,* 344–349.

Friedman, H. (1974). Interrelation of two types of immediate memory in the aged. *Journal of Psychology, 87,* 177–181.

Friedman, W. J. (1991). The development of children's memory for the time of past events. *Child Development, 62,* 139–155.

Friedrich-Cofer, L., & Huston, A. C. (1986). Television violence and aggression: The debate continues. *Psychological Bulletin, 100*, 364–371.

Frisch, R. E., Gotz-Welbergen, A. V., McArthur, J. W. et al. (1981). Delayed menarche and amenorrhea of college athletes in relation to age of onset of training. *JAMA, Journal of the American Medical Association, 246*, 1599.

Fritz, D. (1978). Decision makers and the changing retirement scene. *Aging and Work*, 221–230.

Fritzsche, V., Tracy, T., Speirs, J., & Glueck, C. J. (1990). Cholesterol screening in 5,719 self-referred elderly subjects. *Journal of Gerontology, 45*, M198–M202.

Frodi, A., & Senchak, M. (1990). Verbal and behavioral responsiveness to the cries of atypical infants. *Child Development, 61*, 76–84.

Fromholdt, P., & Larsen, S. F. (1991). Autobiographical memory in normal aging and primary degenerative dementia (dementia of Alzheimer type). *Journal of Gerontology, 46*, P85–P91.

Frydenberg, E., & Lewis, R. (1991). Adolescent coping: The different ways in which boys and girls cope. *Journal of Adolescence, 14*, 119–134.

Fujimura, L. E., Weis, D. M., & Cochran, J. R. (1985, June). Suicide: Dynamics and implications for counseling. *Journal of Counseling and Development, 63*, 612–615.

Fuller, J. R., & LaFountain, M. J. (1987). Performance-enhancing drugs in sport: A different form of drug abuse. *Adolescence, 22*, 969–976.

Furman, E. (1984). Children's patterns in mourning the death of a loved one. In H. Wass & C. Corr (Eds.), *Childhood and death* (pp. 185–203). Washington, DC: Hemisphere/McGraw-Hill.

Furstenberg, F. F., & Spanier, G. (1984). *Recycling the family: Remarriage after divorce*. Beverly Hills, CA: Sage.

Gabennesch, H. (1990). The perception of social conventionality by children and adults. *Child Development, 61*, 2047–2059.

Gadow, S. (1980, December). Medicine, ethics, and the elderly. *Gerontologist, 20*, 680–685.

Gaensbauer, T., & Hiatt, S. (1984). *The psychobiology of affective development*. Hillsdale, NJ: Erlbaum.

Galda, L., & Pellegrini, A. D. (Eds.). (1985). *Play, language, and stories: The development of children's literate behavior*. Norwood, NJ: Ablex.

Gallagher, J. M., & Noppe, J. C. (1976). Cognitive development and learning. In J. F. Adams (Ed.), *Understanding adolescence* (3rd ed.). Boston, MA: Allyn & Bacon.

Gardner, B. T., & Gardner, R. A. (1971). Two-way communication within infant chimpanzee. In A. Schrier & F. Stollintz (Eds.), *Behavior of nonhuman primates* (Vol. 4). New York: Academic Press.

Gardner, B. T., & Gardner, R. A. (1986). Discovering the meaning of private signals. *British Journal for the Philosophy of Science, 27*, 477–495.

Gardner, H. (1983). *Frames of mind*. New York: Basic Books.

Gardner, L. I. (1972). Deprivation dwarfism. *Scientific American, 227*, 76–82.

Garelik, G. (1985, October). Are the progeny prodigies? *Discover Magazine, 6*, 45–47, 78–84.

Garver, D. L., & Zelman, F. P. (1986). Receptor studies in diagnosis and treatment of depression. In A. J. Rush & K. Z. Alshuler (Eds.), *Depression*. New York: Guilford.

Gavazzi, S. M., & Sabatelli, R. M. (1990). Family system dynamics, the individuation process, and psychosocial development. *Journal of Adolescent Research, 5*, 500–519.

Gaylord-Ross, R. J. (1975). Paired associate learning and formal thinking in adolescence. *Journal of Youth and Adolescence, 4*, 375–382.

Gecas, V., & Schwalbe, M. L. (1986). Parental behavior and adolescent self-esteem. *Journal of Marriage and the Family, 48*, 37–46.

Geiger, D. L. (1978). Note: How future professionals view the elderly: A comparative analysis of social work, law, and medical students' perceptions. *Gerontologist, 18*, 591–594.

Geiss, S. K., & O'Leary, K. D. (1981). Therapists ratings of frequency and severity of marital problems: Implications for research. *Journal of Marital and Family Therapy, 7*, 515–520.

Gelb, R., & Jacobson, J. L. (1988). Popular and unpopular children's interaction during cooperative and competitive peer group activities. *Journal of Abnormal Child Psychology, 16*, 247–261.

Gelles, R. J., & Conte, J. R. (1990). Domestic violence and sexual abuse of children: A review of research in the eighties. *Journal of Marriage and the Family, 52*, 1045–1058.

Gellman, E. et al. (1983). Vaginal delivery after Cesarean section. *JAMA, Journal of American Medical Association, 249*, 2935–2937.

Genesee, F. (1985). Second language learning through immersion: A review of U.S. programs. *Review of Educational Research, 55*, 541–546.

George, L., & Gwyther, L. (1984). The dynamics of caregiving burden: Changes in caregiver well-being over time. *Gerontologist, 23*, 249.

George, L. K. (1981). Subjective well-being: Conception and methodological issues. In C. Eisdorfer (Ed.), *Annual review of gerontology and geriatrics* (Vol. 2). New York: Springer.

George, L. K., & Landerman, R. (1984). Health and subjective well-being: A replicated secondary data analysis. *International Journal of Aging and Human Development, 19*, 133–136.

Gerard, L., Zacks, R. T., Hasher, L., & Radvansky, G. A. (1991). Age deficits in retrieval: The fan effect. *Journal of Gerontology, 46*, P131–P136.

Gertner, M. (1986). Short stature in children. *Medical Aspects of Human Sexuality, 20*, 36–42.

Gesell, A. (1934). *An atlas of infant behavior*. New Haven, CT: Yale University Press.

Gesell, A., & Ames, L. B. (1956). *Youth: The years from ten to sixteen*. New York: Harper & Row.

Gesell, A., & Ilg, F. L. (1943). *Infant and child in the culture of today*. New York: Harper.

Gesell, A., & Ilg, F. L. (1946). *The child from five to ten*. New York: Harper.

Ghiselli, E. E. (1966). *The validity of occupational aptitude tests*. New York: Wiley.

Gibson, R. C. (1991). The subjective retirement of black Americans. *Journal of Gerontology, 46*, S204–S210.

Gifford, V. D., & Dean, M. M. (1990). Differences in extracurricular activity participation, achievement, and attitudes toward school between ninth-grade students attending junior high school and those attending senior high school. *Adolescence, 25*, 799–802.

Gilbert, E. H., & DeBlassie, R. R. (1984, Winter). Anorexia nervosa: Adolescent starvation by choice. *Adolescence, 19*, 839–846.

Gilford, R. (1984). Contrasts in marital satisfaction throughout old age: An exchange theory analysis. *Journal of Gerontology, 39*, 325–333.

Gilger, J. W., Geary, D. C., & Eisele, L. M. (1991). Reliability and validity of retrospective self-reports of the age of pubertal onset using twin, sibling, and college student data. *Adolescence, 26*, 41–54.

Gilligan, C. (1977). In a different voice: Women's conceptions of self and of morality. *Harvard Educational Review, 47,* 481–517.

Gilligan, C. (1982). *In a different voice: Psychological theory and women's development.* Cambridge, MA: Harvard University Press.

Gilligan, C. (1984). *Remapping the moral domain in personality research and assessment.* Invited address presented to the American Psychological Association Convention, Toronto.

Gilmore, G. C., Allan, T. M., & Royer, F. L. (1986). Iconic memory and aging. *Journal of Gerontology, 41,* 183–190.

Gispert, M. (1987). Preventing teenage suicide. *Medical Aspects of Human Sexuality, 21,* 16.

Gispert, M., Wheeler, K., Marsh, L., & Davis, M. S. (1985). Suicidal adolescents: Factors in evaluation. *Adolescence, 20,* 753–762.

Giudubaldi, J., & Perry, J. D. (1985). Divorce and mental health sequelae for children. A two-year follow up of a nationwide sample. *Journal of the American Academy of Child Psychiatry, 24,* 531–537.

Glass, J. C., & Grant, K. A. (1983). Counseling in later years: A growing need. *Personnel and Guidance Journal, 62,* 210–213.

Glass, R., & Ericsson, R. (1982). *Getting pregnant in the 1980s.* Berkeley: University of California Press.

Glenn, N. D., & Kramer, K. B. (1987). The marriages and divorces of children of divorce. *Journal of Marriage and the Family, 49,* 811–825.

Glenn, N. D., & McLanahan, S. (1981). The effects of offspring on the psychological well-being of older adults. *Journal of Marriage and the Family, 43,* 409–421.

Glenn, N. D., & Weaver, C. N. (1981). The contribution of marital happiness to global happiness. *Journal of Marriage and the Family, 43,* 161–168.

Glick, P. C., & Lin, S. (1986). More young adults are living with their parents: Who are they? *Journal of Marriage and the Family, 48,* 107–112.

Gnepp, J., & Chilamkurti, C. (1988). Children's use of personality attributions to predict other people's emotional and behavioral reactions. *Child Development, 59,* 743–754.

Goff, J. L. (1990). Sexual confusion among certain college males. *Adolescence, 25,* 599–614.

Gohmann, S. F. (1990). Retirement differences among the respondents to the retirement history survey. *Journal of Gerontology, 45,* S120–S127.

Goldberg, M. (1982). Current thinking on remarriages: Commentary. *Medical Aspects of Human Sexuality, 16,* 151–158.

Goldberg, M. E., & Gorn, G. J. (1977, March). *Material vs. social preferences, parent-child relations, and the child's emotional responses.* Paper presented at the Telecommunications Policy Research Conference, Raleigh House, VA.

Goldberg, S. (1983). Parent-infant bonding: Another look. *Child Development, 54,* 331–355.

Goldman, J. A., Lerman, R. H., Contois, J. H., & Udall, J. N. (1986). Behavioral effects of sucrose on preschool children. *Journal of Abnormal Child Psychology, 14,* 565–577.

Goldman, J. A., Rosenzweig, C. M., & Lutter, A. D. (1980, April). Effect of similarity of ego identity status on interpersonal attraction. *Journal of Youth and Adolescence, 9,* 153–162.

Goldsmith, H. H. (1983). Genetic influences on personality from infancy to adulthood. *Child Development, 54,* 331–355.

Goldsmith, H. H., Buss, A. H., Plomin, R., Rothburt, M. K., Thomas, A., Chess, S., Hinde, R. A., & McCall, R. B.

(1987). Roundtable: What is temperament? Four approaches. *Child Development, 58,* 505–529.

Goldsmith, H. H., & Campos, J. J. (1990). The structure of temperamental fear and pleasure in infants: A psychometric perspective. *Child Development, 61,* 1944–1964.

Goldsmith, H. H., & Gottesman, I. I. (1981). Origins of variation in behavioral style: A longitudinal study of temperament in young twins. *Child Development, 52,* 91–103.

Goldstein, M. J. (1981, October). Family factors associated with schizophrenia and anorexia nervosa. *Journal of Youth and Adolescence, 10,* 385–405.

Goldstine, D. (1977). *The dance-away lover.* New York: Morrow.

Goleman, D. (1980, February). 1,528 little geniuses and how they grew. *Psychology Today, 13,* 28–143.

Goleman, D. (1986, December 2). Major personality study finds that traits are mostly inherited. *New York Times,* pp. 17–18.

Goleman, D. (1989, October 22). Pushing preschoolers may not be a good idea. *Maine Sunday Telegram,* p. 20.

Golinko, B. E. (1984, Fall). Adolescence: Common pathways through life. *Adolescence, 19,* 749–751.

Goodman, G. A., & Haith, M. M. (1987). Memory development and neurophysiology: Accomplishments and limitations. *Child Development, 58,* 713–717.

Goodman, M. J., Stewart, C. J., & Gilbert, F., Jr. (1977). Patterns of menopause: A study of certain medical and physiological variables among Caucasian and Japanese women living in Hawaii. *Journal of Gerontology, 32,* 291–298.

Goodwin, M. P., & Roscoe, B. (1990). Sibling violence and agonistic interactions among middle adolescents. *Adolescence, 25,* 451–468.

Goossens, F. A., & van Ijzendoorn, M. H. (1990). Quality of infants' attachments to professional caregivers: Relation to infant–parent attachment and day-care characteristics. *Child Development, 61,* 832–837.

Gordon, J. S., & Haire, D. (1981). Alternatives in childbirth. In P. Ahmed (Ed.), *Pregnancy, childbirth, and parenthood.* New York: Elsevier.

Goswami, U. (1991). Analogical reasoning: What develops? A review of research and theory. *Child Development, 62,* 1–22.

Gould, R. L. (1972). The phases of adult life: A study in developmental psychology. *American Journal of Psychiatry, 129,* 521–531.

Gould, R. L. (1978). *Transformations: Growth and change in adult life.* New York: Simon & Schuster.

Graham, S. (1986, August). *Can attribution theory tell us something about motivation in blacks?* Paper presented at the meeting of the American Psychological Association, Washington, DC.

Grande, C. G. (1988). Delinquency: The learning disabled students' reaction to academic school failure. *Adolescence, 23,* 209–219.

Grant, C. L., & Fodor, J. G. (1984, April). *Body image and eating disorders: A new role for school psychologist in screening and prevention.* Mimeographed paper, New York University, School of Education, Health, Nursing, and Arts Profession.

Grant, C. L., & Fodor, J. G. (1986). Adolescent attitudes toward body image and anorexic behavior. *Adolescence, 21,* 269–281.

Grant, E. A., Storandt, M., & Botwinick, J. (1978). Incentive and practice in the psychomotor performance of the elderly. *Journal of Gerontology, 33,* 413–415.

Graybill, D. (1978, September). Relationship of maternal child-rearing behaviors to children's self-esteem. *Journal of Psychology, 100,* 45–47.

Green, D. L. (1990). High school student employment in social context: Adolescents' perceptions of the role of part-time work. *Adolescence, 25,* 425–434.

Green, T. H., Jr. (1977). *Gynecology: Essentials of clinical practice.* Boston, MA: Little, Brown.

Greenberg, J. S., Bruess, C. E., & Sands, D. W. (1986). *Sexuality. Insights and issues.* Dubuque, IA: Wm. C. Brown.

Greenberg, M. T., & Crnie, K. A. (1988). Longitudinal predictors of developmental status and social interactions in premature and full-term infants at age two. *Child Development, 59,* 554–570.

Greenberger, E., & Steinberg, L. (1981). The work-place as a context for the socialization of youth. *Journal of Youth and Adolescence, 10,* 185–210.

Greene, A. L., & Grimsley, M. D. (1990). Age and gender differences in adolescents' preferences for parental advice: Mum's the word. *Journal of adolescent research, 5,* 396–413.

Greenfield, P. M., & Savage-Rumbaugh, E. S. (1984). Perceived variability and symbol use: A common language-cognition interface in children and chimpanzees (*Pan troglodytes*). *Journal of Comparative Psychology, 98,* 201–218.

Greenough, W. T., Black, J. R., & Wallace, C. S. (1987). Experience and brain development. *Child Development, 58,* 539–559.

Greer, D., Potts, R., Wright, J. C., & Huston, A. (1982). The effects of television commercial form and commercial placement on children's social behavior and attention. *Child Development, 53,* 611–619.

Greif, G. L. (1985). Children and housework in the single father family. *Family Relations, 34,* 353–357.

Greif, G. L. (1988). Single fathers: Helping them cope with day-to-day problems. *Medical Aspects of Human Sexuality, 22,* 18–25.

Greuling, J. W., & DeBlassie, R. R. (1980, Fall). Adolescent suicide. *Adolescence, 59,* 589–591.

Griffin, N., Chassin, L., & Young, R. D. (1981, Spring). Measurement of global self-concept versus multiple role-specific self-concepts in adolescents. *Adolescence, 16,* 49–56.

Grindstaff, C. F. (1988). Adolescent marriage and childbearing: The long-term economic outcome: Canada in the 1980s. *Adolescence, 23,* 45–58.

Grobstein, C. (1989). When does life begin? *Psychology Today, 23,* 42–46.

Grossman, J. H. (1986). Congenital syphilis. In J. L. Sever & R. L. Brent (Eds.), *Teratogen update: Environmentally induced birth defect risks.* New York: Liss.

Grotevant, H. D., Thorbecke, W., & Meyer, M. L. (1982, February). An extension of Marcia's identity status inteview into the interpersonal domain. *Journal of Youth and Adolescence, 11,* 33–47.

Gruen, R. J., Folkman, S., & Lazarus, R. S. (1988). Dyadic response patterns in married couples, depressive symptoms, and somatic dysfunction. *Journal of Family Psychology, 1,* 168–186.

Gruman, G. J. (1966). A history of ideas about the prolongation of life. The evolution of prolongevity hypothesis to 1800. *Transactions of the American Philosophical Society, 56,* Pt. 9.

Guarnera, S., & Williams, R. L. (1987). Optimism and locus of control for health and affiliation among elderly adults. *Journal of Gerontology, 42,* 594–595.

Gubrium, J. F. (1976). Being single in old age. In J. F. Gubrium (Ed.), *Times, roles and self in old age.* New York: Human Sciences Press.

Guilford, J. P. (1967). *The nature of human intelligence.* New York: McGraw-Hill.

Gullotta, T. P., Steven, S. J., Donohue, K. C., & Clark, V. S. (1981). Adolescents in corporate families. *Adolescence, 16,* 621–628.

Guralnick, M. J., & Groom, J. M. (1987). The peer relations of mildly delayed and non-handicapped preschool children in mainstream playgroups. *Child Development, 58,* 1556–1572.

Gurin, J. (1989). Leaner not lighter. *Psychology Today, 23,* 32–36.

Guthrie, D. M. (1980). *Neuroethology.* New York: Halsted Press.

Gutierrez, J., & Sameroff, A. (1990). Determinants of complexity in Mexican-American and Anglo-American mothers' conceptions of child development. *Child Development, 61,* 384–394.

Gutierrez, J., Sameroff, A. J., & Karrer, B. M. (1988). Acculturation and SES effects on Mexican American parents' concepts of development. *Child Development, 59,* 250–255.

Guttentag, R. E., & Hunt, R. R. (1988). Adult age differences in memory for imagined and performed actions. *Journal of Gerontology, 43,* P107–P108.

Guttmacher, A. F. (1983). *Pregnancy, birth and family planning* (rev. ed.). New York: New American Library.

Guttman, D. V. (1977). *A study of legal drug use by older Americans. NDA services research report.* Washington, DC: U.S. Government Printing Office.

Hadley, J. (1984, July/August). Facts about childhood hyperactivity. *Children Today,* pp. 8–13.

Hagan, P. (1983, May). Does 180 mean supergenius? *Psychology Today, 17,* 18.

Haith, M. M. (1986). Sensory and perceptual processes in early infancy. *Journal of Pediatrics, 109,* 158–171.

Hakuta, K., & Garcia, E. E. (1989). Bilingualism and education. *American Psychologist, 44,* 374–379.

Halgin, R. P., & Leahy, P. M. (1989). Understanding and treating perfectionistic college students. *Journal of Counseling and Development, 68,* 222–225.

Hall, E. G., & Lee, A. M. (1984). Sex differences in motor performances of young children: Fact or fiction? *Sex Roles, 10,* 217–230.

Hall, H. (1986). A pat on the back helps smokers quit. *Psychology Today, 20,* 20.

Hall, G. S. (1891). The contents of childrens' minds on entering school. *Pedagogical Seminary, 1,* 139–173.

Hall, G. S. (1904). *Adolescence: Its psychology and its relation to physiology, anthropology, sociology, sex, crime, religion, and education* (2 vols.). New York: Appleton.

Hall, J. A. (1987). Parent-adolescent conflict: An empirical review. *Adolescence, 22,* 767–789.

Hallfrisch, J., Muller, D., Drinkwater, D., Tobin, J., & Andres, R. (1990). Continuing diet trends in men: The Baltimore longitudinal study of aging (1961–1987). *Journal of Gerontology, 45,* M186–M191.

Halverson, H. (1940). Genital and sphincter behavior of the male infant. *Journal of Genetic Psychology, 56,* 95–136.

Hamacheck, D. E. (1976). Development and dynamics of the self. In J. F. Adams (Ed.), *Understanding adolescence* (3rd ed.). Boston, MA: Allyn & Bacon.

Hamachek, D. E. (1988). Evaluating self-concept and ego development with Erikson's psychosocial framework: A formulation. *Journal of Counseling and Development, 66,* 354–360.

Hamburger, A. C. (1988). Beauty quest. *Psychology Today, 22,* 28–32.

Hammer, T., & Vaglum, P. (1990). Use of alcohol and drugs in the transitional phase from adolescence to young adulthood. *Journal of Adolescence, 13,* 129–142.

Hamon, R. R., & Blieszner, R. (1990). Filial responsibility expectations among adult child–older parent pairs. *Journal of Gerontology, 45,* P110–P112.

Handel, A. (1980, December). Perceived change of self among adolescents. *Journal of Youth and Adolescence, 9,* 507–519.

Hansen, D., & Hill, R. (1964). Families under stress. In H. T. Cristensen (Ed.), *Handbook of marriage and the family.* Chicago, IL: Rand McNally.

Hanson, R. A. (1990). Initial parent attitudes of pregnant adolescents and a comparison with the decision about adoption. *Adolescence, 25,* 629–645.

Harding, G., & Snyder, K. (1991). Tom, Huck, and Oliver Stone as advocates in Kohlberg's just community: Theory-based strategies for moral education. *Adolescence, 26,* 319–330.

Haring-Hidore, M., Stock, W. A., Okun, M. A., & Witler, R. A. (1985). Marital status and subjective well-being: A research synthesis. *Journal of Marriage and the Family, 47,* 947–953.

Harkins, E. B. (1978). Effect of empty nest transition on self-report of psychological and physical well-being. *Journal of Marriage and the Family, 40,* 549–556.

Harkins, S. W., Chapman, C. R., & Eisdorfer, C. (1979). Memory loss and response bias in senescence. *Journal of Gerontology, 34,* 66–72.

Harris, P. L. (1983). Infant cognition. In P. H. Mussen, M. Haith, & J. J Campos (Eds.), *Handbook of child psychology* (4th ed., Vol. 2). New York: Wiley.

Harris, R. (1988). Exercise and sex in the aging patient. *Medical Aspects of Human Sexuality, 22,* 148–159.

Harris, T. G. (1989). Heart disease in retreat. *Psychology in Retreat, 23,* 46–48.

Harrison, A. O., Wilson, M. N., Pine, C. J., Chan, S. Q., & Buriel, R. (1990). Family ecologies of ethnic minority children. *Child Development, 61,* 347–362.

Hart, C. H., Ladd, G. W., & Burleson, B. R. (1990). Children's expectations of the outcomes of social strategies: Relations with sociometric status and maternal disciplinary styles. *Child Development, 61,* 127–137.

Hart, K. E. (1990). Coping with anger-provoking situations: Adolescent coping in relation to anger reactivity. *Journal of Adolescent Research, 6,* 357–370.

Harter, S. (1983). Developmental perspectives on the self system. In P. H. Mussen (Ed.), *Handbook of child psychology* (4th ed., Vol. 4). New York: Wiley.

Harter, S., & Pike, R. (1984). The pictorial scale of perceived competence and social acceptance for young children. *Child Development, 55,* 1969–1982.

Hartley, A. A. (1981). Adult age differences in deductive reasoning processes. *Journal of Gerontology, 36,* 700–706.

Hartley, A. A., & Anderson, J. W. (1983). Task complexity and problem-solving performance in younger and older adults. *Journal of Gerontology, 38,* 72–77.

Hartley, J. T., & Walsh, D. A. (1980). The effect of monetary incentive on amount and rate of free recall in older and younger adults. *Journal of Gerontology, 35,* 899–905.

Hartocollis, P. (1972). Aggressive behavior and the fear of violence. *Adolescence, 7,* 479–490.

Hartsough, C. S., & Lambert, N. M. (1985). Medical factors in hyperactive and normal children: Prenatal developmental and health history findings. *American Journal of Orthopsychiatry, 55,* 190–201.

Hartup, W. W. (1983). Peer relations. In P. H. Mussen (Ed.), *Handbook of child psychology* (4th ed., Vol. 4). New York: Wiley.

Hartup, W. W., Laursen, B., Stewart, M. I., & Eastenson, A. (1988). Conflict and the friendship relations of young children. *Child Development, 59,* 1590–1600.

Harvey, M. A. S., McRorie, M. M., & Smith, D. W. (1981). Suggested limits to the use of the hot tubs and sauna by pregnant women. *Canadian Medical Association Journal, 125,* 50–53.

Hatfield, E., & Sprecher, S. (1986). Measuring passionate love in intimate relationships. *Journal of Adolescence, 9,* 383–410.

Hauck, W. E., & Loughead, M. (1985). Adolescent self-monitoring. *Adolescence, 20,* 567–574.

Haug, M. (1978, July). Aging and the right to terminate medical treatment. *Journal of Gerontology, 33,* 586–591.

Hauser, S. T., Bornan, E. H., Jacobson, A. M., Powers, S. I., & Noam, G. G. (1991). Understanding family contexts of adolescent coping: A study of parental ego development and adolescent coping strategies. *Journal of Early Adolescence, 11,* 96–124.

Havighurst, R. J. (1972). *Developmental tasks and education* (3rd ed.). New York: David McKay.

Hay, D. F., Nash, A., & Pedersen, J. (1983). Interaction between six-month-old peers. *Child Development, 54,* 557–562.

Hayflick, L. (1970). Aging under glass. *Experimental Gerontology, 5,* 291–303.

Hayne, H., Rovee-Collier, C., & Perris, E. E. (1987). Categorization and memory retrieval by three-month-olds. *Child Development, 58,* 750–767.

Hayslip, B., & Brookshire, R. G. (1985). Relationships among abilities in elderly adults: A time lag analysis. *Journal of Gerontology, 40,* 748–750.

Hayslip, B., & Leon, J. (1988). *Geriatric care practice in hospice settings.* Beverly Hills, CA: Sage.

Hazen, N. L., & Black, B. (1989). Preschool peer communication skills: The role of social status and interaction context. *Child Development, 60,* 867–876.

Health services issues AIDS guidelines (1985, November 15). Portland, ME: Portland Press Herald.

Heatherington, L., Friedlander, M. L., & Johnson, W. F. (1989). Informed consent in family therapy research: Ethical dilemmas and practical problems. *Journal of Family Psychology, 2,* 373–385.

Heckhausen, J., & Baltes, P. B. (1991). Perceived controllability of expected psychological change across adulthood and old age. *Journal of Gerontology, 46,* P165–P173.

Heilbrun, A. B. (1984). Identification with the father and peer intimacy of the daughter. *Family Relations, 33,* 597–605.

Heilbrun, A. B., & Loftus, M. P. (1986). The role of sadism and peer pressure in the sexual aggression of male college students. *Journal of Sex Research, 22,* 320–332.

Helwig, C. C., Tisak, M. S., & Turiel, E. (1990). Children's social reasoning in context: Reply to Gabennesch. *Child Development, 61,* 2068–2078.

Hendricks, J., & Hendricks, C. D. (1986). *Aging in mass society: Myths and realities* (3rd ed.). Boston, MA: Little, Brown.

Henker, F. O. (1982, August). Men's concern about penis size. *Medical Aspects of Human Sexuality, 16,* 149.

Hepworth, J., Ryder, R. G., & Dreyer, A. S. (1984). The effects of parental loss on the formation of intimate relationships. *Journal of Marital and Family Therapy, 10,* 73–82.

Herrera, A., & Macaraeg, A. (1984). Physicians' attitudes toward circumcision. *American Journal of Obstetrics and Gynecology, 148,* 825.

Hertzog, C., Raskind, C. L., and Cannon, C. J. (1986). Age-related slowing in semantic information processing speed: An individual difference analysis. *Journal of Gerontology, 41,* 500–502.

Herzberger, S. D., & Tennen, H. (1985). The effect of self-relevance on judgments of moderate and severe disciplinary encounters. *Journal of Marriage and the Family, 47,* 311–318.

Herzog, A. R., Diokno, A. C., Brown, M. B., Normolle, D. P., & Brock, B. M. (1990). Two-year incidents, remission, and change patterns of urinary incontinence in noninstitutionalized older adults. *Journal of Gerontology, 45,* M67–M74.

Hertzler, A. A., & Grun, I. (1990). Potential nutrition message in magazines read by college students. *Adolescence, 25,* 717–724.

Heston, L. L., & Mastri, A. R. (1982). Age at onset of Pick's and Alzheimer's dementia: Implication for diagnosis and research. *Journal of Gerontology, 37,* 422–424.

Hetherington, E. M. (1989). Coping with family transitions: Winners, losers, and survivors. *Child Development, 60,* 1–14.

Hetherington, E. M., Cox, M., & Cox, R. (1979). Play and social interaction in children following divorce. *Journal of Social Issues, 35,* 26.

Hetherington, E. M., Cox, M., & Cox, R. (1982). Effects of divorce and children. In M. Lamb (Ed.), *Nontraditional families: Parenting and child development.* Hillsdale, NJ: Erlbaum.

Heymont, G. (1980, July–August). A star is reborn. *Dynamic Years, 15,* 61–64.

Hicks, M. W., & Williams, J. W. (1981, October). Current challenges in educating for parenthood. *Family Relations, 30,* 579–584.

Hier, S. J., Korboot, P. J., & Schweitzer, R. D. (1990). Social adjustment and symptomatology in two types of homeless adolescents: Runaways and throwaways. *Adolescence, 25,* 761–772.

High school profile report. (1987). Annual. Iowa City, IA: American College Testing Program.

Hill, L. M., Breckle, R., & Gehrking, W. C. (1983). The prenatal detection of congenital malformations by ultrasonography. *Mayo Clinic Proceedings, 58,* 805–826.

Hill, R. D., Storandt, M., & Simeone, C. (1990). The effects of memory skills training and incentives on free recall in older learners. *Journal of Gerontology, 45,* P227–P232.

Hiltz, S. R. (1978, November/December). Widowhood: A roleless role. *Marriage and the Family Review, 1,* 1–10.

Himelstein, S., Graham, S., & Weinter, B. (1991). An attributional analysis of maternal beliefs about the importance of child-rearing practices. *Child Development, 62,* 301–310.

Hinde, R. (1983). Ethology and child development. In P. H. Mussen (Ed.), *Handbook of child psychology* (4th ed., Vol. 2). New York: Wiley.

Hinds, M. D. (1982, May 2). Countries acting on baby formula. *New York Times,* p. 10.

Hite, S. L. (1981). *The Hite report: A nation-wide study of female sexuality.* New York: Dell.

Hite, S. L. (1982). *The Hite report on male sexuality.* New York: Ballantine.

Hjorth, C. W. (1982, April). The self-image of physically abused adolescents. *Journal of Youth and Adolescence, 11,* 71–76.

Ho, D. Y. F. (1989). Continuity and variation in Chinese patterns of socialization. *Journal of Marriage and the Family, 51,* 149–163.

Hobart, C. (1987). Parent-child relations in remarried families. *Journal of Family Issues, 8,* 259–277.

Hobart, C. (1988). The family system in remarriages: An exploratory study. *Journal of Marriage and the Family, 50,* 649–661.

Hobbs, D. F., & Wimbish, J. M. (1977). Transition to parenthood by black couples. *Journal of Marriage and the Family, 39,* 677–689.

Hock, E., McBride, S., & Gnezda, M. T. (1989). Maternal separation anxiety: Mother-infant separation from the maternal perspective. *Child Development, 60,* 793–802.

Hock, R. A., & Curry, J. F. (1983, December). Sex-role identification of normal adolescent males and females as related to school achievement. *Journal of Youth and Adolescence, 12,* 461–470.

Hodgson, J. W., & Fischer, J. L. (1978, December). Sex differences in identity and intimacy development in college youth. *Journal of Youth and Adolescence, 7,* 271–392.

Hoelter, J., & Harper, L. (1987). Structural and interpersonal family influences on adolescent self-conception. *Journal of Marriage and the Family, 49,* 129–139.

Hofer, M. A. (1981). *The roots of human behavior: An introduction to the psychology of early development.* San Francisco, CA: Freeman.

Hofferth, S., Kahn, J. R., & Baldwin, W. (1987). Premarital sexual activity among U.S. teenage women over the past three decades. *Family Planning Perspectives, 19,* 46–53.

Hoffman, V. J. (1984, Spring). The relationship of psychology to delinquency: A comprehensive approach. *Adolescence, 19,* 55–61.

Holden, G. W., & Titchie, K. L. (1991). Linking extreme marital discord, child rearing, and child behavior problems: Evidence from battered women. *Child Development, 62,* 311–327.

Holden, G. W., & West, M. J. (1989). Proximate regulation by mothers: A demonstration of how differing styles affect young children's behavior. *Child Development, 60,* 64–69.

Holding, D. H., Noonan, R. K., Pfau, H. D., & Holding, C. S. (1986). Date, attribution, age, and the distribution of lifetime memories. *Journal of Gerontology, 41,* 481–485.

Hole, J. W. (1987). *Human anatomy and physiology* (4th ed.). Dubuque, IA: Wm. C. Brown.

Holleran, P. R., Pascale, J., & Fraley, J. (1988). Personality correlates of college-age bulimics. *Journal of Counseling and Development, 66,* 378–381.

Holmbeck, G. N., & Hill, J. P. (1991). Rules, rule behaviors, and biological maturation in families with seventh-grade boys and girls. *Journal of Early Adolescence, 11,* 236–257.

Holmbeck, G. N., Waters, K. A., & Brookmen, R. R. (1990). Psychosocial correlates of sexually transmitted diseases and sexual activity in black adolescent females. *Journal of Adolescent Research, 5,* 431–448.

Holt, E. L. (1972). Energy requirements. In H. L. Barnett & A. H. Einhorn (Eds.), *Pediatrics* (15th ed.). New York: Appleton-Century-Crofts.

Hook, E. B., Cross, P. K., & Schreinemachers, D. (1983). Chromosomal abnormality rates at amnioscentesis and in liveborn infants. *JAMA, Journal of the American Medical Association, 249,* 2034–2038.

Hooker, K., & Ventis, D. G. (1984). Work ethic, daily activities, and retirement satisfaction. *Journal of Gerontology, 39,* 478–484.

Hopkins, J., Marcues, M., & Campbell, S. B. (1984). Postpartum depression: A critical review. *Psychological Bulletin, 95,* 498–515.

Hopson, J. L. (1986). The unraveling of insomnia. *Psychology Today, 22,* 62–63.

Horley, J. (1984). Life satisfaction, happiness, and morale: The problems with the use of subjective well-being indicators. *Gerontologist, 24,* 124–127.

Horn, J. C. (1986). When a parent dies. *Psychology Today, 20,* 15.

Horn, J. C (1988). The peak years. *Psychology Today, 22,* 62–63.

Horn, J. C., & Meer, J. (1987). The vintage years. *Psychology Today, 21,* 76, 77, 80–84, 88–90.

Horn, J. L., & Cattel, R. B. (1967). Age differences in fluid and crystallized intelligence. *Acta Psychologica, 26,* 107–129.

Horn, J. M. (1983). The Texas Adoption Project. *Child Development, 54,* 268–275.

Horn, M. E., & Rudolph, L. B. (1987). An investigation of verbal interaction, knowledge of sexual behavior and self-concept in adolescent mothers. *Adolescence, 87,* 591–598.

House, J. S. et al. (1979). Occupational stress and health among factory workers. *Journal of Health and Social Behavior, 20,* 139–160.

Houser, B. B., & Berkman, S. L. (1984). Aging parent/mature child relationships. *Journal of Marriage and the Family, 46,* 245–299.

Howard, D. V., Lasaga, M. I., & McAndrews, M. P. (1980). Semantic activation during memory encoding across the life span. *Journal of Gerontology, 35,* 884–890.

Howell, M. C., Allen, M. C., & Doress, P. B. (1987). Dying and death. In P. B. Doress & D. L. Siegal and the Midlife and Older Women Book Project (Eds.), *Ourselves, growing older* (pp. 392–403). New York: Simon & Schuster.

Howes, C., & Rubenstein, J. (1985). Determinants of toddler experiences in day care: Age of entry and quality of setting. *Child Care Quarterly, 14,* 140–151.

Howes, C., Unger, O., & Seidner, L. B. (1989). Social pretend play in toddlers: Parallels with social play and solitary pretend. *Child Development, 66,* 77–84.

Howes, C., & Wu, F. (1990). Peer interactions and friendships in an ethnically diverse school setting. *Child Development, 61,* 537–541.

How people will live to be 100 or more. (1983, July 4). *U.S. News and World Report, 73,* 74.

Hoyt, D. R., & Creech, J. C. (1983). The life satisfaction index: A methodological and theoretical critique. *Journal of Gerontology, 38,* 111–116.

Hoyt, D. R., Kaiser, M. A., Peters, G. R., & Babchuk, N. (1980). Life satisfaction and activity theory: A multi-dimensional approach. *Journal of Gerontology, 35,* 935–941.

Huber, C. H. (1983). Feelings of loss in response to divorce: Assessment and intervention. *Personnel and Guidance Journal, 61,* 357–361.

Hudson, L. M., & Gray, W. M. (1986). Formal operations, the imaginary audience and the personal fable. *Adolescence, 84,* 751–765.

Hudson, R. B. (1987). Tomorrow's able elders: Implications for the state. *Gerontologist, 27,* 405–409.

Huesmann, L. R., & Eron, L. D. (Eds.). (1986). *Television and the aggressive child: A cross national comparison.* Hillsdale, NJ: Erlbaum.

Hultsch, D. F. (1971). Adult age differences in free classification and free recall. *Developmental Psychology, 4,* 338–342.

Hundleby, J. D., & Mercer, G. W. (1987). Family and friends as social environments and their relationship to youth adolescents' use of alcohol and marijuana. *Journal of Marriage and the Family, 49,* 151–164.

Hunt, M. (1974a). *Sexual behavior in the 1970s.* New York: Dell.

Hunt, M. (1974b, October). Sexual behavior in the 1970s. *Playboy,* p. 204.

Hurley, D. (1985, March). Arresting delinquency. *Psychology Today, 19,* 62–68.

Hurrelmann, K., Engel, U., Holler, B., & Nordlohne, E. (1988). Failure in school, family conflicts, and psychosomatic disorders in adolescence. *Journal of Adolescence, 11,* 237–249.

Hurst, C. D., & Guldin, D. A. (1981). The effects of intra-individuals and inter-spouse status inconsistency on life satisfaction among older persons. *Journal of Gerontology, 36,* 112–121.

Huston, A. C., Siegle, J., & Bremer, M. (1983, April). *Family environment and television use by preschool children.* Paper presented at the biennial meeting of the Society for Research in Child Development, Detroit, MI.

Hyde, J. S. (1985). *Half the human experience.* Lexington, MA: D.C. Heath.

Hyland, D. T., & Ackerman, A. M. (1988). Reminiscence and autobiographical memory in the study of personal past. *Journal of Gerontology, 43,* P35–P39.

Hyson, M. C., & Izard, C. E. (1985). Continuities and changes in emotional expressions during brief separations at 13 and 18 months. *Developmental Psychology, 21,* 1065–1170.

Increasing rates of ectopic pregnancies. (1984, December). *Medical Aspects of Human Sexuality, 18,* 14.

Inhelder, B., & Piaget, J. (1958). *The growth of logical thinking from childhood to adolescence.* New York: Basic Books.

Institute for Social Research. (1985). How children use time. In *Time, goals, and well-being.* Ann Arbor: University of Michigan.

Iosub, S., Bamji, H., Stone, R. K., Gromisch, D. S., & Wasserman, E. (1987). More on human immune deficiency virus embryopathy. *Pediatrics, 80,* 512–516.

Irion, J. C, & Blanchard-Fields, F. (1987). A cross-sectional comparison of adaptive coping in adulthood. *Journal of Gerontology, 42,* 502–504.

Irving, H., Benjamin, M., & Tracme, N. (1984). Shared parenting: An empirical analysis utilizing a large Canadian data base. *Family Process, 23,* 561–569.

Isabella, R. A., & Belsky, J. (1991). Interactional synchrony and the origins of infant–mother attachment: A replication study. *Child Development, 62,* 373–384.

Ishii-Kuntz, M., & Lee, G. R. (1987). Status of the elderly: An extension of the theory. *Journal of Marriage and the Family, 49,* 413–420.

Ishiyama, F. I. (1984, Winter). Shyness: Anxious social sensitivity and self-isolating tendency. *Adolescence, 19,* 903–911.

Istvan, J. (1986). Stress, anxiety, and birth outcomes: A critical review of the evidence. *Psychological Bulletin, 100,* 331–348.

Izard, C. E. (1977). *Human emotions.* New York: Plenum.

Izard, C. E. (1980). The young infant's ability to produce discreet emotion expression. *Developmental Psychology, 16,* 132–140.

Izard, C. E., Hembree, E. A., & Huebner, R. R. (1987). Infants' emotion expressions to acute pain: Developmental change and stability of individual differences. *Developmental Psychology, 23,* 105–113.

Jacobs, J. E., & Potenza, M. (1991). The use of judgment heuristics to make social and object decisions: A developmental perspective. *Child Development, 62,* 166–178.

Jacobs, R., & Krohn, D. L. (1976). Variations of fluorescence characteristics of intact human crystalline lens segments as a function of age. *Journal of Gerontology, 31,* 641–647.

Jacobson, J. E., & Willie, D. E. (1986). The influence of attachment pattern on developmental changes in peer interaction from the toddler to the preschool period. *Child Development, 57,* 338–347.

Jacobson, J. L., Jacobson, S. W., Fein, G. G., Schwartz, P. M., & Dowler, J. K. (1984). Prenatal exposure to an environmental toxin: A test of multiple effects. *Developmental Psychology, 20,* 523–532.

Jacobvitz, D., & Sroufe, L. A. (1987). The early caregiver-child relationship and attention-deficit disorder with hyperactivity in kindergarten: A perspective study. *Child Development, 58,* 1496–1495.

Jakab, I. (1987). Growing up in the 80s: Prescriptions for raising a happy and successful child. *Medical Aspects of Human Sexuality, 21,* 53–63.

Janus, M., Burgess, A. W., & McCormack, A. (1987). Histories of sexual abuse in adolescent male runaways. *Adolescence, 22,* 405–417.

Jaquish, G. A., & Savins-Williams, R. C. (1981, December). Biological and ecological factors in the expression of adolescent self-esteem. *Journal of Youth and Adolescence, 10,* 473–485.

Jellinger, M. S., & Slovik, L. S. (1981). Current concepts in psychiatry: Divorce-input on children. *New England Journal of Medicine, 305,* 552.

Jemmott, L. S., & Jemmott, J. B. III. (1990). Sexual knowledge, attitudes, and risky sexual behavior among inner-city black male adolescents. *Journal of Adolescent Research, 5,* 346–369.

Jencks, C. (1982). Divorced mothers, unite! *Psychology Today, 16,* 73–75.

Jensen, G. F. (1986). Explaining differences in academic behavior between public-school and Catholic-school students. A quantitative case study. *Sociology of Education, 59,* 32–41.

Jensen, L., & Borges, M. (1986). The effect of maternal employment on adolescent daughters. *Adolescence, 21,* 659–666.

Johansson, B., & Berg, S. (1989). The robustness of the terminal decline phenomenon: Longitudinal data from the digit-span memory test. *Journal of Gerontology, 44,* P184–P186.

Johnsen, K. P., & Medley, M. L. (1978, September). Academic self-concept among black high school seniors: An examination of perceived agreement with selected others. *Phylon, 39,* 264–274.

Johnson, B. M., Shulman, S., & Collings, W. A. (1991). Systemic patterns of parenting as reported by adolescents: Developmental differences and implications for psychosocial outcomes. *Journal of Adolescent Research, 6,* 235–252.

Johnson, C., Lewis, C., Love, S., Lewis, L., & Stuckey, M. (1984, February). Incidence and correlates of bulimic behavior in a female high school population. *Journal of Youth and Adolescence, 13,* 15–26.

Johnson, G. M., Shontz, F. C., & Locke, T. P. (1984, Summer). Relationships between adolescent drug use and parental drug behavior. *Adolescence, 19,* 295–299.

Johnson, M. M. S. (1990). Age differences in decision making: A process methodology for examining strategic information processing. *Journal of Gerontology, 45,* P75–P78.

Johnson, R., & Strehler, B. L. (1972). Loss of genes coding for ribosomal RNA in aging bring cells. *Nature (London), 240,* 412–414.

Johnston, L. D., O'Malley, P. M., & Bachman, J. G. (1987). *National trends in drug use and related factors among American high school students and young adults, 1975–1986.* Washington, DC: U.S. Government Printing Office.

Jones, R. E. (1984). *Human reproduction and sexual behavior.* Englewood Cliffs, NJ: Prentice-Hall.

Jones, S. S., & Raag, T. (1989). Smile production in older infants. The importance of a social recipient for the facial signal. *Child Development, 60,* 811–818.

Jose, P. E. (1990). Just-world reasoning in children's immanent justice judgments. *Child Development, 61,* 1024–1033.

Joyce, E. (1984). A time of grieving. *Psychology Today, 18,* 42–46.

Judson, F. (1985). Assessing the number of genital chlamydial infections in the United States. *Journal of Reproductive Medicine, 30*(Suppl.), 269–272.

Jurich, A. P., Polson, C. J., Jurich, J. A., & Bates, R. A. (1985). Family factors in the lives of drug users and abusers. *Adolescence, 20,* 143–159.

Jurich, A. P., Schumm, W. R., & Bollman, S. R. (1987). The degree of family orientation perceived by mothers, fathers, and adolescents. *Adolescence, 22,* 119–238.

Kagan, J. (1984). *The nature of the child.* New York: Basic Books.

Kagan, J., Reznick, J. S., Clarke, C., Snidman, N., & Garcie-Cole, C. (1984). Behavioral inhibitors to the unfamiliar. *Child Development, 55,* 2212–2225.

Kagan, J., Reznick, J. S., & Snidman, N. (1987). The physiology and psychology of behavioral inhibition in children. *Child Development, 58,* 1459–1473.

Kagan, J., Reznick, J. S., Snidman, N., Gibbons, J., & Johnson, M. (1988). Childhood derivatives of inhibition and lack of inhibition to the familiar. *Child Development, 59,* 1580–1589.

Kail, R. (1979). *Memory development in children.* San Francisco, CA: Freeman.

Kail, R., & Bisanz, J. (1982). Information processing and cognitive development. In H. Reese (Ed.), *Advances in child development and behavior* (Vol. 17). New York: Academic Press.

Kaitz, M., Meschulach-Sarfaty, O., Auerbach, J., & Eidelman, A. (1988). A reexamination of newborn ability to imitate facial expressions. *Developmental Psychology, 24,* 3–7.

Kalish, R. A. (1985a). The social context of death and dying. In R. H. Binstock & E. Shanas (Eds.), *Handbook of aging and the social sciences.* New York: Van Nostrand-Reinhold.

Kalish, R. A. (1985b). *Death, grief, and caring relationships* (2nd ed.). Monterey, CA: Brooks/Cole.

Kalish, R. A., & Reynolds, D. K. (1981). *Death and ethnicity: A psychocultural study.* Farmington, NY: Baywood.

Kalmuss, D., & Seltzer, J. A. (1989). A framework for studying family socialization over the life cycle. *Journal of Family Issues, 10,* 339–358.

Kalter, N. (1983). How children perceive divorce. *Medical Aspects of Human Sexuality, 17,* 18–45.

Kamii, C., & deVries, R. (1980). *Group games in early education.* Washington, DC: National Association for Education of Young Children.

Kammer, P. P., Fouad, N., & Williams, R. (1988). Follow-up of a pre-college program for minority and disadvantaged students. *Career Development Quarterly, 37,* 40–45.

Kanchier, C., & Unruh, W. R. (1988). The career cycle meets the life cycle. *Career Development Quarterly, 37,* 127–137.

Kandel, D. B. (1990). Parenting styles, drug use, and children's adjustment in families of young adults. *Journal of Marriage and the Family, 52,* 183–196.

Kangas, J., & Bradway, K. (1971). Intelligence at middle age: A thirty-eight year follow-up. *Developmental Psychology, 5,* 333–337.

Kanin, E. J., & Parcell, S. R. (1977). Sexual aggression: A second look at the offended female. *Archives of Sexual Behavior, 6,* 67–76.

Kaplan, H. B. (1977, March). Increase in self-rejection and self-enhancement in adolescence. *Journal of Youth and Adolescence, 7,* 253–277.

Kaplan, H. B. (1978, September). Deviant behavior and self-enhancement in adolescence. *Journal of Youth and Adolescence, 7,* 253–277.

Kaplan, H. S. (1979). *Disorders of sexual desire.* New York: Simon & Schuster.

Karasawa, A., Kawashima, K., & Kasahara, H. (1979). Mental aging and the medico-psychosocial background in the very old Japanese. *Journal of Gerontology, 34,* 680–686.

Kargman, M. W. (1983). Stepchild support obligations of stepparent. *Family Relations, 32,* 231–238.

Karp, L. (1980). The arguable propriety of preconceptual sex discrimination. *American Journal of Medical Genetics, 6,* 185–187.

Kasari, C., Sigman, M., Mundy, P., & Yirmiya, N. (1988). Caregiver interactions with autistic children. *Journal of Abnormal Child Psychology, 16,* 45–56.

Kastenbaum, R., & Aisenberg, R. (1976). *The psychology of death.* New York: Springer.

Kastenbaum, R., Derbin, V., Sabatini, P., & Artt, S. (1972). The ages of me: Toward personal and interpersonal definition of functional aging. *Aging and Human Development, 3,* 197–211.

Katz, P. H., & Walsh, P. V. (1991). Modification of children's gender-stereotyped behavior. *Child Development, 62,* 338–351.

Kausler, D. H., & Puckett, J. M. (1981). Adult age differences in memory of sex of voice. *Journal of Gerontology, 36,* 44–50.

Keating, N. C., & Cole, P. (1980). What do I do with him 24 hours a day? Change in the housewife role after retirement. *Gerontologist, 20,* 84–89.

Kee, D. W., Gottfried, A. W., Bathurst, K., & Brown, K. (1987). Left-hemisphere language specialization and consistency in hand preference and sex differences. *Child Development, 58,* 718–724.

Keesey, R. E., & Pawley, T. L. (1986). The regulation of body weight. *Annual Review of Psychology, 37,* 109–133.

Keith, P. M. (1979, November). Life changes and perceptions of life and death among older men and women. *Journal of Gerontology, 34,* 870–878.

Keith, P. M. (1986). Isolation of the unmarried in later life. *Family Relations, 35,* 389–395.

Keith, P. M. (1987). Depressive symptoms among younger and older couples. *Gerontologist, 27,* 605–610.

Kellam, S. G., Adams, R. G., Brown, O. H., & Ensminger, M. E. (1982). The long-term evaluation of the family structure of teenage and older mothers. *Journal of Marriage and the Family, 44,* 539–554.

Kelly, C., & Goodwin, G. C. (1983). Adolescents' perceptions of three styles of parental control. *Adolescence, 18,* 567–571.

Kelly, J. B. (1988). Longer-term adjustment in children of divorce: Converging findings and implications for practice. *Journal of Family Planning, 2,* 119–140.

Kendall, P. C., & Brophy, C. (1981). Activity and attentional correlates of teacher ratings of hyperactivity. *Journal of Pediatric Psychology, 6,* 451–458.

Keniston, K. (1970). Youth: A new stage of life. *American Scholar, 39,* 4.

Keyes, S., & Block, J. (1984, February). Prevalence and patterns of substance use among early adolescents. *Journal of Youth and Adolescence, 13,* 1–13.

Kids and contraceptives. (1987, February 16). *Newsweek,* pp. 54–65.

Kidwell, J. S. (1981). Number of siblings, sibling spacing, sex, and birth order: Their effects on perceived parent-adolescent relationships. *Journal of Marriage and the Family, 43,* 315–332.

Kifer, E. (1985). Review of the ACT Assessment Program. In J. V. Mitchell (Ed.), *Ninth mental measurement yearbook* (pp. 31–45). Lincoln: University of Nebraska Press, Buros Mental Measurement Institute.

Kii, T. (1982). A new index for measuring demographic aging. *Gerontologist, 22,* 438–442.

Kilty, K. M., & Behling, J. H. (1985). Predicting the retirement intentions and attitudes of professional workers. *Journal of Gerontology, 40,* 219–227.

Kilty, K. M., & Behling, J. H. (1986). Retirement financial planning among professional workers. *Gerontologist, 26,* 525–530.

King, P. (1989). The (meno)pause that refreshes. *Psychology Today, 22,* 11.

Kinney, D. K., & Matthysse, S. (1978). Genetic transmission of schizophrenia. *Annual Review of Medicine, 29,* 459–473.

Kinsey, A. C., Pomeroy, W., and Martin, C. (1948). *Sexual behavior in the human male.* Philadelphia, PA: Saunders.

Kirkendall, L. (1981, May). The case against circumcision. *Sexology Today,* pp. 56–59.

Kissman, K. (1990). Social support and gender role attitude among teenage mothers. *Adolescence, 25,* 709–716.

Kitson, G. C., & Morgan, L. A. (1990). The multiple consequences of divorce: A decade review. *Journal of Marriage and the Family, 52,* 913–924.

Kitzman, D. W., & Edwards, W. D. (1990). Minireview: Age related changes in the anatomy of the normal human heart. *Journal of Gerontology, 45,* M33–M39.

Klaus, M., & Kennel, J. (1982). *Parent-infant bonding* (2nd ed.). St. Louis, MO: Mosby.

Klaczynski, P. A. (1990). Cultural-developmental tasks and adolescent development: Theoretical and methodological considerations. *Adolescence, 25,* 811–824.

Kleban, H. H., Lawton, M. P., Brody, E. M., & Moss, M. (1976). Behavioral observations of mentally impaired aged: Those who decline and those who do not. *Journal of Gerontology, 31,* 333–339.

Kleinman, J. C., Cooke, M., Machlin, S., & Kessel, S. S. (1983). *Variations in use of obstetric technology* (DHHS Publication No. PHS84-1232). Washington, DC: U.S. Government Printing Office.

Kline, M., Johnston, J. R., & Tschann, J. M. (1991). The long shadow of marital conflict: A model of children's postdivorce adjustment. *Journal of Marriage and the Family, 53,* 297–309.

Knoff, H. M. (1983, Fall). Learning disabilities in the junior high school: Creating the six-hour emotionally disturbed adolescent? *Adolescence, 18,* 541–550.

Knox, D., & Wilson, K. (1981). Dating behavior of university students. *Family Relations, 30,* 255–258.

Knox, D., & Wilson, K. (1983). Dating problems of university students. *College Student Journal, 17,* 225–228.

Kochanska, G. (1990). Maternal beliefs as long-term predictors of mother–child interaction and rapport. *Child Development, 61,* 1934–1943.

Kochanska, G. (1991). Patterns of inhibition to the unfamiliar in children of normal and affectively ill mothers. *Child Development, 62,* 250–263.

Kochanska, G., Kuczynski, L., & Radke-Yarrow, M. (1989). Correspondence between mothers' self-reported and observed child-rearing practices. *Child Development, 60,* 56–63.

Koenig, L. J. (1988). Self-image of emotionally disturbed adolescents. *Journal of Abnormal Child Psychology, 16,* 111–126.

Koff, E., Rierdan, J., & Sheingold, K. (1982, February). Memories of menarche: Age, preparation, and prior knowledge as determinants of initial menstrual experience. *Journal of Youth and Adolescence, 11,* 1–19.

Koff, E., Rierdan, J., & Stubbs, M. L. (1990). Gender, body image, and self-concept in early adolescence. *Journal of Early Adolescence, 10,* 56–68.

Kohlberg, L. (1963). The development of children's orientation toward a moral order. *Vita Humana, 6,* 11–33.

Kohlberg, L. (1966a). A cognitive-developmental analysis of children's sex role concepts and attitudes. In E. Maccoby (Ed.), *The development of sex differences.* Palo Alto, CA: Stanford University Press.

Kohlberg, L. (1966b). Moral education in the schools: A developmental view. *School Review, 74,* 1–30.

Kohlberg, L. (1969). *Stages in the development of moral thought and action.* New York: Holt, Rinehart, & Winston.

Kohlberg, L. (1970). Moral development and the education of adolescents. In R. F. Purnell (Ed.), *Adolescents and the American high school.* New York: Holt, Rinehart, & Winston.

Kohlberg, L., & Gilligan, C. (1971, Fall). The adolescent as a philosopher: The discovery of the self in a postconventional world. *Daedalus,* 1051–1086.

Kohlberg, L., & Kramer, M. S. (1969). Continuities and discontinuities in childhood and adult development. *Human Development, 12,* 93–120.

Kohlberg, L., & Turiel, E. (Eds.). (1972). *Recent research in moral development.* New York: Holt, Rinehart, & Winston.

Kohn, A. (1988). Make love, not war. *Psychology Today, 22,* 34–38.

Kolata, G. (1986). Obese children: A growing problem. *Science, 232,* 20–21.

Kolata, G. (1988). Child splitting. *Psychology Today, 22,* 34–36.

Kolodny, R. C. (1980, November). *Adolescent sexuality.* Paper presented at the annual convention of the Michigan Personnel and Guidance Association, Detroit.

Kompara, D. R. (1980). Difficulties in the socialization process of stepparenting. *Family Relations, 29,* 69–73.

Koop, C. E. (1986). *Surgeon general's reports on acquired immune deficiency syndrome.* Washington, DC: U.S. Department of Health and Human Services.

Kopp, C. B. (1983). Risk factors in development. In P. H. Mussen, M. Haith, & J. J. Campos (Eds.). *Handbook of child psychology* (4th ed., Vol. 2, pp. 1081–1088). New York: Wiley.

Kopp, C. B., & Kaler, S. R. (1989). Risk in infancy: Origins and implications. *American Psychologist, 44,* 224–230.

Kopp, C. B., & McCall, R. B. (1982). Predicting later mental performance for normal, at risk, and handicapped infants. In P. B. Baltes & O. G. Brim (Eds.), *Life-span development and behavior* (Vol. 4). New York: Academic Press.

Korman, S. (1983). Nontraditional dating behavior: Date initiation and date expense-sharing among feminists and non-feminists. *Family Relations, 32,* 575–581.

Korman, S., & Leslie, G. (1982). The relationship between feminists ideology and date expense-sharing to perceptions of sexual aggression in dating. *Journal of Sex Research, 18,* 114–129.

Kosik, K. S. (1989). Minireview: The molecular and cellular pathology of Alzheimer neurofibrillary lesions. *Journal of Gerontology, 44,* B55–58.

Kovar, M. G. (1986). *Aging in the eighties: Age 65 years and over and living alone, contacts with family, friends, and neighbors,* advance data from vital and health statistics, No. 116 (DHHS Publication No. [PHS] 86-1250). Washington, DC: National Center for Health Statistics.

Kozma, A., & Stones, M. J. (1983). Prediction of happiness. *Journal of Gerontology, 38,* 626–628.

Kramer, M. S. (1981). Do breast feeding and delayed introduction of solid foods protect against subsequent obesity? *Journal of Pediatrics, 98,* 883–887.

Krause, N. (1986a). Social support, stress, and well-being among older adults. *Journal of Gerontology, 41,* 512–519.

Krause, N. (1986b). Stress and coping: Reconceptualizing the role of locus of control beliefs. *Journal of Gerontology, 41,* 617–622.

Krause, N. (1986c). Stress and sex differences in depressive symptoms among older adults. *Journal of Gerontology, 41,* 727–731.

Krause, N. (1988). Stressful life events and physician utilization. *Journal of Gerontology, 43,* S53–S61.

Krause, N. (1990). Perceived health problems, formal/informal support, and life satisfaction among older adults. *Journal of Gerontology, 45,* S193–S205.

Krause, N. (1991). Stress and isolation from close ties in later life. *Journal of Gerontology, 46,* S183–S194.

Krause, N. (1991). Stressful events and life satisfaction among elderly men and women. *Journal of Gerontology, 46,* S84–S92.

Krein, S. F., & Beller, A. H. (1988). Educational attainment of children from single-parent families: Differences by exposure, gender, and race. *Demography, 25,* 221–224.

Krieshock, S. I., & Karpowitz, D. H. (1988). A review of selected literature on obesity and guidelines for treatment. *Journal of Consulting and Development, 66,* 326–330.

Kroger, J. A. (1980, Winter). Residential mobility and self-concept in adolescence. *Adolescence, 15,* 967–977.

Krone, R. J., & Hodson, R. (1988). Exercising and the heart. *Medical Aspects of Human Sexuality, 22,* 21–22.

Kroupa, S. E. (1988). Perceived parental acceptance and female juvenile delinquency. *Adolescence, 23,* 171–185.

Krueger, R., & Hansen, J. C. (1987). Self-concept changes during youth-home placement of adolescents. *Adolescence, 86,* 385–392.

Krupka, L. R., & Vener, A. M. (1979). Hazards of drug use among the elderly. *Gerontologist, 19,* 90–95.

Kubler-Ross, E. (1969). *On death and dying.* New York: Macmillan.

Kubler-Ross, E. (1974). *Questions and answers on death and dying.* New York: Macmillan.

Kuczaj, S. A. (1986). Thoughts on the intentional basis of early object word extension. Evidence from comprehension and production. In S. A. Kuczaj & M. D. Barrett (Eds.), *The development of word meaning. Progress in cognitive developmental research.* New York: Springer-Verlag.

Kugler, D. E., & Hansson, R. O. (1988). Relational competence and social support among parents at risk of child abuse. *Family Relations, 37,* 328–332.

Kuhn, D. (1979). The significance of Piaget's formal operations stage in education. *Journal of Education, 161,* 34–50.

Kupersmidt, J. B., & Coie, J. D. (1990). Preadolescent peer status, aggression, and school adjustment as predictors of externalizing problems in adolescence. *Child Development, 61,* 1350–1362.

Kupfersmid, J. H., & Wonderly, D. M. (1980). Moral maturity and behavior: Failure to find a link. *Journal of Youth and Adolescence, 9,* 249–261.

Kurdek, L. A. (1989). Relationship quality for newly married husbands and wives: Marital history, stepchildren, and individual-difference predictors. *Journal of Marriage and the Family, 51,* 1053–1064.

Kurdek, L. A., & Berg, B. (1983). Correlates of children's adjustment to their parents' divorce. In L. A. Kurdek (Ed.), *Children and divorce.* San Francisco, CA: Jossey-Bass.

Kuypers, J. A., & Bengston, V. L. (1973). Social breakdown and competence: A model of normal aging. *Human Development, 16,* 181–201.

Labouvie-Vief, G. (1985). Intelligence and cognition. In J. E. Birren & K. W. Schaie (Eds.), *Handbook of the psychology of aging.* New York: Van Nostrand-Reinhold.

Labouvie-Vief, G. (1986). Modes of knowledge and organization of development. In M. L. Commens, L. Kohlberg, F. A. Richards, & J. Sinnott (Eds.), *Beyond formal operations: Models and methods in the study of adult and adolescent thought* (Vol. 3). New York: Praeger.

Labouvie-Vief, G., & Gonda, J. N. (1976). Cognitive strategy training and intellectual performance in the elderly. *Journal of Gerontology, 31,* 327–332.

Lachenmeyer, J. R., & Muni-Brander, P. (1988). Eating disorders in a nonclinical adolescent population: Implications for treatment. *Adolescence, 23,* 303–312.

Lachman, M. E., & Jelalian, E. (1984). Self-efficacy and attributions for intellectual performance in young and elderly adults. *Journal of Gerontology, 39,* 577–582.

Lackovic-Grgin, K., & Dekovic, M. (1990). The contribution of significant others to adolescents' self-esteem. *Adolescence, 25,* 839–846.

Ladd, G. W. (1990). Having friends, keeping friends, making friends, and being liked by peers in the classroom: Predictors of children's early school adjustment? *Child Development, 61,* 1081–1100.

Ladd, G. W., & Price, J. M. (1987). Predicting children's social and school adjustment following the transition from preschool to kindergarten. *Child Development, 58,* 1168–1189.

Ladd, G. W., Price, J. M., & Hart, C. H. (1988). Predicting preschoolers' peer status from their playground behaviors. *Child Development, 59,* 986–992.

Lagercrantz, H., & Slotkin, T. A. (1968). The "stress" of being born. *Scientific American, 254,* 100–107.

Laing, J., Valiga, M., & Eberly, C. (1986). Predicting college freshman major choices from ACT Assessment Program data. *College and University, 61,* 198–205.

Lamaze, F. (1970). *Painless childbirth.* Chicago, IL: Regency.

Lamb, M. E., Frodi, M., Hwang, C., & Frodi, A. M. (1983). Effects of paternal involvement on infant preference for mothers and fathers. *Child Development, 54,* 450–458.

Landau, S., & Milich, R. (1988). Social communication patterns of attention-deficit-disordered boys. *Journal of Abnormal Child Psychology, 16,* 69–81.

Landers, A. (1985, June 11). Is affection more important than sex? *Family Circle.*

Landry, R. (1987). Additive bilingualism, schooling, and special education: A minority group perspective. *Canadian Journal for Exceptional Children, 3,* 109–114.

Langer, E. J. (1989, April). The mindset of health. *Psychology Today, 23,* 48–51.

Langfeldt, T. (1981). Sexual development in children. In H. Cook & H. Howells (Eds.), *Adult sexual interest in children.* London: Academic Press.

LaRiviere, J. E., & Simonson, E. (1965). The effect of age and occupation on speed of writing. *Journal of Gerontology, 20,* 412, 416.

LaRossa, R. (1988). Fatherhood and social change. *Family Relations, 37,* 451–457.

Larsen, J. W. (1986). Congenital toxoplasmas. In J. L. Sever & R. L. Brent (Eds.), *Teratogen update: Environmentally induced birth defect risks.* New York: Liss.

Larson, J. H. (1984). The effect of husband's unemployment on marital and family relations in blue-collar families. *Family Relations, 33,* 503–511.

Larson, R. (1978). Thirty years of research on the subjective well-being of older Americans. *Journal of Gerontology, 33,* 109–125.

Larson, R., & Richards, M. H. (1991). Daily companionship in later childhood and early adolescence: Changing developmental contexts. *Child Development, 62,* 284–300.

Latham, M. C. (1977). Infant feeding in national and international perspective: An examination of the decline in human lactation, and the modern crisis in infant and young child feeding practices. *Annals of the New York Academy of Sciences, 300,* 197–209.

Lavee, Y., McCubbin, H. I., & Olson, D. H. (1987). The effect of stressful life events and transitions on family functioning and well-being. *Journal of Marriage and the Family, 49,* 857–873.

Lavee, Y., McCubbin, H. I., & Patterson, J. M. (1985). The double ABCX model of family stress and adaptation: An empirical test by analysis of structural equations with latent variables. *Journal of Marriage and the Family, 47,* 811–825.

Lavin, J., Stephens, R., Miodovnik, M., & Bardon, T. (1982). Vaginal delivery in patients with a prior cesarean section. *Obstetrics and Gynecology, 59,* 135–148.

Lawson, J. S., Rodenburg, M., & Dykes, J. A. (1977). A dementia rating scale for use with psychogeriatric patients. *Journal of Gerontology, 32,* 153–159.

Lawton, M. P. (1975). The Philadelphia center morale scale: A revision. *Journal of Gerontology, 30,* 85–89.

Leadbeater, B. (1986). The resolution of relativism in adult thinking: Subjective, objective, and conceptual. *Human Development, 29,* 291–300.

Leboyer, F. (1975). *Birth without violence.* New York: Alfred A. Knopf.

LeBreck, D. B., & Baron, A. (1987). Age and practice effects in continuous recognition memory. *Journal of Gerontology, 42,* 89–91.

LeClair, N., & Berkowitz, B. (1983, February). Counseling concerns for the individual with bulimia. *Personnel and Guidance Journal, 61,* 352–355.

Lederberg, A. J. (1982). A framework for research on preschool children's speech modification. In S. A. Kuczaj, II (Ed.), *Language development: Vol. 2. Language, thought, and culture.* Hillsdale, NJ: Erlbaum.

Lee, D. J., & Markides, K. S. (1990). Activity and mortality among aged persons over an eight-year period. *Journal of Gerontology, 45,* S39–S42.

Lee, G. R., & Ellithorpe, E. (1982). Intergenerational exchange and subjective well-being among the elderly. *Journal of Marriage and the Family, 44,* 217–224.

Lee, V. E., Brooks-Gunn, J., Schnur, E., & Liaw, F. (1990). Are Head Start effects sustained? A longitudinal follow-up comparison of disadvantaged children attending Head Start, no preschool, and other preschool programs. *Child Development, 61,* 495–507.

LeFlore, L. (1988). Delinquent youths and family. *Adolescence, 23,* 629–642.

Legal rights still cloudy for 18-year-olds. (1976, March 8). *U.S. News and World Report,* pp. 27–28.

Lehman, H. C. (1962). The creative production rates of present versus past generations of scientists. *Journal of Gerontology, 17,* 409–417.

Lehman, H. C. (1966). The psychologists most creative years. *Amerian Psychologist, 21,* 363–369.

Leiblum, S., Bachmann, G., Kemmann, E., Colburn, D., & Swartzman, L. (1983). Vaginal atrophy in postmenopausal woman: The importance of sexual activity and hormones. *JAMA, Journal of the American Medical Association, 249,* 2195–2198.

Leifer, M. (1980). *Psychological effects of motherhood: Study of first pregnancy.* New York: Praeger.

LeMare, L. J., & Rubin, K. H. (1987). Perspective taking and peer interaction: Structural and developmental analysis. *Child Development, 58,* 306–315.

Lempers, J. D., & Clark-Lempers, D. (1990). Family economic stress, maternal and paternal support and adolescent distress. *Journal of Adolescence, 13,* 217–230.

Lenneberg, E. H. (1973). *Biological foundation of language* (pp. 128–130). New York: Wiley.

Leo, J. (1987, January 12). Exploring the traits of twins. *Time,* p. 63.

Lerea, L. E., & LiMauro, B. F. (1982). Grief among healthcare workers: A comparative study. *Journal of Gerontology, 37,* 604–608.

Lerner, J. V., Hertzog, C., Hooker, K., Hassibi, M., & Thomas, A. (1988). Longitudinal study of negative emotional states and adjustment from early childhood through adolescence. *Child Development, 59,* 356–366.

Lerner, R. M., Delaney, M., Hess, L. E., Jovanovic, J., & von Eye, A. (1990). Early adolescent physical attractiveness and academic competence. *Journal of Early Adolescence, 10,* 4–20.

LeRoux, R. S. (1977). Communicating with the dying person. *Nursing Forum, 16,* 145–155.

Leslie, L. A., & Grady, K. (1985). Changes in mothers' social networks and social support following divorce. *Journal of Marriage and the Family, 47,* 663–673.

Leslie, L. A., Huston, T. L., & Johnson, M. P. (1986). Parental reactions to dating relationships: Do they make a difference? *Journal of Marriage and the Family, 48,* 57–66.

Lester, B. M. (1987). Prediction of developmental outcome from acoustical cry analysis in term and preterm infants. *Pediatrics, 80,* 529–534.

Lester, B. M., & Dreher, M. (1989). Effects of marijuana use during pregnancy on newborn cry. *Child Development, 60,* 765–771.

Lester, R., & Van Theil, D. H. (1977). Gonad function in chronic alcoholic men. *Advances in Experimental Medicine and Biology, 85A,* 339–414.

Leupnitz, D. A. (1982). *Child custody: A study of families after divorce.* Lexington, MA: Lexington Books.

Levant, R. F., Slattery, S. C., & Loiselle, J. E. (1987). Fathers' involvement in housework and child care with school-age daughters. *Family Relations, 36,* 152–157.

Levin, E., Adelson, S., Buchalter, G., & Bilcher, L. (1983, February). Karen Carpenter. *People.*

Levine, J. B. (1988). Play in the context of the family. *Journal of Family Psychology, 2,* 164–187.

Levinson, D. J. (1977). The midlife transition: A period in adult psychosocial development. *Psychiatry, 40,* 99–112.

Levinson, D. J., Darrow, C. N., Klein, E. B., Levinson, M. H., & McKee, B. (1976). Periods in the adult development of men: Ages 18 to 45. *Counseling Psychologist, 6,* 21–25.

Levinson, D. J., Darrow, C. N., Klein, E. B., Levinson, M. H., & McKee, B. (1978). *The seasons of a man's life.* New York: Alfred A. Knopf.

Levy, J. (1985, May). Right brain, left brain. Fact and fiction. *Psychology Today, 19,* 28–44.

Levy-Shiff, R., Sharir, H., & Mogilner, M. B. (1989). Mother- and father-preterm infant relationships in the hospital preterm nursery. *Child Development, 60,* 93–102.

Lewinsohn, P. M., & Talkington, J. (1979). Studies on the measurement of unpleasant events and relations with depression. *Applied Psychological Measurement, 3,* 83–101.

Lewis, C., & Osborne, A. (1990). Three-year-olds' problems with false belief: Conceptual deficit or linguistic artifact? *Child Development, 61,* 1514–1519.

Lewis, M. (1987). Social development in infancy and childhood. In J. D. Osofsky (Ed.), *Handbook of infant development* (2nd ed.). New York: Wiley.

Lewis, M., & Feiring, C. (1989). Infant, mother, and mother-infant interaction behavior and subsequent attachment. *Child Development, 60,* 831–837.

Lewis, R. A., Freneau, P. J., & Roberts, C. L. (1979). Fathers and postparental transition. *Family Coordinator, 28,* 514–520.

Liang, J. (1982). Sex differences in life satisfaction among the elderly. *Journal of Gerontology, 37,* 100–108.

Liang, J. (1984). Dimensions of the Life Satisfaction Index A: A structural formulation. *Journal of Gerontology, 39,* 613–622.

Liang, J. (1985). A structural integration of the affect balance scale and the Life Satisfaction Index A. *Journal of Gerontology, 5,* 552–561.

Liang, J., Asano, H., Bollen, K. A., Kahana, E. F., & Maeda, D. (1987). Cross-cultural comparability of the Philadelphia Geriatric Center Morale Scale: An American-Japanese comparison. *Journal of Gerontology, 42,* 37–43.

Liang, J., & Bollen, K. A. (1983). The structure of the Philadelphia Geriatric Center Moral Scale: A reinterpretation. *Journal of Gerontology, 38,* 181–189.

Liang, J., Lawrence, R. H., & Bollen, K. A. (1987). Race differences in factorial structures of two measures of subjective well-being. *Journal of Gerontology, 42,* 426–428.

Liang, J., & Warfel, B. L. (1983). Urbanism and life satisfaction among the aged. *Journal of Gerontology, 38,* 797–1006.

Licht, B. G., & Dweck, C. S. (1984). Determinants of academic achievement: The interaction of children's achievement orientations and skill areas. *Developmental Psychology, 20,* 628–638.

Lieberman, A. F., Weston, D. R., & Pawl, J. H. (1991). Preventive intervention and outcome with anxiously attached dyads. *Child Development, 62,* 199–209.

Light, H. K., Hertsgaard, D., & Martin, R. E. (1985). Farm children's work in the family. *Adolescence, 20,* 425–432.

Lin, C. C., & Fu, V. R. (1990). A comparison of child-rearing practices among Chinese, immigrant Chinese, and Caucasian-American parents. *Child Development, 61,* 429–433.

Linn, R. (1991). Sexual and moral development of Israeli female adolescents for city and kibbutz: Perspectives of Kohlberg and Gilligan. *Adolescence, 26,* 59–72.

Linde, E. V., Morrongiello, B. A., & Rovee-Collier, C. (1985). Determinants of retention in 8-week-old infants. *Developmental Psychology, 21,* 601–613.

Lindeman, R. D. (1975). Age changes in renal function. In R. Goldman & M. Rockstein (Eds.), *Physiology and pathology of human aging* (pp. 19–38). New York: Academic Press.

Lipsitt, L. (1986). Learning in infancy: Cognitive development in babies. *Journal of Pediatrics, 109,* 172–182.

Littrell, M. L. D., & Littrell, J. M. (1990). Clothing interests, body satisfaction, and eating behavior of adolescent females: Related or independent dimensions? *Adolescence, 25,* 77–96.

Lockshin, R. A., & Zakeri, Z. F. (1990). Minireview: Programmed cell death: New thoughts and relevance to aging. *Journal of Gerontology, 45,* B135–B140.

Locitzer, K. (1989). Are you at sync with each other? *Psychology Today, 23,* 66.

Locke, J. (1892). Some thoughts concerning education. In

P. H. Quick (Ed.), *Locke on education* (pp. 1–236). Cambridge, England: Cambridge University Press.

Loehlin, J. C. (1985). Fitting heredity-environment models jointly to twin and adoption data from the California Psychological inventory. *Behavior Genetics, 15,* 199–221.

Logan, D. D. (1980). The menarche experience in twenty-three foreign countries. *Adolescence, 58,* 247–256.

Logan, R. D. (1983, Winter). A re-conceptualization of Erikson's identity stage. *Adolescence, 18,* 943–946.

Lohr, M. J., Essex, M. J., & Klein, M. H. (1988). The relationship of coping resources to physical health status and life satisfaction among older women. *Journal of Gerontology, 43,* P54–P60.

Lollis, S. P. (1990). Effects of maternal behavior on toddler behavior during separation. *Child Development, 61,* 99–103.

Longino, C. F., Jr., Jackson, D. J., Zimmerman, R. C., & Bradsher, J. E. (1991). The second move: Health and geographical mobility. *Journal of Gerontology, 46,* S218–S225.

Lorch, E. P., Bellack, D. R., & Augsbach, L. H. (1987). Young children's memory for televised stories: Effects of importance. *Child Development, 58,* 453–463.

Lorenz, K. Z. (1965). *Evolution and the modification of behavior.* Chicago, IL: University of Chicago Press.

Lowenstein, D. A., Amigo, E., Duara, R., Guterman, A., Hurwitz, D., Berkowitz, N., Wilkie, F., Weinberg, G., Black, B., Gittelman, B., & Eisdorfer, D. (1989). *Journal of Gerontology, 44,* P114–P121.

Lowik, M. R. H., Wedel, M., Kok, F. J., Odink, J., Westenbrink, S., & Meulmeester, J. F. (1991). Nutrition and serum cholesterol levels among elderly men and women (Dutch Nutrition Surveillance System). *Journal of Gerontology, 46,* M23–M28.

Ludemann, P. M. (1991). Generalized discrimination of positive facial expression by seven- and ten-month-old infants. *Child Development, 62,* 55–67.

Lund, N. L., & Salary, H. M. (1980, Spring). Measured self-concept in adjudicated juvenile offenders. *Adolescence, 15,* 65–74.

Lundholm, J. K., & Littrell, J. M. (1986). Desire for thinness among high school cheerleaders. Relationship to disordered eating and weight control behavior. *Adolescence, 21,* 573–579.

Lundin, T. (1984). Morbidity following sudden and unexpected bereavement. *British Journal of Psychiatry, 144,* 84–88.

Lupri, E., & Frideres, J. (1981). The quality of marriage and the passage of time. Marital satisfaction over the family life cycle. *Canadian Journal of Sociology, 6,* 283–305.

Luster, T., Rhoades, K., & Haas, B. (1989). The relation between parental values and parenting behavior: A test of the Kohn hypothesis. *Journal of Marriage and the Family, 51,* 139–147.

Luszki, M., & Luszki, W. (1985). Advantages of growing older. *Journal of the American Geriatric Society, 33,* 216–217.

Lyons-Ruth, K., Connell, D. B., & Grunebaum, H. U. (1990). Infants at special risk: Maternal depression and family support services as mediators of infant development and security of attachment. *Child Development, 61,* 85–98.

Maccoby, E. E. (1980). *Social development.* San Diego, CA: Harcourt Brace Jovanovich.

Maccoby, E. E., Depner, C., & Mnookin, R. (1988). *Family functioning in three forms of residence: Maternal, paternal, and joint.* Paper presented at the annual meeting of the American Orthopsychiatry Association, San Francisco, CA.

MacFarlane, A. H., Norman, G. R., Streiner, D. L., Ray, R., & Scott, D. J. (1980). A longitudinal study of the influence of the psychosocial environment on health status: A preliminary report. *Journal of Health and Social Behavior, 21,* 124–133.

Macklin, E. D. (1983). Nonmarital heterosexual cohabitation: An overview. In E. D. Macklin & R. H. Rubin (Eds.), *Contemporary families and alternate lifestyles: Handbook on research and theory* (pp. 49–73). Beverly Hills, CA: Sage.

MacWhinney, B. (1982). Basic syntactic processes. In S. Kuczaj, II (Ed.), *Language development: Vol. 1. Syntax and semantics.* Hillsdale, NJ: Erlbaum.

Madden, D. J., & Harbin, H. T. (1983, July). Family structures of assaultive adolescents. *Journal of Marital and Family Therapy, 9,* 311–316.

Maddox, G. L. (1970). Themes and issues in sociological theories of human aging. *Human Development, 13,* 17–27.

Madison, L. S., Madison, J. K., & Adubato, S. A. (1986). Infant behavior and development in relation to fetal movement and habituation. *Child Development, 57,* 1475–1482.

Mahler, M. S., Pine, F., & Bergman, A. (1975). *The psychological birth of the human infant: Symbiosis and individuation.* New York: Basic Books.

Main, M., & Cassidy, J. (1988). Categories of response in reunion with the parent at age 6: Predictable from infant attachment classifications and stable over a 1-month period. *Developmental Psychology, 24,* 415–426.

Makin, J. W., & Porter, R. H. (1989). Attractiveness of lactating females breast odors to neonates. *Child Development, 60,* 803–810.

Malatesta, C. Z., Grigoryev, P., Lamb, C., Albin, M., & Culver, C. (1986). Emotion socialization and expressive development in preterm and full-term infants. *Child Development, 57,* 316–330.

Malinak, R., & Wheeler, J. (1985). Endometriosis. *Female Patient, 6,* 35–36.

Mallick, M. J., Whipple, T. W., & Huerta, E. (1987). Behavioral and psychological traits of weight-conscious teenagers: A comparison of eating-disordered patients and high- and low-risk groups. *Adolescence, 85,* 157–168.

Manaster, G. J. (1977). *Adolescent development and the life tasks.* Boston, MA: Allyn & Bacon.

Mandler, J. M. (1983). Representation. In J. H. Flavell & E. M. Marman (Eds.), *Handbook of child psychology* (4th ed., Vol. 3, pp. 420–494). New York: Wiley.

Mangelsdorf, S., Gunnar, M., Kestenbaum, R., Lang, S., & Andreas, D. (1990). Infant proneness-to-distress temperament, maternal personality, and mother–infant attachment: Associations and goodness of fit. *Child Development, 61,* 820–831.

Manton, K. B., & Stallard, E. (1991). Cross-sectional estimates of active life expectancy for the U.S. elderly and oldest-old populations. *Journal of Gerontology, 46,* S170–S182.

Manton, K. G., Siegler, I. C., & Woodbury, M. A. (1986). Patterns of intellectual development in later life. *Journal of Gerontology, 4,* 486–499.

Marcia, J. E., & Friedman, M. L. (1970). Ego identity status in college women. *Journal of Personality, 38,* 249–263.

Marcus, D. E., & Overton, W. F. (1978, June). The development of cognitive gender constancy and sex-role preferences. *Child Development, 49,* 434–444.

Marion, R. W., Wiznia, A. A., Hutcheon, G., & Rubinstein, A. (1986). Human T-cell lymphotropic virus type III (HTLV-III) embryopathy. *American Journal of Diseases of Children, 140,* 638–640.

Markides, K. S., & Lee, D. J. (1990). Predictors of well-being and functioning in older Mexican Americans and Anglos: An eight-year follow-up. *Journal of Gerontology, 45,* S69–S73.

Markus, H. J., & Nurius, P. S. (1984). Self-understanding and self-regulation in middle childhood. In W. A. Collins (Ed.), *Development during middle childhood: The years from six to twelve* (pp. 147–183). Washington, DC: National Academy Press.

Maroufi, C. (1989). A study of student attitude toward traditional and generative models of instruction. *Adolescence, 24*, 65–72.

Marshall, J. R. (1978, September). Changes in aged white male suicides: 1948–1972. *Journal of Gerontology, 33*, 763–768.

Martens, R. (1988). Helping children become independent, responsible adults through sports. In E. W. Brown & C. T. Branta (Eds.), *Competitive sports for children and youth: An overview of research and issues* (pp. 297–307). Champaign, IL: Human Kinetics.

Martin, C. L., & Little, J. K. (1990). The relation of gender understanding to children's sex-typed preferences and gender stereotypes. *Child Development, 61*, 1427–1439.

Martin, C. L., Wood, C. H., & Little, J. K. (1990). The development of gender stereotype components. *Child Development, 61*, 1891–1904.

Martin, J. D. (1971). Power, dependence, and the complaints of the elderly: A social exchange perspective. *Aging and Human Development, 2*, 108–112.

Martinez, G. A., Dodd, D. A., & Samaltgedes, J. (1981). Milk-feeding patterns in the United States during the first twelve months of life. *Pediatrics, 68*, 863–868.

Martinez, R., & Dukes, R. L. (1991). Ethnic and gender differences in self-esteem. *Youth and Society, 22*, 318–338.

Martinson, F. M. (1976). Eroticism in infancy and childhood. *Journal of Sex Research, 12*, 251–262.

Maslow, A. H. (1968). *Toward a psychology of being* (2nd ed.). Princeton, NJ: Van Nostrand.

Maslow, A. H. (1970). *Motivation and personality* (2nd ed.). New York: Harper.

Maslow, A. H. (1971). *The farther reaches of human nature.* New York: Viking.

Masselam, V. S., Marcus, R. F., & Stunkard, C. L. (1990). Parent–adolescent communication, family functioning, and school performance. *Adolescence, 25*, 725–738.

Masson, J. M. (1984). *The assault on truth: Freud's suppression of the seduction theory.* New York: Farrar, Straus, & Giroux.

Masters, W. H., & Johnson, V. E. (1966). *Human sexual response.* Boston, MA: Little, Brown.

Mathew, A., & Cook, M. (1990). The control of reaching movements by young infants. *Child Development, 61*, 1238–1257.

Matlin, M. (1983). *Cognition.* New York: Holt, Rinehart, & Winston.

Matter, R. M. (1984, Spring). The historical emergence of adolescence: Perspectives from developmental psychology and adolescent literature. *Adolescence, 19*, 131–142.

Matthews, L. J., & Ilon, L. (1980, July). Becoming a chronic runaway: The effects of race and family in Hawaii. *Family Relations, 29*, 404–409.

Maurer, D., & Salapatek, P. (1976). Developmental changes in the scanning of faces by young infants. *Child Development, 47*, 523–527.

May, J. M. (1986). Cognitive processes and violent behavior in young people. *Journal of Adolescence, 9*, 17–27.

Maylor, E. A. (1990). Recognizing and naming faces: Aging, memory retrieval, and the tip of the tongue state. *Journal of Gerontology, 45*, P215–P226.

Maynard, F. (1974). Understanding the crisis in men's lives. In C. E. Williams & J. F. Crosby (Eds.), *Choice and challenge* (pp. 135–144). Dubuque, IA: Wm. C. Brown.

Maziade, M., Boudréault, M., Cote, R., & Thivierge, J. (1986). Influence of gentle birth delivery procedures and other perinatal circumstances on infant temperament and developmental and social implications. *Journal of Pediatrics, 108*, 134–136.

McCabe, M. P. (1984). Toward a theory of adolescent dating. *Adolescence, 19*, 159–170.

McCarty, W. M., Siegler, I. C., & Logue, P. E. (1982). Cross-sectional and longitudinal patterns of 3 Wechsler Memory Scale subtests. *Journal of Gerontology, 37*, 169–175.

McCauley, E., Kay, T., Ito, J., & Treder, R. (1987). The Turner syndrome: Cognitive deficits, affective discrimination, and behavior problems. *Child Development, 58*, 464–473.

McClelland, D., Constantian, C. S., Regalado, D., & Stone, C. (1978, June). Making it to maturity. *Psychology Today, 11*, 42–53, 114.

McClelland, K. A. (1982). Self-conception and life satisfaction: Integrating aged subculture and activity theory. *Journal of Gerontology, 37*, 723–732.

McCombs, A., Forehand, A., & Smith, K. (1988). The relationship between maternal problem-solving style and adolescent social adjustment. *Journal of Family Psychology, 2*, 57–66.

McCoy, N., Cutler, W., & Davidson, J. (1985). Relationships among sexual behavior, hot flashes, and hormone levels in perimenopausal women. *Archives of Sexual Behavior, 14*, 385–394.

McCrae, R. R. (1982). Age differences in the use of coping mechanisms. *Journal of Gerontology, 37*, 454–460.

McCary, J. L., & McCary, S. P. (1982). *McCrary's human sexuality* (4th ed.). Belmont, CA: Wadsworth Publishing Co.

McCubbin, H. I., Joy, C. B., Cauble, A. E., Comeau, J. K., Patterson, J. M., & Needle, R. H. (1980). Family stress and coping: A decade review. *Journal of Marriage and the Family, 42*, 855–871.

McCulloch, B. J. (1990). The relationships of intergenerational reciprocity of aid to the morale of older parents: Equity and exchange theory comparisons. *Journal of Gerontology, 45*, S150–S155.

McCullers, J. C., & Love, J. M. (1976). The scientific study of the child. In B. J. Taylor & T. J. White (Eds.), *Issues and ideas in America.* Norman: Oklahoma University Press.

McDermott, D. (1984, Spring). The relationship of parental drug use and parents' attitude concerning adolescent drug use to adolescent drug use. *Adolescence, 19*, 89–97.

McGraw, M. B. (1940). Neural maturation as exemplified in achievement of bladder control. *Journal of Pediatrics, 16*, 580–590.

McGrory, A. (1990). Menarche: Response of early adolescent females. *Adolescence, 25*, 265–270.

McHale, S. M., Bartko, W. T., Crouter, A. C., & Perry-Jenkins, M. (1990). Children's housework and psychosocial functioning: The mediating effects of parents' sex-role behaviors and attitudes. *Child Development, 61*, 1413–1426.

McKenry, P. C., Kotch, J. B., & Browne, D. H. (1991). Correlates of dysfunctional parenting attitudes among low-income adolescent mothers. *Journal of Adolescent Research, 6*, 212–234.

McKenry, P. C., Price-Bonham, S., & O'Bryant, S. L. (1981). Adolescent discipline: Different family members' perception. *Journal of Youth and Adolescence, 10*, 327–337.

McKusick, V. A. (1986). *Mendelian inheritance in man* (7th ed.). Baltimore, MD: Johns Hopkins University Press.

McLanahan, S., & Booth, K. (1989). Mothers-only families: Problems, prospects, and politics. *Journal of Marriage and the Family, 51*, 557–580.

McLanahan, S. S., Wedemeyer, N. V., & Adelberg, T. (1981).

Network structure, social support, and psychological well-being in a sole-parent family. *Journal of Marriage and the Family, 43,* 601–612.

McLaren, N. M., & Nieburg, P. (1988, August). Fetal tobacco syndrome and other problems caused by smoking during pregnancy. *Medical Aspects of Human Sexuality, 22,* 69–75.

McLaughlin, B. (1985). *Second language acquisition in childhood: Vol. 2. School-age children* (2nd ed.). Hillsdale, NJ: Erlbaum.

McLoyd, V. C. (1990). The impact of economic hardship on black families and children: Psychological distress, parenting, and socioemotional development. *Child Development, 61,* 311–346.

McMillan, D. W., & Hiltonsmith, R. W. (1982). Adolescents at home: An explanatory study of the relationship perception of family social climate, general well-being, and actual behavior in the home setting. *Journal of Youth and Adolescence, 11,* 301–315.

McMurran, M., & Whitman, J. (1990). Strategies of self-control in male young offenders who have reduced their alcohol consumption without formal intervention. *Journal of Adolescence, 13,* 115–128.

McNally, S., Eisenberg, N., & Harris, J. E. (1991). Consistency and change in maternal child-rearing practices and values: A longitudinal study. *Child Development, 62,* 190–198.

McNeill, D. (1970). Language development in children. In P. H. Mussen (Ed.), *Handbook of child psychology* (3rd ed.). New York: Wiley.

McPherson, J. R., Lancaster, D. R., & Carroll, J. C. (1978). Stature change with aging in black Americans. *Journal of Gerontology, 33,* 20–25.

Mead, M. (1950). *Coming of age in Samoa.* New York: New American Library.

Mead, M. (1974). Adolescence. In H. V Kraemer (Ed.), *Youth and culture: A human development approach.* Monterey, CA: Brooks/Cole.

Mednick, S. S., & Christiansen, K. O. (1977). *Biosocial bases of criminal behavior.* New York: Gardner Press.

Meer, J. (1986a). The smoking diet plan. *Psychology Today, 20,* 12.

Meer, J. (1986b). Yours, mine, and divorce. *Psychology Today, 20,* 13.

Meer, J. (1986c). The reason of age. *Psychology Today, 20,* 60–64.

Mehl, L. E., & Peterson, G. (1981). Home birth versus hospital birth: Comparisons of outcomes of matched populations. In P. Ahmed (Ed.), *Pregnancy, childbirth, and parenthood.* New York: Elsevier.

Meichenbaum, D. (1972). Cognitive modification of test anxious college students. *Journal of Consulting and Clinical Psychology, 39,* 370–380.

Meier, B. (1987, February 5). Companies wrestle with threats to workers' reproductive health. *Wall Street Journal,* p. 21.

Meltzoff, A. N. (1988). Infant imitation after a 1-week delay: Long-term memory for novel acts and multiple stimuli. *Developmental Psychology, 24,* 470–476.

Meltzoff, A. N., & Moore, M. K. (1977). Imitation of facial and manual gestures by human neonates. *Science, 198,* 75–78.

Meltzoff, A. N., & Moore, M. K. (1979). Interpreting "imitative" responses in early infancy. *Science, 205,* 217–219.

Menich, S. R., & Baron, A. (1990). Age-related effects of reinforced practice on recognition memory: Consistent versus varied stimulus–response relations. *Journal of Gerontology, 45,* P88–P93.

Meredith, D. (1986). Day care: The nine-to-five dilemma. *Psychology Today, 20,* 36–44.

Meredith, H. V. (1978). Research between 1960 and 1970 on the standing height of young children in different parts of the world. In H. W. Reese & L. P. Lipsitt (Eds.), *Advances in child development and behavior* (Vol. 12). New York: Academic Press.

Messer, A. A. (1989). Boys' father hunger: The missing father syndrome. *Medical Aspects of Human Sexuality, 23,* 44–50.

Metcalf, K., & Gaier, E. L. (1987). Patterns of middle-class parent and adolescent underachievement. *Adolescence, 23,* 919–928.

Meyers, D. A., Goldberg, A. P., Bleecker, M. L., Coon, P. J., Drinkwater, D. T., & Bleecker, E. R. (1991). Relationship of obesity and physical fitness to cardiopulmonary and metabolic function in healthy older men. *Journal of Gerontology, 46,* M57–M65.

Meyers, J. E., & Nelson, W. M. III. (1986). Cognitive strategies and expectations as components of social competence in young adolescents. *Adolescence, 21,* 291–303.

Mezynski, K. (1983). Issues concerning the acquisition of knowledge: Effects of vocabulary training on reading comprehension. *Review of Educational Research, 53,* 253–279.

Micheli, L. J. (1988). The incidence of injuries in children's sports: A medical perspective. In E. W. Brown & C. F. Branta (Eds.), *Competitive sports for children and youth: An overview of research and issues* (pp. 280–284). Champaign, IL: Human Kinetics.

Miller, A. T., Eggertson-Tacon, C., & Quigg, B. (1990). Patterns of runaway behavior within a larger systems context: The road to empowerment. *Adolescence, 25,* 271–290.

Miller, B. C., & Bowen, S. L. (1982, January). Father-to-newborn attachment behavior in relation to prenatal classes and presence at delivery. *Family Relations, 31,* 71–78.

Miller, B. C., & Sollie, D. L. (1980). Normal stress during the transitions to parenthood. *Family Relations, 29,* 459–465.

Miller, D. (1974). *Adolescence: Psychology, psychopathology, and psychotherapy.* New York: Jason Aronson.

Miller, D. (1991). Do adolescents help and share? *Adolescence, 26,* 449–456.

Miller, E., Cradock-Watson, J. E., & Pollack, T. M. (1982, October). Consequences of confirmed maternal rubella and successive stages of pregnancy. *Lancet,* pp. 781–784.

Miller, H. (1977, September–October). Why we oppose mandatory retirement. *Dynamic Years, 12,* 18.

Miller, J. A., Turner, J. G., & Kimball, E. (1981). Big Thompson flood victims: One year later. *Family Relations, 30,* 111–116.

Miller, J. B., & Lane, M. (1991). Relations between young adults and their parents. *Journal of Adolescence, 14,* 179–194.

Miller, J. P. (1978, Summer). Piaget, Kohlberg, and Erikson: Developmental implications for secondary education. *Adolescence, 13,* 237–250.

Miller, K. E. (1990). Adolescents' same-sex and opposite-sex peer relations: Sex differences in popularity, perceived social competence, and social cognitive skills. *Journal of Adolescent Research, 5,* 222–241.

Miller, L. (1988). The emotional brain. *Psychology Today, 22,* 34–42.

Miller, M. (1978, October). Geriatric suicide: The Arizona study. *Gerontologist, 18,* 488–495.

Miller, M. W. (1985, January 17). Study says birth defects more frequent in areas polluted by technology firms. *Wall Street Journal,* p. 6.

Miller, P. H., & Aloise, P. A. (1989). Young children's understanding of the psychological causes of behavior: A review. *Child Development, 60,* 257–285.

Miller, S. S., & Cavanaugh, J. C. (1990). The meaning of grandparenthood and its relationship to demographic, relationship, and social participation variables. *Journal of Gerontology, 45,* P244–P247.

Mills, C. J. (1981, April). Sex roles, personality, and intellectual abilities in adolescents. *Journal of Youth and Adolescence, 10,* 85–112.

Mills, D. M. (1984). A model for stepfamily development. *Family Relations, 33,* 365–372.

Mills, J. L., Graubard, B. I., Harley, E. E., Rhoads, G. G., & Berendes, H. W. (1984). Maternal alcohol consumption and birth weight: How much drinking is safe during pregnancy? *JAMA, Journal of the American Medical Association, 252,* 1875–1879.

Mills, R. S. L., & Rubin, K. H. (1990). Parents' beliefs about problematic social behaviors in early childhood. *Child Development, 61,* 138–151.

Mistry, J. J., & Lange, G. W. (1985). Children's organization and recall of information in scripted narratives. *Child Development, 56,* 953–961.

Mitchell, D. R., & Lyles, K. W. (1990). Minireview: Glucocorticoid-induced osteoporosis: Mechanisms for bone loss; evaluation of strategies for prevention. *Journal of Gerontology, 45,* M153–M158.

Mitchell, J. (1980, Fall). Adolescent hypocrisy. *Adolescence, 15,* 731–736.

Mitchell, J., & Dodder, R. A. (1980, June). An examination of types of delinquency through path analysis. *Journal of Youth and Adolescence, 9,* 239–248.

Mitchell, J. E., Pyle, R. L., & Eckert, E. D. (1981). Frequency and duration of binge-eating episodes in patients with bulimia. *American Journal of Psychiatry, 138,* 835, 836.

Mitgang, L. (1980, April 28). *Student SAT scores decline for third year.* Portland, ME: Portland Press Herald.

Modell, J., Furstenberg, F. F., & Hershberg, T. (1976). Social change and transitions to adulthood in historical perspective. *Journal of Family History, 1,* 7–32.

Moehle, K. A., & Long, C. (1989). Models of aging and neuropsychological test performance decline with aging. *Journal of Gerontology, 44,* P176–177.

Moffitt, T. E. (1990). Juvenile delinquency and attention deficit disorder: Boys' developmental trajectories from age 3 to 15. *Child Development, 61,* 893–910.

Mom, nine, doing fine. (1986, June 15). *Parade,* p. 15.

Money, J. (1968). *Sex errors of the body.* Baltimore, MD: Johns Hopkins University Press.

Money, J. (1980). *Love and love sickness.* Baltimore, MD: Johns Hopkins University Press.

Monge, R. H., & Gardner, E. V. (1972). *A program of research in adult differences in cognitive performance and learning: Backgrounds for adult education and vocational training* (Final Report, Project No. 6-1963, Grant No. OEG 1-706193-o149).

Montague, A., & Matson, F. (1979). *The human connection.* New York: McGraw-Hill.

Montgomery, J. E. (1982). The economics of supportive services for families with disabled and aging members. *Family Relations, 31,* 19–27.

Moore, D., & Schultz, N. R. (1983). Loneliness at adolescence: Correlates, attributions, and coping. *Journal of Youth and Adolescence, 12,* 95–100.

Moore, J. W., Jensen, B., & Hauck, W. E. (1990). Decision-making processes of youth. *Adolescence, 25,* 583–592.

Moore, K. A., & Stief, T. M. (1991). Changes in marriage and fertility behavior: Behavior versus attitudes of young adults. *Youth and Society, 22,* 362–286.

Moore, K. L. (1982). *The developing human: Clinically oriented embryology* (3rd ed.). Philadelphia, PA: Saunders.

Moore, L. M., Nielsen, C. R., & Mistretta, C. M. (1982). Sucrose taste thresholds: Age-related differences. *Journal of Gerontology, 37,* 64–69.

Moore, S., & Rosenthal, D. (1990). Adolescent invulnerability and perceptions of AIDS risk. *Journal of Adolescent Research, 6,* 164–180.

Mor, V., & Masterson-Allen, S. (1987). *Hospice care systems: Structure, process, costs, and outcome.* New York: Springer.

Moran, G. F., & Vinovskis, M. A. (1986). The great care of godly parents: Early childhood in Puritan New England. *Monographs of the Society for Research in Child Development, 50* (4-5, Serial No. 211).

Morehouse, L. E., & Gross, L. (1975). *Total fitness in 30 minutes a week.* New York: Simon & Schuster.

Morell, P., & Norton, W. T. (1980). Myelin. *Scientific American, 24,* 88–118.

Morgan, M., & Gross, L. (1982). Television and educational achievement. In D. Pearl, L. Bouthilet & J. Lazer (Eds.), *Television and behavior: Ten years of scientific progress and implications for the eighties* (Vol. 2). Washington, DC: U.S. Government Printing Office.

Morgan, R. E. (1968). The adult growth examination: Preliminary comparison of physical aging in adults by sex and race. *Perceptual and Motor Skills, 27,* 595–599.

Moritani, T., & deVries, H. A. (1980). Potential for gross muscle hypertrophy in older men. *Journal of Gerontology, 135,* 672–682.

Moritz, D. J., Kasl, S. V., & Berkman, L. F. (1989). The health impact of living with a cognitively impaired elderly spouse: Depressive symptoms and social functioning. *Journal of Gerontology, 44,* S17–S27.

Morris, J. C., Rubin, E. H., Morris, E. J., & Mandel, S. A. (1987). Senile dementia of the Alzheimer's type: An important risk factor for serious falls. *Journal of Gerontology, 42,* 412–417.

Motenko, A. K. (1989). The frustrations, gratifications, and well-being of dementia caregivers. *Gerontologist, 29,* 166–172.

Mueller, D. P., & Cooper, P. W. (1986). Children of single parent families: How they fare as young adults. *Family Relations, 35,* 169–172.

Mueller, K. E., & Powers, W. G. (1990). Parent–child sexual discussion: Perceived communicator style and subsequent behavior. *Adolescence, 25,* 469–482.

Mueller, J. H., Rankins, J. L., & Carlomusto, M. (1979). Adult age differences in free recall as a function of basis of organization and method of presentation. *Journal of Gerontology, 34,* 375–380.

Mukerji, V. (1988). Peripheral vascular disease. *Medical Aspects of Human Sexuality, 22,* 83–84.

Muller, H. F., & Schwartz, G. (1978). Electroencephalogram and autopsy findings in geropsychiatry. *Journal of Gerontology, 33,* 504–513.

Murdock, B. B., Jr. (1974). *Human memory: Theory and data.* Potomac, MD: Erlbaum.

Murray, A. D. (1988). Newborn auditory brainstem evoked responses (ABRs): Prenatal and contemporary correlates. *Child Development, 59,* 571–588.

Muson, H. (1977). The lessons of the Grant study. *Psychology Today, 11,* 42, 48, 49.

Muuss, R. E. (1985). Adolescent eating disorder: Anorexia nervosa. *Adolescence, 20,* 525–536.

Muuss, R. E. (1988a). Carol Gilligan's theory of sex differences in the development of moral reasoning during adolescence. *Adolescence, 23,* 229–243.

Muuss, R. E. (1988b). *Theories of adolescence* (5th ed.). New York: McGraw-Hill.

Myers, D. A. (1991). Work after cessation of career job. *Journal of Gerontology, 46,* S93–S102.

Myska, M. J., & Pasewark, R. A. (1978, December). Death attitudes of residential and non-residential rural aged persons. *Psychological Reports, 43,* 1235–1238.

Nadi, N. S., Nurnberger, J. L., & Gershon, E. S. (1984). Muscarinic cholinergic receptors on skin fibroblasts in familial affective disorder. *New England Journal of Medicine, 311,* 225–230.

Nagy, M. H. (1948). The child's theories concerning death. *Journal of Genetic Psychology, 73,* 3–27.

Nagy, W., & Anderson, R. C. (1984). The number of words in printed school English. *Reading Research Quarterly, 19,* 304–330.

Nagy, W., Herman, P. A., & Anderson, R. C. (1985). Learning words from context. *Reading Research Quarterly, 20,* 233–253.

National audience demographics. Report 1985. (1985). Northrock, IL: A. C. Nielsen Co.

National Children and Youth Fitness Study. (1984). Washington, DC: U.S. Public Health Service, Office for Disease Prevention and Health Promotion.

National Commission for the Protection of Human Subjects of Biomedical and Behavioral Research. (1978). Institutional review boards: Report and recommendations. *Federal Register, 43,* 56174–56198.

National Commission on Excellence in Education. (1983). *A nation at risk: The imperative for educational reform.* Washington, DC: Department of Education.

National Foundation for the March of Dimes. (1977). *Birth defects: Tragedy and hope.*

National Institute on Alcohol Abuse and Alcoholism (NIAA). (1986). *Media alert: FAS awareness campaign: My baby . . . strong and healthy.* Rockville, MD: National Clearinghouse for Alcohol Information.

National Institute on Mental Health (NIMH). (1982). *Television and behavior: Ten years of scientific progress and implications for the eighties: Vol. 1. Summary Report* (DHHS Publication No. ADM 82–1195). Washington, DC: U.S. Government Printing Office.

Neiger, B. L., & Hopkins, R. W. (1988). Adolescent suicide: Character traits of high-risk teenagers. *Adolescence, 23,* 469–475.

Neimark, E. D. (1981). Confounding with cognitive style factors: An artifact explanation for the apparent nonuniversal incidence of formal operations. In I. Siegel, D. Brodzinsky, & R. Golinkoff (Eds.), *New directions in Piagetian theory and practice.* Hillsdale, NJ: Erlbaum.

Nelson, C., & Keith, J. (1990). Comparison of female and male early adolescent sex role attitude and behavior development. *Adolescence, 25,* 183–204.

Nelson, F. L., & Farberow, N. L. (1980, November). Indirect self-destructive behavior in the elderly nursing home patient. *Journal of Gerontology, 34,* 949–957.

Nelson, K. (1981). Individual differences in language development: Implications for development and language. *Developmental Psychology, 17,* 170–189.

Nemeth, P. (1990, April). Kids on ritalin: Are they better off? *On campus.* Washington, DC: American Federation of Teachers.

Nettles, S. M. (1989). The role of community involvement in fostering investment behavior in low-income black adolescents: A theoretical perspective. *Journal of Adolescent Research, 4,* 190–201.

Neugarten, B. L. (Ed.). (1968). *Middle age and aging: A reader in social psychology.* Chicago, IL: University of Chicago Press.

Neugarten, B. L. (1989). Policy issues for an aging society. *The psychology of aging.* Washington, DC: American Psychological Association.

Neugarten, B. L., Havighurst, R. J., & Tobin, S. (1961). The measurement of life satisfaction. *Journal of Gerontology, 16,* 134–143.

Neugarten, B. L., Havighurst, R. D., & Tobin, S. S. (1968). Personality and patterns of aging. In B. L. Neugarten (Ed.), *Middle age and aging* (pp. 173–177). Chicago, IL: University of Chicago Press.

Neugarten, B. L., Moore, J. W., & Lowe, J. C. (1965). Age norms, age constraints, and adult socialization. *American Journal of Sociology, 40,* 710–717.

Neugarten, B. L., & Neugarten, D. A. (1987). The changing meanings of age. *Psychology Today, 21,* 29–33.

Newcomb, M. D., & Bentler, P. M. (1980). Cohabitation before marriage: A comparison of married couples who did and did not cohabit. *Alternate Lifestyles, 3,* 65–83.

Newcomer, S. F., Udry, J. R., & Cameron, F. (1983). Adolescent sexual behavior and popularity. *Adolescence, 18,* 515–522.

Newell, G. K., Hammig, C. L., Jurich, A. P., & Johnson, D. E. (1990). Self-concept as a factor in the quality of diets of adolescent girls. *Adolescence, 25,* 117–130.

Newman, B. M., & Newman, P. R. (1983). *Understanding adulthood.* New York: Holt, Rinehart, & Winston.

Newman, B. M., & Newman, P. R. (1984). *Development through life: A psychosocial approach* (2nd ed.). Homewood, IL: Dorsey Press.

Nieburg, P., Marks, J. S., McLaren, N. M., & Remington, P. L. (1985). The fetal tobacco syndrome. *JAMA, Journal of the American Medical Association, 253,* 2998–2999.

Niinimaa, V., & Shephard, R. J. (1978). Training and oxygen conductance in the elderly. *Journal of Gerontology, 33,* 354–361.

Nock, S. L. (1988). The family and hierarchy. *Journal of Marriage and the Family, 50,* 957–966.

Norris, F. H., & Murrell, S. A. (1987). Older adult family stress and adaptation before and after bereavement. *Journal of Gerontology, 42,* 606–612.

Northman, J. E. (1985). The emergence of an appreciation for help during childhood and adolescence. *Adolescence, 20,* 775–781.

Norton, A. J., & Glick, P. B. (1986). One-parent families: A social and economic profile. *Family Relations, 35,* 9–13.

Norton, A. J., & Moorman, J. E. (1987). Current trends in marriage and divorce among American women. *Journal of Marriage and the Family, 49,* 3–14.

Norton, W. T. (1963). Toward an adequate taxonomy of personal attributes: Replicated factor structure in peer nomination personality ratings. *Journal of Abnormal and Social Psychology, 66,* 577.

Nurmi, J. A., & Pulliainen, H. (1991). The changing parent–child relationships, self-esteem, and intelligence as determinants of orientation to the future during early adolescence. *Journal of Adolescence, 14,* 17–34.

Nuttal, R. L., Fozard, J. L., Orse, C. L., & Spencer, B. (1971). *The ages of man: Ability, age, personality age, and blood chemistry age.* Proceedings of the 79th annual convention of the American Psychological Association (Vol. 6, pp. 605–606).

Offer, D., Ostrov, E., & Howard, K. J. (1982, August). Family perceptions of adolescent self-image. *Journal of Youth and Adolescence, 11,* 281–291.

Ogundari, J. T. (1985, Spring). Somatic deviations in adolescence: Reactions and adjustments. *Adolescence, 20,* 179–183.

Okun, M. A., & Sasfy, J. H. (1977, Fall). Adolescence, the self-concept, and formal operations. *Adolescence, 12,* 373–379.

Okun, M. A., Stock, W. A., Haring, M. J., & Witter, R. (1984). Health and subjective well-being: A meta-analysis. *International Journal of Aging and Human Development, 19,* 111–132.

Olsen, J. A., Jensen, L. C., & Greaves, P. M. (1991). Adolescent sexuality and public policy. *Adolescence, 26,* 419–430.

Olson, S. L., Bates, J. E., & Bayles, K. (1984). Mother-infant interaction and the development of individual differences in children's cognitive competence. *Developmental Psychology, 20,* 166–179.

Olthof, T., Ferguson, T. J., & Luiten, A. (1989). Personal responsibility antecedents of anger and blame reactions on children. *Child Development, 60,* 1328–1336.

Olvera-Ezzell, N., Power, T. G., & Cousins, J. H. (1990). Maternal socialization of children's eating habits: Strategies used by obese Mexican-American mothers. *Child Development, 61,* 395–400.

Olweus, D. (1977). Aggression and peer acceptance in adolescent boys: Two short-term longitudinal studies of ratings. *Child Development, 48,* 1301–1313.

Openshaw, D. K., Thomas, D. L., & Rollins, B. C. (1983, Summer). Socialization and adolescent self-esteem: Symbolic interaction and social learning explanations. *Adolescence, 18,* 317–329.

Oppenheimer, M. (1982). What you should know about herpes. *Seventeen,* pp. 154, 155, 170.

Orlofsky, J. L. (1982). Psychological androgyny, sex typing, and sex role ideology as predictors of male-female interpersonal attraction. *Sex Roles, 8,* 1057.

O'Sullivan, R. G. (1990). Validating a method to identify at-risk middle school students for participation in a dropout prevention program. *Journal of Early Adolescence, 10,* 209–220.

Ottenweller, J. E., Tapp, W. W., Creighton, D., & Natelson, B. H. (1988). Aging, stress, and chronic disease interact to suppress plasma testosterone in Syrian hamsters. *Journal of Gerontology, 43,* M175–M180.

Otto, L. B. (1988). America's youth: A changing profile. *Family Relations, 37,* 385–391.

Overpeck, M. D. et al. (1989). A comparison of the childhood health status of normal weight birth and low birth weight infants. *Public Health Reports, 104,* 58.

Paccione-Dyszlewski, M. R., & Contessa-Kislus, M. A. (1987). School phobia: Identification of subtypes as a prerequisite to treatment intervention. *Adolescence, 22,* 277–384.

Paddack, C. (1987). Preparing a boy for nocturnal emissions. *Medical Aspects of Human Sexuality, 21,* 15, 16.

Padin, M. A., Lerner, R. M., & Spiro, A. III. (1981, Summer). Stability of body attitudes and self-esteem in late adolescents. *Adolescence, 16,* 371–384.

Page, R. M. (1990). Shyness and sociability: A dangerous combination for illicit substance use in adolescent males? *Adolescence, 25,* 803–806.

Paikoff, R. B. (1990). Attitudes toward consequences of pregnancy in young women attending a family planning clinic. *Journal of Adolescence Research, 5,* 467–484.

Palazzi, S., deVito, E., Luzzati, G., Guerrini, A., & Torre, I. (1990). A study of the relationships between life events and disturbed self-image in adolescents. *Journal of Adolescence, 13,* 53–64.

Paley, V. G. (1984). *Boys and girls: Superheroes in the doll corner.* Chicago, IL: University of Chicago Press.

Palmore, E. (1977, August). Facts on aging: A short quiz. *Gerontologist, 17,* 315–320.

Palmore, E., & Cleveland, W. (1976). Aging, terminal decline, and terminal drop. *Journal of Gerontology, 31,* 76–81.

Papini, D. R., Farmer, F. F., Clark, S. M., Micka, J. C., & Barnett, J. W. (1990). *Adolescence, 25,* 958–976.

Papini, D. R., Roggman, L. A., & Anderson, J. (1990). Early-adolescent perceptions of attachment to mother and father: A test of the emotional-distancing and buffering hypotheses. *Journal of Early Adolescence, 11,* 258–275.

Parcel, G. S., & Luttman, D. (1981). Evaluation of a sex education course of young adolescents. *Family Relations, 30,* 55–60.

Pardeck, J. T. (1990). Family factors related to adolescent autonomy. *Adolescence, 25,* 311–320.

Parfitt, R. R. (1977). *The birth primer.* Philadelphia, PA: Reunion Press.

Parish, J. G., & Parish, T. S. (1983, Fall). Children's self-concepts as related to family structure and family concept. *Adolescence, 18,* 649–658.

Parish, T. S. (1990). Evaluations of family by youth: Do they vary as a function of family structure, gender, and birth order? *Adolescence, 25,* 353–356.

Parish, T. S. (1991). Ratings of self and parents by youth: Are they affected by family status, gender, and birth order? *Adolescence, 26,* 105–112.

Parish, T. S., & Dostal, J. W. (1980, August). Evaluations of self and parent figures by children from intact, divorced and reconstituted families. *Journal of Youth and Adolescence, 9,* 347–351.

Parish, T. S., Dostal, J. W., & Parish, J. G. (1981). Evaluations of self and parents as a function of intactness of family and family happiness. *Adolescence, 16,* 203–210.

Parish, T. S., & Parish, J. G. (1991). The effects of family configuration and support system failures during childhood and adolescence on college students' self-concepts and social skills. *Adolescence, 26,* 441–448.

Parish, T. S., & Taylor, J. C. (1979, December). The impact of divorce and subsequent father absence on children's and adolescents' self-concepts. *Journal of Youth and Adolescence, 8,* 427–432.

Park, K. A., & Waters, E. (1989). Security of attachment and preschool friendships. *Child Development, 60,* 1076–1081.

Parker, W. A. (1980). Designing an environment for childbirth. In B. L. Glum (Ed.), *Psychological aspects of pregnancy, birthing, and bonding.* New York: Human Sciences Press.

Parkinson, S. R., Lindholm, J. M., & Urell, T. (1980). Aging, dichotic memory and digit span. *Journal of Gerontology, 35,* 87–95.

Parlee, M. B. (1978). The rhythms in men's lives. *Psychology Today, 11,* 82.

Parten, M. B. (1932). Social participation among preschool children. *Journal of Abnormal and Social Psychology, 27,* 243–269.

Passuth, P., Maines, D., & Neugarten, B. L. (1984, April). *Age norms and age constraints twenty years later.* Paper presented at the Midwest Sociological Society meeting, Chicago, IL.

Palti, H., Mansbach, I., Pridan, H., Adler, B., & Palti, Z. (1984). Episodes of illness in breast-fed and bottle-fed infants in Jerusalem. *Journal of Medical Sciences, 20,* 395–399.

Paton, S. M., & Kandel, D. B. (1978, Summer). Psychological factors and adolescent illicit drug use: Ethnicity and sex differences. *Adolescence, 13,* 187–200.

Patten, M. A. (1981, Winter). Self-concept and self-esteem: Factors in adolescent pregnancy. *Adolescence, 16,* 765–778.

Patterson, C. J., Kupersmidt, J. B., & Vaden, N. A. (1990). Income level, gender, ethnicity, and household composition as predictors of children's school-based competence. *Child Development, 61,* 485–494.

Patterson, F. (1977). The gestures of a gorilla. Language acquisition in another primate species. In J. Hamburg, J. Goodall, & L. McCown (Eds.), *Perspectives in human evolution* (Vol. 4). Menlo Park, CA: W. A. Benjamin.

Patterson, M. M., & Lynch, A. Q. (1988). Menopause: Salient issues for counselors. *Journal of Counseling and Development, 67,* 185–188.

Pattison, E. M. (1977). *The experience of dying.* Englewood Cliffs, NJ: Prentice-Hall.

Paul, E. L., & White, K. M. (1990). The development of intimate relationships in late adolescence. *Adolescence, 25,* 375–400.

Paul, M. J., & Fischer, J. L. (1980, April). Correlates of self-concept among black early adolescents. *Journal of Youth and Adolescence, 9,* 163–173.

Paulson, S. E., Hill, J. P., & Holmbeck, G. N. (1990). Distinguishing between perceived closeness and parental warmth in families with seventh-grade boys and girls. *Journal of Early Adolescence, 11,* 276–293.

Pearson, J. L., & Ferguson, L. R. (1989). Gender differences in patterns of spatial ability, environmental cognition, and math and English achievement in late adolescence. *Adolescence, 24,* 421–431.

Pearson, J. L., Hunter, A. G., Ensminger, M. E., & Kellam, S. G. (1990). Black grandmothers in multigenerational households: Diversity in family structure and parenting involvement in the Woodlawn community. *Child Development, 61,* 434–442.

Pederson, D. R., Moran, G., Sitko, C., Campbell, K., Ghesquire, & Acton, H. (1990). Maternal sensitivity and the security of infant–mother attachment: A Q-sort study. *Child Development, 61,* 1974–1983.

Pederson, E., Faucher, A., & Eaton, W. W. (1978). A new perspective of the effects of first-grade teacher on children's subsequent adult status. *Harvard Educational Review, 48,* 1–31.

Pedersen, W. (1990). Adolescents initiating cannabis use: Cultural opposition or poor mental health? *Journal of Adolescence, 13,* 327–340.

Pellegrini, A. D., Perlmutter, J. C., Galda, L., & Brody, G. H. (1990). Joint reading between black Head Start children and their mothers. *Child Development, 61,* 443–453.

Perlmutter, M. (1979). Age differences in adults' free recall, cued recall, and recognition. *Journal of Gerontology, 34,* 533–539.

Perlmutter, M. (1987). Aging and memory. In K. W. Schaie & K. Eisdorfer (Eds.), *Annual Review of Gerontology and Geriatrics* (Vol. 7). New York: Springer Publishing Co.

Perlmutter, M., & Nyquist, L. (1990). Relationships between self-reported physical and mental health and intelligence performance across adulthood. *Journal of Gerontology, 45,* P145–P155.

Perper, T., & Weiss, D. L. (1987). Proceptive and rejective strategies of U.S. and Canadian college women. *Journal of Sex Research, 23,* 455–480.

Perris, E. E., Myers, N. A., & Clifton, R. K. (1990). Long-term memory for a single infancy experience. *Child Development, 61,* 1796–1807.

Perry, D. G., Williard, J. C., & Perry, L. C. (1990). Peers' perceptions of the consequences that victimized children provide aggressors. *Child Development, 61,* 1310–1325.

Pestrak, V. A., & Martin, D. (1985). Cognitive development and aspects of adolescent sexuality. *Adolescence, 22,* 981–987.

Pete, J. M., & DeSantis, L. (1990). Sexual decision making in young black adolescent females. *Adolescence, 25,* 145–154.

Petersen, J. R., Kretchner, A., Nellis, B., Lever, J., & Hertz, R. (1983). The playboy readers sex survey. Part 2. *Playboy,* p. 90.

Petersen, L. R., Lee, G. R., & Ellis, G. J. (1982). Social structure, socialization values, and disciplinary techniques: A cross-cultural analysis. *Journal of Marriage and the Family, 44,* 131–142.

Peterson, G. W., & Rollins, B. C. (1987). Parent-child socialization. In M. B. Sussman & S. K. Steinmetz (Eds.), *Handbook of marriage and the family* (pp. 471–507). New York: Plenum.

Peterson, C. C., & Murphy, L. (1990). Adolescents' thoughts and feelings about AIDS in relation to cognitive maturity. *Journal of Adolescence, 13,* 185–188.

Peterson, K. L., & Roscoe, B. (1991). Imaginary audience behavior in older adolescent females. *Adolescence, 26,* 195–200.

Pett, M. B., & Vaughan-Cole, B. (1986). The impact of income issues and social status in post-divorce adjustment of custodial parents. *Family Relations, 35,* 103–111.

Pettit, G. S., Doge, K. H., & Brown, M. M. (1988). Early family experience, social problem solving patterns, and children's social competence. *Child Development, 59,* 107–120.

Pezdek, K. (1987). Memory of pictures: A life-span study of the role of visual detail. *Child Development, 58,* 807–815.

Pfeffer, C. (1987). Suicidal children announce their self-destructive intentions. *Medical Aspects of Human Sexuality, 21,* 14.

Phares, E. J. (1984). *Introduction to personality.* Glenview, IL: Scott, Foresman.

Phifer, J. G., & Norris, F. H. (1989). Psychological symptoms in older adults following natural disaster: Nature, timing, duration, and course. *Journal of Gerontology, 44,* S207–S217.

Phillips, D. A. (1987). Socialization of perceived academic competence among highly competitive children. *Child Development, 58,* 1308–1320.

Phillips, J. S., Barrett, G. V., & Rush, M. C. (Spring, 1978). Job structure and age satisfaction. *Aging and Work,* pp. 109–119.

Phinney, J. S., & Alipuria, L. L. (1990). Ethnic identity in college students from four ethnic groups. *Journal of Adolescence, 13,* 171–184.

Phinney, V. G., Jensen, L. C., Olsen, J. A., & Cundick, B. (1990). The relationship between early development and psychosexual behaviors in adolescent females. *Adolescence, 25,* 321–332.

Piaget, J. (1926). *The language of the child* (M. Warden, Trans.). New York: Harcourt.

Piaget, J. (1948). *The moral judgment of the child* (1932 reprint). Glencoe, IL: Free Press.

Piaget, J. (1950). *The psychology of intelligence.* London: Routledge and Kegan Paul.

Piaget, J. (1954). *The construction of reality in the child.* New York: Basic Books.

Piaget, J. (1962). *Play, dream, and imitation in childhood.* New York: W. W. Norton.

Piaget, J. (1963). *The origins of intelligence in children.* New York: W. W. Norton.

Piaget, J. (1967a). *The child's construction of the world.* Totowa, NJ: Littlefield, Adams.

Piaget, J. (1967b). *Six psychological studies* (A. Tenzer, & D. Elkind, Trans.). New York: Random House.

Piaget, J. (1971). The theory of stages in cognitive development. In D. R. Green (Ed.), *Measurement and Piaget.* New York: McGraw-Hill.

Piaget, J. (1972). Intellectual evolution from adolescence to adulthood. *Human Development, 15,* 1012.

Piaget, J. (1980). Intellectual evolution from adolescence to adulthood. In R. E. Muuss (Ed.), *Adolescent behavior and society: A body of readings* (3rd ed.). New York: Random House.

Piaget, J., & Inhelder, B. (1969). *The psychology of the child.* (H. Weaver, Trans.). New York: Basic Books.

Pichitino, J. P. (1983). Profile of the single father: A thematic integration of the literature. *Personnel and Guidance Journal, 5,* 295–299.

Piers, E. V. (1984). *Revised manual for the Piers-Harris children's self-concept scale.* Los Angeles, CA: Western Psychological Services.

Piers, M. W. (1978). *Infanticide: Past and present.* New York: W. W. Norton.

Pierson, E. C., & D'Antonio, W. V. (1974). *Female and male: dimensions of human sexuality.* Philadelphia, PA: Lippincott.

Pillemer, D. B., Koff, E., Rhinehart, E. D., & Rierdan, J. (1987). Flashbulb memories of menarche and adult menstrual distress. *Journal of Adolescence, 10,* 187–199.

Pillow, B. H. (1988). Young children's understanding of attentional limits. *Child Development, 58,* 38–46.

Pines, M. (1981, September). The civilizing of Genie. *Psychology Today, 14,* 28–34.

Pines, M. (1984). In the shadow of Huntington's. *Science, 84, 5,* 32–39.

Pinneau, S. R. (1961). *Changes in intelligent quotient.* Boston, MA: Houghton Mifflin.

Pinon, M. F., Huston, A. C., & Wright, J. C. (1989). Family ecology and child characteristics that predict young children's educational television viewing. *Child Development, 60,* 846–856.

Pipp, S., & Harmon, R. J. (1987). Attachment as regulation: A commentary. *Child Development, 58,* 648–652.

Pitcher, E. G., & Schultz, L. H. (1983). *Boys and girls at play: The development of sex roles.* New York: Holt, Rinehart, & Winston.

Plemons, J. K., Willis, S. L., & Baltes, P. (1978). Modifiability of fluid intelligence in aging: A short-term longitudinal training approach. *Journal of Gerontology, 33,* 224–231.

Plomin, R. (1989). Environment and genes: Determinants of behavior. *American Psychologist, 44,* 105–111.

Plummer, L. D., & Koch-Hattem, A. (1986). Family stress and adjustment to divorce. *Family Relations, 35,* 523–529.

Plummer, W. (1985, October 28). A school's Rx for sex. *People,* pp. 39–41.

Poehlman, E. T., Melby, C. L., & Badylak, S. F. (1991). Relation of age and physical exercise status on metabolic rate in younger and older healthy men. *Journal of Gerontology, 46,* B54–B58.

Pombeni, J. L., Kirchler, E., & Palmonari, A. (1990). Identification with peers as a strategy to muddle through the troubles of the adolescent years. *Journal of Adolescence, 13,* 351–370.

Pomerantz, S. C. (1979, March). Sex differences in relative importance of self-esteem. Physical self-satisfaction and identity if predicting adolescent satisfaction. *Journal of Youth and Adolescence, 8,* 51–61.

Ponterotto, J. G., Pace, T. M., & Kavan, M. G. (1989). A counselor's guide to the assessment of depression. *Journal of Counseling and Development, 67,* 301–309.

Poon, L. W., & Fozard, J. L. (1978). Speed of retrieval from long-term memory in relation to age, familiarity, and datedness of information. *Journal of Gerontology, 33,* 711–717.

Porjesz, B., & Begleitner, H. (1985). Human brain electrophysiology and alcoholism. In R. Tarter & D. Thiel (Eds.), *Alcohol and the brain.* New York: Plenum.

Porreco, R., & Meier, P. (1983). Trials of labor in patients with multiple previous cesarean sections. *Journal of Reproductive Medicine, 28,* 770–772.

Porter, F. L., Porges, S. W., & Marshall, R. E. (1988). Newborn pain cries and vagal tone: Parallel changes in response to circumcision. *Child Development, 59,* 495–505.

Porter, N. L., & Christopher, F. S. (1984). Infertility: Toward an awareness of a need among family life practitioners. *Family Relations, 33,* 309–315.

Portes, P. R., Dunham, R. M., & Williams, S. (1986). Assessing child-rearing style in ecological settings: Its relation to culture, social class, early age intervention, and scholastic achievement. *Adolescence, 21,* 723–735.

Potash, M., & Jones, B. (1977). Aging and decision criteria for the detection of tones in noise. *Journal of Gerontology, 32,* 436–440.

Powell, D. A., Milligan, W. L., and Furchtgott, E. (1980). Peripheral autonomic changes accompanying learning and reaction time performance in older people. *Journal of Gerontology, 35,* 57–65.

Powers, P. S. (1980). *Obesity: The regulation of weight.* Baltimore, MD: Williams & Wilkins.

Presser, H. B. (1978, Summer). Age at menarche, socio-sexual behavior, and fertility. *Social Biology, 25,* 94–101.

Preston, D. B., & Mansfield, P. K. (1984). An exploration of stressful life events, illness, and coping among the rural elderly. *Gerontologist, 24,* 490–495.

Preston, G. A. N. (1986). Dementia in elderly adults: Prevalence and institutionalization. *Journal of Gerontology, 41,* 261–267.

Price, D. W. W., & Goodman, G. S. (1990). Visiting the wizard: Children's memory for a recurring event. *Child Development, 61,* 664–680.

Price, J., & Feshbach, S. (1982, August). *Emotional adjustment correlates of televising viewing in children.* Paper presented at the meeting of the American Psychological Association, Washington, DC.

Prinz, P. A. (1977). Sleep patterns in the healthy aged: Relationship with intellectual function. *Journal of Gerontology, 32,* 179–186.

Pritchard, J., MacDonald, D., & Grant, N. (1985). *Williams obstetrics* (17th ed.). New York: Appleton-Century-Crofts.

Protinsky, H., & Farrier, S. (1980, Winter). Self-image changes in pre-adolescence and adolescents. *Adolescence, 15,* 887–893.

Pruchno, R. A., & Resch, N. L. (1989). Husbands and wives as caregivers: Antecedents of depression and burden. *Gerontologist, 29,* 159–165.

Puglisi, J. T., Park, D. C., Smith, A. D., & Dudley, W. N. (1988). Age differences in encoding specificity. *Journal of Gerontology, 43,* P145–P150.

Putallaz, M. (1987). Maternal behavior and children's sociometric status. *Child Development, 58,* 324–340.

Pyle, R. L., Mitchell, J. E., & Eckert, E. D. (1981). Bulimia: A report of 34 cases. *Journal of Clinical Psychiatry, 42,* 60–64.

Quayhagen, M. P., & Quayhagen, M. (1989). Differential effects of family based strategies on Alzheimer's disease. *Gerontologist, 29,* 150–155.

Quinn, P., & Allen, K. R. (1989). Facing challenges and making compromises: How single mothers endure. *Family Relations, 38,* 390–395.

Quinn, W. H. (1983). Personal and family adjustment in later life. *Journal of Marriage and the Family, 45,* 57–73.

Quintana, S. M., & Lapsley, D. K. (1990). Rapprochement in late adolescent separation-individuation: A structural equations approach. *Journal of Adolescence, 13,* 371–386.

Rabinowitz, J. C., & Craik, F. I. M. (1986). Prior retrieval effects in young and old adults. *Journal of Gerontology, 41,* 368–375.

Radomski, M. (1981). Stereotypes, stepmothers, and splitting. *American Journal of Psychoanalysis, 41,* 121–127.

Raffoul, P. R., Cooper, J. K., & Love, D. W. (1981). Drug misuse in older people. *Gerontologist, 21,* 146–150.

Raine, A., Hulme, Ch., Chadderton, H., & Bailey, P. (1991). Verbal short-term memory span in speech disordered children: Implications for articulatory coding in short-term memory. *Child Development, 62,* 415–423.

Raloff, J. (1986). Even low levels in mom affect baby. *Science News, 130,* 164.

Ralph, N., & Morgan, K. A. (1991). Assessing differences in chemically dependent adolescent males using the child behavior checklist. *Adolescence, 26,* 183–194.

Ramsey, D. S. (1985). Fluctuations in unimanual hand preference in infants following the onset of duplicated syllable babbling. *Developmental Psychology, 21,* 318–324.

Ramsey, D. S., & Weber, S. L. (1986). Infants' hand preference in a task involving complementary roles for the two hands. *Child Development, 57,* 300–307.

Raphael, D. (1979). Sequencing in female adolescents' consideration of occupational, religious, and political alternatives. *Adolescence, 14,* 73–80.

Rapp, G. S., & Lloyd, S. A. (1989). The role of "home as haven" ideology in child care use. *Family Relations, 38,* 426–430.

Rapp, S. R., & Davis, K. M. (1989). Geriatric depression: Physician's knowledge, perceptions, and diagnostic practices. *Journal of Gerontology, 29,* 252–257.

Raschke, H. J., & Raschke, V. J. (1979, May). Family conflict and children's self-concepts: A comparison of intact and single-parent families. *Journal of Marriage and the Family, 41,* 367–374.

Raskin, P. M. (1990). Identity status research: Implications for career counseling. *Journal of Adolescence, 13,* 375–388.

Rauh, V. A., Achenbach, T. M., Nurcombe, B., Howell, C. T., & Teti, D. M. (1988). Minimizing adverse effects of low birthweight: Four-year results of an early intervention program. *Child Development, 59,* 544–553.

Ravitch, B. (1983, October). The educational pendulum. *Psychology Today, 17,* 62–71.

Reardon, B., & Griffing, P. (1983, Spring). Factors related to the self-concept of institutionalized, white, male, adolescent drug abusers. *Adolescence, 18,* 29–41.

Reaves, J., & Roberts, A. (1983). The effects of the type of information on children's attraction to peers. *Child Development, 54,* 1024–1031.

Rebok, G. W., Montaglione, C. J., & Bendlin, G. (1988). Effects of age and training on memory for pragmatic implications in advertising. *Journal of Gerontology, 43,* P75–P78.

Rees, D. D., & Wilborn, B. L. (1983, February). Correlates of drug abuse in adolescents: A comparison of families of drug abusers with families of nondrug abusers. *Journal of Youth and Adolescence, 6,* 1–9.

Reich, P. A. (1986). *Language development.* Englewood Cliffs, NJ: Prentice-Hall.

Reis, H. T., Nezlek, J., & Wheeler, L. (1980). Physical attractiveness and social interaction. *Journal of Personality and Social Psychology, 38,* 604–617.

Reiss, I. L. (1973). *Heterosexual relationships: Inside and outside of marriage.* Morristown, NJ: General Learning Press.

Reissland, N. (1988). Neonatal imitation in the first hour of life: Observations in rural Nepal. *Developmental Psychology, 24,* 464–469.

Reitzes, D. C., Mutran, E., & Pope, H. (1991). Location and well-being among retired men. *Journal of Gerontology, 46,* S195–S203.

Reker, G. T., & Peacock, E. J. (1981). The Life Attitude Profile (LAP): A multidimensional instrument for assessing attitudes toward life. *Canadian Journal of Behavioral Science, 13,* 264–273.

Reker, G. T., Peacock, E. J., & Wong, P. T. P. (1987). Meaning and purpose in life and well-being: A life-span perspective. *Journal of Gerontology, 42,* 44–49.

Relman, A. S. (1982). *Marijuana and health.* Washington, DC: National Academy Press.

Remley, A. (1988). From obedience to independence. *Psychology Today, 22,* 56–59.

Resman, B. (1986). Can men "mother"? Life as a single father. *Family Relations, 35,* 95–102.

Revicki, D. A., & Mitchell, J. P. (1990). Strain, social support, and mental health in rural elderly individuals. *Journal of Gerontology, 45,* S267–S274.

Reynolds, C. F., III, Mon, T. H., Hoch, C. C., Jennings, J. R., Buysee, D. J., Houck, P. R., Jarrett, D. B., & Kupfer, D. J. (1991). Electroencephalographic sleep in the healthy "old old": A comparison with the "young old" in visually scored and automated measures. *Journal of Gerontology, 46,* M39–M46.

Reznick, J. S., Kagan, J., Snidman, N., Gersten, M., Baak, K., & Rosenberg, A. (1986). Inhibited and uninhibited children: A follow-up study. *Child Development, 57,* 660–680.

Rice, B. (1979a, September). Brave new world of intelligent testing. *Psychology Today, 12,* 27ff.

Rice, B. (1979b, September). The SAT controversy: When an aptitude is coachable. *Psychology Today, 13,* 30ff.

Rice, B. (1981). How not to pick up a woman. *Psychology Today, 23,* 15–17.

Rice, F. P. (1978). *The adolescent: Development, relationships, and culture* (2nd ed.). Boston, MA: Allyn & Bacon.

Rice, F. P. (1979). *The working mother's guide to child development.* Englewood Cliffs, NJ: Prentice-Hall.

Rice, F. P. (1986). *Adult development and aging.* Boston, MA: Allyn & Bacon.

Rice, F. P. (1989a). *Causes of worry in college females attending the University of Maine.* Unpublished study.

Rice, F. P. (1989b). *Human sexuality.* Dubuque, IA: Wm. C. Brown.

Rice, F. P. (1990a). *The adolescent: Development, relationships, and culture* (6th ed.). Boston, MA: Allyn & Bacon.

Rice, F. P. (1990b). *Intimate relationships, marriages, and families.* Mountain View, CA: Mayfield Publishing Co.

Rice, G. E., & Meyer, B. J. F. (1986). Prose recall: Effects of aging, verbal ability, and reading behavior. *Journal of Gerontology, 41,* 469–480.

Richman, C. L., Clark, M. L., & Brown, K. P. (1985). General and specific self-esteem in late adolescent students: Race and gender × SES effects. *Adolescence, 20*, 555–566.

Ricks, S. S. (1985). Father-infant interactions: A review of empirical research. *Family Relations, 34*, 505–511.

Ridley, J. C., Bachrach, C. A., & Dawson, D. A. (1979). Recall and reliability of interview data from old women. *Journal of Gerontology, 34*, 99–105.

Riese, M. L. (1990). Neonatal temperament in monozygotic and dizygotic twin pairs. *Child Development, 61*, 1230–1237.

Riege, W. H., & Inman, V. (1981). Age differences in nonverbal memory tasks. *Journal of Gerontology, 36*, 51–58.

Riegel, K. (1975). Toward a dialectical theory of development. *Human Development, 18*, 50–64.

Riemer, J. W. (1981, Spring). Deviance as fun. *Adolescence, 16*, 39–43.

Rippe, J. M. (1989). CEO fitness: The performance plus. *Psychology Today, 23*, 50–53.

Rissenberg, M., & Glanzer, M. (1986). Picture superiority in free recall: The effects of normal aging and primary degenerative dementia. *Journal of Gerontology, 41*, 64–71.

Ritter, J. M., Casey, R. J., & Longlois, J. H. (1991). Adults' responses to infants varying in appearance of age and attractiveness. *Child Development, 62*, 68–82.

Ritvo, E. R., Freeman, B. J., Mason-Brothers, A., Mo, A., & Ritvo, A. M. (1985). Concordance for the syndrome of autism in 40 pairs of afflicted twins. *American Journal of Psychiatry, 142*, 74–77.

Ritz, S. (1981). Growing through menopause. *Medical Self-Care*, pp. 15–18.

Robbins, D. (1983). A cluster of adolescent suicide attempts: Is suicide contagious? *Journal of Adolescent Health Care, 3*, 253–255.

Roberto, K. A., & Scott, J. P. (1986). Equity considerations in the friendships of older adults. *Journal of Gerontology, 41*, 241–247.

Roberts, A. R. (1982, Summer). Adolescent runaways in suburbia: A new typology. *Adolescence, 17*, 379–396.

Roberts, E., & DeBlossie, R. R. (1983, Winter). Test bias and the culturally different early adolescent. *Adolescence, 18*, 837–843.

Roberts, L. R., Sarigiani, P. A., Petersen, A. C., & Newman, J. L. (1990). Gender differences in the relationship between achievement and self-image during early adolescence. *Journal of Early Adolescence, 10*, 159–175.

Roberts, M. (1988a, May). Heartfelt panic. *Psychology Today, 22*, 13.

Roberts, M. (1988b). Comeback from bypass. *Psychology Today, 22*, 18–20.

Roberts, M. (1988c). School yard menace. *Psychology Today, 22*, 52–56.

Roberts, M. (1989). Minding your health. Mind over cholesterol. *Psychology Today, 23*, 21–33.

Roberts, M., & Harris, T. G. (1989). Wellness at work. *Psychology Today, 23*, 54–58.

Robinson, B. E. (1984). The contemporary American stepfather. *Family Relations, 33*, 381–388.

Robinson, P. (1981, March). Five models for dying. *Psychology Today, 15*, 85–91.

Robinson, S. I. (1983, January). Nader versus ETS: Who should we believe? *Personnel and Guidance Journal, 61*, 260–262.

Rockstein, M., & Sussman, M. (1979). *Biology of aging.* Belmont, CA: Wadsworth.

Rodgers, J. (1988). Pains of complaint. *Psychology Today, 22*, 26, 27.

Rodin, J. (1982). Obesity: Why the losing battle. In B. B. Wolman (Ed.), *Psychological aspects of obesity: A handbook* (pp. 30–87). New York: Van Nostrand.

Roe v. Wade, 410 U.S. 113 (1973).

Rogers, C. R. (1951). *Client-centered therapy: Its current practice, implications, and theory.* Boston, MA: Houghton Mifflin.

Rogers, C. R. (1961). *On becoming a person.* Boston, MA: Houghton Mifflin.

Rogers, C. R. (1980). *A way of being.* Boston, MA: Houghton Mifflin.

Rogers, M. F. (1985). AIDS in children: A review of the clinical, epidemiological and public health aspects. *Pediatric Infectious Disease, 4*, 230–236.

Rogosch, F. A., & Newcomb, A. F. (1989). Children's perceptions of peer reputation and their social reputations among peers. *Child Development, 60*, 597–610.

Rogow, A. M., Marcia, J. E., & Slugoski, B. R. (1983, October). The relative importance of identity status interview components. *Journal of Youth and Adolescence, 12*, 387–400.

Rohner, R. P., & Rohner, E. C. (1981). Parental acceptance-rejection and parental control: Cross cultural codes. *Ethnology, 20*, 245–260.

Rohling, M. L., Ellis, N. R., & Scogin, F. (1991). Automatic and effortful memory processes in elderly persons with organic brain pathology. *Journal of Gerontology, 46*, P137–P143.

Rollins, B. C., & Cannon, K. L. (1974). Marital satisfaction over the family life cycle: A reevaluation. *Journal of Marriage and the Family, 36*, 271–282.

Romaine, S. (1984). *The language of children and adolescents. The acquisition of communication competence.* Oxford: Blackwell.

Romaniuk, J. G., & Romaniuk, M. (1982). Participation of older adults in higher education: The elderhostel experience. *Gerontologist, 22*, 364–368.

Romeo, F. F. (1984, Fall). Adolescence, sexual conflict, and anorexia nervosa. *Adolescence, 19*, 551–555.

Roopnarine, J. L. (1984). Sex-typed socialization in mixed age preschool classrooms. *Child Development, 55*, 1078–1084.

Roopnarine, J. L. (1986, January). Mothers' and fathers' behavior toward the toy play of their infant sons and daughters. *Sex Roles: A Journal of Research, 14*, 59.

Roosa, M. W., Fitzgerald, H. E., & Carlson, N. A. (1982). A comparison of teenage and older mothers: A systems analysis. *Journal of Marriage and the Family, 44*, 367–377.

Roscoe, B., Diana, M. S., & Brooks, R. H. II. (1987). Early, middle, and later adolescents' views on dating and factors influencing partner selection. *Adolescence, 87*, 511–516.

Roscoe, B., Kennedy, D., & Pope, H. (1987). Distinguishing intimacy from nonintimate relationships. *Adolescence, 87*, 511–516.

Roscoe, B., & Kruger, T. L. (1990). AIDS: Late adolescents' knowledge and its influence on sexual behavior. *Adolescence, 25*, 39–48.

Rose, S. A. (1984). Developmental changes in hemispheric specialization for tactual processing in very young children. Evidence from cross-modal transfer. *Developmental Psychology, 20*, 568–574.

Rose, S. A., Feldman, J. F., McCarton, C. M., & Wolfson, J. (1988). Information processing in seven-month old infants as a function of risk status. *Child Development, 59*, 589–603.

Rosel, N. (1978–1979). Toward a social theory of dying. *Omega: Journal of Death and Dying, 9*, 49–55.

Rosenberg, F. R., & Rosenberg, M. (1978, September). Self-esteem and delinquency. *Journal of Youth and Adolescence, 7*, 279–291.

Rosenblith, J. F., & Sims-Knight, J. E. (1985). *In the beginning: Development in the first two years.* Monterey, CA: Brooks/Cole.

Rosenfeld, A., & Stark, E. (1987). The prime of our lives. *Psychology Today, 21*, 62–70.

Rosenstein, D., & Oster, H. (1988). Differential facial responses to four basic tastes in newborns. *Child Development, 59*, 1555–1568.

Rosenthal, D., & Hansen, J. (1980, October). Comparison of adolescents. Perception and behavior in single- and two-parent families. *Journal of Youth and Adolescence, 9*, 407–414.

Rosoff, J. I. (1989, July/August). The Webster decision: A giant step backwards. *Family Planning Perspectives, 21*, 148–149.

Ross, D. M., & Ross, S. A. (1982). *Hyperactivity: Current issues, research, and theory* (2nd ed.). New York: Wiley.

Ross, H. S., & Lollis, S. P. (1989). A social relations analysis of toddler peer relationships. *Child Development, 60*, 1082–1091.

Ross, R. J. (1974). The empirical status of the formal operations. *Adolescence, 9*, 413–420.

Rossie, A. S. (1968). Transition to parenthood. *Journal of Marriage and the Family, 30*, 26–39.

Rothbart, M. K. (1988). Temperament and the development of inhibited approach. *Child Development, 59*, 1249–1250.

Rothenberg, R., Lentzener, H. R., & Parker, R. A. (1991). Population aging patterns: The expansion of mortality. *Journal of Gerontology, 46*, S66–S70.

Rotheram-Borus, M. J. (1990a). Ethnic differences in adolescents' identity status and associated behavior problems. *Journal of Adolescence, 13*, 361–374.

Rotheram-Borus, M. J. (1990b). Patterns of social expectations among black and Mexican-American children. *Child Development, 61*, 542–556.

Rotherarm, M. J., & Armstrong, M. (1980, Summer). Assertiveness training with high school students. *Adolescence, 15*, 267–276.

Rotkin, I. D. (1973). A comparison review of key epidemiological studies in cervical cancer related to current searches for transmissible agents. *Cancer Research, 33*, 1353–1367.

Rousseau, J. J. (1955). *Emile.* New York: Dutton. (Original work published 1762)

Rovee-Collier, C. K. (1987a). Learning and memory in infancy. In J. D. Osofsky (Ed.), *Handbook of infant development* (2nd ed.). New York: Wiley.

Rovee-Collier, C. K. (1987b). Learning and memory in children. In J. D. Osofsky (Ed.), *Handbook of infant development* (2nd ed.). New York: Wiley.

Rowan, R. L. (1982, July). Irrelevance of penis size. *Medical Aspects of Human Sexuality, 16*, 153, 156.

Rubenstein, C. (1981). Money and self-esteem, relationships, secrecy, envy, and satisfaction. *Psychology Today, 13*, 62–76.

Rubenstein, C. (1983, July). The modern art of courtly love. *Psychology Today, 14*, 40–49.

Rubenstein, E. A. (1983). Television and behavior: Research conclusions of the 1982 NIMH report and their policy implications. *American Psychologist, 38*, 820–825.

Rubin, D. H., Craskilnikoff, P. A., Leventhal, J. M., Weile, B., & Berget, A. (1986, August 23). Effect of passive smoking on birth weight. *Lancet*, pp. 415–417.

Rubin, J. (1988, October). Stress: From heart to heart. *Psychology Today, 22*, 14.

Rubin, K. H., Fein, G. G., & Vandenberg, B. (1983). Play. In P. H. Mussen (Ed.), *Handbook of child psychology* (4th ed., Vol. 4). New York: Wiley.

Rubin, L. G. (1979). *Women of a certain age: The midlife search for self.* New York: Harper & Row.

Rubin, Z. (1982). Fathers and sons—The search for reunion. *Psychology Today, 16*, pp. 23ff.

Ruble, D. N., & Brooks-Gunn, J. (1982). The experience of menarche. *Child Development, 53*, 1557–1566.

Ruble, D. N., & Flett, G. L. (1988). Conflicting goals in self-evaluative information seeking: Developmental and ability level analysis, *Child Development, 59*, 97–106.

Ruff, H. A., Lawson, K. R., Parrinello, R., & Weissberg, R. (1990). Long-term stability of individual differences in sustained attention in the early years. *Child Development, 61*, 60–75.

Russell, B., & Russell, A. (1987). Mother-child and father-child relationships in middle childhood. *Child Development, 58*, 1573–1585.

Russell, C. S. (1974). Transition to parenthood: Problems and gratifications. *Journal of Marriage and the Family, 36*, 294–302.

Russell, J., Halasz, G., & Beumont, P. J. V. (1990). Death related themes in anorexia nervosa: A practical exploration. *Journal of Adolescence, 13*, 311–326.

Russell, J. A. (1990). The preschooler's understanding of the causes and consequences of emotion. *Child Development, 61*, 1872–1881.

Rust, J. O., & McCraw, A. (1984, Summer). Influence of masculinity-femininity on adolescent self-esteem and peer acceptance. *Adolescence, 19*, 357–366.

Rutter, M. (1983). School effects on pupil progress: Research findings and policy implications. *Child Development, 54*, 1–29.

Rutter, M., & Schopher, E. (1987). Autism and persuasive developmental disorders: Concepts and diagnostic issues. *Journal of Autism and Developmental Disorders, 17*, 159–186.

Ryff, C. D. (1982). Successful aging: A developmental approach. *Gerontologist, 22*, 209–214.

Sadker, M., & Sadker, M. (1985, March). Sexism in the schoolroom of the 80s. *Psychology Today, 19*, 54–57.

Salk, L. (1974). *Preparing for parenthood.* New York: David McKay Co.

Sanders, R. E., Murphy, M. D., Schmitt, F. A., & Walsh, K. K. (1980). Age differences in free recall strategies. *Journal of Gerontology, 35*, 550–558.

Sanders, R. E., & Sanders, J. C. (1978). Long-term durability and transfer of enhanced conceptual performance in the elderly. *Journal of Gerontology, 33*, 408–412.

Sandler, D. P., Everson, R. B., Wilcox, A. J., & Browder, J. P. (1985). Cancer risk in adulthood from early life exposure to parents smoking. *American Journal of Public Health, 75*, 487–492.

Sands, L. P., & Meredith, W. (1989). Effects of sensory and motor functioning on adult intellectual performance. *Journal of Gerontology, 44*, P56–P58.

Sanfilippo, J. S. (1984, April). Precocious puberty. *Medical Aspects of Human Sexuality, 18*, 196–201.

Sanik, M. M., & Mauldin, T. (1986). Single versus two-parent families: A comparison of mothers' time. *Family Relations, 35*, 53–56.

Sanik, M. M., & Stafford, D. (1985). Adolescents' contributions to household production: Male and female differences. *Adolescence, 20*, 207–215.

Santrock, J. W. (1970a). Paternal absence, sex-typing, and identification. *Developmental Psychology, 6*, 264–272.

Santrock, J. W. (1970b). Influence of onset and type of paternal absence on the first four Eriksonian developmental crises. *Developmental Psychology, 6,* 273–274.

Santrock, J. W., & Wohlford, P. (1970). *Effects of father absence: Influences of, reasons for, and onset of absence.* Proceedings of the 78th annual convention of the American Sociological Association (Vol. 5, pp. 265–266).

Sarason, I. G. (1981). *The revised life experiences survey.* Unpublished manuscript, University of Washington, Seattle.

Sarason, I. G., Johnson, J. H., & Siegal, J. M. (1978). Assessing the impact of life stress: Development of life experience survey. *Journal of Consulting and Clinical Psychology, 46,* 932–946.

Sarigiani, P. A., Wilson, J. L., Petersen, A. C., & Viocay, J. R. (1990). Self-image and educational plans of adolescents from two contrasting communities. *Journal of Early Adolescence, 10,* 37–55.

Sataloff, J., & Vassallo, L. (1966). Hard-of-hearing senior citizens and the physician. *Geriatrics, 21,* 182–186.

Sato, I., Hasegawa, Y., Takahashi, N., Hirata, Y., Shimomura, K., & Hotta, K. (1981). Age-related changes of cardiac control function in man. *Journal of Gerontology, 36,* 564–572.

Sauer, L. E., & Fine, M. A. (1988). Parent-child relationships in stepparent families. *Journal of Family Psychology, 1,* 434–451.

Saul, L. J. (1983). How to cope with adultery. *Medical Aspects of Human Sexuality, 17,* 90–106.

Saunders, J. M., & Edwards, J. N. (1984). Extramarital sexuality, a predictive model of permissive attitudes. *Journal of Marriage and the Family, 46,* 825–835.

Scafidi, F. A. (1986). Effects of tactile/kinesthetic stimulation on the clinical course and sleep/wake behavior of preterm neonates. *Infant Behavior and Development, 9,* 91–105.

Scarr, S. (1984, May). What's a parent to do? *Psychology Today, 18,* 58–63.

Scarr, S. (1985). Constructing psychology: Making facts and fables for our times. *American Psychologist, 40,* 499–512.

Scarr, S., & Weinberg, R. A. (1978, October). The influence of family background on intellectual attainment. *American Sociological Review, 43,* 674–692.

Scarr, S., & Weinberg, R. A. (1983). The Minnesota adoptions studies: Genetic differences and malleability. *Child Development, 54,* 260–267.

Schacter, S., and Singer, J. E. (1962). Cognitive, social, and physiological determinants of emotional state. *Psychological Review, 69,* 379–399.

Schaefer, D., & Lyons, C. (1986). *How do we tell the children?* New York: Newmarket Press.

Schaefer, E. S. (1959). A circumplex model for maternal behavior. *Journal of Abnormal and Social Psychology, 59,* 226–235.

Schaffer, H. R. (1984). *The child's entry into the social world.* Orlando, FL: Academic Press.

Schaffer, R. (1977). *Mothering.* Cambridge, MA: Harvard University Press.

Schaie, K. W. (1977–1978). Toward a stage theory of adult cognitive development. *Journal of Aging and Human Development, 8,* 129–138.

Schaie, K. W. (1978). External validity in the assessment of intellectual development in adulthood. *Journal of Gerontology, 33,* 695–701.

Schaie, K. W., & Labouvie-Vief, G. (1974). Generational versus ontogenetic components of change in adult cognitive behavior: A fourteen-year cross-sectional study. *Developmental Psychology, 10,* 305–320.

Schaie, K. W., Labouvie-Vief, G., & Buech, B. U. (1973). Generational and cohort-specific differences in adult cognitive functioning: A fourteen-year study of independent samples. *Developmental Psychology, 9,* 151–166.

Schallenberger, M. E. (1894). A study of childrens' rights as seen by themselves. *Pedagogical Seminary, 3,* 87–96.

Schatten, G., & Schatten, H. (1983). The energetic egg. *Science, 23,* 28–34.

Schmidt, J. A., & Davison, M. L. (1983, May). Helping students think. *Personnel and Guidance Journal, 61,* 563–569.

Schmitt, J. F., & McCroskey, R. L. (1981). Sentence comprehension in elderly listeners: The factor of rate. *Journal of Gerontology, 36,* 441–445.

Schmitt, N., Gogate, J., Rothert, M., Rovener, D., Holmes, M., Talarcyzk, G., Given, B., & Kroll, J. (1991). Capturing and clustering women's judgment policies: The case of hormonal therapy for menopause. *Journal of Gerontology, 46,* P92–P101.

Schneider-Rosen, K., & Wenz-Gross, M. (1990). Patterns of compliance from eighteen to thirty months of age. *Child Development, 61,* 104–112.

Schonfield, D. (1965). Memory changes with age. *Nature (London), 28,* 918.

Schram, R. W. (1979). Marital satisfaction over the family life cycle: A critique and proposal. *Journal of Marriage and the Family, 41,* 7–12.

Schuckit, M. A. (1985). Genetics and the risk for alcoholism. *JAMA, Journal of the American Medical Association, 254,* 2614–2617.

Schuckit, M. A. (1987). Biological vulnerability to alcoholism. *Journal of Consulting and Clinical Psychology, 55,* 301–309.

Schuckman, T. (1975). *Aging is not for sissies.* Philadelphia, PA: Westminster Press.

Schultz, N. R., Elias, M. F., Robbins, M. A., Streeten, D. H. P., & Blakeman, N. (1986). A longitudinal comparison of hypertensives and normiotensives on the Wechsler Adult Intelligence Scale: Initial findings. *Journal of Gerontology, 41,* 169–175.

Schumm, W. R., & Bugaighis, M. A. (1986). Marital quality over the marital career: Alternative explanations. *Journal of Marriage and the Family, 48,* 165–168.

Schunk, D. H. (1984). Self-efficacy perspective on achievement behavior. *Educational Psychologist, 19,* 48–58.

Schwartz, J. B., Gibb, W. J., & Tran, T. (1991). Aging effects on heart rate variation. *Journal of Gerontology, 46,* M99–M106.

Schwartz, J. I. (1981). Children's experiments with language. *Young Children, 36,* 16–26.

Schwartz, L. L. (1987). Joint custody: Is it all right for all children? *Journal of Family Psychology, 1,* 120–134.

Schwartz, M. A. (1976). *Career strategies of the never-married.* Paper presented at the 71st annual meeting of the American Sociological Association, New York.

Schwarz, J. C. (1979). Childhood origins of psychpathology. *American Psychologist, 34,* 879–885.

Schwartz, R. S., Shuman, W. P., Bradbury, V. L., Cain, K. C., Fellingham, G. W., Beard, J. C., Kahn, S. E., Stratton, J. R., Cerqueira, M. D., & Abrass, I. B. (1990). Body fat distribution in healthy young and older men. *Journal of Gerontology, 45,* M181–M185.

Schweinhart, L. J., & Weikart, D. P. (1985). Evidence that good early childhood programs work. *Phi Delta Kappan, 66,* 545–551.

Sears, R. R., Maccoby, G. P., & Levin, H. (1957). *Patterns of child rearing.* New York: Harper & Row.

Sebald, H. (1984). *Adolescence: A social psychological analysis* (3rd ed.). Englewood Cliffs, NJ: Prentice-Hall.

Sebald, H. (1986). Adolescents' shifting orientation toward parents and peers: A curvilinear trend over recent decades. *Journal of Marriage and Family, 48,* 5–13.

Seefeldt, V. (1982). The changing image of youth sports in the 1980s. in R. A. Magill, M. J. Ash, & F. L. Smoll (Eds.), *Children in sport* (pp. 16–26). Champaign, IL: Human Kinetics.

Segest, E., Mygind, O., Jergensen, W., Bechgaard, M., & Fallov, J. (1990). Free condoms in youth clubs in Copenhagen. *Journal of Adolescence, 13,* 17–24.

Sekuler, R., & Blake, R. (1987). Sensory underload. *Psychology Today, 21,* 48–51.

Selman, R. L. (1977). A structural-developmental model of social cognition: Implications for intervention research. *Counseling Psychologists, 6,* 3–6.

Selman, R. L. (1980). *The growth of interpersonal understanding: Development and clinical analysis.* New York: Academic Press.

Seltzer, J. A. (1990). Relationships between fathers and children who live apart: The father's role after separation. *Journal of Marriage and the Family, 53,* 79–101.

Selye, H. (1976). *The stress of life* (rev. ed.). New York: McGraw-Hill.

Serok, S., & Blum, A. (1982, Summer). Rule-violating behavior of delinquent and nondelinquent youth in games. *Adolescence, 17,* 457–464.

Sessa, F. M., & Steinberg, L. (1991). Family structure and the development of autonomy during adolescence. *Journal of Early Adolescence, 11,* 38–55.

Shafi, M. (1988). Suicidal children. *Medical Aspects of Human Sexuality, 22,* 63.

Shanas, E. (1980). Older people and their families: The new pioneers. *Journal of Marriage and the Family, 42,* 9–15.

Shantz, C. U. (1987). Conflicts between children. *Child Development, 58,* 283–305.

Shapira, J., & Cummings, J. L. (1989). Alzheimer's disease: Changes in sexual behavior. *Medical Aspects of Human Sexuality, 23,* 32–36.

Shapiro, H. D. (1977, February 6). Do not go gently. *New York Times Magazine,* pp. 36–40.

Shapiro, S. H. (1973). Vicissitudes of adolescence. In S. L. Copel (Ed.), *Behavior pathology of childhood and adolescence.* New York: Basic Books.

Sharps, M. J., & Gollin, E. S. (1987). Memory for object locations in younger and elderly adults. *Journal of Gerontology, 42,* 336–341.

Sharps, M. J., & Gollin, E. S. (1988). Aging and free recall for objects located in space. *Journal of Gerontology, 43,* P8–P11.

Shaver, P. (1983, May). Down at college. *Psychology Today, 17,* 16.

Shea, J. A., & Adams, G. R. (1984). Correlates of romantic attachment: A path analysis study. *Journal of Youth and Adolescence, 13,* 27–44.

Sheingold, D. K., & Tenney, Y. J. (1982). Memory for a salient childhood event. In U. Neisser (Ed.), *Memory observed.* San Francisco, CA: Freeman.

Shelton, C. M., & McAdams, D. P. (1990). In search of everyday morality: The development of a measure. *Adolescence, 25,* 923–944.

Shephard, R. J. (1976). Physiology—Comment. In J. G. Allinson & G. M. Andrew (Eds.), *Child in sport and physical activity* (pp. 35–40). Baltimore, MD: University Park Press.

Sheppard, B. J. (1974). Making the case for behavior as an expression of physiological condition. In B. L. Kratonile

(Ed.), *Youth in trouble.* San Rafael, CA: Academic Therapy Publications.

Sherman, B. M., Wallace, R. B., Bean, J. A., Changy, Y., & Schlabaugh, L. (1981). The relationships of menopausal hot flushes to medical and reproductive experience. *Journal of Gerontology, 36,* 306–309.

Shestowsky, B. J. (1983, Fall). Ego identity development and obesity in adolescent girls. *Adolescence, 18,* 551–559.

Shinn, M. W. (1900). *The biography of a baby.* Boston, MA: Houghton Mifflin.

Shock, N. W. (1977). Systems integration. In C. E. Finch & L. Hayflick (Eds.), *Handbook of the biology of aging* (pp. 639–665). New York: Van Nostrand-Reinhold.

Shore, H. (1976). Designing a training program for understanding sensory losses in aging. *Gerontologist, 16,* 157–165.

Short, R. V. (1984). Breast feeding. *Scientific American, 250,* 35–41.

Shuman, E. (1980). Arthritis and the middle years. *Dynamic Years, 15,* 39–42.

Sidney, K. H., & Shephard, R. J. (1977). Maximum testing of men and women in the seventh, eighth, and ninth decade of life. *Journal of Applied Physiology, 43,* 280–287.

Siegel, A., & White, S. H. (1982). The child study movement: Early growth and development of the symbolized child. In H. W. Reese (Ed.), *Advances in child development and behavior* (Vol. 17). New York: Academic Press.

Siegler, I. G., McCarty, S. M., & Logue, P. E. (1982). Wechsler memory scale scores, selective attrition, and distance from death. *Journal of Gerontology, 37,* 176–181.

Siegler, I., Roseman, J., & Harkins, S. (1975, June). *Complexities in the terminal drop hypothesis.* Paper presented at the International Congress of Gerontology, Jerusalem.

Siegler, R. S. (1989). Mechanisms of cognitive development. *Annual Review of Psychology, 40,* 353–379.

Silber, S. J. (1980). *How to get pregnant.* New York: Scribner.

Silber, T. J. (1986). Gonorrhea in children and adolescents. *Medical Aspects of Human Sexuality, 16,* 92H–92X.

Simcock, B. (1985). Sons and daughters—a sex preselection study. *Medical Journal of Australia, 142,* 541–542.

Simmons, R. G. et al. (1978, October). Self-esteem and achievement of black and white adolescents. *Social Problems, 26,* 86–96.

Simon, C. (1989). The triumphant dieter. *Psychology Today, 23,* 48–52.

Simon, C. (1988). One is too much. *Psychology Today, 22,* 10.

Simon, L. (1988). Freud, in his time and ours. *Psychology Today, 22,* 68, 69.

Singer, J. L. (1984). *The human personality.* San Diego, CA: Harcourt Brace Jovanovich.

Singer, J. L., & Singer, D. G. (1983). Implications of childhood television viewing for cognition, imagination, and emotion. In J. Bryant & Dr. R. Anderson (Eds.), *Children's understanding of television: Research on attention and comprehension* (pp. 265–297). New York: Academic Press.

Sinnett, E. R., Goodyear, R. K., & Hanneman, V. (1989). Voluntary euthanasia and the right to die: A dialogue with Derek Humphry. *Journal of Counseling and Development, 67,* 568–572.

Skandhan, K. P., Pandya, A. K., Skandhan, S., & Mehta, Y. B. (1988). Menarche: Prior knowledge and experience. *Adolescence, 89,* 149–154.

Skeen, P., Covi, R. B., & Robinson, B. E. (1985). Stepfamilies: A review of the literature with suggestions for practitioners. *Journal of Counseling and Development, 64,* 121–125.

Skinner, B. F. (1953). *Science and human behavior.* New York: Macmillan.

Skinner, B. F. (1957). *Verbal behavior*. New York: Appleton-Century-Crofts.

Skinner, B. F. (1983). *A matter of consequences. Part 3 of an autobiography*. New York: Alfred A. Knopf.

Slade, A. (1987). A longitudinal study of maternal involvement and symbolic play during the toddler period. *Child Development, 58*, 367–375.

Slater, A., Morison, V., & Rose, D. (1983). Perception of shape by the newborn baby. *British Journal of Developmental Psychology, 1*, 135–142.

Slaughter-Defoe, D. T., Nakagawa, K., Takanishi, R., & Johnson, D. J. (1990). Toward cultural/ecological perspectives on schooling and achievement in African- and Asian-American children. *Child Development, 61*, 363–383.

Slesinger, D. P., McDivitt, M., & O'Donnell, F. M. (1980). Food patterns in an urban population: Age for sociodemographic correlates. *Journal of Gerontology, 35*, 432–441.

Slonim-Nevo, V., Ozaga, M. N., & Auslander, W. F. (1991). Knowledge, attitudes and behaviors related to AIDS among youths in residential centers: Results from an exploratory study. *Journal of Adolescence, 14*, 1–16.

Smart, M. S., & Smart, R. C. (1972). *Children: Development and relationships* (2nd ed.). New York: Macmillan.

Smetana, J. G., Braeges, J. L., & Yau, J. (1991). Doing what you say and saying what you do: Reasoning about adolescent–parent conflict in interviews and interactions. *Journal of Adolescent Research, 6*, 276–295.

Smidt, L. J., Cremin, F. M., Grivetti, L. E., & Clifford, A. J. (1991). Influence of thiamin supplementation on the health and general well-being of an elderly Irish population with marginal thiamin deficiency. *Journal of Gerontology, 46*, M16–M22.

Smilgis, M. (1987, February 16). The big chill: Fear of AIDS. *Time*, pp. 58–59.

Smith, E. (1988, May). Fighting cancerous feelings. *Psychology Today, 22*, 22–23.

Smith, K. R., & Zick, C. D. (1986). The incidence of poverty among the recently widowed: Mediating factor in the life course. *Journal of Marriage and the Family, 48*, 619–630.

Smith, M. C. (1975). Portrayal of the elderly in prescription drug advertising. *Gerontologist, 16*, 329–334.

Smith, P. B., & Pederson, D. R. (1988). Maternal sensitivity and patterns of infant-mother attachment. *Child Development, 59*, 1097–1101.

Smith, P. B., Weinman, M., & Malinak, L. R. (1984). Adolescent mothers and fetal loss, what is learned from experience? *Psychological Reports, 55*, 775–778.

Smith, T. E. (1981). Adolescent agreement with perceived maternal and paternal educational goals. *Journal of Marriage and the Family, 43*, 85–93.

Smith, T. E. (1983). Adolescent reactions to attempted parental control and influence techniques. *Journal of Marriage and the Family, 45*, 533–542.

Smith, T. E. (1988). Parental control techniques. *Journal of Family Issues, 9*, 155–176.

Snodgrass, D. M. (1991). The parent connection. *Adolescence, 26*, 83–88.

Snyder, S. (1991). Movies and juvenile delinquency. *Adolescence, 26*, 121–132.

Sobel, D. (1981, June 29). Surrogate mothers: Why women volunteer. *New York Times*, p. B-5.

Social factors not age are found to affect risk of low birth weight (1984, May/June). *Family Planning Perspectives, 16*, 142–143.

Sohngen, M., & Smith, R. J. (1978). Images of old age in poetry. *Gerontologist, 18*, 181–186.

Solorzano, L., Hague, J. R., Peterson, S., Lyons, D. C., & Bosc, M. (1984, August 27). What makes great schools great. *U.S. News and World Report*, pp. 46–49.

Sommer, B. (1984). The troubled teen: Suicide, drug use, and running away. *Women's Health, 9*, 117–141.

Sostek, A. M., Smith, Y. F., Katz, K. S., & Grant, E. G. (1987). Developmental outcome of preterm infants with intraventricular hemorrhage at one and two years of age. *Child Development, 58*, 779–786.

Southard, B. (1985). Interlimb movement control and coordination in children. In J. E. Clark & J. H. Humphrey (Eds.), *Motor development: Current selected research*. Princeton, NJ: Princeton Book Co.

Spanier, G. B. (1983). Married and unmarried cohabitation in the United States: 1980. *Journal of Marriage and the Family, 45*, 277–288.

Spanier, G. B., Lewis, R. A., & Cole, C. L. (1975). Marital adjustments over the family life cycle: The issues of curvilinearity. *Journal of Marriage and the Family, 37*, 263–275.

Speare, A., Jr., Avery, R., & Lawton, L. (1991). Disability, residential mobility, and changes in living arrangements. *Journal of Gerontology, 46*, S133–S142.

Spearman, C. (1927). *The abilities of man: Their nature and measurement*. New York: Macmillan.

Spencer, M. B., & Markstrom-Adams, C. (1990). Identity processes among racial and ethnic minority children in America. *Child Development, 61*, 290–310.

Spetner, N. B. & Olsho, L. W. (1990). Auditory frequency resolution in human infancy. *Child Development, 61*, 632–652.

Spiro, A., III, Aldwing, C. M., Levenson, M. R., & Bosse, R. (1990). Longitudinal findings from the normative aging study: II. Do emotionality and extraversion predict symptom change? *Journal of Gerontology, 45*, P136–P144.

Spock, B. (1946). *Commonsense book of baby and child care*. New York: Duell, Sloan & Pearce.

Spock, B. (1990, May 30). *Spock would abolish Little League*. Portland, ME: Portland Press Herald.

Spock, B., & Rothenberg, M. B. (1985). *Dr. Spock's baby and child care*. New York: Pocket Books.

Sprague, R. L., & Ullman, R. K. (1981). Psychoactive drugs and child management. In J. M. Kaufman & D. P. Hallahan (Eds.), *Handbook of special education*. New York: Prentice-Hall.

Sprecher, S. (1985). Sex differences in bases of power in dating relationships. *Sex Roles, 12*, 449–462.

Sprecher, S., McKinney, K., Walsh, R., & Anderson, C. (1988). A revision of the Reiss premarital sexual permissiveness scale. *Journal of Marriage and the Family, 50*, 821–828.

Spreen, O., Tupper, D., Risser, A., Tuokko, H., & Edgell, D. (1984). *Human developmental neuropsychology*. New York: Oxford University Press.

Springer, S. P., & Deutsch, G. (1985). *Left brain, right brain*. New York: Freeman.

Sroufe, L. A., Egeland, B., & Kreutzer, T. (1990). The fate of early experience following developmental change: Longitudinal approaches to individual adaptation in childhood. *Child Development, 61*, 1363–1373.

Stacey, C. A., & Gatz, M. (1991). Cross-sectional age differences and longitudinal change on the Bradburn affect balance scale. *Journal of Gerontology, 46*, P76–P78.

Stack, S. (1985, May). The effect of domestic/religious individualism in suicide, 1954–1978. *Journal of Marriage and the Family, 47*, 431–447.

Stager, J. M. (1984). Reversibility of amenorrhea in athletes: A review. *Sports Medicine, 1*, 337.

Stager, J. M. (1988). Menarche and exercise. *Medical Aspects of Human Sexuality, 22,* 118, 133.

Stager, J. M., Ritchie, B. A., & Robertshaw, D. (1984). Reversal of aligo/amenorrhea in collegiate distance runners. *New England Journal of Medicine, 310,* 51.

Stake, J. E., DeVille, C. J., & Pennell, C. L. (1983, October). The effects of assertive training on the performance self-esteem of adolescent girls. *Journal of Youth and Adolescence, 12,* 435–442.

Stanley, B. K., Weikel, W. J., & Wilson, J. (1986). The effects of father absence on interpersonal problem-solving skills of nursery school children. *Journal of Counseling and Development, 64,* 383–385.

Stayton, W. R. (1983). Preventing infidelity. *Medical Aspects of Human Sexuality, 17,* 36C–36D.

Steel, L. (1991). Early work experience among white and non-white youths: Implications for subsequent enrollment and employment. *Youth and Society, 22,* 419–447.

Steele, C. I. (1980, Winter). Weight loss among teenage girls: An adolescent crisis. *Adolescence, 15,* 823–829.

Stefanko, M. (1984, Spring). Trends in adolescent research: A review of articles published in adolescence, 1976–1981. *Adolescence, 19,* 1–14.

Stein, D. M., & Reichert, P. (1990). Extreme dieting behaviors in early adolescence. *Journal of Early Adolescence, 10,* 108–121.

Stein, P. J. (1978). The lifestyles and life chances of the never married. *Marriage and the Family Review, 1,* 3–11.

Stein, P. J. (Ed.). (1981). *Single life: Unmarried adults in social context.* New York: St. Martin's Press.

Stein, R. F. (1987). Comparison of self-concept of non-obese and obese university junior female nursing students. *Adolescence, 22,* 77–90.

Steinberg, L. D. (1981). Transformations in family relations at puberty. *Developmental Psychology, 17,* 833–840.

Steinberg, L. D., Greenberger, E., Garduque, L., Ruggiero, M., & Vaux, A. (1982). Effects of early work experience on adolescent development. *Developmental Psychology, 18,* 385–395.

Steinberg, L. D., Greenberger, E., Jacobi, M., & Garduque, L. (1981, April). Early work experience: A partial antidote for adolescent egocentrism. *Journal of Youth and Adolescence, 10,* 141–157.

Steinman, S., Zemmelman, S., & Knoblauch, T. (1985). A study of parents who sought joint custody and who returns to court. *Journal of the American Academy of Child Psychiatry, 24,* 554–562.

Stern, J. A., Oster, P. J., & Newport, K. (1980). Reaction time measure, hemisphere specialization, and age. In L. W. Poon (Ed.), *Aging in the 80's: Psychological issues.* Washington, DC: American Psychological Association.

Stern, M., Northman, J. E., & Van Slyck, M. R. (1984, Summer). Father absence and adolescent "problem behaviors": Alcohol consumption, drug use, and sexual activity. *Adolescence, 17,* 847–853.

Stern, M., & Zevon, M. A. (1990). Stress, coping, and family environment: The adolescent's response to naturally occurring stressors. *Journal of Adolescent Research, 5,* 290–305.

Stern, P. N. (1982). Affiliating in stepfather families: Teachable strategies leading to a stepfather-child friendship. *Western Journal of Nursing Research, 4,* 76–89.

Sternberg, R. J. (1985). *Beyond IQ.* Cambridge, England: Cambridge University Press.

Sternberg, R. J., & Wagner, R. K. (Eds.). (1986). *Practical intelligence: Nature and origins of competence in the everyday world.* Cambridge, England: Cambridge University Press.

Steuer, J., Bank, L., Olsen, E. J., & Jarvik, L. F. (1980). Depression, physical health, and somatic complaints in the elderly: A study of the Zung Self-Rating Depression Scale. *Journal of Gerontology, 35,* 683–688.

Stevens, J. H., Jr. (1988). Social support, locus of control, and parenting in three low-income groups of mothers: Black teenagers, black adults, and white adults. *Child Development, 59,* 635–642.

Stevens, R., & Pihl, R. O. (1987). Seventh-grade students at risk for school failure. *Adolescence, 22,* 333–345.

Stevenson, H. W., Chen, C., & Uttal, D. H. (1990). Beliefs and achievement: A study of black, white, and Hispanic children. *Child Development, 61,* 508–523.

Stevenson, H. W., Hale, G. A., Klein, R. E., & Miller, L. K. (1968). Interrelations and correlates in children's learning and problem solving. *Monographs of the Society for Research in Child Development, 33*(Serial No. 123).

Stevenson, H. W., Lee, S., Chen, C., & Lummis, M. (1990). Mathematics achievement of children in China and the United States. *Child Development, 61,* 1053–1066.

Stevenson, H. W., Lee, S. Y., & Stigler, J. W. (1986). Mathematics achievement in Chinese, Japanese, and American children. *Science, 231,* 693–699.

Stevenson, J. S. (1977). *Issues and crises during middlescence.* New York: Appleton-Century-Crofts.

Stevenson, M. R., & Black, K. N. (1988). Paternal absence and sex-role developments: A meta-analysis. *Child Development, 59,* 793–814.

Stewart, H. S. (1982, Fall). Body type, personality, temperament, and psychotherapeutic treatment of female adolescents. *Adolescence, 22,* 77–90.

Stigler, J. W., Lee, S., & Stevenson, H. W. (1987). Mathematics classrooms in Japan, Taiwan, and the United States. *Child Development, 58,* 1272–1285.

Stipek, D. J., & Hoffman, J. (1980). Development of children's performance-related judgments. *Child Development, 51,* 912–914.

Stipek, D., & MacIver, D. (1989). Developmental change in children's assessment of intellectual competence. *Child Development, 60,* 521–538.

Stivers, C. (1988). Parent-adolescent communication and its relationship to adolescent depression and suicide proneness. *Adolescence, 23,* 291–295.

Stjernfeldt, M., Berglund, K., Lindsten, J., & Ludvigsson, J. (1986). Maternal smoking during pregnancy and risk of childhood cancer. *Lancet,* pp. 1350–1352.

Stock, W. A., & Okun, M. A. (1982). The construct validity of life satisfaction among the elderly. *Journal of Gerontology, 37,* 625–627.

Stoller, E. P. (1985). Exchange patterns in the informal support networks of the elderly: The impact of reciprocity on morale. *Journal of Marriage and the Family, 47,* 335–342.

Stone, A. A. (1987, November). Moody immunity. *Psychology Today, 21,* 14.

Storandt, M., & Futterman, A. (1982). Stimulus size and performance on two subtests of the Wechsler Adult Intelligence Scale by younger and older adults. *Journal of Gerontology, 37,* 602–603.

Story, M. D. (1982). A comparison of university student experience with various sexual outlets in 1974 and 1980. *Adolescence, 17,* 737–747.

Storz, N. S. (1982, Fall). Body image of obese and adolescent girls in a high school and clinical setting. *Adolescence, 17,* 667–672.

Strang, R. (1957). *The adolescent views himself.* New York: McGraw-Hill.

Strate, J. M., & Dubnoff, S. J. (1986). How much income is enough? Measuring the income adequacy of retired persons using a survey based approach. *Journal of Gerontology, 41,* 393–400.

Strathe, M., & Hash, V. (1979, Spring). The effect of an alternative school in adolescent self-esteem. *Adolescence, 14,* 185–189.

Street, S. (1988). Feedback and self-concept in high school students. *Adolescence, 23,* 449–456.

Streetman, L. G. (1987). Contrasts in self-esteem of unwed teenage mothers. *Adolescence, 23,* 459–464.

Streissguth, A. P., Martin, D. C., Barr, H. M., Sandman, B. M., Kirshner, G. L., & Darby, B. L. (1984). Intrauterine alcohol and nicotine exposure: Attention and reaction time in 4-year-old children. *Developmental Psychology, 20,* 533–541.

Strongman, K. T. (1987). *The psychology of emotion* (3rd ed.). New York: Wiley.

Stroufe, L. A. (1985). Attachment classification from the perspective of infant-caregiver relationships and infant temperament. *Child Development, 56,* 1–14.

Stryker, S. (1980). *Symbolic interactionism.* Menlo Park, CA: Benjamin/Cummings.

Stuck, M. F., & Glassner, B. (1985). The transition drug use and crime to noninvolvement: A case study. *Adolescence, 20,* 669–679.

Stunkard, A. J., Foch, T. T., & Hrubec, Z. (1986). A twin study of human obesity. *JAMA, Journal of the American Medical Association, 256,* 51–54.

Subak-Sharpe, G. J. (Ed.). (1984). Genital herpes. *The physicians manual for patients* (pp. 370–372). New York: Times Books.

Suicide Prevention Center. (1984). *Suicide statistics.* Los Angeles, CA.

Sullivan, J. F. (1987, June 25). Wishes of patient in refusing care backed in New Jersey: Right to die is extended. Rulings in three cases give interests of individuals priority over states. *New York Times, 1,* 8–12.

Sunderland, A., Watts, K., Baddeley, A. D., & Harris, J. E. (1986). Subjective memory assessment and test performance in elderly adults. *Journal of Gerontology, 41,* 376–384.

Svec, H. (1987). Anorexia nervosa: A misdiagnosis of the adolescent male. *Adolescence, 87,* 617–623.

Swanbrow, D. (1989). The paradox of happiness. *Psychology Today, 23,* 37–39.

Sweer, L., Martin, D. C., Ladd, R. A., Miller, J. K., & Karpf, M. (1988). The medical evaluation of elderly patients with major depression. *Journal of Gerontology, 43,* M53–M58.

Sweet, A. Y. (1979). Classification of the low-birth-weight infant. In M. H. & A. A. Fanaroff (Eds.), *Care of the high-risk infant* (2nd ed.). New York: Saunders.

Swensen, C. H. (1983). Post-parental marriage. *Medical Aspects of Human Sexuality, 17,* 171–194.

Swensen, C. H., Eskew, R. W., & Kohlhepp, K. A. (1981). Stage of family life cycle, ego development, and the marriage relationship. *Journal of Marriage and the Family, 43,* 841–851.

Tagatz, G., Gibson, M., Schiller, P., & Nagel, T. (1980). Artificial insemination utilizing donor semen. *Minnesota Medicine, 63,* 539–541.

Talbert, G. B. (1977). Aging of the reproductive system. In C. E. Finch & L. Hayflick (Eds.), *Handbook of the biology of aging* (pp. 318–356). New York: Van Nostrand-Reinhold.

Tamis-LeMonda, C. S., & Bornstein, M. H. (1986). Habituation and maternal encouragement of attention in infancy as predictors of toddler language, play and representational competence. *Child Development, 60,* 738–751.

Tan, L. (1985). Laterality and motor skills in 4-year-olds. *Child Development, 56,* 119–124.

Tanfer, K., & Horn, M. C. (1985). Contraceptive use, pregnancy, and fertility patterns among single American women in their 20s. *Family Planning Perspectives, 17,* 10–19.

Tangney, J. P. (1988). Aspects of the family and children's television viewing control preferences. *Child Development, 59,* 1070–1079.

Tanner, J. M. (1962). *Growth of adolescence.* Springfield, IL: Charles C. Thomas.

Tanner, J. M. (1970). Physical growth. In P. H. Mussen (Ed.), *Carmichael's manual of child psychology* (3rd ed., Vol. 1). New York: Wiley.

Tanner, J. M. (1972). Sequence, tempo, and individual variation in growth and development of boys and girls aged twelve to sixteen. In J. Kegan & R. Coles (Eds.), *Twelve to sixteen: Early adolescence.* New York: W. W. Norton.

Tanner, J. M. (1973, September). *Scientific American.*

Tedesco, L. A., & Gaier, E. L. (1988). Friendship bonds in adolescence. *Adolescence, 89,* 127–136.

Television and your children. (1985). Ontario, Canada: TV Ontario, Ontario Educational Communications Authority.

Tentler, T. N. (1977, October). Death and dying in many disciplines: A review article. *Comparative Studies in Society and History, 19,* 511–522.

Teri, L., Hughes, J. P., & Larson, E. R. (1990). Cognitive deterioration in Alzheimer's disease: Behavioral and health factors. *Journal of Gerontology, 45,* P58–P63.

Terman, L. (1925). *Genetic studies of genius: Vol. 1. Mental and physical traits of a thousand gifted children.* Stanford, CA: Stanford University Press.

Terman, L., & Oden, M. H. (1959). *Genetic studies of genius: Vol. 4. The gifted group at midlife.* Stanford, CA: Stanford University Press.

Terman, M., & Link, M. (1989). Fighting the winter blues with bright light. *Psychology Today, 22,* 18–21.

Teti, D. M., & Ablard, K. E. (1989). Security of attachment and infant-sibling relationships: A laboratory study. *Child Development, 60,* 1519–1528.

Teti, D. M., Lamb, M. E., & Elster, A. B. (1987). Long-range economic and marital consequences of adolescent marriage in three cohorts of adult males. *Journal of Marriage and the Family, 49,* 499–506.

Tew, M. (1978). The case against hospital deliveries: The statistical evidence. In S. Kitzinger & J. A. Davis (Eds.), *The place of birth.* New York: Oxford University Press.

Teyler, T. J., & Fountain, S. B. (1987). Neuronal plasticity in the mammalian brain: Relevance to behavioral learning and memory. *Child Development, 58,* 698–712.

Thayer, R. E. (1988). Energy walks. *Psychology Today, 22,* 12–13.

Thelen, E. (1981). Rhythmical behavior in infancy: An ethological perspective. *Developmental Psychology, 17,* 237, 257.

Thomas, A., & Chess, S. (1977). *Temperament and development.* New York: Brunner/Mazel.

Thomas, A., & Chess, S. (1984). Genesis and evaluation of behavioral disorders: From infancy to early adulthood. *American Journal of Orthopsychiatry, 14,* 1–9.

Thompson, A. P. (1984). Emotional and sexual components of extramarital relations. *Journal of Marriage and the Family, 46,* 35–42.

Thompson, J. K. (1986). Larger than life. *Psychology Today, 20,* 39–44.

Thompson, L., Acock, A. C., & Clark, K. (1985). Do parents know their children? The ability of mothers and fathers to gauge the attitudes of their young adult children. *Family Relations, 34,* 315–320.

Thompson, L., & Spanier, G. B. (1983). The end of marriage and acceptance of marital termination. *Journal of Marriage and the Family, 45,* 103–113.

Thompson, L. W., Breckenridge, J. N., Gallagher, D., & Peterson, J. (1984). Effects of bereavement on self-perceptions of physical health in elderly widows and widowers. *Journal of Gerontology, 39,* 309–314.

Thompson, R. A., Connell, J. P., & Bridges, L. J. (1988). Temperament, emotion, and social interactive behavior in the strange situation: A component process analysis of attachment system functioning. *Child Development, 59,* 1102–1110.

Thompson, W. E., & Dodder, R. A. (1986). Containment theory and juvenile delinquency: A reevaluation through fact analysis. *Adolescence, 21,* 365–376.

Thompson, W. R., & Grusec, J. E. (1970). Studies of early experience. In P. H. Mussen (Ed.), *Carmichael's manual of child psychology* (Vol. 1). New York: Wiley.

Thornburg, H. D. (1975). *Development in adolescence.* Monterey, CA: Brooks/Cole.

Thorndike, R. L., Hagen, E. P., & Sattler, J. M. (1985). *Stanford-Binet* (4th ed.). Chicago, IL: Riverside Publishing.

Thornton, B., & Ryckman, R. M. (1991). Relationships between physical attractiveness, physical effectiveness, and self-esteem: A cross-sectional analysis among adolescents. *Journal of Adolescence, 14,* 85–98.

Thornton, M. C., Chatters, L. M., Taylor, R. J., & Allen, W. R. (1990). Sociodemographic and environmental correlates of racial socialization by black parents. *Child Development, 61,* 401–409.

Thornton, W. E. (1982, Winter). Gender traits and delinquency involvement of boys and girls. *Adolescence, 17,* 749–768.

Thurstone, L. L. (1938). *Primary mental abilities. Psychometric monographs.* No. 1. Chicago, IL: University of Chicago Press.

Thurstone, L. L., & Thurstone, T. B. (1949). *SRA primary and mental abilities.* Chicago, IL: Science Research Associates.

Thurstone, L. L., & Thurstone, T. G. (1953). *Examiner manual for the Primary Mental Abilities for Ages 5 to 7* (3rd ed.). Chicago, IL: Science Research Associates.

Tidwell, R. (1988). Dropouts speak out: Qualitative data on early school departures. *Adolescence, 92,* 939–954.

Tierno, M. J. (1983, Fall). Responding to self-concept disturbance among early adolescents: A psychosocial view for educators. *Adolescence, 18,* 577–584.

Till, A., & Freedman, E. M. (1978). Complementarity versus similarity of traits operating in the choice of marriage and dating partners. *Journal of Social Psychology, 105,* 147–148.

Timnick, L. (1982). How you can learn to be likable, confident, socially successful for only the cost of your present education. *Psychology Today, 16,* 42–49.

Tognoli, J. (1980). Male friendships and intimacy across the life span. *Family Relations, 29,* 273–279.

Tolan, P. (1988). Socioeconomic, family, and social stress correlates of adolescent antisocial and delinquent behavior. *Journal of Abnormal Child Psychology, 16,* 317–331.

Tolson, T. F. J., & Wilson, M. N. (1990). The impact of two- and three-generational black family structure on perceived family climate. *Child Development, 61,* 416–428.

Tooth, G. (1985, February 18). Why childrens' TV turns off so many parents. *U.S. News and World Report,* p. 65.

Torrance, E. P. (1974). *Torrance tests on creative thinking norms—technical manual.* Lexington, MA: Personnel Press.

Tortora, G. J., & Anagnostakos, N. P. (1981). *Principles of anatomy and physiology* (3rd ed.). New York: Harper & Row.

Tower, R. B., Singer, D. G., Singer, L. J., & Biggs, A. (1979). Differential effects of television programming on preschooler's cognition, imagination, and social play. *American Journal of Orthopsychiatry, 49,* 265–281.

Trapped by mutilatory troy? Need help finding dracula's heart? Just call the Nintendo hotline (1990, January 8). *People, 33,* 82.

Treichel, J. (1982). Anorexia nervosa: A brain shrinker? *Science News, 122,* 122–123.

Tribich, D., & Klein, M. (1981). On Freud's blindness. *Colloquium, 4,* 52–59.

Trotter, R. J. (1986). Three heads are better than one. *Psychology Today, 20,* 56–62.

Trotter, R. J. (1987a). Project day-care. *Psychology Today, 21,* 32–38.

Trotter, R. J. (1987b, May). You've come a long way, baby. *Psychology Today, 21,* 34–45.

Trussell, J. (1988). Teenage pregnancy in the United States. *Family Planning Perspectives, 20,* 262–272.

Tschann, J. M., Johnston, J. R., Kline, M., & Wallerstein, J. S. (1989). Family process and children's functioning during divorce. *Journal of Marriage and the Family, 51,* 431–444.

Tucker, L. A. (1982). Relationship between perceived conatotype of body cathexis of college males. *Psychology Reports, 50,* 983–989.

Tucker, L. A. (1983). Muscular strength and mental health. *Journal of Personality and Social Psychology, 45,* 1355–1360.

Tudor, C. G., Petersen, D. M., & Elifson, K. W. (1980, Winter). An examination of the relationship between peer and parental influences and adolescent drug use. *Adolescence, 15,* 783–795.

Tun, P. A. (1989). Age differences in processing expository and narrative text. *Journal of Gerontology, 44,* P9–P15.

Turnbull, S. K., & Turnbull, J. M. (1983). To dream the impossible dream: An agenda for discussion with stepparents. *Family Relations, 32,* 227–230.

Turner, J. S., & Helms, D. B. (1979). *Contemporary adulthood.* Philadelphia, PA: Saunders.

Turner, P. H., & Smith, R. M. (1983). Single parents and day care. *Family Relations, 32,* 227–230.

Tygart, C. (1988). Public school vandalism: Toward a synthesis of theories and transition to paradigm analysis. *Adolescence, 15,* 783–795.

Tygart, C. E. (1991). Juvenile delinquency and number of children in a family: Some empirical and theoretical updates. *Youth and Society, 22,* 525–536.

Ubell, E. (1990, January 14). You don't have to be childless. *Parade Magazine,* pp. 14, 15.

Udry, J. R., & Cliquet, R. L. (1982). A cross-cultural examination of the relationship between ages at menarche, marriage, and first birth. *Demography, 19,* 53–63.

Uhlenberg, P., Cooney, T., & Boyd, R. (1990). Divorce for women after midlife. *Journal of Gerontology, 45,* S3–S11.

Uhr, S., Stahl, S. M., & Berger, P. A. (1984). Unmasking schizophrenia. *VA Practitioner,* 42–53.

Umberson, D. (1989). Relationships with children: Explaining parents' psychological well-being. *Journal of Marriage and the Family, 51,* 499–1012.

Upchurch, D. M., & McCarthy, J. (1989). Adolescent childbearing and high school completion in the 1980s: Have things changed? *Family Planning Perspectives, 21,* 199–202.

U.S. Bureau of the Census. (1980a). American families and living arrangements. *Current population reports* (Ser. P-23,

No. 84). Washington, DC: U.S. Government Printing Office.

U.S. Bureau of the Census. (1980b). *Social indicators III*. Washington, DC: U.S. Government Printing Office.

U.S. Bureau of the Census. (1987a). Who's minding the kids? Child care arrangements: Winter 1984–85. *Current population reports: Household economic status* (Series P-20, No. 9). Washington, DC: U.S. Government Printing Office.

U.S. Bureau of the Census. (1987b). *Statistical abstract of the United States, 1987*. Washington, DC: U.S. Government Printing Office.

U.S. Bureau of the Census. (1988). *Statistical abstract of the U.S., 1988* (108th ed.). Washington, DC: U.S. Government Printing Office.

U.S. Bureau of the Census. (1989). *Statistical abstract of the United States, 1989* (109th ed.). Washington, DC: U.S. Government Printing Office.

U.S. Bureau of the Census. (1990). *Statistical abstract of the United States, 1990*. Washington, DC: U.S. Government Printing Office.

U.S. Department of Agriculture and U.S. Department of Health and Human Services. (1985). *Dietary guidelines for Americans* (Home and Garden Bulletin, No. 232). Washington, DC: U.S. Government Printing Office.

U.S. Department of Health and Human Services. (1979). *The Belmont Report: Ethical Principles and Guidelines for the Protection of Human Subjects of Research* (Publication No. 1983, pp. 81–132, 1305). Department of Health, Education, and Welfare, Washington, DC: U.S. Government Printing Office.

U.S. Department of Health and Human Services. (1980, June). *Marijuana research findings: 1980*. Rockville, MD: National Institute on Drug Abuse.

U.S. Department of Health and Human Services: Office of Human Development (1980, August). *Status of children, youth, and families, 1979* (DHHS Publication No. [OHDS] 80-30274). Washington, DC: U.S. Government Printing Office.

U.S. Department of Health and Human Services. (1981). *Statistics on incidence of depression*. Washington, DC: U.S. Government Printing Office.

Usui, W. M., Keil, T. J., & Durig, K. R. (1985). Socioeconomic comparisons and life satisfaction of elderly adults. *Journal of Gerontology, 40*, 110–114.

Usui, W. M., Keil, T. J., & Phillips, D. C. (1983). Determinants of life satisfaction: A note on race-interaction hypothesis. *Journal of Gerontology, 38*, 107–110.

Vaillant, G. E. (1977a). *Adaptation to Life*. Boston, MA: Little, Brown.

Vaillant, G. E. (1977b). The climb to maturity: How the best and brightest come of age. *Psychology Today, 11*, 34ff.

Valencia, R. R. (1985). Predicting academics achievement in Mexican-American children using the Kaufman Assessment Battery for Children. *Education and Psychological Research, 5*, 11–17.

Valenzuela, M. (1990). Attachment in chronically underweight young children. *Child Development, 61*, 1984–1996.

Vandell, D. L., Owen, M. T., Wilson, K. S., & Henderson, V. K. (1988). Social development in infant twins: Peer and mother-child relationships. *Child Development*, 168–177.

Vandell, D. L., & Wilson, K. S. (1987). Infants' interactions with mother, sibling, peers: Contrasts and relations between interaction systems. *Child Development, 58*, 176–186.

Van Thorre, M. D., & Vogel, F. X. (1985, Spring). The presence of bulimia in high school females. *Adolescence, 20*, 45–51.

Vaughn, B. E., Block, J. H., & Block, J. (1988). Parents' agreement on child rearing during early childhood and the psychological characteristics of adolescents. *Child Development, 59*, 1020–1033.

Vaughn, B. E., Lefever, G. B., Seifer, R., & Barglow, P. (1989). Attachment behavior, attachment security, and temperament during infancy. *Child Development, 60*, 728–737.

Vaughn, B. E., & Waters, E. (1990). Attachment behavior at home and in the laboratory: Q-short observations and strange situation classifications of one-year-olds. *Child Development, 61*, 1965–1973.

Vaughn, V. C. III. (1983). Developmental pediatrics. In R. E. Behrman & V. C. Vaughn III. (Eds.), *Pediatrics*. Philadelphia, PA: Saunders.

Verbrugge, L. M. (1979). Multiplicity in adult friendships. *Social Forces, 57*, 1286–1309.

Verbrugge, L. M., Kepkowski, J. M., & Konkol, L. L. (1991). Levels of disability among U.S. adults with arthritis. *Journal of Gerontology, 46*, S71–S83.

Verduyn, C. M., Lord, W., & Forrest, G. C. (1990). Social skills training in schools: An evaluation study. *Journal of Adolescence, 13*, 3–16.

Vermeulen, A., Rubens, R., & Verdonck, L. (1972). Testosterone secretion and metabolism in male senescence. *Journal of Clinical Endocrinology and Metabolism, 32*, 730.

Vicary, J. R., & Lerner, J. V. (1986). Parental attributes and adolescent drug use. *Journal of Adolescence, 9*, 115–122.

Vinokur, A., & Selzer, M. L. (1975). Desirable versus undesirable life events: Their relationship to stress and mental distress. *Journal of Personality and Social Psychology, 32*, 329–337.

Visher, E., & Visher, H. (1979). *Stepfamilies: A guide to working with stepparents and stepchildren*. New York: Brunner/Mazel.

Vlay, S. C., & Fricchione, G. L. (1987). Ventricular tachyarrhythmia: Helping patients cope with stress. *Medical Aspects of Human Sexuality, 21*, 116–123.

Vollman, R. R. (1977). *The menstrual cycle*. Philadelphia, PA: Saunders.

von Frisch, K. (1953). *The dancing bees: An account of the life and senses of the honeybee*. New York: Harcourt, Brace, & World.

Vontner, L. (1982, August). Herpes: Managing pregnancies. *Sexually Transmitted Disease Bulletin*, pp. 1, 5.

Voorhees, J. (1981, Spring). Neuropsychological differences between juvenile delinquents and functional adolescents: A preliminary study. *Adolescence, 16*, 57–66.

Voth, H. M., Perry, J. A., McCranie, J. E., & Rogers, R. R. (1982). How can extramarital affairs be prevented? *Medical Aspects of Human Society, 16*, 62–74.

Wade, N. L. (1987). Suicide as a resolution of separation-individuation among adolescent girls. *Adolescence, 22*, 169–177.

Wagner, C. (1980). Sexuality of American adolescents. *Adolescence, 15*, 567–580.

Waksman, S. A. (1984a, Spring). Assertion training with adolescents. *Adolescence, 19*, 123–130.

Waksman, S. A. (1984b, Summer). A controlled evaluation of assertion training on performance in highly anxious adolescents. *Adolescence, 19*, 277–282.

Waletzky, L. (1981). Emotional illness in the postpartum period. In P. Ahmed (Ed.), *Pregnancy, childbirth, and parenthood*. New York: Elsevier.

Walker, A. J. (1985). Reconceptualizing family stress. *Journal of Marriage and the Family, 47*, 827–837.

Walker, E., Downey, G., & Bergman, A. (1989). The effects of parental psychopathology and maltreatment on child behavior: A test of the diathesis-stress model. *Child Development, 60,* 15–24.

Walker, L. J., & Taylor, J. H. (1991). Family interactions and the development of moral reasoning. *Child Development, 62,* 264–284.

Wallerstein, E. (1980). *Circumcision.* New York: Springer.

Wallerstein, J. S. (1989, January 23). Children after divorce: Wounds that don't heal. *New York Times Magazine,* pp. 19–21, 41–44.

Wallerstein, J. S., & Kelly, J. B. (1980). *Surviving the breakup: How children and parents cope with divorce.* London: Grant McIntyre.

Wallinga, C., Paguio, L., & Skeen, P. (1987, August). When a brother or sister is ill. *Psychology Today, 21,* 42–43.

Wallis, C. (1984, March 26). Hold the eggs and butter. *Time, 123,* 56–63.

Wallis, C. (1987, February). You haven't heard anything yet. *Time.*

Walsh, A., & Beyer, J. A. (1987). Violent crime, sociopathy, and love deprivation among adolescent delinquents. *Adolescence, 22,* 705–717.

Wang, H. S., & Busse, E. W. (1974). Heart disease and brain impairment among aged persons. In E. Palmore (Ed.), *Normal aging II.* Durham, NC: Duke University Press.

Ward, R. A. (1980, May). Age and acceptance of euthanasia. *Journal of Gerontology, 35,* 421–431.

Ward, R. A., Sherman, S. R., & LaGory, M. (1984). Subjective network assessments and subjective well-being. *Journal of Gerontology, 39,* 93–101.

Warren, L. R., Wagener, J. W., & Herman, G. E. (1978). Binaural analysis in the aging auditory system. *Journal of Gerontology, 33,* 731–736.

Warrington, E. K., & Silberstein, M. (1970). A questionnaire technique for investigating very long term memory. *Quarterly Journal of Experimental Psychology, 22,* 508–512.

Warshak, R. A. (1986). Father-custody and child development: A review of analysis of psychological research. *Behavioral Science and the Law, 4,* 185–202.

Wasik, B. H., Ramey, C. T., Bryant, D. M., & Sparling, J. J. (1990). A longitudinal study of two early intervention strategies: Project CARE. *Child Development, 61,* 1682–1696.

Wass, H., & Corr, C. A. (1984). *Childhood and death.* Washington, DC: Hemisphere Publishing Corp.

Wasserman, G. A., Raugh, V. A., Brunelli, S. A., Garcia-Castro, M., & Necos, B. (1990). Psychosocial attributes and life experiences of disadvantaged minority mothers: Age and ethnic variations. *Child Development, 61,* 566–580.

Wasson, A. S. (1980, Fall). Stimulus-seeking, perceived school environment, and school misbehavior. *Adolescence, 15,* 603–608.

Waterman, A. S. (1982). Identity development from adolescence to adulthood: An extension of theory and a review of research. *Developmental Psychology, 18,* 341–358.

Waterman, A. S. (1990). Curricula interventions for identity change: Substantive and ethical considerations. *Journal of Adolescence, 13,* 389–400.

Waterman, C. K., & Nevid, J. S. (1977, December). Sex differences in the resolution of the identity crisis. *Journal of Youth and Adolescence, 6,* 337–342.

Waters, E., & Stroufe, L. A. (1983). Social competence as a developmental construct. *Developmental Review, 3,* 79–97.

Watkins, H. D., & Bradbard, M. R. (1982). Child maltreatment: An overview with suggestions for intervention and research. *Family Relations, 31,* 323–333.

Watson, J. B., & Raynor, R. R. (1920). Conditional emotional reactions. *Journal of Experimental Psychology, 3,* 1–4.

Watson, R. E. L. (1983). Premarital cohabitation vs. traditional courtship and subsequent marital adjustment: A replication and follow-up. *Family Relations, 36,* 193–196.

Watson, R. E. L., & DeMeo, P. W. (1987). Premarital cohabitation vs. traditional courtship and subsequent marital adjustment: A replication and follow-up. *Family Relations, 36,* 193–196.

Watson, W. H., & Maxwell, R. J. (1977). *Human aging and dying: A study in sociocultural gerontology.* New York: St. Martin's Press.

Watts, W. D., & Wright, L. S. (1990). The relationship of alcohol, tobacco, marijuana, and other illegal drug use to delinquency among Mexican-American, black, and white adolescent males. *Adolescence, 25,* 171–182.

Waugh, N. C., & Norman, D. A. (1965). Primary memory. *Psychological Review, 72,* 89–104.

Waxman, S. R., & Kosowski, T. D. (1990). Nouns mark category relations: Toddlers' and preschoolers' word-learning biases. *Child Development, 61,* 1461–1473.

Waxman, S. R., Shipley, E. F., & Shepperson, B. (1991). Establishing new subcategories: The role of category labels and existing knowledge. *Child Development, 62,* 127–138.

The way singles are changing the U.S. (1977, January 31). *U.S. News and World Report,* pp. 59–60.

Webb, R. A. (1974). Concrete and formal operations in very bright 6- to 11-year-olds. *Human Development, 17,* 292–300.

Webster v. Reproductive Health Services, Inc., 951 F. 2d., at 1079 (1988).

Wechsler, D. (1955). *Manual for the Wechsler adult intelligence scale.* New York: Psychological Corporation.

Wechsler, D. (1967). *Wechsler preschool and primary scale for intelligence.* New York: Psychological Corporation.

Wechsler, D. (1974). *Wechsler intelligence scale for children.* New York: Psychological Corporation.

Wechsler, D. (1981). *Wechsler adult intelligence scale—revised.* New York: Psychological Corporation.

Wehr, S. H., & Kaufman, M. E. (1987). The effects of assertive training on performance in highly anxious adolescents. *Adolescence, 85,* 195–205.

Weiffenbach, J. M., Tylenda, C. A., & Baum, B. J. (1990). Oral sensory changes in aging. *Journal of Gerontology, 45,* M121–M125.

Weigel, R. R., Weigel, D. J., & Blundall, J. (1987). Stress, coping, and satisfaction: Generational differences in farm families. *Family Relations, 36,* 45–48.

Weinraub, M., Clemens, L. P., Sockloff, A., Ethridge, T., Gracely, E., & Myers, B. (1984). The development of sex role stereotypes in the third year: Relationships to gender labeling, gender identity, sex-typed toy preferences, and family characteristics. *Child Development, 55,* 1493–1503.

Weinstein, E., & Rosen, E. (1991). The development of adolescent sexual intimacy: Implications for counseling. *Adolescence, 26,* 331–340.

Weisner, T. S., & Wilson-Mitchell, J. E. (1990). Nonconventional family life-styles and sex typing in six-year-olds. *Child Development, 61,* 1915–1933.

Weiss, M. J., Zelazo, P. R., & Swain, I. U. (1988). Newborn response to auditory stimulus discrepancy. *Child Development, 59,* 1530–1541.

Welsh, M. C., Pennington, B. F., Ozonoff, S., Rouse, B., & McCabe, E. R. B. (1990). Neuropsychology of early-treated phenylketonuria: Specific executive function deficits. *Child Development, 61,* 1697–1713.

Werner, E. E., & Smith, R. R. (1982). *Vulnerable but invincible:*

A longitudinal study of resilient children and youth. New York: McGraw-Hill.

West Berlin Human Genetics Institute. (1987). *Studies on effect of nuclear radiation at Chernobyl on fetal development.* West Berlin: Human Genetics Institute.

Westney, O. J., Jenkins, R. R., Butts, J. D., & Williams, I. (1984, Fall). Sexual development and behavior in black preadolescents. *Adolescence, 19,* 557–568.

Wetherby, A., & Prutting, C. (1984). Profiles of communicative and cognitive-social abilities in autistic chldren. *Journal of Speech and Hearing Research, 27,* 364–377.

Whalen, C. K., Henker, B., Castro, J., & Granger, D. (1987). Peer perceptions of hyperactivity and medication effects. *Child Development, 58,* 816–828.

Whillits, F. K., & Crider, D. M. (1988). Healthy rating and life satisfaction in the later middle years. *Journal of Gerontology, 43,* S172–176.

Whisman, M. A., & Jacobson, N. S. (1989). Depression, marital satisfaction, and marital and personality measures of sex roles. *Journal of Marital and Family Therapy, 15,* 177–186.

White, J. A., McGue, M., & Heston, L. L. (1986). Fertility and parental age in Alzheimer's disease. *Journal of Gerontology, 41,* 40–41.

White, K. M. (1980, Spring). Problems and characteristics of college students. *Adolescence, 15,* 23–41.

White, L. K., & Brinkerhoff, D. B. (1981). Children's work in the family: Its significance and meaning. *Journal of Marriage and the Family, 43,* 789–798.

White, M. J., & Tsui, A. O. (1986). A panel study of family-level structural change. *Journal of Marriage and the Family, 48,* 435–446.

Whitehouse, J. (1981). The role of the initial attracting quality in marriage: Virtues and vices. *Journal of Marital and Family Therapy, 7,* 61–67.

Whitten, P., & Whiteside, E. J. (1989). Can exercise make you sexier? *Psychology Today, 23,* 42–44.

Widmayer, S. M., Peterson, L. M., Larner, M., Carnahan, S., Calderon, A., Wingerd, J., & Marshall, R. (1990). Predictors of Haitian-American infant development at twelve months. *Child Development, 61,* 410–415.

Wilkie, F., & Eisdorfer, C. (1972, December 22). *Terminal changes in intelligence.* Paper presented at the 25th annual meeting of the Gerontological Society.

Willems, E.D., & Alexander, J. L. (1982). The naturalistic perspective in research. In B. Wolman (Ed.), *Handbook of developmental psychology.* Englewood Cliffs, NJ: Prentice-Hall.

Williams, C., & Spark, A. (1988). Identifying and preventing coronary disease in families. *Medical Aspects of Human Sexuality, 22,* 92–98.

Williams, K. (1988). Parents reinforce feminine role in girls. *Medical Aspects of Human Sexuality, 22,* 106–107.

Williams, R. (1989). The trusting heart. *Psychology Today, 23,* 36–42.

Williams, S. A., Denney, N. W., & Schadler, M. (1980). Elderly adults' perception of their own cognitive development during the adult years. *International Journal of Aging and Human Development.*

Williamson, J. A., & Campbell, L. P. (1985). Parents and their children comment on adolescence. *Adolescence, 20,* 745–748.

Willis, L., Thomas, P., Gary, P. J., & Goodwin, J. S. (1987). A prospective study of response to stressful life events in initially healthy elders. *Journal of Gerontology, 42,* 627–630.

Willits, F. K., & Crider, D. M. (1988). Healthy rating and life satisfaction in the later middle years. *Journal of Gerontology, 43,* S172–S176.

Wilson, J., Carrington, E., & Ledger, W. (1983). *Obstetrics and Gynecology.* St. Louis, MO: Mosby.

Wilson, P. T. (1985). *Amount of reading, reading instruction, and reading achievement.* Paper presented at the annual meeting of the National Reading Conference.

Wilson, R., & Matheny, A. (1983). Assessment of temperament in infant twins. *Developmental Psychology, 19,* 172–183.

Wilson, S. M., & Medora, N. P. (1990). Gender comparisons of college students' attitudes toward sexual behavior. *Adolescence, 25,* 615–628.

Wiltse, S. E. (1894). A preliminary sketch of the history of child study in America. *Pedagogical Seminary, 3,* 189–212.

Wingfield, A., Aberdeen, J. S., & Stine, E. A. L. (1991). Word onset gating and linguistic context in spoken word recognition by young and elderly adults. *Journal of Gerontology, 46,* P127–P129.

Wingfield, A., Lahar, C. J., & Stine, E. A. L. (1989). Age and decision strategies in running memory for speech: Effects of prosody and linguistic structure. *Journal of Gerontology, 44,* P106–P113.

Wintre, M. G., Polivy, J., & Murray, M. A. (1990). Self-predictions of emotional response patterns: Age, sex, and situational determinants. *Child Development, 61,* 1124–1133.

Wise, K. L., Bundy, K. A., Bundy, E. A., & Wise, L. A. (1991). Social skills training for young adolescents. *Adolescence, 26,* 233–242.

Witelson, S. F. (1987). Neurobiological aspects of language in children. *Child Development, 58,* 653–688.

Witkin, S., & Toth, A. (1983). Relationship between genital tract infections, sperm antibodies in seminal fluid, and infertility. *Fertility and Sterility, 40,* 805–808.

Witters, W. L., & Jones-Witters, P. (1980). *Human sexuality: A biological perspective.* New York: Van Nostrand.

Wodarski, J. S. (1990). Adolescent substance abuse: Practical implications. *Adolescence, 25,* 667–688.

Wohl, A. J. (1988). Your heart and cholesterol. *Medical Aspects of Human Sexuality, 22,* 83–84.

Wolf, F. M. (1981, Summer). On why adolescent formal operators may not be critical thinkers. *Adolescence, 16,* 345–348.

Wood, B. S. (1981). *Children and communication: Verbal and nonverbal language development* (2nd ed.). Englewood Cliffs, NJ: Prentice-Hall.

Wood, J., Chapin, K., & Hannah, M. E. (1988). Family environment and its relationship to underachievement. *Adolescence, 23,* 283–290.

Wood, N. L., Wood, R. A., & McDonald, T. D. (1988). Integration of student development theory into the academic classroom. *Adolescence, 23,* 349–356.

Woodward, J. C., & Kalyan-Masih, V. (1990). Loneliness, coping strategies and cognitive styles of the gifted rural adolescent. *Adolescence, 25,* 977–988.

Woody-Ramsey, J., & Miller, P. H. (1988). The facilitation of selective attention in preschoolers. *Child Development, 59,* 1497–1503.

Wooley, J. D., & Wellman, H. M. (1990). Young children's understanding of realities, nonrealities, and appearances. *Child Development, 61,* 946–961.

Worobey, J. L., & Angel, R. J. (1990). Functional capacity and living arrangements of unmarried elderly persons. *Journal of Gerontology, 45,* S95–S101.

Wright, J. D., & Hamilton, R. F. (1978, June). Work satisfaction and age: Some evidence for the job change hypothesis. *Social Forces, 56,* 1140–1158.

Wright, L. S. (1985). Suicidal thoughts and their relationships to family stress and personal problems among high school seniors and college undergraduates. *Adolescence, 20,* 575–580.

Wright, R. E. (1982). Adult age similarities in free recall output order and strategies. *Journal of Gerontology, 37,* 76–79.

Wyshak, G. (1981). Hip fracture in elderly women and reproductive history. *Journal of Gerontology, 36,* 424–427.

Yamaura, H., Ito, M., Kubota, K., & Matsuzawa, T. (1980). Brain atrophy during aging: A quantitative study with computed tomography. *Journal of Gerontology, 35,* 492–498.

Yaniv, I., & Shatz, M. (1990). Heuristics of reasoning and analogy in children's visual perspective taking. *Child Development, 61,* 1491–1501.

Yarcheski, A., & Mahon, N. E. (1984). Chumship relationships, altruistic behavior, and loneliness in early adolescents. *Adolescence, 19,* 913–924.

Yearick, E. S., Wang, M. L., & Pisias, S. J. (1980). Nutritional status of the elderly: Dietary and biochemical finding. *Journal of Gerontology, 35,* 663–671.

Young, G., & Gately, T. (1988, June). Neighborhood impoverishment and child maltreatment. *Journal of Family Issues, 9,* 240–254.

Young, K. T. (1990). American conceptions of infant development from 1955 to 1984: What the experts are telling parents. *Child Development, 61,* 17–28.

Younger, A. J., & Piccinin, A. M. (1989). Children's recall of aggressive and withdrawn behavior: Recognition memory and likability judgments. *Child Development, 60,* 580–590.

Youngs, G. A., Jr., Rathge, R., Mullis, R., & Mullis, A. (1990). Adolescent stress and self-esteem. *Adolescence, 25,* 333–342.

Zabin, L. S. (1981). The impact of early use of prescription contraceptives on reducing premarital teenage pregnancies. *Family Planning Perspectives, 13,* 72ff.

Zani, B. (1991). Male and female patterns in the discovery of sexuality during adolescence. *Journal of Adolescence, 14,* 163–178.

Zacks, R. T., Hasher, L., Doren, B., Hamm, V., & Attig, M. S. (1987). Encoding used memory of explicit and implicit information. *Journal of Gerontology, 42,* 418–422.

Zarb, J. M. (1984, Summer). A comparison of remedial failure and successful secondary students across self-perception and past and present school performance variables. *Adolescence, 19,* 335–348.

Zarbatany, L., Hartmann, D. P., & Rankin, D. B. (1990). The psychological functions of preadolescent peer activities. *Child Development, 61,* 1067–1080.

Zarit, S. H., Cole, K. D., & Guider, R. L. (1981). Memory training strategies and subjective complaints of memory in the aged. *Gerontologist, 21,* 158–165.

Zarling, C. L., Hirsch, B. J., & Landry, S. (1988). Maternal social networks and mother-infant interactions in full-term and very low birthweight, preterm infants. *Child Development, 59,* 178–185.

Zarski, J. J., Bubenzer, D. L., & West, J. D. (1986). Social interest, stress, and the prediction of health status. *Journal of Counseling and Development, 64,* 386–388.

Zautra, A., & Hempel, A. (1984). Subjective well-being and physical health: A narrative literature review with suggestions for future research. *International Journal of Aging and Human Development, 19,* 95–110.

Zelkowitz, P. (1987). Social support and aggressive behavior in young children. *Family Relations, 36,* 129–134.

Zellman, G. L. (1982). Public school programs for adolescent pregnancy and parenthood as assessment. *Family Planning Perspectives, 14,* 15–21.

Zelnik, M., & Kantner, J. P. (1980). Sexual activity, contraceptive use and pregnancy among metropolitan-area teenagers 1971–1979. *Family Planning Perspectives, 12,* 230ff.

Zentall, S. A., & Meyer, M. J. (1987). Self-regulation of stimulation from ADD-H children during reading and vigilance task performance. *Journal of Abnormal Child Psychology, 15,* 519–536.

Zeplin, H., Wolfe, C. S., & Kleinplatz, F. (1981). Evaluation of a year-long reality orientation program. *Journal of Gerontology, 36,* 70–77.

Zern, D. S. (1991). Stability and change in adolescents' positive attitudes toward guidance in moral development. *Adolescence, 26,* 261–272.

Zeskind, P. S., & Iacino, R. (1984). Effects of maternal visitation to preterm infants in the neonatal intensive care unit. *Child Development, 55,* 1887–1893.

Zimmerman, D. (1983, December 22). Where are you Captain Kangaroo? *U.S.A. Today,* p. 1D.

Zimmerman, S. L. (1982, April). Alternative in human reproduction for involuntary childless couples. *Family Relations, 31,* 233–241.

Zober, E. (1981, Summer). The socialization of adolescents into juvenile delinquency. *Adolescence, 16,* 321–330.

Zollar, A. C., & Williams, J. S. (1987). The contribution of marriage to the life satisfaction of black adults. *Journal of Marriage and the Family, 49,* 87–92.

Zube, M. (1982). Changing behavior and outlook of aging men and women: Implications for marriage in the middle and late years. *Family Relations, 31,* 147–156.

Zucavin, S. J. (1988). Fertility patterns: Their relationships to child physical abuse and child neglect. *Journal of Marriage and the Family, 50,* 983–993.

Zucker, R. A., & Gomberg, E. S. L. (1986). Etiology of alcoholism reconsidered: The case for a biopsychosocial process. *American Psychologist, 41,* 783–793.

Zuckerman, D. (1985, January). Too many sibs put our nation at risk? *Psychology Today, 19,* 5, 10.

Zusman, J. (1966, January). Some explanations of the changing appearance of psychotic patients: Antecedents of the social breakdown syndrome concept. *Milband Memorial Fund Quarterly,* p. 64.

Zusman, J. U. (1980). Situational determinants of parental behavior: Effects of competing activity. *Child Development, 51,* 792–800.

Zweibel, N. R., & Cassel, C. K. (1989). Treatment choices at the end of life: A comparison of decisions by older patients and their physicians—selected proxies. *Gerontologist, 29,* 615–621.

PHOTO CREDITS

The photos on the following pages are used courtesy of the photographer and are © Lawrence Migdale: pp. 3, 4, 5, 6, 7 (left, right), 9, 12, 14, 25, 26, 41, 49, 59, 64, 69, 70, 73, 79, 80, 81, 89, 90, 91 (left), 93, 98, 101, 102 (top), 105 (bottom), 109 (bottom), 115, 116, 117, 124 (top, bottom), 126, 130, 139, 140, 142, 145, 147, 149, 162, 167, 173, 174, 178, 180, 183, 189, 195, 196, 201, 202, 208, 214, 216, 226, 229, 230, 233, 234, 241, 243, 248, 259, 260, 265 (left, right), 268, 277, 278, 284, 286, 289, 299, 300, 302, 303, 316, 320, 323, 324 (left), 327, 331, 332, 333, 341, 347, 348, 350, 351, 352, 359, 364, 373, 374, 376, 391, 393, 399, 400, 401, 402, 404, 406, 419, 420, 425, 427, 430, 433, 439, 442, 451, 453 (bottom).

Other photos: Part One (p. xxiv), courtesy of Robin Najor; p. 27, © Archiv/Photo Researchers, Inc.; p. 29, UPI/Bettmann; p. 31, TASS from Sovfoto; p. 32, UPI/Bettmann; p. 33, Chuck Painter, Stanford University; pp. 35 and 36, The Bettmann Archive; p. 37, © Bill Anderson/Monkmeyer Press Photo Service; p. 40, Thomas McAvoy/Life Magazine, © 1955 Time Inc.; p. 46, © Chris Migdol; pp. 50, 51 and 53, © Lennart Nilsson/Bonnier Fakta; p. 56, © Hank Morgan, Science Source/Photo Researchers, Inc.; p. 60, Grant Heilman Photography; p. 61, © Michel Tcherevkoff/The Image Bank; p. 65, Suzanne Szasz/Photo Researchers, Inc.: pp. 83, 86, and 91 (right), © Joel Gordon; p. 92, Susan Leavines/Photo Researchers, Inc.; p. 102 (bottom), Scala/EPA/Art Resource; p. 103, Culver Pictures, Inc.; p. 104 (left), The Bettmann Archive; p. 104 (right), © Lewis Hines/The Bettmann Archive; pp. 105 (top) and 106, Culver Pictures, Inc.; p. 107 (top left), The Bettmann Archive; p. 107 (bottom right), Louis Bates Ames/Gesell Institute; p. 109 (top), News Service/Stanford University; p. 141, © Tony Korody/Sygma; p. 155, Dr. Rovee-Collier/Izard; p. 166, © Alan Becker/The Image Bank; p. 177, Photofest; p. 184, Dr. Caroll Izard; p. 188, courtesy of Christine Cardone; p. 217, © Peter Freed; p. 254, © Paul Fusco/Magnum Photos; p. 269, © Kay Chernush/The Image Bank; p. 294, © Tom McKillerick/Impact Visuals; p. 310, © Evan Johnson/Impact Visuals; p. 313, © Hella Hammid/Photo Researchers, Inc.; p. 324 (right), © Stockphotos/The Image Bank; p. 360, courtesy of The American Heart Association; p. 362, © JANEART, LTD./The Image Bank; p. 367, courtesy of Marilyn McMahon; p. 407, © C. Chauvel/Sygma; p. 453 (top), © Andrew Lichtenstein/Impact Visuals; p. 455, © Jim Grace/Photo Researchers, Inc.; p. 459, © Joel Gordon/Joel Gordon Photography; p. 460, © Ray·Ellis/Photo Researchers, Inc.; p. 461, © Rick Reinhard/Impact Visuals; p. 464, © A. Tannenbaum/Sygma; p. 465, © Paul Fusco/Magnum Photos

NAME INDEX

Sigman, M. D., 154, 162
Silber, S. J., 51
Silber, T. J., 310
Silberstein, M., 390
Silvern, L., 10
Simeone, C., 390
Simmons, R. G., 249, 287
Simock, B., 59
Simon, C., 354, 358
Simon, L., 28
Simon, T., 158
Simonson, E., 351
Sims-Knight, J. E., 154
Singer, D. G., 214–216
Singer, J. E., 183
Singer, J. L., 27, 214–215
Singer, L. J., 216
Singh, S., 308, 309
Sinnett, E. R., 467
Sitko, C., 175
Skandhan, K. P., 247
Skeen, P., 206, 220, 460
Skinner, B. F., 32, 142
Slade, A., 210
Slater, A., 93
Slattery, S. C., 205
Slaughter-Defoe, D. T., 196
Slesinger, D. P., 354
Slonim-Nevo, V., 310
Slotkin, T. A., 85
Slovik, L. S., 167, 205
Slugoski, B. R., 232
Small, S. A., 285
Smart, M. S., 182
Smart, R. C., 182
Smetana, J. G., 302
Smidt, L. J., 354
Smilgis, M., 429
Smith, A. D., 389
Smith, D. W., 68
Smith, E., 200, 408
Smith, J., 376
Smith, K., 301
Smith, K. R., 435
Smith, M. C., 349
Smith, P. B., 68, 175
Smith, P. K., 211
Smith, P. T., 382
Smith, R. J., 349
Smith, R. M., 203
Smith, R. R., 41
Smith, T. E., 301
Smith, Y. F., 90
Snidman, N., 71, 184
Snodgrass, D. M., 271
Snyder, K., 234
Snyder, S., 293
Sobel, D., 56
Sockloff, A., 219
Sohngen, M., 349
Sollie, D. L., 332, 432
Solorzanol, L., 165
Somberg, D. R., 213
Sommer, B., 464
Sostek, A. M., 90
Southard, B., 126
Sowarka, D., 376
Spanier, G. B., 332, 425, 431, 437, 438
Spark, A., 359
Speare, A., Jr., 333
Speirs, J., 355
Spencer, B., 350
Spencer, M. B., 188

Spetner, N. B., 93
Spinetta, J., 461
Spiro, A., III, 252, 408
Spock, B., 110, 127–129, 132, 185
Sprague, R. L., 187
Sprecher, S., 279, 309, 427
Spreen, O., 120
Springer, S. P., 120
Sroufe, L. A., 12, 174, 182, 187, 190
Stacey, C. A., 400
Stack, S., 464
Stafford, D., 302
Stager, J. M., 246, 248
Stahl, S. M., 73
Stake, J. E., 288
Stallard, E., 329
Stallsmith, R., 253
Stanley, B. K., 204
Stark, E., 10
Staudt, J., 374
Staundinger, V. M., 376
Stayton, W. R., 437
Steel, L., 234
Steele, C. I., 253
Steelman, L. C., 218
Stefanko, M., 291, 302
Steinberg, L., 286, 316
Steinberg, L. D., 264, 300, 316
Steinbert, L. D., 262
Stein, D. M., 254
Stein, P. J., 420, 424
Stein, R. F., 253
Steingrueber, H. J., 176
Steinman, S., 206
Stenberg, C., 188
Stern, J. A., 126
Stern, M., 282, 290
Stern, P. N., 438
Sternberg, R. J., 159
Steuer, J., 411
Steven, S. J., 301
Stevens, J. H., Jr., 198
Stevens, R., 272
Stevenson, H. W., 165, 167
Stevenson, J. S., 332
Stevenson, M. R., 204
Stewart, C. J., 363
Stewart, H. S., 252
Stewart, M. I., 209
Stief, T. M., 310
Stigler, J. W., 165
Stine, E. A. L., 388
Stine, E. A. L., 389
Stipek, D. J., 188
Stivers, C., 464
Stjernfeldt, M., 67
Stock, W. A., 400, 405, 430
Stoller, E. P., 435
Stone, A. A., 408
Stone, C., 201
Stone, R. K., 67–68
Stoneman, Z., 215
Stones, M. J., 434
Storandt, M., 378, 386, 390, 411
Story, M. D., 308
Storz, N. S., 253
Strang, R., 284
Strate, J. M., 334
Strathe, M., 288
Stratton, J. R., 354
Streeten, D. H. P., 383
Streetman, L. G., 285
Strehler, B. L., 367

SUBJECT INDEX

C